Portugal

written and researched by

Mark Ellingham, John Fisher
and Graham Kenyon

This edition updated by

Matthew Hancock, Francisca Kellet,

Josephine Quintero and Paul Smith

ROUGH
GUIDES

www.roughguides.com

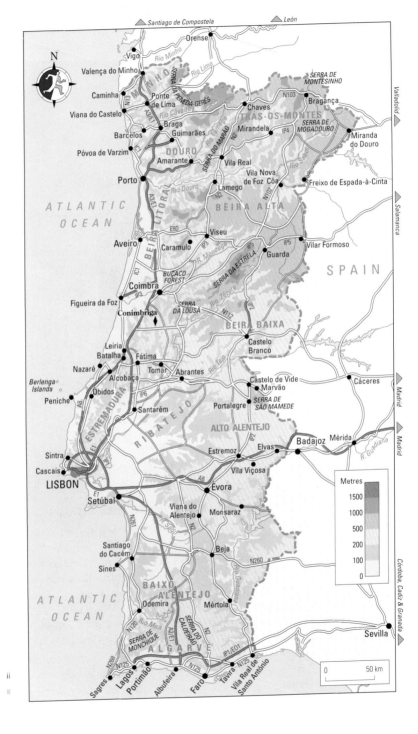

Introduction to

Portugal

Portugal is an astonishingly beautiful country; the rivers, forests and lush valleys of the north are a splendid contrast to its contorted southern coastline of beaches, cliffs and coves. If you've come from the arid plains of central Spain, Portugal's dry southern Alentejo region doesn't promise any immediate relief, but – unlike Spain – you don't have to travel very far to witness so total a contrast that it's hard, at first, to take in. Suddenly the landscape is infinitely softer and greener, with flowers and trees everywhere. Life also seems easier-paced and the people more courteous; the Portuguese talk of their nation as a land of *brandos costumes* – gentle ways.

For so small a country, Portugal sports a tremendous cultural diversity. There are highly sophisticated resorts along the coast around Lisbon and on the well-developed **Algarve** in the south, upon which European tourists have been descending for over forty years. **Lisbon** itself, in its idiosyncratic, rather old-fashioned way, has enough diversions to please most city devotees; the massive development projects that accompanied the 1998 Lisbon Expo firmly locked it into modern Europe without quite jettisoning its most endearing, ramshackle qualities. But in the rural areas – the Alentejo, the mountainous Beiras, or northern Trás-os-Montes – this is often still a conspicuously underdeveloped country. Tourism and European Union membership have changed many regions – most notably in the north, where new road building scythes through the countryside – but for anyone wanting to get off the beaten track, there are limitless oppor-

Fact file

• Portugal is the most south-westerly country in mainland Europe; its only neighbour is Spain with which it shares one of the longest and most established borders in Europe.

• The country occupies an area of approximately 92,000 square kilometres with a surprisingly diverse landscape – from the steep mountains of the north to the arid plains of the Alentejo and the wetlands of the south-east coast. The entire coastline of 1,793km gives on to the Atlantic Ocean.

• Tourism is the country's largest industry, though the greatest proportion of the population works in agriculture. Twenty-six percent of land remains arable, with a further thirty-six percent made up of forests and woodland. Portugal's most important exports are textiles, wine, especially port from the north of the country, and cork – over fifty percent of the world's wine corks come from Portugal.

• Apart from brief periods of Spanish occupancy, Portugal has been an independent country since 1140. It became a republic in 1910 and is now a parliamentary democracy divided into eighteen regions, together with two autonomous regions (the islands of Madeira and the Azores). It joined the EU in 1985 and, despite rapid economic growth, remains one of the EU's poorest countries, with a GDP of around sixty-six percent that of the four leading European economies. Lisbon is officially the European capital with the lowest cost of living.

tunities to experience smaller towns and rural areas that still seem rooted in the last century.

In terms of population and customs, differences between the **north and south** are particularly striking. Above a roughly sketched line, more or less corresponding with the course of the Rio Tejo (River Tagus), the people are of predominantly Celtic and Germanic stock. It was here, in the north at Guimarães, that the Lusitanian nation was born, in the wake of the Christian reconquest from the North African Moors. South of the Tagus, where the Roman, and then the Moorish, civilizations were most established, people tend to be darker-skinned (*moreno*) and maintain more of a Mediterranean lifestyle (though the Portuguese coastline is, in fact, entirely Atlantic). **Agriculture** reflects this divide as well, with oranges, figs and cork in the south, and more elemental corn and potatoes in the north. Indeed, in places in the north the methods of farming date back to pre-Christian days, based on a mass of tiny plots divided and subdivided over the generations.

More recent events are also woven into the pattern. The 1974 **Revolution**, which brought to an end 48 years of dictatorship, came from the south – an area of vast estates, rich landowners and a dependent workforce – while the later conservative backlash came from the north, with its powerful religious authorities and individual smallholders wary of change. But more profoundly even than the Revolution, it is **emigration** that has altered people's attitudes and the appearance of the countryside. After Lisbon, the largest Portuguese community is in Paris, and there are migrant workers spread throughout France, Germany and North America. Returning, these emigrants have brought in modern ideas and challenged many traditional rural values. New ideas and cultural influences have arrived, too, through Portugal's own **immigrants** from the old African colonies of Cape Verde, Mozambique and Angola, while the country's close ties with Brazil are also conspicuously obvious.

The greatest of all Portuguese influences, however, is **the sea**. The Atlantic dominates the land not only physically, producing the consistently temperate climate, but mentally and historically, too. The Portuguese are very conscious of themselves as a seafaring race; mariners like Vasco da

I am very happy here, because I loves oranges, and talks bad Latin to the Monks, who understand it as it is like their own. And I goes into society (with my pocket pistols) and I swims in the Tagus all across at once, and I rides on an ass or a mule and swears Portuguese, and I have got a diarrhoea, and bites from the mosquitoes. But what of that? Comfort must not be expected by folks that go a-pleasuring.

Byron in Portugal, July 1809

The Golden Age

For over a hundred years, in the period spanning the fifteenth to sixteenth centuries, Portugal was one of the richest countries in the world, an economic powerhouse that controlled a trading empire spreading from Brazil in the west to Macau in the east. It was Vasco da Gama's discovery of a sea route to India in 1498 that kick-started the spice trade, shooting Portugal – already doing well from African gold and slavery – into the top league of wealthy nations. Its maritime empire reached a peak during the reign of Manuel I "the fortunate" (1495–1521), the so-called Golden Age that also produced Luís de Camões and Gil Vicente, two of Portugal's greatest writers, along with the new, exuberant Manueline architectural style. Portugal was to hit the jackpot again in the seventeenth century, when enormous gold reserves were discovered in Brazil, but changing markets and over-indulgence soon reduced its financial clout, and after the Great Earthquake of 1755 the country sank into economic obscurity. Nevertheless, the physical legacy of Portugal's empire remains in the surviving buildings and monuments of the Golden Age, such as Lisbon's Torre de Belém and Mosteiro dos Jerónimos, while Portuguese itself is the world's fifth most-spoken language.

Gama led the way in the discovery of Africa and the New World, and until comparatively recently Portugal remained a colonial power, albeit one in deep crisis. Such links long ago brought African and South American strands into the country's culture: in the distinctive music of fado, blues-like songs heard in Lisbon and Coimbra, for example, or the Moorish-influenced Manueline or Baroque Discovery, the style of architecture that provides the country's most distinctive monuments.

This "glorious" history has also led to the peculiar national characteristic of *saudade*: a slightly resigned, nostalgic air, and a feeling that the past will always overshadow the possibilities of the future. The years of isolation under the dictator Salazar, which yielded to democracy after the 1974 Revolution, reinforced such feelings, as the ruling elite spurned influences from the rest of Europe. Only in the last two decades or so, with Portugal's entry into the European Union, have things really begun to change and the Portuguese are becoming increasingly geared toward Lisbon and the cities. For those who have stayed in the countryside, however, life remains traditional – disarmingly so to outsiders – and social mores seem fixed in the past. Women still wear black if their husbands are absent, as many are, working in France, or Germany, or at sea.

Where to go

The obvious place to start a visit to Portugal is the capital **Lisbon**, which contains a selection of just about everything the country has to offer within its vicinity: historical monuments from the Golden Age, superb beaches nearby and a cool hilltop retreat just north in **Sintra**, along with neighbourhood grill houses, hip nightclubs and traditional village quarters. Further north on the River Duoro, and best known for

The Atlantic dominates the land not only physically, but mentally and historically, too.

its port wine lodges and soccer teams, **Porto** is the country's second city and the economic heart of the nation. It certainly beats to a faster work rhythm than the rest of the country but the city nevertheless retains an earthy, typically Portuguese welcome for outsiders.

These are the only cities of any size in Portugal, but the country's cultural and historical past is also reflected in smaller towns, especially the

Food from afar

Portugal's former status as an important trading nation has had a far

greater influence on world cuisine than is often realized. Along with port, the Portuguese are credited with introducing several dishes that today are quintessentially Eastern. The Japanese tempura method of deep-frying food was introduced to the Japanese by sixteenth-century Portuguese traders and missionaries, while the fiery curry-house mainstay vindaloo derives from a *vinho* (wine) and *alho* (garlic) sauce popular with the Christian community in Portuguese Goa. Indeed, the use of chiles in the East only began when the Portuguese started to import them from Mexico. Another, less exotic, Portuguese export is marmalade (although Portuguese *marmelada* is actually made from quince).

Despite this global culinary influence, however, it is only recently that the Portuguese themselves have embraced food with anything other than solid Portuguese ingredients. Nowadays, along with the ubiquitous grilled chicken and sardines, you'll find restaurants serving dishes deriving from Portugal's former colonies, such as Angolan *mufete* (beans with palm oil and fish), chicken *piri piri* (chicken in chile sauce), which originated in Angola and Mozambique, Asian *caril de camarão* (shrimp curry) and Brazilian dishes such as *feijoada* (bean stew).

university towns of **Coimbra** and **Évora**; **Guimarães**, the country's first capital; and **Braga**, the religious centre. But, with its miles of Atlantic coastline, Portugal is most famous for its beaches. The safest and most alluring of these are in the **Algarve**, and though this has led to large-scale development, you can still escape the crowds in the east of the region on the offshore islands around **Tavira** and along the west coast north of **Sagres**. Other less-developed but more exposed beaches can be found up the entire west coast of Portugal, with small-scale, thoroughly Portuguese resorts such as **Milfontes** on the Alentejo coast, **Nazaré** and the Pinhal de Leiria resorts in Estremadura, and the **Costa da Prata** resorts in the Beira Literal. Crowds are even thinner along the Costa Verde around **Viana do Castelo**, but by the time you are this far north the sea is decidedly chilly for much of the year.

Most of Portugal's population lives on the coastline and to see a more rural, traditional side of Portugal involves heading inland. The most dramatic and verdant scenery lies in the north around the sensational

The missing lynx

Portugal's traditional farming techniques, combined with a lack of major industrialization, have historically helped protect the kind of wildlife that has become endangered elsewhere on the continent. A handful of the world's two hundred remaining **Iberian lynx**, for example – a relative of the tiger and Europe's only native big cat – survive in the Serra da Malcata park near the Spanish border, while another rare species, the **Iberian wolf**, lives in the mountainous interior and the north of Portugal. However, as a predatory animal that still arouses fear and suspicion, the latter creature is often shot on sight. Furthermore, as Portuguese agriculture has been modernized in recent years, so the habitats of both these species have become increasingly threatened. Conservation attempts are offering hope, however, ironically, in the tourist areas of the Algarve and

gorge and valley of the river **Douro** and in the wild mountainous national parks of the **Serra da Estrela**, **Peneda–Gerês** and **Montesinho**. Some of the rural villages in **Trás-os-Montes**, **Beira Alta** and **Beira Baixa** still live a startlingly traditional existence firmly rooted in subsistence farming. By contrast, the wide-open plains of the flat **Alentejo** are an agricultural area of endless olive and cork groves scattered with some of Portugal's prettiest whitewashed villages. Here the fierce sun and parched landscape promotes a far more laid-back lifestyle than in the greener hills of the north and centre. All along the border with Spain you'll find fantastic fortified border settlements, from **Valença** in the north to **Elvas** and **Monsaraz** in the south, most of them barely touched by tourism.

Lisbon: a new lynx reserve is planned in the hills of the Algarve to boost numbers of this handsome, spotted cat, while the Centro de Recuperação de Lobo Ibérico north of Mafra, just outside Lisbon, is doing sterling work in conserving the much-feared wolf.

When to go

A weather map of endless suns sums up the situation across the whole of Portugal in summer, certainly between June and September, when the only daytime variation across the country is a degree or two further up the scale from 30°C. At this time, and especially in July and August, Portugal's coastal resorts are at their busiest and prices correspondingly reach their peak.

But, with such a verdant landscape, it should be no real surprise that Portugal also has a fairly high level of rainfall, most of it from November to March. The **north** of Portugal is particularly wet, and in the higher areas showers are possible more or less throughout the year. In **central** and **southern** Portugal, especially on the coast, it is mild all year round and, although it can be cloudy in winter, when the sun does break through it is delightfully warm.

Average temperatures and rainfall

daytime temperatures (°C) and average monthly rainfall (mm)

	Jan	March	May	July	Sept	Nov
Lisbon						
Max °C	14	18	22	27	25	17
Min °C	8	10	13	17	16	12
Rainfall	111	109	44	3	33	93
Porto (Costa Verde)						
Max °C	13	15	19	25	24	17
Min °C	5	7	10	15	14	8
Rainfall	159	147	87	20	51	148
Faro (Algarve)						
Max °C	15	18	22	28	26	19
Min °C	9	11	14	20	19	13
Rainfall	70	72	21	1	17	65

Perhaps the best times of year to visit are in late **spring** – for the dazzling flowers – and early **autumn**, when the weather is warm but not too hot and the summer crowds have thinned out. Swimmers, however, should note that the official swimming season in Portugal lasts from around June to mid-September; outside these months, outdoor pools close and few beaches are manned with lifeguards. Some hotels, restaurants, campsites and water parks also only open from around Easter to September.

In **winter**, in the north things can get pretty chilly, especially inland where snow is common along the mountainous border areas in January and February. But, if you don't mind the odd tourist facility being closed, crisp, sharp sunshine makes winter a highly appealing time to visit the middle and south of the country. In Lisbon, the Alentejo and Algarve there are dramatic reductions in hotel prices and, in February, the almond blossom lights up the countryside. This is the time when you'll see the country at its most Portuguese, with virtually no tourists around.

40

things not to miss

It's not possible to see everything that Portugal has to offer in one trip – and we don't suggest you try. What follows is a selective taste of the country's highlights: outstanding buildings and historic sights, natural wonders and vibrant events. They're arranged in five colour-coded categories, which you can browse through to find the very best things to see and experience. All highlights have a page reference to take you straight into the guide, where you can find out more.

01 Porto's riverfront page **285** • One of Europe's most striking cityscapes; its southern banks are lined by the famous port wine lodges.

02 **Algarve's rock formations** pages **545 & 556** • Explore the Algarve's extraordinary-shaped rocks and grottoes by boat from the historic ports of Lagos or Portimão.

03 **Wines** page **38** • Once you develop a taste for the fruity Portuguese varieties, you may find you want nothing else.

04 **Bom Jesus do Monte** page **369** • Portugal's most photographed church, reached up a series of winding steps.

05
Pilgrimage to Fátima
page **183** •
Every May and October, thousands of devout Catholics descend to a giant square by the basilica to commemorate the Apparitions of the Virgin Mary.

06
Óbidos page **165** • Picture-book walled village that was once the traditional bridal gift of Portuguese kings.

07
Bacalhau
page **37** •
Dried cod is the country's national dish, and with over 365 ways of cooking it, one of them is sure to be to your taste.

ACTIVITIES | CONSUME | EVENTS | NATURE | SIGHTS |

08 Douro valley • Famed for its port wine vineyards, but also boasts spectacular countryside best seen on the Douro train line.

09
Gulbenkian museum
One of Europe's greatest treasure chests of arts from ancient times to the twentieth century.

10 **Pousadas** page **32** • Splash out on a night at a state-run hotel set in a castle or historic building.

11 **FC Porto/Boavista** page **316** • Catch a game with one of Portugal's top clubs in Porto's magnificent stadia.

12 **Conímbriga** page **219** • The most important Roman site in Portugal.

13 **Tram #28, Lisbon** page **65** • The city's best tram route, grinding through all the historic districts.

14 **Mafra convent** page **140** • With 5200 doors and 2500 windows, this lavish buidling nearly bankrupted the country when it was built by a workforce of 45,000 labourers in the eighteenth century.

15 **Monsanto and Sortelha** pages **274 & 280** • Two of the country's most ancient hilltop settlements seem to grow out of the very rocks they are built on.

16 **Serra da Estrela** page **266** • The best region for mountain walks in an area where rare Iberian lynx roam.

17 **Évora** page **463** • UNESCO-protected university town complete with Roman temple, Moorish alleys and medieval walls.

18 **Sintra** page **132** • The hilltop town is one of the most scenic in the country, stuffed with opulent palaces and superb museums.

19 **Citania de Briteiros** page **361** • Step back to pre-Roman times at the magnificent Celtic hill fort.

20 Pastéis de Belém page 110 • Fashionable flaky custard tartlets, best eaten at Belém's *Antiga Confeitaria de Belém*.

21 Beachside beer page 39 • You can't beat an end-of-day beer on the beach – and virtually every stretch of sand in the country has a café to buy one from.

22 Alfama, Lisbon page 88 • A village in the heart of the capital, with streets so narrow and precipitous that few cars can enter.

23 Fundaçao de Serralves, Porto page 301 • Contemporary art from Warhol, Pollock and company in a wonderful building remodelled by Portugal's leading architect, Álvaro Siza.

24 page 522 • **Algarve's sand-spit beaches** Despite the tourist trappings, Algarve's offshore *ilhas* offer some of the best beaches in the country.

25 **Corgo train line** page **431** • Titchy, highly scenic train winding through spectacular gorges to Vila Real in Trás-os-Montes.

26 **Bairro Alto, Lisbon** page **77** • The country's densest concentration of top clubs, bars and restaurants.

27 **Festa de Santo António** page **88** • Saint's day when Lisbon really parties, especially in Alfama, with dancing until dawn.

28 **Ericeira** page **155** • Hang out at this world-championship surfing beach.

29 **Alcobaça** page **172** • An impressive twelfth-century Cistercian monastery.

30 **Feira de Barcelos** page **373** • The country's liveliest and most colourful market shows that rural traditions are alive and well.

31 **Queima das Fitas** page **209** • A rowdy celebration of the end of the academic year in Coimbra, Portugal's main university town.

32 **Convento de Cristo, Tomar** page **189** • Extraordinary former headquarters for the Knights Templars.

33
Alentejo border villages
pages **476, 487 & 488** • The fortified hilltop villages of Monsaraz, Marvão and Castelo de Vide show rural Portugal at its best.

34 Parque Natural de Montesinho
page **446** • Bucolic unspoilt countryside dotted with traditional villages

35
Azulejos
page **90** • Beautiful decorative glazed tiles grace buildings and monuments.

36 Pinhal de Leiria page **177** • Little-visited, pine-fringed coastline with superb wave-battered beaches.

37 Fado page **596** • The embodiment of the Portuguese word *saudade*, fado is very much a living artform. Mariza, pictured, is one of fado's best known and most critically acclaimed performers.

38 Festa de São João page **287** • Expect to be pounded with plastic hammers at one of the country's most important saint's days, especially in Porto.

xxiii

39 **Parque Nacional da Peneda-Gerês** page **403** • Wild mountain terrain for walks and cycling.

40 **Dolphin watching** page **490** • Bottle-nosed dolphins play in the Sado estuary and can be viewed by boat all year.

Contents

Using the Rough Guide

We've tried to make this Rough Guide a good read and easy to use. The book is divided into five main sections, and you should be able to find whatever you want in one of them.

Colour section

The front colour section offers a quick tour of Portugal. The **introduction** aims to give you a feel for the place, with suggestions on where to go. We also tell you what the weather is like and include a basic country fact file. Next, our authors round up their favourite aspects of Portugal in the **things not to miss** section – whether it's great food, amazing sights or a special event. Right after this comes a full **contents** list.

Basics

The Basics section covers all the **pre-departure** nitty-gritty to help you plan your trip. This is where to find out which airlines fly to your destination, what paperwork you'll need, what to do about money and insurance, about internet access, food, security, public transport, car rental – in fact just about every piece of **general practical information** you might need.

Guide

This is the heart of the Rough Guide, divided into user-friendly chapters, each of which covers a specific region. Every chapter starts with a list of **highlights** and an **introduction** that helps you to decide where to go, depending on your time and budget. Likewise, introductions to the various towns and smaller regions within each chapter should help you plan your

itinerary. We start most town accounts with information on arrival and accommodation, followed by a tour of the sights, and finally reviews of places to eat and drink, and details of nightlife. Longer accounts also have a directory of practical listings. Each chapter concludes with **public transport** details for that region.

Contexts

Read Contexts to get a deeper understanding of what makes Portugal tick. We include a brief history, an article on Portuguese music and a detailed further reading section that reviews dozens of **books** relating to the country.

Language

The **language** section gives useful guidance for speaking Portuguese and pulls together all the vocabulary you might need on your trip, including a comprehensive menu reader. Here you'll also find a glossary of words and terms peculiar to the country.

Index + small print

Apart from a **full index**, which includes maps as well as places, this section covers publishing information, credits and acknowledgements, and also has our contact details in case you want to send in updates and corrections to the book – or suggestions as to how we might improve it.

Chapter list and map

Contents

Colour section

Basics

Guide

Contexts

573–608

Language

609–618

Index

619–632

Map symbols

maps are listed in the full index using coloured text

-------	International boundary		⊥	Gardens
- - - -	Chapter division boundary		⊙	Statue/monument
═══════	Motorway		📱	Casa abrigo
═══════	Road		∩	Arch
▓▓▓▓▓▓	Pedestrianized roads		⊠—⊠	Gate
- - - - -	Path		———	Wall
⊞⊞⊞⊞⊞⊞	Steps		Å	Campsite
━━━━━	Railway		🅿	Parking
....	Funicular		✈	Airport
- — -	Ferry route		★	Bus stop
———	Waterway		Ⓜ	Metro station
♦	General point of interest		⛳	Golf course
⚲	Church (regional maps)		@	Internet access
+	Chapel		⊞	Hospital
⌂	Monastery		ⓘ	Tourist office
✡	Synagogue		ℂ	Telephone
∴	Ruins		⊠	Post office
⌒	Cave		⊛	Swimming pool
▲	Peak		▉	Building
⌃⌃	Mountains		⊞	Church (town maps)
↯	Viewpoint		⊡	Cemetery
⌁	Lighthouse		▨	Park
⚘	Waterfall		⁂	Forest
♜	Castle		⠁⠁	Beach
🏛	Stately home			

Basics

Basics

Getting there

Tucked away in the southwest corner of Europe, Portugal is most easily reached by plane; there are regular international services to Lisbon and flights to its two other international airports, Faro in the south and Porto in the north. If you're making Portugal part of a longer European trip, you may want to check out details of the rail passes, which must be purchased in advance of your arrival and can get you by train to Portugal from anywhere in Europe (see p.27 for details).

Air fares always depend on the **season**, with the highest being around June to September when the weather is best; fares drop during the "shoulder" seasons – mid-September to October, mid-March to May and the ten days or so before Christmas – and you'll get the best prices during the low season, just after New Year to mid-March (at Christmas and New Year prices are hiked up and seats are at a premium). Note also that flying on weekends ordinarily adds £35–50/$50–70 to the round-trip fare; price ranges quoted below assume midweek travel.

You can often cut costs by going through a **specialist flight agent** – either a consolidator, who buys up blocks of tickets from the airlines and sells them at cut prices, or a **discount agent**, who in addition to dealing with discounted flights may also offer special student and youth fares and a range of other travel-related services such as insurance, rail passes, car rentals, tours and the like. Some agents specialize in **charter flights**, which may be cheaper than anything available on a scheduled flight, but again departure dates are fixed and withdrawal penalties are high. For some parts of the country, you may even find it cheaper to pick up a bargain **package deal** from one of the tour operators listed below and then find your own accommodation when you get there.

Booking flights online

Many airlines and discount travel websites offer you the opportunity to book your tickets online, cutting out the costs of agents and middlemen. Good deals can often be found through discount or auction sites, as well as through the airlines' own websites.

ⓦ**www.etn.nl/discount.htm** A hub of consolidator and discount agent weblinks, maintained by the nonprofit European Travel Network.

ⓦ**www.geocities.com/Thavery2000** An extensive list of airline toll-free numbers and websites.

ⓦ**www.flyaow.com** Online air travel info and reservations site.

ⓦ**www.cheaptickets.com** Discount flight specialists.

ⓦ**www.cheapflights.com** Bookings from the UK and Ireland only. Flight deals, travel agents, plus links to other travel sites.

ⓦ**www.lastminute.com** Bookings from the UK only. Offers good last-minute holiday package and flight-only deals.

ⓦ**www.expedia.com** Discount airfares, all-airline search engine and daily deals.

ⓦ**www.travelocity.com** Destination guides, hot fares and good deals on car hire and accommodation.

ⓦ**www.hotwire.com** Bookings from the US only. Last-minute savings on regular published fares.

ⓦ**www.priceline.com** Name-your-own-price website. You cannot specify flight times (although you do specify dates).

ⓦ**www.skyauction.com** Bookings from the US only. Auctions tickets and travel packages using a "second bid" scheme. The best strategy is to bid the maximum you're willing to pay, since if you win you'll pay just enough to beat the runner-up regardless of your maximum bid.

ⓦ**www.travelshop.com.au** Australian website offering discounted flights, packages, insurance, online bookings.

From Britain

By far the quickest, easiest way to reach Portugal from Britain is to **fly**. There are various no-frills, schedule and charter flights from airports around the country. If you want

11

to see some of France or Spain en route or want to take your own vehicle there are various **overland** combinations of ferry, rail and road you could choose. Bear in mind though that these will nearly always work out pricier than flying.

Flights

There are **scheduled** year-round flights to Faro (in the Algarve), Lisbon and Porto from London and to Faro from several regional British airports, including Bristol, Manchester and East Midlands. Some of the scheduled flights to Lisbon and Faro are with low-cost **no-frills** airlines which means ticket prices are extremely competitive, especially outside high season. These are often even cheaper than the numerous package companies that also sell **charter** flights (mostly to Faro) from a variety of British regional airports.

Charter deals are sold either with a package holiday or as a flight-only option; they have fixed and unchangeable outward and return dates, and allow a maximum stay of one month. Obviously the more flexible you can be about departure dates, the better your chances of a rock-bottom fare. Last-minute summer flights go for as little as £120 return, occasionally even less, though more realistically you'll pay around £200–250.

Travel agents throughout Britain sell charter flights to Portugal (see opposite for agents' addresses) and even the major high-street chains frequently promote "flight-only" deals, or heavily discount their all-inclusive holidays. The greatest number of flights, however, tends to be from the London airports to Faro; there are fewer charters to Lisbon and Porto. However, the independent Portuguese airline, Portugália, has daily flights from Manchester to Lisbon, a Sunday to Friday service to Porto and a Monday to Saturday service to Faro; all these standard return flights cost from £207 low season to around £330 in high season.

Scheduled flights to Lisbon and Porto (with British Airways, its franchise partner GB Airways, or the Portuguese national airline TAP) can be booked well in advance and remain valid for three months, sometimes longer. To Lisbon and Faro the same airlines' routes have to compete with low-cost air-lines Easyjet, British Midland and Monarch, and very competitive fares are often available. There are various classes of scheduled ticket and occasional special offers, but with most of the cheaper tickets you'll have to stay at least one Saturday night and you won't be allowed to change your flight once it's booked. As with charters, discount deals are available from high-street travel agents, as well as specialist flight and student/youth agencies.

Currently the cheapest scheduled option is Go/Easyjet who offer flights from London Stansted, Bristol and East Midland to Faro from around £100 depending on the availability of tickets – in general the further ahead you book the cheaper the seat. Unsurprisingly, these flights fill up quickly and you'll need to book a couple of months ahead for the summer. Alternatives include Monarch flights to Faro from Luton and Manchester; British Midland flights to Faro from East Midlands; TAP flights from London (Heathrow) to Lisbon, Porto and Faro and from London (Gatwick) to Lisbon; British Airways services to Lisbon from London (Heathrow), and GB Airway services to Lisbon, Porto and Faro from London (Gatwick). Fares vary widely depending on time of year and length of stay; economy-class return fares range from around £100–150 in low season and from £250 to £500 high season.

An alternative is to **fly to Spain** and travel on to Portugal from there. You can pick up scheduled flights by budget airlines such as EasyJet throughout the summer to Bilbao, Madrid or Málaga from as little as £80 return (depending on availability). Train and bus connections from these Spanish cities on to Portugal are simple enough – (see p.19).

Besides the operators above, you can try the classified sections of newspapers like the *Independent* and the *Guardian*, the *Sunday Times* and the *Observer* or, in London, *Time Out*, the *Evening Standard* or *TNT*.

Airlines

British Airways/GB Airways ☎ 0845/773 3377, ⓦ www.ba.com
British Midland ☎ 0870/607 0555, ⓦ www.flybmi.com

EasyJet ☎0870/600 0000, ⊛www.easyjet.com
Go ☎0870/6076543, ⊛www.go-fly.com
Monarch ☎08700/405040, ⊛www.fly-crown
.com
Portugália Airlines ☎0870/755 0025, ⊛www
.pga.pt/atrio
TAP ☎0845/6010932, ⊛www.tap-airportugal.pt

Flight agents

Avro ☎0870/036 0116, ⊛www.avro.com. Good-
value flight-only deals to Lisbon (summer only)
and Faro.
Eclipse Direct ☎08705/010203. Discount fares
from Gatwick to Faro, and packages to Lisbon and
the Algarve.
Flightbookers ☎020/7757 2444,
⊛www.flightbookers.com. Low fares on an
extensive selection of scheduled flights and tailor-
made holidays. Discounted TAP tickets.
North South Travel ☎01245/492882,
⊛www.north-southtravel.co.uk. Friendly,
competitive travel agency, offering discounted
fares to all destinations – profits are used to
support projects in the developing world.
Portugalicia ☎020/7221 0333. Discounted
scheduled flights (BA/TAP from Gatwick and
Heathrow; Portugália from Manchester).
STA Travel ☎0870/160 6070,
⊛www.statravel.co.uk. Specialists in low-cost
travel for under-26s; older customers welcome.

Specialist operators

Abreu Travel ☎020/7229 9905, ©sales@abreu
.co.uk. Portuguese-run agency – good on flights
and accommodation.
Cachet Travel ☎020/8847 3848, ⊛www.cachet
-travel.co.uk. Self-catering apartments and villas.
Caravela Tours ☎020/7630 9223,
⊛www.caravela.co.uk. Various holidays including
stays in pousadas, golf packages, Lisbon city
breaks and fly-drives.
Destination Portugal ☎01993/773269,
⊛www.destination-portugal.co.uk. Discount flight-
only deals, car rental, city breaks, villa and manor
house lets, bird-watching, sailing and hiking
holidays.
Explore Worldwide ☎01252/760000, ⊛www
.exploreworldwide.com. Hiking specialist that
offers small group tours in the Douro, Gerês,
Madeira and the Azores.
HF Holidays ☎020/8905 9558, ⊛www.hfholidays
.co.uk. Walking holidays with flights from Gatwick
and Manchester.
Keytel ☎020/7616 0300, ⊛www.pousadas.pt.

Official UK representative for Portuguese pousadas
(see p.32).
Latitude 40 ☎020/7581 3104, ⊛www.latitude40
.net. Flights, car rental, hotels and villas.
The Magic of Portugal ☎020/8741 1181,
⊛www.magictravelgroup.co.uk. Flights plus villas
and hotels.
Mundi Color ☎020/7828 6021,
⊛www.mundicolor.co.uk. Upmarket packages
including golf holidays and fly-drive deals.
Portugala Holidays ☎020/8444 1857,
⊛www.portugala.com. Villas, hotels, flight only
and fly-drive.
Portuguese Affair ☎020/7385 4775,
⊛www.portugueseaffair.com. High-quality villas
and fly-drive.
Ramblers Holidays ☎01707/331133,
⊛www.ramblersholidays.co.uk. Walking holidays
in Gerês, the Douro, Algarve and Madeira.
Simply Travel ☎020/8541 2207, www.simply
-travel.com. Quality villas and "flying nanny"
service for kids.
Something Special ☎08700/270520,
esomethingspecial.co.uk. Flights and villas.
Style Holidays ☎0870/444 4404 or 4414,
⊛www.style-holidays.co.uk. Flights, car hire and
package holidays.
Sunvil Holidays ☎020/8758 4722, ⊛www
.sunvil.co.uk. Manor houses and hotels, as well as
fly-drive options.
Travel Club of Upminster ☎01708/225 000,
⊛www.travelclub.org.uk. Villas and mostly
four/five star hotels, with flights from London,
Manchester or Birmingham.
Travellers' Way ☎01527/578100, ©travsway@
aol.com. Quality villas plus golfing and riding
holidays.

Package holidays

Although package holidays tend to concentrate on the Algarve, there is a fair range of
other possibilities as well. In addition to
beach-and-villa or beach-and-hotel holidays,
there are companies that arrange rooms in
manor houses and pousadas (see p.32) and
others that operate weekend breaks to
Lisbon or organize sporting (mainly tennis
and golf) holidays.

Standard villa/hotel breaks to the Algarve
start at around £350–400 per person
(including flights) for a week in high season,
although some companies will take only
two-week bookings at this time; in winter,
you can get some very good deals and may

pay around £100 less than this. Specialist holidays come a little pricier, from around £550 for a week's golfing holiday based in a four-star hotel, though a three-night weekend break in Lisbon can be had for as little as £200 in winter, more like £350 to £500 in high season. With package deals most companies will be quite flexible, and a week or two's extension to the flight – allowing you to indulge in some independent travel – shouldn't usually be a problem.

Our list of recommended specialist operators above includes mainly smaller companies, whose holidays tend to be directed towards individuals; all should be able to arrange flights and car rental. For further details of companies offering holidays in Portugal, contact the Portuguese National Tourist Office (see p.20 for website).

By train

To get from London to Lisbon by train is quicker now thanks to the Channel Tunnel, but the journey still takes over 24 hours. A standard class adult return, including necessary seat reservations on the TGV in France and a couchette in Spain/Portugal, is around £275. To bag this fare, especially in high season and at weekends, particularly on Fridays and Sundays, early booking is essential. There are cheaper rates for under 26s and over 60s, and the price can be reduced further by taking a seat instead of a couchette on the Sud Express. Cheaper still (around £220), are tickets that route you via the ferries; setting out from Charing Cross station, crossing the Channel at Dover–Calais, changing trains in Paris (and transferring stations, from Nord to Austerlitz via Metro line #5) and again at the Spanish border (at Hendaye/Irún), takes closer to forty hours. It's a good way to travel if you want to stop off in France or Spain on the way. But even if you qualify for under-26 or over-65 discounts, you are likely to pay more than you would for a flight.

There are two **main train routes** into Portugal: from Paris via Bordeaux, Biarritz,

Irún, San Sebastian, Salamanca and Guarda to Lisbon (change in Guarda for connections to Porto and Coimbra); and alternatively to Madrid from Irún via Valladolid and then through Cáceres to Marvão-Beirã, Abrantes and Entroncamento to Lisbon (or for connections to Coimbra and Porto).

For trains to Faro, in the **Algarve**, the fastest way is via Lisbon; it will almost certainly be cheaper, and quicker, to buy a ticket to Lisbon, then get an express coach on to Faro, which would cost €14 (around £9) one way, far cheaper than the add-on rail price. All the above quoted train tickets are valid for two months and stops are allowed anywhere along the way on a pre-specified route. For other routes into the Algarve from Spain see below.

Train Information

Eurostar ☎ 0870/160 6600, ⓦ www.eurostar.com.
Rail Europe ☎ 0870/584 8848, ⓦ www.raileurope .co.uk.
TrainsEurope ☎ 01354/660222 or 020 8699 3654, ⓔ info@trainseurope.co.uk.

By car, ferry and Le Shuttle

The best way of cutting down on the driving time to Portugal is to take the **ferry to northern Spain**. Brittany Ferries sail from Plymouth (twice weekly March–Nov/Dec; 24hrs) to Santander – although this still leaves you a long day's drive before you reach Portugal itself. Passenger-only prices for a return trip cost around £100, though public transport connections to Portugal are not very convenient. Return fares for a car with four passengers plus cabin accommodation range from around £450 in low season, £700 to £850 mid-season and £850 to £1000 high season (mid-July to Aug); prices also depend on the the duration of the ticket. All passengers are obliged to book some form of accommodation on the ferry itself, seats cost £4 to £6 and berths £21 to £27. In addition, from Portsmouth to Bilbao, P&O runs a ferry though it takes a whopping 30–35 hours and is more expensive. Details and tickets are available from most travel agents or direct from the ferry companies. Note that prices for motorcyclists are signifi-

See page p.27 for details of rail passes.

cantly cheaper – especially if you can find one of the frequent discounted fares advertised in motorcycling publications.

Driving **through France**, your route obviously depends on what you want to see along the way. The quickest route is to take the coast road via Nantes and Bordeaux, entering Spain at Irún. This can be approached from the standard Channel ports (Calais, Boulogne or Dieppe) or, further to the west, off the ferries from Portsmouth–Cherbourg (5hr; P&O); Poole–Cherbourg (2hr 10 min–4hr 15min; Brittany Ferries); Portsmouth–Caen (6hr; Brittany Ferries); Portsmouth–St Malo (8hr 45min; Brittany Ferries), or Plymouth–Roscoff (6hr; Brittany Ferries).

Ferry costs vary enormously and depend on the size of car, number of passengers and, especially, the season – from October to March there are very good deals on all the longer crossings. Full details can be obtained from travel agents, the ferry companies (see below), or on the internet (Ⓦ www.seaview.co.uk).

Shuttle train via the Channel Tunnel for vehicles and their passengers only. The service runs continuously between Folkestone and Coquelles, near Calais, with up to four departures per hour (only one per hour midnight–6am) and takes 35min (45min for some night departure times), though you must arrive at least 30min before departure. It is possible to turn up and buy your ticket at the toll booths (after exiting the M20 at junction 11a), though at busy times booking is advisable. Rates depend on the time of year, time of day and length of stay (the cheapest ticket is for a day-trip, followed by a five-day return); it's cheaper to travel between 10pm and 6am, while the highest fares are reserved for weekend departures and returns in July and August.

Ferry companies and Le Shuttle

Brittany Ferries UK ☎ 0870/901 2400, Ⓦ www.brittanyferries.co.uk. Poole to Cherbourg; Portsmouth to Caen and St Malo; Plymouth to Roscoff and to Santander (March–Nov/Dec).
Eurotunnel (Le Shuttle) UK ☎ 0870/535 3535, Ⓦ www.eurotunnel.com.
Hoverspeed UK ☎ 0870/240 8070, Ⓦ www.hoverspeed.co.uk. 24 daily departures.

Dover to Calais and Ostend; Newhaven to Dieppe.
P&O Portsmouth UK ☎ 0870/242 4999, Ⓦ www.poportsmouth.com. Portsmouth to Cherbourg, Le Havre and Bilbao.
P&O Stena Line UK ☎ 0870/600 0600, Ⓦ www.posl.com. Dover to Calais.

By bus

If you can tolerate the long journey (40–45hr depending on your destination), **Eurolines**, the foreign travel wing of National Express, operates various services to Portugal. The current fare to Lisbon is £120 return (£67 for under-12s); there are no student discounts. You have to change buses in Paris, where there's a lengthy wait between connections. Alternatively, if you make your own way to Paris, there are buses six days a week (not Mon) to Lisbon, and fairly regular services to most other towns in Portugal. Coming back, providing you've made bookings in advance, you can join these buses at any stage. In Paris, tickets are sold at the Porte de Charenton terminus.

Tiring though these journeys are, they're comfortable enough, and broken by frequent rest and meal stops. As long as you take plenty to eat, drink and read, as well as a certain amount of French and Spanish currency to use along the way, you should emerge relatively unscathed.

Another alternative is the **Busabout** service which runs European circuits in summer (fewer in winter), that take in most major cities, including Lisbon, with a link to London and through tickets from elsewhere in Britain and Ireland. Tickets are available in increments of two, three or four weeks; there are also special deals on set itineraries. Busabout also sells Flexipasses, allowing 6, 10 or 15 days' travel within 2 months, 21 days' travel within 3 months, or 30 days out of 4 months.

Bus contacts

Busabout UK ☎ 020/7950 1661, Australia ☎ 1300/301776; New Zealand ☎ 09/309 8824, Ⓦ www.busabout.com. The passes are available from STA Travel in the US.
Eurolines UK ☎ 0870/514 3219, Ⓦ www.eurolines.co.uk. Tickets can also be purchased from any Eurolines or National Express agent (☎ 0870/580 8080, Ⓦ www.nationalexpress.co.uk or Ⓦ www.gobycoach.com).

From Ireland

There are no direct **scheduled** flights from either Dublin or Belfast to Portugal – most airlines, such as TAP and BA, route through London's Heathrow. BA offers good connection times from both Dublin and Belfast, with fares to Lisbon starting at £166 from Belfast (year-round), and at €280 (low season) and €400 (high season) from Dublin. You may find cheaper fares going via a European gateway – with Air France via Paris, or KLM via Amsterdam, for example – though journey times tend to be longer.

If you're heading to the Algarve, seasonal **charters** can be good value and have the advantage of being direct – expect to pay around €200–215 return for summer charters from Dublin to Faro, and around £260 return from Belfast to Faro. Taking a **package holiday** may cut costs, with one week's villa or hotel holiday costing from €380–650 (from Dublin) or around £500 (from Belfast).

If you're really trying to get there in the cheapest way possible, you might find **budget flights** with Go, Ryanair or British Midland to London or East Midlands, plus a last-minute charter or budget flight to Faro, will save you a few pounds, but don't count on it. Buying a Eurotrain ticket from Dublin to London will slightly undercut the plane's price, but by this time you're starting to talk about a journey of days and not hours.

Airlines

Air France Northern Ireland ☎0845/0845 111; Eire ☎01/605 0383; ⓦwww.airfrance.co.uk.
Aer Lingus Northern Ireland ☎0845/973 7747; Eire ☎0818/365000; ⓦwww.aerlingus.ie.
British Airways Northern Ireland ☎0845/773 3377; Eire ☎1800/626747; ⓦwww.ba.com.
British Midland Northern Ireland ☎0870/607 0555; Eire ☎01/407 3036; ⓦwww.flybmi.com.
Go Northern Ireland ☎0870/607 6543; Eire ☎1890/932922; ⓦwww.go-fly.com.
KLM Northern Ireland ☎0870/507 4074, ⓦwww.klmuk.com.
Ryanair Northern Ireland ☎0870/156 9569; Eire ☎01/609 7800; ⓦwww.ryanair.com.
TAP (Air Portugal) Northern Ireland ☎020/7630 0900; Eire ☎01/679 8844; ⓦwww.tap-airportugal.pt.

Specialist agents and tour operators

Abbey Travel Eire ☎01/804 7100, ⓔabbeytvl@indigo.ie. Charter flights, accommodation and packages.
Co-op Travel Care Northern Ireland ☎028/9047 1717. Packages and charters as well as scheduled flights.
Joe Walsh Tours Eire ☎01/676 0991; ⓦwww.joewalshtours.ie. Budget fares agent.
Neenan Travel Eire ☎01/607 9900, ⓦwww.neenantrav.ie. Packages and flights, specializes in city breaks.
Selective Travel Northern Ireland ☎028/9096 2010. Specialists in charter flights from Belfast.
Trailfinders Eire ☎01/677 7888, ⓦwww.trailfinders.ie. Well-informed agents for independent travellers, offering competitive fares out of all Irish airports, plus deals on hotels, tours and car rental.

From North America

The only **direct** non-stop flights between the US and Portugal run from New York to Lisbon: from all other cities you'll need to get a connecting flight via New York. Alternatively, you may find it cheaper to fly on a European airline via its home hub, such as British Airways which flies from various US cities via London, Iberia which flies via Madrid, Lufthansa via Frankfurt, or Air France via Paris. If you want to fly to Porto or Faro, TAP can organize onward flights from Lisbon, while some of the European airlines such as BA, Lufthansa and Air France fly direct to Porto and/or Faro from their home hubs.

From the east coast

There are two airlines with daily non-stop flights **from New York** to Lisbon – TAP (operating a code-share with American Airlines) and Continental. The non-stop flight time from New York to Lisbon is just under seven hours, with Lisbon to Porto or Faro adding an extra 30 to 45 minutes. Fares on the TAP/AA non-stop flight from New York to Lisbon start at $470 (low season) and $700 (high season), while BA fares (via London) start at $500 (low season) and $915 (high season).

From central USA and the west coast

All flights to Portugal from **central USA** and the **west coast** involve changing planes, either in New York or in Europe. Both Continental and American Airlines can book through-flights from a variety of US cities to connect with the New York service, while several European airlines, such as BA, Lufthansa and Air France, can book through-tickets from a variety of US cities via their home hubs. From West Coast cities such as Los Angeles, San Francisco or Seattle, expect to pay around about $250 on top of the New York fare (see above); from Chicago the extra cost is around $200.

From Canada

There are no direct flights from Canada to Portugal, but Air Canada, Continental and United have connecting flights via New York (see above), while several European airlines fly from a selection of Canadian cities via their home hubs. **From Montreal**, Air Canada can book through-flights on the TAP/AA service from New York (10hr 35min) or the Lufthansa service from Frankfurt (11hr 55min), while Continental can book a through-flight, changing planes in New York (10hr 20min). Air France via Paris offers a slightly quicker flight time (10hr 15min). **From Toronto**, the most straightforward option is with Continental via New York (10hr 40min), though taking an Air Canada or United flight to connect with the Continental service from New York gives you a slightly quicker flight time (10hr 20min). **From Vancouver**, Air Canada and United can both book through-flights on the TAP/AA and Continental services from New York to Lisbon, but connection times are appalling and travelling this route can take up to 33 hours. Much quicker (15hr 10min) is the Lufthansa service via Frankfurt, or the Air Canada/British Airways flight via London (14hr 25min). Fares from Montreal and Toronto to Lisbon start at around CDN$1000 (low season) and CDN$1300 (high season), from Vancouver at CDN$1300 (low season) and CDN$1700 (high season).

Airlines

Air Canada ☎1-888/247-2262, www.aircanada.ca.
Air France US ☎1-800/237-2747; Canada ☎1-800/667-2747; 🖰www.airfrance.com.
American Airlines ☎1-800/433-7300, 🖰www.aa.com.
British Airways ☎1-800/247-9297, 🖰www.british-airways.com.
Continental Airlines ☎1-800/231-0856, 🖰www.continental.com.
Iberia ☎1-800/772-4642, 🖰www.iberia.com.
Lufthansa ☎1-800/645-3880; Canada ☎1-800/563-5954; 🖰www.lufthansa.com.
TAP (Air Portugal) ☎1-800/221-7370, 🖰www.tap-airportugal.pt.

Consolidators, discount agents and travel clubs

Council Travel ☎1-800/226-8624 or 617/528-2091, 🖰www.counciltravel.com. Nationwide organization that mostly, but by no means exclusively, specializes in student/budget travel.
New Frontiers/Nouvelles Frontières ☎1-800/677-0720 or 212/986-6006, 🖰www.NewFrontiers.com. French discount-travel firm. Other branches in LA, San Francisco and Québec City.
Now Voyager ☎212/431-1616, 🖰www.nowvoyagertravel.com. Courier flight broker and consolidator.
Skylink US ☎1-800/AIR-ONLY or 212/573-8980, Canada ☎1-800/SKY-LINK. Consolidator.
STA Travel ☎1-800/777-0112 or 1-800/781-4040, 🖰www.sta-travel.com. Specialists in independent travel including student IDs, travel insurance and rail passes.
Travac ☎1-800/872-8800, 🖰www.thetravelsite.com. Consolidator and charter broker.
Travel Avenue ☎1-800/333-3335, 🖰www.travelavenue.com. Full-service travel agent.
Travel Cuts US ☎416/979-2406; Canada ☎1-800/667-2887. Canadian student-travel organization.
Worldwide Discount Travel Club ☎305/534-2642. Discount travel club.

Specialist tour operators

There is a list of further travel agents that specialize in holidays to Portugal on 🖰www.atop.org

4th Dimension Tours ☎1-800/877-1525 or 305/279-0014, ⊛www.4thdimension.com. Specialists in custom-built tours staying in manor house or *pousada* accommodation.

Abercrombie and Kent ☎1-800/323-7308, ⊛www.abercrombiekent.com. Upmarket tours of Portugal.

Abreu Tours ☎1-800/223-1580, ⊛www .abreu-tours.com. Portugal specialists who can organize *pousada* bookings, tailor-made holidays and land/air packages.

Contiki Holidays ☎888/CONTIKI, ⊛www .contiki.com. Spain and Portugal coach tours for 18- to 35-year-olds.

Europe Through the Back Door ☎425/ 771-8303, ⊛www.ricksteves.com. Excellent travel club which publishes a regular newsletter, sells Eurail passes, and runs good-value bus tours to Spain and Portugal.

Homeric Tours ☎1-800/223-5570 or 212/753-1100, ⊛www.homerictours.com. Customized tours and packages in Portugal, plus Lisbon city breaks.

Isram World of Travel ☎1-800/223-7460 or 212/661-1193, ℮info@asram.com. Portugal specialist who can organize flights with Continental and TAP, escorted tours, packages and *pousada* accommodation.

Magellan Tours ☎215/695-0330, ⊛www .magellantours.com. Portugal specialists arranging golfing trips, *pousada* and manor house accommodation, fly/drive holidays, and city breaks.

Maupintour ☎1-800/255-4266, ⊛www.maupintour.com. Offers various tours of Portugal and Spain including *pousada* accommodation.

Petrabax Tours ☎1-800/634-1188, ⊛www .petrabax.com. A variety of escorted tours, plus accommodation vouchers and *pousada* bookings throughout Portugal.

Pinto Basto Tours International ☎1-800/345-0739 or 914/639-8028, ℮info@pousada.com. Fly-drive holidays, flight-only, and customized special interest trips, including hiking and watersports, all featuring small, characterful hotels.

From Australia & New Zealand

There are **no direct flights** from Australia or New Zealand to Portugal: the most straight-forward route is to fly with British Airways/Qantas, changing planes at London's Heathrow. Alternatively, several of the European airlines, such as Air France or Lufthansa, fly via their home hubs, though connection times may not be so good. You may find it cheaper to buy a budget flight to London from a discount agent – on Garuda, for example – then either pick up a cheap charter or budget airline flight (see p.13) or travel overland by road (see p.15) or rail (see "European rail passes" on p.27). However, with the high living and transport costs in northwestern Europe, this rarely works out any cheaper in practice.

Fares vary according to the seasons, which break down as follows: high season (mid-May to Aug & Dec to mid-Jan); shoulder season (March to mid-May & Sept); and low season (mid-Jan to Feb, Oct & Nov). Low-season fares **from Australia** (Sydney, Melbourne and Perth) to Lisbon via London on British Airways currently start at A$2239, mid-season at A$2479 and high season at A$3019. Flight times from Sydney and Melbourne to Lisbon take around 26hrs, 30min, including connections.

From New Zealand flights on BA to Lisbon, via Los Angeles and London, start at NZ$2599 in low-season, $NZ2849 in mid-season, and NZ$3149 in high-season (from both Auckland and Christchurch).

If you are planning several stopovers en route, it may also be worth considering a **Round-the-World** (RTW) ticket, which is valid for a year. BA's "Global Explorer" ticket, in conjunction with Qantas, costs from A$2299/NZ$3099 in low season, and A$2699/NZ$3249 in high season for an itinerary including Portugal.

Airlines

Air France Australia ☎02/9244 2100; New Zealand ☎09/308 3352; ⊛www.airfrance.com.
Air New Zealand Australia ☎132476; New Zealand ☎0800/737 000; ⊛www.airnz.com.
British Airways Australia ☎02/8904 8800; New Zealand ☎0800/274847; ⊛www.ba.com.
Garuda Australia ☎02/9334 9970; New Zealand ☎09/366 1862; ⊛www.garuda-indonesia.com.
Lufthansa Australia ☎1300/655 727; New Zealand ☎09/303 1529; ⊛www.lufthansa.com.
Qantas Australia ☎131313; New Zealand ☎09/661901; ⊛www.qantas.com.au.

Discount agents

Anywhere Travel Australia ℡02/9663 0411,
ⓔanywhere@ozemail.com.au.
Flight Centre Australia ℡02/9235 3522,
℡131600 for nearest office; New Zealand
℡09/358 4310; ⓦwww.flightcentre.com.
STA Travel Australia ℡1300/360960 or 131776;
New Zealand ℡09/309 0458;
ⓦwww.statravelaus.com.au.
Thomas Cook Australia ℡131771 or
1800/801002; New Zealand ℡09/379 3920;
ⓦwww.thomascook.com.au.
Trailfinders Australia ℡02/9247 7666.
Travel.com Australia ℡02/9290 1500,
ⓦwww.travel.com.au.

Specialist operators

Adventure World Australia ℡02/9956 7766 or
1300/363055, ⓦwww.adventureworld.com.au;
New Zealand ℡09/524 5118,
ⓦwww.adventureworld.co.nz. Organized tours
around Spain and Portugal, as well as city breaks
and accommodation throughout the country.
European Travel Office (ETO) Melbourne
℡03/9329 8844; Sydney ℡02/9267 7727. A wide
selection of package holidays and accommodation
from hotels to country inns, palaces and
monasteries.
Ibertours Australia ℡03/9670 8388 or
1800/500016, ⓦwww.ibertours.com.au. Portugal
specialists who book *pousada* and manor house
accommodation, as well as organizing fly-drive
trips and escorted tours throughout the country.
PFM Travel Australia ℡02/9550 0788. Very
helpful agent specializing in flights and holidays to
Portugal, including the Algarve.
Ya'lla Tours Australia ℡1300/362844. Holidays
to Portugal, combined with other European
destinations.

Overland from Spain

If you are combining a trip to Portugal with
Spain, there are easy bus and train connections from Madrid or Málaga, with rewarding
stops en route. If you have your own transport there are numerous other places where
you can cross the border – all the frontiers
are open and unguarded – but if you're in a
rental car remember to check whether
you're covered to take the vehicle between
countries.

From Madrid, the most direct trains leave
from the Estación Atocha, reaching **Lisbon**
(Oriente and Santa Apolónia stations) ten
hours later. Another route is via Badajoz, the
"gateway to Portugal", which is around five
and a half hours from Lisbon, and a close
neighbour of **Elvas** (see p.447), the first stop
the train makes in Portugal. Other stops along
this line, such as the lofty towns of Portalegre
(p.482) and Abrantes (p.194), make this a
recommended route through the country.

From Málaga you are well placed to head
for the **Algarve** and, if you have the time,
you could take in a loop through the great
Andalucian cities of Granada, Córdoba and
Seville (though note that the Málaga–
Granada and Granada–Córdoba journeys
are quicker and easier by bus). At Córdoba,
you're back on the main train line to Seville
from where buses run to the Portuguese
border at Ayamonte–Vila Real de Santo
António and along the coast to Albufeira.
Alternatively, you can get off at the
Portuguese border town of Vila Real, where
you can join the Algarve train line, towards
Faro and Lagos, or catch one of the frequent
local buses.

If you want to explore **central Portugal**,
the line from Salamanca, which enters
Portugal at Vilar Formoso, has useful connections to Guarda (1hr) and Coimbra (3hr)
as well as Lisbon (5hr) and Porto (6hr
40–9hr). From **northern Spain**, trains connect from Vigo in Galicia to the border at
Valença (3hr to Porto, 6hr 30min–9hr to
Lisbon).

Red tape and visas

EU citizens need only a valid passport or identity card for entry to Portugal, and can stay indefinitely. Currently citizens of the US, Canada, Australia and New Zealand can enter for up to ninety days with just a passport, but visa requirements do change, and it is always advisable to check the situation before leaving home.

An **extension to your stay** can be arranged once you're in the country. Extensions are issued by the nearest District Police headquarters or the Foreigner's Registration Service which has branch offices – Serviço de Estrangeiros e Fronteiras – in most major tourist centres. You should apply at least a week before your time runs out and be prepared to prove that you can support yourself without working (for example by keeping your bank exchange forms every time you change money). Extended stay visas are also available through any Portuguese Consulate abroad. Check out one of the following sites for more visa information:

ⓦ www.travel.state.gov/visa_services.html
ⓦ www.travisa.com/visa1.htm

Portuguese consulates and embassies abroad

A full list of Portuguese consulates and embassies

can be found at ⓦ www.Portugal.org/geninfo /missions/missions.html.
Australia 23 Culgoa Circuit, O'Malley ACT ☎ 02/6290 1733, ⓦ www.consulportugalsydney .org.au. Plus consulates in Sydney, Melbourne, Brisbane, Adelaide, Darwin and Fremantle.
Britain 11 Belgrave Square, London SW1X 8PP ☎ 020/7235 5331.
Canada 645 Island Park Drive, Ottawa K1Y 0B8 ☎ 613/729-0883, Ⓔ embportugal@embportugal -ottowa.org. Plus consulates in Vancouver, Montreal and Toronto.
Ireland Knocksinna House, Knocksinna, Fox Rock, Dublin 18 ☎ 01/289 3375.
New Zealand Consulates PO Box 305, 33 Garfield Street, Parnell, Auckland ☎ 09/309 1454; and PO Box 1024, Suite 1 1st floor, 21 Marion Street, Wellington ☎ 04/382 7655.
USA 2125 Kalorama Rd NW, Washington DC 20008 ☎ 202/328-8610, Ⓔ embportwash@ mindspring.com. Plus consulates including New York, Boston and San Francisco.

Information and maps

You can pick up a wide range of brochures and maps, for free, from the Portuguese National Tourist Office in your home country (check ⓦ www.Portugal.org for contact details). Though some of their descriptions are best taken with a pinch of salt, it is worth contacting one of their offices for information before you leave home.

In Portugal itself you'll find a tourist office, or **turismo**, in almost every town and village of any size. Most are detailed in the guide

and are usually helpful and friendly. Aside from the help they can give in finding a room (some will make bookings, others simply

The following sites have English language versions unless otherwise stated.

⦿**www.rtalgarve.pt** The official Algarve tourist board website, good for events listings and general background information.

⦿**geocid–snig.cnig.pt** High resolution satellite and aerial topographic images on the website of the Portuguese National Geographic Information Infrastructure (GEOCID). An in-depth site which also includes useful information on beaches, heritage and even weather reports.

⦿**www.maisturismo.pt** Search engine for hotels throughout Portugal, mostly business-orientated or at the top end of the market.

⦿**www.min-cultura.pt/Agenda/ Agenda.html** The Ministry of Culture's website, with details of events in major towns.

⦿**www.paginasamarelas.pt** Portuguese version of the Yellow Pages, in Portuguese and English.

⦿**www.portugal-hotels.com** A directory of hotels throughout Portugal, though the information is not regularly updated.

⦿**www.portugalinsite.pt** or ⦿**www.portugal.org** The official Portuguese websites with details of tourist attractions and links to accommodation agencies, businesses and directories.

⦿**www.portuguesesoccer.com** Independent soccer magazine in English detailing the latest soccer news, with reports on games, fixtures and links to official club websites.

⦿**www.portugalvirtual.pt** Comprehensive directory of everything from hotels to shops, tourist sites and businesses.

⦿**www.nexus-pt.com** Detailed site dedicated to the Algarve, covering tourist sites to weather and shopping.

⦿**www.rede-almanaque.pt/feiras** List of the country's fairs, *romarias* and special events, though not regularly updated.

⦿**www.townnet.com/world/europe/ portugal.htm** Good general info links, newspapers, weather and exchange rates.

supply lists), they often have useful local maps to supplement the ones in this book and leaflets that you won't find in the national offices. **Opening hours** are given after each office in the text but don't be surprised if you find them closed when they should be open – times of opening are often totally dependent on staff available, especially in small towns and villages.

For all tourist queries, there's an excellent **freephone** telephone number (Linha Verde Turista; ☎800 296 296) – that you can call when you arrive in Portugal – whose English-speaking operators can give you information about museums and their opening times, transport practicalities and timetables, and provide lists of hotels and restaurants, hospitals and police stations, for example. It operates Monday to Saturday from 9am to midnight, and Sundays and holidays from 9am to 8pm.

Maps

The Portuguese National Tourist Office and the turismos in larger towns can provide you with a reasonable **map** of the country (1:600,000), which is fine for everything except mountain roads. If you're doing any real exploration, however, it's worth investing in a good road map. The best maps available abroad are Michelin's 1:400,000 Portugal (#440); or Geo Centre's Euro Map Portugal and Galicia at 1:300,000. Geo Centre also produces a 1:200,000 map of the Algarve and a 1:250,000 map of the Lisbon area; Bartholomew's Algarve Holiday Map 1:100,000 is good, too. If you're planning on spending more than a day or two in Lisbon, the Michelin Lisboa Planta Roteiro is superb. The new Geocid website is certainly worth a visit at ⦿geocid–snig.cnig.pt; the site offers high-resolution satellite and aerial topographic images, and innumerable maps of almost all of Portugal.

More detailed topographic maps for walkers are produced by the Instituto Geográfico do Exercito, Avenida Dr. Alfredo Bensaúde, Olivais Norte ☎218 520 063, ⓦwww.igeoe.pt. You can also find them at the Instituto Geográfico e Cadastral by the Basilica da Estrela in Lisbon, and in Porto at Porto Editora, Praça Filipe de Lancastre 42 ☎222 007 681. Unfortunately, many of these topographic maps are disastrously out of date, although a major updating programme began in 1996: the new versions (scale 1:25,000, so-called Serie M888) are now available for some regions, and are invaluable for hiking.

Map outlets

In the UK and Ireland

Blackwell's Map and Travel Shop 50 Broad St, Oxford OX1 3BQ ☎01865/793 550, ⓦhttp://maps.blackwell.co.uk/index.html.
Easons Bookshop 40 O'Connell St, Dublin 1 ☎01/873 3811, ⓦwww.eason.ie.
Heffers Map and Travel 20 Trinity St, Cambridge CB2 1TJ ☎01865/333 536, ⓦwww.heffers.co.uk.
Hodges Figgis Bookshop 56–58 Dawson St, Dublin 2 ☎01/677 4754, ⓦwww.hodgesfiggis.com.
James Thin Booksellers 53–59 South Bridge, Edinburgh EH1 1YS ☎0131/622 8222, ⓦwww.jthin.co.uk.
The Map Shop 30a Belvoir St, Leicester LE1 6QH ☎0116/247 1400, ⓦwww.mapshopleicester.co.uk.
National Map Centre 22–24 Caxton St, London SW1H 0QU ☎020/7222 2466, ⓦwww.mapsnmc.co.uk.
Newcastle Map Centre 55 Grey St, Newcastle-upon-Tyne, NE1 6EF ☎0191/261 5622.
Ordnance Survey Ireland Phoenix Park, Dublin 8 ☎01/802 5349, ⓦwww.irlgov.ie/osi.
Ordnance Survey of Northern Ireland Colby House, Stranmillis Ct, Belfast BT9 5BJ ☎028/9025 5755, ⓦwww.osni.gov.uk.
Stanfords 12–14 Long Acre, London WC2E 9LP ☎020/7836 1321, ⓦwww.stanfords.co.uk. Maps available by mail, phone order, or email. Other branches within British Airways offices at 156

Regent St, London W1R 5TA ☎020/7434 4744, and 29 Corn St, Bristol BS1 1HT ☎0117/929 9966.
The Travel Bookshop 13–15 Blenheim Crescent, London W11 2EE ☎020/7229 5260, ⓦwww.thetravelbookshop.co.uk.

In the US and Canada

Adventurous Traveler Bookstore 102 Lake Street, Burlington, VT 05401 ☎1-800/282-3963, ⓦwww.adventuroustraveler.com.
Book Passage 51 Tamal Vista Blvd, Corte Madera, CA 94925 ☎1-800/999-7909, ⓦwww.bookpassage.com.
Distant Lands 56 S Raymond Ave, Pasadena, CA 91105 ☎1-800/310-3220, ⓦwww.distantlands.com.
Elliot Bay Book Company 101 S Main St, Seattle, WA 98104 ☎1-800/962-5311, ⓦwww.elliotbaybook.com.
Forsyth Travel Library 226 Westchester Ave, White Plains, NY 10604 ☎1-800/367-7984, ⓦwww.forsyth.com.
Globe Corner Bookstore 28 Church St, Cambridge, MA 02138 ☎1-800/358-6013, ⓦwww.globercorner.com.
Map Link 30 S La Patera Lane, Unit 5, Santa Barbara, CA 93117 ☎805/692-6777, ⓦwww.maplink.com.
Rand McNally ☎1-800/333-0136, ⓦwww.randmcnally.com. Around thirty stores across the US; dial ext 2111 or check the website for the nearest location.
The Travel Bug Bookstore 2667 W Broadway, Vancouver V6K 2G2 ☎604/737-1122, ⓦwww.swifty.com/tbug.
World of Maps 1235 Wellington St, Ottawa, Ontario K1Y 3A3 ☎1-800/214-8524, ⓦwww.worldofmaps.com.

In Australia and New Zealand

Mapland 372 Little Bourke St, Melbourne, Victoria 3000, ☎03/9670 4383, ⓦwww.mapland.com.au.
The Map Shop 6–10 Peel St, Adelaide, SA 5000 ☎08/8231 2033, ⓦwww.mapshop.net.au.
MapWorld 173 Gloucester St, Christchurch, New Zealand ☎0800/627967 or 03/374 5399, ⓦwww.mapworld.co.nz.
Perth Map Centre 1/884 Hay St, Perth, WA 6000, ☎08/9322 5733, ⓦwww.perthmap.com.au.
Specialty Maps 46 Albert St, Auckland 1001 ☎09/307 2217, ⓦwww.ubdonline.co.nz/maps.

Costs, money and banks

The cost of living in Portugal has been edging up ever since its entry into the EC in 1986 but, for tourists, it remains one of the cheapest places to travel in Europe. Accommodation, transport, food and drink are still cheaper than in northern Europe – or North America – and, on the whole, better value than in Spain. The only things that are markedly more expensive are phone calls and petrol.

A European **under-26 card** is well worth having if you're eligible – it'll get you free or reduced admission to many museums and sights, discounts on bus and train tickets, as well as reductions in numerous shops and restaurants (sometimes even hotels). Of much less use is the International Student Identity Card (ISIC), which is rarely accepted, even if you attempt an explanation in Portuguese. Both are available through STA in Britain and Ireland, Council Travel in the US and Travel CUTS in Canada (see the relevant "Getting there" sections for addresses). You will also find the Euro<26 card on sale in Portugal at post offices and banks – ask for a Cartão Jovem. **Over 60s** are also entitled to reductions; see p.48 for details.

Costs

In most places in Portugal you can get by on a **budget** of around £30/$45 a day, which will get you a room for the night, picnic lunch, dinner with drinks in a restaurant, a bus or train ride, and a beer or two. By camping and being a little more frugal, you could reasonably expect to survive on much less than this; while on £35–40/$50–60 a day you'll be living pretty well. It's worth noting that things cost up to twenty percent more in Lisbon and the Algarve.

You should always be able to get a substantial basic meal for around £5/$7.50; even dinner in the smarter restaurants is unlikely to cost more than £20/$30 a head. Drink costs are more than reasonable, too – a bottle of house wine rarely comes to more than £3/$5, a glass of the local brew in a bar around 50p/75¢. Even transport is hardly going to break the bank, especially since most distances you'll travel are fairly short and fares (especially on trains) low. A

second-class train journey from Porto to Lisbon, or Lisbon to the Algarve, for example, costs around £12/$18. See p.31 for details of accommodation costs.

Currency

Portugal is one of the twelve European Union countries to use the **euro** (€). Introduced in January 2002 to replace the escudo, euro notes are issued in **denominations** of 5, 10, 20, 50, 100, 200 and 500 euro, and coins in denominations of 1, 2, 5, 10, 20 and 50 cents and 1 and 2 euro. The exchange rate is around €1.60 to £1 and €1.10 to $1.

Banks and exchange

You'll find a bank in all but the smallest towns. Standard **opening hours** are Monday to Friday 8.30am to 3pm. In Lisbon and in some of the Algarve resorts they may also open in the evening to change money, while some banks have installed automatic exchange machines for various currencies and denominations. Changing cash in banks is easy, and shouldn't attract more than €3 commission. As ever, it's unwise to carry all your money as cash, so consider the alternatives.

By far the easiest way to get money in Portugal is to use **ATMs** (called Multibancos). You'll find them in even the most out-of-the-way small towns and you can withdraw up to €200 per day. Check with your bank to see whether you can use your credit or debit card in Portugal (the major cards are all accepted), and remember that you're usually charged a cash handling fee on credit card withdrawls in addition to the usual currency conversion fee. Most Portuguese banks will also give **cash advances** on credit cards over the counter and will charge a currency conversion fee. **Cards** are also accepted for payment in many hotels and restaurants.

Watch out if using **travellers' cheques**, as banks charge an outrageous commission for changing them (upwards of €13 per transaction). However, more reasonable fees can be had in *caixas* – savings banks or building societies – and some exchange bureaux. Larger hotels are sometimes willing to change travellers' cheques at low commission. It's probably worth taking a supply in case your plastic is lost, stolen or swallowed by an ATM.

Health and insurance

Portugal poses few health problems for the visitor: the tapwater is safe to drink – although most visitors prefer bottled water – and no inoculations are necessary. Mosquitoes can be a menace in the summer, though December and January are usually mosquito-free. Mosquito-repellent lotion and coils are widely sold in supermarkets and pharmacies. Take care to use a high-factor sun cream as the sun is extremely powerful.

For minor complaints go to a **farmácia** (pharmacy). There's one in virtually every village and English is often spoken. Pharmacists are highly trained and can dispense drugs that would be prescription-only in Britain or North America. **Opening hours** are usually Mon–Fri 9am–1pm & 3–7pm, Sat 9am–1pm. Local papers carry information about 24-hour pharmacies and the details are posted on every pharmacy door.

In the case of serious illness, get the contact details of an English-speaking doctor from a British or American consular office or, with luck, from the local tourist office, or a major hotel. There's also a British Hospital in Lisbon (see "Listings", p.123). In an **emergency** dial ☏112 (free).

Travel insurance

As an EU country, Portugal has free reciprocal health agreements with other member states on production of your passport. You don't need a form E111 (available from main post offices) unless you're emigrating. Reassuring as the EU health agreements may sound, however, some form of travel insurance is still worthwhile – and essential for North Americans and Australasians, who must pay for any medical treatment in Portugal.

In many parts of Portugal public health care lags behind much of northern Europe and you may well prefer to get private treatment. Before paying for a new policy, however, it's worth checking whether you are already covered: various credit card companies offer cover for holidays bought on their account. The level of cover varies considerably from card to card, so check with your card-issuer or bank, but it should at least include travel accident cover up to £50,000/$73,000. Some all-risks home insurance policies may cover your possessions when overseas, and many private medical schemes include cover when abroad. In Canada, provincial health plans usually provide partial cover for medical mishaps overseas, while holders of official student/teacher/youth cards in Canada and the US are entitled to meagre accident coverage and hospital in-patient benefits. Students will often find that their student health coverage extends during the vacations and for one term beyond the date of last enrolment.

After exhausting the possibilities above, you might want to contact a specialist travel insurance company, or consider the travel insurance deal we offer (see box). A typical travel insurance policy usually provides cover

Rough Guides travel insurance

Rough Guides offers its own travel insurance, customized for our readers by a leading UK broker and backed by a Lloyd's underwriter. It's available for anyone, of any nationality and any age, travelling anywhere in the world.

There are two main Rough Guides insurance plans: Essential, for basic, no-frills cover; and Premier – with more generous and extensive benefits. Alternatively, you can take out annual multi-trip insurance, which covers you for any number of trips throughout the year (with a maximum of 60 days for any one trip). Unlike many policies, the Rough Guides schemes are calculated by the day, so if you're travelling for 27 days rather than a month, that's all you pay for. If you intend to be away for the whole year, the Adventurer policy will cover you for 365 days. Each plan can be supplemented with a "Hazardous Activities Premium" if you plan to indulge in sports considered dangerous, such as skiing, scuba diving or trekking.

For a policy quote, call the Rough Guides Insurance Line on UK freefone ☎0800/015 0906; US freefone ☎1-866/220-5588, or if you're calling from elsewhere ☎+44 1243/621046. Alternatively, get an online quote or buy online at ⓦwww.roughguides.com/insurance.

for the loss of baggage, tickets and – up to a certain limit – cash or cheques, as well as cancellation or curtailment of your journey. Most of them exclude so-called dangerous sports unless an extra premium is paid: in Portugal this can mean scuba diving, windsurfing and trekking, though probably not kayaking or jeep safaris. Many policies can be chopped and changed to exclude coverage you don't need – for example, sickness and accident benefits can often be excluded or included at will.

If you do take medical coverage, ascertain whether benefits will be paid as treatment proceeds or only after return home, and whether there is a 24-hour medical emergency number. When securing baggage cover, make sure that the per-article limit – typically under £500/$730 – will cover your most valuable possession. If you need to make a claim, you should keep receipts for medicines and medical treatment and, in the event you have anything stolen, you must obtain an official statement from the police (the main police stations are listed for each main centre in the guide).

 # Getting around

Portugal is not a large country and you can get almost everywhere easily and efficiently by train or bus. Trains are often cheaper, and some lines very scenic, but it's almost always quicker to go by bus – especially on shorter or less obvious routes. Approximate times and frequencies of most journeys are given in the "Travel details" section at the end of each chapter; local connections and peculiarities are pointed out in the text. Car rental is also worth considering if time is limited and you want to cover a lot of ground, though you may find you need nerves of steel to drive on some Portuguese roads.

Trains

CP, the Portuguese railway company, operates all trains. Most are designated *regional*, which means they stop at most stations en route and have first- and second-class cars. *Inter-regional* are faster, stopping only at

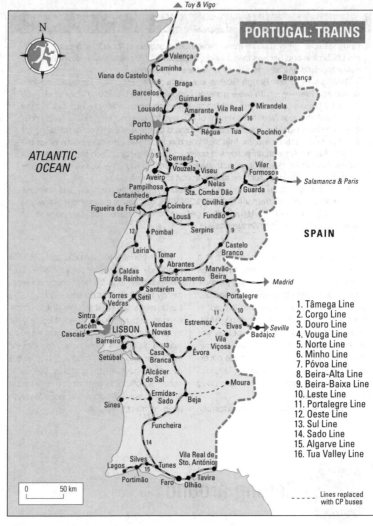

▲ Tuy & Vigo

PORTUGAL: TRAINS

N

Valença
Caminha
Viana do Castelo   6   Braga   ●Bragança
Barcelos   Guimarães
        Lousado Amarante Vila Real Mirandela
Porto   1   16
Espinho   3 Régua Tua Pocinho

ATLANTIC
OCEAN   5   Sernada
        Vouzela Viseu   Vilar
Aveiro   8   Formoso
Pampilhosa   Nelas   → Salamanca & Paris
Cantanhede   Sta. Comba Dão Guarda
        Coimbra Covilhã
Figueira da Foz   Lousã Fundão
        Pombal Serpins   9
12   Castelo
Leiria   Branco   SPAIN
Tomar
Caldas   Abrantes   Marvão-
da Rainha   Beira
Torres Santarém Entroncamento   → Madrid
Vedras Setil   Portalegre
Sintra   11 10
Cacém Vendas Estremoz Elvas → Sevilla
Cascais LISBON Novas   Badajoz
Barreiro   13 Vila
Setúbal   Casa   Viçosa
        Branca Évora
        Alcácer
        do Sal   ●Moura
Sines   Ermidas-
        Sado Beja
        Funcheira
        14
        Vila Real de
Silves   Sto. António
Lagos   Tunes
Portimão 15 Faro Tavira
        Olhão

0   50 km

1. Tâmega Line
2. Corgo Line
3. Douro Line
4. Vouga Line
5. Norte Line
6. Minho Line
7. Póvoa Line
8. Beira-Alta Line
9. Beira-Baixa Line
10. Leste Line
11. Portalegre Line
12. Oeste Line
13. Sul Line
14. Sado Line
15. Algarve Line
16. Tua Valley Line

- - - - - Lines replaced
with CP buses

major stations. On both of these, night trains can be populated with some dodgy characters – stay awake or get someone you trust to keep an eye on your luggage. The next category up, *intercidades*, are twice as fast and twice as expensive, and you need to reserve your seat in advance if using them. The fastest, most luxurious and priciest services are the *rápidos* (known as "*alfa*"), which speed between Lisbon, Coimbra and Porto – sometimes they have only first-class seats.

Both these latter classes charge supplements for rail-pass holders (see below).

Always turn up at the station with time to spare since long queues often form at the ticket desk. On certain trains, even with a rail pass, you'll need to queue up for seat reservations, too. If you end up on the train without first buying a ticket you could be liable for a huge on-the-spot supplement, or be kicked off the train by the guard at the next stop. However, smaller regional stations are sometimes unstaffed, in which case just hop on and pay the ticket inspector on board.

Complete **train timetables** (€4) and timetables for individual lines are available from information desks at main stations, as well as on the internet at ⓦwww.cp.pt. These can also supply information about taking a **car train** (*auto-express*), a service available on the main Lisbon to Porto, Faro, Guarda and Mangualde routes.

Although several of the old narrow-gauge mountain railways of the north have been phased out, the Tâmega, Corgo, Tua Valley and Douro lines are still terrific routes; see the guide for details. Other minor lines have been replaced by buses operated by CP. Regular train tickets and passes are valid on these bus lines.

Lastly, it's as well to be aware that train stations can be some miles from the town or village they serve – Portalegre station and town are 12km distant, for example – and there's no guarantee of connecting transport.

Tickets and passes

Train travel is relatively inexpensive and most visitors simply buy a ticket every time they make a journey; **children** under 4 go free, under-12s pay half price. **Senior citizens** (over-65s) can get thirty percent off travel if they produce ID proving their age and ask for a *bilhete terceira idade* (third-age ticket). It's cheapest to travel on the so-called "Blue Days" – ie avoiding Friday afternoons, Sunday afternoons, Monday mornings, national holidays and the day preceding a national holiday.

If you're planning a lot of train travel, using a **rail pass** might save you money, though note that pass holders pay supplements and reservation fees on *intercidades* and *rápidos*. CP sells its own *bilhete turístico* rail pass (valid for first-class travel on all trains except the Lisbon–Madrid Talgo) for €100 (£65/$91) for 7 days, €170 (£106/$155) for 14 days, and €250 (£160/$230) for 21 days. The same tickets are half-price for under-12s and for **senior citizens** (over-65s). There's also a CP **family card** (*cartão de familia*) and **group tickets** (*bilhetes de grupo*), which offer varying reductions on tickets – more information can be obtained from local stations.

European rail passes

If you're intending to visit Portugal as part of a longer trip to Europe it may well be worth looking into buying a **European rail pass**. There's a huge array of passes available, covering regions as well as individual countries. Some have to be bought before leaving home while some can only be bought in the country itself. Rail Europe is the umbrella company for all national and international rail purchases, and its comprehensive website (ⓦwww.raileurope.com) is the most useful source of information on which rail passes are available; it also gives all current prices.

Eurail passes

A **Eurail pass** is not likely to pay for itself if you're planning to stick to Portugal. The pass, which must be purchased before arrival in Europe, allows unlimited free first-class train travel in Portugal and 16 other countries, and is available in increments of 15 days, 21 days, 1 month, 2 months and 3 months. If you're under 26, you can save money with a **Eurail Youthpass**, which is valid for second-class travel or, if you're travelling with 1–4 other companions, a joint **Eurail Saverpass**, both of which are available in the same increments as the Eurail Pass. You stand a better chance of getting your money's worth out of a **Eurail Flexipass**, which is good for 10 or 15 days' travel within a two-month period. This, too, comes in first-class, under-26/second-class (**Eurorail Youth Flexipass**) and group (**Eurail Saver Flexipass**) versions.

In addition, a scaled-down version of the Flexipass, the **Europass**, is available which allows first-class and youth (second-class) travel in France, Germany, Italy, Spain and Switzerland for any 5 days, 6 days, 8 days, 10 days or 15 days within 2 months; Portugal is one of up to four "associate" countries (the others are Austria/Hungary, Benelux and Greece) that can be included for an additional fee. The **Europass Saverpass** is a version of the Europass for people travelling in groups of two or more that offers a savings of fifteen percent per person on the regular fare.

Details of prices for all these passes can be found on ⓦ www.raileurope.com, and the passes can be purchased from one of the agents listed below.

Inter-Rail pass

These passes are only available to **European residents**, and you will be asked to provide proof of residency before being allowed to purchase one. They come in over-26 and (cheaper) under-26 versions, and cover 28 European countries (including Turkey and Morocco) grouped together in zones, with Portugal zoned alongside Spain and Morocco. The passes are available for 22 days (one zone only) or 1 month and you can purchase up to three zones or a global pass covering all zones. Inter-Rail passes do not include travel between Britain and the continent, although Inter-Rail pass holders are eligible for discounts on rail travel in Britain and Northern Ireland and cross-Channel ferries, plus discounts on other shipping services around the Mediterranean. The Inter-Rail pass also gives a discount on the London–Paris Eurostar service. See ⓦ www.inter-rail.co.uk for details.

Euro Domino pass

Only available to European residents. Individual country passes provide unlimited travel in 28 European and North African countries. The passes allow 3 to 8 days rail travel in one calendar month within Portugal, therefore giving more flexibility than the state railways' *bilhete turístico* (see above) at comparable prices. Standard fares start at £41/$60 for 3 days up to £68/$99 for 8 days. You can buy as many separate country passes as you want; for contact details of agents see below. There is a discounted youth price for those under 26, and a half-price child (age 4–11) fare.

Rail contacts

In the UK

Rail Europe UK ☎ 08705/848848, ⓦ www.raileurope.co.uk.
Discounted rail fares for under-26s on a variety of European routes; also agents for Inter-Rail, Eurostar and Eurodomino.
See p.ooo for further contacts.

In North America

CIT Rail US ☎ 1-800/223-7987 or 212/730-2400; Canada ☎ 1-800/361-7799; ⓦ www.fs -on-line.com. Eurail, Europass, German and Italian passes.
DER Travel US ☎ 1-888/337-7350, ⓦ www.dertravel.com/rail. Eurail, Europass and many individual country passes.
Rail Europe US ☎ 1-800/438-7245; Canada ☎ 1-800/361-7245; ⓦ www.raileurope.com/us. Official North American Eurail Pass agent; also sells Europass, multinational passes and most single-country passes.

In Australasia and New Zealand

CIT World Travel Australia ☎ 02/9267 1255 or 03/9650 5510, ⓦ www.cittravel.com.au. Eurail, Europass and Italian rail passes.
Rail Plus Australia ☎ 1300/555 003 or 03/9642 8644, ⓔ info@railplus.com.au; New Zealand ☎ 09/303 2484. Sells Eurail, Europass, and Britrail passes.
Trailfinders Australia ☎ 02/9247 7666, ⓦ www.trailfinder.com.au. All European passes.

Buses

Buses shadow many of the main train routes as well as linking most of the country's smaller towns and villages. It's almost always quicker to go by bus if you can, though you'll pay slightly more than for the equivalent train ride. Comfortable express buses operate on longer routes, for which you'll usually have to reserve tickets in advance.

All bus services are privatized, though a national network of express coaches (Rede Expressos) has been maintained, combining services from a number of different companies (there's a map of their routes on the internet at ⓦ www.rede-expressos.pt/index _uk.htm). Although the competition brought on by privatization has meant an increase in the number of buses on certain routes, it has also led to the inevitable reduction or phasing out of many local services. The variety of companies can also be a cause of confusion, as two buses going to the same destination may leave from different terminals (in the case of Porto almost all of the twenty companies operate out of different terminals) and companies may be unwilling to volunteer information about rival bus operators.

Local bus stations (detailed wherever possible in the text) are the place to pick up timetables and reserve seats on long-distance journeys but, as companies, addresses and routes change every year, it's advisable to check first with the local turismo – they can usually advise on where to book or catch specific buses. It's as well to be aware that bus services are considerably less frequent – occasionally non-existent – at weekends, especially on rural routes; while at other times, you'll find that departures can be frighteningly early in the morning. This is because bus services are often designed to fit around school and market hours.

Driving, car rental and taxis

With **car rental** rates among the lowest in Europe, driving around Portugal is an option worth thinking about, even for just a part of your travels. **Petrol** (*gasolina*), however, is not so cheap, at around €1 (about 62p/$0.86) a litre for unleaded (*sem chumbo*) petrol, a little less for diesel. Most rental cars run on unleaded. Driving licenses from most countries are accepted, so there's no need to get an international one. Before you set out, however, bear in mind that Portugal has one of the highest accident rates in Europe.

Road surfaces are improving, but even major roads (prefixed EN – *Estrada Nacional* – or just N) are often potholed, narrow and full of dangerous bends. But it's not so much the quality of roads but the driving that is lethal – reckless overtaking being the main problem. Even on motorways, you'll need to check your mirror every few seconds to make sure someone isn't right up your exhaust pipe.

Until the 1990s, Portugal had just one (incomplete) motorway from Lisbon to Porto. Since then, a massive EU-funded road construction programme, now in its final stages, has made previously remote areas of the country such as Trás-os-Montes and Beira far more accessible, via a network of main highways (numbers prefixed "IP"), similar in speed to motorways. The motorway network itself (numbers prefixed with "A") is privately owned by BRISA and is a network of toll roads gradually expanding outwards

from a central spine that links the Algarve with Lisbon and Porto. Be warned, though, that the tolls can add significantly to the cost of your journey – as an indication, the stretch from Lisbon to Porto will set you back £10/$15. The advantages, as usual, are less traffic and a faster journey time.

Traffic on the smaller roads will be much heavier: slow journeys stuck behind trucks are common. In addition, as car ownership has increased massively over recent years, towns can no longer cope with the traffic. Travelling by car in the main resorts in season, you'll have endless problems finding central parking spaces. Only the top hotels have car parks; otherwise you can expect to spend ages looking for a space, often ending up on the outskirts of town and having to walk to the centre. Coimbra is notoriously bad, and has pioneered a park-and-ride scheme in response.

When **parking** in cities, do as the locals do and use the empty spaces pointed out to you by men – often the unemployed. A tip of around €1 will pay them for "looking after" your car.

Traffic drives on the right: **speed limits** are 50kph in towns and villages; 90kph on normal roads; and 120kph on motorways and inter-regional highways. At road junctions, unless there's a sign to the contrary, vehicles coming from the right have priority – a rule that wreaks havoc at roundabouts, effectively giving anyone cutting in the right of way. If you're stopped by the police, they'll want to see your documents – carry them in the car at all times and be courteous to the officers (see "Trouble and the police", p.45).

Motoring organizations

Many car insurance policies cover taking your car to Portugal; check with your insurer while planning your trip. However, you're advised to take out extra cover for motoring assistance in case your car breaks down. Look into the RAC's European Cover or the AA's Five-Star Europe cover. Alternatively, you can get assistance from the Automóvel Clube de Portugal ☏219 429 103, ⊛www.acp.pt which has reciprocal arrangements with foreign automobile clubs.

In the UK and Ireland

AA UK ☎0800/444500, ⓦwww.theaa.co.uk.
AA Travel Dublin ☎01/617 9988,
ⓦwww.aaireland.ie.
RAC UK ☎0800/550055, ⓦwww.rac.co.uk.

Car rental

Car rental agencies can be found in all the major towns and at the airports in Lisbon, Porto and Faro; details are listed in the guide. Local agencies usually charge less than international companies, and contact details for recommended ones are listed in the text. **Rates** are reasonable, from around £30–40/$45–60 a day to £100–120/$150–180 a week for the cheapest car with unlimited mileage, though prices are inflated by around thirty percent in high season. You may find it cheaper to organize car rental from home, or arrange car rental in conjunction with your flights. Several of the specialist holiday companies detailed on pp.13–19 will arrange car rental in conjunction with flights; or call one of the major car rental outfits listed below.

When picking up your car, check such important details as brakes and, if you're renting locally, insurance coverage. As you might have gathered, collision insurance is a good idea and unless you pay a separate supplement the initial several hundred euros' worth of damage may be on your head; if you're given the option of collision damage waiver, take it. Keep the receipts of any repairs you make along the way – you may be able to get some money back from the company.

Finally, it can't be stressed enough that foreign and hire cars are common targets of **theft**. Don't leave anything in an unattended car.

Car rental agencies

In the UK

Autos Abroad ☎0870/066 7788,
ⓦwww.autosabroad.co.uk.
Avis ☎0870/606 0100, ⓦwww.avisworld.com.
Budget ☎0800/181181,
ⓦwww.go-budget.co.uk.
Europcar ☎0845/722 2525,
ⓦwww.europcar.co.uk.

Hertz ☎08708/448844, ⓦwww.hertz.co.uk.
Holiday Autos ☎08704/000099,
ⓦwww.holidayautos.co.uk.
National ☎08705/365365,
ⓦwww.nationalcar.com.
Thrifty ☎01494/751600, ⓦwww.thrifty.co.uk.

In Ireland

Avis Northern Ireland ☎028/9024 0404, Eire
☎01/605 7500, ⓦwww.avis.co.uk.
Budget Northern Ireland ☎028/9023 0700, Eire
☎01/9032 7711, ⓦwww.budgetcarrental.ie or
www.budget-ireland.co.uk.
Cosmo Thrifty Northern Ireland ☎028/9445 2565,
ⓦwww.thrifty.co.uk.
Europcar Northern Ireland ☎028/9442 3444, Eire
☎01/614 2800, ⓦwww.europcar.ie.
Hertz Eire ☎01/813 3416, ⓦwww.hertz.co.uk.
Holiday Autos Eire ☎01/872 9366,
ⓦwww.holidayautos.ie.
SIXT Eire ☎1850/206088,
ⓦwww.irishcarrentals.ie.

In North America

Alamo US ☎1-800/522-9696,
ⓦwww.alamo.com.
Auto Europe US ☎1-800/223-5555; Canada
☎1-888/223-5555; ⓦwww.autoeurope.com.
Avis US ☎1-800/331-1084; Canada ☎1-
800/272-5871; ⓦwww.avis.com.
Budget US ☎1-800/527-0700,
ⓦwww.budgetrentacar.com.
Dollar US ☎1-800/800-6000, ⓦwww.dollar.com.
Europe by Car US ☎1-800/223-1516,
ⓦwww.europebycar.com.
Hertz US ☎1-800/654-3001; Canada ☎1-
800/263-0600; ⓦwww.hertz.com.
National ☎1-800/227-7368,
ⓦwww.nationalcar.com.
Thrifty ☎1-800/367-2277, ⓦwww.thrifty.com.

In Australia

Avis ☎136333, ⓦwww.avis.com.
Budget ☎1300/362848, ⓦwww.budget.com.
Hertz ☎133039, ⓦwww.hertz.com.
National ☎131045, ⓦwww.nationalcar.com.au.
Thrifty ☎1300/367227, ⓦwww.thrifty.com.au.

In New Zealand

Avis ☎09/526 2847 or 0800 655111,
ⓦwww.avis.co.nz.
Budget ☎0800/652227 or 09/976 2222,
ⓦwww.budget.co.nz.
Hertz ☎0800/654321, ⓦwww.hertz.co.nz.

National ☏ 0800/800115 or 03/366 5574,
🌐 www.nationalcar.co.nz.
Thrifty ☏ 09/309 0111, 🌐 www.thrifty.co.nz.

Taxis

Travelling by **taxi** in Portugal is relatively cheap by European standards. It is worth considering for trips across major towns and for shorter journeys in rural areas where other means of transport may be limited. Generally, taxis are metered, with a minimum **fare** of €1.50. Additional charges are made for carrying baggage in the boot, and for travelling between 10pm and 6am and at weekends. Outside major towns, you can negotiate if you want to hire a taxi for a few hours. Unsurprisingly, they're more expensive in the Algarve.

Bikes, mopeds and motorbikes

Bicycles are a great way of seeing the country, though anywhere away from the coast especially north of Lisbon is hilly and you'll find pedalling hard work in mountainous Beira Alta or across the burned plains of southern Alentejo. Bikes can be transported on any *regional* or *inter-regional* train (in other words, not the fast ones) as long as there is space; the charge is usually around €2, or free if the bike is dismantled. Ask in advance which train to take, as not all take bicycles – for example they are not allowed on most of the Algarve line – and it's advisable to arrange it in advance with the baggage office. Several special shops, hotels campsites and youth hostels rent out bikes for around €10 a day; the major ones are listed in the text.

If all that legwork is not to your taste, you can also rent **mopeds**, **scooters** and low-powered (80cc) **motorbikes** in many of the resorts, with hire costs starting at around €25 a day. You need to be at least 18 to hire these (and over 23 to rent larger bikes over 125cc), and to have held a full licence for at least a year. Rental usually includes helmet hire and locks along with third-party insurance. A helmet and valid licence are obligatory. Check all the cables before setting off and go easy.

Accommodation

In almost any Portuguese town you can find a *pensão* (pension) offering a double room for around €16–32 (£10–20/$15–30) – single rooms can be a little cheaper, though not always. The only accommodation that you're likely to find cheaper than this is rooms in a private home; most turismos have lists of those available in the area. You can expect to pay more in Algarve resorts in high season, or in Lisbon. If you have the money to move upmarket, you're often spoilt for choice, with some wonderful manor houses and a network of state-run *pousadas* scattered about the country, and at prices that beat the rest of Europe hands down. See p.32 for details of likely costs for these.

Even in high season you shouldn't have much of a problem finding a bed in most Portuguese regions. However, Lisbon and parts of the Algarve are often a very different matter, with all rooms booked up for days ahead. Try and reserve in advance where you can, especially if you're arriving late.

Rooms, pensões and residenciais

Other than youth hostels and camping (see pp.33 and 34), the cheapest accommodation consists of **rooms** (*quartos* or *dormidas*) let out in private houses. Most commonly available in the seaside resorts, these are sometimes

Accommodation price codes

The **accommodation prices** in this book have been coded using the symbols below. The symbols represent the lowest prices you can expect to pay for a double room in high season. Effectively this means that most rooms in places with a **①** or **②** category will be without private bath or shower, though there's usually a washbasin in the room. In places with a **③** category and above, you'll probably be getting private facilities and often a TV, while many of the cheaper places may also have more expensive rooms with bath/shower if you ask.

Price codes are not given for youth hostels and campsites (see pp.33 and 34 for the rates at those).

❶ under €25	❹ €55–75	❼ €125–150
❷ €25–35	❺ €75–100	❽ €150–200
❸ €35–55	❻ €100–125	❾ over €200

advertised, or more often hawked at bus and train stations. The local turismo may also have a list of rooms available. Rates should be a little below that of a *pensão*, say €13–20 for a double (£8–32/$11–44), though on the Algarve, in high season, you can expect to pay up to twice as much. It's always worth haggling over prices, especially if you're prepared to commit yourself to a longish stay, but don't expect too much success in high season. And always ask where the room is before you agree to take it – in the resorts you could end up miles from the town centre or beach. Get the owner to write down the agreed price too, if possible, to avoid the possibility that they may and overcharge you when it's time to leave.

The main budget travel standby is a room in a **pensão** (plural, *pensões*) – which are officially graded from one to three stars (often, it seems, in a quite random fashion). Many serve meals, but they rarely insist that you take them. *Pensões* that don't serve meals are sometimes called **residenciais** (singular *residencial* or *residência*), though in price and all other respects they are virtually identical, and many establishments use both definitions. Similar to *pensões*, and generally at the cheaper end of the scale, are **hospedarias** or *casas de hóspedes* – boarding houses – which can be characterful places.

Pensão prices for a double room range from around €16–48 (£10–30/$15–42), depending on the season, their location and facilities. Always ask to see the room before you take it, and don't be afraid to ask if

there's a cheaper one (rooms without private showers or bathrooms are often considerably less) – especially if you're travelling alone, in which case you'll frequently be asked to pay more or less the full price of a double. *Tem um quarto mais barato?* ("Do you have a cheaper room?") is the relevant phrase.

Hotels and pousadas

A one-star **hotel** usually costs about the same as a three-star *pensão*, and often don't show any notable differences from *pensões*. Prices for two- and three-star hotels, though, see a notable shift upwards, with doubles running from €32–64 (£20–40/$30–60).

There's a more dramatic shift in rates as you move into the four- and five-star hotel league, where you'll pay anything from €100–300 (£65–200) for a double. *Estalagens* and *albergarias* – **inns** – are other designations of hotels in the same range. The very fanciest places, on the Algarve and in Lisbon, can pretty much charge what they like.

One fairly surprising bargain is the chain of 45 government-run **pousadas** (with more in the pipeline), often converted from old monasteries or castles, or located in dramatic countryside settings. Prices vary considerably depending on the location, size and position of room and season, but expect to pay upwards of £60/$100.

Look out for seasonal promotions, however, especially for over-65s, who can receive discounts of around thirty-five percent. We've detailed most of the *pousadas* in the guide but for a full list contact the Portuguese National Tourist Office in your home country (see p.20), or ENATUR, Av Santa Joana Princesa 10, 1749 Lisbon ☎218-442-001, ⊕218-442-085, ⊛www.pousadas.pt.

Country and manor houses

An increasingly popular alternative in the three- to four-star hotel price range is to stay in one of the many properties throughout Portugal promoted by the tourist board as country and **manor houses** – phrases commonly used are *Turihab, turismo no espaço rural, Solares de Portugal*, and *turismo rural*. Rivals to the *pousadas*, there are now upwards of 150 of them, all of which have had their facilities and accommodation inspected and approved by the government tourist office. In terms of atmosphere and luxury, they are often unbeatable and their equivalent in other European countries would command in excess of double the price. The properties vary from simple **farmhouses** (*casas rústicas*) offering just two or three rooms on a bed-and-breakfast basis to **country manors** (*quintas*) and estate houses (*herdades*) and even **palaces** (*casas antigas*) owned by Portuguese aristocrats who have allowed their ancient seats to become part of the scheme. Their facilities have to conform to certain standards, categorized on a scale of A–C. Rates are currently the same throughout the year: category A doubles are around €100; B €75; and C €60. In high season in certain areas you might find that stays are for a minimum of three nights. Facilities can vary from a simple room in a rustic house to a suite or annexe of a manor house with its own gardens and swimming pool. All properties which have been approved under this scheme are entitled to display a green tree symbol, although there are some unauthorized houses displaying their own symbols.

In general the scheme has given a new lease of life to properties which had begun to fall into decline through changing patterns of economics and lifestyles. The appeal – or not as the case may be – lies in the chance to stay with the owners of the properties. Many will provide typical dinners made from local ingredients, sometimes accompanied by wine and other produce made on the estate, and almost all are founts of advice and information about local matters. Even if dinner is not available – or you prefer not to eat with the family – large breakfasts are invariably included.

Once a property has passed the government inspection, its owners can choose to join one of the private marketing organizations, of which the first and best known is Solares de Portugal (formerly known as Turihab), based in Ponte de Lima where the scheme originated (Praça da República, 4990 Ponte de Lima; ☎258 741 672, ⊕258 741 444, ⊛www.turihab.pt). It has some amazing country houses on its books as well as simpler, more basic properties. You can get a list of theirs and other marketing organizations' properties from the Portuguese National Tourist Office who can send you the short *Guide to Country and Manor Houses*. It's also possible to book in advance with several of the specialist holiday operators detailed on pp.13–19, who can make arrangements for you, or with individual properties directly, the best of which are listed in the guide.

Villas

Virtually every area of the country – certainly near the coast – has some sort of **villa** or **apartment** available for hire, from simple one-room apartments to luxurious five- or six-bed houses complete with gardens and swimming pools. Holiday and tour operators are often the best sources if you want to rent such a place in advance (see pp.13–19). High summer sees the best places booked months in advance; expect to pay at least €50 (£40/$60) a night in high season for an apartment for two people, up to €160 (£100/$150) for a top villa. Outside peak period you should be able to turn up and bag somewhere for around twenty-five percent less, and fifty percent less in winter. The local turismo will probably be able to help.

Youth hostels

There are 41 **youth hostels** (*pousadas de juventude*) in Portugal, most open all year round. The price for a dormitory bed runs from €8–13 a night, depending on the location and season; doubles cost between €17 and €32. Add on a little extra if you need to hire sheets and blankets. The most expensive hostels are in Lisbon, Porto and on the Algarve.

Most have a curfew (usually 11pm or midnight) and all require a valid Hostelling International (HI) card – available from your home-based youth hostel association (see below). In Portugal, the head office of the Portuguese Youth Hostel Association (Movijoven) is at Av Duque de Ávila 137, 1069-017 Lisbon ☏213 596 000, ☏213 596 002, ☏www.pousadasjuventude.pt (Mon–Fri 9.30am–12.45pm & 2–5.45pm).

Among the best hostels in Portugal are those at Vilarinho das Furnas (in the Gerês National Park), Penhas de Saúde (in the Serra de Estrêla), São Martinho do Porto, Areia Branca, Oeiras (on the seafront near Lisbon), Coimbra, Alcoutim (northeastern Algarve), Lagos and Leiria (perhaps the best of the lot).

Youth hostel associations

In England and Wales

Youth Hostel Association (YHA) Trevelyan House, 8 St Stephen's Hill, St Albans, Herts AL1 2DY ☏0870/870 8808, ☏www.yha.org.uk & ☏www.iyhf.org. Annual membership £12.50, for under-18s £6.25.

In Scotland

Scottish Youth Hostel Association 7 Glebe Crescent, Stirling FK8 2JA ☏0870/155 3255, ☏www.syha.org.uk. Annual membership £6, for under-18s £2.50.

In Ireland

An Óige 61 Mountjoy St, Dublin 7 ☏01/8430 4555, ☏www.irelandyha.org.
Adult (and single parent) membership €13, family (2 parents and children under 16) €25, under-18s €5.
Hostelling International Northern Ireland 22–32 Donegall Rd, Belfast BT12 5JN ☏028/9032 4733, ☏www.hini.org.uk. Adult membership £10, under-18s £6, family £20.

In the USA

Hostelling International-American Youth Hostels (HI-AYH) 733 15th St NW, Suite 840, PO

Box 37613, Washington, DC 20005 ☏202/783-6161, ☏www.hiayh.org. Annual membership for adults (18–55) is $25, for seniors (55 or over) is $15, and for under-18s is free. Lifetime memberships are $250.

In Canada

Hostelling International/Canadian Hostelling Association Room 400, 205 Catherine St, Ottawa, ON K2P 1C3 ☏613/237-7884, or 613/237-7884, ☏www.hostellingintl.ca. Rather than sell the traditional 1- or 2-year memberships, the association now sells one Individual Adult membership with a 28- to 16-month term. The length of the term depends on when the membership is sold, but a member can receive up to 28 months of membership for just CDN$35. Membership is free for under-18s and you can become a lifetime member for CDN$175.

In Australia

Australia Youth Hostels Association 422 Kent St, Sydney ☏02/9261 1111, ☏www.yha.com.au. Adult membership rate A$49 for the first twelve months and then A$32 each year after.

In New Zealand

New Zealand Youth Hostels Association 173 Gloucester St, Christchurch ☏03/379 9970, ☏www.yha.co.nz. Adult membership NZ$40 for one year, NZ$60 for two and NZ$80 for three.

Camping

Portugal has around two hundred authorized campsites, many of them in very attractive locations and, despite their often large size (over five hundred spaces is not uncommon), they can get extremely crowded in summer. The most useful campsites are given in the text (unless otherwise stated they are open all year) and you can get the **Roteiro Campista**, a booklet detailing the country's campsites, from most Portuguese tourist offices (€10) as well as from bookshops and newsstands, or from Roteiro Campista, Apartado 3168, 1301-902 Lisbon ☏www.roteiro-campista.pt. Most of the larger campsites have spaces for camper vans and caravans; many also have permanent caravans and bungalows for hire. Charges are per person and per caravan or tent, with showers and parking extra; even so, it's rare that you'll end up paying more than €4 a person although those operated by the

Orbitur chain are usually a little more expensive. For details of their sites, contact Orbitur, Rua Diogo Couto 1-8°, 1149-02 Lisbon ☎218 117 070, ⊛www.orbitur.pt.

There are a few sites in Portugal for which you will have to produce an **international camping carnet**, and if you're planning to do a lot of camping, an international camping carnet is a good investment. The carnet gives discounts at member sites and serves as a useful form of ID. Many campsites will take it instead of making you surrender your passport during your stay, and it covers you for third-party insurance when camping. In the **UK and Ireland**, the carnet costs £4.50, and is available to members of the AA or the RAC (see above), or from either of the following: the **Camping and Caravanning Club**, Greenfields House, Westwood Way, Coventry CV4 8JH ☎024/7669 4995, ⊛wwwcampingandcaravanningclub.co.uk, or the **Carefree Travel Service** ☎024/7642 2024, which provides the CCI free if you take out insurance with them; they also book ferry crossings and inspect camping sites in Europe. In the **US and Canada**, the carnet is available from home motoring organizations, or from **Family Campers and RVers** (FCRV), 4804 Transit Rd, Building 2, Depew, NY 14043 ☎1-800/245-9755, ⊛www.fcrv.org. FCRV annual membership costs $25, and the carnet an additional $10.

Camping outside official grounds is legal, but with certain restrictions. You're not allowed to camp: "in urban zones, in zones of protection for water sources, or less than 1km from camping parks, beaches, or other places frequented by the public". What this means in practice is that you can't camp on tourist beaches, but with a little sensitivity you can pitch a tent for a short period almost anywhere in the countryside. That said, in recent years a number of Portugal's natural parks have banned unofficial camping in an attempt to reduce littering and fire damage. Check first with the relevant park office whether it is permitted or not.

The Algarve is another exception, having banned unlicensed camping altogether. When staying on one of the region's campsites, be warned that **thefts** are a regular occurrence; in the rest of the country, however, you can usually leave equipment without worrying.

Eating and drinking

Portuguese food is excellent, inexpensive and served in quantity. Virtually all cafés, whatever their appearance, will serve you a basic meal for around €8 (£5/$8), while for €24 (£15/$22) you have the run of most of the country's restaurants. Only a handful of top-class restaurants in Lisbon and the Algarve will make more of a dent in your credit card. Do beware, however, of eating anything you haven't explicitly asked for and expecting it to be free, or included: it won't be.

Breakfast, snacks and sandwiches

For **breakfast** it's best to head for a café or *pastelaria* (pastry shop) for a croissant or pastry of some kind washed down with a coffee. The latter is usually taken espresso-style (ask for *uma bica* in the south, or simply *um café* in the north), though the milky version (*um galão*) served in a glass, is also popular at breakfast time.

You'll often find a whole range of dishes served at a **café**, but classic Portuguese snacks include *rissóis de carne* (deep-fried meat patties); *pastéis de bacalhau* (cod fishcakes); and *prego no pão* (steak sandwich), which when served on a plate with a fried egg on top is called a *prego no prato*, while

See p.614 for more food vocabulary.

35

the same with sliced ham is a *prego no fiambre*. In the north you may also find *lanches* (pieces of sweetish bread stuffed with ham) and *pastéis de carne* or *pastéis de chaves* (puff pastries stuffed with sausage meat). If cafés cook in a big way you'll probably see blackboard lists of dishes, or perhaps just a sign reading **Comidas** (meals). Some have signs advertising *petiscos*, bar snacks, usually consisting of plates of *camarões* (prawns), *chouriço* (smoked sausage), *tremoços* (pickled lupin seeds) and *caracois* (snails).

Among sandwiches (*sandes*) on offer, the most common fillings include *queijo* (cheese), *fiambre* (ham), *presunto* (smoked ham) and *chouriço* (smoked sausage). *Sandes mistas* are usually a combination of ham and cheese; grilled, they're called *tostas mistas*. If there's food displayed on café counters and you see anything that looks appealing, just ask for *uma dose* (a portion). *Uma coisa destas* (one of those) can also be a useful phrase.

Markets – often held in indoor covered sites – are always good hunting grounds for snacks. At many of them you'll find stands serving complete meals, or at least some local delicacy. In the north, especially, the most delicious standby is a chunk of *broa* (corn/rye bread) with local cheese and *marmelada* (thick quince spread).

Meals and restaurants

Even those on the tightest of budgets won't need to depend exclusively on snacks and picnics. The country is awash with accessible and affordable restaurants and, in addition, servings tend to be huge. Indeed, you can usually have a substantial meal by ordering a *meia dose* (half portion), or *uma dose* between two. Meals are often listed like this on the menu and it's normal practice; you don't need to be a child.

It is worth checking out the **ementa turística**, too – not a "tourist menu", but the set meal of the day, sometimes with a choice of two starters and two main courses, plus beer or wine. It can be very good value, particularly in *pensões* that serve meals, or in the cheaper workers' cafés. Smarter restaurants, however, sometimes resent the law that compels them to offer the *ementa turística*, responding

with stingy portions, excessive prices or, where there's any deviation from the set fare, declaring your meal to be *à lista* (à la carte) and consequently twice as expensive. If you feel strongly enough to want to make a formal complaint, ask for the **livro de reclamações** (complaints book) – every restaurant, however humble, is obliged to keep one.

Otherwise, the one thing to watch for when eating out in Portugal – especially if you've grown happily complacent in Spain on a regular intake of free tapas – is the **plate of starters** usually placed before you when you take a table and before you order. These can be quite elaborate little dishes of olives, cheese, sardine spread and *chouriço*, or can consist of little more than rolls and butter, but what you eat is counted and you will be charged for every bite. Each item should be itemized on the menu, so you can see what you're spending.

Apart from straightforward restaurants – **restaurantes** – you could end up eating a meal in one of several other venues. A *tasca* is a small neighbourhood tavern; a *casa de pasto*, a cheap, local dining room usually with a set three-course menu, mostly served at lunch only. A *cervejaria* is literally a "beer house", more informal than a restaurant, with people dropping in at all hours for a beer and a snack. In Lisbon they are often wonderful old tiled caverns, specializing in seafood. Also specializing in seafood is a *marisqueria*, occasionally very upmarket, though as often as not a regular restaurant with a superior fishy menu.

Meal times are earlier than in Spain, with lunch usually served from noon–3pm, dinner from 7.30pm onwards; don't count on being able to eat much after 10pm outside the cities and tourist resorts. Simple cafés and restaurants don't charge for service, though you'll have paid a cover charge for bread and appetizers if you had any. People generally leave just small change as a tip in these places, though in more upmarket restaurants, you'll either be charged, or should leave, around ten percent.

Dishes and specialities

It's always worth taking stock of the **prato do dia** (dish of the day) if you're interested in sampling local specialities. They're often considerably cheaper than the usual menu fare as well. Some of the more common dishes are detailed in the food lists on p.614.

Soups are extraordinarily inexpensive (though few restaurants are happy with people only ordering soup), and the thick vegetable *caldo verde* – cabbage and potato broth sometimes with pieces of ham – is as filling as dishes come. The other soup served everywhere is *sopa à alentejana*, a garlic and bread soup with a poached egg in it. Otherwise, fish and shellfish soups are always worth sampling.

On the coast, **fish and seafood** are preeminent: crabs, prawns, crayfish, clams and huge barnacles are all fabulous, while fish on offer always includes superb mullet, tuna and scabbard fish. The most typical Portuguese fish dish is that created from *bacalhau* (dried, salted cod), which is much better than it sounds. It's virtually the national dish with reputedly 365 different ways of preparing it. Running a close second are sardines (*sardinhas*), which – when grilled or barbecued outside – provide one of the country's most familiar and appetizing smells. On the coast, you shouldn't miss trying a *cataplana* – pressure-cooked seafood and strips of ham, named after the copper vessel in which it's cooked – or *arroz de marisco*, a bumper serving of mixed seafood served with a soupy rice. These are nearly always served for a minimum of two people.

On the whole, **meat dishes** are less special, though they're often enlivened by the addition of a fiery *piri-piri* (chilli) sauce, either in the cooking or provided on the table. Simple grilled or fried steaks of beef and pork are common; while chicken is on virtually every menu – at its wonderful best when barbecued (*no churrasco*); certain restaurants specialize in this and little else. Other, more exotic, specialities include smoked hams (*presunto*) from the north of the country (especially Chaves), and the ubiquitous and extremely tasty *porco à alentejana* (pork cooked with clams) – perhaps Portugal's most enterprising contribution to world cuisine – which originated, as its name suggests, in the Alentejo. However, steel yourself for a couple of special dishes that local Portuguese people might entice you into trying: Porto's *tripas* (tripe)

dishes incorporate beans and spices but the heart of the dish is still recognizably chopped stomach-lining; while *cozido à portuguesa*, widely served in restaurants on a Sunday, is a stomach-challenging boiled "meat" stew in which you shouldn't be surprised to turn up a pig's ear or worse. And it's worth paying good money to avoid eating the unspeakable *papas de sarrabulho* (a blood- and bread-based dish).

Accompanying most dishes will be potatoes (generally fried so ask if you want them boiled) and/or rice – calorific overkill is a strong feature of Portuguese meal times. Other vegetables rarely make an appearance, though you might find sliced fresh tomato served with your fish, and boiled carrots or cabbage and the like accompanying meat stews.

If you've had enough rich food, any restaurant will fix a **salada mista** (mixed salad), which usually has tomatoes, onions and olives as a base, and you can ask for it to be served *sem óleo* (without oil), though it's nowhere near as tasty if you do. Otherwise, strict vegetarians are in for something of a hard time outside Lisbon and the Algarve, where there's a bigger choice of non-Portuguese food. Eggs are mostly free-range in Portugal, but out in the sticks you'll soon tire of omelettes or fried eggs, chips and salad – though every restaurant will be happy to prepare this for you if you ask.

Pastries, sweets and cheeses

Pastries (*pastéis*) and cakes (*bolos*) are usually at their best in *casas de chá* (tearooms), though you'll also find them in cafés and in *pastelarias*, which themselves often serve drinks, too. Here, pastries are serious business and enthusiasts won't be disappointed. Among the best are *pastéis de nata* (delicious little custard tarts), the Sintra cheese-cakes (*queijadas de Sintra*), *palha de ovos* (egg pastries) from Abrantes, *bolo de anjo* (angel food cake), and a full range of marzipan cakes from the Algarve. The incredibly sweet, egg-based *doces de ovos* – most infamously from Aveiro – are completely over-the-top.

Unfortunately, few of these delicacies are available in restaurants as **desserts**. Instead, you'll almost always be offered either fresh fruit, the ubiquitous Olá ice cream price list, *pudim flan* (crème caramel), *arroz doce* (rice pudding) or *torta da noz* (almond tart). Cheese is widely available in restaurants, the best being the *queijo da Serra* (from the Serra da Estrela). *Cabreiro* or *queijo de cabra* (often referred to as *queijo seco*, dried cheese) is a goat's cheese like a dry Greek feta; and also worth looking out for are the soft cheeses of Tomar and Azeitão. Travelling in remoter areas, you're also in for a treat – the cheeses of northern Beira and southern Trás-os-Montes being especially worth a mention.

Alcoholic drinks

Portuguese **table wines** are dramatically inexpensive and of a good overall quality. Even the standard *vinho da casa* that you get in the humblest of cafés is generally a very pleasant drink. But it's fortified **port**, of course, and **Madeira** that are Portugal's best-known wine exports – and you should certainly sample both.

Beer choices are far less varied, with just two or three brands available country-wide, while the typical Portuguese measure of spirits is equivalent to at least two shots in Britain or North America, making drunkenness all too easy. Low prices, too, are an encouragement, as long as you stick to local (*nacional*) products.

Wines

Modern wine-making techniques are making fast inroads into Portugal's traditional wine-growing regions, with a corresponding growth in the number of internationally recognized and reputed Portuguese labels, such as Bairrada, from the region between Coimbra and Aveiro, and Ribatejo, Arruda and Leziria from the Ribatejo. Some of the best-known Portuguese table wines are reds from the Dão region, a roughly triangular area between Coimbra, Viseu and Guarda, around the River Dão. Tasting a little like burgundy, and produced mainly by local co-operatives, they're available throughout the country. Among other smaller regions offering interesting wines are Colares (near Sintra), Bucelas in the Estremadura (crisp,

dry whites), Valpaças from Trás-os-Montes, Reguengos from Alentejo and Lagoa from the Algarve.

The light, slightly sparkling **vinhos verdes** – "green wines", in age not colour – are again produced in quantity, this time in the Minho. They're drunk early as most don't mature or improve with age, but are great with meals, especially shellfish. There are red and rosé *vinhos verdes*, though the whites are the most successful. The region was officially demarcated in 1908, and producers are now entitled to use the European VQPRD label. Worth seeking out are *the vinhos verdes de quinta*, which are produced solely with grapes from one property (*quinta*), along the lines of the French chateaux wines: look for labels saying "Engarrafado Pelo Viticultor (or Produtor)" and "Engarrafado Na Propriedade (or Quinta)".

Otherwise, Portuguese rosé wines are known abroad mainly through the spectacularly successful export of Mateus Rosé, said to be Saddam Hussein's favourite tipple. This is too sweet and aerated for most tastes, but other rosés – the best is Tavel – are definitely worth sampling.

Portugal also produces an interesting range of sparkling, champagne-method wines, known as *espumantes naturais*. They are designated *bruto* (extra dry), *seco* (fairly dry), *meio seco* (quite sweet) or *doce* (very sweet). The best of these come from the Bairrada region, north of Coimbra, though Raposeira wines are the most commonly available.

Even the most basic of restaurants usually has a decent selection of wines, many of which are available in half-bottles, too. The *vinho da casa* (house wine) is nearly always remarkably good value, but even ascending the scale and choosing from the wine list, you'll be surprised at the quality wines on offer at very moderate prices. Most wine lists don't just distinguish between **tinto** (red) or **branco** (white); they'll also list wines as either *verdes* (ie, young and slightly sparkling) or *maduros* (mature) – choose from the latter if you're after a red with a kick or a white with no bubbles.

Fortified wines: port and Madeira

Port (*vinho do Porto*) – the famous fortified wine – is produced from grapes grown in the valley of the Douro and stored in huge wine lodges at Vila Nova de Gaia, facing Porto across the Rio Douro. You can visit these for tours and free tastings; see p.303 for all the details. Alternatively, you can try any of three hundred types and vintages of port at the Instituto do Vinho do Porto (Port Wine Institute) bars in Lisbon (p.112) and lodges Porto (p.300). But even if your quest for port isn't serious enough to do either, be sure to try the dry white aperitif ports, still little known outside the country.

Madeira (*vinho da Madeira*), from Portugal's Atlantic island province, has been exported to Britain since Shakespeare's time – it was Falstaff's favourite tipple, known then as sack. Widely available, it comes in three main varieties: Sercial (a dry aperitif), Verdelho (a sweeter aperitif) and Bual or Malmsey (sweet, heavy dessert wines). Each improves with age and special vintages are greatly prized and priced.

Spirits (licor)

The national **brandy** is arguably outflanked by its Spanish rivals – which are sold almost everywhere – but the native spirit is available in two varieties (Macieira and Constantino), each with loyal followings. It's frighteningly cheap. Portuguese gin is weaker than international brands but again ridiculously inexpensive.

Local firewaters – generically known as **aguardente** – are more impressive. They include Bagaço (the fieriest), Figo (made from figs, with which it shares similar qualities when drunk to excess), Ginginha (made from cherries; watch out for the cherry, however, soaked in alcohol for years it has an incredible bite), and the very wonderful Licor Beirão (a kind of cognac with herbs). In the Algarve, the best known firewater is Medronho, a local brandy made from the strawberry tree, which tastes a bit like schnapps. Other local spirits include Algarviana, made from almonds; and brandymel, a honey brandy.

Beer

The most common Portuguese **beer** (*cerveja*) is Sagres in the south or Super Bock in the north, but there are a fair number of local varieties. If you're curious, they can all be tasted at the Silves Beer Festival, held in the Fábrica Inglês in summer (see p.552). For something unusual (and not recommended on a hot afternoon) try the Sagres Preta, which is a dark beer, resembling British brown ale.

When drinking draft beer order *um imperial* (or *um fino* in the north) if you want a regular glass; *uma caneca* will get you a half-litre. And when buying bottles, don't forget to take your empties back: they can represent as much as a third of the price!

Coffee, tea and soft drinks

Coffee (*café*) comes either black, small and espresso-strong (*uma bica* or simply *um café*); small and with milk (*um garoto* or *um pingo* in some parts of the north); or large and with milk but often disgustingly weak (*um galão*). For white coffee that tastes of coffee and not diluted warm milk, ask for "*um café duplo com um pouco de leite*".

Tea (*chá*) is usually plain; *com leite* is with milk, *com limão* with lemon, but *um chá de limão* is hot water with a lemon rind. *Chá* is a big drink in Portugal (which originally exported tea-drinking to England) and you'll find wonderfully elegant *casas de chá* dotted around the country.

All the standard **soft drinks** are available. Tri Naranjus is a good range of fruit drinks (excellent *limão*, lemon), and the fizzy Sumol is extremely fruity and appetizing. Fresh orange juice is *sumo de laranja* – add the word *fresca* to ensure you get the real thing. Lastly, mineral water (*água mineral*) is available almost anywhere in the country, either still (*sem gás*) or carbonated (*com gás*).

Communications

Portuguese postal services and telecommunications are reasonably priced and generally efficient. Hotels and businesses are not all on email, but internet access is becoming widespread.

Internet access

Internet cafés can be found in the larger towns and resorts, most charging around €2.50–4/hr. Most larger **post offices** have internet posts which you can access by debit card (around €2.50/hr), or by buying a prepaid net card with up to six hours' access for around €5.50. A similar setup exists in some municipal **libraries** (often in the town hall). In **Institutos da Juventude** (youth centres), access is generally free but limited to half an hour. See the guide for specific details of where to go online.

Postal services

Post offices (*correios*) are normally open Monday to Friday 8.30am–6pm, larger ones sometimes on Saturday mornings, too. The main Lisbon and Porto branches have much longer opening hours; see "Listings", pp.122–124. **Stamps** (*selos*) are sold at post offices, automatic dispensing machines and anywhere that has the sign of a red horse on a white circle over a green background and the legend *Correio de Portugal – Selos*. To send a card to Europe costs €0.55, €0.62 to anywhere else. Letters or cards take three or four days to arrive at destinations in Europe, and a week to ten days to North America.

You can have **poste restante** (general delivery) mail sent to you at any post office in the country. Letters should be marked Poste Restante, and your name, ideally, should be written with your surname first, in capitals and underlined. To collect, you need to take along your passport – look for the counter marked *encomendas*. If you are expecting mail, ask the postal clerk to check for letters under your first name and any other initials (including Ms, etc) as well as under your surname – filing can be erratic. There's a charge of around €1 per item.

Telephones

All calls, whether local or international, are most easily made using card-operated public phones called **credifones**, which you'll find in all but the most remote villages. Cards cost either €3, €6 or €9, and are available from post offices, newsagents, tobacconists and kiosks. There are also coin-operated phones but these are less convenient unless you have a lot of change.

You'll also find pay phones in bars and cafés (and, increasingly, in turismo offices and newsagents), usually indicated by the sign of a red horse on a white circle over a green background and the legend *Correio de Portugal – Telefone*. If you need quieter surroundings you'd be better off in one of the phone cabins found in most main post offices – simply tell the clerk where you want to phone, and pay for your call afterwards. Except in Lisbon and Porto, most telephone offices are closed in the evening. The cheap rate for international and national calls is between 9pm and 9am Monday to Friday, and all day weekends and holidays.

Reverse charge (collect) calls (*chamada cobrar ao destinatário*) can be made from any phone, dialling ☎120 for a European connection, ☎172 for the rest of the world. If you encounter difficulties, call ☎179.

The media

The two most established Portuguese daily **newspapers** are the Lisbon-based *Diário de Notícias* (⊛www.dn.pt) and the *Jornal de Notícias* (⊛www.jnoticias.pt) from Porto. They have their uses for listings information, even if you have only a very sketchy knowledge of the language. The stylish *Público* (⊛www.publico.pt) has good foreign news and regional inserts as well as fairly easy-to-read listings. For an interesting view of the

numbers

To phone abroad from Portugal

Dial 00 + country code (given below) + area code (minus initial zero) + number

Country codes

Australia 61	France 33	Ireland 353	UK 44
Canada 1	Germany 49	New Zealand 64	USA 1

To phone Portugal from abroad

Dial the international access code (see below) + 351 (country code) + number (nine digits)

International Access Code

Australia 0011	UK 00	New Zealand 00
Ireland 00	Canada 001	USA 001

Portugal's international dial code for mobile phones is 268.

Useful telephone numbers

Directory enquiries 118	Speaking clock 151
Emergency services 112	Tourist enquiries (freephone)
Operator (rest of the world) 179	800 296 296

country's culture, try *JL* (*Jornal de Letras*).

The *International Herald Tribune* and most British newspapers can be bought in the major cities and resorts, usually a day late. One or two domestic English-language magazines and newspapers pop up from time to time on the Algarve, none of them especially informative but occasionally useful for finding work.

Portuguese **television** has four domestic stations, which import many American and British shows – nearly always subtitled rather than dubbed. You also get *telenovelas* – soaps – often from Latin America, and compelling, if trashy, viewing even if you don't understand a word. Most bars and many hotels also have cable and satellite TV stations; sports channels are popular in bars, showing televised bullfights and football.

On the radio, you can pick up the BBC World Service, with hourly news, on 648KHz medium wave and 15.007MHz short wave (note that short-wave frequencies vary depending on the time of day). Voice of America is sporadically audible on 6040 on the 49m short wave band. Portugal also has a plethora of national and local radio stations, many of which play all the latest international hits as well as distinctive local sounds.

Opening hours and public holidays

Most stores and businesses, plus smaller museums and rural post offices, close for a good lunchtime break – usually from around 12.30pm to 2.30 or 3pm.

Banks are a rare exception, opening Monday to Friday 8.30am to 3pm. **Shops** generally open around 9am, and upon re-opening after lunch keep going until around 6pm; except in larger cities, they tend to close for the weekend at Saturday lunchtime. Larger **shopping centres**, however, stay open seven days a week, often until midnight. **Museums**, **churches** and **monuments** generally open from around 10am to 12.30pm and 2 to 6pm, though the larger ones stay open through lunchtime.

Almost all **museums** and **monuments**, however, are closed on Mondays (or Wednesdays for palaces). Restaurants tend to be closed on Sunday evenings or one day during the week.

The other thing to watch out for are **national public holidays** (see box) when almost everything is closed and transport services reduced. There are also local festivals and holidays (see opposite), when entire towns, cities and regions grind to a halt: for example June 13 in Lisbon and June 24 in Porto.

Public holidays

January 1 New Year's Day
Good Friday
April 25 Liberty Day, commemorating the 1974 Revolution
May 1 Labour Day
Corpus Christi Usually early June
June 10 Dia de Camões e das Comunidades

August 15 Feast of the Assumption
October 5 Republic Day
November 1 All Saints' Day
December 1 Celebrating independence from Spain in 1640
December 8 Immaculate Conception
December 25 Christmas Day

Festivals

Portugal maintains a remarkable number of folk customs which find their expression in local carnivals (*festas*) and traditional pilgrimages (*romarias*). Some of these have developed into wild celebrations lasting days or even weeks and have become tourist events in themselves; others have barely strayed from their roots.

Every region is different, but in the north especially there are dozens of village festivals, everyone taking the day off to celebrate the local saint's day or the harvest, and performing ancient songs and dances in traditional dress for no one's benefit but their own. Look out, too, for the great

feiras, especially at Barcelos (p.372). Originally they were markets, but as often as not nowadays you'll find a combination of agricultural show, folk festival, amusement park and, admittedly, tourist bazaar.

The festival list is potentially endless and only the major highlights are picked out

Major popular festivals

Among the biggest and best known of the country's popular festivals are:

January

Epiphany (6 Jan). The traditional crown-shaped cake *bolo rei* (king's cake) with a lucky charm and a bean inside is eaten; if you get the bean in your slice you have to buy the cake next year.

February

Carnaval Many areas are rekindling an interest in Rio-like processions; Lisbon and towns in the Algarve are good destinations.

May

Queima das Fitas (mid-May), celebrating the end of the academic year in Coimbra.

Fátima (May 13), Portugal's most famous pilgrimage; also in October; see p.183.

June

Feira Nacional da Agricultura at Santarém lasts for ten days (starting on the first Fri). Dancing, bullfighting and an agricultural fair; see p.197.

Festa de São Gonçalo in Amarante (1st weekend); see p.197.

Santos Popularos (Popular Saints) – celebrations in honour of Santo António (St Anthony, June 12–13), São João (St John, 23–24) and Pedro (St Peter, 29–29) throughout the country; Lisbon's biggest celebration is for Santo António while Porto's is for São João.

July

Festa do Colete Encarnado in Vila Franca de Xira, with Pamplona-style

running of bulls through the streets (first two weeks); see p.201.

August

Romaria da Nossa Senhora da Agonía in Viana do Castelo (third weekend); see p.382.

September

Romaria da Nossa Senhora dos Remédios in Lamego (pilgrimage Sept 6–8, though events start in last week of Aug and run through to mid-Sept); see p.341.

Feiras Novas, "New Fairs" in Ponte de Lima (2nd & 3rd weekend); see p.398.

October

Feira de Outubro in Vila Franca de Xira (first two weeks); more bull-running and fighting; see p.201.

Fátima (Oct 13); second great pilgrimage of the year; see p.183.

November

Feira Nacional do Cavalo (National Horse Fair) in Golegã; see p.195.

December

Christmas. The main Christmas celebration is midnight mass on December 24, followed by a traditional meal of *bacalhau*.

New Year's Eve. Individual towns organize their own events, usually with fireworks at midnight, and the new year is welcomed by the banging of pots and pans.

above although more of the best ones are listed in the guide. For more details on what's going on around you, check with the local turismo or buy either of the annual *Borda d'Água* or *Seringador* booklets, which are old-style almanacs detailing saints' days, star signs, eclipse predictions, gardening tips and, most importantly, all the country's annual fairs – available from stationers or tobacconists. Alternatively, consult the webpage ⓦ**www.rede-almanaque.pt/feiras**, although it is not regularly updated.

Among major national celebrations, Easter week, St Anthony and St John's Eve (June 12/13 and 23/24) stand out. All are celebrated throughout the country with religious processions. The former is most magnificent in Braga, where it is full of ceremonial pomp, while the latter tends to be a more joyous affair. In Lisbon, the Alfama becomes a giant street party. In Porto, where St John's Eve is the highlight of a week of celebration, everyone dances through the streets all night, hitting each other over the head with plastic hammers.

B

BASICS | Festivals

43

Sports and bullfighting

Portugal is famous as the home of some of Europe's top golf courses and tennis centres. Watersports are also popular, in particular surfing and windsurfing, while, away from the coast, the countryside provides ample opportunity for horse-riding, hiking and fishing. The country's national sport, however, is football and at times during the football season (September to June) more than half the nation will be tuned to the radio or watching that week's big match at a stadium or on TV. Bullfighting too has a loyal following, and the spectacle has a very distinct identity from its Spanish cousin.

Participatory sports

Although Portugal boasts some top-class **golf** courses, exclusivity is often the key word, and green fees are rarely under €60 for 18 holes. The best way to guarantee a round is to go on a special golf-holiday package (see pp.13–14) or stay at one of the hotels or villas attached to golf clubs, which usually charge guests discounted rates. For more information on the country's courses, see the excellent Ⓦwww.portugal-golf.pt and Ⓦwww.algarvegolf.net.

The biggest **windsurfing** (and surfing) destination is Guincho, north of Lisbon (see p.129), though the winds and currents here require a high level of expertise; Ericeira is another centre (see p.155). Windsurf boards are available for rent on most of the Algarve beaches and at the more popular northern and Lisbon coast resorts.

Tennis courts are a common feature of most larger Algarve hotels – their attraction being that you can play year-round. If you want to improve your game, the best intensive coaching is under the instruction of ex-Wimbledon pro Roger Taylor at the Vale do Lobo resort complex.

There are **horse-riding** stables dotted around throughout the country and many offer one hour or full day rides into the surrounding countryside. Prices start from around €15–20 for an hour's trek, rising to around €80–100 for a full day's trek, which usually includes a picnic lunch. For details of Centros Hipicos (riding schools) in a particular area, contact the local tourist office.

Anyone interested in **fishing** should head to the trout streams of the Minho and other northern regions; licences are available from local town halls.

There are several walks detailed in the guide but if you're planning a dedicated **walking holiday** you'd do best to get hold of a copy of *Walking in Portugal* (see p.607). Local tourist offices are another good bet as many produce walking **leaflets**, and can usually supply details of local organized tours.

For further information – and addresses of operators promoting **sporting holidays** – see p.13 and contact the Portuguese National Tourist Office for a copy of their *Sportugal* brochure.

Football

Portuguese **football** has a long and often glorious tradition of international and club teams. The country will host the European Football Championships in 2004, an event that has led to the upgrading or rebuilding of several stadia. The famous Estádio de Luz in Lisbon is due to be rebuilt, and a brand new one is planned for the Algarve.

The leading clubs, inevitably, hail from Lisbon (Benfica and Sporting) and Porto (FC Porto). Just about every Portuguese supports one of these three teams, paying scant attention to the lesser, local teams. Of these, Boavista, Porto's second team, has been most successful in recent years; other teams worth catching are Sporting Braga and Guimarães. If you want to see a league match, the season runs from September through to May. Tickets are inexpensive, and matches given due prominence in the local press. Indeed the national paper *Bola* deals with little else. The spectacle of a packed capacity football stadium puts bullfights somewhat in the shade.

Bullfights

The Portuguese **bullfight** is neither as commonplace nor as famous as its Spanish counterpart, but as a spectacle it's marginally preferable. In Portugal the bull isn't killed, but instead wrestled to the ground in a genuinely elegant, colourful and skilled display. After the fight, however, the bull is usually injured and it is always slaughtered later in any case. There is also a small but growing band of Portuguese bullfight fans who want to follow the Spanish model and have bulls killed in the ring. Indeed Pedrito, a leading Portuguese bullfighter, recently pushed the boundaries – and risked imprisonment or a £250,000 fine – by killing a bull in the ring at Moita, opposite Lisbon, and became a *cause célèbre* when the police threatened to arrest him for the act.

If you choose to go – and we would urge visitors not to support the events put on simply for tourist benefit on the Algarve – these are the basics.

A **tourada** opens with the bull, its horns padded or sheared flat, facing a mounted *toureiro* in elaborate eighteenth-century costume. His job is to provoke and exhaust the bull and to plant the dart-like *farpas* (or *bandarilhas*) in its back while avoiding the charge – a demonstration of incredible riding prowess. Once the beast is tired the *moços-de-forcado*, or simply *forcados*, move in, an eight-man team which tries finally to immobilize it. It appears a totally suicidal task – they line up behind each other across the ring from the bull and persuade it to charge them, the front man leaping between the horns while the rest grab hold and try to subdue it. It's as absurd as it is courageous, and often takes two or three attempts, the first tries often resulting with one or more of the *forcados* being tossed spectacularly into the air.

The great Portuguese bullfight centre is **Ribatejo**, where the animals are bred. If you want to see a fight, it's best to witness it here, amid the local aficionados, or as part of the festivals in Vila Franca de Xira and Santarém. The season lasts from around April to October. Local towns and villages in the Ribatejo also feature bull-running, through the streets, at various of their festivals; see Chapter Two for further details.

Trouble and the police

By European standards, Portugal is a remarkably crime-free country, though there's the usual petty theft in the cities and larger tourist resorts. Although Lisbon is one of the safer European capitals, you should take care in the Alfama and especially in its parks after dark. If you are robbed, whatever you do, don't resist. Hand over your valuables and run. Watch out also for pickpockets on public transport, something for which Lisbon is developing a bit of a reputation. Rental cars, too, are always prey to thieves: remove any rental company stickers and, wherever you park, don't leave anything visible in the car – preferably, don't leave anything in the car at all.

The police

There are three different authorities with which you might come into contact, though, in an emergency, the first policeman you see will be able to point you in the right direction. In Porto and Lisbon, the police force most likely to be of assistance will be the blue-uniformed **PSP** (*Polícia de Segurança Pública*), responsible among other things for incidents involving tourists. Outside these cities, you will have to rely on the **GNR** (*Guarda Nacional Republicana*) for help: they police

In an emergency, dial ☎112 for the police.

the rural areas, patrol the roads and motorways, and are responsible for overseeing all ceremonial occasions, like state visits, at which time they deck themselves out in magnificent dress uniforms. Ordinarily, though, they wear blue-grey uniforms and highly polished knee-length boots. If you require specialist help – work permits and the like – the local office of the **Serviço de Estrangeiros e Fronteiras** is the place to go.

What to do if you are robbed

If you do have anything stolen while in Portugal, you'll need to go to the police – primarily to file a **report**, which your insurance company will require before they'll pay out for any claims made on your policy. Police stations in Lisbon and other major towns are detailed in the various "Listings" sections throughout the guide.

You can't count on English being spoken by most of the local police personnel you may have occasion to meet, and since tourists can usually muster only a few basic words of Portuguese, confusion can easily arise. To this end, showing deference to a police officer is wise: the Portuguese still hold respect dear, and the more respect you show a figure in authority, the quicker you will be on your way.

Travellers with disabilities

Portugal is slowly coming to terms with the needs of travellers with disabilities, but you should not expect much in the way of special facilities. That said, the Portuguese themselves always seem ready to help and people will go out of their way to make your visit as straightforward as possible.

Facilities that do exist include adapted WCs and wheelchair facilities at airports and main train stations; a "dial-a-ride" system for wheelchair users in Lisbon, O Serviço Especial de Transporte de Deficientes (€1 per trip; Mon–Fri 6.30am–10pm, Sat & Sun 8am–10pm; ☎213 613 161, ⒲www.carris.pt), though two days' advance notice and a medical certificate is required; and reserved disabled parking spaces in main cities, where the Orange Badge will be recognized. Portuguese national tourist offices abroad can supply a list of wheelchair-accessible hotels and campsites. Once there, your first port of call in any town should be the local turismo, which will invariably find you a suitable hotel and, in smaller towns, may be able to organize your needs. It's worth bearing in mind that many of the cheap hotels in towns are located on the first floor, and often don't have lifts. All official buildings tend to have good wheelchair access, though some bars and restaurants have access via steps or beaches.

Useful addresses

Portugal

ARAC Rua Dr. António Cândido 8, 1097 Lisbon ☎213 563 836. Provides information on hire companies that have cars with adapted controls.
Secretariado Nacional de Reabilitação Av Conde de Valbom 63, 1000 Lisbon ☎217 936 517. Provides information on transport facilities and Lisbon access, but in Portuguese only.
Secretariado Nacional Para a Reabilitação e Integração das Pessas com Deficiêcia Av Conde Valbom 63 ☎217 929 500, ⒲www.snripd.mts.gov.pt. Government

organization that produces a comprehensive *Accessible Tourism Guide* featuring disabled-friendly travel agents, restaurants, clubs etc.
Wheeling Around the Algarve (Rodando Pelo Algarve) Rua 5 de Outubro 181, Apartado 3421, 8136 Almancil, Algarve ℡289 393 636. Private company organizing holiday accommodation, transport and sporting/leisure activities in the Algarve. All facilities are personally inspected before recommendation.

Britain

Access Travel 6 The Hillock, Astley, Lancashire M29 7GW ℡01942/888844, ⓦwww.access -travel.co.uk. Tour operator that can arrange flights, transfers and accommodation; suitable for disabled travelling in Portugal. ATOL bonded.
Holiday Care Service 2nd floor, Imperial Building, Victoria Rd, Horley, Surrey RH6 7PZ ℡01293/774535, ⓕ784647, ⓦwww.holidaycare.org.uk. Provides free lists of accessible accommodation abroad – European, American and long haul destinations. Information on financial help for holidays available.
ICEP 2nd floor, 22–25a Sackville St, London W1S 3DW ℡09063/640610, ⓔiceplondt@aol.com. Publishes a list of hotels in Portugal that are "without barriers or with few obstacles to wheelchair users".
Tripscope Alexandra House, Albany Rd, Brentford, Middlesex TW8 0NE ℡08457/585641,

ⓦwww.justmobility.co.uk/tripscope. This registered charity provides a national telephone information service offering free advice on UK and international transport for those with a mobility problem.

North America

Mobility International USA 451 Broadway, Eugene, OR 97401, voice and TDD ℡541/343-1284, ⓦwww.miusa.org. Information and referral services, access guides, tours and exchange programmes. Annual membership $35 (includes quarterly newsletter).
Society for the Advancement of Travel for the Handicapped (SATH), 347 5th Ave, Suite 610, New York, NY 10016 (℡212/447-7284 or 0027; ⓦwww.sath.org). Non-profit educational organization that has actively represented travellers with disabilities since 1976.

In Australia and New Zealand

ACROD (Australian Council for Rehabilitation of the Disabled) PO Box 60, Curtin ACT 2605 ℡ 02/6282 4333; 24 Cabarita Rd, Cabarita NSW 2137 ℡02/9743 2699. Provides lists of travel agencies and tour operators for people with disabilities.
Disabled Persons Assembly 4/173–175 Victoria St, Wellington, New Zealand ℡04/801 9100. Resource centre with lists of travel agencies and tour operators for people with disabilities.

Women travellers

The ruralism and small-town life of Portugal make it one of the most relaxed of the Latin countries for women travellers. Which is not to say that the Portuguese machismo is any less ingrained than in Spain or Italy, simply that it gets rather less of an outlet.

Portugal is rarely a dangerous place for women travellers, and only in the following few areas do you need to be particularly wary: parts of Lisbon (particularly around Cais do Sodré and the top end of Avenida da Liberdade at night), the darker alleys near the seafront in Porto and the streets immediately around train stations in the larger towns (tradi-

tionally the red-light districts), and some of the Algarve resorts where, like seaside resorts the world over, men congregate on the pick-up.

On the whole it's a rural country, often intensely traditional and formal to the point of prudishness. People may initially wonder why you're travelling on your own – especial-ly inland and in the mountains, where

47

Portuguese women rarely travel unaccompanied – but once they have accepted that you are a crazy foreigner you're likely to be welcomed, adopted, and even offered food in their homes.

By day **public transport** is good and quite safe; but remember to take the usual precautions at night on Lisbon's Metro and on the Cais do Sodré–Cascais coastal train line. If you are on your own or feel uncomfortable anywhere, you should be able to get around at night by taxi, which are very cheap outside the Algarve.

Local contacts

There are relatively few women's organizations in Portugal. The best contact is the **Comissão para a Igualdade e para os Direitos das Mulheres** Av da República 32-1°, 1000 Lisbon; ☎217 983 000, which maintains a watching brief on all aspects of women's lives in Portugal; members organize conferences and meetings, are very active in areas of social and legal reform, and are linked with feminists throughout the country.

Travelling with children

As in many southern European countries, children have a high profile in Portuguese society which largely revolves round family life. As a result, Portugal is very child-friendly and families will find it one of the easiest places for a holiday. The two main worries for parents in Portugal are cars – which as a rule don't observe pedestrian crossings – and the strong sun. Keep young kids covered up between 11am and 3pm and always apply a high factor sun cream.

Most **hotels and pensões** will happily provide extra beds or cots (ask for *um berço*) for children if notified in advance. There is usually no charge for children under 6 who share their parents' room, while discounts of up to fifty percent on accommodation for 6- to 8-year-olds – and under 12 in some cases – are not uncommon.

Children will be welcomed in most cafés and **restaurants** at any time of the day. Indeed, waiters often go out of their way to spend a few minutes entertaining restless children; toddlers may even find themselves being carried off for a quick tour of the kitchens while parents finish their meals in peace. However, changing facilities in restaurants, cafés and public toilets are non-existent, and when you do find them – such as in larger shopping centres – they are usu-

ally part of women's toilets only. Highchairs and menus specifically for children are scarce – though restaurants happily do half portions. In addition, restaurants rarely open much before 7.30pm, so kids will need to adjust to Portuguese hours; local children are still up at midnight.

For those with **babies**, fresh milk (*leite do dia*) is sold in larger shops and supermarkets; smaller shops and cafés usually stock UHT milk only. Nappies (*fraldas*) are widely available in supermarkets and pharmacies, as are formula milk, babies' bottles and jars of baby food.

Museums and most sights don't usually charge for small children. On **public transport**, under-5s go free while 5- to 11-year-olds travel half price on trains but pay full fare on metros and buses.

Senior travellers

BASICS | Gay travellers • Senior travellers

Senior travellers in Portugal are entitled to a range of benefits. Many sites and museums give generous discounts and it is always worth showing your senior citizen's card when asking for tickets.

Senior citizen's cards are not recognized for discounts on public transport, though they do allow fifty percent off the cost of the state railway's *bilhete turístico* (tourist pass), which allows unlimited transport on Portuguese trains (see p.27 for details).

Look out too for seasonal promotions for over-65s at the country's *pousadas* (state run inns, see p.32), with discounts of around thirty-five percent.

Contacts for senior travellers

In the UK

Saga Holidays ☏0130/377 1111, ⊛www.sagaholidays.com. The country's biggest and most established specialist in tours and holidays aimed at older people.

In the US

American Association of Retired Persons 601 E St, NW Washington, DC 20049 ☏1-800/424-3410 or 202/434-2277, ⊛www.aarp.org. Can provide discounts on accommodation and vehicle rental. Membership open to US and Canadian residents aged 50 or over for an annual fee of US $10 or $27 for three years. Canadian residents only have the annual option.
Saga Holidays 222 Berkeley St, Boston, MA 02116 ☏1-877/265-6862, ⊛www.sagaholidays .com. Specializes in worldwide group travel for seniors. Their Smithsonian Odyssey Tours have a more educational slant.

Gay travellers

Though traditionally a conservative and macho society, Portugal has become increasingly tolerant of homosexuality. However, coming out is still a problem, for many young gays as family attitudes remain predominantly traditional and visible gay scenes are only really present in the larger towns or international resorts. As there is no mention of homosexuality in law, gays have the same rights as heterosexuals by default and the legal age of consent is 16.

The best first point of call is the Lisbon-based Centro Comunitário Gay e Lesbica de Lisboa (☏218 873 918, ⊛www.ilga-portugal .org; Mon–Sat 4–8pm) which organizes gay events, mainly in the capital, but can also help with information and contacts. A good source for gay **listings** is ⊛www.ilga-portugal.org /guia or ⊛www.portugalgay.pt, though on the latter the information – in Portuguese – is not updated regularly.

Lisbon, of course, has a number of gay clubs and local gay beaches (see p.115), plus the *Blue Angel Hotel* (see p.69). The Algarve is probably more tolerant than other more conservative parts of the country and there are a couple of gay-only guest houses including the *Gay Guest House/Residencial Gil Vicente*, Rua Gil Vicente 26, Lagos (☎282 081 150, ✆ggh@netvisao.pt). For other accommodation and holiday details try ⊛www.gaytravel.co.uk, an online gay and lesbian **travel agent**, offering good deals on all types of holiday.

Working in Portugal

Portugal has employment problems of its own, and without a special skill you're unlikely to have much luck finding any kind of long-term work. One realistic option though is teaching English. For this a TEFL certificate is a distinct advantage, though you may find work without one. The biggest demand nowadays is for teaching English to children, especially in the smaller provincial towns. If you're already in Portugal you could just apply to individual schools or advertise your services privately, but even EU citizens should register with the Serviço de Estrangeiros e Fronteiras. Non-EU passport holders must apply for a work permit before they enter Portugal.

Working on the Algarve

As far as temporary jobs go, the most opportunities are in tourist-related work on the **Algarve**, which offer a range of ways of getting money, all of them dependent to some extent on your self-confidence and/or lack of scruples. Most obvious of the jobs is bar work. This is not easy to find – you'll stand the best chance in one of the many British-owned places – and even when you do, it often brings in barely enough money to live on. Better, at least in terms of time involved, is to try your hand walking the streets at night handing out nightclub invitations to holiday-makers. This work is available in most major resorts and is paid solely on commission, but it does leave you free during the day – and much of the night – to seek your own entertainment.

Which leads nicely into the biggest scam in the country – perhaps in Europe – of selling time shares. Here possibilities exist for making really big bucks, though not everyone, of course, strikes it rich. The work involves walking the streets in the major resorts inviting British tourist couples to view time-share resorts and villas. It is extremely tiring, soul-destroying and, at its most successful, pretty disreputable work, but earnings are on commission and this can add up to a fair living if you're the type who enjoys selling your own grandmother. Just ask the people who are already doing the job on the street what to do. They'll tell you how to find work and how depressing it is.

One last option is to head for the huge yacht marina at Vilamoura, which holds around a thousand craft surrounded by international bars and restaurants. You could try some of these, but it's even better to approach the yachties themselves. Almost all boat owners have hundreds of little tasks that need doing and, given the opportunity, will pay a few hundred euros to anyone presenting themselves as a handyman/woman. Mostly it's painting or scrubbing down decks – hardly skilled labour – but if you can convince someone you know what you're doing the quality of work you'll be given may improve. Between late September and early November, however, there's the chance of crewing to the Canaries or the Caribbean; for this sort of angle try the local bars as well as word of mouth. For the more menial odd jobs you just need persistence and a thick skin.

If you do decide to stay on in the Algarve to work, note that non-EU visitors can no longer simply hop over to Spain to get a visa extension, but must leave all European Schengen Treaty countries, and will not be permitted to return until six months after the start of your first stay. The only way to renew your visa, if reliable long-term employment beckons, is to go to one of the Serviço de Estrangeiros offices in Portimão, Albufeira or Faro.

Directory

Addresses Most addresses in Portugal consist of a street name and number followed by a storey number, eg, Rua de Afonso Henriques 34-3º. This means you need to go up to the third floor of no. 34 (US, fourth floor). An "esq" or "E" (standing for *esquerda*) after a floor number means you should go to the left; "dir" or "D" (for *direita*) indicates the apartment or office you're looking for is on the right. R/c stands for *rés-do-chão* (ground floor). *Esquina* means corner or junction. In rural areas, the address may simply consist of a house or building name followed by the area.

Baggage You can often leave bags at a train or bus station for a small sum while you look for rooms. On the whole the Portuguese are highly trustworthy, and even shopkeepers and café owners will keep an eye on your belongings for you. Or try the local turismo, which may agree to look after your bags for a while.

Beaches Beware of the heavy undertow on many of Portugal's western Atlantic beaches and don't swim if you see a red or yellow flag. The EU blue flag indicates that the water is clean enough to swim in – sadly, not always the case at many of Portugal's resorts. The sea is warmest on the eastern Algarve (ie the beaches east of Faro).

Contraception Condoms – *preservativos* – are widely available from street vending machines, as well as in pharmacies and supermarkets. In more rural, traditional places, you may have to ask and the pharmacist will set out an array on the counter, in the best formal Portuguese manner.

Dress Churches often require "modest dress" – which basically just means you shouldn't wear shorts or flimsy tops.

Emergencies Phone ☏ 112 for the emergency services. If you're involved in a road accident, use the nearest roadside orange-coloured SOS telephone – press the button and wait for an answer.

Film Going to the movies in Portugal is extremely cheap, and films are often shown with the original (usually English-language) soundtrack with Portuguese subtitles. Listings can be found in the local newspaper or on boards, invariably placed somewhere in the central square of every small town. Screenings are cheap, with reduced prices at matinées and at all Monday shows.

Laundry There are very few self-service launderettes, but loads of *lavandarias*, where you can get your clothes washed, mended, and ironed (overnight) at a fairly low cost. Some of these offer only a dry-cleaning service.

Swimming pools Every sizeable town has a swimming pool, usually outdoors, but you'll find that they are often closed from September to May.

Time Portugal now follows "British" time, ie GMT in winter and one hour ahead in summer. Clocks go forward one hour at the end of March and back an hour at the end of October.

Tipping Hotels and restaurants include a service charge but porters and maids expect something; cab drivers don't.

Toilets "Ladies" often charge and are clean, "Gentlemen" may look more aesthetic (lots of ironwork) and may be free, but are usually pretty unattractive inside. A sign that says *Retretes*, *Banheiro*, *Lavabos* or WC will head you in the right direction, then it's *homens* or *cabalheiros* for men and *senhoras* or *mulheres* for women. Ask for "*a casa do banho*" or "*um banheiro*" if in doubt.

Guide

Guide

Lisbon and around

CHAPTER 1 # Highlights

✳ **Tram #28** Ride the city's most scenic tram route. See p.65

✳ **Bairro Alto** The "high district" is packed with vibrant bars, clubs and restaurants. See p.77

✳ **Ribeira market** Bustling fresh food market with handicrafts, cooked food and live music. See p.77

✳ **Castelo de São Jorge** There's not much left of Lisbon's castle, but the views from its ramparts are stunning. See p.86

✳ **Alfama** The oldest and most atmospheric quarter; getting lost here is half the fun. See p.88

✳ **Gulbenkian Museum** An awe-inspiring collection of priceless art and antiquities. See p.93

✳ **Mosteiro dos Jerónimos** The magnificent Manueline complex houses the tomb of Vasco da Gama. See p.98

✳ **Lux** Dance till dawn, and beyond at one of Europe's coolest clubs. See p.113

✳ **Sintra** The wooded hilltop retreat is the traditional residence of the city's aristos. See p.132

✳ **A ferry to Cacilhas** Ride over the Tagus for Lisbon vistas and great seafood restaurants. See p.142

Lisbon and around

T here are few cityscapes as startling and eccentric as that of **Lisbon** (Lisboa). Built on a switchback of hills above the broad Tejo estuary, its quarters are linked by an amazing network of cobbled streets with outrageous gradients, up which crank trams and funiculars. Down by the river, you are lured across towards the sea by a vast, Rio-like statue of Christ, arms outstretched, whose embrace encompasses one of the grandest of all suspension bridges and a fleet of cross-river ferries. For visitors, it's hard not to see the city as an urban funfair, a sense heightened by the castle poised above the Alfama district's medieval, whitewashed streets; the fantasy Manueline architecture of Belém; the mosaics of the central Rossio square; and the multitude of Art Nouveau shops and cafés. Gentler than any port or capital should expect to be, almost provincial in feel and defiantly human in pace and scale, Lisbon is immediately likeable.

For much of the last century, the city stood apart from the European mainstream, an isolation that ended abruptly with the 1974 revolution, and still more so with Portugal's integration into the European Community (now the European Union) just over a decade later. Over the past hundred years, central Lisbon's population has more than doubled to over a million, one tenth of all Portuguese, with numbers boosted considerably after the Revolution by the vast influx of **refugees** – *retornados* – from Portugal's former African colonies of Angola, Cabo Verde, São Tomé e Principe, Guinea-Bissau and Mozambique. The *retornados* imposed a heavy burden on an already strained economy, especially on housing, but their overall integration is one of the chief triumphs of modern Portugal. Like the city's Brazilian contingent, the Portuguese Africans have also brought a significant cultural buoyancy. Alongside the traditional fado clubs of its Bairro Alto and Alfama quarters, Lisbon now has superb Latin and African bands, and a panoply of international restaurants and bars.

The 1755 Great Earthquake destroyed many of Lisbon's most historic buildings. The Romanesque **Sé** (cathedral) and the Moorish walls of the **Castelo de São Jorge** are fine early survivors, however, and there is one building from Portugal's Golden Age – the extraordinary **Mosteiro dos Jerónimos** at Belém – that is the equal of any in the country. Several museums demand attention, too: the **Fundação Calouste Gulbenkian**, a combined museum and cultural complex with superb collections of ancient and modern art, and the **Museu Nacional de Arte Antiga**, effectively Portugal's national art gallery. Smaller, but impressive in its own way, is the **Design Museum** in Belém, with an extraordinary collection of contemporary design gems. Another modern highlight is the **Oceanarium** – Europe's largest – at the former Expo site of Parque das Nações. There are numerous smaller museums too,

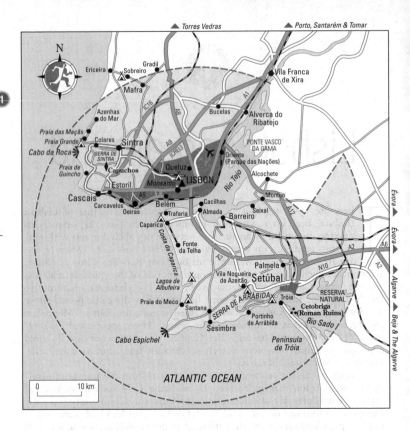

but beyond these sights, it's the central streets, avenues and squares, and their attendant comings and goings, that keep the interest level high; watch out, too, for some adventurous contemporary architecture, such as Tómas Taveira's shopping complex at **Amoreiras** and the award-winning buildings at the **Parque das Nações**.

All of this makes for a city that demands at least a few days out of anyone's Portuguese itinerary. Better still, make the capital a base for a week or two's holiday, taking day trips and excursions out into the surrounding area. The sea is close by, with the beach suburbs of **Estoril** and **Cascais** just half an hour's journey away to the west by train; while to the south, across the Tejo, are the miles of dunes along the **Costa da Caparica**. Slightly further south lies the port of **Setúbal**, featuring one of the earliest Manueline churches, and nearby is the resort of Sesimbra – a popular day trip for Lisboetas. Northwest of the city, again easily reached by train, lie the lush wooded heights and royal palaces of **Sintra**, Byron's "glorious Eden". And, should you have an interest in Portuguese architecture, there are the Rococo delights of the **Palácio de Queluz** and its gardens en route to Sintra, or the extraordinary monastery of **Mafra** – a good first step into Estremadura, the region immediately to the north.

Lisbon

P hysically, central **LISBON** is an eighteenth-century city: elegant, open to the sea and carefully planned. The description does not extend to its modern expanse, of course – there are suburbs here as poor and inadequate as any in Europe – but remains accurate within the old central boundary of a triangle of hills. This "lower town", the **Baixa**, was the product of a single phase of building, carried out in less than a decade by the dictatorial minister, the Marquês de Pombal, in the wake of the earthquake that destroyed much of central Lisbon in 1755.

The **Great Earthquake**, which was felt as far away as Jamaica, struck Lisbon at 9.30am on November 1 (All Saints' Day) 1755, when most of the city's population was at Mass. Within the space of ten minutes there had been three major tremors and the candles of a hundred church altars had started fires that raged throughout the capital. A vast tidal wave swept the seafront, where refugees were seeking shelter and, in all, 40,000 of the 270,000 population died. The destruction of the city shocked the continent, prompting Voltaire, who wrote an account of it in his novel *Candide*, into an intense debate with Rousseau on the operation of providence. For Portugal, and for the capital, it was a disaster that in retrospect seemed to seal an age. Previously, eighteenth-century Lisbon had been arguably the most active port in Europe.

Indeed, the city had been prosperous since **Roman**, perhaps even **Phoenician**, times. In the Middle Ages, as **Moorish** Lishbuna, it thrived on its wide links with the Arab world, while exploiting the rich territories of the Alentejo and Algarve to the south. The country's reconquest by the Christians in 1147 was an early and dubious triumph of the Crusades, its one positive aspect being the appearance of the first true Portuguese monarch **Afonso Henriques**. It was not until 1255, however, that Lisbon took over from Coimbra as the capital.

Over the following centuries Lisbon was twice at the forefront of European development and trade, on a scale that is hard to envisage today. The first phase came with the great Portuguese **discoveries** of the late **fifteenth** and **sixteenth** centuries, such as Vasco da Gama's opening of the sea route to India. The second was in the opening decades of the **eighteenth century**, when the colonized Brazil was found to yield both gold and diamonds. These phases were the great ages of Portuguese patronage. The sixteenth century was dominated by the figure **Dom Manuel I**, under whom the flamboyant national architectural style known as **Manueline** (see box on p.190) developed. Lisbon takes its principal monuments – the tower and monastery at Belém – from this era. The eighteenth century, more extravagant but with less brilliant effect, gave centre stage to **Dom João V**, best known as the obsessive builder of Mafra, which he created in response to Philip II's El Escorial in Spain.

The city in the **nineteenth** and early **twentieth** centuries was more notable for its political upheavals – from the assassination of Carlos I in 1908 to the Revolution in 1974 – than for any architectural legacy, though the **Art Nouveau** movement made its mark on the capital. In the last two decades, however, Lisbon has once more echoed to the sounds of incoming money and reconstruction on a scale not seen for two hundred years. After the influx of EU cash for economic regeneration in the 1980s came the recognition of Lisbon as **European City of Culture** in 1994, with new arts facilities giving

LISBON

ACCOMMODATION

Alegria	21	As Janelas Verdes	29
Avenida Alameda	10	Lapa Palace	27
Britania	16	Lar do Areeiro	1
Canadá	3	Lisboa Plaza	20
Dom Carlos	13	Miraparque	9
Dom Sancho I	18	Monumental	23
Fenix	14	Orion Eden	26
Florescente	22	O Paradouro	11
Impala	4	Pascoal de Melo	8
Imperial	25	Pátria	2
Rex	7	Suiço Atlântico	24
Ritz Four Seasons	12	Tivoli Lisboa	15
São Pedro	5	Veneza	17
		York House	28
		Youth Hostel	6
		13ª da Sorte	19

Map labels: Airport, Roma Metro, Campo Grande & Museu da Cidade, Zoo, Aqueduto das Águas Livres, AREEIRO, PENHA DE FRANÇA, CAMPO PEQUENO, ALAMEDA, ARROIOS, ESTEFANIA, PICOAS, SALDANHA, PARQUE, S. SEBASTIÃO, Entrecampos Station, Praça de Touros, Feira Popular, Culturgest, Bus Station, Museu Dr A. Gonçalves, Esturas, Parque Eduardo VII, Museu Gulbenkian, Centro de Arte Moderna, Fundação Arpad-Szenes, Amoreiras

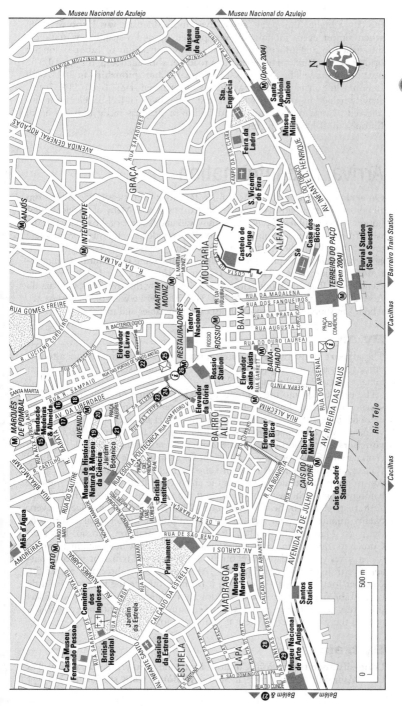

▲ Museu Nacional do Azulejo   ▲ Museu Nacional do Azulejo

▼ Barreiro Train Station

▼ Belém & 27   ▼ Belém

61

the city a higher European profile. Even more dramatic was **Expo** in 1998, when almost every monument was spruced up and a major new transport infrastructure put into place, including the construction of Europe's longest bridge, new rail and metro lines and a road network encircling the capital. The next milestone will be the football **European Championships** in 2004, with Lisbon as the main venue at two newly constructed stadia (see p.119). If this activity helped in some ways to diminish the provincial feel of the city, it also injected a wave of excitement and optimism that has made Lisbon one of Europe's most happening cities.

Arrival and information

On **arrival**, the first place to head for is Rossio, which is easily accessible from all points of arrival, either on foot, by metro, bus or taxi. Many of the city's guest houses (*pensões* and *residenciais*) are within walking distance of the square. On the western side of the adjoining Praça dos Restauradores is the main Portuguese tourist board in the Palácio da Foz (daily 9am–8pm; ☎213 463 314; ⓦwww.portugalinsite.pt) which is helpful in providing **information** on destinations outside Lisbon. The main Lisbon tourist office, the Lisbon Welcome Centre is in Praça do Comércio (see p.73) down by the riverfront, on Rua do Arsenal 15 (daily 9am–8pm; ☎210 312 700, ⓦwww.atl-turismolisboa.pt), which can supply accommodation lists, bus timetables and maps.

By air

The **airport** is just twenty minutes north of the city centre and has a tourist office (daily 6am–midnight; ☎218 450 657), 24-hour exchange bureau and car rental agencies (see "Listings" p.122).

The easiest way into the centre is by **taxi**; depending on traffic conditions a journey to Rossio should cost €70–100. Note that you'll be charged €1.50 extra for baggage, and that fares are slightly higher between 10pm and 6am, at weekends and on public holidays. The tourist office at the airport also sells **taxi vouchers**, priced according to the zone you are travelling to (€110 for the central zone, €140 for zone 2, to Belém for example, and €330 to Estoril and Cascais; extra supplements for each zone for night travel). The vouchers allow you to jump the queue for taxis at the airport and help you establish the cost beforehand but otherwise they work out more expensive than normal rides.

Alternatively, catch the #91 **Aerobus** (☎966 298 558), which departs every twenty minutes between 7am and 9pm from outside the terminal, and runs to Praça do Marquês de Pombal, Praça dos Restauradores, Rossio, Praça do Comércio and Cais do Sodré train station. The **ticket**, which you buy from the driver, gives you one day's travel on the city's buses and trams for €2.30 (available free from the Welcome Desk for TAP passengers), or three days' for €5.50. Cheaper **local buses** (#44 or #45) leave from outside the terminal – a little beyond the Aerobus stop – to Praça dos Restauradores and Cais do Sodré station every ten to fifteen minutes between 6am and midnight and cost €0.85, though these are less convenient if you have a lot of luggage.

By train

Long-distance trains from Coimbra, Porto and northern Portugal, as well as from Madrid and Paris, arrive at **Santa Apolónia train station** (☎218 884

142), from where it's about fifteen minutes' walk west to Praça do Comércio or a bus ride (buses #9, #39, #46 or #90 for Praça dos Restauradores or Rossio). From 2004 it will also be on the Gaivota metro line. At the station there's a helpful information office (Mon–Sat 9am–7pm; ☎218 821 604) and an exchange bureau. An increasing number of trains call at **Oriente** station east of the centre, at the old Expo site, now called the Parque das Nações; on the red Oriente metro line, this station is more convenient for the airport and for the north or east of Lisbon.

There are plans to open a new rail bridge over the Tejo and to extend the commuter rail route under the Ponte 25 de Abril so it links up with the Algarve line, but for the time being trains from the Algarve and the south of Portugal still terminate opposite Lisbon at **Barreiro train station** (☎212 073 028), on the far bank of the river, from where you catch a ferry (included in the price of the train ticket) to the **Fluvial ferry station** (also known as Sul e Sueste), next to Praça do Comércio. Buses #9, #39, #80 and #90 run up from Fluvial to Rossio, through the Baixa. From 2004 Praça do Comércio will also be on the Gaivota metro line.

Local trains – from Sintra or Queluz – emerge right in the heart of the city at **Rossio train station** (☎213 465 022), a mock-Manueline complex with train platforms an improbable escalator-ride above street-level entrances. The station is complete with shops, bank exchange counters and left-luggage cabins. Services from Cascais and Estoril arrive at the other local station, **Cais do Sodré train station** (☎213 470 181), also fairly central – you can either walk the half kilometre east along the waterfront to Praça do Comércio or take any of the buses heading in that direction. The station also has its own metro stop.

By bus

Various bus companies have terminals scattered about the city, but the main terminal is at **Avenida João Crisóstomo** (metro Saldanha; ☎213 545 439), north of the centre, which has an information office that can help with all bus arrival and departure details. This terminal is also where most **international bus services** arrive. You can usually buy tickets if you turn up half an hour or so in advance, though for the summer express services to the Algarve it's best to book a seat (through any travel agent) a day in advance. An increasing number of bus services also use the **Oriente** transport interchange at Parque das Nações on the red Oriente metro line. See "Listings" for other bus terminals in the city, and check with the turismo for the latest details.

By car

Driving into Lisbon can take years off your life, and if it's the beginning or end of a public holiday weekend should be avoided at all costs. Heading to or from the south on these occasions, it can take over an hour just to cross the Ponte 25 de Abril, a notorious traffic bottleneck that the new Vasco da Gama bridge has done little to alleviate. **Parking** is also very difficult in the centre. Pay-and-display bays get snapped up, and many unemployed people earn tips for guiding cars into any available space (give a small tip – a euro should do it – to avoid finding any unpleasant scratches on your car when you return).

You'd be wise to head straight for an official **car park**: central locations include the underground one at Restauradores; Parque Eduardo VII; the underground car parks around the Gulbenkian such as Parking Berna on Rua Marquês de Sá da Bandeira; and the Amoreiras complex on Avenida Eng. Duarte Pacheco. Expect to pay around €8 per day. Wherever you park, do not leave valuables inside: the break-in rate is extremely high.

If you are **renting a car** on arrival, for touring outside Lisbon, the best advice is to wait until the day you leave the city to pick it up; you really don't need your own transport to get around Lisbon. See "Listings" on p.122 for car rental companies and remember to leave plenty of time if returning your car to the airport: paperwork is time-consuming.

City transport

Most places of interest are within easy walking distance of each other, but for those that are further away transport connections by tram, bus, ferry or metro are outlined in the relevant accounts. Taxis are among the cheapest in Europe and a useful complement at all hours. Although Lisbon ranks among one of the safer European cities it too has its share of **pickpockets**, so take special care over your belongings when using the metro and buses, and when walking around the main squares.

Apart from taxis and the metro, **public transport** in the city is operated by Carris (℡213 632 044, ⓦwww.carris.pt). You can buy a day **travel day pass** (*bilhete turístico*) for just €2.50, which allows unlimited travel on buses, trams, *elevadores* and the metro until midnight of that day. You can also buy a three-day *bilhete turístico* for €5.50, but confusingly this is not valid on the metro. The **Passe Turístico** (€9.25 for four days, €13.10 for seven days) is also good value. It's valid on the metro, trams, buses and *elevadores*, and is obtainable – like the one-day pass – at kiosks next to the Elevador Santa Justa, in Praça da Figueira and in Restauradores metro station, among other places. If you're planning some intensive sightseeing, consider a **Lisbon Card** (Cartão Lisboa; €11 for one day, €18 for two, or €23 for three). The card entitles you to unlimited rides on buses, trams, metro and *elevadores* and entry to around 25 museums, including the Gulbenkian and Museu de Arte Antigua, plus discounts of around 25–50 percent to other main sites. It's available from all the main tourist office (see p.62), including the one in the airport. Otherwise, just buy a **single ticket** (*bilhete simples*) each time you ride: all the details are given below.

The metro and local trains

Lisbon's **metro** – the Metropolitano – was radically restructured for Expo 98 and is now the slickest way to reach outlying sights, including the Gulbenkian museum, the zoo, and the Oceanarium. The most central metro stations are those at Restauradores, Rossio and Baixa-Chiado. The **hours of operation** are from 6.30am to 1am and **tickets** cost €0.50 per journey, or €4.50 for a ten-ticket *caderneta* – sold at all stations. If you think you're going to use the metro a lot, buy a **one-day pass** (*bilhete diário*; €1.40) or the mixed-tram/bus/metro options above.

There is a **local train** line originating from Cais do Sodré station, which runs west along the coast to Belém (see p.97) or to Estoril (see p.126) and Cascais (see p.126). You can also by a three-day pass on the **Cascais train line** (€5.10) which is worth considering if you are staying in the resorts of Carcavelos, Estoril or Cascais. Individual tickets to Estoril and Cascais are currently €1.05 one way. The other local train line you're likely to use is the service to Queluz (see p.139; €0.70 one way) and Sintra (see p.130; €1.05 one way), which departs from the central Rossio station.

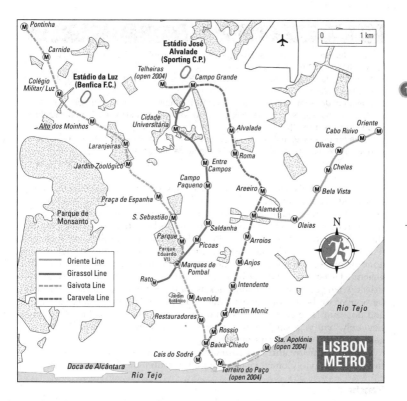

Oriente Line
Girassol Line
Gaivota Line
Caravela Line

LISBON
METRO

Trams, elevadores and buses

At the slightest excuse you should ride one of the city's **trams** (*eléctricos*). Ascending some of the steepest gradients of any city in the world, Lisbon's five tram routes are worth taking for the sheer pleasure of the ride alone. The best route is **#28**, which runs from Largo Martim Moniz to Prazeres, though the most interesting stretch is from São Vicente to the Estrela gardens, passing through Rua da Conceição in the Baixa – possibly the best public transport ride in the city. Other useful (and interesting) routes include the **#12** which circles the Castelo de S. Jorge via the Alfama, Praça da Figueira and Largo Martim Moniz; and the new modern "supertram" **#15** from Praça da Figueira to Algés via Belém. Tram **#18** runs from Rua da Alfândega via Praça do Comércio and Cais do Sodré to the Palácio da Ajuda; and the remaining route, **#25**, runs from Rua da Alfândega to Campo Ourique via Praça do Comércio, Cais do Sodré, Lapa and Estrela.

The three funicular railways and one street lift – each known as an **elevador** – are also exciting forms of transport and offer quick access up to Lisbon's highest hills and the Bairro Alto (see box below for their routes). Otherwise, **buses** (*autocarros*) run just about everywhere in the Lisbon area and can prove valuable for getting to and from the more outlying attractions. Most of the trams, buses and *elevadores* run every ten to fifteen minutes throughout the day, from around 6.30am to midnight: stops are indicated by a sign marked *paragem*, which carries route details.

Elevadores

Elevador da Bica: funicular linking Calçada do Coimbro in Barrio Alto to Rua da Boavista near Cais do Sodré station.

Elevador da Glória: a funicular linking the Bairro Alto with the west side of Praça dos Restauradores.

Elevador de Santa Justa: a lift, rather than a funicular, taking you from Rua do Ouro, on the west side of the Baixa, up to a walkway by the ruined Carmo church; due to reopen shortly.

Elevador do Lavra: funicular linking Rua São José, just off Av da Liberdade, to the back of the Institute of Medicine and Hospital de São José.

Individual **tickets** (*bilhetes*, also known as BUCs, pronounced *books*) for buses, trams and *elevadores* are best value when bought in advance. The same tickets are valid on buses, trams and *elevadores* (though not on the metro or ferries); they can be bought either individually or in blocks of ten from kiosks around the main bus terminals, such as in Praça do Comércio and Praça da Figueira. These cost €0.85 each, and are valid for two journeys within a single travel zone or one journey across two travel zones (such as from the city centre to Belém). Tickets are validated by putting them into the machine next to the driver when you board. Individual tickets for buses, trams and *elevadores* can also be bought on board (the modern tram #15 has an automatic ticket machine and does not issue change). These also cost €0.85, but are valid for one journey only within a single travel zone – much more than those bought in advance. See p.64 for details of passes.

A couple of **tram and bus tours** run during the summer months, departing from Praça do Comércio; for more information see "Listings".

Taxis

Lisbon's cream or (older) black-and-green **taxis** are inexpensive, so long as your destination is within the city limits; there's a minimum charge of €1.80 and an average ride will run to around €4–5. Fares are higher from 10pm to 6am, at weekends and on public holidays. All taxis have meters, which should be switched on, and tips are not expected. A green light means the cab is occupied. Outside the rush hour they can be found quite easily in the street, or alternatively head for one of the ranks in around the centre including outside the stations; at Rossio and Praça da Figueira; at the southern end of Avenida de Liberdade; and Estação Fluvial, though expect to queue during morning and evening rush hours. At night, you're best bet is to ask a restaurant or bar to phone one for you, or phone yourself (which entails €0.80 extra charge): try Rádio Taxis (☎218 119 000), Autocoope (☎217 932 756) or Teletáxi (☎218 111 100).

Ferries

Finally there are the **ferries**, which cross the Tejo at various points and are worth taking for the terrific views of Lisbon alone. From **Praça do Comércio** (Fluvial; due to reopen in 2004 after metro tunnelling is complete), there are crossings to Cacilhas (every 15min: Mon–Fri 6.10am–21.45, Sat & Sun 6.15am–9.50pm; €0.55 one way), Barreiro for train connections to Algarve and the south (every 20–30min, same hours; €1) and Montijo (every 30min: Mon–Fri 6.30am–11.30pm, Sat 7am–10pm, Sun 9.45am–10pm; €1.55). Ferries also run from **Cacilhas** to **Parque das Nações**, the old Expo site (Mon–Fri 6 daily, Sat & Sun 8 daily; €1.10). From **Cais do Sodré**, car ferries also cross to Cacilhas (every 5–10min: daily 5.30am–2.30am; €0.55 one way). From **Belém** there are services to Trafaria (every 30min–1hr: Mon–Sat 6.30am–11.30pm, Sun 7.30am–11.30pm; €0.55 one way), from where you can catch buses to Caparica.

Accommodation

The **airport information desk**, facing you as you pass through customs, or any of the turismos in town, will establish whether or not there's space at a city *pensão* or hotel; they won't reserve the room for you but will supply telephone numbers if you want to phone yourself. For more information on the various types of accommodation available see "Basics" p.31.

Lisbon has scores of small, inexpensive **pensões**, often in tall tenement buildings, in all the central parts of the city. The most obvious and accessible areas, with dozens of possibilities, are around Rossio, Praça dos Restauradores and Praça da Figueira. Among cheaper *pensões*, the most likely to have space during busy times of the year are those on streets parallel to Avenida da Liberdade, such as Rua das Portas de Santo Antão and Rua da Glória. The Baixa grid, to the south, has a fair selection of places, too, with a couple of more upmarket choices in the Chiado's shopping streets. Bairro Alto is the best place to stay to be in the thick of the nightlife, though rooms in its few *pensões* can be both hard to come by and noisy. If you want to stay in the most atmospheric part of town there are a few attractive places on the periphery of the Alfama, climbing up towards the castle. Finally, a number of more expensive **hotels** are located outside of the historic centre: in the prosperous streets in the suburb of Lapa; around Parque Eduardo VII and Saldanha, where many places are geared to the business traveller; or to the east, towards the airport, in the area around Avenida Almirante Reis – in particular the streets between Anjos and Arroios metro stops.

When doing the rounds, be warned that the *pensões* tend to be on upper storeys (leaving one person with all your bags is a good idea if you're in company). **Addresses** – written below as 53-3° and so on – refer to the street number followed by the storey number. Don't be unduly put off by some fairly insalubrious staircases, but do be aware that rooms facing onto the street can be unbearably noisy.

Lisbon has several **youth hostels**, two close to the city centre, one out at Oeiras, overlooking the sea, another over the river at Almada, as well as one more in Sintra. For details of these, and the city's **camping** possibilities, see pp.71–72.

At Easter, and even more so in midsummer, room **availability** is often stretched to the limit, with artificially inflated prices – though August can be less expensive as many people head for the beach. At peak times, be prepared to take anything vacant – within reason – and, if need be, look around the next day for somewhere better, or possibly cheaper. Fortunately, for most of the year you should have little difficulty finding a room, and can even try knocking the price down at quieter times, especially if you're able to summon up a few good-natured phrases in Portuguese.

Metro stops

Metro stops are given in these reviews only when they are the most convenient way to reach the hotel, restaurant or bar. Otherwise, for places that are central, taking a bus or one of the *elevadores*, or walking, is probably the best option.

Rossio and Praça da Figueira

All the hotels and pensões *listed below are marked on the Baixa map on p.74.*

Arco da Bandeira Rua dos Sapateiros 226-4° ☎213 423 478. Friendly pension with half a dozen simple but comfortable rooms, some overlooking Rossio. The separate bathrooms are spotless. The entrance is just through the arch at the southern end of the square. ❸

Avenida Palace Rua 1° de Dezembro ☎213 460 151, ⓔhotel.av.palace@mail.telepac.pt. Lisbon's grandest downtown hotel, tucked away between Rossio and Praça dos Restauradores. Elegant nineteenth-century style with modern touches, and very comfortable rooms sporting high ceilings, traditional furnishings and marble bathrooms. ❽

Beira Minho Praça da Figueira 6-2° ☎213 461 846. Rooms in this *pensão* (with and without bath) are small but clean and some have fine views, though a few of the cheaper ones have no windows. Price includes breakfast. ❸

Coimbra e Madrid Praça da Figueira 3-3° ☎213 421 760, Ⓕ213 423 264. Large, decently run (if faintly shabby) *pensão*, above the *Pastelaria Suíça*. Superb views of Rossio, Praça da Figueira and the castle beyond from – street-honkingly noisy – front-facing rooms, which come with shower or bath. Best choice on the square. Breakfast included. ❹

Residencial Gerês Calçada da Garcia 6 ☎218 810 497, Ⓕ218 882 006. Set on a steep side street just off Rossio. The beautifully tiled entrance hall set the tone of the city's more characterful central guest houses. Varying-sized rooms are simple but clean, all have TVs. En-suite rooms ❹, otherwise ❸

Pensão Ibérica Praça da Figueira 10-2° ☎218 865 781, Ⓕ218 867 412. Central location and lots of rooms, most with TVs, but it's a bit ramshackle and has gloomy, uninspiring decor. The rooms overlooking the Praça are the best, if the noisiest. ❸

International Rua da Betesga 3 ☎213 461 913, Ⓕ213 478 635. You know this is a smart central hotel as soon as you see the red-carpeted lift, and if you get one of the rooms with a balcony overlooking the town, you won't be disappointed. Rooms have air conditioning, TV and a safe. ❹

Metrópole Rossio 30 ☎213 469 164, Ⓕ213 469 166. Turn-of-the-century hotel, very centrally located and with most rooms, and an airy lounge bar, offering superb views over Rossio and the castle beyond. Comfortable en-suite rooms, but you pay for the location, and the square can be pretty noisy at night. ❼

Mundial Rua Dom Duarte 4 ☎218 842 000, ⓦwww.hotel-mundial.pt. Central four-star hotel with nearly 300 plush rooms. Rooftop restaurant, disabled access and all mod cons. ❻

Portugal Rua João das Regras 4 ☎218 877 581, Ⓕ218 867 343. An amazing old hotel that has suffered from an appalling conversion; the high decorative ceilings upstairs have been chopped up under wall partitions. For all that, there are comfortable rooms, a lovely ornate TV room and fine *azulejo*-lined stairs. ❹

Residencial do Sul Praça Dom Pedro IV 59 ☎213 422 511, Ⓕ218 132 697. Entered through a small shop, this is very close to the station, and a good first choice if you want a view of Rossio itself. It's very clean and there are quieter back rooms, though some are windowless. ❸

The Baixa and Chiado

All the hotels and pensões *listed below are marked on the Baixa map on p.74.*

Borges Rua Garrett 108 ☎213 461 951, Ⓕ213 426 617. A traditional hotel in a handy position for Chiado's shops and cafés, though the rooms are very ordinary and the hotel often fills with tour groups. Breakfast included. ❺

Duas Nações Rua da Vitória 41 ☎213 460 710, Ⓕ213 470 206. Classy, pleasantly faded, nineteenth-century hotel in the Baixa grid with a secure entrance and friendly reception. Rooms without bath ❷, en suite ❸

Galicia Rua do Crucifixo 50-4° ☎ & Ⓕ213 428 430. The entrance to this *pensão* is through a shoe repair stall, which you may be in need of once you've been up and down the steep stairs a few times. Small rooms – the best have sunny balconies and wooden floors – but surly owners and dodgy drains. ❷

Insulana Rua da Assunção 52 ☎213 427 625. Reached through a series of underwear shops, this decent *residencial* has smart rooms, each with its own bath. The bar overlooks a quiet pedestrianized street. English-speaking staff. Good breakfasts, too. ❸

Hotel Lisboa Regency Rua Nova do Almada 114 ☎213 256 100, ⓔeregencychiado@ madeiraregency.pt. Stylish hotel designed by Álvaro Siza Viera – the architect responsible for the Chiado redevelopment with eastern-inspired interior decor. The cheapest rooms lack much of a view, but the best ones have terraces with stunning views of the castle – a view you get from the bar terrace too. All rooms have fax, modems and pay TV. ❼

Moderna Rua dos Correeiros 205-4° ☎213 460 818. The stairwell is offputting but rooms in this *pensão* are big, clean and crammed with old furniture. Some have (rickety) balconies overlooking the pedestrianized street. Communal bathrooms. ❷

Prata Rua da Prata 71-3° ☎213 468 908. You need mountaineering experience to climb the stairs to this *pensão*, which offers small rooms in a welcoming, family-run apartment with TV lounge. Some rooms have showers, others share a clean bathroom. It's in a handy location for Praça do Comércio. Book in advance as it's popular. ❷

Bairro Alto and Príncipe Real

All the pensões *listed below are marked on the Bairro Alto map on pp.78–79.*

Blue Angel Hotel Rua Luz Soriano 75 ☎213 478 069. This is the city's first exclusively gay hotel; small and classy with neat rooms right in the heart of the area's nightlife, which can make it noisy. ❸

Residencial Camões Trav. do Poço da Cidade 38-1° ☎213 467 510, ℱ213 464 048. Small *residencial* with a mixed bag of rooms, some with balcony and the more expensive ones with private bathroom. Situated right in the midst of the Bairro Alto action (which can up the noise level). Without bathroom ❷, en suite ❸

Casa de São Mamede Rua da Escola Politécnica 159 ☎213 963 166, ℱ213 951 896. Superb seventeenth-century town house with period fittings, bright breakfast room and even a grand stained-glass window. Rooms are rather ordinary but come with private bathrooms and TVs. ❺

Pensão Duque Calçada do Duque 53, ☎ & ℱ213 463 444. Near São Roque church, down the steps off Largo T. Coelho heading down to Rossio, so clear of the nightlife noise. It has basic but spotless rooms, with shared bathrooms. ❷

Pensão Globo Rua do Teixeira 37 ☎213 462 279. Up Travessa da Cara from the Elevador da Glória and first right. Located in an attractive house, the rooms are simple but clean and reasonably large (though those at the top are a little cramped). It's in a good location, near the clubs but in a quiet street. Cheaper rooms are without shower or windows, more expensive ones have showers and views. ❷–❸

Pensão Londres Rua Dom Pedro V 53 ☎213 462 203, ℱ213 465 682. Great old building with high ceilings and pleasant enough rooms spread across several price ranges and floors. Some rooms come with cubby-hole bathrooms. Breakfast included. ❷–❸

Pensão Luar Rua das Gavéas 101-1° ☎213 460 949. Calm, polished interior and decently furnished rooms (with and without shower), which are some-

what noisy. Some are much larger than others, so ask to see. ❸

Lapa

To reach these superb hotels (marked on the general map of Lisbon on pp.60–61, take bus #40 or #60 or tram #25 from Praça do Comércio.

As Janelas Verdes Rua das Janelas Verdes 47 ☎213 968 143, ℮jverdes@heritage.pt. This discreet eighteenth-century town house, where novelist Eça de Queirós wrote *Os Maios* (see box p.80), is just metres from the Museu Nacional de Arte Antiga. There are well-proportioned rooms with marble-clad bathrooms, period furnishings, and a delightful walled garden with a small fountain. Top-floor rooms have river views. Breakfast is served in the garden. ❼

Lapa Palace Rua do Pau de Bandeira 4 ☎213 99 494, ℮www.orient.expresshotels.com. A stunning nineteenth-century mansion with dramatic vistas over the Tejo. Rooms are luxurious, particularly within the Palace Wing, where the decor is themed from Classical to Art Deco. In summer, grills are served in the gardens by the pool. Disabled access. ❾

Residencial York House Rua das Janelas Verdes 32 ☎213 962 785, ℮yorkhouse @mail.telepac.pt. Installed in a sixteenth-century convent, rooms come with rugs, tiles and four-poster beds. The best rooms are grouped around a beautiful interior courtyard, where drinks and meals are served in summer. The highly rated restaurant is also open to non-residents. ❽

Alfama and Castelo

All the hotels and pensões *listed below are marked on the Alfama and Castelo map on p.84.*

Pensão Ninho das Águias Costa do Castelo 74 ☎218 854 070. Beautifully sited *pensão* in its own view-laden terrace garden on the street looping around the castle. Climb up the staircase and past the bird cages. Rooms are bright, white and light, management capricious. Book in advance. ❸

Pensão São João de Praça Rua de São João de Praça 97-2° ☎218 862 591, ℱ218 881 378. Located immediately below the cathedral in a beautiful town house with street-facing balconies. It's a clean, quiet and friendly choice. Rooms vary from en suite to sharing a shower. Dinner can be provided. ❹

Sé Guest House Rua São João de Praça 97-1° ☎218 864 400, ℱ063 271 612. In the same building as the *Pensão São João de Praça* but slightly more upmarket. Wooden floors and bright, airy rooms with communal bathrooms and a substantial breakfast included in the price. ❹

Albergaria Senhora do Monte Calçada do Monte 39 ℡ 218 866 002, @ senhoradomonte@ hotmail.com. Comfortable, modern hotel in a beautiful location, close to Largo da Graça, with lovely views of the castle and Graça convent from its south-facing rooms – the more expensive rooms have terraces. Breakfast is included. Parking available or tram #28 passes close by. ❻

Avenida da Liberdade, Restauradores and Rua das Portas de Santo Antão

All the hotels and pensões *listed below are marked on the general map of Lisbon on p.60–61.*

Residencial 13° da Sorte Rua do Salitre 13 ℡ & ℻ 213 531 851. Translates as "lucky 13", and it's certainly an attractive option in a good location. The en-suite rooms are well decorated and include TVs and minibars. ❸

Residencial Alegria Praça Alegria 12 ℡ 213 220 670, @ mail@alegrianet.com; metro Avenida. Great position, facing the leafy square, with spacious, spotless rooms with TVs. Those with bath are more expensive than shower-only rooms. ❸

Britania Rua Rodrigues Sampaio 17 ℡ 213 155 016, @ britania.hotels@heritage.pt; metro Avenida. A smart three-star hotel, just to the east of the Avenida, with good-sized rooms and classic 1940s Deco interior designed by Cassiano Branco. Buffet breakfast included. ❽

Hotel Dom Carlos Av Duque de Loulé 121 ℡ 213 512 590, @ dcarlos@mail.telepac.pt; metro Marquês de Pombal. Decent three-star hotel just off Praça Marquês de Pombal, with fair-sized rooms, all with bath, TV and mini bars. There's a downstairs bar, and price includes a good buffet breakfast. ❺

Residencial Dom Sancho I Av da Liberdade 202 ℡ 213 548 648, @ dsancho@iol.pt; metro Avenida. One of the few inexpensive options right on the Avenida, and what's more set in a grand old mansion, with high ceilings and decorative cornices – though front rooms are noisy. Large en-suite rooms come with TVs and air conditioning. Breakfast included. ❹

Residencial Florescente Rua das Portas de Santo Antão 99 ℡ 213 426 609, ℻ 213 427 733. One of this pedestrianized street's best-value *residenciais*, where the many of the rooms are spick-and-span and come with TV and small bathroom (others are windowless and less appealing). Breakfast not included. ❸

Pensão Imperial Praça dos Restauradores 78-4° ℡ 213 420 166. This *pensão* has a fine blue-tiled facade and is situated in a sunny position at the bottom of the avenue (by Rua Jardim Regedor). Enter through an optician's and climb to the top floor for small rooms, some with showers and a view up the avenue. ❷

Hotel Lisboa Plaza Trav. Salitre 7 ℡ 213 218 218, @ plaza.hotels@heritage.pt; metro Avenida. Just off the Avenida, and in front of a theatre park, this bright, polished, four-star hotel has marble bathrooms, bar, restaurant and botanical garden views from rear rooms. Good breakfast included. Disabled access. ❻

Pensão Monumental Rua da Glória 21 ℡ 213 469 807, ℻ 213 430 213. A backpackers' favourite with a mixed bag of rooms in a rambling old building; the hot water supply is a little erratic, but it's in a good position close to the tourist office. ❸

Orion Eden Praça dos Restauradores 18–24 ℡ 213 216 600, @ eden.lisboa@mail.telepac.pt. Four-star studios and apartments sleeping up to four people, in the impressively converted Eden Theatre. Get a ninth-floor apartment with a balcony and you'll have the best views and be just below the rooftop pool and breakfast bar. All studios come with dishwashers, microwaves and satellite TV. ❻ for studios and double apartments; ❼ for larger apartments. Disabled access.

Hotel Suíço Atlântico Rua da Glória 3–19 ℡ 213 461 713, @ h.suisso.atlantico@mail.telepac.pt. Tucked around the corner from the *elevador*, just off the Avenida, this is a clean and modern hotel in a central location. Standard mid-range accommodation; rooms with shower and some with a balcony overlooking the seedy Rua da Glória. The intriguing mock-baronial bar is the best bit. ❹

Tivoli Lisboa Av da Liberdade 185 ℡ 213 198 900, htlisboa@mail.telepac.pt; metro Avenida. Flash five-star hotel with cavernous lobby-lounge. Three hundred sound-proofed rooms, outdoor pool, tennis courts, garden and a top-floor grill-restaurant with superb city views. Breakfast included. Disabled access. ❽

Hotel Veneza Av da Liberdade 189 ℡ 213 522 618, @ 3k.hoteis@mail.telepac.pt; metro Avenida. Built in 1886 by a Portuguese lawyer, the distinguishing feature of this former town house is an ornate staircase, now flanked by modern murals of Lisbon. The rest of the hotel is more ordinary, with standard rooms containing minibars, TVs and en-suite facilities. ❼

Praça Marquês de Pombal to Saldanha

All the hotels and pensões *listed below are marked on the general map of Lisbon on p.60–61.*

Residencial Avenida Alameda Sidónio Pais 4

⑦213 532 186, ⑰213 526 703; metro Parque or Marquês de Pombal. Very pleasant three-star *pensão* with air-con rooms, all with bath and park views. Breakfast included. ❸

Residencial Canadá Av Defensores de Chaves 35-1–4° ⑦213 521 455, ⑰213 542 922; metro Saldanha. Excellent value for money: largish, airy rooms with private bathrooms (and satellite TV) plus a sunny breakfast room and lounge area. Very handy for bus station. ❹

Hotel Fenix Praça do Marquês de Pombal 8 ⑦213 862 121, ⑭h@fenixip.pt; metro Marquês de Pombal. Large four-star hotel on the Rotunda, with double-glazed rooms to keep out the noise. Popular with tour groups, some rooms overlook Rotunda or the park. ❻

Hotel Impala Rua Filipe Folque 49 ⑦213 148 914, ⑰213 575 362; metro Picoas. Interesting choice if you want a longer Lisbon stay, offering small simple apartments sleeping up to four people. *Pensão*-standard bedrooms attached to small kitchen/living rooms with TVs. There are also laundry facilities. ❺

Miraparque Av Sidónio Pais ⑦213 524 286, ⑭miraparque@isoterica.pt; metro Marquês de Pombal or Parque. An attractive building with a traditional feel overlooking Parque Eduardo VII. The reception can be a bit brusque, but there's a decent bar and restaurant. All rooms come with TV. ❹

Pensão Pátria Av Duque d'Ávila 42-4–5° ⑦213 150 620, ⑰213 578 310; metro Saldanha. Situated close to the main bus station; plenty of nice little rooms with clean bathrooms in a cheerful establishment. Some rooms with rooftop views, others with small, glassed-in verandas. ❷

Hotel Rex Rua Castilho 169 ⑦213 882 161, ⑭rex@rex.pt; metro Marquês de Pombal. Smart hotel with in-house restaurant and small but well-equipped rooms, complete with pay TV, minibar and baths. The front rooms have large balconies overlooking Parque Eduardo VII. ❻

Ritz Four Seasons Rua Rodrigo da Fonseca 88 ⑦213 811 400, ⑳www.fourseasons.com; metro Marquês de Pombal. On the west side of Parque Eduardo VII, this vast modern block is one of the grandest – and most expensive – hotels in Lisbon, with huge airy rooms, terraces overlooking the park, and public areas replete with marble, antiques, old masters and overly attentive staff. There's also a fitness centre, highly rated restaurant and internet facilities. Disabled access. ❾

Around Avenida Almirante Reis

All the hotels and pensões *listed below are marked on the general map of Lisbon on p.60–61.*

Pensão Lar do Areeiro Praça Dr. Francisco de Sá Carneiro 4-1° ⑦218 493 150, ⑰218 406 321; metro Areeiro. Respectable, old-fashioned and well-run *pensão*, whose rooms all come with a bath. It's right on the Praça, which means it's noisy; ask for a room at the back. Breakfast included. ❸

Residencial O Paradouro Av Almirante Reis 106-7° ⑦218 153 256, ⑰218 155 445; metro Arroios. Smart, English-speaking *residencial* in a residential neighbourhood, opposite the fine *Portugalia* restaurant. All rooms with TV, some with balconies. Breakfast included. ❸

Residencial Pascoal de Melo Rua Pascoal de Melo 127–131 ⑦213 577 639, ⑰213 144 555; metro Arroios or Saldanha. Spotless and airy, this three-star *residencial* is characterful, with an *azulejo*-lined entry hall. Rooms have bathrooms, TVs and balconies. ❸

Residencial São Pedro Rua Pascoal de Melo 130 ⑦213 578 765, ⑰213 578 865; metro Arroios or Saldanha. Lots of dark wood and heavy furniture gives this place a rather sombre feel, but rooms are clean and comfortable and it's near the bus station. ❸

Youth hostels

Pousada de Juventude da Almada Quinta do Bucelinho, Pragal, Almada. ⑦212 943 491, ⑭almada@movijovem.pt. On the south side of the Tejo – with terrific views back over Lisbon – this is not particularly convenient for sightseeing in the city, but is within striking distance of the Caparica beaches. Also well equipped with games rooms, disabled access and internet facilities. Over twenty dorms with four beds from €12.50, and thirteen twin beds with their own loos from €30.

Pousada de Juventude de Catalazete Estrada Marginal, Oeiras ⑦214 430 638, ⑭catalazete@movijovem.pt. A small, attractive hostel, overlooking the beach at Oeiras, between Belém and Cascais. It is best reached by bus #44 from the airport, or take a train from Cais do Sodré to Oeiras station, then a taxi for the last 2km. Reception is open 6am–11pm and there's a midnight curfew. although you can get a pass to stay out later. Dorm rooms from €10.50, twin rooms from €25.50.

Pousada de Juventude de Lisboa Rua Andrade Corvo 46 ⑦213 532 696, ⑭lisboa@movijovem.pt; metro Picoas. This is the main city hostel, set in a rambling old building, with a small bar (6pm–midnight) and canteen. Thirty rooms sleeping 4 or 6 (with shared bathrooms) for €15 per person; or better value doubles with private shower rooms for €33 per room. There's also a TV room on the top floor. Price includes breakfast. Disabled access.

Lisboa Parque das Nações Rua de Moscavide 47–101, Parque das Nações ☎218 920 890, ℮ liboaparque@movijovem.pt; metro Oriente. Some five minutes' walk northeast of the Torre Vasco da Gama towards the new bridge, this modern youth hostel in Parque das Nações has ten double beds from €25.50 and 18 dorms of four beds, from €11. There's also a pool table and disabled access.

Campsites

Parque Municipal de Campismo Estrada da Circunvalação, Parque Florestal de Monsanto ☎217 623 100, ℗217 623 106. The main city campsite – with disabled facilities, a swimming pool and shops – is 6km west of the city centre, in the expansive, hilltop Parque de Monsanto. The entrance is on Estrada da Circunvalação on the park's west side. Bus #43 runs to the campsite from Praça da Figueira via Belém. Though the campsite is secure, take care in the park after dark.

Orbitur Costa de Caparica Av Afonso de Albuquerque, Quinta de St António, Monte de Caparica ☎212 901 366, ℮info@orbitur.pt. In a good position a short, tree-shaded walk from the beach, this is one of the few campsites in Caparica open to non-members, but tents, caravans and bungalows are crammed in cheek by jowl; facilities are good, but it's not for those looking for solitude.

Orbitur Guincho, N247, Lugar da Areia, Guincho ☎214 870 450, ℮info@orbitur.pt. Attractive campsite set among pine trees close to Guincho beach, served by bus from Cascais (see p.126). The site, with its own tennis courts, minimarket and café, also has bungalows and caravans for hire. Orbitur members get a ten percent discount.

Camping Praia Grande Praia Grande ☎219 290 581, ℮wondertur@ip.pt. Well-equipped campsite less than 1km from the beach at Praia Grande (see p.138), west of Sintra. Bus #441 runs from Sintra train station to here.

The City

Eighteenth-century prints show a pre-quake Lisbon of tremendous opulence, its skyline characterized by towers, palaces and convents. There are glimpses of this still – the old Moorish hillside of Alfama survived the destruction, as did Belém – but these are isolated neighbourhoods and monuments. It is instead Pombal's perfect Neoclassical grid that covers the centre. Giving orders, following the earthquake, to "Bury the dead, feed the living and close the ports", the king's minister followed his success in restoring order to the city with a complete rebuilding. The **Baixa** – still the heart of the modern city – was rebuilt according to Pombal's strict ideals of simplicity and economy; individual streets were assigned to each craft and trade and the whole enterprise was shaped by public buildings and squares.

One of the legacies of this visionary town planning is a city centre in which it could hardly be easier to get your bearings. At the Baixa's southern end, opening onto the Rio Tejo, is the broad, arcaded **Praça do Comércio** (also known as Terreiro do Paço), with its ferry stations for crossing the river, tram terminus for Belém, and grand triumphal arch. At the Baixa's northern end – linked to the Praça do Comércio by almost any street you care to take – stands Praça Dom Pedro IV, popularly known as **Rossio**, the main square since medieval times and the only part of the rebuilt city to remain in its original place, slightly off-centre in the symmetrical design. Rossio merges with **Praça da Figueira** and **Praça dos Restauradores** and it is these squares, filled with cafés and lively with buskers, business people, and streetwise hawkers and dealers, that form the hub of Lisbon's daily activity. At night the focus shifts to the **Bairro Alto**, high above and to the west of the Baixa, and best reached by funicular (the Elevador da Glória) or – when it reopens – by the great street elevator, the Elevador de Santa Justa. Between the two districts, halfway up the hill, **Chiado** is Lisbon's most elegant shopping area, largely rebuilt after being severely damaged in the fire that swept through the Baixa in 1988. East of the

Baixa, the **Castelo de São Jorge**, a brooding landmark, surmounts a still taller hill, with the **Alfama** district – the oldest, most fascinating part of the city with its winding lanes and anarchic stairways – sprawled below.

From Rossio, the main, tree-lined **Avenida da Liberdade** runs north to the city's central park, **Parque Eduardo VII**, beyond which spreads the rest of the modern city: the **Museum Gulbenkian** is to the north; the **Amoreiras** shopping complex to the west; and mundane shopping streets to the east. No stay in Lisbon should neglect the futuristic **Oceanarium** in the Parque das Nações, 5km to the east, or the waterfront suburb of **Belém**, 6km to the west, which is dominated by one of the country's grandest monuments, the **Jerónimos** monastery. En route to Belém lies Lisbon's other main museum, the **Museu de Arte Antiga.**

However, it should be remembered that Lisbon's contemporary interest lies as much in the everyday aspects of the city as in any specific sights. The cafés, markets, trams, ferries across the Tejo: all these are sufficient stimulation for random wanderings, the most rewarding areas being, as you'd expect, the oldest.

The Baixa

At the southern, waterfront end of the Baixa, the **Praça do Comércio** was the climax to Pombal's design, surrounded by classical buildings and centred on an exuberant bronze of Dom José – the reigning monarch during the earthquake and the capital's rebuilding. The metro station (open from 2004) is named **Terreiro do Paço**, after the original royal palace that once stood on this spot (its steps still lead up from the Tejo). Ironically, Portugal's royals came to a sticky end in the Praça; in 1908, alongside what was then the Central Post Office, King Carlos I and his eldest son were shot and killed, clearing the way for the declaration of the Republic two years later. Nowadays the square is one of the city's main venues for New Year's Eve festivities.

At the western side of the square lies Lisbon's **Welcome Centre** (see p.117; daily 9am–8pm), which acts as the tourist office as well as housing a café, internet centre, shops, restaurant and exhibition hall, all buried in a series of rooms between the square and neighbouring Rua do Arsenal, where there is another entrance. A more historic refreshment spot lies at the opposite side of the square, under the arcades – the old-world café *Martinho da Arcada* (see p.110), one of the haunts of Portugal's greatest twentieth-century poet, Fernando Pessoa.

The largely pedestrianized route north from Praça do Comércio along Rua Augusta is marked by a huge arch, **Arco da Rua Augusta**, depicting statues of historical figures, including Pombal and Vasco da Gama, and fronted by a bronze statue dedicated to Pessoa – his head a book – by Belgian artist Folon. North of here, the lower town – the **Baixa** – is very much the heart of the capital, housing many of the country's administrative departments, banks and business offices. Europe's first great example of Neoclassical design and urban planning, it remains an imposing quarter of ramrod-straight streets, cobbled underfoot and much of it given over to pedestrians, street performers and pavement artists. This area was also the site of Lisbon's first settlement; building work on the Banco Comercial Português at Rua dos Correeiros 21 revealed Roman walls and a mosaic floor, which can be viewed from the tiny **Núcleo Arqueológico** museum (book in advance for visits Thurs 3–5pm, Sat 10am–noon & 3–5pm; ☎213 211 700; free).

A major appeal of the Baixa is the survival of tradition. Many of the streets in the Baixa grid take their names from the crafts and businesses as Pombal

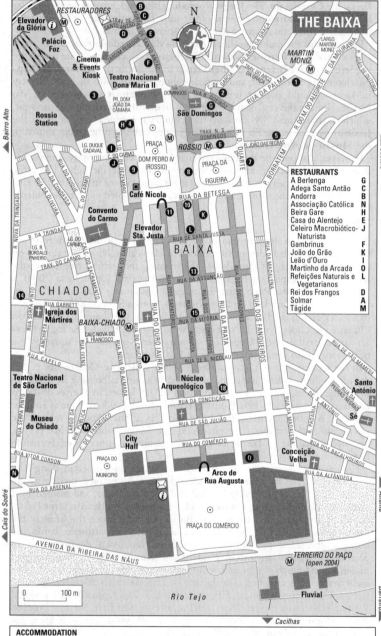

LISBON AND AROUND

THE BAIXA

RESTAURANTS

A Berlenga	G
Adega Santo Antão	C
Andorra	B
Associação Católica	N
Beira Gare	H
Casa do Alentejo	E
Celeiro Macrobiótico-Naturista	J
Gambrinus	F
João do Grão	K
Leão d'Ouro	I
Martinho da Arcada	O
Refeições Naturais e Vegetarianos	L
Rei dos Frangos	D
Solmar	A
Tágide	M

ACCOMMODATION

Arco da Bandeira	11	Coimbra e Madrid	8	Ibérica	7	Metrópole	9	Portugal	5
Avenida Palace	3	Duas Nações	15	Insulana	13	Moderna	12	Prata	18
Beira Minho	6	Galicia	17	International	10	Mundial	1	Residencial do Sul	4
Borges	14	Gerês	2	Lisboa Regency	16				

Development and destruction

In recent years Lisbon has experienced some of the most radical **redevelopment** since the Marquês de Pombal rebuilt the shattered capital after the 1755 earthquake. This phase began with Portugal's relative economic stability – and extensive grants – in the wake of joining the European Community in 1986, when foreign investment poured into the capital. The building boom accelerated in preparation for Expo 98, which saw further chunks of old Lisbon disappearing under new transport links while tramlines were removed to provide space for faster roads. Ironically, it is beyond Pombal's statue at Rotunda that most of the redevelopment work is being done.

Meanwhile, complicated **rent laws** have meant that landlords get insufficient income to maintain properties, making the option of selling up to property developers a tempting one. As a result, many of the city's beautiful pre-war mansions and tenement buildings are either in a state of decay, or have been demolished to make way for office buildings – while new property in Lisbon is some of the most expensive in Europe.

But not all of old Lisbon is lost and at least the **city centre** retains its elegance. EU funding continues to help with the restoration work of many historic buildings, including Lisbon's oldest quarter, the **Alfama**. However, the most obvious sign of renovation is in the streets of the **Chiado**, burned out in the 1988 fire and now beautifully restored to their original design by Portugal's leading architect Álvaro Siza. The riverfront, too, has been given a new lease of life, with former derelict warehouses converted into thriving cafés and clubs, while the Expo 98 site is now the vibrant **Parque das Nações** (see p.101), an attraction in its own right.

devised, such as Rua da Prata (Silversmiths' Street), Rua dos Sapateiros (Cobblers' Street), Rua do Ouro (Goldsmiths' Street, now better known as Rua Aurea) and Rua do Comércio (Commercial Street). These, along with the mosaic-sidewalked squares, are a visual delight, with tiled Art Deco shopfronts and elaborately decorated *pastelarias* still surviving here and there. At the western end of Rua de Santa Justa in the upper reaches of the Baixa, it's hard to avoid Raul Mésnier's **Elevador de Santa Justa** (May–Sept Mon–Fri 8.30am–10.30pm, Sat & Sun 9am–10.30pm; Oct–April daily 9am–7pm; €1 return if you buy a ticket in advance, or €1.70 return for a ticket on board), one of the city's most extraordinary and eccentric structures. Built in 1902 by a disciple of Eiffel, a giant lift whisks you 32m up the innards of a latticework metal tower before depositing you on a platform high above the Baixa. The exit at the top of the *elevador* – which leads out beside the Convento do Carmo (see p.81) – has been closed for some time now for structural work, but this should not deter you from taking the trip up to the rooftop **café** with great views over the city.

Rossio and around

Rossio (Praça Dom Pedro IV) – at the northern end of the Baixa grid – is Lisbon's oldest square, and though shot through with traffic, remains the liveliest. The square itself is modest in appearance, but very much a focus for the city, sporting several atmospheric and popular cafés, most of which have outdoor seating.

The square's single concession to grandeur is the **Teatro Nacional de Dona Maria II**, built along the north side in the 1840s. Here, prior to the earthquake, stood the Inquisitional Palace, in front of which public hangings, *autos-da-fé* (ritual burnings of heretics) and even bullfights used to take place. The nineteenth-century statue atop the central column is of Dom Pedro IV (after whom the square is officially named), though curiously it's a bargain adaptation: cast originally as Maximilian of Mexico, it just happened to be in Lisbon en route from France when news came through of Maximilian's assassination.

São Domingos church, immediately to the east in Largo São Domingos, was where the Inquisition read out its sentences. It was gutted by a fire in the 1950s, but has now been fully restored. The road and square outside the church, at the bottom of Rua das Portas de Santo Antão, is a popular meeting place – the local African population hangs out on the street corner; businessmen get their shoes cleaned at the rank of little metal booths; and Lisbon's lowlife frequent the various **ginginha bars**, which specialize in lethal measures of cherry brandy. Resist the urge to eat the proffered cherry itself – they've been soaked in alcohol for years and provide a kick usually only available from expensive drugs.

South, past the church, the street runs into **Praça da Figueira**, the square adjacent to Rossio. It contains one of the main city bus and tram stops and, like Rossio, is centred on a fountain and lined with shops, though there is less through traffic making it an altogether more relaxing spot to enjoy the cafés with outdoor seating.

Chiado

On the west side of the Baixa, stretching up the hillside towards the Bairro Alto, the area known as **Chiado** – the nom de plume of the poet António Ribeiro – suffered great damage from a fire that swept across the Baixa in August 1988. It destroyed all but the facade of the Grandella department store and many old shops in Rua do Crucifixo, though most buildings are now fully restored. Restoration is very much in keeping with the Chiado's traditions; new, soaring marble facades consciously mimic those destroyed in the fire, though they now shelter smart designer shops and the new Baixa-Chiado metro station.

Chiado remains one of the city's most affluent quarters, focused on the fashionable shops and old café-tearooms of the Rua Garrett. Of these, **A Brasileira**, Rua Garrett 120, is the most famous, having been frequented by generations of Lisbon's literary and intellectual leaders – the very readable Eça de Queirós (see box on p.80) and Portugal's greatest twentieth-century poet, Fernando Pessoa (see box on p.83), among them. While on Rua Garrett, take a stroll past **Igreja dos Mártires** (Church of the Martyrs), which occupies the site of the Crusader camp during the Siege of Lisbon. The church was built on the site of a burial ground created for the English contingent of the besieging army. Music recitals are often held in the church; check the local press for details.

Just beyond, Rua Serpa Pinto veers steeply downhill to the **Museu do Chiado** (Tues 2–6pm, Wed–Sun 10am–6pm, free on Sun until 2pm; €3). Opened in 1994, this stylish building, with a pleasant courtyard café and rooftop terrace, incorporates the former Museum of Contemporary Art, whose original home was damaged in the Chiado fire. The new museum was constructed around a nineteenth-century biscuit factory, which explains the presence of the old ovens. The three floors display the work of some of Portugal's most influential artists since the nineteenth century. Highlights include the beautiful sculpture *A Viúva* (The Widow) by **António Teixeira Lopes** and some evocative scenes of the Lisbon area by Carlos Botelho and José Malhoa. Look out also for the wonderful decorative panels by **José de Almada Negreiros**, recovered from the San Carlos cinema. There is also a small collection of French sculpture, including Rodin's *The Bronze Age*.

Around Cais do Sodré

Ten minutes' walk west of the Baixa grid, along the riverfront or the parallel **Rua do Arsenal** (a road packed with shops selling dried cod, cheap wines, port and brandies) is **Cais do Sodré** station and metro, from where trains run out to Estoril and Cascais, and ferries cross to Cacilhas. It's not the most elegant, or inviting, of areas, but it's certainly bustling. Varinas – fishwives from Alfama – and groups of *retornados* from Cabo Verde and other former colonies bargain for wares and cart off great basketsful of fish on their heads.

Take a look inside the **Ribeira market** too (market Mon–Sat 6am–2pm; flower market Mon–Sat 3pm–7pm; Loja de Artesenato daily 10am–10pm; food stalls daily 10am–11pm; live music Fri–Sat 10pm–1am), located in the domed building on Avenida 24 de Julho, just beyond Cais do Sodré. This is Lisbon's main market, a highly atmospheric array of local characters selling fish and meat of all shapes and sizes, tables full of fruit and vegetables. In 2001, the upper level of the market was opened as a centre for regional arts and gastronomy. Though squarely aimed at tourists, the Loja de Artesenato (craft shop) on the upper level, specializes in art and crafts from Lisbon and the Tejo valley, and doubles as an exhibition space and shop. The upper level also has various food stalls selling gastronomy from various, including superb fresh breads, cheeses, wines and *petiscos* (tapas like snacks); there is also a restaurant specialising in regional food. A central stage hosts live music at weekends, from jazz to folk; at other times, conferences and temporary exhibits are held here.

A short walk behind the market, with its entrance on Rua de São Paulo, is the precipitous **Elevador da Bica** (Mon–Sat 7am–10.45pm, Sun 9am–10.45pm; €1), an atmospheric funicular railway leading up to the foot of the Bairro Alto. Take a left at the top and then the second left down Rua M. Saldanha and you'll reach the **Miradouro de Santa Catarina**, with spectacular views over the city with a handy drinks kiosk with outdoor tables.

Bairro Alto

High above the central city, to the west of the Baixa, **Bairro Alto**, the upper town, is the natural place to spend your evening – in its fado houses, bars, excellent restaurants, or even in the refined and somewhat dauntingly named *Instituto do Vinho do Porto* (Port Wine Institute). By day, the quarter's narrow seventeenth-century streets have a very different character – it's a residential district with children playing and the elderly sitting in doorways. It is well worth a morning or afternoon's exploration, with two of the city's most interesting churches – Carmo and São Roque – on the fringes and a few approaches to the quarter that are a treat in themselves.

Approaches by Elevador

You can approach the Bairro Alto on two amazing feats of engineering in the form of the two funicular-like trams, originally powered by water displacement, and then by steam, until electricity was introduced. A third approach by lift, the Elevador de Santa Justa (see p.75), has its exit at the side of the Convento do Carmo – but this has been closed for structural works for some time. The **Elevador da Bica** (Mon–Sat 7am–10.45pm, Sun 9am–10.45pm; €1 one way) climbs up to Rua Loreto (west of Praça Luis de Camões) from Rua de São Paulo/Rua da Moeda, northwest of Cais do Sodré (see above). The **Elevador da Glória**, (7am to 1am; €1 one way), built in 1885, links the quarter directly with Praça dos Restauradores (see p.72), from where it takes off just behind the tourist office on the left.

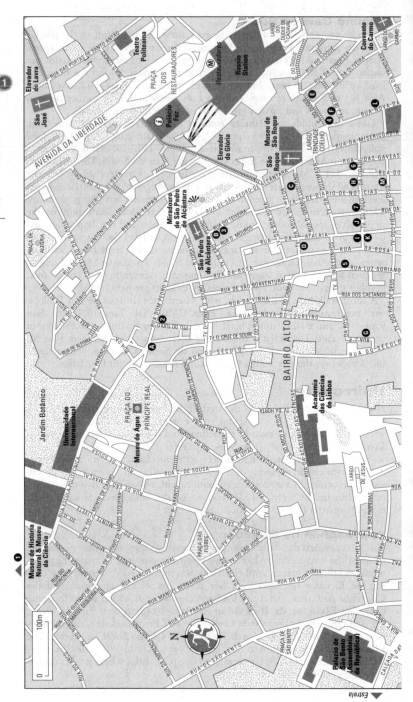

▲ Estrela

Museu de Historia Natural & Museu da Ciência

Jardim Botânico

Universidade Internacional

PRAÇA DO PRINCIPE REAL

Museu de Água

Academia das Ciências de Lisboa

BAIRRO ALTO

Palácio de São Bento (Assembleia da República)

Elevador de Lavra

São José

Teatro Politeama

PRAÇA DOS RESTAURADORES

AVENIDA DA LIBERDADE

Palácio foz

Elevador da Glória

Rossio Station

Museu de São Roque

São Roque

Convento do Carmo

LARGO DO DUQUE DE CADAVAL

Miradouro de São Pedro de Alcântara

São Pedro de Alcântara

LARGO TRINDADE COELHO

N

100m
0

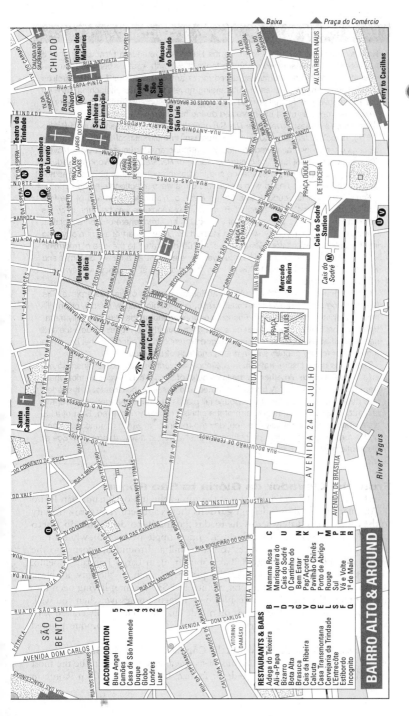

▲ Baixa   ▲ Praça do Comércio

Ferry to Cacilhas

CHIADO

Igreja dos Mártires

Museu do Chiado

Teatro de São Carlos

Baixa-Chiado Ⓜ

Nossa Senhora da Encarnação

Teatro de São Luis

Teatro da Trindade

TRINDADE

Nossa Senhora do Loreto

PRAÇA DOS CAMÕES

Praça Duque de Terceira

Cais do Sodré Station

Elevador de Bica

Mercado da Ribeira

Cais do Sodré Ⓜ

Miradouro de Santa Catarina

PRAÇA DOM LUIS

Santa Catarina

River Tagus

AVENIDA 24 DE JULHO

AVENIDA DE BRASILIA

SÃO BENTO

AVENIDA DOM CARLOS I

BAIRRO ALTO & AROUND

ACCOMMODATION

Blue Angel	5
Camões	7
Casa de São Mamede	1
Duque	4
Globo	3
Londres	2
Luar	6

RESTAURANTS & BARS

Adega do Teixeira	B
Ali-a-Papa	I
Bizarro	D
Bota Alta	J
Brasuca	G
Cais da Ribeira	V
Calcutta	O
Casa Transmontana	E
Cervejaria da Trindade	L
L'Entrecôte	S
Estibordo	F
Incognito	Q
Mamma Rosa	C
Marisqueira do Cais do Sodré	U
O Cantinho do Bem Estar	N
Pap'Açorda	K
Pavilhão Chinês	T
Porto de Abrigo	M
Rouge	P
Sul	H
Vá e Volte	R
1° de Maio	Q

79

Eça de Queirós

Halfway down the Rua do Alecrim, in the Bairro Alto, stands a bizarre statue of a frock-coated, moustachioed man who looks down with a rather bemused expression at the half-naked woman sprawled in his arms. The man is **Eça de Queirós** (1845–1900), who in a series of outstanding novels turned his unflinching gaze on the shortcomings of his native land; the woman is presumably Truth – the quality for which his work was most often praised during his lifetime.

While Eça's earliest novels, like *The Sin of Father Amaro* (1875) and *Cousin Bazilio* (1878), reveal a clear debt to French naturalism in their satirical intent, his mature writings offer a more measured critique of contemporary Portuguese society. Novels like *The Maias* (1888) and *The Illustrious House of Ramires* (1900) work by gradually building up a picture of decadence and inertia, through an assemblage of acutely observed vignettes tinged with a sardonic but always affectionate humour.

Eça's cosmopolitan outlook was both a result of his background and of the fact that he was extremely well travelled. Born out of wedlock, he was brought up by his paternal grandparents in the north of Portugal in an atmosphere of Liberal political ideas. At Coimbra University, where he studied law, he was part of a group of young intellectuals (known as the "Generation of 1870") dedicated to the idea of reforming and modernizing the country. His adult years were spent as a career diplomat and for much of the 1870s and 1880s he was in England, first as consul in Newcastle upon Tyne and then in Bristol.

Oddly enough, it was at Newcastle that Eça wrote much of his masterpiece, *The Maias*, a complex portrayal of an aristocratic, land-owning family unable, or unwilling, to adapt to changing times. Focusing on three generations of male family members, Eça brilliantly conveys what he sees as a peculiarly Portuguese indolence and hedonism that inevitably acts as curb to good intentions – a condition that becomes a metaphor for the country's inwardness and lack of ambition.

The Maias is the Lisbon novel *par excellence*, conjuring up an extraordinarily powerful sense of place. Whether it's the leafy quiet of the Janelas Verdes district where Ramalhete, the Maia family home, is situated, the bustle of the Chiado, or the faded grandeur of the São Carlos Opera House (all places that have changed little over the last 100 years), the essential charm of the city is beautifully conveyed. Best of all is a description of a seemingly carefree, day trip to Sintra, in which a mundane errand and a romantic assignation are poignantly interwoven in a way that reveals Eça at his subtle best.

From the Elevador da Glória to São Roque

The Elevador da Glória drops you at the top of the hill on Rua de São Pedro de Alcântara, from whose adjacent **gardens** there's a superb view across the city to the castle. Immediately across the road is the **Instituto do Vinho do Porto** a good place to stop and taste Portugal's finest tipple (see p.303), while a turn to the left from the *elevador* takes you downhill and round the corner to the **Igreja de São Roque** (daily 8.30am–5pm; free), in Largo Trindade Coelho. From the outside, this looks like the plainest church in the city, its bleak Renaissance facade (by Filipo Terzi, architect of São Vicente) having been further simplified by the earthquake. Nor does it seem impressive when you walk inside until you look at the succession of side chapels, each lavishly crafted with *azulejos* (some emulating reliefs), multicoloured marble, or Baroque painted ceilings.

However, the highlight of a visit is the **Capela de São João Baptista**. It was one of the most bizarre commissions of its age and is estimated to be the most expensive chapel ever constructed, for its size. It was ordered from Rome in

1742 by Dom João V to honour his patron saint and, more dubiously, to requite the pope, whom he had persuaded to confer a patriarchate upon Lisbon. Designed by the papal architect, Vanvitelli, and using the most costly materials available, including ivory, agate, porphyry and lapis lazuli, it was actually erected at the Vatican for the pope to celebrate Mass before being dismantled and shipped to Lisbon. The cost, then, was about £250,000 sterling, which is perhaps its chief curiosity. But there are other eccentricities; take a close look at the four "oil paintings" of John the Baptist's life and you'll discover that they are in fact mosaics, intricately worked over what must have been years rather than months.

Next to the church, the associated **Museu de São Roque** (May–Oct Tues–Sun 10am–5pm; Nov–April daily 10am–noon & 1–5pm; €1, free Sun) displays sixteenth- to eighteenth-century paintings and the usual motley collection of vestments, chalices and bibles bequeathed to the church over the centuries, including treasure from the Capela de São João Baptista.

Convento do Carmo

Further south, it's a couple of minutes' walk down to the pretty, enclosed **Largo do Carmo**, with its outdoor café facing the ruined Gothic arches of the **Convento do Carmo**. Once the largest church in the city, this was half-destroyed by the earthquake but is perhaps even more beautiful as a result. In the nineteenth century its shell was adapted as a chemical factory but these days it houses the splendid **Museu Arqueológico do Carmo** (April–Sept 10am–6pm; Oct–March 10am–5pm; €2.50, free on Sun), whose miscellaneous collection is one of the joys of the city, housing many of the treasures from monasteries that were dissolved after the 1834 Liberal revolution. The entire nave is open to the elements, with columns, tombs and statuary scattered in all corners. Inside, on either side of what was the main altar, are the main exhibits, centring on a series of **tombs** of great significance. Largest is the beautifully carved, two-metre-high stone tomb of **Ferdinand I**; nearby, the tomb of **Gonçalo de Sousa**, chancellor to Henry the Navigator, is topped by a statue of Gonçalo himself, his clasped arms holding a book to signify his learning. Other noteworthy pieces include a fifteenth-century alabaster relief, made in Nottingham, and sixteenth-century Hispano-Arabic *azulejos*. There's also a model of the convent before it was ruined, an Egyptian sarcophagus (793–619BC), whose inhabitant's feet are just visible underneath the lid; and, more alarmingly, two pre-Columbian **mummies** which lie curled up in glass cases, alongside the preserved heads of a couple of Peruvian Indians. Elsewhere there are flints, arrowheads, prehistoric ceramics, coins dating back to the thirteenth century, Roman inscriptions, church architecture and much more.

West of Rua da Misericórdia

Many of the Bairro Alto's most interesting streets, certainly after dark, lie west of **Rua da Misericórdia**, which runs alongside the Igreja de São Roque a couple of blocks west from the Convento do Carmo. Here, a confusing network of narrow, cobbled streets, their buildings liberally defaced with grafitti, have undergone renovation in the last few years and parking and traffic access is now restricted. It's here that you'll find many of the city's best bars, restaurants and fado clubs (see pp.105, 112 and 116). The main streets to get your bearings from are those running north to south: Rua do Norte, Rua Diário de Notícias, Rua da Atalaia and Rua da Rosa. A little further west, steeply downhill towards São Bernto, Rua do Século is one of the city's most historic streets; a sign at number 89 marks the birthplace of the Marquês de Pombal, while the basement of the modernizing minister's former home is now occupied by a restaurant *Consenso*.

Praça do Príncipe Real and around

At the north end of Rua do Século, or a pleasant ten-minute walk uphill from the top of Elevador da Glória along Rua Dom Pedro V, lies the attractive Praça do Príncipe Real, one of the city's loveliest squares, laid out in 1860 and surrounded by the ornate homes of former aristocrats – now largely offices. The central pond and fountain is built over a covered reservoir that forms the **Museu da Água Príncipe Real** (Mon–Sat 10am–6pm; €1). Steps lead down inside the nineteenth-century reservoir where you can admire the water and temporary exhibits from a series of walkways winding among the columns, usually accompanied by ambient music. This is part of a network of underground water supplies that link up with the Aqueduto das Águas Livres (see p.92).

From here it is a short walk along Rua Escola Politécnica to the classical building housing both the **Museu de História Natural** and the **Museu da Ciência**; alternatively take bus #15 or #58 from Cais do Sodré station. The Museu de História Natural (Mon–Fri 10am–noon & 1–5pm, closed Aug; free) exhibits a rather sad collection of stuffed animals tracing the evolution of Iberian animal life, while the adjoining Museu da Ciência (Mon–Fri 10am–1pm & 2–5pm, Sat 3–6pm; closed Aug; free) includes an imaginative interactive section amongst its geological displays. Neither museum, however, is particularly inspiring.

Beyond the museums lies the entrance to the enchanting **Jardim Botânico** (May–Oct Mon–Fri 9.30am–7pm, Sat–Sun 10am–8pm; Nov–April same hours until 6pm; €1.30). Laid out in 1873, the gardens are almost completely invisible from the surrounding streets, and form an oasis of twenty thousand exotic plants from around the world – each one neatly labelled.

Estrela

Situated on another of Lisbon's hills, the district of **Estrela** lies 2km west of Bairro Alto – a thirty-minute walk or a short ride on tram #28 from Praça Luís de Camões in Chiado, or bus #13 from Praça do Comércio. Its main point of interest for the visitor is the **Basílica da Estrela** (daily 8am–1pm & 3–8pm; free), a vast domed church and *de facto* monument to late-eighteenth-century Neoclassicism. Below the church is the **Jardim da Estrela**: Lisbon takes its gardens seriously, even the small patches amid squares and avenues, and these are among the most enjoyable in the city, a quiet refuge occasionally graced with an afternoon band. There's a pool of giant carp, too, and a café with outside tables.

Through the park and on Rua de São Jorge is the gate to the post-Crusader **Cemitério dos Ingleses** (English cemetery; ring loudly for entry) where, among the cypresses, lies Henry Fielding, author of *Tom Jones*, whose imminent demise may have influenced his verdict on Lisbon as "the nastiest city in the world".

A little uphill from here at Rua Coelho da Rocha 16 is the **Casa Museu Fernando Pessoa** (Mon–Wed 10am–7pm, Fri 10am–6pm, Thurs 1–8pm; free), home to Portugal's best-known poet for the last fifteen years of his life (see box opposite). The building is now a cultural centre containing **Almada Negreiros'** famous painting of the writer, a few of Pessoa's personal belongings, such as his glasses and diaries, and exhibits of artists who have been influenced by Pessoa.

Fernando Pessoa

"Whether we write or speak or do but look
We are ever unapparent. What we are
Cannot be transfused into word or book."

Fernando Pessoa (1888–1935) is now widely recognized not just as Portugal's greatest poet of the twentieth century but as one of the major – and strangest – figures of European Modernism. Born in Lisbon, Pessoa spent most of his childhood in Durban, South Africa, where he underwent an English education and wrote his earliest poems – in English. He returned to Portugal in 1905 and spent most of his adult life working as a translator for various commercial firms. The rest of his time was devoted to literature. He founded a short lived artistic magazine *Orpheu* in 1915 with fellow poet Mario de Sá-Carneiro, contributed to several other magazines, and rapidly became a conspicuous figure in the Baixa cafés where he wrote.

Much of Pessoa's work is concerned with the evasive nature of the self and, perhaps in recognition that personality can never be fixed, his work was created under a number of different identities, or "heteronyms". Each of his poetic alter egos had a fully worked out history, vision and style of their own – he even went so far as to have calling cards printed for his English heteronym, Alexander Search. By a marvellous piece of poetic serendipity, "*pessoa*" actually means "person" in Portuguese, a word that in turn derives from "*persona*" – the mask worn by Roman actors. Of the many heteronyms that Pessoa adopted, three were responsible for his finest poems. They are the nature poet, Alberto Caeiro; the classicist, Ricardo Reis; and the ebullient modernist, Álvaro de Campos. All three made their first appearance in 1914, and to some extent their histories intertwine with each other but with Caeiro regarded as the master by the other two. They share an obsessive introspection and a morbid fascination with interior and exterior reality that makes Pessoa one of the most telling of existential artists.

Pessoa died a year after the publication of *Mensagem* (Message), a series of patriotic and mystical poems dealing with Portuguese history. Written for a national competition (which he didn't win), this was the only volume of his Portuguese verse to appear during his lifetime. What he left was a large trunkload of manuscripts and typescripts, often in quite fragmentary form. These include the unclassifiable *Livro do Desassossego* (Book of Disquiet) written under the heteronym Bernardo Soares, a quasi-autobiography, consisting of aphorisms, anecdotes, and philosophical rumination, that has a directness and self-centredness that is both exhilarating and irritating by turns. It is in the piecing together and editing of these scraps of writing that the posthumous reputation of the enigmatic Pessoa has been built.

From the tram stop in front of the Basílica da Estrela you can catch #25 down the steep Rua de São Domingos à Lapa, getting off where the tram veers left into Rua Garcia de Orta. Here, you're only a five-minute walk from the Museu Nacional de Arte Antiga (see p.96); staying with the tram takes you to Praça do Comércio and back into the Baixa.

From Praça do Comércio to the Sé and Castelo

A couple of blocks east of the riverfront Praça do Comércio, along Rua da Alfândega, is the church of **Conceição Velha**, severely damaged by the earthquake but still in possession of its flamboyant Manueline doorway, an early example of the style and hinting at the brilliance that later emerged at Belém. It once formed part of the Misericórdia (almshouse) – you'll find one of these

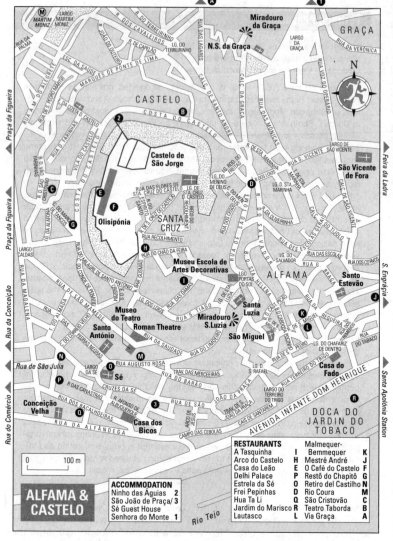

RESTAURANTS

A Tasquinha	I	Malmequer-Bemmequer	K
Arco do Castelo	H	Mestré André	J
Casa do Leão	E	O Café do Castelo	F
Delhi Palace	P	Restô do Chapitô	G
Estrela da Sé	O	Retiro del Castilho	N
Frei Pepinhas	D	Rio Coura	M
Hua Ta Li	Q	São Cristovão	C
Jardim do Marisco	R	Teatro Taborda	B
Lautasco	L	Via Graça	A

ACCOMMODATION

Ninho das Águias	2
São João de Praça	3
Sé Guest House	
Senhora do Monte	1

ALFAMA & CASTELO

impressive structures in almost every Portuguese town or city. Five minutes'
walk further east, at Campo das Cebolas, stands the curious **Casa dos Bicos**
(Mon–Fri 9.30am–5.30pm), set with diamond-shaped stones. The building
was built in 1523 for the son of the Viceroy of India, though only the facade of the
original building survived the earthquake. It sees fairly regular use for cultural
exhibitions; at other times, you can look round the remains of Roman fish preserving tanks and parts of Lisbon's old Moorish walls (demolished in the fifteenth century) which were excavated during renovation work in the 1980s.
On the riverfront just east of here, across the busy Avenida Infante Dom

Henrique, lies the **Jardim do Tobaco** dockland development. Facing one of the broadest sections of the Tejo, the views from the outdoor tables of its restaurants attracts an upmarket and largely local crowd.

The Sé

Lisbon's cathedral – the **Sé** (daily 8.30am–6pm; free) – stands stolidly above the Baixa grid. Founded in 1150 to commemorate the city's reconquest from the Moors, it has a suitably fortress-like appearance, similar to that of Coimbra, and in fact occupies the site of the principal mosque of Moorish Lishbuna. Like so many of the country's cathedrals, it is Romanesque – and extraordinarily restrained in both size and decoration. The great rose window and twin towers form a simple and effective facade, but inside there's nothing very exciting: the building was once splendidly embellished on the orders of Dom João V, but his Rococo whims were swept away by the earthquake and subsequent restorers. All that remains is a group of Gothic tombs behind the high altar and the decaying thirteenth-century **cloister**.

You need to buy tickets for admission to the cloister (Mon & Sun 9am–5pm, Tues–Sat 9am–7pm; €0.50) and the Baroque Sacristia (same hours; €2.50) with its small **museum** of treasures, including the relics of St Vincent, brought to Lisbon in 1173 by Afonso Henriques, having arrived in Portugal from Spain in a boat piloted by ravens. For centuries the descendants of these birds were shown to visitors but the last one died in 1978, despite receiving great care from the sacristan. Nevertheless, ravens are still one of the city's symbols.

Opposite the Sé is the church of **Santo António** (daily 9am–7.30pm, free), said to have been built on the spot where the city's adopted patron saint was born. His life is chronicled in the neighbouring **museum** (Tues–Sat 10am–1pm & 2–6pm; €1).

Up to the Castelo

From the Sé, Rua Augusto Rosa winds upward towards the castle, past sparse ruins of a **Roman theatre** (57 AD), set behind a grille just off to the left at the junction of ruas de São Mamede and Saudade. The finds excavated from the site can be visited at the small adjacent **Museu do Teatro Romano** (entrance on Patio de Aljube; Tues–Sun 10am–1pm & 2–6pm; free), which has multimedia explanations about the theatre's history. Further up the hill you reach the **Igreja da Santa Luzia** and the adjacent **Miradouro da Santa Luzia**, from where there are fine views down to the river.

Just beyond, at Largo das Portas do Sol 2, is the Espírito Santo Silva Foundation, home of the **Museu Escola de Artes Decorativas** (Tues–Sun 10am–5pm; €4.50) a seventeenth-century mansion stuffed with what was once the private collection of banker Ricardo do Espírito Santo Silva, who offered it to the nation in 1953. On display are unique pieces of furniture, major collections of silver and porcelain, paintings, textiles and *azulejo* panels – in short, some of the best examples of seventeenth- and eighteenth-century applied art in the country. The museum also has a courtyard café.

Over the road from the **terrace-café** in Largo das Portas do Sol, the views are tremendous – a solitary palm rising from the stepped streets below, the twin-towered facade of Graça convent, the dome of Santa Engrácia, and the Tejo beyond. Catch your breath here for the final push up to the castle, higher up the hill to the northeast – signposts keep you on the right track as the roads wind confusingly ever higher.

Incidentally, **tram** #28 runs from Rua da Conceição in the Baixa, past the Sé and Santa Luzia, to Largo das Portas do Sol; coming from Rossio, **bus** #37 from Praça do Comércio follows a similar route, cutting off at Santa Luzia and climbing to one of the castle entrances.

The Castelo de São Jorge

A small statue of Afonso Henriques, triumphant after the siege of Lisbon, stands at the main entrance to the **Castelo de São Jorge**. An important victory, leading to the Muslim surrender at Sintra and throughout the surrounding district, this was not, however, the most Christian or glorious of Portuguese exploits. A full account of the siege survives, written by one Osbern of Bawdsley, an English priest and Crusader, and its details, despite the author's judgmental tone, direct one's sympathies to the enemy.

The attack, in the summer of 1147, came through the opportunism and skilful management of Afonso Henriques, already established as "King" at Porto, who persuaded a large force of French and British Crusaders to delay their progress to Jerusalem for more immediate and lucrative. The Crusaders – scarcely more than pirates – came to terms and in June the siege began. Osbern records the Archbishop of Braga's demand for the Moors to return to "the land whence you came" and, more revealingly, the weary and contemptuous response of the Muslim spokesman: "How many times have you come hither with pilgrims and barbarians to drive us hence? It is not want of possessions but only ambition of the mind that drives you on." For seventeen weeks the castle and inner city stood firm but in October its walls were breached and the citizens – including a Christian community coexisting with the Muslims – were forced to surrender.

The pilgrims and barbarians, flaunting the diplomacy and guarantees of Afonso Henriques, stormed into the city, cut the throat of the local bishop and sacked, pillaged and murdered Christian and Muslim alike. In 1190 a later band of English Crusaders stopped at Lisbon and, no doubt confused by the continuing presence of Moors who had stayed on as New Christians, sacked the city a second time.

The Castelo

The **Castelo** (daily: March–Oct 9am–9pm; Nov–Feb 9am–6pm; free) is perhaps Lisbon's most splendid monument, as much through its impressive location as anything else. Beyond the main gates stretch gardens and terraces, walkways, fountains and peacocks, all lying within the old Moorish walls which were scrubbed raw in an over-zealous clean-up operation for Expo 98. At first the Portuguese kings took up residence within the castle – in the *Alcáçova*, the Muslim palace – but by the time of Manuel I this had been superseded by the new royal palace on Terreiro do Paço. Of the *Alcáçova* only a much-restored shell remains. This now houses **Olisipónia** (daily: March–Oct 10am–1pm & 2–6pm; Nov–Feb 10am–1pm & 2–5.30pm; €3), a multimedia exhibition detailing the history of the city. On entry you are given portable headsets which deliver a 35-minute commentary at four booths presenting aspects of Lisbon's development through film, sounds and images. The presentations overlap somewhat and gloss over some of the less savoury chapters of the past – such as slavery and the Inquisition – but are a useful introduction to the city's make-up nonetheless.

The rest of the castle is an enjoyable place to spend a couple of hours, wandering amid the ramparts looking down upon the city. Built into the ramparts, the Tower of Ulysses holds a **Câmara Escura** (daily every 30 minutes, weather permitting, 10am–1.30pm & 2.30–6.30pm; Nov–May until 5.30pm; €2), a

△ Balconies, Rua dos Bacalhoeiros

periscope focusing on sights round the city with English commentary – though the views are almost as good from the neighbouring unadorned towers.

Crammed within the castle's outer walls is the tiny medieval quarter of **Santa Cruz**, still very much a village in itself. This area, despite a few grand old houses, is currently undergoing substantial redevelopment.

Just below the castle's eastern entrance sprawls the old **Mouraria** quarter, to which the Moors were relegated on their loss of the town, stretching to Largo Rodrigues de Freitas from where **tram #12** grinds down to Largo Martim Moniz, a broad square north of the Baixa grid. From Largo Martim Moniz, Calçada da Graça leads up to the Graça district and the **Miradouro da Graça** from where the views across the city are stunning.

Alfama

The oldest part of Lisbon, stumbling from the walls of the castle down to the Tejo, **Alfama** was buttressed against significant damage in the 1755 earthquake by the steep, rocky mass on which it is built. Although none of its houses dates from before the Christian conquest, many are of Moorish design and the kasbah-like layout is still much as Osbern described it, with "steep defiles instead of ordinary streets... and buildings so closely packed together that, except in the merchants' quarter, hardly a street could be found more than eight foot wide".

In Arab-occupied times Alfama was the grandest part of the city, and continued to be so after the Christian reconquest, but following subsequent earthquakes the new Christian nobility moved out, leaving it to the local fishing community. Today, it is undergoing some commercialization, with its cobbled lanes and "character", but although antique shops and an increasing number of fado restaurants are moving in, they are far from taking over. The quarter retains a largely traditional life of its own: you can eat at local prices in the cafés; the flea market (see below) engulfs the periphery of the area twice a week, and this is very much the place to be during the June "Popular Saints" festivals (above all on June 12), when makeshift cafés and stalls appear on every corner.

The steep defiles, alleys and passageways are known as *becos* and *travessas* rather than *ruas*, and it would be impossible (as well as futile) to try and follow any set route. Along all these streets and alleys, life continues much as it has done for years: kids playing ball in tiny squares and chasing each other up and down precipitous staircases; people buying groceries and fish from hole-in-the-wall stores; householders stringing washing across narrow defiles and stoking small outdoor charcoal grills. At some point in your wanderings around the quarter, though, head for the **Rua de São Miguel** – off which are some of the most interesting *becos* – and for the (lower) parallel **Rua de São Pedro**, the main market street leading to the lively **Largo do Chafariz de Dentro**, right at the bottom of the hill. Here you'll find the **Casa do Fado e da Guitarra Portuguesa** (daily 10am–1pm & 2–5pm; €2.50), an engaging museum detailing the history of fado and Portuguese guitar through a series of rooms. Each one has wax models, pictures, sounds and descriptions of leading characters and the stages of history in this very Portuguese musical style – an excellent introduction to the music and worth seeing before you visit a fado house. There's a good shop for fado CDs and a small café.

The Feira da Ladra

The **Feira da Ladra**, Lisbon's rambling and ragged flea market, fills the Campo de Santa Clara, at the eastern edge of Alfama on Tuesdays and Saturdays

(7am–6pm). Though it's certainly not the world's greatest, it does turn up some interesting things: oddities from the former African colonies, old prints of the country, and army-surplus gear. Out-and-out junk – broken alarm clocks and old postcards – is spread on the ground above Santa Engrácia, and half-genuine antiques at the top end of the *feira*. To get here, tram #28 runs from Rua da Conceição in the Baixa to São Vicente (see below), and bus #12 runs between Santa Apolónia station and Praça Marquês de Pombal.

Santa Engrácia and São Vicente de Fora

While at the flea market, take a look inside **Santa Engrácia** (Tues–Sun May–Oct 10am–6pm; Nov–April 10am–5pm; €2, free Sun 10am–2pm), the loftiest and most tortuously built church in the city. Begun in 1682 and once a synonym for unfinished work, its vast dome was finally completed in 1966. Since 1916, the church has been the **Panteão Nacional** housing the tombs of eminent Portuguese figures, including former presidents and the writer Almeida Garrett. You can go up to the dome, and look down on the empty church and out over the flea market, port and city.

More interesting, architecturally, is the nearby **São Vicente de Fora** (Tues–Fri 9am–6pm, Sat 9–7pm, Sun 9am–12.30pm & 3–5pm; free), whose name – "of the outside" – is a reminder of the extent of the sixteenth-century city walls. It is where Afonso Henriques pitched camp during his siege and conquest of Lisbon. Built during the years of Spanish rule by Philip II's Italian architect, Felipe Terzi, its severe geometric facade was an important Renaissance innovation. Through the **cloisters**, decorated with *azulejos*, you can visit the old monastic refectory, which since 1855 has formed the **pantheon of the Bragança dynasty** (Tues–Sun 10am–5.30pm; €2). Here, in more or less complete sequence, are the bodies of all Portuguese kings from João IV, who restored the monarchy, to Manuel II, who lost it and died in exile in England in 1932. Among them is Catherine of Bragança, the widow of Charles II and (as the local guide points out) "the one who took the habit of the fifth o'clock tea to that country". You can enjoy tea and other beverages at the monastery café, which has a roof terrace commanding superb views over the Alfama and the Tagus.

Further east: the Museu Militar, Museu da Água and Museu Nacional do Azulejo

There's not much call to head east beyond the Alfama, unless you're leaving by train from **Santa Apolónia station** or visiting the dockside clubs and restaurants (see p.114). However, there is a trio of museums of varying interest. Opposite the station, on Largo Museu da Artilharia, a couple of blocks south of Santa Engrácia, is the imposing Corinthian facade of the city's military museum, the **Museu Militar** (Tues–Sun 10am–5pm; €2, free Wed), though this is very traditional in layout – old weapons in old cases – and lacks much appeal. However, some ten minutes' walk beyond Santa Apolónia station, or a ride on bus #105 from Praça da Figueira, off Calçada dos Barbadinhos at Rua do Alviela 12, stands the **Museu da Água** (Mon–Sat 10am–6pm; €2), a moderately engaging museum devoted to the evolution of the city's water supply. It is housed in an attractive old pumping station, built in 1880 to pump water up Lisbon's steep hills, and is complete with working nineteenth-century steam engines. While here, you can arrange a visit to the Aqueduto das Águas Livres (see p.92).

About 1.5km east of Santa Apolónia (bus #104 from Praça do Comércio, bus #105 from Praça da Figueira) is the **Museu Nacional do Azulejo**

(Tues 2–6pm, Wed–Sun 10am–6pm; €2.25, free on Sun) at Rua Madre de Deus 4. Installed in the church and cloisters of Madre de Deus, whose own eighteenth-century tiled scenes on the life of St Anthony are among the best in the city, it contains an impressive collection of *azulejos* from the fifteenth century to the present day. The highlight, however, is Portugal's longest *azulejo* – a wonderfully detailed 36-metre panorama of Lisbon, completed in around 1738. Don't miss out on the opportunity of a drink in the lovely garden café here.

Portuguese azulejos

Lisbon has some fine example of **azulejos** – brightly coloured, decorative ceramic tiles – and you can see a variety of styles spanning five hundred years decorating the inside and outside of houses, shops, monuments and even metro stations. The craft was brought over by the Moors in the eighth century – the word "*azulejo*" derives from the Arabic "*al-zulecha*" meaning "small stone". The Koran prevents the portrayal of living forms – hence the typically geometric Moorish designs – and the craft developed using thin ridges of clay to prevent the lead-based colours from running into each other. Early Portuguese tiles were produced using the same techniques – see the early sixteenth-century geometric tiles in the Palácio Nacional in Sintra (see p.132) – and because of these ridges the Catholic Portuguese were able to design figurative images. Portuguese *azulejos* developed their own style around the mid-sixteenth century when a new Italian method – introduced to Iberia by Francisco Niculoso – enabled images to be painted directly onto the clay thanks to a tin oxide coating which prevented running.

At first, religious imagery was the favoured form – such as those in the Igreja de São Roque (see p.80) – but during the seventeenth century decadent and colourful images were all the rage. Wealthy Portuguese began to commission large *azulejos* panels displaying battles, hunting scenes and fantastic images influenced by Vasco Da Gama's voyages to the east. Later, Dutch Delftware techniques made it possible to add much more detail to each tile. Large *azulejos* panels were also commissioned for churches – these often covered an entire wall and became known as *tapetes* (carpets) because of their resemblance to large rugs. Fascinating examples of these can be seen in the Museu Nacional do Azulejo (see above).

By the late seventeenth century, blue and white tiles influenced by Dutch tile-makers, were popular with Portugal's aristocracy, and their favoured images were flowers and fruit – see the Palácio dos Marquêses de Fronteira (see p.95). The early eighteenth century saw artist masters being highly trained to compete with international rivals, producing elaborately decorated multicoloured ceramic mosaics, culminating in Rococo themes which can be seen, for example, in Madre Deus (see above).

After the Great Earthquake, more prosaic tiled facades, often with Neoclassical designs, were considered good insulation devices, as well as protecting buildings from rain and fire. By the mid-nineteenth century, *azulejos* were being mass-produced to decorate shops and factories – such as the tiles on the front of the Fábrica Viúva Lamego (p.121) – while the end of the century saw the reappearance of figurative designs, typified by the work in the Cervejaria da Trindade (p.107). The nineteenth century also heralded the arrival of individualists like Rafael Bordalo Pinheiro (p.95), who used *azulejos* for satirical purposes. Art Deco took hold in the 1920s, while more modern works can be admired in Lisbon's underground stations – Campo Pequeno, Colégio Militar and Cidade Universitária, among others. But though there remain individual artists maintaining the hand-painted tradition, the majority of today's tiles continue to be less impressive mass-produced items, pale imitations of the old figurative or geometric designs.

Avenida da Liberdade, Parque Eduardo VII and Amoreiras

To the north of the Baixa is the city's principal park – the Parque Eduardo VII. The easiest approach is by metro (to Marquês de Pombal or Parque) or bus (to Marquês de Pombal), though you could take an energetic twenty-minute walk up the main **Avenida da Liberdade**, which would give you the chance to make a couple of stops along the way. The bottom end of Avenida da Liberdade, just above the new metro interchange at Restauradores, has some of the city's nicest outdoor **cafés**, with esplanade tables in the green swathes that split the avenue. Running parallel, to the east, the pedestrianized **Rua das Portas de Santo Antão** is well known for the seafood restaurants that line it; their waiters hover by every doorway attempting to entice you in. Despite the obvious tourist trappings, you can still have a good, reasonably inexpensive meal here (see p.108).

Once the Avenida da Liberdade was the exclusive address for some of Lisbon's most respected figures, and heading north, west of Avenida at Rua Rosa Araújo 41, you can experience a taste of this opulence at the **Fundação Medeiros e Almeida** (Mon–Sat 1–5.30pm; €5), set in the former home of art collector António Medeiros (1895–1986). Parts of the museum have been kept as they were when he lived there, other rooms display his priceless collection of works including 2000-year old Chinese porcelain, an important collection of sixteenth to nineteenth-century watches and English and Portuguese silverware. Look out for the sumptuous eighteenth-century *azulejos* in the Sala de Lago, a room filled with fountains.

Parque Eduardo VII

At the top of the avenue, in the formal, elongated **Parque Eduardo VII**, the big attractions are the **Estufas** (daily: April–Sept 9am–5.30pm, Oct–March 9am–4.30pm; €1.10). These are huge and wonderful hothouses at the park's northern end, and are filled with tropical plants, pools and endless varieties of palms and cacti. Rock and classical concerts and an antiques fair are occasionally held in the **Estufa Fria**. Just south of the Estufas, next to a children's play area, is a handy café with tables set up outside. You can walk uphill past the viewpoint, which affords fine views over the city, over the grassy hillock to the Gulbenkian museum (see below), or alternatively take bus #51, which runs from Belém to the museum via the top of the park.

Amoreiras

Leading west of the park from Praça do Marquês de Pombal, Avenida J.A. de Aguiar becomes Avenida E. Duarte Pacheco, on which you will find Lisbon's Post-Modernist shopping centre, **Amoreiras** (daily 10am–midnight), still visible on the city skyline from almost any approach despite the growing number of high-rise blocks around it. The complex, designed by Tomás Taveira in the 1980s, is a wild fantasy of pink and blue, sheltering eleven cinema screens, sixty cafés and restaurants, 370 shops and a hotel. Most of the shops here stay open until midnight (11pm on Sun); the heaviest human traffic is on Sunday, when entire families descend on the complex for an afternoon out. To get here directly by bus, take the #11 from Rossio/Restauradores.

While in the area, head down the narrow Rua das Amoreiras to the delightful **Praça das Amoreiras,** dominated on its west side by the end section of the Aqueduto das Águas Livres (see below) and on the south side by the **Mãe d'Água** water cistern (Mon–Sat 10am–6pm; €1.80), which marks the end of the line for the aqueduct. The interior holds a reservoir contained in a huge, semi-cathedral-like stone building with gothic lion heads along its square roof. Completed in 1843, the chunky, castellated structure nowadays hosts occasional exhibitions.

On the east side of Praça das Amoreiras, set in a former eighteenth-century silk factory, the **Fundação Arpad Siznes-Viera da Silva** (Mon & Wed–Sat noon–8pm, Sun 10am–6pm; €2.50) is a gallery dedicated to the works of two painters and the artists who have been influenced by them: the Hungarian-born Arpad Siznes (1897–1985) and his Portuguese-born wife Maria Helena Viera da Silva. The foundation shows the development of both the artists' works, with Viera da Silva's more abstract, subdued paintings contrasting with the colourful, more flamboyant Siznes, whose *Enfant au cerf-volant* shows the clear influences of Miró.

The Aqueduto das Águas Livres

Bus #11 passes Amoreiras and continues on the kilometre or so west to the **Aqueduto das Águas Livres**. Opened in 1748, the aqueduct brought reliable drinking water to the city for the first time. It stood firm during the 1755 earthquake and later became notorious through one Diogo Alves, a nineteenth-century serial killer who threw his victims off the arches – a drop of 60m. If you'd like to visit it, enquire at the Museu da Água (see p.82), who can arrange walking tours over the aqueduct. Once inside and up, you can make the very scenic walk across the aqueduct to the **Parque Monsanto**. The park, set on a wooded hill, is known as Lisbon's lungs, and though there are some good viewpoints from its heights, it tends to shelter some of Lisbon's less savoury characters and you should certainly avoid it after dark.

The Fundação Calouste Gulbenkian

The **Fundação Calouste Gulbenkian** is the great cultural centre of Portugal – and it is a wonder that it's not better known internationally. Housed in a superb complex, a few minutes' walk north of Parque Eduardo VII, the foundation is set in its own park, and features a museum whose collections seem to take in virtually every great phase of Eastern and Western art – from Ancient Egyptian scarabs to Art Nouveau jewellery, Islamic textiles to French Impressionists. In a separate building, across the park, the **Centro de Arte Moderna** sports excitingly displayed and largely Portuguese works, which touch on most styles of twentieth-century art. The complex has its main entrance at Avenida de Berna 45; to reach it, take **bus** #31 or #46 from Restauradores, #51 from Belém (not weekends), or the **metro** to Praça de Espanha or São Sebastião.

Astonishingly, all the main museum exhibits were acquired by just one man, the Armenian oil magnate **Calouste Gulbenkian** (1869–1955), whose legendary art-market coups included buying works from the Leningrad Hermitage after the Russian Revolution. In a scarcely less astute deal made during the last war, Gulbenkian literally auctioned himself and his collections to the European nations: Portugal bid security, an aristocratic palace home (a Marquês was asked to move out) and tax exemption, to acquire one of the most important cultural patrons of the century.

Today the Gulbenkian Foundation runs an orchestra, three concert halls and two galleries for temporary exhibitions, in the capital alone. It also finances work in all spheres of Portuguese cultural life – there are Gulbenkian museums and libraries in the smallest towns – and makes charitable grants to a vast range of projects. The admissions desk of the museum has a schedule of current activities.

Anyone travelling with children may be equally impressed to know that the Gulbenkian maintains a **Centro Artístico Infantil** in its gardens (entrance just off Rua Marquês de Sá de Bandeira), well stocked with toys and offering free **childcare sessions** for four- to twelve-year-olds between 9.30am and 5.30pm.

The Museu Gulbenkian

The **Museu Gulbenkian** (main entrance on Avenida de Berna; Tues 2–6pm, Wed–Sun 10am–6pm; €3, free on Sun; combined ticket with Museu de Arte Moderna €5) was completely renovated in 2001 which improved the layout and the labelling – now in English and Portuguese – as well as enlarging the exhibition space to allow viewing of items that were previously in storage. The collections aren't immense in number but each contains pieces of such individual interest and beauty that you need frequent unwinding sessions – well provided for by the basement **café-bar** and tranquil gardens.

Classical and oriental art

It seems churlish to hint at highlights, but they must include the entire contents of the small **Egyptian room**, which covers almost every period of importance from the Old Kingdom (2700 BC) to the Roman period. Particularly striking are the bronze cats from 664–525BC and the Head of Sestrostris III from the XIIth dynasty (2026–1785BC). Fine **Roman** statues, silver, glass and intricate gold jewellery and coins from ancient **Greece** come soon after. **Mesopotamia** produced the earliest forms of writing, and two cylinder seals – one dating from before 2500 BC – are on display here, along with architectural sculpture from the Assyrian civilization. **Islamic arts** are magnificently represented by ornamented texts, opulently woven carpets, glassware (such as the fourteenth-century mosque lamps from Syria) and Turkish *azulejos*. There is stunning fourteenth-century Syrian painted glass and some superbly intricate eighteenth-century silk coats from **Persia**. This is followed by remarkable illuminated manuscripts and ceramics from **Armenia**, porcelain from **China**, and beautiful **Japanese** prints and lacquer-work.

European art

European art (Rooms 8–17) includes work from all the major schools, beginning with a group of French medieval ivory diptychs (in particular the six scenes depicting the life of the Virgin) and a thirteenth-century version of St John's prophetic Apocalypse with the commentary of Beregaudus, produced in Kent and touched up in Italy under Pope Clement IX. From fifteenth-century Flanders, there's a pair of panels by van der Weyden, and from the same period in Italy comes Ghirlandaio's *Portrait of a Young Woman*. The seventeenth-century collection yields two exceptional portraits – one by Rubens of his second wife, *Helena Fourment*, and Rembrandt's *Figure of an Old Man* – plus works by van Dyck and Ruisdael. Eighteenth-century works featured include a good Fragonard, and a roll-call incorporating Gainsborough, Sir Thomas Lawrence and Francesco Guardi. Finally Corot, Manet, Monet, Degas and Renoir supply a good showing from nineteenth- to twentieth-century France.

Sculpture is poorly represented on the whole, though a fifteenth-century medallion of *Faith* by Luca della Robbia, a 1780 marble *Diana* by Jean-Antoine Houdon, and a couple of Rodins all stand out. Elsewhere, you'll find **ceramics** from Spain and Italy; **furniture** from Louis XV to Louis XVI; eighteenth-century works from **French goldsmiths**; fifteenth-century Italian bronze **medals** (especially by Pisanello); and assorted Italian tapestries and textiles, including a superb fifteen-century red velvet parasol from Venice. The last room consists of an Art Nouveau collection, with 169 pieces of fantasy jewellery by **René Lalique**; look for the amazing bronze and ivory Medusa paperweight (1902) and the fantastical *Peitoral-libélula* brooch, half woman, half dragonfly, decorated with enamel work, gold, diamonds and moonstones.

Centro de Arte Moderna

To reach the **Centro de Arte Moderna** (main entrance on Rua Dr. N. de Bettencourt; hours as main museum; €3, combined ticket with Museu Gulbenkian €5; free on Sun) walk through the gardens, which are enlivened by some specially commissioned sculptures. The light and well-laid-out centre features some big names on the twentieth-century Portuguese scene, including **Almada Negreiros** (1873–1970), the founder of *modernismo* (look out for his self-portrait, set in the café *A Brasileira*), Amadeu de Sousa Cardoso and Guilherme Santa-Rita (both of Futurist inclinations), and **Paula Rego** (one of Portugal's leading contemporary artists, now resident in England). Next to the museum, don't miss the perennially popular self-service **restaurant** (see p.109).

North of the Gulbenkian

Few visitors explore anything of Lisbon **north** of the Gulbenkian, unless for a trip to the Sporting or Benfica football stadiums. Near the youth hostel, however, there is an interesting house museum, **Casa-Museu Dr. Anastácio Gonçalves** and beyond the Campo Pequeno bullring, out past the Cidade Universitária, are other mildly diverting **museums**, devoted to the city's history and to costume, plus a private **art collection**. They are all on the route of the #1 bus, which runs from Cais do Sodré via Rossio. Over to the northwest of the Gulbenkian, further peripheral attractions are provided by the **Jardim Zoológico** (the city's zoo), and by the nearby **Palácio dos Marquêses da Fronteira**. Buses #31 links Restauradores with the Jardim Zoológico via Praça Marquês de Pombal, or take the metro, to Jardim Zoológico.

Casa-Museu Dr. Anastácio Gonçalves and Campo Pequeno

Close to the city youth hostel (see p.71) near metro Picoas is the **Casa-Museu Dr. Anastácio Gonçalves** (Wed–Sun 10am–6pm, Tues 2–6pm; €2), a little to the southwest on Rua Pinheiro Chagas. Set in the Casa Malhoa, a Neo-Romantic building with Art Nouveau touches – such as its beautiful stained-glass window – the house was constructed for the painter José Malhoa in 1904 and retains many of its original fittings. It now holds the private art collection of ophthalmologist, Dr Antastácio Gonçalves, Calouste Gulbenkian's doctor. When he died in 1964, Gonçalves left a collection not quite as sumptuous as the Armenian, but amongst his 2,000 works of art are paintings by Malhoa himself, Chinese porcelain from the sixteenth-century Ming dynasty, and furniture from England, France, Holland and Spain dating from the seventeenth century.

One kilometre north lies **Campo Pequeno**, beside the metro of the same name. This is the city's bullring, one of the largest in the world with a capacity of nearly 9,000. Built in 1893 with a stunning Moorish-influenced red roof, the bullring also hosts occasional concerts and visiting circuses. It is under going renovation at the time of writing, but is due to reopen in time for the

2003 bullfighting season (see p.119). Just southeast of the bullring, with its main entrance on Rua do Arco de Cego, the huge, futuristic **Culturgest** is one of Lisbon's main auditoriums (see p.118).

The Museu da Cidade, Museu Rafael Bordalo Pinheiro and Museu do Traje

Some 2km north of the Gulbenkian, around 1km north of Campo Pequeno, and just south of metro Campo Grande, the **Museu da Cidade** (Tues–Sun 10am–1pm & 2–6pm; €2, free on Sun and for under 18s) is installed in the eighteenth-century Palácio Pimenta, in the northwestern corner of Campo Grande. Its principal interest lies in an imaginative collection of prints, paintings and models of pre-1755 Lisbon. A death-defying crossing of the road leads you to another lovely mansion housing the **Museu Rafael Bordalo Pinheiro** (Tues–Sun 10am–1pm & 2–6pm; €1.40), dedicated to the nineteenth-century caricaturist and ceramicist. Upstairs exhibits include his amazing collection of ornate dishes crawling with crabs and lobsters, frogs and snakes. The paintings, cartoons and sketches downstairs are of less interest.

The **Museu do Traje** (Tues–Sun 10am–6pm; joint ticket with Museu do Teatro €3, free Sun 10am–2pm) occupies another eighteenth-century palace, the Palácio do Monteiro-Mor, some 2km further north of the Museu da Cidade on Estrada do Paço do Lumiar (reached by bus #1). The museum's extensive collections are drawn upon for temporary thematic exhibitions – excellent if costume is your subject, less gripping if you're not an aficionado of faded fabrics. For more casual visitors, the surrounding **park** is at least as big an attraction – one of the lushest areas of the city, open daily until 5pm and with a good restaurant and café. The small **Museu do Teatro** (Tues 2–6pm, Wed–Sun 10am–6pm; tickets as for Museu do Traje) containing theatrical memorabilia, is also sited in the grounds but is of truly specialist interest.

The Jardim Zoológico

The **Jardim Zoológico**, on Estrada de Benfica 158–160 (April–Sept 10am–8pm; Oct–March 10am–6pm; €10; ⓦ www.zoolisboa.pt) has been spruced up but remains one of the least inspiring of European zoos, exhibiting overheated bears and other unhappy captives. On the other hand much of it is little more than a rambling garden, and makes for an enjoyable afternoon's ramble, with a small *teleferique* or cable car (daily from 11am until closing time), a reptile house (10am–noon & 1–6pm), a boating lake and performing dolphins (at 11am, 3pm & 5pm) as further diversions. You can get there by metro, to Jardim Zoológico, or by bus #31 and #46 from Restauradores.

The Palácio dos Marquêses da Fronteira

Palace enthusiasts might like to visit the seventeenth-century **Palácio dos Marquêses da Fronteira** (tours daily Mon–Sat: June–Sept at 10.30am, 11am, 11.30am and noon; Oct–May at 11am and noon; €5, or €2.50 for the gardens only; reservations advised, ☎217 782 023), Largo de São Domingos de Benfica 1, which is around twenty minutes' walk west from the zoo; bus #46 from Restauradores (via the zoo) passes nearby. After the view of the bland housing development on Rua de São Domingos de Benfica, the fantastic gardens of this small, pink country house, complete with topiary, statues and fountains, feel like an oasis. Inside, there is period furniture along with more stunning *azulejos* dating back to the seventeenth century; those showing the battles during the Restoration Wars with Spain are particularly vivid.

The Museu Nacional de Arte Antiga

The **Museu Nacional de Arte Antiga** (Tues 2–6pm, Wed–Sun 10am–6pm; €3), Portugal's national gallery, certainly stands comparison with the Gulbenkian. The core of the museum – comprising fifteenth- and sixteenth-century Portuguese works by artists such as Nuno Gonçalves – is excellent and well displayed in a beautiful converted seventeenth-century palace; the garden and café (hours as for museum) are worth a visit in their own right. It is situated at Rua das Janelas Verdes 95 in the wealthy suburb of **Lapa**, 2km west of Praça do Comércio. To get there, take bus #40 or #60 from Praça do Comércio, or bus #27 or #49 on the way to or from Belém.

Gonçalves and the Portuguese School

Gonçalves and his fellow painters of the Portuguese school span that indeterminate and exciting period when Gothic art was giving way to the Renaissance. Their works, notably Gregório Lopes' *Martyrdom of São Sebastião*, and those by Frei Carlos, are exclusively religious in concept, and particularly interesting in their emphasis on portraiture – transforming any theme, even a martyrdom, into a vivid observation of local contemporary life. Stylistically, the most significant influences upon them were those of the Flemish, Northern Renaissance painters: Jan van Eyck, who came to Portugal in 1428, Memling and Mabuse (both well represented here) and Rogier van der Weyden.

The acknowledged masterpiece, however, is Gonçalves' **Panéis de São Vicente** (St Vincent Altarpiece; 1467–70), a brilliantly marshalled canvas depicting the saint – Lisbon's patron – receiving homage from all ranks of its citizens. On the two left-hand panels are Cistercian monks, fishermen and sailors; on the opposite side the Duke of Bragança and his family, a helmeted Moorish knight, a Jew (with book), a beggar, and a priest holding St Vincent's own relics (a piece of his skull, which is still displayed in the Sé). In the epic central panels the moustachioed Henry the Navigator, his nephew Afonso V (in green), and the youthful (future) Dom João II, pay tribute to the saint. Among the frieze of portraits behind them, that on the far left is reputed to be Gonçalves himself; the other central panel shows the Archbishop of Lisbon. **Later Portuguese painters** – from the sixteenth to the eighteenth century – are displayed too, most notably António de Sequeira and Josefa de Óbidos (see p.165).

The rest of the collection

After Gonçalves and his contemporaries the most interesting works are by **Flemish and German** painters – Cranach, Bosch (represented by a fabulous *Temptation of St Anthony*) and Dürer – and miscellaneous gems by Raphael, Zurbarán and Rodin. But exhibits more likely to delay you are those in the extensive **applied art** sections. Here, on Level 1, you'll find **Portuguese furniture and textiles** to rival the European selection in the Gulbenkian and, on Level 2, an excellent collection of **silverware** and **ceramics**. Also on Level 2, the **Oriental Art** collection shows the influence of Indian, African and Oriental designs. Other colonially influenced exhibits include inlaid furniture from Goa and a superb series of late sixteenth-century **Japanese screens**, showing the Portuguese landing at Nagasaki, complete with Pinnochio-like noses.

Belém

It was from **Belém** in 1497 that Vasco da Gama set sail for India, and here too that he was welcomed home by Dom Manuel "the Fortunate" (*o Venturoso*). Da Gama brought back with him a small cargo of pepper, but it was enough to pay for his voyage several times over. The monastery subsequently built here – the **Mosteiro dos Jerónimos** – stands as a testament to his triumphant discovery of a sea route to the Orient, which amounted to the declaration of a "golden age". Built to honour the vow Dom Manuel made to the Virgin in return for a successful voyage, it stands on the site of the old Ermida do Restelo or Capela de São Jerónimo, a hermitage founded by Henry the Navigator, where Vasco da Gama and his companions had spent their last night ashore in prayer. The monastery was partly funded by a levy on the fruits of da Gama's discovery – a five percent tax on all spices other than pepper, cinnamon and cloves, whose import had become the sole preserve of the Crown.

The Rio Tejo at Belém has receded with the centuries, for when the monastery was built it stood almost on the beach, within sight of caravels moored ready for expeditions, and of the **Torre de Belém**, guarding the entrance to the port. This, too, survived the earthquake and is the other showpiece Manueline building in Lisbon. Both monastery and tower lie in what is now – despite the road and railway cutting it in half – a pleasant waterfront suburb, 6km west of the city centre, close to a small group of museums, and with some fine **cafés and restaurants**. Make time, in particular, for the *Antiga Confeitaria de Belém*, in Rua de Belém, by the tram stop, which bills itself as the "única fábrica de pasteis de Belém" – *pasteis de Belém* being delicious flaky tartlets filled with custard-like cream.

Belém is easily reached by **tram** (signed Algés) – the fast supertram #15 runs from Praça da Figueira via Praça do Comércio taking about twenty minutes – or by the Oeiras train from Cais do Sodré or bus #51 (not weekends) from the Gulbenkian museum. Note that a *comboio turístico* (**toy train**) departs roughly hourly (10am–noon & 2–5pm) from in front of the Mosteiro dos Jerónimos up to the Torre de Belém and back. If you feel like escaping to a **beach** you can get a **ferry** across the Tejo from Belém to Trafaria, which is only 3km by

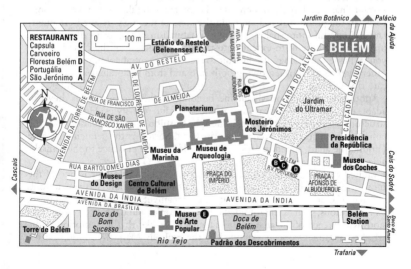

bus from Costa da Caparica (see p.143); (ferries every 30min–1hr, Mon–Sat 6.30am–11.30pm, Sun 7.30–11.30pm; €0.55), from a terminus right by the train station (some five minutes from central Belém). Alternatively, **trains** from here continue to Oeiras where you can change for Cascais (see p.126). When planning your trip keep in mind that quite a few of the sights at Belém are closed on Mondays.

The Mosteiro dos Jerónimos

Even before the Great Earthquake, the **Mosteiro dos Jerónimos** (daily – restricted access on Saturday mornings and during Mass – June–Sept 10am–6.30pm; Oct–May 10am–5pm; free; Cloisters: same hours, €3, free Sun 10am–2pm) was Lisbon's finest monument: since then, it has stood quite without comparison. Begun in 1502 and more or less completed when its funding was withdrawn by João III in 1551, the monastery is the most ambitious and successful achievement of Manueline architecture (see box on p.190). It is less flamboyantly exotic than either Tomar or Batalha – the great culminations of the style in Estremadura – but, despite a succession of master-builders, it has more daring and confidence in its overall design. This is largely the achievement of two outstanding figures: **Diogo de Boitaca**, perhaps the originator of the Manueline style with his Igreja de Jesus at Setúbal, and **João de Castilho**, a Spaniard who took over the construction from around 1517.

It was Castilho who designed the **main entrance** to the **church** (closed during Mass) a complex, shrine-like hierarchy of figures centred around Henry the Navigator (on a pedestal above the arch). In its intricate and almost flat ornamentation, it shows the influence of the then current Spanish style, Plateresque (literally, the art of the silversmith). Yet it also has distinctive Manueline features – the use of rounded forms, the naturalistic motifs in the bands around the windows – and these seem to create both its harmony and individuality. Appropriately, just inside the entrance lie the stone **tombs** of Vasco da Gama (1468–1523) and the great poet and recorder of the discoveries, Luís de Camões (1527–70).

The breathtaking sense of space inside the church places it among the great triumphs of European Gothic. Here, though, Manueline developments add two extraordinary and fresh dimensions. There are carefully restrained tensions between the grand spatial design and the areas of intensely detailed ornamentation. And, still more striking, there is a naturalism in the forms of this ornamentation that seems to extend into the actual structure of the church. Once you've made the analogy, it's difficult to see the six central columns as anything other than palm trunks, growing both into and from the branches of the delicate rib-vaulting.

Another peculiarity of Manueline buildings is the way in which they can adapt, enliven, or encompass any number of different styles. Here, the basic structure is thoroughly Gothic, though Castilho's ornamentation on the columns is much more Renaissance in spirit. So too is the semicircular apse (around the altar), added in 1572, beyond which is the entrance to the remarkable double cloister.

Vaulted throughout and fantastically embellished, the **cloister** is one of the most original and beautiful pieces of architecture in the country. Again, it holds in balance Gothic forms and Renaissance ornamentation and is exuberant in its innovations, such as the rounded corner canopies and delicate twisting divisions within each of the arches. These lend a wave-like, rhythmic motion to the whole structure, a conceit extended by the typically Manueline motifs drawn from ropes, anchors and the sea. In this – as in all aspects – it would be hard to imagine an artistic style more directly reflecting the achievements and preoccupations of an age.

In the wings of the monastery are two museums. The **Museu de Arqueologia** (Tues 2–6pm, Wed–Sun 10am–6pm; €3, free Sun morning), to the west of the main entrance, seems sparse and, apart from a few fine Roman mosaics unearthed in the Algarve, thoroughly unexceptional. In contrast, the enormous **Museu da Marinha** (Tues–Sun June–Sept 10am–6pm; Oct–May 10am–5pm; €2.50), with its entrance opposite the Centro Cultural de Belém, is more interesting, packed not only with models of ships, naval uniforms and a surprising display of artefacts from Portugal's oriental trade and colonies, but also with real vessels – among them fishing boats and sumptuous state barges – a couple of seaplanes and even some fire engines. It also incorporates the **Museu das Crianças**, a children's museum, with imaginative interactive displays designed to raise children's awareness of themselves, other children and adults.

The Torre de Belém

Still washed on three sides by the sea, the **Torre de Belém** (Tues–Sun: June–Sept 10am–6pm; Oct–May 10am–5pm; €3) stands 500m west of the monastery, fronted by a little park with a café. Whimsical, multi-turreted and with a real hat-in-the-air exuberance, it was built over the last five years of Dom Manuel's reign (1515–20) as a fortress to safeguard the approach to Lisbon's harbour – before the Great Earthquake shifted its course, it stood virtually in the centre of the river. As such, it is the one completely Manueline building in Portugal, the rest having been adaptations of earlier structures or completed in later years (see box on p.190).

Its architect, **Francisco de Arruda**, had previously worked on Portuguese fortifications in Morocco and the Moorish influence is very strong in the delicately arched windows and balconies. Prominent also in the decoration are two great symbols of the age: Manuel's personal badge of an armillary sphere (representing the globe) and the cross of the military Order of Christ, once the Templars, who took a major role in all Portuguese conquests. Though worth entering for the views from the roof, the tower's interior is unremarkable except for a "whispering gallery". It was used into the nineteenth century as a prison, notoriously by Dom Miguel (1828–34), who kept political enemies in the waterlogged dungeons.

Back towards the Monumento dos Descobrimentos

Walking back along the waterfront, towards the monastery, you'll pass the **Museu de Arte Popular** (Mon–Sat 10am–12.30pm & 2–5pm; €1.75, free Sun 10am–2pm), a province-by-province display of Portugal's still very diverse folk arts, housed in a shed-like building. Almost adjacent is the **Padrão dos Descobrimentos** (Monument to the Discoveries; Tues–Sun June–Sept 9am–7pm, Nov–May 9am–5pm; €2), an angular slab of concrete in the shape of a caravel which was erected in 1960 to commemorate the 500th anniversary of the death of Henry the Navigator. Henry appears on the prow with Camões and other Portuguese heroes. Within the monument is a temporary exhibition space, with interesting and changing exhibits on the city's history; the entrance fee also lets you climb right up to the top for some fine views of the Tejo and Torre de Belém.

The Centro Cultural de Belém, the Museu do Design and the Museu dos Coches

Across from the monument, on the western side of the Praça do Imperio, an underpass leads to the modern **Centro Cultural de Belém** (Mon–Fri 11am–8pm, Sat & Sun 10am–7pm; ⓦwww.ccb.pt), controversially built in 1992 right by the historic monastery. This puts on regular cultural exhibitions and concerts as well as hosting some live entertainment over the weekend – jugglers, mime artists and the like. For the best views of the surroundings, drop into the café, whose garden esplanade overlooks the river and the Monument dos Descobrimentos.

The Centro Cultural's Exhibition Centre houses the **Museu do Design** (daily 11am–8pm, last entry 7.15pm; €3; ☎213 612 400), which has been cited as having one of the most important collections in Europe. Opened in 1999, the collection is enormous and the exhibits are occasionally rotated, although the most important items usually remain on display. These are displayed chronologically in three sections entitled "Luxo" (Luxury), "Pop" and "Cool" and comprise design classics including furniture, glass and jewellery spanning the period from 1937 to today, all amassed by former stockbroker and media mogul Francisco Capelo. Classics include Charles and Ray Eames' fibreglass chairs, 1970s bean bags and an amazing Joe Colombo Mini Kitchen, while the late twentieth century features Phillipe Starck's chairs, works by the Memphis Group and contemporary designs by Tomas Tavira and Álvaro Siza.

At the corner of Belém's other main square – Praça Afonso de Albuquerque, a few minutes' walk east from the monastery along Rua de Belém – you'll find the **Museu dos Coches** (Tues–Sun 10am–6pm; €3). Housed in the attractive former riding school of the President's palace, it consists of an interminable line of royal coaches – baroque, heavily gilded and sometimes beautifully painted.

East to Ponte 25 de Abril

Heading back over the railway footbridge to the riverside from Praça Afonso de Albuquerque, past the ferry station, it is possible to walk the 2km along the relatively traffic-free gardens all the way from Belém to the towering Ponte 25 de Abril. En route is the extraordinary redbrick **Museu da Electricidade** (Tues–Fri & Sun 10am–12.30pm & 2–5.30pm, Sat 10am–12.30pm & 2–8pm; €3), an early twentieth-century electricity generating station with cathedral-like windows. The electricity museum's highlights include its original enormous generators, steam turbines and winches – all looking like something out of the science-fiction film *Brazil*.

Back north of the railway line, just beyond the high-tech Lisbon Congress Centre on the main Rua da Junqueira 30, it is another ten minutes' walk to the **Museu do Centro Científico e Cultural de Macau** (Tues–Sun 10am–5pm, Sun noon–6pm; €2.50). This museum is dedicated to Portugal's trading links with the Orient and its former colony of Macau, which was handed back to Chinese rule in 1999. There are model boats and audio displays detailing early journeys, and exhibits of Chinese art from the sixteenth to the nineteenth centuries which include porcelain, statuary, silverware and an impressive array of opium pipes and ivory boxes.

Palácio da Ajuda

Jump on bus #14, from central Belém or Calçada da Ajuda behind the Museu dos Coches, for the short ride uphill to the **Palácio da Ajuda** (half-hour tours Mon, Tues & Thurs–Sun 10am–4.30pm; €3, free Sun morning 10am–2pm). The palace was built by those crashingly tasteless nineteenth-century royals,

Dona Maria II and Dom Ferdinand, and like their Pena Palace folly at Sintra (see p.130) is all over-the-top aristocratic clutter. The **banqueting hall**, however, is quite a sight; likewise the lift, decked out with mahogany and mirrors. Next to the palace is the attractive **Jardim Botânico d'Ajuda** (Mon, Tues & Thurs–Sun 9am–dusk; €1.50), one of the city's oldest botanical gardens – a fine example of formal Portuguese gardening boasting some great views over Belém. Tram #18 will get you back from the palace to Praça do Comércio, or take #60 to Praça da Figueira.

Parque das Nações

Now called **Parque das Nações** – the Park of Nations – the former Expo 98 site, 5km to the east of the city, remains a huge attraction for Lisboans who pack out the 2km-long site especially at weekends. The main highlight is the world's second largest **Oceanarium**, one of Lisbon's most impressive landmarks. The **Virtual Reality Pavilion** is another key draw, while the educational exhibits in the **Centre of Live Science** are also highly rewarding. Other attractions include water gardens, a cable-car offering a stunning perspective over the site, a viewing tower, two of Lisbon's largest concert venues and a diverse array of bars, shops and restaurants, many with outdoor seating overlooking Olivais docks and the astonishing 17km-long Vasco da Gama bridge over the Tagus. The park is part of an area of three square kilometres along Lisbon's eastern riverfront, which is slowly being transformed into a large-scale business and residential zone, complete with a mammoth riverside park. The main aim is of redirecting Lisbon's sprawling suburbs in a more planned fashion; completion is due in the next ten years.

Getting there

Stepping off Oriente metro, you arrive in the bowels of the **Estação do Oriente**, a stunning glass-and-concrete bus and train interchange designed by Spanish architect Santiago Calatrava; from the station, there are connecting overland trains to Santa Apolónia station, as well as bus links to towns north and south of the Tagus. See p.142 for details of ferry connections from Cacilhas. As you exit the station, head through the Vasco da Gama shopping centre to the main **Posto de Informação** (information desk; daily 9.30am–8pm; ⓦwww.parquedasnacoes.pt), which has details of current events. For families or if you want to visit more than a couple of sights, it may be worth buying a *Cartão do Parque* here. The card (€11.50, or €28 for a family of four) allows unlimited access to the main sights and discounts at other attractions.

A **toy train** trundles anticlockwise round the whole Parque every 20min (daily 10.30am–7pm; €1), starting and finishing in front of the Atlantic Pavilion. You can also hire bikes (from around €4/hr), a good way to get round the flat, traffic-free lanes. It is not too taxing, however, to walk to the principal attractions, especially if you take advantage of the cable car (see above). Within the Parque, there are ATMs, a post office and countless bars and restaurants, the best of which are reviewed on p.109.

Oceanário de Lisboa

From the park's main entrance turn right along the waterfront and the futuristic **Oceanarium** (daily 10am–7pm; €8.50) is only a five-minute walk. At weekends in particular, hour-long queues to get in are not uncommon, so it is worth getting here early. Designed by Peter Chermayeff, and resembling a set

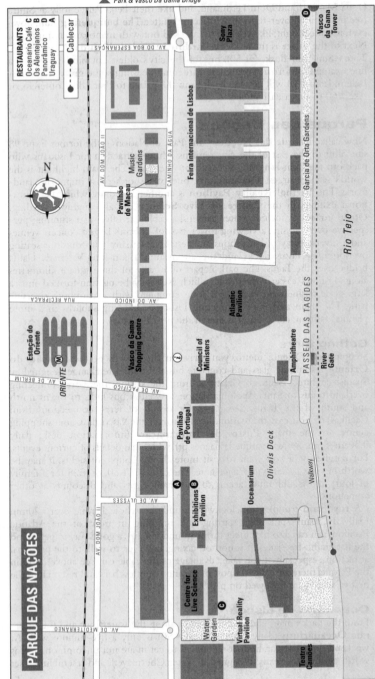

PARQUE DAS NAÇÕES

RESTAURANTS
Oceanário Café   C
Os Alentejanos   B
Panorâmico   D
Uruguay   A

● ─ ─ ─ ● Cablecar

N

▲ Park & Vasco Da Gama Bridge

Estação do Oriente

Vasco da Gama Shopping Centre

Pavilhão de Macau

Music Gardens

Feira Internacional de Lisboa

Sony Plaza

Vasco da Gama Tower D

Garcia de Orta Gardens

Council of Ministers

Atlantic Pavilion

Pavilhão de Portugal

Exhibitions Pavilion A B

Centre for Live Science

Virtual Reality Pavilion C

Water Garden

Teatro Camões

Oceanarium

Olivais Dock

Amphitheatre

River Gate

PASSEIO DAS TAGIDES

Walkway

Rio Tejo

AV. DO BOA ESPERANÇAS

AV. DOM JOÃO II

CAMINHO DA ÁGUA

AV. DO INDICO

RUA RECIPRAÇA

AV. DE BERLIM

ORIENTE

AV. DE PACIFICO

AV. DOM JOÃO II

AV. DE ULYSSES

AV. DOM JOÃO II

AV. DE MEDITERRÂNEO

i

M

▼ Lisbon

from a James Bond film, Europe's largest oceanarium contains some 25,000 fish and marine animals. Its main feature is the enormous central tank, the size of four Olympic-sized swimming pools, which you can look into from different levels to get close-up views of the various creatures that live on the surface, including sharks, down to the rays which live on the sea bed. Almost more impressive, though, are the re-creations of various ocean ecosystems, such as the Antarctic tank containing frolicking penguins, and the Pacific tank, where otters bob about and play in the rock pools. These areas are separated from the main tank by invisible acrylic sheets, which gives the impression that all the marine creatures are swimming together in the same space. On the darkened lower level, smaller tanks contain shoals of brightly coloured tropical fish and other warm water creatures. Find a window free of the school parties and the whole experience becomes the closest you'll get to deep-sea diving without getting wet.

The site and other attractions

Heading back towards Oriente station from the Oceanarium is the **Centro da Ciência Viva** (Centre for Live Science; Tues–Fri 10am–6pm, Sat & Sun 11am–7pm, last entry an hour before closing; €4.50). Run by Portugal's Ministry of Science and Technology (which shares the premises), the centre is great for kids, with permanent interactive exhibits, including holograms and a cybercafé with 30 terminals offering free internet access; there are also temporary exhibits with labelling in Portuguese and English. Behind the centre lies the **Jardim da Água** (Water Garden), crisscrossed by ponds linked by stepping stones, with enough fountains, water gadgets and pumps to keep kids occupied for hours. At the foot of the gardens stands the **Pavilhão da Realidade Virtual** (Virtual Reality Pavilion: daily noon–5.30pm; €8), a fascinating re-creation of the adventures of Luís de Camões's sixteenth-century travels to the new world. The tour round a series of multimedia presentations starts slowly, but culminates in a memorable virtual ride on a caravel through a tempest and pirate attack.

On the riverfront side of the Virtual Reality Pavilion is the **Teatro Camões**, the Parque's main venue for theatre, classical music and opera. Beyond here, a narrow walkway leads across Olivais docks below the **cable car** (daily 11am–7pm; €2.50 one way) which shuttles you to the northern side of the Parque, with commanding views on the way.

The cable car leaves you just beyond the **Jardim Garcia de Orta** (Garcia de Orta garden), a leafy waterside strip displaying plant species from Portugal's former colonies. But the main draw on this side of the Parque is a lift ride to the top of the **Torre Vasco da Gama** (Vasco da Gama Tower; Mon–Thur 10am–8pm, Fri & Sat 10am–10pm; €2.50). A relic from its former incarnation as part of an oil refinery, the viewing platform at the top gives a 360 degree panorama over Lisbon, the Tejo and into the Alentejo to the south. There also a pricey restaurant on the summit (see p.109). Opposite the tower is the **Sony Plaza**, Lisbon's largest purpose-built outdoor arena which hosts concerts and sports events. When there are no events it hosts **Adrenalina**, a small adventure park zone featuring skateboard ramps, climbing walls, trampolines and a Skycoaster, a kind of bunjee swing suspended 35m up; there are also bouncy castles and inflatables for younger children. Opposite here, Lisbon's trade fair hall, the **Feira Internacional de Lisboa** (FIL) hosts various temporary events including a handicrafts fair displaying crafts from round the country (usually in July). At the back of FIL, the mock-colonial **Pavilhão de Macau** (Pavilion of Macau; Tues–Fri noon–6pm, Sat & Sun 3–8pm; €2) is the only international pavilion remaining from Expo 98, and displays traditional and modern aspects of the former Portuguese colony, including a Chinese garden.

Heading back towards Olivais Docks you'll pass the bulk of the **Pavilhão Atlântico** (Atlantic Pavilion), officially Portugal's largest indoor arena and another venue for touring bands and sporting events. Opposite stands one of the most impressive of the many adventurous structures in the Parque, the elegant Pavilhão de Portugal (Portugal Pavilion), the main building facing Olivais docks. Designed by Álvaro Siza Vieira, Portugal's best-known architect, the building now holds Portugal's **Council of Ministers**. From here it is a short walk back to Oriente station, or to the waterfront cafés and restaurants of Olivais Docks.

Eating

Lisbon has some of the best-value **cafés and restaurants** of any European city, serving large portions of good Portuguese food at sensible prices. A set menu (*ementa turística*) at lunch or dinner will get you a three-course meal for €10–13, though you can eat for considerably less than this by sticking to the ample main dishes and choosing the daily specials. **Seafood** is widely available – there's an entire central street, Rua das Portas de Santo Antão, as well as a whole enclave of restaurants across the Rio Tejo at Cacilhas, that specialize in it. This is the only time you'll need to be careful what you eat if you're on a tight budget as seafood is always pricier than other menu items. Several traditional restaurants still survive in Lisbon, most notably beautifully tiled **cervejarias** (literally beer halls) where the emphasis is often as much on drinking as eating; while the capital, naturally, also features some of the country's best (and most expensive) restaurants – specializing for the most part in a hybrid French–Portuguese cuisine. If you tire of all this, Lisbon has a rich vein of inexpensive **foreign restaurants**, in particular those featuring food from the former colonies: Brazil, Mozambique, Angola, Cape Verde, Macão and Goa.

There are plenty of restaurants scattered around the Baixa, a good spot for lunch as there a multitude of set lunches are on offer catering for office employees, and there are some good places, too, in all the other areas in which you're likely to be sightseeing, up in the Alfama and out in Belém. **By night** the obvious place to be is Bairro Alto, which houses several of the city's trendiest restaurants, as well as other more basic value-for-money venues. Metro stops are given for outlying restaurants if this is the best way to reach them.

Note that many restaurants are closed on **Sunday evenings** or **Mondays**, while on Saturday nights in midsummer you may need to book for the more popular places: phone numbers are given below where **reservations** are necessary, or pass by during the day to reserve a table. The following are open daily unless marked. The listings below have been coded into three **price categories**: inexpensive (less than €15); moderate (€15–20); and expensive (above €20). These prices refer to the cost of a two-course meal including wine, but excluding tips. All the places listed accept major **credit cards** unless specifically stated.

You can get snacks and sandwiches in most cafés and bars (see the following section); for locations of **markets** and central **shopping centres**, see pp.121–122.

Vegetarian options

All the following restaurants are reviewed in this chapter – not all of them are purely vegetarian, but all offer good meat-free options.

Celeiro, Baixa, below
Centro de Arte Moderna, Saldanha, p.109
Farah's Tandoori, Lapa, p.107
Centro de Alimentaçao e Saúde Natural, Avenida da Liberdade, p.108
Espiral, Avenida Reis, p.109
Teatro Taborda, Castelo, p.108
Os Tibetanos, Avenida da Liberdade, p.108
Refeições Naturais, Baixa, below

Baixa

The restaurants are marked on the Baixa map p.74.

Andorra Rua das Portas de Santo Antão 82. Occupying a raised bit of the street, the *Andorra* specializes in *açorda* and *arroz de marisco*, plus fresh fish and steaks served at its well-positioned outdoor tables. Not particularly cheap, but inside it's small and cosy. Moderate.

Beira Gare Praça Dom João da Câmara. Long-standing snack-bar restaurant opposite Rossio station serving stand-up Portuguese snacks and cheap lunches and dinners in the back diner. Inexpensive.

A Berlenga Rua Barros Queiróz 29, behind São Domingos church. A *cervejaria*/restaurant with a window stuffed full of crabs and seafood. Early-evening snackers at the bar munching prawns give way to local diners eating meals chosen from the window displays. Moderate–expensive.

Casa do Alentejo Rua das Portas de Santo Antão 58. Extravagantly decorated building which is as much a private club dedicated to Alentejan culture as mere restaurant. The courtyard is stunning, as is the period furniture. The house also holds cultural exhibits, giving a great ambience to the sound Portuguese food. Moderate.

Celeiro Macrobiótico-Naturista Rua 1° de Dezembro 65. Just off Rossio, this health-food supermarket with basement self-service restaurant offers tasty vegetarian spring rolls, quiches and the like. Open till 8pm; closed weekends. Inexpensive.

Gambrinus Rua das Portas de Santo Antão 15 ☎213 421 466. One of Lisbon's top seafood restaurants, serving up dishes like broiled eel with bacon, lobster and dessert crepes in a smart, wood-panelled interior. Expensive.

João do Grão Rua dos Correeiros 220–228. Established Baixa restaurant with *azulejo*-covered interior, outdoor seats, and good, reliable Portuguese dishes and interesting salads. Moderate.

Leão d'Ouro Rua 1° de Dezembro 105 ☎213 469 495. Very attractive, *azulejo*-covered restaurant specializing in seafood and grilled meats. Get there early or book to reserve a table. Moderate–expensive.

Martinho da Arcada Praça do Comércio 3. Beautiful, traditional restaurant, in the arcade, little changed from the beginning of the century when it was frequented by writer Fernando Pessoa. Closed Sun. Expensive.

Refeições Naturais e Vegetarianos Rua dos Correeiros 205, 2°. Atmospheric self-service canteen with a daily changing menu of vegetarian hot and cold meals – usually crepes, rissoles and rice dishes – in second-floor Baixa town house. Closes 7pm and weekends. Inexpensive.

Rei dos Frangos Trav. de Santo Antão 11–18. Also known as *Bom Jardim*, this place has branches on two sides of an alleyway connecting Restauradores with Rua das Portas de Santo Antão. It is the place for spit-roast chicken – whole ones with fries for about €6.

Adega Santo Antão Rua das Portas de Santo Antão 42. Very good value *adega* with a bit of local character: a bustling bar area and tables inside and out offering great grilled meat and fish. Closed Mon. Inexpensive.

Solmar Rua das Portas de Santo Antão 108 ☎213 423 371. A vast showpiece seafood restaurant, with fountain and marine mosaics, though food can be somewhat hit or miss. Expensive.

Chiado

Unless stated the restaurants are marked on the Baixa map p.74.

Associação Católica Trav. Ferragial 1. Go through the unmarked door and head to the top floor for this self-service canteen offering different dishes each day. The chief attractions are the low prices and the fine rooftop terrace with views over the Tejo. Open Mon–Fri noon–3pm. Inexpensive.

L'Entrecôte Rua do Alecrim 121. The place to eat

steaks washed down with fine wines. Relaxed, informal atmosphere in a spacious, wood-panelled interior with soaring ceilings (see Bairro Alto map pp.78–79). Closed Sun lunch. Moderate–expensive.

Tágide Largo Academia das Belas Artes 18–20 ☎213 420 720. One of Lisbon's priciest restaurants, serving superb regional dishes in a dining room with sweeping city views. Book ahead, especially for a window seat. Closed weekends. Expensive.

Around Cais do Sodré

The restaurants are marked on the Bairro Alto map pp78–79.

Cais da Ribeira Armazem A, Porta 2 ☎213 463 611. Attractive converted warehouse with river views around the back of Cais do Sodré serving superior fish, meat and seafood dinners, straight from the market. Evenings only except Sun; closed Mon. Expensive.

Marisqueira do Cais do Sodré Cais do Sodré ☎213 422 105. Big, pricey seafood restaurant by the station, complete with bubbling fish tanks. Try the *caldeirada de tamboril* (monkfish stew), the *caril de gambas* (curried prawns) or the seafood *parrilhada*. Closed last week in Oct. Expensive.

Porto de Abrigo Rua dos Remolares 16–18. Old-style tavern-restaurant serving market-fresh fish at reasonable prices. Closed Mon. Inexpensive–moderate.

Bairro Alto

Unless stated, the restaurants are marked on the Bairro Alto map pp78–79.

1° de Maio Rua da Atalaia 8. Buzzing *adega* at the Chiado end of the road; good-value dishes of the day and sizzling meat and fish dishes. Closed all day Sun and Sat evenings. Inexpensive.

Adega do Teixeira Rua da Teixeira 39. The leafy, streetside outdoor terrace is unusual for this part of town and the main appeal of this tranquil restaurant; all the usual Portuguese dishes and good salads. Closed Sun. Moderate.

Ali-a-Papa Rua da Atalaia 95. Rare Moroccan restaurant with an attractive interior. Good-value couscous and tajine dishes. Closed Tues. Moderate.

Bizarro Rua da Atalaia 133. Unpretentious spot with a limited, but tasty, menu and a TV in the corner. The *ementa turística* is a good deal. Closed all day Sun, and Sat lunch. Inexpensive.

Bota Alta Trav. da Queimada 37 ☎213 427 959. This attractive old tavern with quirky, boot-themed decor (its name means "high boot") attracts queues for its large portions of traditional Portuguese food. It's always packed and the tables

are crammed in cheek by jowl; try to get there before 8pm. Closed Sat lunch and all day Sun. Moderate.

Brasuca Rua João Pereira da Rosa 7 ☎213 220 740. Well-established Brazilian restaurant in a great old building down hill from the Bairro Alto. Dishes include good *feijoada moqueca* (chicken and beans stew), *picanha* (slices of garlicky beef). Closed Mon from Nov–April. Moderate.

Restaurante Calcuta Rua do Norte 17 ☎213 428 295. Very popular Indian restaurant at the foot of the Bairro Alto, with modern decor and a largely young clientele. Lots of chicken, seafood and lamb curries, tandooris, good vegetarian options and a reasonable tourist menu. Closed Sun. Moderate.

O Cantinho do Bem Estar Rua do Norte 46. The decor borders on the kitsch, with fake chickens and a tiled roof over the kitchen, but the "canteen of well-being" lives up to its name with friendly service. Rice dishes and generous salads are the best bet; the passable house wine comes in ceramic jugs. Moderate.

Casa Transmontana Calçada do Duque 39. Tiny place specializing in cuisine from northern Portugal, mostly meat-oriented. Inexpensive.

Comida de Santo Calçada Engenheiro Miguel Pais 39. Rowdy, late-opening Brazilian restaurant serving cocktails and classic dishes. Off Rua das Escola Politécnica, opposite the entrance to the botanical gardens. Expensive.

Estibordo Trav. João de Deus 14. Simple local restaurant with slightly gloomy ship-theme decor. Specialities include prawns or veal in breadcrumbs (*vitela empanada*), served with liberal swathes of mayonnaise. Not for healthy eaters, but very good value. If you fancy something lighter, grab a stool at the bar for a good range of *petiscos*. Closed Sun. Inexpensive.

Faz Frio Rua Dom Pedro V 96. A beautiful, traditional restaurant, replete with tiles and private cubicles. Huge portions of *bacalhau*, seafood paella and daily specials, a five-minute walk north of the Bairro Alto up Rua Dom Pedro V. Inexpensive.

Mamma Rosa Rua do Grémio Lusitano 14. Late-opening pizza and pasta restaurant popular with the student and gay communities; always bustling and good value. Inexpensive.

Pap'Açorda Rua da Atalaia 57–59 ☎213 464 811. Famous restaurant attracting arty celebrities who enjoy the agreeable surroundings of a dining room converted from an old bakery, now hung with chandeliers. *Açorda* – the house speciality – is a sort of bread and shellfish stew, seasoned with fresh coriander and a raw egg. Reservations recommended. Closed Mon. Expensive.

Rouge Trav. dos Fiéis de Deus 28 ☎213 426 372.

Fashionable clientele, eastern-inspired decor and an interesting mix of Thai and Mediterranean cuisine, including decent Greek salads. The most appealing aspect is the outdoor seating – a rarity in the Bairro Alto – on this stepped side street. Closed Mon. Moderate.

Sul Rua do Norte 13. Idiosyncratic restaurant and tapas bar that – as its name suggest – serves all types of food from the South, ie southern Portugal/Spain/Italy, southern Africa and South America. The lower level houses a neat bar with classy wines and bar snacks. Closed Mon. Moderate.

Cervejaria da Trindade Rua Nova da Trindade 20. Huge, vaulted beer hall-restaurant – the city's oldest – with some of the Lisbon's loveliest *azulejos* on the walls. It specializes in shellfish, though other dishes are also good, as is the beer. There's also a patio garden. Moderate.

Vá e Volte Rua do Diário de Notícias 100. Family diner serving large plates of fried/grilled fish or meat; food is not spectacular but prices are thoroughly modest. Closed Mon. Inexpensive–moderate.

Estrela and Lapa

Farah's Tandoori Rua de Santana à Lapa 73. Between Lapa and Estrela, this is one of Lisbon's more reliable Indian restaurants and is good for vegetarians, with dishes such as vegetable tikka massala and palak paneer. Meat dishes are also fragrant and delicious. Closed Tues. Inexpensive.

Flor da Estrela Rua João de Deus 11. Neighbourhood restaurant around the back of the Estrela basilica, serving all the usual dishes and cheap wine. There are a few outdoor tables, but the interior is attractive. Try the *feijoada de marisco*. Closed Sun. Moderate.

Picanha Rua das Janelas Verdes 47, Lapa ☎213 975 401. Just up from the Museu de Arte Antiga, with an intimate, ornately tiled interior, *Picanha* has multilingual service and specializes in *picanha* (thin slices of beef) accompanied by black-eyed beans, salad and potatoes. Great if this appeals to you (as that's all they do) and for a fixed-price you can eat as much of the stuff as you want. Closed Sat lunch & Sun. Moderate.

York House Rua das Janelas Verdes 47, Lapa ☎213 968 143. Inside this sumptuous hotel is a surprisingly moderately priced restaurant serving delicious fish, meat, pasta and vegetarian options. In summer, you can dine in the tranquil courtyard. Closes at 9.30pm. Moderate–expensive.

Around the Sé

The restaurants are marked on the Alfama and Castelo map p.84.

Delhi Palace Rua da Padaria 18–20. Unusual

Indian-run restaurant offering curries, pizza and pasta in traditional, *azulejo*-covered interior; full marks for innovation and pretty good marks for the cooking. Closed Mon. Moderate.

Estrela da Sé Largo S. António da Sé 4. Beautiful, *azulejo*-covered restaurant serving tasty dishes like *alheira* sausage and salmon. Closed weekends. Inexpensive.

Hua Ta Li Rua dos Bacalhoeiras 115 ☎218 879 170. Highly rated Chinese restaurant, particularly popular at Sun lunch when reservations are advised; good-value seafood along with usual Chinese dishes. Moderate.

Retiro del Castilho Rua da Padaria 34. Budget meals in a subterranean vault of paper-topped tables. Good for lunches, and soups are recommended. Inexpensive.

Rio Coura Rua Augusto Rosa 30. A couple of hundred metres up from the Sé, and despite the tourist trappings this place offers good-value meals including rough house wine for around €13, served in a traditional, tiled dining room.

Alfama and around the Castelo

Unless stated, the restaurants are marked on the Alfama and Castelo map p.84.

Arco do Castelo Rua do Chão da Feira 25. Cheerful place specializing in Goan dishes; tempting shrimp curry, Indian sausage and spicy seafood. Closed Sun. Moderate.

O Café do Castelo Castelo de São Jorge. Set inside the castle walls, this offers good-value buffet lunches – all you can eat for €6.50 – and drinks. It's outdoor tables are beautifully positioned under shady trees facing a giant statue of a man with a flowerpot for a head. Inexpensive.

Casa do Leão Castelo de São Jorge ☎218 875 962. Couldn't be better sited, within the castle walls and with outdoor summer terrace, offering a superb city view and slick service – which explains high but not too outrageous prices; tourist menu €28. Expensive.

Frei Pepinhas Rua de São Tomé 13–21. Long, *azulejo*-covered bar-restaurant with checked blue tablecloths and decent Portuguese food; largely the haunt of locals. Closed Sun. Inexpensive.

Lautasco Beco do Azinhal 7 ☎218 860 173. Tucked just off the Largo do Chafariz de Dentro, this lovely outdoor spot has a pretty courtyard with fairy lights, and is particularly good for *cataplana*. Book ahead. Closed Sun and Dec. Expensive.

Malmequer-Bemmequer Rua de São Miguel 23–25, at Largo de São Miguel. Charcoal-grilled meat and fish (try the sole) served up amidst cheery, flowery decor. Tourist menu around €13. Closed all day Sun and Tues lunch. Moderate.

Mercado de Santa Clara Campo de Santa Clara, east of São Vicente de Fora. Above the old market building and by Feira da Ladra, this characterful restaurant offers award-winning cuisine and river views; specializes in beef and meat dishes with small fish selection. Closed all day Mon and Sat & Sun evening. Moderate–expensive.

Mestré André Calçadinha de Santo Estevão 4–6. A fine tavern with a bit of traditional colour about it, superb pork dishes and good *churrasco*. Outdoor terrace seating in summer. Closed Sun. Moderate.

Restô do Chapitô Rua Costa do Castelo 7 ☎218 867 334. The restaurant and attached courtyard of this circus school have dazzling views. There's a bar area downstairs and a spiral staircase leading up to a dining room for a limited menu of daily specials. For details of the esplanade bar, see p.113. Evenings only; closed Mon. Moderate.

São Cristóvão Rua de São Cristóvão 28–30. Wonderful, titchy Cape Verdean restaurant which somehow squeezes in live African music on weekends, while serving dishes such as *galinha caboverdiana* (chicken with coconut milk). Inexpensive.

A Tasquinha Largo do Contador Mor 5–7. Considering its position, on the main route up to the castle, this lovely *tasca* has remained remarkably unaffected by tourism, with a few tables in its traditional interior and a fine outdoor terrace. Closed Sun. Moderate.

Teatro Taborda Costa do Costelo 75. Fashionable theatre cafe-restaurant with fine views from the terrace offering fresh vegetarian dishes and Greek salads. Open from 2pm, closed Mon. Moderate.

Via Graça Rua Damasceno Monteiro 9b ☎218 870 830. Unattractive new building but an interior offering stunning panoramas of Lisbon. Specialities include spider crab and duck with muscatel. Closed all day Sun, and Sat lunch. Expensive.

Santa Apolónia and Doca Jardim do Tobaco

All the restaurants marked below are on the Alfama and Castelo map p.84.

Bica do Sapato Av Infante Dom Henrique, Armazém B, Cais da Pedra à Bica do Sapatas ☎218 810 320. Owned by actor John Malkovich and attracting politicians and glitterati, this is a very swish warehouse conversion with an outside terrace facing the river opposite Santa Apolónia. The menu features a long list of pricey but not outrageously priced fish, meat dishes and sushi. Closed all day Sun & Mon lunch. Expensive.

Casanova Loja 7 Armazém B, Cais da Pedra à Bica do Sapato. If *Bica do Sapato* (see above) is beyond your budget, the more modest *Casanova* next door offers pizza, pasta and crostini with similar views from its outside terrace. It's phenomenally popular and you can't book, so turn up early. Closed all day Mon & Tues lunch. Moderate.

Jardim do Marisco Av Infante Dom Henrique, Doca Jardim do Tobaco Pavilhão AB. Best positioned of the row of warehouse-restaurants in the Doca Jardim do Tobaco docks development. No prizes for guessing the speciality: the counter groans under the weight of crabs, giant prawns and shellfish. There's an outside and upstairs terrace with great river views. Expensive.

Along and around Avenida da Liberdade

Casa da Comida Trav. das Amoreiras 1 ☎213 885 376; metro Marquês de Pombal. Just below perhaps Lisbon's loveliest square sits one of the city's top restaurants, with a long list of salads, pasta and superb fish such as *tamboril com molho de limão e alho frances* (monkfish with leeks and lemon sauce), *crepes de camarão* (shrimp crepes). Closed Sat lunch & all day Sun. Expensive.

Centro de Alimentaçao e Saúde Natural Rua Mouzinho da Silveira 25; metro Marquês de Pombal. Self-service restaurant with light, bright upstairs dining rooms and a summer courtyard. Serves good vegetarian options such as chickpea stew, pepper rice and natural fruit juices. Open Mon–Fri till 6pm. Inexpensive.

Ribadouro Av da Liberdade 155 ☎213 549 411; metro Avenida. The Avenida's best *cevejaria*, with modern *azulejos*, serving a decent range of moderate grilled meat and seafood (but no fish). If you don't fancy a full meal, order a beer with a plate of unforgettable prawns at the bar. Moderate–expensive.

Os Tibetanos Rua do Salitre 117; metro Avenida. Located in the Buddhist Centre, this stripped-pine restaurant has superb, unusual veggie food such as vegetarian paella. Closed Sat and Sun. Inexpensive.

Belém

Rua Vieira Portuense, a block back from the main Rua de Belém, off Praça Afonso de Albuerque, is a terrace of little buildings housing tascas and restaurants, all with outdoor seating. They're packed at lunchtime; expect to wait in line if you want to sit outside. Those further from the monastery tend to be better value.

Càpsula Rua Vieira Portuense 74. Tiled interior with upstairs seating and outside tables catering to tourists tucking into tuna steaks, trout and the like. Closed Mon evening and all day Tues. Moderate.

Carvoeiro Rua Vieira Portuense 66–68. A good-value little *tasca*, with good grilled fish and jugs of wine, served at outdoor tables. Closed Sun evening and all day Mon. Inexpensive.

Floresta Belém Praça Afonso de Albuquerque 1. On the corner with Rua Vieira Portuense, this is one of the best-value places on this stretch, attracting a largely Portuguese clientele especially for weekend lunches. Great salads, grills and fresh fish inside or on a sunny outdoor terrace. Closed Sat. Moderate.

Portugália Edifício Espelho D'Áua, Av de Brasília. Pricey fish, seafood and tasty *petiscos* overlooking the docks adjacent to the Padrão dos Descobrimentos. The airy interior is jollied up with glasses hung in neat rows along the ceiling and walls. Closed Fri and Sat evening and all day Wed. Expensive.

São Jerónimo Rua dos Jerónimos 12 ☎213 648 797. Rustic-style dining by the side of the monastery, with excellent fish dishes and specializing in *migas*, a garlicky bread sauce from the Alentejo region. Closed Sat. Moderate–expensive.

Saldanha Estefânia, Campo Pequeno and Arroios

Centro de Arte Moderna Fundação Calouste Gulbenkian, entrance by Rua Dr. N. de Bettencourt; metro São Sebastião. Join the lunchtime queues at the museum restaurant for good-value hot or cold dishes. There are excellent salads for vegetarians; you get a choice of four or six varieties. Closed Mon and from 5.30pm. Inexpensive.

Restaurante Chimarrão Campo Pequeno 79; metro Campo Pequeno. If you're looking for quantity, €20 spent here gets you unlimited stabs at twelve types of barbecued meat and various salads – you'll need to pace yourself. There are also

branches on Rua 1 de Dezembro 102 (Baixa), Av Roma 90 and at Parque das Nações. Moderate–expensive.

Espiral Praça Ilha do Faial 14a, off Largo de Dona Estefânia; metro Saldanha or Arroios. Inexpensive, self-service macrobiotic restaurant downstairs (including vegetarian, Chinese and fish dishes) with adjacent snack bar and upstairs bookshop. The food isn't that great, but there's often live music at the weekend. Inexpensive.

Cervejaria Portugália Av Almirante Reis 117; metro Arroios. The original beer-hall-restaurant where you can either snack and drink at the bar or eat fine *mariscos* or steak in the dining room. A popular family outing and always busy. Moderate.

Parque das Nações

Os Alentejanos Cais dos Argonautas; metro Oriente. Great wooden barrels and hams dangling from the ceiling and waiters in broad-rimmed Alentejan hats give a jolly feel to a restaurant specializing in regional food from the Alentejo district – tapas (olives, cheeses, *presunto* ham), *açorda* with seafood and thick red wines are the best bets. Moderate.

Oceanario Café Armazém 204. Unpretentious self-service canteen and bar with outdoor tables near the Oceanarium; the buffet food is fresh and good value, with an extensive range of salads, hot dishes of the day and tasty desserts. Inexpensive.

Restaurante Panorâmico Torre Vasco da Gama ☎218 939 550; metro Oriente. Former oil refinery tower now an exclusive restaurant with fantastic views; decent Portuguese and international food at prices as high as the tower. Closed Mon. Expensive.

Restaurante del Uruguay Cais dos Argonautas; metro Oriente. Chance to sample Uruguayan cuisine in modern restaurant near Water Gardens. *Picaña ala parrilla con papa paisana* (thin strips of beef with potatoes, garlic and salsa) is recommended. Moderate.

Cafés, bars and clubs

Lisbon has literally thousands of **bars** and **cafés**, ranging from atmospheric turn-of-the-century artists' haunts and Art Deco wonders to those with trendy minimalist interiors frequented by clubbers in designer clothing. For nighttime drinking, there are a few good places in the **Alfama**, but the densest concentration of designer **bars and clubs** is found in the **Bairro Alto**, traditionally the centre of Lisbon's nightlife, with its cramped streets fado houses and restaurants. As the night progresses, some Lisboetas seek out the nightlife along **Avenida 24 de Julho** around Santos, or a little further west at

Alcântara and **Santo Amaro** docks, the latter right underneath the Ponte 25 de Abril. Further east, the world-famous club Lux typifies the city's most up-and-coming area along the riverfront by **Santa Apolónia** station.

Cafés

All the places listed below are good for breakfast, coffee and cakes or just a beer during the afternoon. Most stay open into the evening, too, with a few – like *A Brasileira* and *Cerca Moura* – also on the late-night bar-crawl circuit. All are open daily unless stated otherwise.

Académica Largo do Carmo, Bairro Alto. Tables in one of the city's nicest, quietest squares, outside the ruined Carmo church. Also does light lunches – the grilled sardines are hard to beat.

Antiga Confeitaria de Belém Rua de Belém 90, Belém. Excellent and cavernous, tiled pastry shop and café with scrumptious *pasteis de Belém*.

Bernard Rua Garrett 104, Chiado. Old-style café with an ornate interior offering superb cakes, ice cream and coffees, and an outdoor terrace on Chiado's most fashionable street. Closed Sun.

A Brasileira Rua Garrett 120, Chiado. Marked by a bronze of Pessoa outside, this is the most famous of Rua Garrett's old-style coffee houses. Livens up at night with a more youthful clientele swigging beer outside until 2am, though the interior is its real appeal.

Casa Chineza Rua Aurea 274, Baixa. Beautifully decorated pastry and coffee shop. Closed Sat evenings & Sun.

Cerca Moura Largo das Portas do Sol, Alfama. Stunning views of the Alfama from its esplanade; a good resting place as you climb up and down the hilly streets. Open till 2am, 8pm on Sun.

Confeitaria Nacional Praça da Figueira. Opened in 1829 and little changed since, with a standup counter selling pastries and sweets below a mirrored ceiling. There's a little side room for sit-down coffees and snacks.

Elevador de Santa Justa Café Rua de Santa

Justa. The drinks and snacks are inevitably overpriced, but a visit is worthwhile for the stunning views of the Baixa from the blowy rooftop platform of this iron latticework lift, built in 1902 (see p.77).

A Linha d'Água Parque Eduardo VII. Modern, glass-fronted café facing a small lake at the top of Lisbon's main park. Decent buffet lunches and a great spot to down a coffee or beer; in summer, kids splash about in the shallow waters in front.

Martinho da Arcada Praça do Comércio 3, Baixa. Traditional, old, stand-up café with outdoor tables under the arches; call in for a coffee and *pastel de nata*. Closed Sun.

Nicola Praça Dom Pedro IV 24. On the west side of Rossio, this grand old place is not quite what it was following restoration in the 1990s, but is still a good stop for breakfast. Outdoor seats are always at a premium. Closed Sat afternoon, and all day Sun.

Pastelaria São Roque Rua D. Pedro V 57c, Bairro Alto. Relaxed, ornate corner café where you can enjoy coffee and croissants below a wonderfully high ceiling.

Suíça Rossio 96. Famous for its cakes and pastries; you'll have a hard job getting an outdoor table here, though there's plenty of room inside – the café stretches across to Praça da Figueira where the best tables are.

Bars and clubs

Lisbon does not immediately strike visitors as a city for **nightlife**, largely because many of its clubs are somewhat discreet, get going late and are concentrated in select areas of the city. But once in the know, you'll find its clubs and bars hard to beat. The **Bairro Alto** hosts one of Europe's biggest weekly street parties, with up to 50,000 people descending on the maze of streets over the weekend, drifting from bar to club before heading out to those at Alcântara and around the docks for the small hours. Several Bairro Alto clubs are extremely low key, revealing their presence simply by a streetlight and a slot in the door for the attendant to inspect customers. Don't be intimidated by this: just knock and walk in – and straight out, if you don't like the look of the place. Also in Bairro Alto, and on its periphery, around **Praça Príncipe Real** and Rato, is much of the city's gay scene. You'll be hard pushed to find a bar

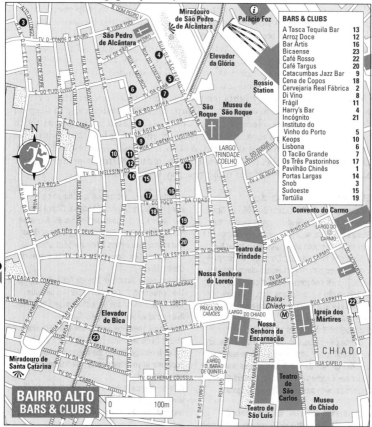

open late at night in the **Baixa**, though things are picking up further east in the **Alfama** and **Graça**, where a growing number of bars cater for the crowds leaving the excellent local restaurants.

Though some of the trendy action still takes place along **Avenida 24 de Julho**, around Santos station, a lot of the nightlife action has moved to the docks, in particular those at **Alcântara** and **Santo Amaro** under Ponte 25 de Abril, which attract the moneyed set, and – more recently – opposite Santa Apolónia station. The shift is partly the result of the local authority's plan to encourage clubs to move out of Barrio Alto into non-residential areas where they can stay open until 6am or later without disturbing the neighbours. Santa Apolónia is close to the centre (and will be on the metro from 2004), but to get to the other docks, you'll need to hop in a taxi or catch a train to **Alcântara Mar** from **Cais do Sodré**, which has a growing number of river-side clubs and bars itself. Committed clubbers, drinkers and low-life enthusiasts might try one of a dozen places along the nearby Rua Nova do Carvalho, which range from atmospheric to downright seedy.

Drinks are uniformly expensive in all fashionable bars and clubs – from €4 for a beer – but the plus-side is that very few charge admission. Instead many places have a "minimum consumption" policy – designed to stop people dancing all night without buying a drink, which many Portuguese would happily do. Sometimes these fees are set, more often they are at the whim of the doorman, who will relax it if it's a quiet night, or whack it up if it's busy or if he doesn't like the look of you. Generally, expect to pay anything from €10 to €50; keep hold of your ticket as drinks will be stamped on it to ensure you consume enough (otherwise you pay on exit).

Friday and Saturday nights tend to be overcrowded and expensive everywhere; while on Sunday, especially in Bairro Alto, places often close to sleep off the weekend excesses. Note that none of the places listed below **opens** much before 10pm unless otherwise stated; all are open until at least 2am, with most doing business much later than that, 3–4am is normal, 7am not unheard of. Unless stated otherwise, the following are open daily. Metro stops are given for places in outlying areas if this is the best way to reach the place.

Baixa and Chiado

Bicaense Rua da Bica Duarte Belo 38–42. Small, fashionable bar on the steep street used by the Elevador da Bica, with jazzy and Latin sounds and a moderately priced list of bar food. Closed Sun.

A Ginginha Largo de São Domingos 8. Everyone should try *ginginha* – Portuguese cherry brandy – once. There's just room in this microscopic joint to walk in, down a glassful and stagger outside to see the city in a new light, though many locals are here daily from 9am.

Café Rosso Galerias Garrett, Rua Ivens 57, entrance on Rua Garrett. Courtyard bar that also serves coffee and snacks in the renovated shop galleries off Rua Garrett, a relaxed spot with seats under huge square canopies. Downstairs there's a huge room with modernist seats and lighting.

Around Cais do Sodré

Irish Pub O'Gilins Rua de Remolares 8. This was the first of a growing band of popular – if pricey – Irish bars with a pleasant, light wooden interior and live music from Thurs to Sat. Pub quizzes on Sun too.

Jamaica Rua Nova do Carvalho 8. Set on a seedy road this is a very characterful club thanks to a mixed bag of clientele from sailors to expats and trendies; music is predominantly retro, with reggae on Tues. Closed Sun.

Poisa Copos Cais da Ribeira. Small bar in a converted warehouse by the river; handy for a pick-me-up at six in the morning; popular with students and a good place for drinks or snacks. Closed Sun & Mon.

Bairro Alto

The map on pp.78–79 shows the whereabouts of the bars and clubs listed below.

Arroz Doce Rua da Atalaia 117–119. Nice, normal bar in the middle of otherwise frenetic nightlife.

Friendly owners and a good spot for an early or late beer; or try "Auntie's" sangria. Closed Sun.

Bar Ártis Rua do Diário de Notícias 95. A relaxed, mildly sophisticated bar wallowing in jazzy decor and music; also serves a fine range of snacks as chicken toasties. Open til 2am (4am at weekends). Closed Mon.

Catacumbas Jazz Bar Trav. da Água da Flor 43. The "catacombs" is a relaxing bar – a pleasant spot for a drink at any time, though gets busy with live jazz at weekends. Closed Sun.

Cena de Copos Rua da Barroca 103–105. Not a club to frequent unless you're under 25 and bursting with energy, though the cheap cocktails at least help anyone feel young. Don't turn up until after midnight.

Di Vino Rua da Atalaia 160. Trendy Bairro Alto wine bar with a warren of small rooms at the back and tasty snacks lined up on the main bar. Closed Sun.

Frágil Rua da Atalaia 126. An icon of trendiness for years before the owner opened *Lux* (see below). Partly gay, definitely pretentious, this continues to be a fashionable club belting them out Thurs–Sat till 4am, quieter on other days. Best after 1am. Ring bell to get in. Closed Sun.

Harry's Bar Rua de São Pedro de Alcântara 57. A tiny front-room bar, with waiter service, bar snacks and an eclectic clientele – often including late-night, slightly older contingent from the nearby gay discos. Ring bell for admission. Closed Sun.

Incógnito Rua dos Poiais de São Bento 37. Appropriately named as only indication is a pair of large metallic doors. The low-lit, plush dance floor downstairs bangs out various tunes. Once within, you'll find the low-lit dance floor downstairs booming with retro sounds, though Wed is more cutting edge. Open Wed–Sat from 11pm.

Instituto do Vinho do Porto Rua de São Pedro de Alcântara 45. Firmly on the tourist circuit, the

Instituto lures in visitors with over three hundred types of port, starting at around €1 a glass and rising to nearly €25 for a glass of forty-year-old JW Burmester. Glasses are served at low tables in a comfortable old eighteenth-century mansion. Waiters are notoriously snooty and the cheaper ports never seem to be in stock, but it's still a good place to kick off an evening. Closed Sun.

Keops Rua da Rosa 157–159. Laid back, friendly music bar with doors open onto the streets, playing latest sounds most nights. A candlelit interior is another draw. Closed Sun.

Lisbona Rua da Atalaia 196. Earthy, local bar with its share of quirky regulars, but its chequerboard tiles covered in soccer memorabilia, old film posters and graffiti also lure in Bairro Alto trendies. Catchy music and inexpensive beer, too. Closed Sun.

Pavilhão Chinês Rua Dom Pedro V 89. A wonderfully decorated bar, completely lined with mirrored cabinets full of ludicrous and bizarre tableaux of artefacts from around the world, including a room full of old war helmets. Drinks include a long list of speciality cocktails.

Portas Largas Rua da Atalaia 105. Atmospheric, black-and-white tiled *adega* with cheapish drinks, music from fado to pop and a varied, partly gay crowd, which spills out onto the street on warm evenings. Often a starting point for clubbers moving on to *Frágil* opposite.

Cervejaria Real Fábrica Rua Escola Politécnica 277. A fifteen-minute-walk north downhill in Rato, this is famous for its own brewed beer, which you can enjoy at the long, curly wooden bar or at smart tables beneath huge mirrors. Good upstairs restaurant, too.

Snob Rua do Século 178. Appropriately named upmarket bar-restaurant towards Principe Real, full of media people. A good spot for cocktails or a late-night light meal (steaks always good); open until 2am.

Sudoeste Rua da Barroca 135. No longer the in-crowd's hangout but a friendly club with small dance floor and areas for chats. Ring for admission. Happy hour 10pm–1am during the week; that's quite an hour. Closed Mon.

O Tacão Grande Trav. da Cara 3. Barn-like bar pulls in young crowd into thumping rock, beer and free popcorn.

Café Targus Rua do Diário de Notícias 40. A popular designer bar that attracts architects, journalists and arty professionals; quietly sophisticated by day – when people come to admire the temporary art exhibits on the walls – people flood in at midnight before moving on to the clubs.

A Tasca Tequila Bar Trav. da Queimada 13–15. Colourful Mexican bar which often opens up way before it's official opening time to cater to a good-time crowd downing tequilas, margaritas and the Brazilian cocktail caiphirinha.

Tertúlia Rua do Diário de Notícias 60. Laid-back café-bar, with inexpensive drinks, papers to read, background jazz and varied art exhibitions that change fortnightly. If you fancy the urge to play, there's a piano for customers too. Open till 4am; closed Sun.

Os Três Pastorinhos Rua da Barroca 111. Welcoming music bar with great dance sounds and an off kilter feel; gets very busy at weekends; closed Mon.

Alfama, Graça and Santa Apolónia

Costa do Castelo Calç. do Marquês de Tancos 1b. Beautifully positioned sunny terrace-café with Baixa views, a long list of cocktails and a restaurant serving mid-price Mozambiquan dishes (see p.107). There's live (usually Brazilian or jazz) music on Thurs and Fri nights, and poetry readings on others. Closed Mon.

Graça Esplanado Caraçol da Graça. Esplanade-bar underneath the Miradouro da Graça, with great views and, as it gets late, pumping music. Great place for a drink at sunset.

Lux Armazéns A, Cais da Pedra a Santa Apolónia. ⓦwww.luxfragil.com This three-storey converted meat warehouse has become not only Lisbon's but one of Europe's most fashionable places to be seen, attracting visiting stars like Prince and Cameron Diaz. Part-owned by actor John Malkovich, it was the first place to venture into the docks opposite Santa Apolónia station. There's a rooftop terrace with amazing views, a middle floor with various bars, comfy chairs and sofas, amazing projection screens and music from pop to jazz and dance. The downstairs dance floor gets frenzied; it's also increasingly on the circuit for visiting bands; closed Mon.

Rêsto do Chapitô Rua Costa do Castelo 7. Multi-purpose venue incorporating a theatre, a circus school restaurant and a tapas bar attracting Lisbon's bohemian set. The outdoor esplanade commands terrific views over the Alfama. For details of the restaurant, see p.108. Open Tues–Fri 7.30pm–1.30am, Sat & Sun noon–1.30am.

Sua Excelência O Marquês Largo Marquês do Lavradio 1. Dark rock bar hidden away in a little square behind the Sé. Live music most nights. Closed Sun.

Avenida 24 de Julho and around

Indústria Rua do Instituto Industrial 6. Popular club in a converted factory with various bars and dance floors echoing to house and dance sounds. It attracts a varied crowd and is liveliest after 3am. Open Fri–Sat midnight–6am.

Kapital Av 24 de Julho 68. Well-established trendy hotspot, with three sleekly designed floors full of *queques* (yuppies) paying high prices for drinks and listening to techno, but watch out for the style police on the door. There's a great rooftop terrace. Wed night is rock night. Open till 6am, until 4am on Sun and Mon.

Kremlin Escadinhas da Praia 5. Another of the established fashionable nightspots, this is packed with flash, young, raving Lisboetas. Tough door rules, and don't bother showing up before 2am. Open till 7am; closed Sun & Mon.

Alcântara

Alcântara Café Rua Maria Luísa Holstein 15. Expensive designer bar-restaurant blending industrial and modern architecture. One of the city's trendiest in decor and clientele. Most people have a drink here and move on to one of the neighbouring clubs. Open 8pm–3am.

Kasino Rua Cozinha Económica 11. Wonderful, big and glitzy spot for house and techno, in half of what was the famous Alcântara-Mar club. Open Wed–Sat 11pm–6am.

Paradise Garage Rua João de Oliveira Miguens 48. Large, ultra-trendy club on a tiny side road off Rua da Cruz à Alcântara offering various sounds from disco to garage. It is also becoming a major venue for visiting bands too. Open Thurs–Sat 11.30pm–4am.

Pillon Rua do Alvito 10. Cape Verdean disco sounds for a relaxed in-crowd. Best night is said to be Tues.

W Rua Maria Luisa Holstein. Recently revamped and renamed club with a laid-back atmosphere and a healthy mix of people out for a fun night. Wed is Ladies' Night, with free drinks for females. Open Wed–Sat 11pm–6am.

Doca de Alcântara

Blues Café R. Cintura do Porto de Lisboa. Attractively converted dockside warehouse serving Cajun food in the restaurant (until 12.30am) in what is claimed to be Lisbon's only blues club.

Live music on Mon and Thurs, club nights on Fri and Sat from 2.30am. Closed Sun.

Cais de Alcântara One of a row of bar-restaurants on boats in the docks, this one with moderately priced food, a pool table and lively music. Closed Sun.

Docks Club Doca de Alcântara. Another thriving warehouse conversion funded by nightclub mogul Pedro Luz; a dance temple for Lisbon's moneyed set. Tues night is Ladies night with free drinks for women; Thurs night features Latin music. Closed Sun.

Indochina R. Cintura do Porto de Lisboa. Another of Pedro Luz's offerings, this is a large, colonial-style club in a converted warehouse. Latin and mainstream pop sounds are the norm, with party nights Thurs–Sat. Closed Sun & Mon.

Queens Rua Cintura do Porto de Lisboa, Armázem H Naves A–B. Pedro Luz launched this club as a "high-tech gay disco", but it has always successfully attracted a large following of beautiful people of all sexual persuasions. It's a huge, pulsating place – there's an excellent sound system – which can hold 2500 people. Tues night is Ladies' Night involving a male strip show; visiting DJs on other nights. Closed Sun & Mon.

Doca de Santo Amaro

Unless otherwise stated, all of the following are clustered around the small Doca de Santo Amaro, beneath Ponte 25 de Abril.

Doca 6 ☎213 957 905 Rated as one of the best bars in the docks and also has good – if pricey – food. Restaurant tables get snapped up so it is best to reserve. Closed Mon from Nov to April.

Doca de Santo Designed by nightclub mogul Pedro Luz, this large, palm-fringed club, bar and restaurant was one of the first places in the docks to attract – and keep – a late-night clientele. The cocktail bar on the esplanade is the latest attraction.

Havana Armazéns 5, Doca de Santo Amaro, Alcântara. Cuban-themed bar-restaurant with wicker chairs, Latin sounds and salsa lessons on request, usually undertaken in the bar area.

Salsa Latina Gare Marítima de Alcântara, Doca de Santo Amaro. A bar-restaurant and club just outside the docks in a fantastic 1940s maritime station, offering salsa Tues to Sat and live music at weekends. Also offers salsa lessons on Tues and Thurs. Alternatively, just come and admire the terrace views. Closed Sun.

Gay and lesbian bars, clubs and discos

Gay nightlife focuses on the Bairro Alto and Praça do Príncipe Real, where a generally laid-back group of clubs and bars attracts gay people of all ages. As at other clubs, the best nights are from Thurs to Sat, with the action kicking off at 9pm and ending well after sunrise. The following bars and clubs are pretty much gay and lesbian only; places which attract a mixed gay and straight crowd are listed in "Bars and clubs" on pp.112–114. For more information on the gay and lesbian scene in Lisbon, see "Listings" p.123.

Bric-a-Bar Rua Cecílio de Sousa 82–84. On a steep road beyond Praça do Príncipe Real, a cruisy gay disco with large dance floor, "dark room" and various bars. Free entry.

Finalmente Rua da Palmeira 38. A well-known and very busy place, with a first-class disco and lashings of kitsch. Weekend drag shows (at 2am) feature skimpily dressed young *senhoritas* camping it up to high-tech sounds. Free entry but minimum drinks consumption of €6.

Katedral Rua de Manuel Bernardes 22. Intimate, relaxed snooker bar attracting lesbian crowd; one of the better places for gay women.

Memorial Rua Gustavo Matos Sequeira 42. One of the few clubs for lesbians, with floor shows some nights; otherwise low-key, with disco and "romantic" sounds. Closed Mon.

Sétimo Ceu Travessa de Espera 54. Real success story of recent years and obligatory stop for beers and caipirinhas served by Brazilian owner. Great atmosphere spilling out onto the street. Closed Sun.

Trumps Rua da Imprensa Nacional 104b. Popular gay disco with a reasonably relaxed door policy. Packed from Thurs to Sat which sees a good lesbian turnout, a bit cruisy midweek. Drag shows on Sun and Wed.

Live music, the arts and other entertainment

Although tourist brochures tend to suggest that **live music** in Lisbon begins and ends with **fado** (see below) – the city's most traditional music – there's no reason to miss out on other forms. Portuguese **jazz** can be good (there's a big annual **International Jazz Festival** at the Gulbenkian in the summer), and **rock** offers an occasional surprise (look out for emerging bands at the March Super Bock Rock festival). For Lisboans, **African music** from the former colonies of Cabo Verde, Guinea Bissau, Angola and Mozambique is the happening sound, as is **Brazilian** music with artists touring frequently.

There's often a crossover between musical styles at many of the places listed below; it's always worth checking the listings magazines (see below) and posters around the city to see what's on. Note, too, that many of the bars listed in the previous section put on live bands on certain nights of the week. There's a charge to get into most live music clubs, which usually covers your first drink, and most of them stay open until around 4am, often later. In addition, big American and British rock bands on tour – not forgetting the top visiting Brazilian singers – play at a variety of **local halls and stadia** (listed below); you can usually get advance tickets from the APEB kiosk (daily 9am–9.30pm) at the corner of Praça dos Restauradores (near the post office), which also has ticket and programme details for all the city's cinemas and theatres. Tickets can also be purchased from FNAC (see p.121) or online from Ⓦ www.ondaticket.com.

Most major **cultural events** in the city – including just about every classical music concert – are sponsored either by the Fundação Calouste Gulbenkian (p.92) or the Centro Cultural de Belém (p.97), both of which have a full annual programme. Classical music aside, there's a fair amount of other cultural entertainment in Lisbon: several **theatres**, countless **cinemas**, three top-flight football teams, summer season **bullfights**, and a host of cultural and traditional **festivals**.

To find out **what's on**, pick up a schedule of exhibitions, concerts and events from the reception desks at the Gulbenkian and the Belém Cultural Centre. The best **listings** magazine is *Agenda Cultural*, a free monthly produced by the town hall which details current exhibitions and shows (in Portuguese). *Follow me Lisboa* is a watered down English language version produced by the local tourist office and also details tourist sites and facilities. All are available from the tourist office. For other **listings and previews** of forthcoming events, concerts, bars, clubs and restaurants, get hold of the Friday editions of the *Diário de Notícias* or *O Independente* newspapers: both have pull-out listings magazines.

Telephone numbers are given below for places where reservations are advised, or where you might like to check out who is playing.

Fado

Fado is often described as a kind of working-class blues, although musically it would perhaps be more accurate to class it as a kind of light operetta, sung to a viola accompaniment. Alongside Coimbra (which has its own distinct tradition), Lisbon is still the best place to hear it, in one of thirty or so nightclubs in the Bairro Alto, Alfama and elsewhere – either at a *casa de fado* or in an *adega típica*. There's no real distinction between these places: all are small, all serve food (though you don't always have to eat), and all open around 8pm, get going toward midnight, and stay open until 3 or 4am.

Their drawbacks are inflated minimum charges – rarely, these days, below €15 – and, in the more touristic places, extreme tackiness. Uniformed bouncers are fast becoming the norm, as are warm-up singers crooning Beatles' songs, and photographers snapping your table. Ask around to discover which are the most authentic current experiences. If you're in Lisbon in February, look out too for the **Fado/Harbour Festival**, which combines fado with music from other port cities from round the world; New Orleans' jazz and rebetika from Athens have featured in recent years. For more on the roots of fado, see p.596. The following venues are open daily unless stated otherwise; metro stops are given when this is the best way to reach a place.

Adega Machado, Rua do Norte 91, Bairro Alto ☎ 213 224 640. One of the longest-established Bairro Alto joints as photo portraits on the wall testify (heads of state included). The fado kicks off at 9.15pm and minimum consumption of €15 builds to around €20 a head if you sample the fine Portuguese cooking. Closed Mon.

Adega Mesquita Rua do Diário de Notícias 107, Bairro Alto ☎ 213 219 280. Another of the big Bairro Alto names, with better-than-average music and meals, air conditioning and traditional dancing as well as singing.

Adega do Ribatejo Rua do Diário de Notícias 23, Bairro Alto ☎ 213 468 343. Great little *adega*, with one of the lowest minimum charges and fado that locals describe as "pure emotion". Enjoyable also for its food, it remains popular with locals. The singers include a couple of professionals, the manager and – best of all – the cooks. There's a minimum charge of €10. Closed Sun.

Clube do Fado Rua de São João da Praça 92–94 ☎ 218 852 704. Intimate and homely place with stone pillars, an old well and a mainly local clientele. Attracts small-time performers, up-and-coming talent and the occasional big names. Minimum charge around €10.

Mercado da Ribeira Av 24 de Julho. The revamped Cais do Sodré market (see p.77) forms the backdrop to Fri and Sat night music sessions (from 10pm) which vary from fado to jazz and folk. Acoustics aren't great and don't expect top performers, but it's an atmospheric place.

Parreirinha d'Alfama Beco do Espírito Santo 1, Alfama ☎ 218 868 209. One of the best fado venues, just off Largo do Chafariz de Dentro, often attracting leading stars and a local clientele. Reservations are advised when the big names appear. Minimum charge around €13, up to around €30 with food.

O Senhor Vinho Rua do Meio à Lapa 18, Lapa

⌬ 213 972 681. Famous club sporting some of the best singers in Portugal, which makes the €20 minimum charge (rising to around €40 with a meal) pretty reasonable. Good decor and relaxed atmosphere; bookings are advised. Closed Sun.
A Severa Rua das Gáveas 55, Bairro Alto ⌬ 213 468 314. A city institution, named after a nineteenth-century gypsy singer who had an affair with a Count,

with big fado names and big prices. Closed Thurs.
Taverna do Embuçado Beco dos Cortumes 10, Alfama ⌬ 218 865 088. Well-established *adega* with a nice feel. Gets some big-name visitors. Closed Sun.
Timpanas Rua Gilberto Rola 24, Alcântara ⌬ 213 972 431. This is one of Lisbon's most authentic options, away from the tourist scene. Closed Wed.

African music

Bleza Largo Conde-Barão 50, Santos. Live music on most nights in this wonderful old venue; dance floor and table service. Closed Sun.
Lontra Rua de São Bento 157, Bairro Alto ⌬ 213 691 083. You'll be hard pushed not to join in the animated dancing in this intimate African club with live music most nights; come after midnight. Closed Mon.
Luanda Trav. Teixeira Júnior 6, Alcântâra. With a smart chrome-and-wood interior, this is one of the

biggest and most popular of African clubs. Big with the Bairro Alto crowd, who like ending a night here. Closed Tues, and Mon–Wed from Oct–April.
Ritz Club Rua da Glória 57 ⌬ 213 425 140; metro Avenida. Temporarily closed for renovation (due to reopen 2004), Lisbon's largest African club occupies the premises of an old brothel-cum-music-hall, one block west of Av da Liberdade. It's a great place, with a resident Cabo Verdean band, plus occasional big-name concerts. Closed Mon.

Brazilian music

Bipi-Bipi Rua Oliveira Martins 6 ⌬ 217 978 924; metro Campo Pequeno. Uptown venue for Brazilian bands, exotic cocktails and dirty dancing. Closed Mon.
Chafarica Calçada de São Vicente 81, Alfama ⌬ 218 867 449. Tiny, pricey old Brazilian bar with live music till late.
Pê Sujo Largo de São Martinho 6–7, Alfama ⌬ 218 866 144 The "dirty foot" is just up from the Sé. There's an outdoor wooden terrace and live bands most nights which can result in massive

table-banging sessions if the audience approves. Closed Mon.
Pintaí Largo Trindade Coelho 22, across the road from the São Roque church. Bouncy Brazilian music and cocktails. Open till 4am; closed Mon.
Salsa Latina Gare Marítima de Alcântara. Set in the superb 1940s maritime station by Doca de Santa Amaro, this is part bar-restaurant, part salsa club, with riotous dancing to live bands serving up Brazilian rhythms, jazz, Dixieland and other infectious sounds.

Rock and pop

Álcool Puro Av Dom Carlos I 59, Santos ⌬ 213 967 467. Different bands every night in this rock bar. Closed Sun.
Anos Sessenta Largo do Terreirinho 21, Mouraria ⌬ 218 873 444; metro Martim Moniz. This small club ("The Sixties") has different rock bands on Fri & Sat; as you would guess, the music is retro. It's a few minutes' walk from Largo Martim Moniz, near the castle.
Bugix Rua D. Fuas Roupinho, Parque das Nações;

metro Oriente. The in-spot in the Parque at present, with live music at midnight and pulsating techno 2–5am Thurs–Sat. The rest of the week it is a relatively quiet restaurant serving moderately priced Portuguese food. Diners pay half the €10 entry fee. Closed Mon.
Paradise Garage Rua João de Oliveira Miguens 38, Alcântara ⌬ 213 955 977. This club (see also p.114) hosts regular gigs, including foreign bands. Open Thurs–Sat.

Jazz

Catacumbas Jazz Bar Trav. da Água da Flor 43, Bairro Alto. Bar with low-key live jazz at weekends. Closed Sun.
Hot Clube de Portugal Praça de Alegria 39, off Av da Liberdade ⌬ 213 621 740; metro Avenida.

The city's best jazz venue – a tiny basement club that hosts local and visiting artists. Closed Mon.
Café Puro Rua do Arsenal 21. The Lisbon Welcome Centre's otherwise sterile café hosts lively music nights, often jazz but also world music

117

and fado. Non-professional but good performers and a lively crowd most nights. Closed Sun. **Speakeasy** Armazém 115, Cais das Oficinas, Doca de Alcântara ☎213 957 308. Docklands jazz bar and restaurant with some big and up-and-coming names usually on Tues–Thurs after 11pm. Closed Sun.

Large venues

Atlantic Pavilion Parque das Nações ☎218 918 440; metro Oriente. Big name stars play at Portugal's largest indoor venue which holds up to 17,000 spectators.

Aula Magna Reitoria da Universidade de Lisboa, Alameda da Universidade ☎217 967 624; metro Cidade Universitaria. The student union venue, which feels like a lecture hall; seating only.

Coliseu dos Recreios Rua das Portas de Santo Antão, Baixa ☎213 240 580. Main city centre indoor rock and pop venue set in a lovely old, domed building.

Estádio José Alvalade ☎217 140 000; metro Campo Grande. The Sporting Lisbon soccer stadium stages concerts by huge international stars, though things may change when the soccer team move into a new stadium next door in 2003.

Sony Plaza Parque das Nações ☎218 919 000; metro Oriente. The Parque's main outdoor venue, holds up to 10,000 people for summer concerts and New Year's Eve extravaganzas.

Classical music, theatre and opera

There are three concert halls (including an outdoor amphitheatre) at the Gulbenkian (see p.92), both a large and small auditorium at the Centro Cultural de Belém (see p.100), and two auditoriums in the enormous, modern Culturgest arts complex at Avenida João XX1 63, near Campo Pequeno (☎217 905 155, ⑩wwwcgd.pt). In addition, regular **classical music** concerts take place at the Teatro Nacional de São Carlos, Rua Serpa Pinto 9, Chiado (☎213 465 914); the Teatro Municipal de São Luís, Rua António Maria Cardoso 40, Baixa (☎213 421 772); the Coliseu dos Recreios, Rua das Portas de Santo Antão, Baixa (☎213 240 580); and at the Teatro Luís de Camões, Avenida Dom João II, Parque das Nações (☎213 427 722); metro Oriente. Tickets range from €3 to €30, though there are also frequent free concerts and recitals at the São Roque church in Bairro Alto, the Sé, the Basílica da Estrela, São Vicente de Fora and the Igreja dos Mártires. The **opera** season runs from September to June at the Teatro Nacional de São Carlos, Rua Serpa Pinto 9, Chiado (☎213 465 914). For details of **ballet** refer to the home page of the renowned Lisbon-based ballet, Companhia Nacional de Bailado, at ⑩www.cnb.pt.

For **theatre**, there are performances of Portuguese and foreign plays at the Teatro Nacional de Dona Maria in Rossio (☎213 472 246). You may also want to check out performances by the Lisbon Players, an amateur English-speaking theatrical group consisting largely of expat actors, at Rua da Estrela 10, Lapa (☎213 961 946).

Cinema

Lisbon and its environs have dozens of **cinemas**, virtually all of them showing original-language films with Portuguese subtitles, and ticket prices are low (around €4; cheaper on Mon). Sadly, however, most of the city's Art Nouveau and Art Deco palaces, often with original period bars, have given way to multiplex centres. The tourist office should be able to tell you what's on, or consult the kiosk at the corner of Restauradores.

Among the most interesting **art-house** venues are Quarteto, Rua das Flores Lima 16 (☎217 971 378), off Avenida Estados Unidos (metro Entre Campos), with four screens; and the Instituto da Cinemateca Portuguesa (☎213 546

279), Rua Barata Salgueiro 39 (metro Avenida), the national film theatre, with twice-daily shows, ranging from contemporary Portuguese films to anything from Truffaut to Valentino. These cinemas also act as the Lisbon venues for the Troia International **Film Festival** in June, which showcases movies from countries which produce fewer than 21 films per year, subtitled in Portuguese. Another annual event is the Gay Film Festival, held at various cinemas in September.

Mainstream movies are shown most centrally at São Jorge, Avenida da Liberdade 174 (☎213 103 400); metro Avenida. At the Amoreiras complex (see p.91; ☎213 831 275) there are no fewer than eleven screens; all, unfortunately, are modest in size. Other large centres include the eight screens in the Edifício Monumental, Avenida Praia da Vitória 71, Saldanha (☎213 142 223); the eleven screens at the top floor of the Vasco da Gama shopping centre in Parque das Nações (☎218 922 280); metro Oriente; and the eleven screens at the vast Colombo Shopping Centre, Avenida Lusíada Letras (☎217 113 200); metro Colégio Militar-Luz.

Sports

Football is the biggest game in Lisbon, and **Benfica** – Lisbon's most famous football team – have a glorious past (the great Eusébio played for the team in the 1960s), though they have been struggling of late to keep up with city rivals Sporting. The famous Estádio da Luz, Avenida Gen. Norton Matos (☎217 266 129, ⓦ www.slbenfica.pt; metro Colégio Militar-Luz), to the north of the city centre, is being rebuilt in preparation for the 2004 European Championships, for which this will be the main venue. In the meantime, Benfica's temporary home is the Estádio Nacional (see below).

Sporting Lisbon (officially called Sporting Club de Portugal), Benfica's traditional city rivals and the more successful in recent years, play at the Estádio José Alvalade (☎217 514 098 or 217 514 000, ⓦ wwwsporting.pt; metro Campo Grande or bus #1 or #36); a new state-of-the-art stadium is due to open next door to the old one in 2003. Top-division action can also be caught at the Estádio do Restelo, home of **Belenenses** of Belém (☎213 010 461).

The Portuguese **Cup Final** is held at the Estádio Nacional (National Stadium; ☎214 197 212), Praça da Maratona, Cruz Quebrada (bus #6 from Algés or train to Cruz Quebrada from Cais do Sodré). The stadium holds up to 55,000 but is pretty run-down and soulless – it's not among the eight stadiums selected as venues for the 2004 European Football.

The daily soccer tabloid *Bola,* available from any newsagent or newspaper kiosk, has fixtures, match reports and news, as do the websites ⓦ www .portuguesesoccer.com and ⓦ www.infodesporto.pt/futebal. To buy advance **tickets** for big games – which cost between €3 and €30 – go to the ABEP kiosk in Praça dos Restauradores (for a small commission), or at kiosks (not the turnstiles) at the grounds on the night.

Bullfights take place most Thursdays (April–Sept) at the principal **Praça de Touros do Campo Pequeno** (metro Campo Pequeno; ☎217 932 093; closed for renovation until 2003), just off Avenida da República; tickets cost €15–60, depending on where you sit, and the spectacle takes place in the evening. There are less frequent fights at Cascais in summer; travel out of Lisbon to Vila Franca de Xira and surrounding towns and villages for more traditional events.

Golf is best enjoyed at the upmarket courses around Estoril (see p.126). Portugal's Formula One **Grand Prix** also takes place in Estoril though the race has been cancelled for the last few years, as the track was considered too dangerous. For those into **water sports**, good surfing opportunities can be found at Caparica (see p.143) and windsurfing at Guincho (see p.129) and Ericeira (see p.155), both of which have previously held world windsurfing championships.

Festivals and events

Lisbon's main **festivals** are in June, with fireworks, fairground rides and street-partying to celebrate the **Santos Populares** – SS António (Anthony; June 13), João (John; June 24) and Pedro (Peter; June 29). Celebrations of each begin on the previous evening; Santo Antonio's is the largest, taking over just about every square in Alfama. Also in June, the **Festas da Lisboa** are a series of city-sponsored events, including free concerts, exhibitions and culinary contests.

On the cultural front, there's the annual **Sintra Music Festival** – which embraces the **Noites de Bailado** ballet festival at Seteais Palace – and **Estoril Festival**, which take place throughout July and August offering – sometimes adventurous – performances by internationally known orchestras, musicians and dance groups. There are also various summer events in Cascais, mostly held in the Parque Palmela. Again at Estoril, and a lot better than it sounds, is the state-run **Handicrafts Fair** (Feira Internacional Artesanato); crafts of all kinds, from every region of the country, are on display – if you buy anything, though, bargain at length. The fair runs through July and August, from around 5pm until midnight, with foodstalls included in the attractions. A similar international handicrafts fair takes place at Feira Internacional de Lisboa (FIL), Lisbon's main exhibitions hall in the Parque das Nações.

Other events in Lisbon include a low-key **carnival** celebration in February or early March; free **street entertainment** in the Baixa as part of the Baixanima festival, July–Sept; the **Oceans Festival** in August, celebrating the city's links with the Ocean through special events, regattas and parades; and more vibrant celebrations on **New Year's Eve**, with fireworks and all-night partying in Praça do Comércio, in Cascais and at the Parque das Nações.

Shops and markets

The more interesting **shopping areas** are detailed in the preceding pages: the Chiado district (p.76); the Amoreiras complex (p.91); and the Alfama flea market (p.88). Some of the better **shops** are picked out below, along with a handful of **markets**. The Bairro Alto is the centre for alternative designer clothes and furniture. Portuguese designers also have outlets in Amoreiras shopping centre and Chiado while international designer names are fast appearing along Avenida da Liberdade.

Shopping hours

Traditional **shopping hours** are Monday to Friday 9am to 7pm (some shops close for an hour at lunch), Saturday 9am to 1am. However, many of the **Bairro Alto** shops are open afternoons and evenings only, usually 2 to 9pm or so. Many larger shops, especially in shopping centres, open all day until 11pm or midnight, some even on Sundays.

Other than traditional **ceramics and carpets**, perhaps the most Portuguese of items to take home is a **bottle of port**: check out the vintages at the *Instituto do Vinho do Porto* (see p.80), where you can also sample the stuff. Alternatively, buy port or the increasingly respected **Portuguese wines** from one of the specialist shops listed below, or from any delicatessen or supermarket. Metro stops are given below when this is the best way to reach a place.

Antiques, arts and crafts

Antique shops are concentrated along **Rua do Alecrim** in Chiado and **Rua Dom Pedro V** in the Bairro Alto. Other interesting shops throughout the city include:

Fábrica Sant'ana Rua do Alecrim 95, Chiado. If you're interested in Portuguese tiles – *azulejos* – check out this factory shop, which sells copies of traditional designs and a great range of pots and ceramics. Closed Sat afternoon and all day Sun.

Fábrica Viúva Lamego Largo do Intendente 25; metro Intendente. Highly rated *azulejo* factory-shop producing made-to-order designs or reproduction antiques. Closed Sat afternoon and all day Sun (plus Sat morning in July and Aug).

Loja de Artesanato Mercado da Ribeira, Av 24 de Julho; metro Cais do Sodré. In 2001, the upper level of Lisbon's main market (see p.77) was turned into a centre for regional arts and gastronomy. Though squarely aimed at tourists, the Loja de Artesanato (craft shop), specializing in art and crafts from Lisbon and the Tejo valley, at least keeps traditional crafts alive and doubles as an exhibition space and shop. Closed Sun.

Ratton Cerâmicas Rua Academia das Ciências 2c, São Bento. Expensive gallery-cum-shop displaying and selling some of the country's classiest ceramics and tiles. Closed weekends.

Santos Ofícios Rua da Madalena 87. Small shop near the Sé stuffed with a somewhat touristy collection of regional crafts including some attractive ceramics, rugs, embroidery, baskets and toys. Closed Sun. There's another branch at the Lisbon Welcome Centre (entrance on Rua do Arsenal; daily 10am–8pm)

Wine and food

Casa Pereira da Conceição Rua Augusta 102–104, Baixa. Fine Art Deco 1930s shop selling aromatic coffee beans and teas. Closed Sat afternoon and all day Sun.

Instituto do Vinho do Porto Rua de São Pedro de Alcântara 45, Bairro Alto. Over three hundred types of port, so you should find something to your taste (see p.303 for further details). Closed Sun.

Manuel Tavares Rua da Betesga 1A, Baixa. On the edge of Rossio, this small, century-old shop has a decent selection of wine, chocolate and national cheeses. Closed all day Sun and Sat after-

noon (Oct–June).

Napoleão Rua dos Fanqueiros 70, Baixa, at the junction with Rua da Conceição. Great range of port and wine, with knowledgeable, English-speaking staff. Closed Sun.

Books and music

Casa do Fado e da Guitarra Portuguesa Largo do Chafariz de Dentro 1. Alfama. The museum shop (see p.88) contains an excellent selection of fado CDs and cassettes, and staff are generally able to give expert advice.

FNAC Rua do Crucifixo 103, Chiado. Branch of the international chain offering a good range of English-language books, along with an extensive music department and computer equipment; also has desk selling tickets to major events (see p.115). There's another branch at Loja 103a, Colombo Shopping Centre (see below).

Livraria Bertrand Rua Garrett 73, Chiado; Loja 1129, Amoreiras (metro Rato); and also Av de Roma 13B (metro Roma). Good general bookshops with novels in English, plus a range of foreign magazines. Closed Sun morning.

Livraria Britânica Rua de S. Marçal 83, Bairro Alto. English-language bookshop, which caters mainly for the British Council nearby, and is well stocked. Closed Sat afternoon and all day Sun.

Livraria Portugal Rua do Carmo 70–74, Baixa. Excellent Portuguese bookshop that features – among other fine books – Rough Guides. Closed Sat afternoon and all day Sun.

Markets

Feira da Ladra Campo de Santa Clara, Alfama. Flea market (see p.88). Tues & Sat 7am–6pm.

Mercado 31 de Janeiro Rua Eng. Vera da Silva; metro Picoas or Saldanha. Once an outdoor affair, this is now housed in a smart new block on two floors. Features everything from fresh fish and flowers to arts and crafts. Mon–Sat 7am–2pm.

Mercado da Ribeira Av 24 de Julho. Just up from Cais do Sodré, one of Lisbon's most atmospheric covered markets; the fish hall is fascinating (see p.77). Mon–Sat: food 5am–2pm; flower market 3pm–7pm; collector's market 9am–1pm.

Numismatists' market Praça do Comércio, Baixa. Old coins and notes from Portugal and its former colonies. Sun morning.

Parque das Nações Estação do Oriente, level 2. Changing markets take place weekly above the metro station. The first Sun of the month sees a Stamps, Coins and Collectibles Fair; the second Sun has handicrafts; the third antiques; and the fourth decorative arts. Sun 10am–7pm.

Praça de Espanha Characterful, downmarket affair near the Gulbenkian Foundation, with stalls selling African music CDs, cheap clothes and general tack. Mon–Sat 9am–6pm.

Shopping centres

The following are all open daily.

Armazéns do Chiado Rua do Carmo 2. This well-designed, traditionally fronted shopping centre on six floors above metro Baixa-Chiado. The top floor has a series of cafés and restaurants, most offering great views over town or Chiado.

Centro Vasco da Gama Av D. João II, Parque das Nações. Three floors of local and international stores under a glass roof permanently washed by running water; top floor restaurants, children's areas and disabled access.

Colombo Shopping Centre Av Colégio Militar-Luz, metro Colégio Militar-Luz. Enormous shopping complex boasts four hundred international and national stores, restaurants, cinemas and kids' areas.

Tivoli Forum Av da Liberdade, opposite Avenida Metro. Flash marble-fronted shopping emporium sheltering the likes of DKNY, French Connection & Adolfo Dominguez. Also has a Pingo Doce supermarket (8.30am–9pm daily), cafés and a juice bar.

Listings

Airlines Air France, Av 5 de Outubro 206 ☎217 900 202; Alitalia, Praça Marquês de Pombal 1–5° ☎213 536 141; British Airways, Av da Liberdade 36–2° ☎213 217 900; Iberia, Rua Rosa Araújo 2 ☎213 558 119; KLM, Campo Grande 220B ☎217 955 018; Lufthansa, Av da Liberdade 192 ☎213 573 722; TAP, Praça Marquês de Pombal 3 ☎213 179 100; Varig, Praça Marquês de Pombal 1 ☎213 136 830.

Airport information ☎218 413 700, ⊛www .lisboa-airport.com.

American Express The local agent is Top Tours, Av Duque de Loulé 108 ☎213 155 885 (metro Marquês de Pombal; Mon–Fri 9.30am–1pm & 2.30–6.30pm).

Banks Most main branches are in the Baixa and surrounding streets. Standard banking hours are Mon–Fri 8.30am–3pm. ATMs can be found throughout Lisbon, and if you have a credit or debit card the best way of obtaining euro. English-language instruction options are usually available.

Buses The main terminal is at Av João Crisóstomo ☎213 545 439 (metro Saldanha) for international and most domestic departures, including express services to the Algarve. There are other bus services from Praça de Espanha (metro Praça de Espanha) for Transportes Sul do Tejo departures to Caparica, Sesimbra and places south of the Tagus; Parque das Nações (metro Campo Oriente) for AVIC services (☎218 940 238) to the northwest coast, and Renex services (☎218 874 871) to the Minho and Algarve; and Campo Grande 5 (metro Campo Grande) for Mafrense Empresa Barraqueiro

services to Mafra and Ericeira. You can buy advance bus tickets from most of the major travel agents, one helpful agency is Marcus & Harting, Rossio 45–50 ☎213 224 550.

Car rental If you're not picking up a car at the airport, ask at the main tourist office; someone who can arrange car rental for you and have the car delivered to your hotel. The main agencies in Lisbon are: Alamo/Guerin Av Alvares Cabral 45b ☎213 882 724/800 201 078; Auto Jardim: Rua Luciano Cordeiro 6 ☎213 549 182, airport ☎218 463 187; Avis: Av Praia da Vitória 12c ☎213 514 560, airport ☎218 435 550; Budget: Rua Castilho 167b ☎213 860 516, airport ☎218 478 803; Europcar: Santa Apolónia station ☎218 861 573, airport ☎218 401 176; Hertz: Rua Castilho 72 ☎213 812 430, airport ☎218 463 154; Nova Rent: Largo Monterroio Mascarenhas 9 ☎213 870 808.

Car trouble Automóvel Clube de Portugal ☎219 429 103, ⊛www.acp.pt has a reciprocal agreement with automobile associations in other EU countries.

Embassies Australia (consulate): Av da Liberdade 198–2° ☎213 101 500 (metro Avenida); Canada (consulate): Av da Liberdade 196–200 ☎213 164 600; Ireland: Rua da Imprensa à Estrela 1–4° ☎213 929 440 (tram 28 to Estrela); UK, Rua de São Marçal 174 ☎213 929 440, ⊛www .uk-embassy.pt (metro Rato); USA: Av das Forças Armadas ☎217 273 300 (metro Jardim Zoológico).

Emergencies ☎112

Fairs There's a permanent fairground, the Feira Popular, opposite the Entrecampos metro station:

eats, rides and a thoroughly Portuguese night out (March–Oct Mon–Fri 7pm–1.30am, Sat & Sun 3pm–1.30am; Dec Tues–Fri 2.30–10pm, Sat & Sun 11am–10pm; closed Nov, Jan & Feb; €2, some rides extra).

Gay & lesbian scene Lisbon's gay and lesbian scene is gradually opening up in a city which was until quite recently fairly conservative. The Centro Comunitário Gay e Lèsbica de Lisboa (Lisbon Gay and Lesbian Community Centre), Rua de São Lazaro 88 ☎218 873 918 (Mon–Sat 4–8pm) organizes gay events and can help with information – check their excellent and comprehensive website (in English and Portuguese) at ⊛www.ilga-portugal.org. The centre also has a bar and internet café. For more gay and lesbian nightlife see p.115, and for accommmodation see p.69.

Hospital British Hospital, Rua Saraiva de Carvalho 49 ☎213 955 067 has English-speaking staff.

Internet The internet is very popular in Lisbon and there are numerous web cafés where you can browse the internet and send or receive emails. Most places charge around €3–4/hr for internet use. Central options include *Ask Me Lisboa*, above the Lisbon Welcome Centre in Praça do Comércio ☎210 312 815; the lively *Web Café*, Rua do Diário de Notícias 16 ☎213 421 181, ✉web1@mail .esoterica.pt (daily 4pm–2am); the bright café-bar *Cyberica*, Rua Duques de Bragança 7 ☎213 421 707, ✉Cyberbica@telepac.pt (Mon–Thur 9am–midnight, Fri 9am–2am, Sat 7pm–2am); and at Forum Picoas building, Av Fontes Pereira de Melo 38 ☎213 142 527, ⊛www.telepac.pt (Mon–Fri 9am–7pm), by metro Picoas.

Language courses Portuguese lessons are given by the Cambridge School, Av da Liberdade 173 ☎213 527 474, or International House, Rua Marquês Sa da Bandeira ☎213 151 496 (metro São Sebastião).

Laundry Lavandaria Saus Ana, in the Centro Comércial da Mouraria, Largo Martim Moniz 9 (metro Socorro), does service washes for €5 (Mon–Sat 9.30am–8pm), or try the self-service Lava Neve, Rua da Alegria 37, Bairro Alto (Mon 9am–1pm & 3–7pm, Tues–Fri 10am–1pm & 3–7pm, Sat 9am–1pm; €4.50 for 5kg).

Left luggage There are 24hr lockers at the airport (in level 1 of car park 1); at Rossio, Cais do Sodré and Santa Apolónia stations (around €2 a day), and a left-luggage office at the bus terminal on Av João Crisóstomo (Mon–Fri 6.30am–8pm, Sat & Sun 9am–1pm & 2–6pm).

Lost property Report any loss to the police station in the Foz Cultura building in Palácio Foz, Restauradores (daily 24 hours, ☎213 421 634) or

phone ☎218 355 403.

Newspapers There are several newsstands around Rossio and Restauradores – such as the one attached to the ABEP ticket kiosk – which sell foreign-language papers, as do the lobbies of many of the larger hotels.

Pharmacies and contraception Open Mon–Fri 9am–1pm & 3–7pm, Sat 9am–1pm. Local papers carry information about 24-hour pharmacies and the details are posted on every pharmacy door. Contraceptives – and even, in some areas, hypodermic syringes – are available from automatic vending machines outside pharmacies.

Police The tourist police station is the Foz Cultura building in Palácio Foz, Restauradores ☎213 421 634 (daily 24 hours). You need to report here in order to make a claim on your travel insurance.

Post Office The main post office is on Praça dos Restauradores 58 (Mon–Fri 8am–10pm, Sat & Sun 9am–6pm), from where you can send airmail and *correio azul* (express mail – the fastest service). There's a 24-hour post office at the airport. Stamps can also be purchased from some – but not all – newsagents.

Public toilets There are very few of these in the street. However, nearly all the museums and main tourist sights have a public toilet (*casa de banho*, *retrete*, *banheiro*, *lavabos* or WC), and it is not difficult to sneak into a café or restaurant if needs be. Gents are usually marked H (*homens*) or C (*cabalheiros*), and ladies M (*mulheres*) or S (*senhoras*).

River cruises Two-and-a-half-hour cruises up the Tejo depart from Estação Fluvial (☎218 820 348; daily 11am & 3pm; €15) past Parque das Nações and Belém. The price includes a drink and a bilingual commentary. At weekends, the boat stops off at both points.

Swimming pools The most central option is the pool in the Atheneum club on Rua das Portas de Santo Antão, next to the Coliseu (Mon–Fri 3.30–4.30pm & 9–10pm, Sat 3.30–7pm; €3.20).

Telephones For international calls there's a telephone office next to the post office in Praça dos Restauradores (see above). There's a second office on the corner of Rossio (no. 65; 8am–11pm). You can also make international calls from any phone booth. See also "Basics" p.40.

Tickets for football matches, films and other spectacles can be bought APEB kiosk (daily 9am–9.30pm) at the corner of Praça dos Restauradores (near the post office), which also has ticket and programme details for all the city's cinemas and theatres. Tickets can also be purchased from FNAC (see p.121) or online from ⊛www.ondaticket.com.

Tram and bus tours You can also take a *tour* in

a revamped turn-of-the-century tram. The Circuito Colinas (Hills Tour) (March–Oct hourly from 9am–6pm; Nov–Feb departures at 11am, 1.30pm & 3.30pm; €15) takes passengers on a ninety-minute ride from Praça do Comércio round Alfama, Chiado and São Bento (information on ☏966 298 558). Carris runs various bus tours in open-top buses. The one-hour Circuito Tejo (hourly 11am–4pm; €12.50) takes passengers round Lisbon's principal sites; a day ticket allows you to get on and off whenever you want. The Oriente Express Tour departs from Praça do Comércio three times daily to Parque das Nações for the same price. Tickets can be bought on board. Information on ☏213 632 021.

Trains See pp.62–63, for details of Lisbon's various stations. Timetables and train information are available from individual stations and on ⓦwww.cp.pt. Always check departure times and stations in advance: many intercity services require a seat reservation (particularly to Coimbra/Porto), which you can do prior to depar-ture, though allow yourself plenty of time.

Travel agencies Marcus & Harting, Rossio 45–50 ☏213 224 550 is a good, central option for bus tickets and general travel information. The well-informed Top Tours is at Av Duque de Loulé 108 ☏213 155 885, near metro Marquês de Pombal. It also acts as American Express agents. USIT Tagus, Rua Camilo Castelo Branco 20 ☏213 525 986, specializes in discounted student tickets and sells ISIC cards.

Walks The *turismo* in Palácio Foz, Praça dos Restauradores (see p.72), is the starting point for a privately run three-hour guided walk through the "medieval" suburbs of Chiado and Bairro Alto. Additional walks through "Old Lisbon" take in Alfama and the castle area, beginning from Casa dos Bicos on Praça da Ribeira. Minimum six people at €13 per person; two weeks' notice must be given. Information on ☏ & ☏213 906 149, ⓔjcabdo@ip.pt.

Around Lisbon

The most straightforward way to escape the city is to head for the string of beach resorts west along the coast from Belém, which can be reached by train from Cais do Sodré. At places like **Oeiras** and **Carcavelos**, and above all at **Estoril** and **Cascais**, the beaches are good even if the water quality isn't. For better sands and a cleaner ocean you'll have to head north to **Guincho**; or cross the Tejo by ferry to reach the **Costa da Caparica**, a 30km expanse of dunes to the south of the capital. Further south, there are also good, clean beaches at Sesimbra and in the Parque Natural da Arrábida, a superb unspoilt craggy reserve, while the large town of **Setúbal** is noted for its Igreja de Jesus, the earliest of all Manueline buildings. There's reasonably priced accommodation at all these places, as well as a youth hostel at Oeiras and campsites at Guincho, Costa da Caparica and Arrábida. But, as you might imagine, all the beach resorts in the Lisbon area get very crowded at weekends and throughout August.

Basing yourself in Lisbon, you also could take in a fair part of the provinces of Estremadura (Chapter Two) and Alentejo (Chapter Eight) on day trips. Indeed, some of those regions' greatest attractions lie within a 50km or so radius of the capital – such as the palaces of **Queluz** or **Mafra** – and are best seen on a day trip. The beautiful town of **Sintra**, the most popular excursion from Lisbon, demands a longer look, and reveals a different side if you stay overnight. However you decide to see them, bear in mind that most of the Sintra palaces are closed on Mondays, and those at Queluz and Mafra on Tuesdays.

West to Estoril and Cascais

Stretching for over 30km west of Lisbon, the **Estoril coast** – from Oeiras to Cascais – makes for an enjoyable day out, drifting from beach to bar and strolling along the lively seafront promenades. Sadly, the water itself has suffered badly from pollution and, though steps are being taken to clean it up, most beaches fail to get a blue flag. Nonetheless, the coast retains its attractions and **Cascais**, in particular, makes a pleasant alternative to staying in Lisbon, and is well placed for trips to Sintra or to the wild Guincho beach.

Access to the resorts could hardly be easier. The Linha de Cascais train leaves every twenty minutes (Mon–Thurs & Sun 5.30am–1.30am, Fri & Sat 5.30am–2.30am; €1.05) from **Cais do Sodré** station, stopping at Oeiras, Carcavelos and stations beyond. You can also pick up a train from Alcântara and Belém, though these stopping trains involve changing at Oeiras. By road, the **N6** is the coastal highway, passing through most of the centres along the seafront, often as the Avenida Marginal; the faster **A5 motorway** (Auto-Estrada da Oeste) is an (inexpensive) toll road running from Lisbon to Estoril – drive west past Amoreiras and follow the signs.

Oeiras to São João

The first suburb of any size after Belém is **OEIRAS**, where the River Tejo officially turns into the sea. The **beach** here has recently been cleaned up, though most people swim in the Ocean Pool alongside the sands; riverside walkways are also being improved. Unless you're staying at the youth hostel (see p.71), however, the only reason for a stop here would be to see the **Palácio do Marquês de Pombal**, erstwhile home of the rebuilder of Lisbon. The house is now an adult education centre and the park is not technically open to visitors. However, if there's nothing special going on, the guard should be able to show you the attractive formal gardens, or you can peer over the walls at its massive grotto.

Carcavelos

The next stop, **Carcavelos**, has the most extensive sandy beach on this part of the coast. Swimmers chance the waters in high summer, and at other times it's a lively spot for beach soccer, surfing and blowy winter walks. To reach the beach, it's a ten-minute walk from the station along the broad Avenida Jorge V. There are plenty of beachside cafés and bars; *Perola*, on the promenade at the west end of the beach, offers inexpensive food and great sea views. Try to visit Carcavelos on Thursday morning, when the town hosts a huge **market**; turn right out of the station and follow the signs. Street upon street is taken over by stalls selling cheap goods, clothes (many with brand-name labels) and ceramics.

São Pedro and São João

Along the last stretch of the Linha de Cascais, the beaches improve rapidly and you reach the beginning of an esplanade that stretches virtually uninterrupted to Cascais. **SÃO PEDRO** has a superb beach, just down from the station, and **SÃO JOÃO** is flanked by two lovely stretches of sand. The whole seafront here is pretty animated in the summer months, swarming with young surfers and Portuguese holidaymakers frequenting the numerous cafés and restaurants.

Estoril

ESTORIL gained a postwar reputation as a haunt of exiled royalty and the idle rich, and it continues to maintain its pretensions towards being a "Portuguese Riviera", with grandiose villas and luxury hotels. It is little surprise, then, that the town's touristic life revolves around an exclusive **golf course** (golf passes are available from the tourist office) and **casino**. The latter requires some semblance of formal attire to get in (daily 3pm–3am; free). Inside you'll find roulette, cards, slot machines, restaurants, shops, nightly shows at 11pm and even an art gallery.

The casino sits at the far end the Parque do Estoril, a lovely stretch of fountains and exotic trees, surrounded by Estoril's nicest bars and restaurants. For a leisurely tour of Estoril, a **toy train** departs from the eastern end of the park (daily every 50min 11am–12.40pm & 2.20–4pm; free). The resort's fine sandy beach is backed by a seafront promenade that stretches all the way to Cascais. A stroll between the two towns is recommended: drifting from beach to bar, the walk takes around twenty minutes. From July to mid-September, a free fireworks display takes place above Estoril's beach, Praia de Tamariz, every Saturday night at midnight.

Practicalities

The **train station** is on Estoril's through-road, with the beach accessible by underpass. Across the main road from the station, at the bottom of the park, you'll find the very helpful **turismo** (Mon–Sat 9am–7pm, Sun 10am–6pm; ☎214 663 813, ⓦwww.estorilcoast-tourism.com) which can give advice on private rooms and details of the area's various golf clubs.

For **accommodation**, there are just a few pensões, of which *Pensão-Residencial Smart*, Rua José Viana 3 (☎214 682 164, Ⓔresidencial.smart @netcabo.pt; ❹), is the best, with pleasant rooms and breakfast included. It's east of the park – turn right out of the station, turning left when you reach Avenida Bombeiros Voluntarios, which runs up behind the *Hotel Paris*. If you want to go upmarket, *Estoril Sol* at Parque Palmela (☎214 839 000, Ⓔsales@hotelestorilsol.pt; ❾) is a top-range old-fashioned highrise between Cascais and Estoril; it offers dazzling views over Cascais bay from many of its rooms. Facilities include a restaurant, inside and outside pool and a health club.

For coffee and cake, a meal or just a late **drink**, it's nice to sit at the outdoor tables at *Frolic* (open till 2am; closed Mon), a restaurant, café and nightclub complex on Avenida Clotilde 2765, overlooking the eastern side of the park. *Jonas Bar*, right on the seafront between Cascais and Estoril, is a fun spot day or night, selling cocktails, juices and snacks. The best place to eat is the *English Bar (Cimas)*, at Avenida Sabóia 9 (☎214 680 413), just west of the square in Monte Estoril (closed Sun). Named after the Englishman who built the mansion in the 1940s, it has sumptuous wood-panelled decor, sea views and top quality fish, meat and game that have attracted politicians, journalists and Spanish royalty.

Cascais

At the end of the train line, and with three fairly good beaches along its esplanade, **CASCAIS** is a major resort, with a flash marina adding to its appeal. It is positively bursting at the seams in summer, especially at weekends, but despite its commercialism it's not too large or difficult to get around and has a much younger, less exclusive, feel than Estoril. It even retains some vestiges of its previous existence as a fishing village. There's a lively **market** every

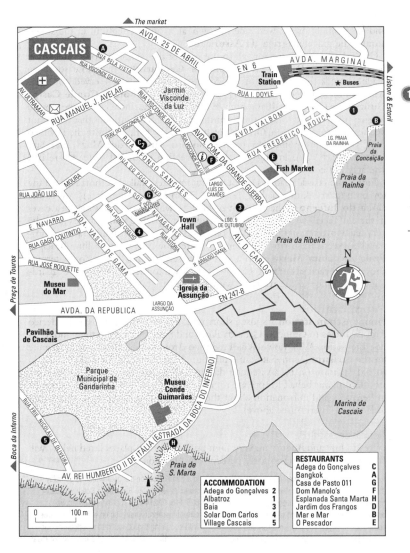

CASCAIS

The market

AVDA. 25 DE ABRIL

RUA BELA VISTA

RUA VISCONDE DA LUZ

AV. ULTRAMAR

RUA MANUEL J. AVELAR

Jarmin
Visconde
da Luz

EN 6

AVDA. MARGINAL

Train
Station

★ Buses

RUA I. DOYLE

Lisbon & Estoril

TRAV. DO VISCONDE DE LUZ

RUA VISCONDE DA LUZ

AVDA. COM. DA GRANDE GUERRA

RUA VISCONDE DA LUZ

AVDA VALBOM

RUA FREDERICO AROUÇA

LG. PRAIA
DA RAINHA

Praia
da
Conceição

RUA AFONSO SANCHES

RUA DO POÇO NOVO

Fish Market

Praia da
Rainha

MOURA

RUA JOÃO LUIS

RUA DOS

LARGO
LUIS DE
CAMÕES

E. NAVARRO

RUA GAGO COUTINHO

AVDA. VASCO DE GAMA

RUA DOS NAVEGANTES

RUA LATINO COELHO

NAVEGANTES

RUA VITORIA

Town
Hall

LGO. 5
DE OUTUBRO

AV. D. CARLOS

Praia da Ribeira

RUA JOSÉ ROQUETTE

Praça de Touros

Museu
do Mar

RUA ARAUJO VIANA

Igreja da
Assunção

EN 247-8

N

AVDA. DA REPUBLICA

LARGO DA
ASSUNÇÃO

Pavilhão
de Cascais

Boca do Inferno

RUA ENG. NICOLAU DE OLIVEIRA

Parque
Municipal da
Gandarinha

Museu
Conde
Guimarães

ESTRADA DA BOCA DO INFERNO

Marina de
Cascais

AV. REI HUMBERTO II DE ITALIA

Praia de
S. Marta

0   100 m

ACCOMMODATION

Adega do Gonçalves	2
Albatroz	1
Baia	3
Solar Dom Carlos	4
Village Cascais	5

RESTAURANTS

Adega do Gonçalves	C
Bangkok	A
Casa de Pasto 011	G
Dom Manolo's	F
Esplanada Santa Marta	H
Jardim dos Frangos	D
Mar e Mar	B
O Pescador	E

Wednesday on Rua do Mercado – head up Alameda C. da Grande Guerra, bear left at the roundabout and it's on the right – and there are Sunday evening **bullfights** during summer in the Praça de Touros Avenida Pedro Alvares Cabral in the west of town.

You'll find the main concentration of **bars and nightlife** – and consequently most of what makes Cascais tick as a town – on Rua Frederico Arouca, the main pedestrian thoroughfare on the east side of the Avenida Combatantes da Grande Guerra, which splits the town. Also in this area and worth a look is the **fish market** that takes place around 8am (Mon–Sat) between the Ribeira and Rainha beaches. For a wander away from the crowds, cross over Avenida Com. Grande Guerra, and stroll up beyond Largo 5 de Outubro into the old, and surprisingly pretty, west side of town, at its most delightful in the streets around the graceful **Igreja da Assunção**.

Cascais' other attractions are all to the west of the centre. Beyond the church lies the pleasant **Parque Municipal da Gandarinha**, in whose southern reaches stands the mansion of the counts of Guimarães, preserved complete with its nineteenth-century fittings as the **Museu Biblioteca Conde Castro Guimarães** (Tues–Sun 10am–5pm; €1.30); most days, there's someone around to give you a guided tour of the furniture, paintings and antiques that the count bequeathed to the nation. On the north side of the park, opposite the Pavilhão de Cascais, signs point you to the modern **Museu do Mar** (Tues–Sun 10am–5pm; €1.30), an engaging little collection of model boats, sea-related artefacts, old costumes and pictures.

Taking the coastal road, it's about twenty minutes' walk or a short ride on the toy train (every 45min daily 11.15am–1.30pm & 3–4.30pm; free) west to the **Boca do Inferno** – the "Mouth of Hell" – where waves crash against caves in the cliff face. The viewpoints above are always packed with tourists (as is the very tacky market on the roadside) but, frankly, the whole affair is rather unimpressive except in stormy weather. En route, however, there's a little beach at **Praia de Santa Marta** with a nice café (see "Eating" below) on a terrace above. The beach sits next to Cascais' fort, closed to the public, but now guarding the entrance to the **marina**, with more shops, cafés and restaurants.

Practicalities

From the **train station** it's just a short walk across to the main Rua Frederico Arouca; **buses** to Guincho, Cabo da Roca and Sintra leave from the stands outside the station. Walk down Rua Frederico Arouca and cross the main avenue for the **turismo** (Mon–Sat 9am–7pm, Sun 10am–6pm; ☎214 868 204), set in an old mansion on Rua Visconde da Luz, where the staff will usually phone around on your behalf for private rooms. There are local bus timetables posted in here, too, and information about the **toy train** that rattles from the station to Boca do Inferno (see above).

Accommodation

Prices in July and August are very high but most of the places listed below will drop room rates by up to forty percent out of season.

Hotel Albatroz Rua Frederica Arouca 100 ☎214 832 821, @albatroz@mail.telepac.pt. Seaside hotels don't come much grander than this – one of the best in the region, with glorious views from some rooms (which you pay extra for) and the restaurant, plus top-of-the-range facilities. Big winter reductions. ❾

Hotel Baia Av Com. Grande Guerra ☎214 831 033, @hotelbaia@mail.telepac.pt. Modern seafront hotel overlooking the beach and harbour. Rooms are very good value out of season, and not bad in summer; it's worth booking ahead for a room with a sea view. ❻

Adega do Gonçalves Rua Afonso Sanches 54 ☎214 831 519. Basic rooms above the restaurant; in a handy location but guaranteed to be noisy. ❷

Solar Dom Carlos Rua Latina Coelho 8 ☎214 828 115, ℗214 865 155. A very attractive sixteenth-century mansion on a quiet backstreet with cool tiling throughout and a welcoming air. Bright, pretty rooms, garden and even an old royal chapel. Breakfast included. ❹

Village Cascais Rua Frie Nicolau de Oliveira ☎214 826 000, @villagecascais@vilagale.pt. Superbly positioned next to Parque da Gandarinha near to an unspoilt part of coast, *Village Cascais* is also one of the area's more tasteful modern developments set in palm-studded grounds. Spacious rooms have satellite TV, minibar and kitchenettes, and there's also a bar and restaurant. ❻

Eating

Bangkok Rua da Bela Vista 6 ☎214 847 600. Sublime Thai cooking in a traditional Cascais town house beautifully decorated with inlaid wood and oriental furnishings. Dishes include lobster in curry paste and assorted Thai snacks; expect to pay upwards of €30. Expensive.

Casa de Pasto 011 Travessa dos Navegantes 11. With just half a dozen tables, this local grill house gets packed thanks to its bargain value and very tasty fish, meat dishes and house wine; service is slow, so sit back and enjoy. Closed Sun. Inexpensive.

Dom Manolo's Av Marginal 13. Busy grill house just down from the turismo, where the alley runs through to Largo Luís de Camões. Superb chicken and chips; add a salad, local wine and home-made dessert and you'll still pay only around €10. Inexpensive.

Esplanada Santa Marta Praia de Santa Marta. Charcoal-grilled fish served on a tiny terrace over-

looking the sea and little beach on the road out to the Boca do Inferno. Moderate.

Adega do Gonçalves Rua Afonso Sanches 54. Traditional *adega* not yet overwhelmed by tourists, serving huge portions of good food at moderate prices; the grilled fish is recommended. Moderate.

Jardim dos Frangos Av Com. da Grande Guerra 66. Permanently buzzing with people and sizzling with the speciality, grilled chicken, which is devoured by the plateload at indoor and outdoor tables. Inexpensive.

Mar e Mar Praia da Conceição. Tiny kiosk serving beach-side grills, kebabs and salads on outdoor tables facing the waves. Closed in bad weather. Moderate.

O Pescador Rua das Flores 18 ☎214 832 054. One of several close to the fish market, this offers superior fish meals. Good food and service but pricey. Closed Sun. Expensive.

Drinking and nightlife

At night, Cascais shows itself off in the smart pubs, bars and cafés along **Rua Frederico Arouca**. More boisterous behaviour goes on in **Largo Luís de Camões**, down the steps on the west side of the main avenue. By day this is a suntrap, none of whose café-bar-restaurants serve particularly memorable meals but are pleasant (if expensive), places to sit and drink. However, on summer nights, the bars throw open their doors, turn up the music and, come closing time at 2am, the square is full of bleary-eyed drinkers dancing and shouting the words to tunes they never realized they knew.

Chequers Largo Luís de Camões 7. Not quite as legendary as it would have you believe, but lively enough English-style pub, especially once the pumping rock music strengthens its grip.

Coconuts Av Rei Humberto II de Itália 7. Disco on the road to Boca do Inferno, attracting an odd mix of trendy locals and clubbing tourists. Theme nights include karaoke and strippers on Wed nights. Closed Sun in winter.

John Bull Praça Costa Pinto 31. Backing onto the

Largo Luís de Camões, another English-style pub which fills up early with a good-time crowd; serves meals, too.

Music Bar Largo da Praia da Rainha. One of the few bars in town with decent sea views, which you can take in sitting at tables on the patio above the beach. Closed Mon.

News Estrada da Malveira da Serra. One of the "in" discos in the area, with a terrace and a lively night guaranteed, especially Fri. Open till 4am.

Praia do Guincho

There are buses every 1–2 hours (daily 7.15am–7.15pm; €1.80) from outside Cascais train station that run the 6km west to **PRAIA DO GUINCHO**, a great sweeping field of **beach** with body-crashing Atlantic rollers. It's a superb place for **surfing and windsurfing** – legs of the World Windsurfing Championships are often held here in August – but also a dangerous one. The undertow is notoriously strong and people are drowned almost every year. To add to that, there's absolutely no shade and on breezy days the wind cuts across the sands. Even if you can't feel the sun, you need to be very careful.

The beach has become increasingly popular over the years and the coastal approach road is flanked by half a dozen large **terrace-restaurants**, all with standard, fish-dominated menus and varying views of the breaking rollers. As nearly everyone comes here on day trips, there's no cheap accommodation, except the campsite (see below). At the deluxe-class *Fortaleza do Guincho* (☎214 870 491, ℮reservations@guinchohotel.pt; ❾) you can stay in a converted fort; there's even a ballroom. Rooms come with satellite TV and minibars. More affordable is *Estalagem O Muchaxo* (☎214 870 221, ℮muchaco@ip.pt; ❹ or ❺ for sea views), showing signs of shabbiness but remaining a highly attractive place, with a sea pool, stone-flagged bar and picture windows looking out across the beach from the restaurant, which is rated as one of the best in the Lisbon area. Pop in for just a coffee or a beer if you don't want to spend around €20 a head on a meal. The well-equipped Orbitur **campsite** see (p.72) is about 1km back from the main part of the beach; follow the signs from the coast road.

Sintra and around

As the summer residence of the kings of Portugal, and the Moorish lords of Lisbon before them, Sintra's verdant charms have long been celebrated. British travellers of the eighteenth and nineteenth centuries found a new Arcadia in its cool, wooded heights, recording with satisfaction the old Spanish saying: "To see the world and leave out Sintra is to go blind about." Byron stayed here in 1809 and began *Childe Harold*, his great mock-epic travel poem, in which the "horrid crags" of "Cintra's glorious Eden" form a first location. Writing home, in a letter to his mother, he proclaimed the village:

... perhaps in every aspect the most delightful in Europe; it contains beauties of every description natural and artificial. Palaces and gardens rising in the midst of rocks, cataracts and precipices, convents on stupendous heights, a distant view of the sea and the Tagus ... it unites in itself all the wildness of the Western Highlands with the verdure of the South of France.

That the young Byron had seen neither of these is irrelevant: his description of Sintra's romantic appeal is exact – and still telling two centuries later. Move mountains and give yourself the best part of two full days here.

The Town

SINTRA loops around a series of green and wooded ravines making it a confusing place in which to get your bearings. Basically, though, it consists of three distinct and separate villages: the drab **Estefânia** (around the train station), **Sintra-Vila** (the attractive main town) and, 2km to the east, the functional but pleasant **São Pedro de Sintra**. It's a ten- to fifteen-minute walk from the station to Sintra-Vila and around twenty minutes from Sintra-Vila to São Pedro.

Before you head into the town centre, it's worth making a small detour 300m northeast of the station to visit the superb **Museu de Arte Moderna** on Avenida Heliodoro Salgado (Tues–Sun 10am–6pm; €3). Built in Sintra's former casino, the 1920s building spreads over three floors, chronologically displaying the main modern movements, including pop art, minimalism, kinetic art and conceptual art. The collection is so huge that exhibits change every two months, but depending on when you visit you can see works by Jackson Pollock, Hockney, Lichtenstein and Warhol, including his Campbell's soup tin and a wonderful portrait of Judy Garland. The top floor contains a café and

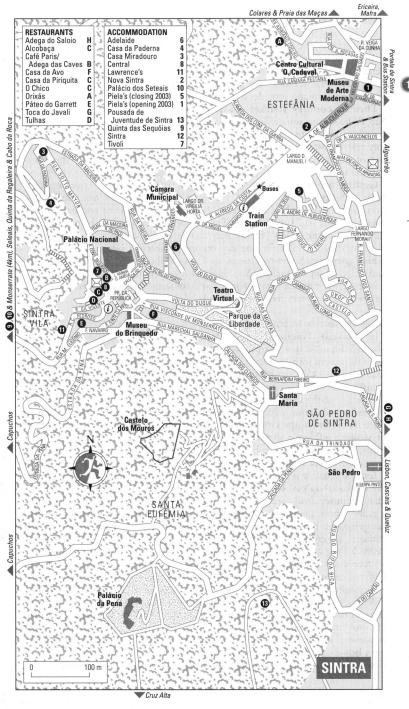

Colares & Praia das Maças ▲
Ericeira, Mafra ▲

Portela de Sintra & Bus Station

RESTAURANTS
Adega do Saloio	H
Alcobaça	C
Café Paris/ Adega das Caves	B
Casa da Avo	F
Casa da Piriquita	C
O Chico	C
Orixás	A
Páteo do Garrett	E
Toca do Javali	G
Tulhas	D

ACCOMMODATION
Adelaide	6
Casa da Paderna	4
Casa Miradouro	3
Central	8
Lawrence's	11
Nova Sintra	2
Palácio dos Seteais	10
Piela's (closing 2003)	5
Piela's (opening 2003)	1
Pousada de Juventude de Sintra	13
Quinta das Sequóias	9
Sintra	12
Tivoli	7

Centro Cultural O. Cadaval

Museu de Arte Moderna

ESTEFÂNIA

Alguierão ▶

① ⑩ & Monserrate (4km), Seteais, Quinta da Regaleira & Cabo da Roca

Câmara Municipal

Palácio Nacional

SINTRA VILA

Teatro Virtual

Parque da Liberdade

Museu do Brinquedo

Capuchos ◀

Capuchos ◀

Castelo dos Mouros

SÃO PEDRO DE SINTRA

Santa Maria

Lisbon, Cascais & Queluz ▶

São Pedro

SANTA EUFÉMIA

Train Station

Buses

Palácio da Pena

N

0   100 m

SINTRA

▼ Cruz Alta

restaurant, with an outdoor terrace offering great views over the Pena Palace.

On the way into town you pass the fantastical **Câmara Municipal** (town hall), but it is the extraordinary landmark of the **Palácio Nacional** (see below), distinguished by its vast pair of conical chimneys, that dominates the central square around which the old town is gathered. Opposite here the turismo (see "Practicalities" on p.136) in Praça da República can help with accommodation and provides a useful map of the surroundings.

There's a **country market** – with antiques and crafts, as well as food – in São Pedro's main square on the second and last Sunday of every month. The town's annual **festa** in honour of St Peter is held on June 28 and 29, and in July and August there's a **music festival**, with classical performances in a number of the town's buildings (see p.120). The end of July also sees the Feira Grande in São Pedro, with crafts, antiques and cheeses on sale.

Getting around Sintra's environs involves a fair amount of travelling. The most useful **bus** service is #434, which takes a circular route from Sintra station to Sintra-Vila, the Castelo dos Mouros, Palácio da Pena and back (daily every 40 mins 10.20am–5.15pm). Tickets can be purchased on board and cost €3. A **day rover ticket** (€6.50) may also be worthwhile if you want to pack it all in; they are valid for one day on any Stagecoach bus, including #403, which goes from Sintra to Cascais via Cabo da Roca. For full details of buses and times, ask in the turismo. You might also want to make use of **taxis**, which cost roughly €8 one way to Pena or Monserrate, though negotiate a fee beforehand as meters aren't always used.

The Palácio Nacional

The **Palácio Nacional** – or **Paço Real** (Mon, Tues & Thurs–Sun 10am–5.30pm; €3) – was probably already in existence under the Moors. It takes its present form, however, from the rebuilding and enlargements of Dom João I (1385–1433) and his fortunate successor, Dom Manuel, heir to Vasco da Gama's inspired explorations. Its style, as you might expect, is an amalgam of Gothic – with impressive roofline battlements – and the latter king's Manueline additions, with their characteristically extravagant twisted and animate forms. Inside, the Gothic–Manueline modes are tempered by a good deal of Moorish influence, adapted over the centuries by a succession of royal occupants. The last royal to live here, in the 1880s, was Maria Pia, grandmother of the country's last reigning monarch – Manuel II, "The Unfortunate".

Today the palace is a museum (it's best to go early or late in the day to avoid the crowds). You pass through the **kitchens** first, their roofs tapering into the giant chimneys, and then on to the upper floor. The first room on this floor is a gallery above the palace chapel, built perhaps on the old mosque. In a room alongside, the deranged Afonso VI was confined for six years by his brother Pedro II; he eventually died here in 1683, listening to Mass through a grid, Pedro having seized "his throne, his liberty and his queen". Beyond the gallery, a succession of state rooms climaxes in the **Sala das Armas**, its domed and coffered ceiling emblazoned with the coats of arms of 72 noble families.

Highlights on the lower floor include the Manueline **Sala dos Cisnes**, so-called for the swans painted on its ceiling, and the **Sala das Pegas**. This last room takes its name from the flock of magpies (*pegas*) painted on the frieze and ceiling, holding in their beaks the legend *por bem* (in honour) – reputedly the response of João I, caught by his queen, Philippa (of Lancaster), in the act of kissing a lady-in-waiting. He had the room decorated with as many magpies as there were women at court in order to satirize and put a stop to their gossiping.

The Museu do Brinquedo and Teatro Virtual

The fascinating private toy collection of João Arbués Moreira is now housed in a former fire station, imaginatively converted into a high-tech **toy museum** (Tues–Sun 10am–6pm; €3) just round the corner from the Palácio Nacional on Rua Visconde de Monserrate. The museum comes complete with internal glass lifts, a café and video units. The huge array of toys over three floors are somewhat confusingly labelled, but look out for the 3000-year-old stone Egyptian toys on the first floor; the Hornby trains from the 1930s, and some of the first ever toy cars, produced in Germany in the early 1900s. Perhaps the most interesting section is that on early Portuguese toys, containing old cars made from papier-mâché, tin-plate animals, wooden trams and trains, as well as a selection of 1930s beach toys, including beautifully painted buckets and the metal fish that appears on the museum brochure.

A hundred metres or so southeast of the toy museum, off Volta do Duche in the leafy slopes of the Parque da Liberdade, the **Teatro Virtual** (June–Sept Tues–Fri 9.30am–12.30pm & 2–6pm, Sat & Sun 2–6pm; Oct–May same hours until 5.30pm; €1.50), is a tiny cinema projecting a virtual recreation of the Portuguese discoverers and their early voyages to Japan, the Portuguese depicted with giant noses, which is how the Japanese saw them.

The Castelo dos Mouros and Palácio da Pena

From near the church of **Santa Maria**, towards São Pedro, a stone pathway leads up to the ruined ramparts of the **Castelo dos Mouros** (daily: June–Sept 10am–7pm; Oct–May 10am–5pm; €3). Alternatively you can catch bus #434 from Sintra station. Captured with the aid of Scandinavian Crusaders by Afonso Henriques, the Moorish castle spans two rocky pinnacles, with the remains of a mosque spread midway between the fortifications. **Views** from here are extraordinary: south beyond Lisbon's bridge to the Serra de Arrábida, west to Cascais and Cabo da Roca (the westernmost point of mainland Europe), and north to Peniche and the Berlenga Islands.

The upper gate of the castle gives onto the road up to Pena, opposite the lower entrance to **Pena park** (daily: mid-June to mid-Sept 9am–7pm; mid Sept–mid June 10am–5pm; €3, or €5 combined ticket with Palácio da Pena), a stretch of rambling woodland, with a scattering of lakes and follies. At the top of the park, about twenty minutes' walk, rears the fabulous **Palácio da Pena** (Tues–Sun: mid-June to mid-Sept 10am–7pm; mid-Sept to mid-June 10am–5pm; €5), a wild fantasy of domes, towers, ramparts and walkways, approached through mock-Manueline gateways and a drawbridge that doesn't draw. A compelling riot of kitsch, it was built in the 1840s to the specifications of Ferdinand of Saxe-Coburg-Gotha, husband of Queen Maria II, and it bears comparison with the mock-medieval castles of Ludwig of Bavaria. The architect, the German **Baron Eschwege**, immortalized himself in the guise of a warrior-knight on a huge statue that guards the palace from a neighbouring crag. Inside, Pena is no less bizarre, preserved exactly as it was left by the royal family on their flight from Portugal in 1910. The result is fascinating: rooms of concrete decorated to look like wood, statues of turbaned Moors nonchalantly holding electric chandeliers. Of an original convent, founded to celebrate the first sight of Vasco da Gama's returning fleet, a chapel and Manueline cloister have been retained.

Above Pena, past the statue of Eschwege, a marked footpath climbs to the **Cruz Alta**, highest point of the Serra de Sintra. Another footpath (unmarked) winds down to the left from Pena, coming out near Seteais (see p.135).

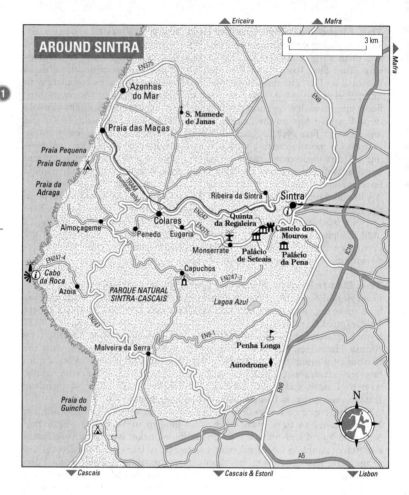

Sights around Sintra

After the castle and Pena, a visit to **Quinta da Regaleira**, the palace of **Seteais** and luxuriant gardens of **Monserrate** are the other obvious goals of a Sintra walk. Enthusiastic hikers can make a circuit of these, via the **Convento dos Capuchos**, known as the "Cork Convent"; otherwise, to see everything, you're looking at a taxi-ride at least one way.

Quinta da Regaleira

Quinta da Regaleira, lying just a five-minute walk out of town on the Seteais–Monserrate road (tours daily: June–Sept every 30 mins 10am–6pm; March–May & Oct–Nov roughly hourly 10am–3.30pm; Dec–Feb roughly hourly 11am–3.30pm; 90min tours must be booked in advance on ☎219 106 650; €10) is one of Sintra's most elaborate private estates and was declared a UNESCO World Heritage site in 1995. The estate was designed by Italian architect and theatrical set designer Luigi Manini for wealthy landowner António Augusto Carvalho Monteiro at the turn of the century. The Italian's sense of the dramatic is obvious: the principal building, the mock-Manueline Palaçio dos Milhões, sprouts turrets and towers, though the interior is sparse apart from some elaborate Rococo wooden ceilings and impressive Art Nouveau tiles. The surrounding gardens are more impressive and shelter fountains, terraces, lakes and grottoes. The highlight is the Initiation Well, inspired by the initiation practices of the Knight Templars and Freemasons. Entering via an Indiana Jones-style revolving stone door, you can walk down a moss-covered spiral stairway to the foot of the well and through a tunnel, which eventually resurface at the edge of a lake.

The Palácio de Seteais

The **Palácio de Seteais** ("Seven Sighs") stands just beyond the Quinta da Regaleira, fifteen minutes' walk west from the centre of town. It is one of the most elegant palaces in Portugal, completed in the last years of the eighteenth century and entered through a majestic Neoclassical arch. Maintained today as an immensely luxurious **hotel** (☎219 233 200, Ⓔhpseteais@mail.telepac.pt; ⓿), it is one of the most expensive places to stay in Portugal. With more modest money to blow, make for the bar and terrace downstairs to the left, past a distinctly unwelcoming reception. Look out, for the summer concerts that are held in the lovely gardens as part of the Sintra Music Festival (see p.120).

Monserrate

Beyond Seteais, the road leads past a series of beautiful private *quintas* (manors or estates) until you come upon **Monserrate** (daily: June–Sept 9am–7pm; Oct–May 9am–5pm; €3) – about another forty minutes' walk away (a taxi costs around €8). With its Victorian folly-like mansion and vast botanical park of exotic trees and subtropical shrubs and plants, Monserrate is one of the most romantic sights in Portugal. It would be easy to spend the whole day wandering around the paths laid out through the woods. The charm of the place is immeasurably enhanced by the fact that it's only partially maintained. The name most associated with Monserrate is that of **William Beckford**, author of the Gothic novel *Vathek* and the wealthiest untitled Englishman of his period. He hired the *quinta* here from 1793 to 1799, having been forced to flee Britain because of homosexual scandal – buggery then being a hanging offence. Setting about improving this "beautiful Claude-like place", he landscaped a waterfall and even imported a flock of sheep from his estate at Fonthill. In this Xanadu-like dreamland, he whiled away his days in summer pavilions, entertaining with "bevys of delicate warblers and musicians" posted around the grounds.

Half a century later, a second immensely rich Englishman, **Sir Francis Cook**, bought the estate. His fantasies were scarcely less ambitious, involving the construction of a great Victorian house inspired by Brighton Pavilion. Cook also spared no expense in developing the grounds and imported the head gardener from Kew to lay out succulents and water plants, tropical ferns and palms, and just about every conifer known. Fernando II, who was building the Pena Palace at the time, was suitably impressed, conferring a viscountcy on Cook for his efforts. **Cook's house** is closed but you can still admire the exterior, with its mix of Moorish and Italian decoration (the dome is modelled on Brunelleschi's Duomo in Florence), and peer into a splendid series of empty salons.

The Convento dos Capuchos

One of the best long walks in the Sintra area is to the **Convento dos Capuchos** (tours every 15–30 mins: Mon–Fri 9.30am–5pm, Sat & Sun 9.30am–5.15pm; advanced bookings essential on ☎219 237 300; €3), an extraordinary hermitage with tiny, dwarf-like cells cut from the rock and lined in cork – hence its popular name of the "Cork Convent". Philip II, King of Spain and Portugal, pronounced it the poorest convent of his kingdom, and Byron, visiting a cave where one monk had spent 36 years in seclusion, mocked in *Childe Harold*:

Deep in yon cave Honorius long did dwell,
In hope to merit Heaven by making earth a Hell.

To get there, the most straightforward approach is by the ridge road from Pena – a distance of 9km. There are other indistinct paths through the woods from Monserrate and elsewhere in the region, but without local advice and a good map, you'll be hard pushed to find your way. Whichever route you take, the surroundings, too, beg a startled reaction: the minor road between Sintra, the convent and Cabo da Roca sports some of the country's most alarming natural rock formations, with boulders as big as houses looming out of the trees.

Coming upon the place after a walk through the woods, however, it's hard not to be moved by the simplicity and seclusion of the place. It was occupied for three hundred years and finally abandoned in 1834 by its seven remaining monks. Some rooms – **penitents' cells** – can be entered only by crawling through 70cm-high doors; here, and on every other ceiling, doorframe and lintel, are attached panels of cork, taken from the surrounding woods. Elsewhere, you'll come across a washroom, kitchen, refectory, tiny chapels, even a bread oven set apart from the main complex.

Practicalities

Trains depart every 15 minutes for Sintra from Lisbon's Rossio station (€1.05 one way). The **train station** in Sintra itself is fifteen minutes' walk from the centre of Sintra-Vila; local **buses** stop across the street from the station, with services to and from Cascais, Colares, Cabo da Roca, the Sintra beaches, Estoril and Mafra; Sintra's main bus station is at Portela, opposite the station of the same name, the stop before Sintra. There are **taxis** outside the train station and in Praça da República, near the Palácio Nacional; check the price first for every journey since the meters aren't always used. You'll find a **post office** and **bank** on Praça da República, too.

Sintra is a popular resort and you should book ahead or turn up early in the day if you intend to stay, especially if you're here during one of the town's festivals (see p.120) when accommodation will definitely be scarce. On the spot, accommodation is best arranged through the efficient and helpful **turismo** (daily: June–Sept 9am–8pm; Oct–May 9am–7pm; ☎219 231 157, ⓔtur @cm-sintra.pt), just off the central Praça da República. There is also a small turismo desk at Sintra station.

Accommodation

There's a fair range of **accommodation** available including a network of private rooms (best booked through the turismo; usually ❷), half a dozen **pensões** and **hotels**, and upmarket bed and breakfast in several local *quintas*, or manor houses. At the opposite end of the range from the top-class *Palácio de Seteais* (see above), there's an attractive **youth hostel** located in the hills above São Pedro de Sintra, while the nearest **campsite** is at Praia Grande (see opposite).

Pensões, quintas and hotels

Residencial Adelaide Rua Guilherme Gomes Fernandes 11 ☏219 230 873. Very clean if spartan rooms with their own bath; quieter back rooms face a back patio. Price does not include breakfast. ❷

Casa Miradouro, Rua Sotto Mayor 55 ☏219 235 900, ✉mail@casa-miradouro.com. Renovated mansion built in 1894, 500m beyond the Palácio Nacional, with terrific views of coast and castle. Five rooms with bath, terraced garden and good breakfast included. ❻

Casa da Paderna Rua da Paderna 4 ☏219 235 053. Highly attractive accommodation in a small old house reached down a steep cobbled track, with en-suite bathrooms, just north of Sintra-Vila. Great views up to Quinta da Regaleira. ❺

Hotel Central Praça da República 35 ☏219 230 963. Characterful and comfortable nineteenth-century hotel, opposite the Palácio Nacional – polished wood and tiles throughout. Triple rooms available, too, and good off-season discounts. Breakfast included. ❺

Lawrence's Hotel Rua Consigliéri Pedroso 38–40 ☏219 105 500, ✉lawrence-hotel@iol.pt. Lays claim to being the oldest hotel in Iberia, opening in 1764 and reopened with five stars by Dutch owners in 1999. Byron stayed here in 1809 and other visitors have included Eça de Queirós and William Beckford. Only eleven spacious rooms and five suites, and a highly-rated restaurant. ❾

Pensão Nova Sintra Largo Afonso de Albuquerque 25 ☏219 230 220, ℗219 107 033. Very smart *pensão* in a big mansion with a raised café-terrace overlooking a busy street. Modern rooms, all with TV, bath and shiny marble floors, plus good breakfasts. ❹

Piela's Rua João de Deus 70–72 ☏219 241 691. On the street behind the train station, this café-*pastelaria* has six simple but spotless double rooms. From 2003, it will move to a renovated town house at Avenida Desiderio Cambournac 1–3 (same phone), where plusher rooms will come with bath, TV and air conditioning – all above a new cybercafé. ❸

Quinta das Sequóias ☏219 230 342, ℗219 230 342. Immaculate manor house with six rooms, out in the Sintra hills beyond Seteais – continue past the Palácio de Seteais for 1km and follow the signposted private road on your left. A lovely, antique-furnished place with superb views, gardens, sauna, jacuzzi and pool. Excellent buffet breakfast included. ❼

Residencial Sintra Trav. dos Alvares, São Pedro ☏219 230 738, ✉pensao.residenciasl.sintra@clix.pt. Fantastic, characterful place with a rambling garden, swimming pool and giant rooms which can easily accommodate extra beds – so great for families or groups. You'll need to book ahead in summer. ❺

Hotel Tivoli Praça da República ☏219 237 200, ✉htsintra@mail.telepac.pt. Modern block sticking out bang in the middle of the historic centre, with fine views from balconies and comfortable rooms with bath, internet access and minibars. There's also an in-house restaurant. Rates drop in winter. ❻

Youth hostel and campsites

Pousada de Juventude de Sintra Santa Eufémia, São Pedro de Sintra ☏219 241 210, ✉sintra@movijovem.pt. The comfortable hostel is a 6km walk from the train station; it's best if you first catch a local bus to São Pedro, from where it's just a 2km walk. Meals are served if you can't face the hike down into town and back. Dorm rooms from €9.50, doubles from €21.

Camping Praia Grande ☏219 290 581, ✉wondertur@ip.pt. Well-equipped campsite less than 1km from the beach at Praia Grande, west of Sintra. Bus #441 runs from Sintra train station to here.

Eating and drinking

There are some fine **restaurants** scattered about the various quarters of Sintra. With a couple of honourable exceptions the most mundane are in the centre, near the palace or around the train station; the best concentration is at São Pedro, a twenty-minute walk from town.

Local specialities include *queijadas da Sintra* – sweet cheese pastry-cakes. If you're out for the day, take a **picnic**: refreshments out of town are exorbitantly priced.

Sintra-vila

Adega das Caves Rua de Pendora 2 (café) & 8 (restaurant). Bustling café-bar beneath *Café Paris*, attracting a predominantly youthful local clientele; the neighbouring restaurant has good value Portuguese grills. Moderate.

Alcobaça Rua das Padarias 7–11. The best central choice for a decent, straightforward Portuguese meal. Plain, tiled dining room with friendly service and large servings of grilled chicken, *arroz de marisco*, clams and steak for around €13 a head. Inexpensive.

Casa da Avo Rua Visconde de Monserrate 46. Basic eating house with few pretensions but the house wine is cheap enough and it's hard to fault dishes like *caldeirada* (fish stew). There's a decent bar attached, too. Closed Thurs. Inexpensive.

Casa da Piriquita Rua das Padarias 1. On the uphill alley across from the *Café Paris*. Quality tearoom and bakery, busy with locals queueing to buy *queijadas da Sintra* and the similarly sticky *travesseiros*. Closed Wed.

O Chico Rua Arco do Teixeira 8. Standard Sintra prices (so fairly high) and food, but come on Thurs in summer for the fado. It's off Rua das Padarias and has outdoor tables on the cobbles. Bar open till 2am. Expensive.

Café Paris Largo Rainha D. Amélia ☏219 232 375. Highly attractive and highest-profile café in town, opposite the Palácio Nacional, which means steep prices for underwhelming food. Great place to sit and nurse a drink in the sun, though.

Páteo do Garrett Rua Maria Eugénia Reis F. Navarro 7. Bar-restaurant with a darkened interior and lovely, sunny patio with great views over the village; standard Portuguese fare, or just pop in for

a drink. Closed Wed and Jan–April. Moderate.

Tulhas Rua Gil Vicente 4, behind the turismo ☏219 232 378. Imaginative cooking in a fine building, converted from old grain silos. The speciality is veal with Madeira. Closed Wed. Moderate–expensive.

Near the station

Orixás Av Adriano Coelho 7. Brazilian bar, restaurant, music venue and art gallery in a lovely building complete with waterfalls and outdoor terrace, on the road behind the Museu de Arte Moderna. The buffet costs around €30, but can last all night. With live Brazilian music thrown in, it's not bad value. Evenings only, closed Mon.

Piela's Rua João de Deus 70–72. Budget meals and late-night drinks, as well as rooms; due to move in 2003 (see above). Inexpensive.

São Pedro de Sintra

Adega do Saloio Trav. Chão de Meninos ☏219 231 422. A fine grill-restaurant with a standard Portuguese menu and hospitable owners. Does a good *arroz de marisco*. Closed Tues. Moderate.

Toca do Javali Rua 1º Dezembro 18 ☏219 233 503. Tables set up outside in summer amidst a lovely terraced garden; superb cooking at any time of year. Wild boar (*javali*) is the house speciality. Expensive. Closed Wed.

Further west: Colares, the beaches and Cabo da Roca

About 6km further west of Monserrate is **COLARES**, a hill village famed for its rich red wine made from vines grown in the local sandy soil – an ancient vine which survived the 19th-century infestation that wiped out many local varieties. The local producer, Adega Regional de Colares, hosts occasional concerts, tastings and exhibitions; ☏219 288 082 for details. Head uphill (signed Penedo) for superb views back towards Sintra. It's easily reached on the Sintra–Cascais bus route #403, with **buses** leaving from outside the train station in both towns. For **food**, there's a smart restaurant and teashop, *Colares Velho* on Largo Dr. Carlos Franca 1–4 (Tues–Sun 11am–11pm) or, if you have your own transport, it is worth making a detour to the excellent *Toca do Júlio* (Tues–Sun; ☏219 290 815) – take the Praia Grande road from the nearby village of Almoçageme. The *Estalagem de Colares* (☏219 282 942, ☏219 282 983; ❹) is a smart inn with comfortable rooms, not a bad alternative base to Sintra for the price.

Continuing west of Colares, the road winds around through the hills to **PRAIA GRANDE**, perhaps the best and safest beach on this section of coast, with a row of handy cafés and restaurants spreading up towards the cliffs. There's a large **campsite** (see p.72), as well as *Hotel Arribus* (☏219 289 050, ✉hotel.arribus@mail.telepac.pt; ❻), a modern three-star plonked ungraciously at the north end of the beach. Rooms are enormous while the hotel boasts sea pools, a restaurant and café-terrace with great sea views.

Just north of Praia Grande is the larger resort of **PRAIA DAS MAÇÃS**, with a broad expanse of sands. You can take bus #441 from Sintra train station or, in summer, there's a **tramline** running from Ribeira da Sintra, just outside Sintra, via Colares. Praia das Maçãs has two good **pensões** – the modern *Oceano* on the main Avenida Eugénio Levy 52 (☎219 292 490, ⓔpensaooceano.pt; ❹) and the more rundown but atmospheric *Real* (☎219 292 002; ❸) right on the seafront. Of its several **bars and restaurants**; *O Loureiro*, Esplanada Vasco da Gama has great-value seafood and overlooks the beach (closed Thurs); or try the cheap and cheerful *Esplanada do Casino* opposite, with a seaside terrace and dishes that include *salada de orelha de porco* – pig's ear salad. Nearby **AZENHAS DO MAR**, around 2km to the north, is a picture-book cliff-top town with a small beach and sea pool, and can also be reached on bus #441 from Sintra.

Cabo da Roca

A popular destination in this region is **CABO DA ROCA**, 14km southwest of Colares; regular buses (#403) from either Sintra or Cascais train stations make the run throughout the year. It's an enjoyable trip, though the cape itself comprises little more than a lighthouse – below which foamy breakers slam the cliffs – a couple of stalls selling shells, a café and a **tourist office** (☎219 280 892). In here, you can buy a certificate recording that you've visited the "Most Westerly Point in Europe" – which indeed you have. A **cross** at the cape carries an inscription by Luís Camões ("Here …where the land ends, and the sea begins"), whose muse, for once it seems, deserted him.

Palácio de Queluz

The **Palácio de Queluz** (Mon & Wed–Sun 10am–5pm; €3) is one of Portugal's most sumptuous palaces, set in superb formal gardens. It lies on the Sintra train line, making it easy to see either on the way out (it's just twenty minutes from Lisbon's Rossio station; €0.70 one way) or on the way back from Sintra. The station is called Queluz-Belas: turn left out of the station and walk down the main road for fifteen minutes, following the signs through the unremarkable town until you reach a vast cobbled square, Largo do Palácio, with the palace walls reaching out around one side. The Largo is also home to a local **turismo** (Fri–Wed 10am–12.30pm & 2–7pm; ☎214 350 039).

The Palace

The building is as perfect a counterpoint to Mafra (see p.140) as you could imagine: an elegant, restrained structure regarded as the country's finest example of Rococo architecture. Its low, pink-washed wings enclose a series of public and private rooms and suites, as well as rambling eighteenth-century formal gardens. Although preserved as a museum, it doesn't quite feel like one – retaining instead a strong sense of its past royal owners. In fact, the palace is still pressed into service for accommodating state guests and dignitaries, and hosts classical concerts in the summer months.

It was built by Dom Pedro III, husband and regent to his niece, **Queen Maria I**, who lived here throughout her 39-year reign (1777–1816), quite mad for the last 27, following the death of her eldest son, José. William Beckford visited when the Queen's wits were dwindling, and ran races in the gardens with the Princess of Brazil's ladies-in-waiting; at other times fireworks displays were held above the ornamental canal and bullfights in the courtyards.

Visitors first enter the **Throne Room**, lined with mirrors surmounted by paintings and golden flourishes. Beyond is the more restrained **Music Chamber** with its portrait of Queen Maria above the French grand piano. Smaller quarters include bed and sitting rooms; a tiny oratory swathed with red velvet; and a **Sculpture Room**, whose only exhibit is an earthenware bust of Maria. Another wing comprises an elegant suite of **public rooms** – smoking, coffee and dining rooms – all intimate in scale and surprisingly tastefully decorated. The **Ambassador's Chamber**, where diplomats and foreign ministers were received during the nineteenth century, echoes the Throne Room in style, with one side lined with porcelain chinoiserie. In the end, though, perhaps the most pleasing rooms is the simple **Dressing Room** with its geometric inlaid wooden floor and spider's web ceiling of radial gilt bands.

The formal **gardens** are included in the ticket price. Low box hedges and elaborate (if weatherworn) statues spread out from the protection of the palace wings, while small pools and fountains, steps and terracing form a harmonious background to the building. From May to October, there is a display of horsemanship here every Wednesday at 11am (€1). You can still enjoy a meal in the Palace's original kitchen, the **Cozinha Velha** (daily from 12.30–3pm & 7.30–10pm; ☎214 350 232), which retains its stone chimney, arches and wooden vaulted ceiling, and sports copper pots, pans and utensils in every niche and alcove. The **food** – classic French-Portuguese – is not always as impressive as the locale, and you're looking at around €25 a head for a full meal (though there is a cheaper café in the main body of the palace). The kitchens are now part of the *Pousada Dona Maria I* (☎212 351 226, ⓦwww.pousadas.pt; ⑧), a **hotel** that gives you the chance to stay in an annexe of the palace; its plush 26 rooms are equipped with satellite TV.

Mafra and around

Moving on from Lisbon or Sintra, **MAFRA** makes an interesting approach to Estremadura. It is distinguished – and utterly dominated – by just one building: the vast **Palace-Convent** (Mon & Wed–Sun 10am–5pm, last entry 4.30pm; €3) which João V – the wealthiest and most extravagant of all Portuguese monarchs – built in emulation of El Escorial in Madrid. Around 5km beyond Mafra, **Sobreiro** is famed for its delightful craft village, a big draw for children.

The Palace Convent
Begun in 1717 to honour a vow made on the birth of a royal heir, **Mafra Convent** was initially intended for just thirteen Franciscan friars. But as wealth poured in from the gold and diamonds of Brazil, João V and his German court architect, Frederico Ludovice, amplified their plans to include a massive basilica, two royal wings and monastic quarters for 300 monks and 150 novices. The result, completed in thirteen years, is quite extraordinary and, on its own bizarre terms, extremely impressive.

In style the building is a fusion of Baroque and Italianate Neoclassicism, but it is the sheer magnitude and logistics that stand out. In the last stages of construction more than 45,000 labourers were employed, while throughout the years of building there was a daily average of nearly 15,000. There are 5200 doorways, 2500 windows and two immense bell towers each containing over 50 bells. An apocryphal story records the astonishment of the Flemish bell-makers at the size of the order: on their querying it, and asking for payment in advance, Dom João retorted by doubling their price and his original require-ment.

Parts of the convent are used by the military but an ingenious cadre of guides marches you around a sizeable enough portion. The **royal apartments** are a mix of the tedious and the shocking: the latter most obviously in the **Sala dos Troféus**, with its furniture (even chandeliers) constructed of antlers and upholstered in deerskin. Beyond are the **monastic quarters**, including cells, a pharmacy and a curious infirmary with beds positioned so the ailing monks could see Mass performed. The highlight, however, is the magnificent Rococo **library** – brilliantly lit and rivalling Coimbra's in grandeur. Byron, shown the 35,000 volumes by one of the monks, was asked if "the English had any books in their country?" The **basilica** itself, which can be seen outside the tour, is no less imposing, with the multicoloured marble designs of its floor mirrored in the ceiling decoration.

Six kilometres north of Mafra on the Gradil road, the **Tapada de Mafra** – the palace's extensive hunting grounds – are also open for ninety-minute tours (Sat, Sun and public holidays at 10am and 3.15pm; €7). For further details, ask at the turismo (see below).

Practicalities

Mafrense buses run hourly from metro Campo Grande in Lisbon or from Sintra station, stopping near the convent. The **town** of Mafra itself is dull, and with frequent buses heading on to the lively resort of Ericeira, 12km away (see p.155), there seems no point in lingering.

If you need to stay, the **turismo** on Avenida 25 de Abril (daily: July–Sept 9.30am–7.30pm; Oct–June 9.30am–6pm; Sat & Sun closed 1–2.30pm; ☎262 812 023) can give details of rooms. For an inexpensive **restaurant** with good food try the *Solar d'El Rei*, Rua Detras dos Quintas, five minutes' walk from the palace.

Sobreiro

The small village of **SOBREIRO**, around 5km northwest of Mafra on the road to Ericeira (see p.155), is home to a **craft village** (daily 10am–6pm) – the Aldeia Típica – established by artist José Franco in 1945. As well as Franco's own work, the showroom sells other reasonably priced ceramics from all over the country, while children will enjoy looking round the traditional bakery, smithy, clockmaker, cobbler, schoolroom, distillery, wind- and water-mills and several other small museum shops, all displaying various tools, furniture and artefacts collected over many years. The *adega* makes a splendid stop for lunch, serving local wine, bread and meals; at weekends, there is also a moderately priced restaurant.

The Lisbon–Mafra–Ericeira **bus** passes by every hour or so, and it's definitely worth a stop if you're driving on to Ericeira from Mafra. There is also a pleas-ant **campsite** should you wish to stay (☎261 813 333).

South of the Tejo: Costa da Caparica, Setúbal and its coast

As late as the nineteenth century, the southern bank of the Tejo estuary was an underpopulated area used as a quarantine station for foreign visitors; the village of Trafaria here was so lawless that the police visited it only when accompanied by members of the army. The huge **Ponte 25 de Abril**, a suspension bridge inaugurated as the "Salazar Bridge" in 1966 and renamed after the 1974 Revolution, finally ended what remained of this separation between "town and country". Since then, Lisbon has spilled over the river in a string of tatty industrial suburbs that spread east of the bridge, while to the west the **Costa da Caparica** has become a major holiday resort. **Setúbal**, 50km south of the capital, sustains one remarkable church and is a pleasant provincial base from which to explore the River Sado and the **Parque Natural da Arrábida**. Its **coastal** surroundings are particularly attractive, with one full-blown resort at **Sesimbra**.

Across the river: Cacilhas and the Cristo Rei

The most enjoyable approach to the Setúbal peninsula is to take a **ferry** from Lisbon's Fluvial station, by Praça do Comércio, to Almada's port, **CACILHAS** (every 10min, Mon–Fri 6.10am–21.45pm, Sat & Sun 6.15am–9.50pm; €0.55). You can also take the car ferry to, and from, **Cais do Sodré** (every 10min, 5.30am–2.30am; €0.55). The blustery ride itself is fun, granting you wonderful views of the city, as well as of the enormous Ponte 25 de Abril bridge, though the **seafood** is as good a reason as any to go over for an evening. *Arroz de marisco* is a speciality in most restaurants, particularly good in the *Escondidinho de Cacilhas* (closed Thurs), immediately on the right as you leave the ferry. More upmarket, but with better views, is the riverside *Cervejaria Farol* (closed Wed). Head towards the bridge along the waterside Cais do Ginjal to two other atmospheric riverside restaurants: the pricey *Atira-te ao Rio* (closed Mon), with Brazilian cuisine, or the marginally cheaper *Ponto Final*, offering Portuguese staples (closed Tues) with great views back to Lisbon.

Just past here is the bottom of the **Elevador Panorâmico da Boca do Vento** (daily 8am–11.45pm; €1 return), a sleek modern lift which whisks you up the cliff face to the old part of **Almada**; if the lift is in the wrong place, the guard will blow his whistle to alert the operator at the other end. From the top there are fantastic views over the river and right over the city, while the surrounding streets are highly atmospheric.

Beyond Almada – best reached by bus #101 from Cacilhas – stands the **Cristo Rei** (daily: June–Sept 9am–7.30pm; Oct–May 9am–6pm; €1.50). Built in 1959, this relatively modest version of Rio's Christ-statue landmark has a lift which shuttles you up the plinth above its church, via a souvenir shop, to a highly dramatic viewing platform, 80m up in the air. On a good day, Lisbon stretches like a map below you and you can catch the glistening roof of the Pena Palace at Sintra in the distance.

From Cacilhas bus station, you can also catch regular **buses** to Costa da Caparica, Setúbal, Sesimbra and Vila Nogueira de Azeitão, for all of which see the relevant sections that follow.

Caparica

Regular buses from Cacilhas (every 15–30min, express buses every 30 min; daily 7am–9pm; €1.75), or from Praça de Espanha (daily 7am–12.45am, every 30min; €1.75), run on to **Caparica**, half an hour from Cacilhas, around forty minutes (or 1hr in rush hour) from Praça de Espanha. Though anything but a pretty place, this is a thoroughly lively Portuguese resort, crammed with restaurants, summer bars and discos and it's here that most locals come if they want to swim or laze around on the sand: there are foreign tourists, too, but they're in a minority. In Caparica town itself, **Rua dos Pescadores** leads up from the central Praça da Liberdade (where you'll find the market, supermarkets and banks) to the beach and is lined on both sides by café-restaurants with outdoor seating.

The **beach** stretches north towards Lisbon and away south into the distance, its initial stretch backed by apartments and more cafés. A promenade with wooden shacks at intervals offering grilled sardines, fresh fish, ice cream and drinks lies alongside the **mini-railway** which runs along the 8km or so of dunes to Fonte da Telha (June–Sept; €2) – if you're after solitude you need only take it this far and walk. However, each of the twenty mini-train stops, based around one or two beach-cafés, has a very particular scene or feel. Earlier stops tend to be family-oriented, later ones are on the whole younger and more trendy, with nudity (though officially illegal) more or less obligatory, especially around Stop 18–19, which is also something of a gay area. The water is of good quality, though watch out for dangerous undertows.

Practicalities

Buses in summer stop at the bus park in town near the beginning of the sands. In winter, buses go to the station in Praça Padre Manuel Bernades, in which case it is best to get off at the first stop in Caparica, on the edge of the leafy square, Praça da Liberdade, five minutes back from the beach. If you arrive here, walk diagonally across the square, turn right and at Avenida da Liberdade 18 you'll find the **turismo** (Mon–Fri 9am–1pm & 2–5.30pm, Sat 9am–1pm; ☎212 900 071).

There are a growing number of **hotels** in Caparica, though they are relatively pricey and often full in summer. *Pensão Real* on Rua Mestre Manuel 18 (☎212 918 870, ☎212 918 879; ❹) is one of the more reasonable central options, some offering sea-facing balconies; or try *Residencial Capa-Rica* (☎212 900 242, ✉benvindo.tours@mail.telepac.pt; ❸), on the main Rua dos Pescadores 9 where bright rooms have their own bathrooms and some face the beach. Accommodation is hardly a problem though, given the frequency of the buses and ferries back to Lisbon. If you really want to stay, talk first to the turismo or aim for one of the string of **campsites**, all of which, again, are pricier than average and crowded in summer. Your best bet is also the nearest, the well-equipped *Orbitur* (☎212 901 366, ✉info@orbitur.pt), complete with café and tennis courts – it's one of the only ones where camping club membership is not required.

Among the dozens of fish and seafood places, a couple of recommended moderately priced **restaurants** are *O Borbas*, Praia da Costa (☎212 900 163; closed Tues evening and all day Wed), at the northern end of the beach with window seats looking out over the sands and bubbling fish tanks inside, and *Primoroso*, further round the seafront towards Lisbon, which has excellent *cataplana* and outdoor tables facing the beach (closed Thurs).

Setúbal and around

Some 50km south from Lisbon, **SETÚBAL** is Portugal's third port and a major industrial centre. It was once described by Hans Christian Andersen as a "terrestrial paradise" and, although most of its visual charm is long gone, its pedestrianized centre and port are enjoyable enough. If you're heading south and have time to break the journey, it's worth stopping at least for a look at the remarkable Igreja de Jesus and the views from the Castelo São Filipe. On a more prolonged visit, the town is a good base for going on local **boat trips**, or to explore some other local vantage points such as the series of excellent **beaches** nearby and the town of Palmela.

The Town

Setúbal's greatest monument is the **Igreja de Jesus** (Tues–Sun 9am–noon & 2–5pm; closed Mon and public holidays) designed by Diogo de Boitaca and possibly the first of all Manueline buildings (see box on p.190). Essentially a late-Gothic structure, with a huge, flamboyant doorway, its interior design was transformed by Boitaca, who introduced fantastically twisted pillars to support the vault. The rough granite surfaces of the pillars contrast with the delicacy of the blue and white *azulejos* around the high altar, which were added in the seventeenth century. The adjacent Convento de Jesus now forms the **Museu de Setúbal** (Tues–Sat 9am–noon & 1.30–5.30pm; free) containing treasures from the church and town, though most of these seem to be permanently in storage; it also hosts temporary exhibits.

Another place to head for is the **Castelo São Felipe**, half an hour's walk to the west of the town; head along Avenida Luísa Todi and keep following the signs, or take a taxi. Built on the orders of Spanish king Felipe II in 1590, it's a grand military structure, harbouring an *azulejo*-lined chapel and protected by sheer walls of overpowering height. Legend has it that a series of secret tunnels connect the castle with the coast, but any proof was lost in the great earthquake. Part of the castle is now a *pousada* (see p.146) but the ramparts and bar are open to non-guests and there are superb views over the mouth of the Sado estuary and the Tróia peninsula.

The rest of town has little to detain you, though the pedestrianized shopping streets in the **old town** around Rua A. Castelões are handsome enough, and there are gardens, a market and port to poke around as well. Near the town tourist office (see below) on Largo Corpo Santo, take a peek, too, into the

Boat trips, dolphin watching and activity sports

The tourist office can supply details of a range of privately organized tours and activity sports in the area including walking trips, jeep excursions, hot-air balloon flights and off-road driving. Highlights include the Cruzeiros – Galeões do Sal cruises up the Sado in sailing boats traditionally used to transport salt – organized by Nautur (℡265 532 914, ⓦwww.nautur.com). The trips leave from the harbour, and departures are daily depending on both the weather and the number of people interested (minimum of ten passengers); phone ahead to check for next sailing. Trips costs €40 per person. Vertigem Azul (℡265 238 000, ⓔvertigemazul@mail.telepac.pt) organize year-round trips to watch bottle-nosed dolphins in the Sado estuary with the chance to go snorkelling too (daily 9.30am and 3pm, dependent on weather; €28 per person). They also organize various other excursions, including all-day jeep safaris taking in dolphin watching and tours of Arrábida, including a visit to the Convento da Arrábida (minimum five people, €60).

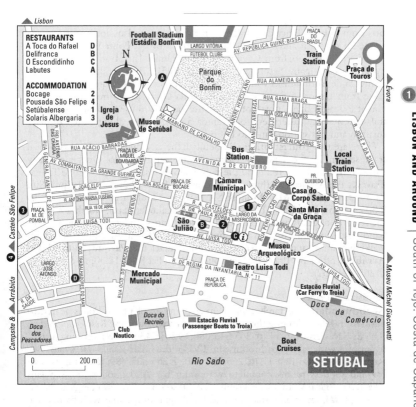

RESTAURANTS
A Toca do Rafael   **D**
Delifranca   **B**
O Escondidinho   **C**
Labutes   **A**

ACCOMMODATION
Bocage   **2**
Pousada São Felipe   **4**
Setúbalense   **1**
Solaris Albergaria   **3**

Lisbon

Football Stadium
(Estádio Bonfim)

LARGO VITÓRIA
FUTEBOL CLUBE

AV. REPÚBLICA GUINÉ-BISSAU

PRAÇA DO BRASIL

Train Station

Praça de Touros

Évora

Parque do Bonfim

RUA ALAMEIDA GARRETT

RUA GAMA BRAGA

RUA DOS AVIADORES

Igreja de Jesus

Museu de Setúbal

AV. MARIANO DE CARVALHO

AV. ALEXANDRE HERCULANO

AV. ALEXANDRE HERCULANO

DR. MANUEL ARRIAGA

R. CAP. ARAÚJO

AVENIDA DA PORTELA

R. DAS ALCAÇARIAS

R. JOSÉ DA SILVA

RUA ACÁCIO BARRADAS

PRAÇA DE MIGUEL BOMBARDA

AVENIDA 5 DE OUTUBRO

Bus Station

Local Train Station

R. FREI ANTÓNIO DAS CHAGAS

RUA GENERAL DANIEL DE SOUSA

AV. COMBATENTES DA GRANDE GUERRA

R. JOÃO ELOY

R. ANTÓNIO MARIA EUSÉBIO

RUA 18 DE ABRIL

AVENIDA 22 DE DEZEMBRO

RUA BOCAGE

PRAÇA DE BOCAGE

Câmara Municipal

PR QUEBEDO

i

Casa do Corpo Santo

Castelo São Felipe

PRAÇA M. DE POMBAL

AV. LUÍSA TODI

R. A. CASTELÕES

R. DR. PAULA BORBA

São Julião

LARGO DA MISERICÓRDIA

Santa Maria da Graça

SANTO ORÃO

R. ANTÃO TRÃO

RUA PEREIRA CÃO

ARRONCHES JUNQUEIRO

BUA JOÃO CARVALHO

i

Arrábida

LARGO JOSÉ AFONSO

R. DOS TRABALHADORES

RUA DO OURO

RUA OCID. DO MERCADO

AV. LUÍSA TODI

Mercado Municipal

R. DE REGIM. DA INFANTARIA N.º 11

PRAÇA DE REPÚBLICA

Museu Arqueológico

Teatro Luísa Todi

AV. LUÍSA TODI

Museu Michel Giacometti

Campsite &

R. DA SAÚDE

Doca dos Pescadores

Doca do Recreio

Club Nautico

Estação Fluvial
(Passenger Boats to Troia)

Estação Fluvial
(Car Ferry to Troia)

Doca

da

Comércio

Boat Cruises

0   200 m

Rio Sado

SETÚBAL

N

Casa do Corpo Santo (Tues–Fri 9.30am–5pm, Sat 9.30am–6pm; free), built in 1714 as part of the Cabedo family's palace and later a fisherman's fraternity. The upper floor has a painted ceiling, Baroque chapel and walls decked in superb *azulejos* showing scenes of São Pedro, patron saint of fishermen. There's a certain amount of interest, too, in the central **Museu Arqueológico**, at Avenida Luísa Todi 162 (Tues–Sat 9am–12.30pm & 2–5.30pm; closed Sun & Mon; also closed Sat in Aug; free) where sparse finds from the city's Roman age are displayed along with dusty historical fishing boats and handicrafts. If you nip into the nearby turismo, too (see below), you can see the foundations of a Roman fish-preserving industry underneath the glass floor. A ten- to fifteen-minute-walk east along Rua Arronches Junqueiro brings you to the **Museu Michel Giacometti** at Largo Defensores da República (Tues–Fri & Sun 9am–noon & 2–6pm; free) a museum of work implements collected by Giacometti – a Corsican ethnologist who was particularly interested in Portuguese culture – in the 1970s. Historical agricultural implements from around Portugal complement exhibits of tools from traditional local trades such as blacksmiths, braziers, basket weavers and canners. Attractively housed in a former canning factory, the museum is worth a detour for anyone interested in Portuguese enthnography.

Practicalities

You can reach Setúbal by **train** via Palmela, though since it involves crossing to Barreiro by ferry and changing (see p63), it's quicker to take the half hourly

bus from Lisbon's Praça de Espanha, which takes around an hour; routes go via Ponte 25 de Abril and Vila Fesca de Nogueira or via Ponte Vasco da Gama. There are buses, too, from Cacilhas (hourly; 50min–1hr). Both routes are run by the bus company Setubalase (☎265 525 051). By **car**, the fast A2 from Ponte 25 de Abril whisks you to Setúbal in around forty minutes; it's about the same from Lisbon airport via Ponte Vasco da Gama. Trains from Lisbon drop you at Praça do Brasil, north of the centre; local trains use Setúbal's more central station at the eastern end of Avenida 5 de Outubro, along which the city turismo and bus station can also be found.

There are two **tourist offices** in Setúbal: the city one across from the local train station in the Casa do Corpo Santo, on Praça do Quebedo (daily 9am–7pm; ☎265 534 402), and the regional one, just off Avenida Luísa Todi at Travessa Frei Gaspar 10 (June–Sept Mon–Sat 9am–12.30pm & 2–7pm, Sun 9am–12.30pm; Oct–May Mon & Sat 9.30am–12.30pm & 2–6pm, Tues–Fri 9.30am–6pm; ☎265 539 120, ✉costa.azul@mail.telepac.pt), worth a visit for the remains of the Roman "fish condiments" factory under its glass floor. Both hand out maps and can help with finding rooms. If you want information on walking tours round Arrábida (see p.148), contact the **Parque Natural Da Arrábida** office on Praça da República (Mon–Fri 9am–12.30pm & 2–5pm; ☎265 524 032).

Accommodation

Accommodation is rarely a problem as there are plenty of hotels geared to business travellers. Among the **pensões** worth trying out are: *Residencial Bocage*, Rua de São Cristovão 14 (☎265 543 080, ℗265 543 089; ❸), offering attractive rooms with private bathrooms and TVs; or the smart *Residencial Setubalense*, Rua Major Afonso Pala 17 (☎265 525 790, ℗265 525 789; ❹), with its own bar and spotless rooms complete with mini bar. Also good value is *Solaris Albergaria,* Praça Marquês de Pombal 12 (☎265 541 770, ✉albergaria.solaris @netc.pt; ❹), set in an attractive tiled building; rooms come with bath, cable TV and minibar. The extremely attractive **pousada**, the *São Filipe* (☎265 523 844, ✉enatur@mail.telepac.pt; ❸) occupies the castle and the front rooms command superb views over the estuary, as does the surprisingly good-value restaurant, which is open to non-guests.

Eating, drinking and nightlife

Good-value fish and seafood **restaurants** abound in the dock area and around the western end of Avenida Luísa Todi. In the former, *A Toca do Rafael*, Rua Trabalhadores do Mar 25–27 (closed Sun), is a characterful tavern with *azulejo*-lined pillars, serving inexpensive fish and grills. For inexpensive baguettes with interesting fillings head for *Delifranca*, Largo Dr Francisco Soveral 20–22, with outdoor seats on the square. *O Escondidinho*, Rua José António Januário da Silva 6, is another inexpensive option with outdoor tables (closed Sun). A smarter option is *Labutes* (Setúbal backwards) Avenida 22 de Dezembro, out by Parque do Bonfim, which serves quality Portuguese dishes. For a more expensive treat, however, head for the restaurant attached to the *Pousada São Filipe* (see accommodation above). There are also plenty of places around the atmospheric fish and vegetable **market**; in midsummer, the market area is considerably expanded with clothes and touristy bric-a-brac.

Nightlife in Setúbal is lively; outdoor tables at the café-bars along Avenida Luísa Todi bustle with activity all evening. Alternatively, for a competely different scene, the *Teatro Luísa Todi* stages shows at weekends and often runs art-house movies during the week.

△ Igreja da Jesus, Setúbal

Tróia

Setúbal's local **beaches**, reached by frequent ferries from the town, are on the **PENÍNSULA DE TRÓIA**, a large sand spit hemming in the Sado estuary. The peninsula was settled by the Phoenicians and subsequently by the Romans, whose town of Cetobriga appears to have been overwhelmed by a tidal wave in the fifth century. There are some desultory remains, including tanks for salting fish, on the landward shore. Originally a wilderness of sand and wild flowers, Tróia must once have been magnificent, but it's now a heavily developed resort with its own golf course. Plans to demolish all but two of the high-rise blocks, and to build a new upmarket complex complete with marina and a casino, have been in the pipeline for some time, but for now be prepared to walk for twenty minutes or so south along the beach to escape the worse of the development. Car **ferries** depart daily from Setúbal (every 15 mins, 6am–11pm; hourly during the night; €1 per person, cars €4.25); expect long queues for cars in summer.

Palmela

The small town of **PALMELA**, around 10km north of Setúbal, is worth a quick visit for the views from its medieval **castle**, which on a clear day encompass Lisbon, Setúbal, the Sado estuary and Tróia. This is the centre of a wine-producing area, hence the town's major event in September: the Festa das Vindimas celebrating the first of the year's wine harvest, with processions, fireworks, grape-treading and running of the bulls.

A fabulous place to stay is the former church in the castle, which has been restored and extended into a *pousada*, the *Castelo de Palmela* (☏212 351 226, ⓔenatur@mail.telepac.pt; ❽). The castle also incorporates a row of handicraft shops selling *azulejos*, cheeses and the highly rated local wines, a café and a **museum** (Tues–Fri 10am–12.30pm & 2–5.30pm, Sat–Sun 10am–1pm & 3–5.30pm; free), which houses a small collection of archeological remains from the area dating back to Moorish times. Opposite the museum is Palmela's **turismo** (Mon–Fri 10am–12.30pm & 2–5.30pm, Sat–Sun 10am–1pm & 3–5.30pm; closes 8pm from June–Sept; ☏212 332 122), which can provide you with details of accommodation options in the area. During the week there are ten **buses** a day with four at weekends from Lisbon's Praça de Espanha; the ride takes forty minutes; and there are buses every twenty minutes, on the ten-to fifteen-minute run from Setúbal.

The Parque Natural da Arrábida

Between Setúbal and Sesimbra lies the **PARQUE NATURAL DA ARRÁBIDA**, whose main feature is the 500-metre granite ridge known as the Serra da Arrábida, visible for miles around and popular for its wild mountain scenery – home to wildcats, badgers, polecats, buzzards and Bonelli eagles. The twisted pillars of Setúbal's Igreja de Jesus were hewn from here. If you want to explore the area on foot, **walking guides** are available from the park's main office in Setúbal (see p.146).

Year-round public transport is limited to those **buses** from Setúbal to Sesimbra, which take the main road, well back from the coast. The bus passes through the town of **VILA NOGUEIRA DE AZEITÃO** where the main highlight is the **José Maria da Fonseca wine vaults and museum** on the main Rua José Augusto Coelho 11–13 (Mon–Fri 9am–noon & 2.15–4.15pm; €2; Sat 10am–12.15pm & 2.15–4.30pm; €3; advanced reservations essential ☏212 198 940). A tour of the vaults, which lasts 45 minutes, includes free tasting, and provides an interesting introduction to the local Setúbal Moscatel. Vila Nogueira de Azeitão can also be reached by **bus** from Lisbon's Praça de Espanha (hourly; 45min). There is a well-equipped **campsite**, *Picheleiros* (☎212 181 322), just outside town, complete with mini-market, café and kids playground.

If you have your own transport, however, you should take the N379–1 from Azeitão to the **Convento da Arrábida** (Wed–Sun 3–4pm; €3; to make an appointment to look round at other times, call in advance ☎212 180 520). Owned by the Fundação Orient, the convent was built by Franciscan monks in the sixteenth century. The convent's white buildings tumble down a steep hillside, offerings stunning ocean views.

Around four kilometres south of the convent, the N10 winds down to the coast and the tiny harbour village of **PORTINHO DA ARRÁBIDA**, which has one of the coast's best beaches – wonderful out of season and often quieter than Tróia. The harbour is guarded by a tiny seventeenth-century fort, now housing the **Museu Oceanográfico** (Tues–Fri 10am–4pm, Sat–Sun 3–6pm; €1.75), displaying marine animals from the region either live – in a small aquarium – or stuffed. At weekends, day-trippers head for the *Restaurant Beira Mar* (closed Wed & Sept–March) on the seafront, serving a good range of moderately priced fish and seafood. Pricey, but attractive, private **rooms** can be rented out above the diving school, the *Centro de Mergulho* (☎212 183 197, ⑤212 183 656), with a couple of double rooms (❸) or a self-catering apartment sleeping up to five (❹). If you hold a diving certificate, the diving school can organize equipment; the waters here are some of the calmest and clearest of the entire Portuguese coast.

Some 2km along the coast towards Setúbal you come to **GALAPOS**, a beautiful stretch of sand with beach cafés. Closer to Setúbal – and correspondingly more crowded – is the wide beach of **Figueirinha**, with the big sea-facing *Restaurante Bar Mar* (open daily) – and the smaller **Praia de Albarquel**, with a beachside café and disco. Just beyond the beach by the main road, *Outão* (☎265 238 318, ⑤265 228 098) is a busy **campsite** set amongst trees. In summer, the coast road is served by three daily **buses** from Setúbal; if driving, expect queues back into town at the end of the day in summer.

Sesimbra

If you get up early enough in **SESIMBRA**, you'll still see the fishermen mending their nets on the town's beach, but you'll see little more of this old fishing town's tradition now that it's a full-blown resort, with apartment buildings and hotels mushrooming in the low, bare hills beyond the steep narrow streets of the old centre.

Sesimbra was an important port during the time of the discoveries. Dom Manuel lived here for a time, and the town's fort, **Fortaleza de Santiago**, was built in the seventeenth century as an important part of Portugal's coastal defenses. In the eighteenth century, Portuguese monarchs used the fort as a seaside retreat; ironically, today it serves as a police station and prison.

Today Sesimbra is largely a day trip destination for residents of Lisbon, though the wealthier ones have bought second homes here for the summer, during which time Sesimbra is extremely busy. Nonetheless, it's still an admirable spot, with excellent swimming from the long **beach** and an endless row of **café-restaurants** along the beach road, each with an outdoor charcoal-grill wafting fine smells across the town. At high tide the beach splits into two, with a strand either side of the waterfront Forte do Santiago; offshore, jet skis and little ketches zip up and down the clear blue sea.

A **Moorish castle** (Sun–Thurs 7am–7pm, Fri & Sat 7am–8pm; free) sits above Sesimbra, a short drive or a stiff half-hour climb from the centre. Within the walls are a pretty eighteenth-century church, café and cemetery, while a circuit of battlements gives amazing panoramas over the surrounding country-side and coastline. Back in the town, the only other main sight lies just off Avenida da Liberdade (take the steps by *Restaurante Xurrex*), the **Museu Municipal** (Mon–Fri 10am–12.30pm & 2–5.30pm; free), which features scant archeological and historical finds from the area, while the best of the church-es, the Manueline **Igreja da Mai**, is on nearby Rua João de Deus.

Give yourself time, too, to see the original fishing port, **Porto de Abrigo**, with its brightly painted boats, daily fish auctions, and stalls selling a superb variety of shellfish. It's a pleasant walk to Porto de Abrigo from the centre, along the seafront Avenida dos Náufragos, where the local anglers try their hand at sea fishing. Departing from here are various **boat trips**; the Clube Naval (☎212 233 251, ⓦwww.naval-sesimbra.pt) offers cruises on a tradition-al sailing boat, the *Santiago*. From May to September, *Aquarama* (☎965 263 157) runs daily "floating submarine" trips in a boat with a glass bottom, either up to Cabo Espichel or on night trips. Tickets cost €15 and can be bought on the boat or from the kiosk on Avenida dos Náufragos.

Practicalities

There are frequent **buses** to and from Lisbon's Praça de Espanha and Setúbal; and half-hourly services to and from Cacilhas. Coming from Lisbon in sum-mer, it's usually much quicker to take the ferry across to Cacilhas (p.142) and pick up a bus there, as the main bridge road is often jammed solid with traffic.

In Sesimbra, you're dropped at the **bus station**, halfway up Avenida da Liberdade, a five-minute walk from the seafront. Walk down to the water, turn right past the fort, and the **turismo** (daily: June–Sept 9am–8pm; Oct–May 9am–12.30pm & 2–5.30pm; ☎212 288 540) is underneath the terrace, a step back from the seafront Avenida dos Náufragos.

Accommodation

Accommodation can be hard to come by in high season, with just a dozen or so *pensões* and pricey hotels. If you haven't booked in advance, your best bet is to try for private rooms through the turismo. Otherwise, head for the very central *Residencial Chic*, Trav. Xavier da Silva 2–6 (☎212 233 110; ❸), just back from the sea on a corner with Rua Candido dos Reis. It has bright rooms, some with restricted sea views. *Residencial Náutico*, steeply uphill on Bairro Infante D. Henrique 3 (☎212 233 233; ❸), is another comfortable place and a little more secluded. The best upmarket choice is *Sana Park*, right on the seafront Avenida 25 de Abril (☎212 289 000, ⓔsanapark.sesimbra@sanahotels.com; ❻, or ❼ with sea views). Plush rooms have minibars, TVs and baths, while the modern hotel has glass lifts, a sauna and pool (open to non guests), restaurant and groovy rooftop bar. There's also a well-located **campsite** at Forte do Cavalo (☎212 233 905; closed Nov–April), just past the fishing port.

Eating

At night, families crowd the line of **restaurants** east of the fort, along Avenida 25 de Abril, and round the little Largo dos Bombaldes. Cheaper places (meals under €13) abound in the backstreets on either side of the central spine, Avenida da **Nova Fortaleza**.

Marisqueira Filipe Avenida 25 de Abril. Extremely popular seafood restaurant, and one of the more expensive places in town – €20 and upwards – but it serves great grilled fish, a bumper *arroz de marisco* plus some decent wines. Closed Wed. Expensive.

Nova Fortaleza Largo dos Bombaldes. On the edge of the square facing the beach with a great terrace, serves well-priced fish and good salads. Moderate.

A Tasca de Ratinho Rua Plinio Mesquita 17. Tucked up a sidestreet behind Largo dos Bombaldes, this cosy place specializes in swordfish cooked in cream and port, with a terrace over-looking the sea. Closed Thurs. Moderate.

Santiago Av dos Náufragos 22. This jolly place offers some of the best sea views from the first-floor restaurant; the food is unspectacular but reliable enough and good value. Moderate.

A Sesimbrense Rua Jorge Nunes 17–19. Bustling local just back from Largo dos Bombaldes (keep going past the *Toni Bar*), serving no-nonsense soups, fish and grills with a TV for company. Closed Tues. Inexpensive.

Toni Bar Largo dos Bombaldes (☎212 233 199) For a quality fish or shellfish meal, the *Toni Bar* at the back of the square is hard to beat. Expensive.

Drinking and nightlife

West of the fort along the avenue is also where most of the **music bars** and **cafés** are found. At some point in the evening, dip into *De Facto*, Avenida dos Náufragos 26; the *Sereia* at no. 22, more of a hippy rock bar; *Bote Douro* (closed Tues) at no. 10, a *cervejaria*-café; or the sleek and booming *Mareante* at no. 13, which sometimes has live music. *A Galé*, Rua Capitão Leitão 5, on a raised terrace overlooking the sea, next to the Safari surf shop, is a popular student hang out.

Clubs with a bit of a summer reputation include *Belle Epoch*, off Largo do Calvario, steeply uphill behind the Sana Park; and two in-places on Rua Prof. Fernandes Marques just off the western seafront: *Bolina* at #3 and *Central* at #11; both get going at midnight.

Cabo Espichel and beaches

Twice a day (both in the afternoon, making a day trip by bus feasible if brief), buses make the 11km journey west from Sesimbra to the **CABO ESPICHEL**, an end-of-the-world plateau lined on two sides by ramshackle arcaded eighteenth-century pilgrimage lodgings, with a crumbling chapel perched above the rocks at one end. The whole place has an appealing desolate air that has made it a popular location for film directors including Wim Wenders for *A Lisbon Story*. Beyond, wild and windswept cliffs drop almost vertically several hundred feet into the Atlantic; appropriately, dinosaur footprints have been found on the nearby Praia dos Lagosteiros.

Four buses a day travel from Sesimbra beyond Cabo Espichel to the southern **beaches** of the Costa da Caparica (see p.143 for the northern section). A few kilometres to the south of Cabo Espichel and up the surprisingly verdant and undeveloped coast is the village of **ALDEIA DO MECO**, with a small, friendly **campsite** at Fetais (☎212 682 978) five minutes walk out of town. A path from here cuts down the superb beach of Praia do Meco. A larger campsite, *Campimeco* (☎219 747 669, ☎219 748 728), complete with tennis courts, restaurant, pool and mini market, lies northwest of here just off Praia das Bicas. Like the other beaches on this coast, both these – which are popular with nudists – are prone to overcrowding in July and August, but can be almost deserted out of season when the main drawback is the strong surf. The calmest strip of beach is by the lagoon at **LAGOA DE ALBUFEIRA**, a little further south; the lake is extremely clean and excellent for windsurfing. There's another campsite, *Parque O Repouso*, 1km back from the lagoon (☎212 684 300; closed Oct–April), while just back from the beach overlooking the lagoon, *O Lagoeiro* (closed Mon) is the best place for grills, drinks or snacks.

Travel details

Trains

See also entries at the end of relevant chapters.
Cais do Sodré to: Belém (every 10min; 7min); Cascais (every 20min; 30min); Estoril (every 20min; 25min).
Fluvial, via Barreiro, to: Faro (4–5 daily; 4hr 45 min–5hr 15min; change for stations to Vila Real); Lagos (change at Tunes; 4–5 daily; 5–5hr 45min); Palmela (every 30min; 40min);Setúbal (every 30min; 55min); Tunes (for connections to western Algarve line; 4 daily; 4hr 15min).
Rossio to: Mafra (11 daily; 50min–1hr 30min); Queluz (every 15min; 20min); Sintra (every 15min; 45–50min).
Santa Apolónia (note some services connect with Oriente trains) to: Abrantes (4 daily; 1hr 50min–2hr 15min); Coimbra (16 daily; 2hr–6hr 15min); Évora (6 daily; 2hr 30min–6hr); Porto (12 daily; 3hr 30min–6hr 40min); Santarém (hourly; 50min–1hr 5min); Tomar (13 daily; 1hr 45min–2hr).

International trains

Santa Apolónia/Oriente to: Badajoz (2 daily; 4hr 30min–5hr 30min); Biarritz (1 daily; 17hr 20min); Bordeaux (1 daily; 19hr 20min); Caceres (1 night train; 6 hr); Madrid (1 night train; 10hr 20min); Paris (1 daily; 22hr 20min); Salamanca (1 daily; 8hr 20min); San Sebastián (1 daily; 14hr 30min).

You can also pick up connections to Galicia in Spain from Porto (see opposite).

Buses

Express buses run daily to all main towns throughout the country; see entries at the end of relevant chapters. Information from the main bus terminal at Avenida João Crisóstomo (see p.63). Other services depart from a variety of termini (see p.65). Local services include:
Lisbon to: Costa da Caparica (every 30min; 40min–1hr); Évora (6–12 daily; 2hr); Fátima (10 daily; 1hr 30min); Ericeira (10 daily; 1hr 50min); Mafra (hourly; 1hr 30min); Nazaré (hourly; 1hr 50min); Palmela (hourly; 40min–1hr); Peniche (9 daily; 1hr 45min); Sesimbra (7–9 daily; 1hr 30min–2hr); Setúbal (every 30min; 45min–1hr); Tomar (2–4 daily; 1hr 45min); Torres Vedras (12 daily; 2hr); Vila Nogueira de Azeitão (hourly; 45min).

Domestic flights

There are internal flights of varying regularity from Lisbon to: Bragança, Chaves, Covilhã, Faro, Porto, Vila Real, Viseu and to Madeira and the Azores.
Fares are reasonable (though expensive compared with coach and train travel); check current schedules at any travel agency.

Estremadura and Ribatejo

N

ATLANTIC
OCEAN

SPAIN

CHAPTER 2   # Highlights

* **Ericeira** Head down to the sands at sunset to watch the surfers riding the Atlantic rollers. See opposite

* **Óbidos** After the coach tours have left, enjoy the atmospheric streets of this unspoilt village. See p.165

* **Nazaré** A classic seaside resort, where you can take a funicular ride to Sítio for tremendous ocean views. See p.169

* **Alcobaça** Check out the twelfth-century monastery at Alcobaça – one of Europe's most impressive Cistercian monuments. See p.172

* **Grutas de Mira de Aire** Visit the most spectacular underground caves in the country. See p.183

* **Fátima** One of the Catholic Church's most popular shrines is the place to visit for its extraordinary atmosphere and kitsch souvenirs. See p.183

* **Tomar** One of the region's prettiest towns, home to the stunning Manueline Convento de Cristo. See p.189

* **Fataca na telha** Head for a seafood joint in Santarém and try this local speciality. See p.200

* **Arruda Dos Vinhos** Lunch at one of the restaurants in the wine country surrounding Arruda Dos Vinhos. See p.201

②

Estremadura and Ribatejo

The **Estremadura** and **Ribatejo** regions have played a crucial role in each phase of the nation's history, and have the monuments to prove it. They are also comparatively wealthy regions, both having received substantial EU grants to help restructure agriculture. Although they encompass a comparatively small area, the provinces boast an extraordinary concentration of vivid architecture and engaging towns: **Alcobaça**, **Batalha** and **Tomar** – with the most exciting buildings in Portugal – all lie within a ninety-minute bus ride of each other. Other attractions are equally compelling: ferries sail from Peniche to the remote **Ilha Berlenga**; Óbidos is a completely walled medieval village; spectacular underground caverns can be visited at Mira d'Aire; and there are tremendous castles at Porto de Mós, Leiria (itself an elegant town), and on Almourol, an islet in the middle of the Rio Tejo.

The Estremaduran coast – the lower half of the Costa de Prata – provides an excellent complement to all this, and if you're simply seeking sun and sand it's not a bad alternative to the Algarve. **Nazaré** and **Ericeira** are justifiably the most popular resorts but there are scores of less developed beaches. For more isolation, try the area around **São Martinho do Porto** or the coastline west of **Leiria**, backed most of the way by the pine forest of **Pinhal de Leiria**.

Virtually all of these highlights fall within the boundaries of Estremadura, which, with its fertile rolling hills, is perhaps second in beauty only to the Minho. Although the flat, bull-breeding lands of **Ribatejo** (literally "banks-of-the-Tejo") fade into the dull expanses of northwestern Alentejo, the Tejo river valley itself boasts some of Portugal's richest **vineyards**, while many of its towns host lively traditional **festivals**. The wildest and most famous of these is the Festa do Colete Encarnado of **Vila Franca de Xira**, with Pamplona-style bull-running through the streets.

Ericeira

Perched on a rocky ledge thirty metres above a series of fine sandy beaches, **ERICEIRA** offers one of the few natural harbours between Cascais and Peniche. As a result, during the last century, the town became a major port,

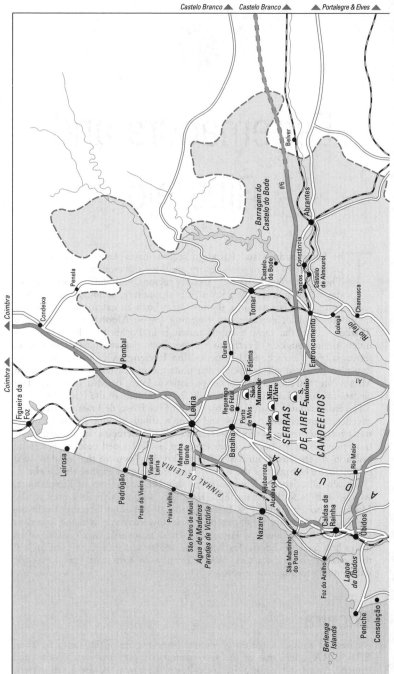

Castelo Branco ▲ Castelo Branco ▲   ▲ Portalegre & Elves ▲

Coimbra ▲

Coimbra ▲

Belver

IP6

Barragem do
Castelo do Bode

Abrantes

Constância

Castelo
do Bode

Tancos

Castelo de Almourol

Penela

Chamusca

Tomar

Golegã

Rio Tejo

Entroncamento

Condeixa

Pombal

Ourém

Fátima

São
Mamede

Mira
d'Aire

S.
António

E.

Figueira da
Foz

Reguengo
do Fetal

Porto
de Mós

SERRAS

A1

Leiria

Batalha

Alvados

DE AIRE E

CANDEEIROS

Leirosa

Marinha
Grande

Pedrógão

Vieira de
Leiria

Ajubarrota

PINHAL DE LEIRIA

A

R

Rio Maior

Praia da Vieira

Alcobaça

D

U

Praia Velha

Nazaré

A

São Pedro de Muel

Caldas da
Rainha

Água de Madeiros
Paredes de Victória

Óbidos

São Martinho
do Porto

Lagoa
de Óbidos

Foz do Arelho

Berlenga
Islands

Peniche

Consolação

156

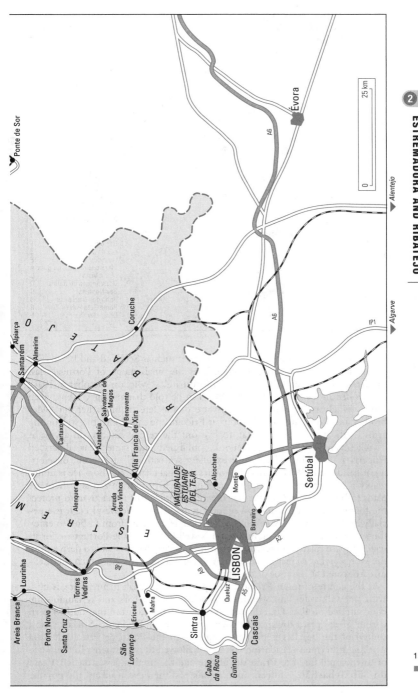

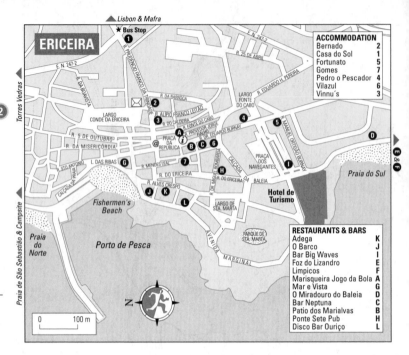

▲ Lisbon & Mafra
★ Bus Stop

ERICEIRA

ACCOMMODATION
Bernado   2
Casa do Sol   1
Fortunato   5
Gomes   7
Pedro o Pescador 4
Vilazul   6
Vinnu´s   3

Praia do Sul

Praia do Norte

Fishermen's Beach

Porto de Pesca

Hotel de Turismo

0   100 m

RESTAURANTS & BARS
Adega   K
O Barco   J
Bar Big Waves   I
Foz do Lizandro   E
Limpicos   F
Marisqueira Jogo da Bola A
Mar e Vista   G
O Miradouro do Baleia   D
Bar Neptuna   C
Patio dos Marialvas   B
Ponte Sete Pub   H
Disco Bar Ouriço   L

from where boats left to trade with countries such as Scotland and Brazil. The town's main claim to fame, though, is as the final refuge of Portugal's last monarch, Dom Manuel II – "The Unfortunate" – who, on October 5, 1910, was woken in his palace at nearby Mafra to be told that an angry Republican mob was advancing from Lisbon. Aware of the fate of his father and elder brother, he fled to the small harbour at Ericeira and sailed into the welcoming arms of the British at Gibraltar, to live out the rest of his days in a villa at Twickenham. Baedeker's guidebook, published the same year, described Ericeira as "a fishing village with excellent sea bathing" and recent development has done little to change the town's original character. The place is undeniably a busy resort – the main square has been pedestrianized and there are plans to build a *pousada* in the seventeenth-century fort (once used to protect the town from Algerian pirates) – but it remains an attractive place. It is especially lively on summer weekends, when people come up from Lisbon to enjoy the surprisingly buoyant nightlife, and is well known to the Portuguese for its seafood (particularly lobsters and crayfish) – its very name is said to derive from the words *ouriços do mar* (sea urchin). You can see the tanks in which the shellfish are reared at the foot of the cliffs.

At the centre of town **Praça da República**, the small main square, is busy with sidewalk cafés and wonderful *pastelarias*, while bars and restaurants are concentrated on Rua Dr. Eduardo Burnay, which leads from the southwestern corner of the praça towards the town's main beach, **Praia do Sul**. The most central of the beaches is the tempting one in the Porto de Pesca, but it's a working fishermen's beach and you're not allowed to swim there. To the north of town you'll find the **Praia do Norte** and the prettier, less crowded, **Praia do São Sebastião**, a fifteen-minute walk past the next headland and popular with surfers. Another option is to take the bus from Praça dos Navigantes to reach the series of untouched local beaches further to the north – the World Surfing Championships have been held at Praia da Ribeira d'Ilhas, 3km out of town. The best local beach, however, is perhaps the one at **São Lourenço**, a peaceful hamlet just 5km north of Ericeira.

Back in town, if the sea is too rough, you can use the pool in the *Hotel de Turismo* (€5) just beyond the pretty Parque Santa Marta, which also has tennis courts. If you want to try **surfing**, equipment can be hired in town from *Ultimar* at Rua 5 de Outubro 25 (☎261 862 371; closed Sun).

Practicalities

Buses run virtually every hour to and from Mafra (see p.140) and Lisbon, making Ericeira a useful first or last stop in Estremadura, and there are also services to Sintra. If you arrive by bus, you will be dropped in town at the top of Rua Prudêncio Franco da Trindade, which leads down to the main square. The **turismo**, at Rua Dr. Eduardo Burnay 46 (daily: July–Aug 9am–midnight; Sept–June 9am–10pm; ☎261 863 122, ⓦwww.ericeira.net), may help with finding **private rooms**, which are advertised throughout town above bars and restaurants. **Internet** access is at *Clube de Video*, Praça da República (daily 11am–1am; €2/hr; ☎261 865 743).

Accommodation

Pensões and hotels are generally good value and pleasant (there's a list of the best below), though most are not open all year round; those that are should be a good deal cheaper in winter. There's an excellent, well-equipped **campsite** at Parque Mil Regos, just beyond Praia do São Sebastião (☎261 862 706), and a second at Sobreiro (see p.141).

Hospedaria Bernado Rua Prudêncio Franco da Trindade 17 ☎261 862 378. Spotless and attractive *pensão*, fairly close to the main square. ❷

Casa do Sol Rua Prudêncio Franco da Trindade 1 ☎261 864 400. A small, but grand, house with shady gardens at the top end of the steep street into town. Rooms are small but some are en suite. ❹

Residencial Fortunato Rua Dr. Eduardo Burnay 7 ☎ & ⓕ261 862 829. Good views of Praia do Sul from the rooms, but a little noisy. There's a range of accommodation and prices; an annexe copes with the overflow. Breakfast included. ❸–❹

Residencial Gomes Rua Mendes Leal 11 ☎261 863 619. An old, rambling building with faded decor, but clean and fresh with friendly, if somewhat eccentric, staff. ❸

Hotel Pedro o Pescador Rua Dr. Eduardo Burnay 22 ☎261 864 302, €hotel.pedro@mail.telepac.pt. Friendly elegant small hotel with colourful tile work, plenty of plants and private patio. ❹

Hotel Vilazul Calçada da Baleia 10 ☎261 864 101, ⓦwww.hotelvilazul.net. Just off Rua Dr. Eduardo Burnay, this plush, good-value hotel is popular with upmarket British tour operators. The rooms have private bathrooms and good views from the balconies. Serves great breakfasts. ❺

Residencial Vinnu's Rua Prudêncio Franco da Trindade 25 ☎ & ⓕ261 863 830. Close to the main square, this is clean, modern and airy with a lively bar to boot. Some rooms have small balconies. ❸

Eating

The lively *pastelarias* around Praça da República are recommended for lunch – or tea-time indulgences. In the **restaurants**, seafood is obviously the thing to go for; the local speciality is *açorda de mariscos*, a sort of shellfish stew with bread.

Adega Rua Alves Crespo 3. A cosy beamed restaurant decorated with black and white tiles and specializing in grilled meats and fish, plus an excellent range of local wines.

O Barco Rua Capitão João Lopes 14 ☎261 862 759. Upmarket pricey seafood restaurant overlooking the harbour; the *ementa turística* is around €15 a head. Closed Thurs & Nov.

Marisqueira Jogo da Bola Moderately priced seafood restaurant on the corner of Rua Provedor Jorge Fialho and Rua Fonte do Cabo.
Mar a Vista Largo das Ribas. This popular place for locals has some tables with sea views; a full meal with wine will set you back €12.50 a head. Closed Wed.

O Miradouro do Baleia Praia do Sul. Great sea views and a wide range of reasonably priced seafood.
Restaurante Patio dos Marialvas Rua Dr. Eduardo Burnay 29. A friendly place with outdoor tables, serving excellent *arroz de marisco* at moderate prices. Closed Mon.

Nightlife

Ericeira after dark is surprisingly animated – its bars, clubs and proximity to the beaches attract an influx of young Lisboetas. In Ericeira itself, the bars are on or around Rua Dr. Eduardo Burnay, but most of the "in" places are to be found out of town.

Bar Big Waves Praça dos Navigantes 22. One of the happening bars on the square near Praia do Sul. The place where locals start off the evening.
Limpicos Foz do Lizandro. This is one of the best of a group of trendy bars in this small beach resort 8km south of Ericeira – part of the night-time circuit for those with their own transport.
Bar Neptuno Trav. J. Mola. A good-time bar with a two-for-one Happy Hour and frequent live music.

Disco-Bar Ouriço Rua Capitao João Lopes 10, next to *O Barco* restaurant. An in-place for the trendies of Ericeira.
Ponto Sete Pub Rua Dr Miguel Bombarda. A hole-in-the-wall bar decorated with old rock memorabilia with jazz and blues jam sessions at weekends.
Virtual South Beach. Summer only disco popular for the surfing crowd.

Torres Vedras

TORRES VEDRAS, 27km to the north and inland from Ericeira, took its name from the Duke of Wellington's famous defence lines (Linhas de Torres) in the **Peninsular War** against Napoleonic France. The "Lines" consisted of a chain of 150 hilltop fortresses, stretching some 40km from the mouth of the Rio Sizandro, directly west of Torres Vedras, to Alhandra, southeast of Torres Vedras, where the Tejo widens out into a huge lake. Astonishingly, they were built in a matter of months and without any apparent reaction from the French. Here, in 1810, Wellington and his forces retired, comfortably supplied by sea and completely unassailable. The French, frustrated by impossibly long lines of communication and by British scorching of the land north of the Lines, eventually retreated back to Spain in despair. Thus from a last line of defence, Wellington completely reversed the progress of the campaign – storming after the disconsolate enemy to effect a series of swift and devastating victories.

The Town

In view of this historical glory, modern Torres Vedras is somewhat disappointing. There are a few ruins of the old fortresses and a couple of imposing sixteenth-century churches, but all this is swamped by a dull sprawl of recent buildings. Yet, from the thirteenth to the sixteenth century, the **castle** (daily 9am–7pm; free) at Torres Vedras was a popular royal residence. It was here, in 1414, that Dom João I confirmed the decision to take Ceuta – the first overseas venture leading towards the future Portuguese maritime empire. The castle was eventually abandoned and then reduced to rubble by the earthquake of 1755.

Booklets and old maps can be read at the **turismo**, Rua 9 de Abril, off Praça 25 de Abril (Mon–Sat 10am–1pm & 2–6pm; ℡261 314 094, ⓦwww.cm-t .vedras.pt). Internet access is at *Cyber Postnet*, Rua Princesa Benedita (daily

8.30am–7.30pm; €2.50/hr; ℡261 336 930), while across Praça 25 de Abril, in the old Convento da Graça, is the **Museu Municipal** (Tues–Sun 10am–1pm & 2–6pm; €0.75), with a room devoted to the Peninsular War. Unless you get hooked on the local wine, there's not much else to keep you in the town.

However, if you decide **to stay**, try the clean but basic *Pensão-Restaurante 1° de Maio*, Rua 1° de Dezembro 3 (℡261 322 875; ❷), or the similar *Residencial Moderna*, opposite the cinema on Avenida Tenente Valadim (℡261 314 146; ❸). For a **meal**, *O Gordo* in Rua Almirante Gado Coutinho 15 (closed Tues) and *Adega Típica Manadinhas*, Rua Capitão Luis Botto Pimental, are good options while a great people-watching **café** is *Havaneza* on Plaça República, which serves coffees, cakes and snacks overlooking the main church.

In general, however, you'd probably be better off taking one of the many buses on to Peniche, Óbidos, or the popular local resort of Praia de Santa Cruz. The **bus station** is just uphill from the **train station** which is located at the end of the central Avenida 5 Outubro.

Praia de Santa Cruz and other beaches

Most people at the modern resort of **PRAIA DE SANTA CRUZ** are locals from Torres Vedras, 13km to the east, and the place has a friendly, easy-going feel, as well as some excellent places to eat. There are two sandy beaches, **Praia Guincho** below the town, and the more secluded **Praia Formosa**, beneath cliffs to the south. In between is a "screaming rock" – partly covered by the tide – where air and water is forced through a hole in the rock at certain times to produce the distinctive sound. **Rooms** are available at the *Pensão-Restaurante Mar Lindo*, Trav. Jorge Cardoso (℡261 937 297; ❹), some with sea views, and at the modern *Hotel de Santa Cruz*, Rua José Pedro Lopes (℡261 937 148; ❹). There's a shady **campsite** north of the village, five minutes' walk from the sea but it fills up quickly in summer.

The quieter resorts below – uncrowded outside public holidays or summer weekends – are to be found to the north of here and are easily reached on buses heading to Lourinhã or Peniche.

Praia de Porto Novo

Five kilometres north of Santa Cruz, is the small bay of **PRAIA DE PORTO NOVO** which is starting to suffer from the surrounding development, although the beach is still relatively unspoilt and there are good walking possibilities inland. In August 1808, British reinforcements were landed here, at the mouth of the River Maceira. They enabled Wellington, in his first serious encounter with the French, to defeat General Junot at the battle of Vimeiro, following which the French sued for peace. Should you want **to stay**, the fanciest hotel is the *Hotel Golf Mar* (℡261 984 157, ℻261 984 621). Alternatively, there are some reasonable pensions, opposite the beach, including *Residencial Promar* (℡261 984 220, ℻261 984727; ❹), which is marginally superior to the rest.

Areia Branca and Consolação

Further north on the Peniche road, 21km from Torres Vedras, lies **AREIA BRANCA** ("White Sand"), a small resort with a congenial campsite (℡261 412 199) and a good beachside **youth hostel** (℡261 422 127). Other **accommodation** options include *Estalagem Areia Branca*, Praia da Areia Branca (℡261 412 491; ❺), near the beach, and *Residencial Restaurante D. Lourenço*, on the way out of town (℡261 422 809; ❹); alternatively, ask at the **turismo** (Mon–Sat 10am–1pm & 2–6pm; ℡61 422 167) for a list of private **rooms**. The

Restaurante Dom Lourenço is the best place for **food**.

Despite the attractive sands here, the sea at Areia Branca is not too clean and it's better to go north to **CONSOLAÇÃO**, just south of Peniche, with its great swathe of beach popular with surfers, although the surrounding gaudily coloured development is decidedly ugly. There are few places to stay the night but you're probably better off moving on to Peniche or Baleal for accommodation. For snacks and drinks, try *Bar Forte Club* in the old fort in the attractive old part of town.

Peniche and the Ilha Berlenga

PENICHE, impressively enclosed by ramparts and one of Portugal's most active fishing ports, is the embarkation point for the **Ilha Berlenga**. As late as the fifteenth century the town was an island but the area has silted up and is now joined to the mainland by a narrow isthmus with gently sloping beaches on either side. Unfortunately, Peniche has burst out of its natural confines and unsightly development now stretches along the coast, but inside the walled town there is more to appreciate. The main attraction is the fortress which dominates the south side of town, and there's also an enjoyable **market** on the *campo*, held on the last Thursday of the month.

The sixteenth-century **Fortaleza** (Tues–Sun 10.30am–12.30pm & 2–7pm; closes at 5pm in winter) was one of the dictator Salazar's most notorious jails. Greatly expanded in the 1950s and 1960s to accommodate the growing crowds of political prisoners, it later served as a temporary refugee camp for *retornados* from the colonies. Today it houses a **museum** (€1), with the familiar mix of local archeology, natural history and craft displays, among which you can still see the old cells (on the top floor), the solitary confinement pens (*segredos*) and the visitors' grille (*parlatório*).

Just outside the city walls, off the fine **north beach** of the peninsula, there's a traditional boat yard. It's fascinating to watch the shipwrights here manoeu-

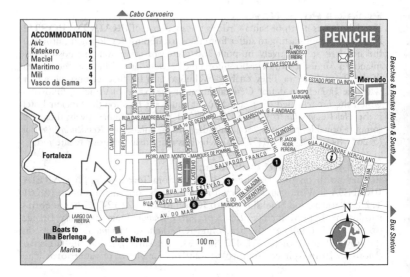

vring huge timbers into position to form the skeletal framework of a new fishing vessel. If you've got more time to spare, you can take a ninety-minute walk (though if you have a car it's a good idea to drive clear of the suburbs first) beyond the fortress – out to the tip of **Cabo Carvoeiro**, the rugged, rock-pillared and lighthouse-topped peninsula, where there's a smart restaurant, the *Nau dos Corvos*, with a superb view and a tourist menu for around €10. Another rewarding walk, a few kilometres to the north of Peniche, is to **BALEAL**, an islet-village, joined to the mainland by a narrow strip of fine sand. This would make a good base in its own right, with a fine beach, not too much development and a few **rooms** for rent. It has a small, but reasonably equipped **campsite** (☎262 769 333) or you could try the friendly *Hospedaria Baleal a Vista* (☎262 769 467; ➌), on the main Peniche road around 4km out of town, the modern *Pequena Baleia* (☎262 769 370; ➌) or the wonderful *A Casa das Marés* (☎262 769 371; ➏).

If you are in Peniche over the first weekend in August, you'll see the **festival** of Nossa Senhora da Boa Viagem (Our Lady of Good Journeys), during which the statue of the Virgin is brought to the harbour by boat to be greeted by candle-bearing locals. After the village priest has blessed the fleet, there are fireworks, bands and dancing in the street.

Practicalities

Buses arriving in Peniche pull in at the station on the isthmus just outside the town walls. It's a ten-minute walk into the centre across the Ponte Velha, which takes you to Rua Alexandre Herculano, where you turn left for the **turismo** (daily: summer 10am–6pm; winter 10am–1pm & 2–5pm; ☎ & ☏262 789 571, ✉turismocmp@sapa.pt). **Internet** access is at *Cybercafe On Line,* Rua Antonio Cervantes, 5 (Mon–Sat 5pm–2am; €2.50/hr; ☎262 783 460), and *Websdot,* Camping Peniche Pria (€2/hr; ☎262 783 460).

Nearly all of Peniche's hotels, bars and restaurants are on or just back from Rua Alexandre Herculano and Avenida do Mar, which leads down to the harbour by Largo da Ribeira.

Accommodation

In summer (particularly in August), **accommodation** can be hard to find; you may be approached by people offering private rooms, but it's best to head for the turismo who can usually help you to find something. Out of season, or early in the day, try one of **residenciais** below. There's a municipal **campsite** (☎262 789 529) on the way into town, after you've crossed the Rio Lagôa, which is well placed for the bus station, and a fine private campsite, *Camping Peniche Praia* (☎262 783 460, ☏262 789 447), complete with pool and restaurant, on the north shore of the peninsula.

Residencial Aviz Ruá Jacob Epereira 7 ☎262 782 153. Centrally located old-fashioned hostel with clean, comfortable rooms and choice of en-suite bathroom. ➋

Katekero Av do Mar 76 ☎262 787 107. Good-value, airy rooms with TVs, some with sea views. ➌

Residencial Maciel Rua José Estêvão 38 ☎262 784 685. The best budget option in town, with excellent, spotless rooms and a central location. ➌

Marítimo Rua José Estêvão ☎262 782 850. Set just back from the harbour, this *residencial* has simple rooms with private bathrooms. ➋

Mili Rua José Estêvão 45 ☎262 783 918. Comfortable, well-located and efficient place with friendly owners. ➍

Vasco da Gama Rua José Estêvão 23 ☎262 781 902, ☏262 781 787. Good value and in a central position. Rooms come with TV and bathrooms and the price includes breakfast. ➍

Eating and drinking

There is a fine array of **restaurants** along Avenida do Mar – most of them good value, and serving huge portions. *Restaurante Gaivota* and *Restaurante Onda Azul*, both by the harbour on Largo da Ribeira, have inexpensive seafood and often set up outdoor barbecues. The wonderful **market snack bar** just off Arq. Paulino Montez is just the place for breakfast or picnic provisions; it's usually full of fishwives in knitted capes and socks, swinging plastic bags of fish as they sip *bicas* and exchange news. Your best bet for a lively drink and a view of the world going by is one of the harbourside **bars**.

Ilha Berlenga

The **ILHA BERLENGA**, 10km offshore and just visible from the cape, is a dreamlike place – rather like a Scottish isle transported to warmer climes. Just two-and-a-half square kilometres in extent, it is the largest island of a tiny archipelago, with a jagged coastline of grottoes, miniature fjords, and extraordinary rock formations. In summer the sea is calm, crystal clear, and perfect for snorkelling and diving – rare in the Atlantic.

The only people permitted to live here are a couple of dozen fishermen, as the whole island has been declared a **Natural Reserve**, the home of thousands upon thousands of sea birds, including gulls, puffins and cormorants, perched in every conceivable cranny and clearly plotting to leave their mark on every possible victim. Makeshift paths are marked out with stones, and guardians watch out for visitors straying into the prohibited areas and disturbing the birds.

The island

Human life revolves around the main **landing dock** with its colour-washed fishing boats and small sandy **beach**. It can get crowded and noisy down here at the height of the season – it takes very few people to make the place seem packed – though the only buildings are a cluster of huts, a couple of basic shops and a mini-market and a lighthouse. If you want **to stay**, it's a choice between the nearby bar-restaurant *Pavilhão Mar e Sol* (T262 750 331; ❺) which offers somewhat pricey **rooms** or, for the tighter budget, the rudimentary **hostel** (T262 785 263; ❶) in the seventeenth-century Forte de São João Baptista, a short walk beyond the lighthouse, on an islet joined by the narrowest of causeways. You have to reserve in advance and bookings are for a minimum of one week and for the hostel you'll need to bring your own food (there is a kitchen) and sleeping stuff. There's also a **campsite** (€2.50 per person), which clings to a strictly limited site on the rocky slopes above the harbour. If you want to stay here, you should try and book in advance at the turismo in Peniche (see p.163).

Rowing boats can be hired at the jetty to explore the intricacies of the coastline, though you may prefer to go in something with a motor if there's any motion on the sea (you can get a guided trip for a few euro). Don't miss the **Furado Grande**, a fantastic tunnel 75m long which culminates in the aptly named **Cova do Sonho** (Dream Cove) with its precipitous cliffs.

Getting there

The **ferry** from Peniche to Berlenga is operated by Viamar and takes one hour – longer if the sea is rough. The service operates from May 15 to September 15; currently, there are three ferries daily in July and August (9am, 11.30am and 5.30pm; return at 10.30am, 4.30pm and 6.30pm) and one daily in May, June and September (10am; return at 4.30pm). A return **ticket** costs €15 and there's a limit of 300 tickets sold each day; one person can buy up to five at a time. In

July and August the ticket office opens at 8pm to take bookings for the next day's ferry; if you want to be sure of a place, get there in good time. Outside these months, it's not usually a problem getting a ticket on the day of travel.

Two other companies, Turpesca (☎262 789 960) and Berlenga Praia (☎262 782 636), operate **boat trips** all year round except December (minimum four people). Tickets are €15 return and the price includes a visit to the caves along the coastline. Both companies, plus Mergulhê (☎966 008 487), can arrange fishing or diving trips, for which equipment can be hired from the Berlenga Sub, Largo da Ribeira 24 (☎262 784 104, ℉262 784 105). Note that you can use Turpesca for overnight stays on the island only between June and September; the rest of the year it will take only day-trippers. All boats to the island are booked from the jetty below the fort.

However, bear in mind that if the weather is difficult, times will change and boats may be cancelled. In any case, be sure to go without breakfast − it's a rough ride, as evinced by the grim collection of buckets under the seats.

Óbidos

ÓBIDOS, 23km east of Peniche, is known as the "The Wedding City", and was the traditional bridal gift of the kings of Portugal to their queens. The custom was begun in 1282 by Dom Dinis and Dona Isabel, and the town can hardly have changed much in appearance since then. It is very small and completely enclosed by lofty medieval walls: streets are cobbled, houses whitewashed with bright blue and yellow borders, and at all points steep staircases wind up to the ramparts, where you can gaze across a lovely rural landscape.

It wasn't always like this. Five hundred years ago, when Peniche was an island, the sea also reached the foot of the ridge on which Óbidos stands and boats were moored below its walls. However, by the fifteenth century the sea had retreated, leaving a fertile green plain and the distant Lagoa de Óbidos with its narrow, shallow entrance to the sea.

The town is touristy, of course, attracting coach loads of daily visitors, while the area around it is becoming built up. However, you can walk right around the town along its perimeter **walls** − a narrow and at times hair-raising walkway with no handrails, and from this vantage point the town still seems to have a private life of its own. If you stay the night, the feeling is reinforced, as the town slowly empties to regain its charm.

The Town

The most striking building in town is Dom Dinis's massively towered **Castelo**, which has been converted to a very splendid *pousada* (see "Accommodation" on p.166). Below the castle, the principal focus of the streets is the parish church, the **Igreja de Santa Maria**, in the central *praça* − chosen for the wedding of the ten-year-old child king, Afonso V, and his eight-year-old cousin, Isabel, in 1444. It dates mainly from the Renaissance period, though the interior is lined with seventeenth-century blue *azulejos* in a homely manner typical of Portuguese churches. On the left-hand wall is an elaborate tomb designed by Nicolas Chanterene, an influential French sculptor active in Portugal in the first half of the sixteenth century. The *retábulo* to the right of the main altar was painted by **Josefa de Óbidos**, one of the finest of all Portuguese painters − and one of the few women artists afforded any reputation by art historians. Born at Seville in 1634, Josefa spent most of her life in a convent at Óbidos. She began her career as an etcher and miniaturist and a remarkable handling of detail is a feature of her later full-scale religious works. Another of her paintings, a portrait, can be seen in the adjacent **museum** in the old town hall (daily 10am–12.30pm & 2–6pm; €1.25).

There's an annual **festival of ancient music** from mid-September to mid-October, held in various venues around the town, including the purpose-built **Casa da Música**, just inside Porta da Vila, the principal town gate at the far end of Rua Direita. The town is also busy on Tourist Day (one of the last two Sun in Aug), when free wine is on offer. If you're on the lookout for things to buy, there's a range of **shops** on the main Rua Direita, from the Casa Mourisco (ceramics, paintings and carvings) to the worthy old people's **handicrafts centre**, which has a good variety of nicely made items.

Practicalities

Buses from Caldas da Rainha (6km to the north) and Peniche (24km west) stop outside the Porta da Vila, which leads into **Rua Direita** where you can find the **turismo** at number 51 (Mon–Fri 9.30am–7pm, Sat & Sun 9.30am–1pm & 2–7pm; ℡262 959 231, ⓦwww.cm-obidos.pt). The **train station** is at the foot of the ridge; there is no ticket office here, so pay once you are on the train. If you are not too heavily laden, you can cross the tracks and climb the steps, which will bring you to the gate by the Castelo *pousada* – at the opposite end of Rua Direita. Otherwise, follow the road and the easier gradients to reach the Porta da Vila.

Accommodation

Accommodation is on the expensive side, unless you get one of the handful of private **rooms** (usually ❸), advertised in the windows of a few houses and sometimes touted at the bus station; alternatively try those at Rua Direita 40 (℡262 959 188). Of the **pensões and hotels** the following represent a good selection:

Pousada do Castelo ℡262 959 105, ⓦwww.pousadas.pt. Relatively small but nevertheless one of the country's finest and priciest *pousadas* – visit for morning coffee or afternoon tea at the very least. Its size means it fills up quickly. ❽

Estalagem do Convento Rua Dr. João de Ornelas ℡262 959 214. A minor convent, converted rather tastelessly into a hotel. Expensive patio dining in summer is the best feature. ❺

Albergaria Josefa de Óbidos Rua Dr. João de Ornelas ℡262 959 228. A modern air-conditioned hotel, outside the walls. Rooms all have TVs and breakfast is included. ❹

Casa D'Óbidos Quinta de São José ℡262 950 924, ℱ262 959 970. A couple of kilometres from town, this is an attractive converted farmhouse.

Price includes an enormous breakfast. ❻

Casa do Poço Trav. da Rua Nova ℡262 959 358. Downhill from the castle, this renovated house retains its Moorish foundations and a well in the courtyard. There are only four double rooms, all en suite, and there's fado in the bar at weekends. ❹

Albergaria Rainha Santa Isabel Rua Direita ℡262 959 323. The carefully preserved facade hides a modern hotel with lounge and bar. Hearty breakfasts included. Some of the rooms have balconies overlooking the main street. ❺

Casa da Relógio Rua da Graça ℡262 959 282. Outside the walls, a former eighteenth-century mansion whose "clock" is in fact a stone sundial on the facade. Six very appealing en-suite double rooms that are real value for money. ❹

Eating

Restaurants are mainly geared towards day-trippers and menus range from predictable fare and chips to traditional local dishes, but prices tend to be slightly higher than elsewhere.

Restaurante Alcaide Rua Direita, opposite the Albergaria Rainha Santa Isabel ☎ 262 959 220. Attractive place serving very good unusual dishes. Arrive early – or book – particularly if you want to eat on the balcony; pricey. Closed Mon & Nov.
Restaurante O Conquistador Rua Josefa de Óbidos, off Rua Direita. Near the Porta da Vila; try the soup and the duck, or eat from the *ementa turística* for around €7.50.
Estalagem do Convento Rua Dr. João de Ornelas. Excellent but expensive patio dining, though the *ementa turística* is quite reasonable at €15.

Café-Restaurante 1° de Dezembro Largo Sao Pedro, next to the church. The best bet for a cheap meal, although service can be slack.
D. João V Lg. do Santuário do Senhor da Pedra ☎ 262 959 134. A special place with old-fashioned elegance where you can expect to pay for the excellent traditional local cuisine.
Casa de Ramiro Rua Porta do Vale. Just outside the walls in an old house, redesigned in Arabic style. It's noted for its aromatic grills and is moderately priced. Closed Thurs & Jan–Feb.

Caldas da Rainha

Six kilometres north of Óbidos, **CALDAS DA RAINHA** ("Queen's Spa") was put firmly on the map by Dona Leonor. Passing by in her carriage, she was so impressed by the strong sulphuric waters that she founded a hospital here, initiating four centuries of noble and royal patronage. That was in 1484 but the town was to reach the peak of its popularity in the nineteenth century when, all over Europe, spas became as much social as medical institutions. The English Gothic novelist, William Beckford, stopping off on his journey to Batalha and Alcobaça (recorded in his *Travels in Spain and Portugal*), found it a lively if depressing place – "every tenth or twelfth person a rheumatic or palsied invalid, with his limbs all atwist, and his mouth all awry, being conveyed to the baths in a chair".

Disappointingly little remains of all the royal wealth poured into the spa, though it is still a pleasant stop on your way to Nazaré or Alcobaça. From the central **Praça da República**, which hosts a fruit market every morning, the **royal spa hospital**, still very much in use, is a short walk downhill. There is a museum (Tues–Sun 10am–12.30pm & 2–5pm; €2) but you can only bathe in the warm, sulphurous swimming pools under doctor's orders. Protruding from the back of the spa is the striking Manueline belfry of **Nossa Senhora do Pópulo**, the hospital church. There's a *Virgin and Child* by Josefa de Óbidos in the sacristy.

In the leafy Parque Dom Carlos I, the **Museu de José Malhoa** (Tues–Sun 10am–12.30pm & 2–5pm; €1.25, free Sun am) displays Malhoa's work and that of other late-nineteenth-century Portuguese painters. There are two other museums at the far edge of the park: the **Atelier Museu António Duarte** (Mon–Fri 9am–1pm & 2–6pm, Sat & Sun 10am–1pm & 2–6pm; €1.25), devoted to the eminent sculptor; and, alongside, the much better **Museu da Cerâmica** (Tues–Sun 10am–12.30pm & 2–5pm; €1.25), which contains some of the original work of local potter and caricaturist Rafael Bordalo Pinheiro – look for his series of life-sized ceramic figures representing the Passion. Indeed, Caldas remains famed for its traditional ceramics (including peculiar phallus-shaped objects) and the **Feira Nacional da Cerâmica** is held here during July or October in the *Expooeste*, an industrial part of town, northwest of the railway tracks.

Practicalities

It's a short walk from either the **bus** or **train station** to **Praça da República**, where you'll find the summer **turismo** (Mon–Fri 9am–7pm, Sat & Sun

10am–1pm & 3–7pm; ☎262 834 511, ✉geizal@cm.caldas.rainha.pt); the main turismo (☎262 839 700, ℉262 839 726) is open all year and is situated next to the town hall in Praça 25 de Abril. If you wish to go online, there's **inter-net** access at the *Biblioteca Municipal*, Rua Vitorino Fróis 60 (Sat–Fri 10am–6pm; €2.50/hr; ☎262 823 773) and at *Valia Mais*, Avenida 1 de Maio 16C (Mon–Fri 10am–9pm, Sat 10am–1pm & 3–6pm;€2/hr; ☎262 823 773).

Accommodation
Due to the presence of the spa, there's a fair amount of **accommodation** around town, most of it reasonably priced, although generally rather characterless.

Caldas Internacional Hotel Rua Dr. Figueirõa Rêgo 45 ☎262 832 307. The smartest, although rather unexciting, option in town. ❺
Residencial D. Carlos Rua de Camões 39a ☎262 832 551, ✉dcarlos.all@netc.pt. Traditional old hotel, well situated near the royal spa hospital and the park. All rooms are en suite and have TVs. ❸
Pensão Central Largo Dr. José Barbosa ☎262 831 914. A pleasant choice and the birthplace of painter José Malhoa. Breakfast included. ❸
Residencial Europeia Rua Almirante Cândido dos Reis 64 ☎262 831 508. Another central, smart choice with heavy wooden furniture, TVs and a bar. ❹
Residencial Rainha D. Leonor Hermicício João Paulo II, 9 ☎262 842 171. A big, modern, soulless block but with satellite TV, private parking and all mod cons. ❹

Eating and drinking
For **food**, it's hard to beat the spit-roasts and grills at the *Zé do Barrete,* at Trav. da Cova da Onça 16–18 (☎262 832 787; closed Sun), midway down Rua Almirante Cândido dos Reis. There are several other good restaurants along this street. *Populus* (closed Mon), on the edge of the park at Rua de Camões, has lovely outdoor seating and serves up good salads and beef dishes at moderate prices. You may also be tempted to visit *Supatra* (☎262 842 920; closed Mon), 1km out on Rua General Amílcar Mota (the Óbidos road) – an unlikely setting for one of the country's most respected Thai restaurants. The cafés around Largo Rainha D. Leonor are a good bet for an evening **drink**, and also for sampling the local, rather sickly, sweets, such as *trouxas de ovos*. One of the most popular is **Pasteleria Baia** on the corner of Rua da Liberdade.

North to Nazaré

Heading **north from Caldas**, buses and trains loop inland, touching the coast only at São Martinho do Porto, 13km south of Nazaré. However, if you have your own transport, you can bear northwest from Caldas along the N360, which takes you past the tranquil **Lagoa de Óbidos**, and then out along the coast via Foz do Arelho on a beautiful clifftop route – a much better option than the busy N8.

Foz do Arelho
At **FOZ DO ARELHO**, 9km from Caldas and the first resort you come to, there's a fine beach and a lagoon where you can swim. There is a **campsite** (☎262 979 197) plus a few decent **places to stay**: the modern *Penedo Furado* (☎262 979 610; ❹); the upmarket, seafront *Foz Praia* (☎262 979 413, ℉262 979 460; ❺), complete with pool, tennis courts and restaurant; and, 1km before the village and only 500m from the lake, the *Quinta da Foz* (☎262 979 369;

⑤) – a lovely sixteenth-century country-house hotel with just five rooms. Good seafood **restaurants** can be found behind the beach, while the smarter *Adega Real Restaurante* on Largo Do Arraial, an attractive pedestrian square, serves fancier food, like stuffed crab and cream of shrimp soup. Green Hill disco, at the northern end of the beach, is the place for diehard boppers to head after dark.

São Martinho do Porto

SÃO MARTINHO DO PORTO is the main resort between Peniche and Nazaré, and one of the more developed spots along the Estremaduran coast, though at least most of the new building is relatively low-rise. In high season, it's probably not worth the struggle to find a room – or even a place in the campsite.

The reason for São Martinho's tourist success is its **beach**: a vast sweep of sand which curls around a landlocked bay to form a natural swimming pool. This shelter makes it one of the warmest places to swim on the west coast, with the sands sloping down into calm, shallow, solar-heated water. For something more bracing – or less crowded – there's a good northern beach on the open Atlantic coastline beyond the bay. (Beware of the Atlantic beaches beyond the bay; they can be dangerous.)

Check with the **turismo**, at the far end of Avenida 25 de Abril (summer Mon–Fri 10am–1pm, 3–7pm; Sat & Sun 9am–1pm & 3–6pm; winter Mon–Fri 10am–1pm & 2–6pm; ☎262 989 110), about the possibility of accommodation in **private rooms**. Alternatively, try *Residencial Atlântica*, at Rua Miguel Bombarda 6 (☎262 989 151 ⑤262 980 163; ④), a popular place two blocks from the seafront with attractive modern decor; or *Residencial Concha*, on Largo Vitorino Froís (☎262 989 220; ⑥, closed Oct–April), which is a comfortable hotel with satellite TV and balconies. There's also a **campsite**, *Colina do Sol* (☎262 989 764), 2km to the north, off the Nazaré road (N242), and a **youth hostel** (☎262 999 506), 4km away and further inland at Alfeizerão, off the Caldas da Rainha/Alcobaça road (N8).

The restaurants all serve solid home-cooked fare; probably one of the better **restaurants** is that attached to the *Residencial Atlântica*. Other good options include: *A Cave*, Rua Conde de Avalar (closed Wed); *O Largo* at Largo Vitorino Froís 21; or the *Café Baia*, Rua Vasco da Gama, behind the turismo. After that, look into the *Bonia Club*, near the *Residencial Concha*, open every night from midnight and with a disco at weekends open until 6am.

Nazaré

After years of advertising itself as the most picturesque seaside village in Portugal, **NAZARÉ** has more or less destroyed itself. In summer, the crowds are way too much for the place to cope with, and the enduring characteristics are not so much "gentle traditions" as trinket stalls and high prices. That said, local traditions are still just about managing to coexist with tourism – you'll see women weaving barefoot through the town bearing immense trays of fish on their heads, and a few fishermen sitting unperturbed on the beach, mending their nets beside brilliantly painted sardine boats. However, most of the boats have disappeared to a new harbour, fifteen minutes' walk from the village, where cranes have replaced the oxen once used to haul them in.

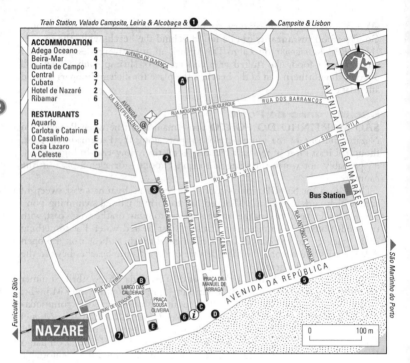

ACCOMMODATION
Adega Oceano   5
Beira-Mar   4
Quinta de Campo   1
Central   3
Cubata   7
Hotel de Nazaré   2
Ribamar   6

RESTAURANTS
Aquario   B
Carlota e Catarina A
O Casalinho   E
Casa Lazaro   C
A Celeste   D

AVENIDA DE OLIVENÇA

RUA DOS BARRANCOS

RUA MOUZINHO DE ALBUQUERQUE

AVENIDA VIEIRA GUIMARÃES

RUA SUB · VILA

RUA SUB · VILA

Bus Station

RUA ADRIÃO BATALHA

RUA GIL VICENTE

RUA ANTÓNIO C. LARANJA

RUA MOUZINHO DE ALBUQUERQUE

PRAÇA DR. MANUEL DE ARRIAGA

AVENIDA DA REPÚBLICA

RUA DO LEIRIA

LARGO DAS CALDEIRAS

TRAV. DE ELEVADOR

PRAÇA SOUSA OLIVEIRA

NAZARÉ

Funicular to Sítio

São Martinho do Porto

0   100 m

The village and beaches

The original settlement was not at Nazaré but at Sítio, 110m up the rock face
above the present sprawl of holiday apartment buildings, a location that was, by
most accounts, the legacy of pirate raids which continued well into the nineteenth century. However, legend has a different explanation, telling of a
twelfth-century knight, Dom Fuas Roupinho, who, while out hunting, was led
up the cliff by a deer. The deer dived off into the void and Dom Fuas was saved
from following by the timely vision of **Nossa Senhora da Nazaré**, in whose
name a church was subsequently built.

You can reach this church, and the surrounding Sítio district, by a **funicular**,
which rumbles up and down almost continuously from 7am to midnight
(€0.50). There is an enjoyable *miradouro* at the top, though the shrine itself is
unimpressive, despite an icon carved by St Joseph and painted by St Luke (a
handy partnership active throughout Europe). The church does, however, host
a well-attended **romaria** (Sept 8–10) with processions, folk dancing, and bullfights. The Sítio bullring also stages Saturday night *touradas* in summer.

Back down below, the area between the funicular and Praça Dr. Manuel de
Arriaga retains an old-world charm which the seafront has all but lost. But the
main disadvantage of staying in Nazaré is that its **beaches** – grand, tent-
studded sweeps of clean sand, stretching out to the north beyond the headland
of Sítio, and south across the narrow Alcôa estuary – are dangerous for swimming. The Atlantic can be fierce along the Estremaduran coast, so, for safety's
sake, stick to the patrolled main beach where the bathers are packed in as tight-
ly as the sardine boats. Alternatively, tramp southwards towards the village of

Gralha, where you'll find a number of small coves and one sheltered beach isolated enough to be a popular spot for nude bathing.

Practicalities

Using public transport, it's simplest to arrive at Nazaré by bus. There are regular connections with most towns in the region, and the **bus station** is centrally located, halfway down Avenida Vieira Guimarães, which meets the main drag, Avenida da República, at right angles at the foot of the hill. The nearest **train station** is at Valado, 6km inland, on the Alcobaça road; buses from Alcobaça call there on the way into town.

Avenida da República runs the length of the beach, and this is where you'll find most of the hotels and restaurants, as well as the **turismo** (daily: July & Aug 10am–10pm; Sept–June 10am–1pm & 3–6pm; ☎262 561 194, ⓦwww.cm-nazar.pt), near the funicular. For **internet** access head for the post office, at Avenida Independência Nacional 2 (Sat–Fri 9am–12.30pm & 1.30pm–6pm; €1.50/hr).

Accommodation

Pensões in Nazaré are heavily booked throughout the summer but **rooms** are plentiful and you'll be approached by their owners at the bus station – expect to pay around €22 in high season. If you have problems finding a place, consult the turismo, which has a list of available rooms. The more promising **pensão** and **hotel** possibilities are listed below. There's a **campsite** on the road to Valado (☎262 561 111; closed mid-Nov to mid-Jan), and another – the well-equipped *Vale Paraíso* (☎262 561 800, ⓔcamping.vp.nz@mail.telepac.pt) – nestling in pine woods 2km out of town on the road to Marinha Grande (N242), complete with pool and bike rental.

Residencial Adega Oceano Av da República 51 ☎262 561 161, ⓕ262 561 790. Right on the beachfront, this is a good-value, cheerful choice offering en-suite rooms with TV and balconies. ❹
Residencial Beira-Mar Av da República 40 ☎262 561 358, ⓔcamaeanazaregap@mail.telepac.pt. Same very pleasant sea view setting the *Oceano*, with large, breezy rooms (some with sea views) and private bathrooms; the price includes breakfast. Closed Nov–Feb. ❼
Quinta do Campo Valado dos Frades ☎262 577 135, ⓔquintadocampo@mail.telepac.pt. Situated in a tranquil setting 6km inland, this *quinta* was founded as an agricultural college by monks in the fourteenth century and makes an excellent base if you have your own transport. The building is set in extensive grounds and offers various sports facilities including a pool and tennis courts. ❻

Pensão Central Rua Mouzinho de Albuquerque 85 ☎262 551 510, ⓕ262 551 542. Old and well managed; book in advance if you can. The rooms facing the courtyard are best. Breakfast included. ❹
Residencial Cubata Av da República 6 ☎262 561 706, ⓕ262 561 700. A great position and good value if you can get a sea view. It's between the turismo and the foot of the funicular. ❹
Hotel da Nazaré Largo Afonso Zuquete ☎262 569 030, ⓕ262 569 038. Upmarket choice with small rooms, simply furnished. The views from the upper floors are splendid, and even better from the rooftop terrace. Closed Jan. ❻
Pensão Restaurante Ribamar Rua Gomes Freire 9 ☎262 551 58, ⓕ262 562 224. Across the road from the turismo, with some rooms overlooking the beach. The bathrooms are tiled with *azulejos* and breakfast is included in the price. ❺

Eating and drinking

The main concentration of **restaurants and cafés** is along Avenida da República and the several squares off the avenue.

Aquário Largo das Caldeiras 13. One of the best of a cluster of places in this pretty square. Outdoor tables and moderate prices.
Carlota e Catarina Rua Adrião Batalha 162. Good

seafood served in an agreeable setting and at reasonable prices, but it's quite a climb to get there and the restaurant is only open July–Sept.
O Casalinho Praça Sousa Oliveira 6. Popular with locals which is recommendation enough for its fish and meat dishes. Service is with a smile and prices are moderate.

Casa Lazaro Rua Adrião Batalho. Good-value seafood and excellent house wine in tiled surroundings by the seafront.

Ã Celeste Av da República 54. Expensive but top-quality seafood overlooking the beach.

Alcobaça

The Cistercian monastery at **ALCOBAÇA** was founded in 1153 by Dom Henrique to celebrate his victory over the Moors at Santarém six years earlier. Building started soon after, and by the end of the thirteenth century it was the most powerful monastery in the country. Owning vast tracts of farmland, orchards and vineyards, it was immensely rich and held jurisdiction over a dozen towns and three seaports. Its church and cloister are the purest and the most inspired creation of all Portuguese Gothic architecture and, alongside Belém and Batalha, are the most impressive monuments in the country. The church is also the burial place of those romantic figures of Portuguese history, Dom Pedro and Dona Inês de Castro.

Aside from the monastery, the only other point of interest in Alcobaça is the **Museu do Vinho** (summer Tues–Sun 9am–noon & 2–5.30pm; winter Mon–Fri, same hours; free), ten minutes' walk from the bus station out on the Leiria road, which gives a fascinating glimpse into the area's wine-making and agricultural past. There are free guided tours, which last about an hour, and you get the chance to purchase some of the local produce.

The Mosteiro de Alcobaça

The **Mosteiro de Alcobaça** (daily: April–Sept 9am–7pm; Oct–March 9am–5pm; €2.50, entry to church free), although empty since its dissolution in 1834, still seems to assert power, magnificence and opulence. And it takes little imagination to people it again with the monks, said once to have numbered 999. Mass was once celebrated here without interruption, but it was the residents' legendary extravagant and aristocratic lifestyles that formed the common ingredients of the awed anecdotes of eighteenth-century travellers.

Even William Beckford, no stranger to high living, found their decadence unsettling, growing weary of "perpetual gormandising. .. the fumes of banquets and incense. .. the fat waddling monks and sleek friars with wanton eyes, twanging away on the Jew's harp." Another contemporary observer, Richard Twiss, for his part found "the bottle went as briskly about as ever I saw it do in Scotland" – a tribute indeed. For all the "high romps" and luxuriance, though, it has to be added that the monks enjoyed a reputation for hospitality, generosity and charity, while the surrounding countryside is to this day one of the most productive areas in Portugal, thanks to their agricultural expertise.

The abbey church

The main **abbey church**, modelled on the original Cistercian abbey at Citeaux in France, is the largest in Portugal. External impressions are disappointing, as the Gothic facade has been superseded by unexceptional Baroque additions of the seventeenth and eighteenth centuries. Inside, however, all later adornments have been swept away, restoring the narrow soaring aisles to their original vertical simplicity. The only exception to this Gothic purity is the frothy Manueline doorway to the sacristy, hidden directly behind the high altar and, as at Tomar and Batalha, encrusted with intricate, swirling motifs of coral and seaweed.

The church's most precious treasures are the fourteenth-century **tombs of Dom Pedro and Dona Inês de Castro**, each occupying one of the transepts and sculpted with a phenomenal wealth of detail. Animals, heraldic emblems, musicians and biblical scenes are all portrayed in an architectural setting of miniature windows, canopies, domes and towers; most graphic of all is a dragon-shaped Hell's mouth at Inês's feet, consuming the damned. The tombs are inscribed with the motto "Até ao Fim do Mundo" (Until the End of the World) and in accordance with Dom Pedro's orders have been placed foot to foot so that on the Day of Judgement the pair may rise and immediately feast their eyes on one another.

Pedro's earthly love for Inês de Castro, the great theme of epic Portuguese poetry, was cruelly stifled by high politics. Inês, as the daughter of a Galician nobleman, was a potential source of Spanish influence over the Portuguese throne and Pedro's father, Afonso IV, forbade their marriage. The ceremony took place nevertheless – secretly at Bragança in remote Trás-os-Montes – and eventually Afonso was persuaded to sanction his daughter-in-law's murder. When Pedro succeeded to the throne in 1357 he brought the murderers to justice, personally ripping out their hearts and gorging his love-crazed appetite for blood upon them. More poignantly, he also exhumed and crowned the corpse of his lover, forcing the entire royal circle to acknowledge her as queen by kissing her decomposing hand.

The kitchen

From one highlight to another. Beckford – Romantic dilettante that he was – stood bewildered by the charms of these tombs when "in came the Grand Priors hand in hand, all three together. 'To the *kitchen*,' said they in unison, 'to the kitchen and that immediately.' They led him past the fourteenth-century chapterhouse to a cavernous room in the corner of the cloisters – a route that you can follow.

Alcobaça's feasting has already been mentioned but this **kitchen** – with its cellars and gargantuan conical chimney, supported by eight trunk-like iron columns – sets it in perspective. A stream tapped from the River Alcôa still runs straight through the room: it was used not only for cooking and washing but also to provide a constant supply of fresh fish, which plopped out into a stone basin. At the centre of the room, on the vast wooden tables, Beckford continued to marvel at:

... pastry in vast abundance which a numerous tribe of lay brothers and their attendants were rolling out and puffing up into a hundred different shapes, singing all the while as blithely as larks in a cornfield. "There," said the Lord Abbot, "we shall not starve. God's bounties are great, it is fit we should enjoy them."

And enjoy them they did, with a majestic feast of "rarities and delicacies, potted lampreys, strange Brazilian messes, edible birds' nests and sharks' fins dressed after the mode of Macau by a Chinese lay brother". As a practical test for obesity the monks had to file through a narrow door on their way to the **refectory**; those who failed were forced to fast until they could squeeze through.

The cloisters and Sala dos Reis

The **Claustro do Silencio** (Cloisters of Silence), notable for their traceried stone windows, were built in the reign of Dom Dinis, the "poet-king" who established an enduring literary and artistic tradition at the abbey. An upper storey of twisted columns and Manueline arches was added in the sixteenth century, along with, in its standard position opposite the refectory, a beautiful hexagonal lavatory.

The **Sala dos Reis** (Kings' Room), off the cloister, displays statues of virtually every king of Portugal up until Dom José, who died in 1777. Blue eighteenth-century *azulejos* depict the siege of Santarém, Dom Afonso's vow, and the founding of the monastery. Also on show here is a piece of war booty which must have warmed the souls of the brothers – the huge metal cauldron in which soup was heated up for the Spanish army before the battle of Aljubarrota in 1385 (for more of which, see "Batalha" on p.178).

The rest of the monastery, including four other cloisters, seven dormitories and endless corridors, is closed to the public; parts of it are currently occupied by an old people's home. For the best overall view of the monastery, make your way to the ruined hilltop **castle**, about five minutes' walk away.

Practicalities

Though Alcobaça is no longer a hive of activity, it's not a bad place to stay. A useful first stop is the **turismo** (daily: summer 10am–1pm & 3–7pm; winter 10am–1pm & 2–6pm; T262 582 377) on the central Praça 25 de Abril, opposite the monastery. It can supply maps of the town and advise on accommodation and transport. For **internet** access head for *Ciber Café*, Rua Dr. Francisco Zagelo (daily 10am–midnight; €2.50/hr; T262 582 274). The **bus station** is five minutes' walk from the centre of town, across the bridge; coming into town, bear right and head towards the abbey towers. There are reasonably frequent connections to Nazaré and Leiria.

Alcobaça has a scattering of inexpensive **pensões and hotels**, just off Praça 25 de Abril. The local **campsite** (T262 582 265) is some ten minutes' walk north of the bus station, on Avenida Manuel da Silva Carolina, near the covered market; there are some trees for shade, but the ground here is hard and barren.

An upmarket option is *Challet Fonte Nova Palacete*, Estrada da Fonte Nova (T262 598 300, W www.challetfontenova.pt; ⑤), located in a restored nineteenth-century palace. In contrast, the *Hotel Santa Maria*, Rua Dr. Francisco Zagalo (T262 597 395, F262 596 715; ④), is a modern hotel facing the monastery. Rooms are equipped with all mod cons and those at the front have good views. Just off the main square, *Hotel Santa Maria*, at Rua Frei António Brandão 39 (T262 582 142, F262 582 14; ③), has large but rather dark rooms, some overlooking an internal courtyard; the restaurant below is well thought of.

In addition to the **restaurants** at the various *pensões*, you could consider eating at the *Celeiro dos Frades* ("monks' barn"), on Arcos de Cister under the arches alongside the abbey, where you can dine well for around €10, or just enjoy a coffee in its atmospheric café. *Restaurante O Telheiro*, Rua da Lavadinha (closed Sat), up the road beyond the *Hotel Santa Maria*, is more expensive but has great views over the abbey. Also worth a try is the huge *Frei Bernardo* on Rua D. Pedro V 17–19, which seats 180 and serves the sort of meals you need to fast after, and at moderate prices – albeit geared to tourists.

Leiria

Thirty-five kilometres north of Alcobaca, a royal castle hangs almost vertically above the large town of **LEIRIA**, whose graceful old town is a place of cobbled streets, attractive gardens, and fine old squares, once you penetrate its drab modern outskirts. If you are travelling around on public transport, you will probably want to make it your base for a couple of nights, as the three big sites of northern Estremadura – Alcobaça, Batalha and Fátima – all make easy day excursions by bus. Not so easy, but still quite feasible, are day trips to Porto de Mós and the caves of Mira de Aire, Alvados and Santo António (see pp.182–183); or to São Pedro de Muel and the coast (see p.177). Leiria also has enough restaurants, bars and nightlife to keep the evenings occupied, with most of the bars being concentrated around the lively Largo Cândido dos Reis.

Leiria's **Castelo** (April–Sept Mon–Fri 9am–6.30pm, Sat & Sun 10am–6.30pm; Oct–March Mon–Fri 9am–5.30pm, Sat & Sun 10am–5.30pm; €1.50) was one of the most important strongholds in Moorish Portugal, reconquered by Afonso Henriques as he fought his way south in 1135. The actual building you see today dates mostly from the fourteenth and eighteenth centuries. Within its walls stands a royal palace, with a magnificent balcony high above the Rio Lis. Leiria was the main residence of Dom Dinis, who gave the town to his beloved Queen Isabel along with Óbidos, Abrantes, Porto de Mós and Trancoso. The walls also contain the **Church of Nossa Senhora da Penha**, erected by João I in about 1400 and now reduced to an eerie, roofless shell. If you have small children with you, beware: there are several precipitous, unguarded points among the buildings and staircases. Nearby, on Largo de Sé, is the town's sixteenth-century **Cathedral**, which was built under the reign of Dom João III and has three naves. It was designed by Afonso Alvares, who worked on the São Roque in Lisbon.

At the heart of the old town is **Praça Rodrigues Lobo**, surrounded by beautiful arcaded buildings and dominated by a splendidly pompous statue of the eponymous seventeenth-century local poet. In fact, Leiria's literary connections go back much further than this – in 1480, the town had one of Portugal's first printing presses, which was run by Jews who printed in Hebrew.

Practicalities

Arriving by **bus**, you'll be dropped at a modern terminal at the near end of Avenida Heróis de Angola, but with another entrance on Praça Paulo VI. Across the Jardim Luís de Camões, on Praça Goa Damão e Dio, is the very helpful **turismo** (daily: summer 10am–1pm & 3–7pm; winter 2–6pm; ☎244 814 748, ⊕www.rt-leiriafatima.pt), which dispenses maps. Round the corner, next to the post office, on Rua Combatentes Grande Guerra, the *Arquivo Coffee Shop*, (daily 9.30am–midnight; €2/hr) offers **internet** access. The **train station** is 4km north of town – a cheap taxi ride away.

Accommodation

For **accommodation**, make your way to Praça Rodrigues Lobo and look around the restaurants and *pensões* both here and on the narrow side streets: try Rua Mestre de Aviz and Rua Miguel Bombarda. More cheap rooms are to be found in Largo Paio Guterres and Largo Cónego Maia, both near the cathedral. There's also a very well-appointed **youth hostel** – one of the most enjoyable in the country – at Largo Cândido dos Reis 9 (☎244 831 868).

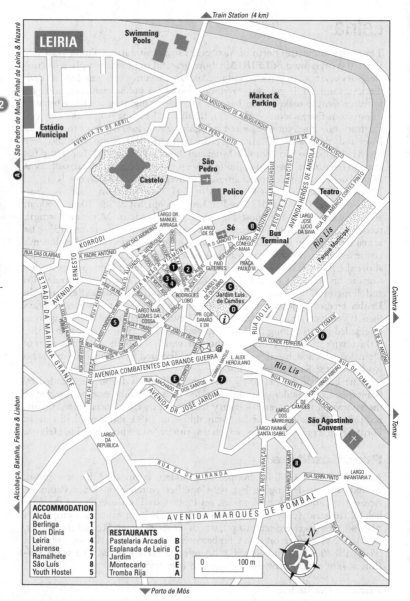

▲ Train Station (4 km)

LEIRIA

Swimming Pools

Market & Parking

Estádio Municipal

Castelo

São Pedro

Police

Sé

Bus Terminal

Teatro

Rio Lis

Parque Municipal

Jardim Luís de Camões

Rio Lis

São Agostinho Convent

ACCOMMODATION

Alcôa	3
Berlinga	1
Dom Dinis	6
Leiria	4
Leirense	2
Ramalhete	7
São Luís	8
Youth Hostel	5

RESTAURANTS

Pastelaria Arcadia	B
Esplanada de Leiria	C
Jardim	D
Montecarlo	E
Tromba Rija	A

0   100 m

N

▼ Porto de Mós

◄ São Pedro de Muel, Pinhal de Leiria & Nazaré

◄ Alcobaça, Batalha, Fátima & Lisbon

Coimbra ►

Tomar ►

Pensão Alcôa Rua Rodrigues Cordeiro 24–26 ☎244 832 690. Smallish but good-value rooms with TVs. Price includes breakfast. There's a good restaurant, too. ❸

Pensão Berlinga Rua Miguel Bombarda 3 ☎244 823 846. Just off Praça Rodrigues Lobo; look for the sign in the corner of the square. A big,

rambling, friendly place. ❸

Residencial Dom Dinis Trav. de Tomar 2 ☎244 815 342, ℻244 823 542. Across the bridge from the turismo and up a steep side road. A modern, popular place with a pleasant roof terrace and parking. ❹

Hostal Leiria Rua Rodrigues Cordeiro 14 ☎244

823 270. Spartan but very cheap, clean rooms, above a workman's cafe-style eatery ❶
Pensão Residencial Leirense Rua Afonso de Albuquerque 6 ☎244 823 054, ⓕ244 823 073. A firm favourite for some years – very central and offering good value for money. Breakfast is included. ❸

Residencial Ramalhete Rua Dr. Correia Mateus 30 ☎244 812 802, ⓕ244 815 099. An efficiently run place; the rooms at the rear are quieter. ❹
Hotel São Luís Rua Henrique Sommer ☎244 813 197, ⓕ244 813 897. Good value and a good location, albeit out of the centre. Breakfast included. ❹

Eating and drinking

September is the best time to sample the region's cuisine, when the **Festival of Gastronomy** fills up the Mercado Santana with row upon row of food stalls. The best place for a **drink** and a snack is at one of the **cafés** or **bars** around Largo Cândido dos Reis which also give you the chance to take in Leiria's lively streetlife – try *Bar Estrebaria* at no. 23, or *Bar Santo Estevão* at Trav. da Paz 9. Alternatively, the *Galeria Bar*, Quinta de Santo António 43, is worth a visit.

Pastelaria Arcadia Praça Rodrigues Lobo. Under the arches in the main square and a good place to enjoy breakfast or a tea stop at the outdoor tables.
Café Restaurante Esplanada de Leiria Jardim Luís de Camões. Just the place for poor deprived vegetarians or those who like plenty of choice, with a daily buffet spread.
Jardim Jardim Luís de Camões. Nice position overlooking the river and the park, serving inexpensive seafood and other specialities; popular with students. Closed Mon.

Restaurante Montecarlo Rua Dr. Correia Mateus 32–34. The best on this street – you can eat for under €6 if you have a *meia dose*, which should be sufficient.
Tromba Rija Rua Professores Portelas 22 ☎244 855 072. Real Portuguese cuisine – expensive, but worth every penny – can be found out of town on the Marrazes road; go west under the N1 and take a left turning after the *Casa da Palmeira*. Closed Sun, Mon lunch & Aug.

The Pinhal de Leiria and its beaches

Some of the most idyllic spots on the stretch of coast west of Leiria are in the **Pinhal de Leiria** (or Pinhal do Rei), a vast 700-year-old pine forest stretching from São Pedro de Muel to Pedrógão. Although there were always trees here, the "Royal Pine Forest" was planned by Dom Dinis, a king renowned for his agrarian reforms, to protect fertile arable land from the menacing inward march of sand dunes. It has since grown into an area of great natural beauty, with sunlight filtering through endless miles of trees and the air perfumed with the scent of resin. The turismo at Marinha Grande, halfway between Leiria and the coast, can supply maps of the forest if you want to make your way through its grid-like tracks on foot.

The **beaches**, for the most part, are superb, and currently the sea is free of pollution from Paredes da Vitória, 12km south of São Pedro de Muel, to Leirosa, 11km south of Figueira da Foz.

São Pedro de Muel

The nearest beach to Leiria is at **SÃO PEDRO DE MUEL**, 22km to the west, where development has remained low-key. Many buildings have been renovated or built in the old style with attractive wooden balconies, making it a pleasant place to stay, though the town gets very busy in high season. If the sea is too fierce to swim in you can try one of the swimming pools situated surreally above the beach.

Buses from Leiria involve a change at Marinha Grande, about halfway. There are regular buses in summer, but the service is less frequent outside the holiday season. If you wish to stay, **accommodation** – even in high season – should be no problem, since there are more than a dozen *pensões* and hotels. The seasonal **turismo** (☎244 599 152)), at the top of the village by the post office, should be able to help. Otherwise, try *Residencial Perola do Oceano* (☎244 599 157; ❸) in Trav. Antigos Armazens, which is virtually on the seafront; it has a large annexe up the hill, too. There are two **campsites**, north of the village. The nearer is the *Orbitur* site (☎244 599 168)), which can get packed; further out but less expensive is the *Inatel* (☎244 599 289; closed mid-Dec to mid-Jan).

Excellent **restaurants** abound, among them the *Brisamar*, Rua Dr. Nicolau Bettencourt, and *A Fonte*, on Praçeta Afonso Lopes Vieira, both of which specialize in seafood, and the upmarket *A Concha*, Rua Duquesa de Caminha 16 (closed Thurs). However, for sunsets and sea views, *Estrela do Mar* (closed Thurs in winter) is hard to beat, situated right above the town beach. For breakfast, try *Café Central* on Rua Dr. Alfonso Leitão, where you can relax on wicker chairs outside.

South of São Pedro, too, you can find sheltered stretches of beach – especially around **PAREDES DA VITÓRIA**, 6km to the south and popular with the Portuguese for camping wild – though here you're no longer in the forest. Another quiet spot is **ÁGUA DE MADEIROS**, 3km south, where the smart *Residencial Água de Madeiros* sits above the wild, often deserted beach (☎244 599 324; ❺).

Praia Velha, Praia da Vieira and Pedrógoã

A couple of kilometres north of the lighthouse at São Pedro, **PRAIA VELHA** is a popular local beach – mainly because of the chance to swim in the small lake behind the beach – though it can get littered in summer. There are a few **rooms** for let at the excellent restaurant, *O Pai dos Frangos* (☎244 599 158; ❹), which has won awards – try its amazing mixed kebabs.

Ten kilometres to the north of Velha, **PRAIA DA VIEIRA** and the main town of **VIEIRA DE LEIRIA** (the latter 3km inland) are on the estuary of the Rio Liz and are notable for their fish restaurants. Praia da Vieira is served by a patchy bus service from Marinha Grande and has grown into quite an unattractive modern resort, though it does have a great beach. Of the several *residenciais*, try first the *Ouro Verde* (☎244 695 931; ❹) or the *Estrela do Mar* (☎244 695 762; ❸). Alternatively, the seasonal **turismo** (☎244 695 230) can recommend places to stay. Among the resort's several **restaurants** is the excellent *Solemar*, on Rua José Botas (☎244 695 404). There's also a municipal **campsite** (☎244 695 354; June to mid-Sept).

PEDRÓGOÃ, 6km further to the north, also has a rash of modern development spread around another fantastic expanse of beach, which is still used by fishermen to launch their high-prowed boats. There's a great **campsite** (☎244 695 403; closed mid-Dec to Jan) in the woods, while in town, there are several restaurants and a seasonal **turismo** (July & Aug Tues–Sun 10am–1pm & 3–7pm; ☎244 695 411), which can give information about **private rooms**.

Batalha and around

Eleven kilometres south of Leiria, the Mosteiro de Santa Maria da Vitória, better known as **BATALHA** (Battle Abbey), is the supreme achievement of

Portuguese architecture – the dazzling richness and originality of its Manueline decoration rivalled only by the Mosteiro dos Jerónimos at Belém, with which it shares UNESCO world monument status. An exuberant symbol of national pride, it was built to commemorate the battle that sealed Portugal's independence after decades of Spanish intrigue.

With the death of Dom Fernando in 1383, the royal house of Burgundy died out, and in its wake there followed a period of feverish factional plotting over the Portuguese throne. Fernando's widow, Leonor Teles, had a Spanish lover even during her husband's lifetime, and when Fernando died she betrothed her daughter, Beatriz, to Juan I of Castile, encouraging his claim to the Portuguese throne. João, Mestre de Aviz, Fernando's illegitimate stepbrother, also claimed the throne. He assassinated Leonor's lover and braced himself for the inevitable invasion from Spain. The two armies clashed on August 14, 1385, at the **Battle of Aljubarrota**, which despite its name was actually fought at São Jorge, 10km northeast of Aljubarrota and just 4km south of present-day Batalha. Faced with seemingly impossible odds, João struck a deal with the Virgin Mary, promising to build a magnificent abbey in return for her military assistance. It worked: Nuno Álvares Pereira led the Portuguese forces to a memorable victory and the new king duly summoned the finest architects of the day.

Today, however, the abbey is rattled by the N1 highway from Lisbon to Coimbra which runs across an embankment perilously close to the abbey and is gradually altering the structure as vibrations and fumes take their toll. There is talk of "moving" the road, though no plans have yet been forthcoming. Furthermore, the abbey is showing its age: built largely of limestone, it's being increasingly affected by acid rain.

The Abbey

The honey-coloured **Abbey** (daily: April–Sept 9am–6.30pm; Oct–March 9am–5.30pm; main church free, cloisters €2.50, both free Sun am) was transformed by the uniquely Portuguese Manueline additions of the late fifteenth and early sixteenth centuries, but the bulk of the building was completed between 1388 and 1434 in a profusely ornate version of French Gothic. Pinnacles, parapets, windows and flying buttresses are all lavishly and intricately sculpted. Within this flamboyant framework there are also strong elements of the English Perpendicular style. Huge pilasters and prominent vertical decorations divide the main facade; the nave, with its narrow soaring dimensions, and the chapterhouse are reminiscent of church architecture in the English cathedral cities of Winchester and York.

The Capela do Fundador

Medieval architects were frequently attracted by lucrative foreign commissions, but there is a special explanation for the English influence at Batalha. This is revealed in the **Capela do Fundador** (Founder's Chapel), directly to the right upon entering the church. Beneath the octagonal lantern rests the joint tomb of Dom João I and Philippa of Lancaster, their hands clasped in the ultimate expression of harmonious relations between Portugal and England.

In 1373, Dom Fernando had entered into an alliance with John of Gaunt, Duke of Lancaster, who claimed the Spanish throne by virtue of his marriage to a daughter of Pedro the Cruel, king of Castile. A crack contingent of English longbowmen had played a significant role in the victory at Aljubarrota, and in 1386 both countries willingly signed the **Treaty of Windsor**, "an inviolable, eternal, solid, perpetual, and true league of friendship". As part of the same political package Dom João married Philippa, John of Gaunt's daughter, and with her came English architects to assist at Batalha. The alliance between the two countries, reconfirmed by the marriage of Charles II to Catherine of Bragança in 1661 and the Methuen Commercial Treaty of 1703, has become the longest-standing international friendship of modern times – it was invoked by the Allies in World War II to establish bases on the Azores, and the facilities of those islands were offered to the British Navy during the 1982 Falklands war.

The four younger sons of João and Philippa are buried along the south wall of the Capela do Fundador in a row of recessed arches. Second from the right is the **tomb of Prince Henry the Navigator**, who guided the discovery of Madeira, the Azores and the African coast as far as Sierra Leone. Henry himself never ventured further than Tangiers but it was a measure of his personal importance, drive and expertise that the growth of the empire was temporarily shelved after his death in 1460.

Concerted maritime exploration resumed under João II (1481–95) and accelerated with the accession of Manuel I (1495–1521). Vasco da Gama opened up the trade route to India in 1498, Cabral reached Brazil two years later and Newfoundland was discovered in 1501. The momentous era of burgeoning self-confidence, wealth and widening horizons is reflected in the peculiarly Portuguese style of architecture known (after the king) as Manueline (see box on p.190). As befitted the great national shrine, Batalha was adapted to incorporate two masterpieces of the new order: the Royal Cloister and the so-called Unfinished Chapels.

The Claustro Real and Sala do Capítulo

In the **Claustro Real** (Royal Cloister), stone grilles of ineffable beauty and intricacy were added to the original Gothic windows by Diogo de Boitaca, architect of the cloister at Belém and the prime genius of Manueline art. Crosses of the Order of Christ and armillary spheres – symbols of overseas exploration – are entwined in a network of lotus blossom, briar branches and exotic vegetation.

Off the east side opens the early fifteenth-century **Sala do Capítulo** (chapterhouse), remarkable for the audacious unsupported span of its ceiling – so daring, in fact, that the Church authorities were convinced that the whole chamber would come crashing down and employed criminals already condemned to death to build it. The architect, Afonso Domingues, could finally silence his critics only by sleeping in the chamber night after night. Soldiers now stand guard here over Portugal's **Tomb of the Unknown Warriors**, one killed in France during World War I, the other in the country's colonial wars in Africa. The **refectory**, on the opposite side of the cloister, houses a military museum in their honour. From here, a short passage leads into the **Claustro de Dom Afonso V**, built in a conventional Gothic style which provides a yardstick against which to measure the Manueline flamboyance of the Royal Cloister.

The Capelas Imperfeitas

The **Capelas Imperfeitas** (Unfinished Chapels) form a separate structure tacked on to the east end of the church and accessible only from outside the main complex. Dom Duarte, eldest son of João and Philippa, commissioned them in 1437 as a royal mausoleum but, as with the cloister, the original design was transformed beyond all recognition by Dom Manuel's architects. The portal rises to a towering fifteen metres and every centimetre is carved with a honeycomb of mouldings: florid projections, clover-shaped arches, strange vegetables; there are even stone snails. The place is unique among Christian architecture and evocative of the great shrines of Islam and Hinduism: perhaps it was inspired by the tales of Indian monuments that filtered back along the eastern trade routes. It is a perfect illustration of the variety and uninhibited excitement of Portuguese art during the Age of Discovery.

The architect of this masterpiece was Mateus Fernandes, whose tomb lies directly outside the entrance to the Capela do Fundador. Within the portal, a large octagonal space is surrounded by seven hexagonal chapels, two of which contain the sepulchres of Dom Duarte and his queen, Leonor of Aragon. An ambitious upper storey – equal in magnificence to the portal – was designed by Diogo de Boitaca, but the huge buttresses were abandoned a few years later in 1533.

Practicalities

The Batalha stands alone, the huddle of cottages that once surrounded it swept away and replaced by a bare concrete expanse. There's a **turismo** (summer: daily 10am–1pm & 3–7pm; winter daily 2–6pm; ☎244 765 180), but not much else here except a sprinkling of tourist shops, bars and restaurants, which all do brisk business during the Fátima weekend in early October, when the place is packed. **Buses** stop on the central Largo 14 de Agosto de 1385.

Accommodation is limited and the best idea is to see Batalha on a day trip from Leiria. If you do want to stay, try: *Casa do Outeiro*, Largo Carvalho 4 (☎244 765 806; ❹), near the town hall, a charmingly converted small house with a swimming pool; *Residencial Batalha* on Largo da Igreja (☎244 767 500, ℱ244 767 467; ❹), a modern, comfortable option, or the cheaper *Residencial Gladius*, Praça Mouzinho de Albuquerque 7 (☎244 765 760; ❸). For leisured luxury, the *Pousada do Mestre Afonso Domingues*, Largo Mestre Afonso Domingues (☎244 765 260, ⓦwww.pousadas.pt; ❻), is impossible to better. For good-value Portuguese **food**, try *Os Carlos*, near the square on Largo Goa, Damâo e Diu.

Around Batalha

The busy N1 highway carries heavy traffic from Batalha to the small town of **São Jorge**, 4km to the south and site of one of Portugal's most important battles. Just beyond here the quieter N243 branches off to **Porto de Mós**, with its distinctive castle and the added attraction of being the nearest base from which to visit the fabulous **underground caves** at Mira de Aire – which lie within the wild and craggy **Parque Natural das Serras de Aire e Candeeiros**, a good spot to do some **walking**. The N362 provides an alternative scenic route through the park, running from Porto de Mós in the north all the way to Santarém, though the caves themselves are located in the more wooded eastern half of the park.

São Jorge: the battle site

The Battle of Aljubarrota was fought on a plain 10km northeast of Aljubarrota itself, at the small hamlet of **SÃO JORGE**, just 4km south of Batalha. When the fighting was over a **chapel** was built and it still stands today. The battle lasted only one hour, but it was a hot day and the commander of the victorious Portuguese forces, Nuno Álvares Pereira, complained loudly of thirst; even today, a jug of fresh water is placed daily in the porch of the chapel in his memory. Legend has it that Aljubarrota itself was defended by its baker, Brites de

A walk in the Serras de Aire e Candeeiros National Park

The **Serras de Aire e Candeeiros** is a small but scenic national park to the south of Porto de Mós, which contains a mix of rugged limestone hills, crags and upland farmland divided by ancient stone walls. This 10km circular trail – known as the **Algar do Pena** – is well marked with yellow equal signs and begins at Vale da Trave on the southern boundary of the national park. To get there take the bus from Porto de Mós to Mira de Aire and ask the driver to let you off at the junction for Barreiras and Vale da Trave. A 3km walk from the junction brings you to the village Vale da Trave. You should bring along lots of water and a picnic, as no supplies are available along the route.

To begin the walk, take the gravel track that leads from a stone cross in the middle of Vale da Trave, ignoring signs for the Grutas da Pena and keep on the lane to the right. After half a kilometre, the trail forks; at a signpost for the Algar do Pena circuit keep right, following the route through cork and olive groves until you reach an olive tree to the right of the lane, marked with a red equal sign. Turn right here, and 20m down the path a second marked olive tree signals the point where the route threads down along a little-used track between two more prominent lanes. Although overgrown in parts, the trail is well marked and easy to follow to the outskirts of the village of **Cortiçal**, 2km on from Vale da Trave. From here, it swings sharply uphill and to the left, passing a quarry and winding through a series of traditionally built farm buildings hewn from local limestone. Once on top of the barren plateau, **views** open out to the south. For the next 3km, the trail passes several quarries and an old well, eventually going over the brow of a hill and arriving at the **Grutas da Pena** – large caves, similar to the Grutas de Mira de Aire, but not open to casual visitors.

The broad track back from the caves to Vale da Trave leaves from behind the information centre (☎243 999 480), and follows a shallow valley downhill. Several less prominent paths strike off from the route, but you should ignore these and stick to the marked track. After a couple of kilometres, a marked post signals a smaller track off to the left, which leads 50m to a huge iron grate covering the entrance to a large **cavern** – Algar da Aderneira. Several of the bat species found in the park live inside, and a twilight visit may be rewarded with the sight of **bats** emerging for a night's hunting. From here, keeping to the same little track, it's only 1km to Vale da Trave, where you can purchase a cool drink at either of the village's two bars, one of which doubles as a barber.

Almeida, who fended off the Castilian army with her baking spoon. This fearsome weapon dispensed with seven soldiers, whom Brites then proceeded to bake in her oven.

Also in São Jorge, the **Museu Militar** (Tues–Fri 2–5pm, Sat & Sun 10am–noon & 2–5pm) deals with the battle itself and the contemporary political intrigue, while nearby there's a frieze commemorating the battle with carved blocks of stone representing, it is said, the archers and foot soldiers.

None of this is particularly any reason to come, though you can always break your journey here on the way to or from Porto de Mós (see below), 5km to the south; indeed, you may have to change buses in São Jorge anyway.

Porto de Mós

High above the expanding and uninspiring village of **PORTO DE MÓS**, 8km south of Batalha, a grandiose thirteenth-century **castle** stands guard. It was given to Nuno Álvares Pereira in 1385 by the grateful Dom João I in recognition of his victory at Aljubarrota – significantly, the Portuguese army had rested here on the eve of the battle – and was later turned into a fortified palace reminiscent in scale of that at Leiria. Severely damaged in the earthquake of 1755, the castle (Tues–Sun 8am–5pm; free) has been renovated piecemeal since then; restoration continues on the electric-green conical towers. Just below the castle is the town's small **archeology and geology museum** (Tues–Sun 10am–12.30pm & 2–5.30pm; free), which boasts locally collected dinosaur bones amongst its displays.

The town's bus terminal is on Avenida Dr. Francisco Sá Carneiro. On weekdays, there are around three **buses to Porto de Mós** from Leiria, via Batalha, and others from Alcobaça, Santarém and Nazaré (summer only), or from Batalha itself. At other times, you could catch one of the long-distance buses from Leiria or Batalha to Alcobaça or Caldas da Rainha and ask to be set down at São Jorge, just off the main N1, and take a local bus from there to Porto de Mós. The **turismo** (summer daily 10am–1pm & 3–7pm; winter Mon–Sat 10am–1pm & 3–6pm; ☎244 491 323) is on Alameda D. Afonso Henriques in the local public gardens. If you plan **to stay**, there is a campsite, 15 km east at Mendiga (☎244 450 555). Alternatively, in town there is the friendly *Residencial O Filipe*, Largo do Rossio 41 (☎244 401 455, 𝔽244 402 246; ❸); and the *Quinta do Rio Alcaide* (☎244 402 124; ❹), a converted mill with self-catering apartments and a swimming pool, around 1km out of the village on the road to the caves (the N243). Cafés and **restaurants** are grouped around the bus terminal.

The caves
The largest, most spectacular and most accessible caves in Portugal are the **GRUTAS DE MIRA DE AIRE** (daily: Oct–May 9.30am–5.30pm; June & Sept 9.30am–7pm; July & Aug 9.30am–8.30pm; €3.50; ☎244 440 322), ten minutes' walk from the bus stop in the drab textile town from which they take their name. There are three daily **buses** to Mira de Aire from Porto de Mós, at 12.05pm, 2.30pm and 5.20pm. The only return bus leaves from Mira de Aire town at 4.15pm. On weekends, there are buses at 12.05pm and 5.20pm, but no return service: a return trip by **taxi** from Porto de Mós should cost around €13, including a two-hour wait while you visit the caves. Known locally for years but only open to the public since 1974, the caves comprise a fantasy land of spaghetti-like stalactites and stalagmites and bizarre rock formations with names like "Hell's Door", "Jelly Fish" and "Church Organ". Rough steps take you down and the excellent 45-minute guided tour (in French or Portuguese, or even English on occasion) culminates in an extravagant fountain display in a natural lake 110m underground. You might have to wait some time for a group of acceptable size to gather. At the end of the tour, you emerge beside an aquatic park (summer only; use of its pools and slides is included in the entry fee for the caves), a great place to cool off and admire the views.

Fátima and around

FÁTIMA is the fountainhead of religious devotion in Portugal and one of the most important centres of pilgrimage in the Roman Catholic world. Its cult is founded on a series of six **Apparitions of the Virgin Mary**, in the first of which, on May 13, 1917, three peasant children from the village were confronted, while tending their parents' flock, with a flash of lightning and "a lady brighter than the sun" sitting in the branches of a tree. According to the memoirs of Lúcia, who was the only one who could hear what was said – and the only one of the children to survive into her teens – the Lady announced, "I am from Heaven. I have come to ask you to return here six times, at this same hour, on the thirteenth of every month. Then, in October, I will tell you who I am and what I want."

News of the miracle was greeted with scepticism, and only a few casual onlookers attended the second appearance, but for the third, July 13, apparition, the crowd had swollen to a few thousand. Although only the three children could see the heavenly visitor, Fátima became a *cause célèbre*, with the anticlerical government accusing the Church of fabricating a miracle to revive its flagging influence, and Church authorities afraid to acknowledge what they feared was a hoax. The children were arrested and interrogated but refused to change their story.

By the date of the final appearance, October 13, as many as 70,000 people had converged on Fátima where they witnessed the so-called **Miracle of the Sun**. Eyewitnesses described the skies clearing and the sun, intensified to a blinding, swirling ball of fire, shooting beams of multicoloured light to earth. Lifelong illnesses, supposedly, were cured; the blind could see again and the dumb were able to speak. It was enough to convince most of the terrified witnesses. Nevertheless, the three children remained the only ones actually to see the Virgin, and only Lúcia could communicate with her.

To her were revealed the three **Secrets of Fátima**. The first was a message of peace (this was during World War I) and a vision of Hell, with anguished, charred souls plunged into an ocean of fire. The second was more prophetic and controversial: "If you pay heed to my request," the vision declared, "Russia will be converted and there will be peace. If not, Russia will spread her errors through the world, causing wars and persecution against the Church" – all this just a few weeks before the Bolshevik takeover in St Petersburg, though not, perhaps, before it could have been predicted. After decades of speculation, the third secret was revealed in May 2000 by the Vatican. It had apparently predicted the attempt on Pope John Paul II's life in 1981, fortelling of a "bishop clothed in white" who "falls to the ground, apparently dead, under a burst of gunfire". The announcement was made in Fatima during an emotional ceremony in front of more than 60,000 people. The complete text will apparently be published after "appropriate" preparation.

The Basilica and the Town

To commemorate the extraordinary events and to accommodate the hordes of pilgrims who flock here, a shrine has been built, which has little to recommend it but its size. The vast white **Basilica**, completed in 1953, and its gigantic esplanade are capable of holding more than a million devotees. In the church the **tombs of Jacinta and Francisco** – Lúcia's fellow witnesses, both of whom died in the European flu epidemic of 1919–20 – are the subject of constant attention in their chapels. Long Neoclassical colonnades flank the basilica and enclose part of the sloping esplanade in front. This huge area, reminiscent of an airport runway, is twice the size of the piazza of St Peter's in Rome. On its left-hand side the original oak tree in which the Virgin appeared was long ago consumed by souvenir-hunting pilgrims; the small **Chapel of the Apparitions** now stands in its place, with a new tree a few yards away.

Whatever your feelings about the place, there is an undeniable atmosphere of mystery around it, perhaps created by nothing more than the obvious faith of the vast majority of its visitors. It's all at its most intense during the great **annual pilgrimages** on May 12–13 and October 12–13. Crowds of up to 100,000 congregate, most arriving on foot, some even walking on their knees in penance. Open-air Mass is celebrated at 5am and an image of the Virgin is paraded by candlelight as priests move among the pilgrims hearing confessions. The fiftieth anniversary of the apparitions attracted one-and-a-half million worshippers, including Pope Paul VI and Lúcia – who is still alive, a Carmelite nun in the Convent of Santa Teresa near Coimbra. Lúcia was again part of the vast crowds that greeted John Paul II here in 1982 and 1991.

A multitude of hotels, car parks, hospices and convents have sprung up in the shadow of the basilica. Inevitably the fame of Fátima has resulted in its commercialization and some of the town's last surviving old houses and mansions are under threat of demolition to make way for further developments. (The latest plan is to build a covered area to shelter up to ten thousand people during open-air Mass.) As each year goes by, the grotesquely kitsch souvenirs on sale move into hitherto unexplored territories of tastelessness – look out for the Fátima ballpoint pens, which tilt to reveal the Virgin in Glory. Business is particularly brisk on Sunday, when thousands of local families converge by bus, car, lorry and cart, often just for a family picnic – yet the shrine itself is not yet swamped. Make sure you catch the daily torchlit procession at dusk, which can be uplifting whatever your religious feelings; the procession is largest on the twelfth day of each month.

The town's other attractions include the **Museu de Cera** (Wax Museum; daily: April–Oct 9.30am–6.30pm; Nov–March 10am–5pm; €3.50) on Rua Jacinta Marto, which relates the story of the miracle in 28 scenes filled with somewhat grotesque wax figures. There is also a pleasant walk from the Rotunda de Santa Teresa de Ourém, on the outskirts of town, up to the place of the "**Apparitions of the Angel**", along which pilgrims follow the Stations of the Cross.

Practicalities

There are regular **bus services** to Fátima from Leiria (25km to the northwest) and Tomar (35km east) making it an easy day trip. Coming **from Batalha** (20km west) on the N356, you'll pass Reguengo do Fétal, another pilgrimage site that's host to a torchlit procession (lit by burning oil carried in shells) up to a hilltop sanctuary around October 3. If you arrive **by train**, you'll need to get a local bus (there's not always an immediate connection) from Estação de Fátima, a hefty 25km east of town; the station is on the main Lisbon–Porto line. The **turismo** (daily: May–Oct 10am–1pm & 3–7pm; closes at 6pm in winter; ☎249 531 139, ⓦwww.rt-leiriafatima.pt) is just off the main esplanade and through-road, the Avenida D. José Alves Correia da Silva. If you'd like to go online, there's **internet** access at *Centro de Copias,* R.S. João de Deus, Edif. Varandas de Fátima 13 (daily 10am–7pm; €2.50/hr; ☎249 532 260).

The basilica and its huge esplanade cut the town in half; on the west side of the basilica is Rua Jacinta Marto, while to the east the main street becomes Rua Francisco Marto. *Pensões* and restaurants abound in Fátima, but during the pilgrimages (when most accommodation is booked up months in advance) people camp all around the back and sides of the basilica. However, outside the major pilgrimages – and weekends – there's enough **accommodation** to go round, since many of the older boarding houses are built on monastic lines, with over a hundred rooms and private chapels; the huge modern hotels which abound can be bargains in low season. Otherwise, try *Residencial Santo Amaro,* Rua Francisco Marto 59 (☎249 530 171, ⓕ249 532 904; ❸), with modern, comfortable rooms but away from the main area of restaurants and bars; *Residencial São Paulo,* Rua de São Paulo 10 (☎249 531 572, ⓕ249 533 257; ❷), another modern giant, but friendly and welcoming; or, best of all, *Irmãs Dominicanos*, Rua Francisco Marto 50 (☎249 533 317, ⓕ249 532 688; ❹), one of the few remaining attractive old buildings.

One of the best **restaurants** is *Santa Cruz*, on the corner of Rua Jacinta Marto and Rua de São José, with a pleasant outlook and reasonably priced dishes. Other possibilities are *O Zé Grande*, Rua Jacinta Marto 32, or *Restaurante O Truão* (☎249 521 542), 4km out of Fátima at Boleiros but worth the trip.

Grutas da Moeda

Six kilometres west of Fátima, the labyrinthine **Grutas da Moeda** (daily: April–Sept 9am–6pm; Oct–March 9am–5pm; €3; ☎044 704 302, ⓦwww.Fatimavirtual.com/GrutasMoeda) at **SÃO MAMEDE** are well worth seeing, not least because one of the chambers has been converted into a bar with rock music, subtle lighting and stalactites nose-diving into your glass of beer. With haggling, you should be able to arrange a reasonably priced taxi, though you may have to wait for a group to form before you can enter the caves.

Ourém

If you have your own transport, you may prefer to visit Fátima from the quieter base of **OURÉM**, 12km east, staying at *Pensão Ouriense*, Avenida D. Nuno Álvares Pereira ☎249 542 202; ❷). Although the new town, Vila Nova de Ourém, is nothing special, Ourém **castle** (no set hours; free) is just 2km above it, sitting on a hilltop within an impressive medieval walled town. The town's heyday was in the fifteenth century, when the fourth count of Ourém, Don Afonso, built several grand monuments and converted the castle into a palace. The castle was virtually destroyed by Napoleon's forces, but is now largely restored; walk around its parapet, and you'll get stunning views, with the basilica in Fátima to the west. The well-signed history trail round the old town will lead you to the **cisterns** (daily 3–6pm), which, according to local legend, have never run dry. Look out also for the fifteenth-century **fountain** by the town gates. The **turismo**, to your right as you enter the old town (Tues–Sun: May–Sept 10am–1pm & 3–7pm; Oct–April 2–6pm; ☎249 544 654) can provide maps and also arrange guides for visits to the small archeological **museum** (☎249 540 900; free).

Tomar

The Convento de Cristo at **TOMAR**, 34km east of Fátima, is an artistic *tour de force* which entwines the most outstanding military, religious and imperial strands in the history of Portugal. The Order of the Knights Templar and their successors, the Order of Christ, established their headquarters here and successive Grand Masters employed experts in Romanesque, Manueline and Renaissance architecture to embellish and expand the convent in a manner worthy of their power, prestige and wealth.

In addition, Tomar is an attractive town in its own right, well worth a couple of days of slow exploration. Built on a simple grid plan, it is split in two by the Rio Nabão, with almost everything of interest on the west bank. Here, Tomar's old quarters preserve much of their traditional charm, with whitewashed,

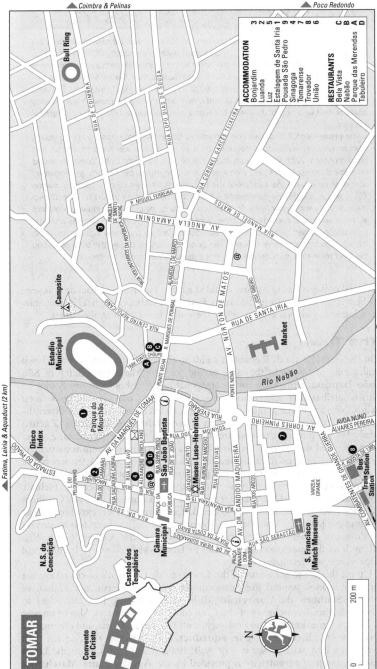

TOMAR

▲ *Coimbra & Pelinas* ▲ *Poco Redondo*

Bull Ring

RUA DE COIMBRA
RUA LOPO DIAS DE SOUSA
RUA CORONEL GARCES TEIXEIRA

R. MIGUEL FERREIRA
PRAÇA DE SANTO ANTÓNIO-ANDRÉ
AV. ANGELA TAMAGNINI
RUA MANOEL DE MATOS
ALMEDA TE MARCO
RUA JOSÉ RIBEIRO
RUA UTILITARISTAS DA REPUBLICA

Campsite
Estadio Municipal
RUA CENTRO REPUBLICANO
R. MARQUES DE POMBAL
RUA DE SANTA IRIA

@

Parque do Mouchão
TRAV. FONTE CHOUPO
PONTE VELHA
A B C
AV. NORTON DE MATOS

Market

Disco Index
ESTRADA DO PRADO
▲ *Fatima, Leiria & Aquaduct (2 km)*

PONTE NOVA
Rio Nabão

i
AV. DR. MARQUES DE TOMAR
RUA EVERARDO

▶ *Santarém, Castelo do Bode, 9 & Reservoir*

Disco Index
L. DO PELOURINHO
AV. DR CAMARÃO
RUA DR. CAMARÃO
RUA MAGALHÃES
SILVA
RUA SACADURA CABRAL
RUA GIL AVÔ
RUA ALEXANDRE HERCULANO
RUA SERPA PINTO
RUA DOS MOINHOS
AV. TORRES PINHEIRO

N.S. da Conceição

Castelo dos Templários

Convento de Cristo

São João Baptista
Museu Luso-Hebraico
RUA DOS
RUA D. JOAQUIM JACINTO
RUA DE S. JOÃO
RUA PEDRO DIAS
RUA D. AURORA DE MACEDO
RUA INFANTARIA 15
AV. DR. CANDIDO MADUREIRA

Câmara Municipal
PRAÇA DA REPUBLICA
@

AVDA NUNO ALVARES PEREIRA
Bus Station
R. AGOSTA DE 1385
Train Station
AV. COMBATENTES DE GRANDE GUERRA

VARZEA GRANDE

i
PRAÇA INNANTE DOM HENRIQUE
RUA DR VIEIRA GUIMARÃES
RUA DA COSTA BAIXO
RUA SÃO SEBASTÃO

S. Francisco (Match Museum)

N

0 200 m

The Festa dos Tabuleiros

Tomar is renowned throughout the country for its **Festa dos Tabuleiros** (literally, the Festival of the Trays). Its origins can be traced back to the saintly Queen Isabel who founded the Brotherhood of the Holy Spirit in the fourteenth century, though some believe it to derive from an ancient fertility rite dedicated to Ceres. Whatever its origins, it's now a largely secular event, held at three- or four-yearly intervals. The next one is likely to happen in July 2003, but check with the local turismo. It's a five-day affair, at the beginning of July, with the highlight – the parade of "trays" – on the final Sunday.

The **procession** (Procissão dos Tabuleiros) consists of four hundred or so young women wearing white, each escorted by a young man in a white shirt, red tie and black trousers. Each woman carries on her head a tray with thirty loaves threaded on vertical canes, intertwined with leaves and colourful paper flowers, and crowned with a white dove – the symbol of the Holy Spirit. The resulting headdress weighs 15kg, and is roughly person-height – hence the need for an escort to lift and help balance it. As with other festivals, there's music and dancing in the streets, fireworks at dawn and dusk, and a bullfight the night before the procession. The day after the procession, bread, wine and beef are distributed to the local needy, following Isabel's injunction to "give bread to the poor" – needless to say, the bulls providing the beef have their own procession, three days before that of the *tabuleiros*.

terraced cottages lining narrow cobbled streets. This pleasing backdrop is seen to best effect during Tomar's famous **Festa dos Tabuleiros**, held at intermittent intervals (see box above), when the entire town takes to the streets.

The Town

On the central Praça da República stands an elegant seventeenth-century town hall, a ring of houses of the same period, and the Manueline church of **São João Baptista**, remarkable for its octagonal belfry, elaborate doorway, and six panels attributed to Gregório Lopes (1490–1550), one of Portugal's finest artists. Nearby at Rua Joaquim Jacinto 73 is an excellently preserved fifteenth-century synagogue, now the **Museu Luso–Hebraico Abraham Zacuto** (daily 10am–7pm; free), named after the Spanish astronomer, Abraham Zacuto, who prepared navigational aids for Vasco da Gama. The museum is particularly interesting in a town dominated for so long by crusading Defenders of the Faith, and its stark interior, with plain vaults supported by four slender columns, houses a collection of thirteenth- to fourteenth-century Hebraic inscriptions. In 1496 Dom Manuel followed the example of the Reis Católicos (Catholic Kings) of Spain and ordered the conversion or expulsion of all Portuguese Jews. The synagogue at Tomar was one of the very few to survive so far south – there's another at Castelo de Vide in the Alentejo (see p.487). Many Jews fled northwards, especially to Trás-os-Montes where Inquisitional supervision was less hawk-eyed.

Up on the hill to the north of the Convento de Cristo, it's worth taking the time for a look around the unassumingly beautiful Renaissance church of **Nossa Senhora da Conceição** (daily 11am–6.45pm). It is attributed to Diogo de Torralva, architect of the Convento's Great Cloisters. Also of interest is the town **market**, held on Fridays, just off Rua de Santa Iria, and the impressive seventeenth-century Pegões **aqueduct**, built to supply the convent with water; the best place to see it – or walk along it – is 2km out on the Leiria road. A touch of eccentricity is provided by the **Aguiles Lima Matchstick**

Museum (daily 10am–noon & 2–4pm), inside the Convento de São Francisco, which claims to have the largest match collection in Europe.

The Convento de Cristo

The **Convento de Cristo** (Tues–Sun: June–Sept 9.15am–12.30pm & 2–6pm; Oct–May 2–5pm; €2.50) is set among pleasant gardens with splendid views, about a quarter of an hour's walk uphill from the centre of town. Founded in 1162 by Gualdim Pais, first and grandest Master of the **Knights Templar**, it was the headquarters of the Order and, as such, both a religious and a military centre.

One of the main objectives of the Templars was to expel the Moors from Spain and Portugal, a reconquest seen always as a crusade – the defence of Christianity against the Infidel. Spiritual strength was an integral part of the military effort and, despite magnificent additions, the sacred heart of the whole complex remains the **Charola** (also known as the Rotunda or Templars' Apse), the twelfth-century temple from which the Knights drew their moral conviction. It is a strange place, more suggestive of the occult than of Christianity. At the centre of the sixteen-sided, almost circular, chapel stands the high altar, surrounded by a two-storeyed octagon. Deep alcoves, decorated with sixteenth-century paintings, are cut into the outside walls. The Templars are said to have attended mass on horseback. Like almost every circular church, it is ultimately based on the Church of the Holy Sepulchre in Jerusalem, for whose protection the Knights Templar were originally founded.

Dom Manuel's additions

By 1249 the reconquest in Portugal was completed and the Templars reaped enormous rewards for their services. Tracts of land were turned over to them and they controlled a network of castles throughout the Iberian peninsula. But as the Moorish threat receded, the Knights became a powerful political challenge to the stability and authority of European monarchs.

Philippe-le-Bel, King of France, took the lead by confiscating all Templar property in his country, and there followed a formal papal suppression of the Order in 1314. In Spain this prompted a vicious witch-hunt and many of the Knights sought refuge in Portugal, where Dom Dinis coolly reconstituted them in 1320 under a different title: the **Order of Christ**. They inherited all the Portuguese property of the Templars, including the headquarters at Tomar, but their power was now subject to that of the throne.

In the fifteenth and sixteenth centuries, the Order of Christ played a leading role in extending Portugal's overseas empire and was granted spiritual jurisdiction over all conquests. Prince Henry the Navigator was Grand Master from 1417 to 1460, and the remains of his **Palace** in the Convento de Cristo can be seen immediately to the right upon entering the castle walls. Henry ordered two new cloisters, the **Claustro do Cemitério** and the **Claustro da Lavagem**, both reached via a short corridor from the Charola and attractively lined with *azulejos*.

Dom Manuel succeeded to the Grand Mastership in 1492, three years before he became king. Flush with imperial wealth, he decided to expand the convent by adding a rectangular **nave** to the west side of the Charola. This new structure was divided into two storeys: the lower serving as a chapterhouse, the upper as a choir. The **main doorway**, which leads directly into the nave, was built by João de Castilho in 1515, two years before Dom Manuel appointed him Master of Works at Belém. Characteristically unconcerned with structural matters,

Manueline architecture

With the new-found wealth and confidence engendered by the "Discoveries", came a distinctly Portuguese version of late Gothic architecture. Named after King Manuel I (1495–1521), the **Manueline style** is characterized by a rich and, often, fantastical use of ornamentation. Doors, windows and arcades are encrusted by elaborately carved stonework, in which the imagery of the sea is freely combined with both symbols of Christianity and of the newly discovered lands.

The style first appeared at the Igreja de Jesus (1494–98), in **Setúbal** (see p.144), where each of the columns of the nave are made up of three strands of stone seemingly wrapped around each other like rope. This relatively restrained building is the work of Diogo Boitac, who later supervised the initial construction of the great Jéronimos monastery at **Bélem**, a few miles downstream from Lisbon (see p.98). Commissioned by the king, this is a far more exuberant structure with an elaborately carved south portal opening onto a nave where the vaulting ribs seem to sprout out of the thin, trunk-like columns like leaves from a palm tree. Bélem was the point from which many of the Portuguese navigators set forth, and the new building was largely subsidized by the new, lucrative spice trade.

The Jéronimos monastery is the most unified expression of the new style, but Manuel I also commissioned lavish extensions to existing buildings, like the Convento do Cristo at **Tomar** (see p.189). This is arguably the most brilliant and original expression of Manueline decoration. In particular, the famous sacristy window is a riot of virtuosic stone carving, in which twisted strands of coral, opulent flower heads and intricately knotted ropes are crowned by the royal coat of arms, the cross of the Order of Christ and two armillary spheres.

The armillary sphere – a navigational instrument – became the personal emblem of King Manuel, and frequently appears in Manueline decoration. It can be seen at the great abbey at **Batalha** (see p.179) in the screens set within the top half of the arches of the Claustro Real (Royal Cloister). The intricate tracery of these screens suggest Islamic filigree work and may well have been directly influenced by buildings in India. Beyond the church is a royal mausoleum begun by King Duarte and continued by King Manuel I but never completed. This octagonal building with seven radiating chapels is entered through a vast trefoil-arched portal that is smothered in a profusion of ornament (including snails and artichokes) that seems to defy the material from which it's carved. Work on the chapels was stopped in 1533, leaving the great stumps of the half-built piers stranded and abandoned to the elements.

Not all Manueline architecture was ecclesiastical: there were also palaces, like that of the Dukes of Bragança at **Vila Viçosa** (see p.474), and castles, like the one at **Évora Monte** (see p.470) where the whole of the exterior is bound by a single stone rope. Most famous of all secular constructions is the **Torre de Bélem** (see p.99), a fortress built on an island in the Tagus which incorporates Moorish-style balconies, domed look-out posts, battlements in the form of shields, and even a carving of a rhinoceros.

Manueline architecture did not continue much beyond the fourth decade of the sixteenth century. In the reign of Manuel's successor, King João III, a more austere religious atmosphere prevailed in which the decorative excesses of the Manueline style were replaced by the ordered sobriety of Italian classicism.

the architect profusely adorned the doorway with appliqué decoration. There are strong similarities in this respect with contemporary Isabelline and Plateresque architecture in Spain.

The crowning highlight of Tomar, though, is the sculptural ornamentation of the windows on the main facade of the **chapterhouse**. The richness and self-confidence of Manueline art always suggests the Age of Discovery, but here the

△ Convento de Cristo, Tomar

connection is crystal clear. A wide range of maritime motifs is jumbled up in two tumultuous window frames, as eternal memorials to the sailors who established the Portuguese Empire. Everything is here: anchors, buoys, sails, coral, seaweed and especially ropes, knotted over and over again into an escapologist's nightmare.

The windows can only be fully appreciated from the roof of the **Claustro de Santa Bárbara**, adjacent to the Great Cloisters, which unfortunately almost completely obscure a similar window on the south wall of the chapterhouse.

A new style: João III

João III (1521–57) transformed the convent from the general political headquarters of the Order into a thoroughgoing monastic community, and he endowed it with the necessary conventual buildings: dormitories, kitchens and no fewer than four new cloisters (making a grand total of seven). Yet another, much more classical, style was introduced into the architectural melange of Tomar. So meteoric was the rise and fall of Manueline art within the reign of Dom Manuel that, to some extent, it must have reflected his personal tastes. João III on the other hand had an entirely different view of art. He is known to have sent schools of architects and sculptors to study in Italy, and his reign finally marked the much-delayed advent of the Renaissance in Portugal.

The two-tiered **Great Cloisters**, abutting the chapterhouse, are one of the purest examples of this new style. Begun in 1557, they present a textbook illustration of the principals of Renaissance neoclassicism. Greek columns, gentle arches and simple rectangular bays produce a wonderfully restrained rhythm. At the southwest corner a balcony looks out on to the skeletal remains of a second chapterhouse, begun by João III but never completed.

Practicalities

The **train** and **bus stations**, on Avenida Combatentes da Grande Guerra, are within easy walking distance of the centre. Head directly north and you'll soon hit Avenida Dr. Cândido Madureira, at the top end of which there's a **turismo** (daily: April–Sept 10am–7pm; Oct–March 9.30am–6pm; ℗249 322 427, Ⓔgeral.rrtemplários@ip.pt), which can give details of local walks round the Sete Montes National Forest. The turismo faces a fierce statue of Infante Dom Henrique and the gates of a park, which once formed the gardens of the Convento de Cristo, however there is talk of a relocation. There's also a **regional tourist office** at the bottom of Rua Serpa Pinto (Mon–Fri 9.30am–12.30pm & 2–6pm; ℗249 329 000). The Biblioteca Municipal offers **internet** access at Rua Gualdin Pais, as does *Residencial Luz*, Rua Serpa Pinto 144 for €2 per hour.

Accommodation

Tomar has a good range of **accommodation** and finding a room should be pretty straightforward. The only time when it could be tricky is during the Festa dos Tabuleiros (see box on p.188). There's a pleasant municipal **campsite** (℗249 322 608, Ⓕ249 322 608), out towards the football stadium and an even nicer site 14km out of town at Castelo do Bode (℗249 849 262, Ⓕ249 849 244), served by two buses daily from Tomar. It's set amid pine woods by the reservoir and you can rent out boats to visit the islands in the lake. The pleasant campsite *Campismo Rural* (℗249 301 814, in the small village of Pelinos, 7km out of town on the road to Coimbra, rents out **mountain bikes** and can arrange **canoeing** trips; but beware that the sporadic buses here from Tomar can take up to two hours. There is another campsite – even further out – at Poço Redondo, 10km east of Tomar (☎ & ℗ 249 376 421).

Pensão Bonjardim Praçeta de Santo André ☎ 249 313 195, ℗ 249 316 136. Basic but adequate, though some way out, across the river. ❸

Residencial Luanda Av Marquês de Tomar 15 ☎ 249 315 153, ℗ 249 322 145. Modern and comfortable *pensão* facing the river. All the rooms come with bath. ❹

Residencial Luz Rua Serpa Pinto 144 ☎ 249 312 317, ℗ 249 312 753. Simple, old-fashioned rooms but can be good value, especially those for four to six people. ❸

Estalagem de Santa Iria Parque do Mouchão ☎ 249 313 326, ℮ estalagem.iria@clix.pt. In the park, by the river, Somerset Maugham once stayed here – but then he was rich. Its restaurant, however, is good value. ❻

Pousada São Pedro Castelo do Bode ☎ 249 381 159, ☯ www.pousadas.pt. Overlooking the reservoir, 13km from Tomar, this is a great place to

unwind if you have the funds. ❻

Residencial Sinagoga Rua Gil Avô 31 ☎ 249 323 083, ℗ 249 322 196. Near the town hall, this smart place has air conditioning and satellite TV in all rooms. ❹

Pensão Tomarense Av Torres Pinheiro 13 ☎ 249 312 948, ℗ 249 323 419. Not a first choice, but cheap. Rooms are spartan and, at the front, noisy, but there are fine views of the convent from the rear rooms. Breakfast included. ❷

Residencial Trovador Rua de Agosto de 1385 ☎ 249 322 567, ℗ 249 322 194. Light and airy modern *residencial* facing the bus station. ❹

Residencial União Rua Serpa Pinto 94 ☎ 249 323 161, ℗ 249 321 299. Central and very popular; in July and Aug advance booking is essential. Nice rooms around a courtyard, all with private bath or shower. ❹

Eating, drinking and nightlife

Many of the *pensões* in Tomar have **restaurants** attached. Midday, the busiest **cafés and bars** are on Avenida Dr. Cândido Madureira and around the Varzea Grande; on a summer's evening there's more action on the riverside. The liveliest **dance venue** is *Index* on Estrada do Prado 2.

Bela Vista Trav. Fonte Choupo 6. Justifiably the town's most renowned restaurant, by the river, with full meals for around €10; try the chicken curry. Closed Mon evening, Tues & Nov.

Restaurante Nabão Trav. Fonte Choupo 3. Standard Portuguese favourites at moderate prices and with a river view. Closed Wed.

Restaurante Parque das Merendas Situated by

the river, this has a somewhat limited menu, but it's cheap and in a lovely position, with a lively café attached.

Restaurante Tabuleiro Rua Serpa Pinto 140. Elegant restaurant on pedestrian street serving traditional Portuguese food with an emphasis on grilled meats and yummy desserts. Closed Tues.

East along the Tejo to Abrantes

Eighteen kilometres south of Tomar, the N110 road and the railway both divide at the dull town of Entroncamento. From here, one branch of the railway swings east to follow the Rio Tejo past **Tancos** and the remarkable castle at **Almourol**, meeting the Rio Zêzere at **Constância**, one of the most attractive towns on the Tejo. By road, an alternative route to Constância is via Castelo do Bode, which will also take you across the dam (Barragem do Castelo do Bode). From Constância, the Tejo retains its rural hue for the 12km east to **Abrantes**, a town with a historic centre and the last significant stop on the river, beyond which road and rail routes branch out for Spain or north and south for the rest of the country.

Almourol and Tancos

As if conjured up by some medieval-minded magician, the **castle of Almourol** stands deserted on a tiny island in the middle of the Tejo. Built by the Knights Templar in 1171, it never saw military action – except in sixteenth-century romantic literature – and its double perimeter walls and ten small towers are perfectly preserved. It's military property but there's no objection to visitors, and once inside you'll be granted a beautiful rural panorama from the tall central keep.

The train line hugs the northern banks of the Tejo at this point and there are two convenient stations, Tancos and Almourol, thirty and fifteen minutes' walk respectively from the island. The latter is stuck in the middle of nowhere but **TANCOS** is actually a small village with a couple of bars catering to a nearby army barracks. To reach the castle from Tancos, you'll need to take a taxi; the river banks are an impassable forest of eucalyptus trees, cacti and assorted bushes.

Constância

CONSTÂNCIA, 3km upstream from Almourol, is a convenient place to stay the night after a visit to the castle. A sleepy, incredibly picturesque, whitewashed town, arranged like an amphitheatre around the Tejo and the mouth of the Rio Zêzere, it is best known in Portugal for its association with **Luís de Camões**, Portugal's national poet. In fact, Camões was here for only three years (1547–50), taking refuge from the court of Dom João III, whom he had managed to offend by the injudicious dedication of a love sonnet to a woman on whom the king himself had designs. Constância, however, is said to have remained dear to the poet's heart until the end of his life. In more troubled times, the town served the Duke of Wellington in 1809: he amassed his forces here and prepared for the Battle of Talavera in Spain. Nowadays, Constância is at its liveliest during the **Festa dos Barqueiros**, on Easter Monday, with parades and traditional boats on the Tejo.

For Constância, get off the **train** at Praia do Ribatejo-Constância, the stop after Almourol. If you want **to stay**, ask for *dormidas* in the central cafés or try one of the following: the spotless *Residencial Casa João Chagas*, on Rua João Chagas near the main square (☎249 739 403, ⓕ 249 739 458; ❸); the fantastic Privetur property, *Casa O Palácio* (☎249 739 224; ❹), by the water's edge; or the very pleasant rural *Quinta de Santa Bárbara* (☎249 739 214, ⓕ249 739 373; ❺), 1km out of town, off the road to Abrantes. There is a **campsite** (☎249 739 546) by the river beach, next to the Horto de Camões gardens, which are based on the gardens described in Camões' epic poem, *Os Lusíadas*. An alternative campsite is in an attractive lakeside setting at Castelo do Bode 9km to the north, up the Rio Zêzere (see p.192).

Abrantes

ABRANTES is perched strategically above the Tejo, 15km upstream of Almourol. The pretty streets and *praças* here are at their best in spring and summer when the flowers on Rua da Barca and in the Jardim da República are in bloom; the views are also impressive. Additionally, the town has useful train connections linking up with the lower Beiras and the Alto Alentejo.

The high point – in all respects – is the town's battered **Castelo** (Mon–Fri 9am–noon & 1–5pm, Sat & Sun 10am–1pm & 2–6pm), constructed in the early fourteenth century. As at Santarém (see p.197), Romans and Moors established strongholds here, and the citadel was again sharply contested during the Peninsular War. The chapel of **Santa Maria do Castelo**, within the fort, houses a motley archeological museum, its prize exhibits being three tombs of the Almeidas, Counts of Abrantes. From the battlements there's a terrific view of the countryside and the rooftops of Abrantes and the gardens around its old town walls. The two large, whitewashed churches visible from here were both rebuilt in the sixteenth century.

Practicalities

The **turismo** (Mon 9am–noon & 2–6pm, Tues–Thurs 9am–6pm, Fri, Sat & Sun 10am–1pm & 2–6pm; ☎241 362 555) is in the town hall on Largo 1 de Maio. Tejo **buses** stop a kilometre or so down the hill, in a separate depot on the way to the IP6 highway. There are two local **train stations**, both out of town. The main one is 2km south, across the Tejo, and all trains stop there; you could walk into the centre from here, but it's uphill all the way – shared taxis aren't too expensive.

If you want to **stay**, there are three decent *pensões* in the old centre: first choice for atmosphere is the old and very pleasant *Pensão Central*, Praça Raimundo Soares 15 (☎241 362 422; ❷); the *Pensão Aliança*, Largo do Chafariz 50 (☎241 362 348; ❸), owned by the same proprietor, is slightly less characterful but has better facilities, with showers in some rooms. *Pensão Lírios*, Praça Barao da Batalha 31 (☎241 362 142; ❸), is another reliable choice. A kilometre out of town, just off the road to the IP6 highway, is the more modern *Hotel de Turismo* (☎241 361 261, ✉hotelabrantes@eol.pt; ❺), with its own tennis courts and pool. Abrantes' nearest **campsite** (☎241 333 550) is in Rossio ao Sul do Tejo, 5km away over the bridge on the south side of the Tejo.

There are a number of reasonable **restaurants** in Abrantes: *Fumeiro* at Rua do Pisco 9 (closed Sun) serves good Portuguese staples, while *Nova Grelha*, Rua Montéiro de Lima, is the place for good-quality, chunky, grilled food. The locals' favourite is *A Cascata* (closed Mon), 3km out of town, at Alferrarede, near the second train station. *Tasquinha do Américo* (☎241 333 884), at Rossio ao Sul do Tejo, is highly recommended for those with transport, or if you're staying at the campsite.

Ribatejo: along the east bank

Seven kilometres south of Entroncamento, the attractive town of **Golegã** is one of the main crossing points to the east bank of the Rio Tejo – bull-breeding territory, full of rich plains and riverside marshes. This side of the river isn't as accessible by bus or train but, with your own transport, the N118 from here marks the most attractive route along the river, taking in several small historic towns, villages and *quintas* worth passing by en route to Lisbon or the Alentejo coast. Accommodation isn't particularly plentiful, but then you're unlikely to want to stop for any great length of time, except during their energetic annual **festivals**, when accommodation gets booked up in advance.

Golegã

GOLEGÃ, on the west bank of the Tejo, midway between Tomar and Santarém, is a very pleasant town, best known for its **Feira Nacional do Cavalo** (National Horse Fair), held during the first two weeks in November. The fair incorporates celebrations for St Martin's Day on November 11, when there's a running of the bulls and a grand parade in which red-waistcoated grooms mingle with gypsies. Culinary diversions include roasted chestnuts and barbecued chickens, accompanied by *água-pé* (literally "foot water") – a light wine made by adding water to the crushed grape husks left after the initial wine production. During the evening, people crowd into the *Restaurante Central*, on Largo da Imaculada Conceição, both to eat and to mingle with haughty *cavaleiros* who have survived the bullfighting.

Golegã also boasts two museums: the **Museu Municipal de Pintura e Escultura Martins Correia** (Tues–Sun: June–Sept 11am–12.30pm & 3–5pm; Oct–May 10am–12.30pm & 3–6pm; free), opposite the Igreja Matriz, which houses an impressive collection of contemporary art and sculpture; and the amazing **Casa-Museu de Fotografia Carlos Relvas**, at the top of Rua José F. Relvas (same hours; free). Carlos Relvas was father of the Republican José Relvas (see below) and, ironically, godfather to King Carlos, who was assassinated by Republicans in 1908. The museum is an archive of Relvas's interest in the newly discovered art of photography and contains some thirteen thousand glass negatives. The house itself is worthy of being a museum piece; it's a fantastic fairy-tale building designed by Henrique Carlos Afonso and set in landscaped gardens. Other attractions in Golegã include the sixteenth-century **Igreja Matriz**, with its Manueline door, and the nearby Reserva Natural Parque do Paúl do Boquilobo, 5km out of Golegã off the road to Azinhaga, where you may be lucky enough to spot some otters.

If you want **to stay** in Golegã, *Restaurante Central* (☎249 976 345) is your best bet, with a few rooms to rent, though they'll almost certainly be occupied during the fair. There's also a lovely **campsite** (☎249 976 222) very close to the Igreja Matriz. Otherwise, if you're continuing south along the west bank, you could stay at the *Casa de Santo António da Azinhaga*, Rua Nova de Santo António (☎249 957 162, ⓕ 249 957 122; ⓪), in the attractive stream-side village of Azinhaga, 12km southwest from Golegã, where you can also find *Patio do Burgo*, a popular local restaurant serving traditional fare.

Chamusca

Across the Tejo from Golegã and 9km by road, **CHAMUSCA** is the most northerly of the east bank's bullfighting towns. Its **Festa da Ascensão** – six days of bull-running and bullfighting – is held during the week incorporating Ascension Day (ie, forty days after Easter) and also features a craft fair. Outside these times, the town remains attractive enough for a brief stopover: the 1930s-style **Casa Rural Tradicional** (summer daily 10am–8pm; winter Mon–Fri 9.30am–7.30pm; €1.25) – a country house reconstructed with traditional furnishings – and the municipal swimming pool, both in the park alongside Largo 25 de Abril, are the main attractions.

Alpiarça

ALPIARÇA, on the east bank 18km south of Chamusca (and just 10km east of Santarém), boasts the **Casa Museu dos Patudos** (Mon–Fri 10am–5.30pm, Sat & Sun 10am–1pm & 2–5.30pm; €2.50), on Rua José Relvas south of town, which was originally the home of José Relvas (1858–1929). Musician, art collector, landowner, bullfighter, diplomat and politician, José is best known as the man who proclaimed the Portuguese Republic in Lisbon in 1910. The exterior of the house, designed by Raul Lino, is striking, with a colonnade and outdoor staircases to the first floor. Inside, you'll find priceless collections of Portuguese paintings, porcelain, furniture, tapestries and over forty carpets from Arraiolos, including one embroidered in silk and dating from 1701. The

turismo in the town hall (☎243 559 100) may be able to help with renting **rooms**; otherwise, there's a French owned **campsite** (☎243 557 040) beyond the museum and off the Almeirim road.

Almeirim and Salvaterra de Magos

Seven kilometres south of Alpiarça lies **ALMEIRIM**, whose golden days were during the reign of the House of Avis (1383–1580), when the royal family – ensconced at Santarém, just 7km to the northwest – hunted from a summer palace on the riverside here. Nothing remains of the palace today but the town does boast an **ethnographical museum** (Mon–Fri 9am–12.30pm & 2–4pm; free) with moderately interesting insights into local traditions. *Restaurante Tonçinho*, on Rua de Timor 2 (closed Thurs) is a good place both for lunch and to sample the local wines, considered some of the best in the region. If you want to visit the **vineyards**, the eighteenth-century *Quinta da Alorna*, (☎243 570 700, ☏243 577 079; €5 per person), 1km from Almeirim on the Lisbon road, offers daily tours and tastings. Reservations must be made in advance.

SALVATERRA DE MAGOS, 29km south of Almeirim, retains rather more of its historical relics and has a fine, sandy river beach nearby. A palace built for the Bragança monarchs is long gone, but the palace **chapel** with its outstanding golden altarpiece still survives, as does the **Palácio da Falcoaria** (Falconry Palace), whose 310 niches once housed the royal falcons. In its eighteenth-century heyday, the palace contained a theatre and a bullring, though after the noble Count of Arcos was killed during a bullfight here, Pombal banned the sport – it was only legally reinstated in 1920.

Santarém

SANTARÉM, capital of the Ribatejo, rears high above the Rio Tejo, commanding a tremendous view over the rich pasturelands to the south and east. It ranks among the most historic cities in Portugal: under Julius Caesar it became an important administrative centre for the Roman province of Lusitania; Moorish Santarém was regarded as impregnable (until Afonso Henriques captured it by enlisting the aid of foreign Crusaders in 1147); and it was here that the royal *Cortes* (parliament) was convened throughout the fourteenth and fifteenth centuries. All evidence of Roman and Moorish occupation has vanished but, with its two exquisite churches, modern Santarém remains a pleasant place to stay and a visit will also be rewarded by the famous view from the *miradouro* known as the **Portas do Sol**.

If you can, it's worth planning your stay to coincide with one of the many **festivals** held in the town. The thinly populated agricultural plain above which Santarém stands is the home of Portuguese **bullfighting**: here, the very best horses and bulls graze in lush fields under the watchful eyes of *campinos*, mounted guardians dressed in the traditional bright costume. Agricultural traditions, folk dancing (especially the fandango) and bullfighting all come together in the great annual **Feira Nacional da Agricultura**, held at Santarém for two weeks starting on the first Friday in June, while dishes from every region in Portugal are sampled at the **Festival de Gastronomia** (10–12 days, ending early Nov). For a fixed price you can eat as much as you like during this event. There are also **street markets** on the second and fourth Sunday of every month.

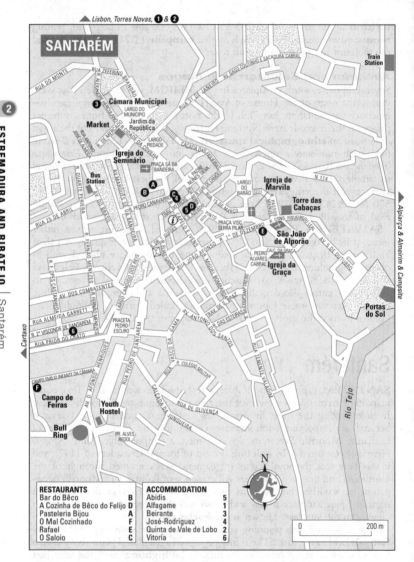

SANTARÉM

❸ Câmara Municipal

Market

Igreja do Seminário

Bus Station

Igreja de Marvila

Torre das Cabaças

São João de Alporão

Igreja da Graça

Portas do Sol

Campo de Feiras

Youth Hostel

Bull Ring

Train Station

▲ Cartaxo

▲ Alpiarça & Almeirim & Campsite

Rio Tejo

N

RESTAURANTS		ACCOMMODATION	
Bar do Bêco	B	Abidis	5
A Cozinha de Bêco do Felijo	D	Alfagame	1
Pasteleria Bijou	A	Beirante	3
O Mal Cozinhado	F	José-Rodriguez	4
Rafael	E	Quinta de Vale de Lobo	2
O Saloio	C	Vitória	6

0   200 m

The Town

At the heart of the old town is **Praça Sá da Bandeira**, overlooked by the many-windowed Baroque facade of the Jesuit **Seminário** (1676), which serves as the town's cathedral. Rua Serpa Pinto or Rua Capelo e Ivens lead from here towards the signposted Portas do Sol, about fifteen minutes' walk, with the best of the churches conveniently en route.

First of these is the Manueline **Igreja de Marvila** (Tues–Sun 9am–12.30pm & 2–5.30pm, Sat & Sun open till 6.30pm) at the end of Rua Serpa Pinto, with its brilliant seventeenth-century *azulejos* and lovely stone pulpit comprising eleven miniature Corinthian columns. From here, Rua J. Araújo, at right angles to the side of the church, descends a few yards to the architectural highlight of Santarém: the early fifteenth-century **Igreja da Graça** (Tues–Sun 9.30am–12.30pm & 2.30–5.30pm). A spectacular rose window dominates the church and overlapping blind arcades above the portal are heavily influenced by the vertical decorations on the main facade at Batalha. Pedro Álvares Cabral, discoverer of Brazil in 1500, is buried within, but his rather austere tomb-slab is overshadowed by the elaborate sarcophagus of Pedro de Menezes, the first Governor of Ceuta, who died in 1437.

Continuing toward the *miradouro*, a third sidetrack is to the twelfth-century church of **São João de Alporão**, now an **archeological museum** (Tues–Sun 9.30am–12.30pm & 2–5.30pm; €1). Take a look at the flamboyant Gothic tomb of Duarte de Menezes who met his gruesome fate in 1464 – so comprehensively was he butchered by the Moors in North Africa that only a single tooth was recovered for burial. Avenida 5 de Outubro eventually finishes at the **Portas do Sol** (Gates of the Sun), a large garden occupying the site of the Moorish citadel. Modern battlements look down on a long stretch of the Tejo with its fertile sandbanks and, beyond, a vast swathe of the Ribatejo disappears green and flat into the distance.

Practicalities

The **train station** lies a couple of hundred metres below the town. There are half-hourly buses into the centre, or you can take a taxi or walk. The **bus station** is more central, on Avenida do Brasil; and Rua Pedro Canavarro, across the gardens opposite, leads into Rua Capelo e Ivens, the main pedestrian street of the old town. Excellent free maps are available from the **turismo** at no. 63 (Mon–Fri 9am–7pm, Sat & Sun 10am–12.30pm & 2.30–5.30pm; ☎243 391 512).

Accommodation

Finding a place to stay can be hard during festival times, when your best bet is to turn up early and see if the turismo can find you a **private room**. There should be little problem at other times of year; try one of the **hotels** or **pensões** listed below. The cheapest beds are at the *Pousada de Juventude* (**youth hostel**; ☎243 333 486, ℗243 327 855) at Avenida Madre Andaluz; while the nearest **campsite** is across the river, 9km to the east, at Alpiarça (☎243 557 040; see p.197).

Residencial Abidis, Rua Guilherme de Azevedo 4 ☎243 322 017/8. A slice of nineteenth-century style with close on thirty rooms, though only six have a bath. Highly recommended and excellent value, with breakfast included. ❷

Hotel Alfageme Av Bernardo Santaremo 38, just off the Torres Novas road ☎243 370 870, ℗243 370 850. Modern hotel whose rooms are all en suite, air conditioned and double-glazed. Breakfast included. ❺

Residencial Beirante Rua Alexandre Herculano 3/5 ☎243 322 547, ℗243 333 845. Moderately priced rooms, all with private bath. ❸

Pensão José Rodrigues Trav. do Frois 14 ☎243 323 088. A clean, basic *pensão*, on a quiet alleyway just off Rua Capelo e Ivens. ❷

Quinta de Vale de Lobo Azóia de Baixo, 6km north of town on the Lisbon and Torres Novas road ☎243 429 264. This pleasant house (where the historian Alexandre Herculano spent the last years of his life) is surrounded by gardens and has a pool. ❺

Residencial Vitória Rua 2º Visconde de Santarém 19 ☎243 309 130, ℗243 328 202. Fifteen minutes' walk from the centre, with decent, if small, rooms – all with bath. Breakfast included. ❹

Santarém has a range of **restaurants**, especially around Rua Capelo e Ivens, behind the market, or near the bullring on the road to Cartaxo. Among local fish specialities look out for *fataça na telha*, mullet cooked on a tile.

Bar do Bêco Bêco da Cacaimba 9–10 ☎ 243 322 937. Tucked down a cul-de-sac this cozy bar-restaurant offers a soup and dish of the day, as well as toasted sandwiches and snacks.

A Cozinha de Bêco do Feleijo Bêco do Feleijo ☎ 243 327 722. Classy small restaurant serving traditional local dishes with a nouvelle twist.

Pastelaria Bijou Praça Sa da Bandeira. Perfect croissant-and-coffee spot opposite the Seminário, with outdoor tables from where you can watch the world go by.

O Mal Cozinhado Campo de Feiras ☎ 243 323

584. Small place where you may need to reserve a table, particularly on Fri, which is fado night. Some of the meat comes from bulls recently on duty in the nearby bullring – and, despite the odd restaurant name ("badly cooked"), dishes are good, if expensive.

Restaurante Rafael Rua 1° Dezembro 3. Good tourist menu in a friendly, family-run place.

O Saloio Trav. do Montalvo 11, off Rua Capelo e Ivens. Popular with local families, this cheap *tasca* is good value for money.

The west bank: wine towns and Vila Franca de Xira

The western bank of the Rio Tejo is highly developed south of Santarém, though away from the river it doesn't take long to get into the rolling hills and vineyards. It's around an hour's journey on the fast A1 motorway from Santarém to Lisbon but, if you have a passing interest in **wines**, there are several worthy detours on your way west including *quintas* and museums where you can sample the stuff. In addition, the west bank hosts two of Portugal's most distinctive festivals in the city of **Vila Franca de Xira**, which sits at the edge of the important wetlands of the **Reserva Natural do Estuario do Tejo**.

Wine towns

Some of the Ribatejo's finest vineyards are found on the west bank (see box below) and a good place to start exploring the wine trade is **CARTAXO**, 14km south of Santarém. The town is uninspiring but it has a fine **Museu Rural e do Vinho** (Tues–Fri 10.30am–12.30pm & 3–5.30pm, Sat & Sun 9.30am–12.30pm & 3–5.30pm; €7.50), in a *quinta* on Rua José Ribeiro da Costa, with a couple of traditional houses where you can taste and buy the local, full-bodied, fruity wine.

Ribatejo wines

Wine has been produced on the banks of the Tejo for around 2000 years, but it is only recently that modern wine-making techniques have ensured that the result is appreciated not only in local tascas but throughout Europe. The highly respected wines from the five denominations in the Ribatejo region – Almeirim, Cartaxo, Chamusca, Coruche and Santarém – can now be found in supermarkets outside Portugal, marketed under labels such as Ribatejo, Arruda and Liziria. Ribatejan **whites** are typically from the Fernão Pires or Trincadeira-das-Pratas grapes, which give rise to a dry, lemon-coloured and fruity wine. **Reds** tend to be from the Periquita, Tincadeira Preta and Castelão Nacional grapes, though Cabernet Sauvignon produces some of the best-tasting wines.

AZAMBUJA, 13km to the south, is known for its great reds made from the Periquita grape, but the town itself only really comes alive with the bull-running during its Feira do Maio, held during the last weekend in May. The Marquês de Pombal built a 26km long canal – the Vala de Azambuja – parallel to the river here, to drain the land when the Tejo was in flood – at its mouth are the ruins of the **Palácio das Obras Novas**, used as a staging post for the steamers plying from Lisbon north to Constância (see p.194) in the nineteenth century.

Perched on a hillside 17km to the southwest, **ALENQUER** sits in a major wine area; its refreshing, lemony-flavoured whites are particularly worth tasting. There is little else to delay you apart from the attractive upper town spreading up a steep hillside and boasting a **Franciscan convent** as its most prominent building. Founded in 1222 by Dona Sancha, daughter of Dom Sancho I, the convent is the oldest Franciscan house in Portugal and was built during the lifetime of St Francis of Assisi. It features a fine thirteenth-century doorway and Manueline cloisters, the latter added in 1557. Sadly it is open only on the first Sunday of the month between morning and evening Mass.

However, it is in the valleys below the windmill-topped hills around **ARRUDA DOS VINHOS**, 16km south of Alenquer, that the region's vineyards are at their most attractive. The fresh, beaujolais-style Arruda (also known as Arruta) red wines produced here are available throughout Europe, and are one of the reasons why Lisboans come to the village in their droves on Sundays. Many have lunch at the *adega-restaurante O Fuso* (☎263 975 121), where vast slabs of meat and *bacalhau* are grilled over crackling open fires – if you can't get in there, *Restaurante Nazareth* opposite is a good alternative.

Vila Franca de Xira

VILA FRANCA DE XIRA, 45km downriver from Santarém, makes a rival claim to be the capital of the Ribatejo, but it's largely a drab, industrial city – a poor second when it comes to cultural attractions. Its riverside location made it the favoured home for English Crusaders, who named it Cornogoa after Cornwall. Now Vila Franca is the central point of interest for aficionados of the Portuguese bullfight: the rearing of bulls and horses dominates the local economy. The two great annual events are the **Festa do Colete Encarnado** ("Red Waistcoat Festival", a reference to the costume of the *campinos*) held over several days in the first two weeks of July; and the **Feira de Outubro** (October Fair), in the first two weeks of the month. On both occasions there are bullfights and a Pamplona-style running of the bulls through the streets – leading to the usual casualties among the bold (and drunk).

Accommodation is difficult to find during festivals – its advisable to book well in advance or visit on a day trip from Santarém or Lisbon; the **turismo**, Avenida Pedro Victor 88 (☎063 260 31, ⓕ063 270 788), may be able to help. Places to stay in town include the *Residencial Ribatejana*, Rua da Praia 2 (☎263 272 991; ❷), next to the station, and the *Residencial Flora*, Rua Noel Perdigão 12 (☎263 271 272, ⓕ263 276 538; ❸), one block from the station and with a good restaurant. There's a shaded **campsite** (☎263 276 031) on the outskirts, near the municipal swimming pool, but it's only open in the summer months.

For **eating**, *O Copote* in the station square, on the first floor above a bar, is inexpensive; *Restaurante O Redondel*, Praça de Touros (near the bullring on the Lisbon side of town; closed Mon), is also recommended, though the full works here can cost around €10 per person.

The Reserva Natural de Estuario del Tejo

South and southeast from Vila Franca de Xira, the banks of the Tejo are classified as the **Reserva Natural de Estuario del Tejo**, providing protection for
the thousands of wild birds that gather in the estuary. It is Portugal's most
important wetland, but was somewhat disrupted by the construction of the
enormous Vasco da Gama bridge (see p.101). The reserve's headquarters are
35km south of Vila Franca in **ALCOCHETE**, right on the waterfront on the
south side of the bridge at Avenida Combatentes 1 (℡212 341 742), from
where information and advice are dispensed. With your own transport, the best
approach to the reserve is from Alcamé, south of the N10 Vila Franca–Porto
Alto road, or – better still – from Pancas, west of the N118. Otherwise, take the
ferry from Lisbon (hourly from Praça do Comércio) to Montijo, a fifty-minute
journey. Once there, it's a 5km bus or taxi ride to Alcochete.

Between October and April, you can book **tours** of the wetlands from the
reserve's headquarters in Alcochete. This is the best time to see the migrating
bird species such as flamingoes, teal and avocet. During the summer, you'll
catch nesting species such as black-winged stilt, purple heron and marsh harriers.

You can also arrange a tour of the reserve from the Tejo estuary itself by **renting a boat** (or a place in a boat). Contact Domingos Chefe (℡212 360 278)
a day in advance. You'll also need to obtain permission to visit from the reserve
headquarters. The boat can take up to nine people and trips are available on
weekends only throughout the year.

Travel details

Trains

Abrantes to: Castelo Branco (6 daily; 1hr
30min–2hr); Covilhã (5 daily; 2hr 30min–3hr
30min); Elvas (3 daily; 2hr 30min); Lisbon (8 daily;
1hr 35min–2hr 30min); Portalegre (4 daily; 1hr
35min).

Caldas da Rainha to: Figueira da Foz (7 daily; 1hr
30min–2hr 20min); Leiria (7 daily; 45min–1hr);
Lisbon (9 daily; 1hr 15min–2hr); São Martinho do
Porto (5 daily; 9–20min); Torres Vedras (9 daily;
30–50min).

Leiria to: Caldas da Rainha (5 daily; 45min–1hr
10min); Figueira da Foz (6 daily; 45min–1hr
20min); Lisbon (4 daily; 2–3hr 20min); São
Martinho do Porto (5 daily; 40–55min); Torres
Vedras (4 daily; 1hr 14min–2hr 14min).

Lisbon to: Caldas da Rainha (9 daily; 1hr
15min–2hr); Leiria (5 daily; 2hr–3hr); Torres Vedras
(9 daily; 45min–1hr 15min).

Santarém to: Castelo Branco (5 daily; 2hr
25min–3hr 10min); Covilhã (5 daily; 3hr
30min–4hr 20min); Lisbon (hourly; 1hr); Tomar (8
daily; 1hr).

Tomar to: Lisbon (7 daily; 2hr); Santarém (7 daily;
1hr);

Torres Vedras to: Caldas da Rainha (9 daily;
30–50min); Figueira da Foz (4 daily; 2hr 15min);
Leiria (5 daily; 1hr 20min–2hr); Lisbon (8 daily; 40
min–1hr 10min).

Vila Franca de Xira to: Lisbon (hourly; 30 min);
Santarém (hourly; 40min); Tomar (hourly; 1hr
30min).

Buses

Abrantes to: Coimbra (1 daily; 2hr 45min); Fátima
(3 daily; 1hr 30min); Leiria (1 daily; 2hr); Lisbon (8
daily, 2hr 30min); Santarém (4 daily; 1hr 25min);
Tomar (2–4 daily; 1hr 10min).

Alcobaça to: Batalha (5 daily; 30min); Leiria (4
daily; 45min); Lisbon (3 daily; 2hr); Nazaré (8 daily;
35min).

Batalha to: Fátima (4 daily; 25min); Leiria (5 daily;
15min); Lisbon (5 daily; 2hr).

Caldas da Rainha to: Foz do Arelho (9–10 daily;
20min); Leiria (4 daily; 1hr 55min); Lisbon (6 daily;
1hr 45 min); Nazaré (7 daily; 40min); Óbidos (6
daily; 20min).

Ericeira to: Lisbon (7 daily; 1hr 25min); Sintra (12 daily; 45min).

Fátima to: Coimbra (5 daily; 1hr–1hr 30min); Leiria (9 daily; 25min); Lisbon (6 daily; 1hr 45min–2hr 15min); Porto (4 daily; 2hr 30min–3hr 30min).

Leiria to: Abrantes (1 daily; 1hr 50min); Alcobaça (4 daily; 50min); Batalha (3 daily; 15min); Coimbra (10 daily; 50min); Fátima (9 daily; 25min); Lisbon (9 daily; 1hr–2hr 10min); Porto de Mós (3 daily; 35min); Tomar (3 daily; 1hr 30min).

Nazaré to: Alcobaça (6 daily; 20min); Caldas da Rainha (7 daily; 40min); Leiria (10 daily; 1hr 10min); Lisbon (6 daily; 2hr); Óbidos (3 daily; 1hr); São Martinho do Porto (3 daily; 20min).

Óbidos to: Caldas da Rainha (10 daily; 20min); Nazaré (7 daily; 1hr); Peniche (7–8 daily; 25–40min).

Peniche to: Areia Branca (6 daily; 30min); Caldas da Rainha (7 daily; 45min); Consolação (12 daily; 15min); Lisbon (9 daily; 1hr 45min); Óbidos (7–8 daily; 25–40min); São Martinho do Porto (3 daily; 1hr); Torre Vedras (8 daily; 50min).

Santarém to: Abrantes (6 daily; 1hr 25min); Fátima (9 daily, 1hr); Lisbon (12 daily; 1hr 15min); Ourem (1 daily; 1hr 10min); Tomar (2–6 daily; 1hr); Vila Franca (2–5 daily; 1hr 35min–2hr 20min).

Tomar to: Abrantes (2–4 daily; 1hr 10min); Coimbra (2 daily; 2hr); Fátima (2–4 daily; 45min); Leiria (2 daily; 1hr 10min–2hr); Lisbon (2–4 daily; 1hr 15min–2hr); Santarém (2–4 daily; 1hr 5min).

Vila Franca de Xira to: Évora (1 daily; 2hr); Lisbon (hourly; 50min); Santarém (2–5 daily; 40min–1hr 25min).

3

Coimbra & the Beira Litoral

ATLANTIC
OCEAN

SPAIN

N

CHAPTER 3　Highlights

* **Coimbra** Wander the cobbled lanes of this ancient university town. See opposite

* **Coimbra fado** The city's instrumental fado is best listened to in a smoky bar, drink in hand. See p.218

* **Roman ruins at Conímbriga** Rove amongst Portugal's finest Roman remains. See p.219

* **Serra da Lousã** Hike through abandoned villages in this little-visited mountain range. See p.222

* **Buçaco Forest** Explore the revered forest and stop for a drink in the luxurious *Hotel Palace do Buçaco*. See p.226

* **Rio Dão valley** Home to some of the country's finest red wines. See p.228

* **Museu do Automóvel** An incongruous but superb museum in the hilltop town of Caramulo. See p.229

* **Figueira da Foz** Be a proper tourist and bronze your limbs on this great swathe of beach. See p.231

* **Seafood in Aveiro** The simple *adegas* in Aveiro's fish market are a great spot to enjoy the region's fresh seafood. See p.240

3

Coimbra & the Beira Litoral

The province of Beira Litoral is dominated by the city of Coimbra, which, with Guimarães, Lisbon and Porto, forms the quartet of Portugal's historic capitals. Situated on a hill above the Rio Mondego, it's a wonderfully moody place, full of ancient alleys and lanes, spreading around the country's oldest university. As a base for exploring the region, the city can't be beaten, with Portugal's most extensive Roman site, Conímbriga, 16km to the southwest, the castle at Montemor-o-Velho 32km west on the road to Figueira da Foz, and the delightful spa town of Luso and ancient forest of Buçaco under an hour's journey to the north.

Beira's endlessly sandy coastline, from Figueira da Foz north as far as Porto, has been dubbed the **Costa de Prata** ("Silver Coast"). Although slowly succumbing to development, most noticeably around **Praia de Mira**, it remains one of the least spoiled coasts in Portugal, backed by rolling dunes and pine forests. The only resort of any real size is **Figueira da Foz** and even this remains thoroughly and enjoyably local in character. Inland, the villages and towns of the fertile plain have long been conditioned by the twin threats of floodwaters from Portugal's highest mountains, and silting caused by the restless Atlantic. Drainage channels were cut to make cultivation possible and houses everywhere are built on high ground. At **Aveiro**, positioned on a complex estuary site, a whole network of canals was developed to cope with the currents, and to facilitate salt production and the harvesting of seaweed – still the staple activities of the local economy.

The Beira region also hints at the river valley splendour to come, in the Douro and Minho, further north. Following the delightful **Rio Mondego** upstream from Coimbra, you'll come to see why it has been celebrated so often in Portuguese poetry as the "Rio das Musas" – River of the Muses. An equally beautiful road journey trails the **Rio Vouga**, from Aveiro, up to the town of **Vouzela** and the spa of **São Pedro do Sul**.

Coimbra

COIMBRA was Portugal's capital for over a century (1143–1255) and its famous **university** – founded in 1290 and permanently established here in

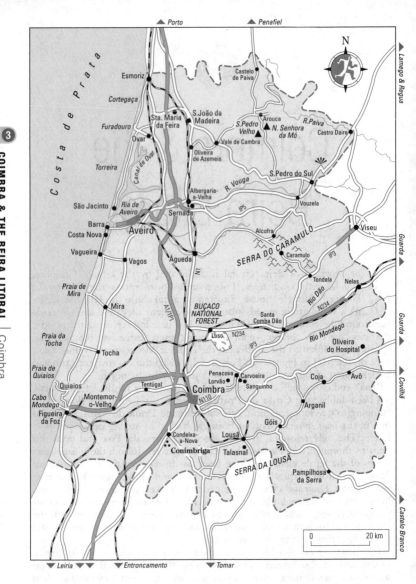

▲ Porto   ▲ Penafiel

N

Costa de Prata

Esmoriz
Cortegaça
Castelo
de Paiva
Furadouro
Sta. Maria
da Feira
S.João da
Madeira
Arouca
R.Paiva
S.Pedro
Velho
N. Senhora
da Mó
Castro Daire
Ovar
Vale de Cambra
Torreira
Oliveira
de Azemeis
S.Pedro do Sul
Albergaria-
a-Velha
R. Vouga
São Jacinto
Ria de
Aveiro
Canal de Ovar
Sernada
IP5
Vouzela
Barra
Costa Nova
Aveiro
Alcofra
SERRA DO CARAMULO
Viseu
Vagueira
Vagos
Águeda
Caramulo
IP3
Praia de
Mira
Tondela
Nelas
Mira
N234
Rio Dão
Praia da
Tocha
BUÇACO
NATIONAL
FOREST
Santa
Comba Dão
Tocha
Luso
N234
Rio Mondego
IP3
Oliveira
do Hospital
Praia de
Quiaios
Quiaios
Tentúgal
Penacova
Lorvão
Carvoeira
Sanguinho
Coja
Avô
Cabo
Mondego
Montemor-
o-Velho
Coimbra
N110
Arganil
Figueira
da Foz
Góis
Condeixa-
a-Nova
Lousã
Conímbriga
Talasnal
SERRA DA LOUSÃ
Pampilhosa
da Serra

Lamego & Regua
Guarda
Guarda
Covilhã
Castelo Branco

0   20 km

▼ Leiria ▼ ▼   ▼ Entroncamento   ▼ Tomar

1537 after a series of moves back and forth to Lisbon – was the only one in Portugal until the beginning of the last century. It remains highly prestigious and provides the greatest of Coimbra's monuments and buildings, most notably the renowned Baroque library. In addition, there are a remarkable number of other riches: two cathedrals, dozens of lesser churches, and scores of ancient mansions, one housing the superb **Museu Machado de Castro**.

This roll-call of splendours is promoted zealously by the inhabitants of what – when all is said and done – is little more than a small, provincial town. There's an air of self-importance that whistles through city and citizens, bolstered by Coimbra's long academic tradition and fed by shops, galleries and cafés that would sit easily in Lisbon. For visitors, this means that Coimbra can be a lot of fun: it's a very manageable size, with a population of around a hundred thousand, its streets packed with bars and taverns, at their busiest when the students are in town. The liveliest time to be here is in May, when the end of the academic year is celebrated in the **Queima das Fitas**, with late-night concerts, parades and graduates ceremoniously tearing or burning their gowns and faculty ribbons. Although the student's alcohol-fuelled antics can get rather excessive, this is when you're most likely to hear the genuine **Coimbra fado**, distinguished from the Lisbon version by its mournful pace and romantic or intellectual lyrics.

Arrival, information and city transport

There are three **train stations** – Coimbra A, Coimbra B and Coimbra Parque. Riverside **Coimbra A** (often just "Coimbra" on timetables, and known as Estação Nova) is right at the heart of things; express trains call only at **Coimbra B** (Estação Velha), 3km to the north, from where you pick up a local train into Coimbra A – just follow everyone else across the platform (you don't need another ticket). **Coimbra Parque**, southeast of the centre, is for services to and from Lousã, to the south (see p.221).

The main **bus station** is on Avenida Fernão de Magalhães, about fifteen minutes' walk northwest of the centre. Almost all long-distance buses operate from here, as do international services to Spain, France and Germany. AVIC buses, operating along the Costa da Prata to and from Praia da Mira, stop at the station at Rua João de Ruão 18, on the way in from the main bus station. AVIC also runs buses to and from Condeixa-a-Nova (for Conímbriga), which also make a stop at the top of Avenida Emídio Navarro, just before Coimbra A station.

Drivers should beware that driving into Coimbra can be a nightmare, since most of the central streets are closed to cars. It's best to use one of the signposted car parks (marked on the map on pp.210–211) or stay at a hotel with car parking and then walk into town.

Information and transport

For a free map, call in at the **turismo** on the triangular Largo da Portagem, facing the Ponte Santa Clara (Mon–Fri 9am–6/7pm, Sat & Sun 10am–1pm & 2.30–5.30pm; ☎239 855 930; ⓦwww.turismo-central.pt). There are also tourist offices on Largo Dom Dinis (☎239 832 591) and Praça da República (☎239 833 202), both open the same hours as the main office, and a small information kiosk on the platform of Coimbra B.

You'll get most out of **walking** around the old quarter of Coimbra; indeed, you'll have no choice given the complexity and inaccessibility of most of the hillside alleys and streets. Tickets for **town buses** (which include services out to the youth hostel; see p.213) are sold on board or more cheaply from kiosks in Largo da Portagem, Praça 8 de Maio and Praça da República. Marginally better value are the five- or ten-ticket strips (called *senhas*) which you buy from automatic machines dotted around town. There's one in front of the Bank of Portugal in Largo da Portagem, and they all have an English-language option. Click your ticket in the machine by the driver as you board. For a cheap bus **tour** of the city, #1 and #3 take in most of the sights. Information on bus routes and timetables is available from the riverside café in front of the *Hotel Astória*, or the kiosk a little further up. If you prefer to get around by **taxis**,

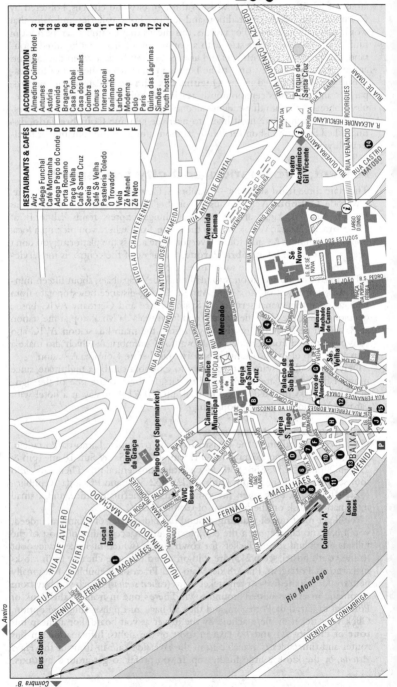

RESTAURANTS & CAFÉS
Aviz	K
Adega Funchal	F
Café Montanha	J
Adega Paço do Conde	D
Porta Romano	C
Praça Velha	H
Café Santa Cruz	B
Sereia	A
Café Sé Velha	G
Pasteleria Toledo	J
O Trovador	E
Viela	F
Zé Manel	I
Zé Neto	F

ACCOMMODATION
Almedina Coimbra Hotel	3
Antunes	14
Astoria	13
Avenida	16
Bragança	8
Casa Pombal	4
Casa dos Quintais	18
Coimbra	10
Dómus	6
Internacional	11
Kanimambo	1
Larbelo	15
Moderna	7
Oslo	5
Paris	9
Quinta das Lágrimas	17
Simões	12
Youth hostel	2

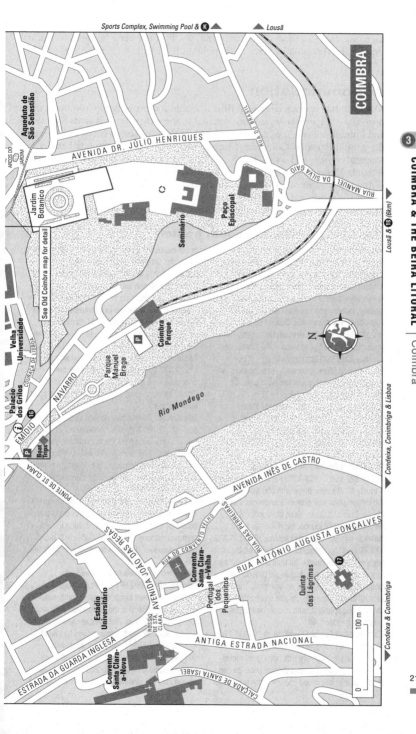

Sports Complex, Swimming Pool & K ▲   ▲ Lousã

COIMBRA

Aqueduto de São Sebastião

ARCOS DO JARDIM

AVENIDA DR. JÚLIO HENRIQUES

RUA DO BRASIL

Jardim Botânico

See Old Coimbra map for detail

Seminário

Paço Episcopal

P

RUA MANUEL DA SILVA GAIO

▶ Lousã & 18 (6km)

Velha Universidade

COURAÇA DE LISBOA

Palácio dos Grilos

EMÍDIO

NAVARRO

Parque Manuel Braga

Coimbra Parque

P

N

Rio Mondego

▶ Condeixa, Conimbriga & Lisboa

Boat Trips

PONTE DE ST. CLARA

AVENIDA INÊS DE CASTRO

RUA DO CONVENTO VELHO

RUA DAS FERREIRAS

Convento Santa Clara-a-Velha

Portugal dos Pequenitos

RUA ANTÓNIO AUGUSTA GONÇALVES

Quinta das Lágrimas

17

▶ Condeixa & Conimbriga

ESTRADA DA GUARDA INGLESA

Estádio Universitário

AVENIDA JOÃO DAS REGAS

ROSSIO DE STA. CLARA

AVENIDA JOÃO DAS REGAS

ANTIGA ESTRADA NACIONAL

Convento Santa Clara-a-Nova

CALÇADA DE SANTA ISABEL

100 m

0

there are ranks outside all the train stations, by the police headquarters near Praça 8 de Maio, and in Praça da República. To call a cab, ring Politaxis (☎239 484 045).

Accommodation

Much of the city's **accommodation** is within a short walk of Coimbra A station. The cheaper *pensões* are concentrated in the rather sleazy Rua da Sota (left and immediately right out of the station) and the little streets between here and the central Praça do Comércio. More expensive places line Avenida Fernão de Magalhães (left and immediately left out of the station) and the riverside Avenida Emídio Navarro (directly ahead of the station). What you won't find is much choice in the hilly streets of the old town. There is no longer a campsite in Coimbra, and the **youth** hostel is a fair way from the centre. Note that all accommodation reviewed below is marked on the map on pp.210–211.

Pensões, hotels and youth hostel

Almedina Coimbra Hotel Av Fernão de Magalhães 199 ☎239 855 500, ✉geral@residencial-almedina.pt. Situated next to a fire station on a race-track main road. Double-glazing keeps the noise down, but the rooms lack charm. Nearby parking, though, and breakfast is included. ❺

Residencial Antunes Rua Castro Matoso 8 ☎239 854 720, ✉Residencialantunes@mail.pt. Quiet, polished and good value – the rooms are decently sized with bathrooms and TV. It's near Praça da República, a fair walk from the old town, though close to a couple of excellent bars. ❹

Hotel Astória Av Emídio Navarro 21 ☎239 853 020, ✉almeidahotels.com. Perfectly placed (look for the landmark dome), classically upmarket and wonderfully old fashioned, exhibiting a strange blend of Art Nouveau and 1930s decor. The best rooms overlook the river. ❻

Residencial Avenida Av Emídio Navarro 37 ☎239 822 156, ℻239 822 155. On the riverside, a musty Art Nouveau place with characterful rooms complete with broken chandeliers, sturdy old furniture and small, clean bathrooms. Bar, restaurant and TV lounge, too. ❹

Hotel Bragança Largo das Ameias 10 ☎239 822 171, ✉email.hbraganza@mail.telepac.pt. If you were staying any nearer the train station, you'd be in it – which given the *Bragança's* pseudo-Soviet brutalist exterior might be no bad thing. Things pick up inside, where rooms are inoffensively modern and spacious, with marble bathrooms; breakfast included. ❺

Casa Pombal Rua dos Flores 18 ☎239 835 175, ℻239 821 548. Higgledy-piggledy Dutch-run town house near the university with lashings of atmosphere, a tiled dining room and small patio-garden. Breakfast is splendid and you can order good vege-

tarian meals, too. Thoroughly recommended. ❹

Casa dos Quintais at Assarfage, 6km south of Coimbra ☎239 438 305. Small private house with a delightful garden and fine views of Coimbra; follow signs to Carvalhais de Cima and then signs for "Casa Rurale". There are just three double rooms with a common lounge area, and an excellent breakfast is served; call ahead to reserve a room. ❺

Residencial Coimbra Rua das Azeiteiras 55 ☎239 837 996. Pleasant choice on a busy pedestrianized street in the heart of the city. Smart, en-suite rooms, friendly service and good breakfasts. ❹

Residencial Dómus Rua Adelino Veiga 62 ☎239 828 584, ℻239 838 818. On the nicest of the narrow streets across from the train station, this homely place (entrance hidden next to a rug store) has a wide variety of rooms and friendly owners keen to show them off. The best rooms have shower and TV. ❸

Residencial Internacional Av Emídio Navarro 4 ☎239 825 503. Facing the river, this once-grand hotel has divided up its rooms, making them a bit cramped, although very comfortable with nice new bathrooms. Rooms at the front can be rather noisy. ❸

Residencial Kanimambo Av Fernão de Magalhães 484 ☎239 827 151. Upstairs in a modern apartment block, this is a slightly more salubrious choice near the bus station, with nicely furnished rooms (with and without shower) spread across two dark floors and accessed by lift. ❸

Residencial Larbelo Largo da Portagem 33 ☎239 829 092. Close to the main turismo; you can't miss the lime green facade. It's simply furnished and has new bathrooms (pay extra), but it's

gloomy and – for single travellers at least – rather overpriced. Rooms facing the Largo are noisy. ❸
Moderna Rua Adelino Veiga 49 ☎239 825 413, ☏239 829 508. Set in an unlikely block of shops off a busy pedestrian street, the reception and corridors are gloomy, but the rooms are well furnished and comfortable, with bath and TV. ❸
Hotel Oslo Av Fernão de Magalhães 25 ☎239 829 071, ✉hoteloslo@sapo.pt. Pleasant, modern hotel with a restaurant and bar on the top floor. Despite the Scandinavian style, the rooms facing the street feature traditional Portuguese late-night noise. ❹
Residencial Paris Rua da Sota 41 ☎239 822 732, ☏239 820 569. Laid-back guesthouse a block back from the river, with a friendly owner who is happy to haggle over prices. Many of the decent-sized rooms have bathrooms, and the place is resplendent with plastic flowers and doilies. ❸

Quinta das Lágrimas off Rua António Augusta Gonçalves ☎239 802 380, ⓦwww.supernet.pt/hotelagrimas. Situated across the river, this is Coimbra's grandest and most atmospheric choice. A plush stately house set in the infamous gardens and counting Wellington amongst its former guests. ❻
Simões Rua Fernandes Tomás 69 ☎239 834 638. Cheapest choice in the old town, with simple, clean, monastic lodgings on a cobbled street that climbs from the Arco de Almedina. The ground-floor rooms are noisy but cheaper than in the rest of the building. ❶
Youth hostel Rua Henrique Seco 14 ☎239 822 955, ✉coimbra@movijovem.pt (daily: reception open 8am–noon & 6pm–midnight). Above the Parque Santa Cruz, this is a decent modern hostel with nice rooms, patio, kitchen and TV room. It's about twenty minutes' walk, or take buses #29 or #46 from Coimbra A.

The City

Old Coimbra straddles a hilly site, with the university crowning its summit, on the north bank of the Rio Mondego. Its slopes are a convoluted mass of ancient alleys around which the modern town has spread, and most of interest is concentrated on the hill itself or in the largely pedestrianized commercial centre at its foot. Chances are you'll get lost as soon as you start to climb past the remains of the city walls, but that's half the fun. It's probably best to start your exploration of Coimbra with the **Velha Universidade**, not least because it's the easiest place to find, and from its balcony the city is laid out below you like a map. You can see right across the river to the twin **Santa Clara** convents, a visit to which is the only time you need leave the confines of the old city. If you don't feel like walking, bus #1 takes you up to the Museo Machado de Castro and the university buildings.

Into the old town

The old town is bounded on its western side by the pedestrianized main street which runs north from the café-filled Largo da Portagem to the Igreja de Santa Cruz. Here, in the **Baixa**, along **Rua Ferreira Borges** and its continuation **Rua Visconde da Luz**, are most of the fashionable shops and cafés; off to the west, the narrow rat-runs and alleys that cut down to the train station contain budget restaurants, canteens, grocery stores, workshops, butchers and bakers.

Heading up into the old town involves a steep climb, with perhaps the nicest approach being halfway along the main street, through the Arco de Almedina, an arch cut through the old city wall. Stepped streets climb beyond into the heart of old Coimbra, with attractive alleys off to either side. Down Rua Sub Ripas, to the left, is the Palácio de Sub Ripas, sporting a fine Manueline doorway – the Renaissance windows and stone medallions are from the workshop of the French sculptor Jean de Rouen (João de Ruão), which used to be nearby. Almost any other turn you care to make reveals more interest: hidden courtyards, flower-decked balconies, cobbled dead-ends and glimpses of sky and lower town through unexpected gaps in the crumbling walls.

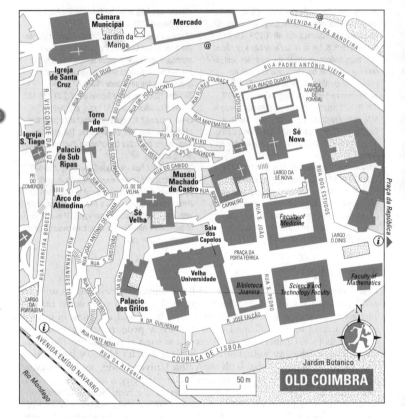

Câmara Municipal · Mercado · AVENIDA SÁ DA BANDEIRA · Jardim da Manga · Igreja de Santa Cruz · RUA DO CORPO DE DEUS · R. DO COLÉGIO NOVO · RUA FLORES · COURAÇA DOS APÓSTOLOS · RUA PADRE ANTÔNIO VIEIRA · PRAÇA MARQUÊS DE POMBAL · RUA DR. JOÃO JACINTO · RUA INACIO DUARTE · R. VISCONDE DA LUZ · Torre de Anto · RUA MATEMÁTICA · Sé Nova · Igreja S. Tiago · Palacio de Sub Ripas · RUA DOS COUTINHAS · RUA BOA VISTA · RUA DO LOUREIRO · R. DE S. SALVADOR · PR. DO COMERCIO · RUA SUB RIPAS · RUA DO CABIDO · Museu Machado de Castro · LARGO DA SÉ NOVA · RUA DOS ESTUDOS · Praça da República · Arco de Almedina · LG. DE SÉ VELHA · RUA BORGES · CARNEIRO · RUA S. JOÃO · Faculty of Medicine · Sé Velha · RUA FERREIRA BORGES · RUA JOÃO ANTÓNIO DE AGUIAR · RUA FERNANDES TOMAZ · Sala dos Capelos · LARGO D.DINIS · CRISTÓVÃO · RUA · PRAÇA DA PORTA FÉRREA · Faculty of Mathematics · LARGO DA PORTAGEM · R. DA ILHA · RUA DOS ESTEIROS · Palacio dos Grilos · Velha Universidade · Biblioteca Joanina · RUA S. PEDRO · Science and Technology Faculty · RUA FONTE NOVA · R. DR. GUILHERME · R. JOSÉ FALCÃO · Rio Mondego · AVENIDA EMÍDIO NAVARRO · RUA DA ALEGRIA · COURAÇA DE LISBOA · Jardim Botanico · N · 0 50 m · OLD COIMBRA

The Sé Velha

The **Sé Velha** (Mon–Thurs & Sat 10am–6pm, Fri 10am–2pm, Sat 10am–5pm, closed Sun), an unmistakable fortress-like bulk, squats about halfway up the hill in its own steeply shelving square. Begun in 1162, it's one of the most important Romanesque buildings in Portugal, little altered and seemingly unbowed by the weight of the years. The one significant later addition – the Renaissance Porta Especiosa in the north wall – has, in contrast to the main structure, almost entirely crumbled away. Solid and square on the outside, the cathedral is also stolid and simple within, the decoration confined to a few giant conch shells holding holy water and some unobtrusive *azulejos* from Seville around the walls. The Gothic tombs of early bishops and the low-arched cloister (€0.75) are equally restrained.

The Velha Universidade

The main buildings of the **Velha Universidade** (daily: summer 9am–7.30pm; winter 9.30am–12.30pm & 2–5.30pm; €4 for university, library and Sala dos Capelos) lie further up the hill, and date from the sixteenth century when João III declared its establishment at Coimbra permanent. The buildings are set around the **Pátio das Escolas** (also known as Praca da Porta Ferrea), a court-yard dominated by the Baroque clock tower nicknamed "A Cabra" – the goat – and a statue of the portly João III.

The elaborate stairway to the right of the main court leads into the administrative quarters and the **Sala dos Capelos**; tickets are sold here for visits to each of the main sections of the university. The hall itself – hung with portraits of Portugal's kings – is used for conferring degrees and has a fine wood-panelled ceiling with gilded decoration in the Manueline style. The highlight of this part of the building, though, is the narrow catwalk around the outside walls. The central door off the courtyard leads past the **Capela**, not the finest of Coimbra's religious foundations but one of the most elaborate – covered with *azulejos* and intricate decoration including twisted, rope-like pillars, a frescoed ceiling, and a gaudy Baroque organ.

To the left is the famous library, the **Biblioteca Joanina**, a Baroque fantasy presented to the faculty by João V in the early eighteenth century. Its rooms telescope into each other, focusing on the founder's portrait in a disconcertingly effective use of trompe l'oeil. The richness of it all is impressive, such as the expanse of cleverly marbled wood, gold leaf, tables inlaid with ebony, rosewood and jacaranda, Chinese-style lacquer work and carefully calculated frescoed ceilings. The most prized valuables, the rare and ancient books, are locked away out of sight and, despite their impressive multilingual titles, the volumes on the shelves seem largely chosen for their aesthetic value; no one seems likely to disturb the careful arrangement by actually reading anything.

Sadly, the other faculty buildings of the university are almost completely devoid of interest. Their lofty position atop the narrow, cobbled streets notwithstanding, too many are mere concrete excrescences dating from a modernization programme under Dr. Salazar. The wide spaces in between are tempered by modern sculpture of dubious quality, and only the lure of the student-frequented pavement cafés on **Praça da República** – down the steep steps from Largo Dom Dinis – merit the diversion. The **Parque de Santa Cruz**, stretching uphill from the praça, is best avoided after dark.

The Jardim Botânico

Just down the hill from Largo Dom Dinis, ten minutes or so to the south, the **Jardim Botânico** is worth a brief visit. Founded in the eighteenth century, these botanical displays once enjoyed a worldwide reputation and, even if they've seen better days, it's still very pleasant to stroll among the formally laid out beds of plants from around the world, but note that you're not allowed to picnic here. Nearby are the impressive remains of the sixteenth-century **Aqueduto de São Sebastião**.

The Museu Machado de Castro and Sé Nova

Back up on the hill, after the old university buildings, is the **Museu Machado de Castro** (closed until autumn 2003; check with the tourist office for details), just down Rua de São João. The museum, named after an eighteenth-century sculptor, is housed in the former archbishop's palace, which would be worth visiting in its own right even if it were empty. As it is, it's positively stuffed with treasures: sculpture (see especially the little medieval knight riding home with his mace slung over his shoulder), paintings, furniture, and ceramics. Underneath all this is the Roman **Cryptoportico**, a series of subterranean galleries probably used by the Romans as a granary and subsequently pressed into service for the foundations of the palace.

Across the way stands the unprepossessing **Sé Nova**, or New Cathedral (Tues–Sat 9.30am–12.30pm & 2–6.30pm; free), a seventeenth-century Jesuit foundation which replaced the Sé Velha as cathedral in 1772.

Igreja de Santa Cruz

The last old-town stop is right at the bottom of the hill, at the northern end of Rua Visconde da Luz, and restraint and simplicity are simply not the words that spring to mind when considering the **Igreja de Santa Cruz** (Mon–Sat 9am–noon & 2–5pm, Sun 4–6pm; cloister €1), the church of the monastery that was founded on the site by São Teotónio. The church predates even the Sé Velha, but nothing remains that has not been substantially remodelled – its exuberant facade and strange double doorway setting the tone. In the early sixteenth century Coimbra was the base of a major sculptural school that included the French artists Nicolas Chanterene and Jean de Rouen (João de Ruão), as well as the two Manueline masters João de Castilho and Diogo de Boitaca, all of whom had a hand in rebuilding Santa Cruz.

These artists designed a variety of projects: **tombs** to house Portugal's first kings, Afonso Henriques and Sancho I; an elaborate **pulpit**; and, most famously, the **Cloister of Silence**. It is here that the Manueline theme is at its clearest, with a series of airy arches decorated with bas-relief scenes from the life of Christ. From the cloister a staircase leads to the raised *coro*, above whose wooden benches is a frieze celebrating the nation's flourishing empire.

Around the back of the church, the small **Jardim da Manga** faces the main road. More cloister than garden, it was at one time surrounded by orange trees, and today still retains a cupola and fountain; there's a handy café at the rear of the garden.

The Santa Clara convents

It was in Santa Cruz that the romantic history of Dom Pedro and Inês de Castro (see "Alcobaça", p.173) came to its ghoulish climax. Pedro, finally proclaimed king, had his lover exhumed and set up on a throne in the church, where his courtiers were forced to pay homage to the decomposing body.

Inês had originally lain in the **Convento de Santa Clara-a-Velha**, a twenty-minute walk away from the main town across the river, her tomb placed alongside the convent's founder and Coimbra's patron, the saint-queen Isabel. Isabel was married to Dom Dinis, whom she infuriated by constantly giving away his wealth to the poor. She performed one of her many miracles when, confronted by her irate husband as she smuggled out yet another cargo of gold, she claimed to be carrying only roses: when her bag was opened that was exactly its contents. The Gothic hall church she built, over time, became almost entirely covered by silt from the River Mondego, but the ruin is slowly being restored.

The two tombs have long since been moved away, Inês's to Alcobaça and Isabel's to the **Convento de Santa Clara-a-Nova** (daily 8.30am–6pm; cloister €0.50) higher up the hill and safe from the shifting river. The new convent, built in 1650, doesn't have much of the charm of the old and the fact that the nuns' quarters now house a Portuguese army barracks doesn't help. Its two saving graces, which make the climb worthwhile, are **Isabel's tomb** – made of solid silver collected by the citizens of Coimbra – and the vast **cloister**, heady with honeysuckle, which was financed by João V, a king whose devotion to nuns went beyond the normal bounds of spiritual comfort. The army's presence exerts itself in a small, uninteresting **military museum** (daily 10am–noon & 2–5pm; €1.25), displaying bits and bombs retrieved from World War II.

Portugal dos Pequenitos

Between the two convents extends the parkland site of **Portugal dos Pequenitos** (March–June 10am–7pm; July–Sept 9am–8pm; Oct–Feb

10am–5pm; €4), a 1950s theme park where scale models of many of the country's great buildings are interspersed with "typical" farmhouses and sections on the overseas territories, heavy with the White Man's Burden. Historically and architecturally accurate it's not, but the place is great fun for kids who can clamber in and out of the miniature houses.

A short distance beyond is a somewhat more sombre little park, the **Quinta das Lágrimas** (Garden of Tears), in which, so legend has it, Inês de Castro was finally tracked down and murdered.

Eating

The city's **cheapest meals** are to be found in the dives along Rua Direita in the Baixa, where if you're not too bothered about your surroundings – basement saloons and rough tables – you can eat for under €5. For a tad more sophistication, search out the atmospheric little cafés and restaurants tucked into the tiny alleys between Largo da Portagem, Rua da Sota and Praça do Comércio – Rua das Azeiteiras, in particular, has several good possibilities. Local specialities to try out are *chanfana* – kid goat roasted in wine, a little fatty for some tastes – and Santa Clara pastries. For **breakfast**, the cafés and coffee houses in the Baixa are best; see p.218 for more details.

Restaurante Aviz Rua do Brasil 185. Bustling good-time local eating place, a five-minute taxi ride east of the centre and serving later than most in town. Best known for its seafood, though it also does great (and cheaper) steaks – try the *bifé à Aviz*, cooked in cream and coffee. Around €15.

Adega Funchal Rua das Azeiteiras 18. Just off Praça do Comércio, this reasonably priced place serves generous helpings of chicken or mutton stew and the like in agreeable rustic surroundings. Under €10.

Adega Paço do Conde Rua Paço do Conde 1. Great, locally renowned *churrasqueiria* of cavernous proportions, with a dining room either side of a covered terrace. Around €7.50 for grilled meat or fish, salad, wine and coffee. Closed Sun.

Porta Romano Rua João Jacinto 18–20. Excellent pizzeria where everything is fresh and the chef is happy to conjure up special requests; you'll pay around €5–8. Open till 11pm.

Sereia Rua Henriques Seco 1. Café-bar close to the youth hostel with a popular range of grills, egg dishes and stews, although prices are higher than elsewhere. Open till midnight.

O Trovador Largo da Sé Velha 17. Next to the old cathedral, this lovely wood-panelled and ceramic-tiled restaurant is surprisingly good value – around €12–17 – if rather limited in choice and a little touristy. There are regular fado sessions here, too. Closed Mon.

Viela Rua das Azeiteiras 35. Simple tiled dining room with good food, overseen by a friendly proprietor. The *carne de porco* is delicious and a gluttonous bargain at €7 – splitting the enormous full portions means a meal shouldn't top €10 or so.

Zé Manel Beco do Forno 12. Tiny, atmospheric place, tucked away in a quiet street behind *Hotel Astória*. The walls are adorned with cartoons and poems; the service is brisk and friendly; and the simple food excellent – don't miss the superb *feijoada*. If you don't want to queue, be sure to turn up by 7pm.

Zé Neto Rua das Azeiteiras 8–12. A similar list of Portuguese grills and fries to that served up at *Adega Funchal* but at budget prices, washed down with some of the cheapest house wine in town. Last orders around 9.45pm.

Drinking and nightlife

At some stage of the day, you should visit one of the traditional **cafés** and **coffee houses** along Rua Ferreira Borges and Rua Visconde da Luz, filled with package-laden shoppers. Praça da República, across town by the Parque de Santa Cruz, is also surrounded by cafés, this time popular with students and staying open until 2am. Other trendy **bars** are scattered across old and new parts of town, and the best are reviewed below; all stay open until 2am unless otherwise stated. Coimbra's **clubs** remain open much later; in some, you can expect the music to keep going until 6am. As a rule, you'll pay a minimum entrance fee of €2.50–4 in the clubs, and in bars where there's a DJ or live music.

You're most likely to catch **fado** during the student celebrations in May, though there are year-round performances in bars like *Diligência* (see below) and even in some restaurants; those around the Sé Velha are good bets. For up-to-the-minute news on **concerts** and events, watch for fly posters stuck up all over university buildings.

Cafés

Café Montanha Largo da Portagem. Best-sited of the square's cafés with a good view of the passing parade and bridge traffic. There's live music or poetry some evenings.

Café Santa Cruz Praça 8 de Maio. Coimbra's most atmospheric and appealing café, set in part of the monastery buildings. It's hard to say which spot is more attractive – the vaulted stone interior or the outside tables.

Café Sé Velha Rua Joaquim António d'Aguiar 132. At the top of a particularly exhausting flight of steps a stone's throw from the cathedral, with outdoor terrace seating.

Pasteleria Toledo Largo da Portagem. Busy little café serving sandwiches, filling soups and divine cinnamon-dusted *pastel de nata*.

Praça Velha Praça do Comércio. Tables outside in a veritable suntrap of a square, just down the steps from the main street.

Bars

Académico Praça da República. Just next to the ever-popular Tropical (see below), this new, fashionable spot gets busy with a young studenty crowd.

Aqui Há Rato Largo da Sé Velha 20. Bar with dance floor and DJ spinning pop-dance hits from 10pm until 4am.

Bar Quebra Costas Rua Quebra Costas 47. Small, stylishly laid-back bar tucked away on the steps leading down from the Sé Velha.

Boémia Bar Rua do Cabido 6. Upmarket wood-and-tile jazz/blues bar, which packs in the students at weekends; just off Largo da Sé Velha. Has fado on some Friday and Saturday nights. Closed Sun.

Cartola Esplanada Bar Praça da República. Student favourite, next to the turismo, with esplanade seats, interior chrome fittings and boombox acoustics.

Diligência Bar Rua Nova 30, between Rua Direita and Rua da Sofia. There's food, drink and fado every night in this atmospheric joint with cobblestone walls and candles, though the feelings of *saudade* (loss and longing), from which the music draws its spirit, will also be felt in your wallet.

De Sjoelbak Rua do Brasil 93 Dutch bar with lashings of lager and a boisterous crowd swinging to R&B and Sixties' classics; eat at the *Aviz* (see p.217) and pop in here afterwards. Closed Sun.

Tropical Praça da República, corner of Rua Alexandre Herculano. Split-level bar packed with students at the weekends. The pavement tables soon get swamped, while the barman roves around with trays of ice-cold Super Bocks.

Clubs

Clube Dux Av Alfonso Henriques. Fashionable club favoured by the well-heeled glamour crowd, swinging their slender hips to house music.

Scotch Quinta da Ínsula. Young and lively club pumping out the latest dance tunes to a cheerful, studenty crowd.

Via Latina Rua Almeida Garrett 1. Youthful, disco hi-jinks near Praça da República. Similar crowd to Scotch, with hard house and techno music. Open till 4am; closed Sun.

Listings

Banks and exchange Banks are grouped along the avenidas west and east of Coimbra A station, Avenida Emídio Navarro and Avenida Fernão de Magalhães. The *Hotel Astória*, Av Emídio Navarro 21 (close to Largo da Portagem), will change currency outside bank hours, as will *Hotel Tivoli*, Rua João Machado.

Boat trips Basófias runs 75min trips up the Rio Mondego (departing from beside Parque Dr. Manuel Braga, ☏239 826 815), giving you a duck's-eye view of the old city. In summer, trips depart Tues–Sun at 3pm, 4.30pm & 6pm, with additional 11.30am & 7.30pm services at weekends; in winter, 3pm & 4.30pm, additional 6pm service at weekends. O Pioneiro do Mondego also arrange downriver kayak trips from the nearby town of Penacova to Coimbra – for details, see p.224. More information from the turismo.

Buses Most services use the main bus station at the top end of Av Fernão de Magalhães (information ☏239 855 270). AVIC, Rua João de Ruão 16 ☏239 823 769, ✉avic.mondego@mail.telepac.pt, runs to the Costa de Prata resorts, Figueira da Foz, Aveiro and Condeixa-a-Nova (for Conímbriga); Moisés Correia de Oliveira, Rua Rosa Falcão 10 ☎239 828 268, ✉moises.lda@nect.pt, runs to Montemor-o-Velho and other villages on or close to the Coimbra–Figueira da Foz road (N11) and direct to Figueira itself. For services to Mountain Beiras and the north, contact Rodo Norte ☎239 825 190, ✉www.rodonorte.pt.

Car breakdowns Automóvel Club de Portugal (ACP), Av Emídio Navarro 6 ☎239 852 020, ✉www.acp.pt.

Car rental Avis, Coimbra A station ☎239 834 786, ✉www.avis.com; Hertz,Rua Padre Estevão Cabral ☎239 834 750, ✉www.hertz.com; Hervis, Rua João Machado 94 ☎239 824 062; Salitur, Rua Padre Estevão Cabral ☎239 838 983.

Cinema Cine Avenida, Av Sá da Bandeira ☎239 855 630; also has a rooftop bar and great city views. Teatro Academico Gil Vicente, Praça da República ☎239 829 372, has an arts cinema as well as a gallery, café and occasional classical and jazz concerts.

Hospital Hospital da Universidade de Coimbra, Praça Professor Mota Pinto ☎239 400 400.

Internet *Central Modem*, Escadas do Quebra Costas (daily 9am–4pm; €2/hr; ✉www .centralmodem.com). *ECTEP*, Galerias Avenida shopping centre, Avenida Sá da Bandeira (Mon–Sat 10.30am–midnight, Sun 1pm–midnight; €2/hr; ✉www.ectep.pt). *Postnet*, Rua Antero de

Quental 73 (Mon–Fri 9am–midnight, Sat & Sun 3pm–midnight; €2.50/hr; ☎239 841 025).

Markets The recently refurbished main food market is on Rua Nicolau Rui Fernandes, above the post office. On Saturday mornings, there's an open-air antiques market in Praça do Comércio.

Police Main HQ at Rua Olímpio Nicolau Rui Fernandes, across from the post office (☎239 822 022).

Post office The main post office is at Av Fernão de Magalhães 223, near Largo do Arnado (Mon–Fri 8.30am–6.30pm, Sat 9am–12.30pm); other central offices are on Rua Nicolau Rui Fernandes, just below the market, and on Praça da República (both same hours as main post office).

Swimming pool The Piscina Municipal (summer 10am–1pm & 2–7pm; winter 12.30–1.30pm; ☎239 701 605) is at the Estádo Municipal São José sports complex, east of the centre: take bus #5 from Largo da Portagem.

Telephones Use a street pay phone with a phone card (see p.40) or call from the main post office or the branch across from the market.

Train information ☎239 834 998, ✉www.abren.pt.

Travel agencies Abreu, Rua da Sota 2 ☎239 855 520, and Intervisa, Av Fernão de Magalhães 11 ☎239 823 873, both sell international bus and flight tickets. Or try Viagens Mondego, Rua João de Ruão 16 ☎239 822 555, ✉www .viagensmondego.com.

Around Coimbra

There are several sights within easy reach of Coimbra that are worth a day trip or a little more. Close by is the Roman city of **Conímbriga** with some exceptional mosaics, while west towards the coast stand the impressive ruins of a castle at **Montemor-o-Velho**. **Lousã**, to the southeast, also has a castle, although it is the distinctive Serra countryside which makes a trip here worthwhile. To the northeast of the city the kayaking possibilities on the **Rio Mondego** and the attractive scenery around the town of **Penacova** are similarly enticing.

Conímbriga

The ancient city of **CONÍMBRIGA** (daily: summer 9am–8pm; winter 9am–6pm; €3), 16km southwest of Coimbra, is by far the most important Roman site in Portugal. It was almost certainly preceded by a substantial Celto-Iberian settlement, dating back to the Iron Age, but the excavated buildings nearly all belong to the latter days of the Roman Empire, from the second to the fourth century AD. Throughout this period Conímbriga was a major stopping point on the road from Olisipo (Lisbon) to Bracara Augusta (Braga). Although by no means the largest town in Roman Portugal, it has survived better than any other – principally because its inhabitants abandoned

Conímbriga, apparently for the comparative safety of Coimbra, and never resettled it. That the city came to a violent end is clear from the powerful wall thrown up right through its heart, a wall thrown up so hurriedly and determinedly that it even cut houses in two.

The site

It is the **wall**, with the **Roman road** leading up to and through it, that first strikes you. Little else, indeed, remains above ground level. In the urgency of its construction anything that came to hand was used and a close inspection of the wall reveals pillars, inscribed plaques and bricks thrown in among the rough stonework. Most of what has been excavated is in the immediate environs of the wall; the bulk of the city, still only part-excavated, lies in the ground beyond it.

What you can see is impressive enough though. Houses with exceptional **mosaic floors**, some now covered to protect them from the elements, **pools** whose original fountains and water-ducts have been restored to working order (drop €0.50 into the machine in front of the fountains to watch them play), and a complex series of **baths** with their elaborate under-floor heating systems have been revealed. In one part of the grounds, two skeletons lie partly exposed beneath the dust covering a Visigoth burial site. Beyond the wall, less work has been undertaken, but here, too, are evocative remains, particularly of the **aqueduct**, which fed the city with water, and the **forum**, with its shop entrances, and nearby **temple**. At the edge of the site, on a bluff above the steep valley – for many years Conímbriga's main defence – a series of **public baths** enjoy a stupendous view.

There are some explanatory notes in English posted across the site, but to make sense of it all, it's worth investing in the official **guidebook** sold at the entrance. In the summer you may find students on site to explain the finer points.

The museum

The Conímbriga entrance fee (hang onto your ticket) includes entry to the excellent **Museo Monográfico de Conímbriga** (summer: Tues–Sun 10am–8pm; winter: Tues–Sun 10am–6pm), opposite the site entrance. On display are fascinating finds from the dig, presented thematically in cabinets detailing various trades (glass-making, ironmongery, weaving, even house-building) and aspects of daily life: in the section on health and hygiene, scalpels and needles wink wickedly in the light, while nearby is a lovely collection of carved jade rings. The other side of the museum shows how the finds relate to the site itself, by means of photographs and diagrams. Here, too, are displayed the larger spoils – statues of torsos, carved lintels, gargoyles from temples, monochromatic mosaics, remarkably bright mural fragments, and slabs, pillars and tombstones from the necropolis. The only drawback to this fascinating museum is that there's no English-language labelling whatsoever. Make sure you end up with a visit to the **café** with terrific views from its terrace down into the valley.

Practicalities

There are regular buses to **CONDEIXA-A-NOVA**, a nearby market town, from the AVIC bus station in Coimbra (see p.209). The bus drops you by the church at the edge of the main square and it's a 2km walk from here to the site at Conímbriga – follow the signposts. The last bus back leaves at 8.05pm. The town is a pleasant little place, with several cafés and bars around the square – *O Regional* does decent meals at reasonable prices. For something more upmarket there's the restaurant in the elegant *Pousada de Santa Cristina* (☎239 941 286, ⓦ www.pousadas.pt; ❼). Condeixa is also the centre of the Beira's **hand-painted ceramics** industry and numerous local factories are open for visits – you'll pass a couple on the walk out along the main road to the site.

Montemor-o-Velho

Thirty-two kilometres west of Coimbra, the **castle** (10am–12.30pm & 2–5pm; closed Mon; free) at **MONTEMOR-O-VELHO** broods over the flood plain of the Mondego. From the train, or driving along the N111, to Figueira da Foz (see p.231), its keep and crenellated silhouette rival that of Óbidos, as does its early history. First the Romans, then the Moors, fortified this conspicuous rocky bluff; finally taken from the Moors at the end of the eleventh century, it became a favoured royal residence. It was here in 1355 that Dom Afonso IV met with his council to decide on the fate of Inês de Castro, and here, thirty years later, that João de Avis received the homage of the towns-people on his way to Coimbra to be acclaimed king Dom João I.

Despite this royal attention, the town itself never prospered, and today there's little enough to see inside the castle walls either, though the views from the walkways are stunning. The main attraction within the walls is the Manueline **Igreja de Santa Maria de Alcáçova**, said to have been designed by Diogo de Boitaca of Belém fame; it has a beautiful wooden ceiling, fine twisted columns and Moorish-style *azulejo* decoration.

If you can, aim to visit on the second or fourth Wednesday of the month, when Montemor's vast **market** spills across the plain in the lee of the castle. Families swarm in from the surrounding countryside, some still by donkey and cart, though most by car and scooter, which soon clog up the congested central streets.

Practicalities

The **train station** is a 1km walk from town and castle; **buses** from Coimbra drop you much more centrally. There's no particular reason to stay, given the proximity of Coimbra or indeed Figueira da Foz, just 13km further west. That said, the *Residencial Abade João*, Rua Combatentes da Grande Guerra 15 (☎239 689 458; ❸), a beautiful, converted period town house, may persuade you to stop; it's just up the street to the left as you face the large, white town hall in the central Praça da República. The **turismo**, within the walls of the castle (Tues–Sun 10am–12.30pm & 2–5.30pm; ☎239 680 380), could doubtless drum up more reasons to hang around, though there's no better excuse than a **meal** at the *Restaurante Ramalhão*, Rua Tenente Valadim 24 (closed Sun evening, Mon, & Oct), where all the dishes – eel stew, chicken with rice, duck or rabbit – use ingredients grown, reared or caught around the town. You'll get away with spending €10–15 depending on your appetite.

Lousã and the Serra da Lousã

Another popular day trip from Coimbra is to **LOUSÃ**, 25km to the southeast, with its attractive ruined castle and surrounding **Serra countryside**. You can get there by train (Coimbra Parque station) or by bus (Mon–Fri). There are two train stations at Lousã: get off at the first, **Lousã A**. From here, take the road at right angles to the rail line and walk uphill to the centre. To reach the castle, you'll need to continue on past the church until you see a sign for "C.P. Prado", which you follow until reaching the *Café Lousanese* – at the fork here, it's left for the castle ("Castelo e Ermidas"), right for *A Cave* restaurant (see p.223).

A hike around the Serra da Lousã's abandoned villages

This hike in the **Serra da Lousã** provides marvellous views and a sequence of eerie sights in the range's abandoned mountain villages, deserted in the 1950s as a result of rural emigration. It's quite an unsettling experience to wander through the empty streets and into the open rooms. In the first and third villages you come to (Casal Novo and Talasual); some of the houses have been renovated and can be rented for the night. Ask at the turismo in Lousã for contact details.

Intermittently marked with blue and yellow paint blazes, this three-hour, 8km circular hike begins at Lousã's ruined castle and climbs steeply through the woods to the villages. The 1:25,000 map (no.252) available from the IGeoE in Lisbon, or from Porto Editora in Porto (see p.316), covers this walk, but it's a bit out of date and you may also find the map handed out at Lousã's turismo helpful.

From the *Burgos* restaurant near the pools below the castle, walk up the stone steps to the end of the picnic area, and take steep, rocky path marked by paint blazes. After one kilometre, take the right-hand path at a junction; here, the landscape becomes barren, charred by regular forest fires. After 700m or so along the path, turn left at a dirt forestry track and continue uphill. The track changes from dirt to gravel as you reach a T-junction with another gravel track; ignore the latter and go straight ahead up a narrower rocky path until you reach **Casal Novo**. Turn right at the top of the village, then immediately left onto a dirt track. Take the left-hand turn at a dusty road 1km later to arrive at **Chiqueiro**. The village is still inhabited by shepherds and farmers and there's a drinking fountain here.

Leave the village on a stony track clearly marked with paint blazes, then turn right on joining a broad track which quickly peters out. Head steeply downhill to join the dusty road visible below, turn right on reaching it, and another kilometre brings you into **Talasnal**, probably the most beautiful of the range's villages with a harmonious mix of ruined and restored cottages amidst stunning mountain views. Continue through the village along an old stony path, and turn left when you join a track at the bottom of the village. Head over an old stone bridge and follow this good, easily navigable path all the way back to the river pools, keeping an eye out for occasional burnt-out logs blocking the path and the dizzy drop to your right. A well-earned dip in the pools below the castle makes a refreshing end to the walk.

Development in the last few years has transformed Lousã from a diminutive village into a sprawling town, though the compact and attractive old centre remains fairly unchanged. Wandering around the older streets, you pass a succession of intricately decorated **chapels** and **casas brasonadas** (heraldic mansions), while in the handsome town hall, a little museum doubles as the **turismo** (Mon–Fri 9am–12.30pm & 2–5.30pm, Sat 10am–12.30pm & 2.30–4pm, Sun 10.30am–1pm & 2.30–4pm; ☎239 990 376, ⓦwww .cm-lousa.pt). Customarily helpful, this can supply you with a sketch map of the Serra da Lousã, vital if you want to explore, and useful, too, for the walk up to the castle.

Follow the path up from the village through the pine trees, and you pass springs midway, bubbling beautifully clear water that locals drive up to collect. After around 2km (30min), you emerge at a spot where a tributary of the Mondego curls around a narrow gorge between two splendid wooded hills. On one sits a miniature **castle**, whose stone keep provides views across the valley; on the other is a small hermitage dedicated to **Nossa Senhora da Piedade**. Pilgrims mingle with picnickers and the swimmers who come to bathe in the chilly river pool between the two. The *Burgos* **restaurant** (closed at time of writing, but due to reopen; ☎ & ⓕ239 991 162) has a lovely setting, with a dining room overlooking the river.

Practicalities

The village has two central **pensões**, both pleasant and moderately priced: the *Residencial Martinho*, Rua Forças Armadas (☎239 991 397, ℗239 994 335; ❷), whose rooms all have bathrooms; and *Pensão Bem Estar* at Avenida Coelho da Gama 11 (☎239 991 445, ℗239 993 915; ❷), where the back dining room serves typical country dishes at reasonable prices – all rooms are bright and clean, with TV and telephone, though only some have bathrooms. There is also a **campsite** (☎ & ℗239 991 052; open March–Nov), ten minutes' east of the centre and signposted from the town hall.

Apart from *Burgos* by the castle, the best **eating** options are *Casa Velha*, a good, homely restaurant despite the blaring TV, in the modern plaza behind the market, or the unlikely-looking *A Cave* (closed Tues) a modern building set among new housing fifteen minutes' walk from the centre in Barrio do Penedo, on the way to the local paper factory. It dishes up huge portions of local cooking – the *leitão* (suckling pig) is excellent, though there's also lamb, *chanfana* and even *coq au vin*. During your stay, try the shockingly alcoholic **Licor Beirão** – herb-flavoured "firewater" – which is made locally from a secret recipe developed by a pharmacist from Lousã.

Penacova

Northeast of Coimbra, the hilly, wooded valley of the **Rio Mondego** is a delight. The river is trailed by the minor N110 road, along which run regular buses from Coimbra, while for six months of the year it's possible to rent a **kayak** to travel downriver from Penacova to Coimbra (see below).

The drive is lovely, the **N110 road** keeping high above the river for the most part, affording the occasional sweeping view of glistening water and improbably perched hamlets. At Penacova, the road forks and drivers can make the most of the scenic surroundings by heading up the equally attractive **N235 to Luso** (see p.227). The **IP3**, meanwhile, sticks initially with the Mondego and forges on for Viseu, via Tondela (p.228), a roller coaster of a main road with some very fast sections and more fine views.

Penacova

PENACOVA, 22km northeast of Coimbra, is a small town of some antiquity set high above the river, with stunning views of the valley – spoiled only by the sweep of the motorway which cuts through on the opposite hillside. There is little enough to the place itself – a pint-sized square, a couple of cafés and restaurants, and the surrounding river and woods – though an oddity is the highly elaborate **toothpicks** (*palitos*) on sale. These are hand-carved from willow by local women and are beautiful artefacts; the more delicate ones are like feathered darts. You can inspect these – and buy them, too, if you wish – at the **turismo** (Mon–Fri 9am–5pm, Sat & Sun 10am–1pm & 2–5pm; ☎239 470 300, ⓦwww.fish.pt/cm-penacova) in the town hall in the main square.

If you fancy a night in these quiet surroundings, there are three **places to stay**: 100m uphill, past the town hall and turismo, is *Casa do Repouso* (☎ & ℗239 477 137; ❸), a lovely old house with a beautiful garden and the best views in town. Otherwise, try the friendly, traditional *Pensão Avenida*, Avenida Abel Rodrigues da Costa (☎239 477 142; ❷), on a bluff as you drive into town, with a polished wood interior, sun-terrace and restaurant; or the newer *Residencial São João* (☎ & ℗239 477 545; ❸), a modern building across the road from the *Avenida*. For meals, the *O Panorâmico* **restaurant** – next to the town hall and turismo – has a glorious view down the valley; full meals cost around €13–17.

A walk around Penacova

This leisurely 11km, three-hour stroll starts near the campsites on the outskirts of Penacova and threads through farmland, woodland and hamlets that remain peaceful and tourist-free even in July and August. You might want to take along a copy of the IGeoE 1:25,000 map (no. 231) available from the IGeoE in Lisbon (see p.22), or from Porto Editora in Porto (see p.316).

From the campsite to the right of the bridge in Penacova, turn left to walk down a tarmac road, turning right after 100m onto another paved but usually car-free road that follows a river valley to the tiny village of **Sanguinho**, 2km away. At the village, turn right to follow the cobbled road uphill, then left at the last house along a good, uphill forestry track that affords excellent views of Penacova and the Mondego valley. Two kilometres along, there's a pronounced fork in the track; turn right here. Take a right turn at a T-junction 100m later, and right again 50m further on. After heading downhill for 400m, you arrive at the hamlet of **Cume do Soito**; on joining a T-junction with a tarmac road, turn right, then immediately right again down a stony track. After 300m, this meets another paved road where you turn right. Another 300m and the road bends sharply to the left; take the right-hand forestry track 50m after this bend. Once the forestry track becomes paved and turns another left-hand bend, take the forestry track which strikes off to the right and you'll arrive back at the top of Sanguinho after a 1km walk through forest. The woodland here has been devastated in parts by indiscriminate logging, and monotonous swathes of pine and eucalyptus alternate with bare patches of badly eroded land.

Leave Sanguinho along the same road, but instead of following the road back to the campsite, turn left 150m after the village along a dirt track which follows the bottom of the valley, narrowing and eventually crossing over the stream via a small concrete bridge. An intricate network of tiny fields awash with sunflowers during the summer, the valley is also dotted year-round with bizarre scarecrows. Keep a lookout for birds of prey circling the fields for prey. The path emerges at the village of **Carvoeira** – a tiny, beautifully preserved collection of narrow cobbled streets and stone archways with a bar and a small grocery shop. At the other end of Carvoeira, you'll reach a main road; turn right here and it's a 200m walk back to the campsite.

There's a municipal **campsite** 3km away at Vila Nova (℡239 477 946, ⓦwww.fish.pt/cm-penacova), where you can fish in the river. To get there, turn left after you cross the bridge below town; if you turn right instead of left after the bridge, you'll find a second campsite (℡239 477 664; closed mid-Dec to mid-Jan). From here, O Pioneiro do Mondego arranges downriver **kayak trips** to Coimbra (April to mid-Oct daily; €13 per person), leaving Penacova at 11am. It's a 25km (3–4hr) trip back to Coimbra. You'll need to book in advance (English-speaking: call ℡239 478 385), and if you've reserved there's a free minibus from Coimbra at 10am to get you to Penacova in time for departure; more information is available from the turismo in Coimbra. Sportmargens (℡239 477 143, ⓔsportmargens@net.sapo.pt) rent out canoes and bicycles for the day.

The Buçaco Forest and Luso

The **Buçaco Forest** is something of a Portuguese icon. The country's most famous and most revered woods were a monastic domain throughout the Middle Ages, and the site in the Peninsular War of a battle that saw Napoleon's first significant defeat. Today, they are a little uncared for and overvisited, but remain an enjoyable spot for rambling.

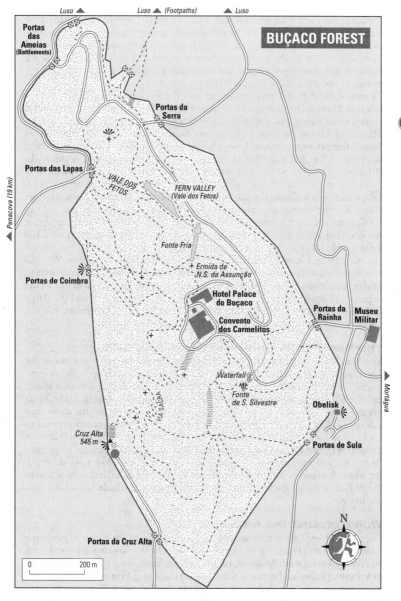

BUÇACO FOREST

Luso ▲   Luso ▲ (Footpaths)   ▲ Luso

Portas
das
Ameias
(Battlements)

Portas da
Serra

▲ Penacova (19 km)

Portas das Lapas

VALE DOS
FETOS

FERN VALLEY
(Vale dos Fetos)

Fonte Fria

Portas de Coimbra

+ Ermida de
N.S. da Assunção

Hotel Palace
do Buçaco

Portas da
Rainha

Museu
Militar

Convento
dos Carmelitos

▲ Mortágua

Waterfall

VIA SACRA

Fonte
de S. Silvestre

Obelisk

Cruz Alta
545 m

Portas de Sula

N

Portas da Cruz Alta

0   200 m

Benedictine monks established a hermitage in the midst of Buçaco Forest as early as the sixth century, and the area remained in religious hands right up to the dissolution of the monasteries in 1834. The forest's great fame and beauty, though, came with the **Carmelite monks** who settled here in the seventeenth century, building the walls which still mark its boundary.

In 1643 Pope Urban VIII issued a papal bull threatening anyone who

damaged the trees with excommunication; an earlier decree had already protected the monks' virtue by banning women from entering. The monks,
meanwhile, were propagating the forest, introducing varieties new to Portugal
from all over the world. Nowadays there are estimated to be more than seven
hundred different types of tree, but the most impressive remain some of the
earliest – particularly the mighty Mexican cedars.

From Coimbra it is easy enough to visit the forest as a day trip, or en route
to Viseu. Entry is free during the winter (walls enclose the area and access is via
a number of gates), but you pay €2.50 if you want to go in by car between
May and October. All non-express buses from Coimbra to Viseu take a short
detour from the spa town of **Luso** (40min from Coimbra), through the forest,
stopping at the old royal forest lodge, now the swanky **Hotel Palace do
Buçaco**, and again by the **Portas da Rainha**. Alternatively, you could stay
overnight in the *Hotel Palace* itself (☎231 937 970, ✆bussaco-palace@clix.pt;
❼), which was built on the site of the old Carmelite monastery as a summer
retreat for the Portuguese monarchy. However, as it was completed only in
1907, three years before the declaration of the Republic, it saw little royal use.
An enormous imitation Manueline construction, it charges upwards of €100
for a double room in low season and around €150 in high season, but anyone
can stroll in and have a drink (their wine cellar is superb) or a meal. You can
also view what remains of the **Convento dos Carmelítas** (daily except
Friday 9am–noon & 2pm; €0.50), and admire the Afonso Mucha prints or the
sequence of *azulejos* depicting the Portuguese conquest of Ceuta and the Battle
of Buçaco (see below). If your budget won't stretch to the *Hotel Palace*, you can
find less expensive accommodation in Luso itself (see opposite).

The Battle of Buçaco and the Museu Militar

The **Battle of Buçaco** (1810) was fought largely on the ridge just above the
forest, and it marked the first serious reverse suffered by Napoleon in his campaigns on the Peninsula. The French under Massena launched a frontal assault
up the hill on virtually impregnable Anglo-Portuguese positions, sustaining
massive losses in what for the Duke of Wellington amounted to little more than
a delaying tactic, which he exploited in order to give himself time to retreat to
his lines at Torres Vedras. A small **Museu Militar** (Tues–Sun 10am–12pm &
2–5pm; €1), outside the forest near the Portas da Rainha, contains maps, uniforms and weapons from the campaign. Just above it, a narrow road climbs to
the **obelisk** raised as a memorial to the battle, with vistas inland right across to
the distant Serra da Estrêla, from where the **Portas de Sula** leads back into
the forest.

Walks around the forest

Buçaco is a lovely place to wander around, if not always the haven of peace the
monks strove to create – at weekends and holidays the woods are packed with
picnicking Portuguese. Walks are laid out everywhere: along the delightful **Vale
dos Fetos** (Valley of Ferns) to the lake and cascading **Fonte Fria**, for example, or up Avenida dos Cedros to the **Portas de Coimbra**. But you can wander freely anywhere in the forest, and in many ways it's at its most attractive
where it's wildest, away from the formal pathways and tour groups.

The **Via Sacra**, lined with seventeenth-century chapels in which terracotta
figures depict the stages of Christ's journey carrying the cross to Calvary, leads
from the *Hotel Palace* to the **Cruz Alta**, a giant cross at the summit of the hill.
From here, as from the Portas de Coimbra, there are magnificent panoramas of
the surrounding country.

Luso

LUSO lies just 3km downhill from the forest. A spa town for the past hundred years or so, it still draws crowds of Portuguese, taking the waters as a cure for rheumatism and other complaints. As such places go, it's pretty enjoyable, with a series of elegant spa buildings, a wonderful nineteenth-century *salão do chá* – all white wicker, potted palms and Art Nouveau decor – and a casino along the main street.

Taking the waters (☎231 937 444, @agua.luso@mail.telepac.pt; closed Nov–April) can be fun, too. Massages, hydrotherapies and other treatments cost from €5–12 a go; the only serious expenditure is incurred if you see one of the spa's consultants. There's also a fine, Olympic-sized **swimming pool**, attached to the central *Grande Hotel de Luso* (see below), whose somewhat stiff admission fee (€13; closed mid-Sept to mid-July) is more than recompensed by a few hours' basking. Most locals, though, are here to picnic in the surroundings, taking the opportunity to fill bottles and plastic containers for free with spa water from the outdoor **Fonte de São João** (which also has its own *casa do chá*).

Practicalities

There are several trains a day from Coimbra which stop near Luso, but it is a 5km hike from the station. Far more convenient are the buses which stop first at Luso and then at Buçaco. There are six daily buses, leaving from Coimbra bus station between 7.35am and 7.20pm; the last returning bus leaves at 6.18pm from Buçaco and 6.28pm from Luso.

The **turismo** (summer Mon–Fri 9am–7pm, Sat & Sun 10am–1pm & 3–5pm; winter Mon–Fri 9.30am–12.30pm & 2–6pm, Sat & Sun 10am–1pm & 3–5pm; ☎231 939 133) is just up from the bus stop on Avenida Emídio Navarro, near the post office, and can help you find a **room** or provide a list of local accommodation.

There are several good **places to stay** in Luso: *Pensão Portugal*, Rua Marinha Pimenta (☎231 939 158; ❷), is quite a climb from the town centre – on the way to the turismo, turn left off Avenida Emídio Navarro along Rua Alvaro Castelões; it's fairly unprepossessing but undeniably value for money. More expensive but still good value are: *Pensão Astória*, Avenida Emídio Navarro (☎231 939 182; ❸), which has a certain faded charm and is located beyond the turismo, almost opposite the *Grande Hotel*; *Pensão Alegre*, also on the *avenida* (☎231 930 256; ❹), up past the *Hotel Eden*, an impressive building full of nineteenth-century style which was once the residence of the Conde Graciosa; and the friendly, family-run *Residencial Imperial* (☎231 937 570, ⓕ231 937 579; ❸), opposite the *Hotel Eden*, in a modern building with very comfortable rooms filled with sturdy old furniture – all have new bathrooms and TV. Top of the range is, of course, the *Grande Hotel de Luso*, Rua dos Banhos (☎231 937 937, @hoteluso@clix.pt; closed Nov & Dec; ❺), with its unmissable yellow exterior. Inside, it's splendidly furnished with a heated indoor pool. There's also a campsite about 2km out of town on the way to the football ground (☎231 930 916).

Most of the *pensões* and hotels have **restaurants** attached, one of the best being that of the *Pensão Alegre*, on Avenida Emídio Navarro. The plain and popular *Cesteiro*, on Rua Lúcio Pais Abranches, on the way out towards the train station, serves decent meals for around €12.50. A more upmarket choice is *Lourenços*, a smart regional restaurant serving good value meals for around €15.

The Dão Valley and the Serra do Caramulo

The route northeast from Coimbra to Caramulo leads through the **valley of the Rio Dão**, heart of the region where **Dão wines** – some of the country's finest and richest reds – are produced. Where they're not covered with vineyards, the slopes are thickly wooded with pine and eucalyptus trees, but all too often there are bare tracts where forest fires have raged. It's a fine ride and though there's no overwhelming point of interest en route, you might stop for coffee at least in the small market town of **SANTA COMBA DÃO**, a little over 50km from Coimbra.

Beyond here, the views from the main IP3 are of the spectacular **Serra do Caramulo**, breaking to the northwest. Tondela (see below) marks the eastern turn-off point for the mountains, accessed along the minor **N230** which winds tortuously through a succession of tiny villages at the heart of the mountain range, before descending to Águeda, from where the fast main road runs due south to Coimbra. With your own transport, you could describe the circle from Coimbra, seeing Luso and Buçaco Forest on the way. By **bus**, the same circuit is possible, though it's a much more complex affair and one which will entail a night in the mountains, at the pretty village of Caramulo – no great hardship.

The Serra do Caramulo

Most of the Serra villages are little more than hamlets, of interest principally for their environs, full of rhododendrons, brightly coloured azaleas and thick green shrubs growing wild on the hillside. If you feel like staying off the beaten track, places like **Cambarinho** and **Alcofra** have **rooms** to rent, but perhaps the best base is the main village, **CARAMULO**, a twisting 19km from Tondela and the highway. Coming **from Coimbra**, there are three daily buses to Caramulo, via Águeda. **From Luso**, you need first to take the Viseu bus as far as **TONDELA**, where you should be able to pick up one of the two daily buses on to Caramulo/Águeda, a majestic if rather bumpy drive straight across the centre of the Serra do Caramulo. If you're detained by choice or necessity in Tondela, the *Residencial Tondela* (☎232 822 411; ❸) in the main square is good value. For **eating**, there's a decent restaurant, *O Solar*, on the other side of the square.

An alternative approach to Caramulo, from the north, is **from Vouzela** (see opposite) in the Vouga valley. On weekdays, one bus a day runs between Vouzela and Caramulo. If you are approaching from the south, Vouzela is an obvious next destination after Caramulo.

Caramulo

Tucked beneath the peaks of the high Beiras Serra, **CARAMULO** is a great walking base – the loftiest Serra de Caramulo peak, **Caramulinho** at 1075m, is less than an hour's hike away. It's also a striking village, a diminutive, rather ghostlike place, which makes an almost surreal setting for a couple of very fine museums.

At the **Museu do Caramulo** (daily 9am–12.30pm & 2–6pm; €5), the principal display is the **Museu de Arte**, a wonderfully jumbled art collection, with everything from primitive religious sculpture to sketches by the greatest modern masters – minor works by Picasso and Dalí among them. There's an exquisite series of sixteenth-century Tournai tapestries depicting the earliest

Portuguese explorers in India, full of weird animals and natives based on obviously very garbled reports. A painting by British portraitist Graham Sutherland, donated to Portugal by the Queen, and symbolizing the long alliance with Britain, is accompanied by its letter of authenticity from Buckingham Palace. Elsewhere there's a large *John the Baptist*, painted by Grão Vasco, and quantities of furniture and china. Downstairs, and continuing next door, is the even more incongruous **Museu do Automóvel**, a superb collection of vintage cars and motorcycles, including some of the earliest Benz, Buggatti and Fiat models, an elegant series of Rolls-Royces and a pack of 1950s Harley Davidsons.

The **turismo** was closed at the time of writing – the best source of information at present is the Tondela turismo (℡232 811 110). Finding cheap **accommodation** can be tricky. The town's only *pensão* closed recently, but there are some **private rooms** for rent. The best bet is to ask at the *Mercado Serrano*, a local grocery shop, where the owner is often willing to help – walk up the main road past *Restaurante Marte*, and the take the left fork opposite the Galp petrol station; the shop is past the chemist on the left. With more money to spend, first choice is the excellent *Hotel Caramulo*, Avenida Dr. Abel Lacerda (℡232 860 100, Ⓦ www.hotel-caramulo.com; **❻**), with superb amenities (including jacuzzi and hydrotherapy facilities) and unbeatable views towards the Serra da Estrela. You can also book mountain activities such as canyoning, canoeing and mountain-biking through Desafios Caramulo (℡232 860 155), which is based in the *Hotel Caramulo*. The six-bedroom **pousada**, *São Jerónimo* (℡232 861 291, Ⓦ www.pousada.pt; **❻**), a kilometre along the Tondela road, pales in comparison but is cheaper than most in the chain and has a swimming pool and great views. The *Café-Restaurante Marte*, on the main road through the village, has surly service but affordable **meals**; just up the hill, locals while away the hours under the trees at the *Café Avenida*.

Along the Rio Vouga

The **Rio Vouga** is one of the most beautiful, somnolent rivers in the country and a fine route to follow if you feel like taking in a little of backwater Portugal. Coming from Coimbra or Aveiro, you can get a train as far as **Albergaria-a-Velha**, where you change to a CP bus. The old Vouga train line along the river has been replaced by a bus service which stops at various rural spots en route. You probably won't want to get off until **Vouzela** (see below), though drivers will feel compelled to pause now and again to take in the views. Alternatively, you can approach from the south, from Caramulo, or from Viseu, to the east, from where the minor N337 makes a particularly memorable approach.

Vouzela

VOUZELA is one of the most immediately attractive of Beira towns, a small place with an almost palpable sense of civic pride. The locals boast of the peculiar sweet cakes, or *pasteis de Vouzela* (only for the most sweet-toothed), richly flavoured traditional dishes such as *vitela de Lafões*, and the heady local *vinho Lafões* (similar to *vinho verde*).

The old centre is built around a sluggish stream, bordered by lilies and overhung with weeping willows, which serves as the backdrop to the main morning activity – washing clothes. Beneath a low **Romanesque bridge**, garments are spread to dry on the tall grass and soap suds run blue in the clear water.

Houses clustered around the bridge are all of the small-town manor type, with granite steps and balconies and whitewashed plaster work. Topping this scene, a viaduct gracefully loops its way across the rooftops, while beyond it the Serras of Arada and Caramulo rise up, dark and green, to north and south.

Just off the main through-road, at the top of the lane down to the river, the **turismo** (Tues–Sun 10am–12.30pm & 2–5pm; ☎232 771 515) is housed in a former prison in the Largo Morais de Carvalho. On the floor above, there's a **museum** (free) offering insights into local weaving, photography and painting. It contains a small, rather odd collection, ranging through anthropological and historical exhibits, traditional craftwork and Romanesque fragments, to an array of old dolls. Nearby, up in Praça da República, is the thirteenth-century **parish church** and the town **Pelourinho**, popularly referred to as the *forca* or scaffold, from its days as a site of executions during the Inquisition.

There's a **feira** on May 14 when flowers are strewn in the streets in honour of **São Frei Gil**, and everyone drives up into the hills to witness the blossoming of the rare *loendros*, a type of rhododendron peculiar to this area and which is now protected by law. Otherwise, note that there's a **street market** every first Wednesday in the month, a good time to be in town.

Practicalities

Buses drop you at the station just up from the centre – to get to the main street, walk down the hill, take the first right followed by the first left. The **turismo** is on the square off to the left. Unfortunately, finding a **room** can be a problem. Just out of town, *Casa de Fataunços* (☎232 772 697; ❺), 3km from Vouzela in the village of the same name, is a beautifully restored manor house with lovely rooms, gardens and a pool. Otherwise for budget options try *Residencial Ferreira*, Rua Barão da Costeiro 7 (☎232 771 650; ❷), a little way up from the turismo on the main road, although it's often full. There is also a municipal **campsite** with fine views (☎232 771 847, ℱ232 771 513), 4km up the road towards Mortágua and **Senhora do Castelo**, a low hill which is the location for much merrymaking and picnicking on the first Sunday after August 5. There's a signpost pointing the way from Praça da República.

There are a handful of decent **restaurants**, including *Restaurante Chafariz* or *Restaurante Paulo* on Rua Mousinho de Albuquerque, off Praça da República.

Termas de São Pedro do Sul

Four kilometres northeast of Vouzela is the thermal resort area of **TERMAS DE SÃO PEDRO DO SUL**, possibly the oldest spa in Portugal. It was a great favourite with the Romans, a popular haunt of Portuguese royalty – Dom Afonso Henriques is said to have bathed his wounded leg here after the battle at Badajoz – and remains among the grandest and most attractive in the country. Its position beside the Vouga, with pine trees all around, certainly lend it charm, and the resort makes for a pleasant stop between buses or an afternoon trip from Vouzela. The **spa** (☎232 723 060, ☜www.fish.pt/cm-spsul) is open all year for those who want to sluice themselves in its foul-smelling waters and avail themselves of the usual range of treatments.

You can get here by **bus** from Viseu (Mon–Fri 6 daily, weekends 1–2) or Vouzela (Mon–Fri 5 daily); for information on onward bus travel ask at the Quiosque das Termas facing the spa. The **turismo** (Mon–Sat 9am–1pm & 2.30–5.30pm, Sun 9am–1pm; ☎232 711 320), just across the bridge from the spa, has a list of *pensões* and can help with **rooms** in private houses. If you plan to stay, you'd be wise to book ahead since the **hotels** and **pensões** stacked up above the river are frequently full. Among the best options – all easily found and often signposted – are the family-run *Pensão Romana* (☎232 711 524; ❸; closed Dec & Jan), on a pleasant little cobbled street; the *Pensão David* (☎232 723 053; ❸), which has cheaper rooms in an annexe beyond the main building (❷); the *Hotel Vouga* (☎232 723 063; ❺); and the modern *Hotel do Parque* (☎232 723 461, ❺232 723 047; ❺). In high season, these and the other places may insist on your paying for full board. The resort's **youth hostel** is situated in an unattractive high-rise overlooking the centre (reception open 8am–midnight; ☎232 724 543, ❸spedrosul@movijovem.pt); it also has double rooms available (❸). There's also a **campsite** (☎232 711 793; June–Sept) on the eastern outskirts of town, signposted from the stone bridge. There are fewer **places to eat** that you'd expect, although the hotels and *pensões* often have restaurants attached – try the one at *Pensão David*. Another popular choice is the *Nunes Pinto*, up the hill behind the spa, serving up good value meals including excellent fresh fish.

The town of **SÃO PEDRO DO SUL** itself is another 3km to the northeast, an unremarkable spread of buildings either side of a busy main road, at the confluence of the Sul and Vouga rivers. You can pick up more bus connections here to Viseu and Lamego, if you're unlucky in Termas. For details of the extraordinary driving route between here and **Arouca** to the northwest, see p.245.

Figueira da Foz

FIGUEIRA DA FOZ is one of the liveliest towns on the west coast, a major resort and deep-sea fishing port. Sited at the mouth of the Mondego, roughly equidistant from Lisbon and Porto and just over an hour by train from Coimbra, it attracts people from all over the country to its superb beaches and surf. That said, it's not the most initially alluring of beach resorts: there's a somewhat industrial approach from the south, and the town itself is resolutely modern with its long promenade backed by a line of anonymous apartment blocks. But it's as close to a typical Portuguese resort as you'll find. Most of the action, in fact, takes place away from the sands in the atmospheric backstreets, where a bubbling good humour prevails, even when the town's packed to the gills.

Arrival, information and accommodation

The **train station** is a long 20- to 25-minute walk from the centre and beach. Keep walking along the river until you see the ocean and then cut into the town – a useful beachfront landmark is the concrete clock tower, close to the tourist office. AVIC **buses to Buarcos** – a fishing village at the northern end of the bay, which has become more or less part of Figueira – leave from directly outside the train station (Mon–Sat every 30min until 11pm, or 8.10pm off season; hourly on Sun). The **bus station** is slightly closer in, though it's still a fair walk down to São Julião church and the municipal gardens, from where the streets run straight to the beach.

If you need help with anything, the **main turismo** (daily: Sept–June 9am–12.30pm & 2–5.30pm; July & Aug 9am–midnight; ☎233 402 820, ❸www.cm-figfoz.pt) is in Edifício Atlântico on Avenida 25 de Abril and is even more helpful than most; there's another in Buarcos at Largo de Buarcos (summer daily 9am–8pm; winter Mon–Fri 9am–5.30pm; ☎233 433 019), which is served by regular buses along the seafront. If you stay some way out

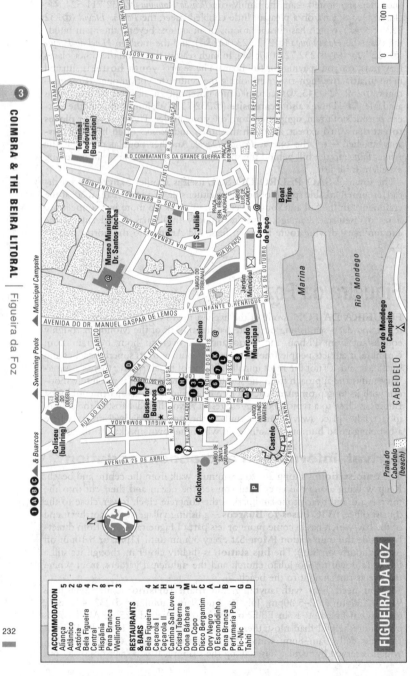

FIGUEIRA DA FOZ

RUA VASCO DA GAMA
RUA 28 DE INFANTARIA
RUA 10 DE AGOSTO
RUA DOS HERÓIS DO ULTRAMAR
RUA DO HOSPITAL
R.D.COMBATENTES DA GRANDE GUERRA
R. D. RESTAURAÇÃO
RUA MAURÍCIO PINTO
BOMBEIROS VOLUNTÁRIOS
RUA DOS
RUA FERNANDES COELHO
Museu Municipal
Dr. Santos Rocha
Police
S. Julião
PRAÇA
GEN. FREIRE
DE ANDRADE
LARGO
LUÍS DE
CAMÕES
PRAÇA
8 DE MAIO
RUA DA REPÚBLICA
AV. DE SARAIVA DE CARVALHO
PRAÇA
Boat
Trips
Casa
do Paço
RUA DO PAÇO
LARGO DO
TRIBUNAL
Jardim
Municipal
RUA 5 DE OUTUBRO
Marina
Rio Mondego
Terminal
Rodoviário
(Bus station)

Municipal Campsite ▲

Swimming Pools ▲

AVENIDA DO DR. MANUEL GASPAR DE LEMOS
PÇ. INFANTE D. HENRIQUE
AVENIDA DO DR. MANUEL GASPAR DE LEMOS
RUA DR. LUÍS CARIÇO
RUA DA FONTE
RUA SÃO LAURENÇO
RUA DE SOUSA
Casino
Mercado
Municipal
RUA FRANCISCO A. DINIS
RUA CÂNDIDO DOS REIS
RUA A. MAGALHÃES
RUA DA CALÇADA
R. MAESTRO DE SOUSA
RUA DE BUARCOS
R. MIGUEL BOMBARDA
RUA DO VISO
LARGO DO
COLISEU
Coliseu
(bullring)

Buses to
Buarcos

D E F G
1 3 J
8 K L
5 6 7
4 M
2

LARGO DE
SANTA CATARINA
LARGO
ANTUNES
MARTINS

Clocktower
Castelo
AVENIDA 25 DE ABRIL
AVENIDA DE ESPANHA
P
Praia do
Cabedelo
(beach)
CABEDELO
Foz do Mondego
Campsite

& Buarcos ▲

1 A B C ◄

N

0   100 m

ACCOMMODATION
Aliança   5
Atlântico   2
Astória   6
Bela Figueira   7
Central   4
Hispânia   8
Pena Branca   1
Wellington   3

RESTAURANTS
& BARS
Bela Figueira   4
Caçarola I   K
Caçarola II   H
Cantina San Loven   E
Cristal Taberna   J
Dona Bárbara   M
Dom Copo   F
Disco Bergantim   C
Dory Negro   A
O Escondidinho   L
Pena Branca   B
Perfumaria Pub   I
Pic-Nic   G
Tahiti   D

of town, you might want to **rent a bike** from the municipal campsite; it costs around €8 per day; **car rental** can be arranged through Marco Viagens, Rua Maestro David de Sousa (☎233 425 113). The Museu Municipal Dr. Santos Rocha offers free **internet access** (Tues–Fri 9.30am–5.15pm, Sat & Sun 2.15pm–5.15pm). Otherwise, there are two internet cafés in town: *Café Nau* (☎233 422 678) next to the Town Hall, and *E Leclerc* (☎233 402 380) in the shopping centre by the casino.

Accommodation

It can take time to find a room in Figueira in high season, but with persistence you should be able to get something. In high season, you might well be met at the train station by people offering **private rooms**, which – provided they're reasonably central – will be the best bargains in town. Otherwise, there are a couple of cheap *pensões* just in front of the train station on Rua Fernandes Tomás and Rua da República, but these are a long way from the beach. It's much better to head for the centre, where both **Rua Bernardo Lopes** and **Rua da Liberdade** are lined with possibilities, though many are booked well in advance. You'll also find that **prices** – already comparatively high in Figueira – tend to shoot through the roof in summer, particularly in July and August.

Hotels and pensões

Residencial Aliança Rua Miguel Bombarda 12 ☎ & ℉233 422 197. Newly renovated, friendly place. The rooms are brightly furnished with polished wooden floors, smart bathrooms and TV. There's also a restaurant on the ground floor. ❸

Hotel Apartmento Atlântico Av 25 de Abril ☎233 403 910. Very good upmarket option in a modern high-rise with pool. En-suite rooms with all mod cons. ❻

Pensão Astória Rua Bernardo Lopes 45 ☎233 422 256. Not as nice as the *Central*, opposite, but a decent fall-back with a restaurant below. ❸

Pensão Bela Figueira Rua Miguel Bombarda 13 ☎233 422 728, ℉233 429 960. Near the main beach and town centre. It can be noisy; many of the unremarkable rooms come with shower and TV. ❸

Pensão Central Rua Bernardo Lopes 36 ☎233 422 308. Airy *pensão* approached up a flight of side-steps. Rooms have high ceilings and nice old furniture, and a couple share a grand street-facing balcony, though these are noisy. ❹

Hotel Hispânia Rua Dr. Francisco António Dinis 61 ☎233 422 164, ℉233 429 664. A rambling old hotel, one of the few right in the centre with private parking. Closed Jan. ❹

Residencial Pena Branca Rua 5° de Outubro 42 ☎233 432 665, ℉233 421 892. In Buarcos, near

the turismo, and just outside the city wall. Splendid, high-quality set-up with private bathrooms, phone, TV, fridge and balcony; breakfast included. There's a good regional restaurant below. ❹

Hotel Wellington Rua Dr. Calado 23–27 ☎233 426 767, ✉hotelwelligton@mail.telepac.pt. Three blocks from the beach, the once shabby Wellington has moved into the flash modern building next door. The rooms are very comfortable, if a little anonymous, all with bathroom and with cable TV. ❺

Campsites

Parque Municipal de Campismo ☎233 402 810. Large and well equipped, with a swimming pool (though you have to pay to use it) and tennis courts. It's 2km inland – follow the signs from town and beach, or take a taxi from the station.

Foz do Mondego ☎233 402 740. Across the river mouth, and close to Cabadelo beach, this is by far the cheapest in the area (closed Dec & Jan).

Orbitur ☎233 431 492 Mata de Lavos, Gala, 4km to the south, across the estuary. The most expensive – though the ocean is much cleaner for swimming here. Take the AVIC "Cova Gala" bus (Mon–Fri every 30min till 8.10pm, Sat hourly till 6.10pm, Sun every two hours till 6.10pm) from the Mercado Municipal. *Carrossel*, at Largo da Beira-Mar near the campsite, serves good food.

The Town and beaches

The town doesn't offer much in the way of sightseeing – the most impressive sights are the beaches – but there are a couple of places to scout around once you tire of the sands. On the edge of the town park, Parque Abadias, the

Museu Municipal Dr. Santos Rocha (Tues–Fri 9.30am–5.15pm, Sat & Sun 2.15pm–5.15pm; €1.25), Rua Calouste Gulbenkian, has an impressive archeological section, as well as a large number of photographs of nineteenth-century bathing belles. Meanwhile, the inside walls of the **Casa do Paço** (Mon–Fri 9.30am–12.30pm & 2–5.30pm; free), on the waterfront by the marina, are covered with thousands of Delft tiles, part of a ship's cargo which somehow got stranded in Figueira.

Apart from this, you can check out Figueira's central streets which form a tight little grid set back from the eastern end of the beach. Many are pedestrianized, brimming with pavement cafés and strolling holidaymakers, while back along the river, on Rua 5° de Outubro, is the **market** (summer Mon–Sat 7am–6pm; winter Mon–Fri 7am–4.30pm, Sat 7am–1pm), good for food and just about anything else you might need.

The beaches

Figueira's **town beach** is enormous, not so much in length as in width: it's a good five-minute walk across the sand to the sea and unless you wear shoes or stay on the wooden walkways provided, the soles of your feet will have been burned long before you get there. There are cafés along the whole length of the beach, but since the busy main road and promenade are set well back from the water, there's no great sense of place. Best spot is probably at the **Buarcos** end of the beach, 2km away, where a huddle of pastel-coloured fishermen's houses sit amidst a rash of new concrete high-rises behind what remains of the old defensive wall.

If it's **surfing** you're after, then just step around the promontory at Buarcos, where fans gather to admire the breakers. By contrast, **Cabadelo beach**, behind the mole on the Mondego river mouth's south bank, is small, sheltered and good for families – though to reach it you have to go right out through the town and over the bridge by bus.

The only problem in recent years has been that of pollution; the EU blue flag, denoting water acceptable to swim in, does not always fly over all of Figueira's beaches. If this concerns you, an up-to-date appraisal of the water quality at each of the beaches is posted outside the turismo – tests are carried out weekly in summer.

You can always have a dip instead in the fee-paying **swimming pools** on the north side of town: the nearest is Piscina de Santa Catarina, a fifteen-minute walk along Rua Joaquim Sotto Mayor, in a park on the right. Further along, there's another pool in the Ginásio Club next to the municipal stadium.

Eating

The centre of town is packed with **places to eat**, with any number of snack bars, cafés and seafood restaurants offering *ementas turísticas* at reasonable prices.

Aquário Alto do Forno, Buarcos. One of several good seafood places in Buarcos, with a great *cataplana*, and fado on Fridays.

Bela Figueira Rua Miguel Bombarda 13. The *pensão*'s restaurant serves fine Indian and Portuguese food. Try the shrimp and rice curry – and eat on the terrace (where prices are slightly higher). Around €10.

Caçarola I Rua Cândido dos Reis 65. Basement shellfish restaurant with daily specials chalked on the board. To keep costs down, you could just sit at the bar and have a plate of prawns and a beer.

Caçarola II Rua Bernardo Lopes 85–87. Sister restaurant to *Caçarola I* and just as good, if not better. Open till 4am.

Cristal Taberna Rua Académico Zagalo 28. Great little rustic restaurant serving good, simple fare at cheap prices. Friendly service and English-language menus too.

Dory Negro Largo Caras Direitas 16, Buarcos. On the edge of Buarcos, this is a good place to come for fish, with dishes around the €8 mark. It's hidden out of sight from the sea, but has a little covered patio. Closed Tues in winter.

O Escondidinho Rua Dr. Francisco António Dinis 62. Hidden away (as the name suggests), this is worth seeking out for superb and inexpensive Goan food. The entrance is through a doorway opposite *Hotel Hispânia*, leading to a courtyard. Under €10 if you pick and choose. Closed Sun night and Mon.

Pena Branca Rua 5° de Outubro 42, Buarcos. With windows overlooking the beach at Buarcos, this is the best place for an *arroz de sardinha* and

caldeirada. Other fish and meat specials, too, and full meals for €15.

Pic-Nic Rua de São Lourenço, at junction with Rua David de Sousa. Well-priced menu (under €12.50 for a full meal), with plenty of fish and a lovely roof-terrace to eat it on.

Tahiti Rua da Fonte 86. Nice little backstreet restaurant, away from the central bustle, with friendly English-speaking staff, great prices and decent food – which extends to English break-fasts and fish and chips for the criminally unad-venturous.

Nightlife, entertainment and events

Nightlife centres on the **casino** at Rua Bernardo Lopes 1 (3pm–3am; take your passport for entry), for which semi-formal dress and an initial outlay on chips are compulsory. The casino also houses a couple of **cinemas**, which gen-erally have up-to-date releases. In the first couple of weeks of September the casino hosts an **International Film Festival** – a little uneven in its organiza-tion, but always with a good selection of new films shown in their original lan-guage; ask at the turismo for more information.

Alternatively, there are several central **pubs** and **bars**, like *Perfumaria*, Rua Dr. Calado 37; *Dom Copo*, Rua São Lourenço 13; and *Dona Bárbara*, Rua A. Zagalo, all of which play the same kind of rock and pop until around 4am. For cock-tails, head to *Cantina San Lorenzo*, on Rua São Lourenço just next door to Dom Capo, a cheerful Mexican-themed place specialising in Margaritas. Of the **discos**, *Disco Bergantim*, Rua Dr. Lopes Guimarães 28, is a long-standing favourite. If you have transport you could make a late-night trip out to *Flashen,* hidden in pine trees outside the village of Quiaios, 8km north of Figueira. Discos do not get going till around midnight, but they don't close till 4am and all-nighters are not unheard of in summer.

One of the best of the year's parties is **St John's Eve** (June 23 and 24) with bonfires on the beach and a "Holy Bathe" in the sea at dawn; while **bullfights** are often held during the summer season.

North of Figueira: to Praia de Mira

The coastline immediately **north of Figueira** is remarkable only for its air of total desertion. Beyond Buarcos, there's very little, and for long stretches hard-ly even a road. Off the main north–south road (N109) you can get to the coast at just three points before Aveiro: at **Quiaios, Tocha** and **Mira**, each with their respective beaches, all of them flying blue flags declaring them clean enough to swim in. If you're driving **on to Aveiro** (see p.236), stick with the minor coastal route beyond Praia de Mira, a pleasant run through farmland with dunes to one side and river to the other; this way, you'll pass through probably the nicest of this coast's small resorts, **Costa Nova** (see p.241).

Praia de Quiaios and Praia da Tocha

With a car you can find virtually empty beaches around either **QUIAIOS** or **TOCHA**, though the low-lying coastal plain offers no protection against the Atlantic winds. For more sheltered leisure pursuits, aim for the inland lakes between the two beaches, particularly the large, pine-fringed **Lagoa da Vela**, where there are scores of picnic areas, and windsurfing and sailing schools.

Buses run every hour or so from Figueira bus station up the N109, stopping at both Praia de Quiaios (25min) and Praia da Tocha (40min). There isn't any accommodation once you get to either beach other than the excellent **campsites**, *Praia de Quiaios* (☎233 910 499; July–Sept), which has its own swimming pool, and *Praia da Tocha* (☎231 441 143; June–Sept).

Praia de Mira

Set on a small lagoon – the southernmost point of a system of waterways and canals centered around Aveiro – **PRAIA DE MIRA** is the focus of increasing development. Seven kilometres west of the inland town of Mira, it is rather more accessible than the beaches at Quiaios or Tocha, with half a dozen buses a day from either Figueira, Coimbra or Aveiro. There's a lot more accommodation, too, the downside being that you may not want to stay. You couldn't exactly describe Praia de Mira as a beautiful place – its one extremely long main street, Avenida Cidade de Coimbra, spears towards the sea, lined by new apartments and dusty building sites. But the beach that stretches around it is seemingly endless and backed by dunes: ideal if your aims extend no further than beach-lounging and walks.

Many places offer cheap, basic *dormidas* along the main street – look out for the signs, or ask in any bar. The **turismo**, in the boathouse-like building beside the lagoon (☎231 472 566) may be able to help with rooms, but is itself often closed out of season. **Pensões** aren't cheap and if you're going to stay in one, it might as well be one with a sea view from its balconies: immediately on the left at the end of the main street, the modern *Arco Íris* on Avenida do Mar (☎234 471 202; ③) is a passable spot with a restaurant. Far preferable is the *Miratlântico* (☎231 471 262; ③) three hundred metres further along the seafront. It has pleasant, airy rooms with TV and bath – the front rooms are the best, with private balconies overlooking the beach.

There are two official **campsites** a short way from the village – the municipal site (☎231 472 173; May–Sept) is closer and considerably cheaper, though less well equipped, than the Orbitur site (☎231 471 234, ℗231 472 047; closed Dec & Jan), for which you go up the main street, turn left at the seafront and continue for a kilometre. Directly opposite the Orbitur site is a **youth hostel** with its own campsite (reception 8am–noon & 6pm–midnight; ☎231 471 199, ⓔmira@movijovem.pt; hostel open all year, campsite June–Sept). The *A Cozinha* **restaurant**, one of several on Avenida Barrinha – the road backing the lagoon – has windows overlooking the water and, among other dishes, serves a buttery grilled squid and tasty *porco à alentejana*.

Aveiro and around

Most visitors to **AVEIRO** are intent on getting straight out again, to the series of excellent **beaches** to north and south and into what a tourist brochure describes as the "virile, iodine-bearing sea". However, Aveiro itself is also a place of some antiquity and interest. It was a thriving port throughout the Middle Ages, up until the 1570s, when the mouth of the Vouga silted up, closing its harbour and creating vast, fever-ridden marshes. Recovery began only in 1808 when a canal was cut through to the sea, reopening the port and draining much of the water; only the shallow lagoons you see today were left. These form the backbone of a modern economy based on vast **saltpans**, fishing, and

△ *Moliceiro* boat

the collection of seaweed (*molico*) for fertilizer. The occasional pungent odour wafting across town, seemingly from the lagoon, is actually from the large paper factory nearby.

The town's big annual event is the **Festa da Ria**, celebrated in the last two weeks of August with boat races, folk dances, and competitions for the best decorated *barcos moliceiro*, the flat-bottomed lagoon boats used to collect seaweed. The other major celebration is the **Festa de São Gonçalinho**, held in honour of the patron saint of fishermen and single women in the second week of January. Those who have made vows during the year, either for the safe return of a fisherman or for the finding of a husband, climb to the top of a chapel and throw down loaves of bread to the crowd below; the aim is to catch as much as possible.

The Town

Aveiro casts off its rather dowdy first appearances as soon as you reach the central praça and bridge over the main canal. The traditional industries here are celebrated by imposing statues of the local workers on the bridge – the *marnoto* and the *salineira*, the latter with her salt tray. Handsome, pastel-coloured houses (of which the turismo is one) line Rua João Mendonça, and in the narrow little streets behind the **fish market** tiled houses face each other across arms of the canal. Lagoon boats with raised prows lie tied up along the quaysides.

True, there's only one sight of real note, the fifteenth-century **Convento de Jesus**, across the central canal and five minutes' walk up on the right. This now houses the **town museum** (Tues–Sun 10am–5.30pm; €1.50), whose finest exhibits all relate to Santa Joana, a daughter of Afonso V who lived in the convent from 1475 until her death in 1489. She was barred from becoming a nun because of her royal station and her father's opposition, and was later beatified for her determination to escape from the material world (or perhaps simply from an unwelcome arranged marriage). Her tomb and chapel are strikingly beautiful, as is the convent itself, and there's a fine collection of art and sculpture – notably a series of naive seventeenth-century paintings depicting the saint's life.

Once you've seen this you may as well cross the road to the **cathedral**, whose exterior concrete loggia and interior breeze-block walls make it resemble a municipal swimming pool. Infinitely more pleasing is the **Misericórdia** church, back down towards the canal, whose seventeenth-century facade features blue snowflake-design tiles. The **town hall**, a century older, stands opposite, both buildings facing a declamatory **statue** of Aveiro's famous son, the nineteenth-century politician José Estevão Coelho de Magalhães.

Beyond these few attractions, the main local interest is in the surrounding beaches and lagoons, for which see p.241. There's a certain fascination, too, in hanging around in the **cafés**, watching life on the Ria: try some of the celebrated local sweets, especially *ovos moles*, candied egg yolks.

Practicalities

Aveiro is on the main Lisbon–Porto rail line, with the **train station** at the northeastern end of town; most **buses** (including services to and from Praia de Mira) use the train station forecourt and adjacent streets as their terminus. From the station, walk straight down the broad main street in front of you – Avenida Dr. Lourenço Peixinho – and you'll eventually hit Praça Humberto Delgado and the bridge, a fifteen-minute walk.

The **turismo** is just up from the bridge on the right in a beautiful Art

RESTAURANTS & BARS
Alexandre	D
Cervejaria Rossio	H
Estrondo	A
Neptuno	I
Salpoente	B
Sonatura	C
O Telheiro	G
Zé da Parreirinha	F
Zico	E

ACCOMMODATION
Arcada	8
Beira	2
A Brasileira	7
Estrela	3
Imperial	5
Mercure Aveiro	1
Palmeira	6
Hospedagem Rossío	4

Nouveau building at Rua João Mendonça 8 (June–Sept daily 9am–8pm; Oct–May Mon–Sat 9am–7pm; ☎234 420 760, ⓦ www.rotadaluz.aveiro.pt). It supplies free maps and local bus timetables and can help with finding accommodation. **Bicycles** are a good way to explore the town and are available free from the *BUGA* kiosk on the main square. You need to show your passport to get a bike, but are then free to use it around the town for a whole day. *Aveiro Digital*, in the modern building opposite the Town Hall, offers free **internet access** (Mon–Sat 10am–8.30pm).

Accommodation

You shouldn't have much trouble finding a **room in Aveiro**, except perhaps during the Festa da Ria in August, when you'd be wise to book ahead. There are several places immediately down from the train station, but they're a little far from things; in the centre, try the backstreets around the fish market, particularly Rua das Marnotos, for inexpensive *dormidas*. Those with transport have the option of staying **out of town** at one of the lagoon- or beach-resorts (see pp.241–242) – although the beaches themselves are accessible by public transport, the nicer places to stay tend to be more off the beaten track.

The local **campsites** are also way out of town, at São Jacinto to the north (see p.242), or to the south at Praia da Barra, Costa Nova and Praia da Vagueira (see p.241).

Hotel Arcada Rua de Viana do Castelo 4 ☎234 423 001, ℻234 421 886. Small, unexciting rooms, though pleasant staff and a central location in a grand building by the bridge with views over the canal. All rooms with either shower or bath, breakfast and TV. ❹

Beira Rua José Estevão 18 ☎234 424 297. Clean and welcoming *residencial* just off the praça, with breakfast included. The rooms are bright and homely, furnished with sturdy wooden furniture; some have bathrooms and all have cable TV. It's often full, so call ahead. ❸

A Brasileira Rua Tenente Resende 47 ☎234 428 634. One of a handful of *dormidas* places near the fish market, this place is rather depressing, although the small rooms are clean and fine for a night. ❷

Pensão Residencial Estrela Rua José Estevão 4 ☎234 423 818. An old, converted house whose plant-filled staircase and polished wooden corridor are rather grander than the smallish, but cool and comfortable, rooms. Friendly, English-speaking owners, and big discounts out of season. ❹

Hotel Imperial Rua Dr. Nascimento Leitão ☎234 380 150, ☏www.ciberquia.pt/hotel-imperial. Modern building, not far from the Convento, with fine views of the lagoon from the top-floor bar; breakfast included. At the top of its price range. ❺

Hotel Mercure Aveiro Rua Luís Gomes de Carvalho 23 ☎234 404 400, ℮h2934 @accor-hotels.com. Very comfortable rooms (with bath and TV) in a gracious, quiet town house, recently taken over by the Mercure chain. Near the station and with its own parking. ❺

Palmeira Rua da Palmeira 7–11 ☎234 422 521, ℮residencial.palmeira@netc.pt. Pretty, modern, tiled town house with attached dining room, in the old quarter between the praça and the Canal de São Roque. Bright rooms, some with shower or bath, and most with TV. ❹

Hospedagem Rossío Rua Dr. Barbosa de Magalhães 24 ☎234 429 857. Good central location off the canalside park, and about as cheap as you'll find, though the fairly spartan rooms are as gloomy as the proprietor; separate bathrooms. ❷

Eating

There are some excellent restaurants in Aveiro, with **local specialities** including eels and shellfish from the lagoons and powerful Bairrada wine. The cheapest eats are in the little *casas de pasto* in the old town streets around the fish market, though there are also several regular restaurants in this area, too.

Alexandre Cais do Alboi 14, near Largo Conselheiro Queirós. A short walk along the canal, this is a well-regarded snack bar and adjacent restaurant with good meals for around €10. Closed July.

Neptuno Rua Mendes Leite 1. Decent little grill house serving large portions of chicken, home-made sausage, chops or fish. Around €10 for a *dose*. Closed Sun.

Salpoente Canal São Roque 83. Ten minutes' walk north along the canal, this superior fish restaurant is set inside a renovated salt barn. Crabs, fish and eels at medium-to-high prices, served Mon–Sat noon–2.30pm & 7.30–10.30pm.

Sonatura Rua Clube dos Galitos 6. Vegetarian wholefood self-service restaurant serving daily

specials of varying size – the food isn't particularly good, but at least it offers veggies a change from omelette and chips. Mon–Sat 12–6.30pm.

O Telheiro Largo da Praça do Peixe 20–21. Excellent *adega* with wooden benches and tiled tables, and food cooked any way you like as long as it's chargrilled. *Lulas grelhados* (grilled squid) is superb; add a fish soup, wine and coffee and you'll pay around €12. Closed Sat.

Zé da Parreirinha Trav. do Lavadouro 10. Rough-and-ready *casa de pasto* with full meals for under €5. Just off Largo do Praça da Peixe. Closed Wed.

Zico Rua José Estevão 52. Very popular local spot, with most dishes around €7. Menu changes daily, but there are always grills, local fish and good wine. Closed Sun.

Drinking

The liveliest place in town is the area immediately around the fish market, where young people crowd into the bars and spill out onto the tables scattered across the cobbles. Although there are five or six fashionable spots, these don't have names and open when the punters arrive, making them great places for informal bar hopping. Some alternatives include:

Estrondo Canal São Roque 73. Polynesian-style bar on the canal and just down from *Salpoente*, open till 2–3am for cocktails and drinks. Closed Mon.

Cervejaria Rossío Largo da Rossio 8a. Central

cervejaria serving beer and good steak sandwiches until 2am. Closed Mon.

Salpoente Canal São Roque 83. The restaurant has an enjoyable bar which opens at 11.30pm and has live music on Fri and Sat until 2.30am. Closed Sun.

Around Aveiro: the lagoon and beaches

There's no beach in Aveiro itself but the coast north and south is a more or less continuous line of sand, cut off from the mainland for much of the way by the meandering **lagoon**. Although developers have long caught on, the whole sand bar is still little spoilt, and offers ample opportunity for beach lounging as well as fascinating walks along the lagoon's swampy edge, which boasts abundant birdlife. Note that the pine forests shelter several military bases, so stick to the roads and don't camp outside official sites.

From May to September, two-hour **boat trips** by *moliceiro* around the lagoon leave from Rua Joâo Mendonça in front of the turismo. Check at the turismo for prices. At any time of year a group of people can rent a boat to tour the river; again, information is available from the turismo.

Praia da Barra and Costa Nova

The most easily accessible coastal points from Aveiro are **PRAIA DA BARRA**, at the mouth of the Vouga, and **COSTA NOVA**, a little further on; but be warned that both are enormously crowded on summer weekends. Local **buses** from Aveiro (hourly 7.10am–8.10pm; €1.75) depart from outside the train station, also stopping on Rua Clube dos Galitos, across the bridge from the turismo and about 150m down the canal on the right. They call at Barra first, then Costa Nova.

Praia da Barra, though less charming than Costa Nova, has a greater choice of **accommodation**, as well as more restaurants and nightclubs, but prices in all three can be steep. The pick of the cheaper accommodation options is: *Pensâo Farol da Barra* (☎234 390 600, ℱ234 390 606; ❹), situated above a cool and pleasant café and billiards room at the end of the main road and overlooked by Portugal's tallest lighthouse; *Residencial Marisqueira*, Avenida João Corte Real (☎234 369 262; ❸); and the *Hotel Barra*, Avenida Fernandes Lavrador 18 (☎234 369 156, ✉hotel-barra@clix.pt; ❺), which has a pool. There's also a municipal **campsite** (☎234 369 425; closed Dec).

Costa Nova is a highly attractive ensemble of candy-stripe wooden buildings (plus the ubiquitous spread of newer concrete blocks), stuffed into the strip between beach and lagoon. There are two places **to stay**: the excellent *Residencial Azevedo*, Rua Arrais Ançã 16 (☎234 390 170, ℱ234 390 171; ❹), and the huge **campsite** 1km to the south (☎234 369 822, ℱ234 360 008), complete with supermarket and disco.

Vagueira

Around 15km south of Aveiro but still accessible by bus, **VAGUEIRA** faces the lagoon, though it is actually situated on the mainland, just 1km from the ocean beaches. The summer **turismo**, on Largo Parracho Branco at the north end of the beach where the bus drops you, can help with **rooms**. Alternatively, there are tiny bungalows for rent, 1500m to the south on the Mira road (☎234 797 732, ⓦwww.costasitur.com; ❷) next to the entertaining Vaga Splash aqua park. There's also an excellent **campsite** here (☎234 797 618, ℱ234 797 093) where you can rent bikes.

São Jacinto

If you want more than just a beach, then you need to head north of Aveiro to **SÃO JACINTO**. Boats from Aveiro leave from Rua B. Bachado (a five-minute walk from Largo do Rossio) and take just over half an hour (Mon–Fri every two hours from 7.05am–12.45am; €1.30). Unlike its neighbours along the coast, Sao Jacinto is not really a resort at all, but rather a thriving little port with a handful of dockside café-restaurants. With a military base at one end and a forest of cranes cluttering the skyline, it's not beautiful, but there is an enormous – and undeveloped – dune-fringed **beach** twenty minutes' walk away: off the boat, walk to the right past the post office and, at *Restaurant Ferraz* (the best place to eat), turn left. The beach is straight up the improbably long road ahead, where you'll also find the *Restaurante Marluci*, which has a few **rooms**, some with kitchens (☏234 331 074; ❶, with kitchen ❷). If your budget is a little higher and you have your own transport, head along the road to Torriera to the *Pousada da Ria*, Bico do Muranzel (☏234 860 180, ⓦwww.pousadas.pt; ❻), a mid-priced *pousada* with swimming pool, tennis courts and lagoon-view balconies. There's a municipal campsite (☏234 331 220) 2.5km out on the Torriera road and a substantial Orbitur **campsite** (☏ & ⓕ234 331 220; closed mid-Nov to mid-Jan) with good facilities a further 2.5km on.

São Jacinto backs onto an extensive **bird reserve**, where you can join a guided tour (summer: Mon–Wed, Fri & Sat 9am–noon & 1.30–5pm; winter hours erratic; €1), though this may depend on numbers; for more information and for times of tours in winter, contact the reserve office (☏234 331 282, ⓕ234 831 063). It's 1km out of town, along the main road to Torriera: turn left at the post office, walk up to the main road and head right. Adjacent to the reserve office is a small scrap of beach overlooked by the *Portelas* bar-restaurant.

Torreira

In summer, buses run the 13km north from São Jacinto to **TORREIRA**, a lively little resort with several small *pensões*. The best hotel is the four-star *Estalagem Riabela*, at the north end of town (☏234 838 137, ⓕ234 838 147; ❺); if you can't quite stretch to that, there's the slightly cheaper *Residencial Albertina*, Trav. Arraias Faustino (☏234 838 306, ⓕ234 838 206; ❹), a popular, modern hotel by the beach with air-conditioned rooms and a bar. You can rent bikes here, too.

For **eating**, the restaurant *Casa Passoiera*, on the main road, is highly recommended. The *Estalagrem Riabela* also has a decent grill-restaurant and live music. The buses at this point loop back round to Aveiro; to head onwards to Furadouro (see below), you have to make a detour through Ovar.

Ovar, Furadouro and Santa Maria da Feira

The distinctive Ria countryside comes to an end around **Ovar**, 25km to the north of Aveiro, and there's no great reason to delay the drive or train ride straight to Porto. But Ovar itself is worth at least a coffee break, while the beach to the west at **Furadouro** is as good as anything that's gone before. Further inland, **Santa Maria da Feira** boasts a splendid castle and a good interactive science park.

Ovar and Furadouro

OVAR is on the main train line to Porto. If you're lucky, there'll be a bus waiting to take you into the centre of Ovar; failing that, it's a fifteen-minute walk. There are direct buses, too, from São Jacinto and Torreira.

An attractive market town, Ovar is 5km away from a fine beach at Furadouro, to which there's a regular bus. The **turismo** (Mon–Fri 9.30am–12.30pm & 2–5pm, Sat 10am–12.30pm; ☎256 572 215) is near the main square, on Rua Dr. Manuel Arala. Just off the square itself you'll find the surprisingly good **Museu Ovar** (Mon–Sat 10am–noon & 2–6pm; €1.50), with an international collection of dolls, plus traditional clothing and the usual folklore displays. Perhaps more compellingly, while you're here try some of the local *pão-de-ló* sponge cake – every bit as good as it looks, and available at the main market behind the church on Rua Gomes Freire, which also offers a vast selection of fruit, vegetables and flowers. The nicest **accommodation** in town is provided by the modern *Hotel Meia-Lua*, Quinta das Luzes (☎256 575 031, ℻256 575 232; ⑤), and the large, four-star *Albergaria São Cristóvão*, at Rua Aquilino Ribeiro 1 (☎256 575 105, ℻256 575 107; ⑥). At the budget end of the scale, the flash **youth hostel** (reception 8am–midnight; ☎256 591 832, ⓔovar@movijovem.pt) is about 2km out of town on Avenida Dom Manuel I (the N327 "ring-road" around Ovar: to get on it, head towards Furadouro and turn right at the roundabout).

The rather unglamourous resort of **FURADOURO** marks pretty much the northern extent of the system of waterways, and like its neighbours to the south boasts a long stretch of pine-backed dunes. The only place to stay is at the signposted **campsite**, a pleasant forested site with a restaurant (☎256 596 010, ⓦwww.clubecampismo-sjm.pt).

Santa Maria da Feira

At **SANTA MARIA DA FEIRA** (or, more simply, Feira), easily reached by bus from Aveiro or Espinho (see p.317), at first sight one of the most spectacular castles in Portugal – the **Castelo da Feira** (daily: summer 9am–noon & 2–6pm; reduced hours in winter; €1.25) – looms on a hillside beyond the town, its skyline a fanciful array of turrets. A sunken gateway leads into the castle's interior – part dilapidated, part over zealously restored. The principal room is the **Great Hall**, a magnificent Moorish structure. Beyond the keep, a tunnel links the two parts of the castle in such a way that no direct or easy access can ever have been offered to intruders – arrow slits and hidden entrances emphasize the point. In some of the walls you can see stones marked with Roman inscriptions, and you can make out the familiar straight Roman road through the wooded hills above. It's a fifteen-minute climb up the hill to the castle.

On the way down from the castle, you pass the grand **Convento de Loios** (now a conference centre). Feira's newest attraction, the Europarque **Visionarium** (Mon–Fri 9am–6pm, Sat & Sun 10am–8pm; ☎256 370 609, ⓦwww.visionarium.pt; €6.50, discounted family tickets) is Portugal's largest science museum, located 3km out of town in the opposite direction to the castle. The impressive, interactive displays (in both Portuguese and English) cover subjects ranging from the Portuguese voyages of discovery to the insides of microchips.

The best time to visit Feira is undoubtedly during the annual **Festa das Fogaceiras** (Jan 20), when files of little girls parade through the town carrying castle-shaped *fogaça* cakes. It's a custom – much revived in recent years – which dates back to the plague of 1750 when the Infante Pedro made a *vota* to Santa Maria that cakes in the shape of his castle would be baked in thanksgiving for those who survived.

Practicalities

There's a smart new **turismo** (Mon–Fri 9am–6pm, Sat 10am–5pm, closed Sun; ☎256 372 032, ⓦwww.cm-feira.pt) on Praça da República – turn left in front of the church at the bottom of the castle road, and it's straight ahead. If you want **to stay**, try *Residencial Tony*, Rua Jornal Correio da Feira 22 (T 256 372 593; ②), five minutes' walk from the bus station, which offers clean en-suite rooms. With more money to spend, the best option is the outstanding *Casa das Ribas* (T & F 256 373 485; ④), a stunning eighteenth-century manor house with large antique-filled rooms and gorgeous gardens, right next to the castle. Decent and inexpensive **meals** are to be had at the *Charrete* restaurant on the street at the bottom of the road up to the castle, where there are several other little cafés, too. *Fair Play,* on the same street, is a more upmarket alternative with a stylish interior and pricier local specialities, including a good *feijoada.*

Arouca and the Serra da Arada

Picking up the N224, it's a splendid drive from Feira to **Arouca**, 20km to the east, a winding route through forested hills and small terraced slopes of tumbling vineyards, the air heady with the scent of pine resin and eucalyptus. There are regular buses from Feira, and although there are no public transport links south from Arouca, through the magnificent **Serra da Arada** (see opposite), buses do run on north to Porto.

Arouca

AROUCA is a small town entirely overshadowed by the vast **Convento da Arouca** (Tues–Sun 9.30am–noon & 2–5pm; €1.75), whose imposing walls loom across the busy main road that cuts through town. It was founded as early as 1091, though most surviving parts are from rather later medieval times. In the kitchen there are huge fireplaces along Alcobaça lines; the vast Baroque church (which you can see without buying a ticket; enter from the main road) holds richly carved choir stalls and a great organ with 1352 notes, played on rare occasions by one of the country's few experts; while off the central courtyard there's an airy Sala Capítula, where the abbesses once held court, lined with *azulejos.*

The convent peaked in importance when Queen Mafalda, of whose dowry it had formed a part, found her marriage to Dom Henriques I of Castile annulled and retired here to a life of religious contemplation. In the extensive **museum** upstairs, you can see some of Mafalda's most prized treasures, including an exquisite thirteenth-century silver diptych, along with a series of paintings by Josefa de Óbidos (see p.165) and Diogo Teixeira. In 1792, four centuries after Mafalda's death, villagers claimed to have witnessed her saving the convent from the ravages of a terrible fire. She was promptly exhumed and beatified.

The rest of town struggles to make a mark in the face of its prize exhibit, but it's a handsome little place with a certain sleepy appeal. The central square holds a couple of cafés with pavement seats, while in the medieval backstreets there are some beautiful old houses decked with wisteria. Stay for the night if you can: Arouca is at its quietest and best during the somnolent evenings or in the early morning when shrouded in rising mist from the surrounding hills.

Local heart rates increase slightly during the annual **Festa de Nossa Senhora da Mó**, when the whole town turns out for a picnic on the crown of the hill 8km east of the town. **Holy Week** processions are a big deal here, too, starting on the Wednesday and culminating on the Saturday night, when most of the inhabitants parade behind the local saints' statues to the Misericórdia church, with candles lit in all the town's windows.

Practicalities

Buses stop at the new station at the entrance to the town on the main road. The main square, Praça Brandão de Vasconcelas, is opposite the convent, with the **turismo** on the right-hand side (Mon–Fri 9.30am–12.30pm & 2–5.30pm, Sat 9.30am–12.30pm, closed Sun; ☎256 943 575, ⓔarouca.rotadaluz @inovanet.pt).

There are two **places to stay** in town, although neither is cheap. The *Residencial São Pedro*, Avenida Reinaldo de Noronha (☎256 944 580, ⓕ256 943 054; ❹), is five minutes' walk from the square – walk up the main road and take the left fork. Although the rooms are rather musty and overpriced, the staff are very friendly, and some of the front rooms have balconies with views over the town and convent. A better choice is the rustic *Quinta do Bóco* (☎ & ⓕ256 944 169; ❹), in a lovely old farmhouse with a pool; turn left at the town hall at the end of the main street and drive for about five minutes – it's on the left hand side.

For a **meal**, the *Restaurante Parlamento*, Travessa da Ribeira 2 is a smart option. There are a couple of *casas de pasto* around town, too, while *Residencial São Pedro* has a good restaurant.

The Serra da Arada

If you have your own transport, consult the turismo in Arouca for information on places to visit in the nearby **Serra da Arada**, whose beautiful countryside is terraced like the Minho and abundantly littered with dolmens, crumbling villages and waterfalls with ancient bridges. Whitewater rafting, mountain biking and other mountain activities are also on offer – contact the Arouca turismo in advance to arrange these activities.

Perhaps the most extraordinary route over the peaks is the drive **south**, heading for São Pedro do Sul and Vouzela (see p.229). Initially, you need to follow the minor road out of Arouca which climbs to the radio mast on the heights of **São Pedro Velho** (1100m), from where views of the valley are tremendous. Then head for Albergaria das Cabras, from where São Pedro do Sul is signposted. The route can be hard to find but you can get a map from the Arouca turismo. On the way, tiny hamlets cling to the hillside, vines grow on precipitous terraces, while the road snakes first through pine forest and then high across the heather-dotted moorland.

At **MANHOUCE**, a mean, medieval hamlet, the road disappears altogether for an instant and degenerates into cart-rutted cobbles worn by centuries of use. If you want to stay and enjoy the pine forests and rocky uplands of the Serra, the beautifully restored *Quinta das Uchas* (☎232 700 800, ⓕ232 700 807; ❺), about 1km from the village on the right, is the perfect base. Staff can supply information or organize trips around the Serra and also rent mountain bikes. Just before Manhouce, the attractive one-horse settlement of **ALBERGARIA DAS CABRAS**, with its sporadically closed **campsite** (☎256 947 723) and **restaurant**, makes another good base for exploring the Serra. Beyond Albergaria or Manhouce, there's another 12km of incredible bends and views before emerging onto the N227 – a 43-kilometre journey that takes ninety minutes to negotiate. It's a spectacular drive but be prepared to take evasive action along the whole route, against other drivers or, occasionally, against wandering cattle.

There is – incredibly – a bus service along this route, though it's geared towards market and school times and consequently isn't conducive to day trips or connections to anywhere reasonable. However, if you fancied extensive

hiking and camping in the forests, you could just strike out from any of these places, providing you were properly equipped: there are endless paths and tracks connecting all the hamlets along the way.

Travel details

Trains

Aveiro to: Coimbra (hourly; 45min–1hr); Espinho (hourly; 35–50min); Lisbon (hourly; 2hr 30min–4hr 50min); Ovar (hourly; 25–40min); Porto (hourly; 50min–1hr 30min).

Coimbra to: Aveiro (hourly; 45min–1hr); Figueira da Foz (hourly; 1hr–1hr 20min); Guarda (8 daily; 3hr–3hr 20min); Lisbon (17 daily; 2hr–3hr 20min); Lousã (Mon–Fri 18 daily, Sat 12 daily, Sun 8 daily; 50min); Luso-Buçaco (5 daily; 45min); Ovar (hourly; 50min–1hr 30min); Porto (hourly; 1hr 20min–2hr).

Figueira da Foz to: Caldas da Rainha (7 daily; 1hr 25min–2hr 25min); Coimbra (hourly; 1hr–1hr 20min); Leiria (7 daily; 1hr–1hr 15min); Torres Vedras (7 daily; 2hr–3hr 25min).

Buses

Arouca to: Porto (Mon–Fri 10 daily, Sat & Sun 2 daily; 1hr 30min); Santa Maria de Feira (Mon–Fri 10 daily, Sat & Sun 2 daily; 40min).

Aveiro to: Arouca (Mon–Fri 6 daily; 2hr 50min); Figueira da Foz (6 daily; 1hr 15min); Ilhavo (8–10 daily; 30min); Lisbon (4–6 daily; 4hr); Porto (Mon–Fri 8 daily; 2hr 45min); Praia da Barra (every 30min; 30min); Praia de Mira (6 daily; 45min); Praia da Tocha (4–6 daily; 50min).

Coimbra to: Braga (6–7 daily; 2hr 40min–3hr); Caramulo (3 daily; 2hr); Condeixa-a-Nova (Mon–Fri 7am–12.05am every 30min; reduced service weekends; 30min); Covilhã (4 daily; 2hr 50min–3hr 25min); Fátima (8 daily; 1hr–1hr 25min); Figueira da Foz (10 daily; 1hr–1hr 45min); Guarda (4 daily; 2hr 40min–3hr); Leiria (8 daily; 1hr); Lisbon (16

daily; 2hr 20min); Luso (Mon–Fri 5 daily, Sat & Sun 2 daily; 45min); Mira (9 daily; 1hr–1hr 30min); Montemor-o-Velho (3–9 daily; 1hr 10min); Penacova (6 daily; 45min); Peso da Régua (2–4 daily; 2hr 30min); Porto (7–12 daily; 1hr 30min–2hr 45min); Santa Maria de Feira (2 daily; 2hr 30min); Tondela (5–7 daily; 1hr 40min); Vila Real (2–4 daily; 3hr 20min); Viseu (2–8 daily; 1hr 20min–2hr 20min).

Figueira da Foz to: Aveiro (5 daily; 1hr 30min); Coimbra (Mon–Fri 9 daily, Sat & Sun 4–6 daily; 1hr–1hr 45min); Leiria (10 daily; 1hr 15min); Lisbon (3 daily; 2hr 45min); Mira (6 daily; 1hr); Montemor-o-Velho (Mon–Fri every 30min, Sat & Sun 4–8 daily; 30min); Tocha (7 daily; 40min).

Luso to: Coimbra (Mon–Fri 5 daily, Sat & Sun 2 daily; 45min); Viseu (Mon–Fri 5 daily, Sat & Sun 2 daily; 1hr 50min).

Penacova to: Coimbra (6 daily; 45min).

Praia de Mira to: Aveiro (6 daily; 45min); Coimbra (9 daily; 1hr–1hr 30min); Figueira da Foz (6 daily; 1hr).

Santa Maria de Feira to: Arouca (Mon–Fri 10 daily, Sat & Sun 2 daily; 40min); Coimbra (2 daily; 2hr 45min); Porto (every 30min; 35min).

São Pedro do Sul to: Sernada do Vouga (9–10 daily; 1hr 45min) for trains to Aveiro and Espinho; Viseu (9–10 daily; 1hr).

Termas de São Pedro do Sul to: Viseu (Mon–Fri 4–5 daily, Sat & Sun 1–2 daily; 1hr); Vouzela (Mon–Fri 2 daily; 10min).

Vouzela to: Sernada do Vouga (9–10 daily; 1hr 35min) for trains to Aveiro and Espinho; Varzielas (Mon–Fri 2 daily; 30min); Viseu (9–10 daily; 1hr 10min).

Mountain Beiras

ATLANTIC
OCEAN

SPAIN

N

CHAPTER 4

Highlights

* **Viseu** The dignified little streets and leafy squares of this elegant old town are perfect for a stroll. See opposite

* **Trancoso** Wander between the fascinating facades of ancient Jewish houses in this ancient village. See p.258

* **Fortified walls of Almeida** The extraordinary fortifications are built in the form of a twelve-pointed star. See p.262

* **Serra da Estrela** The extraordinary boulder-strewn moonscape makes for excellent walking territory. See p.264

* **Parque Natural de Serra da Estrela** View the high peaks and hike through desolate plains, resin-scented forests and sleepy villages. See p.266

* **Queijo da serra** Try the pungent local cheese in the range's highest village, Sabugeiro. See p.268

* **Roast wild boar** Feast on the local delight in the beautiful walled village of Sortelha. See p.276

* **Monsanto** An ancient village where houses hewn out of granite cling to a misty, boulder-strewn hillside. See p.280

Mountain Beiras

Composed of two provinces, the Beira Alta (Upper) and Beira Baixa (Lower), the Mountain Beiras region features some of the least explored country in the Iberian peninsula, as well as some of the most spectacular: the enormous boulders which lie strewn across much of the region limit agriculture and have instead favoured a pastoral culture of rugged hamlets (*aldeias*). Arguably, it is also the most quintessentially Portuguese part of the country. Little touched by outside influence, it is historically the heart of ancient Lusitânia, where Viriatus the Iberian rebel (a symbol of the spirit of independence in Neoclassical literature) made his last stand against the Romans. You'll see many signs of this patriotism in the fine old town of Viseu, in Beira Alta, where every other café or hotel is called the Viriato or Lusitânia. Here, too, in the heights of the wild and beautiful Parque Natural da Serra da Estrela, lies the source of the Rio Mondego, that most Portuguese of rivers: the only one (bar the insignificant Zêzere) to begin and end in Portugal rather than crossing the border from Spain. The whole region in and around the park is excellent walking country, especially if you strike off from one of the two main routes which cross the range. For useful regional information, visit Ⓦ www.rt-serradaestrela.pt.

Guarda is perhaps the most fascinating of the Beira Alta towns. Though diminutive in size, it has one of the highest locations of any provincial capital in the country and it bristles with life, especially on *feira* days. To the north and east stretch a whole series of high-sited castle-towns and some of the country's most remote villages, of which **Sortelha** is perhaps the outstanding example. Over to the south lies the more sombre plain of the **Beira Baixa** with its capital at **Castelo Branco** and, its most obvious highlight, the ancient hilltop town of **Monsanto**.

The whole Mountain Beiras region is little visited by tourists and travellers: if you've spent some days in the fleshpots of Lisbon, Porto or the Algarve, you'll find a very different **atmosphere** here – and almost exclusively Portuguese company. Bear in mind that – out of season at least – many hotels and restaurants shut sporadically; you'll rarely have trouble finding a bed for the night, but if you have a particular establishment in mind, be sure to phone ahead.

Viseu

From its high plateau, **VISEU** surveys the surrounding countryside with the air of a feudal overlord; and indeed, this dignified little city is capital of all it

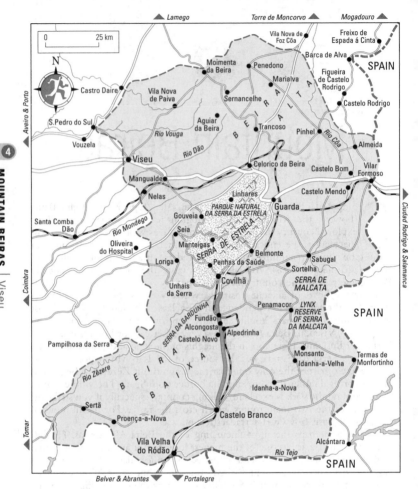

can see. It's also a place of great antiquity. There was a Roman town here, and on the northern outskirts you can still make out the remains of an encampment claimed to be the site where Viriatus (Viriato in Portuguese) fought his final battle. In fact, it was almost certainly a Roman fortification and, aside from a statue of Viriatus, there's not much there. The heart of the medieval city has changed little, though it's now approached through the broad avenues of a prosperous provincial centre. Parts of the walls survive and it is within their circuit, breached by two doughty gateways, that almost everything of interest lies.

The liveliest event in Viseu's calendar is the **Feira de São Mateus** which takes place from mid-August until its climax on September 21 (Dia do São Mateus) – it's largely an agricultural show, but is enlivened by occasional bull-fights and folk-dance festivals. The showground is at the top end of Avenida Dr. António José de Almeida, beyond the bus station and across the Rio Paiva.

The Old City

A good place to start exploring is the old quarter around the **Praça da Sé**. The approach, from the central **Praça da República** (also known as Rossio), up through the Porta do Soar, or along the shop-lined Rua Dr. Luís Ferreira, exhibits a certain amount of "beautification", but the jumble of alleys immediately behind the cathedral remains virtually untouched. You suddenly come upon sixteenth-century stone mansions proudly displaying their coats of arms in the middle of a street of rundown houses.

The cathedral square itself is lined with noble stone buildings, most striking of which is the **Igreja da Misericórdia** with its white Baroque facade. Silhouetted against a deep blue sky it looks like a film set without substance – you expect to walk around the back and find wooden props holding it up. There's some truth to that feeling: behind the symmetry of the facade, it's a very ordinary, rather dull church.

There's nothing two-dimensional, however, about the **Sé** (daily 9.30am–noon & 2–5.30pm), a weighty, twin-towered Romanesque base on which a succession of later generations have made their mark. The granite frontage, remodelled in the seventeenth century, is stern and makes the church look smaller than it actually is – inside it opens out into a great hall with intricate vaulting, twisted and knotted to represent ropes. The cathedral's Renaissance **cloister**, of which you get no intimation from outside, is one of the most graceful in the country. The rooms of its upper level look out over the tangled roofs of the oldest part of the town and house the treasures of the cathedral's art collection, including naive sculptures, two thirteenth-century Limoges enamel coffers and a twelfth-century Bible.

Museu de Grão Vasco

The greatest treasure of Viseu is the **Museu de Grão Vasco** in the Paço dos Três Escalões – once the Bishop's palace. **Vasco Fernandes** (known always as Grão Vasco, The Great Vasco) was born in Viseu and became the key figure in a school of painting which flourished here in the first half of the sixteenth century. The style of these "Portuguese primitives" was influenced heavily by Flemish masters and in particular by van Eyck, but certain aspects – the realism of portraiture and richness of colour – are distinctively their own. Vasco and his chief rival Gaspar Vaz have a fair claim to being two of the greatest artists Portugal has produced.

Closed for remodelling at the time of writing, the museum is due to reopen in 2003; check with the tourist office (see below) for the latest information. During this time, a proportion of the collection has been moved to the north wing of the Igreja da Misericordia, opposite the cathedral (Tues 2–6pm, Wed–Sun 10am–6pm; €1.50, free Sunday mornings; Ⓦwww.ipmuseus.pt /portu/museus/vasco.htm). The centrepiece is the masterly *St Peter on His Throne*, one of Grão Vasco's last works and painted, it is said, to rival Gaspar Vaz's treatment of the same theme for the church at São João de Tarouca (see p.345). It shows considerably more Renaissance influence than some of the earlier paintings but its Flemish roots are still evident, particularly in the intricately – and sometimes bizarrely – detailed background.

Also worth a visit is the tiny **Museu Almeida Moreira** (Mon–Fri 9.30am–12.30pm & 2–5.30pm; €1.50) on the edge of the Jardim das Mães. This traditional house displays furniture and pottery from the seventeenth to nineteenth century, and is named after the founder of the Grão Vasco museum.

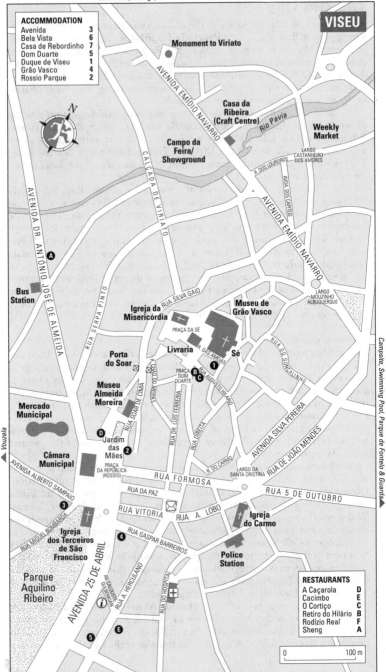

▲ *Aveiro, Lamego, Chaves & Vila Real*

VISEU

ACCOMMODATION
Avenida	3
Bela Vista	6
Casa de Rebordinho	7
Dom Duarte	5
Duque de Viseu	1
Grão Vasco	4
Rossio Parque	2

Monument to Viriato

Casa da Ribeira (Craft Centre)

Rio Pavia

Weekly Market

AVENIDA EMÍDIO NAVARRO

LARGO CASTANHEIRO DOS AMORES

R. DOS LOUREIROS

AVDA DOS CAPITÃES

Campo da Feira/ Showground

CALÇADA DE VIRIATO

AVENIDA DR. ANTÓNIO JOSÉ DE ALMEIDA

RUA SERPA PINTO

A

Bus Station

RUA SILVA GAIO

Igreja da Misericórdia

Museu de Grão Vasco

PRAÇA DA SÉ

LARGO MOUZINHO ALBUQUERQUE

Livraria

R. DAS AMEIAS

Sé

RUA DO GONÇALINHO

Porta do Soar

1

PRAÇA DOM DUARTE

B
C

RUA AUGUSTO HILÁRIO

RUA SOAR DE CIMA

Museu Almeida Moreira

RUA DR. LUÍS FERREIRA

RUA DIREITA

AVENIDA SILVA PEREIRA

Mercado Municipal

D

Jardim das Mães

2

R. DO CARMO

RUA DE JOÃO MENDES

Câmara Municipal

PRAÇA DA REPÚBLICA (ROSSIO)

RUA FORMOSA

LARGO DA SANTA CRISTINA

RUA 5 DE OUTUBRO

AVENIDA ALBERTO SAMPAIO

RUA DA PAZ

3

RUA VITÓRIA

RUA A. LOBO

RUA MIGUEL BOMBARDA

Igreja dos Terceiros de São Francisco

4

RUA GASPAR BARREIROS

Igreja do Carmo

Parque Aquilino Ribeiro

AVENIDA 25 DE ABRIL

AV. GALIBET GUENNAN

RUA A. HERCULANO

RUA DO HOSPITAL

Police Station

i

5

E

RESTAURANTS
A Caçarola	D
Cacimbo	E
O Cortiço	C
Retiro do Hilário	B
Rodízio Real	F
Sheng	A

0   100 m

▼ **6**, **F**, @ & Coimbra   ▼ **7**, @ & Nelas

◀ *Vouzela*

Campsite, Swimming Pool, Parque de Fontelo & Guarda ▶

Practicalities

Viseu is no longer on the rail line, though CP **buses** still operate along the old routes, linking the town with Guarda, Coimbra and Lisbon on the Beira Alta line at Nelas (30min south of Viseu) and with the Coimbra–Aveiro–Porto line at Sernada do Vouga (2hr 45min west of Viseu). Coming from Porto, an alternative approach is to take the Douro train line to Peso da Régua (2hr) and then the bus via Lamego, Castro Daire and Carvalhal (2–3hr). The **bus station** in Viseu is on Avenida Dr. António José de Almeida, a short walk from the centre.

The **turismo** (Mon–Fri 9am–12.30pm & 2.30–6pm, Sat 10am–12.30pm & 2.30–5.30pm, Sun 10am–12.30pm; Jan–March closed weekends; ☎232 420 950, ⓦ www.rt-dao-lafoes.com) is situated just south of Rossio on Avenida Calouste Gulbenkian, and can provide maps and information on the Beira Alta region as a whole. There are two **internet cafés** in Viseu: the *Metal Bar* (Mon–Sat 2.30pm–2am; €2/hr), on Praça de Gôa, south of Pargue Aquilino; and *Cyber Café* (daily 11am–midnight; €1.50/hr), on Quinta do Galo, to the southwest of the centre.

Accommodation

The best **hotels and pensões** are in the old quarter, but Viseu is short on budget accommodation. There's a well-equipped *Orbitur* **campsite** (☎232 436 146, ⓕ232 436 120; closed mid-Dec to mid-Jan) in the Parque do Fontelo, ten minutes' walk east from Rossio, and a municipal swimming pool 500m away, on Avenida José Relvas.

Avenida Av Alberto Sampaio 1 ☎ & ⓕ232 423 432. A fairly pleasant hotel in a good location near the Parque Aquilino Ribeiro, with a few cheaper rooms. ❹

Bela Vista Rua Alexandre Herculano 510 ☎232 422 026, ⓕ232 428 472. Functional *pensão* in a street up from the turismo; has some cheaper rooms without baths. ❸

Casa de Rebordinho Rebordinho ☎232 461 258, ⓕ232 461 258. Situated 6km south on the N231 Nelas road, this ANTER property is in a converted seventeenth-century manor house on a farm estate. ❺

Dom Duarte Rua Alexandre Herculano 214 ☎232 421 980, ⓕ232 424 825. Pleasant *residencial* despite the gloomy grey walls; all rooms with bath, TV and air conditioning. ❸

Duque de Viseu Rua das Ameias 22 ☎232 421 286. A converted town house right by the cathedral. Somewhat lacking in character, with small rooms and tiny bathrooms, but the owners are friendly and the location couldn't be better. ❸

Grão Vasco Rua Gaspar Barreiros ☎232 423 511, ⓕ232 426 444. Viseu's finest hotel – a grand central hotel with bar and swimming pool, but overpriced. ❺

Rossio Parque Praça da República 55 ☎232 422 085. An old hotel that has seen better days but it's in an excellent location. Some rooms are small and cramped; others have no window or shower – prices vary accordingly. There's a pleasant, if slightly musty, dining room. ❸

Eating and drinking

Viseu is well known for its gastronomic delights, and wherever you eat or drink, bear in mind that locally produced **Dão wines**, especially the reds, are some of the best you'll find in the country. For provisions, there's a **weekly market** on Tuesday, on the ring road by Largo Castanheiro dos Amores, and a weekday market in the **Mercado Municipal**, just west of Rossio. Most of Viseu's **nightlife** is to be found in the old town around Rua Augusto Hilário, Rua Dom Duarte and the Sé. The **restaurants** listed below are all very popular locally; you may have to wait for a table.

A Caçarola Trav. Major Teles 3, just off Rossio. Big and cheap portions of traditional fare in a place that gets packed at lunchtimes.

Cacimbo Rua A. Herculano. Good value and very popular, with a wider choice of meat dishes than other restaurants.

O Cortiço Rua Augusto Hilário 45 ☎ 232 423 853. In the old town near the cathedral, just down from the statue of Dom Duarte, this is popular enough for tables to be at a premium. Food and decor are *típicos*, but the service can be a bit sullen. Around €13 a head.

Retiro do Hilário Rua Augusto Hilário 55 ☎ 232 426 499. Good Portuguese food in a nice atmosphere with live fado every night – the owner is a musician himself. Open till 2am.

Rodízio Real Bairro Santa Eulália ☎ 232 422 232. Out in the suburbs in Repeses, on the N2 (Coimbra direction). Diners come from far and wide to sample its Brazilian cooking; up to €18.

Restaurante Sheng Av Dr. António José de Almeida. A cheap and tasty Chinese option opposite the bus station.

East to Guarda

East of Viseu, the high and austere territory of the **Serra da Estrela** spreads as far as the eye can see: a landscape of great jagged boulders and rough, dry grass – often singed in patches by summer fires. The wilderness of the area, as so often in mountain regions, belies its inhabitants, who, though a little abrupt, have none of the suspicion of outsiders often encountered in Portuguese cities and coastal regions.

The fast IP5 highway from Aveiro cuts east right through, skirting Viseu and running on to **Guarda**. Train travellers have to backtrack south to Nelas from Viseu in order to follow the **Beira Alta rail line** from Santa Comba Dão to Guarda. By road or rail, the only realistic stop before Guarda is at **Celorico da Beira**, which lies at a nexus of routes, with bus connections to Linhares (p.266), perhaps the most attractive of the *serra* villages.

Celorico da Beira

CELORICO DA BEIRA, 50km east of Viseu, is an unprepossessing town; its one claim to fame is as the birthplace of the aviator Sacadura Cabral. It is certainly not the most attractive *serra* base – a major road and bus interchange for people heading to the *planalto* north of Guarda, the town is also split by heavy traffic along the east–west road from Spain and the north–south route to Lisbon. It does, however, have a pretty enough old town hugging the slopes around the fine castle and, if you're passing through at the right time, it's the best place to pick up a pungent *queijo da serra*, the famed round cheese of the Serra da Estrela district.

It is no longer possible to enter the **Castelo**, although the views from below the walls are stunning; all around stretches the extraordinary wasteland of the mountains, split only by a small river and a couple of highways. The castle has a long military history, forming, together with Trancoso and Guarda, a triangle of defensive fortifications against Spain.

Feiras – held on alternate Fridays for cheese, and on Tuesdays for the ordinary covered market – are the times to catch the town's cheery provinciality. People come in form the mountains to sell their *queijo da serra* – market-going being the only source of income to support their impoverished hilltop farms. If you miss the cheese market, visit the excellent old cheese shop on the main road through town, just down from the post office. A visit on June 13 will give you the chance to join in the Santo António **festivals** when the whole village enjoys a riverside picnic; ask at the turismo for details of other summer festivals, when locals indulge in the traditional game of climbing a greased pole to try and retrieve a flask of wine and some *bacalhau*.

Practicalities

Celorico's **train station** is 6km north of town at Celorico Gare; bus connections are erratic, so you'll probably need to take a taxi (if you can find one) or walk. If you find yourself walking from the station, look out for the forked rocks near Espinho – 1km west of the road – which were once used to hang criminals, and the megalithic stone necropolis at nearby São Gens. It's more convenient to arrive in Celorico by **bus** as many long-distance services pass through: there are bus stops outside the *Residencial Parque* and the *Café Central* on the town's main road has information about services. There is a helpful **turismo** (Tues–Fri 9am–1pm & 3–6pm, Sat 10am–1pm & 3–6pm; ☎271 742 109) on the edge of town on the Coimbra road – look out for the modern hut on the roadside.

If you want to **stay**, the town's best and most central *pensão* is the friendly *Residencial Parque,* Rua Andrade Corvo 48 (☎271 742 197, ⓕ271 743 798; ❸), located slightly south of the centre. There's also a hotel on the road to the turismo, the modern *Hotel Mira Serra,* Bairro de Santa Eufémia (☎271 742 604, ⓕ271 741 382; ❺), with magnificent views from some of the bedrooms. Just beyond the turismo, on the same road, there are rooms above the *Nova Estrela* (☎271 741 241; ❶), whose **restaurant** is excellent, as is the *Boa-Hora*, next door. There is a possible freelance **campsite** by the Rio Mondego, near the station. Seven kilometres further upstream, off the Guarda road, there's an official site, *Parque Ponte do Ladrão* (☎271 742 645; open April–Sept), at Lajeosa do Mondego.

Guarda

Twenty-two kilometres southeast of Celorico da Beira, **GUARDA**, at an altitude of over 1000m, is claimed by its inhabitants to be the highest city in Europe – an assertion to be taken with a pinch of salt. It is high enough, though, to be chilly and windswept all year round and to offer endless views, especially to the east into Spain. The city was founded in 1197 by Dom Sancho I, to guard (as the name implies) the borders against both Moors and Spaniards. It was a heftily fortified place and, despite the fact that castle and walls have all but disappeared, it still has something of the grim air of a city permanently on a war footing. Fortunately, nowadays, the presence of a polytechnic injects a fair amount of life into the town. Guarda is known in Portugal as the city of the four Fs: *Fria, Farta, Forte e Feia* – cold, rich, strong and ugly. However, the city fathers – unhappy with the last of these – have launched a "five Fs" campaign to replace *Feia* with *Fiel* (loyal) and *Formosa* (beautiful). Oversensitive perhaps, though it is true to say that the centre of Guarda, with its arcaded streets and little praças, can be distinctly picturesque.

Numerous **festivals** take place in the Guarda area. The biggest events are the great **feiras** (June 24 and October 4), extended markets full of life and character. The **Festas da Cidade** (held during the summer months on different dates each year) are cultural affairs with exhibitions and folk-dancing, but a little too highly organized for their own good.

The Town

At the heart of it all dominating the Praça Luís de Camões (or Praça Velha) is the dour grey **Sé** (Tues–Sun 9–11.30am & 2.30–5pm), one of those buildings which took so long to complete (1390–1540) that several architectural styles came and went during its construction, all of them incorporated into the work somewhere. The castellated main facade, with its two heavy octagonal towers,

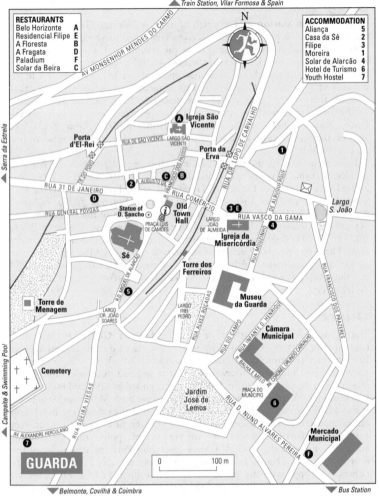

looks like the gateway of some particularly forbidding castle, but around the sides the design is lightened by flying buttresses, fantastic pinnacles and grimacing gargoyles – the ones facing Spain are particularly mean-looking. Inside, it's surprisingly long and lofty, with twisted pillars and vaulting influenced by the Manueline style of the later stages of its development. The huge carved stone **retábulo** is the work of João de Ruão, a leading figure in the sixteenth-century resurgence of Portuguese sculpture at Coimbra.

Apart from the cathedral, there's little else to see in Guarda: the displays of local archeology, art and sculpture in the **Museu da Guarda** (Tues–Sun 10am–12.30pm & 2–5.30pm; €2, free on Sun mornings; Ⓦ www.ipmuseus .pt/portu/museus/guarda.htm) on Rua Alves Roçadas are, frankly, dull, and of the castle, on a bleak little hill nearby, only the plain square keep, the **Torre de Menagem**, survives, while the walls are recalled by just three remaining gates

– the most impressive of them the **Torre dos Ferreiros** (Blacksmiths' Tower). The cobbled streets of the old town, though, are fascinating in themselves, and the tangled area between the other two portals – the **Porta da Erva** and **Porta d'El-Rei** – can have changed little in the past 400 years.

Like Celorico, Guarda has a covered **market** on Rua D. Nuno Álvares Pereira, busiest on Saturdays, where you'll find delicious *queijo da serra*. On the other side of town, below Avenida Monsenhor Mendes do Carmo, is the open-air Feira Ao Ar Livre, held on the first and third Wednesday of every month and attracting agricultural folk from all around.

Practicalities

Guarda's **train station** is 3km north of the town centre but there's usually a bus to meet all the major arrivals. The **bus station**, alongside Rua D. Nuno Álvares Pereira, is fairly central and ultra-efficient. Services are operated by a variety of companies to most of the neighbouring villages, the only problem being that many buses leave early in the morning and often don't return until late in the afternoon. The **turismo** is in the old town hall building, just across from the Sé on Praça Luís de Camões (Mon–Sat 9am–12.30pm & 2–5.30pm; ☎271 205 530, ⓦwww.domdigital.pt/cm-guarda). The building also holds a large **internet café**, offering free access (daily 9am–12.30pm & 2–5.30pm). There is also a **Serra da Estrala information office** 100metres away at Rua D. Sancho 1 (☎271 225 454).

Accommodation

You should have no trouble getting a room at one of the **pensões** and **hotels** detailed below, or try the **youth hostel** on Avenida Alexandre Herculano (daily: reception 8am–noon & 6pm–midnight; ☎ & ⓕ271 224 482, ⓔguarda@movijovem.pt). Guarda's **campsite** (☎271 221 200) is in a park a short way from the castle; beware that in spring and autumn the nights can get extremely cold. The town's heated swimming pool is 500m further on.

Aliança Rua Vasco da Gama 8a ☎271 222 235, ⓕ271 221 451. Just down the hill from the *Filipe*, this modern, welcoming *pensão* also has a restaurant and bar. ❷

Casa da Sé Rua Augusto Gil 17 ☎271 212 501, ⓦwww.casa-da-se.com. Small, bright characterful rooms with bathrooms and TVs. Good value and centrally located off the Praça Luís de Camões. ❷

Filipe Rua Vasco da Gama 9 ☎271 223 659, ⓕ271 221 402. A more upmarket hotel, opposite the Igreja da Misericórdia. Some of the rooms are a little cramped, but all have TV and private facilities. Breakfast included. ❸

Residencial Moreira Rua Mouzinho de Albuquerque 47 ☎271 214 131. Central and good-value option; all rooms have bathrooms. ❷

Solar de Alarcão Rua Dom Miguel de Alarcão 25–27 ☎271 214 392. Magnificent granite manor house dating back to the seventeenth century, with wonderful rooms. Book ahead. ❹

Hotel de Turismo Praça do Município ☎271 223 366, ⓕ271 223 399. Guarda's grandest and part of the Best Western chain: big and reasonably well run but without the charm and character of the *Solar de Alarcão*. ❺

Eating

Most of the town's **restaurants** are to be found in the area between the Porta da Estrela and the Igreja de São Vicente.

Belo Horizonte Largo de São Vincente 1. Set in a pretty square opposite a church, this is a good place to try local dishes such as rabbit and sausages.

Residencial Filipe Rua Vasco da Gama 9. The first-floor dining room is a shade too florid, but

there's no arguing with the generous portions of good food. You'll pay around €10 for a meal.

A Floresta Rua Franciso dos Passos 40. Reasonably priced and serves enormous portions – grills are the house speciality, and the *ementa turística* is a bargain at €5.

Restaurante A Fragata Rua 31 de Janeiro 17. Popular place near the cathedral serving recommended standard Portuguese dishes. Daily specials costs around €6.

Restaurante Paladium Rua Francisco dos Prezeres 23. On the way to the bus station (and near the *Hotel de Turismo*), this serves daytime snacks and a full menu in the evening. Meals for around €10; the chicken dishes are especially good.

Solar da Beira Rua Francisco dos Passos 9. Highly recommended option around the corner from Praça Luís de Camões with main courses for around €6. Try the *cabrito de ensopado* (stewed kid goat) or *lombo grelhado* (grilled pork loin). Closed Thurs.

North of Guarda: the Planalto of Beira Alta

North and east of Guarda stretches a rough and barren-looking territory known as the **Planalto** – tableland – of the Beira Alta. Villages are far apart, with much of the land between untamed by agriculture, strewn with boulders and great slabs of granite. There is the odd fertile valley, though, and a speciality of the local settlements is roast or dried chestnuts. Once a replacement for potatoes, and now a dessert, they come from vast, shady trees growing beside the roads on almost any approach to a village.

In medieval times, the region's Jewish settlements such as **Trancoso** and **Sernancelhe** prospered, though their merchant trade went into decline from the Age of Discovery onwards as business moved to the coast. In successive centuries, the *planalto* towns became closely associated with Portuguese independence from Spain, and in particular with Afonso Henriques's march south down the length of the country. Today, their **castles** are the highlight of the region. **Penedono**'s Castelo Roqueiro is especially magnificent, with seventeenth-century reconstructions on top of the original. Impressive, too, are the star-shaped fortress at **Almeida**, the site of the penultimate battle in the Peninsular Wars against Napoleon and, in its own understated way, the town of **Pinhel**, with its untouched atmosphere and architecture.

If you're travelling in **winter**, take to heart the proverb that "*O frio almoça em Penedono, merenda em Trancoso e ceia na Guarda*" (The cold lunches in Penedono, takes tea in Trancoso and dines in Guarda), and come suitably prepared. You will at least be rewarded by some extraordinary landscapes: the frost (*sincelo*) can have an extraordinary effect on the *planalto*, with massive trees linked by boughs of crystal and metre-long icicles hanging from every house.

Trancoso

Forty-four kilometres north of Guarda, **TRANCOSO**, still largely contained within a circuit of medieval walls, is an atmospheric little town, full of dark alleyways and interesting architectural details. The presence of a large **Jewish community** during the Middle Ages is apparent from the facades of the more ancient homes. Each has two doorways – a broad one for trade and a narrow one (leading to the first floor) for the family – and above the carefully crafted and bevelled stonework, some have clumsy crosses, inscribed by the Inquisition to indicate the family's conversion to Christianity. The most striking – although in need of restoration – is the former **rabbi's house** (known as the Casa do Gato Negro), next to the restaurant *São Marcos*, which is decorated with the Lion of Judea, the Gates of Jerusalem and a figure of *Preguiça,* which some translate as "Sloth".

Bandarra, the cobbler-prophet

Trancoso takes its place in Portuguese history through the legend of one **Bandarra**, a shoemaker-prophet who lived in the town in the fifteenth century. The cobbler began his prophetic career with local horoscopes and poems, but after a while moved to more national matters – foretelling, among other things, the end of the Portuguese kingdom. In an age of religious dilemma and disillusionment with monarchical rule his prophecies struck a chord, and attracted the attention of the authorities. Their circulation was banned and Bandarra condemned to death – a sentence commuted after popular outcry to a punishment of walking barefoot around town carrying a massive candle until it burned to the wick.

There the matter might have rested, but twenty years after Bandarra's death, Dom Sebastião did indeed die (along with most of the Portuguese nobility) in the battle of Alcácer-Quibir in Morocco, leaving no heir to the throne. Portugal subsequently lost independence to Spain, and Bandarra was pronounced the Nostradamus of his time.

At the centre of the fortifications is the **castle**, with its squat, almost triangular, tower – a distinctive silhouette visible from many miles away, yet paradoxically rather difficult to find once within the town walls. It's a Moorish design and a reminder of the Saracen domination of the town in the tenth century, following the town's conquest by al-Mansur. The following two centuries saw frequent siege and battle, with the fortress taken by Fernando Magno in 1033, and finally by Afonso Henriques and Egas Moniz in 1139 – an event celebrated by the construction of the monastery at São João de Tarouca (see p.345). Trancoso's later military history includes the usual invasions and billeting during fourteenth-century Castillian troublemaking and the nineteenth-century Peninsular War – look out for the charming corner house with an open stone stairway on the central square, which has the tellingly British name, Quartel do General Beresforde.

An equally historic site is the small **Capela de São Bartolomeu**, on the side of the dusty avenue leading into town, where Dom Dinis married the twelve-year-old Isabel of Aragon in 1282; he later gave her the entire town as a gift. Outside the walls from here, in front of the law courts, **Celtic tombs** attest to very early origins indeed.

Feiras are held on Fridays, with the big annual bash, the **Feira de São Bartolomeu**, on August 8–14, followed by the **Festa de Nossa Senhora da Fresta** on August 15.

Practicalities

Buses to Lamego pass twice a day during the week, stopping in the square in front of the main gates. There are one or two buses daily to Lisbon via Coimbra and Celorica, where you can also catch connections to Viseu or Guarda. You can buy tickets from the café next to the **turismo** (Mon–Sat 10am–12.30pm & 2–5.30pm; ☎271 811 147); the latter is opposite the main gates to the walled town and can point you in the direction of **private rooms** (❶).

The town offers a choice of three **pensões**: cheapest is the *Pensão Vale a Pena* (☎271 811 951; ❷), a genial place above a garage, just outside the walls near the hospital on Largo Senhora da Calçada – breakfast is included in the rates. The best place to stay is the *Residencial Dom Dinis* (☎271 811 525; ❷), also outside the walls above the post office, at Campo das Viúvas 2, with English-speaking owners. If that's full, try the *Residencial Saõ Bartolomeu* (☎271 812 129, ❷), another modern choice on the main road out to Guarda. For **eating**, the

Café Bandarra, near the main gateway, serves a wide range of dishes; more expensive, but value for money and very popular with the locals, is *O Brasão* on Rua Adriano Mountinho.

Sernancelhe

Sited 30km northwest from Trancoso, a couple of kilometres off the Guarda–Lamego road, **SERNANCELHE** is not exactly the hub of Beira Alta, but it's a quietly impressive place, in the manner of Trancoso, with further reminders of the area's Jewish past and a fine riverside location. The village is also said to produce the *planalto's* finest chestnuts and its approach is dominated by the broad-boughed trees spreading across the road. Carnivals, love songs, recipes, and folk tales all centre on the fruit, and if you coincide with the **Festa de Nossa Senhora de Ao Pé da Cruz** on May 1 you'll witness a curious mixture of religious devotion, springtime merrymaking and, above all, folkloric superstition. There's a dance of the chestnuts, a blessing of the trees, and the exchange of handfuls of blossom by local lovers, aside from the religious procession.

Should you want to know more about the town, the local cultural expert, Padre Cândido Azevedo, is more than pleased to welcome a stranger into his majestic, castle-like home overlooking the town. The walk up there takes you through the **old quarter** of town, now only semi-populated and coming alive only for the weekly Thursday market. En route, along the main road, you pass the **Igreja Matriz**, an attractive Romanesque church with a curious facade. Fixed into twin niches on either side of the main doorway are six weathered apostles – said to be the only free-standing sculptures of the period in the whole of Portugal. Inside the church are several sixteenth-century panels, including a magnificent *John the Baptist*.

A wander around the old quarter will also reveal the same features of medieval **Jewish settlement** as in Trancoso – canted lintels, pairs of granite doorways of unequal size, the occasional cross for the converted. Equally noticeable are a number of large **town houses**, dating from the sixteenth and seventeenth centuries. One of these is the supposed birthplace of the Marquês de Pombal, another is the birthplace of Padre João Rodrigues, an influential missionary who founded a series of mission houses in Japan in the sixteenth century. Japanese tourists often make the pilgrimage here to see the building.

There are basic **rooms** above the *Café Flora* (☎254 595 304; ❷). Alternatively, you could put up a tent by the river, just outside Sernancelhe, or at the **Barragem do Tavora**, a man-made barrage 3km to the north. **Buses** on to Lamego (see p.340) leave from the N226, 4km away – there are two a day in the week, none at weekends. There are also daily buses (Mon–Fri) to Penedono and Trancoso, departing from the same place.

Penedono

Sixteen kilometres to the northeast of Sernancelhe, **PENEDONO** is another one-horse town, but again a likeable place, and with a fantastic **Castelo Roquiero** – visible from miles around. The *roqueiro* ("rock") part of the name is due to the castle's emergence from its granite base, as if the rock and the walls were one and the same. From the top, as you might imagine, there are grand views, with the village's old quarter laid out below. Keys are available from the village shopkeeper, who will warn you to rattle the castle doors first in order to get the pigeons in the air – rather than have them flying straight at your face.

The castle, in times of war, and the **Solar dos Freixos** (now the town hall), in times of peace, were supposed to have been home to Álvaro Gonçalves Coutinho, the legendary **King Magriço** ("Lean One"), sung of in Camões's *Os Lusíadas*. It's a claim fought over fiercely with the inhabitants of Trancoso, who likewise are prepared to swear he is their man. According to Camões, the Magriço led eleven men to England to champion the cause of twelve noble English ladies, who found themselves without knights, and fought a joust on their behalf. Such tales of chivalry made them the subjects of numerous allegorical murals and panels of *azulejos* around the country.

The village has one **pensão**, the clean *Residencial Flora* (☎254 504 411; ❷). With a little more to spend, the new *Estalagem de Penedono* (☎254 509 120, ⓕ254 509 129; ❺), directly opposite the castle, has excellent rooms and as good a **restaurant** as you'll find in this part of Portugal – their *bacalhau*, in particular, is superb. *Café Avenida*, on the main road, is a cheaper alternative serving very good meals. **Feiras** are held every other Wednesday, and there's a **romaria** on September 15–16. **Buses** continue (Mon–Fri) to Vila Nova de Foz Côa, and to Trancoso.

Marialva and Pinhel

If you've got your own transport, it's worthwhile driving from Penedono to Pinhel via the tiny village of **MARIALVA**, dominated by the crumbling remains of a massive ruined **castle** built by Dom Sancho I in 1200. Despite, or perhaps because of, its remoteness and state of disrepair, this is among the most atmospheric of all the region's many ruins, although it is currently being restored. A ruined and deserted old village is contained within the castle walls; the only intact building is the sixteenth-century Igreja Matriz (not open to visitors). There is no accommodation in the village.

PINHEL itself is big enough to run both a wine co-operative (producing an excellent red) and a cake factory (churning out *cavaca* sweetmeats). But, consumables apart, it's also small enough to have left the narrow lanes of the old centre of town virtually untouched inside its crumbling walls. From one corner of the walls you look down on the shell of a ruined **Romanesque church**, whose facade alone merits closer inspection. On another stretch sits what is left of the original **fortress**, a soaring tower with an intricately carved Manueline window.

Down in the town further architectural pleasures are in store, with numerous **manor houses** clustered about magnificent gardens. One of the largest is now the **Câmara Municipal** – the small office to the right of the entrance hall acts as a **turismo** and can help with rooms. An adjacent building houses the town **museum** (closed at time of writing – check at the Câmara for details), with a pile of **Celtic tombstones** on the ground floor and, upstairs, remnants of a local convent.

Pinhel has two modest-priced **pensões**: *Pensão Skylab*, on Rua Silva Gouveia (☎271 412 494, ❷), just down from the Câmara, with a restaurant and bar; and the *Hoteleiro Falcão*, Avenida Carneiro Gusmão 25 (☎271 413 969; ❸). The more upmarket *Hotel Paris*, 12km away in Pínzio on Rua Pínzio (☎271 947 121; ❹) offers all the mod cons. If you want to **camp**, no one seems to object to tents being pitched around the castle walls. **Buses** leave from the centre of the municipal gardens – ask in the museum or nearby shop for schedules. One useful connection is the daily bus operated by Rodorvaria Beira Interior, which you can flag down at 4.30pm to go to Almeida or on to Figueira de Castelo Rodrigo (see p.339), and there are between two and four daily buses which connect Pinhel with Almeida and Guarda. The local **Festa de Santo António** is held on the Sunday closest to June 13.

Almeida

Perhaps the most attractive of all the fortified border towns, **ALMEIDA** is a beautifully preserved eighteenth-century stronghold. Its **walls** are in the form of a twelve-pointed star, with six bastions and six curtain walls within ravelins – a Dutch design, influenced by the French military architect Vauban. To fully appreciate the shape, take a look at the aerial shot postcards sold around town. A four-kilometre walk around the walls – now overgrown with grass – takes in all the peaks and troughs. If you stay overnight, there's an irresistible charm in watching the sun go down and the lights come on in a hundred tiny villages across the plateau of the Ribacôa.

This was one of the last stretches of land to be recognized as officially Portuguese in the Treaty of Alcañices with the Spanish in 1297, and it's easy to see why boundaries were not clearly staked out in the broad, flat terrain. Indeed, it was occasionally reoccupied by Spain – the last time was in 1762, after which the present stronghold was completed. The original two double **gates** are among the town's most splendid features – long, shell-proof tunnels with emblazoned entrances and sizeable guardroom. In the outer guardroom of the São Francisco gateway there is a small **museum** (closed at time of writing), while the larger guardroom houses a **turismo** office. The **Casamatas** (daily 9am–noon & 2–5pm; free), or barracks, is second in size only to Elvas, with a capacity for five thousand men and their supplies. Its layout explains how it withstood lengthy sieges. With its own water supply, rubbish chute, breathing holes, hidden escape routes, munitions chamber (there's a range of cannonballs and gunshot still on view), and dormitory space, the possibilities were limitless.

One other curiosity, opposite the *pousada* gateway in the walls, is an inscription on the side of a small house declaring it to be the dumping ground for illegitimate children. At the **Rodo dos Eispostos** (literally the "Circle of the Deserted"), anyone could come and claim an unwanted child for themselves – a convenient arrangement for both mother and foster parent.

Inevitably, perhaps, tourism has been catching up with Almeida – the number of cafés in town has risen from three to twenty or more within the last decade, while the arrival of the *pousada* in 1987 necessitated the hacking out of

Almeida in the Peninsular War

Almeida played a key role in the **Peninsular War** (1807–14). In January 1808 it fell to the French General Junot, whom Napoleon subsequently made Governor of Portugal. Later, when the French retreated unscathed following the infamous Convention of Sintra of August 1808, the Portuguese reoccupied the town. The Napoleonic army returned in 1810 and, en route to Buçaco and Torres Vedras, occupied Ciudad Rodrigo in Spain and besieged Almeida. The Luso-Britannic forces held out for seventeen days and then on July 26 the unforeseen happened. A leaky barrel of gunpowder, carried from the cathedral-castle in the centre of town to the Praça Alta (an artillery platform on the northern walls), left a fatal trail of powder. Once ignited, this began a fire which killed hundreds, and the survivors gave themselves up to the French. Wellington, on his victorious return from Torres Vedras, defeated the French on May 11, 1811, at Fuentes d'Onoro and subsequently took the fortress at Almeida with no bloodshed. The French army scuttled away during the night, probably making use of one of three *portas falsas* – narrow slits in the ramparts allowing for a discreet exit.

a new gateway in Almeida's fortifications, though the result wasn't as outrageous as feared. The locals seem intrigued by the phenomenon of rich tourists turning up in their long-forgotten town to fork out more than a villager's daily earnings to ride in a souped-up pony cart, or to pay through the nose for a coffee on the balcony overlooking the humble dwellings below. If you can possibly do so, try to visit during one of the twice-monthly **feiras** (on the eighth day and last Saturday) or – best of all – come at Pentecost (fifty days after Easter) for the grand picnic in the grounds of the **Convento da Barca**, a former Franciscan monastery with a distinctively Tuscan feel about its domed chapel and setting. It's the only time you can visit the convent grounds, which are now privately owned, but at other times of the year you can sample the excellent red wine, apples, peaches, nuts and various other produce for which it is famous, at shops in town.

Practicalities

Apart from the luxurious *Pousada Senhora das Neves* (☎271 574 290; ❻), there are two Turismo Espaço Rurals which let out **rooms** in the old town: *Casa Pátio da Figueria* (☎919 469 170, ❷) and *Casa Do Cnatinho* (☎271 574 224,❷). You could also ask about accommodation at the *Casa da Amelinha*, where *ginginha* (morello cherry liqueur) has been served since 1883, or at the **turismo** within the town walls (Mon–Fri 9am–12.30pm & 2–5.30pm, Sat & Sun 10am–12.30pm & 2–5.30pm; ☎271 570 020).

Otherwise, there are two modern *residenciais* by the crossroads outside the fort, both comfortable and friendly – *A Muralha* (☎271 574 357; ❸), with its own pleasant restaurant, and *Morgado* (☎271 574 412; ❸), alongside which, and under the same management, is the *Restaurante A Tertúlia*. A second good **restaurant**, just outside the main gate, is the *Granitus*, where a cheerful couple serve up solid meals. For **camping**, make your way to the Rio Côa, a 2km stroll downhill on the Pinhel road. Just above the old Romanesque bridge (and its present-day equivalent), you'll find some idyllic spots.

Buses for the north come from Vilar Formoso three times daily (Mon–Fri) and go as far as Figueira de Castelo Rodrigo; the Rodorvaria Beira Interior-operated bus stops on the main road, 200m from the gates to the old town, near the two *residenciais*, at about 4.30pm every afternoon. Going south there are local services as far as Vilar Formoso, which has trains to Guarda and Spain, and three daily buses to Sabugal and Castelo Branco. There is also one daily bus to Guarda (Mon–Fri) operated by Rodoviária Nacional, via Castelo Mendo and Castel Bom, leaving at 8.30am, and a daily bus to Pinhel. Ask in either of the *residenciais* for bus information. At weekends, public transport is virtually non-existent.

Vilar Formoso, Castelo Bom and Castelo Mendo

From Almeida, it's 12km south to **VILAR FORMOSO**, an uninteresting town on the Spanish border that has good bus and rail connections to Guarda and elsewhere, as well as about a dozen hostels if you find yourself stuck there overnight. Seven kilometres west of Vilar Formoso, on the old N16 to Guarda, **CASTELO BOM** is a small village with some old fortifications and **rooms** available at *Restaurante Lurdes* (☎271 513 653; ❶). There's also a **campsite** shortly before you reach the village, at Café Rio Côa on the N16 beside the river – a very pretty spot, although somewhat marred by the large bridge for the new IP5 highway. From Castelo Bom, it's a further 4km along the N16 to

CASTELO MENDO, one of the prettiest of the region's fortified villages and well worth a visit if you have your own transport. Otherwise, the daily bus from Almeida to Guarda passes at about 9.50am, with the eastbound bus to Vilar Formosa and Almeida returning at 5.20pm. The walk along the N16 between the two villages is pleasant and there's very little traffic, as most cars take the newer IP5 instead.

The Serra da Estrela

The peaks of the **Serra da Estrela** – the highest mountains in Portugal and the last of the four central Iberian *serras* – rise to the southwest of Guarda. The range is basically a high plateau cut by valleys, from within which emanate two of Portugal's greatest **rivers**: the Rio Mondego flows north to Celorico da Beira before swinging southwest to Coimbra and the sea at Figueira da Foz; while the Rio Zêzere flows southwest from near Guarda until it joins the Rio Tejo at Constância. Over the last few decades the *serra* landscape has changed. Once, farmers lived in stone houses with straw roofs, dotted across the peaks and valleys, but they have now moved to more modern dwellings on the valley floor. Originally, too, the whole area was heavily forested, but these days the pines are widely cultivated for timber and shepherds now graze their sheep on the higher ground. Rye is grown lower down, where the land is more fertile.

For visitors, most of the interest is in the mountain region known as the **Parque Natural da Serra da Estrela**, established in 1976 to preserve the rural character of the *serra* villages and landscape. In 1990, all land over 1200m was designated "protected countryside", which means in effect that you're not allowed to camp wild, light fires or pick flowers. However, there are three major (and several minor) **trails** through the park, which take in various authorized campsites and villages with accommodation and other facilities. The best time to walk the trails is from May to October; some of them are featured in the box on p.266. If you're interested in staying in rural properties in the park, contact ADRUSE, Avenida de Bombeiros Voluntários, Gouveia (☎238 490 180, ✉adruse@ip.pt), who can provide details and handle reservations.

Park approaches and information

Public transport into the area is erratic at the best of times. **Buses** serve the main towns of Seia, Gouveia, Celorico, Guarda and Covilhã, which form a circle around the range, but since privatization almost all local services into the more interesting mountain villages have been cut back or axed completely. The best place to check for up-to-date bus times is at the turismo or the bus station in Guarda. However, **taxis** are not quite as prohibitive as you might expect; Covilhã–Penhas costs around €15 and even the longest journey won't set you back more than €25. **Hitching** is another possibility, especially in winter when Penhas de Saúde has Portugal's only skiing facilities.

If you're coming from the west and north **by car**, you can follow the N17 down from Celorico da Beira, branching off on minor roads to enter the park at the quirky village of **Linhares**, or via the larger (and less interesting) towns of **Gouveia** and **Seia** and the traditional settlement of **Sabugeiro**. Alternatively, from the east and south, the railway and N18 road (between Guarda and Castelo Branco) skirt the eastern slopes, with access to the park from **Belmonte** and **Covilhã**. If you're intent on serious hiking, the best base is **Penhas da Saúde**, just northwest of Covilhã. Penhas has the region's only

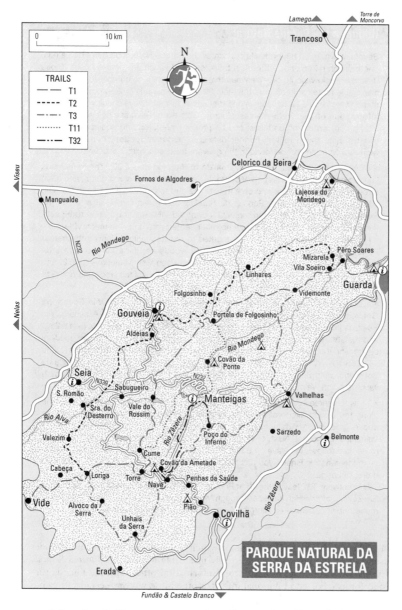

TRAILS

— — T1
- - - - T2
—·— T3
········ T11
—··— T32

0   10 km

N

Lamego ▲

Torre de Moncorvo ▲

Trancoso ●

Celorico da Beira ●

Fornos de Algodres ●

Mangualde ●

Viseu ◀

N232

Rio Mondego

Lajeosa do Mondego

Nelas ◀

Linhares ●

Folgosinho ●

Pêro Soares
Mizarela ●
Vila Soeiro ●

Guarda ▲ ⓘ

Videmonte ●

Gouveia ⓘ ▲

Aldeias ●

Portela de Folgosinho

Rio Mondego ▲

Covão da Ponte

Seia ⓘ

S. Romão ●

N339

Sabugueiro ●

N232

Rio Zêzere

Manteigas ⓘ

Valhelhas ▲

Sra. do Desterro

Vale do Rossim

Poço do Inferno

Sarzedo ●

Belmonte ⓘ

Rio Alva

Valezim ●

Cume

Covão da Ametade

Cabeça ●

Loriga ●

Torre Nave

Penhas da Saúde

Vide ●

Alvoco da Serra ●

Pião

Covilhã ⓘ

Rio Zêzere

Unhais da Serra ●

PARQUE NATURAL DA
SERRA DA ESTRELA

Erada ●

Fundão & Castelo Branco ▼

youth hostel and offers easy access to the valleys north to **Manteigas** or south to **Unhais da Serra**.

For specific details about the *parque natural*, there are **information offices** in Manteigas, Guarda, Gouveia and Seia; the details are given in the relevant sections. At each, you'll be able to buy several useful **guidebooks**, invaluable if you intend to delve into the region in any depth: the best of these is the English-language *Discovering the Region of the Serra da Estrel*. It costs €4.25 and

Several waymarked **hiking trails** cut across the Parque Natural de Serra da Estrela. The map on p.265 shows the main trails, some of which are detailed here. Those described below would take between three and four days to complete, but shorter, alternative routes spin off from the main trails, while each is broken down into segments which could be tackled as half-day or day hikes. Always check with the **park information offices** (in Manteigas, Guarda, Gouveia or Seia; see below, p.268 and 272) before setting off on hikes; and be properly prepared and equipped for what can be quite tough routes. Further details of **accommodation, campsites and facilities** en route can be found in the relevant town and village accounts.

• T1 (waymarked in red) runs **from Guarda to Vide** (on the N230). The route leads you across high land, first to Videmonte, an inhabited farming area, and then through Portela de Folgosinho on a forest road and to the dammed lake at Rossim. You then reach Torre (see "Penhas da Saúde", p.271), via Cume, after which the route ends either at Loriga (on the N231) or at Vide (N230). You'll need to be self-sufficient after Videmonte; there are no other settlements until you reach Vide.

An alternative route, the T11 (waymarked in red and yellow), leaves the trail at Portela de Folgosinho and cuts through pine woods and farm land to Covoa da Ponte, where there's a campsite. From there you can visit Manteigas (p.272) and return to the T1 at Cume. T14 leaves the trail at Torre instead and runs down to Penhas da Saúde and Covilhã, by way of the Pião campsite.

• T2 (waymarked in yellow) runs from west and then south, **from Vila Soeiro via Gouveia to Loriga**, along the western edge of the Serra da Estrela. Access to Vila Soeira is from Guarda along the T1, after which the route runs to Linhares (see below) and the atmospheric mountain village of Folgosinho; there's a grocery store, medical centre, and rooms to rent in O *Albertino*, a traditional granite house in the centre (℡238 745 266/104). At Gouveia there's a campsite; then the route runs through Cabeça de Velha and on to Senhora do Desterro (grocery store), Castro de São Romão (superb vantage point), Valezim – a sizeable village on the N231 – and finally to Loriga.

• T3 (waymarked in yellow) runs **from Videmonte via Valhelhas to Loriga**, this time along the eastern slope of the *serra*, crossing the Mondego and Zêzere rivers. As above, you reach Videmonte from Guarda along the T1 and then walk on to Valhelhas (campsite). Next, at Poço do Inferno, there's a spectacular waterfall; the route then follows the Nave de Santo António, a sandy alluvial plain supporting cattle in the summer. Finally, you pass through Alvoco da Serra on the N231 and, from there, to Loriga.

Alternatively, T32 leaves the T3 at Poço do Inferno and takes the forest road to the Rio Zêzere, after which it passes through Manteigas to the Covão da Ametade (summer campsite), before rejoining the T3 at the Nave de Santo António.

describes the hiking trails – some of which are outlined above – and includes useful maps and cross-sections. Equally invaluable is the *Carta Turística Serra da Estrela* 1:50, 000 map, available from information offices and the Guarda turismo for €6. For good regional information, visit Ⓦwww.rt-serradaestrela.pt.

Linhares

LINHARES, 20km southwest of Celorico da Beira, perches on a slope overlooking the Rio Mondego valley, and is one of the most accessible of the *serra* villages, with a trio of attractions in its castle, series of troglodyte-like dwellings, and stretch of Roman road. To get here, take the Celorico da Beira–Gouveia **bus** and stop at Carrapichana, from where it's a two-kilometre walk to the village.

The lofty keep of the **Castelo** (Mon–Fri 9am–noon & 2–5.30pm; free) presides over its surroundings and for good reason: it dates from 1169 when Linhares, then more of a town, was claimed for Portugal. Afonso Henriques realized its potential as a defensive post, and soon the men of Linhares were trained up and equipped to carry out such feats of bravery as the rescue of Celorico da Beira from the Spaniards in 1198. In the walls are traces of the *cisternas* which gave the village a constant supply of water during times of siege. You can still see the course of the spring which now runs along the gully beneath the great slabs of rock on which the castle was constructed.

Although the stone houses of the village have been spruced up with neat, green street signs, Linhares still feels ancient. If you arrive in the early morning the village appears deserted; its only sounds of life are the animals grunting and kicking their stable doors to be let out. Later in the day you'll see the donkeys being brought in from the fields and, depending on the time of year, seeds laid out to dry in the sun, wine casks being washed for the next year's vintage and, whatever the season, village gossips on their doorsteps, keen as ever to meet a stranger.

A little-known secret of the village's **church** is that it contains three paintings almost certainly executed by **Grão Vasco** and belonging to a larger series which is now lost. Propped up behind vulgar wooden statues and, in one case, stuck in one of the side aisles, the panels, *Adoration of the Magi*, *Descent from the Cross* and *Annunciation*, shine out in the obscurity. They reveal all the qualities of the great painter – his skill as a portraitist and his deft handling of tone and colour, particularly in the depiction of clothing and folds of material.

Near the schoolhouse in Linhares a path branches off towards Figueiró da Serra. Following it, you'll soon realize that you are walking along an old **Roman road** – part of the one which ran to Braga – with heavy slabs of rock for paving stones looking like something out of an Asterix cartoon. The walk is a beauty, the hedgerows lined with flowers in the spring and blackberries in the autumn.

If you want to **stay**, you'll have to head 4km out on the Carrapichana road to the attractive and friendly *Tascinha Serrano* (☎275 752 770; ❷). There's a restaurant, bar and pool (open at weekends only), and all the rooms have private facilities. Alternatively, you may be able to pitch your tent above the village near the football pitch.

Gouveia

Another 20km southwest of Linhares by road, **GOUVEIA** has lost the rural *serra* feel that once constituted its charm, as it has developed into a fair-sized provincial town.

However, it boasts several fine buildings, the most outstanding being the **Câmara Municipal**, on Avenida 25 de Abril. Open-air concerts are held in its courtyard during the summer months, but you are generally free to walk in. Incongruously, the town also has a modern art museum, in the same building as the Câmara Municipal, the **Museu de Abel Manta** (Tues–Sun 9.30am–12.30pm & 2–6pm; free), with a broad selection of contemporary Portuguese pictures donated by Gouveia-born artist Abel Manta (1888–1982).

If you can, it's worth timing your visit to take in Gouveia's Thursday **market** and if you have your own transport or are happy to make the 4km walk, the *Adega Cooperativa de São Pāio* (Mon–Fri 9.30am–noon & 2–5pm; free; ☎238 492 101) welcomes visitors to try its Dão wines.

Practicalities

Buses drop you by the bridge; walk up and veer right and you'll reach the centre of town. The **turismo** (daily: 9am–12.30pm & 2–5.30pm, occasionally closed Sun & Mon; ℡238 492 185) is in Jardim Lopes da Costa (if there's no one around try the helpful reception in the Câmara Municipal) and staff will hand out maps of the town. Walkers may also want to call in at the **information centre** of the Parque Natural de Serra da Estrela, around the corner at Rua dos Bombeiros Voluntários 8 (Mon–Fri 9am–12.30pm & 2–5.30pm; ℡238 492 411), which has further maps and leaflets on the area. For a hiking route in the park that passes through Gouveia, see the box on p.266.

Gouveia offers a handful of **accommodation** possibilities, none of which are particularly appealing. *Pensão Estrela*, Rua da República 36 (℡238 492 171; ❸), is a run-down old hotel with modern prices – pay the extra for private facilities, as the shared bathrooms are distinctly grotty. It has a **restaurant** with a good reputation. The town's most upmarket option is the *Hotel de Gouveia*, Avenida 1° de Maio (℡238 491 010; ❹), with decent if not very characterful rooms and a pool. The local **campsite** (℡238 491 008) is at Curral do Negro, around 3km from the centre of town; to get there, turn right immediately after the Câmara Municipal, then right again, before finally forking to the left for 2km.

Seia and Sabugeiro

Cut out **SEIA** (16km southwest of Gouveia) from your itinerary and you would miss little, but like Gouveia, it can be a useful jumping-off point, providing bus connections to Coimbra and access to the Estrela *parque natural*. If you stay, you could try one of the three upmarket **hotels**: the excellent *Hotel Camelo*, Rua 1° de Maio 16 (℡238 310 100, ✉hotelcamelo@mail.telepac.pt; ❹); the *Estalagem de Seia*, Avenida Dr. Afonso Costa (℡238 315 866, ℻238 315 538; ❺); or the *Albergaria Senhora do Espinheiro*, Rua Senhora do Espinheiro (℡ & ℻238 312 073; ❹). A less expensive option is the *Residência Serra da Estrela*, in the centre of town on Largo Marquês da Silva (℡238 315 566; ❸).

With enough time, or transport, however, it's better to press on into the park, after first visiting the **information centre** at Praça da República 28 (Mon–Sat 9am–12.30pm & 2–5.30pm; ℡238 310 440). There's also a **turismo** in Praça da República (Tues–Fri 9am–noon & 2–6pm, Sat 9am–noon & 2–8pm; ℡238 317 762).

If you don't have the time for an extended trip, you can always make a fleeting visit to **SABUGEIRO**, 10km east of Seia, said to be Portugal's highest village and one of the more interesting in the *serra*. As well as making a good base for walking, Sabugeiro offers the chance to see rye bread, local spice sausage and Estrela cheese being made, and plenty of Serra puppies for sale. Although the main road has succumbed to a rash of souvenir shops selling cheese, ham and leather tat, much of the village remains essentially agricultural and traditional. Most of the **accommodation** is in rooms above the souvenir shops, but other options are the traditional country houses in the old village: the *Casa do Cruzeiro*, *Casa Nova* and *Casa da Sofia* (all on ℡238 312 825; ❸). Other options include the *Residencial du Sabugeira* (℡238 313 485; ❷), on the Seia road, and *Monte Estrela* (℡238 312 984, ❸), just down the hill, with superb views from its back rooms.

From Sabugeiro you can continue southeast on the N339 to Penhas da Saúde and Covilhã; or take the minor road northeast to the N232, which runs from Gouveia to Manteigas, Valhelhas and Belmonte – for all of which, see below.

There is no regular transport on these routes, but you can usually make do with a mix of walking and hitching. Alternatively, buses cover the southern route to Covilhã. Take the bus from Sabugeiro to Seia (Mon–Fri 8am) and then on from Seia to Covilhã (Mon–Fri 6.20pm).

Belmonte

Twenty kilometres south of Guarda, the small and rather remote **BELMONTE** has the honour of being the birthplace of Pedro Álvares Cabral, the discoverer of Brazil, and is a village of considerable interest, commanded by a heavily restored thirteenth-century **castle** (Tues–Sun 10am–12.30pm & 2–5pm; free). Pedro Cabral was actually born in the castle when it was his family's residence; his tomb is next to the thirteenth-century **Igreja de São Tiago**, just below the walls. Inside the newer **Igreja Matriz**, at the foot of Rua 25 de Abril, there's an image of Nossa Senhora da Esperança, said to have accompanied Cabral on his first visit to Brazil. The castle is now equipped with a bar and modern amphitheatre for summer concerts; there are also plans for an archeological museum to display findings from recent excavations.

A little-known fact about Belmonte is that it has one of Portugal's largest Jewish communities, with up to 120 families living in the village. Records show there was a thirteenth-century synagogue in the town, but this fell into ruins after the Inquisition, when many Jews fled the country or were forced to convert to being "New Christians". However, many of the Jews continued to practise their faith in secret, using a town house on Rua Chafariz do Areal as a makeshift synagogue up until the 1970s. Only since the 1974 Revolution have the Jews felt secure enough to "out" their religion, and in the mid-1990s were finally able to build a brand-new synagogue on the site of the old town house.

Practicalities

Belmonte is a pleasant stopping-off point on the route south; for those with transport, it provides access to the *parque natural* as well as to the barren and medieval region of the Beira Baixa (covered later in this chapter). There are **bus** services to the two main Beira Baixa towns of Fundão and Castelo Branco, and a daily Rodoviaria Nacional bus (Mon–Fri) to Sabugal and the fortress-village of Sortelha. Most of the long-distance buses to Lisbon, Coimbra and Porto stop at Gingal junction, 2km below the town, at the foot of the hill. For details of times for onward connections, ask at the helpful **turismo** just next to the castle (daily 9.30am–12.30pm & 2.30–5.30pm; ℡275 911 488).

If you want **to stay**, try the basic *Pensão Altitude* on Rua Pedro Álvares Cabral (℡275 911 170; ❷), beyond the park at the western end of the village. For more comfort there's the *Hotel Belsol* (℡275 912 206, ℻275 912 315; ❹), which has a swimming pool – it's about 3km from town, back down on the main N18 road between the junction and the turn-off for Valhelhas and Manteigas (N232). The best (and most expensive) place to stay is the brand new *pousada,* in the old Convento de Belmonte (℡275 910 300, ℻275 910 310; ❻). **Buses** for Manteigas pass through at around 6pm daily.

Covilhã

Another 20km beyond Belmonte, **COVILHÃ** lies immediately below the highest peaks of the *serra*, and is the most obvious base for exploring the *parque natural*. In summer, weekend picnickers and campers spread across the hillsides; in winter, ski enthusiasts take over, using Covilhã as a base for trips to the

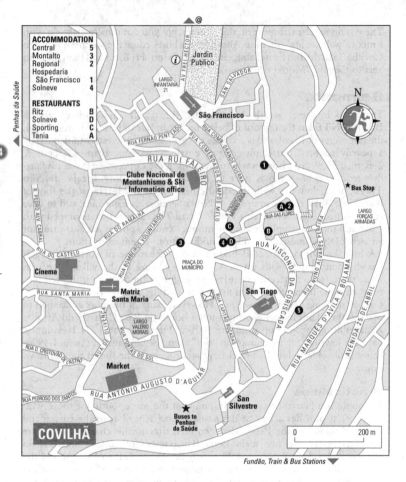

ACCOMMODATION
Central   5
Montalto   3
Regional   2
Hospedaria
  São Francisco   1
Solneve   4

RESTAURANTS
Ritz   B
Solneve   D
Sporting   C
Tania   A

Penhas da Saúde

Jardin
Publico

LARGO
INFANTARIA
21

São Francisco

RUA FERNAO PENIX

RUA RUI FALEIRO

Clube Nacional de
Montanhismo & Ski
Information office

R. PEDRO ALV. CABRAL

RUA DO RAMALHA

RUA BOMBEIROS VOLUNTARIOS

RUA DO CASTELO

Cinema

RUA SANTA MARIA

Matriz
Santa Maria

RUA DE OLIVENÇA

LARGO
VALÉRIO
MORAIS

RUA PORTAS DO SOL

RUA D. CRISTOVÃO DE CASTRO

RUA PEDROSO DOS SANTOS

Market

RUA ANTÓNIO AUGUSTO D'AGUIAR

San
Silvestre

Buses to
Penhas
da Saúde

COVILHÃ

AV. FREI HECTOR

SAN SALVADOR

RUA COMENDADOR CAMPOS MELO

RUA COMP. GRANDE GUERRA

RUA DAS FLORES

RUA VISCONDE DA CORTIÇADA

PRAÇA DO
MUNICÍPIO

San Tiago

RUA CAPITÃO ROÇADAS

RUA NUNO ÁLVARES PEREIRA

RUA MARQUÊS D'ÁVILA E BOLAMA

AVENIDA 25 DE ABRIL

Bus Stop

LARGO
FORÇAS
ARMADAS

N

0   200 m

Fundão, Train & Bus Stations

slopes. It's a steeply terraced town with every thoroughfare looking out across the plain below or up to the crags of the Serra da Estrela. A market town since the Middle Ages, it developed a textile industry in the seventeenth century using wool from the local sheep, who also provide the milk for the renowned local *queijo da Serra*. After industrialization, the woollen industry began to harness water power from the mountain streams; factories today, down on the plain below town, are powered by hydroelectricity.

Covilhã's favourite son is **Pêro de Covilhã**, who set out in 1487 on behalf of Dom João II, to search for Prester John (legendary Christian priest and king) in what is now Ethiopia. However, having reached Cairo, de Covilhã sailed instead to India before returning to Cairo and then heading south on his original errand. He never found Prester John and never returned to Portugal, though Vasco da Gama found his report about India useful when he made his own celebrated voyage there, around the Cape of Good Hope, in 1498. In front of the town hall there's a huge, polished granite slab depicting Pêro de Covilhã's voyages and a decidedly queasy-looking statue of the man himself.

Practicalities

The **train station** is 4km from the town, at the foot of the hill, as is the new **bus station**. From here, catch a local bus into town or take a taxi; otherwise, it's a stiff uphill walk. The **turismo** (Mon–Fri 9am–6pm, Sat & Sun 9am–noon & 2–5.30pm; ☎2275 319 560) is in the pink building opposite the Jardim Publico. Further north and opposite the university is the Cyber Centre, on Avenida Frei Heitor Pinto, offering free **internet access**.

Other than the campsite on the road to Penhas da Saúde (see below), the cheapest **accommodation** is to be found between Largo São João and Praça do Município. Some good options include: *Pensão Central,* Rua Nuno Álvares Pereira 14 (☎275 322 727; ❷), old, basic and as characterful as the perky old lady who runs it; *Residencial Montalto,* Praça do Município 1 (☎275 327 609, ℱ275 315 424; ❸; rooms with bath ❹), which has seen better days, but is in a brilliant position; *Pensão Regional,* Rua das Flores 4–6 (☎275 322 596; ❸), a tranquil place tucked away in a side street and with an inexpensive restaurant underneath; the reasonably priced *Hospedaria São Francisco,* Rua Almeida Eusebio 35 (☎275 322 263; ❶), downhill from the centre in a quiet street; and *Residencial Solneve,* Rua Visconde da Coriscada 126 (☎275 323 001, ℱ275 315 497; ❹), a smart option with its own garage parking – there are some cheaper rooms on the top floors (❸) and prices drop dramatically between the main summer and winter seasons.

For **food**, the *pensão* restaurants are usually the best bet. Alternatively, *Restaurante Tania,* in the same street as *Pensão Regional,* serves good, reasonably priced meals, while *Restaurante Ritz,* above a bar of that name on Praça do Município, is an excellent budget option. *Restaurante Solneve,* below the eponymous *residencial,* is another good choice with efficient, friendly service. *Restaurante Sporting,* on Rua Comendador Mendes Veiga, has a limited menu but its main attraction is its outdoor terrace.

Hikers or skiers intending to move on should contact the Club Nacional de Montanhismo, Rua Rui Faleiro (office hours; ☎275 323 364), for up-to-date details of local conditions. Covilhã also has plenty of shops for stocking up on **provisions**.

Penhas da Saúde and around

PENHAS DA SAÚDE is another good base for hiking, right at the heart of the *serra* and close to the highest, most spectacular ground. Getting here in the first place, however, is somewhat problematic. You can either hike the 11km up the glacial valley from Covilhã or catch the bus from beside Covilhã's market (July–Sept only, daily at 8.50am, the bus back leaves at 5.10pm; however, you should check bus times with the turismo before you travel, as they change frequently). If you're hiking, after 4km you'll pass the *Pião* **campsite** (☎275 314 312; open all year), followed a couple of kilometres further on by the swanky *Hotel Varanda dos Carqveijas* (☎275 319 120, ℯvc@turistrela.pt; ❻), which offers breathtaking views over the Beira Baixa far below and has a restaurant (meals under €10) and swimming pool. Further on, you pass the ruins of several large fin-de-siecle sanatoria, one of which is being converted into a *pousada* (check with the Covilhã turismo), before reaching the rather desolate-looking Penhas da Saúde.

If you want to stay at Penhas, try the 112-bed **youth hostel** (daily: reception 8am–noon & 6pm–midnight; ☎ & ℱ275 335 375, ℯpenhas@movijem.pt), at the crest of a rise as you enter Penhas on the Covilhã road and with superb views across the plain to the Serra de Malcata. Just below the youth hostel is

the overpriced *Hotel Serra da Estrela* (☎275 310 300, ✉hse@turistrela.pt; ❺).
In July and August there's also large-scale unofficial **camping** across the hillside, but the site is unpleasant and litter-strewn and you're much better off staying at *Pião* (see above). Bear in mind that, despite the accommodation here,
Penhas da Saúde is not really a village and, apart from a few cafés, there are not
many facilities.

Torre

From Penhas, you are within striking distance of the chief beauty spots of the
serra, with the highest peak in Portugal – **Torre** at 1993m – 10km up the road
to the northwest. The stone *torre* (tower) here was added in the last century, on
the orders of Dom João VI, to raise the height to a more impressive 2000m.
You can easily walk up from Penhas, but the road gets busy in summer so you
may prefer to drive or hitchhike right to the top. However, any sense of natural beauty and grandeur at the summit has been severely reduced by the dis-
figuring array of buildings, litter and broken-down skilifts, all in various stages
of decay. One, however, is a café, which may be welcome if you've walked up.
 En route you will pass the vast statue of **Nossa Senhora da Boa Estrela**,
carved into a niche in the rock, to which there's a massive procession from
Covilhã on the second Sunday in August. A little northeast of Torre, on the
road to Manteigas, is the narrow rock cone known as the **Cântaro Magro**
(Slender Pitcher), which conceals the source of the Rio Zêzere; there's an
excellent summer **campsite** below it at Covão d'Ametade. One of the park's
hiking routes passes by Torre and through Penhas and Covilhã; see "Hiking in
the Parque Natural" on p.266.

Caldas de Manteigas and Manteigas

A few kilometres beyond Penhas, you can strike **north** at Nave de Santo
António, between Penhas and Torre, and follow the glacial **valley of the Rio
Zêzere** down to the spa of **CALDAS DE MANTEIGAS**. Here the gushing
spa waters run past a lovely old water mill (now a hotel training school), and
the village spreads along one road on the bottom of the river valley, where
you'll find **places to stay**. *Residencial Miralapa* (☎275 982 098; ❸) has modern comfortable rooms (each with a TV) and a decent restaurant. Further along
the same road is the excellent *Do Manel* restaurant (☎275 981 104; ❷), which
also has rooms; and then, further still and off to the left, the well-run, modern
Berne Albergaria (☎275 981 351, ✉albergaria-berne@hotmail.com; ❹).
 Caldas de Manteigas virtually merges with the larger *serra* town of
MANTEIGAS, whose whitewashed houses and red roofs run along the con-
tour above the Rio Zêzere. It is another good option as a base for exploring
the *serra* and for hiking, with two of the *parque's* official walks passing through.
Joalto run **buses** to and from Guarda, 45km to the northeast, passing through
Belmonte and via the campsite at Valhelhas (see p.269), but check times with
the turismo in Guarda. The bus stops on the main street, Rua 1º de Maio, setting you down outside the *parque's* **main information office** (Mon–Sat
9am–12.30pm & 2–5.30pm; ☎275 980 060), where you can buy guidebooks;
nearby, next to the small park below the Galp service station, there's a regular
turismo (Tues–Sat 9.30am–noon & 2–6pm; ☎275 981 129), which has a
leaflet of circular walks from Manteigas, including the one detailed opposite.
 As for **accommodation**, at the same end of the village as the turismo but
high above the main street, is the *Pensão Estrela*, Rua Dr. Sobral 5 (☎275 981
288; ❹), boasting fine views across the valley but overpriced, and with some

A hike from Manteigas to the Poço de Inferno

There's a lovely round walk from **Manteigas** to the waterfall of **Poço de Inferno** and back via Caldas de Manteigas, which takes around five to six hours. Begin at the Galp petrol station, and take the small road which goes steeply down to the right of the main road, behind the turismo. Follow this road downhill, bearing right, until you cross a small bridge. Bear left and you will start to pick up the yellow marker arrows which head right into the woods. Keep your eyes peeled as these are not always easy to spot, but the arrows will eventually lead you to Poço de Inferno, 'hell's well', which is a great spot for a picnic and has good swimming potential. From here, continue along the paved road and you will arrive back in town at the top of Caldas de Manteigas.

poky rooms. A little way along Rua 1º de Maio, *Pensão Serradalto* (☎275 981 151; ❷) has good simple rooms above a reasonable restaurant. Drivers (or energetic hikers) could continue beyond Manteigas, 12km to the west and all uphill, to the marvellous *Pousada de São Lourenço* (☎275 982 450, ℱ275 982 453; ❻); it has only 22 rooms, most with spectacular views, so don't turn up without a reservation.

Apart from the hotel **restaurants**, there's the reliable, but less ambitious, *Santa Luzia*, on the way out of town beyond the turismo; the *Antiga Casa Anita*, near the Santa Maria church on Rua Dr. Sobral, serving dull dishes at a fast pace; and *A Cascata* on Rua 1º de Maio, just up from the Galp station, a cheap option with great views.

Sabugal, Sortelha and Serra da Malcata

The area **east of Covilhã**, over towards the Spanish border, is worth exploring for the chance to visit **Sabugal** and, more particularly, **Sortelha**, whose amazing circuit of walls rises amid one of the bleakest locations in all Portugal – undulating highland plateau strewn with giant glacial boulders, desolate but for a few trees and the shepherds who make their living here. If you're dependent on buses, you'll need to pick up connections from Guarda or Belmonte, but with your own transport the two towns make an easy side trip from Covilhã, and you can continue into the **Serra da Malcata** – wild terrain which, believe it or not, harbours a **lynx reserve**.

Sabugal

SABUGAL, like most towns in Beira Alta, has a **castle**. It's a good one, too, with massively high walls, a vast hollow centre, and a pentagonal tower with three arched chambers piled one on top of the other. Trust the rickety staircase and you could be on top of the world; trust the wobbly stonework and you could walk right around the walls. Having explored the castle, there's very little reason to hang around Sabugal, which is modern and dull. Should you need to stay over, the village has a couple of **pensões**: the basic and rundown *Residencial Robalo* (☎271 753 594; ❷) by the roundabout 50m from the closed *Hotel Paliz*; and the modern *Residencial Sol Rio*, down by the bridge (☎271 753 197; closed October; ❷) which also rents out pedalos. There's no official campsite, but nobody should object if you put a tent up by the river, on its out-of-town stretch.

There's a **festa** (June 24) and a grand **feira** (June 29); at other times of year it's all pretty quiet. If you're heading for the Serra da Malcata (see p.276), pay a visit to the *Reserva Natural* office on Largo de São Tiago, near the castle.

Buses leave from the new bus station, behind the defunct *Hotel Paliz*. There are up to six daily services to Guarda, and daily services to Belmonte, Vilar Formoso, Penamacor and Castelo Branco on weekdays, but these buses are few and far between at weekends. Public transport **to Sortelha** is limited to the early-morning bus (Mon–Fri) to Belmonte. Otherwise, there are school buses, which run in the late afternoon (and, obviously, not during the holidays). You may have to walk, though that's no bad thing as the boulder-strewn scenery is as bizarre as it is breathtaking.

Sortelha

SORTELHA is isolated and rather eerie – probably the most atmospheric town in the region, especially when mist drifts down from the *serra*. It is an ancient town, with Hispano-Arabic origins, and was also the first *castelo roqueiro* ("rock fortress") to be built this side of the Côa. Mystery and legend have grown up with the castle and its fortifications (*sortelha* means "ring"), with stories spun around the figure of an old lady (*a velha*) whose profile you can see on rocks from outside the top gates. At first sight the town seems nothing special. Walk uphill from the new quarters, however, and you arrive at the fantastically walled old town, a tight web of cobbled lanes wending between squat stone houses. Take a look at the **Igreja Matriz** (keys from the house next door) with its beautiful ceiling, executed by medieval Moors. Arabic script can be seen, too, on several house lintels near the top of town.

During the summer there's an interesting **antique shop** on the road up to the castle, and a **carpet workshop** on the route back down towards Sabugal, both offering insights into the way life used to be, but above all showing a healthy attitude to present-day tourism. Even if their continuing existence depends entirely on the foreign visitor, you never get the feeling that the show is laid on just for you. The chance to work with the fine materials and coloured wools seems to be enjoyed by all in the workshop, and the antique dealer is as happy to chat about the curious customs and folk tales as strike a bargain.

Sortelha's major event is a **bullfight**, which takes place on August 15, once every two or three years, when the local council has money to stage it. It retains the ancient and peculiar custom of the *forca* – a rudimentary defence against the bull, using branches – which has been handed down from generation to generation. The order of events for the day begins with a *forca* involving all the young boys of the village – at least 25 of whom are needed to carry the device to prevent it from being tipped up by the bull. Later, solo performers strut the stage with their red capes to take the bull's charges. Onlookers are also frequently involved – many a young bull has hopped up onto the terrace of rocks, only to find himself sniffing at discarded hats and bags while nervous laughter rises up from behind the safety of the nearest wall. In non-bullfight years there's still a **festa** on August 15, and a **romaria** in honour of Santo António takes place on June 13.

Practicalities

Sortelha has a superb traditional stone house to stay in on the outskirts of the village: *Casa do Pátio* (℡271 388 113; ❹); advance booking is recommended, especially in summer. It is replete with massive walls, wooden furniture, hot

△ Sortelha

baths, cobwebs – all in all, a splendid mix of modern comforts and medieval surroundings. If you want to stay in the old walled town itself, your best bet is to ask at the *Restaurante Alboroque* (see below) which sometimes has rooms to rent in nearby cottages and also acts as a kind of unofficial booking office for the houses mentioned above. The *Casa do Campanário* (☏271 388 198; ❹), Rua Mesquita, at the top of the old village, also has rooms and lovely views from its leafy terrace. There is a **turismo** signposted near the top of the village, but it's more often closed than open.

Alternatively, there are any number of promising areas to pitch **camp** above and beyond the old town, where the terrain is rocky and sheep take shelter beneath massive boulders. For **meals**, there's the classy but expensive *Restaurante Dom Sancho I*, just inside the main gate, which often has *javali* (wild boar) on the menu. A cheaper alternative is the *Restaurante Palmeiros*, along the road to Belmonte. **Buses** back to Sabugal leave at 8am and 5.25pm Mon–Fri, but it's a good idea to check times the day before at one of the restaurants.

The Serra da Malcata

The **Serra da Malcata** has its reserve's headquarters at Penamacor, 33km south of Sabugal. The staff are full of advice about how to approach the area and where best to go at different times of the year. The **lynx** – a graceful spotted feline with the build of a domestic cat but the dimensions of a labrador – is notoriously difficult to see, especially without the aid of the park keepers, but the countryside is compensation enough if you don't get a sighting. If you're fortunate you might also see a wild boar disappearing into the forests of black oak. The reserve also contains a dam, currently a scar on the landscape, though it will hopefully heal in time; it has good swimming spots.

Penamacor

PENAMACOR's medieval **castle** may not be as impressive as those in Sabugal and Sortelha but it offers great views over the Serra da Malcata towards Spain, and the town itself makes a good base from which to explore the area. You can whet your appetite beforehand in the municipal **museum** (daily 9am–12.30pm & 2–5.30pm; free) – look out for the stuffed lynx here as it's probably the only glimpse you'll get of one. There's also a collection of local archeological finds, agricultural tools, coins and notes (including an unexplained US dollar) and the obligatory Singer sewing machines.

The **reserve's headquarters** can be found on Rua Dr. Ribeiro Sanehes 60 (☏277 394 467). The turismo has closed, but the office in the museum may be able to help with town information. If you're making Penamacor your base, a good budget option is **to stay** in one of the rooms at *Café Caninhas*, Rua de São Estevão 20, just up from the Galp station, or you can rent a room above the Romância shop on Rua 25 Abril, opposite the Glap station (both ❶). The wonderful *Estalagem Vila Rica* (☏277 394 311; ❸), 500m west of the centre on the main road, offers a more sumptuous alternative; the views from this ivy-cloaked eighteenth-century *solar* are marvellous and the rooms comfortable.

Markets are held every first and third Wednesday of the month, and **feiras** on May 10, August 28, September 21, October 15 and November 30.

South from Covilhã: Serra da Gardunha

Fundão and the neighbouring villages of **Alpedrinha** and **Castelo Novo** lie sunk into a ridge, the **Serra da Gardunha**, south of Covilhã. All have magnificent views and are healthy, rural places, with delicious local fruit and, at Castelo Novo, healing waters. Without your own transport, a route through Fundão is an easier approach to Monsanto (see p.280) than cutting across country from Sabugal and Penamacor.

Fundão

FUNDÃO, 17km south of Covilhã by road or rail, is the largest town in the area and has little to merit a visit, although it is a good place to stock up on supplies. As far as sights are concerned, even the local tourist pamphlet admits that the town has "no monuments of note", although Fundão's glorious abundance of fresh fruit and vegetables does much to make up for its touristic shortcomings. The villages around the *serra* are celebrated for their produce and this is the local market centre. In season you'll find cherries, apples, pears, grapes and chestnuts – add to this a visit to the cheese and sausage shops in the Centro Comercial Cidade Nova, at the top of Avenida da Liberdade, and you've got an excellent picnic.

If you want to **stay overnight**, your only budget option is the rather down-at-heel *Pensão Tarouca*, at Rua 25 de Abril 37 (☎275 752 168; ❷) – turn left along Rua Jornal do Fundão, off Avenida da Liberdade. Alternatively, you could try the five-storey *Hotel Samasa*, Rua Vasco da Gama (☎275 751 299, ℉275 751 809; ❹), also off the *avenida*, or the eighteenth-century ANTER property *Casa dos Maias*, Praça do Município 11 (☎275 752 123; ❺). The **turismo** on Avenida da Liberdade (Mon–Sat 9.30am–12.30pm & 2.30–5.30pm; ☎275 752 770) might be able to help with **rooms**; or there's a small all-year **campsite** (☎275 753 118), 2km west of town on the N238, with some shade and a swimming pool.

There are plenty of **restaurants** and cafés to choose from – some of the better ones include the *Marisqueira* fish restaurant on Travessa Das Oliveiras 12, or the popular but expensive *Hermínia Restaurante* at Avenida da Liberdade 123. **Bars** are more limited: *Praça Velha*, off Rua Jornal do Fundão is open till late, as is the pleasant designer joint *O Alaúde Bar*, on Trav. das Oliveiras.

Most local **bus** services depart from the bus station at the bottom of the *avenida*; regional services operated by Rodoviária do Beira Interior leave from Rua Conde Idanha-a-Nova, parallel to the *avenida* and on the same side as the bus station.

Alpedrinha

ALPEDRINHA is set into the side of the *serra*, overlooking fields of olives and fruit trees and is easily reached by any bus from Fundão to Castelo Branco. In spring the hillside flowers, fruit-tree blossoms and spring water oozing from every crack in the road make it as idyllic a spot as you could hope to find – notwithstanding the rumbling lorries crashing through the village on the main road to the south.

A good first stop is at the museum in the former **Paços do Concelho**, which displays a collection of tradesmen's tools – from cobbler to baker to tinsmith – and traditional clothing, including a striking black wedding dress, the customary colour in this part of the world. A short way beyond, the **Capela do Leão**, in the courtyard of the Casa de Misericórdia, provides Alpedrinha with its current talking-point. Something of a mystery surrounds the present whereabouts of a series of valuable sixteenth-century panels that disappeared from the chapel during its renovation and which were last spotted at a Primitivist exhibition in Lisbon.

At the top of the same street, above the plain **Igreja Matriz**, is the elaborate fountain known as the **Chafariz de Dom João V**. When the king passed through in 1714 he found the water so good that he commissioned the *chafariz* as a sign of royal approval. The little village flourished and grand houses such as the now-deserted **Palácio do Picadeiro**, which towers above the fountain, were constructed during the eighteenth century. In front of this spectre of a palace, the old **Roman road** begins to wind its cobbled way up the side of the *serra* toward Fundão.

A further point of interest is the **furniture workshop**, situated below the main road on the way out of town toward Castelo Branco. Ask inside and someone will show you around António Santos Pinto's **sala de arte**, with some of the most consummate single-handed marquetry ever produced. Pinto moulded Louis XV chair legs to Napoleonic dressers and threw the odd carved African pageboy into his structures for good measure. There's even a set of tableaux depicting the first six cantos of Camões's *Lusíadas* – all in the most incredible detail.

Practicalities

Information on **buses** is available from the newspaper kiosk on the side of the main through-road. The Alpedrinha **train station**, a ten-minute walk on the plain below, is unstaffed but you can buy tickets on the trains.

The best **accommodation** in town is the *Casa de Barreiro*, Largo das Escolas (☎275 567 120; ❹), a turn-of-the-century house with luxurious rooms and magnificent views, set amid rambling gardens at the north end of town. Cheaper options include the recommended *Pensão Clara* (☎275 567 391; ❷), run by a sprightly old lady of the same name (there's no sign, but it's on the right as you enter the village on the E802 from the north – ask at one of the town's cafés if you're having trouble finding it), and *Pensão Sintra da Beira*, Rua Francisco Dias 14 (☎275 567 858; ❶), which is reasonable enough and has a good restaurant. You can unofficially **camp** near the spectacularly situated swimming pool, which has its own bar (open June–Sept), about 1km north of town on the main Fundão road.

The town hosts a tremendous **feira** (market), on the first Sunday in every month, and a full-blown festival, the **Festa do Anjo da Guarda**, each August 3.

Castelo Novo

In northern Portugal **CASTELO NOVO** is best known as the source of *Alardo*, a bottled mineral water reputed to possess healing properties. At the **spa**, marked by just a single café-restaurant, the water gushes from every crack in the earth's surface. The only **accommodation** is the manor house, *Quinta do Ouriço* (☎ & ℱ275 567 236; ❺), but there's scope for camping – and no shortage of sparkling clear water.

The village proper, like Alpedrinha, has ancient origins, and a few crumbling remains to prove it: a **castle**, an attractive **Paços do Concelho** (above the main square), and a Manueline **pelourinho**. Off to the sides of the square, narrow alleyways and heavy stonework constitute the village's principal charm. Although there is no **bus** to the village, four daily run along the main N18 road (between Fundão and Castelo Branco); you can be dropped or picked up at the crossroads, 4km out.

Into the Beira Baixa

After the rugged beauty of most of Beira Alta, the flat plain of the lower province, **Beira Baixa**, can come as something of an anticlimax. Yet the monotonous, parched landscape has it's own mysterious beauty, dotted with cork and carob trees or the occasional orchard. If you are here over Christmas, you may see burning logs outside each church; these are traditionally kept alight until Twelfth Night. From **Castelo Branco**, the capital of the Beira Baixa and its only sizeable town, you can make rewarding and fairly easy excursions to two strange and atmospheric villages – **Monsanto** and **Idanha-a-Velha**.

Castelo Branco

Not much of **CASTELO BRANCO** has survived the successive wars of this frontier area and today it appears as a predominantly modern town. Set out around sweeping boulevards, squares and parks, it has an air of prosperity and activity in contrast with the nearby somnolent villages.

What's left of the **old town** is confined within the narrow cobbled alleyways and stepped side streets leading up to the ruins of the **Castelo**. Around its twelfth-century walls, a garden-viewing point, the **Miradouro de São Gens**, has been laid out. Nearby is the **Palácio Episcopal** (Tues–Sun 10am–12.30pm & 2–5.30pm; €2), the old bishop's palace, with its formal, eighteenth-century garden, a sequence of elaborately shaped hedges, Baroque statues, little pools, fountains and flowerbeds. The balustrades of the two grand staircases are peopled with statues – on one, the Apostles; on the other, the kings of Portugal. Two of the latter are much smaller than the rest: the hated Spanish rulers, Felipe I and II. Elsewhere in the gardens other statues represent months of the year, signs of the zodiac, Christian virtues and the then-known continents.

The palace itself houses the **Museu Tavares Proença Júnior**, a regional museum whose collections roam through the usual local miscellany, save for a large and splendid display of finely embroidered bedspreads, or *colchas*, a craft for which the town is known throughout Portugal. The museum has been closed for a few years for renovations but is due to reopen shortly. The same is true of the elegant sixteenth-century **Câmara Municipal** in the Praça Luís de Camões, though you can still view the exterior and those of the several seventeenth- and eighteenth-century mansions in the streets around it.

Practicalities

There is a **turismo** (Mon–Fri 9.30am–5.30pm, Sat & Sun 9.30am–1pm & 2.30–6pm; ☎272 330 339, ✉turismo.cmcb@mail.telepac.pt) right in the centre of Castelo Branco, in a little park off the Alameda da Liberdade. The **bus station** is on the corner of Rua Rebelo and Rua do Saibreiro, the latter leading straight up to the Alameda. It's a little further to the **train station**, but equally simple – straight down the broad Avenida de Nuno Álvares.

As the regional capital, the town has a number of **pensões** (ten or more), though less than half of these merit recommendation. *Residencial Lusitânia* (☎272 344 214; ❷), above a chemist shop at Rua Sidónio Pais 7, the northern extension of the Alameda, is the most central, though distinctly tattered. For more comfort, try the well-run *Residencial Arraiana*, Avenida 1° de Maio 18 (☎272 341 634, ☏272 341 634; ❸); otherwise, the turismo can point you towards inexpensive *dormidas* behind the Alameda (❶). The municipal

campsite (☎272 330 361) is 3km north of town along the N18; it has recently been revamped with new bungalows and a pool.

For somewhere decent to **eat**, head for the *Restaurante Arcadia*, Alameda da Liberdade 19 (next to *Residencial Lusitânia*). It's open daily and particularly crowded with locals at the weekend, paying up to €10 for a fine spread. Further up towards the castle (along Rua Sidónio Pais), there's an equally popular Chinese restaurant, *Grande Muralha*, at Rua da Sé 28. Opposite, *Café Beirão* has pleasant outdoor tables facing the cathedral. For your own supplies, there's a large covered **market** on Avenida 1° de Maio.

Monsanto

MONSANTO, 48km northeast of Castelo Branco (buses twice daily bound for Termas de Monfortinho), claims to be the most ancient settlement in Portugal. The old village – there's a newer settlement at the bottom of the hill where the bus drops you – looks as though it has barely changed in centuries. The houses huddle between giant granite outcrops, their walls carved from and moulded around the grey boulders, appearing to have grown organically from the hillside. It's all strikingly beautiful – flowers tumble from windows and the streets, barely wide enough for a mule, are cut out of the rock.

The **castle**, too, is impressive, though ramshackle. As you climb up through the village you're quite likely to meet someone who'll insist on guiding you up, showing you the views and expounding some of the legends. A big celebration takes place every May 3, when the village girls throw baskets of flowers off the ramparts. The rite commemorates an ancient siege when, in desperation and close to starvation, the defenders threw their last calf over the walls: their attackers, so disheartened at this evidence of plenty within, gave up and went home.

Practicalities

Adega Tipica O Cruzeiro (☎277 314 528; ❸), an attractive bar on Rua Fernando Namora 6, has a couple of lovely upstairs **rooms** with great views (although the back rooms are windowless) – you'll almost certainly have to book ahead as the only other accommodation in town is the *Pousada de Monsanto* (☎277 314 471, ℻277 314 481; ❺) with ten rooms. Otherwise, you could walk or take the twice-daily bus to Penha Garçia, 8km east, where the *Café Isaias* (☎277 366 171; ❷), on Rua da Tapada, serves good meals and occasionally rents out rooms.

In Monsanto, the only **restaurant** is at the *pousada*, where you can taste stewed wild boar or braised kid goat for around €18. However, the service is surly and the food a disappointment – you might be better off having a drink and snack at the *Adega Tipica O Cruzeiro*.

Idanha-a-Velha

IDANHA-A-VELHA is another tiny backwater, situated a few kilometres from Monsanto. It sees two buses a day from Idanha-a-Nova, where there are connections to Castelo Branco; however, if you don't have transport, you could try the walk cross-country from Monsanto, but make sure you get good directions before heading off. The village is certainly worth a little effort to reach. It's possibly of a similar age to or even older than Monsanto, but has a considerably more illustrious history. Known as Igaetania, it was once a major Roman city and, subsequently, under Visigothic rule, was the seat of a bishopric –

which endured even Moorish occupation. Wamba, the legendary King of the Goths, is said to have been born here. During the reign of Dom Manuel, however, early in the fifteenth century, it is said that a plague of rats forced the occupants to move to Monsanto or nearby Idanha-a-Nova.

The village looks much as it must have done when the rats moved in, and not far different from when the Romans left, either. It retains a section of massive Roman wall, the **Roman bridge** is still in use, and odd Roman relics lie about everywhere. In the very ancient **Basilica**, which is at least part Visigothic, there's a collection of all the more mobile statues and lumps of inscribed stone found about the place; another small chapel contains an exhibition of coins, pottery and bones, all found more or less by accident. Ask in the village café for the key to the basilica, if it is locked. Another oddity, whose history nobody seems to know, is a Moorish-inspired balconied mansion.

Termas de Monfortinho

Nestling among pine trees on the banks of the River Erges, **TERMAS DE MONFORTINHO**, 20km east of Monsanto right on the Spanish border, is a tranquil wooded spa resort which, with your own transport, makes an attractive base for exploring the surrounding area and nearby Alcántara and Cáceres, over the border in Spain. It has been a popular resort since Roman times, though up until the 1930s it was not connected by road with the rest of Portugal and so was used mostly by the Spanish, who waded across the River Erges and camped among the pine trees. The town has a relaxed atmosphere and pleasant riverside walks, although since the construction of a bridge over the Erges in 1993, connecting the resort to Spain, things have become more lively.

The **thermal baths** (daily 8am–1pm & 4.30–7pm; ☎277 430 320) are north of the turismo, hidden away down by the river and surrounded by woods; you may wish to try out one of the treatments or a massage as the waters are among the most mineral-rich in Portugal. The town also boasts three **swimming pools** and several **tennis courts**; **mountain bikes** are also available for hire from the *Hotel Fonte Santa*.

Practicalities

The **turismo** (☎277 434 223) is two blocks down on the main road, next to the municipal swimming pool. There's no shortage of places **to stay** in Monfortinho. In the modern part of town, the *Beira Baixa* (☎277 434 115; ❷), on Rua das Fragueiras, is comfortable and cheap but not particularly welcoming, while the friendlier *Pensão Boavista* (☎ & ☎277 434 213; ❸) has TV and telephone in all its rooms. In the old town, there's a cluster of inexpensive, attractive but slightly run-down *pensões* in the woods, by the river; take the road towards the thermal baths and turn right at the fork in the road. However, the best place to stay – if you can afford to splash out – is the peaceful *Hotel Fonte Santa* (☎277 430 104; ❺), with beautiful rooms and an attractive swimming pool set in landscaped gardens. There are plenty of **restaurants** and **cafés** along the Castelo Branco road, of which *O Garfo* is particularly good.

For onward transport, there are two **buses** daily to Monsanto and Castelo Branco, which leave early in the morning from outside the GALP petrol station near the turismo.

Travel details

Trains

Castelo Branco to: Abrantes (5–6 daily; 1hr 20min–2hr); Covilhã (5–7 daily; 1hr 25min); Lisbon (6 daily; 4hr 5min).
Celorico da Beira to: Coimbra (5 daily; 2hr 50min); Guarda (5 daily; 50min); Lisbon (4 daily; 4hr 15min); Vilar Formoso (2 daily; 2hr).
Covilhã to: Abrantes (5 daily; 2hr 25min–3hr 15min); Castelo Branco (5–7 daily; 1hr 25min); Guarda (3 daily; 1hr 15min); Lisbon (5–6 daily; 3hr 20min–4hr 30min).
Fundão to: Castelo Branco (6 daily; 1hr 5min–1hr 30min); Covilhã (7 daily; 25min); Porto (6 daily; 4hr 15min–5hr 15min).
Guarda to: Coimbra (5–8 daily; 2hr 30min–3hr 40min); Covilhã (2 daily; 1hr 15min); Lisbon (5 daily; 5hr–7hr 50min); Vilar Formoso (4–5 daily; 50min).
Vilar Formoso (Spanish border) to: Guarda (4–5 daily; 50min); Lisbon (1–3 daily; 6hr 30min); Salamanca, Spain (2 onward connections from Portugal daily; 2hr 30min).

Buses

Almeida to: Guarda (1 daily; 2hr).
Alpendrinha to: Castelo Branco (Mon–Fri 5 daily; 30min); Covilhã (2–3 daily; 2hr 35min); Fundão (2–3 daily; 15–25min); Guarda (4 daily; 1hr 20min); Lisbon (5 daily; 4hr 30min).
Belmonte to: Guarda (3 daily; 45min).
Castelo Branco to: Coimbra (3–4 daily; 3hr); Covilhã (4–6 daily; 40min–1hr 5min); Guarda (hourly; 1hr 55min); Lisbon (4–6 daily; 3hr 45min–4hr 10min); Termas de Montefortinho (2 daily; 2hr 30min); Viseu (2 daily; 3hr 30min).

Celorico da Beira to: Coimbra (3 daily; 2hr 25min); Covilhã (5–6 daily; 1hr 15min); Guarda (4 daily; 1hr 30min); Lamego (Mon–Fri 3 daily; 3hr 5min); Lisbon (2 daily; 5hr); Viseu (4 daily; 50min–1hr).
Covilhã to: Castelo Branco (4 daily; 1hr 5min); Fundão (4 daily; 20min); Guarda (9 daily; 50min); Lisbon (2–4 daily; 5hr 30min); Penhas da Saúde (August only: Sat 2 daily, Sun 3 daily; 35min); Viseu (7 daily, 2hr 10 min).
Guarda to: Almeida (1 daily; 2 hr); Alpedrinha (4 daily; 1hr 20min); Belmonte (3 daily; 45min); Braga (3 daily; 4hr 20min); Castelo Branco (8–12 daily; 1hr 55min); Covilhã (14 daily; 50min); Fundão (9 daily; 1hr 5min); Lisbon (4 daily; 5–6hr); Pinhel (4 daily; 1 hr); Trancoso (3 daily; 1hr 30min); Vilar Formoso (4 daily; 50min); Viseu (2–5 daily; 2hr 15min).
Seia to: Celorico (5 daily; 45min); Coimbra (5 daily; 1hr 40min); Guarda (4 daily; 1hr 15min).
Trancoso to: Braga (1 daily; 4hr 10min); Bragança (2 daily; 3hr); Celorico da Beira (1–2 daily; 1hr 25min); Covilhã (1–2 daily; 1hr 45min); Guarda (1–3 daily; 1hr); Lamego (1–2 daily; 2hr); Lisbon (2 daily; 6hr 10min); Pocinho (2 daily; 1hr 20min); Viseu (2 daily; 1hr 50min).
Vilar Formoso to: Guarda (4 daily; 50min); Lisbon (4 daily; 5hr 40min–6hr).
Viseu to: Belmonte (Ginjal) (2 daily; 1hr 50min); Celorico da Beira (6 daily; 50min–1hr); Coimbra (8 daily; 1hr 25min); Covilhã (7 daily; 2hr 15min); Faro (9 daily; 11hr 35min–12hr 20min); Guarda (8 daily; 1hr 20min); Lisbon (9 daily; 4–5hr); Porto (10 daily; 1hr 50min); São Pedro do Sul (Mon–Fri 4–5 daily, 1–2 daily at weekends; 1hr); Sernancelhe (3 daily); Trancoso (2–3 daily; 1hr 25min).

Porto & the Douro

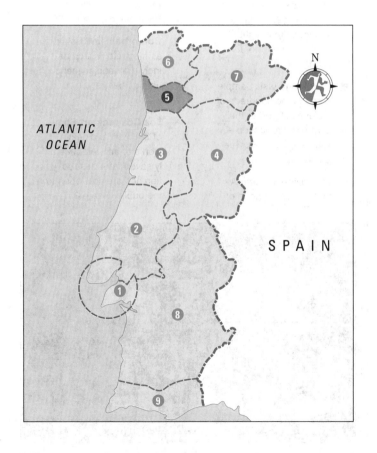

ATLANTIC
OCEAN

N

SPAIN

CHAPTER 5

Highlights

❋ **Porto's old town** The cramped timeless streets and alleyways of the riverside area are an ideal introduction to this beguiling city. See p.297

❋ **Fundação de Serralves** Housed in a building by Portugal's leading architect, the gallery has a collection to delight all fans of contemporary art. See p.301

❋ **Port lodge visit** Sample some of the hundreds of varieties of port in the centre of production – Vila Nova de Gaia. See p.303

❋ **FC Porto/Boavista** A match involving one of Portugal's top clubs in Porto's magnificent football stadia is a must for all fans of the game. See p.316

❋ **Douro river cruise** Watch the countryside drift by on a trip along the country's historic River of Gold. See p.316

❋ **Douro train line** Relax as the region's increasingly dramatic scenery unfolds before you. See p.325

❋ **Foz Côa rock art** Some of the world's oldest works of art were recently saved from destruction and are now open to the public. See p.337

5

Porto & the Douro

Portugal's second-largest city, **Porto**, is dramatically situated at the mouth of the Douro River, its old quarters scrambling up the rocky north bank in tangled tiers. It's a massively atmospheric city, almost Dickensian in parts, though rather unfairly the attention of many visitors is focused firmly on the port-producing suburb of **Vila Nova de Gaia**, across the river. For excellent beaches, you don't have to head too far north; those at the resorts of **Vila do Conde** and **Póvoa de Varzim** offer a taste of what's to come as you head into the Minho.

Above all, it's the **Rio Douro** ("river of gold") that dominates every aspect of this region: a narrow, winding gorge for the major part of its long route from the Spanish border, with port wine lodges dotted about the hillsides and a series of tiny villages, visited by few except for the seasonal wine trade workers. The valleys and tributaries form some of the loveliest and most spectacular landscapes in the whole of Portugal, and even though the wine no longer shoots down the river's rapids in barges, as it once did, a trip up the valley remains one of the most scenic routes in the country. The capital of the Alto Douro province is **Peso da Régua**, a growing town with more scope for visiting wine lodges; just 13km south of here is the delightful Baroque town of **Lamego**, the home of Portugal's champagne-like wine, Raposeira, and the magnificent shrine of Nossa Senhora dos Remédios.

If you're driving, you can follow minor roads along the river practically all the way from Porto to the border crossings at Miranda do Douro (see p.451). Taking the **train**, though, is probably more fun, and certainly more scenic. The **Douro line** joins the course of the river about 60km inland from Porto and sticks to it from then on, cutting into the rock face and crisscrossing the water on a series of rickety bridges: one of those journeys that needs no justification other than the trip itself. To the east, narrow gauge rail lines follow the river's tributaries north into Trás-os-Montes: the **Tâmega line** runs to the beautiful riverside town of **Amarante**; the **Corgo line** connects with Vila Real, a useful bus terminal for exploring Trás-os-Montes; while the **Tua line** goes from Tua to Mirandela in central Trás-os-Montes, from where you can catch buses to Bragança in the northeast.

Porto

Although the capital of the north, **PORTO** (Oporto) is a very different city from Lisbon – unpretentious, inward-looking, and unashamedly commercial.

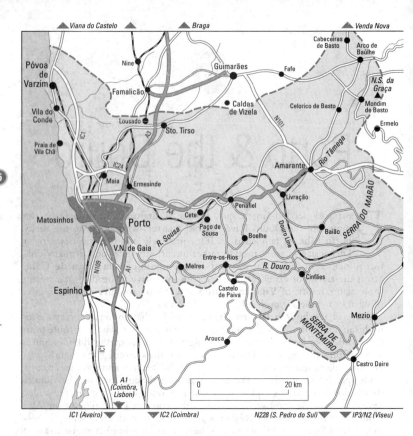

As the local saying goes: "Coimbra studies; Braga prays; Lisbon shows off; and Porto works." The city's most obvious sights are its five bridges: three modern, two nineteenth-century, and all of them spectacular. The older ones are the defunct metalwork Maria Pia railway link, designed by Eiffel, and the dizzying, two-tiered Ponte Luís I, which connects the city with **Vila Nova de Gaia**, home of the port wine lodges.

In the city proper, there is a handful of buildings around which to direct your wanderings: the landmark **Torre dos Clérigos** and the **Sé**, the ornate interiors of the **Bolsa** and church of **São Francisco**, and a clutch of good **museums**. But the fascination of Porto lies very much in the day-to-day life of the place, with its prosperous business core surrounded by both well-to-do suburbs as well as depressed housing estates, tempered by a heart of cramped streets and ancient alleys wholly untouched by the planners.

In 2001, Porto, jointly with Rotterdam, was declared **European City of Culture**. This was the signal for massive urban redevelopment designed to further enhance the city's reputation as an attractive and laid-back destination. The areas around **Batalha**, **Cordoaria** and **Dom João 1** are being pedestrianized and many of the city's historic buildings are finally receiving the restoration work that they have been crying out for many years. The historic **Ribeira** – a **Unesco World Heritage Site** – is receiving a clean-up and there will be a stunning new

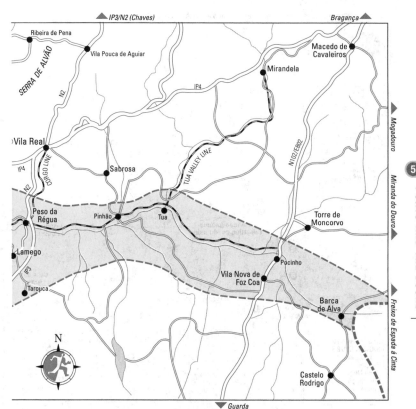

maritime promenade linking **Avenida Boavista** with the ocean. The major urban works were still causing significant chaos at the time of going to print.

It's hard not to like the city, or to respond to the crowds, tiny bars and antiquated shops. If you can, plan your visit to coincide with **St John's Eve** (the night of June 23–24), when the place is at its earthiest and finest for the riotous celebration of São João. On this night, seemingly the entire population takes to the streets, hitting each other over the head with squeaky, plastic hammers, or anything else to hand, letting off illuminated balloons and generally having a good time. See box on p.312 for more information on festivals in Porto.

Arrival

Buses #56 and #87 (every fifteen to thirty minutes Mon–Sat 6am–9pm; €1 one way) shuttle between the **airport**, 13km north of the city, and Jardim da Cordoaria, by the Universidade building; the journey usually takes forty minutes, but allow an hour at peak times of day. There's also the AeroBus (every 30min 7.45am–7.15pm; €2.50 although free if you fly with TAP; ☎800 200 166), which drops you off at your hotel if possible, or at an appropriate bus stop (the ticket remains valid for unlimited use on local buses until midnight).

Taxis from the airport into the centre cost €12–17. Airport banks are open

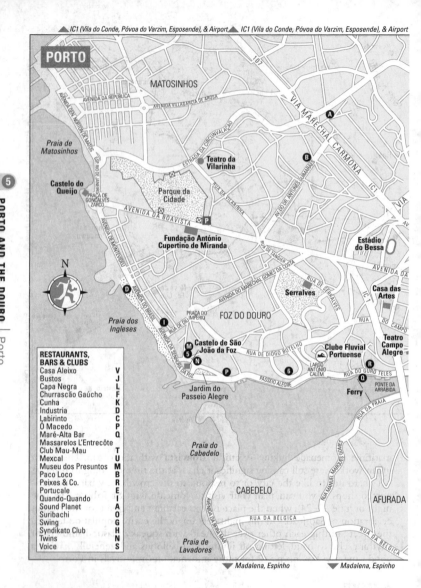

PORTO

MATOSINHOS

AVENIDA DA REPÚBLICA

AVENIDA VILLAGARCIA DE AROSA

Praia de
Matosinhos

Castelo do
Queijo

PRAÇA DE
GONÇALVES
ZARCO

AVENIDA DA BOAVISTA

Teatro da
Vilarinha

Parque da
Cidade

Fundação António
Cupertino de Miranda

Estádio
do Bessa

AVENIDA DA

PRAÇA DO
IMPÉRIO

Praia dos
Ingleses

FOZ DO DOURO

Serralves

Casa das
Artes

Teatro
Campo
Alegre

Castelo de São
João da Foz

Clube Fluvial
Portuense

Jardim do
Passeio Alegre

PASSEIO ALEGRE

Ferry

PONTE DE
ARRABIDA

Praia do
Cabedelo

CABEDELO

AFURADA

RUA DA BÉLGICA

RUA DA BÉLGICA

Praia de
Lavadores

**RESTAURANTS,
BARS & CLUBS**

Casa Aleixo	V
Bustos	J
Capa Negra	L
Churrascão Gaúcho	F
Cunha	K
Industria	D
Labirinto	C
Ó Macedo	P
Maré-Alta Bar	Q
Massarelos L'Entrecôte	
Club Mau-Mau	T
Mexcal	U
Museu dos Presuntos	M
Paco Loco	B
Peixes & Co.	R
Portucale	E
Quando-Quando	I
Sound Planet	A
Suribachi	O
Swing	G
Syndikato Club	H
Twins	N
Voice	S

daily 8am–8pm, and there's also an information counter (daily 8am–11.30pm; ☎ 229 412 534, ℻ 229 412 534).

Coming into Porto by train or bus, you'll find yourself deposited fairly centrally, though the various terminals can cause a little confusion (see box on p.290). Arriving from the south, **trains** drop you at the **Estação de Campanhã** (☎ 225 364 141), a few kilometres east of the centre on Rua da Estação; change here for a local train into the more central **Estação de São Bento** (☎ 222 002 722), on Praça Almeida Garrett – it takes about five min-

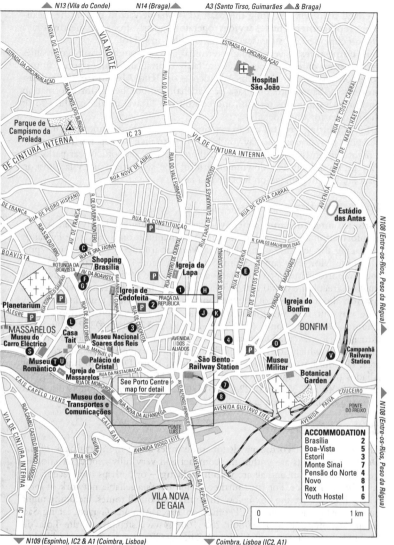

ESTRADA DA CIRCUNVALAÇÃO

Hospital
São João

Parque de
Campismo da
Prelada

IC 23

VIA DE CINTURA INTERNA

DE CINTURA INTERNA

Estádio
das Antas

RUA DA CONSTITUIÇÃO

R. CARLOS MALHEIRO DIAS

Shopping
Brasília

Igreja da
Lapa

BOAVISTA

ROTUNDA DA
BOAVISTA

Igreja de
Cedofeita

PRAÇA DA
REPÚBLICA

Igreja do
Bonfim

Planetarium

BONFIM

MASSARELOS

Casa
Tait

Museu do
Carro Eléctrico

Museu Nacional
Soares dos Reis

Campanhã
Railway
Station

Museu
Romântico

Palácio de
Cristal

São Bento
Railway Station

Museu
Militar

Igreja de
Massarelos

Botanical
Garden

See Porto Centre
map for detail

PONTE
DO FREIXO

Museu dos
Transportes e
Comunicações

AVENIDA GUSTAVO EIFEL

PONTE
LUÍS I

VILA NOVA
DE GAIA

AVENIDA DIOGO LEITE

ACCOMMODATION	
Brasília	2
Boa-Vista	5
Estoril	3
Monte Sinai	7
Pensão do Norte	4
Novo	8
Rex	1
Youth Hostel	6

0   1 km

utes and there should never be more than a twenty-minute wait. The Duoro
line from the east runs directly to São Bento, as do trains from Viana do Castelo
in the Minho (via Barcelos) or from Braga (via Nine). The train service to
Guimarães was indefinitely suspended at the time of writing. **Estação da
Trindade**, on Rua Alferes Malheiro just to the north of Avenida dos Aliados,
once the arrival point for trains from the north coast (Vila do Conde/Póvoa
de Varzim) is closed until 2004 when it will become a major hub in Porto's
ongoing **metro development**. The metro is scheduled to replace the former

overland train services along the coast to Póvoa de Varzim but, in the meantime, **replacement bus services** operate regularly from the nearby Praça Dona Felipe de Lencastre (see "Travel Details" on p.346).

Bus companies have no single terminal and, although various companies operate from different streets, they are fairly central, and many operate from a common terminal – Garagem Atlântico – on **Rua Alexandre Herculano** (just east of São Bento, off Praça da Batalha). See box below for information on Porto's various bus termini, and consult the "Travel details" at the end of this chapter for route details.

If you're hiring a **rental car** to explore the surrounding countryside, it might be better to wait until the day you leave Porto to pick one up. **Parking** can be a nightmare in the centre of town as there are very few official car parks and they fill up quickly. The downtown grid of one-way streets and Vila Nova de Gaia are best negotiated on foot or in a taxi.

Information

Porto has three **turismos**, where you can pick up large-scale city plans as well as information about port lodges. The most helpful is on Rua Clube Fenianos 25, facing the left side of the Câmara Municipal (July–Sept daily 9am–7pm; Oct–June Mon–Fri 9am–5.30pm, Sat & Sun 9am–4.30pm; ☎223 393 470, Ⓦwww.portoturismo.pt). It contains a new Loja de Mobilidad (same hours as turismo; freephone ☎800 220 905), a "transport shop" that can provide **information** about all forms of city transport, including bus and train timetables. A little way out, near the *Ribeira* in the old town, is a second turismo at Rua Infante Dom Enrique 63 (Mon–Fri 9am–5.30pm; ☎222 009 770, Ⓔturismo.ribeira@mail.telepac.pt). It has a similar collection of leaflets to the main office, which are very helpful when you're exploring the old riverside area. The third, partly privatized turismo is on Praça Dom João I, just east of Aliados (Mon–Fri 9am–7.30pm, Sat & Sun 9.30am–3.30pm; during Aug Sat & Sun 9.30am–7.30pm; ☎222 057 514, Ⓕ222 053 212), and offers discounts on some of the more expensive hotels.

City transport

Although modern Porto sprawls for some miles along the north bank of the Douro, most sights are within the compact and very hilly centre, six kilometres from the ocean, and all are within **walking** – or perhaps more accurately climbing – distance. For trips further afield, there's a reliable network of local STCP **buses** – see the box below. **Information** on all routes, including night buses, can be had at the STCP office on Praça Almeida Garrett, facing São Bento station (freephone ☎800 200 166, Ⓦwww.stcp.pt), or the Loja de Mobilidad (see "Information" above). The STCP provides an invaluable bus route map, the *mapa geral*; and also the *mapa da madrugada*, detailing the night buses; both also available from the turismo.

City bus terminals in Porto

Avenida dos Aliados	Praça da Liberdade
Bolhão	Praça da República
Cordoaria	Rotunda da Boavista
Praça Almeida Garrett	Rua Nova da Alfândega
Praça da Batalha	Rua Sá da Bandeira

Single **tickets** cost €1 on the bus, but only €0.50 in advance from the newsagents, stationers, or kiosks at all the main bus stops. The kiosks also sell ten-journey tickets for €4.20 (€5.80 including the Foz do Douro and Boavista). If you plan to travel a lot, however, you might consider buying one of the city's numerous **travel passes** (available on the bus): a one-day city pass, Diário Porto, costs €2, and the Diário Geral, which includes Vila Nova de Gaia, costs €2.50. The Bilhete Porto 2001, valid in all zones, covers travel on city buses, trams and the Aerobus and costs €5 for three days. If you are interested in exploring the cultural aspects of the city, it may be worth investing in a Passe Porto tour pass. Available for one day (€4) or two days (€5.50), they offer free entrance to eight museums and monuments and discounts on several others, in addition to the standard unlimited free travel. They are available from the main turismo near the Câmara Municipal or the *Ribeira* turismo.

There are ten main bus terminals in the city centre for bus routes mentioned in the text (as listed in the box opposite). Services cease or are much reduced after around 9pm: there is an extensive night bus network, running approximately hourly until 5am, covering fourteen routes (#1, #7, #11, #12, #15, #19, #29, #33, #54, #59, #76, #83, #91 and #94) and all passing through Praça da Liberdade. Buses to Rotunda da Boavista – 1.5km northwest of the centre – include #3, #20, #23, #34, #36, #52, #82 and #84.

Central Porto has two, much reduced, **tram routes**, with a flat fare of €0.45 (Mon–Sat 8.30am–7.30pm) which are worth a trip just for the ride alone. #1E runs from Infante on the Cais de Ribeira, along the coast as far as Passeio Alegre. Due to building works it no longer continues along the Avenida Boavista via the Castelo do Quiejo, but there are plans to reinstate this route once the works are finished. Similarly #18 is truncated in its route, only running from Carmo to the Tram Museum on the river-front. For up-to-the-minute information ask at the Loja de Mobilidade in the main turismo. Another option is to take an organized tram trip or a sightseeing **tour** on a double-decker bus (April–Sept only). You have a choice of a hop-on, hop-off ticket, which gives you the option of spending time at the sights themselves, or a one-and-a-half-hour return trip with commentary in English. Tickets cost €12.50 and are available from most travel agents, or call Diana Tours on ☎ 223 771 230. For details of **river cruises**, see "Listings", p.316.

In 1999 work began on an ambitious, partly underground, **metro** system, which is scheduled for completion in May 2004. A section of the first line should be open by the end of 2002, connecting Trindade station with Senhora da Hora (home of the huge Norteshopping centre) in the northwest, and continuing on to Senhor de Matosinhos. The tourist office will be able to give you up-to-date information on the progress of the line.

Besides walking, the easiest way to negotiate Porto is by **taxi**; they are cheap and there are ranks in most squares, or alternatively call Raditáxis on ☎ 225 073 900. Fares are metered, and shouldn't cost more than €4–5 for a ride in the centre, often much less. The *carros de aluguer* – distinguishable by an "A"– do not run on a meter and are best used for longer distances. Fares are usually quite reasonable, but negotiate a price beforehand.

Accommodation

Porto's **accommodation** is generally good value. The least expensive rooms in the city are in the area south and east of São Bento station but it's a particularly good idea to use the recommendations below around these areas as some establishments are decidedly grotty; for rather more salubrious places, your best

CENTRAL PORTO: ACCOMMODATION

8

Prelada, Campsite, Centro Comercial Brasília, Boavista Stadium & Serralves

Cedofeita, Rotunda da Boavista,

▲ Palácio de Cristal, Solar do Vinho do Porto

ACCOMMODATION

Residencial dos Aliados	18
Belo Sonho	21
Hotel da Bolsa	27
Brasília	2
Duas Nações	15
Estoril	3
Europa	6
Girassol	20
Grande Hotel do Porto	14
Garden Court	23
Inca	4
Infante de Sagres	16
Internacional	17
Malaposta	7
Mercure Batalha	24
Monte Sinai	25
Pensão do Norte	8
Pão de Açúcar	13
Peninsular	22
Pensão de Paris	19
Paulista	11
Porto Novo	26
Porto Rico	12
Portuguesa	5
Rex	1
São Marino	10
Vera Cruz	9

RUA GONÇALO CRISTOVÃO

RUA DO BONJARDIM

RUA GUEDES AZEVEDO

RUA DA FIRMEZA

RUA DE SÁ DA BANDEIRA

RUA DA FIRMEZA

RUA DE SANTA CATARINA

TOMÁS

Mercado Bolhão

RUA DE SÁ DA BANDEIRA

RUA DO BOLHÃO

RUA FERNANDES TOMÁS

RUA FORMOSA

RUA DE PASSOS MANUEL

Coliseu

Ateneu

R. AT COM

PORTO

Estação da Trindade

RUA DO BONJARDIM

RUA DE CAMÕES

RUA DE FERNANDES TOMÁS

RUA DE SÁ DA BANDEIRA

PRAÇA DE D. JOÃO I

RUA DO ALFERES MALHEIRO

RUA TRINDADE

Câmara Municipal

R. RODRIGUES SAMPAIO

RUA DO BONJARDIM

Rivoli Teatro Municipal

PRAÇA DA REPÚBLICA

Igreja da Trindade

PRAÇA DA TRINDADE

R. DR. H. DELGADO

AV. DOS ALIADOS

RUA DO ALMADA

Trindade Cinema

RUA RICARDO JORGE

R. DR. ORTIGÃO

RUA E. MELO

AV. DOS ALIADOS

6 **5**

11

9

13

18

R DE ÁLVARES CABRAL

1

2

RUA DO ALMADA

12

RUA DA PICARIA

PRAÇA FILIPA DE LENCASTRE

17

R DA FABRICA

16

19

RUA DOS MÁRTIRES DA LIBERDADE

R. PINHEIRO

Bus Station - North

RUA CEUTA

VIZELA

DE PARIS

RUA DE STA. TERESA

RUA DE MIRANTE

PRAÇA CORONEL PACHECO

R. GEN. SILVEIRA

RUA DA CONCEIÇÃO

4

7

RUA JOSÉ FALCÃO

SÁ DE NORONHA

G.G. FERNANDES

PRAÇA DE

R. STA. TERESA

RUA

Livraria Lello & Irmão

PR. GOMES

15

TRAVESSA DE CEDOFEITA

Auditório Nacional Carlos Alberto

10

PRAÇA CARLOS ALBERTO

RUA DE CEDOFEITA

RUA DO CARMO

Igrejas do Carmo & Carmelitas

RUA DE CEDOFEITA

RUA DO BREYNER

3

RUA PROF VICENTE JOSÉ CARVALHO

MENÉRES

RUA PROF VICENTE JOSÉ CARVALHO

Hospital Santo António

RUA DE MIGUEL BOMBARDA

RUA CLEMENTE

Museu Nacional Soares dos Reis

RUA DO ROSARIO

R. D. MANUEL II

N

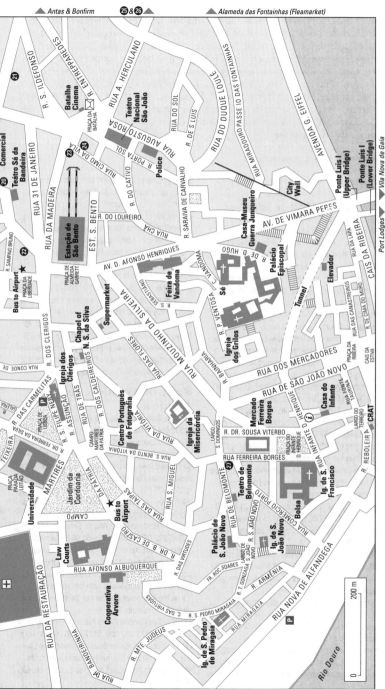

Antas & Bonfirm ▲ 25 & 26 ▲ Alameda das Fontainhas (Fleamarket)

5 PORTO AND THE DOURO | Porto

Massarelos & Foz do Douro ▲

293

bet is to ignore bargainers at the stations and head for the *pensões* and hotels detailed below, in areas west or east of the central thoroughfare, Avenida dos Aliados. In winter, it's worth investing in more expensive rooms than you might otherwise choose, or you'll freeze, as few budget hotels have any heating; turismos have lists of places with central heating.

If you want to stay by the **sea** then Foz do Douro, west of the centre, is a good option. You can reach Foz do Douro on bus #1 from Praça Almeida Garrett or Rua Nova da Alfândega, or alternatively bus #24 from the Cordoaria. All places are shown on the Central Porto map on pp.292–293 unless stated otherwise.

Hotels and pensões

West of Avenida dos Aliados

Residencial dos Aliados Rua Elísio de Melo 27–2º ☎222 004 853, ℻222 002 710. Comfortable *pensão* that fills quickly in summer; book ahead. Rooms at the back are better, those at the front tend to be noisy; breakfast included. ❸

Hotel da Bolsa Rua Ferreira Borges 101 ☎222 026 768, ℻222 058 888. Great three-star hotel with all mod cons. Service is polite and friendly and there are facilities for the disabled. ❹

Pensão Residencial Duas Nações Praça Guilherme Gomes Fernandes 59 ☎ & ℻222 081 616, ✉duasnacoes@mail.teleweb.pt. This simple modern *residencial* has good clean rooms with English-speaking staff, free internet access and a laundry service. Books up early, so call ahead. ❷

Pensão Europa Rua do Almada 396 ☎222 006 971. A bit gloomy, but with a lively bar and good restaurant. The cheaper rooms come without showers. ❶

Hotel Infante de Sagres Praça Dona Filipa de Lencastre 62 ☎222 008 101, ℻222 054 937. Luxurious five-star hotel lavishly furnished with Persian carpets, Carrara marble and stained-glass windows. Today it also houses the Peruvian consulate. Has a good restaurant too. ❾

Hotel Internacional Rua do Almada 131 ☎222 005 032, ℻222 009 063. Modern three-star hotel, with air conditioning, TVs, private bathroom and phones in all rooms. ❹

Hotel Residencial Malaposta Rua da Conceição 80 ☎222 014 352, ℻222 006 295. Modern with clean, comfortable rooms, private bathrooms and breakfast included. ❸

Pensão Pão de Açucar Rua do Almada 262 ☎222 002 425, ℻223 050 239. Stylish 1930s hotel with quiet rooms and private bathrooms; book ahead in summer. ❹

Pensão de Paris Rua da Fábrica 27–29 ☎222 073 140, ℻222 073 149. Popular *pensão* with friendly, helpful owners. Recently renovated, the building is very atmospheric with high ceilings in the en-suite rooms. A limited breakfast is included and served in a restaurant overlooking a small garden. ❸

Residencial Porto Rico Rua do Almada 237 ☎223 394 690. Small, adequate rooms – the quieter ones are at the back. Rooms without facilities are cheaper; breakfast included. ❷

Pensão São Marino Praça Carlos Alberto 59 ☎223 325 499 or ☎ & ℻222 054 380 Located in a pleasant garden square near the Torre dos Clérigos, this friendly *pensão* offers clean rooms all with shower and most with a TV; breakfast included. ❷

Pensão Vera Cruz Rua Ramalho Ortigão 14 ☎223 323 396, ℻223 323 421. This elegant little hotel is close to the tourist office and has pleasant, efficient service; breakfast included in the price. ❸

East of Avenida dos Aliados

Pensão Belo Sonho Rua de Passos Manuel 186, facing the Coliseu ☎222 003 389, ℻222 012 850. Basic but acceptable and reasonable value – principally for its good location. The more expensive rooms have en-suite bathrooms. ❶–❷

Residencial Girassol Rua de Sá da Bandeira 133 ☎222 001 891, ℻222 081 892. A good place offering en-suite rooms – some with TVs. Also has a good restaurant. Breakfast included. ❷

Grande Hotel do Porto Rua de Santa Catarina 197 ☎222 076 690, ℻222 051 061. Claiming to be the oldest hotel in Porto, this large three-star still retains a touch of grandeur in its chandeliers, polished marble columns and uniformed staff. Rooms are air conditioned with TVs and phones. It's on the pedestrianized part of the street and car parking is available. ❺

Holiday Inn Garden Court Praça da Batalha 127–130 ☎223 392 300, ℻222 006 009. An ugly pink edifice on Praça da Batalha opposite the cinema. Typical Holiday Inn: modern and comfortable with TVs in its rooms and facilities for disabled. ❺

Hotel Mercure Batalha Praça da Batalha 116 ☎222 000 571, ℱ222 002 468. Similar standard to the *Holiday Inn*, with brighter rooms and some very kitsch decoration. Disabled facilities and car parking. ❺

Pensão Monte Sinai Rua Alexandre Herculano 146 ☎222 008 218, ℱ222 018 861; shown on the Porto map. No-frills place offering fairly big rooms, some with baths and TVs. Extremely cheap – although it can be noisy and is a little dingy. ❶

Pensão do Norte Rua de Fernandes Tomás 579 ☎222 003 503; shown on the Porto map. On the junction with Rua de Santa Catarina (opposite an extravagantly tiled church), this pleasant, rambling old place has masses of rooms, with and without bathrooms. The best rooms have balconies overlooking the street, though these can be noisy. ❶

Pensão Paulista Av dos Aliados 214–2° ☎222 054 692, ℱ222 005 730. Well placed, and with comfortable en-suite rooms with TVs. Can be noisy so ask for a room at the back. Breakfast included. ❷

Hotel Peninsular Rua de Sá da Bandeira 21 ☎222 003 012, ℱ222 084 984. Central (just uphill from São Bento station) and comfortable two-star pension with a range of rooms. The *azulejos* in the entrance reveal it to have once been an outbuilding of the nearby church. Breakfast is included. ❸

Residencial Porto Novo Rua Alexandre Herculano 185 ☎222 055 739; shown on the Porto map. Clean, bright, comfortable rooms with TVs, those on the top floor also have balconies affording magnificent views over the river. Friendly staff, although no English spoken. ❷

North towards Praça da República

Residencial Brasília Rua de Álvares Cabral 221 ☎222 082 981, ℱ223 395 529; shown on the Porto map. There are only ten rooms in this very friendly hotel, so ring ahead. Self-contained rooms have TVs, phones and air conditioning. Breakfast is included. Parking €4 per day extra. ❷

Pensão Estoril Rua de Cedofeita 193 ☎222 002 751, ℮estoril@usa.net; shown on the Porto map. Rooms of varying sizes (and sometimes odd shapes) in a friendly and well-maintained *pensão*, with a café on the ground floor. Some rooms have balconies, all have TVs. It's on the pedestrianized section of the street, and overlooks a garden. ❷

Hotel Inca Praça Coronel Pacheco 52 ☎222 084 151, ℮hotelinca@mail.telepac.pt. Modern hotel with small, clean en-suite rooms with TVs and air conditioning. ❹

Residencial Portuguesa Trav. Coronel Pacheco 11, corner with Rua Martires da Liberdade ☎222 004 174. A converted house, some way out near Praça Coronel Pacheco, and consequently quiet, although its cheapness is offset by the inconvenience of extra travel. ❶

Residencial Rex Praça da República 117 ☎222 074 590, ℱ222 074 593; shown on the Porto map. At the top end of Rua do Almada, facing the garden square, this *residencial* has the feel of a grand hotel, with spacious, functional rooms. Highly recommended, although it can be noisy. Parking available and breakfast included in the price ❷

Foz do Douro

Hotel Boa-Vista Esplanada do Castelo 58, Foz do Douro ☎226 180 083, ℱ226 173 881; shown on the Porto map. Lovely old grand hotel at the mouth of the Douro, where the more expensive front rooms have magnificent views over the river, ocean and Castelo de São João da Foz. There's also a good rooftop restaurant and bar. ❺

Youth hostel and campsites

Porto's popular **youth hostel**, the *Pousada da Juventude*, is at Rua Paulo da Gama 551, 4km west of the centre in the *bairro* of Pasteleira overlooking the mouth of the Douro (reception 9–10am & 6pm–midnight; ☎226 177 257, ℱ226 177 247; ❶); buses #35 from Praça Almeida Garrett, Cordoaria, or Praça da Batalha, and #36 from Rotunda da Boavista pass by, or catch buses #1 or #24 and get off at bus stop "Fluvial", and the youth hostel is only a four-hundred-metre walk. Single-sex dorms are available on request, or there are mixed dorms plus some double rooms (❷). Facilities include a kitchen, bar and arrangements for disabled guests; food is also available. You'll need to book ahead in summer.

The closest **campsite**, *Parque de Campismo da Prelada*, Rua Monte dos Burgos (☎228 312 616), is 3km northwest of the centre but – with 650 pitches – is not exactly intimate; get there on buses #54 from the Cordoaria, #87 from the airport or #6 from Avenida dos Aliados. On the south side of the river, there are two sites near the mouth of the Douro: to get to the *Parque de Campismo de Salgueiros*, at Rua de Salgueiros, Canidelo (May–Sept; ☎227 810 500, ⓕ227 810 500), take a Santos and Irmãos bus marked "Paniceiro" from Rua Augusto Rosa, just off Praça da Batalha; for the Orbitur site (open all year; min stay 2 days or 1 week in July & Aug; ☎227 122 520, ⓕ227 152 534), 500m from Praia da Madalena, which has a swimming pool, tennis and volleyball courts, some caravans to rent and a mini-market, take bus #57 from either the airport or Praça Almeida Garrett.

The City

The centre of Porto is perhaps best regarded as **Avenida dos Aliados**, the commercial hub of the city, fronted by banks and offices. **Praça da Liberdade** marks the bottom end of this sloping avenue and a little further south, across the busy road (reached via a pedestrian underpass), is the **Estação de São Bento**, the main train station. South of São Bento, a labyrinth of medieval streets and seedy-looking alleyways tumble below the **Sé**, or cathedral, down to the waterfront **Cais da Ribeira**, which is lined with restaurants, bars, clubs and cafés. Here, the lower of the two tiers of **Ponte Luís I** runs across the river to the port wine suburb of **Vila Nova de Gaia**.

The streets leading off Avenida dos Aliados are the city's major shopping areas: to the west, the busy **Rua da Fábrica** with its stationers and bookshops; to the east, **Rua de Passos Manuel**, which runs into **Praça Dom João I**, and beyond into **Rua de Santa Catarina**, full of clothes and shoe shops. The only other areas of interest are to the west of the centre: you can walk as far as the **Jardim do Palácio de Cristal** and the *Solar do Vinho do Porto*, but you'll need to use public transport to reach Porto's world-class museum of modern art, **Serralves** (also called the Museu de Arte Contemporânea).

For those with a particular interest in architecture, a free pamphlet "Porto Tours" is available in English from the turismo. This details four **city walks**, each focusing on a particular architectural style from Medieval, through Baroque and Neoclassical to Azulejo. If you're interested in modern architecture, ask for their list of buildings by the Oporto school including works by Siza and Souto de Moura. All the major city sights are included, but be prepared for a lot of climbing involved so non-enthusiasts may find the walks a little hard going.

From Avenida dos Aliados to Cordoaria

The central **Avenida dos Aliados** is as good a starting point as any for exploration, though other than a quick squint up the avenue to the Câmara Municipal (most impressive at night when its façade is lit) at the very top and a coffee at the pavement tables of one of the cafés at the bottom, there's little reason to linger. If you didn't arrive by train, you may as well cut down briefly to the **Estação de São Bento**, one of the city's grandest buildings in its own right, with magnificent *azulejos* by Jorge Colaço in the entrance hall. These, somewhat arbitrarily, take on two great themes – the history of transport and the battle of Aljubarrota.

Also in this area is the **Mercado Bolhão** (Mon–Fri 8am–5pm, Sat 8am–1pm), three blocks east along Rua Formosa, a nineteenth-century wrought-iron construction with three main themes – meat and fish, flowers and fruit and vegetables. On **Rua Formosa** itself, look for the few surviving **bacalhau and port wine shops**, delightfully antiquated places that hang their wares outside. The *bacalhau* (dried, salted codfish) is also bundled up in stacks all around the counter, alongside just about every type of port available. Two blocks south of Bolhão, the **Ateneu Comercial do Porto**, at Rua de Passos Manuel 44, is an opulent nineteenth-century building housing the headquarters of Porto's commercial association, as well as temporary exhibitions of earthenware, postage stamps and paintings in its gloriously decorated halls (daily 2–7.30pm; free).

The stifled streets of the old town make it difficult to get your bearings, so it's a good idea to climb the Baroque **Torre dos Clérigos** (summer Mon–Sat 10am–7pm, Sun 10am–noon & 2–7pm; winter Mon–Sat 10am–noon & Sun 2–5pm; €1), 400m west of São Bento, for an aerial view of the city. This landmark was designed, like the curious oval **Igreja dos Clérigos** beneath it (Mon–Sat 8.45am–12.30pm & 3.30–7pm, Sun 10am–1pm and 9pm–11.30pm), by the Italian architect Nicolau Nasoni. It was once the tallest structure in Portugal and the dizzying vistas from the top take in the entire city, as well as south across the river to Vila Nova de Gaia and sometimes even to the distant mouth of the Douro.

The area immediately below the tower comprises the older sections of the university and the gardens of the **Jardim da Cordoaria**. This area is a fairly prestigious quarter of town, housing, for example, most of the city's commercial **art galleries**, which are grouped together on Rua Galeria de Paris and Rua Miguel Bombarda, north of the Cordoaria. Worth a particular mention here is **Cooperativa Árvore**, Rua Azevedo de Albuquerque 1, west of Torre dos Clérigos (☎222 057 235), a co-operative of painters, sculptors and designers who run their own art school in close competition with the official Escola das Belas Artes (itself housed in a nearby mansion). The artists pride themselves on the vitality of the teaching and the freedom they allow their pupils – the results of which are on view in a punchy summer show in June and July.

The Sé and down to the Cais da Ribeira

Set on a rocky outcrop a couple of hundred metres south from São Bento station, Porto's cathedral, the **Sé** (April–Oct daily 8.45am–12.30pm & 2.30pm–7pm; Nov–March closes 6pm; free), is a bluff, austere fortress. Despite attempts to beautify it in the eighteenth century, it retains the hard, simple lines of its Romanesque origins – more impressive from a distance than close up. Inside it's depressing, even the vaunted silver altarpiece failing to make much impression in the prevailing gloom. For €2, however, you can escape into the neighbouring **cloisters** (daily: April–Oct 9am–12.15pm & 2.30–6pm; Nov–March 9am–12.15pm & 2.30–5.15pm) and climb a Nasoni-designed staircase leading up to a dazzling chapterhouse, with more views from the casement windows over the old quarter. There are fine views over the rooftops, too, from the broad flagged courtyard in front of the cathedral.

Beside the Sé stretches the fine facade of the **Archbishop's Palace** (not open to the public), while around the back, at Rua Dom Hugo 32, is the beautiful **Casa-Museu Guerra Junqueiro** (Tues–Sat 10am–12.30pm & 2–5.30pm, Sun 2–5.30pm; €0.75, free Sat & Sun). This is the former home of the poet, who spent a lifetime collecting Islamic art, especially from Iberia. The fruits of his endeavours, such as Seljuk pottery, miniatures and glassware, are exhibited in rooms recapturing the atmosphere of the poet's last home in Porto.

Opposite the museum is a new **3D exhibition** "Historia do Porto" (every 45min Tues–Sat: May–Sept 10.30am–6.15pm; Oct–Apr 2.30pm–5.30pm; €2;

ⓦwww.emrelevo.com) at Rua Dom Hugo 15. Consisiting of a half-hour 3-D cinematic introduction to Porto's colourful history in several languages, it is an interesting way to start your tour of the city.

Back at the Sé, Rua de Dom Hugo curls back around to the Sé to merge with the crumbling, animated old alleys which lead down to the riverside. From the prancing statue of Vimara Peres, **Calçada de Vandoma** plunges downwards through the most fascinating and atmospheric part of the city: a medieval maze of backstreets that would have been demolished or prettified in most other cities of Europe, and have only recently undergone restoration. Tall, narrow and rickety, the houses have grown upwards into every available space, adapting as best they can to the terrain, while children try their best to play ballgames on the steep staircases.

Not much commerce goes on down at the waterfront since the big ships stopped calling here at the beginning of the last century, but along the **Cais da Ribeira** old men still sit around as if they expect to be thrown a line or set to work unloading some urgent cargo, while local children cool off in the summer by leaping into the foul waters of the Douro. The iron *elevador* (free) at the eastern end of the Cais climbs up to a good viewing point, achingly close to the top of the Bairro da Sé, but as it's fenced in you won't be able to disembark. There's some bustle around the weekday fruit and vegetable market down here but, otherwise, it's at night that the riverfront comes alive, with dozens of cafés, clubs and restaurants (see pp.308–313) to tickle the sensations. Heading west past the **Praça da Ribeira** – where a controversial 1970s cube tops an eighteenth-century fountain – you reach Rua da Alfândega, which leads away from the water. If you double back along Rua Infante Dom Henrique you pass the **Casa do Infante** (Mon–Fri 10am–noon & 2–5pm; free), where Prince Henry the Navigator is said to have been born. It's an impressive mansion, which has in its time been the City Customs Hall and a Mint; it currently functions as the headquarters of the city's archives, but at least half the building is open to visitors.

East of the Sé

Compared with the area west of the station there's little of interest **east of the Sé**, however, the sunny **Praça da Batalha** is pleasant enough during the day; it's at the top end of Rua 31 de Janeiro, or up Rua da Madeira beside São Bento station. The square is dominated by the gorgeous **Teatro Nacional São João** (see p.314), which replaced an older theatre that burned down in 1909. At the north end of the Praça, the **Igreja de Santo Ildefonso** has some lovely *azulejo* panels in its Baroque facade, and inside conceals a *retábulo* attributed to the Italian master-carver Nasoni. Heading east from the Praça along Avenida Rodrigues de Freitas, a fifteen-minute walk (or buses #35 or 80 from Praça da Batalha) brings you to the **Museu Militar do Porto**, Rua do Heroísmo 329 (Mon–Fri 10am–1pm & 2–5pm, Sat afternoon only; €1.50 adults). Situated in the former headquarters of the hated political police (PIDE) – disbanded after the 1974 revolution – the museum contains firearms and vehicles from the fifteenth century to the present day. If museum fatigue hits you, there is a very soothing **botanical garden** hidden away around the corner on Rua Barão de Nova Sintra 285 (Mon–Fri 9am–noon & 2–5pm; free), bus #35 from Praça da Batalha, although it is not signposted and is easily missed.

The Bolsa and around

Also on Rua Infante Dom Henrique, Porto's stock exchange – the **Palácio da Bolsa** – faces a statue of the Infante Henry himself, the centrepiece of an eponymously named square. The building is a pompous nineteenth-century edifice with a vast Neoclassical facade and its keepers are inordinately proud of the place. On the half-hour **guided tours** (May–Oct daily 9am–6.30pm; Nov–March daily 9am–5.30pm; €5) they dwell, with evident glee, on the enormous cost of every item, the exact weight of every piece of precious metal, and the intimate details of anyone with any claim to fame ever to have passed through the doors; President Kennedy, apparently, was one. The tour's nadir is the Arab Hall, an oval chamber that misguidedly attempts to copy the Moorish style of the Alhambra; here the guide's superlatives achieve apotheosis. Should you not want to bother with the tour you can see the main courtyard, easily the most elegant part, without having to buy a ticket.

Adjoining the Bolsa is the **Igreja de São Francisco** (daily: March–Oct 9am–6pm; Nov–Feb 9am–5pm; €2.50), perhaps the most extraordinary (albeit deconsecrated) church in Porto. From its entrance on Rua de São Francisco it looks an ordinary enough Gothic construction, but the interior has been transformed by a fabulously opulent eighteenth-century refurbishment. Altar, pillars, even the ceiling, drip with gilded Rococo carving which reaches its ultimate expression in an interpretation of the Tree of Jesse on the north wall. Don't miss the church's small **museum**, housed in the catacombs below – although the entrance is opposite the church – which consists of artefacts salvaged from the former monastery. Beneath the flags of the cellar is an *ossário* – thousands of human bones, cleaned up and stored to await Judgement Day. Until 1845 public cemeteries didn't exist in Portugal and the dead were buried in and around churches in an effort to bring them closer to God. Naturally this contributed to the spread of disease and a Health Law introduced by Costa Cabral in 1866 finally brought the practice to an end.

Two other churches in this neighbourhood have small museums. Pride of the **Igreja da Misericórdia** (church: Sun 9am–noon; museum: Tues–Sun 9am–12.30pm & 2–5.30pm; €1.50 for both museum and church), a couple of blocks to the north on Rua das Flores, is a remarkable *fons vitae*, depicting King Manuel I with his wife Leonor and eight children, richly clothed, kneeling before the crucified Christ. It's an exceptional example of fifteenth-century Portuguese realism – a style which was heavily influenced by Flemish painters like van Eyck and van der Weyden. Over to the west, in the **Igreja de São Pedro de Miragaia**, there's another fine fifteenth-century triptych; the church is kept locked but someone with a key is usually near at hand.

Northwest from Cordoaria

One hundred metres north of the Jardim da Cordoaria, on the corner of Rua do Carmo and Praça Carlos Alberto, lies the eighteenth-century **Igreja do Carmo** (Mon–Fri 8am–12.30pm & 3–6pm, Sat 8am–noon, Sun 8am–1pm) with its deliriously over-the-top *azulejos*. The older and rather more sober **Igreja das Carmelitas** (daily 8am–12.30pm & 2.30–7pm) is almost adjacent, but not quite, as a law stipulated that no two churches were to share the same wall (in this case perhaps to hinder amorous liaisons between the nuns of Carmelitas and the monks of Carmo). As a result, what is probably the **narrowest house in Portugal** – barely a metre wide – was built between them, and remained inhabited until the 1980s.

Heading west past Santo António hospital, you'll pass the **Museu Nacional Soares dos Reis**, on Rua de Dom Manuel II (Tues 2–6pm, Wed–Sun 10am–6pm; €3), Portugal's first designated national museum – dating from 1933. It occupies the former royal Palácio das Carrancas, which served as the

French headquarters in the Peninsular War. The museum contains excellent collections of glass, ceramics and a formidable display of eighteenth- and nineteenth-century Portuguese art. Highlights include the paintings by Henrique Pousão and sculptures by Soares dos Reis (*O Desterrado* – "The Exiled" – is probably his best-known work) and his pupil, Teixeira Lopes.

Follow the road for 100m or so past the Museu Soares dos Reis, or take a bus (#3, #20, #35 and #37 all go this way), and you reach the **Jardim do Palácio de Cristal** (daily 8am–9pm; free), a beautiful stretch of park dominated by a huge domed pavilion, which was built in the 1950s to replace the original "Crystal Palace" and now serves as a sports arena. There's a wealth of activities for children with a safe playground and various hands-on activities with an environmental theme (daily 9am–5.30pm; free; information on all activities: ☎226 099 941 or 226 093 192), including a paper recycling centre, gardening, painting, a "sound centre" with interactive recordings of natural sounds and instruments, and the great Laboratório Micro-Mundo Vivo with its micro-scopic views of fungi, bacteria, bugs and algae. The park also houses a Quaker animal hospital and, in summer, hosts hockey matches, pop and classical con-certs in its bandstand, and exhibitions. However, for the less energetic, the main attraction lies in peaceful shaded strolls, along the wooded paths which, even when the park is busy, remain pleasantly deserted.

Around the back of the park, near the bottom end of the steeply cobbled Rua de Entre-Quintas, stands the **Quinta da Macieirinha**, which houses both the **Museu Romântico** (Tues–Sat 10am–12.30pm & 2–5.30pm, Sun 2–5.30pm; €0.75, free on Sun), a collection of mid-nineteenth-century fur-niture and art works, and – on the ground floor with a separate entrance – the **Solar do Vinho do Porto** (Mon–Sat 2pm–midnight; ☎226 094 749, Ⓦwww.ivp.pt). Relaxing in the comfortable lounge, or on the floral terrace overlooking the river, you can sample one of hundreds of varieties of **port wine**, from around €1 a glass. It's a good prelude to a visit to the port lodges across the river in Vila Nova de Gaia (see p.303) and serves more than enough different varieties of port to keep connoisseurs happy for an evening. For further information about port and the lodges visit the **Instituto do Vinho do Porto** (☎222 071 600) on Rua Ferreira Borges (off Praca Infante Dom Henrique).

Opposite the *Quinta*, at Rua de Entre-Quintas 219, is **Casa Tait** (Mon–Fri 10am–noon & 2–5pm, Sat & Sun 2.30–6pm; free), which, as well as boasting attractive shaded botanical gardens, contains a **numismatic museum**, tracing the history of Portugal through the coins of successive invaders, from the Greeks and Romans to the Moors and Spanish.

Boavista and the Igreja de Cedofeita

From the Palácio de Cristal, the wide Rua de Julio Dinis runs north up to Praça Mouzinho de Albuquerque, popularly known as the **Rotunda da Boavista**. Buses to here include #3, 20 or 52 from Praca da Liberdade or Cordoaria, #23, #82 or #84 from Praça da Liberdade and #34, #82 or #84 from Bolhão or Praça da República. The Rotunda is overlooked by a huge col-umn bearing a lion astride a much flattened eagle, erected to celebrate the vic-tory of the Portuguese and British over the French in the Peninsular War. Three blocks to the east of the Rotunda, you pass the very simple **Igreja de Cedofeita** on Rua Aníbal Cunha (Mon–Sat 9am–noon & 4–7.30pm, Sun 9am–noon), whose name derives from *cedo feita* meaning "built quickly". It's reputed to be the oldest Christian building in the Iberian peninsula (though the people of Balsemão – p.344 – dispute this) and was supposedly built by the

Suevian king Theodomir in 556AD, though the current building is a twelfth-century Romanesque refashioning.

The Fundação de Serralves

The best of the museums outside the centre is the highly contemporary art museum, the **Fundação de Serralves** (Tues–Sun 10am–7pm, closes 10pm on Thurs; €4 museum and park, €2.50 park only, free Sun 10am–2pm; ⓦwww.serralves.pt; bus #3, #19, #21, #35, #78) on Rua de Serralves, 2km west of the Rotunda da Boavista, with exhibits from the 1960s to the present day, including works by international artists like Christian Boltanski and Richard Serra. The exhibits are housed in an ultra-modern building, designed by renowned local architect Álvaro Siza. Temporary exhibitions are held in the nearby 1930s Art Deco Casa de Serralves. The grounds, both formal gardens and natural farmland, are worth a visit too, and are dotted with modern sculptures and usually some installations: there's also a tea shop. Don't miss the inventive scarecrows in the farm at the far end of the park, which appear towards the end of summer; made by schoolchildren from household garbage, they are ceremonially burned in October after the harvest period. Additionally, there's a summer sequence of **jazz concerts** held in the gardens: Jazz no Parque (☎226 180 057 for details).

Museu do Carro Eléctrico and Planetarium

Near the Ponte de Arrábida, in an area known as "Massarelos", is the **Museu do Carro Eléctrico** (Tram Museum), situated in the tram shed on Alameda de Basílio Teles 51 (Tues–Sun 9.30am–1pm & 3–6pm; €1.80). There are various public transport options: bus #1 from Praça Almeida Garrett or Rua Nova da Alfândega; #23 from Praça da Batalha or Rua Nova da Alfândega, or #24 from Cordoaria; tram #18 terminates right outside. The museum will delight kids and enthusiasts alike. Almost all the trams were phased out in the 1970s – apart from trams #18 and #1E (see p.291 for details of their route), but the authorities are talking about phasing them back in, although no timetable has yet been drawn up. In summer on Thursdays, the museum also hosts concerts known as the "Noites de Massarelos", these are mostly of classical chamber music but include some jazz too; ask at the museum or turismo for details. Don't bother with the museum's own tram trips – they run exactly the same route as the #18, but cost considerably more.

Close to the museum on the Rua das Estrelas is the **Planetarium** (☎226 089 863, ⓦwww.astro.up.pt; bus #33, #36, #37 and #39). Intended primarily for schoolkids, it has screenings for the public in Portuguese at weekends (Sat 4pm & 9pm, Sun & holidays 4pm & 5pm; €6). There's also a bar and multimedia library.

West to the coast

Continuing 2km down Avenida da Boavista from Avenida Marechal Gomes da Costa, or 4km from Rotunda da Boavista, you come to the main entrance of the **Parque da Cidade** (daily: winter 9am–6pm; summer 9am–8pm) on the right, before hitting the coast. During the absence of a functioning tram route in Boavista, take bus #24 from Rotunda da Boavista towards Castelo do Quiejo. The park is the largest remaining public space in Porto and perfect for an afternoon's ramble, with several duck ponds, woods and children's playgrounds. The other entrance is to the north, off Estrada da Circunvalação – the ring road which divides Porto from Matosinhos. At the shore is the **Castelo do Queijo** (Tues–Sun 1.30pm–7pm; €0.25), which literally means "Cheese Castle", the reason being that it was built upon boulders that apparently looked like cheese. Although inaccessible at the time of writing because of extensive roadworks, it is sure to reopen on completion of the project. The castle is a typical star-shaped Vaubanesque fort and is still a military establishment but visitors are welcome and there's a small bar, and good views. South of here to the resort of Foz do Douro lie Porto's beaches. The whole coastal area was the recipient of investment as part of Porto 2001, most of this being in the form of a coastal promenade project designed to attract more tourists to the beaches. During the building work the beaches are still accessible, although somewhat spoiled by the presence of bulldozers. Until it is completed you are more likely to be drawn here for the superb beachfront cafés and bars along the Avenida do Brasil, which are unaffected by the building, and become the hub of Porto's nightlife in summer.

Foz itself has a superb hotel (the *Boa-Vista*, see p.295), several nightclubs and classy restaurants (p.295); take bus #1 from Praça Almeida Garrett or Rua Nova da Alfândega, or #24 from Cordoaria. Buses follow the river back towards the centre of town, passing close to the **youth hostel**, the **swimming pools** at Clube Fluvial (p.316), and several more restaurants, including some ultra-cheap *adegas* along Rua do Ouro.

Vila Nova de Gaia

The suburb of **Vila Nova de Gaia** (commonly just Gaia), which is actually a city in its own right, is dominated by the port trade. As you walk across the **Ponte Luís I** from central Porto, the names of the old **port wine lodges**, spelled out in huge white letters across their roofs, dominate the view. The most direct route to the wine lodges is across the bridge's lower level from Cais da Ribeira, or take buses #32, from Avenida dos Aliados or Praça da Batalha, or #57 or #91 both from Praça Almeida Garrett. However, if you've a head for

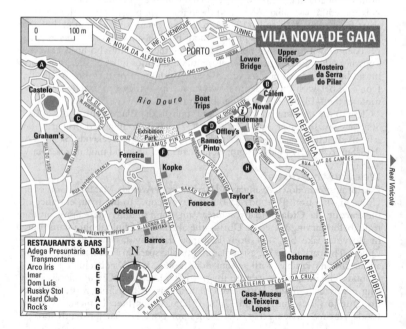

302

heights it's an amazing sensation to walk over the upper level some 60m above the river, or take buses #82 or #83 from Avenida dos Aliados or Praça Almeida Garrett, or #84 from Praça da Batalha or Praça Almeida Garrett. There's a beautiful view of the tiered ranks of Porto's old town from here and an even better one from the terrace of the **Mosteiro da Serra do Pilar** high above the bridge. From this former convent, Wellington planned his surprise crossing of the Douro in 1809 and it's a barracks again today. The round church is open to the public on Saturday afternoon and Sunday morning, but sadly the unusual circular cloister rests in a sort of no-man's-land between church and army territory and cannot be easily visited. Ask about details for visiting it at the **turismo** on the waterfront at Avenida Diogo Leite 242, next door to Sandeman (June–Sept Mon–Sun 10am–7pm; Oct–May Mon–Fri 10am–6pm; ☎223 703 735), where you can also pick up a useful map of Gaia port wine lodges.

The port wine lodges

Most of the **port wine lodges** were established in the eighteenth century, in the wake of the Methuen Treaty of 1703 (see box on p.304), and although on the whole they have long since been bought by multinational companies, they still try hard to push a family image. Almost without exception, they offer **tastings and tours**, with a view to enticing you to buy their produce – worthwhile if you want top-quality stuff but you'll probably find it cheaper to buy the more basic ports in town. If you're with children, a more fun way of doing the tour is via a 45-minute **mini-train ride**, which includes a visit to Offley's wine cellars (daily April–Sept; see "Listings" p.316). The companies which allow visits are listed on pp.304–305. Where no winter times are given, phone or check with the turismo.

Making port wine

Grapes from vines in the demarcated region are **harvested** from mid-September to mid-October and then crushed – mechanically nowadays and not by foot, despite the claims of the various lodges. The grape juice ferments for a couple of days and then, when the natural sugar level is sufficiently reduced, the **fermentation** process is arrested by the addition of grape brandy – in a ratio of four parts wine to one part brandy. The wine then stands in casks in the *armazém* (cellar) of the company **quinta** (estate) until the following March, when it's transported downstream to the shippers' lodges at Vila Nova de Gaia, where it matures.

There are four basic **types of port** – *branco* (white), *tinto* (red), *tinto aloirado* (ruby) and *aloirado* (tawny) – which spend varying times maturing. **Vintages** are only declared in certain years, when a *quinta*'s wine is deemed to be of a sufficiently high quality; when this happens, the wine spends only two years in the cask before being bottled and left to mature. A vintage wine is ready to drink between ten and fifteen years after bottling; it's a darker colour than the other wines, because of the time it spends in the bottle, and needs to be decanted to separate it from sediment. The label on the bottle will show the company, the vintage year, the year it was bottled, and sometimes the name of the *quinta*. **Late-bottled vintage wine** (LBV) is wine that's not of vintage quality, but still good enough to mature in bottles, to which it's transferred after five or six years in the cask when it is already good enough to drink. All other ports are made from blends of wines, and most are kept in the cask for much longer — at least seven years for a tawny. Wines designated 20-, 30- or 40-year-old port are also blended with the age being the average time that the blended ingredients have spent in the cask. During storage, they gradually lose their original red colour, becoming lighter with age.

The origins of the port wine trade

The distinction between **port wine** and the other Portuguese wines was first made at the beginning of the eighteenth century. Many British merchants, engaged in importing English cloth and Newfoundland cod to Portugal, were already living in Porto and were familiar with Portuguese wines. When Britain prohibited the import of French wines from 1679 to 1685 and later during the War of the Spanish Succession (1702–14), Portuguese wines became increasingly popular in Britain, with wines from the Douro region being particularly fashionable.

The **Methuen Treaty** of 1703 between Britain and Portugal reduced the duty paid on Portuguese wine in return for the removal of Portuguese restrictions on British woollen goods. As a consequence, the port wine trade became so profitable and competitive that inferior wines, often adulterated and artificially coloured, were passed off as the genuine article – giving port itself a bad name. This led the future Marquês de Pombal to found the Companhia Geral de Agricultura dos Vinhos do Alto Douro in 1756 while, at the same time, demarcating the area from which port wine could legitimately come. The monopoly and demarcation were contentious for many years; the area was regularly extended, but only recently was permission granted for port to mature elsewhere than at the lodges at Vila Nova de Gaia. Even now, strictly speaking, the demarcated area lies on either side of the Douro from Barrô, 8km downstream of Peso da Régua, to the Spanish frontier at Barca de Alva and on the Portuguese bank north to Freixo de Espada à Cinta and beyond.

It's interesting to contrast one of the large manufacturers, such as **Sandeman** (which has its own museum), with the smaller, more traditional lodges such as **Cálem** – a bit of a hike uphill – where the organizers give a very informative talk on the processes and are happy to take just a couple of visitors at a time. There are distinct contrasts, too, between the "British" names and the Portuguese-founded establishments, such as **Ramos Pinto**. It was **Real Companhia Velha** who led the first Portuguese challenge to the British port monopoly in the nineteenth century and their lodge contains numerous warehouses storing casks for the rich and famous (Generalísmo Franco's descendants among them), as well as a 6km tunnel, which was intended to form part of a rail link but, having turned out to be built at the wrong angle, now serves as a cold storage for Velha's famed sparkling wines and vintage ports. Opening times and structures of tours change frequently, so it is advisable to call ahead or check with the turismo. Entrance is free unless otherwise stated.

Barros Rua Dona Leonor de Freitas 182 ☎ 223 752 320, ℻ 223 751 939; Mon–Fri 10.30am–5.30pm. One of only a handful of remaining family-owned port companies. Renowned as a specialist in Tawnies and vintage dates Colheita Ports.

Cálem Av Diogo Leite 25–42 ☎ 223 746 660, ℻ 223 759 555; Mon–Sat daily 10am–6pm. Frequent and highly organized tours of this small and traditional lodge founded in 1859; informative but lasting no more than ten minutes.

Cockburn Rua Dona Leonor de Freitas ☎ 223 794 031, ℻ 223 750 550; Mon–Fri 10am–noon & 2–4pm. Founded in 1815, the most English (English-owned and run) of the lodges offering personalized visits (1 hour); small groups only.

Ferreira Rua da Carvalhosa 19–103 ☎ 223 746 100, ℻ 223 759 732; Mon–Fri 9.45am–12.30pm & 2–5pm; €2.49 redeemable against the price of a bottle. Founded in 1751 and worth a visit for its lovely *azulejo*-decorated tasting hall alone.

Graham's Rua Rei Ramiro 514 ☎ 223 776 330, ℻ 223 796 301; Mon–Fri 9.30am–1pm & 2–5.30pm. Founded in 1820, this lodge has an impressive stone-arched reception supporting a wooden roof. Tasting terrace overlooks the river.

Ramos Pinto Av Ramos Pinto 480 ☎ 223 707 000, ℻ 223 793 121; Mon–Fri 9am–1pm & 2–5pm. Tastings of vintage wine, exhibits of photographs, trinkets and posters from the end of the nineteenth century. Lodge founded in 1880.

Real Vinícola (Real Companhia Velha) Rua

Azevedo Magalhães 314 ℗ 223 775 100; June–Sept Mon–Fri 9.30am–1pm & 2–6pm, Sat & Sun 9.30am–1pm; closed Oct–May. Founded by Dom José I in 1756; exhibits of oil paintings from his reign are on display – look for the one of the Marquês de Pombal.

Sandeman Largo Miguel Bombarda 3, ℗ 223 740 500, ℉ 223 708 607 Mon–Fri 9am–1pm & 2–5pm; €2.50 redeemable against the price of a bottle. One of the largest companies, founded in 1790 by George Sandeman, and includes a small museum of wine-related artefacts.

Taylor, Fladgate and Yeatman Rua do Choupelo 250, ℗ 223 719 999, ℉ 223 708 607; Mon–Fri 10am–5pm, July–Aug also Sat 10am–6pm. Founded in 1692, the lodge retains a rustic-style tasting room and has panoramic views from the salon. The talk on the processes is very informative.

Casa-Museu de Teixeira Lopes

A more sober visit in Vila Nova de Gaia could be made to the **Casa-Museu de Teixeira Lopes** (Tues–Sat 9am–12.30pm & 2–5.30pm; July–Sept plus Sun 3–7pm; free) – a very steep hike up Rua Cândido dos Reis from the waterfront or a taxi-ride of €2.50 Lopes was Soares dos Reis's principal pupil and formed the centre of an important artistic and intellectual set that lived in Gaia at the end of the nineteenth century. The circle is well represented in the second part of the museum's display, the first being devoted to Lopes's work – much of it preoccupied with the depiction of children. His masterpiece is considered to be the enigmatic portrait of an Englishwoman, *A Inglesa*.

Walks in and around Vila Nova de Gaia

To get a good feel of the town's historical past **walk** up Rua Costa Santos, turn right into Rua Barão de Forrester, then back to the river down Rua Serpa Pinto along cobbled streets and under trailing vines. Another rewarding excursion is the walk 3km downriver past the port houses to the small fishing village of **Afurada**, which used to be engaged in the *bacalhau* trade until stocks were overfished and it became cheaper to import from countries like Norway. Cod was formerly strung out to dry in fields and along the shore all the way from here to the river's mouth at Cabedelo 2km away, where there's a huge sandbar across much of the river and strange boulders strewn around its edges. Small **ferries**, bedecked with Sandeman hoardings and pursuing erratic courses against the currents, cut across the rivermouth between Afurada and Rua do Ouro near the Porto suburb of **Foz do Douro** (fairly frequent throughout the day; tickets on board).

Eating

You may not be over the moon to discover that the Porto's speciality is *tripas* (tripe) and that people are affectionately referred to by the rest of the country as *tripeiros* – tripe eaters. The story goes that the inhabitants selflessly gave away all their meat for the expeditions to Ceuta (Sebta) in North Africa in the late fourteenth century, leaving themselves only the tripe, and that it's been on the menu ever since. Don't let this put you off, if you don't fancy stomach lining then there are always plenty of other choices. Another typical Portuense dish is the *francesinha* ("little French thing"), a hot sandwich containing beef, sausage and ham covered with melted cheese and peppery tomato sauce – quality varies depending on whether canned or real sausages and ham are used.

If you choose carefully, you can eat both well and cheaply, though for the best bargains (well under €5 a head, including drinks) you have to be prepared to dig into less salubrious areas, notably along the riverfront west of Alfândega. At the basic level, Porto has **workers' cafés** galore, all with wine on tap and often with a cheap set menu for the day. They are mainly lunchtime places, though

Prelada, Campsite, Centro Comercial Brasília, Boavista Stadium & Serralves

Cedofeita, Rotunda da Boavista,

Palácio de Cristal, Solar do Vinho do Porto

CENTRAL PORTO: RESTAURANTS, CAFÉS, BARS & NIGHTCLUBS

RESTAURANTS & CAFÉS

Arcádia	M
Atenéia	O
A Brasileira	J
Taberna de Bebobos	Z
Churrasqueira Brasil	Q
Café na Praça	N
A Canastra	bb
Carlos Alberto	E
Casa Cardoso	V
Casa de Chá Actos	C
Chez Lapin	W
Chinês	T
Confeitaria do Bolhão	D
Cunha	B
Dom Tonho	X
Escondidinho	K
Filha da Mãe Preta	aa
Café Guarany	F
Café Majestic	G
Casa Meia Lua	R
Monte Carlo	L
Ginjal do Porto	A
Miradouro	Y
Churrasqueira Papagaio	S
Pinguim	U
Postigo do Carvão	H
Regaleira	P

BARS & NIGHTCLUBS

Academia	a
Aniki Bóbó / Está-Se Bem / Porto Feio / Ribeira Negra	f
Downing Street	d
Meia Cave	e
meu Mercedes é maior que o teu	g
Real Feytoria	b
Ryan's Irish Pub	c
Taberna da Ribeira	h

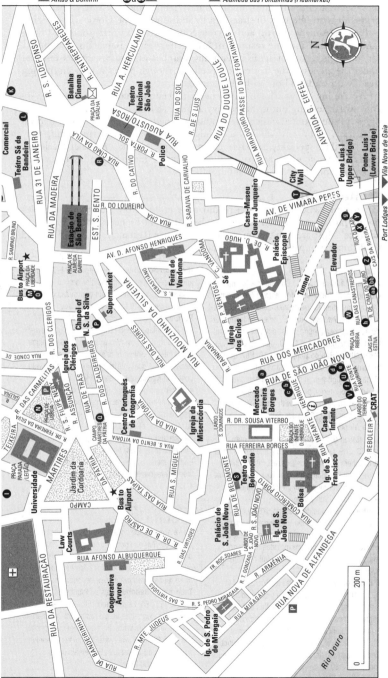

▲ Antas & Bonfirm   ㉕ & ㉖ ▲   ▲ Alameda das Fontainhas (Fleamarket)

N

▼ Vila Nova de Gaia

Port Lodges ▼

RUA DE S. ILDEFONSO

R. S. ILDEFONSO

R. ENTREPAREDES

RUA A. HERCULANO

RUA DO SOL

R. DE S. LUIS

RUA AUGUSTO ROSA

RUA DO DUQUE LOULÉ

RUA MIRADOURO PASSE IO DAS FONTAINHAS

AVENIDA G. EIFFEL

Batalha
Cinema ✉
K

PRAÇA DA
BATALHA

Teatro
Nacional
São João

L Comercial

Teatro Sá da
Bandeira

RUA 31 DE JANEIRO

RUA DA MADEIRA

R. SAMPAIO BRUNO ★

Bus to Airport

M **O**
PRAÇA DA
LIBERDADE

N
PRAÇA DE
LISBOA

R. DO CATIVO

R. PORTA SOL

RUA CIMA DA VILA

R

Police

Casa-Museu
Guerra Junqueiro

R. SARAIVA DE CARVALHO

RUA CHÃ

R. DO LOUREIRO

EST. S. BENTO

Estação de
São Bento

PRAÇA DE
ALMEIDA
GARRETT

AV. D. AFONSO HENRIQUES

Feira de
Vandoma

R. S. SEBASTIÃO

RUA DE D. HUGO

Palácio
Episcopal

Sé

City
Wall

T

AV. DE VIMARA PERES

Ponte Luis I
(Upper Bridge)

Ponte Luis I
(Lower Bridge)

Elevador

Tunnel

Igreja
dos Grilos

RUA DOS MERCADORES

Supermarket

Chapel of
N.S. da Silva

P

Igreja dos
Clérigos

R. DOS CLÉRIGOS

RUA CONDE DE

RUA DAS FLORES

RUA MOUZINHO DA SILVEIRA

RUA DA BAINHARIA

R. P. VENTOSA

R. VANDOMA

Igreja
da Silva

P

Igreja da
Asunção

R. DE TRAS

R. DOS CALDEIREIROS

Centro Português
de Fotografia

RUA DA VITÓRIA

Igreja da
Misericórdia

LARGO
S. DOMINGOS

RUA DR. SOUSA VITERBO

RUA DE SÃO JOÃO NOVO

Mercado
Ferreira
Borges

a
c **b**
d
e

V
i
RUA DA FONTE
TAURINA

Casa do
Infante

CRAT

RUA DAS CANASTREIROS

R. DE CIMA DO MURO

PRAÇA DA
RIBEIRA

CASA DA
ESTIVA

W

h

X
g **Y**

Z
aa PRAÇA DA
ALFÂNDEGA

RUA DA LADA

CAIS DA RIBEIRA

R. PLANTA DA SILVA

R. DAS CARMELITAS

R. S. FILIPE NERI

GALERIA

TEIXEIRA

PRAÇA PARADA
LEITÃO

I Universidade

Jardim da
Cordaria

CAMPO
DA PÁTRIA

MÁRTIRES

Bus to Airport ★

RUA DAS TAIPAS

RUA S. MIGUEL

R. S. BENTO DA VITÓRIA

RUA DE BELOMONTE

Teatro de
Belomonte

Palácio de
S. João Novo

RUA DR. B. DE CASTRO

RUA AFONSO ALBUQUERQUE

Law
Courts

RUA DA RESTAURAÇÃO

✚

Cooperativa
Árvore

RUA DAS VIRTUDES

FR. ROÇ SOARES

LARGO DE
S. JOÃO
NOVO

R. S. JOÃO NOVO

Ig. de S.
João Novo

RUA DE COMÉRCIO PORTO

Bolsa

Ig. de S.
Francisco

RUA DE S. INFANTE D. HENRIQUE

LARGO DO
TERREIRO

R. REBOLEIRA

RUA NOVA DE ALFÂNDEGA

R. T. GONZAGA

R. ARMÉNIA

FR. ROÇ SOARES

R. DAS VIRTUDES

C. DAS VIRTUDES

R. S. PEDRO MIRAGAIA

RUA MIRAGAIA

R. MTE. JUDEUS

RUA DR. BANDEIRINHA

Ig. de S. Pedro
de Miragaia

P

Rio Douro

0   200 m

307

◀ Massarelos & Foz do Douro

most serve an evening meal until around 7.30pm and a few stay open later; prime areas are the grid of streets north and south of the Cordoaria: especially Rua do Almada (north) and Rua de São Bento da Vitória (south). Moving more upmarket, into the **restaurant** league, the Cais da Ribeira is hard to beat for atmosphere or for its fish, with any number of café-restaurants installed under the arches of the first tier of dwellings, though prices have been moving steadily upwards and out of budget range.

If you're buying your own food, check the central **markets** listed on p.316. Also worth seeking out is the **bakery** at Travessa de Cedofeita 20b, one of the oldest in the country, which uses traditional methods such as burning *carqueja* – a variety of broom which reaches high temperatures while producing very little ash. The speciality is *pão-de-ló*, a round sponge cake. Another local speciality is *broa de mel*, a sort of fruit cake mixture made into a biscuit, which makes a good cheap snack at about €0.25.

Restaurants

Unless otherwise stated, all the **restaurants** listed below are open daily; telephone numbers are given for those where it might be necessary to reserve in advance. Most are marked on the Central Porto: Restaurants, Cafés, Bars and Clubs map on pp.306–307 – exceptions are noted.

Central Porto

Adega Vila Meã Rua dos Caldeireiros 62, near Clérigos ☎222 082 967. Modest old restaurant with a reputation for fresh, well-cooked food: various fish and *bacalhau* dishes, an exceptional *cozido à portuguesa* (Thurs), roast octopus (Tues) and roast veal (Fri). Under €12.50. Closed Sun & Aug.

A Brasileira Rua do Bonjardim 118. Next door to its famous café, this is one of the oldest and most elegant (though aging) of Porto's restaurants, with an Art Deco interior, pavement café, stand-up bar and smallish dining room with attentive waiter service. Around €15. Closed Sun.

Casa Aleixo Rua da Estação 216, by Campanhã train station ☎225 370 462; see Porto map pp.288–289. Long-established place with a good atmosphere and an excellent reputation; choose from fish fillets, octopus, roast veal, or roast pork chops. Half-portions (enough for one) under €7.50. Closed Sun & Aug.

Cunha Rua Guedes de Azevedo 676; see Porto map pp.288–289. Famed traditional old pastry shop, which also has a pretty decent snack-bar and restaurant. Basic fare includes roast pork, roast chicken and dorado fillets, but helpings are huge. Around €10.

O Escondidinho Rua de Passos Manuel 144 ☎222 001 079. Hardly hidden (*escondidinho* means "the little hidden place"), this place has a cluttered, country-house interior and excellent French-influenced cuisine, but it's expensive. The menu is unusual: try the hake in Madeira sauce and a kirsch omelette if you have €18 to spend; more like €30 for a feast. Closed Sun.

Ginjal do Porto Rua do Bonjardim 724–726. Tripe and other Portuguese specialities served in a no-frills setting, but don't expect gourmet cooking. Cheap – under €5 for the *prato do dia*.

Portucale Rua da Alegria 598 ☎225 370 717; see Porto map pp.288–289. At the top of a tower block with views over Porto and a 1960s sophisticated interior. Specialities include lobster gratin, *bacalhau*, kid goat, partridge with chestnuts, wild boar and mango and pheasant in almond sauce and there's a good wine list, too. Expensive (mains €30 plus) but highly recommended.

Regaleira Rua do Bonjardim 87, around the corner from Praça Dom João I. One of the best places for fish and seafood, including platefuls of *perceves* (barnacles) and lamprey in season. The English menu can be a little perplexing, but it's worth perservering. Mains cost from €5 to €12.50.

Cais da Ribeira and around

There are unfussy cheap eats at the nameless places on Rua da Fonte Taurina nos. 44 and 78, and elsewhere in the sidestreets back from the river. Nearer the water things become decidedly more touristy and prices rise accordingly.

Taberna de Bebobos Cais da Ribeira 24–25 ☎222 053 565. Established in the nineteenth century, this *taberna* has an old *tasca* feel with barrels of wine lining the walls. Fish and regional specialities – try the pork with wine sauce. Very popular, so book ahead if possible. Full meals up to €17.50. Closed Mon.

A Canastra Cais da Ribeira 37 ☎ 222 080 180. Another highly recommended homely under-the-arches option, but cheaper and more local than its neighbours.

Casa Cardoso Rua da Fonte Taurina 60. One of the cheaper options, with some excellent fish dishes – try the swordfish. Main dishes from €3.50 to €8.50. Closed Sun.

Chez Lapin Rua das Canastreiros 40 ☎ 222 006 418. Under the arches, this deceptively large place is rather expensive and is becoming something of a tourist trap. However, it's still popular with locals, particularly on Sun when many other places are closed (advance reservations necessary), but unfortunately the food doesn't always live up to the price tag. And, yes, one house speciality is rabbit.

Chinês Av de Vímara Peres 38–40 ☎ 222 008 915. Some of the city's best Chinese food – served in a modern building with a stunning interior by the top-level entrance to Ponte Luís I. Allow around €10 for the *ementa turística* but all portions are large and you'd do well to get through three courses.

Dom Tonho Cais da Ribeira 13–15 ☎ 222 004 307. Typical of the move upmarket for the Cais da Ribeira area is this high-class chrome-and-glass restaurant owned by *pimba* pop star Rui Veloso, overlooking the river. Mainly serves seafood with unusual specials like duck and goat and there's a hip bar on the lower level. The tunnel entrance at the far end was once a secret passage between the Sé and Ribeira.

Filha da Mãe Preta Arcos do Douro 2–3, Cais da Ribeira ☎ 222 055 515. Built into the arches, the *azulejo*-decorated upper floor gives you a view over the river to Gaia. An excellent *ementa turística* features a change from the usual dishes although it is rather pricey. The name ("daughter of the black mother") comes from the original establishment here, *Mãe Preta*, which was popular with charcoal makers from upriver. Not to be confused with the nearby and similarly named no-nonsense taverna, which is a little grim and definitely an acquired taste. Closed Mon.

Miradouro Cais da Ribeira, on the arches by the entrance to the bridge. Always bustling with locals, this little spot serves up great pizzas, *bifanas*, *francesinhas* and huge salads. Closed Wed.

Postigo do Carvão Rua da Fonte Taurina 24–26 ☎ 222 004 539. Restaurant and snack bar open to 2am with live music at weekends (fado, folklore, Brazilian). Good for cheap *pratinhos* (try the flame-grilled *chouriço assado*, cheese boards or smoked meats); they also do grilled lobster and fondue. Closed Mon.

Around Praça da Batalha

Casa Meia Lua Rua Cimo da Vila 151. Small and friendly place where you can eat well for around €5. You may have to share tables.

Monte Carlo Rua de Santa Catarina 17. Hidden away up on the second floor, this looks like a badly neglected 1930s tearoom, but has views over Praça da Batalha, a buzzing television, food that veers from good to indifferent and, particularly at Sun lunchtime, very noisy locals. Not everyone's cup of tea, but good value.

Suribachi Rua do Bonfim 136–140, 800m east of Praça da Batalha ☎ 225 106 700; see Porto map pp.288–289. Cheap and cosy macrobiotic and mainly vegetarian restaurant, accessed through a health food shop – not a greasy chip in sight although fish and seafood are on the menu. Inventive tofu dishes among others. Mon–Sat 8.30am–9.30pm.

Cordoaria to Praça de Carlos Alberto

Churrasqueira Brasil Campo dos Mártires da Pátria 136. Very cheap workers' diner on the square immediately south of the gardens. Open until 10pm.

Carlos Alberto Praça de Carlos Alberto 89. Friendly, cheap traditional restaurant. Closed Sat.

Churrasqueira Papagaio Trav. do Carmo 32. Appealing, tiled interior, with good grills and an inexpensive *ementa turística*.

West of the centre

The following are all shown on the Porto map on pp.288–289 unless otherwise stated.

Capa Negra Rua do Campo Alegre 191, between Boavista and Palácio de Cristal; buses #35, #37, #78, #93 or #96 from Cordoaria. Huge, bright and busy operation with good local dishes. Famed city-wide for its *francesinha* meat sandwiches (€6–8), you can also choose fish and lobsters directly from the big bubbly tanks. Snacks from €4, full meals €7.50–15. Open to 2am; closed Mon.

Casa de Chá da Boa Nova Leça da Palmeira ☎ 229 951 785; buses #1 or #19 to Matosinhos port, then walk or catch a cab north for the remaining 1km. Famous café and restaurant by the ocean, designed by Álvaro Siza Vieira, with sweeping views and a small fishermen's chapel beside it. A bit of a way from the centre, but worth it if you take your food (or your architecture) seriously.

Churrascão Gaúcho Av da Boavista 313 ☎ 226 091 738; buses #34 from Praça da República, or #82 or #84 from Bolhão or Praça da Batalha. Sophisticated Brazilian place – speciality is both fish and *rodízio* (€17), which involves waiters carving slices off skewers of grilled lamb and beef onto your plate until you beg them to stop. Closed Sun.

Massarelos L'Entrecôte Rua da Boa Viagem 3, Massarelos, behind the tram museum, ☎ 226 008 732; buses #1 or 23 from Praça Almeida Garrett or Rua Nova da Alfândega, #24 from Cordoaria, or tram #18. Beautiful conversion of the former headquarters of the Portuguese Legion, with balcony views over the Douro. The house speciality is beef steak; mains around €12.50.

Museu dos Presuntos Rua Padre Luís Cabral 1070, Foz do Douro ☎ 226 106 965; buses #1 from Praça Almeida Garrett or Rua Nova da Alfândega, or #24 from Cordoaria; tram #18. Surreal junk-shop-decorated place with a pub-like feel that's popular with students. The decor aside (the dining room is hung with gilt-framed smoked hams), the main draws are the unusual *pratinhos* (small dishes), including stewed chicken innards, pickled *bacalhau* and smoked ham (*presunto*). Around €7 for a full meal.

Ó Macedo Rua do Passeio Alegre 552, Foz do Douro ☎ 226 170 166; buses #1 from Praça Almeida Garrett or Rua Nova da Alfândega, or #24 from Cordoaria; tram #18. Pleasantly refined establishment offering various dishes including onion tart, *bacalhau*, even English roast beef, plus a good wine list. Arrive early for the tables with views over the mouth of the Douro. Closed Sun, and for a fortnight in Aug.

Paco Loco Av do Dr. Antunes Guimarães 1217, 1km north of Av da Boavista ☎ 226 189 480; bus #3 from Praça da Liberdade or Cordoaria. Hot Mexican and Texan food in suitably colourful sur-roundings, with music to match. Good eats but low on authenticity. Closed Sun.

Peixes & Co. Rua do Ouro 133, on the river west of Arrábida bridge ☎ 226 185 655; buses #1 from Praça Almeida Garrett or Rua Nova da Alfândega, or #24 from Cordoaria; tram #18. Friendly and elegant atmosphere in a renovated town house, with views over the river. Different kinds of fish, depending on the day's catch – expect to pay around €15 for the works. Closed Sun.

Vila Nova de Gaia

The following are all shown on the Vila Nova de Gaia map on p.302.

Adega Presuntaria Transmontana Rua Cândido dos Reis 132 and Av Diogo Leite 78 ☎ 223 714 264. Lovely cool dining room with stone walls, and a dozen smoked hams hanging over the bar. Refined but expensive – a full meal costs over €18. Two entrances, the one on the waterfront is the most easily accessible.

Arco Íris Rua Cândido dos Reis 75–79. Popular *pão quente* ("hot bread") place, which has fresh, warm bread all day, as well as very reasonably priced snacks and full meals.

Imar Av Diogo Leite 56 ☎ 223 792 705. Highly recommended, with big portions, reasonable prices, and a predominantly local crowd. If the sun is shining, take a table outside and watch the *barcos rabelos* sailing along the river in front of you.

Dom Luís Av Ramos Pinto 266. The *ementa turística* is worth every cent at €10, or you can go à la carte and sample the speciality – tripe. Good value.

Russky Stol Av Diogo Leite 454. Russian restaurant cum vodka bar with a limited but unusual menu including sausages from €8. Closed Mon.

Cafés, tea and cake shops

Cafés in Porto rival Lisbon's, with some lovely old Art Deco survivors in the main shopping streets. All serve alcohol, snacks and cakes as well as coffee. There is also a handful of pavement cafés on Praça da Ribeira, packed with tourists in summer. The following are marked on the Central Porto: Restaurants, Cafés, Bars and Clubs map on pp.306–307, unless stated otherwise.

Arcádia Praça da Liberdade 63. Long-established sweet shop, famous for its chocolate bonbons, *ovos moles* (sticky UFO-shaped egg confectionery) and regional specialities.

Ateneia Praça da Liberdade 58. For serious addicts: exquisite chocolates from the Costa Moreira company, quince *marmelada*, boiled sweets and cakes, with a cosy raised Art Deco seating area at the back in which to indulge your passion.

A Brasileira Rua de Sá da Bandeira 75. A sister branch to the one in Lisbon, with pavement seats and a good stand-up bar for breakfast and refuelling during the day. Open till 8pm, closed Sun.

Café na Praça Praça de Lisboa. Trendy chrome and glass place popular at all hours. The outdoor tables are a great place to sit and soak up the surroundings, and the *espetada de lulas* (squid kebab) is worth a try. DJs most weekend nights; daily 10pm–4am.

Casa de Chá Actos Rua Sá Noronha 76-1º. Offers a large variety of teas, plus cakes, tarts and even scones. It has unusual hours 4–8pm shift for a genteel atmosphere, followed by 10pm–2am, when it plays host to students and more arty types. Hosts temporary exhibitions.

Confeitaria do Bolhão Rua Formosa 339, opposite the entrance to the Bolhão market. Tranquil cake and coffee shop, kitschly repainted in Art Nouveau style, and rather popular with old ladies. They do good value *pratos do dia* in the restaurant above too. Open daily.

Guarany Av dos Aliados. Less stylish than *A Brasileira*, but bright and airy. Another café that's popular with old ladies at tea-time. Cheap food, but watch the overpriced soft drinks. Open till 10pm.

Majestic Rua de Santa Catarina 112. The most known and most expensive of the old Belle Epoque cafés, with perfectly preserved decor, outside tables and excellent coffee. The grand piano features in out-of-season recitals. Closed Sun.

Pinguim Rua de Belomonte 65–67. A laid-back arty venue, with live Brazilian or Portuguese music Fri evenings starting at 11pm, and poetry readings on Mon at the same time.

Drinking, nightlife and entertainment

As with restaurants and cafés, you're spoilt for choice when it comes to drinking, clubbing and – as a result of investment lavished on the arts during the 2001 City of Culture celebrations – entertainment.

Bars

Trendier than cafés, dozens of modish late-night **bars** are found in the streets around the Cais da Ribeira, as well as along the river in Gaia, in Foz do Douro and up the coast facing Praia dos Ingleses, the last being the main evening drag in summer. The following are marked on the Central Porto: Restaurants, Cafés, Bars and Clubs map on p.306–307, unless stated otherwise.

Aniki Bóbó Rua Fonte Taurina 36–38, Ribeira, ☎ 223 324 619. Cool and spacious. Sometimes features live music and occasionally alternative theatre on Thurs, but call in advance to see if anything is going on. Tues–Sat 10pm–4am. €2.50 cover charge.

Downing Street Praça da Ribeira 10. A more refined ambience than most serving up port wine in the glass-fronted bar.

Está-Se Bem Rua da Fonte Taurina 70–72, Ribeira. A nice little *tasca* where the arty crowd hang out, probably because it's cheap and there's no cover charge. It's also popular with a pre-club crowd. Mon–Sat 9pm–4am.

Labirinto Rua Nossa Senhora de Fátima 334, off Rotunda da Boavista ☎ 226 063 665; see Porto map pp.288–289; night bus #76 to Rotunda. Very pleasant, friendly bar in a converted house, with a shaded back garden and unpretentious gallery space. Occasional live music, poetry recitals and drama (usually starting at midnight). Daily 10pm–4am.

O meu Mercedes é maior que o teu Rua da Lada 30, Ribeira. Hands-down winner of the world's silliest bar name contest ("My Mercedes is bigger than yours") – although there's no name on the door – but happily, a small and friendly bar inside which tends to attract regulars. Evenings only.

Porto Feio Rua da Fonte Taurina 52–54. Hi-tech bar with an art gallery open from 4–10pm, followed by the bar until 2am. Ring the bell for admittance. Closed Sun–Wed.

Quando-Quando Av do Brasil 60, Foz do Douro; see Porto map pp.288–289; night bus #1 from Praça Almeida Garrett. Popular waterfront hotspot for the in-crowd. Tues–Sat 10pm–5am. Closed Sun–Mon.

Taberna da Ribeira Praça da Ribeira. In a prime riverside location, this place has outdoor tables, *chouriço assada* (grilled with alcohol at your table) and home-made sangria to wash it down with. The perfect spot to while away a whole afternoon without realizing it. Open till 2am.

Ribeira Negra Rua Fonte Taurina 66–68. Proof that Porto has it all: an *upmarket* grunge bar.

Ryan's Irish Pub Rua do Infante Dom Henrique 18. Ain't no city in the world without one: Irish music, Guinness (bottled), Jamesons and Bushmills, and Irish prices to match. Thurs & Sun 10pm–2am, Fri 9pm–4am, Sat 5pm–4am. €2.50 entrance after 11pm.

Solar do Vinho do Porto Museu Romântico, Rua de Entre-Quintas; see Porto map pp.288–289. Laid-back venue for port-drinking in civilized surroundings, with views over the Douro and elegant waiter service; see p.300.

Syndikato Club Rua do Bonjardim 836, two

Popular traditions – feiras, festas and romarias

Passion Sunday (March/April; the second Sun before Easter) Celebrated with a feast, special market and procession near Jardim de São Lázaro opposite the church of Nossa Senhora da Esperança, east of Praça da Batalha.

Easter Day (March/April) Effigies of Judas are burnt in several locations around the Sé.

Corpus Christi (May/June) Processions of administrative and religious authorities through the centre of the city.

Santo António (closest Sat to June 13) Religious services in the churches of Massarelos and Bonfim districts in honour of the protector of brides and newlyweds.

São João (June 23–24) The biggest popular tradition of festivals (São João is the patron saint of lovers), which sees performances of folk and choral music, a marathon, and *cascata* competitions (these are displays of dolls depicting Santo António, São João and São Pedro, usually arranged in shop-window displays, complete with miniature houses, trains and cars). The evening of June 23rd culminates with fireworks and riotous celebrations, especially in Ribeira.

São Pedro (June 29) Street decorations, music and dancing celebrate the Saint's day of the first Christian Pope.

São Bartolomeu (Sun after Aug 24) Procession in Foz do Douro of "puppets dressed in paper clothes", culminating in a health-giving bath (*banho santo*) in the rather polluted sea.

Senhora da Boa Fortuna (last weekend in Aug) In the parish of Vitória, west of Ribeira near Torre dos Clérigos/Rua de Ceuta, a procession of young children dressed as angels carry plastic baby dolls to the image of Nossa Senhora in Rua dos Caldeireiros.

Nossa Senhora de Campanhã (closest Sun to Sept 8) Market stalls are set up near Campanhã train station and there's live folk music and dancing.

Nossa Senhora do Ó (last Sun in Sept) A solemn procession from the Capela Nossa Senhora da Piedade do Cais to the river west of Alfândega in honour of the pregnant Virgin.

São Nicolau (Dec 6) Children wait for Santa Claus's arrival by boat at the Cais de Estiva in Ribeira, and then escorted him along Rua da Alfândega to a ceremony at the Igreja de São Francisco.

Nossa Senhora da Conceição (Dec 8 – national holiday) Feast held in Foz do Douro, centred on the Capela da Nossa Senhora da Conceição, followed by a night procession though Foz's streets.

Modern festivals

For details of exact dates, times and various venues, check with one of Porto's turismos or on their website ⓦ www.portoturismo.pt/en/eventos.

February Fantasporto international film festival at the Coliseu and other venues, ⓦ www.caleida.pt/fantasporto.

May–June Book Festival at the Palácio de Cristal; International Festival of Youth Theatre in various open-air venues.

June Beer festival at Jardim do Passeio Alegre, Foz do Douro.

July World Music Festival at the Palácio de Cristal; International Folklore Festival, various venues.

August Rock Festival at the Palácio de Cristal.

October–November Fado Festival at the Coliseu; Jazz Festival at Auditorio Nacional Carlos Alberto.

October–December Contemporary Art Festival, various venues.

November–December European Cinema Festival, various venues.

December Crafts Festival (two weeks) at the Palácio de Cristal; Puppet Festival at Auditorio Nacional Carlos Alberto.

blocks east of Praça da República ☏ 222 084 383. The city's main gay bar, with drag acts for a discerning public. Also popular is *Bustos*, nearby at Rua Guedes de Azevedo 203-1° ☏ 222 054 876. (Both are on the Porto map pp.288–289).

Discos and clubs

Porto's discos are highly regarded, although most are way outside the centre – we've mentioned night buses (usually hourly) for these ones. As with Lisbon, the majority of the clubs really only get going well after midnight, and most stay open until 4–5am or later, with a standard €5–7.50 admission fee (fees are mentioned if cheaper); the entrance ticket acts as a voucher for drinks, not that it'll last long – with beers and soft drinks averaging €2–2.50, and spirits €4, most people drink in bars before hitting the clubs. Ring ahead to check weekday opening times, as these change frequently enough. Unless stated otherwise, the following are marked on the Porto map on pp.288–289.

Academia Rua de São João Novo 80, Ribeira ☏ 222 005 737; see the Central Porto: Restaurants, Cafés, Bars and Clubs map pp.306–307. Modish disco-bar with pretensions, attracting students. Cover €2. Daily 10pm–2am.

Batô Largo do Castelo 13, Leça da Palmeira, north of Matosinhos ☏ 229 953 405; night bus #76. High-camp pirates' galleon interior, just needs Errol Flynn sliding down one of the masts to complete the effect. Tues–Sat 11pm–4am.

Club Mau-Mau Rua do Outeiro 4, west of Palácio de Cristal ☏ 226 076 660; night bus #1 from Praça Almeida Garrett to Massarelos. Restaurant and pavement café Tues–Sat 8pm–4am, disco open Fri–Sat 11pm–6am. Weird mix of music, touching on punk and heavy metal, but still pretty friendly – usually has live music Thurs.

Hard Club Cais de Gaia, Vila Nova de Gaia ☏ 223 753 819; night bus #91; see Vila Nova de Gaia map p.302. Porto's main venue for DJs and live music, including a good number of British and Stateside acts. Fri is more poppy. Worth ringing to see what's coming up.

Industria Av Do Brasil 843, Foz do Douro; night bus #1 from Praça Almeida Garrett. Beach club in Foz packed during the summer months and attracting a youthful clientele. Fri–Sun 11pm–6am.

Maré-Alta Bar Alameda Basílio Teles, a floating teepee moored on the river bank west of Ponte da Arrábida ☏ 226 162 540 (night bus #1 to "Gás"). Trendy mix of music, leaning on Brazilian. Tues–Sun 2pm–6am. Sun "House Breakfast" (7am–2pm) is usually accompanied by a live band. €2.50 cover.

Meia Cave Praça da Ribeira 6 ☏ 223 323 214; see the Central Porto: Restaurants, Cafés, Bars and Clubs map pp.306–307. Drum'n'bass and breakbeat. 10pm onwards with prices going up after 2am. Open Fri & Sat only.

Mexcal Rua da Restauração 39 ☏ 226 009 188; night bus #1 to Massarelos. Very danceable mix of Latin American music. Wed–Sat 10pm–4am; cover €3.50–5 (women free on weekdays).

Real Feytoria Rua Infante Dom Henrique 20 ☏ 222 000 718; see the Central Porto: Restaurants, Cafés, Bars and Clubs map pp.306–307. Daily 9pm–2am. In a great location, with two floors, one with pop, rock and Brazilian, the other playing house. Cover €2.

Rock's 228 Rua Rei Ramiro, Vila Nova de Gaia ☏ 223 751 208; see Vila Nova de Gaia map p.302. Built in old port cellars, with a terrace overlooking the Douro, and barbecues in summer. Thurs–Sat 10pm–4am. Night bus #91.

Sound Planet Av Fontes Pereira de Melo 449 ☏ 226 107 232. Popular venue playing a mixture of pop and house music. Closed Sun–Wed.

Swing Rua Júlio Dinis 766, near Rotunda da Boavista ☏ 226 090 019; night bus #19 or #76. The disco-goers number one; five bars (one gay – the main venue in Porto) and lively clientele. Busiest Fri, also good on Mon. Open 12.30–6am.

Twins Rua do Passeio Alegre 994, Foz do Douro ☏ 226 185 740; night bus #1 from Praça Almeida Garrett. Lively mix of music popular with a younger crowd. Tues to Sun, 10pm to 4am, later on Fri & Sat.

Voice Rua da Boa Viagem 1, next to Museu dos Carros Eléctricos ☏ 226 067 815 (night bus #1 to Massarelos). An old customs warehouse attracting trendies Sat nights. Thurs–Sat 11pm–4am.

Theatre, music, dance and cinema

Listings are given in the free monthly arts listings booklet, *cultura.norte*, and in the quarterly, *Agenda do Porto*, both available at the turismos, and on the website Ⓦ www.agendadoporto.pt. Porto's leading paper, the *Jornal de Notícias*, and the local edition of the weekly *Público* are also useful sources of information on events.

After a shaky period following the 1974 revolution, during which time much of the underground dissident tradition of **theatre** lost ground to musicals, theatre has undergone a renaissance in the past decade. Of the major venues there are: Rivoli Teatro Municipal (also known as "Culturporto") on Praça Dom João I (☎ 223 392 201); and Teatro Nacional São João on Praça da Batalha (☎ 222 086 634, Ⓦ www.tnsj.pt), as well as the Auditório Nacional Carlos Alberto (see below). Smaller, more intimate venues include the Teatro Universitário do Porto (TUP) Rua Jorge Viterbo Ferreira 120, off Rua Dom Manuel II (☎ 226 090 103); Teatro da Vilarinha, Rua da Vilarinha 1386 at the corner with Circunvalação (☎ 226 108 924), bus #52 from Cordoaria, and the superb auditorium at Teatro Campo Alegre, Rua das Estrelas (☎ 226 001 000), bus #31 from Rotunda da Boavista. Another smaller venue is the excellent Casa das Artes, Rua Ruben 210 (or Rua António Cardoso), off Rua do Campo Alegre (☎ 226 006 153, Ⓕ 226 006 152), bus #78 from Cordoaria or Bolhão, which is the centre of the city's alternative arts scene, and screens art-house movies daily. Finally, the Teatro de Belomonte, Rua de Belomonte 57 (☎ 222 083 341) is a **puppet theatre** – ring for details of performances. Call the theatres directly or ask at the turismo for details.

Dance and other musical events, including major **pop and rock concerts**, usually take place in the Coliseu do Porto, Rua de Passos Manuel 137 (☎ 222 059 136, Ⓔ coliseu.do.porto@mail.telepac.pt; closed at time of writing – estimated date for reopening is late 2003). **Classical music concerts** are held regularly in the Auditório Nacional Carlos Alberto, Rua das Oliveiras 43 (☎ 222 004 540, Ⓔ anca@portugalnet.com), which also stages theatre and dance. The home of the Orquestra Nacional do Porto is the former monastery of São Bento da Vitória, Rua de São Bento da Vitória (☎ 222 006 549, Ⓕ 222 052 111). Porto has a limited number of **fado houses** (Mon–Sat), and usually showing music at dinner time only. These include *Casa da Mariquinhas* Rua São Sebastião (☎ 222 056 083) and *Mal Cozinhado* ☎ 222 081 319) on Rua Outeirinho, 13, which are both rather touristy.

Listings

Adventure sports Canoeing and kayaking: Associação Naútica do Douro, Av Diogo Leite 150–2º, Vila Nova de Gaia ☎ 223 798 297, or the Federação Portuguesa de Canoagem, Rua António Pinto Machado 60–3º ☎ 226 066 227, Ⓕ 226 095 424. Mountain climbing, rafting and hill-walking: Trilhos, Rua de Belem 94 ☎ 225 020 740. Windsurfing: Clube Surf do Porto, Rua de Santa Catarina ☎ 225 364 559, Ⓕ 226 178 436; Associão Portuguesa de Windsurf, Rua D. João Iv ☎ & Ⓕ 225 364 559. Sailing and water skiing: Yate Clube do Porto, Molhe Norte, Leixões docks, Leça da Palmeira, Matosinhos ☎ & Ⓕ 229 965 586. Horse-riding: Centro Hípico do Porto e Matosinhos, Lugar de Gonçalves, Leça da Palmeira, Matosinhos ☎ 229 952 133, and the Quinta de São Salvador, Rua Silva Tapada 200, Quebrantões, Vila Nova de Gaia ☎ 223 702 575, Ⓕ 223 703 621. Mountain biking: Montes d'Aventura, Alameda Dr. Antonio Macedo 19 ☎ 228 304 147.

Airlines Air France Av da Boavista 1203–4º ☎ 226 078 982, Ⓕ 226 078 989, airport 229 413 131; Alitalia airport ☎ 229 416 848, Ⓕ 229 416 851; British Airways airport ☎ 229 486 315, or freephone 800 212 125; Ibéria airport ☎ 229 490 723; KLM airport ☎ 229 439 747, Ⓕ 229 486 433; Lufthansa airport ☎ 229 437 900, Ⓕ 229 416 375; Portugália Av Boavista 1361–4º ☎ 226 004 766, Ⓕ 226 008 283, airport ☎ 229 412 075; Sabena airport ☎229 413 112, ☎229 413 111; TAP Praça Mouzinho de Albuquerque 105 ☎226 080 227, ☎226 080 233.

Airport information Call ☎229 432 400.

American Express c/o Star Travel, Av dos Aliados 210 ☎222 050 695.

Banks and exchange The main branches of the banks are concentrated around Praça da Liberdade (Mon–Fri 8.30am–3pm). Better commission and opening hours at Portocâmbios, Rua Rodrigues Sampaio 193, next to the Câmara Municipal (Mon–Fri 9am–6pm, Sat 9am–1pm), and at Intercontinental, Rua Ramalho Ortigão 10, around the corner from the main turismo office (Mon–Fri 9am–noon & 2–6pm, Sat 9am–noon). ATMs are everywhere, particularly around Praca Almeida Garrett at the lower end of Av dos Aliados.

Books There are English-language bookshops in Rua da Picaria and Rua José Falcão. Try also: Bertrand Livreiros, Rua 31 de Janeiro 65; Editorial Estampa, Rua Escola do Exercito 9; Livraria Clássica in Clérigos Shopping, next to the tower; or the lovely Livraria Lello & Irmão second-hand shop at Rua dos Carmelitas 144. Livraria Academica, Rua Martires da Liberdade 10, is a delightful antiquarian bookshop.

Buses Porto has many bus companies, most of which operate out of different terminals; check first with the turismo as to the timetable and departure point for your destination, and see the "Travel details" at the end of this chapter for destinations and appropriate companies. The main companies and their terminals are as follows: Asa Douro, Rua Alexandre Herculano 225; Auto Viação de Espinho, Rua Alexandre Herculano 366; Auto Viação do Minho, Praça Dona Filipa de Lencastre 218; Auto Viação do Tâmega, Rua Alexandre Herculano 68; Auto Viação Landim, Rua Gueses de Azevedo 218; Auto Viação Mondinense, Av Rodrigues de Freitas 405; Auto Viação Pacense, Praça General Humberto Delgado 329; Caima, Rua Alexandre Herculano 366; EVA, Rua Alexandre Herculano 366; Internorte, Praça da Galiza 96; Joalto, Campo Mártires da Pátria 171; João Ferreira das Neves, Praça D. Filipa de Lencastre 193–195; Linhares, Rua José Falcão 198–204; Marquês, Praça Guilherme Gomes Fernandes 71; Rede Expressos, to the north from Praça D. Filipa de Lencastre, to the south from Rua Alexandre Herculano 366; REDM (Rodoviária d'Entre Douro e Minho), Praça Dona Filipa de Lencastre; Renex, Rua das Carmelitas 32; Rodonorte, Central Shopping, Campo 24 de Agosto; Resende, Rua das Carmelitas 183; Santos de Freixo, Central Shopping, Campo 24 de Agosto; Turilis, Rotunda da Boavista/Rua da Meditação; Valpi, Praça General Humberto Delgado 339. See p.290 for further details.

Car rental Most companies maintain offices at the airport, where cars can usually be booked on the spot. Of the multinationals, Europcar is good value: Rua de Santa Catarina 1158 (☎222 057 737, ☎222 000 170) with saloons from €33 per day including TW/CDW over a week. A cheap local company is Roditur, Rua Dr. Alfredo de Magalhães 114 (☎222 053 357, ☎222 087 724), offering the same from €25 per day. Other companies include Hertz, Rua de Santa Catarina 899 (☎222 052 393, ☎222 081 287, booking line freephone ☎800 238 238); Optima, Rua Visconde de Bóbeda 38 (☎225 103 427, ☎225 105 145); and Guerin, Rua do Bolhão 182 (☎222 084 704, ☎222 081 964).

Cinemas You're most likely to find Portuguese and Brazilian films at the Cinema Batalha 47 (and Sala Bebé), Praça da Batalha (☎222 022 407). Art-house movies are screened at the Casa das Artes, Rua do Antonio Cardoso (☎226 006 153) and Terço, Rua João Pedro Ribeira 680 (☎225 507 254). Big-screen blockbusters, often in English, are screened at Cinema Charlot, Centro Comercial Brasilia, Rotunda da Boavista ☎226 097 210; Cinema Passos Manuel, Rua Passos Manuel 137 ☎222 030 706; Nun'Álvares, Rua Guerra Junqueiro 485 ☎226 092 078; Central Shopping, Rua de Santos Pousada (six screens) ☎225 102 785); and Cidade do Porto, Shopping Centre Cidade do Porto, Rua Gonçalo Sampaio, Boavista ☎226 009 164. Film listings can be found in weekly local edition of *Público*.

Consulates UK, Av da Boavista 3072 ☎226 184 789; USA, Av da Boavista 3523 ☎226 186 606, ☎226 186 625.

Crafts The best place for regional crafts is the Centro Regional de Artes Tradicionais (CRAT), on the riverside at Rua da Reboleira 33–37 (Mon–Fri 10am–noon & 1–6pm, Sat & Sun 1–7pm) ☎223 320 076. It also stages temporary exhibitions, and runs week-long arts courses (around €75). More touristy are Canjirão, Rua Santo Ildefonso 215 ☎222 008 523; the Artesanato dos Clérigos, next to the tower at Rua da Assunção 33–34 ☎222 000 257, and Fernando Dias Santos at Rua dos Clérigos 45 ☎222 006 053. For designer objects (including items by architect Álvaro Siza, among others), seek out the Casa de Ferragens Carvalho e Baptista (☎223 392 122) on Rua do Almada 79–83.

Excursions and trips (see also "river cruises"). Diana Tours, Rua Francisco Alexandre Ferreira 96A, Vila Nova de Gaia (☎223 771 230, ☎223 791 508) runs: a two-hour combined cruise and trip by toy train at night in Porto (15 June–15 Sept only, daily except Sat; departs 9pm & 10pm from Gaia turismo office; €9); a one-hour bus trip around Porto with commentary in English (April–Sept daily departing from Sé at 9am, 11am, 3pm & 5pm, Sat & Sun 9am & 11am; €9); and a four-hour Porto and Gaia tour leaving from the turismo in Praça Dom João (Mon–Fri, 2.30pm; €29) which includes a port wine lodge visit. Rent-a-Cab tours will pick you up at your hotel and offer a variety of itineraries. Call ℡ 222 001 530 for information. The Mini-tren (March–Oct only; €5) departs from the Sé and includes a visit to Offley's port cellar ℡ 800 203 983.

Football The city's principal soccer team, Futebol Clube de Porto (℡ 225 570 400, ⓦ www.fcporto.pt), plays at the 60,000-capacity Estádio das Antas, off Av Fernão Magalhães; take buses #6 or #78 from Cordoaria. Boavista F.C. (℡ 226 071 000), whose Estádio do Bessa is on Rua 1º de Janeiro, off Av da Boavista, has recently been more successful (buses #3, #24 or #78, from the Cordoaria). With the European football Championships due to be held in Portugal in the summer of 2004, the stadia are due for renovation. FC Porto will move to an adjacent, and as yet unnamed, stadium after the competition.

Hospital Hospital Santo António, Largo Professor Abel Salazar ℡ 222 077 500 or 222 084 601. For emergencies call 112. Hospital Pedro Hispana on Rua Dr. Eduardo Torres ℡ 229 391 000 is in Matosinhos.

Internet cafés Portweb, Praça General Humberto Delgado 291, is a cheap internet café near the Câmara Municipal (€0.50/hr until 4pm, €1.20 thereafter; closed Sun). If you want to go online its best to arrive early as by the afternoon there is often a large waiting list. More expensive options exist inside the Rivoli theatre and at the Casa das Artes (p.314;€1.25/30min).

Left luggage The only coin-operated lockers are at Campanhã train station (€0.75/24hr; maximum 72 hours).

Library Biblioteca Pública Municipal, Jardim de São Lazaro, Rua Dom João IV ℡ 225 193 480 ℱ 225 193 488; Biblioteca Municipal Almeida Garrett, Rua D. Manuel II ℡ 226 057 000. Both have free, but restricted, internet access.

Maps A series of excellent regional topographic walking maps covering the whole of Portugal are published by the Instituto Geográfico do Exercito, and are available from Porto Editora (℡ 222 007 681), at Praça Filipa Lencastre 42. Prices begin at €6.

Markets The former fruit and flower market by Rua Ferreira Borges is now an exhibition space. There's a general daily market in the Mercado do Bolhão on Rua Sá da Bandeira, behind the main post office, a must for self-caterers and picnic buyers. On weekdays a fruit and veg market operates along the Cais da Ribeira. A weekly flea market is held on Sat mornings along Rua das Fontainhas down to Alameda das Fontaínhas, at the east end of Rua Alexandre Herculano overlooking the river. A few of the stalls sell fruit or home-made foods, but most have a spread of unremitting if fascinating junk. There's a summer flower market on Sun at Praça da Liberdade (April–Oct 9am–5pm).

Pharmacies Late-night and 24hr pharmacies (both called farmácias de serviço) operate on a rota basis. Details in the rear of the Jornal de Notícias, or call ℡ 118 for information.

Police Main headquarters of the Polícia de Segurança Pública do Porto (PSP) are at Rua Augusto Rosa, off Praça da Batalha, next to the Teatro Nacional de São João (℡ 222 088 518 or 222 055 558). There's a station at the southwest corner of the Mercado Ferreira Borges, Rua Mouzinho da Silveira. Call ℡ 118 for information.

Post office The main post office is opposite the town hall in Praça General Humberto Delgado (Mon–Fri 8am–9pm, Sat 9am–6pm); poste restante mail is held here, and you can also make international phone calls and use the internet.

River cruises (see also "Excursions and trips"). Short fifty-minute "five bridges" boat trips along the Douro leave from the Cais da Ribeira and Cais de Gaia in Vila Nova de Gaia (€7.50); details of schedules (much reduced in winter) are available from any turismo. Of these Via d'Douro, on the Gaia side (daily except 1–14 Jan) ℡ 229 388 816, ℱ 229 388 139 has the edge using a souped-up barco rabelo; it also runs one-day journeys to Peso da Régua and Entre-os-Rios. Longer trips are operated by Rota do Douro, Av Diogo Leite 250–2º, Vila Nova de Gaia ℡ 223 759 042, ℱ 223 759 043, who run one-day trips to Régua (€75), Pinhão (€88) and Entre-os-Rios (€65), and a two-day trip (€200). In summer, they also do a two-hour five bridges cruise at night (€7.50).

Swimming pools Piscina de Campanhã at Rua Dr. Sousa Ávides (℡ 225 372 041) and Piscinas da Constituição at Rua Almirante Leote do Rego (℡ 225 506 601); each has a gym as well. Better than either, but more expensive, is the pool at Clube Fluvial Portuense, Rua Clube Fluvial Portuense 13 (℡ 222 054 357), on the riverbank in Pasteleira district near the youth hostel on the way to Foz do Douro.

Telephones You can make international calls at the post office in Praça General Humberto Delgado and at the Telecom office in Praça da Batalha.

There's a further phone office at Praça Liberdade 62. Phonecards are widely available at kiosks and newsagents and card-phones can be found on most streets. Coin-phones are available, but many have an alarming habit of swallowing money without registering it.

Trains See "Arrival" p.287 for destinations from the various Porto stations. São Bento station information office (9am–8pm) has timetables for all trains routed from Campanhã; they can tell you the connection you'll need to make from São Bento.

Campanhã's own information office has the same hours. If you're leaving Porto on an international connection – Paris especially – in the summer, be sure to reserve a seat several days in advance. For general train information call ☎808 208 208 (8am–11pm).

Travel agencies Jumbo Expresso Viagens, Rua Ceuta 47 (☎223 393 320), is useful for budget/student travel. A good general travel agent is Star Turismo, at both Av dos Aliados 210 (☎222 050 695) and Rua Manuel II (☎226 067 251).

Around Porto: the coast

The coastline immediately **south of Porto** was once one of the worst polluted in Europe but, thanks to a major clean-up operation, many of the beaches have now been awarded **blue flag** status, indicating that they are safe to swim. For a list of the blue flag beaches in the area contact the turismo in Porto (see p.290), but if in doubt it is recommended that you don't swim until you reach **Espinho**, **Esmoriz** or, better still, **Cortegaça** or Furadouro. The coast **to the north** of the city is still not the cleanest, and you should certainly not swim off Matosinhos, the country's second largest port. However, press on a few kilometres further north to **Vila do Conde** or **Póvoa de Varzim** and you may well be tempted to stay; indeed, in summer, you might prefer to visit Porto while based at one of these resorts.

South of Porto

Access to the major resort of Espinho, Esmoriz and Cortegaça from Porto is either by **train** (hourly from São Bento) or **bus** (Auto Viação do Espinho departing from Rua Alexandre Herculano 366). En route it's well worth stopping at the small settlement of **MIRAMAR**, 10km south of Porto, to see the Capela do Senhor da Pedra, a seventeenth-century chapel bizarrely situated on a rocky, wave-beaten headland jutting out from the beach. The pleasant fishing village of **AGUDA**, two stops before Espinho on the train, has been transformed by the presence of a marine research station, on the coast just to the west of the train station. Of particular interest are a fishery museum documenting the change in fishing methods over the years, and including an impressive model of the town's fishing fleet; and the public aquarium (both daily 9am–6pm; €2.50 combined ticket), which gives a fascinating underwater profile of native marine life.

Espinho

ESPINHO, 18km south of Porto, is a decaying 1970s-style beach resort, littered with several modern, ugly, high-rise edifices. Windswept and deserted in the winter, hot and overcrowded in the summer, it has a feeling of a suburb rather than a town, with a casino, golf course, hordes of tourist shops, a dull grid of numbered rather than named streets and a railway line right through the centre. You'll find the **turismo** at Rua 6, no. 709 (June–Sept Mon–Fri 9am–9pm, Sat & Sun 10am–noon & 3–6pm; Oct–May Mon–Fri 9.30am–12.30pm & 2–5.30pm, Sat 9.30am–noon; ☎227 335 872). **Swimmers** might want to use the pool at the northern end of the esplanade; the Ministry of Health has blacklisted the Silvade beach to the south of town and, although a series of breakwaters has gone some way to alleviating pollution, it is still not a good idea to swim. **Surfing** is possible, however – get advice from Omni Surf Shop in the Centro Comercial California. If you'd rather steer clear of the water altogether, you can arrange **horseback** rides through the Sociedade Hípica de Espinho, Rua Professor Dias Afonso 129, Corredoura (☎227 344 958, ⓕ227 342 060).

Staying overnight is quite pricey but for a night in a dedicated beach resort there are various alternatives. The cheapest accommodation is the *Hotel Mar Azul*, Avenida 8, no. 676 (☎227 340 824, ⓕ227 312 636; ❷ or ❸ including breakfast), with comfortable rooms and reasonable facilities. Under the same management is the older *Residencial Espinho*, Rua 19, no. 326 (☎227 340 002, ⓕ227 312 636; ❸), which has a similar range of rooms at slightly higher prices. The plushest option is the modern, five-star *Hotel Solverde* at the northern end of town (☎227 313 144, ⓕ227 313 153; ❻), which has its own pool and health club as well as a casino, or try the eight-storey *Hotel Praia Golfe* on Rua 6 (☎227 331 000, ⓔpgolfe@mail.telepac.pt; ❻). There's a **campsite**, *Lugar dos Mochos* (☎227 343 718), inland, on the northern edge of town.

You'll have no problem finding somewhere to **eat**, but be aware that prices tend to increase the closer you get to the sea. The most famous place is *Casa Marreta* on the esplanade at Rua 2, nos. 1355–61, which serves excellent fish and seafood dishes. The *Casa do Pescador* in the fisherman's quarter at the southern end of town, just beyond Rua 2, is more basic but also does superlative seafood. There's surprisingly little to do in terms of **nightlife**. In summer you'll find a number of shoreline bars trying to attract clubbers, including *Disco Double O* near the swimming pool, but out of season it is something of a ghost town after 9pm. The casino at the *Solverde* (☎227 313 154) stages a tacky cabaret as well as temporary art exhibitions – a more worthy option is the **poetry recitals** held every Wednesday at 9.30pm at *Livramar*, Rua 62, no. 136 (☎227 314 705).

Esmoriz and Cortegaça

The beaches at **ESMORIZ** (6km south of Espinho) and **CORTEGAÇA** (a further 2km south) offer a restful contrast to Espinho, primarily because the road and railway start to move inland as they head further south. This leaves you a walk of a couple of kilometres or so to reach either beach. The beaches are backed by sand dunes and groves of pine and eucalyptus, although new developments are increasingly encroaching onto them; both also have all-year **campsites** – *Esmoriz* (☎256 752 709, ⓕ256 753 717) and *Cortegaça* (☎256 752 199, ⓕ256 755 177). Just to the north of Praia de Esmoriz there's a small lagoon – one of the reasons that the road and railway were forced inland in the first place – and here you can expect to see waders, ducks, herons and marsh harriers. From both Esmoriz and Cortegaça, frequent trains continue south to Aveiro (see p.236).

North of Porto

The stretch of coast around the mouth of the Douro is severely polluted, and you need to head beyond Cabo do Mundo to **VILA CHÃ**, 18km north of Porto, for a dip in the ocean. Despite increasing development, Vila Chã still retains a fishing village identity, and has a fine sandy beach with pools at low tide. There's a **campsite** at Praia de Vila Chã (☎229 283 163), Rua do Sol 150,

3km west of the station and well signposted from the main N13 road. Buses run frequently from Praça Filipa de Lencastre, to Vila Chã, before moving on to the larger resorts of Vila do Conde and Póvoa de Varzim.

Vila do Conde

VILA DO CONDE, 27km north of Porto, has become quite a significant resort over recent years, but the town has lost refreshingly little of its character in the process. The old part of Vila do Conde retains an active fishing port, and an atmospheric medieval quarter, which juts towards the sea beside the Rio Ave. For shoppers, a bustling Friday **market** sells everything from farm produce to shoes whilst the antiques market on the third Sunday of every month is rather more refined). The town's ship-building industry is amongst the oldest in Europe and traditional boat-making skills are still used to construct fishing boats reminiscent of fifteenth-century caravels. It was here that a replica of Bartolomeu Dias's caravel was constructed in 1987 as part of the 500th anniversary celebrations of his epic voyage around the Cape of Good Hope.

Much of the compact centre has survived intact, helped along by some excellent restoration work on buildings that other town councils might simply have demolished. The narrow cobbled alleys, beautiful town houses, whitewashed buildings and churches all make Vila do Conde an attractive place to wander. Dominating the **fishing quarter** is the white dome of the Capela do Socorro, built in 1603 and renovated in 1989. Inside, the *azulejos* depicting the Adoration of the Magi are notable for the presence of Moorish figures – further testament to the large population of Moors throughout Portugal who chose to stay and convert to Christianity during the Inquisition. Vila do Conde's narrow streets are at their best on **saints' days**, when the little street-corner votive chapels are illuminated by candles.

Overlooking everything, on a rise behind, is the enormous bulk of the **Convento de Santa Clara** (daily 9am–noon & 2–5.30pm), now a reformatory for boys but still open for visits: just knock on the door. One of the inmates will be designated to show you around its early Gothic church, which contains fine relief carvings, especially on the tombs of the founders. There's an elegant cloister, too, with a fountain fed by the long aqueduct – now partly ruined – which stretches from here into the hills. Below, back in the centre of town, the sixteenth-century **Igreja Matriz** is a beauty, with a soaring, airy interior and – thanks to the Basque workmen who helped with its construction – an unusual but very effective mix of Spanish and Portuguese styles. Like the Capela do Socorro, the church sports a distinctly Moorish dome.

Vila do Conde is also known for its lace – you can visit the **Bobbin lace-making school and museum** (Mon–Fri 9am–noon & 2–6pm, Sat & Sun 3–6pm; free) at Rua de São Bento 70, and there is work for sale in the turismo at Rua 5 de Outubro. If you have a particular interest in Portugal's regional crafts, there's a bonus in the town's annual **Feira Nacional de Artesanato** (crafts fair), held in the last week of July and the first week of August. Vila do Conde also boasts the **Museu Vivo da Comutação Manual** (Telephone Exchange Museum; Tues & Thurs 10am–noon & 2–4pm; free), on Rua Alberto Moreira Soutelo, which, unsurprisingly, claims to be the only one of its kind in Europe. The **Casa de José Régio**, at Avenida José Régio 132 (Tues–Sat 10am–12.30pm & 2–6pm, Sun 2.30–6pm), is also worth a visit, displaying popular art collected by this famous writer. The **Auditório Municipal** shows temporary exhibitions of photography and local arts and crafts as well as film, theatre and dance; it's housed in the renovated eighteenth-century Casa dos Vasconcelos on Praça da República (Tues–Fri 3–11pm, Sat & Sun 3pm–

midnight) and also has a pleasant bar to recommend it further. For cinephiles, there's a six-day short-film festival held here (Festival Internacional de Curtas Metragens), which begins on the first Sunday of July.

The town's newest attraction is the fascinating **Life Science Centre** (Tues–Sun 10am–6pm; €2.50) on Avenida Bernardino Machado 96, about five minute's walk north of the river in the centre. Worth a visit for its bizarrely shaped glass-roofed building alone, it offers a series of themed interactive and educational exhibits in English and Portuguese that will appeal to children and curious adults, as well as free internet access.

Vila do Conde's **beaches** (and all their attendant development) are a couple of kilometres west of town. Here, long stretches of fine sand, with drinks, kiosks and restaurants to hand, have been steadily developed right up the coast to become gradually swamped by the shameless commercialism of Póvoa do Varzim. **Guia** and **Cadeira** are the nearest places to swim, both a fifteen-minute walk from the centre with calm waters and a stumpy fortification – the Forte de São João (now a luxury hotel) – between the two. For a totally different tune, and in stark contrast to the largely peaceful air that prevails through the rest of the year, the revving of racing cars can be heard in the first weekend of June and the second weekend of July, as Vila do Conde gears up for the annual **car races** held in the town – streets are sheathed in red and white crash barriers and the beach sprouts grandstands.

Practicalities

Up to six daily Linhares and Auto-Viação **buses** from Porto arrive (and depart from) opposite the smaller **turismo** in Rua 5 de Outubro (Tues–Fri 10am–7pm, Mon & Sat 10am–1pm & 3–7pm, Sun 3–6pm; ☎252 642 700). This branch has only limited information, but the **main** turismo, an attractive ivy-clad house, is just around the corner on Rua 25 de April 103 (Oct–Apr Mon–Fri 9am–6pm Sat–Sun 2.30–5.30pm; May–Sep Mon–Fri 9am–6pm Sat–Sun 10am–1pm & 2.30–6pm; ☎252 248 473, ℱ252 248 422). Both turismos have free maps, but the latter is the best for information about accommodation and day trips in the region. There are 5–10 daily Linhares buses between Vila do Conde and Santo Tirso, and hourly services (Auto-Viação do Minho and Linhares) from and to Viana do Castelo. The train station is now defunct, although the town will be linked to Porto as part of the metro system that is expected to be operational by the end of 2004.

Vila do Conde has a wide selection of **accommodation** to fit every budget, but at peak times the rooms fill quickly. In the summer, if you haven't booked ahead, you will probably need to contact the main turismo for their list of private **rooms** (❶). The nearest **campsite** (☎252 633 225, ℱ252 643 593) is 3km south of town, on Rua do Cabreiro near the beach at Árvore.

Estalagem do Brasão Avenida Dr. João Canavarro ☎252 642 016, ℮estralagem-brazao@mail.telepac.pt. Lovely four-star hotel set in a seventeenth-century town house with period furnishings. ❺

Forte de São João Avenida Brasil ☎222 240 600, ℮info@hotelfortesjoao.com. Newly converted from the town's pentagonal fortress, this small luxury hotel offers various-sized, comfortable en-suite rooms. ❽

Residencial Manco D'Areia Praça da República 84 ☎ & ℱ252 631 748. Recently renovated with a mixed bag of rooms: some are rather dingy, while the front ones have nice views over the river. Rooms with shared bathroom are slightly cheaper. ❸

Pensão Patarata Cais das Lavandeiras 18 ☎252 631 894. Pleasant *pensão* with big, airy rooms in a nice location overlooking the waterfront. ❸

Pensão Princesa do Ave Rua Dr. António José Sousa Pereira 261 ☎252 642 065, ℱ252 632 972. An excellent cheap option with satellite TV in every room. ❷

Hotel Sant'Ana Monte de Sant'Ana ☎252 641

717, ✉ hotel.santana@clix.pt. On the south side of the river by the bridge, all the rooms in this friendly hotel have en-suite bathrooms and river-view balconies; there's also an indoor swimming pool, sauna and solarium. ❸

Hospedaria Venceslau Corner of Rua das Mós and Rua 5 de Outubro ☎252 646 362. Modern, comfortable rooms, most with TVs. Some way from the town centre but conveniently located for the beaches. ❷

Le Villageois Praça da República 94 ☎252 631 119. Above the restaurant of the same name. Easily the best budget option in town with clean, well-furnished, en-suite rooms, although some lack windows. The restaurant is excellent too. ❶

Of the **restaurants**, the most established is the one at *Le Villageois* (closed Mon), a pretty place serving huge portions (with skate a speciality) and with a few tables outside. Expensive but certainly recommended is *Restaurante São Roque* in Rua do Lidador 128 (closed Mon); while more reasonable is the *Restaurante Rendilheira* at Cais dos Lavandeiras 48, where regional specialities are served up within an odd modern art decor. Also good, with a value-for-money *prato do dia* (€6), is *Restaurante Ramon* (closed Tues), near the small turismo in Rua 5 de Outubro. The unnamed café at Rua de Santo Amaro 6, three doors down from the Casa de José Régio, used to be the favourite haunt of Régio and other artistic dissidents, and is still a good place for food at reasonable prices.

There's not much **nightlife** to speak of, though *Tota Bar* – next to the *Estalagem do Brasão* on Avenida Dr. João Canavarro – is packed most nights from around 10pm. Try also *Danalf*, Rua de São Bento, which has a more studenty feel, or *Café Concerto* piano bar (7pm–2am), rather oddly placed in the Centro Municipal de Juventude on Avenida João Graça. Live music (anything from grunge to salsa) can be found at *Azenha Dom Zameiro Bar* (Thurs–Sat), a 3km taxi ride out of town at Ponte d'Ave, Vilarinho.

Póvoa do Varzim

PÓVOA DO VARZIM is about 4km to the north of Vila do Conde (frequent buses along the main highway and coast road) but the two couldn't be more different. Although Póvoa, too, retains a small harbour, along with the ruins of an eighteenth-century fortress, it is very much a resort, aimed firmly at beach-loving sun-worshippers. A casino and a line of concrete hotels open onto the 8km-long **beach** (partly pebbly, so bring flip-flops or sandals), which is crowded throughout the year with Portuguese holidaymakers. The local council seems well aware of Póvoa's shortcomings and has embarked on a series of projects to prettify the town, such as the state-of-the-art fountains in the Largo do Passeio near the *Grande Hotel*, which "dance" to music during the summer.

That said, the crowds help to create a lively, enjoyable seaside feel, restaurants are plentiful and excellent value, there's plenty of nightlife, and there usually seems to be enough accommodation to go round. If you feel the need for culture, check out the **Museu Municipal de Etnografia e História**, on Rua Visconde de Azevedo (Tues–Sun 10am–12.30pm & 2.30–6pm; €1), which has well-presented displays of local archeological finds, including some from Terroso (see p.323), as well as an exhaustive collection of anything and everything connected to local seafaring through the ages.

An international classical music festival is held here in July, and there is a series of traditional **festivals** throughout the summer, the best of which is the Romaria de Nossa Senhora da Assunção on August 15, when local fishermen carry life-sized images of Our Lady of the Assumption to the quayside to bless those who have perished at sea; the whole event is accompanied by fireworks let off from fishing boats. A similar event occurs at the end of September for Our Lady of Sorrows. Monthly details of cultural events are listed in the *Agenda Municipal*, available at the turismo. A wander down to the **marina** will allow you to cast a jealous eye over the yachts moored there, but it is also the venue of frequent events and activities aimed at tourists. Ask at the turismo for details.

Practicalities

The helpful **turismo** (July 15–Sept 15 daily 9am–9pm; Sept 16–July 14 Mon–Fri 9am–1pm & 2–7pm, Sat & Sun 9.30am–1pm & 2.30–6pm; ☎252 298 120, ℱ252 617 870), in an unusual turreted building on Praça Marquês de Pombal on the way in from Vila do Conde, has maps, lists of rooms, and a leaflet detailing bus timetables. **Buses** operate from the central Praça do Almada the more out of the way Central do Camiomagem on Rua de D. Maria I, north of the centre. Trains are out of action until the town is linked to Porto's forthcoming metro system, officially scheduled to be completed by the end of 2004. The beach can be reached from almost anywhere in town by simply heading east, with all roads eventually funnelling towards the coastal Avenida dos Banhos. You can **rent cars** from OTM on Rua Dr. Leonardo Coimbra (☎252 682 240) and Atlas on Avenida Vasco da Gama (☎252 682 922). **Bicycles** can be hired in summer from people who hang around the north end of the port at the south end of Passeio Alegre.

There are plenty of smart hotels around, while cheaper **pensões** are to be found mostly along Rua Paulo Barreto, which is the main Porto road and runs from Praça do Almada to Praça Marquês de Pombal, next to the market. The best inexpensive option is *Hospedaria Jantarada*, Rua Paulo Barreto 8 (☎252 622 789; ❷), clean, friendly and above a popular restaurant. *Residencial Gett*, on the tree-lined Avenida Mouzinho de Albuquerque 54 (☎252 683 206, ℮ residencial.gett@clix.pt; ❸), is a pleasant, modern place, with friendly and efficient staff and satellite TV in all rooms, while *Pensão Avô Velino*, Avenida Vasco da Gama 15 (☎252 681 628; ❸), is a bit out of the way, on the Viana road, but otherwise a good choice. Functional but charmless comfort can be had at *Hotel Luso-Brasileiro*, Rua dos Cafés 16 (☎252 690 710, ℱ252 690 719; ❸), 100m from the beach. If you want somewhere with a swimming pool, your only choice is the expensive and ugly *Novotel Vermar*, a high-rise complex on Rua da Imprensa Regional, 2km north on the seafront (☎252 298 900, ⓦ www.novotel.com; ❺). The nearest **campsite** is the *Orbitur* at Rio Alto, 8km to the north (☎252 615 699; open all year).

Póvoa is endowed with well over fifty **restaurants** ranging from Chinese to seafood or pizzas; most are within a block or two of the seafront. If you're into fish, Póvoa is a treat – there's huge choice and the competition keeps prices keen. The local speciality is *pescada à poveira* (slices of boiled whiting served with turnip leaves, eggs, potatoes and bread soused in olive oil, onion and paprika), while the adventurous might seek out *buchos de pescada* (boiled whiting stomachs stuffed with chopped whiting liver, onion and parsley), best eaten with olives. Good places for seafood include the *São José* on Largo do Passeio Alegre 118, which also has a fine view, the *31 de Janeiro* on the Rua of the same name, which is otherwise strong on grills, or the *Belo Horizonte* at Tenente Valadim 63, which serves a great *açorda de marisco* (seafood soup). Alternatively, sample the local atmosphere and excellent marinated sardines and fish stews at the *Adega Firmino* at Rua Caetano de Oliveira 100, two blocks back from the beach off Avenida Mouzinho de Albuquerque. More sophisticated is *Brook's* on Praça Dom João XXIII (closed Sun), serving a wide variety of grilled fish, kid goat and other meats.

The liveliest **bars** are the youthful *J.B.* on Rua Caetano de Oliveira, *IT Bar* on Avenida dos Banhos and *Enseada Café* on Passeio Alegre, in front of the *Grande Hotel*. The best **disco** is at *Novotel Vermar*, which hots up on Fridays and Saturdays. No surprises at the **Casino da Póvoa**, Avenida da Braga (nightly dinner 8.30pm, floor show 11pm; ☎252 615 151), situated at the southern end of the esplanade – it's the usual concoction of tacky cabaret shows and games (minimum bet €1), but its known countrywide and for many it remains the main reason to visit the town.

Around Póvoa de Varzim

There are four reasonably accessible sites located in or near villages close to Póvoa, which, given a spare day and rented bikes, or a car, would make a rewarding circuit – maps and information leaflets are available from the turismo in Póvoa de Varzim. **LAÚNDOS**, 7km to the northeast, is notable for the windmills which stand on São Félix hill. Further on is **RATES**, boasting a splendid eleventh-century Romanesque church (São Pedro) built by the Benedictines in granite for Henry, Count of Burgundy, supposedly on the site of the martyrdom of the first Bishop of Braga. The three naves are timber-roofed while, inside, a series of fine pillars with carved capitals are lit by a colourful rose window. **RIO MAU**, 8km east of Póvoa, is the site of a smaller, but even better decorated, Romanesque church (São Cristovão), also granite and completed in 1151. The carvings on the capitals are reminiscent of those in Braga cathedral and, in this case, are thought to illustrate the Song of Roland, a medieval French epic glorifying Charlemagne (Charles the Great).

The oldest of the settlements on this circuit is **TERROSO**, just 5km northeast of Póvoa de Varzim. A *citânia* similar to the better-known ones at Sanfins (see p.324) and Briteiros (see p.361) was excavated at the beginning of this century and the double ring of ramparts can still be traced. The spring here once fed the eighteenth-century aqueduct which carried water over 999 arches to the Convento de Santa Clara in Vila do Conde (see p.319).

Santo Tirso and around

Travelling **northeast** from Porto towards the southern Minho towns of Guimarães and Braga, you pass through attractive, rolling countryside: a mix of market gardening in the valleys, vines on the gentle slopes, and wooded hill tops. The textile town of Santo Tirso is the minor capital of this area, a riverside town which serves as a base for visiting the Romanesque church at nearby Roriz and the *citânia* of Sanfins de Ferreira.

Santo Tirso

Just under 30km northeast of Porto, **SANTO TIRSO** lies on the steep southern bank of the River Ave, which flows west to meet the sea at Vila do Conde. At the foot of the slope, by the bridge linking the town to its train station, is the former Benedictine monastery and church of São Bento, which now houses an agricultural college and a small **municipal museum** (Mon–Fri 9am–12.30pm & 2–6pm, Sat 2.30–6pm). This is less than gripping, fielding the usual motley collection of local archeological finds, but take the opportunity to visit the church, whose cloister features a fine double row of galleries dating from the fourteenth century. On the plateau cresting the slope is the town hall, a charmless concrete block; the **turismo** (Mon–Fri 9am–12.30pm & 2–5.30pm; ☎252 830 411) occupies an ugly tiled annexe, and provides a series of leaflets detailing walks in the surrounding area.

Santo Tirso is served by Linhares **buses** from Póvoa (8–18 daily, more in summer), and Mondinense and Landim buses from Porto; both drop you at the station on Rua Infante Dom Henrique. You're unlikely to need to stay – **accommodation**, in any case, is limited and expensive – but if you do, try the homely *Pensão Caroço* at Largo Coronel Baptista Coelho 48 (☎252 852 823; ❷), or the more expensive *Pensão Carvalhais*, in the ugly modern block at the top of town on Praça Rodrigues Ferreira (☎252 857 910; ❸).

Roriz

RORIZ, 10km east of Santo Tirso, is much prettier, but poorly served by public transport. Any bus on the Santo Tirso–Guimarães route can set you down just after Rebordões, leaving a 4km walk to the church of São Pedro, at the top of the village.

The village itself is a mixture of old, rough granite cottages, whitewashed houses and several fairly kitsch creations built by returned emigrants – one is straight out of Disneyland, a Seven Dwarfs' cottage with brown concrete thatch. The date of the elegant Romanesque **Igreja de São Pedro** is disputed, but it's said to stand on the foundations of a Roman temple, later destroyed by the Moors. It was originally the church of the Benedictine monastery that once stood alongside, of which only one building still stands – and that's in private hands. The fine west door is embellished with an early Gothic rose window, adjacent to the solitary bell tower.

The Citânia de Sanfins de Ferreira

Another 4km beyond the Igreja de São Pedro, along a track through shady woods and up a gentle slope (badly signposted), are the ruins of the Celtic **Citânia de Sanfins de Ferreira** (Mon–Fri 9am–6pm, Sat & Sun 10am–7pm; free), dating from the second century BC. It's a splendidly atmospheric place – perched atop its hill, the skyline to the south appears infinite and even at the height of summer, the only sound is that of the broom pods popping out their seeds. Though smaller than Briteiros, Sanfins is no less impressive, with several rings of protective walls and the foundations of 160 circular huts, arranged in family compounds and separated by wide streets. One of the compounds (the *núcleo familiar* or "family nucleus") has been rebuilt, complete with thatched roof. If you want to go inside, ask for the guardian at the café next to the site, who has the key. He's also happy to show you the site's other attractions – a replica *basto* statue of a warrior (the original is in the archeological museum in Lisbon) standing guard on the crest of the hill, and the ruins of a bathhouse at one of the sources of the Rio Leça, whose engraved *pedras formosas* ("beautiful stones") are housed in the site **museum**, a glorious seventeenth-century Baroque mansion inconveniently located 3km out of Sanfins, 1km from the village of Sanfins de Ferreira (summer Tues–Sun 10am–noon & 2–6pm; winter Tues–Sun 10am–noon & 2–5pm; free). Aside from the *pedras*, and a much older slab engraved with a hunting scene, the museum's other draws include three gravestones engraved with Celtic crosses, identical to those found in Ireland.

Porto to Penafiel

One of the surviving northern inland train routes – the **Douro railway line** (Linha do Douro) – heads east, out of Porto, although for the initial 40km it runs alongside the Rio Sousa and not the Rio Douro. If you're on one of the slow trains, it will stop at Cête, a dozen stations out of Porto and just a kilometre or so away from the village of **PAÇO DE SOUSA**, which can also be reached by bus from Penafiel (Mon–Fri 6 daily, Sat 2 daily). This was the former headquarters of the Benedictines in Portugal and, set beside the Rio Sousa, is a popular picnic spot for Porto locals.

The principal sight, inevitably, is the old **abbey church**, a dank and dark medieval building. In one corner is the **tomb of Egas Moniz**, tutor and adviser to the first king of Portugal, Afonso Henriques, and a great figure of loyalty in Portuguese history. In 1127, shortly after Afonso Henriques had broken away from his grandfather, the king of León, Egas was sent to negotiate a settlement, thus enabling Afonso to concentrate his efforts on defeating the Moors in the south. Within three years, the king of León considered the treaty to be broken on the Portuguese side and threatened all-out war. Egas made his way to León, presented himself and his family and, as can be seen on the panels around the tomb, offered to receive the punishment due to his master. Impressed by his loyalty, mercy was granted and the king sent the minister home unscathed.

There are a couple of **cafés** in the village and an excellent old-fashioned *adega*, O Moleira, which serves wine straight from the barrel. You'll find plenty of possible **camping** spots but should you prefer a bed, it's not much further down the line to Penafiel.

Penafiel and around

At Penafiel, 35km from Porto, you enter *vinho verde* country. The wine's origins lie with the Benedictine monks, who were famed in this region for their laborious terracing of the valley slopes. A further legacy of the Benedictine presence is a dozen of the finest **Romanesque churches** in the country, each gorgeously sited in hamlets hidden away in folds of the countryside. South of Penafiel, the Barragem de Torrão offers excellent swimming opportunities, or there's the more relaxing option of a river trip from Torrão itself.

Penafiel

Despite the motorway in the Sousa valley to the west, **PENAFIEL** itself is still split by main road traffic, around which most of the attractions are conveniently situated. The train station, 3km down the hill, was undergoing renovation at the time of writing. Although the station itself is still in operation, the local bus service that once linked it to the town has been suspended indefinitely. It is possible to walk to the town from the station, although it's hard going as much of it is uphill and along main roads; much the best option is to take a taxi (around €4) from the station car park. If coming from Porto, it's preferable to arrive by bus, which stops by the kiosk outside Penafiel's central turismo and further along by the Igreja Matriz. The town itself, known as Arrifana de Sousa until 1770, is a pretty place with a laid-back atmosphere and a fabulous local **wine**. You'll find it everywhere in bottles but to get it straight from the *cuba* (barrel) you'll either have to go to the *adega* near the train station or to the charming **Quinta da Aveleda** (Mon–Fri 9.15–11.30am & 1–4.30pm; €3), where the stuff is made. To get there, go 2km down the Porto road, cross the motorway and turn right at the sign – it's 1km further on from this point. Their guided tours include wine and cheese tasting, and the gardens are delightful. Next to the turismo building on Avenida Sacadura Cabral, the **Museu Municipal de Penafiel** (Mon–Fri 9.30am–noon & 2–5.30pm, Sat 9.30am–12.30pm) is worth a brief visit for its archeological and ethnological displays, mainly from the Celtic *castro* (fortified hilltop settlement) site at Mozinho, as well as some wonderful gold bracelets. The collection is small but attractively laid out with eerie mannequins dressed in traditional farming attire bringing the displays to life.

Practicalities

Accommodation is limited but a complete list is available from the turismo. The best options are the good-value, friendly *Casa João da Lixa* (℡255 213 158; ❶) in Largo do Padre Américo; *O Cedro*, Rua do Cedro (℡255 213 551; ❷); and the *Penahotel* (℡255 711 420, 🅕255 711 425; ❸) in Parque do Sameiro, opposite the modern Santuário de Nossa Senhora da Piedade. If you are interested in exploring the area's churches, call in at the **turismo** at Avenida Sacadura Cabral 90 (Mon–Fri 9am–12.30pm & 2–5.30pm; ℡255 712 561), and ask them to mark the locations on a map. They have a small collection of leaflets in English, although many of these are now seriously out of date. Beneath the turismo, there's a fine covered **market** (Mon–Sat). Just downhill from here, at Rua Engenheiro Matos 67, *Restaurante Relógio do Sol* serves good **food** (for around €7.50 a head) and has a fine view over the Sousa valley. *Churrasqueira Central* on Avenida Sacadura Cabral between the turismo and Igreja Matriz has tasty grilled chicken, and *O Cedro*'s *Churrascaria,* next to the *residencial*, is an equally lively place to eat. Popular **bars** include *Momentos* at Rua Zeferino de Oliveira 29, and for occasional live music, *Bar Jar d'Agua* at Avenida Sacadura Cabral next to Nova Rede bank.

For **onward transport**, VALPI runs buses to Amarante and Porto from its garage near the Igreja da Misericórdia; Santos, for services to Boelhe and Termas de São Vicente, has an office at Avenida Egas Moniz 69–71; and Asa Douro at no. 125 operates services to Torrão and Paço de Sousa.

South of Penafiel

The local **churches** are most easily reached by hire car. Although buses run to most areas of interest, they invariably leave at inconvenient times, making it difficult to visit more than one or two in a day. The most accessible by bus (Mon–Fri 6 daily) from Penafiel is at **BOELHE**, some 10km southeast along the N312 minor road to Entre-os-Rios. São Gens is reputedly the smallest Romanesque church in the country: a simple building, without much architectural detail, which gains its power from a stunning position on the brow of a hill overlooking the Tâmega valley. If it's closed, ask for the key at the nearest house. Note that the last bus back to Penafiel leaves Boelhe at 2.05pm. At **ABRAGÃO** (buses Mon–Fri 7 daily, Sat–Sun 2–3 daily, last bus to Penafiel 6pm), 10km southeast along the N320 from Penafiel, all that survives of the Igreja de São Pedro is the vaulted chapel and transept arch with its rose window, while the Igreja de São Salvador or Cabeça Santa (Holy Head) at **GANDRA** (buses approximately every half hour from 6am, last bus to Penafiel 9.05pm, 8.45pm at weekends), east off the N106 midway between Penafiel and Torrão, gets its name from the holy skull that used to be kept there.

A trip easily made by bus from Penafiel is to the tiny spa town of **TERMAS DE SÃO VICENTE** about 5km further along the N312 from Boelhe, where it meets the main N106. En route you'll pass the **Barragem de Torrão** and its reservoir (see below). The turn-of-the-century spa has all the usual treatments but hours vary so check with the turismo in Penafiel before setting out. The last bus back leaves at 5.25pm or you can stay overnight in one of the good self-contained rooms at the *Pensão Regional* (☎255 615 036; ❶).

Five kilometres from here, south along the N106, Entre-os-Rios faces **TORRÃO** across the confluence of the Douro and Tâmega. Buses regularly make the journey from Penafiel to Torrão (Mon–Fri 7 daily) and the last one back leaves at 6pm. A good way to see some of the area is to take a **river trip** from Torrão (daily at 4pm & 5pm; 1hr; €7.50), operated by the Quinta dos Agros (☎255 581 473): cross back over the bridge towards Entre-os-Rios, bear right and then turn right at the war monument – it's at the bottom of the road. Should you want to stay overnight, the best choice is the *Casa Defronte*, a beautiful town house on the N108 in Entre-os-Rios (☎255 613 484; ❸), offering simple but comfortable stone-walled rooms and an ideal base from which to explore the area on foot.

The Tâmega: Amarante and beyond

At **LIVRAÇÃO**, about an hour east from Porto, the Tâmega train line cuts off for Amarante (see below), hugging the ravine of the **Rio Tâmega**, a tributary of the Douro. There is scarcely more than the station at Livração, so if you're intending to change trains, keep your eyes open. The Tâmega line trains – quaint, single carriage, tram-like contraptions – terminate at Amarante, from where four buses daily run up into the Serra do Marão – following the course of the Rio Tâmega – to **Celorico de Basto** and on to the next crossroads at Fermil, where a local bus picks up passengers for **Mondim de Basto**. To really explore the valley though, the best idea is to take a bus to Celorico and walk along the overgrown tracks to Mondim: a pleasant two-hour hike, through woods and over viaducts.

If your time is limited, the half-hour trip from Livração to Amarante is worthwhile in itself. From the start it's an impressive, scenic ride, with pine woods and vines clinging to steep slopes, and goats scrambling across the steep terrace walls to nibble at haystacks hanging from the branches of trees. For the most part it is a stunning journey, although the new motorway running alongside part of the rail line has tempered it somewhat.

Amarante

AMARANTE is immaculately set in a gorge of the Tâmega River, with the wooden balconies of its old houses leaning over the water. Much of the history of the town revolves around the thirteenth-century hermit **Gonçalo**, later to become São Gonçalo. He is credited with just about everything positive about the town and most of the attractions bear his name or have some link to him. It's a fine place to stop, with innumerable bars and cafés along the south side of the **river** and a wide choice of good value accommodation. Sadly, the polluted river beaches can no longer be recommended for swimming – though in summer you'll see some brave souls risking it – but *guigas* (pedal boats) or rowing boats can be hired for an hour or two's dawdling and there's a swimming pool complex on the south bank with enough slides and water chutes to keep kids and adults happy for a while. Just past the pool, on the south side of

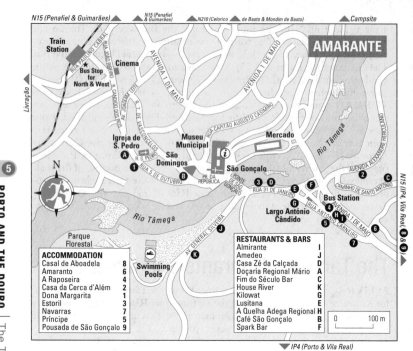

the river, is the peaceful, forested **Parque Florestal** which makes the perfect spot for a picnic. There's also a year-round Wednesday and Saturday morning **market** held beside the river.

The church and former monastery of **São Gonçalo**, beside the very elegant town bridge, is Amarante's most prominent monument. Legend has it that the church marks the spot where Gonçalo's hermitage once stood, although it is almost certainly much older. It formed the heart of an ancient fertility cult – probably with pagan origins – which still persists here at the grand **Romaria de São Gonçalo**, celebrated on the first weekend (Fri–Sun) in June, with the large Sunday procession being the highlight of the festivities. At this time, traditionally, the local unmarried youth exchange phallic cakes as tokens of their love. In the church, the saint's tomb is said to guarantee a quick marriage to anyone who touches it – his face, hands and feet have been almost worn away by hopeful suitors. In another chapel, devoted to Gonçalo's healing miracles, the practice is to offer wax models of every conceivable part of the body along with entire artificial limbs and bottles full of gallstones, although the offerings are removed at the end of each day. Alongside São Gonçalo is another interesting Baroque church with a grand tower – **São Domingos** – which contains a small museum of sacred art (free entry).

Around the side of the church, in the cloister of the former monastery, is the town's municipal library and the **Museu Municipal Amadeo de Souza Cardoso** (Tues–Sun 10am–12.30pm & 2–5.30pm; €1). Dominated by the Cubist works of local boy Amadeo de Souza Cardoso (1887–1918), one of the few Portuguese painters to achieve international renown, this is a surprising exhibition to find out in the sticks. Work by modern painters is displayed in the mini-gallery.

Bridge over troubled water

The north and south parts of town are linked by the **Ponte São Gonçalo**, scene of a heroic stand-off in spring 1809 between the Portuguese, under General Francisco da Silveira, and the retreating French, under Marshall Sault. Fleeing Porto, having lost their brief tenure of Portugal, the French were ransacking villages along the way but when they reached Amarante they met with unexpected resistance. The bravery of the Portuguese army held up the French at the bridge, temporarily halting their rampage and allowing the people of the town to escape to safety. For two weeks there was a stalemate but on the night of May 2, under cover of darkness, the French planted explosives close to the Portuguese lines. The resulting explosions eventually caused enough panic to allow the French to cross the bridge and continue their plundering, but by then the people were safe. Today, canvases hanging inside the church still bear French bayonet marks from soldiers searching for treasure that may have been hidden behind.

For **regional crafts**, Artesania, in Rua Teixeira de Vasconselos, is a good shop, selling shoes, rugs, weavings, and even string instruments.

Practicalities

The **train station** is ten minutes' walk northwest of the centre, while **buses** pull in a little closer but on the other side of the river at the bus station on Rua Antonio Carneiro. When leaving Amarante for the north and west buses leave from outside the train station on Rua Paulino Antonio Cabral. For information, and help with accommodation during summer when rooms can be hard to come by, head for the **turismo** (daily 9am–12.30pm & 2–5.30pm; ☏255 420 246, ℗362 420 203), housed in the Câmara Municipal, next to the Museu Municipal.

Accommodation

There's a good range of **accommodation** in Amarante itself, as well as some lovely *turismo rural* places in the area – ask at the turismos for details. The municipal **campsite** is on the river bank 1.5km upstream at Penedo da Rainha (☏255 437 630).

Residencial A Raposeira Largo António Cândido 53 ☏255 432 221. Clean and comfortable en-suite accommodation above a good cheap restaurant; back rooms have great views over the river. Very close to the central bus station, though surprisingly quiet. Breakfast included. ❶

Casal de Aboadela 9km east of town along the N15 at Aboadela ☏255 441 141. A homely, good-value farmhouse with central heating, log fires and some self-catering apartments (minimum 2-night stay for the latter). ❸

Hotel Residencial Amaranto Av 1º de Maio ☏255 410 840 ℮hotelamaranto@mail.telepac.pt. Large, modern and rather uninspiring hotel and restaurant on the south side of river, with satellite TV and air conditioning in all rooms. ❸

Casa da Cerca d'Além Av Alexandre Herculano, 200m east of the new bridge ☏255 431 449. The

most atmospheric lodgings in town in a converted manor house on the south bank of the Tâmega: beautifully decorated with antique furniture and boasting magnificent views. ❸

Albergaria Dona Margarita Rua Cândido dos Reis 53 ☏255 432 110, ℗255 437 977. Comfortable and pleasantly situated overlooking the river, this hotel was once the budget mainstay but has acquired some pretensions after a renovation, as well as kitchens in all its rooms. ❸

Residencial Estoril Rua 31 de Janeiro 49 ☏255 431 291, ℗255 431 892. A friendly place by the old bridge, and a good choice for budget accommodation. Back rooms have superb views of the river. ❷

Hotel Navarras Rua António Carneiro, beyond the *Príncipe* on the south side of the river ☏255 431 036, ℗255 432 991. A friendly, modern option with a good restaurant. ❸

Residencial Príncipe Largo António Cândido 53, on the south side ℡255 432 956. Cheap option in the modern part of town near the bus station, the front rooms here have balconies, although the views aren't up to much. ➊

Pousada de São Gonçalo Curva do Lancete, Ansiães ℡255 461 113, ℻255 461 353.

Twenty kilometres east of Amarante and just off the IP4 to Vila Real. Perched on a clifftop, the views over the nearby Serra do Marão (walking trips can be arranged) are unbeatable. However, the service sometimes fails to live up to expectations. ➎

Eating, drinking and nightlife

Local specialities include *empadas de frango* (chicken pasties) and *cozido à portuguesa* (boiled meats), but the town is most famous for its **egg pastries**: the charming *Doçaria Regional Mário* on Rua Cândido dos Reis (℡255 433 044) has the lot. For something more substantial to eat, Amarante has a number of good **restaurants**, most clustered on the south bank of the river, around the bus station. The well-spiced dishes at *A Quelha Adega Regional*, immediately south of the bus station on Rua de Olivença, are a meat-eater's dream, especially when washed down with jugs of the rich local wine. A little further north on Largo António Cândido, is *Almirante* an upmarket place specializing in shellfish. Almost adjacent to the bus station itself and below the *residencial* of the same name is *Restaurante A Raposeira*, which serves huge portions of basic fare at very reasonable prices. Heading towards the river on Rua Cândido dos Reis is *Kilowat*, a good cheap *tasca* with hams hanging from the roof and main meals for under €5, while on the river itself at Rua 31 de Janeiro, *Lusitana* is well worth a visit – try the *bacalhau à Narcisa* or roast veal – on the river terrace. *Casa Zé da Calçada,* also on Rua 31 de Janeiro, is a little closer to the bridge. It too has a river terrace and is decidedly pricey, but worth every euro for its friendly service, local specialities and excellent wine list. Across the bridge, *Café São Gonçalo*, on Praça da República alongside the church, serves reasonably priced evening food and has outdoor tables for drinks and snacks.

For **nightlife**, try any of the bars and discos on the south side of the river, whose riverside terraces stay open till late in summer. Currently popular places are *House River* and *Amedeo* on Avenida General Silveira, *Spark Bar* on Avenida Alexandre Herculano, and *Fim do Século Bar* at Caminho de Santo António.

Into the Serra do Marão:
the Basto villages

Beyond Amarante you really feel the climb into the **Serra do Marão** on the approach to the towns of Celorico and Mondim de Basto, both set astride the Tâmega with the Serra do Alvão rising immediately to the east. To the north – and technically in the Minho region – is the larger, provincial town of Cabeceiras de Basto, which provides a useful transport link to Braga and then the Peneda-Gerês national park (see Chapter Six). Together, these three towns and their districts form the **Terras de Basto**, a region of fertile countryside that produces a strong *vinho verde*. The name ("basto" meant "I claim") comes from a group of Celtic statues, symbols of power which were laid horizontally on warrior's graves and have been found in several local spots. Beautifully incised with Celtic emblems on its torso and the shield placed on its belly, one of the finest of these is in the Museu de Arqueologia in Lisbon (see p.99).

Celorico to Mondim de Basto

Thirty kilometres northeast of Amarante, **CELORICO DE BASTO** is proud of its neatly laid out lawns, formal flowerbeds, sweeping views into the Serra do Alvão and annual round of festivals: **Festa de São Tiago** (July 23–25), **Feira de São Caetano** (August 7), **Romaria de São Bartolomeu** (August 24) and **Feira de Santa Catarina** (November 25). Celorico de Basto has only a single **pensão** – the *Progresso* – in Praça Albino Alves Perreira (☎255 321 170; ●), and there's an excellent **restaurant** 1km north of town, the *Quinta do Forno*, set in an old farmhouse and specializing in homebred *vitela* (veal). For a brief foray into the woods, a labyrinth of paths head off from behind the village church, while in the distance lies the prospect of Monte Farinha, the highest peak in the region (see p.332). The mountain is more easily approached from the village of Mondim de Basto, which is accessible from Celorico on frequent Mondinense buses (the station is 200m north of Pensão Progresso).

On the main road, halfway between Celorico and Mondim, lies the small, pleasant village of **Fermil**; buses on their way between Cabeceiras and Amarante pass through three to four times daily. The main attraction is a wonderful turismo rural property, *Casa do Barão de Fermil* (☎255 361 211; ●), a slightly decaying mansion with its own swimming pool and elderly, English-speaking owners.

MONDIM DE BASTO, 9km along the main road northeast of Celorico, is a little more exciting than Celorico, with a small, well-preserved old town in the centre of a modern sprawl. You might consider making Mondim de Basto a base for exploring the **Parque Natural do Alvão** (see p.430); there's an information office (☎255 381 209) 800m down the Celorico road by the Barrio primary school. **Guided walks** in the park can be arranged through Os Tamecanos (☎255 302 637), which also offers rafting, canoeing and canyoning. The **turismo** (daily: summer 9am–9pm; winter 9am–12.30pm & 2–5.30pm; ☎255 381 479) on Praça 9 de Abril provides maps, a list of hotels, information on local turismo rural properties and somewhat illegible hand-written sheets detailing local walking routes.

In town, **places to stay** include two modern, good-value options: the *Residencial Arcadia*, Avenida Dr. Augusto de Brito (☎255 381 410; ●), which can be a touch noisy as it's above a café and games arcade, and the very friendly *Residencial Carvalho (*also called *Residencial Sossego*), by the petrol station on the same road (☎255 381 057; ●), where the spotless, self-contained rooms come equipped with TV and minibar. There's also an excellent **campsite** (☎255 381 650; closed mid-Dec to mid-Jan) – about 1km from the centre along the N304 Vila Real road near the banks of the Rio Cabril; the river water is clean enough to swim in. Rua Velha is the main place for both **bars** and **restaurants** – good, cheap options include the *Adega Santiago* and *Adega Sete Condes*, while *Restaurante Escondidinho* is more upmarket. On Avenida da Igreja, *Churrasqueira Chasslik* is a busy chips-with-everything sort of place, or try *O Transmontano* on the same road for specialities from beyond the Serra do Alvão; try the *feijoada* (bean stew with bits of pork). The main **nightlife** focus is *Bar da Vinha* on Rua Velha, and *Koton Club* at Vilar de Viando, 1km out towards Vila Real. There's an **internet café**, *Bar Net's*, on Avenida da Igreja.

Mondim's bus station is by the central Mercado Municipal and there are regular **bus connections** to Vila Real, a spectacular ride, skirting the Parque Natural de Alvão (Mon–Sat 7am, 12.30pm & 5.30pm), as well as to Guimarães, Coimbra and Lisbon. Alternatively, you could catch a bus to Fermil, and then on to the lively provincial town of Cabeceiras de Basto (see below), from where there are regular buses to Braga.

Monte Farinha and the Cabril Valley

The 996-metre-high **Monte Farinha** is surprisingly easy to climb – less than three hours' easy walking – and, if the times coincide, you can get a head start by taking the bus to the foot of the ascent, three-and-a-half kilometres from Mondim. Walking, follow the N312 Cerva road east out of Mondim, then take a path up to the right shortly after Pedra Vedra. Once on the mountain, follow the road which zigzags to the summit (Mondim's turismo has a map). An alternative but more tiring route is to take the mountain track towards Carazêdo, turning left after 2km onto the path for Pegodinhas. At the hamlet of Campos, a further 2km on, turn left again and continue north to Pegodinhas, after which you've a good ninety-minute hike up steep terrain to join the zigzags to the top. The panoramic views well repay your efforts, though, and at the top is the attractive late eighteenth-century parish church of **Nossa Senhora da Graça**, centre of a major *romaria* on the first Sunday in September. Another *romaria* is held on July 24, in honour of São Tiago. There's also a **restaurant** next to the church, the *Alto da Sonhora da Graça* (☎255 381 404) – call ahead if you plan to eat here.

Another good hike from Mondim is into the **Cabril valley**. Only about twenty minutes beyond the village campsite, the Cabril – more a stream than a river – is crossed by a Roman bridge, impressive in itself and set near a little **waterfall** where there's a good swimming hole. From here, follow the Cabril upstream to a working watermill or take the stone track (about 200m upriver) along what must have been a Roman road. Follow this, cross a road, and you're at the start of a maze of small paths cutting between the fields and vineyards of the Cabril valley, and leading higher into the slopes.

Cabeceiras de Basto

At the heart of the Terras de Basto, **CABECEIRAS DE BASTO** is the largest and most interesting Basto village. If you can, time your visit to coincide with the **Monday feira**, when traders sell clothes and food in the square above the bus station, while the **Feira** and **Romaria de São Miguel** (September 19–30) centres on traditional choirs, dancing, and a market, with a colourful procession on the last day.

The town's old centre is dominated by the twin towers of the Baroque **Mosteiro de São Miguel de Refojos** (daily, roughly 7am–8pm), a former monastery now used as a church, that contains a startlingly lifelike image of Jesus crouching in a darkened corner. Though you should be able to organize access if your Portuguese is good, staff at the **turismo** on the other side of the Praça da Republica (Sept 15–June 14 Mon–Fri 9am–12.30pm & 2–5.30pm; June 15–Sept 14 daily 9am–12.30pm & 2–5.30pm; ☎253 669 100, ℱ253 662 726) may well be more successful in convincing the busy *padre* to let you visit the monastery's locked treasury (a collection of statues and religious garments) and access the clock tower, from which you can view the church's highlight – the *zimbório* (dome). The monastery was most likely founded early in the seventh century by the Visigoths, just before the first Moorish invasion.

Opposite the monastery, in the immaculate gardens of the Praça da República, is a rather curious *basto* figure that probably covered the tomb of one **Hermígio Romarigues**, successful defender of Cabeceiras de Basto from Moorish attacks on three occasions. The *basto's* original head disappeared somewhere along the line (no one's sure where or when), and the figure stood headless for many years until 1892, when somebody added a dapper moustachioed head complete with French-style kepi hat and a new pair of legs and boots.

On the hill above the town is the new **Centro de Educacão Ambiental** (daily 9am–noon & 2–5.30pm; park always open; free). Half complete, it contains a small zoo of native wildlife, along with picnic areas, a children's park and some sports facilities. The second phase of development is the construction of an equestrian centre in the eastern part of the park (ask at the tourist office for more details).

Most of Cabeceiras de Basto's **accommodation** is in the newer part of town, close to the bus station, though the compact nature of the town means that nothing is more than a short walk away. A reliable, inexpensive option is the *Residencial São Miguel*, above the equally good restaurant on Largo Barjona de Freitas (☎253 661 034; ❶), on the road connecting the market square with the Praça da Republica; opposite and more expensive, though no better, are the rooms above *Restaurante A Cafrial* on Avenida General Humberto Delgado (☎253 662 690; ❷). Four kilometres from Cabeceiras, off the road to Venda Nova at Riodouro, there's a small, thirty-pitch **campsite**, *Clube de Campismo Valsereno* (☎253 662 047). The site is close to a small river and has its own bar and swimming pool. More characterful accommodation can be found in a number of farmhouses in the region (all ❸); ask at the turismo for details of *turismo rural* properties. Back in town, good cheap **meals** can be had at the *Cozinha Real Basto*, Avenida Sá Carneiro, a short way up the road to Arco de Baúlhe from the monastery. Classier and more expensive is *Restaurante Barão*, at the narrow end of Praça da República and facing the monastery.

Leaving from the central terminus by the market in the new section of town, **buses** connect Cabeceiras with Celorico and Mondim de Basto, Póvoa de Lanhoso in central Minho, Braga and Porto (Mon–Sat only). Change in Arco de Baúlhe for Chaves. For details of **tours** in the region, pick up the beautifully produced *Guia das Aldeias* booklet from the turismo (free).

Along the Douro: to Peso da Régua and on to the Spanish border

Leaving Porto **by road** and heading for Peso da Régua and port wine country, there are two possibilities: either take the motorway eastwards, leaving it at Penafiel or Amarante, or – with more time – follow the EN108 southeast. This road hugs the north bank of the Douro River until Entre-os-Rios (where the Tâmega meets the Douro), after which it forks, allowing you to drive along either river bank. The north bank road is quicker; the south bank more attractive. As for the Linha do Douro **train from Porto**, this shadows the motorway, and passes close to Penafiel, but shortly after Livraçao the line finally turns south to reach the Douro and then heads upstream. At Mesão Frio, the river temporarily leaves its confined channel and broadens into the little plain commanded by the port wine town of **Peso da Régua**. East of here, trains continue as far as **Pocinho**, though to travel any further – and to cross the border into Spain – you'll need to take buses or your own transport. You could always cut north from Régua instead, up the Corgo line, a brief excursion through marvellous vine and granite landscape to Vila Real (see p.424). Régua is also the jumping-off point for buses to the pilgrimage centre of **Lamego**, 13km to the south, at the tip of Beira Alta and, since this is by far the easiest link with the town, Lamego is covered here, along with its immediate region.

River, rail and ribbon lakes

In the eighteenth century, when the port-producing area was first demarcated (see p.304), the **Rio Douro** could not be navigated by the traditional *barcos rabelos* (barges) beyond the rapids of Cachão de Valeira. By the end of the century, engineering works had circumnavigated the worst of the rapids and opened up the Douro as far east as Pocinho, but travel was still slow – it took three days to float wine down from Peso da Régua to Porto. The arrival of the **railway** at the end of the nineteenth century accelerated transport up and down the valley: the track reached Régua in 1880 and arrived at the Spanish border in 1887, with the branch lines up the river's tributaries completed by 1910. Later, road transport replaced rail and the river itself became something of a backwater until the 1970s, when dams were planned along the length of the Douro.

With the completion of the fifth dam in 1985, the river was turned into a series of **ribbon lakes** and, thanks to locks along the route, it's now possible to cruise via Régua from Porto to Barca de Alva on the Spanish border, a distance of just over 200km; for details, see Porto "Listings" p.316.

Peso da Régua

PESO DA RÉGUA (usually just Régua) is an expanding provincial town that was known for over two centuries as the "Capital of the Upper Douro" because of its role in the port industry. In fact, the centre for quality port wines has shifted to Pinhão, half an hour further east; Régua is simply the junction and the depot through which all the wine must pass on its way to Porto. Dominated by a semi-complete motorway that will eventually link Bragança with Viseu in Beira Alta, Régua is not a pretty place. Local government is attempting to rectify this, starting with the construction of a riverside promenade. Here, the ornamental *barcos rabelos* anchored on the river, and the sombre Sandeman cutout on the horizon, are a reminder of Régua's previous importance as the first capital of Pombal's demarcated port-producing region.

The small **turismo** (Sept 1–June 30 Mon–Fri 9am–12.30pm & 2–5.30pm; July 1–Aug 31 daily 9am–12.30pm & 2–5.30pm; ☎254 312 846, ⓕ254 322 271) is on Rua da Ferreirinha, 1km west of the train station – turn right and head downhill along the river until you reach a large fountain roundabout. Turn right here and the tourist office is facing you at the next junction. Staff will hand out an excellent map of wine-related sites along the Douro – the "*Rota de Vinho do Porto*" – which locate several dozen wine lodges and working *quintas* (farms) that are open to the public (see box on p.303 for more on port wine production). For more information about the local **port lodges** there is an office of the *Instituto do Vinho do Porto* (Mon–Sat 2pm–midnight; ☎254 320 145) on Rua dos Camilos between the turismo and the train station. The nearest is **Quinta de São Domingos** (Mon–Fri 9am–12.30pm & 2–5pm; free; ☎254 320 100), which offers a more personalized and interesting tour than its Vila Nova de Gaia equivalents. To get there, turn left from the train station and follow the signs; it's about five minutes' walk. Next door to the port institute, you can also visit the entrance hall of the Casa do Douro on Rua dos Camilos, the headquarters of the port growers' organization, to see the medieval-style stained-glass window by Lino António.

Apart from the alcoholic diversions, there's not much to do in Régua except wander through the upper town, take a **river trip** to some of the *quintas* around town (summer only; contact the turismo for more information), or

335

△ *Barcos rabelos*

book canoeing and mountain biking trips with Aventuridouro Rua do Souto (☎254 321 496).

You probably won't want to stay the night here, so be sure of your train connection or the next bus out. Leaving from outside the train station, **buses** to Lamego run every hour up until 8pm, and there are five trains daily to Vila Real (last one leaves at 7.15pm). If you do need **accommodation**, the high-rise *Residencial Império*, Rua Vasques Osório 8, at the corner of Largo da Estação (☎254 320 120, ℱ254 321 457; ❸), is close to the train station. Rooms are comfortable, with air conditioning, TVs, heating and minibar, and excellent breakfasts are included. *Pensão Borrajo* on Rua dos Camilos (☎254 213 396; ❶) is a basic option in an old tiled building above a restaurant. The classiest choice is the brand-new *Hotel Régua Douro*, on Avenida da Galiza by the train station (☎254 322 999 or 254 320 700; ❹), which has an outdoor pool, jacuzzi and health club. There are plenty of **restaurants** along the riverfront; elsewhere, try *O Maleiro*, a friendly, bustling place on Rua dos Camilos – which also offers accommodation, a little way out of town, at *Residencial Dom Quixote* (☎254 321 151; ❶). If you ask at the restaurant they will be happy to take you out there. The understated, family-run *Restaurante Arco Íris* on Avenida Sacadura Cabral, west from the turismo, offers superlative cooking at good prices (up to €10) and has a number of awards to its name.

East to the border

Just beyond Régua, and past the massive dam of a hydroelectric power station, as you head into the *Terra Quente* (hot lands) the climate gets noticeably warmer, the landscape more Mediterranean and you begin increasingly to see the terraced slopes where the **port vines** are grown. They're at their best in August, with the grapes ripening, and in September, when the harvest has begun. Quotas for wine production have been in force around here since the mid-eighteenth century, and some terrace walls from that period have withstood the assault of the diggers and dynamite that are used nowadays to clear the way for the vineyard tractors. Grape-treaders and the traditional *barcos rabelos* have also been replaced by machines and cistern lorries, though there's still a demand for large groups of hand-pickers (*rogas*) when there's a bumper crop.

Pinhão to Pocinho

The country continues craggy and beautiful, with the softer hills of the interior fading dark green into the distance, past **PINHÃO**, the main centre for quality ports. Trains pull in at the east end of town near to the river, an area awash with the advertising signs of port lodges. There are a couple of large *pensões* in Pinhão so **accommodation** shouldn't be a problem. *Pensão Douro*, facing the train station (☎254 724 404; ❷), is the more modern of the two, with TVs and air conditioning in the rooms. *Pensão Restaurante Ponto Grande* (☎254 732 456; ❷), two doors down at Rua Central 103–105, offers the same in-room facilities but is fractionally cheaper and has a good restaurant. However, if your budget can stretch to it, opt for the *Quinta de la Rosa* (☎254 732 254, ℯmail@quintadelarosa.com; ❺), a working wine estate 1.5km west of Pinhão, with six double rooms (breakfast is included) and a swimming pool as well as wonderful river views and the chance to see at first hand the early processes of port wine making.

From Pinhão, you could drive (or get a taxi) to the village of **Panascal** and visit the 250-year-old *Quinta do Panascal* (Mon–Fri 10am–7.30pm; ☎254 732

321), a Fonseca port wine company property which offers free tours of the grounds and a chance to sample some local port.

The Douro continues on its journey eastwards, through the village of **TUA**, where buses run up the Tua valley to Mirandela in Trás-os-Montes (see p.432). The train continues on to its terminus, 45km east of Pinhão, at the isolated station of **POCINHO**, where it is met by buses to Torre de Moncorvo (11.30am and 6.30pm), 10km northeast (see p.454). Pocinho is little more than a railway station and a couple of restaurants, so be sure of your onward connection before arrival, as it's 10km uphill to Torre de Moncorvo and 8km, through rather more pleasant surroundings, to Vila Nova de Foz Côa. The last bus to Vila Nova de Foz Côa leaves at 6.30pm, but stay alert as it doesn't hang around.

Vila Nova de Foz Côa

Sitting high above the Côa valley 8km south of Pocinho, **VILA NOVA DE FOZ CÔA** is a small and pleasant place, which was awarded the status of a city on account of an astonishing collection of **Paleolithic rock art**, discovered nearby in 1992. Rescued from imminent submersion under a proposed dam, three of the sites are now open to the public (see the box on p.338), and merit a visit in their own right. Other than the **Igreja Matriz**, with its impressive Manueline doorway, leaning walls and pillory outside, there's little else to Foz Côa. Good dates to coincide with include the self-explanatory Onion Fair (May 8), a municipal holiday on May 21 with parades and music performances, the *Festa de Nossa Senhora da Veiga* on August 8, and the *Feira de São Miguel* on September 29. A monthly market is held on the first Tuesday of each month, and the blossoming of almond trees draws the crowds in late February and early March.

Practicalities

Foz Côa is most easily reached by the Douro train to Pocinho, from where connecting **buses** pass through town on the way to Castelo Rodrigo (going back to Pocinho or Torre de Moncorvo, buses leave Mon–Fri at 9am & 4.30pm, Sat 9am & Sun 4.30pm). For information on other services to the Mountain Beiras and Lisbon, ask at *Café Luís* on Avenida Gago Coutinho, where the buses drop you. The friendly **turismo** (daily 9am–12.30pm & 2–5.30pm; ☏279 765 243), which supplies maps and can help with accommodation, is inconveniently situated 2km from the town centre on the road to Castelo Melhor and Vilar Formosa; from the archeological park office on Avenida Gago Coutinho in the centre of town (see box, p.338), walk down Rua da Portela, and turn right on to Largo da Conceiçao, from where it's a 1.5km hike along Rua do Poco Novo; they also have a small display of local crafts and archeology. **Hotels** in town include *Residencial Avenida*, Avenida Gago Coutinho 8 (☏271 762 175; ❷), the friendly *Residencial Marina* next door (☏271 762 112; ❷), which has satellite TV in the rooms, and *Residencial Cifrão*, Rua do Mercado (☏271 762 452; ❷), around the corner from the park office. A little further up is *Albergaria Vale do* Côa (☏279 760 010; ❸) offering bog standard rooms, although most have the attraction of a balcony. There's also a **youth hostel** (☏279 768 190, ℻279 768 191) on a windswept site with great views, 1.5km northwest of town off the Pocinho road: from the Igreja Matriz, walk down Rua Dr. Silverio de Andrade and turn right after 1km. There are washing machines, a kitchen, a restaurant and disabled facilities, and some double rooms (❶). Good **food** can be had at *Restaurante A Marisqueira* on Rua Juiz Moutinho de Andrade 35, the eastern

The rock art of Foz Côa

The River Côa near Vila Nova de Foz Côa became the centre of one of the greatest archeological finds in recent memory with the discovery in 1992 of the **most extensive array of outdoor Paleolithic art in Europe**. Engravings of horses, deer, goats and other animals (some extinct, such as the auroch, a type of wild ox), as well as later, Neolithic, images of people, were found along 17km of the river's steep, rocky schist valley. The engravings themselves are of a similar style to those found in caves across Europe, but their uniqueness lies in the fact that they are outside on exposed rock faces and invariably near water. With the oldest dated at around 22,000 years, it is remarkable that the engravings survived to be discovered at all, but even more remarkable perhaps is that they continued to survive after their discovery.

The proposed building of a controversial dam, designed to meet increasing electricity demand in the surrounding area, threatened to submerse the site, and the engravings, under 90m of water. The threat increased public awareness of the art and, as interest grew, more and more discoveries came to light as a result, and the site's importance became clear. Archeologists and environmental groups joined forces with local people (who also feared the loss of 16,000 hectares of prime-quality vineyards) and schoolchildren and students from across the country in an incredible "people's **campaign**" against the proposed dam, pressurizing EDP, Portugal's then state-owned electricity monopoly, to abandon the project. Success came in 1995 when the sites were declared a National Monument. The **Parque Arqueológico do Vale do Côa** was created the following year, and in December 1998 became a UNESCO World Heritage site.

To arrange a guided visit, you must contact the park authorities in advance at Av Gago Coutinho 19A, 5150 Vila Nova de Foz Côa (Tues–Sun 9am–12.30pm & 2–5.30pm; ☏279 768 260, ⍟www.ipa.min-cultura.pt/coa). Three sites are open to the public (Tues–Sun; €5 per site): Canada do Inferno and Ribeira de Piscos can be visited in the morning (tours from 9.30am–5pm), and Penascosa in the afternoon (tours 2–5pm). Without your own transport, Canada do Inferno (2hr visit including 1km mountain hike) – the site of the half-built dam – is the easiest option, as you're picked up from the park office in Foz Côa. For the other sites, you have to make your own way to the respective **visitors' centres**, each with its own cafeteria. For the Penascosa site (1hour 30min visit), make your way to Castelo Melhor interpretation centre, on the road to the village of Castelo Rodrigo, which has a ruined castle and a couple of café-restaurants. The interpretation centre for Ribeira de Piscos (2hr 30min including 2km mountain hike) is in Muxagata, off the road to Guarda, with a bar and not much else. There are no helpful bus services to either site, so your only option is to take a taxi. The visits themselves are made in 4WD vehicles, with a maximum of 8 visitors accompanied by each guide (be aware that Portuguese transport laws forbid children under 3 years old from travelling in 4WD vehicles).

Bear in mind that it can get very hot in the sheltered valley, especially at Ribeira dos Piscos, and there is some walking involved, so it's a good idea to bring a hat, sun cream and plenty of water. If you suspect that it may rain, bring a raincoat as umbrellas are prohibited. Visits are restricted to preserve the sites, but if you call in advance then you shouldn't have too much trouble in reserving a place on a tour. In summer it is recommended that you call at least two or three days in advance.

continuation of Avenida Gago Coutinho. For a little **nightlife**, karaoke beckons at *Gaitero Bar*, Avenida Gago Coutinho 12; if you fancy a dance, try either *Pub Discoteca Visage* at Rua Carlos Lacerda 4, or *Discoteca A Rupestre* in Rua do Olho 35.

Onwards to Barca de Alva and the border

Following the last, uppermost reaches of the Portuguese Douro is impossible by road, as on both sides they veer well away from the river. However, the roads converge again over the bridge at Barca de Alva, where the river finally enters Portuguese territory after skirting the border for over 100km. Local Senhor Lopes buses run the two-hour journey to Barca de Alva from Pocinho (Mon–Fri 2pm & 6.30pm, Sat 2pm, Sun 6.30pm) passing through both Vila Nova de Foz Côa and the small, sleepy town of **FIGUEIRA DE CASTELO RODRIGO**, where you'll be dropped in the large Largo Mateus de Castro. There are a couple of basic **pensões** here, the better, but least characterful, of which is *Pensão Figueirense* (☎271 312 517; ❷), just south of the Largo on Avenida 25 de Abril, where breakfast is included. Slightly cheaper is *Pensão Transmontano da Beira*, Rua Osório de Vasconcelos (☎271 312 244, ☏271 312 237; ❷). There is also a regional office for the Parque Natural do Douro Internacional (see p.456) at Rua Artur Costa 1 (☎ & ☏271 313 382), where staff can provide park maps and advice about visiting the park. However, despite a glut of restaurants and a large but simple Romanesque church, the town itself isn't the main draw: about 2km away, on an isolated hill, is the much older, medieval settlement of **CASTELO RODRIGO** (€2.50 by taxi), a site that has been permanently occupied since around 500 BC, when the Turdulos people arrived. It is now inhabited only by a few dozen families settled around the ruins of its castle and is a pleasant place to spend an afternoon – the views are superb and there's a very good restaurant, *O Cantinho dos Avós*, which also has rooms (☎271 312 643; ❷). If you're heading south from Figueira de Castelo Rodrigo, there's one daily bus at 8.20am (except Sat) to Lisbon via Guarda, Viseu and Coimbra: information and tickets from the kiosk in the southwestern corner of the Largo, in front of the *Transmontano* café.

Twenty kilometres to the north and less than 2km from the Spanish border is the last Portuguese village along the Douro, **BARCA DE ALVA**. The route is a delight – defiantly unmodernized agricultural land dotted with boulders, storks' nests and conical, stone-roofed houses – and Barca itself is an attractive place, overlooked by mountains on all sides and with a row of whitewashed cottages facing the river. It is the final destination of some of the river cruises from Porto (see p.316), but it's looking a little neglected now since the railway line across the border was discontinued in the 1980s: if you're brave enough you can risk the rickety old metal railway bridge into Spain (beware of rotten sleepers).

Barca's main appeal is the tranquil atmosphere and attractive countryside, part of the Parque Natural do Douro Internacional (see p.456), which also makes it a good local hiking base. A lovely walk along a quiet road starts by crossing the road bridge into Trás-os-Montes; then you can follow the Douro through olive and orange groves, and past the terraced vineyards still providing grapes for the port companies in Porto.

Accommodation in Barca de Alva is at the *Baga d'Ouro* (☎279 315 126; ❶), above the restaurant on the main road along the river; the *Casa de Pasto*, a few doors along, also has cheap rooms. The *Baga d'Ouro* is also a good place **to eat**, and does a fine set meal and excellent breakfasts of coffee, fresh bread and local honey. **Onward transport** is restricted as there are no bus services north to Freixo de Espada à Cinta; if you want to continue on to Trás-os-Montes your only option (unless you want to hitch the twenty-odd kilometres to Freixo de Espada à Cinta) is to catch a Senhor Lopes bus back to Pocinho (Mon–Fri 7.30am & 4.30pm, Sat 7.30am, Sun 4.30pm), from where there are three daily buses to Torre do Moncorvo and beyond.

Lamego and around

Although technically in Beira Alta, the beautiful town of **LAMEGO** is isolated at the tip of its mountain province, and much more accessible from Régua and the Douro. The town itself has more in common with the Douro region, too, spreading over gentle slopes of the rich agricultural land fed by the river, a terrain which the locals put to good use in the production of such delights as hams and melons, as well as *Raposeira* – the closest thing to champagne you will find in Portugal.

Lamego is a wealthy place, and long has been, as evidenced by the graceful white *quintas* and villas on the hillsides, and the luxuriant architecture of the centre. Here Baroque mansions seem to stand on every corner and lavish decorations are found within even the smallest chapel. Much of the wealth stems from the town's geographical position, with access to the mountains of the north and standing on a valuable trade link between the east and west of the country. In 1143 it was also the site of Portugal's first Parliament, a group of clergy and noblemen assembling to recognize Afonso Henriques officially as the first king of Portugal. Later the town accrued more wealth from the trade in satin and velvet, as well as, of course, the wine trade. Most spectacularly though, Lamego has one of the very greatest Baroque structures in Europe – the shrine of **Nossa Senhora dos Remédios**, which, with its monumental stairway, dominates the west–east axis of the town.

The Town

For all the architectural histrionics of the shrine, it's Lamego's **Sé** that clearly delineates the centre of town (daily 8am–1pm & 3–7pm). It's basically a Renaissance structure, though a thirteenth-century tower survives from a previous building. The mixture works well and the cloister is a beauty. Facing the cathedral, occupying an eighteenth-century palace, is the town's excellent **Museu de Lamego** (Tues–Sun 10am–12.30pm & 2–5pm; €2, free Sun), whose exhibits include five of the remaining panels of a polyptych commissioned from Grão Vasco by the Bishop of Lamego in 1506. Judging by the lack of correlation between the various panels – for instance, the *Creation of the Animals* and the prodigiously executed *Annunciation* – some of the work must be attributed to the great man's school. Also on show are a series of huge sixteenth-century Flemish tapestries (including a marvellous *Life of Oedipus* sequence), three curious statues of a conspicuously pregnant Virgin Mary (a genre peculiar to this region), a fine assembly of *azulejos*, piles of ecclesiastical treasure from the Episcopal Palace, and a group of chapels rescued from the decaying sixteenth-century **Igreja das Chagas**. The museum is rarely packed and you may well be lucky enough to have the place almost to yourself.

Across the square, Rua da Olaria, a narrow street of tiny shops, leads into Rua de Almacave, which follows the walls of the old inner town. The route takes you past the **Igreja de Santa Maria Maior de Almacave** (daily 7.30am–12.30pm & 4–7.30pm), a very ancient foundation said once to have been a mosque, to Praça do Comércio. From here you can pass through the walls of the **Old Citadel** and climb up to the **Castelo** (mid-June to end Sept: Tues–Sun 10am–noon & 3–6pm; Oct–May Sun 10am–noon only; free), surrounded by a cluster of ancient stone houses. This has been pressed into service as the local scout headquarters and the boys do have a fairly legitimate claim on the place, having – so they say – cleared eighteen lorryloads of garbage away in the 1970s and saved the building from ruin. You can look

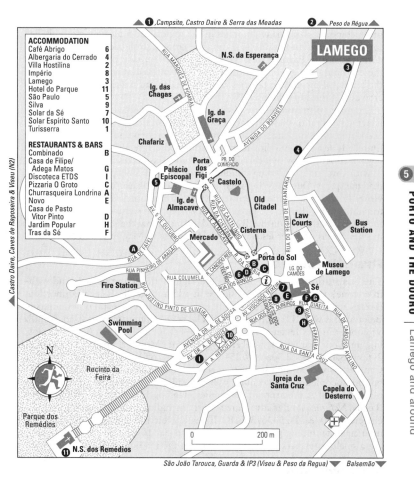

ACCOMMODATION

Café Abrigo	6
Albergaria do Cerrado	4
Villa Hostilina	2
Império	8
Lamego	3
Hotel do Parque	11
São Paulo	5
Silva	9
Solar da Sé	7
Solar Espírito Santo	10
Turisserra	1

RESTAURANTS & BARS

Combinado	B
Casa de Filipe/ Adega Matos	G
Discoteca ETDS	I
Pizzaria O Groto	C
Churrasqueira Londrina Novo	A
Casa de Pasto Vitor Pinto	E
Jardim Popular	D
Tras da Sé	H
	F

Castro Daire, Caves de Raposeira & Viseu (N2)

N.S. da Esperança

Ig. das Chagas

Ig. da Graça

Chafariz

Porta dos
Figi
Palácio
Episcopal

PR. DO COMÉRCIO

Castelo

Old Citadel

Ig. de Almacave

Cisterna

Law Courts

Bus Station

Mercado

Porta do Sol

Museu de Lamego

Fire Station

RUA COLUMELA

RUA DOS BANCOS

LG. DO CAMÕES

Sé

Swimming Pool

Recinto da Feira

Igreja de Santa Cruz

Capela do Desterro

Parque dos Remédios

N.S. dos Remédios

0   200 m

around the castle, providing a spare scout is available to show you around – if the wigwams and scout banners inside don't grab you, climb the rickety stairs onto the roof for some stunning views. Nearby, is the odd thirteenth-century **Cisterna** which still bears the marks from the original stonemasons – sadly, it's closed to the public.

Nossa Senhora dos Remédios

The celebrated shrine of **Nossa Senhora dos Remédios** (daily: summer 7.30am–8pm; winter 8am–6pm) is a major point of pilgrimage – a reputation for healing miracles draws devotees from all over the country. Standing on a hill overlooking the city, at the end of a wide avenue of shady chestnut trees, it's approached by a magnificently elaborate eighteenth-century stairway, modelled on the one at Bom Jesus near Braga (see p.369). Its 611 steps – which the most committed pilgrims ascend on their knees – are punctuated by a *via santa* of *azulejos*-lined devotional chapels and allegorical fountains and statues. After the approach, and its own facade, the church is surprisingly bright and airy, more colourful than many churches in the region and a pleasant assembly hall for the ever-present faithful. To escape the crowds, stroll back along the forested tracks of the **Parque dos Remédios** on either side of the steps; early in the morning the air is filled with cuckoo calls and warbling birdsong, although the arrival of picnicking families later in the day can make the park almost as crowded as the steps themselves.

The great **pilgrimage** here peaks on September 6–8, although the accompanying celebrations last several weeks, starting on the last Thursday in August and continuing into mid-September. At 8am on September 6, the image of Our Lady leaves Remédios in procession to the Igreja das Chagas, where it stays in adoration for two days. The main procession takes place on September 8, with cavalcades of young children in white, and bulls pulling the carriage that transports Our Lady between the Igreja das Chagas and Igreja de Santa Cruz. In addition to the pilgrimage, there's a traditional "Battle of Flowers", torchlit parades, dances, car races, performances from some of the country's top rock bands and a fair on the Recinto da Feira, below the sanctuary. The turismo has details of other festivals which take place in May, June and November.

Practicalities

The **bus station** is behind the museum, right in the centre of town and within a stone's throw of the main sights. In addition to the Régua connections (hourly until 8.15pm), there are daily services linking Viseu and other points in Beira Alta, as well as Lisbon and Porto. The very helpful **turismo** is on Avenida Visconde Guedes Teixeira (July–Sept Mon–Fri 10am–12.30pm & 2–6pm closing an hour earlier at weekends; Oct–June Mon–Fri 10am–12.30pm & 2–6pm, Sat 10am–12.30pm; ☎254 612 005), just off the main square, Largo de Camões. As well as the usual lists of accommodation and sights, they also dole out photocopied sheets detailing walking trails in the region – see the box on p.345. As well as the array of companies plugging Douro cruises from nearby Régua, *Naturimont* offer adventure tourism including canoeing, rafting and orienteering (☎ & ℱ254 613 918). If that's a bit too energetic for you, the municipal swimming pools (April–Sept Mon–Sat 10am–6pm; €2.50), including a small water park, are near the steps on the road out to Viseu.

Accommodation

Accommodation in Lamego can be tricky to find and is on the expensive side. Booking ahead is strongly advised, though if you turn up on spec, the turismo may be able to sort you out a **private room**; possibilities include rooms at Rua de Santa Cruz 15 (❶) or those above *Café Abrigo* on Rua dos Bancos (☎254 612 432; ❷). Turismo staff can also provide you with details of *Solares de Portugal* and similar rural properties, though for these you'll need your own transport. The local **campsite** (June–Sept; ☎969 081 507) is 4km north of town in Turisserra, by the *Motel Turisserra* (see below). There are no buses to the campsite; take the road marked to Avões until you see the signs.

Albergaria do Cerrado on the Régua road, 400m from the Sé ☎254 613 164, ℱ254 615 464. Lamego's main business-class hotel is modern and well equipped but a bit characterless. ❸ Pensão Império Trav. dos Loureiros 6, off Av Visconde Teixeira ☎254 612 742, ℱ254 613 238. Above the restaurant of the same name, with pleasant if somewhat fusty rooms that can be noisy. ❸

Hotel Lamego Quinta da Vista Alegre, about 2km out of town on the Régua road ☎254 656 171, ℱ254 656 180. Modern, and well run with two pools (one indoor), tennis courts and a health club. Rooms have air conditioning and satellite TV and there are disabled facilities. A little out of the way if you don't have your own transport. ❹

Hotel do Parque by the church of Nossa Senhora dos Remédios ☎254 609 140, ℱ254 615 203. An unbeatable location and a lovely hotel, set in its own gardens. ❸
Residencial São Paulo Av 5 de Outubro 22 ☎254 613 114, ℱ254 612 304. A modern building with friendly staff and its own parking spaces; breakfast is included. ❷
Pensão Silva Rua Trás-da-Sé 26 ☎254 612 929. As this is next to the Sé, the bells might disturb, although they are not as loud as you might expect. However, the rooms are decent, if a little antiquated, the French-speaking owner is friendly and it's the cheapest in town. Shared bathrooms. ❶
Residencial Solar da Sé Av Visconde Teixeira ☎254 612 060, ℱ254 615 928. Less characterful than *Silva* but smart, and a fraction further from the Sé clock, though still with fine views over the cathedral. ❷

Residencial Solar Espírito Santo Rua Alexandre Herculano ☎254 655 391, ℱ254 656 233. Comfortable, modern hotel with a facade reminiscent of a giant meringue. Street-facing rooms have balconies. ❸
Motel Turisserra 4km out on the Estrada Florestal ☎254 655 882, ℱ254 656 152. A modest motel (and very good restaurant), occupying a lofty position on the Serra das Meadas, by the campsite. ❸
Villa Hostilina 2km out off the Peso da Régua road in Almacave ☎254 612 394, ⓦwww .minotel.com. A well-signposted Privetur property set in vineyards and orchards, this is a grand nineteenth-century house furnished in Victorian-style clutter, contrasting oddly with its ultra-modern health club, tennis courts and pool. Food is available by arrangement. ❹

Eating, drinking and nightlife

At first glance, Lamego's **restaurants** may seem expensive, especially in the centre of town where guaranteed tourist trade has loosened standards, so you might consider assembling a **picnic**: from the turismo, head up the steep Rua da Olaria, where a selection of grocers sell excellent bread and cheese, as well as Lamego's famed *presunto* (ham) and smoked *salpicão* sausages. If you don't mind a more earthy ambience, there are a number of very cheap and characterful *adegas casas de pasto* scattered around and if the weather is hot you could always sip a cold drink in the shade of the chestnut trees in one of the numerous outdoor cafes on Avenida Dr. Alfredo de Sousa. Best cheap eats are in the streets immediately surrounding the Sé, but these quickly fill with locals at meal times.

Lamego's **nightlife** is somewhat limited; there's a saloon-door bar at the top of Rua de Almacave on the way to the castle, or try the *taberna* on Rua do Castelinho 25 – though both close at 9pm. There are more bars scattered along either side of Avenida Dr. Alfredo de Sousa, which forms the hub for summertime evening drinkers. For younger company, try *Discoteca ETDS* on Avenida Dr. Alfredo de Sousa, at the foot of the steps to the shrine.

Casa de Filipe and Adega Matos Rua Virgílio Correia, immediately behind the Sé. Very basic *casas de pasto*, but good and cheap.
Casa de Pasto Vitor Pinto Rua da Olaria 61. Very cheap eats, with fine *presunto* figuring strongly. Closed Sun.
O Combinado Rua da Olaria 84. A good local *tasca* where you can eat well for under €5. Try *lombos de porco* (grilled pork chops) or the trout. Closed Sun in winter.
Pizzaria O Groto Rua da Olaria. The menu of pizza, pasta and hamburgers is aimed mainly at tourists, but it fills the gap if you have a craving – you'll pay €7.50–10 a meal.
Jardim Popular Rua da Perreira ☎254 655 636. Around the corner from *Pensão Silva*, this is a

rather strange construction in a walled garden but the grills and salads are good. Around €12.50. Closed Mon.
Churrasqueira Londrina Rua de Fafel. Behind the fire station, an unassuming modern place with very reasonable prices and outstanding grills.
Restaurante Novo Largo da Sé 9. Cheap and cheerful with a few outdoor tables overlooking the Sé. Closed Sat in winter.
Tras da Sé Rua Virgilio Correia. As the name suggests, right behind the cathedral. Excellent cheap food (three courses and wine for around €10) and usually packed with locals. The walls are adorned with messages of congratulations for the chef from hundreds of satisfied customers. Closed Wed evening.

Around Lamego: Balsemão and the Caves da Raposeira

At the hamlet of **BALSEMÃO**, a 3km hike from the back of the Lamego cathedral, is a seventh-century chapel founded by the Suevi. The route requires three left turns in all: the first is at the Capela do Desterro down into the old quarters of town and across a bridge; the second, a fork on to the hillside road. The third comes a little later, taking you down into the valley and above a rushing river. After three large curves, a village school, a collection of outhouses and the **Capela de São Pedro** chapel appear (Tues 2–5.30pm, Wed–Sun 9.30am–12.30pm & 2–5.30pm, closed on the third weekend of the month). You might want to check the erratic opening hours with the turismo in Lamego or call the chapel on ☏254 655 656. Some believe São Pedro to be on the site of the oldest Christian temple in the Iberian peninsula, erected by the Visigoths, though the present foundations were laid in the ninth century during the *Reconquista*. The undistinguished granite facade and dark interior give it the air of a family vault, an impression strengthened by the imposing fourteenth-century **sarcophagus** of the Bishop of Porto, Dom Afonso Pires, who was born in Balsemão. The florid capitals encircling the tomb make the few remaining Suevi curls on the archway into the choir seem subdued by comparison. Look out for the restored, profoundly pregnant statue of Nossa Senhora do Ó (that's Ó as in the shape of her belly, though others ascribe it to the exclamation uttered when seeing it: *Ó! Nossa Senhora, Mãe de Deus. . .*).

The other main attraction near Lamego is a visit to the **Caves da Raposeira** (☏254 655 003; Mon–Fri 10am–12.30pm & 2–4.30pm), 1km out of town on the Castro Daire road. These are open for free guided tours around the cellars and tasting of Portugal's "champagne", but call in advance to make sure that tours are going ahead, as it's a long thirsty walk back if they are not.

South from Lamego

Continuing **south from Lamego**, in the direction of Guarda and Viseu, the country of the **Leomil** and **Montemuro** ranges is high, wild and sparsely

---

The Entrudo de Lazarim – Shrove Tuesday

A right turn off the Lamego–Tarouca road on the outskirts of Tarouca leads to the small and normally unremarkable village of **Lazarim**. Sleepy for 364 days of the year, it plays host to one of the oddest rituals to survive in Portugal, the **Entrudo dos Compadres**, or carnival, which has taken place every Shrove Tuesday since the Middle Ages. Revellers celebrate the end of winter and the beginning of spring (Lent in the Christian calendar) by taking to the streets wearing beautifully carved wooden masks, symbolic of the event's licentiousness. However, despite the lewd masquerades, Entrudo dos Compadres is also a time of castigation for the year passed: from a balcony on the Largo do Padrão, two colourful dolls loaded with fireworks are presented to the crowd – the *compadre*, carried by two young women, and *comadre*, toted by two young men. The couples proceed to recite insulting rhymes centring on sexual behaviour, which, in the manner of Punch and Judy, are often maliciously aimed at certain unnamed people in the crowd below. After the recital, the fireworks are lit and the dolls disintegrate in an explosive fury of smoke and flame, marking the end of the festival and the old year and the beginning of the new. A *feijoada* (bean and meat stew) is then served to the waiting crowd. If you like the masks, ask for the carpenter José António Costa: they cost upwards of €75.

The Institute of Cultural Affairs

The **Montemuro** district, between Lamego and Castro Daire, suffers enormously from unemployment and depopulation, but sports a long tradition of local handicraft industries, including weaving, knitting, basketry, honey and cheese production, pottery and cape-making. There's still a thriving cultural life, too – from theatre and folk dance to religious festivals – which occupies a central place in Montemuro life.

The **Instituto dos Assuntos Culturais** (IAC) is an international development organization with a staff of foreign and Portuguese workers supporting the initiatives of local people. Some twenty villages, with a total population of about 11,000, are currently involved with the IAC's work. It's based at the village of **Mezio**, about 20km southwest of Lamego on the N2 Castro Daire road.

If you're interested in having a look at what the Institute does – and it seems there's not much it doesn't take an interest in – you might like to stop en route between Lamego and the Mountain Beiras and stay for a day or two: visitors are actively encouraged. Facilities are basic, but there are showers and toilets and plenty of organic food. Costs vary from €7.50 per person for bed and breakfast or for camping with meals, to around €15, which is pretty much all-inclusive. If you want to make enquiries in advance, contact the IAC at Rua Central 47, Mezio, 3600 Castro Daire (☎ & ℱ254 689 246).

Whether or not you choose to stay, you may find the IAC pamphlet *Hiking Trails in the Montemuro* useful (the turismo in Lamego has photocopies). It describes ten half-day **walks** in the region (though they are pretty strenuous); the IAC can also provide guides and transport for arranged walking circuits for around €15–20 per person per tour. Alternatively contact *Arrepio* (☎228 301 915, ℠www.arrepio.com), a Porto-based company that lays on various adventure activities from climbing and rafting to walks tailored to individual requirements.

inhabited. This territory was among the earliest to fall to Afonso Henriques, the first king of Portugal, in his march south against the Moors. It is said that he laid the first stone of the monastery of **São João de Tarouca** after his victories at Trancoso and Sernancelhe in Beira Alta. The region's three other rewarding sights – the monastery of **Salzedas**, the fortified bridge at **Ucanha** and the church at **Tarouca** – were also founded at this time.

São João de Tarouca

The small village of **SÃO JOÃO DE TAROUCA**, off the southeast route from Lamego to Guarda, was the site of the first Cistercian monastery to be founded in Portugal (1169). Only the **Romanesque church** remains fully intact, its simple and austere interior suffused with a subtle light. Inside, four large panels of early eighteenth-century *azulejos* depict the founding of the monastery, and the original painted Baroque choir pews are still in place. So too is the tomb of Dom Pedro, Count of Barcelos and illegitimate son of Dom Dinis, who made his name as a writer in the early fourteenth century. However, the highlight is Grão Vasco's celebrated painted altarpiece of St Peter, similar to the one in Viseu's Sé. There are usually students working on the site during the summer who might be persuaded to show you around. There's a pleasant spot for rest and recuperation – and a nice **café** – down by the river, not two minutes' walk from the church. Regular EAVT **buses** (Mon–Fri 9 daily, 3–4 at weekends) make the 25-minute journey here from Lamego's bus station.

Ucanha

In **UCANHA** – north of Tarouca, on the opposite side of the EN226 – life revolves around the water. Down below the main road, two ingenious ducts have been made to tap the river upstream in order to provide adequate washing facilities in the centre of the village. The wash houses are practically in ruins, but the system of one tank for suds and another for rinses, common to the Mediterranean, has been preserved. Running below the pools, the river looks so tempting that on a sunny day, regardless of what trash might be floating by, village children are constantly splashing around.

The real beauty of the scene stems from the majestic **tollgate** and single-arched **bridge**. They date from the 1160s, when the diocese of Salzedas was awarded to Teresa Afonso, erstwhile nursemaid to Afonso Henriques's five sons and heirs and widow of Egas Moniz, the first king's tutor and closest adviser. Besides marking and protecting the border of her domain, these structures were also, of course, an ostentatious mark of manorial power. Today, clothes are hung out to dry under the arches.

Salzedas

SALZEDAS lies 4km further along the Ucanha road, past Murganheira, another "champagne" co-operative and a rival to Raposeira. The **Monastery** here was once the greatest of its kind, grander even than São João de Tarouca. In 1168, when the order was Augustinian, the complex was rebuilt with money donated by Teresa Afonso; it became Cistercian during a later period of administration from Alcobaça.

Unfortunately, eighteenth-century renovation has largely altered its original appearance into a clumsy mixture of Baroque and pseudo-Classical styles. The monastery's main facade presides over the small square of the diminutive village. As at Tarouca, students work here in the summer and, though they may seem surprised to see casual visitors, they will follow you around and open the relevant doors. The smell of decay is strong inside and the two dark and dusty **paintings** of *St Peregrine* and *St Sebastian* by Grão Vasco, either side of the choir, are easily overlooked. More conspicuous are the fifteenth-century tombs of the Coutinho family – dominant nobles in these parts in the early years of the Portuguese nation – near the entrance. Out through a side door, a succession of courtyards, once fronting formal gardens, bear the scars of a period of extensive pillage and decay, which began in 1834 with the dissolution of the monasteries.

Travel details

Trains

Amarante to: Livração (7–9 daily; 25min); Porto (8–9 daily; 1hr 40min–2hr).

Espinho to: Coimbra (15–19 daily; 1hr 5min–1hr 40min); Lisbon (9 daily; 3hr 35min–4hr); Porto (15–19 daily; 20–40min).

Penafiel to: Livração (14–17 daily; 25min); Peso da Régua (12–13 daily; 1hr 20min); Pocinho (4 daily; 3hr 15min); Porto (15–18 daily; 45min–1hr 10min); Tua (5 daily; 2hr 10min).

Peso da Régua to: Pocinho (3 daily; 1hr 30min); Porto (14–15 daily; 2hr 10min–2hr 40min); Tua (6–7 daily; 45min); Vila Real (5 daily; 1hr).

Pocinho to: Penafiel (3–4 daily; 2hr 50min); Peso da Régua (4 daily; 1hr 30min); Porto (4 daily; 3hr 30min); Tua (6–7 daily; 40min).

Porto to: Aveiro (roughly every 30min; 1hr 20min); Coimbra (15–19 daily; 2hr); Espinho (15–19 daily; 20–40min); Faro (1 nightly Tues, Thurs & Sun, summer only; 9hrs); Lisbon (12 daily; 3hr–4hr 20min); Livração (15–18 daily; 1hr 15min–1hr 40min);

Braga (10 daily; 1hr 10min); Penafiel (15–18 daily; 45min–1hr 10min); Peso da Régua (14–15 daily; 2hr 10min–2hr 40min); Pocinho (4 daily; 3hr 30min–4hr 50min); Tua (6–7 daily; 3hr 15min–3hr 35min); Viana do Castelo (7 daily; 1hr 36min–2hr).

Train services north to the Costa Verde and Guimarães are currently suspended, pending completion of the city's metro system

Tua to: Mirandela (5 daily; 1hr 50min).

Buses

Destinations from Porto are followed by an abbreviation of the company who operates the service. Where more than one company is given, the order reflects frequency of service. For departure points of the various companies see "Listings" on p.315. Abbreviations are as follows: Asa Douro (AD); Auto Viação de Espinho (AVE); Auto Viação do Minho (AVMi); Auto Viação Mondinese (AVM); Auto Viação do Tâmega (AVT); Caima (C); EVA; Joalto (J); João Ferreira das Neves (JFN); Linhares (L); Marquês (M); Rede Expressos (RE); Renex (Rx); Resende (Rs); Rodonorte (R); Santos de Freixo (SF); Turilis (T); Valpi (V).

Amarante to: Braga (Mon–Fri 5–8 daily, Sat–Sun 1–3 daily; 1hr 20min); Cabaceiros de Basto (3–4 daily; 1hr 35min); Celorico de Basto (Mon–Sat 5 daily; 40min); Fermil (3–4 daily; 1hr); Guimarães (Mon–Fri 5–8 daily, Sat–Sun 1–3 daily; 50min); Porto (3–7 daily; 1hr); Vila Real (Mon–Fri 17–18 daily, Sat–Sun 8 daily; 1hr 40min).

Lamego to: Braga (1 daily; 2hr 50min); Celorico da Beira (Mon–Fri 3 daily; 3hr); Lisbon (2–4 daily; 6hr); Penafiel (3–5 daily; 1hr 40min); Peso da Régua (19 daily; 30min); Porto (4–6 daily; 4–4hr 30min); Sernancelhe (Mon–Fri 6 daily, Sat & Sun 2 daily; 2hr); Tarouca (Mon–Fri 9 daily, Sat & Sun 3–4 daily; 30min); Trancoso (1–2 daily; 2hr); Viseu (5–7 daily; 1hr 20min–2hr).

Penafiel to: Amarante (3–9 daily; 30min); Boelhe (Mon–Fri 6 daily; 45min); Entre-os-Rios (Mon–Fri 7 daily; 40min–1hr 25min); Lamego (3–5 daily; 1hr 40min); Porto (28 daily; 30min–1hr 20min); Torrão (Mon–Fri 7 daily; 45min–1hr 30min).

Peso da Régua to: Coimbra (1–2 daily; 3hr 40min); Guarda (1 daily; 2hr 30min); Lamego (16

daily; 25min); Vila Real (hourly; 40min); Viseu (Mon–Fri 6 daily, Sat & Sun 1–2; 1hr 30min).

Pocinho to: Bragança (2 daily; 1hr 40min); Celerico da Beira (2 daily; 1hr 45min); Coimbra (2 daily; 4hr 55min); Lisbon (2 daily; 7hr 25min); Torre de Moncorvo (3 daily; 30min); Trancoso (Mon–Fri 2 daily; 2hr 30min); Viseu (2 daily; 2hr 45min).

Porto to: Abrantes, R (1 daily; 4hr 35min); Amarante, AD, AVT, R (Mon–Fri 10 daily, Sat & Sun 5 daily; 1hr 10min–1hr 25min); Aveiro, C (4 daily; 2hr 30min); Barcelos, L (Mon–Sat 7 daily; 1hr 45min); Braga, Rx, Rs, RE, C (17 daily; 1hr 20min); Bragança, R (3 daily; 1hr 50min–3hr 50min); Caminha, AVMi (Mon–Fri 7 daily, Sat & Sun 1 daily; 2hr); Chaves, AVT, R (6–12 daily; 3hr 10min–5hr); Coimbra, RE, R, AVT (8–10 daily; 1hr 30min); Fátima, R (6 daily; 3hr 30min); Guarda, M, J, R (7 daily; 2hr 10min–3hr 20min); Guimarães, JFN (12 daily; 2hr); Lamego, AD (3–5 daily; 4hr–4hr 30min); Leiria, R (6 daily; 1hr 40min–2hr 30min); Lisbon, Rx, RE, EVA (hourly; 3hr–3hr 30min); Melgaço, AVMi (2 daily; 3hr); Mirandela, R, SF (2–4 daily; 2hr 45min); Monção AVMi, T, R (7 daily; 2hr 45min–3hr); Mondim de Basto, AVM (7 daily; 3hr 30min); Penafiel, V, AVT (24 daily; 55min–1hr); Póvoa de Varzim, L, AVMi (16 daily; 40–55min); Tomar, R (1 daily; 4hr); Valença do Minho, AVMi, T, R (5 daily; 2hr 30min–2hr 45min); Viana do Castelo, AVMi, L (12–14 daily; 1hr 15min–2hr); Vila do Conde, AVMi, L (16 daily; 35–55min); Vila Real, AVT, R (9 daily; 2hr); Viseu, M, R, & J (8 daily; 2hr).

Póvoa de Varzim to: Barcelos (4–5 daily; 45min); Braga (9 daily; 1hr 15min); Esposende (9–12 daily; 40min); Guimarães (9–11 daily; 1hr 45min); Santo Tirso (Mon–Sat 12 daily, Sun 6 daily; 1hr); Viana do Castelo (Mon–Fri 24 daily, Sat 17 daily, Sun 11 daily; 1hr 5min); Vila do Conde (every 15min; 15min).

Domestic flights

Porto to: Faro (2 daily; 2hr 15min–3hr); Funchal, Madeira (6 weekly; 2hr); Lisbon (19 daily; 45min); Ponta Delgada, Açores (1 daily; 3hr 15min); Porto Santo, Madeira (2 weekly; 4hr 30min); Terceira, Açores (1 daily; 3hr 15min–4hr 45min).

The Minho

CHAPTER 6

Highlights

✳ **Guimarães** The country's first capital is an attractive maze of cobbled streets, medieval monuments and hidden squares. See p.353

✳ **Citânia de Briteiros** Step back to pre-Roman times at the magnificent Celtic hill fort. See p.361

✳ **Braga** Portugal's answer to Rome is at its best during the Easter celebrations. See p.363

✳ **Bom Jesus** Join the pilgrims and the penitents on the wonderful Baroque stairway to heaven. See p.369

✳ **Feira de Barcelos** The spectaclar Thursday *feira* is one of Europe's biggest weekly markets. See p.373

✳ **Beaches of the Costa Verde** There's always space to lay your towel on the kilometres of golden sand on the rugged Atlantic coast. See p.377

✳ **Valença do Minho** Gaze across the Rio Minho to Spain from the ramparts of the ancient walled town. See p.390

✳ **Vinho verde country** Follow the Vinho Verde Route or simply stroll through the endless vineyards and sample the young wine. See p.392

✳ **Peneda-Gerês National Park** A wild and solitary corner of the country offering spectacular hikes and outdoor pursuits. See p.403

6

The Minho

With good reason, many Portuguese consider the **Minho** – the province north of Porto – to be the most beautiful part of their country. A wild rolling province of lush river valleys, forested hillsides, trailing vines and long, sandy beaches, it is immensely pleasing on the eye, while much is made of the Minho's traditional aspect, especially in the mountainous east, where you can still see wooden-wheeled ox-carts creak down cobbled lanes. Here age-old customs are maintained at dozens of huge country markets, *festas* and *romarias*. In summer, especially, you're likely to happen upon these carnivals, though it's worth trying to plan your trip around the larger events if you're keen to experience Minho life at its most exuberant – the main markets and principal festivals are detailed where appropriate throughout the chapter.

As you travel around the region, you'll see signs of new building in even the smallest and most isolated villages; things are starting to change. This is explained by the many new initiatives which are springing up making the most of the tourism potential of the region but also by the new-found prosperity of returned emigrants keen to put something back into their home towns. Starting in the late 1950s, Minho, more than any other area of Portugal, suffered severe depopulation as thousands migrated to France, Switzerland, Germany and even the United States in search of more lucrative work. The tide of emigration has slowed in recent years as Portugal reaps the financial benefits of membership of the European Union, but there are still many who choose to at least start their careers abroad.

The largest towns are concentrated in the southern Minho and any trip should allow time to examine the competing historic claims of **Guimarães**, first capital of Portugal, and neighbouring **Braga**, the country's ecclesiastical centre. Between them lie the extensive Celtic ruins of the **Citânia de Briteiros**, one of the most impressive archeological sites in Portugal, while from Braga it's also easy to visit **Barcelos**, site of the best-known (and biggest) of the region's weekly markets. It takes place on Thursdays, though for the full experience reserve a room in advance and arrive on Wednesday evening.

At Barcelos, you're only 20km from the **Costa Verde**, the Minho coast, which runs north all the way to the Spanish border. This has some wonderful beaches along the way, though the weather is as unpredictable as the sea, with cool temperatures possible even in midsummer. The principal resort is **Viana do Castelo**, an enjoyable and lively town with an elegant historic core though, if you're seeking isolation, there are strands to the north and south that scarcely see visitors. The coast ends at **Caminha**, beyond which the **Rio Minho** runs inland, forming the border with Spanish Galicia. This is a delightful region, featuring a string of compact fortified towns flanking the river on the Portuguese side, their fortresses, in various stages of disrepair, staring across at Spain.

Inland from Viana, the Minho's other major river, the beautiful **Rio Lima**, runs east through a succession of gorgeous small towns where there's little to do but soak up the somnolent scenery. On the whole, much of the Minho is outrageously picturesque and full of quiet charm and interest. In fact it was in the Lima valley, and particularly around the town of **Ponte de Lima**, that TURIHAB first exploited the beauty of the countryside to the benefit of tourists by offering accommodation in local manor houses, old farms and country estates (see p.33). Further east, the gentle Minho scenery eventually gives way to the mountains, waterfalls, river gorges, reservoirs and forests of the protected **Parque Nacional da Peneda–Gerês**, Portugal's only national (as opposed to natural) park. This is superb camping and hiking territory, stretching from the main town and spa of **Caldas do Gerês** north as far as the Rio

Minho and the Spanish border and east into Trás-os-Montes. It's possible to dip into the park from a couple of easily accessible towns, but you really need to devote several days if you're going to see the more isolated regions as bus services are limited; even by car the going's slow and on foot you could spend weeks exploring the trails.

Southern Minho

The **southern Minho**'s two chief towns, **Guimarães** and **Braga**, are both small enough to walk around in a busy day's sightseeing, though a night's stay has greater rewards. This is especially true if you want to explore the series of religious attractions around Braga, none more extraordinary than the pilgrimage site of **Bom Jesus do Monte**; while you'll need to set aside another half-day at least to see the **Citânia de Briteiros**. However, for shoppers, the best overnight stop is undoubtedly at **Barcelos**, provided you can find a room on a Wednesday night before the weekly market.

Braga is on a branch of the main **train route** from Porto to Viana do Castelo; for non-direct trains you'll need to change at Nine. There are currently no trains operating on the Guimarães branch of the main line, but there are vague plans to reinstate the service although no date has been set. Regardless of all this, it is far quicker to use the direct **bus** between Braga and Guimarães rather than fiddle about with connections between the train lines.

Guimarães and around

GUIMARÃES never misses an opportunity to remind you of its place in Portuguese history. Birthplace of the first king, Afonso Henriques, in 1110 and first capital of the fledging kingdom of Portucale, it has every right to be proud of its role in the formation of the nation. It was from here that the reconquest from the Moors began, leading to the subsequent creation of a united kingdom which, within a century of Afonso's death, was to stretch to its present borders. Although Guimarães subsequently lost its pre-eminent status to Coimbra – which became the Portuguese capital in 1143 – it has never relinquished its sense of self-importance, something that's evident from the careful preservation of an array of impressive medieval monuments and the omnipresent reminder "Portugal nasceu aqui" (Portugal was born here). Today, despite its industrial outskirts, the centre of Guimarães retains a grandeur and a tangible sense of history in the labyrinth of narrow streets, which makes it one of the most attractive towns in the country.

If you can afford to stay at one of the two local *pousadas* – one in the centre, the other in a former monastery at **Penha**, 5km southeast – then the experience is complete. Otherwise, decent budget accommodation is hard to come by, though this matters little since Braga (24km), or even Porto (55km), are close enough to be used as base to visit Guimarães on a day trip. Unless you

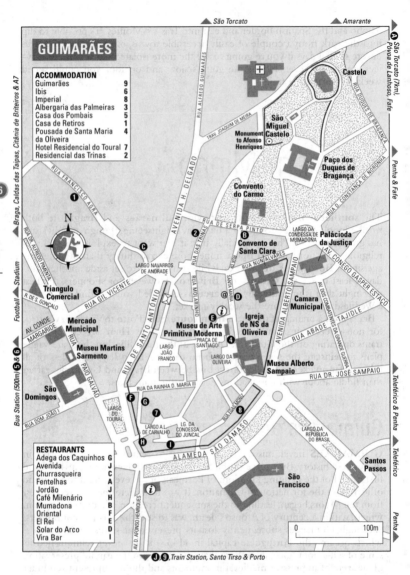

GUIMARÃES

ACCOMMODATION
Guimarães	9
Ibis	6
Imperial	8
Albergaria das Palmeiras	3
Casa dos Pombais	5
Casa de Retiros	1
Pousada de Santa Maria da Oliveira	4
Hotel Residencial do Toural	7
Residencial das Trinas	2

RESTAURANTS
Adega dos Caquinhos	G
Avenida	J
Churrasqueira	C
Fentelhas	A
Jordão	J
Café Milenário	H
Mumadona	B
Oriental	F
El Rei	E
Solar do Arco	D
Vira Bar	I

book well in advance, you may have no other choice, especially if you visit during either of the town's festivals.

The major event is the **Festas Gualterianas** (for São Gualter, or St Walter), which has taken place on the first weekend in August every year since 1452. If you miss this you can catch most of the same stallholders, and something of the atmosphere, the weekend after in Caldas de Vizela, a spa town 10km south of Guimarães. Next in importance is the long-established *romaria* to **São Torcato**, 6km northeast of town, on the first weekend in July, which, in the curious language of the turismo leaflet, "includes a procession with archaic choirs of virgins". A well-timed visit in winter will enable you to see one or more of the festivals of **Nicolinas** (Nov 29–Dec 7), **Nossa Senhora da Conceição** (Dec 8) and **Santa Luzia** (Dec 13).

Arrival and information

Guimarães' **train station** is ten minutes' walk south of the centre; to get into town, bear left from the station and take the first right down Avenida Dom Afonso Henriques, which takes you on to Alameda São Damaso – the main **turismo** is on your right at number 83 (Mon–Fri 9.30am–12.30pm & 2–6.30pm; ☎253 412 450, ⊛www.cm-guimaraes.pt). It produces the *Manual de Informação Turística* (available in English), a work of biblical proportions containing almost every piece of contact information that a visitor could ever need (although you will have to ask for one as they are in short supply). There's a second turismo above an exhibition room at Praça de Santiago 37 (Mon–Fri 9.30am–6.30pm, Sat 10am–6pm, Sun 10am–1pm; ☎253 518 790, ⓔturismo .cmg@mail.telepac.pt). Both are helpful, and supply maps and informative colour booklets on museums and sights, as well as information on hotels and *turismo rural* properties. **Internet** access is available at the funky *Bar Carramão*, next door to the municipal library on Rua de Santa Maria, and costs around €2.60 per hour.

The **bus station** is fifteen minutes' walk southwest of the town centre at the bottom of Avenida Conde Margaride – as part of the Guimarães shopping complex it's unmarked, but identifiable by the Continente supermarket or McDonald's sign above the entrance. For the ten-minute walk from the bus station into the town centre, turn right and walk up Conde Margaride as far as the market (Mercado Municipal); from here you can continue along Rua Gil Vicente, or turn right along Rua Paio Galvão towards Largo do Toural and the main turismo. There are express bus services from Porto and Lisbon, and regular weekday connections with Braga, Amarante, Cabeceiras and Mondim de Basto, and Póvoa do Lanhoso. **Taxis** can be hailed in the street, or called on ☎253 522 522.

Accommodation

Inexpensive **accommodation** is scarce in town, even more so during Guimarães' main festivals – nearby Braga (p.363) has a much better choice of budget accommodation. It's best to book ahead – especially if you're planning a splurge in the *pousadas*, or in one of a number of superb manor houses in the vicinity: the turismo has details of these (ask for *turismo rural*). There are two **campsites** in the locality – the nearest is the *Parque de Campismo da Penha* (☎253 515 912, ⒻAX253 516 569), a pleasant site with a small swimming pool and some bungalows for rent (❷), on the slopes of Penha and accessible by the cable car at the end of Rua de Doutor José Sampaio. Though it's officially open between April and October, it's worth ringing ahead at other times. Seven kilometres northwest of Guimarães, *Caldas das Taipas* (☎253 576 274; June–Sept), by the banks of the Rio Ave off the N101, is pricier but arguably more attractive, with a swimming pool and a thermal spa nearby.

In Town

Casa dos Pombais Av de Londres ☎253 412 917. Opposite the bus station, this eighteenth-century Solares de Portugal manor house is an oasis in a built-up part of town, a lovely old building with attractive gardens. There are only two guest rooms, which have received mixed reports from readers. Conveniently located though, so book well ahead. ❹

Casa de Retiros Rua Francisco Agra 163 ☎253 511 515, ⒻAX253 511 517. A pilgrim's hostel and as a result one of the cheaper places in town. If you wish to stay expect to lead a simple existence with spartan surroundings, bland breakfasts and an 11.30pm curfew. At peak times may be booked up by groups. Rates – per person – are in private rooms or dormitory accommodation, and include breakfast. ❷

Hotel de Guimarães Rua Dr. Eduardo Almeida, 100m from the train station ☏ 253 424 800, ✉ hg@Hotel-guimaraes.com. The top modern choice with four-star comforts, including health club, jacuzzi, pool, sauna and restaurant. ❻

Hotel Ibis Av Conde Margaride ☏ 253 424 900, ℻ 253 424 901. Reasonable if rather generic chain hotel located conveniently next to the bus terminal. ❸

Pensão Imperial Alameda São Damaso 111 ☏ 253 415 163. This gloomy, rundown *pensão* is overpriced by any but Guimarães' standards, but offers some of the cheapest beds in town. ❷

Albergaria das Palmeiras Centro Comercial das Palmeiras, Rua Gil Vicente ☏ 253 410 324, ℻ 253 417 261. Part of a commercial mall, which can make it difficult to find (and enter after shopping hours), but it's modern, with a restaurant and parking facilities. ❸

Pousada de Santa Maria da Oliveira Rua de Santa Maria ☏ 253 514 157, ℻ 253 514 204. Converted from a row of sixteenth-century houses and brilliantly located right in the medieval centre, this sixteen-room *pousada* is beautifully furnished and worth every euro. ❼

Hotel Residencial do Toural Largo do Toural, entrance in Largo A.L. de Carvalho at the back ☏ 253 517 184, ✉ hoteltoural@netc.pt. Once an elegant town house, this has been completely renovated into an ultra-modern four-star establishment – not cheap, but very comfortable. ❺

Residencial das Trinas Rua das Trinas 29 ☏ 253 517 358, ℻ 253 517 362. Situated in the old town,

this *residencial* has eleven top-notch rooms, and is one of the best of the cheaper options. Rooms have private bathrooms, satellite TV and telephone. Those at the back can be noisy, but the rates are good and include breakfast. ❸

Outside town

Casa de Sezim Nespereira, 6km south of Guimarães off the Santo Tirso road – turn right at Covas ☏ 253 523 000, ℻ 253 523 196. Delightful aristocratic country estate – owned by the same *vinho verde*-producing family for over six centuries. The buildings, plastered powder pink, are in a mixture of styles, and have six rooms in the main 18th-century *solar* (manor), each equipped with Murano chandeliers and varied objets d'art. There's a swimming pool, and four-poster beds in many rooms. Walking and horse-riding trips are on offer. ❻

Paço de São Cipriano Taboadelo, 6km south of Guimarães off the Santo Tirso road – turn left at Covas ☏ 253 565 337. Architecturally stunning eighteenth-century country palace, complete with chapel and medieval tower, which contains the five guest rooms. Orchards, vineyards and a swimming pool complete the unforgettable ambience. Closed Nov–March. ❻

Pensão da Penha at the top of the *teleférico* ☏ 253 414 245, ℻ 253 512 952. A perfectly good, if unspectacular, option should you want to stay at the top of Penha. ❷

Pousada de Santa Marinha da Costa at the foot of Monte Penha, 2km along Rua Dr. José Sampaio ☏ 253 511 249, ℻ 253 514 459. Occupying a convent, parts of which date from the ninth century, this is reckoned to be one of the top *pousadas* in the country; ask for one of the original rooms, which have far more character than the new additions. ❽

The Town

The old centre of **Guimarães** is an elongated kernel of small, enclosed squares and cobbled streets dominated by warm, honey-coloured buildings. Bounded at its southern end by the town gardens and overlooked from the north by the imposing castle, it is an enduring symbol of the emergent Portuguese nation. In between lie a series of medieval churches, convents and buildings that lend an air of dignity to the streets – two of the convents provide an impressive backdrop to a couple of the country's more illuminating museums. The presence of the University of the Minho gives the local cafés and bars a lively, student-orientated feel, particularly in the old town.

Around the Castelo

The imposing **Castelo** (June–Sept 9.30am–12.30pm & 2–5.30pm; free) was built in the tenth century by the countess of Mumadona to protect the people of Guimarães from attack by Moors and Normans. It was extended to approximately its modern size by **Afonso Henriques**, who established the first Portuguese court here in the twelfth century. After falling into disrepair and being used as a debtor's prison in the nineteenth century, the castle was rebuilt in the 1940s. Afonso is reputed to have been born in the great square keep, which is surrounded by seven fortified towers. You can wander around the ramparts and check out the views of town, or climb the 77 steps to the top of the central **keep** (€0.50), which opens out onto a narrow tower, but take care as the stonework is uneven and narrow in places. The castle is juxtaposed with the diminutive Romanesque chapel of **São Miguel do Castelo** (9am–12.30pm & 2–5pm; free), on the grassy slope below, in whose font Afonso is traditionally said to have been baptised.

Just across from the chapel is the **Paço dos Duques de Bragança** (July–Aug 9.30am–12.30 & 2–7pm; Sept–June 9.30am–12.30pm & 2–5.30pm; €3, free Sunday mornings). Built in the fifteenth century by the illegitimate son of King Dom João I, Dom Afonso, it was constructed along Burgundian lines by a French architect, reflecting Afonso's cosmopolitan tastes. It served as the medieval palace of the all-powerful Bragançan duchy until it fell into decline at the end of the sixteenth century. Under the Salazar dictatorship, its ruins were "restored" as an official residence for the president (the second floor is still reserved for this function), but today, it looks rather ludicrous – like a mock-Gothic Victorian folly. Inside is an extensive collection of portraits (including a whole room of colourful paintings and sculptures by modern artist José de Guimarães), tapestries, furniture, weapons and porcelain, around which lengthy guided tours perambulate. Free concerts are occasionally held here on summer weekends as part of the annual "Encontros da Primavera" season of concerts; enquire at the turismos for details.

Outside the castle, a number of shops sell **children's toys**, hammered out from old tin and no doubt lethal, but beautiful objects nonetheless; there's a café here, too.

Along Rua de Santa Maria

From the castle, **Rua de Santa Maria** leads down into the heart of the old town, a beautiful thoroughfare featuring iron grilles and granite arches. Many of the town's historic buildings have been superbly restored, and as you descend to the centre you'll pass one of the loveliest – the sixteenth-century convent of Santa Clara, with its Baroque facade, which today acts as the **Câmara Municipal**. Many of its furnishings were removed after the dissolution of the monasteries, and now reside in the Museu Alberto Sampaio (see below).

On a much more intimate scale are the buildings ranged around the delightful central squares at the end of the street, **Praça de Santiago** and **Largo da Oliveira**. The latter is dominated by the **Igreja de Nossa Senhora da Oliveira** (daily 7.15am–noon & 3.30–7.30pm; free), a convent-church built (like the great monastery at Batalha) to honour a vow made to the Virgin Mary by João I prior to his decisive victory over Castile at Aljubarrota. Its unusual dedication to "Our Lady of the Olive Tree" dates from the fourteenth century, when an olive tree from the shrine of São Torcato was replanted in the monastery to provide oil for the lamps of the church. The tree died and remained lifeless until September 8, 1342, when a cross, hung from one of its branches, made it grow again. Before it stands a curious Gothic **canopy-shrine**, erected in 1340 to commemorate the Battle of Salado, another one of many disagreements with the Castilians. It also marks the legendary spot where

Wamba, unwilling king of the Visigoths, drove a pole into the ground swearing that he would not reign until it blossomed. Naturally, in keeping with the remarkable growth patterns hearabouts, it sprouted immediately. João I, feeling this to be a useful indication of divine favour, set out to meet the Castilian forces from this very point.

Next door is the convent's simple Romanesque cloister with varied, naively carved capitals. This, and the rooms off it which formerly comprised the Colegiada (college), now house the **Museu Alberto Sampaio** (Tues–Sun 10am–12.30pm & 2–5.30pm; €2, free Sunday mornings; ☎253 423 910, ⓔmuseu.asampaio@clix.pt), essentially the treasury of the collegiate church and convent but, for once, outstandingly exhibited and containing pieces of real beauty. The highlight is a brilliantly composed silver-gilt *Triptych of the Nativity*, said to have been found in the King of Castile's tent after the Portuguese victory at Aljubarrota in 1385, although it was more probably made from melting down the King's silver measuring weights. Close by is the tunic worn by João I in the battle, now beginning to show its age.

Opposite the museum and housed in a heavy arched structure that was formerly the council chambers, the **Museu de Arte Primitiva Moderna** (Mon–Fri 9am–12.30pm & 2–5.30pm; free) contains over 300 works by self-taught artists which provide a fascinating excursion through daily, secular and ritual life and range from pure kitsch to the odd masterpiece.

The Museu Martins Sarmento and the Igreja de São Francisco

Across to the west, over the main Largo do Toural, the **Museu Arqueológico Martins Sarmento** (Tues–Sun 10am–noon & 2–5pm; €1.50) is another superb collection, also housed in a former convent and named after Martins Sarmento, an archeologist, born in the town who discovered the Celtic *citânia* of Briteiros (see p.361). His body lies in the churchyard of the nearby hamlet of Briteiros. Finds from the site are displayed in the fourteenth-century Gothic cloister of the Igreja de São Domingos. They include a remarkable series of bronze votive offerings (among them, a "coach", pulled at each end by men and oxen), and ornately patterned stone lintels and door jambs from the huts; while most spectacular of all are the **Pedras Formosas** ("beautiful stones"). Once taken to be sacrificial altars or the portals to funerary monuments, it's now agreed that these were most likely to have been taken from the interior of bath houses. The **Colossus of Pedralva**, a vast granite hulk of a figure with arm raised aloft and an oversized phallus, once the museum's prize exhibit, now stands guard at the pedestrian precinct outside the bus station. More enigmatic and considerably more ancient than the Pedras Formosas, it shares the bold, powerfully hewn appearance of the stone pigs found in Trás-os-Montes (see p.443), and, like them, may date from pre-Celtic fertility cults of around 1500 to 1000 BC.

Among the numerous other churches scattered about the centre of Guimarães, the finest is the **Igreja de São Francisco** (Tues–Sat 9.30am–noon & 3–5pm, Sun 9.30am–1pm, Mass 12.30pm; free), on the south side of the town gardens. Constructed in 1220 on the orders of Dona Urraca, wife of Dom Afonso II, it features a series of huge eighteenth-century *azulejos* of St Francis preaching to the fish, and an elegant Renaissance cloister and fountain. Once again, the church was attached to a monastery of considerable size until the 1834 dissolution.

Penha and Santa Marinha da Costa

Two kilometres southeast of Guimarães on the slopes of **Penha** (617m) stands the region's best-preserved medieval building, the former monastery – and now *pousada* – of **Santa Marinha da Costa**. It can be reached by taking the São Roque bus (Mon–Sat 6am–10pm, Sun 6am–8pm; every 30min) from the main turismo; get off at "Costa" and follow the signs.

The monastery was founded in 1154 by order of Dona Mafalda, the wife of Afonso Henriques, in honour of a vow to Santa Marinha, patron saint of pregnant women. Originally Augustinian, the foundation passed into the hands of the Order of St Jerome in the sixteenth century. In the **chapel** (official hours July–Sept 9am–1pm & 2–7pm but often inexplicably closed), Jerome's twin emblems of the skull and the lion are recurring motifs. They are surrounded by an oddly harmonious mixture of styles – tenth-century doorways on the south wall, sixteenth-century panels in the sacristy (including one depicting Jerome beating his breast with a stone against the temptation of women), and an eighteenth-century organ and stone roof in the choir. A disastrous fire hit the monastery in 1951, but careful restoration and its transformation into a *pousada* have returned it to some of its former glories. Strictly speaking, the rest of the monastic buildings are off limits except to guests of the *pousada* (see p.356), but you can peek into the magnificent **cloister**, with its Mozarabic doorway, while the beautiful **gardens** are open to the public, too. If you intend to have more of a look around it would be diplomatic to buy a meal, or at least a drink at the bar.

The peak of Penha is crowned by a statue of Nossa Senhora – by far the most fun way to reach it is to take the ingenious **Teleférico da Penha** cable car, whose hi-tech bubbles leave from the end of Rua de Doutor José Sampaio (Mon–Fri 11am–7pm, Sat & Sun 10am–8pm; €2.50 return).

Eating and drinking

Guimarães has no shortage of places to **eat and drink** which, in contrast to much of the accommodation, is mostly quite reasonably priced. Local specialities to look out for – or avoid – include *chispalhada de feijão* (beans, sausage and pig's trotters), *papas de sarabulho* (a blood and bread stew) and *rojões de porco* (roast pork, sausages and potatoes). Desserts include *melindres* (honey cakes), *aletria* (like vermicelli) and *toucinho do céu* ("heavenly bacon", actually a supersweet concoction of sugar, almonds, eggs and lemon).

Adega dos Caquinhos Travessa da Arrochela between Largo A.L. Carvalho and Rua Rainha D. Maria III. A friendly, traditional *adega* whose name reflects its decor – walls covered in broken crockery (*caquinhos*). The food is good and reasonably priced, at around €8 for a full meal and drinks.

Avenida Av Dom Afonso Henriques. Unassuming place near the main turismo. Eat at tables (you may have to share) or at the bar. No frills, and cheap: under €10 for your meal and drinks.

Churrasqueira Rua Francisco Agra 30. Excellent fresh grilled meat served in basic (and smoky) surroundings. Very cheap at under €5.50 for a meal and drinks.

Fentelhas Rua Pedro Homem de Melo, 7km out of town off the road to São Torcato ☎ 253 551 292. Traditional Portuguese cooking with specialities that

include *galo de cabidela* (on the menu as "rooster rice") and *bacalhau com presunto e broa* (bachalau with ham and corn bread). Closed Sun eve.

Jordão Av Dom Afonso Henriques 55, near the train station. Mid-range regional specialities such as roast veal and *rojões*. Closed Mon eves and Tues all day.

Café Milenário Largo do Toural. Large and airy traditional café serving reasonable snacks; popular with young and old alike.

Mumadona, corner of Rua Serpa Pinto and Rua Santa Maria, near Largo Condessa de Mumadona. Reliable, inexpensive stand-by, with two-course set menus at €7.50–10. Closed Sun.

Oriental Largo do Toural. Excellent budget option serving very good regional specialities as well as more usual fare: try the *truta grelhada com* *presunto* (grilled trout stuffed with ham). Offers superb views over the square. Under €7.50.

Pousada de Santa Maria da Oliveira Rua de Santa Maria ☎253 514 157, 🌐www.pousadas.pt. When on form, this is the best restaurant in town, with traditional Minho dishes served in a wonderful antique dining room or at outside tables in summer. You'll need to reserve a table in advance. From €18 a head.

El Rei Praça de Santiago 20a. Small cosy restaurant in a prime location, serving consistently good-quality food at moderate prices. Closed Sun.

Solar do Arco Rua de Santa Maria 48–50, by the arch. Welcoming restaurant in a prime position, but priced accordingly. Try the unusual *feijoada de camarões* (bean stew with shrimps), or any of the home-made desserts. Around €10–15. Closed Sun.

Vira Bar Largo Condessa do Juncal 27. A well-regarded, church-like place with stained-glass windows, stone walls, a barrel-vaulted ceiling and a subdued ambience. €13–20 will get you the full works. Closed Sun.

Entertainment and nightlife

Outside festival time, at the beginning of July and August, the only time the town erupts into spontaneous celebration is when the local **soccer** team, FC Guimarães (consistently one of Portugal's better teams), wins at home. The stadium, undergoing improvements for the 2004 European Championships, is located to the northwest of the centre, along Rua de São Gonçalo. You'll find a number of **bars** in and around the central Praça de Santiago and the adjacent Largo da Oliveira, most aimed at a youthful clientele, but all with outdoor tables and very popular, particularly on summer nights. The *Ultimatum Jazz Café* on Rua St Rei do Pegu is an atmospheric café-cum-restaurant that metamorphoses into a disco after hours. As for **clubs**, the two mainstays are *Penha Clube*, at the foot of the *teleférico,* which is busiest at weekends (10pm–4am) and has occasional live bands. Popular with all ages, *Seculo XIX* (Wed–Sun 10pm–4am) is 1.5km north of town on Rua Teixeira de Pascoais, just off the continuation of Rua Capitão Alfredo Guimarães (look out for the signs). Other clubs make mayfly-like appearances in the summer months, only to disappear without trace in winter – ask at the turismos for details, or – more reliably – collar a student at one of the Largo da Oliveira's many bars.

East towards Trás-os-Montes

Heading **east towards Trás-os-Montes**, the minor N206 runs across country towards the Rio Tâmega, a region covered in the previous chapter. Buses along this route are frequent as far as **FAFE** (up to 17 daily, run by Auto-Viação Landim), 14km away and little more than an overgrown bus station (you'll almost certainly need to change here for Trás-os-Montes destinations, and may have to stay the night). Fafe has three *pensões* and a large revolutionary statue of a worker violently clubbing his bowler-hatted boss. The best place to stay is probably the *Comfort Inn* on Avenida do Brasil (☎253 595 222; ❸), which, as its name suggests, is comfortable and clean but rather unmemorable.

Beyond Fafe lies some magnificent countryside, dotted with huge boulders, though you'll really need your own transport to get the most out of the region as bus services are less than regular. If you're driving, you might want to stop at **GANDARELA**, 17km east of Fafe, which is famed for its topiary, while at **ARCO DE BAÚLHE**, 10km further, a road splits off 7km north to Cabeceiras de Basto (see p.332). A dozen kilometres or so further east you finally reach the Tâmega River itself, where you're just 30km from the main Vila Real–Chaves road.

The Citânia de Briteiros

Midway between Guimarães and Braga is one of the most impressive and exciting archeological sites in the country, the **Citânia de Briteiros**. *Citânias* – Celtic hill settlements – lie scattered throughout the Minho: remains of 27 have been identified along the coast, plus sixteen more in the region between

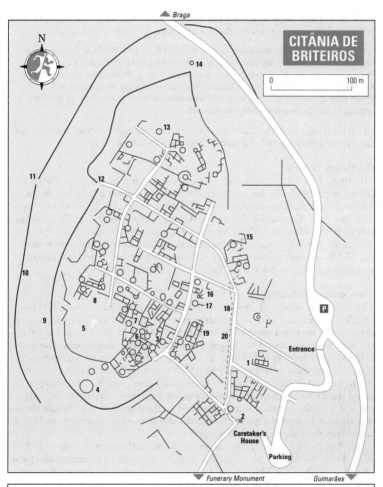

1 Area reserved for cattle	11 Gateway
2 Early fountain	12 Gateway
3 Cross and Christian cemetery	13 Well for water provision
4 Circular house belonging to community	14 Single, isolated house outside inner walls
5 Chapel of S.Romão	15 Water source (now defunct)
6 House with helix	16 Houses with stone benches
7 Houses reconstructed by Martins Sarmento	17 Law courts (?), prisons (?)
8 Small paved area	18 Ingenious method of transporting water
9 Inside wall	19 House with various rooms
10 Second (of four) walls	20 Cistern

Braga and Guimarães alone. Most date from the arrival of northern European Celts in the Iron Age (c.600–500 BC), though some are far older, having merged with an existing local culture established since Neolithic times (c.2000 BC). The site at Briteiros, straddling the boulder-strewn hill of São Romão, was probably the last stronghold of the Celt-Iberians against the invading Romans, finally being taken around 20BC and eventually abandoned in 300AD.

The Roman historian Strabo gave a vivid description of the northern Portuguese tribes, who must have occupied these *citânias*, in his *Geographia* (c.20 BC). They organized mass sacrifices, he recorded, and inspected prisoners' entrails without removing them. Otherwise, they liked to:

live simply, drink water and sleep on the bare earth ... two-thirds of the year they live on acorns, which they roast and grind to make bread. They also have beer. They lack wine but when they have it they drink it up, gathering for a family feast. At banquets they sit on a bench against the wall according to age and rank ... When they assemble to drink they perform round dances to the flute or the horn, leaping in the air and crouching as they fall.

Entrails aside – and they may have been literary licence – none of this seems far removed from the Minho and Trás-os-Montes of recent memory.

Getting there

The Braga **bus** leaves Guimarães every thirty minutes and stops in the pleasant spa town of Caldas das Taipas, from where you can get a local bus the 5km southwest to the *citânia* or take a taxi (€5). Alternatively, catch one of the buses that run from Guimarães through Caldas das Taipas to Póvoa do Lanhoso (Mon–Fri 10.45am & 1.30pm Sat 9am) – which pass through Santo Estevão (Briteiros), just over 1km southeast of the site itself. Leaving the *citânia*, hitching a lift from other visitors, either to Braga or Guimarães, should be fairly easy, and there's also a bus back from Santo Estevão at 2pm (Mon–Sat).

The excavations

The site **excavations** (☎253 415 969; daily 9am–noon and 1–5pm; €1) have revealed foundations of over a hundred and fifty **huts**, a couple of which have been rebuilt to give a sense of their scale and design. Most of them are circular, with benches around the edges and a central stone that would have provided support for a pole holding up a thatched roof. A few are rectangular in shape, among them a larger building which may have been a prison or meeting house – it is labelled the *casa do tribunal*. There's also a clear network of paved streets and paths, two circuits of town walls, plus cisterns, stone guttering and a public fountain (the *fonte*). Most of these features are identifiable as you wander around the place, though the site is more evocative in its layout and extent than for any particular sights.

One feature not to be missed, however, is the **bathhouse** or cistern (a fair walk down the hill to the left of the settlement), with its geometrically patterned stone doorway. This was believed to be a funerary chamber until recently, when it was pointed out that as much of the hill's run-off flowed into the site, it wouldn't have been the best place to put dead bodies. Similar remnants of construction, along with carved lintels from the huts and other finds from the *citânia*, are displayed at the Museu Martins Sarmento in Guimarães (see p.358). These indicate that the settlement was abandoned as late as 300 AD and – unlike Conímbriga, another Celtic site near Coimbra – shows little Roman influence other than the presence of coins.

Braga

BRAGA is a city with ecclesiastical pretensions. Even the turismo pamphlet hails it as the Portuguese Rome, although the Portuguese Canterbury might be more appropriate. One of the country's most ancient towns, it was probably founded by the Bracari Celts (hence the name), later falling into Roman hands and being named Bracara, capital of Roman Gallaecia. Its history is then one of conquest and reconquest, being occupied at various times by the Suevi, Visigoths and eventually the Moors. Braga was an important Visigothic bishopric and by the end of the eleventh century its archbishops were pressing for recognition as "Primate of the Spains", a title they disputed bitterly with archbishops of Toledo and Tarragona over the next six centuries.

The city is still Portugal's religious capital; look around and you'll soon become aware of the weight of Church power, embodied by an archbishop's palace built on a truly presidential scale. At **Easter**, Braga is the scene of spectacular celebrations, with eerie torchlit processions and hooded penitents – while its outlying districts boast a selection of important religious buildings and sanctuaries, including that of **Bom Jesus**, one of the country's most extravagant Baroque creations. The city also has a reputation as a bastion of reactionary politics. It was here, in 1926, that General Gomes da Costa appealed to "all citizens of dignity and honour" to overthrow the democratic regime, kickstarting the process that eventually led to Salazar's dictatorship, while in the more recent past, after the 1974 Revolution, the Archbishop of Braga personally incited a mob to attack local Communist offices.

The city is an enjoyable place to stay and makes a good base for touring the southern Minho. Desperate to escape its traditionally conservative image, it is looking to acquire a new energy that reflects less of the Church and more of its position as a fast-growing commercial centre. This is most clearly evident in the scores of fashion houses, scattered liberally amongst the churches and stores peddling religious paraphernalia. However, the appearance of a network of fast roads, underpasses and big, modern tower blocks in and around the ancient town has angered many residents who feel that the old centre of Braga (the phrase "as old as the Cathedral of Braga" is the Portuguese equivalent of "as old as the hills") should have been better preserved. The uneasy alliance of old and new is never more apparent than when driving – the confused one-way system does its best to keep you in the town when you're trying to leave and to keep you out if you're trying to enter. But the most controversial action has been the digging up of the gardens around Praça da República and Avenida Central to make an underground car park. The excavations uncovered, and promptly destroyed, a number of Roman houses.

In addition to the **Semana Santa** (Holy Week) celebrations, the whole city is illuminated for the **Festas de São João** (June 23–24), which provides the excuse for ancient folk dances, a fairground and general partying. There's also a festival of *gigantones* (giant carnival figures; June 18–20). The main **pilgrimage to Bom Jesus** (see p.369) takes place over Whitsun (six weeks after Easter). Braga also has a regular **Tuesday market**, held at the exhibition park in Avenida Pires Gonçalves, at the end of Avenida da Liberdade.

Arrival, information and accommodation

Braga is a fair-sized city, though the old town – an oval of streets radiating out from the Sé – is a compact area. From the **train station** (☎253 263 665), west of the centre, it's a 15–20 minute walk to the old town, reached down Rua

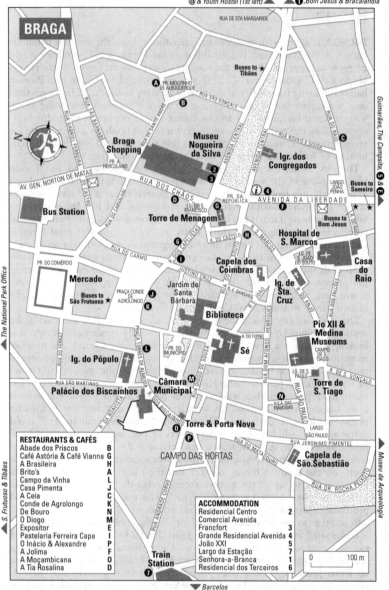

BRAGA

RUA DE STA MARGARIDE

@ & Youth Hostel (1st left) ▲   ▲ ❶ Bom Jesus & Bracalândia

Buses to ★
Tibães

Ⓐ PR. MOUZINHO
DE ALBUQUERQUE

RUA SÃO GONÇAL

Ⓑ

RUA DE SANTO ANDRÉ

Braga
Shopping

RUA GABRIEL PEREIRA DE CASTRO

RUA SÃO BARNABÉ

Museu
Nogueira
da Silva

RUA NOVAIS E SOUSA   Ⓒ

AVENIDA CENTRAL

AVENIDA CENTRAL

Igr. dos
Congregados

Guimarães, The Campsite, 5 & 6 ▶

LARGO
JOÃO
PENHA

Buses to
Sameiro

AV. GEN. NORTON DE MATOS

PR. A.
HERCULANO

RUA DOS CHÃOS

Ⓓ

PR. DA
REPÚBLICA

❷
❸

ⓘ Ⓐ

AVENIDA DA LIBERDADE

Ⓕ

Buses to
Bom Jesus

RUA DO RAIO

★
★

Bus Station

RUA DO CARVALHO

LG. DO S.
FRANCISCO

Torre de Menagem

Ⓖ

R. S. MARCOS

Hospital de
S. Marcos

RUA DO CASTELO

Ⓗ

Casa
do
Raio

RUA DO CARMO

RUA DO CAPELISTAS

❻

Ⓘ

JUSTINO CRUZ

Capela dos
Coimbras

LG. DE
S. JOÃO
DO SOUTO

RUA DO ANJO

RUA DOS FALCÕES

Mercado

PR. DO COMÉRCIO

Buses to ★
São Frutuoso

PRAÇA
CONDE
DE
AGROLONGO

Ⓙ

Ⓚ

Jardim de
Santa
Bárbara

R. F. SANCHES

Biblioteca

R. S. JOÃO

Ig. de
Sta.
Cruz

Pio XII &
Medina
Museums

RUA DO TERRAZ

Ⓛ

PR. DO
MUNICIPIO

Ⓜ

R. DO FORNO

Sé

RUA DOM AFONSO HENRIQUES

CAMPO
DE
S. TIAGO

R. DE S. GONÇAL

Ig. do Pópulo

PRAÇA TORRES DE ALMEIDA

RUA SÃO MARTINHO

Palácio dos Biscaínhos

Câmara
Municipal

RUA DOS BISCAÍNHOS

LG. DE S.
PAULO

RUA SÃO PAULO

Torre de
S. Tiago

R. DA BRAVIA

Ⓝ

R.S.A. DAS
TRAVESSAS

LARGO
SÃO PAULO

Ⓞ

Torre & Porta Nova

Ⓟ

RUA JÉRONIMO PIMENTEL

CAMPO DAS HORTAS

RUA DO MATADOURO

Capela de
São.Sebastião

Museu de Arqueologia ▶

RUA DR. ROCHA PEIXOTO

RESTAURANTS & CAFÉS
Abade dos Priscos   B
Café Astória & Café Vianna   G H
A Brasileira   A
Brito's   L
Campo da Vinha   J
Casa Pimenta   C
A Ceia   K
Conde de Agrolongo   N
De Bouro   M
O Diogo   E
Expositor   I
Pastelaria Ferreira Capa   P
O Inácio & Alexandre   F
A Jolima   O
A Moçambicana   D
A Tia Rosalina

ACCOMMODATION
Residencial Centro
Comercial Avenida   2
Francfort   3
Grande Residencial Avenida 4
João XXI   5
Largo da Estação   7
Senhora-a-Branca   1
Residencial dos Terceiros   6

RUA ANDRADE CORVO

Train
Station
❼

0   100 m

▼ Barcelos

Andrade Corvo. The main **bus station** (☏ 253 277 003) is 5–10 minutes' walk from the centre; turn right along Avenida General Norton de Matos, cross the small Praça Alexandre Herculano before following Rua dos Chãos into Praça da República. Here you'll find the **turismo** (Mon–Fri 9am–7pm, Sat 9am–12.30pm & 2–5.30pm; ☏ 253 262 550), housed in a wonderful Art Deco building on the corner of Praça da República and Avenida da Liberdade; it offers an impressive large-scale map of the city and displays of bus and train timetables. At the time of writing, many of Braga's attractions were undergoing renovations of undetermined length and were closed to the public. Provisional reopening dates were given rather vaguely as "2003", but check with the tourist office for the latest information. Braga also has an unofficial **website**, ⓦhttp://s700.uminho.pt/braga.html.

If you're heading for the Peneda-Gerês national park, it's worth calling in at the **national park headquarters** – a large, white house on Avenida António Macedo in the Quinta das Parretas suburb (Mon–Fri 9am–12.30pm & 2–5.30pm; ☎253 203 480, ⓕ253 613 169), a twenty-minute walk from the centre, where you can buy a useful map and booklet, and pick up information on walking trails (*trilhos*).

Accommodation

Braga has plenty of hotels and *pensões*, though it's unwise to turn up without a reservation during religious events and local festivals (see above). There's an excellent **youth hostel** at Rua de Santa Margarida 6, off Avenida Central (☎ & ⓕ253 616 163; reception 9am–noon & 6pm–midnight), which is very popular in summer with hikers and has some double rooms (❶), as well as a good noticeboard, lockers for valuables, a kitchen and a common room with satellite TV and a pool table. The **campsite**, *Camping Parque da Ponte* (☎253 273 355; April–Oct only), is a 2km walk from the centre, down Avenida da Liberdade and right next to the municipal swimming pool. Officially, you need an international camping carnet. Alternatively, if none of the Braga options appeals, you can stay at Bom Jesus (see p.370), 5km from the centre.

Residencial Centro Comercial Avenida Av Central 27–37 ☎253 275 722, ⓕ253 616 363. On the second floor of the Braga Shopping complex, which is open late for easy access. Big, comfortable rooms with TVs and baths, although some at the back lack windows and can be a bit dingy. Nonetheless handy located for the cinema below. ❸

Pensão Francfort Av Central 1–7 ☎253 262 648. Just across from Praça da República and opposite the main turismo, this charming and friendly place dates from 1879 but, like its owner, is beginning to show its age. Simple rooms, some with bath, make this one of the best bargains in town. ❸

Grande Residencial Avenida Av da Liberdade 738–2° ☎253 609 020, ⓕ253 609 028. Fine old *pensão* in a great location. Once grand, it too is beginning to fade a little these days, but remains good value for money. Rooms at the rear are quieter than those overlooking the underpass and the Avenida. It fills quickly and reservations are advisable in summer. ❷

Hotel João XXI Av João XXI 849 ☎253 616 630, ⓕ253 616 631. Off Avenida da Liberdade, on the way out of town, this six-storey hotel has a top-floor restaurant and neat, en-suite rooms. Good value. ❸

Hotel Largo da Estação Largo da Estação 13 ☎253 218 381, ⓕ253 276 810. According to the brochure, this modern block next to the train station will give you a "feeling of peace and eternity"; the jacuzzis in some rooms may go some way to achieving this, even if the occasional daytime train tries to throw a spanner in the works. ❹

Albergaria da Senhora-a-Branca Largo da Senhora-a-Branca 58 ☎253 269 938, ⓕ253 269 937. Facing a garden and attractively furnished, this is one of Braga's smarter choices – there's parking space too. It's about a kilometre from the centre; keep going out of town down Avenida Central. ❸

Residencial dos Terceiros Rua dos Capelistas 85 ☎253 270 466, ⓕ253 275 767. A well-located modern place; rooms all have TV and private bathroom. ❸

The City

The obvious point from which to start exploring Braga is **Praça da República**, a busy arcaded square at the head of the old town, marked by an impressive trio of fountains. It's backed by the former town keep, the **Torre de**

Menagem, while in the arcade itself you'll find two fine coffee houses which look out down the length of the long central square. From here, almost everything of interest is reached down narrow **Rua do Souto**, the main pedestrianized street which runs past the Sé. The street is also Braga's principal shopping district, though few commercial centres are like this one, where shoe shops rub shoulders with places selling candles and religious icons.

The Sé

The old town centre is dominated by the **Sé**, a rambling structure founded on the site of a Moorish mosque in 1070 after the Christian reconquest. The original Romanesque building encompasses Gothic, Renaissance and Baroque additions, though the cathedral's south doorway is a survival from the building's earliest incarnation, carved with rustic scenes from the legend of Reynard the Fox. The most striking element of the cathedral, however, is the intricate ornamentation of the roofline, commissioned by Braga's great Renaissance patron, Archbishop Diogo de Sousa, and executed by João de Castilho, later to become one of the architects of Lisbon's Mosteiro dos Jerónimos – the greatest of all Manueline buildings.

Inside, the cathedral complex is disorientating and, with the exception of the Baroque organs, somewhat disappointing: you enter through a courtyard fronting three Gothic chapels, a cloister and, most prominently, a ticket desk, where you can gain access to the **Museu de Arte Sacra** and Capela dos Reis (daily 8.30am–6.30pm; €2). The *museu* is essentially the cathedral's treasury and one of the richest of such collections in Portugal, containing representative pieces from the tenth to the eighteenth century but visits are accompanied by a guide, who locks every room behind you, and offers a rather cursory commentary on the age and value of each piece. After several rooms of very similar, unlabelled and confusingly arranged displays, light relief comes with the shoes of the diminuitive Archbishop Dom Rodrigo de Maura-Teles. Measuring just 1m 20cm high, he commissioned 22 monuments during his term of office at the beginning of the eighteenth century, among them the fabulous shrine at Bom Jesus. Eventually you emerge alongside the magnificent Baroque twin organs in the **Coro Alto**, supported by life-sized figures of satyrs, mermen and monstrous fish. From here you can gaze down into the cathedral proper – unexpectedly small and, when you descend, remarkably uninteresting.

Of the three outer chapels, the fourteenth-century **Capela dos Reis** (King's Chapel) is the most significant, built to house the tombs of the cathedral's founders, Henry of Burgundy, first Count of Portucale, and his wife Teresa – the parents of Afonso Henriques. Exposed beside them is the mummified body of Archbishop Lourenço, found "uncorrupt" when his tomb was opened in the seventeenth century. He had fought in the great victory over the Castilians at Aljubarrota in 1385, riding around bestowing indulgences on the ranks, and there sustained a scar on his cheek – which he himself is said to have carved proudly on his effigy.

The rest of the old town

Opposite the cathedral, across Rua do Souto, is the old **Archbishop's Palace**, a great fortress-like building, which in medieval times covered a tenth of the city. Since it was devastated by fire in 1866, it has been used for a variety of purposes, today it easily accommodates the impressive municipal **library** (Mon–Fri 9am–noon & 2–8pm) and various faculties of the university. Inside you can inspect the ornate ceilings of the medieval reading room and the Sala do Doctor Manuel Monteiro. Unless you have an academic interest, you're unlikely to find Braga's other 35-odd **churches** very inspiring: most, like the cathedral, were stripped and modernized in the late-seventeenth and eighteenth centuries. Probably the most authentic is the **Capela de Conceição** on Largo São João de Souto, with its crenellated tower. Located just east of the Sé and built in 1625, it houses magnificent statues of St Anthony and St Paul, as well as *azulejos* telling the story of Adam and Eve.

On the whole, more appealing are the numerous **mansions** from earlier ages, with their extravagant Baroque and Rococo facades. The **Câmara Municipal** and **Casa do Raio** are both by André Soares da Silva, the archbishop's architect; look out, too, for the apostle-clad roofline of the **Hospital de São Marcos**, adjacent to the Casa do Raio. Best of all, though, is the mid-seventeenth-century **Palácio dos Biscaínhos** (☎ & ℉253 217 645; Tues–Sun 10am–12.15pm & 2–5.30pm; €2), whose flagstoned ground floor was designed to allow carriages through to the stables. Nowadays, it houses a small museum of decorative arts, paintings and sculpture from the seventeenth to nineteenth centuries, mostly Rococo and Baroque, in line with the decoration of the house. The pretty landscaped gardens out back, complete with a 200-year-old Virginian magnolia tree, were also designed by Soares da Silva.

On the southern side of town, in Campo de Santiago, a former seminary has been turned into the **Museu Medina e Pio XII** (Tues–Sun 9am–noon & 2–5pm; €1.25; closed for refurbishment at time of writing), which consists of two distinct collections: the Pio XII, housing dusty religious regalia from the eleventh to seventeeth centuries, and the Medina, named after the Portuguese painter and donated on the understanding that it would be housed separately from any other exhibits. Save your energy for the collection of fonts and capitals gathered in a courtyard like standing stones, or for the small excavation of a first-century Roman water tank – and try persuading the guide to hold back on a few of the endless locked doors. There's also a small collection of Stone and Bronze Age tools. Further archeological exhibits, from Paleolithic stone tools to Roman and medieval items, will be housed at the new **Museu de Arqueologia Dom Diogo de Sousa** when construction work is completed (only the library is currently open). It's situated beside some Roman excavations on Rua dos Bombeiros Voluntários, the southern continuation of Rua Jeronimo Pimentel (bus #7; ☎253 273 706, ℉253 612 366) – ask at the turismo for details.

Eating, drinking, entertainment and nightlife

The city's most characterful locales are its nineteenth-century **cafés** – busy throughout the day and into the evening. In all of these you can get sandwiches, snacks and often full meals, though Braga is also well endowed with tempting **restaurants**; a selection of the best is listed below. Local specialities include *caldo de castanhas* (chestnut soup), or *charutos de chila* (cigar-shaped squash pastries) and *rabanadas* (fried slices of milk-soaked bread with a sweet cinnamon sauce) for dessert. Phone numbers are given where it might be necessary to book ahead.

For details of local **cultural events**, get hold of a copy of the daily *Correio do Minho* newspaper; the turismo generally has one on the counter and is happy to offer advice. There are a number of commercial art galleries staging temporary **exhibitions**: try Galeria Belo Belo, Avenida Central 191 (☎253 217 656); or Galeria Sépia, Avenida da Liberdade 505 (☎253 277 447). Also worth a look-in is the city-run **Museu da Imagem** on Largo São Joaquim (Tues–Sun 9am–12.30pm & 2–5pm; free), which stages both permanent and temporary photography exhibitions.

During summer, there's popular entertainment in the **Bracalândia** theme park (10am–midnight; €10; ⓦwww.bracalandia.com), 1km out of town on the Bom Jesus road (any bus to Bom Jesus will stop here).You'll find an assortment of low-tech fairground rides, including a Ferris wheel and helter-skelter.

There's a fair **club scene** in Braga with most of the action taking place at the bottom end of Avenida da Liberdade, around the *Hotel Turismo*. Venues change hands and names reasonably regularly but the current favourites include *Sardinha Biba Bar* (with a swimming pool), nearby at Rua dos Galos; and *Populum Bar* in the centre of Braga at Praça Conde de Agrolongo 115. All play a staple mix of 1980s disco interspersed with a little modern samba and 1990s techno sounds. Less trendy, but no less fun is *Salsa*, on Rua de Diu, which frequently has live samba music.

Cafés

Café Astória Praça da República. The best of the old coffee houses, mahogany-panelled and with cut-glass windows, going very beautifully to seed. Occasional live music and invariably tasty snacks add to its attraction.

A Brasileira Largo Barão de São Marinha. A superb old-style café, at the top of Rua do Souto, full of crusty old waiters dealing out brandies to a similarly aged clientele. In summer, you can sit in the open window-terrace – virtually on the street.

Pastelaria Ferreira Capa Rua dos Capelistas 38–50. Tasty pastries and coffee.

Café Vianna Praça da República. One of Braga's best, adjacent to *Astória*. A gorgeous Art Nouveau turn-of-the-century establishment in a prime location, with outside tables and a wide snack menu including good beef sandwiches (*pregos*).

Restaurants

Abade dos Priscos Praça Mouzinho de Albuquerque 7. Reliable and affordable Portuguese cuisine – try the *bacalhau* gratin or prawn curry. Closed Sun, Mon lunch, and all of July.

Alexandre Campo das Hortas 10. Family run restaurant with traditional fare, served in friendly no-frills atmosphere. Closed Mon.

De Bouro Rua Santo António das Travessas 30–32. Tucked away in the old centre, this pleasantly restored Cistercian monastic lodging house claims to continue the monks' tradition of serving food to "enhance spiritual and contemplative heights". All the traditional favourites mixed with a few Minho specialities. Around €12.50.

Brito's Praça Mouzinho de Albuquerque 49. Specializes in old-style cooking from ancient recipes, including *bacalhau* and salmon in shellfish sauce. Home-made desserts, and a good wine list. Closed Wed.

Campo da Vinha Praça Conselheiro Torres de Almeida 5–6, just off Praça Conde de Agrolongo. Cheap, popular and cheerful: try the *frango*.

Casa Pimenta Praça Conde de Agrolongo 46. A consistently good bet, especially for the fine set menu at around €12.50. Specialities include *papas de sarabulho*, roast kid goat and veal.

A Ceia Rua do Raio 331, off Av da Liberdade. This excellent restaurant is always crowded with locals, so arrive early, especially at weekends, or you'll have to eat at the bar. Spit-roast chickens and steaks are served up in enormous portions at moderate prices, and there's a fine wine list. Closed Mon.

Conde de Agrolongo Praça Conde de Agrolongo 74. Typical Portuguese restaurant serving good rice dishes for under €10. Head for the large, cool basement rather than the deserted ground floor.

Expositor Parques de Exposições, on the right at the end of Av da Liberdade. Huge portions of traditional Minhota cooking, heavy on grilled meat and fish (displayed in window cases). Closed Tues.

O Diogo Rua Dom Diogo da Sousa. Traditional food, including roast kid, served in a friendly atmosphere. Closed Sun.

O Inácio Campo das Hortas 14. Through the town gate at the end of Rua do Souto and off to the left, this is a pricey and rather cosmopolitan restaurant that doesn't limit itself to Portuguese dishes. It's in an old stone house with rustic decor – and costs around €15 a head and upwards. Closed Mon.

A Jolima Av da Liberdade 747, near the turismo. Cheap self-service cafeteria, from ice cream and

pizza to local dishes. Around €3.50 a plate.
A Moçambicana Rua Andrade Corvo 8.
Moderately priced option just outside the town
gate, at the end of Rua do Souto. As the name
suggests, a spattering of African dishes feature on

a menu that includes a rather rough house wine.
A Tia Rosalina Rua dos Chaos 25–31. Long
established purveyor of regional food with a good
reputation and moderate prices.

Listings

Airline TAP, Rua Dr. Justino Cruz 154–2° ℡ 253
616 205, or freephone 800 213 141.
Ambulance ℡ 253 262 470 or 253 264 077.
Books and newspapers English-language books
can be found at Livraria Bertrand, Rua Dom Diogo
Sousa 113, and at Livraria Cruz, on the same
street at no.129. International newspapers are
available from the tobacconists at Rua Dr. Justina
Cruz 149.
Exchange Caravela Travel on Rua Francisco
Sanches 47 ℡ 253 200 500 offers reasonable
rates of exchange and doesn't usually charge
commission.
Hospital São Marcos, Largo Carlos Amarante
℡ 253 603 800.
Internet *Netstation* on Rua de Santa Margarida
13, just past the HI hostel (€3/hr).
Outdoor sports River canoeing and hiking tours

are offered by Gota Verde, at the Instituto da
Juventude, Rua de Santa Margarida 215, sala 8
℡ 253 616 836, Ⓕ 253 616 835. Walking trips in
Peneda–Gerês are run roughly once a week, and
cost €25 per person, including transport.
Police ℡ 253 613 250.
Swimming pools Both are 2km from the centre:
the Complexo Desportivo da Rodovia, at the junction of the main ring road and Av João Paulo II
before Bracalândia (most easily reached down Av
Central, turning right onto Av Padre Julio Fragata);
℡ 253 616 773; and the municipal Piscina da
Ponte (July only) at the far end of Av da Liberdade
by the campsite ℡ 253 264 424.
Taxis Central Rádio Táxi, ℡ 253 614 019.
Travel agents Abreu, Av Central 171 ℡ 253 200
540; Atlas, Praça Conde de Agrolongo 129 ℡ 253
613 731.

Bom Jesus, São Frutuoso and Tibães

Having soaked up the religious atmosphere in Braga itself, there's a number of
fascinating sites within easy reach. The Baroque stairway and pilgrim church of
Bom Jesus do Monte, 5km east of Braga, is a good enough reason to come
in the first place and is within striking distance of the massive, if distinctly
oppressive, **Santuário do Sameiro**; while a similar distance to the northwest
is the Visigothic church of **São Frutuoso** and a ruined Benedictine monastery
at **Tibães**.

Buses (#2) to Bom Jesus leave Braga at 10 and 40 minutes past the hour
from Avenida da Liberdade, close to the post office. Those for São Frutuoso
leave every thirty minutes from Praça Conde de Agrolongo (they are marked
"Sarrido"); get off at the hamlet of São Jerónimo Real, from where it is a five-
minute walk. For Tibães, hourly buses, marked "Padim da Graça", leave from
Avenida Central. If you want to make things easy you could rent a **taxi** for a
few hours (see above).

Bom Jesus do Monte and Santuário do Sameiro

BOM JESUS DO MONTE is one of Portugal's best-known images. Set in
the woods high above the city, the glorious ornamental stairway of granite and
white plaster is a monumental homage, commissioned by Braga's vertically
challenged archbishop Maura-Teles in 1723, and taking 60 years to complete.
There is no particular reason for its presence – no miracle or vision – yet it
remains the object of devoted pilgrimage, with many penitents climbing up on

369

AROUND BRAGA

0   5 km

their knees. It is a very pleasant place to spend an afternoon or, best of all, early evening. There are wooded gardens, grottoes and miniature boating pools behind the church and, at the far end, just outside the park up the hill, horse rides are available at negotiable rates.

Buses run the 3km from Braga to the foot of the stairway. At weekends they are packed, as seemingly half the city piles up to picnic in the woods. Most of the local families, armed with immense baskets of food, ride straight to the top in a rickety hydraulic **funicular** (8am–8pm; every 30min and usually timed to coincide with buses; €1). If you resist the temptation to ride the funicular and make the climb up the stairway, Bom Jesus's simple allegory unfolds. Each of the **stairway** landings has a fountain: the first symbolizes the wounds of Christ, the next five the Senses, and the final three represent the Virtues. At each corner, too, are chapels with crumbling, larger-than-life wooden tableaux of the Life of Christ, arranged chronologically, leading to the Crucifixion at the altar of the church. As a design it's a triumph – one of the greatest of all Baroque architectural creations – and was later copied at Lamego.

The domed **Santuário do Sameiro**, 2km up at the top of the hill, is impressive for its size and grimly monolithic monumental stairway, which affords fantastic views across the city. Although built in 1837, it bears the heavy marks of interference during Salazar's regime in its swathes of concrete and enormous statues. Like it or loathe it, it's a powerful monument to the might and authority of the Roman Catholic Church in Portugal, and the church is the second most venerated shrine in the country after Fátima (see p.183). There's a very good, if somewhat pricey, restaurant here too, the *Restaurante Sameiro*.

Practicalities

There's a good range of **places to stay** up on the mount, which makes a peaceful and attractive place to spend the night. At the budget end of the scale, the friendly *Pensão Águeda* (☎253 676 521; ❷), behind the park at the back of the church, has basic rooms (separate bathrooms), but breakfast is included and the downstairs restaurant is excellent. There are several more expensive options, one of the best being the *Casa dos Lagos* (T & F 253 676 738; ❸), a lovely old Solares de Portugal house on the road just below the top of the steps, with a very hospitable owner and offering fantastic views; it also has three apartments for rent. The *Hotel do Parque* (T 253 603 470, F 253 603 409; ❺) is another excellent option – a superb nineteenth-century pile furnished in 1920s style, situated next to the church and facing the amusing concrete grotto. The nearby *Hotel Elevador* (T 253 603 400, F 253 603 409; ❺), under the same management, is of a similar standard.

There is a handful of lively **restaurants** on the Monte, which come into their own on Saturdays, when they're filled with parties from a constant stream of weddings. Note, however, that most open only at weekends during winter. A good option is *Restaurante Águeda*, beneath the *pensão* of the same name, which is cheap, popular and serves large portions. *Restaurante Portico*, just beyond the bottom of the steps, is a traditional-style building serving quality food, but at high prices.

São Frutuoso and Tibães

Three and a half kilometres northwest of Braga is another worthwhile church excursion: to **São Frutuoso** (Tues–Sun 9am–noon & 2–5pm; keys are kept in a nearby house), built by the Visigoths in the seventh century, adapted by the Moors, and then restored to Christian worship after the reconquest. It's a gem of a church, flanked by an eighteenth-century chapel but unfortunately its previously tranquil setting has now been engulfed by Braga's ever-expanding suburbs. The approach is from São Jerónimo Real.

Half a kilometre beyond the São Frutuoso turning, to the left of the main road, a paved track leads to the monastery of **Tibães** (Tues–Sun 9am–noon & 2–5pm; free), formerly the grandest Benedictine establishment in the land. A vast and partly ruined hulk, its abandoned medieval buildings, cloisters and rambling gardens were once occupied by gypsy families. Now, however, it is state-owned, and recently reopened to the public after extensive renovation. A small local-history museum (Tues–Sun 10am–12.30pm & 2–6pm; €2) provides a fascinating window on the past, while exhibition rooms house temporary displays of photography and art throughout the year. Guided tours of the monastic buildings are available but you are also allowed to explore the gardens and the ruins of the stables and kitchens at your own leisure.

Póvoa do Lanhoso and the road to Gerês

Heading **east from Braga** along the N103 to the Peneda-Gerês park (see p.403), after 16km you come to the turning for **Póvoa do Lanhoso**, which lies 3km south of the main road. If you have transport, and time to spare, this small provincial town is worth a detour for its castle and Romanesque church. Another sight, revered in Portugal though perhaps of more peripheral interest to visitors, is the shrine of **Nossa Senhora da Abadia**, to the north of the Braga–Gerês road, turning off at Santa Maria do Bouro.

Póvoa do Lanhoso

The town of **PÓVOA DO LANHOSO** is famed for its gold jewellery, produced in traditional workshops (*ourivesarias*) and bearing clear traces of Moorish influence, especially in the filigree work. This aside, the modern quarters of the town haven't much to offer, but they do lie sandwiched between two ancient sites. At the northern end of town (the approach from Braga), a steep mound – the Monte do Pilar – rises up to one of the smallest **castles** in Portugal and a scattering of chapels and picnic tables. In the fourteenth century, the lord of the shire was reported to have locked up his adulterous wife, her lover and their servants in the castle and ordered it to be burned; it was substantially rebuilt in the eighteenth century. The *Panorâmico* **restaurant** nearby keeps a set of keys and offers reasonable food and good views, if you can squeeze in between their regular parties of christening and wedding guests. In the opposite direction, 3km out of town, the small church of **Fonte Areada** is a short walk from the main road (past the white statue). The simple interior, characteristic of the Romanesque style, is in marked contrast to the complications of the doorway with its centrepiece relief of a large sheep. If you have your own transport or can hire a taxi, it's worth paying a visit to one of two local **Vinho Verde quintas** that welcome visitors and offer free tastings and tours: *Quinta do Minho* (contact Maria Teresa Martins on ☎253 633 240); or *Quinta Villa Beatriz* in Santo Emilião (☎253 631 523 or 253 631 292), an imposing blue-tiled four-towered mansion in the "Brazilian" style of the early twentieth century, constructed by emigrants who made their fortune in the New World. There are superb gardens, as well as cows and horses for children to admire.

The town provides useful transport links to the east into Trás-os-Montes; south to the Douro, via Cabeceiras de Basto; and to Porto, via Famalição. Regular **buses** also connect with Braga, Caldas do Gerês and Guimarães. To pick up a bus to Montalegre and Chaves (5–7 daily), you have to walk the 3km north to Pinheiro, on the main N103.

Nossa Senhora da Abadia

With your own transport, an alternative route into Gerês is the minor N205–4 via Amares, after which the road becomes the N308. Some 13km along you come to **SANTA MARIA DO BOURO** (Bouro to the locals) – which has a shell of a monastery and a large Baroque church. Turning off from here, you arrive at the shrine of **Nossa Senhora da Abadia**. This is said to be the oldest sanctuary in Portugal and, like Bom Jesus, is a centre of pilgrimage: the main festival is on August 15. The focus of devotions is a twelfth-century wooden statue of the Virgin and Child and, while the church itself was largely rebuilt in the eighteenth century, outside are two earlier, elegant wings of monks' cells and, usually, some market stalls. There's no accommodation here but you can **eat** well with the pilgrims at the sizeable *Restaurante Abadia*, which can seat up to 500 people.

Barcelos

It's worth making plans to arrive in **BARCELOS**, 20km west of Braga, for the Thursday market, the **Feira de Barcelos**. The great weekly event of southern Minho, it takes place from around dawn until late afternoon on the Campo da República – known colloquially as the Campo da Feira – a vast open square in the centre of town. There are traditional events at other times of the year, too: the Festa das Cruzes (Festival of the Crosses) on May 3 and, on the last Saturday of July, a renowned **folklore festival** in Barcelinhos, on the opposite bank of the river, with live music and fireworks.

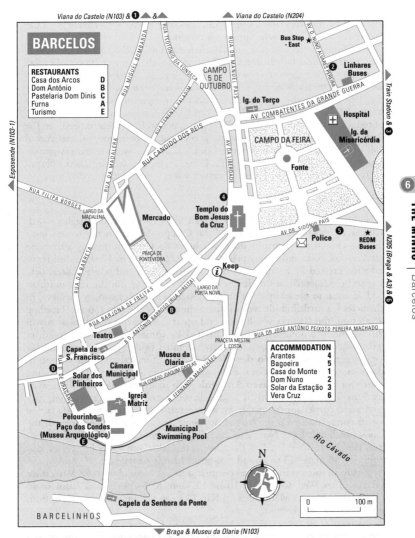

BARCELOS

RESTAURANTS

Casa dos Arcos	**D**
Dom António	**B**
Pastelaria Dom Dinis	**C**
Furna	**A**
Turismo	**E**

◀ Esposende (N103-1)

▲ Bus Stop - East

2 **Linhares Buses**

▶ Train Station & ➍

CAMPO 5 DE OUTUBRO

Ig. do Terço

AV. COMBATENTES DA GRANDE GUERRA

Hospital

CAMPO DA FEIRA

Ig. da Misericórdia

Fonte

RUA CANDIDO DOS REIS

RUA DR. MANUEL PAIS

AV. DA LIBERDADE

RUA TENENTE VALADIM

RUA TEOTONIO DA FONSECA

RUA MIGUEL BOMBARDA

AV. D. NUNO ÁLVARES PEREIRA

6

THE MINHO | Barcelos

RUA FILIPA BORGES

LARGO DA MADALENA

A

Mercado

④ **Templo do Bom Jesus da Cruz**

AV DR. SIDÓNIO PAÍS

⑤ ✉ **Police**

★ **REDM Buses**

▶ N205 (Braga & A3) & ➏

RUA DA BARBEIA

RUA DA MADALENA

PRAÇA DE PONTEVEDRA

ⓘ **Keep**

LARGO DA PORTA NOVA

RUA BARJONA DE FREITAS

Teatro

C

R. D. ANTÓNIO BARROSO (RUA DIREITA) **B**

RUA DR JOSÉ ANTÓNIO PEIXOTO PEREIRA MACHADO

PRAÇETA MESTRE L COSTA

Capela de S. Francisco

D

RUA DE BRAGANÇA

Câmara Municipal

Solar dos Pinheiros

Museu da Olaria

RUA CONEGO JOAQUIM GAIOLAS

R. FERNANDO MAGALHÃES

Igreja Matriz

ACCOMMODATION

Arantes	**4**
Bagoeira	**5**
Casa do Monte	**1**
Dom Nuno	**2**
Solar da Estação	**3**
Vera Cruz	**6**

Pelourinho

Paço dos Condes (Museu Arqueológico)

E

Municipal Swimming Pool

Rio Cávado

N

Capela da Senhora da Ponte

BARCELINHOS

0   100 m

▼ Braga & Museu da Olaria (N103)

The Feira de Barcelos

The Minho's markets are always interesting, and the **Feira de Barcelos**, one of the largest in Europe, is the pick of the bunch. As a spectacle and crash course in the region's economics, it is hard to beat, and even the most conservative budget shoppers are sure to find something that arouses their interest. In addition to row upon row of village women squatting behind baskets of their own produce, there are stalls selling virtually everything – sausage skins, delicious fresh bread, whole avenues of ducks and rabbits, plus less traditional lines in counterfeit sportswear and CDs. The Minho is made up of hundreds of tiny, walled smallholdings, rarely more than allotments, and many people here are just selling a few vegetables, some fruit, eggs, and maybe even cheese from the family cow. It all looks refreshingly wholesome.

Apart from produce, clothes and kitchen equipment, the *feira's* big feature is local **pottery and handicrafts**, for Barcelos is at the centre of Portugal's most active *artesanato* region. The pottery ware – *louça de Barcelos* – is characteristically brown with distinctive yellow dots, and has been highly acclaimed since the 1950s when the imaginative earthenware figurines of Rosa Ramalho (marked RR) began to be collected throughout Europe. In comparison, most of today's pieces look as if they fell off a production line (some, indeed, are Far Eastern imports), but there are some good items to be found, sold at around half the price of outlets elsewhere. Look out for the work of Rosa's granddaughter, Júlia Ramalho, marked JR. Other crafts, too, are impressive – especially the basketwork, traditionally carved yokes (*cangas*) and wooden toys.

The Town

In addition to its festivities, Barcelos has a few more permanent sights worth visiting. At the southwest corner of the Campo da Feira is the town's most striking church, the **Templo do Bom Jesus da Cruz**, fronted by a Baroque garden of obelisks and highly pruned box-hedges. Built in 1704, its distinctive exterior, created by a simple contrast of dark granite and white plasterwork, was to be influential in the design of churches throughout the region. It's an odd addition to the old part of town, though, which is essentially medieval in character – a small, hillside web of streets spun above the Rio Cávado. Heading south from the Campo, you'll soon end up at the **river**, as beautiful as any in the Minho, overhung by willows, fronted by gardens with Gothic pillories (*pelourinhos*), and spanned by a fourteenth-century bridge. Just above the bridge loom the ruins of the **Paço dos Condes**, the former Palace of the Counts of Barcelos, wrecked by the Great Earthquake of 1755 and, since 1920, providing a shell for the outdoor **Museu Arqueológico** (daily: summer 9am–7pm; winter 9am–5.30pm; free). This is a miscellaneous assembly of gravestones, gargoyles and cornerstones, notable for a sixteenth-century crucifix locally famed for its connection with the legend of *Senhor do Galo* – the Gentleman of the Cock (see box below). Note also the religious tombstone emblems of the various peoples to have lived in Barcelos: both Celtic and Catholic crosses, six-point Jewish Stars of David, and five-point Islamic pentagrams. If you wanted to pursue an interest in the local ceramic wares, you could visit the **Museu de Olaria** (Tues, Wed & Fri–Sun 10am–12.30pm & 2–6pm, Thurs 10am–6pm; €2), in the Casa dos Mendanhas on Rua Conego Joaquim Gaiolas, 300m from the archeological museum.

The Barcelos cock

A stone cross in Barcelos's archeological museum depicts the legend of the **Galo de Barcelos**, a miraculous roast fowl which rose from the dinner table of a judge to crow the innocence of a Galician pilgrim the judge had wrongly condemned to the gallows. The pilgrim, having wisely proclaimed "As surely as I am innocent will that cock crow if I am hanged", got his reprieve, although it was a close run thing. He was already in the noose when the bird stepped in but, by luck or maybe divine intervention, the knot caught and he survived. It's a story that occurs in different forms in northern Spain, but the Barcelos rooster has taken a special hold on popular folk art, becoming a national symbol of Portugal and now, usually in pottery form, the ubiquitous emblem of Portuguese tourism.

375

△ Barcelos market

Practicalities

The **train station** (℡253 811 243) is at the drab eastern edge of town; follow Avenida Alcaides de Faria straight ahead for fifteen minutes until it becomes Avenida Combatentes da Grande Guerra, and you'll emerge on the Campo da Feira. There are two main **bus** companies: Linhares, Rua Dr. Julio Vieira Ramos (℡253 811 517), for local services within Minho and to Vila do Conde and Póvoa do Varzim; and REDM, Avenida Dr. Sidónio Pais 245 (℡253 808 300), facing the Campo, for main towns in the region and beyond (also agents for Rede Express, Renex and Internorte for long-distance services). Both run frequent services to Braga. The **turismo** (March–Oct Mon–Fri 9am–12.30pm & 2.30–6pm, Sat 10am–12.30pm & 2.30–5.30pm, Sun 2.30–5.30pm; Nov–Feb Mon–Wed & Fri 9am–12.30pm & 2.30–5.50pm, Thurs 9am–5.30pm, Sat 10am–5pm; ℡253 811 882, ℱ253 822 188) is housed in the **Torre da Porta Nova**, just off the Campo. In addition to its information counter, it features a permanent display and sale of Barcelos handicrafts. The river is too polluted for **swimming** but there are municipal pools just upstream from the bridge on Rua Rosa Ramalho.

Accommodation

There's no really cheap accommodation in Barcelos, so budget travellers should consider staying in Braga. You'll definitely need to book ahead if coinciding with the market (Wed & Thurs nights), as rooms fill up quickly.

Residencial Arantes Av da Liberdade 35–1° ℡253 811 326, ℱ253 821 360. An eccentric mix of modern rooms in this family-run place on the west side of the Campo da Feira, above a good *pastelaria*; avoid the cell-like rooms overlooking a central well. Cheaper rooms are without facilities, but the shared bathrooms are clean. Breakfast is included. ❷

Pensão Bagoeira Av Dr. Sidónio Pais 495 ℡253 811 236, ℱ253 824 588. Facing the Campo, this is a real old market inn. The rooms, all with bathrooms, have recently been modernised and are bright, clean and comfortable. ❸

Casa do Monte Abade de Neiva, 3km west of Barcelos on the N103 Viana do Castelo road ℡ & ℱ253 811 519. Delightful country house belonging to the Solares de Portugal scheme, and deco-

rated with beautiful Alentejo furniture. Large gardens and a verandah give wonderful panoramic views over Barcelos and the valley. ❸

Residencial Dom Nuno Av Dom Nuno Álvares Pereira 76 ℡253 812 810, ℱ253 816 336. A fancy but characterless place, off to the right as you approach Campo da Feira from the station. All rooms have bath, telephone and TV. ❸

Residencial Solar da Estação Largo da Estação ℡253 811 741. By the railway station, the large, spotless, modern rooms have shower and TV; rates include breakfast. ❷

Pensão Vera Cruz Av Dr. Sidónio Pais 371 ℡253 811 333. 100m from *Bagoeira* next to GALP, above a modern if not too salubrious café. Recently renovated rooms are clean and comfortable, but nothing special. ❷

Eating, drinking and nightlife

There is a row of three bargain-basement café-restaurants around the corner from the Campo, in the alleyway opposite the Templo; the central one is best value. The main **nightclub** is the trendy *Vaticano Club*, Rua Cândido da Cunha 188 (℡253 812 962), with house and techno Thursdays, and more Latin sounds on Saturdays.

Bagoeira Av Dr. Sidónio Pais 495 ℡253 811 236. Old market inn full of atmosphere, be sure to have lunch here on market day, when a constant stream of stallholders bring in pots and pans for take-aways. It's open in the evening, too, and meals –

mostly stews, steaks and grills – are excellent value.

Casa dos Arcos Rua Duques de Bragança. Set in a traditional old stone house, and serving unusual regional specialities such as suckling

The miracle of Moure

If you want to witness a **miracle**, head for the **Igreja de Moure**, 7km southwest of Barcelos off the road to Vila Nova de Famalicão and reachable on REDM buses from Barcelos (see Practicalities opposite). The church has become a minor centre of pilgrimage since May 18, 1996, when a ghostly "shadow of the top half of Christ" first appeared. The miracle has since returned every year on May 18, and during its 1998 appearance the congregation entered "total delirium and nervosity" according to a newspaper report: some circled the image, others clapped, while others begged forgiveness for their sins. Sadly, the archbishop of Braga pooh-poohed the miracle, declaring to the press "it is a singular event generated from sentiments of faith and piety but explainable by the laws of optical physics". Further tests concluded that the "miracle" was indeed caused by a mere trick of the light. However, science has not dissuaded the faithful, who still flock here every May to witness what the *Diário de Notícias* calls the "marvellous half-bodied manifestation of Moure".

pig. Expensive but wholesome meals. Closed Mon.

Dom António Rua Dom António Barroso 87. Rather tourist-orientated, but reasonably priced, with huge portions sufficient for two. Wild boar from Montesinho features occasionally, and boiled chestnuts are served in season. Good *rojões*. Under €10.

Pastelaria Dom Dinis Rua Dom António Barroso 100. Pleasant pastry shop with outdoor tables, serving very sweet egg-and-peanut sweets among other goodies.

Furna Largo da Madalena 105. You'll see the queues for takeaway chickens stretching out of the door, which gives a good clue as to its best dish – superb chicken (€3.25 for a whole bird). Closed Mon.

Restaurante Turismo at the foot of Rua Duques de Bragança. This bar, overlooking the river, is the perfect place for a beer while catching the last of the day's sun. Don't be put off by the name.

The Costa Verde

Spurred by the flow of foreign currency into the Algarve, the Regional Tourist Board is energetically trying to promote the Minho's miles of sandy coastline as the **Costa Verde**. So far, the seaside element of the campaign hasn't quite worked for, despite the enticing promises of "unpolluted beaches with a high iodine content … health for the whole year", Costa Verde is green for a reason. It can be drizzly and overcast even in summer and the Atlantic here is never too warm. That said, pick almost any road, any village, and you'll find a great **beach** virtually to yourself.

The coast between Póvoa de Varzim and Caminha is virtually one long beach, with the road running, for the most part, 1km or so inland. There are at least four **buses** a day in each direction, most using the resort of **Viana do Castelo** – very much the main event on this coast – as an axis. The town is also the main **train** terminus in the western Minho, with regular services north to Valença via Caminha, and inland south towards Barcelos and on to Porto.

North from Porto to Viana

Heading north along the picturesque Atlantic coast can be a slow business. Six daily **buses** chug north from Porto to Viana do Castelo, via Póvoa, Ofir, Esposende and São Bartolomeu do Mar. **Trains** north from Porto run inland via Barcelos and do not reach the coast until Viana. This stretch of coastline is fantastically beautiful in parts, and much of it is protected from development by law, including the 18km from Apúlia to the mouth of the River Neiva which has been designated **Área de Paisagem Protegida do Litoral de Esposende** (Esposende Protected Coastal Area). Along this stretch and beyond, the local people have perfected the art of dune agriculture. Small "fields" are created by digging out depressions in the sand dunes, which trap moisture from the Atlantic mists and protect crops from wind. Dried seaweed is used as fertilizer, which over the centuries has created a soil so fertile that many believe these dune fruits and vegetables to be among the best in the country. For more information on the coastal ecosystem, contact the reserve's headquarters in Esposende, at Rua 1° de Dezembro 65 (℡253 965 830, ℻253 965 330).

Esposende

ESPOSENDE, a breezy, sunbleached seaside resort, is easily reached by public transport. Located 20km north of Póvoa on the estuary of the Rio Cávado, and 2–3km from the ocean, it's a more intimate chill-out spot than touristy Viana do Castelo (see p.380). Passing the rather drab sprawl of buildings on the town's outskirts, things brighten up in the compact centre, which has some lovely old buildings and squares, including a small **museum** on Largo Dr. Fonseca Lima (Tues–Fri 10am–noon & 2–8pm, Sat 3–6pm; free), which contains displays of local ethnography, items from nearby *antas* (megalithic Bronze Age tombs), and ceramics and tools from the 2000-year-old *castro* of São Lourenço, a Bronze Age settlement.

The town's **beach** is 2km to the north, accessed via the lighthouse which protrudes from the late-seventeenth-century Forte de São João Baptista. Much less enticing is the beach at **OFIR**, 6km by road on the south side of the estuary, where impressive pine-backed dunes have been ruined by three ugly high-rise buildings.

Practicalities

Buses drop you at the Largo do Mercado on the riverfront beside the market. Two hundred metres south along the river is the **turismo** (Mon–Sat 9.30am–12.30pm & 2.30–6pm, Sun 9.30am–12.30pm; winter closed Sun; ℡ & ℻253 961 354), which gives out a good map that includes Ofir and Fão, as well as leaflets containing directions to various local *antas* and to the *castro* of São Lourenço. It also publishes an excellent guidebook to the district ("*Esposende – A privilege of nature*"; free), whose amusing English-language version contains gems like the caption under a photo of two women entitled "One pair of Seaweeds" and the equally abstract "Small place with Brazilian taste" below a picture of a huge mansion house. There's a modern **swimming pool** complex on the riverbank opposite the turismo (daily 10am–10pm; €5), with waves in its indoor pool and great views from the outdoor one. **Canoeing** and **rafting** are organized by the Associação de Defesa do Ambiente do Rio Neiva (℡253 872 562): rafting costs €25 including transport. You can get **internet access** (daily; €2.50/hr) at Estúdio Internet's two branches: Rua Narciso Ferreira 88 (daily 9am–8pm, open until 1am in summer) and at the municipal swimming pools (daily 2.30–8pm).

Accommodation

The only really cheap accommodation is the **youth hostel** at Fão, 3km away on the south bank of the Cávado (T & F 253 981 790), which has a kitchen, bar, disabled facilities, bicycles for rent, and can arrange canoeing trips – double rooms (①) are also available. Fão also has a decent **campsite** (open all year; T 253 981 777). The turismo may be able to help you find rooms in private houses. Note that during the slow season, (mid-Sept to mid-June), room rates are often reduced by as much as fifty percent.

Residencial Acrópole Praça Dom Sebastião, near the turismo T 253 961 941, F 253 964 238. The only cheapish option – very comfortable rooms with TVs and telephones, and excellent breakfasts are included. ②

Clube Pinhal da Foz Rua João Ferreira da Silva, 1km north of the turismo T 253 961 098, F 253 965 937. Self-catering apartments with TVs, phones and access to a swimming pool, although at a cost. ④

Estalagem Zende on the N13, 1km from the turismo T 253 964 663, F 253 965 018. Modern, with a pleasant lounge, but poor location. A good restaurant specializing in shellfish and a summer disco might help compensate a little. ③

Residencial Mira Rio on the N13, 1km south of the turismo T 253 964 430, F 253 964 429. Ten rooms, each with bathroom, satellite TV and telephone, close to the river but a good 3km from the beach. There's a restaurant on site. ③

Hotel Nélia Av Valentim Ribeiro T 253 966 244, F 253 964 820. Three blocks behind the turismo, a nondescript but well-facilitated 3-star hotel with air conditioning, an indoor swimming pool, gym, squash courts and nightclub. ④

Hotel Suave Mar Rua 27 de Maio T 253 969 400, F 253 969 401. Large resort hotel that's the closest of any to the beach (though still 1km away). Rooms have air conditioning, satellite TV, balconies, safes and telephones, and there's a huge restaurant, outdoor swimming pool, tennis court and gym on site. ⑤

Eating and drinking

The main local speciality is *arroz de lampreia* (lamprey cooked with rice, *chouriço*, wine, onion, pepper and cloves). For dessert, try *clarinhas de Fão*, pastries filled with sweet marrow (*chila*) vermicelli. Recommended **restaurants** include *Dom Sebastião*, Rua 19 de Augusto near the *Residencial Acrópole*; and *Papa Fino*, on Rua Conde de Castro. Set in Largo Fonseca Lima, a pleasant square facing the museum, *Adega Regional O Barrote* has outdoor tables and also serves snacks and drinks. Also worth a try for regional dishes is *Foz do Cavado* on Avenida Arantes Olivira. Aside from the hotel nightclubs, the main **nightlife** venues are two late-night bars: *Quanto Baste* at Rua da Senhora da Saúde 34, and *Bar Bigosses* (also worth trying during the day), near Clube Pinhal da Foz.

São Bartolomeu do Mar

North of Ofir, you probably won't see another tourist all the way to the little fishing village of **SÃO BARTOLOMEU DO MAR**, on the N13 1km back from one of the best stretches of the Costa Verde. It's just 15km south of Viana do Castelo, but there is still refreshingly little to the place: just a church, shop and café (with a few **rooms** to let), and good unofficial camping amid the pines. As well as fishing, the local economy revolves around gathering **seaweed**. Traditionally, whole families harvest it on the beach using huge shrimping nets, which are then hauled across the sands by beautiful wooden carts pulled by oxen. Although the methods are changing and tractors are supplanting beasts, the seaweed is still stacked at the edge of the village to dry before being spread as fertilizer on the coastal fields.

If you're here on August 24, you'll catch the **romaria** that takes place at the end of the Festas de São Bartolomeu. The festivities draw thousands of people from the area, many of them families with sick children who come in the hope that they will be cured by taking the traditional Banho Santo – a bizarre ritual in which the child circles the church three times with a black cockerel tied to his or her head before being thrown into the ocean three times by an attendant. The **menhir** (standing stone; believed by many archeologists to be a fertility symbol) in the field immediately behind the church (it's hidden by corn in summer) is widely believed to have something to do with the roots of the ritual, as many Portuguese parish churches tended to be built adjacent to pre-Christian ritual sites, or else were constructed on top of them.

Viana do Castelo

VIANA DO CASTELO is the Minho's main resort town, and it's all the more appealing for it. A lively, attractive place, it has a historic old centre, above-average restaurants and, some distance from the town itself, one of the best beaches in the north. It's also beautifully positioned, spread along the north bank of the Lima estuary and shaped by the thick wooded hill of Monte de Santa Luzia, which is strewn with Celtic remains and crowned by an imposing basilica. If this wasn't enough of an incentive to come, Viana's **romaria** at the end of August (see p.382) is the biggest and most exciting festival in the Minho.

The Town

Viana has long been a prosperous seafaring town. It produced some of the greatest colonists of the "discoveries" under Dom Manuel, was a departure point for fishing expeditions to Newfoundland's Great Banks and, in the eighteenth century, was the first centre for the shipment of port wine to England. The most interesting buildings are a throwback to these times where, unusually for the north, you'll notice Manueline mouldings around the doors and windows of Viana's mansions.

At the heart of Viana's old town is the distinctive **Praça da República**, a wonderful square enclosed by an elegant ensemble of buildings. You'll see copies of its showpiece Renaissance fountain in towns throughout the Minho, but few structures as curious as the old **Misericórdia** (almshouse) that lines one side of the square. Built in 1589, this is one of the most original and successful buildings of the Portuguese Renaissance, its upper storeys supported by deliberately archaic caryatids. The adjacent sixteenth-century **Câmara Municipal** has been brightly restored, and stands foursquare above a medieval arcade, while just off the square is the **Igreja Matriz**, Viana's parish church, which retains a Gothic door of some interest as well as some unusual sculpturework on the towers.

The **Museu Municipal** (Tues–Sun 9am–noon & 2–5pm; €2) adds further to these impressions of Viana's sixteenth- to nineteenth-century opulence. At the far end of Rua Manuel Espregueira, ten minutes' walk east from the square, the museum is housed in an eighteenth-century palace. The interior has been maintained close to the original, and beautifully displays a large collection of ceramics and furniture, alongside more modern temporary exhibitions, and some simple paintings of nineteenth-century Viana.

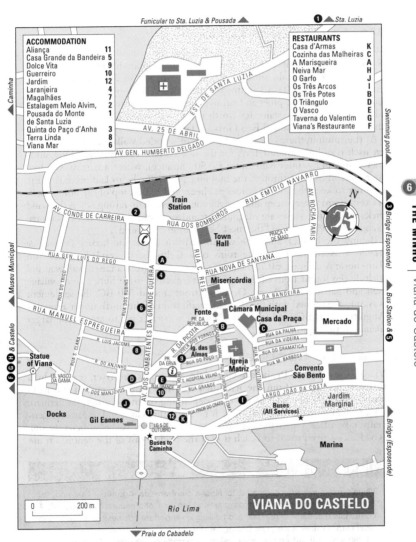

ACCOMMODATION
Aliança 11
Casa Grande da Bandeira 5
Dolce Vita 9
Guerreiro 10
Jardim 12
Laranjeira 4
Magalhães 7
Estalagem Melo Alvim,
Pousada do Monte 1
de Santa Luzia
Quinta do Paço d'Anha 3
Terra Linda 8
Viana Mar 6

RESTAURANTS
Casa d'Armas K
Cozinha das Malheiras C
A Marisqueira A
Neiva Mar H
O Garfo J
Os Três Arcos I
Os Três Potes B
O Triângulo D
O Vasco E
Taverna do Valentim G
Viana's Restaurante F

VIANA DO CASTELO

Funicular to Sta. Luzia & Pousada ▲ Sta. Luzia ①
EST. DE SANTA LUZIA
AV. 25 DE ABRIL
AV. GEN. HUMBERTO DELGADO
Caminha ◄
◄ Museu Municipal
Swimming pool ▶
AV. CONDE DE CARREIRA
② Train Station
RUA DOS BOMBEIROS
RUA EMÍDIO NAVARRO
AV. ROCHA PARIS
N
Town Hall
PRAÇA 1º DE MAIO
③ Bridge (Esposende) ▶
RUA GEN. LUIS DO REGO
Ⓐ
④
RUA NOVA DE SANTANA
Misericórdia
RUA DA BANDEIRA
Bus Station & ⑤ ▶
RUA DO TRIGO
RUA DOS RUBINS
RUA MANUEL ESPREGUEIRA
⑥
⑦
AV. DOS COMBATENTES DA GRANDE GUERRA
Fonte
PR. DA REPÚBLICA
Ⓑ
Câmara Municipal
Casa da Praça Ⓒ
RUA DA PALHA
Mercado
RUA DA VIDEIRA
RUA DA GRAMÁTICA
RUA M. BARBOSA
◄ Museu Municipal
R. S. CLARA
⑧
R. LUIS JACOME
R. DO ANJINHO
R. DA PICOTA
PR. DA ERVA
Ig. das Almas
⑨
Igreja Matriz
Ⓓ
Statue of Viana
IG. VASCO DA GAMA
R. DOS MANJOVOS
Ⓔ
⑩
RUA GRANDE
RUA GRANDE
T. HOSPITAL VELHO
ⓘ
RUA ALHORDA DO TIMAR
Convento São Bento
LARGO JOÃO DA COSTA
Jardim Marginal
◄ F G Ⓗ & Castelo
Docks
Gil Eannes
⑪ ⑫ Ⓚ
ⓘ
Buses (All Services) ★
Bridge (Esposende) ▶
Buses to Caminha
LG. 5 DE OUTUBRO
Marina
0   200 m
Rio Lima
▼ Praia do Cabadelo

If you continue past the museum, you'll eventually reach the **Castelo de Santiago da Barra**, commissioned by Philip II of Spain for the defence of the port. Outside the walls, in the area known as Campo do Castelo, Viana's **Friday market** takes place; it's much smaller than the famous one at Barcelos but attracts many of the same stallholders, and always turns up a few surprises.

On the waterfront, moored in the dock off Largo 5 de Outubro, is the *Gil Eannes*, Portugal's first hospital ship. Although there has been talk of conversion into hostel-style accommodation for years, it currently acts as a floating museum dedicated to the ship's history (Sat & Sun 9am–noon & 2–7pm; €1.50).

Monte de Santa Luzia

Wherever you stand in Viana, the twentieth-century basilica atop **Monte de Santa Luzia** makes its presence felt. The old **funicular** that once hauled people to the top during the summer months no longer runs, and the track is rusted and overgrown. It's a lengthy, yet pleasant, walk along the Estrada Santa Luzia, up through the pines and eucalyptus trees, but shorter and far more punishing if you take the stairs. It's worth it though for, once you get to the top, the views of the coast and Rio Lima are fantastic.

At the summit, there's a café and plenty of wooded walks. While the **basilica** itself is of little interest, look for the side entrance (marked *Zimbório*; summer 8am–7pm; winter 8am–5pm; €0.50 entrance), where a narrow winding staircase climbs right through the building, past traffic lights laid on during the summer to keep the tourist hordes in check, and out on top of the dome itself. It's very narrow, very steep and – at the top – pretty hair-raising when the wind picks up, but the views are magnificent, and were once described by National Geographic Magazine as "the most beautiful in the world".

Behind the basilica, amid the woods and just below the luxury *Pousada do Monte de Santa Luzia*, lie the ruins of a Celto-Iberian **citânia** (Tues–Sun 9am–noon & 2–5pm; €0.70). The ruins are viewed from a raised walkway and include the foundations of dozens of small, circular stone huts, a thick village wall and partly paved streets. Occupied from around 500 BC, the settlement was only abandoned with the Roman pacification of the north under Emperor Augustus (c.26 BC) and is worth a look if you can't get to any of the larger *citânias* in the region.

Praia do Cabedelo

Viana's town beach, **Praia do Cabedelo**, lies across the river, reached by a **ferry**, which leaves from the harbourside at the southern end of the main avenue (daily May–Oct 8.45am–8pm depending on the weather; €1 return); it's a five-minute crossing, but there is no strict timetable, and departures generally take place when the captain considers his boat to be sufficiently full. Road access from town to beach is over the bridge, east of the centre, a route

The Viana romaria

Viana's main *romaria*, dedicated to **Nossa Senhora da Agonía** – Our Lady of Sorrows – takes place for three days around the weekend nearest to August 20. A combination of carnival and fair, and fulfilling an important business function for the local communities, it's a great time to be in town.

Events kick off with an impressive **religious parade** on the Friday. But the best day is probably **Saturday**, when there's a massive parade of floats with every village in the region providing an example of a local craft or pursuit: a marvellous display of incongruities, with threshers pounding away in traditional dress while being pulled by a new Lamborghini tractor. If you want a seat in the stands, get a ticket well in advance.

On each of the three days there are lunchtime **processions** with *gigantones* (carnival giants), folk dancing, loud drum bands, pipe bands and, needless to say, concerted drinking. The blessing of the fishing boats on Monday morning is rather moving – women in the fishing quarter decorate their streets with pictures in coloured sawdust on religious and quotidian themes, and there are spectatcular nightly **firework displays** too.

served by infrequent buses (6 daily Mon–Fri, last bus back to Viana leaving at 5.10pm). More frequent buses, direct to Cabadela, can be caught across the river from Viana, at the end of the bridge. These also run at weekends, and are the best option out of season.

Given sun, the beach is more or less perfect – a low, curving bay with good (but not wild) breakers and a real horizon-stretching expanse of sand. Praia do Cabedelo is ideal for watersports – several companies rent out equipment (see "Listings", p.386). In August, local authorities make the beach accessible to people with disabilities, laying on thick-wheeled buggies for the journey from sand to sea. There's a bar, *Aquarío*, at the windsurf school, and a couple of others close to where the ferry docks, but beyond here there is nowhere to buy food or drink, so take a picnic. From Viana, the beach extends northwards, virtually unbroken, to the Spanish border at Caminha, and south to Póvoa de Varzim. For the energetic, either of these routes makes a memorable and enjoyable hike; for details of the northern route, see p.386.

Practicalities

The **bus station** is inconveniently located at the top end of Rua da Bandeira, twenty minutes' walk northeast of the centre. Outside *festa* time, you might find it easier to catch services from more central bus stops along Avenida Combatentes da Grande Guerra, at the southern end of Largo 5 de Outubro, or further east by the marina. **Buses to Spain** head up the coast to Vigo in Galicia, and leave Monday–Saturday at noon and 5.30pm. The **train station** is at the north end of the main Avenida Combatentes da Grande Guerra, which runs right through the town and down to the river at Largo 5 de Outubro. There's a summer **turismo** stand at the station (June 20–Aug 20 Mon–Sat 9am–6pm, Sun 9.30am–12.30pm), but the main office is in the centre on Rua do Hospital Velho, off Praça da Erva (Mon–Sat 9am–12.30pm & 2.30–6pm, Sun 9.30am–12.30pm; ☎258 822 620, ℱ258 827 873): walk down the avenue and look for the sign pointing to the left. The building dates from 1468 and was first used by pilgrims travelling to Santiago de Compostela in Spain; later it became a hospital. Staff at the main office will hand out a good mapbooklet and a pamphlets detailing **walks** in the city and the surrounding countryside.

Accommodation

Pensões – mostly ranged down and off the main avenue – are easy enough to find, although in summer, and particularly during the *romaria*, private **rooms** offer the best deals and are generally of good quality; chances are you'll be offered rooms on arriving in Viana – otherwise, look for signs in the windows of houses, or try the turismo, which has a limited list of *moradias turísticas*. During the festival, you can expect to pay between €25 and €40 for a private room, though they're more like €15 for the rest of the year. Note that streetfront rooms can be loud in summer, especially at weekends, thanks mainly to Viana's substantial motorbiking community. You might also ask the turismo about accommodation at **farms** and **manor houses** in the surrounding villages – an ideal way to get to know the countryside, provided you have transport; a couple are listed below.

The town's **campsite** (☎258 322 167, ℱ258 321 946; closed Dec 1 to Jan 15), run by Orbitur, is overcrowded in summer (there's a minimum stay of one week in July and August, and two days at other times) and overpriced for what you get (the facilities are no better than at other Orbitur sites). However, it does at least have the advantage of an attractive, pine-shaded location on the Praia do Cabedelo, and also has also some six-bed bungalows for rent (❷). The summer bus (May to mid-Sept) to the beach passes the site, or you can take the ferry across the river and walk from there. Another campsite in Cabedelo, run by *INATEL* (☎258 322 042) is for members only; call for membership details.

Hotel Aliança Av Combatentes da Grande Guerra ☎258 829 498, ℻258 825 299. Eighteenth-century building retaining some of its period charm and with pleasant, comfortable rooms. ❸

Casa Grande da Bandeira Largo das Carmelitas 488, Rua da Bendeira ☎258 823 169. This charming seventeenth-century Solares de Portugal house near the bus station has a small enclosed garden containing camelias and Chinese black bamboos. Only three rooms so book ahead. ❺

Residencial Dolce Vita Rua do Poço 44, opposite the turismo ☎258 824 860. Excellent value, spacious rooms, many with bathrooms, above a great pizza restaurant (see opposite); breakfast is included. ❶

Pensão Guerreiro Rua Grande 14–1º ☎258 822 099, ℻258 820 402. Down-at-heel place at the bottom of the main avenue. All rooms have shared bathrooms but, despite being a bit run-down, it's friendly, and the restaurant (see opposite) is good. ❶

Residencial Jardim Largo 5 de Outubro 68 ☎258 828 915, ℻258 828 917. Overlooking the river, at the bottom of town, with spotless, well-furnished rooms with bath and TV. Rooms with a balcony have good views but can be noisy in summer; excellent value, especially considering the huge breakfasts. ❸

Residencial Laranjeira Rua General Luís do Rego 45 ☎258 822 261, ℻258 821 902. A reasonable choice, just off the main avenue, with small, but pleasant rooms, all with bath. Friendly, fresh and comfortable, and with breakfast included in the price. ❸

Residencial Magalhães Rua Manuel Espregueira 62 ☎258 823 293. Twin and triple rooms, with or without bath, furnished in the best Minho tradition, with dark, carved headboards on the beds. Avoid the rooms at the back which can be noisy. ❷

Estalagem Melo Alvim Av Conde da Carreira 28 ☎258 808 200, ℻258 810 822. Sixteenth-century *solar* superbly renovated in modern minimalist style. Excellent service and a good restaurant too. ❼

Pousada do Monte de Santa Luzia Monte de Santa Luzia ☎258 828 889, 🖥www.pousada.pt. Showpiece *pousada* at the top of the hill just behind the basilica, refurbished in Art Deco style. It's the priciest place in town, and the best equipped, though the restaurant is disappointing and it lacks the uncluttered style of *Melo Alvim*. ❼

Quinta do Paço d'Anha Vila Nova de Anha ☎258 322 459, ℻258 323 904. A Solares de Portugal property 3km south of town on the N3 road to Esposende, and once a hiding place for King Dom Antonio from the invading Spanish. The house is on an estate that produces and bottles its own wine; there are four apartments with kitchenettes in the outhouses. ❺

Residencial Terra Linda Rua Luís Jácome 11–15 ☎258 828 981. Average and adequate, but tries hard to please. Rooms without bath are cheaper. ❶

Pensão Viana Mar Av Combatentes da Grande Guerra 215 ☎258 828 054, ℻258 828 962. Another reasonably good place, with warm rooms in winter and a sunken bar. More expensive rooms have baths; the summer overflow of guests is accommodated in two nearby annexes. ❷

Eating

There's a wide choice of places to eat in town, as you might expect from a busy resort. Some are lunchtime workers' cafés, while there's also a full range of tourist **restaurants**, many of which serve extremely good food since they cater mostly for demanding Portuguese visitors rather than foreigners. There are a number of cheap **cafés** and restaurants with outdoor tables in Rua Prior do Crato, one road back from the river. Several of the *pensões* also incorporate restaurants, open to non-residents; a couple of them are definitely worth considering. For general provisions, there is a permanent **market** at the eastern end of town, on Rua Martim Velho.

Casa d'Armas Largo 5 de Outubro 30 ☎258 824 999. A quality restaurant in a lovely building, but high prices as a result.

Conde do Camarido at the *Estalagem Melo Alvim*, Av Conde da Carreira 28 ☎258 808 200. Good regional dishes with specialities including *arroz de pato a Antiga* and sole.

Cozinha das Malheiras Rua Gago Coutinho 19 ☏ 258 823 680. Top-quality food and service, and not that expensive – main courses are €7.50–10. Serves a number of local specialities. Try roasted wrasse (when available), kid goat, *arroz de marisco* or *papas de sarrabulho* with fried pork (*rojões*). Closed Tues.

Dolce Vita Rua do Poço 44 ☏ 258 824 860. Excellent pizzas and a good pasta and wine, too. Opens 7pm, and there are queues by 8pm.

Pensão Guerreiro Rua Grande 14. This deceives with its unsubtle pictorial tourist menu; the food is actually very good and fairly inexpensive, and features a bumper serving of *porco à alentejana*. The goat in red wine is good too, as is the squid. Closed Thurs.

A Marisqueira Rua General Luís do Rego 36. Carefully cooked, generous dishes go some way towards making up for the somewhat lacklustre service.

Neiva Mar Largo Infante D. Henriques 1. Great for seafood, off the road on the seafront near the castle. *Bacalhau* dishes are well worth a try.

O Garfo Largo 5 de Outubro 28. Friendly, cosy place built into the arches on the waterfront. Offers a fantastic tourist menu – three courses plus wine for €10.

Os Três Arcos Largo João Tomás da Costa 25 ☏ 258 824 014. Facing the Jardim Marginal, this is perhaps the best restaurant in town, with excellent food, a full list of *vinhos verdes*, and a bar where you can eat much more cheaply from the same menu – it's mostly seafood, but other dishes are also good. If you want a table, call in earlier to book. Closed Mon.

Os Três Potes Beco dos Fornos 7 ☏ 258 829 928. Housed in a converted sixteenth-century bakery, this restaurant is incredibly popular in high season, with national costumes and music at weekends. Good traditional food, but relatively pricey, with full meals running to at least €15. Try the *polvo* (octopus). Book ahead in summer. Closed Mon.

O Triângulo Rua dos Manjovos 14. Quiet, pleasant seafood and snack joint.

O Vasco Rua Grande. Simple, tasty Portuguese dishes at reasonable prices. Closed Sun.

Taverna do Valentim Rua Daniel Machado 180. Great seafood restaurant housed in a former fisherman's tavern. Often busy. Closed Sun.

Viana's Restaurante Rua Frei Bartolomeu dos Mártires 179, off Av Campo do Castelo. The place to pursue an interest in *bacalhau* dishes.

Drinking, nightlife and entertainment

Romaria time aside, there's not an awful lot going on after dark in Viana. But a couple of **cafés** at the bottom of the main avenue are good places for a beer or late-night coffee, and if you're feeling energetic, there are a couple of clubs worth checking out. For **cultural** events, consult the *Agenda Cultural*, a monthly diary issued by the Câmara Municipal; the turismo should have a copy, and can also provide information on regional events.

Aquario Bar Praia do Cabedelo. Late night disco bar with loud music and expensive drinks.

Pastelaria Brasileira Rua Sacadura Cabral. Nearly 100 years old, this café-cum-pastry shop is good for a stand-up coffee.

Girassol Café Jardim Marginal. A lovely spot for a *bica*; though it closes at 7pm.

Glamour Rua da Bandeira 177–183. Very stylish and trendy bar-cum-nightclub with fittingly fashionable soul, blues and salsa.

Pastelaria Paris Av Combatentes da Grande Guerra. Great cakes, a pool room and decent toilets for a once.

Sports Bar Av Combatentes da Grande Guerra. Down towards the river, serves good food and drink, and is the perfect place for a beer after a hard day sightseeing. The link to sports is a little tenuous and seems to be based largely on a TV invariably showing football matches.

Disco-Pub-Clube-Viana Sol Rua dos Manjovos, off Largo Vasco da Gama by *Hotel Viana Sol*. A very youthful crowd packs into this place in summer. Open from the afternoon until 3am; 4am on Saturday nights.

Listings

Banks Main banks are on Praça da República and along the main avenue.

Boat trips Departures from the pier at the bottom of the avenue for trips up the Rio Lima; prices are negotiable but expect to pay around €15 per person.

Books and newspapers English-language books are available at Livraria Bertrand, Rua Sacadura Cabral, and international newspapers are sold in the newsagents on the corner of Praça da República.

Car rental Avis, Rua do Gontim ☎258 817 540; Hertz, Av Conde da Carreira ☎258 822 250.

Hospital Santa Luzia Estrada Santa Luzia ☎258 829 081.

Internet The post office (see below) has public online access.

Pharmacy Nelsina, Praça da República; Central, Rua Manuel Espregueira. The turismo has details of late-night openings.

Police Headquarters at Rua de Aveiro ☎258 822 022.

Post office Opposite the train station on Av dos Combatentes da Grande Guerra 66; you can make phone calls from the Portugal Telecom office next door.

Sports Several companies rent **surfing gear** at around €25 per day with wetsuit; of these, try the Associação de Windsurf do Norte, which sets up a stand at Praia do Cabedelo on weekends; Omni Surf Shop, Rua do Poço 38–42 ☎258 826 522, which also rents mountain bikes; and the Surf Club de Viana, Centro Comercial 1° Maio, Praça 1° de Maio ☎966 221 092 (mobile), ✉joaoza-

smith@nortnet.pt, which also offers individual lessons for €10/hr. **Sailing and canoeing** can be arranged through Amigos do Mar (Associação Cívica Internacional para a Defesa do Mar), Apartado 533, 4900 Viana do Castelo (€15 membership; bring two passport photos entitles you to free activities – ring two days before to book), ☎965 841 520, ✉amigos.mar@mail.telepac.pt, and Clube Naútico de Viana, Lugar de Argaçosa, Meadela ☎258 842 165 or 258 827 652. **Biking trips** are run by Puraventura, Rua da Pedela, Vila Nova de Anha ☎253 251 287. **Go-karting** takes place at the Kartodromo, 4km outside Viana on Av do Atlantico near to Praia da Amorosa; ☎258 320 080, ✉kartingviana@iol.pt.

Swimming pool The municipal pool is at Av Capitão Gaspar de Castro, 700m along the eastern continuation of Rua Emídio Navarro. The Foz Health Club, Cabadelo, also has a pool ☎258 331 274.

Taxis Available from ranks along Av Combatentes da Grande Guerra. To call Taxi Vianeses try one of three numbers: ☎258 826 641, ☎258 822 322 or ☎258 822 061.

Viana to Moledo

North of Viana the train line follows the coast all the way to Caminha. Two trains a day, in both directions, stop at all the villages en route – notably at Carreço, Afife, Gelfa, Vila Praia de Âncora and Moledo do Minho – offering easy access to a sequence of largely deserted beaches. Buses cover the same route with fourteen services daily (Mon–Fri) and five daily at weekends. It is possible to **walk** the same route, covering the whole stretch in a couple of days, camping overnight among the sheltered dunes at Afife, 10km north of Viana.

Carreço, Afife and Gelfa

The small village of **CARREÇO** lies a couple of kilometres east of its beach, where there's a café-bar, toilets and showers. **AFIFE**, another 2km further north, is also a good goal with a fort, several cafés and a casino. The modern *Residencial Compostela* (☎258 981 590, ℱ258 981 244; ❷) is on the main road just north of the turning to the beach; it also has a restaurant, although the two on the beach are preferable. If you're looking for a more dramatic place to stay, *Casa do Penedo* (April–Oct only; ☎258 980 000, ℱ258 980 009; ❸) is a typical Minho home, an attractive stone property with a garden, 1km south of the station, up a hillside with sea views. The dunes – and a particularly wonderful expanse of beach – are fifteen to twenty minutes' walk from the village, the least frequented parts being to the south.

At **GELFA**, between Afife and Vila Praia de Âncora, there's a **campsite** in the pine woods (☎258 911 537; mid-March to mid-Oct daily; rest of year weekends only), but it's on the inland side of the train station and hence some distance from the beach.

Vila Praia de Âncora

Six kilometres up the coast from Afife, the next major stop on the train line is **VILA PRAIA DE ÂNCORA**, a large resort that's popular with locals at weekends and in summer. Sitting on the basin of the River Âncora, there is a superb beach right alongside the train line, sheltered by the surrounding hills and drifting back into the river's estuary. Here you can swim enjoyably even when the Atlantic breezes are blowing towels around the sands. For good measure there are two **forts** guarding the bay: the Fortim de Cão, south of the estuary, and the better-preserved Forte de Lagarteira, to the north by the little fishing harbour. Legend has it that the river, and indeed the town, owe its unusual name to a punishment doled out to the adulterous Queen Urraca of Navarre, drowned in the river by her jealous husband King Ramiro II of Asturias, Galicia and Leon with an anchor (*âncora*) around her neck.

The **train station** for Vila Praia is called Âncora-Praia, and is the only station between Viana do Castelo and Caminha at which express trains stop. Just down the road on Largo da Estação, the well-signposted **bus station** also houses the **turismo** (Mon–Sat 9.30am–12.30pm & 2–6pm; ☎258 911 384, ℱ258 911 338), from where you can get leaflets detailing a 5km walking circuit to the **Cividade de Âncora**, the ruins of a first-century AD Bronze and Copper Age settlement; the walk starts from the main square of Santa Maria de Âncora, 2km inland. Finding **accommodation** for a few days here shouldn't be hard. The turismo has a list of **private rooms** (❶–❷), while other choices include the popular, mid-range *Hotel Meira*, at Rua 5 de Outubro 56 (☎258 911 488, ℯhotel.meira@mail.telepac.pt; ❹) and the more reasonably priced *Albergaria Quim Barreiros*, on the seafront behind the train station Avenida Dr. Ramos Pereira (☎258 959 100, ℱ258 959 109; ❸). Apart from **camping** unofficially by the Fortim de Cão, there's the *Parque de Campismo do Paço* (☎258 912 697, ℱ258 951 228; reception open 8am–12.30pm & 2–10pm; closed mid-Oct to mid-March), 1.5km from town on the south bank of the Rio Âncora, which also has canoes and rafting.

Restaurants are plentiful, as is fresh fish. *Restaurante Fonte Nova*, along Rua Miguel Bombarda from the church, and the *Restaurante Central*, opposite the train station on Praça Republica, are both good, serving meals for around €10; while *Restaurante Mar Gelfa* (open July–Sept), twenty minutes' walk south down the beach, is recommended for food (try the lamprey) and sunsets.

Moledo do Minho

Four kilometres north of Vila Praia de Âncora, **MOLEDO DO MINHO** is the train traveller's last chance to swim in the sea. Very much in the same mould as Vila Praia, it too has a fort – this time half-ruined, guarding the river from a long, sandy spit – and is predominantly a Portuguese family resort, with a reputation for attracting the nouveaux riches. If you're heading for Caminha, Valença, or even Spain, you could easily stop off here, wander down to the beach, and catch the next train. Should you want **to stay**, the unnamed *Pensão* (☎258 921 622; ❷) on the main road through to Vila Praia might tempt you; alternatively, the seafront **turismo** (Mon–Fri 9.30am–12.30pm & 2.30–6pm) can help find a room. You can **eat** at the good *Restaurante O Lagar* on the seafront, where you'll also find a number of bars serving snacks.

Along the Rio Minho

At Moledo, the train line moves inland along the south bank of the **Rio Minho**, which meanders northeastwards forming the country's border with Spain. **Caminha** is the first river town, a pleasant stopover, either for a night or for a meal between trains. Beyond here, several small fortified towns guard the Portuguese side of the river, with the Minho train line terminating in perhaps the best of the lot, **Valença do Minho**. This is also the site of a splendid weekly market and a major crossing-point into Spain. However, the most scenic section of the river, from Valença east to **Monção** and **Melgaço**, can only be reached by bus, but is well worth the extra effort. Both towns are also minor border crossings, with buses onwards from the Spanish side.

Caminha

At the mouth of the Rio Minho, and straddling the Rio Coura, **CAMINHA** is a quiet river port that was at its peak in the seventeenth century. A few reminders of more prosperous days remain though, principally in the main square, Praça Conselheiro Silva Torres (known locally as Largo Terreiro) and the area around. Here a battlemented town hall, a Renaissance clock tower and a large fountain vie for your attention. Caminha's most distinguished building, though, is the magnificent **Igreja Matriz**, a couple of minutes' walk from the main square towards the river; take the street through the arch by the clock tower, past the **turismo** (Mon–Sat 9.30am–12.30pm & 2–5.30pm; ☎ & ℻ 258 921 952), which gives out good town maps. The church was built towards the end of the fifteenth century, when the town was reputed to rival Porto in trade, and it still stands within part of the old city walls. Inside there's a magnificent inlaid ceiling, intricate *azulejos* and a carved granite pulpit. Note also the figures carved on the two Renaissance doorways, one on the north side giving the finger to Spain across the river! A small **museum** (9.30am–2.30pm & 2–6pm; free) houses a collection of items plundered from local archeological sites.

A couple of kilometres south of town, the island of **Fortaleza da Ínsua** makes an enjoyable trip – local fishermen run trips across on Sundays from the spit of sand at Foz do Minho, on the river side of its fine beach. If you want to arrange something during the week (for the next morning), ask in the *Café Valadares* for directions to António Garrafão's house. He will go only if there is a reasonably large – or affluent – group gathered. For **watersports**, contact Afluente Desporto e Natureza, Lugar da Sentinela, 5km east at Lanhelas (☎258 727 017, ✉safari@afluente.com), which offers boat trips, "canoe safaris" (daily at 10am & 3pm), mountain biking, rafting, sailing and surfing – each activity costs €25.

Practicalities

The town's best **accommodation** is in the modern, four-star *Hotel Porta do Sol* (☎258 722 340, ℻258 722 347; ❹) with swimming pools and tennis courts, on Avenida Marginal at the southern entrance to town. Otherwise, there is a handful of **pensões** in the centre of town: the *Residencial Arca Nova*

(☎258 721 757; ❸), near the train station in Largo Sidónio Pais, is a little over-priced for what it offers; the older and better-value *Pensão Rio Coura* (☎258 921 142; ❷), in Avenida Saraiva de Carvalho; and the friendly *Residencial Galo d'Ouro*, Rua da Corredoura 15 (☎258 921 160; ❷), just off the main square. Alternatives include a few **private rooms** in houses (ask at the turismo or the *Pêro de Caminha* restaurant; see below), and the *Casa do Esteiró* (☎258 721 336, ⓕ258 921 356; ❸), a small Solares de Portugal property at the entrance to town which has two rooms to rent in lovely gardens.

There are two **campsites** nearby. The better of them is a little inland at *Vilar de Mouros* (☎258 727 472, ⓔpnvm.anta@cartaopostal.com), which is nicely positioned by a small river gorge, and has a swimming pool, tennis court and some bungalows for rent (❷–❸); there are two buses daily (Mon–Fri) to the site from outside the café, 200m left out of the train station. The other, which tends to be crowded in summer, is an Orbitur site (☎258 921 295, ⓕ258 921 473; closed Dec 1–Jan 15), 2km to the south of town between the river and the sea, opposite the Fortaleza da Ínsua; three daily buses (Mon–Fri) from the town hall stop close by.

Several of the best **cafés** and **restaurants** are found in the main square: the *Solar do Pescado* specializes in fish dishes; the cheerful *Pêro de Caminha* serves pizzas amongst other things; and the *Confeitaria Colmeia* is the place for break-fast. There's good, if more expensive, food too at the *Adega do Chico* on Rua Visconde de Sousa Rego 30 (head up the right-hand side of the main square, away from the clock tower). **Bars** tend to be concentrated along the Rua Ricardo Joaquim de Sousa, which heads from the main square down towards the Igreja Matriz.

The town has a **ferry** link to La Guardia in Spain, which leaves from beside the bridge over the Rio Coura. There are services daily throughout summer (on the hour 8am–7pm; €0.60; cars €2.50) but winter times are variable.

Vila Nova de Cerveira

Up to seven daily trains run along the banks of the Rio Minho to **VILA NOVA DE CERVEIRA**, 11km to the northeast of Caminha. This small walled town has a car and passenger ferry (actually little more than a floating platform) which drifts every half-hour across the river to Goyan in Galicia. The **ferry** (summer 8.30am–8.55pm; winter 8.30am–7.25pm; passengers €0.40, cars €1.50) has turned the village into something of a shopping centre for Spaniards, but it remains a pleasant and accessible place and in many respects is more enticing than the bigger and better known Valença further upstream. The town is also home to an art school, hence the surprising prevalence of modern works around town.

The **Solar dos Castros** on Praça da Liberdade was once a manor house and now serves as a cultural centre. At the back, facing a beautifully well-kept gar-den, is the **turismo** (Mon–Sat 8.30am–12.30pm & 2–6pm, Sun 9am–12.30pm; ☎251 708 023, ⓕ251 708 024), while alongside, in a small gar-den, is a striking sculpture of a tripod holding aloft a rock. This has become the symbol of the **arts festival** held here every two years in August and September; the remarkable statue depicting men talking, which won first prize in 1984, is displayed just inside the front door of the Solar dos Castros.

Although there is little in the way of accommodation, there is something to fit every budget. The cheapest option is the pleasant **youth hostel** at Largo 16 de Fevereiro 21 (T & F 251 796 113), which boasts its own kitchen and a terrace, and also has double rooms with private or shared bathroom (①). If you have money to burn, you can do no better than stay in the excellent *Pousada de Dom Dinis* (T 251 795 601, W www.pousadas.pt; ②), built within the sixteenth-century fortress walls overlooking the ramparts. Although not a historic building itself, this would provide a memorable first or last night in Portugal; not surprisingly, it also has the best restaurant in town featuring Minho specialities. In between these two extremes, standard accommodation is on offer at the *Residencial Rainha de Gusmão*, Rua Herois do Ultramar (T 251 796 227, F 251 795 604; ③), some of whose rooms have fine river views. For **food**, the *Café Restaurant Central*, on Largo 16 de Fevereiro, is one of several good places to eat, while *Cerva Bar* and *Barril Bar*, off the main square, are where much of the evening action takes place.

Valença do Minho and around

The border town of **VALENÇA DO MINHO** (usually just referred to as Valença) has bustling modern surroundings to its absurdly quaint old town area clumped amid perfectly preserved, multi-layered seventeenth-century ramparts on a hillock above the river. The fortress has repelled innumerable Spanish and French invasions over the centuries but, more recently, it has proved unable to resist the invasions of bargain-hunting tourists from over the border. But despite the summer hoardes, there are great walks here, both down by the river and along the **ramparts** (watch out for hidden stairwells), the design of which was influenced by the work of the seventeenth-century French military architect, Vauban.

On foot, you're likely to approach the old town from the Largo da Esplanada roundabout at the bottom of the hill, where Rua das Antas – which runs from the train station – enters the new part of town. Climb the hill straight ahead, turn right at the top, and you enter through the **Portas da Coroada**, further along from which a causeway leads over a dry moat to the **Portas do Meio**, the bastion's middle gates. An alternative approach is to turn right at the Largo da Esplanada, and left just before the turismo. Throughout the area around Largo de São João, you'll notice a rich diversity of buildings lining the narrow, cobbled streets, with sudden views of the surrounding countryside appearing over the lower reaches of the walls. During the day, these charms are exploited by a myriad of souvenir shops, catering for the day-trippers who cross the border from Spain to pick up Portuguese linen, ceramics and electrical goods. Increasingly, the extent of this commercialism is reducing the appeal of the town and even the regional tourist office describes Valença as "the shop window of the Upper Minho" – Tuy, across the river in Spain, is probably nicer. By late afternoon, though, the crowds are gone and at night the old part of Valença is almost a ghost town. Apart from the old town itself, the only visitable attraction here is the **Museu do Bombeiro**, Largo 7 de Julho, in the old town near the Praça da República (Mon–Fri 10am–noon & 2–5.30pm, Sat 2–5.30pm; €1), which is full of old firefighting equipment and regalia.

The newer part of town, to the south of the ramparts, has nothing of historical interest but it's here that you'll track down all the basic necessities. Come on Wednesday and you'll encounter the huge weekly **market**, held on the wooded slopes below the walls. Apart from the rows of tourist shops in the old town, the best place for **shopping** is Garrafeira Vasco da Gama on Largo da Esplanada in the new town, to stock up on wines, cheeses, port or chocolate.

Practicalities

Now that European cross-border controls have been removed, arriving in Valença **from Tuy in Spain**, over the river, is a simple matter of staying on the train for another few minutes as it rattles over the bridge (there are two daily trains to and from Vigo to Valença), or simply walking over from Tuy. Domestic **trains** from Viana do Castelo end their run in Valença; to head further east or south you'll have to take a local **bus**, which arrives at and departs from in front of the train station. There are no obvious signs to the old town, but it's easy enough to find: turn right at the avenue that leads away from the station, then head uphill after the crossroads. You'll see the **turismo** (Mon–Sat 9.30am–12.30pm & 2.30–6pm (winter closes 5.30pm), Sun 9.30am–12.30pm; ☏ 251 823 329, Ⓕ 251 823 374) in a wooden shack opposite a small park town; the free town map is helpful, and you can also buy an information pack (€2.50, also available at some other turismos) detailing Romanesque churches and monuments along the Rio Minho. A slightly more exciting way of seeing the region is via Minho Infernal (Lugar da Pedreira 6, Ganfei; ☏ 966 501 329 (mobile), Ⓕ 251 824 771), the town's main **adventure sports** operator, offering rafting, canyoning, biking and four-wheel-drive trips.

Accommodation

Private rooms are available in the old town; ask at the restaurants. Otherwise try the following:

Casa do Poço Trav. da Gaviarra 4 ☏ 251 825 235, Ⓕ 251 825 469. This former doctor's home has been converted into a luxurious Privetur property and is worth every euro. It's in the old, walled town next to the *pousada*, which it equals for views and surpasses in atmosphere and furnishings. There are only five rooms so it's advisable to book ahead. ❻

Hotel Residencial Lara Rua de São Sebastião, 300m uphill from Largo da Esplanada ☏ 251 824 348, Ⓕ 251 824 358. A smart, efficient place in the new town, facing the walls. All rooms have a balcony and TV. ❸

Hotel Valença do Minho Av Miguel Dantas, 500m from the train station ☏ 251 824 211, Ⓕ 251 824 321. Large and impersonal hotel offering rooms with all mod cons and a restaurant and swimming pool. ❸

Residencial Ponte Seca Av Dr. Tito Fontes ☏ 251 822 580. To the east on the edge of the new town,

this is spotless and good value, if a little out of the way. Back rooms overlook fields with the mountains beyond. ❸

Residencial Rio Minho Largo da Estação ☏ 251 809 240, Ⓕ 251 809 248. Opposite the train station, this is probably the cheapest option in town, with simple, airy, newly renovated rooms and a pleasant restaurant; breakfast is included. ❷

Pousada de São Teotónio ☏ 251 824 392, Ⓔ enatur@mail.telepac.pt. Located inside the fortress itself, though much of the building is modern. If you don't want to stay, a drink in the bar – or lunch in the excellent restaurant (around €15–20 a head) gives you a taste of the surroundings. ❻

Residencial Val-Flores Rua de São Sebastião, 200m uphill from Largo da Esplanada ☏ 251 824 106, Ⓕ 251 824 129. A friendly, modern high-rise with spotless rooms; all have baths and satellite TVs. ❸

Eating

You should be able to eat well in any of the old town's restaurants, where competition keeps prices down, though in summer, sharing the experience with the tourists hordes can make it anything but peaceful. **Specialities** include *lampreia* (lamprey), *cabrito à Sanfins* (a goat dish prepared at Easter time), *sável frito* (fried shad) and *enguias à moda da Raposeira* (eels).

Restaurante Baluarte Rua Apolinario da Fonseca. Reasonably priced meals in the old town, with a fine range of *bacalhau* dishes.

Fortaleza Rua Apolinário da Fonseca 5. Just outside the Portas do Meio, this is not as pricey as it looks. It specializes in goat, among other things, which you can enjoy at its outdoor tables.

Mané Edifício São Sebastião, Av Miguel Dantas, by Largo da Esplanada ☎251 823 402. On the road from the station towards the old town. Very good

reputation but expensive; try the *arroz de lampreia* (lamprey with rice).

Monumental built into the walls, just inside the Portas da Coroada. Serves a wonderful, spicy *arroz de marisco* and is reasonably priced.

Os Gallegos Rua Acceso Zona Escolar. As the name suggests, serves more of a Spanish menu and is popular with day-trippers from across the border who turn their nose up at the more basic, traditional Portuguese fare.

Crossing to Spain: Tuy

Just a mile from Valença, across an iron bridge designed by A.G. Eiffel, Spanish **TUY** is an ancient, pyramid-shaped town with a grand battlemented parish church. It, too, is partly walled and it looks far sturdier than Valença, though the first English guidebook to Portugal (*Murray's* in 1855) reported that "the guns of Valença could without difficulty lay Tuy in ruins". If you're not planning to go on to Spain, at least walk across the frontier bridge to explore Tuy's old quarter by the river. There's no passport control: walking from the centre of one old town to the other takes around thirty minutes. By **road** and **train** you can go direct from Valença to Vigo, which is within easy reach of Santiago de Compostela, the ancient and beautiful pilgrimage town of Galicia.

Inland: Paredes de Coura

PAREDES DE COURA, 28km south of Valença, claims to be the oldest village in Portugal, an assertion that's rendered a little hard to believe by the new emigrant-financed houses surrounding what's really quite a sizeable town. Still, if you're headed for Ponte da Barca or Ponte de Lima, it warrants a detour. You can climb up to the top of the town for views over an almost Swiss landscape, with chalet-style houses and white church spires, or follow the track down beyond the football field to the river for the town's best swimming spot. Every year, over the first weekend in August, there's a **festival** – the *Festas do Conselho* – featuring the usual Minho mix of dance, costumed procession and music.

On Mondays to Fridays, there is one daily **bus** to the town from Valença, one from Monção, and two to five daily from Ponte de Lima. Buses stop on Rua 25 de Abril in the east of town. The best **place to stay** is the *Pensão Miquelina*, on the central Rua Miguel Dantas (☎251 782 103; ❷), where you will also find a number of good restaurants; try *Arcada* for huge portions of good local fare. The **turismo** (Mon–Sat 9.30am–12.30pm & 2.30–6pm; ☎251 782 105) is housed in an old prison in Largo Visconde Mouzelos in the east of town, off the Rua Conselheiro Miguel Dantas.

Monção and around

MONÇÃO, 16km east of Valença, is home to yet another **border fortress**, though it doesn't quite make the grade – there being little more than a doorway, a section of walling above the bus station and a high defensive walkway that runs along the northern, river-facing, side of town. The rest was demolished to make way for a road. Perhaps for this reason, Monção has escaped much of the daytime tourist attention that bedevils the towns to the west; the liveliest day to visit is Thursday, market day. But there's an attractive old centre, which always rewards a stroll as well as an old riverside spa bath popular with elderly holidaymakers.

The town's history, in which two local women played a prominent part, provides a colourful backdrop to the surviving fortifications and buildings. The principal figure involved is **Deu-la-Deu Martins** (the name means "God gave her"), a mayor's wife, who is commemorated by a statue and fountain in Largo da Loreto. Her tale, similar to a number of other accounts across Portugal and Spain, recalls a crucial moment in the fourteenth century when the Spanish troops had besieged the townspeople to the point of starvation. With their food store almost exhausted, surrender seemed the only option, but the Spanish had not accounted for the resilience of Deu-la-Deu. With the town's remaining flour stocks mustered together, she baked some cakes and had them presented to the Spanish camp with an offer to "make more if they needed them". Fortunately for the town, the Spanish had eaten all the bread they could handle and the psychological effect of the bluff was so great that they promptly gave up and went away. Local *pãozinhos* (little bread cakes) are still baked in her honour; her birthplace is off the Praça, above the butcher's shop on the arched side road.

A second Spanish siege, in the seventeenth-century Wars of Restoration, was relieved in 1659 when the **Countess of Castelo Melhor**, perhaps inspired by earlier example, resorted to psychological warfare once again. Aware that the Spanish were unlikely to fall for the bread trick again, she negotiated a ceasefire on condition that full military honours be given to her men. When the Countess relinquished her 236 surviving fighters to the Spanish army, the enemy, oblivious of the town's two thousand fatalities, assumed they had been kept at bay by this paltry platoon and duly retreated in shame.

In the town, there are a couple of interesting older places that reward a visit. The seventeenth-century **Igreja da Misericórdia** on Praça Deu-la-Deu contains some magnificent *azulejos*, as does the Romanesque **Igreja da Matriz** – at the centre of a maze of ancient streets – which houses various tombs, including that of Deu-la-Deu herself. The local **festivals** of Corpo de Deus (Corpus Christi; June 18) and Nossa Senhora das Dores (Sept 19–22) are interesting times to visit if you can manage it (though you are unlikely to be able to find any accommodation then). In the former, the procession is followed by a hilarious mock battle between an unconvincing St George and an elaborately painted wooden dragon (the "*coca*") manoeuvred by several locals.

Practicalities

The local **bus station**, for services to Melgaço, Valença and Viana do Castelo, is on the outskirts of town at Veiga Velha (℡251 651 996). AVIC (for Parades de Coura) is at Praça da República; Turilis (Mon–Fri, 3 daily), for services to Porto along the Rio Minho, is off Largo do Loreto at Rua da Independência 8; and Auto Viação do Minho services to destinations within Minho and to Porto depart from the office on the Arcos road by the Galp petrol station. There's a **turismo** (Mon–Sat: summer 9am–12.30pm & 2–7pm, winter 9.30am–12.30pm & 2–6pm; ℡ & ℻251 652 757) in Praça Deu-la-Deu, further on from Praça da República. For travellers to Spain, there's a **road bridge** across to Salvaterra in Spain.

Accommodation

The turismo has details of reasonably priced **private rooms** to rent, including those above *Casa Constantino*, Rua da Independência 24 (℡251 653 624:

1), where a couple of the rooms overlook the river. The nearest **camping** is at the free riverside *Caldas de Monção* campsite (**☎** 251 652 434), next to the spa, but you have to be prepared to go back to basics: there's a pit latrine, no showers and no electricity.

Albergaria Atlântico and Residencial Mané
Rua General Pimenta de Castro 15 ☎ 251 652 355 or 251 652 490, ⓕ 251 652 376. The town's upmarket (if rather bland) modern choice, split into two separate hotels. Rooms in both have TVs, telephones and minibars. The *Atlântico* is more expensive on account of its air conditioning, whilst the *Mané* has discos weekend nights. **3**

Casa de Rodas just out of town at Lugar de Rodar ☎ 251 652 105. A lovely, low eighteenth-century *turismo rural* building with only four guest rooms set in wonderful gardens and surrounded by woodland. The turismo will find out if there's

space and give you directions. **3**

Café Croissanteria Raiano Praça Deu-la-Deu 34 ☎ 251 653 534. Modern, good-value rooms (some self-contained) above the café; the best ones look out over the square to Spain. **2**

Residencial Deu-la-Deu Rua 1 Dezembro ☎ 251 651 996. Good value, clean rooms in a quiet area. **2**

Residencial Esteves Rua General Pimenta de Castro ☎ 251 652 386. Near the station and reasonably priced, with smart, modern rooms – all have bathrooms and TVs. The entrance is on Rua de Santo António. **1**

Eating and drinking

The local wine from Monção and Melgaço, the finest *vinho verde* in the country, is available on draft in a couple of bars off the main square; the most delicious bottled variety is *Palácio da Brejoeira*, which, as a Monção tourist leaflet one-liner puts it, "someone in France once classified as being the best in the world". It's made from the Alvarinho grape, which produces a full bodied wine with a much higher alcoholic content than other *vinhos verdes* (around 12.5 percent), and consequently has the ability to age. It goes well with strong-tasting fish, especially the local eels (*enguias*), shad (*savel*) and the rich, eel-like lamprey (*lampreia*) which is in season between January and March; Minho trout and salmon are always tremendous too. Praça Deu-la-Deu is the best place to start looking for bars; cheap drinks are available at *Ninho do Pardal* on the northern side of the square. The nearest disco is *Beebop* in the hamlet of Cortes 2km to the west.

Probably the best bet for **food** in Monção is the *Restaurante Terra Nova*, in Praça da República, which does tasty trout and salmon at very reasonable prices. There are a few good restaurants around the Praça Deu-la-Deu as well, including *Firmino's*, on the south side.

The spa, Cortes and Lapela

The close proximity of a **thermal spa**, 1500m to the east of Monção (follow the walls), has turned the town into something of a resort for Spanish day trippers and Portuguese weekenders. Aside from the dubious pleasures of the alkaline water, there's a park and a free campsite by the river. However, this is not exactly the most luxurious of spas, and the Victorian cells – each of which contains a cast-iron bath and assortment of frightening-looking equipment – are rather unsettling.

Further afield, to the west of the town, a pleasant walk trails off into the woods from the bus stop at Senhora da Cabeça to the hamlet of **CORTES**, which was Monção's medieval site. About 3km further west is **LAPELA**, whose river beach is safer for swimmers. The village is dominated by a lofty tower, all that remains of a fortress destroyed in 1706 to provide materials for the restoration of the battered walls of Monção.

East to Melgaço

An historic incident in Anglo–Portuguese relations took place on the fragile-looking bridge over the Rio Mouro just before **CEIVÃES**, 10km along the road from Monção to Melgaço. This is the spot where John of Gaunt, the Duke of Lancaster, arranged the marriage of his daughter Philippa to King Dom João I in 1386, an arrangement that resulted in the signing of the **Treaty of Windsor** between the two countries. It gave rise to an alliance lasting over six hundred years and to the naming of numerous public places in honour of "Filipa de Lencastre".

Thermal spa enthusiasts might want to stop at **PESO** (also known as **Termas de Melgaço**), another 10km to the east (and just 4km short of Melgaço). This is a tiny spa town, spread along the old main road (the new one passes just below) and looking down on a magnificent curve of the river. The **spa** (☎251 403 282; baths open summer Mon–Sat 8am–noon & 4–7pm) itself is a delight, with its shaded, landscaped gardens and fountain room. There's a **campsite** by the spa (☎251 403 282, ℗251 402 647; open all year), which also has bunga-lows (❸) for rent. The only **hotel** is the plush, modern *Albergaria Boavista* (☎251 416 464, ℗251 416 350; ❸), which has a swimming pool, fabulous views and a good **restaurant**. On the other side of the road, the *Adega do Sossego* (☎251 404 308; evenings only) is also an excellent place to eat.

Melgaço

MELGAÇO – the country's northernmost outpost – is a small border town sit-ting high above the Rio Minho. Though the town's rural origins are somewhat obscured by the modern developments that sprawl along the main road, at its heart, not much has really changed. Try to arrive for the **Friday market** when chickens, ducks, sticky buns, furniture, pottery, cabbages and corsets cover the stretch of road around the old walls. Otherwise, the only major event is the three-day *Festa da Cultura*, starting on the second Friday of August, when a dis-play of tractors, an array of the town's long-reputed smoked hams (*presunto*), a craft exhibition and a performance from the school banjo band are organized.

At other times, the most likely reasons for visiting Melgaço are that it is so obviously off the tourist track, and that it gives easy access to the northern part of the Parque Nacional da Peneda-Gerês and to Spanish Galicia (see p.396 for access details). Its one historic feature is the ruined **fortress**, dating from 955AD and much fought over during the Wars of Restoration, but now little more than a tower and a few walls handy for hanging out washing.

Short **excursions** from Melgaço might include the two thirteenth-century **Romanesque churches** of **PADERNE** (3km west, off the road to Monção) and Nossa Senhora da Orada (1km east, off the road to the border). Melgaço Radical (☎251 402 155, ℗251 402 429) offers rafting, canoeing on the Rio Minho and canyoning in Peneda-Gerês National Park in addition to its rather over-subscribed walking trips. Costs are around €25 per activity.

Practicalities

The town's helpful **turismo** (Mon–Sat 9.30am–12.30pm & 2.30–6pm; closed Wed in winter; ☎251 402 440) is just out of town on the road to Monção in the stone Casa Castreja. It has details on local *vinho verde quintas* (estates) which welcome visitors, leaflets detailing walks in Peneda-Gerês national park (pp.397–417), and can provide details of inexpensive **rooms** in private houses. Near the turismo on Rua Rio do Porto, those in the home of Maria Helena

Morais are good (☎251 402 188; ❶). The only **pensões** are *Pensão Pemba* on Praça Amadeu Abilio Lopes (☎251 402 555; ❶), and the *Residencial Miguel Pereira* at Rua da Calçada 5, near the cinema (☎251 402 212; ❶–❷), which offers a range of budget and mid-range rooms. The nicest rooms around are at the old stone *Quinta da Calçada* (❸), 1km from the turismo; you book through Solares de Portugal in Ponte de Lima (see p.398).

In the alleys below the fort, a couple of **café–restaurants** offer good food at reasonable prices and there's a café in the attractive castle gardens overlooking the Minho valley. But best of all is *Restaurante Panorama* (☎251 410 400) in the Mercado Municipal, whose unexceptional decor belies top quality food (mains under €10): try the roast pork leg with pineapple, or lamprey cooked in rice. Apart from fish, another local dish is *bifes de presunto de cebolada* (gammon steak fried with onions). For dessert, try *bucha doce*, made with eggs and port wine and traditionally served at carnival time. In the newer part of town there are a couple of pizzerias and *Adega Regional Sabino*, on Largo Hermenegildo Solheiro, which serves generous portions of local food.

Buses leave for Monção daily and connect with services to Braga, Coimbra, Porto and Lisbon. There are also direct services to Porto, Coimbra and Lisbon. Auto Viação Melgaço buses (Mon–Fri) to Lamas de Mouro and Castro Laboreiro for the Peneda-Gerês park leave at 7.30am (with an additional 12.50pm service on Fri). Their buses to São Gregório, for the Spanish border, leave four times a day, in the afternoon and early evening. All services leave from Largo da Calçada.

The Spanish border

The **Spanish border post** is at **PONTE BARXAS**, 1km east of **SÃO GREGÓRIO**, which itself is 10km east of Melgaço. Other than taking one of the buses outlined above in "Practicalities", the only way to get there is by taxi, which is reasonably inexpensive.

Across the frontier, buses leave twice daily (Mon–Fri) for Ribadavia and Orense. Ribadavia (along the Minho and with superb local red wine) and Celanova (on a different route to Orense and dwarfed by a vast medieval monastery) must be two of the most lovely and characteristic towns of Spanish Galicia. The Minho itself – or Miño as it becomes known – is more placid in the further reaches, as it is dammed shortly after the point when both of its banks are within Spain.

The Lima Valley and Parque Nacional da Peneda-Gerês

The **Rio Lima**, whose valley is perhaps the most beautiful in Portugal, was thought by the Romans to be the Lethe, the mythical River of Oblivion. Beyond it, they imagined, lay the Elysian Fields; to cross would mean certain destruction, for its waters possessed the power of the lotus, making the traveller forget country and home. The forces of Roman Consul Decimus Junius Brutus were so convinced of this that they flatly refused to cross, despite having trekked across most of Spain to get there. Brutus had to seize the standard and plunge into the water shouting the names of his legionaries from the far bank – to show his memory remained intact – before they could be persuaded to follow.

There are roads along both banks of the Lima from **Viana do Castelo** (see p.380), where the river meets the sea. Travelling from Viana on the main N202, regular bus services pass through two highly attractive towns – **Ponte de Lima** and **Ponte da Barca**. These are both excellent bases for exploring the wild, dramatic countryside and small villages, often with Romanesque churches.

Further east, the Lima runs into the heart of the astonishingly beautiful **Parque Nacional da Peneda-Gerês National Park**. The easiest points of access are from **Braga** to the central section of the park, **Arcos de Valdevez** and **Ponte da Barca** to the north of the park, and from **Melgaço** to the far north. Access to the eastern section is problematic, but probably simplest from Montalegre in Trás-os-Montes. If you're planning a lot of hiking, you should visit the park offices located in Braga or Ponte da Barca (see p.401).

Ponte de Lima

An hour's ride east of Viana do Castelo, **PONTE DE LIMA** is typical of the cluster of peaceful little towns on the banks of the Lima and its tributaries. It's a delightful place, whose old centre – as is often the way – has no specific attraction other than its air of sleepy indifference to the wider world. You might disagree if you visit in July or August, when Ponte de Lima begins to show worrying signs of midsummer tourist strain, a phenomenon that the local authorities have tried to capitalize on by building an eighteen-hole golf complex. Outside these times though, Ponte de Lima remains one of the most pleasing towns in the region, and visitors are seldom disappointed.

The town takes its name from the low stone bridge that crosses the river, rebuilt in medieval times but still bearing traces of its Roman origin. It is said to mark the path of the first hesitant Roman crossing of the river and was part of a military route leading from Braga to Astorga.

Besides the bridge, the town's main focus is a long, riverside **Alameda** (Passeio 25 de Abril), shaded by magnificent plane trees, leading to the rambling old convent of Santo António (Tues–Sun 2–5.30pm; free), which contains a small **museum** of ecclesiastical treasures within its church. Across the bridge lie the attractive **Jardims Tematicos** and the small **Museu Rural**

(Tue–Sun 2–6pm; free), which houses a rather dull collection of tools and farming acoutrements from over the years.

The surrounding countryside offers some fantastic opportunities for walking. To the east, however, the motorway sharply curtails any exploration after a kilometre or so, but wandering through some of the villages on both sides of the river is a joy. More energetic walkers can climb to **Santo Ovídio chapel** (about half an hour to the top) – a bizarre shrine to the patron saint of ears – for glorious views of the Lima valley, before ambling back to Ponte de Lima along cobbled and vine-covered lanes. The turismo in Ponte de Lima has a few illustrated leaflets detailing attractive local **walks**.

The river at Ponte de Lima would offer fine swimming were it not so polluted; however, there is a municipal **pool** in Rua Francisco Sá Carneiro (Mon–Fri 10am–10pm, Sat & Sun 9am–noon & 5pm–10pm; ☎258 900 412), or you can still take to the river on a **canoe** (€2.50 for two hours) rented from the Clube Naútico (☎258 944 849), 2km from the Alameda on the other side of the river by the new bridge. The river's wide sandbank beaches also provide the venue for the town's bimonthly Monday **market**, the oldest in Portugal, held since a charter was first granted in 1125. A ramshackle collection of items is on sale, from mobile phone accessories to live trussed chickens and local cheeses. Also held here is the curiously named "**New Fair**" (second and third weekend of September), a tremendous festival and market, seemingly attended by half of the Minho, with fireworks, a fairground, wandering accordionists, *gigantones* (enormous carnivalesque statues), and a large brass band competition. More tradition is on display in early June, with the **Vaca das Cordas** festival (see box opposite).

In the town, spare an hour to glance around at the handsome buildings: there are several sixteenth-century **mansions** with stone coats of arms, and interesting remains of the old fourteenth-century **keep** – the *Torre da Cadeia* – used up to the 1960s as a prison (the occupants were allowed to hang cups down from the windows for money and cigarettes). It now houses a small craft shop and the **turismo** (see below).

Practicalities

The **bus station** is behind the market, just a minute or so from the river. There are several daily services to Arcos de Valdevez, Viana do Castelo, Barcelos, Ponte da Barca, Paredes de Coura, Braga and Porto. A few minutes' walk along the riverbank, the **turismo**, in the Torre da Cadeia (Mon–Sat 9.30am–12.30pm & 2.30–6pm, Sun (summer only) 9.30am–12.30pm; ☎258 942 335, ℱ258 942 308), is extremely helpful, and will provide a free map of the town as well as more information on accommodation and walks. The Solares de Portugal headquarters are located in the same building (see below). Internet access is available for €3 per hour at the tiny *SA Bar* on Beco das Selas, off Rua Inacio Perestrelo.

Accommodation

Easily the nicest places to stay are the Turismo Rural properties for which the town is famous. Bookings can made in advance through the central TURI-HAB office by fax or email (ℱ258 931 320, ℮info@turihab.pt), or through several organisations directly: the Solares de Portugal office at Praça da República (☎258 742 827, ℮turihab@mail.telepac.pt) and Privetur, at Rua Sa Carmeiro in the north of town (☎258 743 923, ℮privetur@mail.telepac.pt). Some of the best options from both organizations are given below; note that you will need your own transport to reach the properties.

The Vaca das Cordas

If you're in Ponte de Lima in early June (the day before Corpus Christi), you might witness the rather odd spectacle of the **Vaca das Cordas** (literally, "Cow of the Ropes"), which involves an enraged and rather reluctant bull being dragged down through the town's streets to the beach.

Like Pamplona's famous *Corrida*, this is one of many bovine-related Iberian traditions that stem back to pre-Christian times, with its origins in the ancient Egyptian cults brought to the Iberian peninsula by the Phoenicians a few centuries before Christ. According to mythology, Jupiter, angry that his attempts to kidnap the beautiful Io had been repelled by her mother, turned his love into a cow and commanded a bumble bee to repeatedly sting her. Understandably perturbed, Io fled to Egypt, where she regained her human form, and promptly married the god Osiris. In her honour, the Egyptians erected altars to Isis in the image of an errant cow, a symbol which became a popular goddess of fertility in both Egypt and, later on, in Portugal. The Igreja Matriz in Ponte de Lima was presumably erected over such a temple, after which time the newly converted Christian citizens – to show their renunciation of idols – dragged their old bovine image around town until finally it fell into pieces. Since then, a live cow – actually now a bull – has been used.

Echoes of the original rite still remain: at around 3pm, the bull is led to the church, where it is stabbed with a small dart in order to madden it. At 6pm, two millers arrive, tie the bull by its horns and lead it three times around the church – a common feature of pre-Christian rituals – whilst jabbing it with goads in reference to the mythical bee described above. Following this, and depending upon whether anyone can keep a grip on its ropes, the unfortunate animal then stumbles or charges through the town's streets (mimicking Io's flight to Egypt) before finishing up at the beach. It is then led off to the abattoir, as the good people of Ponte de Lima prepare for the more sedate procession of **Corpo do Deus** the following day, which sees the streets covered with flowers carefully arranged into ornate patterns.

At the lower end of the price scale, there are plenty of good *pensões* in town; alternatively, you could **camp** (unofficially) just out of town on the riverbank, but be warned that the police will move you on from the New Fairs site during the festival. The nearest official site is at Viana do Castelo (see p.383).

In town

Pensão Beira Rio, on the Alameda ☎ 258 943 471. Cheap but somewhat gruff place on the waterfront, with grandstand views of the comings and goings for the Monday market. ❶

Casa das Pereiras Largo das Pereiras ☎ 258 942 939, ☏ 258 941 493. Wonderful eighteenth-century stone *solar* (book through Privetur – see above) with a pool and splendid dinners served every Friday evening. The garden contains 100-year-old camellia shrubs. Open June–Oct. ❹

Hotel Império do Minho Av Dom Luís Filipe (aka Av dos Plátanos), on the riverfront ☎ 258 741 510, ☏ 258 942 567. The largest and most modern place in town offering fifty en-suite rooms with TVs. There's also a spacious bar and a swimming pool. ❹

Pensão Morais Rua da Matriz 8 ☎ 258 942 470. Basic, traditional rooms, some with balconies overlooking a quiet street. ❷

Pensão São João Largo de São João ☎ 258 941 288. Near the bridge, this is excellent value and serves good food downstairs in its restaurant. Most rooms have bathrooms. Front rooms can be noisy because of traffic. ❷

Outside town

Casa de Crasto 1km out of town along the N203 to Ponte de Barca ☎ 258 941 156. A seventeenth-century Solares de Portugal property, which – legend has it – was partly demolished by the owner in 1896 while looking for hidden treasure. The kitchen and tower managed to evade his attention. ❺

Casa do Outeiro Arcozelo, 2km from Ponte de Lima ☎ 258 941 206. This stately Solares de Portugal manor house dates from the sixteenth century and is surrounded by a garden and woods. Has a swimming pool, and two twin rooms plus a small apartment for rent. ❺

Azenha de Estoräos Estoräos, 7km from Ponte de Lima ☏258 941 546. A Solares de Portugal property occupying a converted seventeenth-century water mill. The location is beautiful – next to a Romanesque bridge and with walking, fishing and swimming all at hand. If you want a double room, book in advance as there's only one. Open mid-May to mid-Oct. ❺

Paço de Calheiros Calheiros, 7km from Ponte de Lima ☏258 947 164, ☏258 947 294. This elegant seventeenth-century mansion is the country retreat of none other than the Count of Calheiros, original founder of the TURIHAB scheme (see

p.33). Set in beautifully landscaped gardens with views over the Lima valley, it has nine tastefully decorated bedrooms and six apartments, and a swimming pool and tennis courts too. ❻

Quinta da Roseira 1km out of town on the Darque road ☏258 941 354. A lovely nineteenth-century farm, set among vineyards and fruit trees, with its own swimming pool and horses.Views over Ponte de Lima are exceptional. ❺

Solar de Pessegueiro 7km out of town at Vitorino da Donas ☏ & ☏258 731 644. Fairly large *residencial* with well-equipped rooms including TV and on-site café and games room. ❸

Eating and drinking

There are a few inexpensive **cafés** and **restaurants** along the riverfront, especially in Praça de Camões, by the old bridge. Local dishes include *arroz de sarabulho com rojões* (rice cooked with blood and pieces of roast pork) and lamprey (at its best Jan–March). For **sweets**, try *madalenas* or the dry *biscoito requife*. *Cervejaria Rampinha* and *Bar S.A. Galeria*, with its exhibitions, both at the foot of Rua Formosa, are popular evening **bars**. Good music can be heard at the two unnamed bars on the more northern of the two alleys off Largo das Pereiras. To sample *vinho verde* straight from the barrel, try either the *Tasca de Isac* in Largo São João, facing the hotel, or *Tasca de Gasparinho*, off the Largo on Rua do Arrabalde de São João.

Alameda Largo da Feira, by the bridge on the town side of the river. In a nice position with splendid views, and photographs of Ponte de Lima at New Fairs time. Full meals are under €8.50. Closed Wed.

O Brasão Rua Formosa 1 ☏258 911 890. Good service in an old stone building. Delicious *arroz de marisco* and a long wine list. Closed Wed.

Encanada on the Alameda. A good place to eat tasty, moderately priced local food such as *sarabulho*, close to the market and with a terrace overlooking the river. Closed Thurs.

Fu Man Quinta do Olho Marinho. Chinese with weekday lunchtime menus under €6, and take-

away. Head south from Praça da República and follow the *avenida* as it forks to the left. Open daily from 11.30am to 3.30pm and 7pm to midnight.

Marina Centro Nautico de Ponte de Lima ☏258 944 158. Luxury option across the river and part of the sailing club. Food is good but you're definitely also paying for the attractive surroundings.

Parisiense on the Alameda. This simple *tasca* has a limited menu but a good view of the river from its first- and second-floor tables.

São João Largo de São João. At lunchtime, this place is heaving with locals tucking into the huge, regional dishes, such as *rojões à minhota* – a very tasty mix of roast pork, sausages and roast potatoes.

East to Ponte da Barca

From Ponte de Lima, the N203 runs 18km east to **Ponte da Barca**, another Minho market town with a bridge so attractive it, too, has been incorporated into the town's name. The Barca part refers to a boat that once ferried pilgrims across the Rio Lima, presumably before the bridge was built. On the way, call a halt at the small hamlet of **BRAVÃES**, 14km east of Ponte de Lima, home of the fine Romanesque **Church of São Salvador**, just to the left of the road. Its two sculpted doorways are perhaps the best in the country, filled with carvings of doves, griffins, monkeys and two of the local wide-horned oxen. If the church is locked ask at the cottage behind and the doors will be flung open for you, lighting up medieval murals of St Sebastian and the Virgin. The church is one of several in the Lima region that is simple and rustic in design but features beautiful, naive carvings on the doorways and columns. Most of these churches were built in the twelfth and thirteenth centuries under the supervision of Cluniac monks, who brought their architecture to Spain and Portugal along the pilgrimage routes to Santiago de Compostela in Galicia; the main Portuguese route ran through Braga and so Minho has the highest concentration.

There's a **bar** in Bravães where local transport-users can debate the chances of getting a bus going on to Ponte da Barca, 4km further east; it's probably quicker to walk.

Ponte da Barca

If you ignore the modern suburbs of **PONTE DA BARCA**, and head for the river, the old town is a treat. The Lima is spanned here by a lovely sixteenth-century bridge, beside which there's a superb fortnightly **Wednesday market** (it alternates with Arcos de Valdevez), spreading out by the river in an almost medieval atmosphere, and drawing hundreds of people from outlying hamlets. Just across from the bridge is the shaded Jardim dos Poetas, dedicated to sixteenth-century brothers Diogo Bernardes and Agostinho da Cruz, monastic poets who were born in the town. A statue of them in full garb is situated at one end of the square. It's also worth noting that the town's annual **Feira de São Bartolomeu** takes place on August 19–24, with the big day on August 24; don't expect to get any sleep once the party starts. The whole period sees a crafts fair in Praça da República, and there's a linen festival and secular parade on August 23.

From the bridge, Rua Conselheiro Rocha Peixoto runs east to the triangular Praça da República, passing the small Largo da Misericórdia and its helpful **turismo** (May–Sept Mon–Sat 9.30am–12.30pm & 2.30–7pm, closed Sun; Oct–Apr Mon–Fri 9.30am–12.30pm & 2.30–5.30pm, Sat 9.20am–12.30pm, closed Sun; ☎258 452 899), where you can get a town map and lots of brochures. Next door is the headquarters of **ADERE Peneda-Gerês**, the regional development association for the Peneda-Gerês National Park (☎258 452 250, ⓦwww.adere-pg.pt), which is a treasure chest of information on everything from local customs, handicrafts and gastronomy to places to stay, helping you book accommodation in farmhouses (*casas abrigos*), and providing leaflets detailing **walks** (*trilhos*) throughout the park. It also has details (there are photocopies at the turismo) of two circuits in Ponte de Barca district: one around Ermida, the other from São Miguel (Entre-Ambos-os-Rios) via Germil and the wonderfully unspoilt village of Sobredo. If you're staying in Ponte de Barca itself, you'll need to arrange transport to the start points which are about 10km away. The instructions are somewhat out of date, so a compass and a good map would be useful, and you should bring your own food and drink.

Buses to and from all destinations drop you at the corner of Rua Diogo Bernardes and Rua Conselheiro Rocha Peixoto, around the corner from the bridge. There are connections to Lindoso (2 daily), Arcos de Valdevez and Braga (both hourly).

One of the nicest places to **stay** is the quaint *Pensão Maria Gomes*, Rua Conselheiro Rocha Peixoto 13 (☎258 452 288; ❶ including breakfast), overlooking the river and bridge, where a huge breakfast is served on the balcony; it's worth phoning ahead. Another fine option is the homely *Residencial Fontaínhas*, further along on Rua António José Pereira at Praça da República (☎258 452 442; ❷). *Pensão Os Poetas*, Jardim dos Poetas, in a converted town house near the bridge (☎258 453 568, ⓕ258 453 766; ❸), has plenty of cool marble and large clean rooms with TVs. On the north bank of the river, opposite the town, the Solares de Portugal property *Quinta da Prova* (☎258 452 163, ⒻF258 431 186; ⓖ) has nine rooms, some with kitchenettes and a delightful terrace with river views.

For **meals**, you could do far worse than eat upstairs at *Pensão Maria Gomes*, or try the pricier *Restaurante Bar do Rio*, close to the Praia Fluvial – a beach on the left bank of the river – which is an excellent place to dine while watching the sunset. Another good option is *Restaurante Varanda do Lima* (closed Thurs), near the bridge, where, if you fancy fish, you can choose a victim from the tank by the door. A meal here will set you back around €15, but specialities, like lamprey, are available at more reasonable prices than elsewhere. Cheaper eats at places doubling as **bars** can be found all along Rua Conselheiro Rocha Peixoto, notably at *Café Cantinho* at the corner with Rua Diogo Bernardes, which is very busy at lunchtimes (under €5). Other bars include *Pelourinho* (all day) and *Poetas*, which are open weekday evenings and all day at the weekends, and have occasional live music. Both are on Jardim dos Poetas by the bridge. You could also try *Euzébius*, on Rua Conselheiro Rocha Peixoto, and *A Doca Bar*, Rua Dr. António Veloso, whose DJs attract a more youthful crowd on Friday and Saturday nights.

Arcos de Valdevez

The Rio Vez, a tributary of the Minho, is overlooked by the charming hillside town of **ARCOS DE VALDEVEZ**, located just 5km north of Ponte da Barca. Scene of a seventeenth-century fire that wiped out most of its most interesting buildings, its main appeal lies in its sleepy nature, though it shows its true Minho colours during the fortnightly Wednesday **market**. As at Ponte de Lima and Ponte da Barca, it only really comes alive during its annual festival, in this case the three-day **Festas do Concelho**, held over the second week in August, featuring *gigantones* (giant figures), *zés pereiras* (red-caped drummers), horse races and noisy fireworks. Traditionally these celebrations should take place on the last weekend of the holiday month, but they've been shifted to take account of local emigrants who return to work abroad at the end of August; one of the festival days is actually named the Dia do Emigrante in their honour.

Practicalities

The friendly and well-stocked **turismo** is 200m north of the bridge on the west bank of the river (June–Sept daily 9.30am–12.30pm & 2.30–6pm; Oct–May Mon–Sat 9.30am–12.30pm & 2.30–6pm; ☎ & ⒻF258 516 001). The staff will dole out maps (make sure you get the one with street names marked – the other is useless), brochures covering the Rota do Vinho Verde (wine-related attractions throughout the Minho) and information on *turismo rural* accommodation in the region, and there's also a room with local crafts for sale.

Like Ponte da Barca, Arcos de Valvedez is a useful point of departure for the Parque Nacional da Peneda-Gerês, and there's a **park information office** (☎258 515 338) at Rua do Padre Manuel Himalaia – turn uphill from the river at the new fountain – where you can buy a **map** (€2). The turismo, however, has much more information, including leaflets (in Portuguese) detailing numerous walks.

For information on the **bus** service to Soajo and Lindoso (1–3 daily

Mon–Fri), ask at the turismo, or try the Salvador office (☎258 521 504) on Rua Soares Pereira, off Largo da Lapa. Bear in mind, though, that the service isn't completely reliable and times change frequently. You can catch the Salvador buses to Soajo and Lindoso at the stops along Avenida Marginal, between the bridge and *Pensão Dom António*. The **bus station** itself is 2km northeast of town near the river, and has regular connections with Braga, Monção, Ponte de Lima and Viana do Castelo.

The town has a few reasonably priced **pensões**. In the best position, overlooking the river on the east side of the old bridge, is the rebuilt *Pensão Ribeira* (☎258 515 174; ❷). On the west side of the river are the characterful and inexpensive *Pensão Floresta* (☎258 515 163; ❶) and *Pensão Brasileiro* (☎258 515 245; ❶), both above boozy *casas de pasto*-cum-bars on Rua Amorim Soares, just up from the bridge. Neither are for the fussy, and they're often full around the time of the fortnightly market. More salubrious is the small and unpretentious *Flôr do Minho* in Largo da Valeta, at the end of Rua de São João off Largo da Lapa (☎258 525 216; ❶), while expensive options include the *Residencial Tavares* (☎258 516 253, ℻258 522 851; ❸), just off Largo da Lapa on Rua Padre Manuel José da Cunha Brito, which has modern, if a bit gloomy, apartments with TV and kitchen; breakfast is included. The large, well-equipped *Pensão Dom António* (☎258 521 010, ℻258 521 065; ❸), at the south end of Rua Marginal, has brighter rooms with TV; some have phones and minibars.

There's a cluster of reliable **restaurants** off Largo da Lapa in Rua de São João, notably *Churrascaria Arco dos Caneiros*, which is good and cheap, offering mainly pork and *bacalhau*, with *tripas à moda de Porto* (tripe) on Wednesdays. Other local places that recommend themselves include the *Minho Verde*, Rua Mário J.B. da Costa, up behind the turismo (try the grilled squid), and *O Morais*, Rua Dr. Antonio Caldas, which also serves a few vegetarian dishes.

Parque Nacional da Peneda-Gerês

The magnificent **PARQUE NACIONAL DA PENEDA-GERÊS** is hardly a secret. Caldas do Gerês (known simply as Gerês), the main centre of the park, attracts more tourists than anywhere else in the Minho, with the possible exception of Viana do Castelo and, at weekends, when Portuguese campers arrive in force, parts of it can seem a bit too close to civilization. The park as a whole, though, is large enough to absorb the great numbers of visitors. It's split into three distinct parts: the central area, based around the spa town of **Caldas do Gerês**, the wilder northern section around the **Serra da Peneda**, and the far eastern section of **Serra do Gerês**, which spans the border into Trás-os-Montes. Both Serras remain largely undiscovered, especially in the eastern reaches of the Serra do Gêres where the spectacular mountain terrain feels largely impenetrable.

Vestiges of early human occupation are scattered around the park. Most common are *antas* (or dolmens), tombs constructed from upright stones that were topped with roof slabs and then covered with soil; unexcavated *anta* mounds are called *mamoas*. Less frequent are *menhirs* (tall standing stones with a phallic appearance that archeologists inevitably ascribe to fertility cults), *cromeleques* (stone circles) and *arte rupestre* (rock art, usually engraved symbols such as concentric circles, little cup-like depressions possibly used for sorting or crushing seeds, boxed crosses and hand axes). The locations of some are marked, very approximately, on the park's maps.

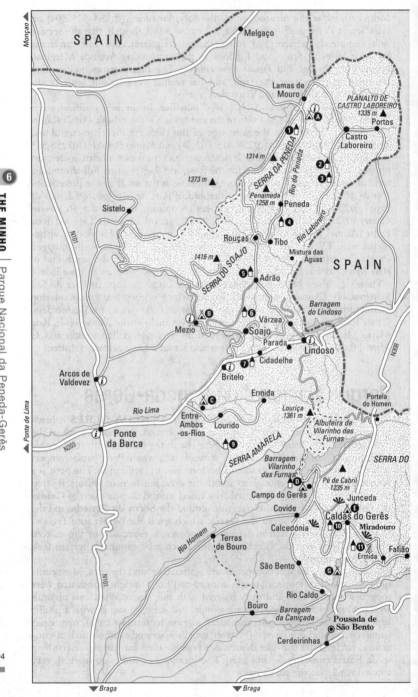

SPAIN

Monçao ▲

Melgaço ●

Lamas de Mouro

PLANALTO DE CASTRO LABOREIRO 1335 m ▲

Portos ●

Castro Laboreiro ●

SERRA DA PENEDA

1314 m ▲

Rio da Peneda

1373 m ▲

Penameda 1258 m ▲

Peneda ●

Rio Laboreiro

Sistelo ●

N101

Rouças ●

Tibo ●

Mistura das Aguas

SPAIN

1416 m ▲

SERRA DO SOAJO

Adrão ▲

Barragem do Lindoso

Várzea ●

Mezio ●

Soajo ▲

Parada ●

Lindoso ●

N308

Arcos de Valdevez ●

Cidadelhe ●

Britelo ●

Ermida ●

Portela do Homen

Rio Lima

Ponte da Barca ●

Entre Ambos-os-Rios ●

Lourido ●

Louriça 1361 m ▲

Albufeira de Vilarinho das Furnas

SERRA DO

SERRA AMARELA

N203

Ponte de Lima ▲

Barragem Vilarinho das Furnas

Pé de Cabril 1235 m ▲

Campo do Gerês ●

Junceda

Covide ●

Caldas do Gerês

Miradouro

Calcedónia ●

Rio Homem

Terras de Bouro ●

São Bento ●

Ermida

Fafião ●

Bouro ●

Rio Caldo ●

Barragem da Caniçada

N101

Pousada de São Bento ◉

Cerdeirinhas ●

▼ Braga   ▼ Braga

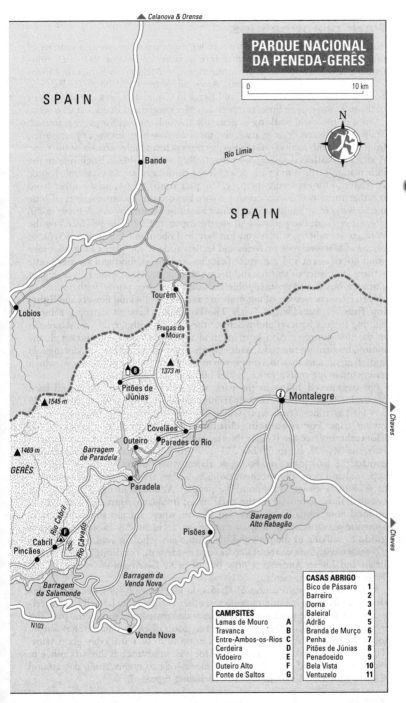

PARQUE NACIONAL
DA PENEDA-GERÊS

0   10 km

N

▲ Celanova & Orense

SPAIN

Bande

Rio Limia

SPAIN

Lobios

Tourém

Fragas da
Moura

▲ 1373 m

Pitões de
Júnias

▲ 1545 m

Covelães

Outeiro   Paredes do Rio

Barragem
de Paradela

▲ 1469 m

GERÊS

Paradela

i Montalegre

▶ Chaves

Barragem do
Alto Rabagão

Pisões

Rio Cabril

Cabril
Pincães

Rio Cávado

Barragem da
Venda Nova

Barragem
da Salamonde

N103

Venda Nova

▶ Chaves

CAMPSITES
Lamas de Mouro	A
Travanca	B
Entre-Ambos-os-Rios	C
Cerdeira	D
Vidoeiro	E
Outeiro Alto	F
Ponte de Saltos	G

CASAS ABRIGO
Bico de Pássaro	1
Barreiro	2
Dorna	3
Baleiral	4
Adrão	5
Branda de Murço	6
Penha	7
Pitões de Júnias	8
Penadoeido	9
Bela Vista	10
Ventuzelo	11

Park practicalities

You can see a great deal of the park under your own steam, along a number of pretty decent roads, but note that **bus** services are limited and often non-existent at weekends. The main connections are: Melgaço to Lamas de Mouro and Castro Laboreiro in the north; Arcos de Valdevez and Ponte da Barca to Soajo and Lindoso in the centre; and Braga to Caldas do Gêres. For the far east of the park, the nearest buses run between Montalegre and Braga and vice versa.

Once in the park, **walking** is generally the only option for getting around. Trails and paths cover large areas, and there are dozens of hiking opportunities, from short strolls to two- and three-day treks across whole sections of the park. A series of **leaflets** detailing footpaths (*trilhos*) are available in English from the information centres and park offices listed below, and are an invaluable source of reference for exploring the park. The park **map** (€2.64) on the other hand is rather more confusing: showing roads, but omitting footpaths, it is of little use to walkers, although it may suffice for those visiting by car. A more useful alternative (with footpaths listed) are the topographical maps produced by the Portuguese military, which you can buy in Lisbon and Porto (see p.316), or online at ⓦ www.igeoe.pt. Maps and leaflets aside, if you plan a long hike, take good boots, warm and waterproof clothes, a compass, food and a water bottle – there are plenty of streams and the water is pretty clean, especially at higher altitudes, but if you're susceptible to stomach upsets, purify with iodine or chlorine tablets. Beware of fog in spring and winter. Picking flowers and **lighting fires** are forbidden in Gerês. The Portuguese have an alarming habit of lighting them whenever and wherever they picnic, with terrible consequences in the dry summers. Also bear in mind that night falls a lot quicker in the mountains than on the coast, temperatures can drop quickly in fog, during rain and at night, and that in winter you're likely to find plenty of snow, which makes following trails a much riskier business

For **organized hikes** in the park, with vehicle transport there and back (around €25 per person), contact Trilhos, Rua de Belém 94, Porto (ⓣ & ⓕ 025 504 604, ⓔ trilhos@trilhos.pt), which also offers canoeing, rafting, biking and caving trips. For **mountain climbing**, contact the Clube Nacional de Montanhismo, Secção Região Norte, Departamento de Montanhismo, Rua Formosa 303–2°, Porto (ⓣ 223 321 295). To hire your own **private guide**, contact the park office in Ponte da Barca, where there is a list of officially approved and generally excellent candidates. Fees are around €10 per person, or €75 for a group (minimum five people). Although hiring a guide is not essential, those approved by the park are an invaluable source of information on local flora, fauna and history and, like anywhere, it's also advisable to have someone accompanying you in case of an accident. An excellent **written guide** to walking in the park and the Minho as a whole is available online for £5 at ⓦ www.sunflowerbooks.co.uk/costaverde.htm, consisting of the text of Brian and Eileen Anderson's now out of print *Landscapes of Portugal: Costa Verde, Minho, Peneda-Gerês*.

Apart from the main centre of Caldas do Gerês (see p.408), **accommodation** is limited to a handful of *pensões* in other villages (which we list in the relevant section of the guide), and camping at designated sites run by the park and by private operators. If you can muster a group of eight, renting *casas abrigos*, four-bedroom converted farmhouses, can prove to be remarkably good value. These must be booked and partly paid for well in advance at the park office in Ponte da Barca and there is a minimum stay of two nights. You'll pay around €40 in winter, and €65 in summer, including firewood.

△ *Espigueiro*

Information on the park can be obtained both from **visitor centres** situated at the park entrances, and at the four park offices in towns surrounding the park. The centres are geared toward their immediate vicinity, with photo displays and information on local agriculture, flora and fauna. Most have books for sale, but can be short on leaflets, and don't count on finding maps there either. The **park offices** are generally more useful, and better stocked with maps, brochures and leaflets detailing signposted walks. You can also find park information on the **internet** at ⓦ www.adere-pg.pt (the park's official site), and ⓦ www.di.uminho.pt/~esteves/turismo/parques1.html and ⓦ www .infocid.pt/areas/ (in Portuguese).

The main **park office** is in **Braga**, at Avenida António Macedo, Quinta das Parretas (Mon–Fri 9am–12.30pm & 2–5.30pm; ☎253 203 480, ⓕ253 613 169), and is an excellent starting point before venturing into the wilderness. Very helpful too is the one in **Ponte da Barca**, at Largo da Misericórdia 10 (Mon–Fri 9am–12.30 & 2.30–6pm; ☎258 452 450 or 258 452 250, ⓔaderepg@mail.telepac.pt), which is also the place to contact if you need to book *casas abrigo* accommodation. The office in **Arcos de Valdevez**, on Rua do Padre Manuel Himalaia (Mon–Fri 9am–12.30 & 2–5.30pm; ☎258 515 338, ⓕ258 522 707) is rather useless in comparison – you'll find more information at the town's turismo. There's also an office in **Montalegre**, at Rua do Reigoso 17 (Mon–Fri 9am–12.30pm & 2–5.30pm; ☎ & ⓕ276 512 281), which concerns itself with the eastern section of the park.

The **visitor centres** all close on Wednesdays. In summer, they open Mon–Tues & Thurs–Fri 10am–12.30pm & 2–6pm, Sat 10am–noon & 2.30pm to 6pm, Sun 10am–noon & 2.30–5pm; in winter, Mon–Tues & Thurs–Fri 9.30am–12.30pm & 2–5.30pm, Sat 10am–12.30pm & 2–5pm, Sun 10am–12.30pm & 2–4.30pm. They are located at Britelo, on the road from Ponte da Barca (☎258 576 160); in Caldas do Gerês at Avenida Manuel Francisco da Costa (☎253 390 110, ⓕ253 391 496); in Lamas de Mouro, on the Melgaço–Peneda road (☎251 465 563); and in Mezio, on the road in from Arcos de Valdevez (☎258 526 751). The Mezio office number is also a 24-hour emergency telephone service. Limited park information is available at the castle in Lindoso (p.414).

The central section: around Caldas do Gêres

The national park is centred on the old spa town of **CALDAS DO GERÊS** (usually referred to simply as Gerês), which can be reached easily from Braga by bus – a ninety-minute journey (operated by Empresa Hoteleira do Gêres). The town consists of little more than two roads running either side of a babbling brook and, weekends aside, when Portuguese picnickers arrive en masse, it's a relaxed and very elegant base. "The Spa of Gerês" became fashionable in the early years of the nineteenth century – an epoch convincingly evoked by a row of grand Victorian hotels (many now in a derilict state) along the sedate old main street, Avenida Manuel Francisco da Costa. The **spa** (☎253 391 113, ⓕ253 391 184) still functions, attracting the infirm in the summer season, though most visitors nowadays are younger and healthier, up from the northern cities to picnic in the woods or, in the case of eccentric foreigners, to hike.

Life in the Parque Nacional de Peneda-Gerês

The **Parque Nacional de Peneda-Gerês** was established in 1971 not only to pro-tect the diversity of landscape and wildlife in the region, but also to safeguard the traditional rural way of life of its inhabitants. Unique domestic animals – primitive breeds long extinct elsewhere like *cachena* and *barrosa* cattle, *bravia* goats, *garra-no* ponies and the powerful *Castro Laboreiro* sheepdog – continue to be the main-stay of the local economy. In distant forested corners, remnants of the wildlife that once roamed all Europe still survive: wild boar, otters, polecats and some of the con-tinent's last surviving wolves exist side by side with more familiar species like badg-ers, foxes and roe deer. Birds are numerous in both numbers and breeds, from majestic raptors such as goshawks, eagles and kites to mountain passerines like rock buntings and aquatic dippers, while on the ground lizards and snakes, though common, are rarely seen.

The variety of vegetation that gives the park its lush greenness is equally impres-sive. A total of eighteen plant species – including the Serra do Gerês iris – are found nowhere else on earth. In the valleys oak and laurel line the riverbanks, replaced by holly, birch, pine and juniper at higher elevations.

But whilst the park boundaries can afford some security to the natural wonders, the traditional communities are less easily protected. The lure of the city proves irre-sistibly attractive to many youngsters, and village populations throughout the region are slowly shrinking. They are also ageing; in some areas as many as three-quarters of the inhabitants are of pensionable age. Tourism may go some way towards pro-viding incentives for locals to stay in the area and thereby preserving ancient cus-toms and traditions, but with the influx of tourists comes a responsibility to protect the delicate ecosystems and uniqueness of the environment. Time will tell if the right balance can be achieved.

There have been a lot of recent development in town, but it's not all bad and you'll probably appreciate the public outdoor swimming pool (reached through the park), tennis courts, boating lake and countless cafés. Pick up information either at the **turismo** (9am–noon & 2–6pm; closed Tues & Sun; ☎253 391 133, ⓕ253 391 282), at the top end of the main avenue, or at the national park office, just around the corner (see above).

Accommodation

Gerês is awash with **pensões** and some – even in the height of summer – are reasonably priced. Note, however, that many are open from May to October only; prices are often halved at those open during the winter, but their restau-rants are usually closed. Much of the accommodation is along the main street, though there's a string of large, modernized *pensões* across the other side of the river in Rua do Amassó, which afford ever better views up the valley. The best-value options, however, are found strung out at reasonably regular intervals along the 8km down the valley to Rio Caldo. The closest **campsite** is *Vidoeiro* (☎253 391 289; open all year) on the edge of town by the river – it's well maintained and has good facilities. *Ponte de Saltos* campsite (☎253 391 394; July–Sept) is 3km south of Caldas by the reservoir at Vilar da Veiga, but it can get crowded – you'll find more room at the *Quinta dos Moinhos* (☎253 391 581), almost adjacent to it, which also sells its own *vinho verde*.

Pensão Adelaide Rua do Amassó ☎253 390 020, ⓕ253 390 029. A comfortable option, high up at the top end of the road; the balconies have correspondingly fine views. **❸**
Pensão Casa da Ponte Rua Boavista, turn right at the roundabout at the southern end of town

253 391 125. A long-established place by the river, friendly and welcoming if a bit dated. Breakfast is included. ❸

Pensão Flôr de Moçambique Rua do Amassó ☎ & ℱ 253 391 119. Clean and amiable. The modern rooms all have baths, TVs and balconies and there's a restaurant with an outdoor terrace. ❸

Pensão O Horizonte do Gerês Rua do Amassó ☎ 253 391 260. Near the *Flôr de Moçambique*, with less impressive views but slightly cheaper rates; breakfast is included. ❷

Pensão Mira Flor Av Manuel Francisco da Costa (no telephone). Handily placed next to a mini-market

and virtually opposite the main bus stop. Clean, modern, bright rooms with TV and nice views. ❷

Pensão São Miguel do Gerês Rua do Amassó ☎ 253 391 360. This has large, airy rooms with bathrooms and stunning outlooks. Good value and breakfast is included. ❷

Hotel Universal Av Manuel Francisco da Costa ☎ 253 391 141, ℱ 253 391 102. Gerês' finest and one of the two surviving old-style grand hotels. The other is its sister *Hotel Termas do Gerês* on the same street ☎ 253 391 141, which is a little more downmarket. Both ❸.

Eating

The restaurants attached to most of the *pensões* offer good-quality if unmemorable food, with portions healthy enough to satisfy the most ravenous hiker. Alternatively, try those below.

Churrasqueira Geresino uphill on the left at the top of town at Lugar do Vidoeiro. An excellent, unpretentious place with great food including outstanding barbecued chicken, which is also available to take away (€2 for half-chicken).

Novo Sol along the main street near the bottom of

town. Service can be surly, but it serves a good-sized *ementa turística* for around €10.

Restaurante Pedra Bela Av Manuel Francisco da Costa. A limited but reasonable choice, with outdoor tables on the attractive verandah.

Hiking in central Gerês

The main reason, of course, for staying in Caldas do Gerês is to explore the national park. From the spa town, there are several interesting and accessible hikes though, frustratingly, the **central Gerês** section is not well equipped with footpaths and walking off the tracks can be difficult and painful, with small shrubs slashing your legs. For all the following routes, a good **map** is essential – see p.406. For the section between Caldas do Gerês and Campo do Gerês, get hold of the *Orienteering Map: Campo do Gerês* (€1), available from the Gerês park office or the turismo.

Southeast to the Miradouro

An hour's walk to the southeast of Caldas do Gerês, the **Miradouro do Gerês** is *the* destination for Portuguese weekend picnickers. And small wonder, with its site overlooking the vast reservoir of Caniçada and a good part of the Gerês range. The only catch, if you're intent on following suit, is the extent of local enthusiasm. This is not a road to walk unless you're immune to inhalation of exhaust fumes and dust; a better bet may be to take a taxi or hitch up and then start hiking. The quickest approach to the Miradouro is to follow the road behind the service station at Gerês, where it becomes an uphill path. The most obvious, and probably the most attractive, route to follow beyond the Miradouro is to **Ermida** (see p.415). Just before arriving here, there's a sign pointing you to the Cascata do Arado, left off the main track; follow this and a brief walk leads to the magnificent **Arado waterfalls**, with its refreshing pools for swimming.

Northwest to Campo do Gerês via Vilarinho das Furnas

This is an exhausting and long day's hike (10–12hr) but a good one, taking you along the Roman road that began at Braga. The route also runs alongside the

Vilarinho das Furnas reservoir, with obvious swimming potential. In the height of summer you can see the submerged village of Vilarinho das Furnas itself – turn right after crossing the dam.

Setting out from Caldas do Gerês, follow the road north towards **PORTELA DO HOMEM**, the Spanish–Portuguese border post where there's a café and a collection of Roman milestones. It's 13km from Gerês, and locals often hitch up here to swim in the nearby **river pool** at the bottom of the Minas dos Carris valley. However, to get to Campo de Gerês, you don't need to go as far as Portela de Homem; instead, veer left off the road beyond the defunct campsite at Albergaria after roughly 8km, following signs to Campo do Gerês and the reservoir. There is a path off to the reservoir, but the main track heads southwest along the water's eastern edge – first along gladed paths and then suddenly into the open, following stretches of the old Roman road. Staying with the road (past an old stone building housing a weaving project run by the park), you come into **CAMPO DO GERÊS** (to which there are daily buses from Braga, operated by Empresa Hoteleira do Gerês).

Here, the friendly *Residencial Stop* (☎253 351 291; ❷) attracts a young and active crowd. The *Cerdeira* **campsite** (☎ & ℉253 351 005; open all year) also lets out bungalows, which sleep up to eight people (roughly €10 per person), and rents bicycles; it has its own restaurant, too. Nearby is the *Vilarinho das Furnas* **youth hostel** (☎253 351 3 39), named after the village which was submerged in 1972 under the nearby dam. The construction workers stayed here (some double rooms are also available; ❷), and there's a swimming pool, tennis court and disco. Through any of these establishments you can contact various local companies that organize a myriad of **activities** including horse-trekking trips, canoeing, mountain biking and climbing: Equicampo (☎ & ℉253 357 022, ✉equicampo@sapo.pt), Gerês Equi'Aventura (☎ & ℉253 352 622) and Planalto (☎253 351 005).

South of Campo do Gerês and heading toward Rio Caldo you come to the crucifix of São João do Campo. Turn left off the road here onto a dirt track which takes you around the southern tip of the mountain west of Gerês. Apart from the occasional obsessive car driver, you'll be pretty much alone – eerily so at times, amid the boulders. After about 3km, there's a signpost on your right for the 3km, two-hour *trilho* to **Calcedónia**, a Celtic and Roman *citânia* with an impressive cave, and boulders scattered all around. This stretch can be hard-going in the midday heat, as there is no shelter, so save it for the late afternoon. Retracing your footsteps to the sign, continue around the mountain in an anti-clockwise direction, following the signs back to Gerês.

South: to Caniçada reservoir, Rio Caldo and São Bento da Porta Aberta

The best base for the **Caniçada reservoir** is the village of **RIO CALDO**, on its west bank and just 8km south of Caldas do Gerês; change here for buses from Caldas to São Bento. There are numerous **water sports** available locally at the reservoir, with possibilities for both windsurfing and waterskiing; swimming is fine, too. For water-sports equipment, contact the English-run AML (☎253 391 740 or mobile ☎968 021 142, ✉aguamontanha@mail.telepac.pt), which rents canoes (€3.50/hr), motorboats (€22.50/hr), mountain bikes and walking gear. There are plenty of places to **stay** along the edge of the reservoir, as well as along the road to Caldas do Gerês – a good bet is the *Pensão Pontes do Rio Caldo* (☎253 391 540, ℉253 391 195; ❷), a stone building with a garden bar at the road junction with the bridges. More modern, but in an unbeatable reservoir location, is the friendly *Casa Beira Rio* (☎253 391 197; ❷), on the north side of the bridge to Gerês, where rooms have bathrooms and TVs. Alternatively, you could catch a bus uphill towards Cerdrinhas to the *Pousada de São Bento* (☎253 647 190, ℗253 647 867; ❻), in a superb position overlooking the reservoir from the east. This timber-beamed former hunting lodge has its own swimming pool and a superb restaurant, with great views.

Three kilometres beyond Rio Caldo, in the Covide direction, **SÃO BENTO DA PORTA ABERTA** is a small village, high above the reservoir, commanding superb views. Its austere sanctuary is a favourite spot with pilgrims, who gather here at the beginning of July and again a month later (and on most Sundays throughout the year) – at such times the traffic and fumes make it a place best avoided. The former monastery, hidden under an ugly modern facade, is now the *Estalagem de São Bento da Porta Aberta* (☎253 391 106, ℗253 391 117; ❸), a little severe inside but nevertheless comfortable and with a good restaurant. Cheaper **rooms** may be available in the *Restaurante Mira Serra* at the western end of the village (☎253 391 362; ❷), and at the charming turn-of-the-century *Pensão São José*, halfway between São Bento and Rio Caldo (☎253 391 120; ❷).

The northern section: Serra da Peneda

Thanks mainly to restrictive public transport and scant accommodation choices, the wild **Serra da Peneda**, in the north of the park, sees far fewer tourists than the central zone around Caldas do Gerês, and this sense of isolation can be an advantage. You'll often have the prehistoric sites, steep forested valleys, and exposed, wind-blown *planaltos* dotted with weird rock formations entirely to yourself – not to mention the marvellous views.

Weekday **buses** leave Melgaço for Lamas de Mouro and Castro Laboreiro at 7.30am (with an additional 12.50pm service on Fridays) and return at around 6.30pm – check times with the parcel depot in Melgaço, just around the corner from the *Pensão Pemba*, or ask at the turismo.

Lamas de Mouro, Castro Laboreiro and Peneda

The only accommodation in **LAMAS DE MOURO**, 19km southeast of Melgaço, is the beautifully situated **campsite** just inside the park, past the visitor centre (☎251 465 494; ring ahead in winter). It is one of four run by the park itself with hot showers, a bar, a nearby natural pool for swimming and a restaurant. There's also a good **guide** here, who covers the *Trilho da Peneda*, a four-hour, 8.2km circuit northwest of Peneda village (access by jeep), in addition to several other trails in the park. For **food**, the *Churrasqueiria Vidoeiro* nearby is slightly pricey but has generous portions.

The left-hand fork at Lamas takes you up to the ancient village of **CASTRO LABOREIRO** (8km further), a place that's best known for the breed of mountain dog to which it gives its name. Once used to protect sheep from marauding wolves, it has become rarer as wolf numbers have declined and is now hardly ever seen outside the region. Before the arrival of tourism, the village was practically deserted every summer when the pastoral community would leave to find greener fields and build *brandas* (temporary homes with stone walls and "soft" roofs made of branches and twigs) elsewhere for the warmer months, returning in winter to their *inverneiras* (winter houses) in Laboreiro. There are some superb **walks** around here, especially to the east and south. The *Trilho Castrejo* leaflet (in Portuguese), available from the turismo in Melgaço, is helpful here. The best **accommodation** is at *Miradouro do Castelo* (☎251 465 469; ❶), at the far end of the village overlooking a magnificent valley and dominated by the castle. You'll also find good, modern rooms at *Casa São José* (T251 465 134; ●), 500m out on the Lamas road. For **eating**, the *Miradouro do Castelo* has a good restaurant, or try the *cabrito serrano* (mountain kid goat) in the *Restaurante da Serra* opposite.

To reach the ruins of the town's **castle**, you have a steep twenty-minute walk: left at the roundabout on the other side of the village, then left up a path where the road drops to the right, past a large rock known as the *Tartaruga* (Tortoise), and through heather and between boulders, with sheer drops to each side and steps hacked out of the rock face.

Nine kilometres south of Lamas de Mouro, along a stunning forested valley topped on either side with vertiginous boulders, you arrive at the small village of **PENEDA**, most famous for the **Sanctuário da Nossa Senhora da Peneda**, a miniature version of Bom Jesus, and full of devotees at the beginning of September (especially on September 7 and 8), but pretty much deserted for the rest of the year. The original focus of adoration was a curious stone which natural forces had sculpted into the form of a woman, who some say was pregnant. Come Christianity, the cult and its stone was adopted as the Virgin Mary, and was duly incorporated into the late eighteenth-century church. There she remained until the 1930s, when somebody stole her; a gaudy plastic replacement now stands in place of the original.

The village itself has cafés and religious artefact shops clustered around the main square. There are good **rooms** in a modern house 100m before Peneda: contact Isolina Domingues Fernandes at the *Casa de Artigos Religiosos*, in the main square (T251 465 139; ●). Otherwise, ask at *Café Star* in the main square (T251 465 568 or 251 465 275; ●) where there are dorm bunks usually used by pilgrims. There's also a classy *turismo rural* property, the *Anjo da Guarda* (no phone; ●), in the main square.

The moderately difficult four-hour, 8.2km *Trilho da Peneda* **walking circuit** (leaflets in Portuguese from the ADERE office in Ponte de Barca) takes you west up the side of the valley into the windblown Serra da Peneda and to the 1258m peak of **Penameda**, where there are freshwater lagoons and fine views across the whole of the park. From here, the track turns north and then east, eventually dropping back down to the Lamas de Mouro road, about 1km north of Peneda by the signpost for the same route in reverse.

Heading south from Peneda, there's a dramatic and attractive **walk** of 20km or so following the well-signposted and fairly quiet road that leads south; bear left at the fork in the road just before the village of Adrão and you'll eventually join the Soajo–Lindoso road.

Soajo, Lindoso and Parada

Midway between the northern and central sections of the park, the traditional villages of **Soajo**, **Lindoso** and **Parada** are fine centres for hiking, as well as attractive destinations in themselves. Soajo is reached most easily from Arcos de Valdevez; **buses** leave Arcos at 5.45pm from Monday to Friday, with extra services at 12.20pm on Mondays and Fridays, and at 8.30am and 2pm on Wednesdays. There are also buses from Arcos, via Ponte da Barca, to Lindoso and Parada (Mon–Sat noon, Sun–Fri 6.10pm, plus extra services on Wed at 8.30am and 2pm). Times for both routes change frequently, and you'd be wise to contact the Salvador office in Arcos before travelling (see p.403). A taxi to either place will set you back around €12.50.

Approaching from Ponte da Barca, you enter the park at **ENTRE-AMBOS-OS-RIOS**, where's there's a **campsite** (T258 588 361). From Arcos de Valdevez, you enter at **MEZIO**, which has a **visitor centre** (see p.408) and a new campsite, 3km away at Travanca (no phone). There's an excavated *anta* tomb at the roadside, and the staff can give you details on a half-day excursion to see the prehistoric rock art in the vicinity. **Horse-riding** is offered at the Centro Hípico do Mezio, 1km into the park at Vilar de Suente (☎258 526 452, ⓕ258 526 088); lessons cost €37.50 for five sessions; trail riding €10–35, and a two-day guided ride costs €115 – the price includes food and accommodation.

Soajo

SOAJO is a small village tucked into the folds of a hilly landscape. Its highlight is a collection of eighteenth- and nineteenth-century **espigueiros** (grain houses), over twenty of which are clumped together on a stony platform, their roof-crosses (intended to bless the annual crop) giving them the look of a graveyard. In addition to providing a ready-made, breezy threshing ground, the *espigueiros* site offers a degree of protection from rats, though the tall stone mushrooms that raise the houses from the ground do not appear to keep vermin entirely at bay. Their grouping together is a vestige of the days when the isolated village depended heavily on communal effort for its survival. Even now there are several flocks of sheep and goats that belong to the whole community and are tended by the village shepherds. If you set off on a hike at the crack of dawn you will walk up into the hills to the sound of small brass bells.

Changes are not accepted easily and the village takes its traditions very seriously. You'll notice that more women than usual observe the custom of wearing black after bereavement; widows wear it for the rest of their lives, while the death of a mother means four years of mourning, and that of children or siblings, two years. Folkloric groups are maintained by those who stay behind, while the emigrants all try to inculcate a sense of *minha terra* (my homeland) into their modern-minded (and in many cases American) offspring. The local **festival** (August 13–15) has a special feel, with the fun and games spontaneous. Owing to a lack of horses, the *corrida* is a race on foot – balancing blue plastic urns full of water on their heads, the contestants compete for the honour of being ceremoniously drenched by all the others. Large, home-made fireworks are set off all over the place without warning.

Staying in Soajo is no longer a problem since ten private homes joined together in a pioneering *Turismo de Aldeia* scheme. Each has its own character and costs upwards of €27.50 for a double room or €70 for a two-bedroom house. Especially recommended are the charming *Casa Do Souto* on Largo do Souto do Bairros and the rustic, homely *Casa dos Videiras* on Lugar de Riobom. You can book at the park office in Ponte da Barca (see p.408), or contact ADERE-Soajo (Mon–Fri 10am–7pm, Sat 10am–1pm; ☎ & ⓕ258 576 427) – ask at the supermarket. There's also a luxurious *turismo rural* property, the *Casa do Adro* (☎258 576 327; ❸), offering rooms in a beautiful eighteenth-century house – book well ahead at festival time. Of the **restaurants**, try either *O Espigueiro*, which specializes in goat, or the *Vidreira* on Lugar de Eiro.

Lindoso and Parada

Close to the Spanish border and set high above a hydroelectric reservoir on the Rio Lima, **LINDOSO** is one of the most attractive villages in Peneda-Gerês, and is most easily reached from Ponte da Barca. Like Soajo, Lindoso is dominated by a cluster of *espigueiros* and, again, life here is intensely traditional. The rearing of **livestock** is central; every morning starts with the lowing of cows or the clattering of the communally herded sheep and goats, and the smell of animals lies thick in the air. The traditional method of baking bread in these parts involved removing hot coals from the oven and sealing the door with an ash and dung mixture, and it's a technique still in use in the old part of the village. If you're interested, there's one of these ovens still in place in the heavily restored **Castelo** (summer Tues–Fri 10am–12.30pm & 2–6pm, Sat 10am–noon & 2.30–6pm, Sun 10am–noon & 2.30–6pm; winter Tues–Fri 9.30am–12.30pm & 2–5.30pm, Sat 10am–12.30pm & 2–5pm, Sun 10am–noon & 2–4.30pm; €1), whose museum details the results of local excavations – you can also get general park information from here.

Luxurious but expensive *Turismo de Aldeia* properties such as Casa do Amparo and Casa da Fonte da Tornada (❺) offer the best accommodation in Lindoso. Book these through the park office in Ponte de Barca (see p.408). For those on a budget, the only cheap **rooms** are at the *Lindo Verde*, 1km east of Lindoso on the road to Spain (☏258 578 010; ❷), which has eight modern rooms with bathrooms over its restaurant, notable for the somewhat bizarre speciality dish of crocodile. There's also a bar, which has a loud disco at weekends.

PARADA, clinging to the hillside 3km west of Lindoso, is perhaps an even more attractive place, with two clusters of *espigueiros*, and vines draped over its cobbled streets. There's a superb two-hour, 4km **walking circuit**, the *Trilho do Penedo do Encanto*, which heads uphill behind the village passing age-old houses and forests of chestnut and cork. For some of the way up, it follows a rocky stream bed, remarkable for the ruts worn into the stones over the centuries by ox carts. After about 1km, with forest plunging down to your right, look for a rusty metal gate straight in front of you, and a wall to your right covered with bundles of branches. Hop over the wall some 40m before the gate, and walk 30m straight on through the bushes. The large flat boulders in the clearing (not visible from the track) are the **Peneda do Encanto** (the "enchanted rocks"), of which the largest is covered with numerous (but faint) Bronze Age engravings. Mainly concentric circles and circular depressions, these are most visible about two hours before sunset, when the shadows are long. No one knows for sure what they represent, though similar designs can be found elsewhere in Minho and in Trás-os-Montes. Further up, the track loses itself in an exposed rocky area with superb views. To descend back to Parada, hug the forest wall to your right.

Accommodation is limited to *Café Mó* (☏258 576 150; ❶), on the main road 1km west of Parada, which has six modern but musty rooms with ancient TVs, shared bathrooms, and a macho ambience in the bar, though the owner and his family are friendly. Nearby is a natural pool for swimming, popular with local kids.

The eastern section: Serra do Gerês

Despite its proximity to Caldas do Gerês (2–3hrs on foot) and the Miradouro (30min on foot), **ERMIDA** has an air of isolation about it – be warned that driving there and beyond involves some extremely steep sections, in parts badly pitted by floods. If you're looking for a quiet base for hiking or else just soaking up the mountain atmosphere, this could be a good choice: there's good accommodation and food at *Casa do Criado* (☏253 391 390; ❶; phone ahead), a scattering of *dormidas*, an orchard to camp in and a couple of cafés, but it is still very much a farming community.

Continuing **east from Ermida**, along a bramble-lined lane, you'll pass a gorgeous group of small waterfalls – paradise to swim in – and cross a distinctly unsafe-looking (and sounding) bridge before coming to **FAFIÃO**, a tiny farming hamlet. There's a restaurant here, the *Retiro do Gerês*, which also has rooms (☎253 658 236; ❶). Past here, the countryside becomes more fertile, terraced with vines and maize, the road winding down to another hamlet, **PINCÃES**, and through it (turn right at the end of the houses) to the slightly larger village of Cabril.

A lovely, isolated place, sat on the Rio Cabril and surrounded on all sides by mountains, **CABRIL** flaunts odd attempts at modernity, though its centre is still sauntered through by oxen, goats and flocks of sheep. Parts of the locality have been submerged because of the Salamonde dam near Fafião. Consequently, the old bridge is half under water and makes for great swimming, through the bridge arch. There's a **campsite** here, *Outeiro Alto* (☎253 659 860), 1km out on the Pincães road, which is fine provided it's not too busy – there are only two toilets. It also rents out bicycles and canoes and offers horse-riding. You can get a good **meal** at the *Restaurante Ponte Novo*, by the bridge, which serves a warming meat stew; the *Café 1º de Maio*, further up the road, also serves food but usually needs advance warning.

On to Montalegre and the Trás-os-Montes: Paradela and Venda Nova

From Cabril, if you're hiking or driving, you could go on to Paradela, Outeiro, Paredes do Rio, Covelães and Pitões das Júnias, the latter with a decaying monastery nearby. Any of these settlements would make an ideal base for a leisurely exploration of this little-known corner of the Minho. With enough time, you could leave Portugal at Tourém, and hook back round through Spain to re-enter either at Portela do Homem (for Caldas do Gerês) or Lindoso for the northern section of the park. There's no public transport along this route, and infrequent traffic, but the gorgeous countryside is well suited for walking, and people are friendly.

In particular, the signposted path from Cabril to Paradela – around 23km – is stunningly dramatic, winding along the river valley through the handsome villages of Sirvozelo, Lapela and Xertola. At **PARADELA**, a particularly attractive mountain village whose cobbled streets are lined with vines, you're rewarded by fine views over the dam and mountains from a clutter of cafés and **hotels**. The modern *Restaurant Sol Rio* (☎276 566 167; ❷) has ten rooms, most with views, bathrooms and TVs. More characterful and set in shaded gardens with views 200 metres down the road to Cabril, *Pensão Pousadinha* (☎276 566 165; ❷) has the feel of an English B&B, with some self-contained rooms and excellent breakfasts included in the rates. The *Pousadinha* is also the base for **horse-riding trips** run by Trote Gerês. A further 100m along the road is the cool and friendly *Hospedaria Restaurante Dom Dinis* (☎276 566 253; ❷), where all rooms have views, TVs, showers and heating, and breakfast is included. The homely **restaurant** here is good, too, with Barrosã specialities like veal and *cozido* in winter.

The small village of **OUTEIRO**, 4km north of Paradela, is home to a bizarre seventeenth-century twin-towered church with an heavily-decorated facade. Accommodation is at the upmarket *Estalagem Vista Bela* (☎276 560 120, ⊕276 560 121; ❸), with sweeping views over the dam, and good meals (around €15) – try the veal or roast goat for dinner (breakfast is included).

PAREDES DO RIO, 3km east, is the next stop, notable for the excellent *Hospedaria Rocha* (☎276 566 147; ❷). All rooms have bathrooms, but the restaurant is the main draw, cooking meat from its own farm. Meals cost around €7.50 (breakfast is included in room rates): try the duck, or *cavidela de frango* – chicken cooked with blood and rice. In winter, go for the *feijoada* or *cozido*. They can also arrange 4–6 hour **walking trips** to Pitões de Júnias for the price of a picnic, or can lend you photocopies of maps with the route marked on. On the hill above the *hospedaria* is the rustic *Casa da Travessa* (☎276 566 121; or book via the park office in Ponte da Barca, see p.408; ❸), which has only two rooms, offering bikes if your legs are up to it, horse-riding and fishing.

After Paredes, **Covelães** is useful only for picking up the key for the *casa abrigo* (see p.406) in **PITÕES DE JÚNIAS**, 10km northwest, set in one of the remotest corners of Portugal, close to the Spanish border. This is lovely walking country, with a ruined monastery and waterfall nearby, and the jagged peaks (*pitões*) of Gerês tantalizingly close to the west. The monastery was founded in the ninth century, and the following century became part of the Cistercian Order; the Romanesque façade and most of the walls still stand. There's modern family-run accommodation at the *Casa do Preto* (☎276 566 158; ❶), which also houses one of Pitões' two excellent restaurants, the other being the *Pitões do Gerês*.

Alternatively, from Cabril or Paradela you can move on to **Montalegre**, via another vast reservoir. Montalegre itself (see p.440) provides a suitably remote and dramatic link with the Trás-os-Montes region, and can be reached by bus from Venda Nova or from Braga. The appeal lies as much in the road there as in the place itself. Bumpy and narrow, it makes for one of those journeys that seem to trigger madness in bus drivers, simultaneously delighting and terrifying unaccustomed passengers.

This route takes you through **VENDA NOVA**, which has two rather pricey **accommodation** options: the better of the two is the purpose-built *Estalagem do Morgado*, 4km west of Venda Nova by the reservoir at Lugar de Padrões (☎253 659 906, ✉mtempo@mail.telepac.pt; ❸), with a swimming pool, tennis courts, water sports marina and shaded gardens. Cheaper is the *Motel São Cristóvão* (☎253 659 387; ❸), an ugly modern building at the corner of the reservoir, 1km beyond Venda Nova at the junction to Salto, which also has tennis courts, and rents out boats.

There are some lovely walks in the vicinity and exceptionally bracing swimming. Buses from Braga pass through Venda Nova to Montalegre and Chaves, passing the hydroelectric plant of **Pisões** in this otherwise very remote region.

Travel details

Trains

Barcelos to: Valença do Minho (7 daily; 1hr 15min–1hr 50min); Viana do Castelo (11–12 daily; 30–40min).

Braga to: Nine – change for Viana and Valença (12–15 daily; 12–28min); Porto (11–14 daily, some change at Nine; 1hr–1hr 45min).

Caminha to: Valença do Minho (7–8 daily; 20–40min); Viana do Castelo (6–8 daily; 20–40min).

Valença do Minho to: Afife (4–6 daily; 55min); Barcelos (7–8 daily; 1hr 15min–2hr); Caminha (6–8 daily; 20–45min); Nine – change for Braga (5–7 daily; 2hr 20min); Vigo, Spain (4 daily; 1hr 10min; connections to Santiago de Compostela

and La Coruña); Vila Nova de Cerveira (6–8 daily; 12–18min); Vila Praia de Âncora (6–7 daily; 20min–1hr).

Viana do Castelo to: Afife (4 daily; 20min); Barcelos (12 daily; 25–45min); Caminha (7–8 daily; 20–40min); Porto (10–12 daily; 1hr 36min–2hr); Vila Nova de Cerveira (7 daily; 30min–1hr); Vila Praia de Âncora (7 daily; 15–35min).

Vila Nova de Cerveira to: Valença do Minho (6–8 daily; 12–18min); Viana do Castelo (6–7 daily; 30min–1hr).

Buses

Arcos de Valdevez to: Braga (2–4 daily; 1hr 15min); Lindoso (Mon–Fri 1–3 daily; 30min–1hr);

Ponte de Lima (5–8 daily; 50min); Porto (2–4 daily; 2hr); Soajo (Mon–Fri 1–3 daily; 30min); Viana do Castelo (5–8 daily; 1hr 45min).

Barcelos to: Braga (Mon–Fri every 30min, Sat & Sun hourly; 50min); Chaves (Mon–Fri 13 daily, Sat & Sun 3–6 daily; 6hr); Ponte de Lima (Mon–Fri 8 daily, 1–2 at weekends; 40–55min); Porto (Mon–Sat 9–12 daily, Sun 1–2 daily; 1hr 45min).

Braga to: Arcos de Valdevez (10–12 daily; 1hr 30min); Barcelos (Mon–Fri every 30min, Sat & Sun hourly; 30–50min); Bragança via Porto (3–5 daily; 6hr); Cabaceiras de Basto (4–5 daily; 1hr 45min); Caldas do Gerês (Mon–Fri hourly, Sat & Sun 8–10 daily; 1hr 30min); Campo do Gerês (3–7 daily; 1hr 30min); Cerdeirinhas (5–9 daily; 45min); Chaves (4 daily; 4hr); Coimbra (6 daily; 2hr 40min); Covide (3–4 daily; 1hr 10min); Guimarães (every 30 min; 30min–1hr); Leiria (6–9 daily; 4hr 5min); Lisbon (8–11 daily; 5hr 30min); Monção (3–5 daily; 2hr 20min); Montalegre (4–7 daily; 2hr 40min); Pisões (4–5 daily; 2hr 15min); Ponte da Barca (4 daily; 1hr 15min); Ponte de Lima (Mon–Fri 9 daily, Sat 5 daily, Sun 1 daily; 1hr); Porto (every 30min; 1hr 10min); Póvoa do Lanhoso (5–7 daily; 35min); Póvoa do Varzim (11 daily; 1hr 25min); Terras do Bouro (3–7 daily; 50min); Venda Nova (5–10 daily; 1hr 50min); Viana do Castelo (4–10 daily; 1hr 40min).

Caldas do Gerês to: Braga (6–10 daily; 1hr 30min).

Campo do Gerês to: Braga (3–6 daily; 1hr 20min).

Guimarães to: Braga (every 30 mins; 30min–1hr); Cabeceiras de Basto (6–8 daily; 1hr 15min); Lisbon (4–6 daily; 5hr 30min–6hr); Mondim de Basto (2 daily; 1hr 5min); Porto (6–8 daily; 2hr 30min–3hr); Vila Real (Mon–Fri 5–7 daily, Sat & Sun 1–3 daily; 1hr 30min).

Melgaço to: Castro Laboreiro (Mon–Fri 1 daily; 1hr); Coimbra (1–3 daily; 5hr); Lamas de Mouro (Mon–Fri 1 daily; 40min); Lisbon (1–3 daily; 6hr);

Monção (Mon–Fri 5 daily, Sat & Sun 1 daily; 40min); Porto (1–3 daily; 3hr); São Gregório (Mon–Fri 3 daily; 30min).

Monção to: Braga (3–6 daily; 1hr 45min); Melgaço (Mon–Fri 5 daily, Sat & Sun 1 daily; 40min); Viana do Castelo (5 daily; 1hr 20min).

Ponte da Barca to: Arcos de Valdevez (hourly; 15min); Braga (14 daily; 1hr); Lindoso (2 daily; 45min); Ponte de Lima (3–4 daily; 20–30min); Viana do Castelo (6–8 daily; 1hr 30min).

Ponte de Lima to: Arcos de Valdevez (5–8 daily; 50min); Barcelos (Mon–Fri 8 daily, 1–2 daily at weekends; 40–55min); Braga (Mon–Fri 10 daily, Sat 6, Sun 3; 1hr); Paredes de Coura (2–5 daily; 1hr 20min); Ponte de Barca (3–4 daily; 20–30min); Porto (7 daily; 2hr); Valença (1 daily; 1hr); Viana do Castelo (Mon–Fri 21 daily, Sat & Sun 9 daily; 50min).

Valença do Minho to: Lisbon (4 daily; 6hr 30min); Melgaço (8 daily; 40min); Monçao (10 daily; 20min); Ponte de Lima (1 daily; 1hr); Porto (7 daily; 2hr 30min); Viana do Castelo via Caminha (7 daily; 1 hr); Vila Nova de Cerveira (6 daily; 15min); to Spain: Sat to Vigo/Santiago (2hr/4hr 15min); Tues, Thurs and Fri via Monção and Melgaço for Ponte Barxas.

Viana do Castelo to: Afife (5–14 daily; 15min); Arcos de Valdevez (3–7 daily; 1hr 50min); Braga (4–8 daily; 1hr 40min); Caminha (Mon–Fri 13 daily, Sat & Sun 5 daily; 35min); Esposende (Mon–Sat 7–13 daily, Sun 4 daily; 40min); Lisbon (2 daily; 6hr); Moledo do Minho (Mon–Fri 13 daily, Sat & Sun 5 daily; 30min); Ponte da Barca (6–8 daily; 1hr 30min); Ponte de Lima (Mon–Fri 21 daily, Sat & Sun 7 daily; 50min); Porto (Mon–Sat 10–14 daily, Sun 4 daily; 2hr 5min); Póvoa de Varzim (Mon–Sat 10–15 daily, Sun 4 daily; 1hr 5min); Vila do Conde (Mon–Sat 7–13 daily, Sun 4 daily; 1hr 40min); Vila Praia de Âncora (Mon–Fri 13 daily, Sat & Sun 5 daily; 30min).

Trás-os-Montes

ATLANTIC
OCEAN

N

SPAIN

CHAPTER 7

Highlights

✳ **Solar de Mateus** Picture yourself on a bottle of wine at the palace made famous by Mateus Rose. See p.426

✳ **Parque Natural do Alvão** Wander in peace through the wilds of Portugal's smallest natural park. See p.430

✳ **The Corgo river** The dramatic river valley north from Vila Real is a verdant land of small villages and vineyards. See p.431

✳ **Chaves** Stroll across the Roman bridge, still doing its job after almost 2000 years. See p.436

✳ **Bragança citadel** The ancient Cidadela has a bird's eye view over the vast expanse of the Parque Natural de Montesinho. See p.443

✳ **Parque Natural do Douro** Internacional Portugal's newest, frontier-spanning natural park is home to some of the country's rarest flora and fauna. See p.456

Trás-os-Montes

RÁS-OS-MONTES – literally "Beyond the Mountains" – is Portugal's Lost Domain. For centuries this remote, rural province has been a place to hide and practise one's beliefs in peace: its peculiar traditions and dialects have been formed by a diversity of populations, from the prehistoric tribes who carved the *porcas* (stone pigs) to Jews who sought refuge here from the Inquisition. For the majority, life here is hard, the landscape forcing people to eke a living from *minifundia* (small holdings) and, as a result, emigration is high. In the more remote areas whole villages are populated by people of pensionable age as the youngsters head for the cities in search of a better life.

A sharp natural divide cuts across the province. In the south is the fertile territory officially entitled the Upper Douro, but known unofficially as the **Terra Quente** (Hot Land), which encompasses the terraced stretches of the rivers Douro, Corgo and Tua. Here the landscape, as well as the climate, is distinctly Mediterranean, peppered with olive groves and vineyards, as well as farms growing peaches, oranges, melons and almonds that flourish in the red soils. By contrast, the bitter winters of the wild and rugged north have earned it the name of **Terra Fria** (Cold Land). The extremity of the climate – "Nine months of winter and three months of hell", as the local proverb puts it – and the aridity of much of its land have kept Trás-os-Montes well apart from the mainstream. Even today, with some industry coming to the major towns, the province has a population half the size of that of the Minho in almost twice the area. But change is afoot: transport links are continually being improved – largely thanks to European Union funding – opening up the province to such a degree that, in many areas, the traditional way of life is coming under threat; the World Bank has invested heavily in the agricultural sector and several of the province's larger population centres are undergoing urban renewal projects aimed at making them more attractive to residents and tourists alike.

Travelling into the province is easy, with fast daily bus services from Porto to the main towns of Vila Real, Chaves, Mirandela and Bragança, though travel within the region can be a slow business, with few remaining train services, and buses generally operating on weekdays only, being as much for the benefit of local schoolchildren as paying customers. However, almost any route in Trás-os-Montes has its rewards, and the fortified frontier towns of **Chaves** and **Bragança** should feature on any itinerary of northern Portugal. For the most part though, Trás-os-Montes' sights are defiantly rural: a succession of hard-working mountain or valley villages, and small, fortified settlements – **Mirando do Douro** (whose almond trees draw weekenders for their fleeting blossoming in late February and early March), **Mogadouro** and **Freixo de**

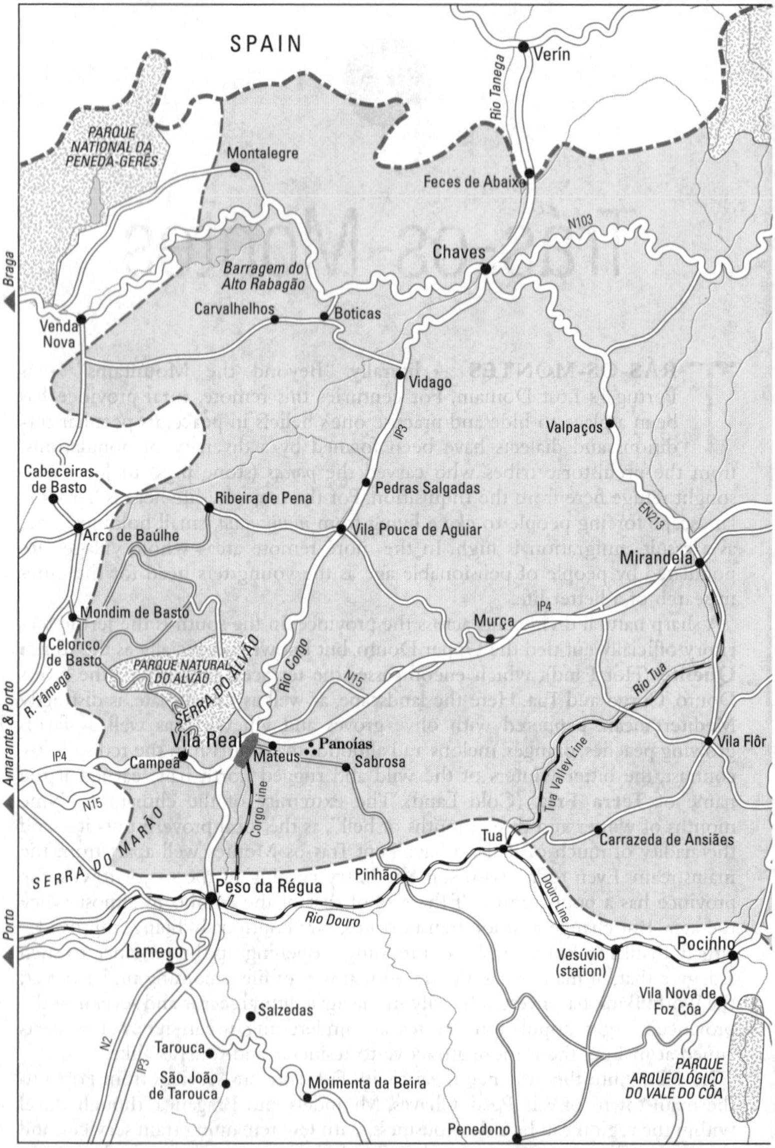
SPAIN
PARQUE NATIONAL DA PENEDA-GERÊS
Montalegre
Verín
Rio Tanega
Feces de Abaixo
N103
Chaves
Barragem do Alto Rabagão
Braga
Carvalhelhos
Boticas
Venda Nova
Vidago
IP3
Valpaços
Cabeceiras de Basto
Pedras Salgadas
Ribeira de Pena
EN213
Arco de Baúlhe
Vila Pouca de Aguiar
Mirandela
IP4
Mondim de Basto
Murça
Celorico de Basto
PARQUE NATURAL DO ALVÃO
SERRA DO ALVÃO
Rio Corgo
N15
Rio Tua
R. Tâmega
Amarante & Porto
Vila Real
Panoías
Mateus
Sabrosa
Vila Flôr
IP4
Campeã
Tua Valley Line
N15
Corgo Line
SERRA DO MARÃO
Tua
Carrazeda de Ansiães
Pinhão
Douro Line
Peso da Régua
Rio Douro
Porto
Lamego
Vesúvio (station)
Pocinho
Vila Nova de Foz Côa
Salzedas
N2
Tarouca
IP3
São João de Tarouca
Moimenta da Beira
PARQUE ARQUEOLÓGICO DO VALE DO CÔA
Penedono
Castro Daire & Viseu
Trancoso & Guarda
Guarda

Espada à Cinta – guarding the border with Spain. The appeal of these towns lies above all in their timeless isolation and, as with much of the rest of the province, the feeling that you are the first foreign visitor to set foot there.

One of the few towns of any real size in the entire region is **Vila Real** – a good starting point for a tour of the province, especially for hikers, with its access to the dramatic granite scenery of the **Parque Natural do Alvão**. A

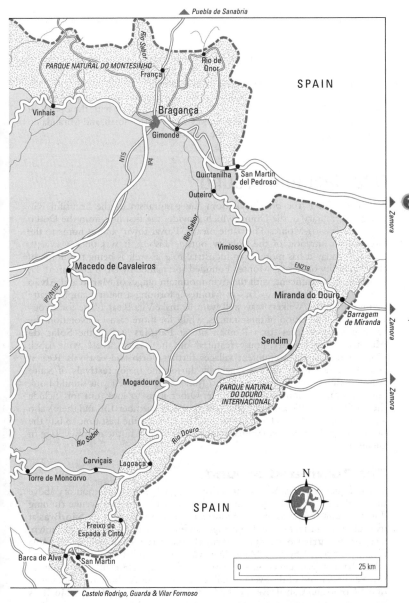

Castelo Rodrigo, Guarda & Vilar Formoso

second natural park hugs the border with Spain in the far north of the province, beyond Bragança, in the **Serra de Montesinho**, where walkers can experience Trás-os-Montes at its most rural and remote; while a third, the **Parque Natural do Douro Internacional**, has been designated in the east of the region where the Douro and its tributary, the Rio Águeda, skirt the Spanish border.

Chaves can be reached, a little tortuously, from Braga and the Peneda-Gerês national park (see p.403), but the most obvious approach to the region is from the Douro, whose eastern reaches (covered in Chapter Five) are technically a part of the province. From the main Douro train line, which runs from Porto to Pocinho, the **Corgo line** branches off to the north through a spectacular winding gorge from Peso da Régua to **Vila Real**, from where you can catch buses north to Chaves and most other destinations; while the **Tua Valley line**, from Tua to **Mirandela** affords equally spectacular scenery, with the option of onward bus connections to Bragança and Chaves in the north, and Miranda do Douro and Torre de Moncorvo in the east.

Vila Real and around

VILA REAL is the one break from the pastoralism of the beautiful Rio Corgo, a tributary of the Douro which provides the first link from the Douro region to Trás-os-Montes. The name means "Royal Town" and, as home to the largest concentration of the nobility outside Lisbon, it was once very apt, although today it has more of an industrial role, as well as being the home of the University of Trás-os-Montes. Founded and named by Dom Dinis in 1829, its setting is magnificent, with the twin mountain ranges of **Marão** and **Alvão** (the so-called "Gateway to Trás-os-Montes") forming a natural amphitheatre behind the town. Walkers may well want to make Vila Real a base for a couple of days' exploration of these ranges, while, for more casual exploration, the town gives easy access to a Roman site at **Panóias** and to the **Solar de Mateus** – the country house featured on the Mateus Rosé wine label. Compared with the somnolent villages further north and east, Vila Real is actually quite a lively place – especially during the major **festivals** of Santo António (June 13–21) and São Pedro (June 28–29), when you should book your accommodation well in advance. Other *feiras* to look out for include those of São Brás (February 3) and Santa Luzia (December 13), and there's also a procession for Corpus Deus on June 3. The *feiras* are the best time to buy the distinctive pewter-grey **earthenware crockery** made in the nearby village of Bisalhães.

The Town and around

The old quarter of Vila Real is attractive enough, built on a promontory above the confluence of the Corgo and Cabril rivers, with the main avenue running down its spine; the view from the fourteenth-century **Capela de São Brás** at its southern end is not one for vertigo sufferers. There's little to see in town, save for the **turismo** building – formerly the palace of the Marquês of Vila Real, and fronted by four Manueline windows – and the **Sé**, over the way, which has modern stained-glass windows and a simple, fifteenth-century interior. At the far end of the avenue, built on a promontory above the confluence of the Corgo and Cabril rivers, is the fourteenth-century **Capela de São Brás** which affords magnificent views of the waterways below. Back at the bottom of the hill by the **Câmara Municipal**, a plaque on the wall of the café opposite commemorates the birthplace of Diogo Cão, who discovered the mouth of the Congo River in 1482. Slightly east of the Largo de Camoes, on Rua do Rossio, there is a small **museum** (Tues–Fri 10am–12.30pm & 2.30–6.30pm, Sat & Sun 2.30–6.30pm; free) specializing in the rarely twinned pursuits of archaeology and numismatism. The main attractions are a selection of

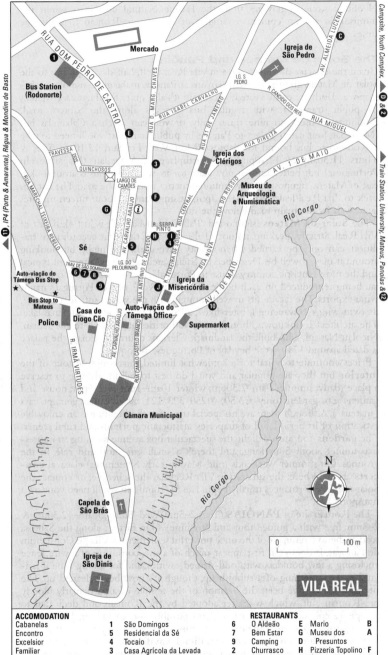

VILA REAL

ACCOMODATION			
Cabanelas	1	São Domingos	6
Encontro	5	Residencial da Sé	7
Excelsior	4	Tocaio	9
Familiar	3	Casa Agrícola da Levada	2
Mira Corgo	10	Casa da Campeã / Casa da Cruz	11
Casa de Hóspedes Mondego	8	Casa da Quinta de São Martinho	12

RESTAURANTS			
O Aldeão	E	Mario	B
Bem Estar	G	Museu dos	A
Camping	D	Presuntos	
Churrasco	H	Pizzeria Topolino	F
O Espadeiro	C	O Transmontano	J
Café Excelsior	I		

Map labels:
- @, Lordelo
- A B & Cabanelas Bus Office & Parque Natural de Alvão
- Campsite, Youth Complex D & 2
- Train Station, University, Mateus, Panóias & 12
- RUA DOM PEDRO DE CASTRO
- Mercado
- Bus Station (Rodonorte)
- TRAVESSA DOS QUINCHOSOS
- RUA MARECHAL TEIXEIRA REBELO
- IP4 (Porto & Amarante), Régua & Mondim de Basto
- Igreja de São Pedro
- AV. ALMEIDA LUCENA
- LG. S PEDRO
- R CANDIDO DOS REIS
- RUA MIGUEL
- RUA D MARG CHAVES
- RUA ISABEL CARVALHO
- RUA 31 DE JANEIRO
- RUA DIREITA
- RUA CENTRAL
- Igreja dos Clérigos
- AV. 1 DE MAIO
- Museu de Arqueologia e Numismática
- RUA DO ROSSIO
- Rio Corgo
- LARGO DE CAMÕES
- R SERPA PINTO
- RUA CARVALHO ARAUJO
- Sé
- LG. DO PELOURINHO
- TRAV DE SÃO DOMINGOS
- RUA ANTÓNIO DE AZEVEDO
- RUA TEIXEIRA DE SOUSA
- RUA NOVA
- AV. 1 DE MAIO
- Igreja da Misericórdia
- Auto-viação do Tâmega Bus Stop
- Bus Stop to Mateus
- Police
- Casa de Diogo Cão
- Auto-Viação do Tâmega Office
- Supermarket
- RUA CAMILO CASTELO BRANCO
- RUA IRMÃ VIRTUDES
- Câmara Municipal
- Rio Corgo
- N
- 0 100 m
- Capela de São Brás
- Igreja de São Dinis

Neolithic stone engravings from the Parque Natural do Alvão, whilst the numismatic section contains examples of coins from Roman to Visigothic times.

The Solar de Mateus and Panóias

Given the paucity of things to do in Vila Real itself, half-day **trips** out to the Solar de Mateus and the Roman remains at Panóias make good use of a night's stopover. Both are easily visited by car, and it's also quite feasible to see Mateus by public transport, with regular **bus** services along the Sabrosa road. Rodonorte buses run nine times daily, or you can catch a Cabanelas bus (Mon–Sat; four daily). To get to Panóias by public transport you'll need to take a Rodonorte bus bound for Sabrosa (Mon, Wed, Fri–Sun 12.10pm, Tues & Thurs 11.30am & 12.10pm), the birthplace of Magellan (Magalhães in Portuguese) but better known nowadays for its wine. The site is around 6km east of Mateus, signposted a few hundred metres north of the road. The last bus back to Vila Real leaves Sabrosa at 3pm, passing Panóias about fifteen minutes later; wait by the main road below the site.

The **Solar de Mateus** (signposted "Palácio de Mateus") is just 4km east of Vila Real. Strictly speaking, it's not a Palácio at all, a title that, according to tradition, can only be earned when royalty have spent the night, but looking around it may as well be. Described by Sacheverell Sitwell as "the most typical and the most fantastic country house in Portugal", it's certainly the most familiar, being reproduced on each bottle of Mateus Rosé, one of Portugal's major wine exports. The facade fits in well enough with the wine's soft-focus image, its twin wings "advancing lobster-like", as Sitwell put it, across a formal lake. The architect is unknown, though most authorities attribute it to the Italian, Nicolau Nasoni, who built the landmark Clérigos church in Porto; the palace is dated around 1740 – the heyday of Portuguese Baroque.

Prices continue to spiral for a somewhat limited thirty-minute tour of the **interior** but they are popular and you'd do best to call in advance to reserve a place (daily: summer 9am–7.30pm; winter 10am–1pm & 2–6pm; house and gardens €6, gardens only €3.50; ☎259 323 121, ⓦwww.utad.geira.pt/casa _mateus/). Although there are no special treasures, the building is an enjoyable evocation of its period, full of draperies, aristocratic portraits and rural scenes. The **gardens**, too, are a delight, the spectacular box avenue forming an impressive tunnel about 50m long, and there's a small gift shop and café in the grounds. On summer weekends (mid-May to early September) classical **concerts** are held here: the turismo in Vila Real has the schedule, or contact the Solar itself. Performances usually begin late (9–10pm), so you'll need your own transport.

The Roman site of **PANÓIAS** (Tues 2–5pm, Wed–Sun 9.30am–12.30pm & 2–5pm; free with a guided tour and brochure), 6km further along the Sabrosa road, is the sole remnant of the once powerful settlement of Vila de Constantim de Panoyas. It doesn't at first appear much of a site, consisting of a wire fence enclosing a few boulders with odd-shaped cavities, and for a long time it languished as something of a rubbish tip, though it's now been cleaned up. The site appears to have been the location of the temple of a particularly bloody pre-Roman cult, which was later adopted by the Romans and dedicated to Serapis (a cult of Egyptian origin), and possibly also to Jupiter. The rickety viewing tower (closed at the time of writing) at the top end gives you a good view of the three coffin-shaped **sacrificial cavities** on the largest boulder, which used to have a filter system for the blood and viscera created by the offerings; the much eroded inscriptions to this effect on nearby boulders are in a strange mixture of Greek and Latin, lending weight to the theory that the temple may have been constructed well before the Romans arrived.

Practicalities

Vila Real is the hub of Trás-os-Montes' regional transport with frequent buses leaving to all major destinations. Rodonorte operates from their **bus station** beside the *Hotel Cabanelas* on Rua dom Pedro de Castro, just north of the centre (☎259 323 234); all other regional buses stop outside here. Cabanelas, who also act as agents for Santos (for services eastwards to Mirandela, Miranda do Douro and Torre de Moncorvo) has its office at Avenida Dom Dinis (☎259 325 256), while for services to Chaves and Bragança, Auto-Viação do Tâmega's office can be found at Avenida Carvalho Araújo 26, near the Camâra Municipal (☎259 322 928). The **train station** is 500m east of the centre, on the opposite bank of the river; to reach the town centre from here, follow the road into town, over the bridge, and turn left. From Vila Real there are five trains daily on the Corgo line to Peso da Régua with the last train leaving at 7.30pm (see p.334).

The **turismo** (summer Mon–Fri 9.30am–7pm, Sat & Sun 10am–noon & 2–5pm; winter Mon–Fri 9.30am–12.30pm & 2–5pm; ☎259 322 819, ⓦwww.cm-vilareal.pt) is on the central Avenida Carvalho Araújo, at no. 94. Helpful as ever, it can provide transport and accommodation details, including advice on the various *turismo rural* properties in the area. More information on the region (including the Serra do Alvão and the Serra do Marão) is available from the **regional tourist office** at Avenida 1° de Maio 70–1° (Mon–Fri 9am–12.30pm & 2–5.30pm; ☎259 322 819, ⓕ259 321 712); those planning a visit to the **Parque Natural do Alvão** (see p.430) should head for the park headquarters at Largo das Freitas behind the Camâra Municipal (Mon–Fri 9am–12.30pm & 2–5.30pm; ☎259 302 831, ⓕ259 302 831). For unlimited **internet** access try *Cyber Centre* on Rua Dr. Cristavão Madeira Pinto, about ten minutes walk north of the Rodonorte bus station, where online access costs €2 per hour.

Accommodation

The pick of the town's **pensões and hotels** are reviewed below but be warned that the more basic places can get distinctly chilly and damp in winter. The cheapest hostel-type accommodation is at the *Instituto da Juventude* youth complex on Avenida Dr. Manuel Cardona (☎259 323 551), and there's a pleasant **campsite** with a swimming pool down by the river (☎259 324 724). To get there from the centre, follow Avenida 1° de Maio and its continuations Avenida Aureliano Barrigas and Rua Dr Manuel Cardona. It's about a fifteen-minute walk; if you're coming from the train station, turn right after crossing the bridge. There's adequate shade, but arrive early if you want a riverside pitch.

In town

Hotel Cabanelas Rua Dom Pedro de Castro ☎259 323 153, ⓕ259 374 181. Modern functional comforts next to the bus station, fractionally cheaper than the *Mira Corgo* but lacking a pool. ❸

Casa de Hóspedes Mondego Trav. de São Domingos 11 ☎259 323 097, ⓕ259 322 039. Near the Sé, this has some of the cheapest rooms in town, but the plumbing is somewhat archaic, and it gets very hot in summer and cold in winter. ❶

Encontro Av Carvalho Araújo 76–78 ☎259 322 532. Family-run *residencial*, inexpensive with a

mixed bag of rooms above a restaurant. It's near the turismo, and can be a bit noisy at night. Breakfast included. ❷

Excelsior Rua Serpa Pinto ☎259 322 422. Next to the café of the same name, this *pensão* has a few basic rooms, most without bathrooms. ❶

Familiar Praça Luís de Camões 36 ☎259 322 100. Good cheap rooms, clean if a little basic, some with bathrooms. ❶

Mira Corgo Av 1° de Maio 76–78 ☎259 325 001, ⓕ259 325 006. Vila Real's swankiest hotel is an ugly modern block but its rooms overlook the stepped terraces of the Corgo, far below, and there's an indoor swimming pool and solarium. There's also a disco, guaranteed to disturb many a peaceful night. ❹

São Domingos Travessa de São Domingos 33 ☎ & ⓕ 259 322 039. A nice, friendly *pensão*, operated by the same family as the *Mondego*. Gets a bit stuffy in summer. ❷

Residencial da Sé Trav. de São Domingos 19–23 ☎ 259 324 575. Next to the *Mondego*, this place has private facilities attached to most of the rooms, and a restaurant below. ❷

Tocaio Av Carvalho Araújo 45–55 ☎ 259 323 106, ⓕ 259 371 675. Large and rather dark 1950s hotel, long since demoted to *pensão* status. All rooms come with a private bathroom (but not always hot water), and the reception area comes with a stuffed wild pig. ❸

Outside town

Casa Agrícola da Levada 2km northeast at Timpeira ☎ 259 322 190, ⓕ 259 346 955; or reserve through Solares de Portugal, see p.33. Take the Mateus bus or follow Avenida 1º de Maio towards Bragança for 2km until the road descends towards a stone bridge; on the left you'll see this impressive farmhouse set in its own grounds and

with an attached chapel. The owners breed wild boar and produce their own sausages and honey. ❹

Casa da Campeã 10km west, 2km before Campeã, just off the IP4 ☎ 259 979 604, ⓕ 259 979 760. Modern chalet-cum-motel set-up with a pool and good restaurant, though the main attraction is the activities offered in the nearby Vale da Campeã (Serra do Marão), including rafting, paragliding, bungee jumping and of course hiking. ❸

Casa da Cruz Campeã, 12km west along the road to Mondim ☎ 259 979 422, ⓕ 259 972 995. Three simple rooms with lovely carved beds in this eighteenth-century granite farmhouse, overlooking the Vale da Campeã. Rustic sitting room, and free use of kitchen. Fishing and cycling trips can be arranged. ❸

Casa da Quinta de São Martinho 4km east at Mateus, 300m from the Solar de Mateus ☎ & ⓕ 259 323 986; or reserve through Privetur. Seventeenth-century granite country house with a comfortable clutter of old and new furniture, nothing fancy but charming in its way. Two bedrooms, two apartments, and a pool. Also port wine tasting in the bar. ❸

Eating, drinking and nightlife

For inexpensive local **meals**, try any of the cafés in the streets behind the turismo. There's also a timeless (and nameless) *adega* – dark, cave-like and festooned with hams and plastic wine jars – at Travessa de São Domingos 17. If you're planning day trips out of Vila Real you can stock up on your own **food supplies** at the weekday market opposite the Rodonorte bus station, or at the **supermarket** hidden in the shopping centre next to *Hotel Mira Corgo* on Avenida 1º de Maio. There's a good **wine shop** on Largo do Pelourinho.

The liveliest **nightspots** are the bars along Largo do Pelourinho and Rua Serpa Pinto, notably *Café Excelsior* at nos. 30–36 on the latter, which has a huge pool hall featuring the strangest timing meters for your game you'll ever see.

Restaurants

Local dishes worth looking out for include roast kid goat and veal, *cozido à portuguesa*, and – if you hadn't eaten your fill in Porto – *tripas aos molhos* ("sheaves" of tripe, no less). For those with a sweeter tooth, **pastries** to ask for are *pastéis de Santa Clara* (stuffed with very sweet egg goo), *toucinho do céu* ("heavenly bacon", because it supposedly looks like it), and *tigelinhas de laranja* ("orange bowls"). Also worth a try is the delicious *nata do céu*, a very sweet, cheesecakelike dessert, drizzled with a sugary egg mixture.

O Aldeão Rua Dom Pedro de Castro 70. Popular and very reasonably priced, with a changing daily menu of standards: meals upwards of €7.50.

Bem Estar Av Carvalho Araújo, opposite the turismo. Family-run, basic, and inexpensive.

Churrasco Rua António de Azevedo 24 ☎ 259 322 313. Simple place offering pretty much normal

fare except for the wonderful spit-roast chicken. Around €8.50. Closed Sun.

O Espadeiro Av Almeida Lucena ☎ 259 322 302. Highly reputed regional restaurant that's been going for over 30 years. Trout stuffed with ham, and the roast kid are both good, though the desserts lag behind; meals cost €12.50 upwards.

429

△ Wine-grower, Douro valley

Good wine list. Closed Wed, and late Sept.
Museu dos Presuntos Av Cidade Orense 43
☎259 326 017. Trendy place near the new
teepee-styled church 1km to the north, great for
pratinhos ("small dishes") – ham, cod-fish balls,
grilled *chouriço*, chicken sweetmeats and tripe.
Closed Tues.

Pizzeria Topolino Rua António de Azevedo, off the
Praça de Camões. A pleasant interior with good
options for vegetarians.
O Transmontano Rua da Misericórdia 37. Caters
for big groups and can be a bit touristy, but good
value nonetheless, specializing in *bacalhau*.

The Parque Natural do Alvão

Portugal's smallest natural park, the boulder-strewn and pine-covered
PARQUE NATURAL DO ALVÃO, can be glimpsed when travelling by
road between Vila Real and Amarante along the IP4, but you'll see more from
the N304, which branches off the IP4 towards Mondim de Basto and goes
through the park itself, around Ermelo. This route is served by buses (from Vila
Real: Mon–Fri 8am, 1.20pm & 6pm, Sat 8am & 1.20pm; from Mondim de
Basto: Mon–Fri 7am, 12.30pm & 5.30pm, Sat 7am & 12.30pm), and is the easiest approach if you're coming by public transport since there's none on the
eastern side of the park. With a car, you might prefer to take the minor N313
from north of Vila Real to Mondim de Basto that cuts right through the park
via Lamas de Ôlo.

Visits to the park aren't made any easier by the lack of **accommodation** (the
turismo in Vila Real has a list of accommodation on the park's outskirts);
camping is prohibited to avoid the very real risk of forest fires. Serious walkers
intending to cross the whole reserve should obtain maps in advance from Porto
or Lisbon and consult the **park headquarters** in Vila Real (see p.427) or the
park office in Mondim de Basto (see p.331). You can buy leaflets detailing
walking circuits from both of these offices (€0.35–0.70) but these are currently
available only in Portuguese. For **organized tours**, contact Realvitur at Largo
Pioledo 2 in Vila Real (☎259 321 800, ℗259 374 353), who offer tailor-made
trips by Land Rover into the park; or Os Tamecanos in Mondim de Basto
(☎255 302 637).

Despite these difficulties, the park itself is a delight, and one of the few places
in Portugal where you really feel you're in the wild. There is only a handful of
settlements, mostly constructed on rocky terrain to conserve the little arable
land available, and almost everywhere you'll have your nostrils filled with the
scent of pine. Locals remove the bark on parts of the tree trunks and use a series
of channels to collect the sap in sticky plastic bags for use in solvent production. **Birds** to look out for include golden eagles, buzzards, screech owls and
the remarkable dipper, a sparrow-sized diving bird that makes its living on tur-
bulent rocky streams. Other **wildlife** isn't so easy to spot and you'd be
extremely lucky to see any of the wolves, roe deer or wild boar that live in the
park. You're also unlikely to see snakes, as they tend to disappear at the sound
of approaching footsteps.

Without your own transport, the easiest **circuit** – giving you gorgeous views
of mountains, pine trees and plunging valleys (allow 5–7 hours) – is in the west:
take the early morning bus from Vila Real or Mondim to the junction for
ERMELO (1km off the main N304), a sleepy little hamlet with the proud title
of "largest village in the park". Ermelo comes alive for two days a year (August
7–8) for the *Feira de São Vicente*, a joint celebration also marking the annual
return of Ermelo's emigrants from Porto and abroad. From here, a track leads
up the mountain, running high above the left bank of the **Rio Ôlo** – a tributary of the Tâmega – past the hamlet of **Fervença** (a 3km detour from here

takes you to **Barreiro**, with superb views westwards), before crossing the river at **Varzigueto**. It then runs back to Ermelo, where you can catch the late-afternoon bus back to Vila Real or Mondim (check at Vila Real or Mondim turismo for times). For an alternative circuit (also 5–7hr), take the track 1km west of Ermelo on the main Vila Real–Mondim road (signposted "Fisgas"), and head uphill along the forestry track, with the Rio Ôlo hidden in the ravine to your right. A couple of kilometres along, a right turn by a restaurant-café takes you on a 2km detour to a spectacular rocky ledge overlooking the waterfalls of **Fisgas de Ermelo**. Back at the restaurant, the track continues uphill among more rugged terrain for another 3km before joining the track from Varzigueto back to Ermelo.

To explore the eastern side of the park, catch a bus from Vila Real towards Chaves, getting off after 5km at the turning for the N313 to Mondim de Basto. From here it's a strenuous few hours hike to **LAMAS DE ÔLO**, a quiet rural hamlet around 1000 metres above sea level, notable for its peculiar granite houses with tent-like thatch roofs (many now abandoned) and, above the village, a watermill with a primitive aqueduct. It's a beautiful walk, though, and at weekends you may be able to hitch a lift with other visitors. A particularly attractive walking circuit (around 3hr) begins in **AGAREZ**, 4km from Lamas de Ôlo, looping anticlockwise via **Galegos da Serra** on the Arnal stream, with its working watermill and waterfall, past a school for ecologists (which may have **rooms** for the night – enquire at the park office in Vila Real), and upstream to **Arnal**, where a women's cooperative produces **linen** clothing and sheets for sale. From Arnal, there's a minor road back to Agarez.

Northeast: routes to Chaves and Bragança

Beyond Vila Real, Trás-os-Montes begins in earnest, with two main routes heading **northeast**, either to Chaves (64km) or to Bragança (136km). The IP3 (formerly the N2) to Chaves is a particularly fine route, the road constrained by the twists and turns of the **Corgo river valley**, but although there are several spa towns along this route, **Vidago** is the only one really worth an overnight stop. The longer roads to Bragança (the EN82 or the new, faster IP4) have more of interest to delay you, with a possible stopover halfway at medieval **Mirandela** in the **Tua valley** (from where the minor N213 cuts north to Chaves); from here, there are also diversions **south** along the N213/N214 to intriguing towns like Vila Flôr and Carrazeda de Ansiães.

The Corgo Valley and Vidago

From Vila Real, Auto-Viação do Tâmega buses run regularly along the IP3 through the spectacular **Corgo river valley**, where everything from cowsheds to vine posts is made from granite, and where the luscious green of the vines belies the apparent barrenness of the earth. En route, you'll also see the strange *espigueiros* or corn sheds, long and improbably thin granite constructions perched atop stone or wooden stilts to protect the contents from rats. It's a less dramatic ride than that once provided by the old Linha do Corgo train line, long since abandoned to the elements, but it's handsome enough, the road following the valley fairly closely as far as the village of **VILA POUCA DE AGUIAR**, 28km from Vila Real, which is famous in the north for its bread.

Besides the Pedras Salgadas Spa (☎259 434 102; June–Sept only), whose waters are apparently good for disorders of the digestive system, there's not much reason to stay here, though if you get stuck, there are a handful of similar-priced *residenciais* along the main road, including the homely *Residencial Califa* (☎259 417 560; ❷). Beyond here, the road cuts through the edge of the Serra da Padrela, before reaching the upper valley of the Tâmega River at Vidago, which it then traces for the rest of the route to Chaves.

Vidago

The spa town of **VIDAGO**, about 12km south of Chaves, is easily the most interesting stop along the way, with some lovely walks in the pine-forested surroundings and the opportunity to splash about in the local rivers. It's important to note, however, that the spa closes in winter, as do most of the hotels and *pensões*. Buses drop you by the summer **turismo** (9am–noon & 2–6pm; ☎276 907 470) on the main road and from here it's only a short walk to the spa and hotels – follow the flurry of signs.

The **spa** itself (mid-June to mid-Oct Mon–Sat 8am–noon & 4–7pm) is set in the beautiful grounds of the four-star *Vidago Palace Hotel* (☎276 990 900; ❻), an astonishingly opulent Edwardian pile and without doubt one of Portugal's finest hotels. The pump room is magnificent, and there's also a bandstand amid the trees, a boating lake and bikes for rent (for residents only), not to mention the pool, tennis courts and nine-hole golf course. Its restaurant is worth a visit, too, with less scary prices than you may imagine (under €12). *Hotel do Parque*, Avenida Teixeira de Sousa (☎276 907 157, ℻276 909 666; ❸), is a modern rival to the *Vidago Palace*, with tennis courts and a pool, but lacks its grace and character. The best of the less expensive options include *Pensão Alameda*, Rua Padre Adolfo Magalhães 2 (☎276 907 246; ❶), a small, friendly, family-run place, with breakfast thrown in; and *Pensão Primavera* (☎276 907 230, ℻276 999 444; ❶), at Avenida Conde de Caria 2, facing the *Vidago Palace*, a good-value and attractive *pensão* with a wide range of rooms and its own restaurant.

Mirandela and the Tua Valley

It's 71km along the N15 (or 65km along the fast IP4) from Vila Real to **MIRANDELA**, an odd little town with a few remnants of a medieval centre, a scattering of Baroque mansions and a modern art gallery, as well as some horrible concrete constructions. It's not to everyone's taste, and is certainly not as attractive as some of the nearby towns, but it has enough positive points to warrant a visit. The town's most striking feature is undoubtedly its **Roman bridge**, renovated in the fifteenth century and stretching a good 200m across seventeen arches. It's open only to pedestrians, with traffic forced to use the new concrete bridge beside it, or the Ponte Europa upstream. Kayaks and pedalos can be hired in summer to splash up and down here, and the riverside gardens and lawns are pleasant places to loaf around.

Much of the **old town** is decaying or has been demolished, and attempts at renovation have yielded mixed results. The chapel near the Câmara Municipal, at the summit of the ancient citadel, simply fell down in 1985. Scavengers pilfered the best of the stonework, and what was left was rebuilt in a four-square style topped with an ugly glass pyramid that contrasts awkwardly with the grandiose **Câmara Municipal** itself. Formerly the Palácio dos Távoras, this was one of several flamboyant town houses associated with the **Távora** family, who controlled the town between the fourteenth and seventeenth centuries. The modern art gallery, the **Museu Armindo Teixeira Lopes** (Mon–Fri 10am–12.30pm & 2–6pm; free), is combined with the town's library and displays modern sculptures and paintings, with one section dedicated to local artist Armindo Teixeira Lopes's images of Mirandela and Lisbon.

The best time to visit Mirandela is during the **Festa da Senhora do Amparo** (July 25 to the first Sunday in August), one of the longest *festas* in Portugal. The final Saturday is the big day, with a procession and fireworks, although things also get hot on Friday night (the *Noite das Bombas*, or "Night of the Drums"), also with fireworks and a parade. Traditional music and dance can be sampled at the **Festa dos Reis** (January 6) at Vale de Salgueiro, 12km north on the Vinhais road, where a "king" visits the village's houses distributing *tremoços* (pickled beans) and wine to the sound of bagpipes. Weekday **markets** are held in Mirandela as close as possible to the 3rd, 14th or 25th of every month.

Practicalities

Buses arrive at the terminal next to the train station. To get to the town centre turn right, then right again and with the river on your left it's a five-minute walk to the Roman bridge, from where the road veers into Rua da República. The **turismo** (Mon–Fri 9.30am–12.30pm & 2–6pm; ☎278 200 200 ext. 272) is located here in the market building, and has a handy free booklet containing information about the town and driving circuits in the area.

With half a dozen **pensões and hotels**, rooms in Mirandela are pretty easy to find, except during the *festa*. Cheapest are the reasonable *Pensão Sá Moreno*, off Rua da República at Rua das Amoreiras 71 (☎278 262 434; ❶), with shared bathrooms; the characterful if basic *Pensão Praia*, Largo 1° de Janeiro 6, also off Rua da República (☎278 262 497; ❶–❷), which has a mixed bag of rooms (some en suite) and attractive lake views from its upper floor; and the self-contained rooms at the friendly pine-furnished *Pensão O Lagar*, Rua da República 120 (☎278 262 712; ❷). *Residencial Globo*, Rua Cidade de Ortês (☎278 248 210, ℗278 248 871; ❷), over the old bridge near the hospital, has better facilities and is good value, while *Residencial Mira-Tua*, at Rua da República 20 (☎278 200 140, ℗278 265 003; ❸), is a decent and well-appointed high-rise. The local **campsite** (☎278 263 177) is 3km north of town on the Bragança road, and has a swimming pool (open to the public June–Sept).

For **meals**, try the ample portions in the restaurant at *Pensão Sá Moreno*, or *O Pomar* on Avenida Dr. Francisco Sá Carneiro (closed Tues). You shouldn't miss trying Mirandela's famed *alheira* **sausages**, a legacy of the Jewish community that has since disappeared. Made primarily from chicken and bread (though pork is now also added), they're cooked quickly and served with rice or potatoes.

On to Bragança: Macedo de Cavaleiros

At Mirandela the Tua valley broadens and the Bragança road veers east along the Rio Azibo, past **MACEDO DE CAVALEIROS**, home of the *solar* of the Marais Sarmento de Vasconcelos family. Unless the shooting and fishing parties at the exclusive *Estalagem do Caçador* on Largo Manuel Pinto de Azevedo (☎278 426 366 or 278 426 381; ❹) are your bag, this is not much of a place to linger. If you want a lunch-stop from driving, or get stranded trying to make a bus connection southeast to Mogadouro, you might sample the delicious

pizzas at the *Pizzeria d'Itália* at Rua Fonte do Paço 5. There are inexpensive **rooms** (with shared bath) at the central *Restaurante Residencial Flórida* (☎278 421 342; ❶), facing the Câmara Municipal on Rua Dr. Francisco Sá Carneiro; more upmarket are *Residencial Nova Churrasqueira*, Rua Pereira Charula 8 (☎278 421 731; ❷), with some en-suite rooms, and *Residencial Muchacha* opposite (☎278 422 658; ❷, breakfast included). You can buy **bus tickets** from the kiosk outside the *Estalagem do Caçador*, and there's a small **turismo** on Praça das Eiras (Mon–Fri variable hours; ☎278 426 034).

Vila Flôr and Carrazeda de Ansiães

Travelling by road between Mirandela and the Douro, the main route (IP2) runs to the southeast of the Tua valley, past **Vila Flôr** and **Carrazeda de Ansiães**. Both are rewarding halts, and are connected by bus to each other, Tua, Mirandela and Torre de Moncorvo.

Vila Flôr

Like so many of the towns in the area, **VILA FLÔR** (Town of Flowers), 24km south of Mirandela, was given its name in the thirteenth century by Dom Dinis who, on his way to meet Isabel of Aragon, was clearly in a romantic frame of mind. His favouritism was short-lived, though, for soon Vila Flôr was forced to contribute a third of its revenue to rebuilding the walls of rival Torre de Moncorvo, 30km to the south. Vila Flôr still has a piece of old wall known as the *Arco Dom Dinis* and a so-called "Roman" fountain.

With its tree-lined squares, attractive location and striking church, the town warrants at least a night's stay, and the eccentric **Museu Municipal de Berta Cabral**, just south of the main square (Mon & Wed–Sun 10am–12.30pm & 2–5.30pm; free), certainly merits a visit. Three eminent Vilaflôrians donated the contents of their houses to the museum when it was founded in 1946, and the result is an incredible hodge-podge: a much-glued stone *porca* and a few dusty pictures by Manuel Moura being the only items of value. The enveloping clutter includes typewriters, the town's first telephone, sewing machines, snake skins, a vicious set of walking sticks doubling as swords and guns, an embalmed Angolan rat, a set of broken percussion instruments, religious sculptures, teacups, stuffed animals and an ensemble of zebra-hide furniture. You'll have to ask the staff to open the rooms downstairs, which are normally kept closed.

An extensive **street market** is held on the weekday closest to the 15th and 28th of every month, and the town **festa** runs from August 22 to 28, with live music and open-air stalls on the last weekend: the main day is the 24th. There's also some activity on the night of São João (June 23–24), but the main event in the region is the **Romaria de Nossa Senhora da Assunção**, which takes place every August 15 to the hilltop sanctuary of Vilas Boas, 8km northwest of Vila Flôr. Held on the site of an apparition of the Virgin in 1673, this is one of the largest *romarias* in Trás-os-Montes, where ten saintly images are carried through the multitude, headed by an image of Nossa Senhora carried on the backs of over a hundred men.

Practicalities

The Carrazeda–Vila Flôr **bus station** is on Avenida Marechal Carmona; there are regular weekday services to Torre de Moncorvo and Mirandela, but weekends are very restricted with no Saturday service and only one or two buses on

Sundays. The town's **turismo** (Mon–Fri only) is opposite the Museu Municipal, but is generally only open for a few hours in the afternoon.

There are two **pensões** at the new, upper end of town, of which *Pensão Campos,* on Avenida Marechal Carmona 43–45 (℡278 516 852; ❷, breakfast included), is the most pleasant, with big rooms, most with bathrooms and TV. The *Casa Roças,* a little further up at Avenida Marechal Carmona 4 (℡278 512 324; ❶), is closer to the bus station, and cheaper too, with some balconied rooms over its café. With your own transport, head for the *Quinta da Veiguinha* (℡278 512 771, ℗278 511 041; ❸), 6km northwest on the Mirandela road at Vilas Boas, close to the Rio Tua and with lovely views over its valley. In addition to the five rooms in the main house, there's also a three-bedroomed self-catering villa (€300 per week) available. A stay here will also give you the chance to sample the owner's home-made bread, cheese and sausages. Vila Flôr's **campsite** (℡278 512 350, ℗278 512 380), 2km to the southeast along the N215 Torre de Moncorvo road, is one of very few in this area, and is right next door to the municipal outdoor swimming pool (free) and a small zoo.

For **meals**, the best bet is the *Pensão Campos,* or *Restaurante Tony* next door; otherwise, you can find sustenance at one of the cafés down by the museum. The local red **wines** from the Adega Cooperativa are regarded as among the best in the country. For **nightlife**, try the modern *Sol da Noite* discotheque (Fri–Sun from 10pm), 1km down the Bragança road.

Carrazeda de Ansiães

CARRAZEDA DE ANSIÃES, 16km southwest of Vila Flôr, is a modern town of little intrinsic interest. However, three and a half kilometres to the south (a taxi should cost around €2.50 each way) are the intriguing ruins of a medieval **walled town**, known as Ansiães. Little remains within the perimeter of walls except rocks and boulders, but two chapels stand outside, the better preserved of which – the twelfth-century **São Salvador** – has a Romanesque portal, extravagantly carved with leaves, animals and human figures. Local myth has it that a tunnel connects Ansiães to another castle beyond the Douro, 12km away; a gaping, fly-ridden hole beneath an impressive slab is the principal piece of supporting evidence. What is undoubtedly true, however, is that the town was a base for five different kings, including the King of Léon and Castile, before Portuguese independence; they're listed by the gateway on a plaque unveiled by Mário Soares in February 1987.

The last inhabitants of old Ansiães left in the mid-eighteenth century. The gradual depopulation resulted from the decision, in 1734, of a gentleman named Francisco de Araújo e Costa, to transfer the official council seat to the new town below (known by then as Carrazeda de Ansiães). In response to local protests he ordered the castle *pelourinho* to be destroyed; with this symbol gone and deprived of a sufficient supply of water, the hill community had no hope of putting up effective resistance. The medieval town went into decline and was soon totally abandoned.

A good time to visit Carrazeda de Ansiães is on January 3 for the *Cantar os Reis* (night-long music and dance in honour of the Three Kings) or, in the summer, for the **Festa de Santa Eufémia** (August 15–16), in which pilgrims stuff themselves with weaned sow and the local wine, the latter famed for its supposed ability to be imbibed in vast quantities without the drinker falling over. If it reneges on its promise, you can always collapse at the *Pensão de Alfredo Pereira* (℡278 617 167; ❶), on Praça Dom Lopo Sampaio.

Chaves

CHAVES stands just 12km from the Spanish border and its name, which means "keys", reflects a strategic history of occupation and ownership. Founded by the Romans in AD78, their name for the town, Aquae Flaviae, comes from a dual reference to the famous spa waters, and Flavio Vespasianus, who was emperor at the time. Between 1128 and 1160 the town was an Islamic enclave, and in the following seven centuries it was fought over in turn by the French, Spanish and Portuguese. One of its greatest overlords, **Nuno Álvares Pereira**, was awarded the "keys" of the north by João I for his valiant service at the battle of Aljubarrota, and from him the town passed into the steady hands of the House of Bragança. However, as recently as 1912, Chaves bore the brunt of a Royalist attack from Spain – two years after Portugal had become a republic.

Today, Chaves is considerably less significant, though it's still a market centre for the villages of the fertile Tâmega plain – the richest agricultural lands in the province – and regional capital for northern Trás-os-Montes. For visitors, its principal attractions are its **spa**, together with its splendid setting, a modest array of monuments, and its gastronomy: Chaves is famed in Portugal for its smoked hams, delicious meat cakes (*bolas de carne*), sausages and a strong red wine. The town centre also boasts a wonderful medieval jumble of streets, many of whose houses support wooden verandahs on their crumbling facades.

Festivals are another feature of Chaves; the town hosts an important winter fair, held on November 1, as well as the annual ten-day **Feira de Artesanato**, held in the Jardim Público in mid-August, and featuring the crafts, music and food of the Alto Tâmega region and neighbouring Spanish Galicia. The **Festas da Cidade** (July 8) coincide with the *Jogos do Eixo Altântico* (July 6–10), a kind of mini-Olympics for northern Portugal and Galicia. The turismo can give details of the **Feira de Velherias**, the antiquities fair that takes place one Saturday a month from May to November.

The Town and spa

The old quarter of Chaves is highly compact, grouped above the river, with the spa just below the old walls to the west. Here, in the centre, the town's military past is still much in evidence. There are two seventeenth-century fortresses, built in the characteristic Vaubanesque style of the north: the **Forte de São Neutel** is closed for visits but occasionally hosts concerts (check with the turismo for details); while the **Forte de São Francisco** has been converted into a luxury hotel (see p.438), worth visiting for a drink or meal to enjoy its beautiful interior and the magnificent views from the ramparts. The **Castelo**, overlooking the spa, has a fourteenth-century keep, the Torre de Menagem, which houses a small **military museum** (Tues–Fri 9am–12.30pm & 2–5.30pm, Sat & Sun 2–5.30pm; €0.50). The highlight of the collection is the battle colours of the infantry regiment that repulsed the Royalist attack from Spain in 1912, but the real attractions of the place are the castle gardens and the views from the battlements, accessed by a back-breakingly tiny door on the top floor of the museum.

The better town museum is the **Museu da Região Flaviense** (Tues–Fri 9am–12.30pm & 2–5.30pm, Sat & Sun 2–5.30pm; €1) on Praça de Camões, a haphazard assortment of material tracing the history of the town and its customs, including quite an assembly of remains from the old Roman spa settlement. The town was an important point on the imperial road from Astorga, in Spanish León, to Braga. In the first century AD it was the army

CHAVES

0   200 m

ACCOMMODATION

Aquae Flaviae	6
Flávia	3
Forte de São Francisco/ Cozinha do Convento	1
Pensão Juventude	5
Restaurante Kátia	4
Quinta de Santa Isabel	7
Trajano	2

RESTAURANTS

Carvalho	F
Casa Costa	H
Dionisyos	E
Adega Faustino	D
Jing-Huá	G
O Lelo	B
Liborio	A
Pote	I
Hotel Trajano	C

headquarters under Aulus Flaviensis, who was responsible for developing the thermal stations here and elsewhere in the region – at Vidago, Carvalhelhos and Pedras Salgadas.

The bathing facilities are no longer open to casual visitors, but you can still drink the waters at the Chaves **spa** (9am–noon & 5–7pm; ☎276 332 445). Built around the *nascente* (spring) near the river below the city walls, the water emerges at a piping 73°C and is not very tasty (loaded as it is with sodium bicarbonate), though the spa is generally full of old ladies with crocheted mug-holders taking a swig. It's reckoned to be particularly good for gout, obesity, rheumatism and senility, although some would argue that, having tasted it once, you'd be mad to want to do so again. Unfortunately, the river itself is polluted, though the gardens are well kept and attractive, and you can take a pedalo ride up and down its banks to view the traces of the Roman past in the form of the **Ponte Trajano** – the Roman bridge – and its ancient milestones. If you feel the urge to swim, the indoor **swimming pool** (daily 2.30–8.30pm; €2) is adjacent to the spa and, though it cannot boast the same health benefits as the spa, it's certainly a better bet than risking the river. The two churches in Praça de Camões are worth a look, too: the **Igreja Matriz**, which is partly Romanesque, and the **Igreja da Misericórdia**, distinguished by vast *azulejo* panels.

The area around Chaves boasts several **Paleolithic and Roman sites**; if you have your own transport, you may want to pick up the *Circuitos Turísticos* pamphlet from the turismo (see below) in which these sites and other possible day trips into the surrounding area are detailed. Alternatively, a number of **outdoor pursuits** are offered by English-speaking guides at *Rotas de Terra* (℡914 876 923, ⓦwww.rotasdeterra.web.pt) including hiking, bird-watching and orienteering.

Practicalities

Rodonorte **buses** for Vila Real and Braga operate from outside their office on Rua da Familia de Camões (℡276 333 491). The Auto-Viação do Tâmega bus station (for Vila Real and Bragança; ℡276 332 352) is five minutes' walk north of the centre around the back of the supermarket next to the old train station; if you're coming into town from here, follow the main road directly ahead, bear left at the roundabout, and you'll emerge near the **turismo** (Mon–Sat 9.30am–12.30pm & 2–6pm, Sun 2–6pm; closed Sun in winter; ℡276 340 661, Ⓕ276 321 419). The regional tourist board – **Região de Turismo do Alto Tâmega e Barroso** – is nearby at Avenida Tenente Valadim 39–1° (℡276 340 660, Ⓔrturismoatb@mail.telepac.pt). **Internet** access is available at *NetPlace* off Largo do Arrabalde and costs €1.25 for half an hour.

Accommodation

Accommodation is plentiful but can be pricey in the summer months, when space is restricted, and intensely cold in winter if you're in an inexpensive, unheated room. At the cheaper end of the budget, *Casa Costa*, on Rua do Tabolado (℡276 323 568) can fix you up with rooms in **private houses** (❶). The nearest **campsite** is *Quinta de Rebentão* in Vila Nova, 5km down the Vila Real road (℡276 322 733).

Hotel Aquae Flaviae Praça do Brasil ℡276 309 000, Ⓔhotelaquaeflaviae@mail.telepac.pt. Adjacent to the spa itself, this is Chaves' largest and ugliest hotel – four-star with pool and tennis courts. ❹
Hospedaria Flávia Trav. Cândido dos Reis 12 ℡276 322 513. Friendly but basic, opposite the *Hotel Trajano*, this has a pleasant, vine-draped courtyard. Same price for single and doubles. ❶

Forte de São Francisco ℡276 333 700, Ⓔwebmaster@forte-s-francisco-hoteis.pt. Chaves' best luxury option has a superb setting in a seventeenth-century fortress with spectacular views. The conversion is a sensitive blend of old and new, with all the trappings you'd expect of a four-star hotel – pool, café, excellent restaurant, and even mini-golf. ❻
Pensão Juventude Rua do Sol 8 ℡276 326 713.

One of many budget options above restaurants along the same street. Clean, although slightly shabby and with bizarrely sloping rooms. OK if you can get over the feeling that you're staying in The House that Jack Built. ❶

Quinta de Santa Isabel Santo Estévão, 7km east of Chaves ☎ & ⓕ 276 351 818. A traditional Trás-os-Montes country house with vineyards, 500m off the

N103 to Bragança. Queen Isabel is said to have slept here the night before she married Dom Dinis. ❸

Hotel Trajano Travessa Cândido dos Reis ☎ 276 301 640, ⓕ 276 327 002. Modern, comfortable and a bit dull, though some of the pleasant rooms have traditional local furniture and good views. There's a renowned restaurant in the basement (see below). ❸

Eating

Some of the *pensões* and hotels have reasonable **restaurants** attached, but wherever you eat you shouldn't have any difficulty finding good Chaves smoked ham, tasty local sausages and fine red wine. The restaurants along Rua do Sol near the river tend to be particularly cheap and serve good hearty portions. Over Christmas, look out for the traditional speciality of **octopus** (*polvo*), brought up dried from the coast, then boiled with potatoes and greens. For coffee and cakes try *Café Geraldes*, at Rua Santo António at the corner with Largo do Arrabaide.

Adega Faustino Trav. Cândido dos Reis. Next to the *Hospedaria Flávia*, this old converted wine cellar, filled with huge wooden barrels, serves great bean salads and a selection of *petiscos*, which you can turn into an inexpensive meal. And, of course, it has terrific wine. There is also an art gallery in one corner.

Carvalho Largo das Caldas ☎ 276 321 727. Some of Portugal's best food is served here, as testified by the numerous awards on the walls. Service is excellent – efficient and unobtrusive – and prices are keen: a meal costs around €12.50. Recommended. Closed Thurs.

Casa Costa Rua do Tabolado. Excellent place serving huge portions of good homely cooking; the speciality is *bacalhau à Costa*. Has a pleasant, vine-covered rear garden.

Cozinha do Convento at the *Forte de São Francisco* hotel. Offers the most elegant setting you'll find in Chaves and serves up a variety of

unusual dishes including wild boar and partridge. Under €17 per head.

Dionisyos Praça do Município 2, opposite the Torre de Menagem. Serves huge portions at reasonable prices (with a cheap *prato do dia*). Try the local speciality, *folar*, an interesting and wholesome pork bread. There are tables outside in summer.

Hotel Trajano Trav. Cândido dos Reis. A very slick operation in the basement and not too expensive; just the place for Chaves ham and local trout. Closes 9.30pm.

Jing-Huá Rua do Tabolado. Reasonable Chinese food for around €9.

Liborio Estrada de Outeiro Seco. A good bet for decent Portuguese dishes, but it means trekking out to near the football stadium.

Pote 1km out on the Bragança road. Serves up generously sized local dishes to an enthusiastic clientele. Closed Mon.

Bars and nightlife

Despite the number of elderly spa-clients in town, there are several trendy **bars** in Chaves. Many of them line the Largo das Caldas, including the *Pórtico Bar*, which plays mainly Latin music until 2am. Local students frequent the cosy *Sá Cristia Bar*, near the Castelo in Rua da Misericórdia, while for a more Stateside experience there's the *Bar Garage* on Travessa Cândido dos Reis, which has bits of cars protruding from the walls. Opposite, the town's only central **nightclub**, *Vanity*, is true to its name, attracting the town's fashion-conscious. *Triunfo*, the main club, is 4km out of town on the road to Valpaços – take a taxi or get a ride with other clubbers from around the Largo dos Caldas at around 10pm.

Routes on from Chaves: Montalegre and Vinhais

Chaves has useful bus connections west to Braga and the Peneda-Gerês national park via **Montalegre** (45km); east to **Vinhais** (65km) and Bragança; and southeast to Mirandela (53km). However, it's worth noting that Saturday services to Bragança are few and far between and that there is no bus at all from Chaves to Mirandela on Saturday. Heading **into Spain**, you could pick up an express bus to Orense, via Verin, on a Thursday or Sunday (originating in Porto, these pass through Chaves in the afternoon; book ahead at Chaves bus station if possible), or else, catch one of the frequent services (marked "Fronteira" – border), and then a Spanish bus on the other side.

West to Montalegre

West of Chaves, **MONTALEGRE** – a 10km detour off the N103 – looms up suddenly, commanding the surrounding plains. Looking at its isolated position on the map, you might expect this frontier town, with a history rooted in past centuries, to be relatively untouched. In fact, there is a fair amount of modern development, caused by the nearby Pisões dam, and it's gradually encroaching on the medieval centre and fourteenth-century **castle** (Tues–Sun 9am–12.30pm & 2–5.30pm; free). However, it makes an enjoyable, atmospheric stopover, especially in winter when snow covers the Serra do Larouco to the north. The town is set in fantastic hiking country, scattered with dolmens and the odd Templar and Romanesque church. For organized walking tours and outdoor activities contact *NaTurBarroso* (☎276 511 337, ✉naturbarroso @hotmail.com).

A ten-minute walk uphill from the **bus station** brings you to the main square, the Praça do Município, and the **turismo** (Tues–Fri 9am–12.30pm & 2–5.30pm, also Sat 9am–12.30pm & 2–5.30pm in summer; ☎276 510 200), which have a map of the district and booklets for sale on archeology (most in Portuguese). There's an office of the Peneda-Gerês National Park (see p.403) at Rua Reigoso 17 (Mon–Fri 9am–12.30pm & 2–5.30pm).

Montalegre has three good **hotels**, all with clean, en-suite rooms with TV. Nearest the bus station on Rua Ponte do Moinho is the modern *Restaurante Hospedaria Girrasol* (☎276 512 715; ❶–❷, breakfast included), with the rooms with shared bathrooms the cheapest. More central are the large *Albergaria Pedreira*, two hundred metres off the Praça at Rua Dom Afonso III 41 (☎276 512 501; ❷, breakfast included), and the friendly *Fidalgo*, uphill from the Praça at Rua da Corujeira 36 (☎276 512 462; ❷), with good views over the valley. The **restaurant** at *Albergaria Pedreira* is excellent; order ahead for its specialities of wild boar, stuffed kid and *cozido à moda de Barroso* – a stew of different meats. Uphill from the *Fidalgo* is the *Restaurante Floresta*, where it's worth paying the higher than usual prices for good food and views. The *Brasilieiro*, on the southwest side of Praça do Município, and the charming *Restaurante Muralha Terra Fria* on Rua Reigoso, are also good bets for an excellent meal.

You might ask at the local bars about *Vinhos dos Mortos* – **Wines of the Dead** – so called because of the practice of maturing the wine in bottles buried underground at the nearby villages of the Serra do Barroso. The practice originated in 1809 when villagers, keen to protect their wine stocks from the invading French hordes, hid their bottles underground, only to find that they tasted considerably better when they dug them up again. Meat-eaters are also in for a treat – the Barroso region is famed for its **smoked meats** (*fumeiros*) and ham (*presunto*), best bought at the shop opposite GALP fuel station, down from Praça do Município, or at the **market** (Mon, Tues & Thurs) below the bus station. Montalegre's annual **Feira do Fumeiro e Presunto** takes place in the fourth week of January.

There's a minor border crossing into Spain north of Montalegre, at Tourém, which is also on the Trilho do Longo Curso (see p.406).

East to Vinhais

The twisting 96km white-knuckle ride from Chaves to Bragança takes in some of the most awe-inspiring scenery in the world. The route passes through broad-leaved forest, pine forest and, at its greatest altitude, rocky moorland, blanketed by yellow gorse and purple heather at certain times of year. Interspersed amongst these are the smallholdings of traditional farmers, with tiny fields still ploughed with the assistance of reluctant donkeys,

Two-thirds of the way along the route is the pleasant village of **VINHAIS**. Its main sight is the Baroque convent of **São Francisco**, a vast building incorporating a pair of churches in its facade. It is situated at the Chaves end of the main street, which runs for 1km or more, and offers staggering views away to the south. A new **turismo** (Mon–Fri 9.30am–12.30pm & 2–6pm; ☎273 770 300, ℱ273 771 108) has opened next door to the bus station on the main street. Chic and well stocked, it can provide you with information about the adjacent Parque Natural de Montesinho, as well as handing out a rather unwieldy map of the village.

Should you get stuck in Vinhais, there are a couple of good **places to stay**: *Pensão Ribeirinha*, Rua Nova 34 (☎273 771 490; ❶–❷), halfway between the main square and the convent, has lovely old en-suite rooms, some with TV and balconies overlooking the valley. More upmarket, and currently a bargain, is the brand-new *Residencial Dom Afonso*, 200 metres west of the *Ribeirinha* on the right (☎273 770 110; ❷). For **food**, *Restaurante Comercial* at the corner of the main street and Rua da Corujeira has a good menu, as does the *Ribeirinha*, and there are several other restaurants as you head out of town on the Chaves road. If hiking hasn't tired you out, there's the weekend *Discoteca do Nordeste*, 1km from the centre on the Chaves road.

If you have the chance, try to visit on Ash Wednesday or the second weekend of February, when Vinhais' *Festa das Fumeiros* takes place, with smoked meats and *presunto* ham galore.

For onward travel, the **bus** office is on the main street, just west of *Restaurante Comercial*. If you have your own transport, you can take the minor road from Vinhais that leads into the Parque Natural de Montesinho (see p.446) – for more information on the park, ask at the Delegação do Parque at the Casa do Povo (Mon–Fri 9am–12.30pm & 2.30–5pm; ☎273 772 416).

Bragança

On a dark hillock above **BRAGANÇA**, the remote capital of Trás-os-Montes, stands a small circle of perfectly preserved medieval walls, rising to a massive keep and castle, and enclosing a white medieval village. Known as the Cidadela, this is one of the most memorable sights in Portugal, seemingly untouched by the centuries, with a hamlet whose size is wonderfully at odds with the royal connotations of the town's dynastic name. The Bragançans were the last line of

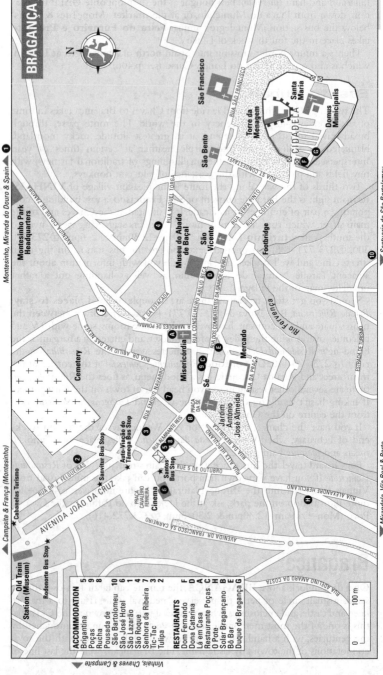

BRAGANÇA

N

Montesinho, Miranda do Douro & Spain

Montesinho Park Headquarters

São Francisco

CIDADELA

Torre da Menagem

Santa Maria

Domus Municipalis

São Bento

São Vicente

Museu do Abade de Baçal

Mercado

Sé

Misericórdia

Jardim António José José Almeida

Cemetery

Auto-Viação do Tâmega Bus Stop

Santos Bus Stop

Cinema

Rodonorte Bus Stop

Old Train Station (Museum)

Campsite & França (Montesinho)

Cabanelas Turismo

Salvitur Bus Stop

Rio Fervença

Footbridge

Santuário de São Bartolomeu

Mirandela, Vila Real & Porto

Vinhais, Chaves & Campsite

RUA SÃO FRANCISCO

RUA ST CONSTÁVEL

RUA SERPA PINTO

RUA T COELHO

RUA MIGUEL TORGA

AVENIDA CIDADE DE ZAMORA

RUA DA ESTACADA

RUA DR. ABÍLIO VAZ DAS NEVES

RUA CONSELHEIRO ABÍLIO BEÇA

RUA DOS COMBATENTES DA GRANDE GUERRA

RUA MARQUES DE POMBAL

RUA EMÍLIO BIEL

RUA ALMIRANTE REIS

RUA DA PRAÇA

PRAÇA DA SÉ

RUA ALFA HUMANA

RUA DA REPÚBLICA

RUA 5 DE OUTUBRO

PRAÇA CAVALEIRO FERREIRA

AVENIDA JOÃO DA CRUZ

AVENIDA DR. FRANCISCO SÁ CARNEIRO

RUA ALEXANDRE HERCULANO

RUA ADELINO AMARO DA COSTA

RUA DR. F. FELGUEIRAS

ESTRADA DE TURISMO

0   100 m

ACCOMMODATION
Brigantina   5
Poças   9
Rucha   8
Pousada de
São Bartolomeu   10
São José Hotel   6
São Lazarão   1
São Roque   4
Senhora da Ribeira 7
Tic-Tac   3
Tulipa   2

RESTAURANTS
Dom Fernando   F
Dona Catarina   D
Lá em Casa   A
Restaurante Poças   C
O Pote   H
Solar Bragançano   B
Bó Bar   E
Duque de Bragança   G

Portuguese monarchs, ruling from 1640, when they replaced the Spaniards, until the fall of the monarchy in 1910. To the British, the name is most readily associated with Catherine, queen to Charles II, who, according to legend, introduced the concept of afternoon tea to Britain. For the Portuguese, however, the town represents the defence of the liberty of the people, because the Bragançans were the first to muster a popular revolt against Junot in 1808, and have always defended their power to make their own decisions.

The citadel, along with an excellent museum, provides the principal reason for a visit to the town. However, for anyone interested in a bit of wilderness hiking, the nearby **Parque Natural de Montesinho** (see p.446) is an additional draw, while the **Festa de Nossa Senhora das Graças** (August 12–22) offers another very good reason to be in town, with lots of cultural events and traditional music. Shortly after, on August 24, there's the religious **Romaria de São Bartolomeu**. Other notable dates include the **Feira das Cantarinhas** (May 2–4), a crafts fair dedicated to the clay water jug (*cantarinha*) which was once used to store the gifts given to a bride on her wedding day; and **Ash Wednesday** (usually February or early March), when people dressed as devils run around whipping penitents – its origins probably lie in an ancient fertility cult, when it was believed that Pan impregnated women simply by smacking them.

The Cidadela

At the heart of the **Cidadela** stands the thirteenth-century council chamber, the **Domus Municipalis**. Very few Romanesque civic buildings have survived, and no other in Europe has this pentagonal form. Its meetings – for solving land disputes and the like – took place on the arcaded first floor; below was a cistern. Ask around for the key at the nearby houses if peering through the keyhole isn't enough for you. Rising to one side, and almost blocking the doorway of the Domus, is the **Igreja de Santa Maria** (daily 10am–noon & 2–5pm), whose interior is distinguished by an eighteenth-century, barrel-vaulted, painted ceiling – a feature of several churches in Bragança.

Facing these buildings is the town keep, the **Torre de Menagem** (Mon–Wed & Fri–Sun 9am–noon & 2–5pm; €1.50, free Sun morning), which the royal family rejected as a residence in favour of their vast estate in the Alentejo. It was one of the first works of restoration by the Society of National Monuments in 1928, and now houses a collection of military odds and ends as well as offering great views from the top. At the side of the keep, a curious **pelourinho** (pillory) rises from the back of a prehistoric granite pig. The town's museum has three more of these crudely sculpted **porcas**, but their most famous representative is to be seen at Murça, halfway between Vila Real and Mirandela. They are thought to have been the fertility idols of a prehistoric cult, and it's easy to understand the beast's prominence in this province of wild boars and chestnut forests, where the staple winter diet is smoked sausage.

To get a sense of the true spirit of the place, it is worth visiting again in the early evening, when the Torre has closed and the crowds are gone. Peace returns and, with only the residents for company, you could almost imagine that you had stepped back in time. Looking out over the furthest walls of the castle you'll see the Parque Natural de Montesinho stretching to Spain. One group who made the most of this isolation were the **Jews**, who escaped over the border in the sixteenth century from the terrors of the Inquisition in Spain. Despite the common rule by Spaniards over the two countries during this period, the Inquisition in Portugal was relatively inefficient – administered in municipalities, the organization spread slowly northwards with ever-decreasing zeal. The Jewish community has left its mark in the names of local families and in the town's cuisine (notably the *alheira* sausage), but the once-thriving synagogue is no more.

You can get a superb **view** of the Cidadela from the bottom of the steps of the church of São Bartolomeu; to get there, follow the signs to the *pousada*, which is next to the church – a half-hour walk from the town centre.

The rest of the town

Modern Bragança, set along the valley below the Cidadela, is a pleasant enough place, despite an eruption of concrete apartment blocks on the outskirts. At the time of writing various areas of the town were being remodelled to ease traffic congestion on access roads. The area around Avenida Dr. Francisco Sá Carneiro and Avenida João da Cruz in particular is likely to be affected by these projects until at least the end of 2003.

From the Cidadela, the narrow, stepped Rua Serpa Pinto leads to the **Igreja de São Vicente**, where Dom Pedro I claimed to have secretly married Inês de Castro (see p.173); while a small diversion east of here, along Rua São Francisco brings you to the **Igreja de São Bento**, the town's finest church – a simple Renaissance structure with three contrasting ceilings.

Continuing into town, along Rua Conselheiro Abílio Beça, you will find the **Museu do Abade de Baçal**, the town's distinguished museum (Tues–Fri 10am–5pm, Sat & Sun 10am–6pm; €1.25, free Sun morning), installed in the eighteenth-century former Bishop's Palace. In its gardens Celtic-inspired medieval tombstones rub shoulders with a menagerie of *porcas*; while, inside, the collection of sacred art and the topographical watercolours of Alberto Souza are the highlights, along with displays of local costumes – especially the dress of the *Pauliteiros* ("stick dancers"), who hail from the area around Bragança and Miranda do Douro. Work is currently underway to expand the museum to include more furniture, paintings and manuscripts. Further down the street is a fine Renaissance-style **Misericórdia** dating from 1873.

One last, incidental sight, which rail buffs will want to check out, is the tiny **transport museum** at the old train station on Avenida João da Cruz. This is closed while the exit road is being completed, but there are plans to improve and expand it whenever it reopens. It features the first steam train operative in northern Portugal, and the royal carriage of Portugal's penultimate king, Dom Carlos, both brought here from Arco de Baúlhe, following the closure of the upper reaches of the Tâmega train line.

Practicalities

Bragança is well connected by public transport with most major towns. The majority of **buses** operate from Avenida João da Cruz, although building work in the area has caused the temporary relocation of their offices to prefabs in a car park west of the centre on Avenida Dom Sancho 1 (where many arriving buses also terminate). Contact details given here are for the offices on Avenida João da Cruz which they are scheduled to reoccupy after the work is completed: Rodonorte (℡273 331 870), for services to Mirandela, Vila Real, and south of Trás-os-Montes, has a kiosk here next to the old train station; and Santos (℡273 326 552), which runs to Miranda do Douro and Mirandela, is based at no. 5 (also agents for Alfandeguense buses to Lisbon). Sanvitur (℡273 331 826) – agents for Rede Expressos services further afield – can also be found on the *avenida*. For onward travel to Vinhais or Chaves, Auto-Viação do

Tâmega has an agent, Cabanelas Turismo, at Rua Guerra de Junqueiro 111 (☎273 323 582). In the event of any problems with contacting the bus companies, check the details with the turismo (see below). For details of travel into the Parque Natural de Montesinho, see p.446, and for **crossing the border** into Spain, see p.446. You can **hire cars** at Nurocar, Rua 5 de Outubro (☎273 331 507). **Taxis** are cheap charging €0.30 per kilometre and are useful for visiting surrounding villages if you don't have your own transport. Try *Linha Azul* (☎273 331 279).

From Avenida João da Cruz it's a short walk south to Praça da Sé, essentially the centre of town. From here it's a couple of hundred metres north to the very helpful **turismo** (May–Sept Mon–Fri 9am–7pm, Sat to 6pm; Oct–April Mon–Fri 9am–12.30pm & 2–5pm; ☎273 381 273, ⊛www.bragancanet.pt/braganca/) on Avenida Cidade de Zamora, a wide boulevard split by gardens. Another 200m down the avenue, in a modern development on the left, is the head office of the **Parque Natural de Montesinho** at Apartamento 90, Lote 5, Bairro Salvador Nunes Teixeira (Mon–Fri 9am–12.30 & 2–5.30pm; also Sat & Sun noon–9pm during summer; ☎273 381 234), who can provide you with information about visiting the park.

Accommodation

Pensões and hotels are scattered around town. The nearest **campsite** (☎273 331 535; April–Sept) is 6km north of town on the França road, and has pretty sparse facilities. Eight kilometres west of town, on the N103 Vinhais road, there's a private campsite, *Cepo Verde* (☎273 999 371; April–Sept), with better facilities, including a pool. A couple of large, **new hotels** are in the pipeline: the huge *Hotel São Lazarão* on the road out to Miranda do Douro is nearing completion and an *Ibis Hotel* is also under development.

Hospedaria Brigantina Rua Almirante Reis, next to the post office ☎273 324 321. The cheapest option in Bragança and quite acceptable, with shared bathrooms. ❶

Residencial Poças Rua Combatentes da Grande Guerra 200 ☎273 331 428. For many years a reliable and cheap city-centre option, though pick your room with care – some are very bare and in winter this place is freezing. Rooms with or without bathroom available. Prices are per person (€10 with shared bath), so very good value for singles. Check in at the restaurant next door. Breakfast included. ❶

Pensão Rucha Rua Almirante Reis 42 ☎273 331 672. More of a family home than a *pensão*, run by an elderly couple and including a hearty breakfast; you'll have to look hard to spot the sign. Some of the eight rooms (with shared bath) are a bit airless, and it can be noisy. Breakfast included. ❷

Pousada de São Bartolomeu Estrada de Turismo ☎273 331 493, ⊛www.pousadas.pt. South of the river, about 1km by road from the centre – follow the signs off Rua Alexandre Herculano. Purpose-built in 1959, it's got wood panelling, cork ceilings, great views and a good restaurant. ❻

Pensão São José Av Dr. Sá Carneiro 11 ☎273 331 578, ℗273 331 242. Box-like concrete structure above the cinema that's popular with visiting businessmen. It's comfortable, well run and most rooms have air conditioning and TV. ❸

Residencial São Roque Rua Miguel Torga 26–27, Zona da Estacada ☎273 381 481, ℗273 326 937. Large modern hotel with well-furnished rooms, attentive service and good views of the citadel from the dining room and upper floors. Breakfast included. ❷

Residencial Senhora da Ribeira Travessa do Hospital ☎273 300 550, ℗273 300 555. On an alley off Rua Almirante Reis, offering comfortable en-suite rooms; opposite a noisy games arcade, so get a room at the back. ❸

Pensão Tic-Tac Rua Emídio Navarro 85 ☎273 331 373, ℗273 331 673. Small and spotless modern rooms with TV and AC set above a reasonable restaurant. Breakfast included. ❷

Residencial Tulipa Rua Dr. Francisco Felgueiras 8–10 ☎273 331 675, ℗273 327 814. Clean, simple but overpriced place near the train station with cramped rooms (with TV). Nevertheless, is highly sought after in summer so arrive early or book ahead. There is also a reasonable restaurant. ❷

Eating, drinking and nightlife

Bragança has a promising array of **bars** and **restaurants**. For the town's rather limited **nightlife**, the places to go are *Bô*, a late-night bar with good music on Rua Combatentes da Grande Guerra, and *Duque de Bragança* (where you might have to ring the bell to get in), a more upmarket but lively place inside the walled town, which sometimes has live music, or magic and poetry evenings and is open until 2am.

Dom Fernando Cidadela 197. Good location just inside the walls of the old town, although the quality of the food and service varies. There's a lively bar downstairs, too.

Dona Catarina Rua Abílio Beça, facing Museu Abade Baçal. One of Bragança's top restaurants, with fine regional dishes at around €15. Also has a *pastelaria* and tea room.

Lá em Casa Rua Marquês de Pombal 7. A convivial place near the Igreja da Misericórdia. Don't be put off by the over-rustic decor. Full meals from €12.50.

Restaurante Poças Rua Combatentes da Grande Guerra 200 ☏ 273 331 428. Excellent and inexpensive food in the restaurant below the *residencial* – family-run and popular enough to fill a couple of floors.

O Pote Rua Alexandre Herculano. Good cheap *tasca*, also does *petiscos* of *chouriço*, ham, cheese, olives, and *bacalhau* fish balls.

Solar Bragançano Praça da Sé 34 ☏ 274 323 875. An upmarket but excellent *casa típica*, where you dine in oak-panelled rooms to the accompaniment of classical music. Unusual specialities include hare (under €10), and partridge cooked with grapes (under €20). There's a nice bar, too.

Crossing to Spain

The easiest way to get to Spain from around here is on the Internorte **express bus**, which runs to Zamora and Valladolid and on to Madrid, on Mondays, Tuesdays, Thursdays and Fridays; you can get tickets from the Rodonorte bus station. Failing that, take a Rodonorte bus to the Portuguese border post at **QUINTANILHA**, 34km away (1–2 daily). At the Spanish frontier village of San Martin del Pedroso, there's a single, combined *pensão* and restaurant, the *Evaristo*, and an early-morning bus to Zamora.

An alternative crossing is to take the road through the Parque Natural de Montesinho (see below), through the border villages of **PORTELO** (Portugal) and Calabor (Spain) to the Spanish town of Puebla de Sanabria, which has onwards bus and train services and accommodation. Using public transport, you can catch Rodonorte buses to Portelo (1–2 daily during school times only) and then irregular Spanish buses (Mon–Fri) between Calabor and Puebla de Sanabria, but you'll have to walk or hitch the 6km between Portelo and Calabor.

The Parque Natural de Montesinho

Occupying the extreme northeastern tip of Portugal, the **Parque Natural de Montesinho** is the only sector of the Terra Fria where the way of life and the appearance of villages have not yet been changed by the new wealth of the emigrant workers. The park has a population of 9000 within its 751 square kilometres, distributed between 92 villages, many of which retain their old Roman or Visigothic names. The Terra Fria's predominantly barren landscape is here disrupted by microclimates which give rise to the Serra de Montesinho's heather-clad hills, wet grass plains and thick forests of oak. Another curious feature of the region is the round *pombal* or pigeon house – a structure which, no matter how well established its position, invariably seems to have dropped in from another world. Today most are deserted, despite efforts

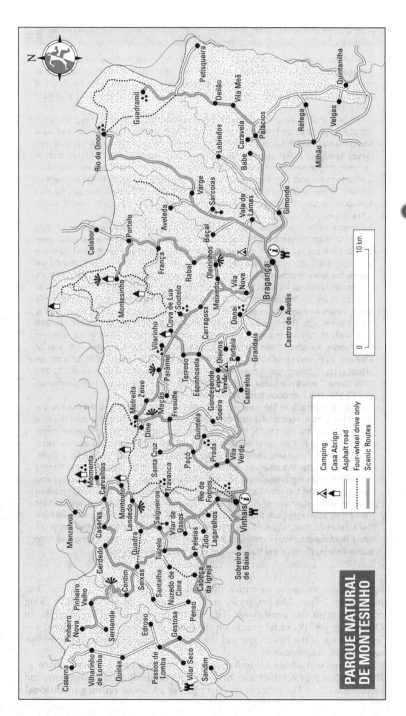

PARQUE NATURAL DE MONTESINHO

0   10 km

Camping
Casa Abrigo
Asphalt road
Four-wheel drive only
Scenic Routes

One of the nicest places to start if you want to do some walking is the village of **França**, 10km north of Bragança and in the heart of the park. The village has a small shop, café and a bar, as well as a pony trekking and mountain bike rental centre, but no accommodation; the nearest official campsite is 6km south on the Bragança road (see p.445).

The best **trail** in the area is a moderately easy two-day walk beginning and ending at França. Start by turning left off the main road, just past a small bar, and walk along the track which follows the Rio Sabor. This track is rarely used by vehicles and winds through a steep gorge, where you can spot many species of birds and, in summer, maybe some wild boar. The track passes a hydroelectric power station and a trout farm (on your left), then after about 4km there's a turning off to the left marked Soutelo. If you have only a short time, take this track and follow it through the picturesque villages of **Soutelo** and **Carragosa**; it will lead you back to França within a few hours.

If you're doing the longer walk, ignore the turning and continue for about 6km along the track towards the isolated reservoir, **Barragem de Serra Serrada**, near the Spanish border. There's a mountain hut for spending the night – just past the reservoir take a right-hand path signposted *Lama Grande*. Alternatively, about 2km before the reservoir, there's a turning off to the left, signposted **MONTESINHO**: it's a worthwhile detour – signs clearly point the way – to see a traditional mountain village. Look out for the inscriptions on the doors of the houses, and the blacksmith's forge, which has been here since the sixteenth century and stopped working only fifteen years ago. There's also a good café here – the *Café Montesinho* (℡273 919 219) – which can do snacks, or meals if given enough notice, and which also has local honey for sale. There are also some nice rooms to rent (some with use of kitchen), all in traditional stone houses (doubles ❸–❹, or around €50 for a house sleeping four), though you'll need to book ahead: contact *Tia Maria Rita* (℡273 919 229), *Dona Constância* (*Casa da Eira*; ℡273 919 227) or the *Casa das Escaleirichas* (℡273 919 248) – or book through the *Café Montesinho*.

To rejoin the track to the reservoir, you can leave Montesinho via the road at the top of the village, next to the bar, and follow any of the narrow paths over the hills until you rejoin the main track; this should take around half an hour. However, many of the smaller paths are quite overgrown and difficult to navigate, so you may find it easier to retrace your steps back to the Montesinho junction and join the track there.

About 2km after the reservoir, the track splits in two; take the right-hand turning for the mountain hut (see above) and the left-hand turning – signposted França and Soutelo – to start the return journey to França. The track leads over a high plateau covered with expanses of heather and rock formations, and giving spectacular views over to Bragança in the distance. Follow the track, descending steadily for a few kilometres, then take a left-hand turning. A couple of kilometres further on, you'll see a right-hand turning – clearly signposted to França – take this turning and after about 4km you'll rejoin the track in França where the walk started.

by the conservationists to entice the birds back. The pigeons, it seems, like many from Trás-os-Montes, prefer an easier existence in the cities than eking out a living in the countryside. The ethnographic museum in Miranda do Douro (see p.451) can fill you in on these and other aspects of traditional village life, such as the black cape and the cloaks of straw – as much a protection against heat as against cold.

For leaflets and advice for walkers, contact the **Montesinho park office** in Bragança (see p.445), which also has brochures on the local flora and fauna and maps for walkers. The office is also the place to ask about **renting traditional**

houses (*casas abrigos*), which are scattered throughout the small villages in the park – prices range from around €50 a night for a studio sleeping two, to €210 for much larger properties. All houses must be booked in advance through the park office and come with a set of rules for their occupancy. **Camping** in the park is prohibited and the only two official sites are located on the southern boundary of the park (see p.445) near **Cepo Verde** and **Vale de Lamas**.

The most useful **bus links from Bragança** are to França/Portelo, due north of Bragança (1–2 Rodonorte buses daily during school times only), and to Rio de Onor, to the northeast (2–3 STUB buses daily; see below). It is not too hard to hitch on the França road in summer, and walking beyond here, alongside the **Rio Sabor**, is idyllic, with wonderful and deserted spots for swimming. **Walking** the 15km to **Rio de Onor** is also an option if you have the energy but, if not, taxis are relatively inexpensive.

Rio de Onor

RIO DE ONOR, right on the Spanish border, 25km north of Bragança, provides perhaps the most fascinating insight into village life in the Serra de Montesinho. There are in fact two Rio de Onors – one in Spain (called Riohonor de Castilla) and one in Portugal – but two stone blocks labelled "E" and "P", and a change from cobbles on the Portuguese side to smooth concrete on the Spanish, are all that delineate the frontier. The villagers have come and gone between the two for generations, intermarrying and buying goods, and operating essentially as an independent state. Both sides spoke, until recently, a hybrid Portuguese–Spanish dialect known as *Rionorês* and even their music is unique, relying heavily on the *gaitero*, a bagpipe-like instrument that shows a distinct Celtic influence (see p.594). Their extreme isolation encouraged the evolution of systems of justice and mutual co-operation that are independent of their respective nations, and were considered so unusual that they inspired an anthropological study in the 1950s. The ageing villagers (most of the youth have left for the cities) share land, flocks, winepresses, mills and ovens, and communal meetings fined troublemakers and miscreants in wine.

The two villages are set on either side of a stream: the granite steps and wooden balconies of rough schist houses line narrow alleyways, and straw creeps out across the cobbles. The bar in the Portuguese "half" of the village contains a long stick on which locals once marked the number of cattle and sheep they owned. Rio de Onor's *Festa dos Reis* – mainly an excuse to feast on *chouriços* – is on January 6. More traditional though is the **Lenha das Almas** ("Firewood of Souls") celebration on November 1, where the boys of the village gather firewood, which is then traditionally hauled into the village by ox carts (though more commonly now by tractors), and auctioned off, the proceeds going to the "souls" of the dead (ie the church). The ritual has its roots in a pre-Roman cult of ancestors, as well as marking the time when boys become adults, and ends with a communal feast and binge on roast chestnuts.

If you want to **stay**, there's the possibility of basic shelter in the *Casa do Povo* (parish rooms) provided you contact the village *presidente* on arrival, but don't count on it. STUB **buses**, fluctuating according to local school and market timetables, connect the village with Bragança: buses currently leave Bragança daily at 5.50pm (plus additional services on Sat at 1.35pm and schooldays at 2pm), returning from Rio de Onor at 7.10am, 2.40pm and 6.50pm (not Sat) – all of which means a day trip by bus is not a realistic option. But you could always **walk** the 13km here from Varge, with its traditional stone houses; the Bragança–Varges bus leaves at 12.33pm daily. The route indicates very clearly how isolated Rio de Onor is – the road has existed for only twenty years, before which time the locals had to walk across open country to and from Bragança. Alternatively, if you don't mind the extra expense in exchange for the convenience, a return trip by taxi costs around €18. Try *Linha Azul* in Bragança (☎273 331 279).

Southeast to Miranda do Douro

From Bragança, the N218 southeast to Miranda do Douro runs across the **Planalto Mirandês**, a breathtaking journey in late February and early March, when the sudden blossoming of the almond trees transforms the countryside. Some say that it was the beauty of this vista – and Miranda do Douro itself – that decided Afonso Henriques, the future first king of Portugal, to turn against his Spanish kinsmen, refortify the border and begin his victorious sweep across Lusitânia at the start of the twelfth century. The route offers the chance for stop-offs in some extremely attractive towns and villages on the way; if you don't have your own transport, you can take one of the Rodonorte or Santos buses that make the trip one to three times daily (although often at inconvenient times).

Seven kilometres out of Bragança is **GIMONDE**, a rural village of traditional wooden houses beautifully sited on the edge of the Montesinho park which would make a fine base should you want to stay somewhere quieter than Bragança. The rivers Onor, Sabor and Igrejas all meet here near a Romanesque bridge, a favourite spot for stork-watching in early summer. There are **rooms** above the *Restaurante 4* (☎273 381 649; ❶), slightly out of town on the Bragança road.

Fifteen kilometres beyond Gimonde, the N218 branches away from the main cross-border road and runs another 10km south to **OUTEIRO**, a once-grand village with a disproportionately huge church, Santo Cristo, built in 1755. Outeiro's erstwhile status as defender of Portugal's eastern tranches is confirmed by the presence of a ruined **castle** on the hill above the village. The small bar on the green by the church contains a sketch of this in its heyday, before it was destroyed in the wars with Spain. The local water hereabouts is believed to cure breathing problems, its miraculous powers supposedly enhanced after a visitation by Nossa Senhora de Fátima on June 11, 1848. The **Festa de São Gonçalo** (January 10) is a Christian version of an ancient bread cult, where an enormous bread "statue" (the *Charolo*) is paraded through town. When it arrives outside the church, the statue is auctioned off, and pieces are then distributed to the crowd by the buyer to the sound of bagpipes.

Between Outeiro and **VIMIOSO**, 22km south, the countryside becomes ever more mountainous and dramatic. The town itself is renowned for its marble and spectacularly set, with some pretty, traditional houses on the steep streets around the Igreja Matriz, though this aside, there's little of interest in Vimioso, much of which is swamped by *emigrante*-financed development. There are two *pensões*: the *Centro* (☎273 512 539, ☎273 512 254; ❶) and, signposted off the main Bragança road, the more upmarket *Charneca* (☎273 512 192; ❶), both with a mix of shared bath and en-suite rooms – but you'd do far better to press on to Miranda do Douro, only another 30km to the southeast.

Miranda do Douro

Facing Spain across the deep rocky gorge of the Douro, **MIRANDA DO DOURO** played a key role in all of the country's wars subsequent to Afonso Henriques' conquest of Lusitânia in the early twelfth century. After valiant service in the Independence, Spanish Succession and Seven Years wars, it ended its fighting days in 1762 when an explosion during a Spanish attack destroyed the castle and the town, and killed 400 inhabitants.

Today, the old town of Miranda seems scarcely more than a village. After the explosion, Miranda remained a neglected outpost for nearly two centuries until the huge Douro dam was built in 1955, breathing some new life into the town. Yet Miranda retains the status of a city, and a sturdy sixteenth-century **Sé** (closed in winter) overlooks its cobbled streets and low white houses. The cathedral and the city status are a throwback to a decision by the Portuguese church authorities to make Miranda the capital of the diocese to counteract the feudal power of the House of Bragança in Trás-os-Montes. At the end of the eighteenth century, however, the see was transferred to the larger of the two towns, turning Miranda cathedral into a rather cumbersome memento of past glory. To the bitter comment "The sacristy is in Bragança, but the cathedral is in Miranda", the astute Bragançans reply, "If ever you go to Miranda, see the cathedral and come home."

The cathedral aside, Miranda has a certain neat charm, despite its modern sprawling outskirts and a rather off-putting rash of frontier tourist shops. The tidied-up ruins of its Episcopal Palace, now a café, and the medieval facades along **Rua da Costanilha** set the tone, and there is a small medieval bridge, too, over the diminutive Rio Fresno. Beyond here you reach an eighteenth-century fountain, the **Fonte dos Canos**.

However, the main focus of interest in town is the **Museu da Terra de Miranda** on Praça Dom João III, just off Rua da Costanilha (Mon & Tues 2–6pm, Wed–Sun 9.30am–12.30pm & 2–6pm; €1.25). Located in a seventeenth-century building which formerly housed the town hall and later the district prison, the museum is literally bursting with curiosities, from pistols to children's balloons made out of sheep's stomachs, and features a couple of reconstructed rooms in traditional Mirandês style – an illustration of local life that's inaccurate only in that the agricultural labourers of the region generally live, sleep and die in a single room. The collection is small but unusual, spoiled only by the shadowy presence of an official who follows you through the displays to make sure that you don't get into mischief.

The turismo has details of **river trips**, or you can contact *Europarques Portugal* (☎273 432 396, ✉info@europarques.com), which offers one or two excursions a day. Trips travel the length of the river that marks the border between Spain and Portugal and run throughout the year with a minimum group size of eight people, or fewer if you are willing to pay the equivalent cost.

If you can, try to time your visit to coincide with one of the local **festa** periods: *Santa Bárbara* on the penultimate weekend of August, is marked by a crafts fair and a special appearance by the **Pauliteiros**, Miranda's famous stick dancers. Local men in traditional outfits dance around clacking wooden sticks together rhythmically, a performance which is today more often seen at large nationwide festivals than in their home town. Also worth catching are *Romaria Nossa Senhora do Nazo* (September 7–8) or the *Festa dos Rapazes* (children's festival) on Christmas eve, held in honour of Santo Estêvão, in which firewood is collected in front of the cathedral and lit after midnight Mass. There's also a **feira** held on the first weekday of every month.

Practicalities

The **turismo**, on Largo do Menino Jesus da Cartolinha (summer Mon–Sat 9am–12.30pm & 2–8pm; winter Mon–Fri 9am–12.30pm & 2–5pm; ☎273 431 132, ⓕ273 431 075), will help with **accommodation**. Marginally the cheapest option is the characterful *Santa Cruz*, in the old town at Rua Abade de Baçal 61 (☎273 431 374, ⓕ273 431 335; ❷), with a family atmosphere and a good restaurant. Other hotels are in the modern part of town, all with self-contained rooms and little to distinguish them, though the ones on Rua do Mercado have views over the reservoir: try *Residencial Morgadinha* at nos. 57–59 (☎273 438 050, ⓕ273 438 051; ❷), *Residencial Flor do Douro* at nos. 7–9 (☎273 431 186; ❷) or *Pensão Vista Bela* at no. 63 (☎273 431 054; ❷). Of a similar standard, but lacking the views, are *Residencial Planalto*, Rua 1° de Maio 25 (☎273 431 362, ⓕ273 432 780; ❷) and *Hotel Turismo*, Rua 1° de Maio 5 (☎273 438 030, ⓕ273 431 335; ❸). The local *pousada*, *Santa Catarina* (☎273 431 005, ⓦwww.pousadas.pt; ❺), is just off Largo Menino Jesus da Cartolinha; its twelve balconied rooms overlook the huge Miranda do Douro reservoir but the *pousada* itself is modern and unexceptional. There's a **campsite**, *Santa Luzia* (☎273 431 273, ⓕ273 431 075; June–Sept), on the southern side of town by the stadium and municipal swimming pools; it's run by the municipality and is free. A small regional office for the Parque Natural do Douro Internacional (Mon–Sun 9am–12.30pm & 2–5.30pm; ☎ & ⓕ273 431 457) is located around the corner just past the Cathedral at Rua do Convento.

In addition to the hotel **restaurants**, good food is available at *O Mirandês* (from €7.50) on Largo do Moagem in the new town, or *Buteko* in the old town at Largo Dom João III, which serves excellent wine and a local *posta à mirandesa* (grilled veal steak) that will feed two or three. The *São Pedro* at Rua Mouzinho de Albuquerque 20 in the old town is also good value, serving excellent *tamboril* and prawn kebabs. For **nightlife**, try the *Taberna Fim do Seclo* just inside the west gate of the old town, or *Bar Atalaia* on Largo do Castelo.

Crossing to Spain

The Spanish border lies just 3km to the west of Miranda, across the **Barragem de Miranda**, at 528m the highest hydroelectric dam in the country and the last before the Portuguese Douro becomes the Spanish Duero. If you have your own transport, this crossing is a good point from which to approach Zamora.

Mogadouro, Torre de Moncorvo and Freixo de Espada à Cinta

For much of its journey southwest from Miranda do Douro to the border with Spain the N221 runs along the western fringes of Portugal's newest and largest nature reserve, the **Parque Natural do Douro Internacional** (see p.456), visible as tantalizing glimpses of water and forested valleys to the east. From **Mogadouro**, almost 50km away, there are onward travel options south to **Freixo de Espada à Cinta** – a good base from which to explore the natural park – or southwest to **Torre de Moncorvo** and Pocinho (see p.337).

Halfway between Miranda and Mogadouro is the pleasant, workaday town of **SENDIM**, where the only real reason to stop off is to sample some great cooking at the *Restaurante Gabriela*. The restaurant is run by Alicia, an award-winning celebrity chef but, sadly, if she's not there, the food can be average and overpriced (around €12). Should you strike lucky, and proceed to eat and drink your fill, you may be glad of the **rooms** at the restaurant (☎273 459 180; ❶), or those around the corner at the *Galego* (☎273 459 202; ❶).

Mogadouro

For an unkempt and authentic picture of town life in the Terra Fria, you need look no further than **MOGADOURO**, specifically its **castle**. This is unexceptional as a monument, but the ground in front is common land where children play and farmers sort out their produce. During the harvest period the area is stacked high with dried *tremoços* bushes, whose seeds are consumed as beer-time snacks and used in soups. The castle hill also commands terrific views over a long, low horizon and a patchwork of fields and *pombais*. The **Câmara Municipal** occupies a former convent, but the square outside is treated by the townspeople as their own backyard, for herding cows home in the evening and playing at tossing coins for hours at a time.

The main tree-lined Avenida Nossa Senhora do Caminho has a sports complex and views over the hills on one side, and a row of shops and cafés on the other. The avenue ends at Praça Duarte Pacheco and the adjacent Largo Trindade Coelho, where **buses** drop you, with the old town and ruined castle beyond. There is a small **turismo** at Largo de Santo Cristo (Mon–Fri 9am–12pm & 2–6pm; ☎279 343 756) which has limited information and even less in English, and the **information office** of the Parque Natural do Douro Internacional at Rua de Santa Marinha (Mon–Sun 9am–12.30pm & 2–5.30pm; ☎279 340 030, ✉pndi@icn.pt) which produces an excellent map for €1 and should be your first point of call if you intend to visit the park.

Should you want **to stay** in Mogadouro, the best hotel is the three-star *Hotel Trindade Coelho* on the Largo (☎279 340 010, ℱ279 340 011; ❸), with a bar and restaurant. Several other places lie just off the square: there are reasonable balconied rooms and a restaurant at *Pensão Russo* (☎279 342 134; ❶), the first of three *pensões* along Rua das Eiras, the continuation of Rua Francisco Antonio Vicente. Other choices include *Residencial A Lareira*, Avenida N.S. do Caminho 58 (☎279 342 363; closed Jan; ❷), with a renowned restaurant (closed Mon); *Residencial Nossa Senhora do Caminho*, nearby at no. 48 (☎279 342 771; ❷); and the modern three-storey *Residencial Estrela do Norte*, Avenida de Espanha 65 (☎279 342 726; ❷). Apart from the hotel **restaurants**, *Restaurante Kalifa* (☎279 342 115), on Rua Santa Marinha, off the Largo, is recommended for its steak and superb red wine. Opposite, and with a second entrance on Rua da República, *Kalifa* **bar** serves as the main evening focus. Local **pastries** can be sampled at *Pastelaria Santa Cruz* on Rua da República.

Be warned that the town is busy (and rooms at a premium) in August, when the emigrants are back home with their families. There is an annual **festa** at this time, in honour of Nossa Senhora do Caminho (August 7–23), with a special *emigrante* weekend on the last weekend of August, before they leave the country again. There's more entertainment in mid-June, with processions, music and exhibitions for the **semana cultural**; the tourist office should have details near the time.

Onward travel

Twenty-five kilometres south of Mogadouro along the N221 is **LAGOAÇA**, a very old village whose houses feature Manueline stone-arched windows, and where some of the older women still wear traditional dress. Pass through the village, beyond the cemetery, and there's a superb viewing platform, looking over the deep Douro valley into Spain. A further 6km along, the road divides: the N221 continues south to Freixo de Espada à Cinta, while the N220 branches off southwest to Torre de Moncorvo. If you're heading to Moncorvo with your own transport, stop off in **CARVIÇAIS** for one of Trás-os-Montes' best restaurants, *O Artur* (T279 939 284; closed Mon), famed for its genuine *alheira* sausages – almost the only place left in Portugal which hasn't succumbed to mixing pork into the stuffing. They also have a few en-suite **rooms** available (❷).

Torre de Moncorvo

Aside from its imposing sixteenth-century Igreja Matriz – the largest church in Trás-os-Montes, taking a century to build – there's little to see in **TORRE DE MONCORVO**, 58km southwest of Mogodouro, though its network of handsome, narrow medieval streets makes the town a pleasant place to spend the night. The **turismo**, hidden away behind the Camâra Municipal on Travessa Campos Monteiro 21 (Mon–Fri 9am–12.30pm & 2–5.30pm; T279 252 265, F279 200 240), has limited information for tourists and functions more as a small museum, being housed in the **Casa da Roda**, a reconstructed dwelling complete with its own underground well. Staff can, however, advise you on how to track down the remains of the old town walls, though more complicated questions may see you directed to the library. The town's main attraction is its almond trees, the blossoming of which draws crowds of Portuguese in late February and early March. Later, the nuts are gathered and sugared, and sold locally; a good place to try is Flormêndoa at Largo Diogo Sá 5–7, by the Igreja Matriz. Local **festivities** include the *Festa de Nossa Senhora da Assunção* (second weekend of August), the *Feira do Ano* (December 23), and the *Feira das Cerejas* (May 10), in honour of Moncorvo's locally produced cherries.

There are three **bus** connections a day from Mogodouro to Moncorvo (as it's known locally), which then continue on to Pocinho, 10km to the southwest, where they meet the trains running along the Douro line (see p.333). Buses also run from Moncorvo to Freixo de Espada à Cinta (see below) and there's a daily connection south to Vila Nova de Foz Côa, in Beira Alta, which continues to Lisbon. Buses to Porto run on Tuesdays and Thursdays. All these buses arrive in and depart from the bus station on Estrada 220, next to the telecom building near the hospital.

Accommodation should be no problem. The cheapest options are the *Residencial Café Popular*, Rua Tomas Ribeiro 66, off the main Praça Francisco Meireles (T279 252 337; ❶), and *Residencial Caçula* (T279 254 218; ❷), on Travessa das Amoreiras beside the Igreja Matriz. More upmarket are the unexciting *Residencial Campos Monteiro*, Rua Visconde de Vila Maior 55 (T& F279 254 055; ❸), and *Residencial Brasília* (T & F279 254 094; ❸), 1km north on the N220, which has the benefit of a swimming pool. *Casa da Avó*, Rua Manuel Seixas 12, a cosy town house built in 1880, has much more charm, with four en-suite rooms and a shaded garden (T279 252 401; ❸; Feb–Nov), while the lovely *Quinta das Aveleiras*, 300 metres from the bus station on the Pocinho road in a large estate (T279 258 280, F279 252 652; ❸), has spacious rooms in two old farmhouses, each with kitchenettes, and bicycles and horses for rent. They also make their own wine.

For **food**, good cheap options include *Restaurante Regional* at Rua do Hospital 16 (around €7.50) and *Café Pizzaria Jardim*, Avenida Enginheiro Duarte Pacheco, in a small garden overlooking a vast and deep valley – the latter also does whole roast chicken with garlic potatoes and salad (€7). Much more expensive is the formal restaurant in *Campos Monteiro*.

Freixo de Espada à Cinta

The southernmost town in Trás-os-Montes, **FREIXO DE ESPADA À CINTA**, is served by four daily buses operated by Santos (℡279 652 188), from Miranda do Douro and Mogadouro. The name is something of a mouthful, translating as "ash-tree of the sword" and supposedly referring to Dom Dinis hacking at a nearby ash tree as he announced the founding of the town. It feels end-of-the-worldish as the bus climbs down to its valley, hidden on each side by wild, dark mountains, a backdrop against which you might glimpse the occasional hawk or black kite. You're unlikely to come across any other travellers on the road; in fact the town was once considered so remote that prisoners who had been granted an amnesty were allowed to settle here – it's this sense of isolation that makes the town worth a visit.

Curiously for such a remote outpost there is a very rich parish church, the **Igreja Matriz** – part Romanesque, part Manueline – with a *retábulo* of paintings by Grão Vasco (see Viseu, p.249). The church is at the heart of the town's **Romaria de Sete Paços**, which takes place at midnight on Good Friday; a sombre cortege of hooded penitents dressed in black with their faces covered proceed from the church and wend their way through the town, chanting. Across the way from the church is a magnificent heptagonal **keep** (Mon–Fri 9am–12.30pm & 2–5.30pm; free), a landmark for miles around, which affords great views from its bell tower for those who brave the very steep steps. Another, unpublicized, attraction is a mansion in Largo do Outeiro that maintains a garden of mulberry bushes complete with worms for silk production; ask around and you may be taken for a look.

The town's small **turismo** (variable hours; ℡279 653 480) is on Avenida do Emigrante. Amongst the ring of dull new buildings surrounding the town are some **places to stay**, such as the modern *Hospedaria Santo António* (℡279 653 104; ❶), a little distance from Avenida 25 de Abril where the bus drops you and facing the Capela de Santo António. The *Cinta de Ouro* (℡279 652 550, ℻279 653 470; ❷), opposite the new municipal market on the way out of town to the south, is very good (if a little bland) with TV and private bathrooms in each room. Its restaurant has an outdoor patio and is the place for **meals**, though you'll find there's a strong Spanish influence in the cooking. For typical Portuguese dishes try the *Bom Retiro*, 100 metres further along, which is also cheaper. There's a **campsite**, *Congida*, just over 4km east on the banks of the Douro (℡279 653 371); follow the signs or take a taxi. The complex also houses the municipal swimming pool, a couple of cafés and a restaurant. There is a **regional office** for the Parque Natural do Douro Internacional at Largo do Outiero (Mon–Sun 9am–12.30 & 2–5.30pm; ℡ & ℻279 658 130) which is worth a visit if you plan to visit the park.

To the south, the N221 follows a beautiful stretch of the Douro to Barca de Alva, 20km southwest (see p.339), but you'll need your own transport as there are no buses along this route.

The Parque Natural do Douro Internacional

Designated in May 1998, the **Parque Natural do Douro Internacional** covers a vast tract of land along the west bank of the Douro as it flows along the Spanish border from Miranda do Douro in the north (p.451) to Barca de Alva (p.339) – the point at which the river officially enters Portuguese territory – as well as a stretch of the Rio Águeda further south in Beira Alta.

The upper Douro is ecologically important because it has a Mediterranean microclimate, in marked contrast to the harsher, mountainous terrain of the Terra Fria which encloses it. The combination of mild winters and its isolation from both large human populations (the mountains saw to that) and the Mediterranean zone proper has led to the survival of a number of animal and plant species now extinct in the south. To the visitor, this quirk of geology is most visible in the region's famous **almond trees**, explained in a legend of a Moorish prince who married a northern European princess. Though happy in summer, she grew sad and wistful in winter, and ached for the snow-clad hills of her homeland. The prince hurried to the Algarve, from where he brought back the almond trees, so that from then on, every February when the trees blossomed, the princess beheld white as far as the eye could see.

Despite some river pollution (mild in comparison with further downstream) and industrial sand extraction on the Spanish side, the area has been left largely untouched by the more damaging aspects of twentieth-century agriculture and industry, and preserves a rich, if endangered, local **flora and fauna**, including rare mammals such as wolves, wild cats and otters, as well as various species of bats and amphibians. The area is also an ornithologist's dream, home to over **170 bird species**, including rare peregrine falcons, black storks and, in summer, Europe's largest concentration of Egyptian vultures.

In common with all natural parks, its success depends on achieving a fine balance between the encouragement of much-needed investment in the agricultural infrastructure on its margins, and the development of ecotourism within the park itself to benefit the local population, which has one of the highest unemployment rates in the country. The main **park office** is in Mogadouro (see p.453), which produces an excellent map (€1) with a brief rundown of the points of interest in the park on the reverse side (in Portuguese). Other park offices are at Miranda do Douro (see p.451), Freixo de Espada à Cinta (see p.455) and Figueira de Castelo Rodrigo (see p.339). For ecological tourism, *Impactus* (℡962 838 261, ⊛www.impactus.com) operates out of Vila Nova de Foz Côa and offers a wide variety of nature walks and activities in the park. If you are slightly more energetic, *Sabor, Douro e Aventura* (℡279 258 270, ⊛www.terravista.pt/nazare/1030/SaborDouroAventura.html), based in Torre de Moncorvo, is an **adventure tour operator**, with activities including rock-climbing and canoeing. **Visiting the park** is a simple matter of choosing one of the towns in the area as a base – Mogadouro being the obvious choice as home of the park headquarters, but Miranda do Douro, Freixo de Espada à Cinta and Barca de Alva are also good – (see the relevant accounts in the text for details of accommodation). You might also consider staying in Vila Nova de Foz Côa (see p.337), which has frequent transport links to towns in the park as well as the added attraction of the Parque Arqueologico do Vale do Côa. Alternatively, **camping** in the park is permitted in designated areas.

Travel details

Trains

Peso da Régua to: Livraçao (for Amarante; 11–13 daily; 1hr 15min); Pocinho (3–4 daily; 1hr 30min); Porto (11–13 daily; 2hr–2hr 30min); Tua (6 daily; 40min); Vila Real (5 daily; 1hr).
Pocinho to: Livraçao (3–4 daily; 2hr 20min–3hr 20min); Peso da Régua (3–4 daily; 1hr 30min); Porto (3–4 daily; 3hr 45min–4hr 45min), via Tua (3–4 daily; 45min).
Tua to: Livraçao (5 daily; 1hr 50min); Mirandela (5 daily; 1hr 50min); Peso da Régua (5 daily; 45min); Pocinho (3–4 daily; 45min); Porto (5 daily; 3hr–4hr).
Vila Real to: Peso da Régua (5 daily; 50min).

Buses

Hours of operation and journey times change frequently. It's advisable to check exact timetables with the turismos or relevant bus companies given in the accounts of each destination.
Bragança to: Braga (3–5 daily; 6hr); Chaves (Mon–Fri & Sun 3 daily, Sat 1 daily; 2hr 10min); Coimbra (2–3 daily; 6hr 50min); Lamego (2–3 daily; 4hr); Lisbon (2–4 daily; 9–10hr); Macedo de Cavaleiros (5 daily; 35–45min); Miranda do Douro (1–3 daily; 1hr 30min–2hr 15min); Mirandela (Mon–Fri 9 daily, Sat & Sun 5–7 daily; 1hr); Mogadouro (Mon–Fri 1 daily; 1hr 40min); Peso da Régua (2–3 daily; 3hr 45min); Porto (2–6 daily; 5hr–5hr 20min); Sendim (Mon–Fri 1 daily; 2hr 10min); Vila Nova de Foz Côa (2 daily; 2hr); Vila Real (Mon–Fri 9 daily, Sat & Sun 5–7 daily; 2hr); Vinhais (2–3 daily; 35min); Viseu (2–4 daily; 5hr 15min).
Chaves to: Braga (Mon–Fri 5–6 daily, Sat & Sun 1 daily; 3hr); Bragança (Mon–Fri & Sun 3 daily, Sat 1 daily; 2hr); Coimbra (4–6 daily; 2hr 40min); Fronteira (3–6 daily; 1hr); Lamego (3–4 daily; 2hr); Lisbon (4–7 daily; 8–10hr); Mirandela (Mon–Fri & Sun 1–2 daily; 2hr); Montalegre (Mon–Fri 5 daily; 1hr 20min); Porto (3–8 daily; 3hr); Vila Real (6–12 daily; 1hr 10min–2hr).
Freixo de Espada à Cinta to: Mogadouro (4 daily; 2–3hr).
Miranda do Douro to: Bragança (1–3 daily; 1hr 30min); Freixo de Espada à Cinta (4 daily; 3hr); Mirandela (1 daily Mon–Fri; 1hr 30min); Mogadouro (3–4 daily; 1hr).
Mirandela to: Bragança (10 daily; 1hr 25min–2hr 45min); Chaves (Mon–Fri & Sun 1–2 daily; 2hr); Miranda (1–2 daily Mon–Fri; 2hr–2hr 30min); Vila Flôr (3 weekly; 40min); Vila Real (Mon–Fri 7 daily, Sat & Sun 3 daily; 1hr 10min).
Mogadouro to: Freixo de Espada à Cinta (4 daily; 2–3hr); Miranda do Douro (2 daily; 50min); Pocinho (3 daily; 1hr 30min); Torre de Moncorvo (3 daily; 1hr).
Montalegre to: Braga (4–6 daily; 2hr 40min); Chaves (Mon–Fri 5 daily; 1hr 20min).
Vila Flôr to: Carrazeda (Mon–Fri 4 daily, Sun 2 daily; 1hr); Mirandela (4 weekly; 40min); Moncorvo (Mon–Fri 2 daily; 1hr); Tua (Mon–Fri 4 daily, Sun 1 daily; 1hr).
Vila Real to: Amarante (Mon–Fri 13 daily, Sat & Sun 8 daily; 1hr 25min); Braga (Mon–Fri 5–8 daily, Sat & Sun 1–3 daily; 2hr); Bragança (Mon–Fri 9–10 daily, Sat & Sun 5–6 daily; 2hr); Chaves (4–8 daily; 1hr 10min); Coimbra (4–6 daily; 3hr 20min); Guimarães (Mon–Fri 5–8 daily, Sat & Sun 1–3 daily; 1hr 30min); Lamego (4–6 daily; 1hr 30min); Lisbon (2–4 daily; 7hr); Mirandela (Mon–Fri 9–10 daily, Sat & Sun 5–6 daily; 1hr); Peso da Régua (7–9 daily; 45min); Porto (Mon–Fri 13 daily, Sat & Sun 8 daily; 1hr 40min); Viseu (4–6 daily; 1hr 45min).

8

Alentejo

ATLANTIC
OCEAN

SPAIN

N

CHAPTER 8

Highlights

✳ **Monsaraz** Stay in the ancient cottages in this fortified hilltop village. See p.476

✳ **Museu do Guy Fino** See Portalegre's finest tapestries – huge reproductions of classical paintings. See p.482

✳ **Dolmen** Enjoy a country walk from Crato, towards Aldeia de Mata, passing the best-preserved dolmen in the country. See p.486

✳ **Castelo de Vide** Charming village with a fascinating old Jewish quarter. See p.487

✳ **Marvão** Watch sunset from this medieval village with stunning valley views. See p.488

✳ **Serpa** Visit the fabulous castle in one of Alentejo's most delightful small towns. See p.495

✳ **Pulo do Lobo waterfall** Picnic alongside Wolf's Leap waterfall. See p.497

✳ **Mértola** The castle ramparts offer a bird's eye view of the kestrels that nest here. See p.498

✳ **Porto Côvo** Enjoy the catch of the day in dishes like *arroz de marisco* or grilled squid. See p.500

Alentejo

The huge, sparsely populated plains of Alentejo are overwhelmingly agricultural, dominated by vast cork plantations – the one crop that is well suited to the low rainfall, sweltering heat and poor soil. This is one of the poorest parts of Europe, much of whose sparse population still derives a living from the huge agricultural estates, known as latifúndios. However, despite the tedium of the interior landscape, there are unexpected surprises throughout the region, from the strong rural traditions still expressed in a variety of local festivals, to the wealth of ornithological interest – Alentejo is home to hundreds of species of birds, from black storks to great bustards, all finely adapted to the mix of varied agriculture and marginal wilderness.

For most visitors, understandably, the region's major draws are its few towns and cities, with the outstanding attraction being historic, and highly atmospheric, **Évora**, whose Roman temple, medieval walls and cathedral – not to mention good transport connections – have put it very much on the tourist map. Elsewhere in **Alto Alentejo** (Upper Alentejo), few towns see more than a handful of visitors in a day. Yet there is much to see and enjoy: the spectacular fortifications of **Elvas**; the hilltop sites of **Monsaraz**, **Évora Monte** and **Marvão**; and the marble towns of **Estremoz**, **Borba** and **Vila Viçosa**, northeast of Évora, where even the humblest homes are made of fine stone from the local quarries, so abundant are they in this otherwise expensive resource. This region is also scattered with **prehistoric remains**, including over a dozen megalithic sites with dolmens, standing stones and stone circles.

South of Évora, the plains of **Baixo Alentejo** (Lower Alentejo), have rather less appeal. The towns can seem rather dull, with the notable exceptions of **Beja** – once an important Moorish stronghold – and **Serpa**, a market town that has been occupied at various times by Celts, Romans, Moors and Spaniards, leaving it with a superb castle as an inheritance. But the Alentejo **coastline** is almost as extensive as the Algarve's and more than compensates for the lack of urban pleasures. Whipped by the Atlantic winds, its **beaches** can seem pretty wild, but in summer at least the sea is warm enough for swimming, and very few of the resorts attract more than weekend crowds. Particularly enticing are the lagoons of **Melides** and **Santo André** – between Setúbal and the industrial port of Sines – and the long beaches further south at **Ilha do Pesseguiero**, **Vila Nova de Milfontes** and **Zambujeira do Mar**. If you want to head straight for these southern resorts, there are express buses in summer from Lisbon. Accommodation is somewhat limited, but there are plenty of campsites strategically positioned along the coast.

Alto Alentejo

Unless you are heading south to the beaches, **Évora** provides the easiest starting point in Alentejo, with frequent and fast buses, or rather slower trains, from Lisbon. From here, you're within striking distance of **Estremoz** and the marble

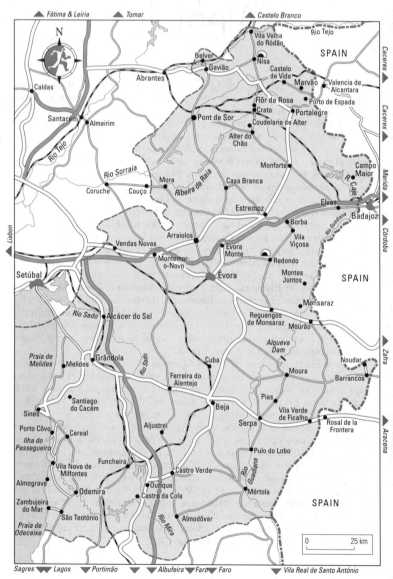

Land reform in Alentejo

The Alentejo's structure of **land ownership** has been in place since Roman times, when the new settlers established massive agricultural estates – *latifúndios* – on which they grew imported crops, such as wheat, barley and olives. Handed down from generation to generation, these estates remained feudal in character, employing large numbers of farm labourers with no stake in the land they worked. In the wake of the 1974 Revolution, much of the land in Alentejo – then a Communist stronghold – was collectivized. However, the workers possessed neither the financial means nor the technical know-how to cope with a succession of poor harvests, and increasingly the original *latifúndio* owners have been clawing back their estates at depressed prices. Jobs today are scarcer than ever, as mechanization has done away with much casual farm labour – a move hastened by European Community grants for modernization programmes and the introduction of new agricultural methods. Only the Beja district, known in Portugal as the reddest region of the country, has a government still controlled by the Communists, who have gradually lost sway in the rest of Alentejo.

towns, beyond which, to the east, lie the superbly preserved walls of **Elvas**, close to the Spanish frontier. The northern part of Alto Alentejo is characterized by more fortified towns – **Portalegre**, **Castelo de Vide** and **Marvão** – the last two, in particular, would make a splendid night's stopover on your way to points further north.

Évora

ÉVORA is one of the most impressive and enjoyable cities in Portugal, its relaxed provincial atmosphere forming a perfect setting for a range of memorable monuments. A Roman temple, Moorish alleys, a circuit of medieval walls, and a rather grand sixteenth-century ensemble of palaces and mansions are all in superb condition, spruced up by a long-term restoration programme and placed under UNESCO protection. Inevitably, they attract a great number of summer tourists but, despite the crowds, the city is far from spoiled. It still plays its part in the agricultural life of the region, with a morning produce market on the second Tuesday of the month; the university, re-established here in the 1970s, adds an independent side to city life.

Évora's big annual event is the **Feira de São João**, a folklore, handicraft, gastronomic and musical festival, whose origins date from pre-Christian times and which takes over the city during the last ten days of June.

Arrival and information

Évora's **train station** is 1km southeast of the centre; if you follow Rua da República, straight ahead, you'll reach **Praça do Giraldo**, the city's main square. CP **buses** to and from Estremoz, Vila Viçosa and Reguengos de Monsaraz use the train station as a depot; others operate from the main **bus terminal** which is about a kilometre out from the walls along the Lisbon road. There are regular green buses running from it to Praça Giraldo. If you're **driving**, you'll have to park in one of the many car parks at the walls and walk in on foot, as the centre is pedestrianized.

The **turismo** on Praça do Giraldo 73 (summer Mon–Fri 9am–7pm, Sat &

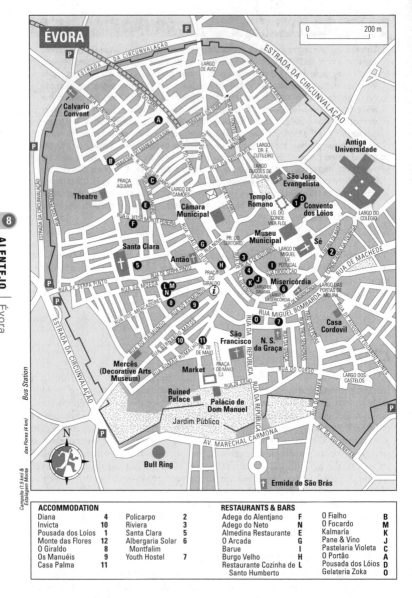

ÉVORA

0   200 m

Calvario Convent

Antiga Universidade

LARGO DE AVIZ

ESTRADA DA CIRCUNVALAÇÃO

Theatre

PRAÇA AGUIAR

São João Evangelista

Templo Romano

Convento dos Lóios

LARGO DO COLÉGIO

Câmara Municipal

Museu Municipal

Sé

Santa Clara

Antão

Misericórdia

RUA DE MACHEDE

Casa Cordovil

Mercês (Decorative Arts Museum)

São Francisco

N. S. da Graça

Market

LARGO DOS CASTELOS

Ruined Palace

Palácio de Dom Manuel

Jardim Público

AV. MARECHAL CARMONA

Bull Ring

Ermida de São Brás

N

Bus Station

Campsite (1.5 km) & Estalagem Monte das Flores (4 km)

ESTRADA DA CIRCUNVALAÇÃO

ACCOMMODATION				RESTAURANTS & BARS			
Diana	4	Policarpo	2	Adega do Alentjano	F	O Fialho	B
Invicta	10	Riviera	3	Adego do Neto	N	O Focardo	M
Pousada dos Loíos	1	Santa Clara	5	Almedina Restaurante	E	Kalmaría	K
Monte das Flores	12	Albergaria Solar	6	O Arcada	G	Pane & Vino	J
O Giraldo	8	Montfalim		Barue	I	Pastelaria Violeta	C
Os Manuéis	9	Youth Hostel	7	Burgo Velho	H	O Portão	A
Casa Palma	11			Restaurante Cozinha de	L	Pousada dos Lóios	D
				Santo Humberto		Gelateria Zoka	O

Sun 9am–12.30pm & 2–5.30pm; winter daily 9am–12.30pm & 2–5.30pm;
☎266 702 671, ℉266 702 950) has maps of the city and province, which
include some excellent walking routes. It can also provide information about
bicycle tours (alternatively contact Turaventur ☎266 743 134,
Ⓔturaventur@mail.telepac.pt), a good way to visit the megalithic sights in the
surroundings (see p.469). The tours cost around €30 per day, and include a

picnic and a knowledgable guide. For the less energetic, there are bus trips to the megaliths for €18 per person; ask at the turismo or call Policarpo (☎266 746 970/1, ⓕ266 746 984) for details.

For **internet** access try the Ciber Cafe, Rua de Serpa Pinto (Mon–Sat 10am–2pm & 5–10pm; €2.50/hr) or Oficina@bar, Rua da Moeda 27 (Mon–Sat 8–2am, Sat 9–2am; €2.50/hr; ☎266 707 312).

Accommodation

Hotel and pensão prices in Évora are higher than in the rest of the Alentejo, and are more or less comparable with Lisbon. In summer you're advised to book at least a day in advance for any of the places listed below; **private rooms** (❷) can be arranged through the turismo. Évora's Orbitur **campsite**, (☎266 705 190, ⓕ266 709 830) is 2km southwest of town on the N380 Alcáçovas road and open all year. If you can't face the 45-minute trudge, you can either catch bus number 5 or take a taxi here which will cost around €2.50. The campsite itself is clean and well equipped, with a restaurant and swimming pool. The **youth hostel** (☎266 744 848, ⓕ266 744 843; ❷) is centrally located at Rua Miguel Bombarda 40 – though, as always, book well in advance.

Residencial Diana Rua Diogo Cão 2 ☎266 702 008, ⓕ266 743 101. Adequate rooms in an atmospheric old house between the Sé and Praça do Giraldo; price includes breakfast. ❷

Pensão Invicta Rua Romão Ramalho 37A ☎266 702 047. Évora's cheapest, with clean but dingy rooms; some have good views over the Igreja de São Francisco. ❷

Pousada dos Lóios Largo do Conde de Vila Flor ☎266 704 051, ⓦwww.pousadas.pt. One of the country's loveliest *pousadas*, housed in the cloistered Convento dos Lóios and with a good open-air restaurant. ❽

Pensão Monte das Flores 2km south of the Orbitur campsite on the N380 ☎266 705 018, ⓕ266 707 564. A guest house in a rural setting offering lots of activities including horse-riding as well as tennis courts, pool plus a decent restaurant. ❹

Pensão O Giraldo Rua dos Mercadores 27 ☎266 705 833. Very pleasant rooms, some with bath; also some overspill rooms available, which are not as nice but much cheaper. ❷

Residencia Os Manuéis Rua do Raimundo 35–1° ☎266 702 861. Decent rooms just west of Praça do Giraldo. ❸

Casa Palma Rua Bernardo Matos 29A ☎266 703 560. First-floor rooms in a scrupulously clean family house stuffed with antiques and assorted china. ❷

Residencial Policarpo Rua Freiria de Baixo 16 ☎266 702 424, ⓕ266 702 424. One of the best places to stay in Évora, this former ducal summer palace has beautiful views, a cosy lounge with a fire in winter, 16th-century *azulejos* and bags of charm; excellent value. ❹

Residencial Riviera Rua 5 de Outubro 49 ☎266 703 304, ⓕ266 700 467. A reasonable if unexciting *pensão* between the Sé and Praça do Giraldo. ❷

Hotel Santa Clara Trav. da Milheira 19 ☎266 704 141, ⓔhotelsantaclara@mail.telelpac.pt. Just east of Santa Clara, this modern hotel is bland but functional; all rooms with bath, TV and air conditioning. ❸

Albergaria Solar Monfalim Largo da Misericórdia 1 ☎266 702 031, ⓕ266 742 367. A restored summer palace formerly belonging to the Dukes of Monfalim – elegant, spacious and relaxed. Breakfasts are taken on the verandah, which has superb views. ❹

The City

Évora was shaped by its **Roman** and **Moorish** occupations: the former is commemorated by a temple, the latter by a characteristic tangle of alleys, rising steeply among the whitewashed houses. Most of the city's other monuments, however, date from the fourteenth to the sixteenth century, when Évora prospered under the patronage of the ruling **House of Avis**. To them are owed the many noble palaces scattered about the city, as are the Jesuit **university**, founded in 1559 by Cardinal Henrique, the future "Cardinal King"; and the wonderful array of Manueline and Renaissance buildings.

That the city's monuments have survived intact is due, in large part, to Évora's decline after the Spanish usurpation of the throne in 1580. Future Portuguese monarchs chose to live nearer Lisbon, and the university was closed down; for the next four hundred years, Évora drifted back into a rural existence as a provincial market centre. Even today, the 50,000-strong population is only half its medieval number.

The Templo Romano and Convento dos Lóios

The graceful **Templo Romano** stands at the very heart of the old city. Dating from the second century AD, it is the best-preserved temple in Portugal, despite its use as an execution-ground during the Inquisition and a slaughterhouse until 1870. The stark remains consist of a small platform supporting fourteen granite columns with Corinthian capitals and a marble entablature. Its popular attribution to Diana is apparently fanciful; Jupiter is the more likely alternative.

Directly opposite the temple, the magnificent fifteenth-century **Convento dos Lóios** has been converted into a top-grade *pousada*. Its cloisters now serve as a dining area in summer, and the hotel staff can be sniffy about allowing in non-residents (or non-diners) to look around. However, dress up as formally as you can – a tie is a help for men – and walk in regardless. The dual horseshoe arches, slender twisted columns and the intricate carvings on the doorway to the chapterhouse are fine examples of the so-called Luso-Moorish style and have been attributed to Francisco de Arruda, architect of Évora's aqueduct and the Belém tower in Lisbon.

To the left of the *pousada* lies the former conventual church, dedicated to **São João Evangelista** (Tues–Sun 9.30am–2.30pm & 2.30–5.30pm; €2.50). This is still the private property of the Ducal Cadaval family, who occupy a wing or two of their adjacent ancestral palace. Just hang around for a few minutes and one of the three guides will let you in to see the floor-to-ceiling *azulejos* within, the masterpiece of one António Oliveira Bernardes and created early in the eighteenth century. Other highlights include a Moorish cistern (the church and convent were built over an old castle), a grisly ossuary containing the bones of the convent's monks, and a magnificent Manueline altar.

The Sé and Museu Municipal

Right in the centre of town, Évora's cathedral, the **Sé** (daily 9am–12.30pm & 2–5pm), was begun in 1186, about twenty years after the reconquest of Évora from the Moors. The Romanesque solidity of its original battlemented towers and roofline contrasts sharply with the pointed Gothic arches of subsequent and less militaristic additions, such as the porch and central window. The interior is more straightforwardly Gothic, although the choir and high altar were remodelled in the eighteenth century by the German, Friedrich Ludwig, architect of the Convent at Mafra. For a nominal fee you can clamber onto a terrace above the west entrance and take an unusually close look at the towers and the *zimbório* (the lantern above the crossing of the transepts). Don't miss the cathedral **museum** (Tues–Sun 9–11.30am & 2–4.30pm; €2), either: it's stuffed with treasures and relics, the prize exhibits being a reliquary studded with 1426 stones and a carved statue of the Madonna, whose midriff opens out to display layered scenes from the Bible.

Immediately adjacent to the Sé is the former archbishop's palace, now the

Museu Municipal (Tues 2.30–5.30pm, Wed–Sun 9.30am–12.30pm & 2.30–5pm; €2), housing important collections of fifteenth- and sixteenth-century Flemish and Portuguese paintings assembled from the city's churches and convents. These provide a good illustration of the significance of Flemish artists in the development of the "Portuguese School", and reflect the strong medieval trade links between the two countries. Frei Carlos, probably the most important Flemish artist known to have worked in Évora, is well represented, but the centrepiece of the museum is a series of thirteen panels – once the cathedral altarpiece – by an anonymous fifteenth-century Flemish artist, portraying scenes from the life of the Virgin.

Up behind the museum, a quick stroll to the north will take you to the beautiful entrance courtyard of the **Antiga Universidade**, with its brazilwood ceiling and *azulejos*, which you wander around at will, although there is a small charge to see the cloister. The university was closed down by the Jesuit-hating Marquês de Pombal during the eighteenth century but since its reopening in the 1970s it is now one of the liveliest corners of the city.

The Igreja de São Francisco and the Capela dos Ossos

Situated on the eastern side of Praça de Maio, the **Igreja de São Francisco** contains perhaps the most memorable monument in Évora – the **Capela dos Ossos** (Chapel of Bones; daily 9am–1pm & 2.30–5.30pm; €1). A timeless and gruesome memorial to the mortality of man, the walls and pillars of this chilling chamber are entirely covered in the bones of more than 5000 monks. During the fifteenth and sixteenth centuries, there were 42 monastic cemeteries in town which took up much-needed space. The Franciscans' neat solution was to move all the remains to one compact, consecrated site. There's a grim humour in the ordered, artfully planned arrangement of skulls, tibias and vertebrae around the vaults, and in the rhyming inscription over the door which reads *Nós ossos que aqui estamos pelos vossos esperamos* (We bones here are waiting for your bones). Such macabre warnings can be encountered in a couple of other locations in Portugal – at Campo Maior, northeast of Évora, and at Faro in the Algarve.

Another interesting feature of this fifteenth-century church is its large **porch**, which combines pointed, rounded and horseshoe arches in a manner typical of Manueline architecture. Appropriately enough, the restored **Palácio de Dom Manuel** – the king who gave his name to the style – lies no more than a minute's walk away, in the Jardim Público. Early sixteenth century, it too incorporates inventive horseshoe arches with strange serrated edges.

The rest of the city

As well as artists and writers such as Gil Vicente and Garcia, great Portuguese and European architects also gravitated to Évora, and the **Ermida de São Brás**, just outside the city walls on the road to the train station, has been identified as an early work by Diogo de Boitaca, pioneer of the flamboyant Manueline style. Its tubular, dunce-capped buttresses and crenellated roofline bear scant resemblance to his masterpieces at Lisbon and Setúbal, but they certainly foreshadow the style's uninhibited originality.

No less bizarre is the mid-sixteenth-century facade of the **Igreja Nossa Senhora da Graça**, out behind the bus station. At each of the corners of its Renaissance pediment, grotesque Atlas-giants support two globes – the emblem of Dom Manuel and his burgeoning overseas empire.

Other buildings worth seeing in Évora include the lavish Neoclassical

Theatre of Garcia de Redende on Praça Aguiar; the **Misericórdia**'s baroque bas-reliefs and *azulejos*, on Largo da Misericórdia; the **Calvario Convent**, built by the Infanta Dona Maria in 1570, at the far end of Rua Candido dos Reis; and the **Church and Convent of Santa Clara**, on Rua Serpa de Pinto, for its beautiful gilded altar. Lastly, it's worth following **Rua do Cano**, north of the old centre, behind the Câmara Municipal. Here, you can travel the course of the medieval **Aqueduto do Água Prata** (Silver Water Aqueduct), into whose arches a row of houses has been incorporated.

Eating and drinking

When the students aren't around, Évora goes to bed pretty early, as if exhausted by the attentions of the tour groups. Finding a place to eat, however, is no problem, with a range of decent **restaurants** to suit most budgets located around the centre; we've listed some of the best below. For **picnic** supplies try the municipal market (Tues–Sun) on Praça 1 de Maio, finishing off your feast with mouth-watering cakes and pastries from Pastelaria Violeta, Rua José Elias Garcia 47, on the corner of Praça Aguiar. For a late-evening **drink** in summer you'll find a couple of outdoor cafés in Praça do Giraldo or, just off the square on Rua João de Deus, there's the cavernous 1930s *O Arcada*, and the very pleasant *Gelateria Zoka* at Rua Miguel Bombarda 10. In term-time, you could try the student circuit which starts at *Barue* – the inexpensive union bar at Rua Diogo Cão 21, or the *Diplomata Pub*, Rua do Apóstola 4, which has live music most weekends. The action continues at Evoras's only **disco**, *Kalmaria*, on Rua de Valdevinos (Mon–Sat until 7am; entrance €2.50 includes two drinks).

Adega do Alentejano Rua Gabriel Vitor do Monte Pereira 21A. Traditional, well-cooked fare served in a delightful old *adega* adorned with giant amphorae. The à la carte menu is a bargain at €10 including wine. Closed Mon.

Almedina Restaurante Trav. de Santa Martha 5 (off Praça Aguiar). In cosy Moorish-style surroundings, this restaurant serves excellent main courses for around €8, including succulent *migas alentejanas* and *bacalhau almedina* (cod fried with marinaded onions).

Burgo Velho Rua de Burgos 10. Serves a comprehensive range of the more common Alentejan dishes for under €6, as well as a tasty shark soup.

Restaurante Cozinha de Santo Humberto Rua da Moeda 39 ☎ 266 704 251. Top-notch establishment highly recommended by locals, on a street which runs downhill from Praça do Giraldo; there's only a small sign. Downstairs, in a converted cellar, you can eat from a fine menu of local dishes for around €20 a head; try the *chispe assado de Santo Humberto* (knuckle of pork). Closed Nov.

O Fialho Trav. das Mascarenhas 16 ☎ 266 703 079. Up a cobbled alley off Praça Aguiar, this is reckoned to be one of the ten best restaurants in Portugal, so reservations are advised. Starters, particularly, are superb, the wine list is good and prices, unsurprisingly, are high. Closed Mon.

O Focardo Rua dos Mercadores 62. Best of a quartet of modestly priced restaurants in this central old city street; good prices and solid quality.

Adego do Neto Rua dos Mercadores 46. No-nonsense Portuguese cooking in intimate surroundings; always busy with locals. A meal with wine will set you back less than €8.

Pane & Vino Patio do Salema (entrance on Rua Diogo Focardo, visible from Rua 5 Outubro). Once the stables of a town house, this restaurant serves up a wide range of Italian dishes – the pizzas are especially good – in a brick-walled, vaulted interior. Very popular with the locals and booking is advised to avoid a long wait.

O Portão Rua do Cano 27. Local haunt next to the aqueduct, popular with students for good, inexpensive food (it does a very decent *porco alentejana*). A full meal with wine will rarely cost more than €8.

Pousada dos Lóios Largo do Conde de Vila Flor. Elegant, upmarket, classic Portuguese dining in the monastery's cloisters. Meals from €20 upwards.

Around Évora

The administrative district of Évora contains over a dozen **megalithic sites** dating from around 3000 BC. The dolmens, standing stones and stone circles found here have their origins in a culture which flourished in the peninsula before spreading north as far as Brittany and Denmark. Two of the most accessible sites lie to the west and northwest of Évora in the Serra de Monfurado, which makes them possible visits in conjunction with the carpet town of **Arraiolos**. An additional attraction in the district, en route to Estremoz from Évora, is Évora Monte, with its superb Renaissance castle.

Os Almendres

One of the sites nearest to Évora is the **stone circle** and three-metre-high **menhir** (upright stone) at a cork plantation called **OS ALMENDRES**. It's located west of the city, about 3km out of Guadalupe, just south of the N114 Évora–Montemor road. Ask for directions in the village and expect a stiff uphill walk through wild country. The legend goes that this stone is the tomb of an enchanted Moorish princess, who appears once a year on the eve of São João and can be seen combing her hair. Those with ornithological interests will have the additional pleasure of seeing the **hoopoes** of the area.

Montemor-o-Novo

Back on the N114, 30km northwest of Évora, lies the white town of **MONTEMOR-O-NOVO**, birthplace of São João de Deus, patron saint of the sick. This large, sleepy town has a dearth of spectacular monuments though it does boast the **castle** (Mon–Sat 10am–5pm; free), where Vasco da Gama finalized his plans for opening up the sea route to India, and a **convent** founded at the end of the fifteenth century by São João de Deus. In the town's main square stands a statue of him carrying an injured beggar in need of care.

The **turismo** is on Largo Calouste Gulbenkian (Mon–Fri 9am–6pm, Sat 9.30am–6pm; ☎266 898 103, @cmmn.tursmo@mail.telepac.pt). There is **internet** access at *Fonte de Letras*, Rua das Flores 10 (Mon–Sat 10am–2pm & 5–10pm; €1.50/hr; ☎266 899 855). **Accommodation** is plentiful if unexciting. Pleasant and inexpensive **rooms** can be found at Rua do Poço do Paço 34 (☎266 892 357; ●); while the pick of the **pensões** include the modern *Residencial Monte Alentejano*, Avenida Gago Coutinho (☎266 899 630, ℗266 899 631) and the rather rundown *Pensão Ribetejo*, Rua do Passo 8 (☎266 892 362; ❷). For **restaurants**, try any of the cluster along the Arraiolos road twenty minutes' walk north of town, or the more upmarket *Residencial Sampaio* restaurant, across the road from the *residencial*.

Twelve kilometres to the south of town are the Neolithic caves of **Escoural**, their weird leathery stalacmites alone worth the visit, and 6km east of the caves, at **São Brissos**, is another dolmen chapel similar to that of São Dinis at Pavia (see below), and just as impressive.

Arraiolos and Pavia

ARRAIOLOS, 22km north of Évora (and connected to it by bus twice a day), is the birthplace of Dom Nuno Álvares Pereira and home of the "noiva de Arraiolos", a legendary bride who took a fortnight to adorn herself only to appear at her wedding in a shepherd's cloak. But the real source of Arraiolos' fame, and fortune, lies with its superb **carpets**, which have been handwoven here since the thirteenth century. Based on elaborate Persian imports, the designs tend to be simpler and more brightly coloured. The most luxuriant eighteenth-century creations hang on the walls of Queluz Palace, near Lisbon (p.139).

There are plenty of carpet shops around town, including *Fracoop Cooperativa* on Praca Lima e Brito 4, reputedly the oldest in town, and *Tapetes de Arraiolos Kalifa*, Rua Alexandre Herculano 34A. The carpets are expensive, but a lot less so than elsewhere. Arraiolos is a typical Alentejo village with its ruined hilltop castle, whitewashed houses and sixteenth-century pillory. The **turismo** on Praça Lima e Brito (daily 9am–12.30pm & 2–5.30pm; ☎266 499 105) can help with **accommodation**. For **food** try the excellent *O Alpendre* restaurant on Bairro Serpa Pinto.

In the hamlet of **PAVIA**, 20km north of Arraiolos along the N370, is a massive **dolmen**, within which the tiny sixteenth-century chapel of São Dinis was built. The effect is a bit grotesque and out of keeping with Pavia's traditional Alentejan architecture, but impressive nonetheless.

Évora Monte

Twenty-nine kilometres northeast of Évora, along the N18, the sixteenth-century **castle** at **ÉVORA MONTE** stands on fortifications going back to Roman times and occupies a spectacular position, atop a steep mound. Its keep is constructed in Italian Renaissance style, with four robust round towers, and is adorned with a simple rope-like relief of Manueline stonework (see p.190). Within are three vaulted chambers, each displaying intricately carved granite capitals. The town – predominantly medieval in appearance – rings the castle mound.

It was here in 1834 that the regent Miguel was finally defeated and the convention signed that put Pedro IV on the Portuguese throne. Legend has it that the signing took so long that there was only stale bread left to eat, causing the invention of the well-known Portuguese dish *açorda* (a soup of bread, water, coriander, garlic and olive oil).

There is a **turismo** on Rua de Santa Maria s/n (daily 10am–2.30pm & 4–7.30pm; ☎268 959 227, ℉268 950 021). If you want to **stay** overnight, try *Monte da Fazenda* (☎268 959 172, ✉montefazendater@mail.telepac.pt; ❹) in a fabulous rural setting on the outskirts of the village, with use of a swimming pool. There are five en-suite rooms and two bungalows which are mostly used for longer lets. For **food**, the *Restaurante A Convento*, at Rua de Santa Maria 26–30, next to the castle, is the town's best bet, with specialities including *bacalhau alentejana*; a full meal costs upwards of €13. There are also a few rooms for let above the restaurant.

Estremoz and the marble towns

Northeast of Évora, quarry trucks and tracks announce your entry into marble country. Around **Estremoz**, 46km from Évora, the area is so rich in marble that it replaces brick or concrete as a building material, giving butchers' stalls and simple cottages the sort of luxurious finish you generally see only in churches and the grandest houses. Estremoz itself, and **Borba** and **Vila Viçosa**, are all distinctive marble towns, and the latter has an additional attraction in its ducal palace – the last residence of the Portuguese monarchy.

Estremoz

ESTREMOZ is the largest and liveliest of the three marble towns, and comes into its own every Saturday when the **market** takes over the Rossio, the main square of the **lower town**. This is a classic marketplace of huge dimensions, surrounded by bars, restaurants and churches, and selling – among other things – what are renowned as some of the best cheeses in Portugal, mainly made from ewe's and goat's milk. Estremoz's annual festival takes place in the Rossio on the first weekend in September, with bull-running, concerts and roll-baking contests. At the start of May it sees a cattle and handicraft fair, including displays of the **earthenware pottery** for which the town has been celebrated since the sixteenth century. The pottery is characterized by simple floral and leaf patterns, sometimes inlaid with marble chips, and is on sale at the weekly market; the most distinctive products are the porous water coolers known as *moringues*, globe-shaped jars with narrow bases, two short spouts and one handle. Although nowadays largely ornamental, the pottery used to play an important role in gypsy weddings: the procession would march into town, whereupon the bride made a sudden dash for freedom across the market place, hotly pursued by the groom. When the groom finally caught up with his bride, a fine Estremoz dish was thrown into the air. The couple were pronounced man and wife at the moment that the dish fell to the ground in pieces.

Arriving by bus, you'll be dropped in the east of town on Avenida 9 de Abril at the old train station. From here, it's a short walk west down Avenida Condessa da Cuba to the Rossio, dominated by the twin-towered marble facade of the eighteenth-century **Câmara Municipal**, which now houses the police station. At no. 62 on the Rossio, the **Museu Rural** (Mon–Sat 10am–12.30pm & 2–5.30pm; €0.50) features a display of earthenware fig-urines from the town potteries, and has an illuminating ethnographic collec-tion of locally produced artefacts in clay, wood, rush, straw, cork, textile and metal. Nearby, to the north of the square at Rua de Serpa Pinto 87, is a **Museu Agricultura** (Mon–Fri 8.30am–12.30pm & 2–4pm, Sat & Sun 2–5pm; €1) with a surprisingly fascinating display of old kitchen equipment.

In its heyday, the population of Estremoz – now around fifteen thousand – was ten times its current size and the town was once one of the most strong-ly fortified in the country. An army garrison is still stationed here, and the inner star-shaped **ramparts** of the **upper town** are well preserved. On the hill within these fortifications stands a white, prison-like building; despite its external austerity, it was once a palace of Dom Dinis, the king famous for his administrative, economic and military reforms. It is now a *pousada* (see p.473), but you're free to wander in and look around; there's a splendid panoramic view from the thirteenth-century **Torre das Três Coroas** (Tower of the Three Crowns), so called because three kings took part in its construction, including Afonso III and Dom Dinis. With its Islamic-style battlements and Gothic balconies, it bears a close resemblance to the great tower of Beja, its exact contemporary. From this part of town the castle of Évora Monte is clearly visible on the horizon, 15km to the southwest. Opposite the tower, in an old almshouse, is a small **Museu Municipal** (May–Sept Tues–Sun 9am–12.30pm & 3–6.30pm; Oct–April Tues–Sun 9am–12.30pm & 2–5.30pm; €1), with more displays of Estremoz pottery and Alentejan life.

Practicalities

The **turismo** (daily 9.30am–12.30pm & 2–6pm; ☎268 333 541, ⓔc.m.estremoz@mail.telepac.pt) is at Largo da República 26. Unless you're

ALENTEJO | Estremoz and the marble towns

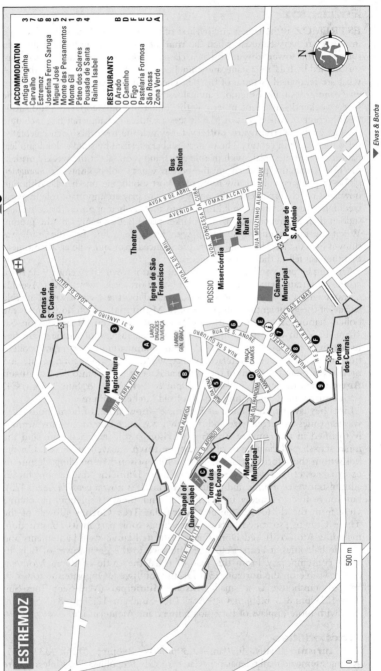

ESTREMOZ

◀ *Évoramonte & Lisbon* ② ▶

▶ *Elvas & Borba* ②

ACCOMMODATION
Antiga Ginginha 3
Carvalho 7
Estremoz 6
Josefina Ferro Saruga 8
Miguel José 5
Monte das Pensamentos 2
Monte Gil 1
Páteo dos Solares 9
Pousada de Santa 4
Rainha Isabel

RESTAURANTS
O Arado B
O Cantinho D
O Figo F
Pastelaria Formosa E
São Rosas C
Zona Verde A

stopping over on Friday night, before the market, **accommodation** should be easy enough to find. For inexpensive **rooms** try *Josefina Ferro Saruga*, Rua Brito Capelo 27A (☎268 332 463; ❷), or *Antiga Ginginha*, Rua 31 Janeiro 4 (☎268 322 643; ❶), run by an energetic elderly *senhora* who rents out her two spare rooms. In the same price range, there's the characterful *Residencial Miguel José*, Travessa da Levada 8 (☎268 322 326; ❸), and the clean but shabby *Residencial Carvalho*, next to the tourist office at Largo da República 27 (☎268 339 370; ❷). Slightly more upmarket but still good value is the *Pensão-Restaurante Estremoz*, at Rossio Marquês de Pombal 14–15 (☎268 322 834; ❷), breakfast included, with a marble staircase and good views over Rossio. Recently opened in a wonderful old manor house, the *Páteo dos Solares* (☎268 338 400; ❻) provides atmosphere at a price. The grandest option in town is the *Pousada de Santa Rainha Isabel* (☎268 332 075, ⓦwww.pousadas.pt; ❻) occupying the lavish thirteenth-century palace of Dom Dinis in the old castle. Lastly, there are a couple of upmarket rural hotels just outside town, both with modern facilities: *Monte das Pensamentos* (☎268 333 166, ⓕ268 332 409; ❹) is an *ANTER* property 4km west of Estremoz on Estrada da Estação do Ameixal; the less expensive *Monte Gil* (☎268 332 996; ❸) is at Fonte Nova, 3km north on the Sousel road.

Estremoz's best **restaurant** is the *São Rosas*, Largo de D. Dinis 11, opposite the castle keep (☎268 333 345; booking advised). Once a medieval inn, now beautifully restored and run by the Cabaço family, this restaurant serves excellently cooked meals and an *ementa turística* at €15; wines, although uniformly good, can be expensive. For good-value budget *ementas turísticas* try the *Café-Restaurante Zona Verde*, Largo Dragões de Olivença 86, or the very basic *O Cantinho*, Rua do Marmelo 2. The *Cervejaria Restaurante O Figo*, Rua da Restauração 36, is worth visiting for its specialities (around €5 a dish), including an excellent *arroz de marisco*, and the *O Arado*, Rua Narciso Ribeiro 7, serves reasonably priced, excellent local dishes. For **picnic** supplies, the place to go is the Saturday-morning market on the Rossio where a wide array of cheeses, spicy sausages and olives are on sale; for **snacks** and pastries, visit the Pastelaria Formosa, just off the Rossio at 16B Largo da República, which sells home-made specialities.

Borba

Eleven kilometres east of Estremoz is **BORBA**, a dazzlingly white little place, where just about anything not whitewashed is made of white marble. The town seems not to have exploited the wider commercial possibilities of its quarries, though, and with the exception of a fine eighteenth-century fountain there are no particular signs of wealth, no extravagant mansions or remarkable churches. All this only serves to make more extraordinary the extensive use of marble in the most commonplace cottages, shops and streets. Borba is an unassuming town with an unusually high concentration of antique shops where one might easily spend an afternoon's browsing. Its other main attributes are the magnificent **wines** produced by the local co-operative, which are receiving increasing plaudits from the rest of Europe; phone the *Adega Cooperativa de Borba* (☎268 894 264, ⓕ268 890 285), who speak little English but some Spanish and French, or contact the **turismo**, located in the town hall on Rua do Convento das Servas (Aug & Sept 10am–1pm & 2–8pm; rest of year 10am–1pm & 2–6pm; ☎268 894 113), to arrange a tour of the winery. For **accommodation** try the *Residencial Inarmos*, just up from the bus stop, at Avenida do Povo 22 (☎268 894 563; ❷), or the spacious *Residencial Vila Borba*,

Rua da Cruz 8 (T & F 268 894 377; ❷) with breakfast included. The *Restaurante Lisboeta* at Rua de Mateus Pais 31 serves a decent *ementa turística* for €9.

Vila Viçosa

The road from Borba to **VILA VIÇOSA**, 6km to the southeast, is lined on either side with enormous marble quarries, and in town everything from the pavements to the toilets in the bus station are made of the local stone. The town is justly famous, too, for its Paço-Ducal, the last palace-residence of the **Bragança dynasty**. The dukes of Bragança were descended from the illegitimate offspring of João I of Avis and established their seat here in the fifteenth century. For the next two centuries they were on the edge of the Portuguese ruling circle but their claims to the throne were overridden in 1580 by Philip II of Spain. Sixty years later, while Spanish attention was diverted by a revolt in Catalonia, Portuguese resentment erupted and massive public pressure forced the reluctant João, eighth Duke of Bragança, to seize the throne; his descendants ruled Portugal until the foundation of the Republic in 1910.

The Paço Ducal and palace square

Despite a choice of sumptuous palaces throughout Portugal – Mafra, Sintra and Queluz are the most renowned – the Bragança kings retained a special affection for their residence at Vila Viçosa, a relatively ordinary country home, constructed in various stages during the sixteenth and seventeenth centuries. Dom Carlos spent his last night here before his assassination on the riverfront in Lisbon in 1908, and it was a favourite haven of his successor, Manuel II, the last king of Portugal.

The **Paço Ducal** (Tues–Sun 9am–1pm & 3–5.30pm; 1hr guided tour; €5, €2.50 extra for the Castelo and coach house) has a simple, rhythmic facade. Entrance is through the Porta do Nó – a stone gateway formed into the knot symbol of the Bragança family. Inside, the standard regal trappings of the more formal chambers are tedious, but the private apartments and mementos of Dom Carlos and his wife Marie-Amélia have a *Hello!* magazine fascination. Faded family photographs hang on the walls, changes of clothing are laid out, and the table is set for dinner: the whole scene seems to await the royals' return. In reality, Dom Duarte, heir to the nonexistent throne, spends his days in experimental eco-farming at his estate near Viseu.

On the south side of the palace square stands the **Convento das Chagas**, used as a mausoleum for the duchesses of Bragança. Their husbands were buried opposite the palace in marble tombs in the chapel of the **Mostéiro dos Agostinhos**, adjacent to one of the most attractive of Vila Viçosa's 22 churches, **Nossa Senhora de Conceição**, worth a visit for its beautiful eighteenth-century *azulejos*.

The old town and castle

The **old town**, still enclosed within walls on its hilltop site, was built by Dom Dinis at the end of the thirteenth century and reinforced four centuries later. Originally the population of Vila Viçosa was based within these walls and a few of the cottages are still lived in. The **Castelo** (Tues–Sun 9am–1pm & 2–5.30pm; 45min guided tour; €2.50), in one corner of the town, was the seat of the Braganças before the construction of their palace. Its interior has been renovated beyond recognition and houses an indifferent archeological museum. However, from the roof there's a good view of the Braganças' old **Tapada**

Real (Royal Hunting Ground), set within its eighteen-kilometre circuit of walls.

Practicalities

Buses park at the elongated Praça da República, from where the old town is straight ahead of you, and the Paço Ducal beyond. Vila Viçosa is a quiet town and despite its attractions there's very little available **accommodation**. Your best bet is to arrange **private rooms** through the **turismo** (daily 9am–12.30pm & 2–4pm; ☎268 881 101, ⓦ www.cm/vila-vicosa.pt) in the town hall on Praça da República. Try those with Maria da Conceição Paixão at Rua Dr. Couto Jardim 7 (☎268 980 169; ❸) just off the square. With more money, your options extend to the anitque-laden seventeenth-century mansion house *Casa dos Peixinhos* (☎268 980 472, ⓕ268 881 348; ❺), 1km out of town (follow the signs for Alandroal), or, at the top of the price range, the *Pousada de D. João IV*, on the south side of Terreiro do Paço (☎268 980 742, ⓦ www.pousadas.pt; ❾), which is converted from a convent dating from 1514. However, when all's said and done, the town's pleasant enough but it is probably better to make a day trip from Évora or Estremoz or to stay in nearby Borba. There are plenty of **restaurants** around the Praça da República and near the football field, the best of which are the *Ouro Branco* at Campo da Restauração 43 and *Os Cucos*, at Mata Municipal, which both serve good regional specialities. **Internet** access is at the post office on Avenida Bento da Jesús Caracas facing the castle (Mon–Sat 9am–12.30pm & 2–4pm; €1.50/hr).

Southeast to Monsaraz

The road **southeast from Vila Viçosa** provides great insights into the rural nature of the Alentejo, taking you past Moorish Alandroal and Terena, both quite prosperous villages set below a castle, before entering a region of scattered farming communities. A couple of buses cover the route daily, with numerous diversions along crumbling back roads.

Reguengos de Monsaraz

One of the better targets is the town of **REGUENGOS DE MONSARAZ** (which is also connected by the dull N256 with Évora, to its west). It's known for its fine local Terras del Rei white and red wines, and you can visit the *adega* just outside town where the wine is bottled: officially you need written permission, but if you just turn up you may find someone willing to take you around. For more information contact the **turismo** (Mon–Fri 9am–12.30pm & 2–5.30pm, Sat & Sun 10am–12.30pm & 2–5.30pm; ☎266 503 315 ext 121, ⓕ266 503140) in the Câmara Municipal on Rua 1° de Maio.

From Reguengos, there are two daily buses 17km further east to the dramatic fortified village of Monsaraz, as well as six daily buses to Évora, leaving from the square off Rua de São Marcos do Campo. Given this, it's unlikely you'd get stranded in Reguengos, but it's not a bad place to spend the night in any case. There are **rooms** at *Pensão Gato* (☎ & ⓕ266 502 353; ❸) on the main Praça da Liberdade, and at the cheaper *Pensão Filhão* (☎266 502 246; ❷), next door, where the rooms are basic but clean. A better bet might be the rooms advertised in the beautiful old house *Casa das Palmeiras* at Praça de Santo António 1 (☎266 502 362; ❷). Good-value **restaurants** include the *Café Central* on Praça da Liberdade and *A Grelha*, on Rua do Covalinho, behind the church

and on the left. The best place to sample the local wine is at the *Adega D'el Rei*
bar opposite the market (up the road by the cinema); it's filled with huge barrels, from which the barman dispenses €0.50 glasses of wine.

Monsaraz

MONSARAZ – known to the locals as "Ninho das Águias" (Eagles' Nest) –
is perched high above the border plains, a tiny village, fortified to the hilt and
entirely contained within its walls. From its heights, the landscape of Alentejo
takes on a magical quality, with absolutely nothing stirring amid a sensational
panorama of sun-baked fields, neatly cultivated and dotted with cork and olive
trees. To the east, you can make out the Rio Guadiana, delineating the frontier
with Spain.

There's something peculiarly satisfying, too, about such a small village. From
the clock tower of the main gateway, the only real street, Rua Direita, leads past
a bar (unmarked, on the left, next to the post office) to the village square. Here
you'll find an unusual eighteenth-century pillory topped by a sphere of the
universe.

The **Torre das Feiticeiras** (Witches' Tower) looms from the castle at the far
end of the village, part of a chain of frontier fortresses continued to the south
at Mourão, Moura and Serpa, and to the north at Alandroal, Elvas and Campo
Maior. When the Moors were ejected in 1167 the village was handed over to
the Knights Templar, and later to their successors, the Order of Christ; their fort
has now been converted into a bullring.

Practicalities

Buses to Reguengos leave at least three times daily, where you can pick a connection to Évora. The **turismo**, on Largo Dom Nuno Álvares (daily
10am–1pm & 2–6pm; ☎266 557 136), can help with **accommodation**.
Alternatively, try the homely rooms, opposite the parish church, at *Casa Pinto*
(☎266 557 388; ❷), or the attractive rooms at *Casa Dom Nuno*, Rua do Castelo
6 (☎266 557 146, ℱ266 557 400; ❸). Both places include breakfast in the
price and fill up quickly in summer; out of season you can probably negotiate
a reduction in the room rate. There's also a rather fancy **hotel**, the *Estalagem de
Monsaraz*, with a pool and restaurant, at Largo São Bartolomeu 6 (☎266 557
112, ℯestmonsaraz@hotmail.com; ❺), in the settlement below the castle walls,
while below the village, heading north towards the tiny village of Barrada,
you'll find *Monte Saraz* (☎266 557 385, ℱ266 557 485; ❹) – a very pretty
cluster of converted farmhouses with a swimming pool and ornamental gardens; advance booking is recommended. The *Lumumba*, on Rua Direita 12, is
the most reasonably priced **restaurant** with a nice patio and good views; a
more upmarket option with even better views is *Restaurant O Alcaide*, at Rua
São Tiago 15, which also caters to vegetarians, on request.

Menhirs around Monsaraz

There are two giant menhirs close to Monsaraz, just off the Reguengos road:
at **Outeiro**, and at **Bulhoa**, where the stone is covered with symbolic engravings. Further menhirs lie at **São Pedro do Corval**, 12km west of Monsaraz
along the Reguengos road, which is known by locals as the Lovers' Rock, and
at **MONTE DO XAREZ**, between Monsaraz and the Guadiana River. This
later one is four metres high, surrounded by a square of standing stones, and
was probably the site of Neolithic fertility rites.

Elvas and around

The hilltop town of **ELVAS**, 40km east of Estremoz, was long one of Portugal's mightiest frontier posts, a response to the Spanish stronghold of Badajoz, just 15km to the east across the Rio Guadiana. Its star-shaped walls and trio of forts are among the most complex and best-preserved military fortifications surviving in Europe. If you make a special detour to see just one Alentejo castle, Elvas is the natural choice; in addition, the town itself is a delight – all steep cobbled streets and mansions.

Elvas was recaptured from the Moors in 1230 and withstood periodic attacks from Spain throughout much of the following three centuries. It succumbed just once, however, to Spanish conquest, when the garrison was betrayed by Spanish bribery in 1580, allowing Philip II to enter and, for a period during the following year, establish his court. The town subsequently made amends during the war over the succession of Philip IV to the Portuguese territories. In 1644, the garrison resisted a nine-day siege by Spanish troops, and in 1658, with its numbers reduced by an epidemic to a mere thousand, saw off a fifteen-thousand-strong Spanish army.

During this period, the fortifications underwent intensive rebuilding and expansion, and they were later pressed into service twice more: in 1801, when the town withstood a Spanish siege during the War of the Oranges, and ten years later, during the Peninsular War, when the fort provided the base from which Wellington advanced to launch his bloody but successful assault on Badajoz. Perhaps out of tradition as much as anything, a military garrison is still stationed in the town.

Elvas's fortnightly event is its **Monday market** – a vibrantly chaotic affair attracting people from miles around, held just outside town behind the aqueduct. Otherwise, the town's big annual bash is its **Festa de São Mateus**, which lasts for six to eight days, starting on September 20, and encompasses a programme of agricultural, cultural and religious events, including the largest procession in southern Portugal. It's well worth coming at this time, although accommodation is at a premium.

Arrival and information

The walls make Elvas a pretty easy place to get your bearings. Arriving by **bus**, you'll find yourself right in the centre of town, in Praça da República; the **turismo** (Mon–Fri 9am–5.30/6pm, Sat & Sun 9am–12.30pm & 2–5.30pm; ℡268 622 236, ℻268 622 191) is next door. Shuttle buses also run from the local **train station**, 4km down the Campo Maior road at Fontaínhas to Praça da República; the station is on the Lisbon–Badajoz line. **Crossing from the Spanish city of Badajoz**, 15km to the east, is in fact easiest by train, with at least two daily services taking fifteen minutes. Buses from and to Badajoz arrive and leave from Praça da República four times daily, but take at least an hour and you'll have to change from a Spanish bus at the border.

There is **internet** access at the post office on Rua de Sao Francisco and at a bookshop, *O Livreiro*, Rua de Ollvença 4 (Mon–Sat 9.30am–3.30pm & 5–7pm; €2.50/hr).

Accommodation

Most of the mid- to upper-range accommodation tends to be situated on the outskirts of Elvas, while in the old town budget rooms abound, of varying

ELVAS

ACCOMMODATION
António Mocisso	4
Casa Coelho/Mocisso	3
Dom Luís	5
Monte de Amoreira	2
Pousada de Santa Luzia	6
Luso-Espanhola	1

RESTAURANTS
A Coluna	D
Canal 7	A
Centro Artístico Elvense	C
Café O Grémio	B
Pousada de Santa Luzia	E

▲ Badajoz (N4)

▲ ② Train Station ▲

◀ Forte da Graça ▲

▶ Forte da Santa Luzia ▼

◀ ① & Portalegre (N246) ▲

▼ Campsite N4

▼ Estremoz N4

▼ Cidade Jardim

0 — 200 m

N

Aqueduto da Amoreira

Jardim Municipal

Portas de São Vicente
Portas da Esquina
Portas de Olivença

Castelo
Pelourinho
Igreja dos Terceiros
Igreja de São Pedro
Igreja de N.S. da Assunção
Igreja de N.S. da Consolação
Chapel of São Lourenço
Igreja de São Domingos
Câmara Municipal
Military Prison
Torre Fernandina
Theatre
Bus Station
Library
Cinema
Market
O Livreiro

Largo de Santa Clara
Praça da República
Largo de S. Domingos

RUA DE OLIVENÇA
RUA ALCAMIM
RUA DA CARREIRA
RUA DOS CHILÕES
RUA DE CADEIA
RUA DE S. FRANCISCO
RUA JOÃO CASQUEIRO
RUA GARCIA DE ORTA
AV.ª 14 DE JANEIRO
AV.ª DE BADAJOZ
AV.ª DA LIBERDADE
AV.ª DO TABOLADO

A B C D

③ ④
① ② ③ ④ ⑤ ⑥
E ⑥

quality; some (listed below) are excellent value. There's also a **campsite**, *Piedade* (May–Sept; ☎268 628 997), on the outskirts of town on the N4 to Estremoz.

António Mocisso Rua Aires Varela 5 ☎268 622 987. Just a couple of simply furnished basic rooms but good value. **②**

Casa Coelho/Mocisso Rua Aires Varela 5 ☎268 622 126. Large, well-appointed rooms in the Moorish quarter, well-signposted from Praça da República; highly recommended. **②**

Hotel Dom Luís Av de Badajoz ☎268 622 756, ⓕ268 620 733. One of several modern hotels situated beyond the old walls on the major Spain-to-Portugal highway. The rooms are good, but the location has little going for it. **③**

Residencial Luso-Espanhola Rua de Melo ☎268 623 092. Functional *residencial* a couple of

kilometres out of town on the N246 towards Portalegre. Mainly has singles but a few doubles as well. **②**

Monte de Amoreira Estrada de Barbacena ☎268 625 912. A small and reasonably priced rural property, 6km northeast of town. **③**

Pousada de Santa Luzia Av de Badajoz ☎268 622 194, ⓦwww.pousadas.pt. The country's first *pousada* (established 1942) but one of the more missable. A modern building, outside the town walls, on the fume-filled N4 – though the rooms are comfortable and it has a good restaurant (see below). **⑥**

The Town

Any exploration of Elvas has to start with its **fortifications**. The earliest stretches of the walls date from the thirteenth century, but most of what you see today is a result of the Wars of Succession with Spain in the seventeenth century. Under the direction of the great French military engineer, Vauban, the old circuit of walls was supplemented by extensive moats and star-shaped ramparts, their bastions jutting out at irregular but carefully judged intervals to maximize the effects of artillery crossfire. Echoes of these designs are to be seen at Estremoz and throughout Portugal. Further chains in the fortifications were provided by the **Forte da Graça**, a couple of kilometres north of Elvas, and the superb star-shaped **Forte de Santa Luzia** (Tues–Sat 10am–1pm 3–7pm; free), a few minutes' walk to the south of the town. The Forte de Graça is still used by the military and visits can only be arranged in advance by contacting the turismo (see below).

The Aqueduto da Amoreira

With its jagged and ungainly course, the **Aqueduto da Amoreira**, at the entrance to the town, looks at first like a bizarre extension of the fortifications. Despite its stark and awkward appearance, it is an imaginative and original feat of engineering: monstrous piles of masonry, distinctive cylindrical buttresses and up to five tiers of arches support a tiny water channel along its 7km course, until it is finally discharged at the fountain in Largo da Misericórdia. It was built between 1498 and 1622 to the Manueline designs of Francisco de Arruda.

The town centre

Arruda was also responsible for the **Igreja de Nossa Senhora da Assunção** (daily except Tues 9.30am–12.30pm & 2.30–7pm; closes at 5.30pm in winter), dominating Praça da República, which was the cathedral until Elvas lost episcopal status in 1882. Alterations in the seventeenth and eighteenth centuries left a ragged hodge-podge of styles, but its original Manueline inspiration remains evident on the south portal and in the unusual painted conical dome above the belfry.

Behind the church lies **Largo de Santa Clara**, a tiny, cobbled square built on a slope around a splendid sixteenth-century **pelourinho**. Criminals were chained from the four metal hooks toward the top but, aside from the grisly technicalities, it's also a work of art, with a typically Manueline twisted column and rope-like decorations. Directly opposite stands the strange and beautiful church of **Nossa Senhora da Consolação** (Tues–Sun 9.30am–12.30pm & 2.30–7pm; closes at 5.30pm in winter). From the outside, it's nothing more than a whitewashed wall with a mediocre Renaissance porch, but the interior reveals a sumptuous octagonal chapel: richly painted columns support a central cupola and virtually all the surfaces are decorated with magnificent seventeenth-century *azulejos*. The chapel was built between 1543 and 1557, on the site of a Knights Templar chapel – providing the inspiration for its octagonal design.

Largo de Santa Clara tapers upwards to a restored tenth-century archway flanked by fortified towers and surmounted by a **loggia**, or gallery. Originally part of the old town walls, this was built by the Moors, who occupied Elvas from the early eighth century until 1226. The street beneath the gateway leads to the **Castelo** (daily 9am–5pm), also constructed by the Moors on an old Roman fortified site, but strengthened by Dom Dinis and João II in the late fifteenth century.

Eating, drinking and nightlife

Elvas has a good selection of **restaurants**, covering all price ranges; those in the old town tend to have the best atmosphere. If you want to put your own **picnic** together, the place to buy supplies is a small, early morning food market held Monday to Saturday at the bottom of Rua dos Chilões.

A Coluna Rua do Cabrito 11. Locally considered one of Elvas's best restaurants, and deservedly so. Housed in whitewashed old stables, it's cavernous but still intimate, and specializes in cod dishes; the *ementa turística* (which invariably includes *bacalhau*) goes for €7.

Canal 7 Rua dos Sapateiros 16, off the main square. The best of the budget places, always popular; €6 for a greasy fill-up.

Centro Artístico Elvense Praça da República, next to the bus station. Reasonably priced café-restaurant with outdoor tables overlooking the praça; the *arroz de marisco* is very good.

Café O Grémio Praça de República. Simple place with outside tables and basic, no-nonsense food.

Pousada de Santa Luzia Av de Badajoz. Not the nicest of settings, but the food is certainly worth the €25 or so it costs to eat here. Serves a range of typical Alentejano dishes such as a delicious *porco alentejana*.

Drinking and nightlife

Elvas is not a late-night town, but if you do want to make a night of it head for cosy *Não Sei* bar at Rua Sa da Bandeira 52a, which is open until 2am and serves great Portuguese tapas. For something more energetic try *Discoteca Luigi*, in the square facing the castle, or *Cidade Jardim*, a complex of four bars and a disco – *Eric's* – a couple of kilometres out of the old town past the Jardim Municipal.

Campo Maior

Eighteen kilometres to the north of Elvas lies the fortress town of **CAMPO MAIOR**. The road from Elvas passes through olive groves and sunflower fields and it's a pleasant enough trip, though the town itself would be unremarkable were it not for the presence of its **Capela dos Ossos** (Mon–Sat 9am–7pm), a diminutive version of the Chapel of Bones in Évora. This stands immediately to the right of the large parish church just off Rua 1º de Maio: ask for the key

△ Pillory, Elvas

in the church or try the door next to the chapel. Adding to the surreal effect, the entrance is through a neat local government office.

The walls and vaults in the claustrophobic chapel interior are completely covered in human bones, while two skeletons hang from the walls, and three rows of skulls are positioned on the window ledge to inspect passers-by. The chapel is dated 1766 and its purpose is indicated by two verses from the Book of Job traced out in collarbones near the window: "My bone cleaveth to my skin and to my flesh, and I am escaped with the skin of my teeth." Job is complaining of his horrific physical and mental suffering, but takes solace in the knowledge that "though after my skin worms destroy this body, yet in my flesh shall I see God".

The chapel may have been "furnished" following the disaster which devastated Campo Maior in 1732, when a gunpowder magazine in the town's castle was struck by lightning, killing 1500 people and destroying 823 houses. Today the castle is little more than a ruin, though with fine views over the borderlands.

Practicalities

The **bus** journey from Elvas takes just 35 minutes, making it an easy side-trip. There's a **turismo** on Rua Major Talaya (Mon–Fri 9am–12.30pm & 2–5.30pm; ☏268 688 936). If you want **to stay**, try *Pensão Ponto Final* on Avenida da Liberdade (☏268 686 564; ❷), near the bridge of the same name, or the more upmarket *Hotel Santa Beatriz*, on Avenida Combatentes da Grande Guerra, off Praça da República (☏268 680 040, ✉hotel.s.beatriz@ mail.telepac.pt; ❻). There's also Parque de Camping Barragal, a **campsite** (☏268 689 493) just a five-minute walk west of the town. For **food**, try *O Ministro*'s affiliated restaurant at Rua 13 de Dezembro 41, or the pleasant *O Faisão* on Rua 1º de Maio opposite the parish church.

Portalegre

PORTALEGRE is the capital, market centre and transport hub of Alto Alentejo. It is an attractive town, crouched at the foot of the Serra de São Mamede where there are good hiking possibilities (see box on p.484), and is endowed with the province's usual contingent of whitewashed and walled old quarters, along with some interesting reminders of its industrial history. These include a cork factory, whose great twin chimneys greet you on the way into town, and the **Fábrica Real de Tapeçarias** on Rua Gomes Fernandes – the town's single surviving tapestry factory and the last remnant of a great textile industry that peaked in the seventeenth and eighteenth centuries. In its studios and weaving hall over five thousand shades of wool are used in the reproduction of centuries-old patterns. At present the factory is not open to the public, however, the new tapestry museum, **Museu do Guy Fino** (daily 9.30am–12.30pm & 2.30–6pm) has a magnificent display of classical tapestries, including paintings. The museum is housed in the eighteenth-century Casa Nobre dos Castelo Branco in Rua da Figueira.

The wealth produced in the town's boom years, in particular from the silk workshops, has a further legacy in the collection of grand mercantile mansions and town houses, which give the town an air of faded affluence. It is especially apparent as you walk up Rua 19 de Junho – the main thoroughfare of the old town – which is lined by a spectacular concentration of late Renaissance

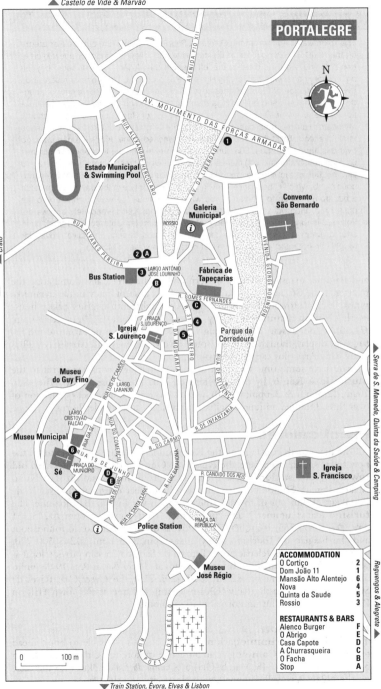

PORTALEGRE

N

▲ Crato

Castelo de Vide & Marvão

AV. MOVIMENTO DAS FORÇAS ARMADAS

AVENIDA PIO XII

RUA ALEXANDRE HERCULANO

AV. DA LIBERDADE

Estado Municipal & Swimming Pool

RUA ÁLVARES PEREIRA

ROSSIO

Galeria Municipal
i

Convento São Bernardo

AVENIDA GEORGE ROBINSON

2 A

3 LARGO ANTÓNIO JOSÉ LOURINHO

Bus Station
B

Fábrica de Tapeçarias

R. GOMES FERNANDES
C

PRAÇA S. LOURENÇO

Igreja S. Lourenço

RUA 31 DE JANEIRO

DA MOURARIA

4

5

Parque da Corredoura

RUA DE OLIVENÇA

Museu do Guy Fino

RUA LUÍS DE CAMÕES

LARGO LARANJO

R. DE INFANTARIA

LARGO CRISTOVÃO FALCÃO

RUA DA SÉ

RUA DO COMÉRCIO

R. DO CARMO

Museu Municipal

6

RUA 19 DE JUNHO

RUA LUIZ BARAHONA

Igreja S. Francisco

Sé

PRAÇA DO MUNICÍPIO

D
RUA DE ELVAS
E

R. CANDIDO DOS REIS

F
RUA DA SANTA CLARA

i

Police Station

PRAÇA DA REPÚBLICA

Museu José Régio

RUA POETA JOSÉ RÉGIO

ALENTEJO | Portalegre

8

▶ Serra de S. Mamede, Quinta da Saúde & Camping

Reguengos & Alegrete ▶

ACCOMMODATION	
O Cortiço	2
Dom João 11	1
Mansão Alto Alentejo	6
Nova	4
Quinta da Saúde	5
Rossio	3

RESTAURANTS & BARS	
Alenco Burger	F
O Abrigo	E
Casa Capote	D
A Churrasqueira	C
O Facha	B
Stop	A

0 ___ 100 m

483

Hiking into the Serra de São Mamede: from Portalegre to Marvão

The 16km walk begins from the *Quinta da Saúde* campsite, 3km outside **Portalegre** on the N246-2. Turn right out of the campsite and follow the road for a few kilometres until you see a signpost to the left marked São Julião. Turn left here, then left again shortly afterwards, following signs to Porto Espada. You'll pass a reservoir on the left-hand side of the road after about 3 or 4km; you'll also see plenty of abandoned farmhouses and buildings, a result of the flooding caused by the construction of the reservoir. On reaching the small village of **Rasa**, turn right, then shortly afterwards, as the road bends sharply to the left, take the dirt track that leads straight ahead. This track emerges at a whitewashed stone bridge – turn right to go over this, then after about 50m turn left. Continue along here for about five minutes until you reach a main road; there are several cafés and restaurants here, where you can rest before tackling the long slog uphill to Marvão. If you're not up to the strenuous climb, which is best done early in the morning or late in the day, you can catch a bus from here up to Marvão. If you want to continue the walk, turn left onto the main road, then right straight after the bridge and right immediately afterwards. Follow this road for a few hundred metres, then turn left up a cobbled track soon after a group of houses. Follow the track upwards through the olive groves for roughly an hour and you will arrive just outside the walls of Marvão.

and Baroque mansions. At the western end of the street, and dominating the quarter, is the **Sé**, an austere building save for a flash of fancy in the pyramidal pinnacles of its towers. To one side of this an eighteenth-century palace houses the **Museu Municipal** (daily except Tues 10am–12.30pm & 2–6pm; €1.50). It's not exactly a compelling visit, with much routine furniture and fittings on display, though there are some lovely ceramics and ivories as well as some early Arraiolos carpets (see p.469).

If you have some time to kill in town, you may also consider a visit to the **Museu José Régio**, by the cemetery on Rua Poeta José Régio (Tues–Sun 10am–12.30pm & 2–6pm; €1.50), where you can see the poet's collection of over three hundred antique crucifixes, altarpieces and powder horns.

Practicalities

All the main roads converge on the **Rossio**, a large square at the centre of the new town. Uphill from here, the Rua 5º de Outubro runs into the walled **old town**. The **bus station** is just a few blocks from the Rossio on Rua Nuno Álvarez Pereira. Shuttle buses to and from here meet **trains** at the Estação de Portalegre, 10km out of town to the south, on the Lisbon–Badajoz line. The **turismo** (daily: summer 10am–7pm; winter 10am–1pm & 3–6pm; ☎245 331 359, ℱ245 330 235) is in the Palácio Póvoas on the main Rossio roundabout and the Região de Tourismo (daily 10am–2pm & 3–6pm; ☎245 300 770, ℰrt.s.mamede@mail.telepac.pt), at Estrada de Santana 25, can provide local as well as regional information. **Internet** access at *Alenco Bar*, at Rua 19 de Junho 38 (daily 10am–midnight; €2/hr; ☎245 205 715), the *Cyber Cafe*, Rives de Sousa, behind the castle (daily 9.30am–10pm) and free at the Town Hall on Plaça da República during normal working hours.

Accommodation

There is limited **accommodation** available, and it's advisable to book ahead to be sure of a bed. **Camping** is an attractive option; the Orbitur site (☎245 331 736, ℱ245 202 848; March–Oct) at *Quinta da Saúde*, 3km into the hills, on the N246-2, is well equipped, with electricity and showers.

O Cortiço Rua Dom Nuno Álvares Pereira 17 ☎245 202 176. Has a few reasonable rooms upstairs. You can usually find the owner in the bar downstairs. ❸
Hotel Dom João III Av da Liberdade ☎245 330 192, ⓕ245 330 444. A dull, overpriced hotel, opposite the Jardim Municipal in the new town. ❸
Mansâo Alto Alentejo Rua 19 de Junho 59 ☎245 202 290, ⓔmansaoaltoalentejo@netc.pt. A pleasant hotel in a traditional building tucked down a side street in the old town. ❸
Pensão Nova Rua 31 de Janeiro 28–30 ☎245 331 212, ⓕ245 330 493. Friendly hostel, with the

same management as the nearby *Pensão São Pedro*, at Rua da Mouraria 14 ☎245 331 212. Both ❷
Quinta da Saúde Estrada de São Mamede, 3km out of Portalegre next to the campsite ☎245 202 324, ⓕ245 207 234. An attractive property with a great view over the surrounding hills and a good rooftop restuarant. ❸
Residencial Rossio Rua Dom Nuno Álvares Pereira 10, next to the bus station ☎245 201 975. The budget rooms on offer, some windowless, are somewhat small and stuffy but adequate for a night. ❶

Eating and drinking

By day the Rossio is the liveliest place for a drink, but in the evening the action, such as it is, switches to the old town; try the *Café Central* on Largo Frederico Laranjo or the *Cervejaria Lusitania*, close by at Rua Luís de Camões 43.

Cervejaria O Abrigo Rua de Elvas 74. Serves inexpensive Alentejan dishes; the *ementa turística* costs around €7.50.
Café-Bar-Restaurante Alenco Burger Rua 19 de Julho 38. 24-hour fast-food restaurant which serves inexpensive fried food and offers internet access for €1/hr.
Casa Capote Rua 19 de Junho 56. Friendly restaurant whose walls are hung with tapestries and paintings; a reasonable full meal will set you back around €10.
Cervejaria A Churrasqueira Rua Guilherme

Gomes Fernandes 29, just off the Rossio. The cheapest option in town serves an excellent set menu for €5, with most main dishes between €7.50 and €10.
Residencial O Facha Largo António José Lourinho 3–5. Wide choice of expensive dishes (more international than regional) served in glorious glass and brass Art Deco surroundings.
Restaurante Stop 11–15 Rua Dom Nuno Álvares Pereira. One of the better options, just off the Rossio, serving typical Alentejan cuisine in pleasant surroundings; a slap-up meal will cost under €10.

Crato, Flôr da Rosa and Alter do Chão

Directly to the west of Portalegre, **Crato** has small-town charms and, nearby, an impressive **dolmen**, as well as the beautiful honey-stone convent of **Flôr da Rosa**. Horse enthusiasts may also want to make the 13km detour south of Crato to **Alter do Chão**, home of a prestigious *coudelaria* (stud farm).

Buses run intermittently from Portalegre to both Crato and Alter do Chão, while the **Estação de Crato** gives access to the Lisbon–Badajoz train line, with connections west to Abrantes and east to Elvas.

Crato

CRATO – 21km west of Portalegre – is an ancient agricultural town which has clearly seen better days and larger populations. A trio of imposing, ornate churches and the elegant **Varanda do Grão Prior** in the main square attest, like Portalegre's monuments, to the textile boom years of the sixteenth century. The *varanda* is the most interesting of the structures – built for the outdoor celebration of Mass. Also worth a look is a town mansion a couple of streets away, by the public gardens, which houses a small **museum** (erratic hours) of Alto Alentejo handicrafts and domestic traditions. Well into the last century, alms were handed out to the local poor from a balcony-chapel upstairs.

The town **castle** was once among the mightiest in the Alentejo, but today it's a pastoral ruin, overrun by farm animals, fig trees and oregano plants. It is normally locked, but keys are generally kept beneath an abandoned blue cart in the field in front; if they're not there, ask at one of the nearby farm dwellings. From the ramparts, there is a splendid view over the town and across the countless rows of olive trees to the hills of Portalegre.

For a good rural walk from Crato, follow the N363 northwest towards Aldeia da Mata. On the left-hand side of the road, about 5km from town, is what is reckoned to be the best-preserved **dolmen** in Portugal. On the corner of the road leading out of town, you'll find an excellent **adega**, with delicious home-cooking and a crowded bar where everyone plays *belho* – a kind of miniature version of *boules*.

The town has no accommodation of any kind, so you'll need to plan a day trip from one of the surrounding towns or villages. If you arrive at the train station, 3km south of town, the station master will telephone for a taxi, which is not expensive.

Flôr da Rosa

Two kilometres north of Crato lies the village of **FLÔR DA ROSA**, traditionally a centre for **pottery**, with as many as seventy families engaged in the trade in the early part of this century. Today the distinctive *olaria* of the region is made in only two workshops, whose shared kiln is near the convent, high above the broad streets and low houses. Their methods of manufacture haven't changed in centuries, though the clay – yellow for waterproofing, grey for ovenware – has to be sought further and further afield. Purchases break easily, but it's nice to know that these functional (and inexpensive) pieces aren't designed for the tourist trade.

The **Convento de Flôr da Rosa**, founded in the fourteenth century and much endowed over the next two hundred years, was abandoned in 1897, due to leaking roofs and a decaying structure. After extensive state restoration (begun in 1940), the fortress monastery finally reopened in 1995 as a *pousada* (☎245 997 210, ⓦwww.pousadas.pt; ❸). Although the building is magnificent, unfortunately the quality of decor and finish seems better suited to a third-rate hotel. It's still worth a look, though, and around the main building you can trace the plan of the gardens, laid out in the insignia of the Order of Malta, in honour of the warlord **Nuno Álvares Pereira**, whose father founded the monastery.

Father Pereira's tomb (dated 1382) is prominent in the narrow, soaring convent church. Adjoining it, on the ground floor, is the sixteenth-century **Sala do Capítulo**, distinguished by fine brickwork, fan vaulting and a Gothic cloister. On the first floor are the monks' **dormitories**, whose open casements offer sweeping views across acres of olive trees.

If you need to stay in the village and can't afford the *pousada*, the more cosy *Palacete Florida Rosa*, on Rua da Cruz (☎245 996 451, ⓕ245 997 286; ❹), is a cheaper option.

Alter do Chão

ALTER DO CHÃO, 13km to the south of Crato, is another town that did well from textiles, particularly during the sixteenth century, as indicated by its attractive Renaissance marble fountain and an array of handsome town houses. There is a **castle**, too, whose central tower can be climbed for an overview of the region, but the chief reason for a visit is the Coudelaria de Alter-Real stud farm, 3km out of town.

The **Coudelaria de Alter-Real** (☎245 610 060, ☏245 610 090) was founded in 1748 by Dom João V of the House of Bragança, and remained in the family until 1910 when the War Office took it over. Today, maintained by the state, it is open for public visits (daily 9am–5.30pm), though to see the horses in action it's best to arrive in the morning: between 10am and noon when you can watch them filing in from the fields to feed, accompanied to the ringing of forty bells. In the town itself you may be lucky enough to see the Coudelaria coach and horses when they come to collect the mail.

The tours of the stud are also interesting, with a museum display of carriages and horse regalia, through which you are conducted at a stately pace by a cavalry officer. Alter-Real horses have been sought after since the stud's foundation – one is depicted in the equestrian statue of Dom José in Lisbon's Praça do Comércio, for example – and they remain the favoured breed of the Portuguese mounted police and the Lisbon Riding School at Queluz.

If you can time a visit, April 24 is the best day to be at the Coudelaria, when the **annual sale** takes place. The town's main festival – the **Festa de Nossa Senhora da Alegria** – occurs on the following day.

Practicalities

Several **pensões** are clustered in the road opposite the castle in Alter do Chão, including the *Pensão Ferreira* (☎245 612 254; ❷) above the *Snack Bar Avenida* on Avenida Dr. João Pestana. For **meals**, the *Páteo Real,* Avenida Dr. Joâo Pestana 37, serves good local cuisine and there are tasty cakes at the nearby *Pastelaria Ateneia*. Daily **buses** connect the town with Portalegre and Crato.

Castelo de Vide and Marvão

The upland district **north of Portalegre** is a bucolic landscape, with tree-clad mountain ranges and a series of gorgeous hilltop villages. Among these, the best targets are **Castelo de Vide** and **Marvão**, both with castles, and the former with a spa. Castelo de Vide is the most easily accessible, connected by bus five times daily with Portalegre; Marvão has three daily services, Monday to Friday only. Getting between the two, one morning and one late afternoon bus from Castelo de Vide to Portalegre connects with buses to Marvão at the main road junction of Portagem.

Castelo de Vide

CASTELO DE VIDE covers the slopes around a fourteenth-century castle, its blindingly white cottages delineated in brilliant contrast to the greenery around. Arriving by bus, you'll be dropped at the *pelourinho* outside the **turismo** (daily: summer 9am–7pm; winter 9am–12.30pm & 2–5.30pm; ☎245 901 361, ⓦwww.cm.castelo-vide.pt) in the centre of town. From here, half a dozen parallel streets make a sharp climb up to the aptly named **Praça Alta** on the edge of town. The main road, meanwhile, peters out into a narrow path, descending past a tranquil Renaissance fountain to the twisting alleyways of the **Judairia** – the old Jewish quarter. Amid the cottages, most of which still have Gothic doorways and windows, is a thirteenth-century **synagogue** (daily 9am–6pm), the oldest surviving one in Portugal. From the outside it doesn't look very different from the cottages, so you will probably need to ask for directions.

On a hill above the Judairia, the **Castelo** (daily: summer 9am–7pm; winter 9am–12.30pm & 2–5.30pm; free) squats within the wider fortifications of the original medieval village.

Practicalities

Given its size, the town has a surprising amount of **accommodation**. Of the budget options, the best value is provided by the friendly, English-speaking *Casa de Hóspedes Melanie*, Largo do Paço Novo 3 (T245 901 632; ➋). Other options in the same price range include the modern, spotless, *Casa Machado*, Rua Luis de Camões 33 (T245 901 515). With more money, your best bet is one of the elegant rooms – breakfast included – in the *Albergaria El Rei Dom Miguel*, Rua Bartolomeu Álvares da Santa (T245 919 191, F245 901 592; ➌) or the slightly blander *Sol e Serra*, Estrada S. Vincente 73 (T245 900 000, F245 900 001), with all mod cons. The restaurant at the *Cantinho Particular*, at Rua Miguel Bombarda 9, is basic but good; for a splurge (around €20) try the excellent *Restaurante Marino's* on Praça Dom Pedro, which specializes in Italian and regional dishes. The *Restaurante São João*, on the road to Portalegre, and *Don Pedro V*, Praça Dom Pedro V, are also very good. The perfect place for snacks is the *Pastelaria Sol Nascente* at Rua de Olivença 31, which has a wonderful selection of pastries. There's **internet** access at *Artitudo Cybercafe*, Rua Mouzinha da Silveira 14 (Mon–Sat 9.30am–midnight; €2/hr; T245 908 085, Egaleria@artitudo.com).

Marvão

Beautiful as Castelo de Vide is, **MARVÃO** surpasses it. The panoramas from its remote eyrie site are unrivalled and the atmosphere even quieter than a population of less than a thousand would suggest. No more than a handful of houses – each as scrupulously whitewashed as the rest – lies outside the seventeenth-century walls. Originally the village seems to have been an outlying suburb of Medobriga, a mysterious Roman city which vanished almost without trace. Its inhabitants fled before the Moorish advance in around 715 but later returned to live under Muslim rule, when the place was renamed after Marvan, the Moorish Lord of Coimbra. It fell to the Christians in 1166 and the **castle** was rebuilt by Dom Dinis around 1229 as another important link in the chain of outposts along the Spanish border. The castle stands at the far end of the village, its walls blending into the sharp slopes of the *serra*. It's dauntingly impenetrable and was indeed captured only once, in 1833, when the attackers entered through a secret gate. Also worth a visit is the **municipal museum** in the Church of Santa Maria, which has an interesting range of Roman remains and other local finds.

The village makes a superb night's stop, as several houses within the walls are rented out under a scheme organized by the **turismo**, on Rua Dr. António Matos Magalhães (daily 9am–12.30pm & 2–5.30pm; T245 993 886, Wwww.em-marvao.pt). In some of these you can get just a room, while others are rented out as a unit; prices, consequently, are extremely varied. Additional **accommodation** is provided by *Restaurante O Seve,* Portagem (T245 993 318, F245 993 458; ➋), which rents out pleasant rooms, the characterful *Dom Dinis* on Rua Dr. António Matos Magalhães (T245 993 957, F245 993 959; ➌) and the attractively converted *Pousada de Santa Maria* (T245 993 201, Wwww .pousadas.pt; ➐) at Rua 24 de Janeiro 7.

For **meals**, the *Restaurante Varanda do Alentejo*, in Praça do Pelourinho, is good and you can also eat and drink at *Bar da Casa do Povo* or *Bar Marcelino*, both

8

just off the square. The *pousada*'s restaurant serves meals at around €25 per head which, even allowing for the grand views, is still rather pricey.

Marvão-Beirã: on into Spain

Lisbon–Madrid trains stop at the station of **MARVÃO-BEIRÃ**, 9km north of Marvão village. Heading for Spain by public transport, this is the easiest way to go, although services, especially outside summer, can be infrequent; check with the turismo for current times. The road border at **GALEGOS**, 14km east of Marvão, is open to traffic but very few cars use it. In addition, there's at least one daily **bus** from Portalegre direct to the Spanish border town of Valencia de Alcántara.

Belver Castle

Travelling northwest from Portalegre, the N18/N118 roads take you up to the Tejo valley and, of course, the Alentejo border. The most interesting targets on this route are the castles of Abrantes and Almourol in Ribatejo (see p.194), and **Belver**, which, although sited with its town on the north bank of the Tejo, is technically a part of Alentejo. If you are dependent on public transport, it is easiest to take a train or bus to Abrantes, and approach Belver from there.

BELVER CASTLE is one of the most famous in the country, its fanciful position, name and tiny size having ensured it a place in dozens of Portuguese legends. The name comes from *belo ver* (beautiful to see), the supposed exclamation of some medieval princess, waking up to look out from its keep at the river valley below. It dates from the twelfth century, when the Portuguese frontier stood at the Tejo, the Moors having reclaimed all the territories to the south, save Évora, that Afonso Henriques had conquered for his kingdom. Its founder was Dom Sancho I, who entrusted its construction and care to the knight-monks of the Order of St John.

The walls form an irregular pentagon, tracing the crown of the hill, with a narrow access path to force attackers into single file. If you find the castle locked, search out the guard who lives at no. 1 on the main square in Belver village. For a small fee, he will even unlock the **chapel** as well to show you its formidable fifteenth-century reliquary. All the pieces of bone were stolen during the French invasions in the nineteenth century, but fortunately for the villagers there was a casket of "spares" hidden away by the priest, and these substitutes are today paraded at the **Festa de Santa Reliquária**, held around August 18.

You're very likely to track down the castle guard sharing a few jokes over a glass of *bagaceira* (Portugal's cheapest hangover) in Belver's single **café-restaurant-pension**. Rooms (❶) are usually available, outside the August festival times.

Buses leave from the *praça* or from the street above the **train station**, which is directly below the village beside the river. If you take the train north along the valley towards Castelo Branco, look out for the striking rock faces before Vila Velha de Ródão, known as the **Portas do Ródão** (Gates of Ródão).

Baixo Alentejo

The hot, dry inland routes of Baixo Alentejo have little to offer beyond a stop at **Beja** – the most interesting southern Alentejo town – en route to the Algarve or, if you're heading for Spain, at the frontier towns of **Serpa** or **Mértola**. The coastline, however, is another matter, with resorts like **Vila Nova de Milfontes**, **Almograve** and **Zambujeira do Mar** providing an attractive alternative to the summer crowds on the Algarve. Their only disadvantage – and the reason for a very patchy tourist development – is their exposure to the Atlantic winds, which at times create huge breakers and dangerous swimming conditions. But as long as you're prepared to spend occasional days out of the water, they are enjoyable places in which to take it easy for a few days by the sea.

All the beaches are situated along minor roads, but there are local **bus services** from Santiago do Cacém and Odemira. Alternatively, coming from Lisbon, you can take the express bus direct to Vila Nova de Milfontes, Almograve and Zambujeira do Mar; it leaves Lisbon twice a day from the main bus terminal (p.122) and, as with all *expressos*, it's wise to buy tickets in advance.

Southeast from Lisbon

Heading southeast into the Alentejo from Lisbon or Setúbal, the main road (and bus) loops around the **Rio Sado estuary**, through **Alcácer do Sal**, at the mouth of the river, and on through the agricultural town of **Grândola**. Heading **towards Beja**, drivers could travel instead directly east from Alcácer do Sal, cutting across a succession of country roads and past a couple of huge reservoirs before meeting the main Évora–Beja road.

Alcácer do Sal

Fifty-two kilometres from Setúbal, **ALCÁCER DO SAL** is one of Portugal's oldest ports, founded by the Phoenicians and made a regional capital under the Moors – whence its name (*al-Ksar*, the town) derives. The other part of its name, *do Sal*, "of salt", reflects the dominance of the salt industry in these parts; the Sado estuary is still fringed with salt marshes. Alcácer today is slightly seedy-looking, but quite attractively so, particularly along its waterfront promenade. A couple of roads back from the promenade at its western end is a charming quarter of mainly medieval houses, centred around Rua Rui Salem. Further uphill, above the town, stands the part-ruined Moorish **castle** (daily 10am–noon & 2–5pm; free), from where there are striking views of the lush green paddy fields which almost surround the town, and of the storks' nests on the church rooftops.

Practicalities

The helpful **turismo** is in the old quarter on Rua da Republica 66 (Mon–Sat 9.30am–6pm; ☎965 610 070). A good place for something **to eat** is the *Café-Restaurant Sado*, at the eastern end of the promenade, past the bus depot at Largo Luís de Camões – try the house speciality of prawns, beer and buttered toast. Next door is one of the town's best bakeries, *Pasteleria Gaby*, where you can sample *pinhoadas,* a honey and pinenut toffee. For a more substantial meal try *Restaurant O Campinho* on Avenida dos Aviadores or splash out at the *parador.* If you decide to **stay the night**, there are modern and functional rooms at *Residencial Cegonha,* Largo do Terreirinho (☏265 612 294, ℗265 612 330; ❶), or eco-enthusiasts may prefer *A Cabana Do Pai Do Tomás* (☏265 532 979, ℮milandancas@mail.telepac.pt; ❸), a few kilometres south of town towards Comporta. Here the self-sufficient hotel offers bright, well-decorated rooms plus the use of a kitchen, garden and bicycles. If you can't stretch to the fabulous *Pousada de Alcácer do Sal* (☏265 613 070, ⓦwww.pousadas.pt; ❽), stop by for a drink at least to ogle the valley view.

At the beginning of October, for around three days, the town hosts a **regional fair** featuring an assembly of agricultural machinery, a couple of bullfights and acres of stalls. It's one of the most enjoyable fairs in the south.

Grândola

At **GRÂNDOLA**, 24km south of Alcácer do Sal, the roads diverge: southwest to the coast; east to Beja, Serpa and, ultimately, Spanish Andalucía. As well as the main road through Alcácer to Grândola, there's an enjoyable alternative approach for drivers from Setúbal who can take the ferry to Tróia and make their way down the long, sand-fringed **Peninsula de Tróia** along the N253. The town was made legendary through the song *Grândola vila morena,* the broadcasting of which was the prearranged signal for the start of the 1974 Revolution. There's precious little reason to stop in town, though it has a few decent restaurants – the pricey *Picapu* on Rua Dom Nuno Álvares Pereira has the best reputation – and there are a couple of average hotels, should you be stuck.

East towards Beja: Viana do Alentejo

Heading **east** instead from Alcácer do Sal, the minor N5 runs to Torrão, curving around the Rio Sado, past the **Barragem de Vale do Gaio**. Sited on the edge of the reservoir is the *Pousada de Vale do Gaio* (☏265 669 610, ⓦwww.pousadas.pt; ❻), a fairly simple conversion of the lodge used by the dam engineers.

Continuing east, along the N383, you pass through **VIANA DO ALENTEJO**, a sleepy and typically southern Alentejan village which preserves a highly decorative **castle**, full of Mudejar and Manueline features (Tues–Sun 10am–12.30pm & 2–5pm; closed Aug). The castle walls were built on a pentagonal plan by Dom Dinis in 1313, and the interior ensemble of buildings was expanded under Dom João II and Dom Manuel I in the late fifteenth century. To this latter period belong a sequence of elaborate battlements and the beautiful parish church, part of a striking group of buildings within the walls, encompassing a Misericórdia, town hall, cistern and *pelourinho.* Viana also boasts a very good restaurant, the expensive *Bernadino Santos Banha,* at Rua António I Sousa 36 (☏266 953 116). **From Viana**, the N384 runs 30km east, past another huge reservoir, to meet the main Évora–Beja road.

Beja

On the inland route through southern Alentejo, **BEJA** appears as a welcome oasis amid the sweltering, featureless wheat fields. Commanding this strategic position in the centre of the plains, it has long been an important and pros-perous city. Founded by Julius Caesar in 48BC it was named Pax Julia, in honour of the peace accord signed here between Rome and the Lusitanians, but later became Pax Augusta and then just Pax, from which it gradually corrupted to Paca, Baca, Baju, and finally Beja.

South of Évora, it's the most interesting stop on the way to the Algarve, and once past the modern suburbs Beja reveals an unhurried old quarter with a cluster of peculiar churches, a beautiful convent and a thirteenth-century castle. You can take in most of the sights in this compact historic centre in half a day, though in summer the heat will probably turn you towards a bar within an hour or so.

If you visit the town during May, you'll witness the town celebrating the **Festas da Cidade** – a month-long jamboree of music, dance, gastronomy and bullfighting.

The Town

In Portugal Beja is best known for the love affair of a seventeenth-century nun who lived in the **Convento de Nossa Senhora da Conceição**, just off Largo dos Duques de Beja. Sister Mariana Alcoforado is believed to have fallen in love with Count Chamilly, a French cavalry officer, and is credited with the notorious (in Portugal anyway) *Five Love Letters of a Portuguese Nun*, first published in Paris in 1669. The originals have never been discovered, and a scholarly debate has raged over the authenticity of the French "translation". Nonetheless, English and Portuguese editions soon appeared and the letters became internationally famous as a classic of romantic literature.

Sentimental associations aside, the convent is an impressive building. Founded in the fifteenth century, it has a panoply of Manueline fripperies, with elaborate portals and a rhythmic roofline decorated with balustrades and pinnacles. The walls of the cloisters and chapterhouse are completely covered with multicoloured sixteenth- and seventeenth-century *azulejos*, and present one of the finest examples of this art form. The other highlight is a magnificent Rococo chapel, sumptuously gilded and embellished with flying cherubs. The convent was dissolved in 1834 and today houses the **Museu Regional** (Tues–Sun 9.45am–1pm & 2–5.30pm; €0.50, free on Sun). Compared with the architecture of the building, the museum pieces are comparatively lacklustre, though they include a wide-ranging display on the town's past eras – including items as diverse as Roman and Visigothic stone, fifteenth- to eighteenth-century Dutch and Portuguese painting, and the grille through which the errant nun first glimpsed her lover.

Beja's **Castelo** (Tues–Sun: summer 10am–1pm & 2–6pm; winter 9am–noon & 1–4pm) rises decoratively on the edge of the old quarter. It was built – yet again – by Dom Dinis and is remarkable for the playful battlements of its Torre de Menagem, which costs €1 to climb up.

In the shadow of the keep stands the Visigothic basilica of **Santo Amaro**, today a small archeological museum. The building is a rare survival from pre-Moorish Portugal; the interior columns are carved with seventh-century geometric motifs.

Among other churches in Beja, the most distinctive is the mid-sixteenth-century **Misericórdia** in Praça da República; its huge projecting porch served originally as a meat market and the stonework is deliberately chiselled to give a coarse, rustic appearance. Earlier, fortress-inclined Gothic elements are to be seen on the church of **Santa Maria**, in the heart of the old quarter, and on

Ermida de Santo André

Évora & Lisbon

Train Station

Serpa

RUA DA LAVOURA

RUA GEN. TEOFILO DA TRINDADE

RUA DE LISBOA

RUA C. MENESES

R. ANTERO DO

Santo Amaro

Castelo

Sé

RUA GEN. TEOFILO DA TRINDADE

A

RUA DOS PINTORES

R. FREI MANUEL DO CENÁCULO

LARGO DR LIMA

LARGO DO LIDADOR

LARGO DO LIDADOR

B

Misericórdia

RUA INFANTE D. HENRIQUE

R. BRANCA

PR. DA REPÚBLICA

LARGO DE SANTA MARIA

R. DA CASA PIA

RUA DOS DUQUES DE BEJA

1

Santa Maria

LARGO DOS DUQUES DE BEJA

Salvador

C

R. DOS INFANTES

R. DO TOURO

D

Convento de N. S. da Conceição

RUA DA LIBERDADE

RUA S. SEMBRANO

R. CONDE DA BOAVISTA

Jardim Publico

E

RUA ANTÓNIO SARDINHA

RUA 5 DE OUTUBRO

RUA CAPITÃO J.F. DE SOUSA

PRAÇA DIOGO FERNANDES

i 2 F

4

R. MÉRTOLA

5

3 G

RUA D. NUNO ÁLVAREZ PEREIRA

Faro

RUA HERÓIS DE DAORA

6 H

RUA LUÍS DE CAMÕES

Market

RUA AFONSO HENRIQUES

@

N

Bus Station

RUA BENTO DE JESUS CARAÇA

AV. DO BRASIL

RUA BAILÃO DE ALMEIDA

RUA DE SÃO JOÃO

Stadium

AVENIDA VASCO DA GAMA

CIDADE DE S. PAULO

AVENIDA DA BOAVISTA

0   100 m

✕ Campsite

ACCOMMODATION

Bejense	2
Cristina	6
Hotel Melius	7
Casa de Hóspedes Pax Julia	1
Casa de Hóspedes Rocha	5
Santa Bárabar	4
Pousada de São Francisco	3

RESTAURANTS

A Esquino	B
Alentjano	D
Ciudade Asia	H
Luís da Rocha	F
Pandora Disco	A
O Portão	C
Pena	E
Pousada de São Francisco	G

8

ALENTEJO | Beja

Mertola & Castro Verde

the fifteenth-century **Ermida de Santo André**, on the road out to Lisbon, which is endowed with gigantic tubular buttresses.

Practicalities

The old quarter is a circular tangle of streets, enclosed within a ring road which has replaced the town walls. At its heart is a pair of interlocking squares – Largo de Santa Maria and Largo dos Duques de Beja. The **bus station** lies five minutes' walk southeast of this quarter; the **train station** five minutes northeast. A very helpful **turismo** (May–Sept Mon–Sat 9am–8pm; Oct–April Mon–Sat 10am–6pm; ⓣ & ⓕ 284 311 913) is located just south of the central squares at Rua Capitão J.F. de Sousa 25. If you're looking for **internet** access, head for the Biblioteca Municipal, on Rua Luís de Camões (Mon–Fri 10am–2pm & 5–7pm, Sat 10am–2pm; ⓣ 284 311 900) or *Só Café*, Centro Comercial Pax Júlia Loja 16 (daily 9am–midnight; €2/hr; ⓣ 284 327 541).

Beja has good **transport connections** to the rest of central and southern Portugal, as well as a bus link to Seville via Rosal de La Fronteira. In most cases you have a choice of bus or train: for Lisbon and the western Algarve take the train, whereas for Évora, Vila Real de Santo António (for the eastern Algarve) and Santiago do Cacém (for the western Algarve) it's quicker to go by bus.

Accommodation

Most of the town's **accommodation** is to be found within a few blocks of the turismo. In summer and during the Festas da Cidade (see p.492) it is well worth booking ahead. The municipal **campsite** (℡284 324 328, Ⓕ284 327 225) is located on the south side of town, past the stadium on Avenida Vasco da Gama. It's fairly pleasant and shaded, and adjoins the local swimming pool.

Residencial Bejense Rua do Capitão J.F. de Sousa 57 ℡284 311 570, Ⓕ284 311 579. Situated close to the turismo, this attractive *residencial* with its bourgainvilla-clad frontage has en-suite doubles and cheaper singles (without bath). Breakfast included. ❸

Residencial Cristina Rua de Mértola 71 ℡284 323 035, Ⓕ284 320 460. A rather soulless, modern hotel, but comfortable enough. ❸

Hotel Melius, Ruá Fialho de Almeida ℡284 321 822, Ⓕ284 321 825. Modern hotel on the edge of town, complete with gym, solarium and sauna. ❸

Casa de Hóspedes Pax Julia Rua Pedro Victor 8 ℡284 322 575. One of the least expensive options in town, with clean, comfortable rooms. ❷

Casa de Hóspedes Rocha Largo Dom Nuno Álvares Pereira 12 ℡284 324 271. Friendly, decrepit old hotel facing the *pousada* offering tatty but clean rooms. ❷

Residencial Santa Bárbara Rua de Mértola 56 ℡284 322 028, Ⓕ284 321 231. Reasonably priced modern rooms, with breakfast included. ❸

Pousada de São Francisco Largo Dom Nuno Álvares Pereira ℡284 328 441, ⓦwww .pousadas.pt. Imposing *pousada* inside the convent of São Francisco, where rooms are in former monastic cells. Also open for non-residents to have a wander. ❾

Eating, drinking and nightlife

Although Beja has a relatively wide selection of restaurants, only a small number serve really good traditional Portuguese food. Beja has no fewer than four Chinese restaurants, which is rather unusual for Portuguese towns. At night, the Beja youth congregate at the enormous *Pandora* **disco** close to the train station at Rua General Teófilo da Trinidade 4 (Wed–Sat 10pm–4am; €5 cover charge), whose five dance floors should have something to please every taste.

Restaurante A Esquina Rua Infante Dom Henrique 26. Located in the west of town and popular with locals, serving up the enormous portions of mainly meat and fish dishes.

Restaurante Alentejano Largo dos Duques de Beja 7. A popular, local restaurant. where most main courses come in at around €7.

Cidade Asia Rua Luís de Camoes 25. Moderately priced and the best of the Chinese restaurants in town. They have menus from €8, which include favourites such as sweet and sour pork; they will be as familiar as the flock wallpaper and lantern decor.

Luís da Rocha Rua do Capitão J.F. de Sousa 63. An immensely popular café serving a wide range of Alentejan fare and a great selection of inexpensive wines. Specials include grilled squid and rack of lamb. There's an *ementa turística* for around €8. Great pastries too.

Restaurante O Portão Trav. da Audiença 1 (off Rua dos Infantes). Not an enormous choice, but excellent quality and great value – the *ementa turística* is €8 – served in an old *adega*.

Restaurante Pena Praça de Diogo Fernandes de Beja 19a. Modest prices and dependable cooking, with fish a speciality. It's between the pedestrian shopping district and the castle.

Pousada de São Francisco Largo Dom Nuno Álvares Pereira ℡284 328 441, ⓦwww.pousadas .pt. The *pousada* offers by far the highest quality traditional Portuguese cuisine in town, though you'll have to pay around €20–25 for a full meal.

Serpa and around

Thirty kilometres east of Beja, the small market town of **SERPA** offers the classic Alentejan attractions – a walled centre, a castle and narrow, whitewashed streets – and makes an enjoyable stop if you are heading towards Spain, or feel like a roundabout but scenic approach to the Algarve, via Mértola. The town has at various times been occupied by Celts, Romans, Moors and Spaniards, and inevitably is dominated by its **Castle** (Tues–Sun 9am–12.30pm & 2–5.30pm; free), predominantly Moorish, and with spectacular vistas of the plain to the north and the hills to the south. There is a tiny archeological museum in the keep and, close by, the thirteenth-century church of **Santa Maria** (open Sun only), containing an altarpiece of intricate woodcarving, surrounded by seventeenth-century *azulejos*.

From the castle, you can track the course of the well-preserved eleventh-century **aqueduct**, although at the time of research it was closed for renovation. If open, though, it is well worth a look from close up, with the remnants of a chain-pump at one end. If you have time to fill, you might also wander down to the **Museu Etnográfico** (Tues–Sun 9am–noon & 2–5pm; free), near the hospital, which offers an interesting account of the changing economic activity of the area, with exhibits such as agricultural implements, olive presses and local costumes.

Practicalities

Serpa's **turismo** is at Largo Dom Jorge de Melo 2 (daily 9am–5.30pm; ☎284 544 727), and the **bus station** is on the Avenida de Paz in the southwest of town; there are six connections a day to Beja. The rail bus also connects with Beja (and Moura) three times a day, but drops you on the main road, well outside Serpa. *Cybercafe*, at Rua Dr Couardo Fernandez de Oliveira 18 (daily 10am–2pm; €1.50/hr; ☎284 548 066) offers access to the **internet**.

You may well find private rooms advertised around the largo but official **places to stay** in town are limited. There's the smart *Residencial Beatriz*, at Largo do Salvador 10 (☎284 544 423, ℗284 543 100; ❷), near São Salvador church; the *Residencial Serpinia*, in the northwest of town on Rua de Santo António (☎284 544 055, ℗284 544 961; ❸), though the disco below may put you off; or the centrally located *Casa da Muralha*, Rua das Portas de Beja 43 (☎284 543 150 ℗284 543 151; ❸), a beautiful country house furnished with antiques and set in a flower-filled garden. A good out-of-town option is the modern *pousada*, the *São Gens* (☎284 544 724, ℗284 544 337; ❼), 2km to the south, on a hill known as Alto de São Gens; it has a swimming pool and wonderful views. Serpa's well-equipped **campsite** (☎284 543 290, ℗284 544 290) is at the southwest corner of town near the swimming pool complex.

Among Serpa's **restaurants**, the *Cervejaria Vila Branca*, Avenida da Paz 4, is highly recommended for its excellent *cataplanas* and seafood, while *O Zé*, at Praça da República 10, serves a decent *gaspacho* and delicious local cheese. Opposite, the Art Deco *Café Alentejano* has a very good, if slightly pricey, restaurant above it; alternatively there's the more reasonable *Restaurant Molho-Bico* at the top of Rua Quente (closed Wed).

Around Serpa

Situated 15km and 30km to the north of Serpa respectively, the wine-producing village of Pias and the spa town of Moura make for interesting destinations in the area, with Moura offering the best options for an overnight

The Alqueva Dam

In February 2002 the floodgates opened on the controversial **Alqueva Dam** project, started decades ago under the Salazar regime. At 250 square metres (of which 69 square kilometres is in Spain), Alqueva will be Europe's largest reservoir. The government claims it will provide reliable irrigation waters in this arid region, satisfy the increasing need for domestic water supplies in the neighbouring Algarve and provide much needed jobs in the agricultural and tourism industries. There are many who dispute these claims and the issue has become a political battleground, pitting environmentalists and UNESCO against the Portuguese government and the EU. Dissenters dispute the viability of the claims and strongly decry the destruction of over a million Holm oak and cork trees, threats to the habit of golden eagles and the even rarer Iberian Lynx, plus the submerging of over 200 prehistoric sites. It is claimed that, in contravention of EU law, no environmental impact assessment was carried out; the World Wildlife Fund has described the project as an ecological disaster.

Having lost the initial battle to stop the reservoir, campaigners are now pushing for a top water level of 139 metres, which they say will save half of the threatened trees, and many precious wildlife habitats. While the debate rages the waters continue to rise and the residents of the soon-to-be-submerged hamlet of Luz have been moved to a facsimile of their village above the waterline. Built at a cost of £20 million, the replica reproduces all 221 buildings in the same street plan, alongside the relocated village cemetery, football pitch and bullring. Whilst villagers struggle to come to terms with the impact of the dam on their lives, the effect of the project on the fragile ecosystem of the region is only beginning to become apparent.

For more information on the campaigns see http://lynxpardinus.naturlink.pt /alqueva_appeal_%20eng.htm.

stay. If you have your own transport, it's also an easy half-day trip to the Pulo do Lobo waterfall, sited amid stark, rocky scenery 18km south of Serpa.

Pias

The village of **PIAS** is well known hereabouts for its red wine, Margaça and Encostas – the Sociedade Agrícola de Pias, Rua Santo António 8 (☎285 858 222), can arrange tours of the vineyards and winery. There are no particular sights, and the local train station has closed down, but if you're driving it makes a worthwhile detour for anyone who wants to examine what is still a very traditional, low-key, Alentejan village. Pias also has a surprisingly good **restaurant**, the *Arroz Doce* in Rua Luís de Camões – try the *migas*. If you just want a **drink**, head for the local favourite, *Canseras Bar* on Rua de João Tiágo Coelho 79. In the unlikely event you want to stay overnight, the only accommodation in town is at the pleasant enough, *Rua do Outeiro* (☎284 858 714, ⓕ284 858 709).

Moura

A further 15km north, the thermal spa town of **MOURA** is an opulent place full of grand mansions, houses and pretty squares. The Moors occupied the town from the eighth century until 1233 – an Arabic well still survives in the old town – and the town is named after a Moorish maiden, Moura Saluquia, who ostensibly threw herself from the castle tower in despair when Christians murdered her betrothed and overran the town. But it was the discovery of the **thermal springs** that prompted Moura's later wealth; located beside the Jardim Doutora Santiago, they are still in use (Mon–Sat 10am–5pm; €0.50 a bath). The key to the adjacent **castle**, built by Dom Dinis over a Moorish castle and largely destroyed by the Duke of Osuna in 1701 (though one Moorish tower survives), is at the Câmara Municipal. Outside the gardens stands the sixteenth-century Manueline **Igreja de São João Batista**, its chapel decorated with Sevillian *azulejos*. Behind the castle lies the ruined Renaissance **Convento do Carmo**, where you can still see statues and beautiful frescoes.

Moura is connected to Beja three times a day by **bus**, via Serpa, which drops you at the southern end of town, and daily to Évora, arriving at the central Praça Cabral. There is free **internet** access here in the *Biblioteca Municipal*, Praça Cabral (Mon–Fri 10am–12.30pm & 2.30–6.30pm, Sat 10am–12.30pm). The **turismo** is on Largo Santa Clara (Mon–Fri 9am–1pm & 2–5pm, Sat & Sun 10am–1pm; ☎285 251 375), and may be able to help with private **rooms**. Alternatively, try the *Pensão Alentejana*, at Largo José Maria dos Santos 40 (☎285 250 080, ℱ285 250 089; ❸), which has large and rambling rooms but is often full, or *A Casa Da Moura*, Largo Dr. Rodrigues Acabado (☎ & ℱ285 251 264; ❷), offering very pleasant, modern rooms. The town's upmarket option is the *Hotel de Moura*, on the peaceful Praça Gago Coutinho (☎285 251 090, ℱ285 251 091; ❸), a superbly ornate building complete with *azulejos*, patios, mirrored doors and a rambling garden. There are plenty of **restaurants** in town; *O Trilho*, Rua 5 de Outubro 5 (closed Mon), serves good regional dishes. In the upper town, try *O Arco* by Porta Nova, with its huge range of *aguardiente* liquors. For **nightlife**, there's *Discoteca Shahazade* by the ruined convent and the pub *Caprixus* at 14 Rua da Mollejas (just off Praça Cabral).

The Pulo do Lobo waterfall

The **Pulo do Lobo** (Wolf's Leap) waterfall lies in a deep gorge carved through the hills by the river and the valley has some strikingly eerie rock formations. You'll probably have the falls all to yourself; to get there from Serpa, follow the road which is signposted behind the Jardim Botanico. It's well surfaced as far as the village of **São Brás** (6km) but as it climbs into the mountainous countryside, it deteriorates suddenly to a rough track, which becomes narrow and vertiginous as it leads down, around the 16km mark, to a stream – a tributary of the Guadiana. Following the track, after a couple of kilometres you can turn left to arrive very close to the Pulo do Lobo. Beware that swimming around around the waterfall or in the river is strongly discorouged; there have been several deaths in recent years.

South to the Algarve

There are three main routes **south from Beja to the Algarve**. The most interesting and enjoyable is the **N122** to Vila Real de Santo António (there are several daily buses), on the eastern border of the province with Spain; this passes through the old Moorish fortress town of **Mértola** and a scenic stretch of the Guadiana river valley. Alternatives, more convenient if you are heading for western or central Algarve, are to take the N391 across the plains to **Castro Verde**, then the fast E1 to **Albufeira**, or the more mountainous N2 to **Faro** (at least three buses daily).

Via Castro Verde

If you're a bird fancier, you may consider the route from Beja to **CASTRO VERDE** (46km south) a must, for the chance to see **great bustards** winging across the plains. This apart, the road has few attractions, with a handful of small agricultural towns set amid interminable parched tracts of wheat fields. Following the N2, directly south of Castro Verde, the route continues in similar vein until you hit the lush greenery of the **Serra do Malhão** and the **Serra do Caldeirão** around Ameixial – just across the border in the Algarve.

To the west, the N264 provides faster access to the Algarve, as well as an interesting detour in the **Castro da Cola**, the remains of a small, Romano-Celtic village, similar to the *citânias* of the north. This is located to the west of the road, a few kilometres beyond the village of Aldeia dos Palheiros. There is a pilgrimage to the site on September 7–8.

Via Mértola

The N122 gets a green edge on the Michelin map as it approaches **MÉRTOLA** – a sure sign of rising gradients and an escape from the plains. The town is as beautifully sited as any in the south, set high above the Rio Guadiana, around the extensive ruins of a Moorish frontier castle. It's a quiet, isolated place, certainly worth a night's stopover – more if you feel like a walking or bird-watching base. The region is home to the rare black stork.

The obvious focus for a visit is the **Castelo**, views from whose keep sweep across the Guadiana valley. To the north, you may be able to make out the copper mines a few kilometres down the Serpa road at Mina de São Domingos. Until recent decades, these were the principal source of the town's employment, and until World War II they were owned by a British company, which employed a private police force and treated the workers with appalling brutality. Back in town, take time to look around the **Igreja Matriz**, which started life as a Moorish mosque and retains its *mihrab* (prayer niche) behind the altar on the eastern wall. Also worth searching out is the little **Museu Arqueológico** (Mon–Sat 9am–12.30pm & 2–5.30pm; €2.50), a well-presented collection of recoveries from local digs, notably Roman pottery, jewellery and needles, plus a set of strange-looking religious figures retrieved from the castle.

Practicalities

Orientation is straightforward, with **buses** (to and from Beja and Vila Real de Santo António) stopping at the bus station, a five-minute walk along Rua Dr. Ferreo Martins from the **turismo**, on Largo Vasco de Gama (Mon–Fri 9am–12.30pm & 2–5.30pm, Sat & Sun 10am–12.30pm & 2–5.30pm; ☎286 612 573). **Accommodation** options include the *Residencial Beira Rio*, Rua Dr. Afonso Costa 18 (☎286 612 340; ❷), which has the edge on *Residencial San Remo*, Avenida Aureliano Mira Fernandes (☎286 612 132; ❷), in character and situation. For a little more, you could stay at the *Casa das Janelas Verdes*, Rua Dr. Manuel Francisco Gomes 38–40 (☎286 612 145; breakfast included; ❸) – a traditional Alentejan house. The *Restaurante Boa Viagem*, opposite the bus stop, offers a good and inexpensive selection of **meals**.

Santiago do Cacém and around

Heading south on the main route from Lisbon or Setúbal, **Santiago do Cacém** is the first place that might, realistically, tempt you to stop. A pleasant little provincial town, it is overlooked by a castle, and has on its outskirts – half an hour's walk away – the fascinating Roman ruins of **Miróbriga**. In addition, it's only a short bus journey from the **Santo André** and **Melides lagoons**, forming two of the Alentejo's finest beaches.

Santiago do Cacém

The Moorish **Castle** (Mon–Fri 8.30am–4.30pm, Sat 8.30am–1pm) in **SANTIAGO DO CACÉM** was later rebuilt by the Knights Templar but now serves as a cemetery. There are splendid views over to the sea from the battlements, whose crumbling masonry provides the habitat for a curious species of large golden beetle. It's also worth making your way to the **Museu Municipal**, facing the municipal gardens off Avenida Pereira (Tues–Fri 10am–noon & 2–5pm, Sat & Sun 2.30–5pm; free), one of the most interesting of its kind and housed in one of Salazar's more notorious prisons in a small park just northeast of the centre. A suitably political strain pervades its display: one of the spartan prison cells has been preserved while two others have been converted into a "typical country bedroom" and "a rich bourgeois bedroom". The drawing section devoted to the local primary school shows a child's impression of the "Great Revolution" of 1974.

The archeological section in Santiago's museum should whet your appetite for a visit to Roman **Miróbriga** (Tues–Sun 9am–12.30pm & 2–5.30pm; closes at 4.30pm in winter; €1.50). From the centre, follow Rua de Lisboa (N120) for about 1km up the hill, then take the marked turning to the right and, after another ten-minute walk, turn left at a sign marking the entrance to the site, which lies isolated amid arcadian green hills. At the highest point of the site a **Temple of Jupiter** has been partly reconstructed, overlooking a small forum with a row of shops built into its supporting wall. A paved street descends to a **villa and bath complex** whose underground central heating system is still intact.

Practicalities

Staying in Santiago shouldn't be a problem, but be warned that, out of season, bus services to the coast can be annoyingly irregular. The **turismo** in Largo do Mercado (Mon–Sat 9am–12.30am & 1.30–4.30pm, Sat 9am–1pm & 2–6pm; ☎269 826 696/887, ⊛www.costa-azul.rts.pt) might be able to help with **rooms**, otherwise try *Porto das Covas* (☎269 822 766, ℱ269 826 902; ❷), a newsagent just off Largo 25 Abril. **Pensões and hotels** include: *Pensão/Restaurante Covas*, by the bus station, at Rua Cidade de Setúbal 8–10 (☎269 822 675; ❸); *Residencial Hotelagoa*, Lagoa de Santo André (☎269 749 117; ❷), both of which are comfortable enough; *Residencial Gabriel*, Rua Professor Egas Moniz 24 (☎269 822 245, ℱ269 826 102; ❸), with modern, comfortable rooms and helpful staff; and *Albergaria D. Nuno*, Avenida D. Nuno Álvares Pereira (☎269 823 325, ℱ296 823 328; ❸), with swimming pool and parking. Best of all, however, is the *Pousada de São Tiago*, Estrada Nacional (☎ & ℱ269 822 459; ❻), 1km out of town on the Lisbon road – a simple but pleasant *pousada*, with a pool and a decent restaurant serving hearty regional specialities around €25 a head.

However, the best **restaurant** in Santiago is the *Pensão/Restaurante Covas*, which specializes in seafood and has a great-value *ementa turística* for €8. Alternatively, try *Refúgio Do Mirante*, opposite the Moróbriga ruins which dishes up tasty local fare, or the friendly, modestly priced *Restaurante Praceta*, Largo Zeca Afonso (behind the bus station), serving fish and chicken cooked on coals outside. There's also a fine covered **market** in the centre of town, next to the turismo, useful for stocking up for a stay at one of the beaches, as many have no facilities.

The Santo André and Melides lagoons

In summer there are five buses a day from Santiago do Cacém to **LAGOA DE SANTO ANDRÉ**, and it's a short walk from there along the shore to **LAGOA DE MELIDES**. These two **lagoon beaches**, separated from the sea by a narrow strip of sand, are named after the nearest inland towns, but each has its own small, laid-back community entirely devoted to having a good time on the beach. The **campsites** at both places are of a high standard and there are masses of signs offering rooms, chalets and houses to let. Space is at a premium in July and August, but at other times accommodation should be no problem.

At either place, the social scene centres around the beach-cafés and ice-cream stalls. Beyond these is the sand – miles and miles of it, stretching all the way to Comporta in the north and to Sines in the south. The sea is very enticing with high waves and good surf, but be warned and take local advice on water conditions: the undertow can be fierce and people drown here every year.

Sines and south to Pessegueiro

Like many Portuguese towns, the outskirts of **SINES** are not its strong point. Vasco da Gama was born here, but he'd probably turn in his grave if he could see the massive oil refinery and the sacrifice of the environment to new roads, railways, pipelines and wells. The centre of town has remained relatively unspoiled, however, and is dominated by a castle where, just inside the entrance, you can find the **turismo** (Mon–Sat 10am–1pm & 2–6pm; ☎269 634 472, ⓦwwwcosta-azul.rts.pt). The *Biblioteca Municipal*, Largo do Poeta Bacage, opposite the Parish Church (Mon–Fri 10am–2pm & 5–10pm, Sat 10am–2pm) offers free **internet**. There are plenty of bars and cafés in the old part of town, as well as some excellent **seafood restaurants**, including *Varanda Oceano* on Largo Nossa Senhora Salvas, serving fresh shellfish in 1930s-style surroundings. If you need to **stay the night** here, try the *Residencial Carvalho*, Rua Gago Coutinho 13 (☎269 632 019; ❶), or the friendly *Pensão Fredemar*, Rua Cândido dos Reis 31–35 (☎269 632 122; ❷).

Moving south from Sines there's a whole set of untouched little **beach** settlements easily accessible from the main road. All the beaches are named; particularly recommended is the **Praia do Somouqueira** named after the extraordinary rock formations and great at low tide when temporary new beaches are created. More good beaches are in the area around Ilha do Pessegueiro, including Praia da Ilha and Praia de Oliveirinha, reached from the road heading down to Porto Côvo – which is served by several daily buses from Sines.

Porto Côvo

The centre of **PORTO CÔVO** is a simple, unassuming, whitewashed place with a small cove harbour, a few *pensões, bars* and restaurants, some rooms to let and a camping site. However, developers have discovered Porto Côvo with a vengeance over the last decade or so and the land behind the village has been engulfed into one large building site. Despite this, it remains a lively and pleasant place to base yourself, not least for the series of beautiful coves stretching along the coast and the Ilha do Pessegueiro within easy walking distance.

The summer-only **turismo** (10am–1pm & 2–5pm; ☎269 905 460, ⓦwww.costa-azul.rts.pt) is on the main square and offers **internet** facilities for around €2.50 per hour. **Buses** connect Porto Côvo at least twice daily with Almograve, Vila Nova de Milfontes and Praia Zambujeira, and once or twice daily with Odemira and Santiago do Cacém. There are several services daily to and from Sines. **Accommodation** isn't a problem, except at the height of summer when advance booking is recommended. There is a new, year-round **campsite** on the approach road to town (☎069 905 136, ℻069 905 239) with good facilities and a pleasant site. The *Pensão Boa Esperança*, Rua Conde Bandeira (☎269 905 109; ❷), offers no-frills accommodation with shared bathrooms. Apartments are also for rent at nos. 6 and 7 Rua da Farmacía (☎269 905 125; €50 for 4), with number 6 having the edge owing to its congenial owner. Outside town on a housing estate is the bland but comfortable three-star *Porto Côvo Hotel* (☎269 905 017, ℮portocovo.hotel@ mail.telepac.pt; ❹). There are several **restaurants** on the main street, including *La Bella Vita Pizzeria*, on Rua Vasco da Gama 8, offering a tastier than most pizza and pasta choice in a scrubbed pine setting. On the same road at number 14 is *Restaurante Os Rosas*, which is popular with locals for its seafood and a variety of rice dishes, including *arroz de marisco*. For a good selection of **snacks** and pastries, you need look no further than the popular *Gelateria/Cafèteria Marques* at the opposite end of the square to the turismo.

Ilha do Pessegueiro

ILHA DO PESSEGUEIRO (Peach Tree Island) can be reached from the Porto Côvo–Vila Nova de Milfontes road, but the nicest approach is to walk, following the coastal path south from Porto Côvo. It's only a couple of kilo-metres and en route you'll pass the remains of a Bronze Age burial site.

The resort's name actually applies to the mainland beach; the island itself is less than a kilometre offshore and reachable on local fishing boats. On the mainland, there's the wonderful *Restaurante A Ilha* (☎269 905 113), a small sea-side **fort**, a rural hotel *Herdade Agro Turística do Pessegueiro* (apartments €50 for 4 in high season; bookings through *A Ilha*) and a **campsite** (☎269 905 178). If you're feeling energetic you could walk the 20km or so south from here to Vila Nova de Milfontes, a good half-day's walk along the beach and cliffs – take enough water for the whole journey.

Southern Alentejo resorts and Odemira

On the southern half of the Alentejo coast, **Vila Nova de Milfontes** is the main beach resort, with **Almograve** and **Zambujeira do Mar**, further south, being quieter, less developed seaside villages. **Odemira** – about 15km from the coast – makes a good inland base, and offers local bus connections to the coast.

Vila Nova de Milfontes

VILA NOVA DE MILFONTES lies on the estuary of the Rio Mira, whose sandy banks gradually merge into the coastline. It is an advantageous spot for sailors (the port is reputed to have harboured Hannibal and his Carthaginians during a storm) and swimmers: if the waves of the Atlantic are too fierce you can always swim in the estuary, though beware of very strong currents.

The resort is not exactly undiscovered – the Germans, especially, built villas here through the 1980s – and it is perhaps the most crowded and popular resort in the Alentejo. The old town, however, huddled around a striking, ivy-

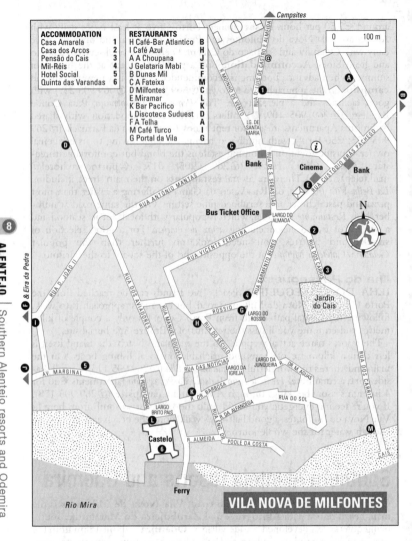

ACCOMMODATION
Casa Amarela	1
Casa dos Arcos	2
Pensão do Cais	3
Mil-Réis	4
Hotel Social	5
Quinta das Varandas	6

RESTAURANTS
H Café-Bar Atlantico	B
I Café Azul	H
A A Choupana	J
J Gelataria Mabi	E
B Dunas Mil	F
C A Fateixa	M
D Milfontes	C
E Miramar	L
K Bar Pacifico	K
L Discoteca Suduest	D
F A Telha	A
M Café Turco	I
G Portal da Vila	G

VILA NOVA DE MILFONTES

wreathed castle, remains a pretty enough place; while Portuguese families on holiday from the big cities of the north give it a homely atmosphere quite distinct from the cosmopolitan trendiness of the Algarve. If you want to escape some of the crowds, take the ferry from the little jetty to the far side of the estuary to beaches nearby.

Practicalities

Arriving by **bus**, you'll be dropped off in a small lot near the **turismo** on Rua António Mantas (summer daily 10am–7pm; ☎283 996 599). Buses run several times daily (Mon–Fri), but less frequently at weekends to Odemira, Alcácer do Sal, Porto Côvo and Zambujeira do Mar. If you're Algarve-bound, catch the bus to Cercal and transfer onto the Portimão express from Lisbon – the **ticket office** for all buses from Vila Nova is on Largo Almada. The *Casa Amarela* on Rua D. Luis de Castro e Almeida offers **internet** facilities (daily 10am–midnight; ℡283 996 632) for around €2 per hour. A range of activities including fishing and scuba diving can be arranged through the turismo, alternatively, **horse-riding** is offered by the English-run Companhia Caminhos do Alentejo (℡283 998 106, ℻283 998 206; €10/hr); **boat rental** is available from Aquadrilos (℡283 997 157), while details of **river trips** to Casa Branca and Odemira can be obtained from Milaventuras on (℡283 998 388).

Accommodation

Finding a place to stay should pose no problems out of season but it's advisable to book ahead in summer. If you turn up without a reservation ask at the turismo for a list of available **rooms** or look for others advertised in windows around town. Most of the newer **hotels** are situated in modern developments to the west of town – they usually have excellent facilities and can be very good value if you don't mind staying on a building site. Many of the new streets do not yet have names, but the hotels are well signposted. There are two **campsites** just north of town: the massive *Parque de Milfontes* (℡ & ℻283 996 104) has excellent facilities, while the nearby *Campiférias* (℡283 996 409, ℻283 996 581; closed Dec) is more modest.

Casa Amarela Rua D. Luís de Castro e Almeida ℡283 996 632. A small pension with rooms for up to four people (€55 for four). All rooms come with bathroom and terrace. ❷

Casa dos Arcos Rua dos Carris ℡283 996 264, ℻283 997 156. A very pleasant small hotel near the estuary with balconies in most rooms and breakfast is included. ❸

Pensão do Cais Rua dos Carris 9 ℡283 996 268. Very friendly hotel, full of Portuguese in summer (advance booking advised). Modern, spacious rooms, some with beautiful views over the estuary. ❷

Castelo de Milfontes ℡283 996 108, ℻283 997 122. Vila Nova's best lodgings, inside the fortress – cross the drawbridge to enter. The owner offers full board and is very picky about her guests, so dress well. Breakfast included. ❻, full board ❼

Duna Parque Rua Eira da Pedra ℡283 996 451, ℻283 996 459. A ten-minute walk from the centre is Milfontes' largest complex, with very well-equipped rooms; all rooms sleep up to four people and minimum stay is one week. ❹

Mil-Réis Actividades Hosteleiras Ltd Largo do Rossio 2 ℡283 998 233, ℻283 998 328. On the corner with Rossio, an old-fashioned pension with kindly owners, offering smart, clean rooms with TV. ❸

Hotel Social Av Marginal ℡283 996 517, ℻283 996 517. Attached to the *Misericórdia de Odemira* and with a rather muted atmosphere. Friendly management, however, and good rooms, some with verandahs overlooking the estuary. Has an inexpensive, if institutional-looking, restaurant – a reasonable meal will set you back around €8.50. ❸

Quinta das Varandas Eira da Pedra ℡283 996 155, ℻283 998 102. Part of an uninspiring complex by the dunes, follow the coast up from *A Choupana*. Good value, though, in family-run apartments, all mod cons with breakfast included. ❸

Eating

A Choupana Av Marginal. At far western end on Praia do Farol. Serves excellent grilled fish, is good value and popular with the locals.

Restaurante-Marisqueira Dunas Mil To the right off Av Marginal. Top quality fish restaurant where a meal will set you back €12 plus, but the food and service are well worth it. Especially recommended is the *açorda de marisco*.

A Fateixa Rua dos Carris. Popular place with a superb location on the riverbank; moderately

priced, with a grilled fish a speciality.

Churrasqueira Milfontes Rua António Mantas. Popular takeaway serving inexpensive, local fare but only open at weekends.

Café-Restaurante Miramar Largo Brito Pais. Good place to sit over a coffee or light snack on a large terrace overlooking the castle.

Churrasqueira A Telha Rua da Pinhal 3. Simple menu of local specialities with takeaway charcoal grilled chicken.

Portal da Vila Largo do Rossio. The Portuguese food in this family-run restaurant, served among greenery in a beautifully tiled interior, is unbeat- able for the price. The baked fish dishes are particularly good. A meal with wine will set you back about €10.

Drinking and nightlife

Café-Bar Atlantico on the Porto Côvo road (follow Rua Custódio Brás Pachego). A friendly late-night drinking den.

Café Azul Rossio 20. Relaxed bar playing a mix of jazz, rock and blues. Reasonably priced drinks include fine frozen tequila margaritas. Busy Fri and Sat and open till 4am.

Gelataria Mabi Rua Custódio Brás Pachego, next to the Post Office. A combined ice-cream parlour and bar, attracting a mixed clientele.

Bar Pacífico Rua Dr. Barbosa. Dance-bar playing a mixture of chart, techno and reggae music. Open 10pm–6am (closed Oct & Nov).

Discoteca Suduest on northern continuation of Rua dos Aviadores. Plays the latest in rave and dance music.

Café Turco Rua Dom João II. A place where it's easy to think you're in Lisbon; trendy, mock-Moorish café-bar with live acoustic music at the weekend when its full of Lisbonites (only open Sat & Sun in winter).

Almograve

The coast south of Vila Nova de Milfontes becomes ever more rugged and spectacular. At the tiny resort of **ALMOGRAVE**, 5km west of the Odemira–Vila Nova de Milfontes road, huge waves come crashing down on the rocks and for most of the day swimming is impossible. It can get very crowded at high tide, too, when the beaches are reduced to thin strips with occasional waves drenching everybody's belongings; but, for all that, it's an exhilarating place.

There are several **bars** and **restaurants** including the reasonable *Restaurante Duna Praia,* Avenida da Praia. The bus service from Odemira is just right for a day trip but should you wish **to stay** overnight, head for the *Pensão Paulo Campos*, Rua Antónia Pachecho 9 (☎283 647 118; ❸; May–Oct). If you can stretch to it though, the best option is the pleasant, new *Residencial, Duna Praia* (☎283 647 115, ☞283 647 112; ❹), conveniently situated on the way to the beach and with a restaurant grill.

Odemira

In summer, the southern Alentejo resorts can get quite crowded, so you may prefer to stay in **ODEMIRA** and take day trips to the seaside – be warned, though, that the bus services can be erratic. The town is pretty enough, set around the River Mira, and has several **pensões**, best of which are the very good *Residencial Rita*, Largo do Poço Novo (☎283 322 531; ❸), and *Residencial Idálio*, Rua Eng. Arantes Oliveira 28 (☎283 322 156; ❷), both off to the left when you come out of the bus station. The new **turismo** (Mon–Fri 10am–6pm; ☎283 320 900, ☞283 327 168) located in the central Praça da Repubública, might also be able to help with finding a room. Among **restaurants**, try *O Tarro*, near the main road junction, where €8 will get you a hearty meal, and for a drink head to *O Cais*, a terrace-bar down by the river, with live music at weekends (turn left over the bridge, then left again).

Zambujeira do Mar and on to the Algarve

At the village of **ZAMBUJEIRA DO MAR**, south of Odemira and 7km west of the main road, a large cliff provides a dramatic backdrop to the beach, which, like that of Vila Nova de Milfontes, can get very crowded in July and

August. The scenery more than compensates for the winds and the sea – which can get positively chilly, even in summer – but can't disguise the rundown state of the village and the encircling villas. If you need to **stay** – and the bus schedule from Odemira makes a day trip impossible – try any of these rather basic options: the *Residencial Mira Mar* (T & F283 961 352; ❸), the modern *Residencial Ondazul* (T283 961 450; ❸), or the *Residencial Mar-e-Sol* (T283 961 171; ❷) which backs onto the market. There's also a reasonable **campsite** (T283 961 172, F283 961 320), about 1km from the cliffs, which has showers and a café-bar, or the more up-market São campsite (T282 947 145, F282 947 245), 15 km due south of the town with tennis courts and a pool. The best **restaurants** are the *Taberna Ti Vitório*, on Largo Mira Mar, which serves wonderful grilled fish, and the *Cervejaria A Marisqueira da Praia*, on Rua Mira Mar 14, which does a good *arroz de marisco* among other dishes. The popular and tacky late-night joint is the *Bar/Discoteca Clube da Praia*, on the beach.

Zambujeira is the southernmost Alentejo beach, and an attractive road twists its way into the hills of the Algarve from the river crossing at Odeceixe. For the most dramatic approach, however, take the road from Odemira through the **Serra de Monchique**, descending to the Algarve coast at Portimão.

Travel details

Trains

Alcácer do Sal to: Lisbon (3 daily; 1hr 45 min–2hr 45 min).
Beja to: Évora (3 daily; 1hr 25min–2hr); Faro (3 daily; 3hr 10min–4hr); Lisbon (4 daily; 2hr 25min–3hr 20min).
Belver to: Lisbon (2 daily; 2hr 35min–3hr).
Crato to: Lisbon (3 daily; 3hr 35 min–3hr).
Elvas to: Lisbon (3 daily; 4hr 50min–5hr 10min); Portalegre (3 daily; 50min).
Évora to: Beja (6 daily; 1hr 40min–2hr 35min); Faro (2 daily; 5hr 10min–5hr 20min); Lisbon (5 daily; 2hr 20min–5hr 25min).
Portalegre to: Crato (3 daily; 15min); Elvas (3 daily; 50min); Lisbon (4 daily; 3hr 55min–4hr 10min).

Buses

Alcácer do Sal to: Lisbon (3 daily; 1hr 30min).
Almograve to: Lisbon (2 daily; 4hr 10min); Porto Côvo (16 daily; 1hr); Vila Nova de Milfontes (2 daily; 35min).
Alter do Chão to: Lisbon (2 daily; 3hr 20min); Portalegre (1 daily; 35min).
Beja to: Albufeira (hourly; 2hr 15min); Elvas (1 daily; 2hr 50min); Évora (hourly; 1hr); Faro (1 daily; 3hr 10min); Lisbon (hourly; 2hr 40min); Moura (2 daily; 1hr 25min); Portalegre (2 daily; 4hr); Serpa (5 daily; 45min).
Borba to: Elvas (6 daily; 30min); Estremoz (2 daily;

15min); Évora (2 daily; 1hr); Lisbon (3 daily; 3hr).
Castelo de Vide to: Portalegre (2 daily; 20min).
Crato to: Lisbon (1 daily; 3hr 50min).
Estremoz to: Borba (2 daily; 15min); Évora (hourly; 45min); Lisbon (2 daily; 3hr); Portalegre (2 daily; 1hr).
Évora to: Albufeira (4 daily; 3hr 10min); Beja (hourly; 1hr 10min); Borba (2 daily; 50min); Coimbra (1 daily; 4hr 35min); Elvas (5 daily; 1hr 35min); Estremoz (hourly; 45min); Faro (4 daily; 3hr 50min); Lisbon (hourly; 1hr 45min); Monsaraz (2 daily; 55min); Moura (23 daily; 1hr 30min); Portalegre (21 daily; 1hr 45min); Santarém (2 daily; 2hr).
Mértola to: Lisbon (2 daily; 3hr 50min).
Moura to: Évora (1 daily; 1hr 30min); Lisbon (1 daily; 3hr 45min).
Odemira to: Lisbon (4 daily; 3hr 30min); Vila Nova de Milfontes (2 daily; 20min).
Portalegre to: Alter do Chão (1 daily; 35min); Beja (2 daily; 3hr 50min); Castelo do Vide (2 daily; 20min); Estremoz (2 daily; 1hr); Évora (36 daily; 1hr 45min); Lisbon (3 daily; 4hr); Portalegre train station (3 daily; 15min); Viseu (2 daily; 5hr).
Porto Côvo to: Almograve (4 daily; 40min); Lisbon (6 daily; 3hr 15min); Santiago do Cacém (4 daily; 1hr); Vila Nova de Milfontes (7 daily; 30min).
Santiago do Cacém to: Lisbon (8 daily; 2hr 15min); Porto Côvo (5 daily; 1hr); Sines (5 daily; 45min); Vila Nova de Milfontes (6 daily; 1hr 25min).
Serpa to: Beja (23 daily; 35min); Lisbon (hourly; 4hr).

Sines to: Beja (2 daily; 2hr 50min); Lisbon (hourly; 3hr 10min); Odemira (1 daily; 1hr 10min); Porto Côvo (5 daily; 25min); Santiago do Cacém (5 daily; 35min); Zambujeira do Mar (4 daily; 1hr 30min).
Vila Nova de Milfontes to: Almograve (2 daily; 15min); Lisbon (hourly; 3hr 35min); Porto Côvo (2 daily; 25min); Zambujeira do Mar (2 daily; 40min).
Vila Viçosa to: Borba (hourly; 10min); Elvas (2 daily; 35min); Estremoz (3 daily; 25min); Évora (3 daily; 1hr); Lisbon (2 daily; 3hr).
Zambujeira do Mar to: Almograve (2 daily; 25min); Lisbon (1 daily; 4hr 35min); Porto Côvo (2 daily; 1hr 15min); Santiago do Cacém (1 daily; 2hr 15min); Sines (4 daily; 1hr 40min); Vila Nova de Milfontes (2 daily; 40min).

The Algarve

ATLANTIC
OCEAN

SPAIN

N

CHAPTER 9

Highlights

* **Cataplana** The classic Algarve dish – seafood cooked in a *cataplana*. See p.37

* **Ilha de Tavira** An enormous stretch of dune-backed beach; getting there is half the fun. See p.526

* **Parque Natural da Ria Formosa** Protected wetlands, home to the bizarre web-footed poodles. See p.527

* **The Guadiana** The river marking the border with Spain offers some of the region's least spoilt scenery. See p.531

* **West coast beaches** A stunning variety of wave-battered sandy swathes between Sagres and Odeceixe. See p.532

* **Silves** The historic Moorish capital of the Algarve is overlooked by the grandest of castles. See p.551

* **The Serra de Monchique** The woods around Monchique's mountains offer superb walking terrain. See p.553

* **Museu Municipal, Lagos** An eclectic jumble of architectural remains, cultural highlights and curios. See p.559

* **Boat trips** Explore extraordinary rock formations and grottoes from Lagos or Portimão. See p.562

The Algarve

With its long, sandy beaches and picturesque rocky coves, the **Algarve** has attracted more tourist development than the rest of the country put together. In some areas the development and crowds overwhelm the charms that made the Algarve popular in the first place, at least in high season. The strip of coast from Faro west to Albufeira has suffered most, with its endless villa complexes creating a rather depressing Mediterranean-style suburbia. On the fringes, though, especially around Sagres and Tavira, things are far better, with small-scale and relaxed resorts near superb beaches or island sandbanks. Out of season, warm sunshine and fewer visitors make the whole region far more appealing.

The coastline in fact has two quite distinct characters. To the **west of Faro** you'll find the classic postcard images of the province – a series of tiny bays and coves, broken up by weird rocky outcrops and fantastic grottoes. They're at their most exotic around the major resort towns of **Lagos** and **Albufeira**. For fewer crowds, alternative bases include the former fishing villages of **Salema** or **Burgau**, the historic cape of **Sagres** – site of Henry the Navigator's naval school – or one of the string of villages along the rougher west coast as far as **Odeceixe**.

East of Faro, there's a complete change as you encounter the first of a series of sandy offshore islets, the *ilhas*, which front the coastline virtually all the way to the Spanish border. Overall, this is the quieter section of the coast and it has the bonus of much warmer waters than those further west. First-choice bases along this stretch would be Faro itself, **Olhão** and **Tavira**, all of which offer access to the sandbank islands.

Inland Algarve is still relatively undeveloped, especially around **Alcoutim** on the Spanish border, and there are scattered attractions in the Roman ruins of **Estói** and the market town of **Loulé**, both north of Faro, and the old Moorish town of **Silves**, easily reached from Portimão. The outstanding area, however, is the **Serra de Monchique**, the highest mountain range in the south, with cork and chestnut woods, remote little villages and a beautiful old spa in **Caldas de Monchique**.

The Algarve is an all-year-round destination, with sunny and relatively mild winters. In many respects the region is at its best in **spring** or **winter**. Most *pensões* and restaurants stay open, so rooms are easy to find. Indeed, **off-season travel** in the Algarve will get you some of the best deals in the country, with luxury hotels offering all-in packages at discounts of up to seventy percent; check out the latest deals at the local tourist offices.

Early summer has the added attraction of the Algarve's **International Music Festival**, sponsored by the Gulbenkian Foundation and hosting major classical

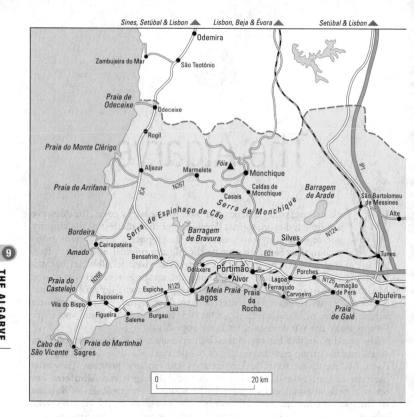

artists. But if you come in high **summer**, without a booking, finding accommodation can be a real struggle, though you'll usually find something. Be prepared for very high summer prices relative to the rest of the country. One of a dozen tourist-orientated Algarve home pages on the **internet** worth investigating is Ⓦwww.nexus-pt.com/index.htm, with links to hotels, golf courses, general information and directories.

Transport

Getting around by **public transport** is easier here than anywhere else in Portugal and, since the coastline is only 240km long from east to west, you can see an awful lot in just a few days. The **Algarve rail line** runs from Lagos in the west to Vila Real de Santo António on the Spanish border, calling at most major towns en route (though you may have to change at Faro and Tavira to do the whole route); **buses** link all the resorts and main inland villages. The two main bus companies running services are EVA and Frota Azul, which link together in the western Algarve to offer a *Passe Turístico* (valid for three consecutive days; €14.50), giving unlimited bus travel between Lagos and Loulé, covering all the main resorts in between (except Faro). You can buy a pass from any bus station in the region.

Driving is useful, especially if you want to reach the more out-of-the-way inland villages and inaccessible cove beaches (or head further into Portugal).

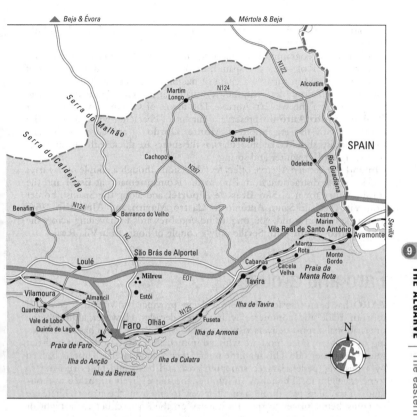

The east–west highway from Albufeira to the Spanish border offers fast and easy access to most of the region, avoiding the dreadful east–west N125, which is one of the most dangerous roads in Portugal (which itself has the highest accident rates in the EU). Two new legs of the highway – west to Lagos and north from Albufeira to Lisbon – are due to open in late 2002.

The eastern Algarve

All flights to the Algarve land at **Faro**, the administrative capital of the region and by far the largest town along the coast. Although no great holiday destination in itself, the centre of the town is considerably more attractive than the concrete suburbs might suggest and there are some fine beaches and interesting local villages within easy reach. It's also not a bad place to start or finish a tour of the rest of the Algarve: Faro is connected with Lisbon by fast express coaches and offers efficient access to most Algarve towns by bus and – a little slower – on the Algarve rail line.

Faro marks a geographical boundary on the Algarve. The **coastline** east from here to Manta Rota, near the Spanish border, is protected by thin stretches of mud flats, fringed in turn by a chain of magnificent, long sandbanks, or *ilhas*. Often accessible only by boat, they're usually far less crowded than the small rocky resorts of the western Algarve. The towns of **Olhão**, **Tavira** and **Vila Real de Santo António** preserve a fair bit of character, while most of the resorts – with the exception of **Monte Gordo** – are fairly small-scale. Ornithologists should take binoculars, as the shores are thick with various types of wading bird in winter and spring.

Inland, the eastern Algarve offers few diversions, though a couple of day trips provide some distraction: from Faro to the Roman remains at **Estói** and the small country town of **São Brás de Alportel**; and along the Spanish border from Vila Real de Santo António to **Castro Marim** and **Alcoutim**. With longer detours in mind, you might find equal rewards in travelling across the frontier **into Spain**, with Seville only a couple of hours from Vila Real.

Faro and around

FARO has been transformed from a sleepy provincial town into a centre of tourism, trade and commerce within three decades. However, although the international airport delivers visitors right to its door, the town has a job holding on to them, since most are whisked immediately away to the out-and-out resorts on either side. This is a little unfair: there's an attractive harbour, backed by a bustling, pedestrianized shopping area, and boats and buses run out to some excellent local **beaches**. In summer, too, there's lively **nightlife**, as thousands of travellers pass through on their way to and from the airport. There are certainly better places to spend a holiday on the Algarve, but for a night or two's stay at either end, it can be an enjoyable enough base.

Faro's Roman predecessor was 8km to the north, at Ossonoba (see p.519); the present city was founded by the Moors, under whom it was a thriving commercial port, supplying the regional capital at Silves. Following its conquest by the Christians, under Afonso III in 1249, the city experienced a chequered few centuries, surviving a series of conquests and disasters. Sacked and burned by the Earl of Essex in 1596, and devastated by the Great Earthquake of 1755, it is no surprise that the modern city has so few historic buildings. What interest it does retain is contained within the **Cidade Velha** (Old Town), which lies behind a series of defensive walls, across the harbour from the main part of town.

Arrival and information

In the summer months, flights land at Faro's international **airport**, 6km west of the town centre, 24 hours a day. Here, you'll find a police and first-aid post, bank, post office and tourist office (daily 10am–midnight; ☏289 818 582), and though the airport is rapidly expanding, there is little else apart from a poor self-service canteen. A number of **car rental** companies (see "Listings", p.518) also have offices at the airport.

One of the quickest ways of getting into the centre is by **taxi**, which should cost about €8, plus €1.50 for any luggage that goes in the boot; there's also a twenty percent surcharge between 10pm and 6am, and at weekends. From June

RESTAURANTS

Aliança	F
Adega Dois Irmãos	D
Cidade Velha	J
Gardy	G
Faro e Benfica	I
Fim do Mundo	E
Ginásio Clube Naval	H
Adega Nova	B
Sol e Jardim	C
Taska	A

ACCOMMODATION

Adelaide	3
Alameda	8
Algarve	2
Eva	7
Madalena	4
Oceano	6
Pinto	5
Samé	10
São Filipe	1
Youth hostel	9

FARO

N

200 m
0

Olhão, Vila Real & Spain

Soccer Stadium

Mercado

Police Station

Igreja de São Pedro

Igreja do Carmo

Museu Regional

Igreja de São Francisco

Museu Arqueológico

CIDADE VELHA

Sé

Bishops Palace

Arco da Vila

Jardim Manuel Bivar

Bus Terminal

Bus to Campsite & Airport

Museu Marítimo

Doca (harbour)

Centro Ciência Viva

Jetty

Train Station

EN125 Lisbon, Lagos & Airport

Ferries to Farol & Ilha Deserta

Street names:
Rua de Berlim
Avenida Dr. Julio Almeida Carrapato
Rua do Bom Joas
Rua Pedro Nunes
Avenida 5 de Outubro
Rua Antero de Quental
Rua Ataíde de Oliveira
Rua General Humberto
Rua Dr. José de Matos
Rua da Policia de Segurança
Rua do Bernardo de Passos
Rua Nova
Largo do Pé da Cruz
Rua de Portugal
Rua de Mota
Rua de Cáçadores
Rua Conselheiro Bívar
Rua Infante D. Henrique
Avenida da República
Rua Com Francisco Manuel
Largo da Sé
Rua 1° de Dezembro

to October there is also a **Aerobus** service operated by EVA (Mon & Wed–Sun hourly from 9am–8pm), which takes only thirteen minutes. The aerobus runs to Faro's bus station, and is free to flight ticket holders – simply show your ticket when taking the aerobus into the centre or coming back to the airport (from the bus station Mon & Wed–Sun hourly 8.15am–8.15pm). Two local **buses** also run from the airport to the centre, a twenty-five-minute ride, costing €1: the #16 (daily roughly every 45 minutes 8am–8.30pm; July to mid-Sept until 11pm), and the rather less frequent #14. Both stop outside the bus terminal in town (see below) and, further on, at the Jardim Manuel Bivar (*Jardim* on the timetables) by the harbour. There are timetables posted at the airport bus stop; buy tickets on board.

The **bus terminal** is located on Avenida da República, behind the *Hotel Eva*, just across the harbour from the old part of town. The **train station** is a few minutes' walk further north up the avenue, facing Largo da Estação. The compact town centre is simple to negotiate **on foot**, and all the *pensões* and hotels are extremely central. There is a **town bus service**, but you'll need it only to get to the beach and campsite (for which, see below) and the airport.

Faro's main **turismo** is close to the harbour front at Rua da Misericórdia 8 (May–Sept daily 9.30am–7pm; Oct–April Mon–Fri 9.30am–5.30pm, Sat & Sun 9.30am–12.30pm & 2–5.30pm; ☎289 803 604). The turismo provides maps of the town and has noticeboards which deal comprehensively with local and long-distance bus, boat and train timetables, too. The regional tourist office – **Região de Turismo do Algarve** – east of the old town at Avenida 5º Outubro (Mon–Fri 9.30am–12.30pm & 2–5.30pm; ☎289 800 400, 🌐www.rtalgarve.pt) is another source of information on the area as a whole. For **internet access**, head to PapaNET, Rua Dr Justino Cúmano 38 (Mon–Fri 10am–7pm; €2.50/hr; ☎289 804 338) just west of the market building.

Accommodation

Like most of the Algarve, Faro's accommodation is stretched to the limit in summer. If you fly in without a reservation, it's worth asking the airport tourist office to try and help you book you a place – though it's not officially part of their job and you'll have to pay for any calls they make on your behalf; otherwise the main turismo and regional tourist office in town (see above) can give you an idea of where to look for **rooms**. Most of the city's **pensões** and **hotels** – the best of which are picked out below – are concentrated in the area just north of the harbour. The town's **youth accommodation centre** is a quiet place, located next to the gardens at Rua da Policia de Segurança Pública (PSP), on the left past the police station (☎289 826 521, 📠289 801 413). You'd be advised to book well in advance as it's often filled with groups. You'll need a hostel card, and prices are €10 for beds in dorms of four or six people, or €21 for a double room without bath, €23 with bath; all prices include breakfast.

In summer, Faro's inexpensive but basic **campsite** at Praia de Faro is always full and very cramped, with tents and caravans wedged onto a sandy dune back from the beach around ten minutes walk east of the main beach car park; if you want to stay, phone or fax ahead (reception 8.30am–9.30pm; ☎289 817 876, 📠289 819 101). Prices are €0.40 per person plus €0.40 per tent. Take bus #14 or #16, either direct from the airport or from the stop opposite the bus terminal in town; the site is a ten-minute walk from the bus stop at Praia de Faro.

Casa de Hóspedes Adelaide Rua Cruz das Mestras 7–9 ⊺ 289 802 383, ⨍ 289 826 870. Clean, very basic rooms, some with their own bathroom, presided over by a friendly owner; some rooms are in an annexe round the corner. ❸

Residencial Alameda Rua Dr. José de Matos 31 ⊺ 289 801 962, ⨍ 289 804 218. A bit removed from the action in a modern part of town, but tidy small rooms all come with en-suite facilities and some boast balconies facing a small park. ❸

Residencial Algarve Rua Infante Dom Henrique 52 ⊺ 289 895 700, ⓔ reservas@residencialalgarve.com. This brand new *residencial* is by far the most comfortable in town, built in traditional style. Spruce rooms come with spotless bathrooms and cable TV. ❺

Hotel Eva Av da República 1 ⊺ 289 803 354, ⨍ 289 802 304. The town's best hotel offering rooms with balconies looking across to the old town or the marina. There's a rooftop pool and restaurant, and a courtesy bus to the local beach. ❼

Pensão Madalena Rua Conselheiro Bivar 109 ⊺ 289 805 806, ⨍ 289 805 807. A mixed bag of rather en-suite characterless rooms with phones and TVs. ❸

Pensão-Residencial Oceano Trav. Ivens 21–1° ⊺ 289 823 349, ⨍ 289 805 590. Clean – if fairly bland – *pensão*; rooms with bathrooms and TVs. ❹

Residencial Pinto Rua 1° de Maio 27, ⊺ 289 807 417. Welcoming and spotless *residencial* with spartan but characterful rooms. Communal bathrooms. ❸

Residencial Samé Rua do Bocage 66 ⊺ 289 824 375, ⨍ 289 804 166. Small rooms in a modern block just outside the old town. Some have balconies and all come with bathrooms and TV. ❹

Pensão São Filipe Rua Infante Dom Henrique 55–1° ⊺ & ⨍ 289 824 182. Clean, reasonable rooms with high ceilings, wooden shutters and TVs. Communal bath. ❸

The Town

The only part of town to have survived the various violent historic upheavals is the **Cidade Velha**, across the harbour, an oval of cobbled streets and brightly painted restored buildings set within a run of sturdy walls. It is entered through the eighteenth-century town gate, the **Arco da Vila**, next to the turismo. From here, Rua do Município leads up to the majestic Largo da Sé, flanked by the cathedral and a group of palaces – including the former bishop's palace – and lined with orange trees. The **Sé** itself (Mon–Sat 10am–12.30pm & 1.30pm–5pm, Sun open for Mass at 10am & noon; €1) is a squat, white mismatch of Gothic, Renaissance and Baroque styles, all heavily remodelled after the 1755 earthquake. It's worth looking inside, though, mainly for the fine eighteenth-century *azulejo* tiling. Climb up the bell tower for superb views over the old town and the mud flats beyond.

More impressive is the **Museu Arqueológico** (May–Sept Mon & Sat 2.30–6pm, Tues–Fri 10am–6pm; Oct–April Mon & Sat 2–5.30pm, Tues–Fri 9.30am–5.30pm; €2) installed in a sixteenth-century convent with a beautiful cloister – one of the oldest in Portugal – in nearby Praça Afonso III; in front of the building stands a forthright, crucifix-carrying statue of the conqueror Afonso himself, king between 1249 and 1279. The most striking of the museum's exhibits is a superb third-century AD Roman mosaic of Neptune surrounded by the four winds, unearthed near the train station. Other items include a collection of Roman statues from the excavations at Estói (see p.519), and a selection of local paintings, military artefacts and naive sixteenth-century multicoloured tiles, upstairs in the art gallery. Sadly much of the museum seems to be under permanent restoration and not all the exhibits can be viewed.

In the rest of the old town, it's well worth wandering around some of the cobbled side streets, whose houses are fronted by decorative balconies and tiling – the odd one serving as an antique shop or art gallery.

The **harbour** is Faro's most vibrant area: the town gardens and a cluster of outdoor cafés overlook the rows of sleek yachts and at the end of the day much of Faro gathers to promenade here. Continuing round the harbour to the west you'll pass the small **Museu Marítimo** (Mon–Fri 2.30–4.30pm; free), a modest maritime museum showing displays of model boats and local fishing techniques. Heading southwards on Rua Comandante Francisco Manuel, along the foot of the harbour, you can follow the railway line for an attractive walk along the seafront, with the town walls on one side and the mud flats on the other; a small arch through the old town walls offers another approach to the Cidade Velha (see p.515). From the jetty opposite here, ferries depart to the local sandspit beaches (see below).

Just before the jetty, the **Centro Ciência Viva** (July to mid-Sept Tues–Sun 4pm–11pm; mid-Sept to June Tues–Fri 10am–5pm, Sat & Sun 3–7pm; €2, children under 12 €0.50; ☎289 890 920), in Faro's former electricity station, makes a good wet weather spot for kids. There are several low-tech interactive exhibits that explain scientific principles; permanent displays include a rock pool and a flight simulator and several temporary exhibits. Most of the displays are labelled only in Portuguese.

Elswhere, in the backstreets around **Rua de Santo António**, shops, bars and restaurants do their best to keep you off the local beach. At the end of Rua de Santo António, on Praça de Liberdade, is the most intriguing of Faro's museums, the **Museu Regional** (Mon–Fri 9am–noon & 2–5pm; €2), which has a display of local crafts and industries, including reconstructions of typical cottage interiors, and models of the net systems still used for tuna fishing.

By far the most curious sight in town, however, is the twin-towered, Baroque **Igreja do Carmo** (Mon–Fri 10am–1pm & 3–6pm; Oct–April until 5pm; Sat 10am–1pm, Sun only for mass at 9am; free, chapel of bones €1), near the central post office on the Largo do Carmo. A door to the right of its altar leads to the sacristy where you buy a ticket to view the macabre **Capela dos Ossos** (Chapel of the Bones), set in an overgrown garden out back. Like the one at Évora (see p.467), its walls are decorated with human bones – in this case disinterred from the adjacent monks' cemetery. Nearby, in Largo de São Pedro, the sixteenth-century **Igreja de São Pedro** is infinitely more attractive as a church, its finest decorative work an altar (to the left of the main altar) whose central image is a gilded, wooden *Last Supper* in relief.

The beaches

Faro's "town beach" – **Praia de Faro** – is typical of the sandspit *ilha* beaches of the eastern Algarve: a long sweep of beautiful sand with both a sea-facing and a more sheltered land-facing side. It's less characteristic in being both overcrowded and overdeveloped, with bars, restaurants, villas and a campsite jammed onto a sandy island too narrow to cope in the height of summer. Still, if you just want a few hours away from the centre of Faro, it's more than adequate; out of season you'll probably have the sands to yourself. The beach is situated on the Ilha de Faro, southwest of the town; buses #14 and #16 run from the harbour gardens, or the stop opposite the bus station, calling at the airport en route (every 45 minutes, 8am–8.30pm, July to mid-Sept until 11pm; €1), stopping just before the narrow bridge to the beach itself.

Alternatively, **ferries** shuttle through narrow marshy channels to a couple of other local sandbar beaches, between Faro and Olhão. They depart from the jetty below the old town, either to **Farol** (described on p.522) on the Ilha da Culatra (June to mid-Sept 4 daily, first boat 9.30am, last return 7pm; €3.50 return), or to the so-called **Ilha Deserta** (June to mid-Sept 4 daily; €10 return) part of the Parque Natural da Ria Formosa. The name is actually a misnomer, as there are cafés and plenty of other sun worshippers for company; the island's official name is Ilha da Barreta.

Eating, drinking and nightlife

The heart of the town is a modern, pedestrianized shopping area on either side of Rua de Santo António, where you can find innumerable **restaurants**, **cafés** and **bakeries** – the latter stocked with almond delicacies, the regional speciality. Most of the pavement restaurants have similar menus (and similar prices); if you're prepared to scout around the backstreets, you can often find cheaper, better food, though without the accompanying streetlife that makes central Faro so attractive. As you'd expect, the cuisine is predominantly seafood-based, including the ubiquitous and often expensive *arroz de marisco* (a stew of shellfish and rice).

Cafés and restaurants

Café Aliança Rua F. Gomes 6–11. Once the favoured haunt of the literary set, this faded coffee house is said to be one of the oldest cafés in Portugal, dating from 1908. It has seats outside, and a full menu of breakfasts, burgers, salads, omelettes, pastries and ice cream.

Cidade Velha Rua Domingos Guieiro 19 Simple café in the old town, serving drinks, soups and inexpensive snacks. Closed weekends.

Adega Dois Irmãos Largo Terreiro do Bispo 13–15. One of the oldest of the city's fish and seafood restaurants, a moderately priced place which specializes in tasty *cataplana* (served for two only). Try the sardines, too.

Marisqueira Faro e Benfica Doca de Faro. One of the town's best spots for a splurge on fish and seafood, with tables facing the town across the harbour. Pricey specialities include *cataplana*, *feijoada* and various rice dishes. Closed Tues.

Fim do Mundo Rua Vasco da Gama 53. Bustling place mostly filled with locals enjoying good value grilled fish and meats – the *frango piri-piri* is the house speciality. Closed all day Mon & Tues lunch.

Gardy Rua de Santo António 16. Popular local *pastelaria* where seats are always at a premium – excellent cakes, pastries and coffee.

Restaurante Ginásio Clube Naval Doca de Faro. Set on a raised terrace right on the harbour, this is one of the few places in town where you can dine with a view over the tidal mud flats. A great place to enjoy moderately priced fish and grilled meats at sunset. Closed Mon.

Adega Nova Rua Francisco Barreto 24. Near the train station, this is an old-fashioned *adega* with classic Portuguese food and jugs of wine. An inexpensive choice if you steer clear of fish and seafood.

Sol e Jardim Praça Ferreira de Almeida 22–23. A junk shop turned restaurant with all manner of oddities suspended from the ceiling of a barn-like "garden" dining room serving moderately priced Portuguese fare. Live folk music at weekends.

Taska Rua do Alportel 38. Friendly place serving traditional Algarve fare to a mostly Portuguese crowd. Averagely priced house specialities, including corn mash with cockles and prawns, accompanied by an excellent range of regional wines. Closed Sun.

Bars and discos

The best of Faro's **nightlife** is concentrated along two or three central pedestrianized and cobbled streets – in particular **Rua Conselheiro Bivar** with its café-bars with outdoor seating, and the parallel **Rua do Prior**, where many of the bars and clubs feature DJs, live bands and video screens; there are rarely cover charges. Few places open much before 11pm and things get going around midnight; soon afterwards, as the bars fill up, drinkers spill out onto the cobbled alleys to party. Faro also occasionally hosts big-name rock and pop **gigs** at the football stadium – check posters around town, or ask at the turismo.

O Cofre Rua Conselheiro Bivar 54. Café-*pastelaria* by day, youth hang-out by night.

Columbus Jardim Manuel Bivar, corner with Rua João Dias. Jazzy local haunt with outdoor seats under arcades opposite the harbour gardens. There's a dartboard inside too. Closed Mon.

Conselheiro Rua Conselheiro Bivar 72–78. Disco bar with a minimum consumption of €25 most nights, with indoor tables, swirling lights and occasionally some good sounds.

Diesel Bar Travessa São Pedro. Chilled-out bar with Aztec-style decor, in a small, dark street off Ruo do Prior. Offers a wide selection of shots and cocktails.

Gothic Rua da Madelena 38, near the Igreja de São Pedro. Gothic/industrial sounds and cheap beer in a dark setting. Pretty unique for the Algarve. Closed Sun.

Kingburger Bar Rua do Prior 40. A small and relaxed bar, one of the first to open up along here, and one of the last to close.

Millennium III Rua do Prior 21. Large club with industrial-warehouse feel, playing all the latest sounds, good DJs and regular performances by local bands. One of the better venues. Open 11pm–5am.

O Prior Ruo do Prior 41. Run by the same management and with a similar clientele as

Universidade, but less cheesy music in a slightly smaller venue, and no live bands.

Universidade Rua de São Pedro 19–23. At the end of Rua do Prior – regular live bands and a post-11pm Happy Hour for cheap beer make this a popular student hang-out.

Upa Upa Rua Conselheiro Bivar 51. Laid back and relatively early opening music bar with a mixed clientele spilling onto outdoor tables on the widest stretch of this pedestrianized street.

Versailles Rua Ivens 7–9. Restaurant-bar that's good for a drink post-restaurant/pre-club, with outdoor seating and – later on at least – a youthful, local crowd. Open until midnight.

Listings

Airlines British Airways (airport ☎289 818 476); Lufthansa (airport ☎289 800 751); TAP, Francisco Gomes 8 ☎289 800 200.

Airport Flight information on ☎289 800 800.

Bus terminal Av da República 106 (information, ☎289 899 700/706). There's an English-speaking information office inside the terminal, though it is not always staffed.

Car rental Auto Jardim airport ☎289 800 881, ☏289 587 780; Avis airport ☎289 810 120, ☏289 818 540; Europcar Av da República 2, ☎289 823 778; airport ☎289 818 777, ☏289 818 393; Hertz Rua Infante D. Henrique 91A, ☎289 803 956, ☏289 803 957; airport ☎289 810 150, ☏289 810 152.

Cinema Cinema Golden City (☎289 820 308) has four small screens in the giant Faro Shopping complex on the airport road (N125).

Consulate The only British consulate in the Algarve is in Portimão (p.547). In Faro itself, there's also a Canadian consulate (Rua Frei Lourenço de Santa Maria 1–1°; ☎289 803 757).

Football The Algarve's top soccer team, Farense, plays at the Estádio São Luís (☎289 894 020), in the north of Faro. Tickets (from €15–20) can be purchased on match days from the office at the back of the stadium or, for big games, from the

Loja Farense on Praça Ferreira de Almeida.

Hospital Hospital Distrital de Faro (☎289 891 100), behind Farense football stadium. In emergencies ☎112.

Left luggage At the bus terminal (Mon–Fri 9am–1pm & 2–6pm; €2.50 per item per day).

Listings A comprehensive free monthly listing of cultural events in Faro can be found in *Agenda*, produced by Faro Town Council in Portuguese only, and available from the tourist office, cultural centres and larger hotels.

Police Rua da Polícia de Segurança Pública 32 (☏289 822 022).

Post office Largo do Carmo (Mon–Fri 8.30am–6.30pm, Sat 9am–12.30pm); also has *poste restante* facilities.

Railway station ☎289 803 090.

Taxis There's a rank in Praça Dr. Francisco Gomes, by the town gardens, otherwise phone ☎289 822 275 or 289 895 795.

Telephones You can make international calls from the post office.

Travel agencies Abreu, Av da República 124 ☎289 870 900, ✉faro@abreu.pt; Top Tours, Edifício Hotel Eva, Doca de Faro ☎289 895 349, ✉faro@toptours.pt.

North of Faro: Estói and São Brás de Alportel

Apart from the beach, other worthwhile day trips from Faro are to the couple of villages in the gentle hills to the north. At **Estói**, you can divide your time between a delightful eighteenth-century country estate and the remains of a Roman settlement at **Milreu**, just below the village. Further north, the hilltop town of **São Brás de Alportel** also makes a pleasant excursion. Travelling by bus, unless you make a fairly early start, it's difficult to see both villages on the same day. However, if you feel reasonably energetic it's perfectly feasible to take the bus to São Brás and walk the 7km down to Estói, catching the late-afternoon bus back to Faro from there.

Estói

Regular buses make the twenty-minute journey 11km north of Faro to **ESTÓI**, which basically consists of a main street, a little square and a small white church. Buses drop you in the square, just off which is the delightful peach-coloured **Palácio do Visconde de Estói**, a diminutive version of the Rococo palace of Queluz near Lisbon (see p.139). At present, only the attractive grounds are open to the public (Tues–Sat 9am–12.30pm & 2–5.30pm; free); the palace is earmarked to become a *pousada*.

The main reason for a visit to Estói, however, is the Roman site at **Milreu** (Tues–Sun: April–Sept 9.30am–12.30pm & 2.30–6pm; Oct–March 9.30am–12.30 & 2–5pm; €1.30), a ten-minute walk downhill from the square. Known to the Romans as Ossonoba, the town that once stood here predated Faro and was inhabited from the second to the sixth century AD. The surviving ruins are associated with a peristyle villa – one with a gallery of columns surrounding a courtyard – and dominated by the apse of a temple, which was converted into a Christian basilica in the third century AD, making it one of the earliest of all known churches. The other recognizable remains are of a bathing complex southwest of the villa, which had underfloor heating, with fragments of fish mosaics, and the *apodyterium*, or changing room, with its stone benches and arched niches below for clothes. The site was finally abandoned in the eighth century AD, after which date the Moors founded Faro to the south.

Back in the village, there's good **food** at *Casa do Pasto Victor's*, Rua Vasco da Gama 41 (closed Sun), just off the square on the Olhão road, where you'd be hard pushed to spend more than €8 a head. There are also no fewer than eleven **bars** along and around the main street; the two on the main square are good bets.

São Brás de Alportel

Seven kilometres north of Estói, **SÃO BRÁS DE ALPORTEL**, in a valley of the Serra do Caldeirão, also makes an appealing detour for those with a couple of hours to spare. Buses pull up in the dull main square and, just off it, at Rua Dr. José Dias Sancho 61, lies the **Museu Etnográfico do Trajo Algarvio** (Tues–Fri 10am–1pm & 2–5pm, Sat & Sun 2–5pm; €0.80). Housed in an old mansion, the museum is quite the best reason to come to São Brás, its alcoves and corridors full of traditional costumes and farming and domestic equipment. If you're the only person there (which is quite likely), you'll be given a personal tour, which consists of the ticket seller walking behind you saying "meat" and "cork" as you stare at various agricultural implements.

From the museum, cut down Rua Nova de Fonte to **Jardim da Verbena** (May–Sept 8am–8pm; Oct–April 8am–5pm; free), a wonderful little garden with an open-air **swimming pool** (hours as park; free). Just west of here lie the narrow streets of the oldest part of town, clustered round the church of **Senhor dos Passos** (signposted *Igreja Matriz*), from where there are lovely views of the surrounding valleys.

Practicalities

There is not much reason to stay in São Brás, unless you're tempted by the **accommodation** offered by one of the Algarve's two *pousadas*, which is 2km to the north. The views from the very comfortable *Pousada de São Brás* (☎289 845 171, ⓦwww.pousadas.pt; ❼) are splendid, and there's an (expensive) restaurant, too; advance booking is essential in summer. In town, the best bet is *Residencial São Brás*, Rua Luís Bivar 27 (Ⓣ & Ⓕ289 842 213; ❸), which runs off the main square, with shared baths and large if musty rooms in a fine old town house.

Restaurants are sparse but try the *Savoy* (closed Sun evening), on Rua Luís Bivar 40, past the *Residencial São Brás*, which offers well-cooked international cuisine and boasts a kids' menu. There are also plenty of café-bars round the main square, all of average quality.

Olhão and its ilhas

OLHÃO, 8km east of Faro, is the largest fishing port on the Algarve and an excellent base for visiting the surrounding sandbank *ilhas*. Once past the built-up outskirts, Olhão is quite an attractive town. There are no sights as such, but the flat roofs, outdoor stairways and white terraces of the old town are striking and give a North African look to the place. No surprise, then, that Olhão has centuries-old trading links with Morocco, as well as a small place in history for its uprising against the French garrison in 1808. Following the French departure, the local fishermen sent a small boat across the Atlantic to Brazil to transmit the news to the exiled king, João VI. The journey, completed without navigational aids, was rewarded after the king's restoration to the throne by the granting of a town charter.

The best view of the whitewashed houses is from the bell tower of the seventeenth-century parish church of **Nossa Senhora do Rosário** (Tues–Sun 9.30am–noon & 3–6pm), right in the middle of town. Outside, at the back of the church, an iron grille protects the chapel of **Nossa Senhora dos Aflitos**, where townswomen traditionally gathered when there was a storm at sea to pray for their sailors amid candles and curious wax ex-voto models of children and limbs.

The other obvious focus of the town is the **market**, held in the two modern redbrick buildings on the harbourside at the bottom of town at the centre of the attractive riverside gardens. Open from the crack of dawn (Mon–Sat), there's meat, fruit and vegetables on one side, fish on the other, the latter hall full of such delights as swordfish heads propped up on the marble counters and squid ink running off the tables into the gutter.

Practicalities

The **train station** is at the northeastern edge of town, off Avenida dos Combatentes da Grande Guerra; the **bus terminal** is a few minutes away on Rua General Humberto Delgado. From either, it's a quick walk down to the main Avenida da República, a wide boulevard which leads into the city centre, a further five minutes' walk away. At the parish church, the avenue forks into two: follow Rua do Comércio, and at the fourth on the right you'll find the **turismo** at the top of Rua Olhanense (June to mid-Sept Mon–Fri 9.30am–5.30pm; mid-Sept to May Mon–Fri 9.30am–1pm & 2–5.30pm; Ⓣ289 713 936), which can provide a town map, advice on accommodation and sailing times of boats to the *ilhas*. For **internet access**, the post office on the main Avenida da República (Mon–Fri) has a *Netpost* terminal; prepaid cards can be bought from the counter.

Accommodation

Accommodation can be hard to find in the height of summer, despite a fair scattering of **pensões**; ask for details of private rooms in the tourist office if the following are full. The nearest **campsite**, *Camping Olhão* (☎289 700 300, Ⓔ sbicamping@mail.telepac.pt; €3.20/person, from €2.60/tent), is at Pinheiros de Marim, 3km east of town next to Quinta da Marim (see below). The upmarket site, served by regular bus from Olhão, is set in substantial grounds with its own pool, playground, tennis courts, mini-market, restaurant and bars.

B & B City Lodge Rua da Verdade 6, off Av 5 de Outubro ☎289 706 607, Ⓕ289 723 709. Just down from the market near the waterfront, this small, friendly guest house has some rooms with balconies overlooking the market as well as a communal kichen. ❷

Pensão Bela Vista Rua Teófilo Braga 65–67 ☎ & Ⓕ289 702 538. The town's best choice with a range of bright rooms arranged around a tiled, flower-filled courtyard; from the turismo, turn left, then left again, and its sign is directly opposite. ❸

Bicuar Rua Vasco da Gama 5 ☎289 714 816. Well-positioned *pensão* in the centre, near Av da República, with balconies and smart communal areas but shared baths. ❸

Pensão Boémia Rua da Cerca 20, off Rua 18 de Junho ☎ & Ⓕ289 714 513. Another good choice, slightly further out of the centre near the bus station. Rooms come with shower and balcony. ❸

Ria Sol Rua General Humberto Delgado 37 ☎289 705 267, Ⓕ 289 705 268. A decent two-star hotel with its own bar and small rooms right by the bus station. ❹

Pensão Vasco da Gama Rua Vasco da Gama 6 ☎289 702 785. Right opposite the *Bicuar*, but slightly more basic; shared facilities but rock-bottom prices. ❷

Eating and drinking

There are plenty of inexpensive **cafés and bars** around the market buildings, while the riverfront Avenida 5 de Outubro is lined with more expensive **fish restaurants**. Up by the ferry stop lie another clutch of budget cafés and fast-food restaurants. The best place for a meal is *A Bote*, west of the market on Avenida 5 de Outubro 122 (closed Mon), which does superb grilled meat and fish. For something a little cheaper and simpler, *Restaurante Bela Vista*, near the tourist office on Rua Dr Teofilio Braga 59 (closed Sundays), does stonking portions of grilled meats.

Quinta da Marim

Three kilometres east of Olhão, just off the N125 Olhão–Tavira road (and served by regular bus from Olhão and Fuzeta), **Quinta da Marim** (daily 9.30am–12.30pm & 2.30–5.30pm; €1.50) is an environmental educational centre within the Parque Natural da Ria Formosa in an area of scrubby dunes and mud flats dotted with pines and gorse. It's a lovely quiet spot well worth a half-day's visit.

The reserve is best known for being the refuge for bizarre **aquatic poodles**, web-footed dogs that were bred to dive into the water to help chase fish into the fishermen's nets. Unfortunately, the aquatic poodles were abandoned for more modern methods in the 1950s, though the shaggy dogs still thrive here in their pure-bred form. The poodles can be seen as part of a 3km long **nature trail** that leads from the car park past a range of attractions including a tidal mill and the remains of Roman salt pans. There's also a visitor centre with a café, and in summer you can take a trip on the waters in a restored tuna fishing boat.

The ilhas: Armona and Culatra

Separate **ferries** leave for the *ilhas* of Armona and Culatra from the jetty at the eastern end of Olhão's municipal gardens, five minutes' walk from the market. There's a timetable posted at the kiosk; if it isn't open, you can buy tickets on the ferries. The **Ilha da Armona**, a fifteen-minute ride away, is reasonably accessible all year round as are the villages of Culatra (35min) and Farol (45min), on the **Ilha da Culatra**, though in summer you may prefer to get the boat to Farol from Faro; see p.516.

Ilha da Armona

Ferries (June to early Sept 9–11 departures daily; July & Aug first departure 7.30am, then hourly 9am–8pm; late Sept–May one daily, three on Saturdays; €0.90 return) drop their passengers at the southern end of the single settlement on **Ilha da Armona** – a long, crowded strip of holiday chalets and huts that stretches right across the island on either side of the main path. It's a fifteen-minute walk to the ocean, where the beach disappears into the distance; a short walk will take you to attractive stretches of sand and dune – the further you go, the greater the privacy. Continue east for two hours up the beach and you end up at the facilities opposite Fuzeta (see below).

There are a few **bar-restaurants** by the jetty, though most close out of season when it's best to stock up on supplies from Olhão's market. There are no *pensões* or hotels on Armona and camping on the beach is frowned upon, but *Orbitur* (☎289 714 173; ❸; April–Oct) operates a series of holiday **bungalows** on the island – it is best to book ahead.

Ilha da Culatra

Regular year-round ferries run to **Ilha da Culatra** (June & Sept 6 daily; July & Aug 7 daily; rest of year 4 daily; €1 to Culatra, €1.20 to Farol return), another huge sand spit, though very different in character from Armona, its northern shore dotted with a series of fishing settlements, mixed with an incongruous sprinkling of holiday chalets. The ferry's first port of call, **Culatra**, is the largest settlement, though **Farol**, the second stop, is far more agreeable. It's a mixture of fisherman's huts and holiday homes gathered below a lighthouse, edged by beautiful tracts of beach on the ocean side, though the mainland-facing beach is rather grubby. In Farol, *A-do-João Restaurant* serves some fine seafood dishes such as *cataplana*, as well as less expensive snacks and sandwiches. If you're considering **staying**, the best you can do is to ask around in the market where you might be able to pick up a private room for approximately €30; camping is not allowed.

Fuzeta

Around 10km east of Olhão, and served by regular bus as well as the main Algarve rail line, the fishing town of **Fuzeta** (or Fuseta) consists of a straggle of backstreets on a low hill facing the lagoons, sheltered by the eastern extremity of Ilha da Armona. Its waterfront of modern shops and apartments faces broad gardens largely taken over by the town's campsite. Beyond this lies a **river beach**, a fine bendy stretch of white sands weaving up to a wooden lifeboat house. In summer many people splash about in the calm waters of the river, though more exhilarating and cleaner waters can be had over the river at **Praia da Fuzeta** on the Ilha da Armona, reached by a regular ferry from the fishing quay behind the campsite (April–Oct roughly every 15 minutes;

Nov–March four daily; €1 return). Here, the **beach** immediately opposite the ferry stop gets fairly crowded in high summer, but you only have to walk ten minutes or so either way from the holiday beach huts to have beautiful, low dune-backed sands all to yourself.

Accommodation is limited in Fuzeta, with most visitors staying at the waterside **campsite**, *Parque de Campismo da Fuzeta* (☎289 793 459; €1.80/person, from €1.80/tent), beautifully positioned under trees with its own mini-market, but it gets pretty chock-a-block in high summer. Otherwise options are limited to **rooms** in private houses or the very basic *Pensão Liberdade*, on Rua da Liberdade 130 (☎289 793 297; ❷), with a mixed bag of gloomy rooms out by the train station. There are plenty of places to **eat and drink** on and around the main Rua da Liberdade. *Restaurante Skandinavia* (closed Tues and Nov–March), on Rua Tenente Barrosa 10, close to the covered market on the riverside, does decent grills on an outdoor terrace, while out on Praia da Fuzeta, *Restaurante Caetano* serves excellent salads, snacks and full meals just back from the sands.

Tavira and around

Situated 30km east of Faro, **TAVIRA** is one of the most beautiful towns in the Algarve and a clear winner if you are looking for a base on the eastern stretch. It's sited on both sides of the broad Rio Gilão, which is overlooked by ancient balconied houses and straddled by two low bridges, one of Roman origin. This is an eminently attractive ensemble, which persuades many to stay longer than planned – particularly those intent on lounging around on the superb island beach of the **Ilha de Tavira**, which lies within easy reach of the town by year-round ferry. There are also several quieter spots in the area, such as **Pedras d'el Rei**, a holiday village nearby and, for some excellent seafood, the tiny fishing village of **Santa Luzia**. Despite ever-increasing numbers of visitors and encroaching development, Tavira continues to make a living as a fishing port, and fish dinners at restaurants along the palm-lined river are in themselves a powerful incentive to stop.

The Town

Founded as long ago as 400 BC, Tavira was an important port trading with North Africa until the earthquake of 1755, when the town was largely rebuilt with the graceful eighteenth-century town houses and mansions that you see today. In the old town streets on both sides of the river, numerous houses retain fine old doorways and coats of arms.

From the arcaded **Praça da República**, by the river, it's a short climb up into the old town following Rua da Galeria. Ahead of you stands the **Igreja da Misericórdia** with its once fine (now badly worn) carved stone doorway from 1541, which depicts a series of mermaids, angels and saints, including Peter and Paul, though the most visible carvings are a couple of lute-playing figures in the doorframe. Inside there's a striking *azulejo* interior showing scenes from the life of Christ, below a wooden vaulted ceiling, but unfortunately the church is almost always locked. Turn left here and a couple of hundred metres up the cobbled street are the ruins of the **Castelo** (Mon–Fri 8am–5pm, Sat & Sun 9am–5.30pm; free), half hidden amid landscaped gardens on a low hill in the centre of town. From the walls you can look down over

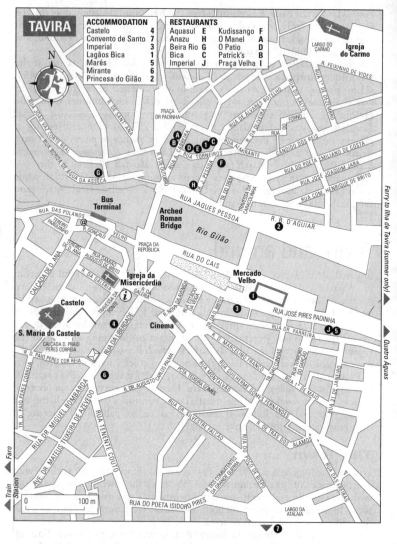

TAVIRA

ACCOMMODATION	
Castelo	4
Convento de Santo	7
Imperial	3
Lagâos Bica	1
Marés	5
Mirante	6
Princesa do Gilão	2

RESTAURANTS			
Aquasul	E	Kudissango	F
Anazu	H	O Manel	A
Beira Rio	G	O Patio	D
Bica	C	Patrick's	B
Imperial	J	Praça Velha	I

the peculiarly hipped terracotta rooftops and the town's numerous church
spires. Adjacent to the castle, the impressive, whitewashed **Santa Maria do
Castelo** is open daily, and contains the tomb of Dom Paio Peres Correia, who
reconquered much of the Algarve, including Tavira in 1242, from the Moors.
Fittingly, the church stands on the site of the former mosque.

With its tranquil vistas and leafy, palm-lined gardens, the **riverfront** is the
best part of Tavira for a wander. Gardens lined with cafés run from south of
Praça da República as far as the **old market** (*mercado velho*) building, which
has been converted into a "cultural and shopping centre" – a handful of small
boutiques and appealing waterfront cafés. The old market walls are also used for
temporary exhibitions, usually the works of local artists and photographers.

Beyond the old market are moored the fishing boats that still operate out of the river port. This is a great place to explore, among the nets and marine clutter, stopping at one of the restaurants or more basic fishermen's bars. Just before the flyover, **ferries** depart for the sandspit beach in high season (see p.526). Head under the bridge and you'll see the large new town **market** (Mon–Sat 8am–1.30pm), housed in a dull concrete box but still retaining a bustling interior filled with an array of vegetables and sea creatures of all shapes and sizes.

Practicalities

Tavira's **bus terminal** is by the river, from where it's a two-minute walk to the old bridge and Praça da República. The **train station** is 1km from the centre of town, straight up the Rua da Liberdade and at the end of Avenida Dr. Mateus Teixeira de Azevedo. Up the steps just off Praça da República is the **turismo**, at Rua da Galeria 9 (May–Oct Mon & Fri–Sun 9.30am–1pm & 2–6pm, Tues–Thurs 9.30am–7pm; Nov–April Mon–Fri 9.30am–1pm & 2–5pm; ☎281 322 511). For accesss to the **internet**, head to *Café Bela Fria*, Rua das Polanos 1 (closed Sun; €1/15min), opposite the bus station.

A leisurely way round town is to take the **toy train** which trundles from the main Rua da Liberdade up to the castle, along the riverfront and out to Quatro Águas (see p.527), every hour or so between 10am–9.30pm (until midnight in July and Aug) for €2 per person. Alternatively, **bikes** can be rented from *Rent-a-Bike*, Rua do Forno, 22 (☎281 321 973, ✉exploratio@hotmail.com) on the other side of the river; the company also organizes cycling tours to the Nature reserve of Ria Formosa and the countryside around Tavira. **Taxis** line up in the *praça*.

Accommodation

As throughout the Algarve, be warned that places are at a premium during high season; if a tout offers you a room, take it, at least for the first night, and look around on your own later on. The tourist office can help with **private rooms** if you have no luck at any of the *pensões* listed below. The nearest **campsite** is on the Ilha de Tavira, for which see p.526.

Pensão do Castelo Rua da Liberdade 22 ☎281 320 790, ☏281 320 799. Very centrally located, and recently renovated, it's a rambling place with clean en-suite rooms and TVs; disabled access. ❸
Convento de Santo António Rua de Santo António ☎281 321 573, ☏ 281 325 632. Book well ahead (by fax only) for one of the seven elegant double rooms in a converted convent with swimming pool and roof terrace, located 1km out of Tavira in a residential suburb. Minimum stay four nights in summer; two in winter. Closed Jan. ❽
Residencial Imperial Rua José Pires Padinha 24 ☎ & ☏281 322 234. Small *residencial* next to the restaurant (see below); opt for rooms overlooking the gardens and river rather than the noisy street-facing ones. Breakfast included. ❸
Residencial Lagâos Bica Rua Almirante Cândido dos Reis 24 ☎281 322 252. Situated on the north side of the river, this has attractive simple rooms

clustered round a rooftop patio above the top-notch budget restaurant, *Bica* (see below). ❸
Residencial Marés Rua José Pires Padinha 134–140 ☎281 325 815, ✉maresresidencial@mail.telepac.pt. Extremely pleasant rooms, some facing the river, with tiled floors and *azulejos* in the bathrooms; there's also a roof terrace and sauna. Breakfast included. Rates drop in the winter. ❺
Residencial Mirante Rua da Liberdade 83 ☎281 322 255. Opposite the post office, this *residencial* with a faded tiled facade has large, high-ceilinged rooms; those overlooking the street are a bit noisy. ❸
Residencial Princesa do Gilão Rua Borda d'Água de Aguiar 10–12 ☎ & ☏281 325 171. A white modern building with *azulejo*-decorated interior right on the quayside. Small rooms, but go for one at the front, with a balcony overlooking the river. Breakfast included. ❸

Eating, drinking and nightlife

A succession of **cafés** and **restaurants** front the gardens along the riverbank, while further down, on Rua José Pires Padinha, tables edge out on to the riverside. For some of the best cakes in town, try *Tavirense*, an old-fashioned *pastelaria* on Rua Marcelino Franco 19, opposite the cinema. As for **drinking**, there are a couple of cafés in the main square, plenty of nameless backstreet **bars** with matchstick-chewing old-timers for company, and a couple of trendier spots north of the river, including the *Arco Bar* (closed Mon) on Rua Almirante Cândido dos Reis 67 – a gay-friendly place attracting a laid-back crowd. For something a bit different there's *Malfado,* at Rua Dr. Augusta da Silva Carvalho 22 (closed Sun), where you can get down to African and Brazilian sounds on the small dance floor till 4am, fuelled by inexpensive drinks.

Tavira's only **disco**, *UBI*, is reached by following Rua Almirante Cândido dos Reis to the outskirts of town; it's housed in the huge metallic warehouse on the right. Playing a mix of house, Latin and techno grooves, it's open Friday and Saturday from midnight to 8 or 9am (Tues–Sun from May to Sept); the locals warm up with a few pre-clubbing drinks in the *Bubi Bar* in the same building (open from 10pm).

Restaurants

Anazu Rua Jacques Pessoa 11–13. Large bar-restaurant on the riverfront – a good place to sit out at sunset.

Aquasul Rua Torneiros 11–13 (evenings only; closed Mon). Reasonably priced, French-owned restaurant on the north side offering healthy salads and pasta. Closed Dec–Feb.

Beira Rio Rua Borda da Àgua de Assêca 46–48. This riverside bar-restaurant with tree-shaded tables is a tranquil venue for inexpensive pizza, pasta and salads; closed Nov.

Bica Rua Almirante Cândido dos Reis 22–24. Excellent inexpensive Portuguese meals on the north side of the river, under the *Residencial Lagôas Bica*. Tourist menu around €7.50.

Imperial Rua José Pires Padinha 22. Just back from the riverside gardens, the *Imperial* is well known for its moderately priced seafood, including clams and tuna.

Kudissango Rua Dr Augusta da Silva Carvalho 8 (closed Tues & Thurs lunch). Excellent spot to sample well-priced cuisine from Portugal's former colonies. There is a good range of vegetarian food, as well as the speciality – boiled mandioca fish with *escabeche*.

O Manel Rua Almirante Cândido dos Reis 6 (closed Tues). Decent if unexciting Portuguese grill restaurant near the *Bica* with most meals around €10.

O Patio Rua Dr. António Cabreira 30 (evenings only; closed Sun). Pricey fish restaurant with French-influenced dishes and attractive summer roof terrace.

Patrick's Rua Dr. António Cabreira 25–27 (closed Sun). Welcoming *adega*-style, English-run bar-restaurant. Full English breakfasts served until 3pm. The house speciality is the mouthwatering *piri-piri* prawns; otherwise there's an inexpensive daily menu.

Marisqueira Praça Velha Mercado Velho (closed Tues). One of the more classy if pricey new places round the old market, serving tasty seafood and *cataplana*. There is a neat little inside room along with pleasant outdoor tables spreading onto the square.

Ilha de Tavira

The **Ilha de Tavira** stretches southwest from Tavira almost as far as Fuzeta, some 14km away (see p.522). For most of its length the landward side of the island is a dank morass of mud flat, but at the eastern tip the mud disappears and the *ilha* ends in an expanse of sand and sea. The beach is enormous, backed by tufted dunes, and over the years its growing popularity has led to a certain amount of development: at the end of the main path, which runs from the jetty through a small chalet settlement, there are water sports facilities, beach umbrellas and loungers, and half a dozen bar-restaurants facing the sea. But, rather than spoiling things, this has fostered something of a good-time feel at the beach. The **campsite** (☎281 324 455; April to mid-Oct), a minute from the sands and with a well-stocked mini-market, shelters a youthful crowd, and the bars pump out music into the night. On the beach, the *Sunshine Bar* serves a tasty tuna steak, and has a full breakfast menu and vegetarian options, too.

From July to mid-September, **boats** to the island depart from the quayside in Tavira, at the town side of the flyover (daily 8am–7.30pm; last return 8pm; €1 return).

At other times of the year you have to pick up a ferry from **Quatro Águas**, 2km east of town. **Buses** (July to mid-Sept Mon–Fri 8am–7.45pm roughly hourly) leave from the bus station in Tavira, stopping outside the train station, for the ten-minute trip to the jetty at Quatro Águas. At other times, you can also catch the toy train to the jetty (see p.525), or you've the choice of a half-hour walk from the town (along the river, past the market, and just keep going) or a taxi. Here there's a snack bar and the very swish *Quatro Águas* seafood restaurant – highly regarded by locals (closed Mondays).

The **ferries** from Quatro Águas to the island (every 15min: June 8am–10pm; July & Aug 8am–midnight; April, May & Sept 8am–9pm; roughly hourly Oct–March 9am–dusk; €0.75 return) take just five minutes. The frequency of departures during winter depend a lot on the weather – ask the ferryman on your way over what time the last boat returns.

Santa Luzia, Pedras d'el Rei and Barril

Along the coastal road from Tavira, regular weekday buses (three on Sat) run the 3km west to the fishing village of **SANTA LUZIA**, a satisfying side-trip which has a cluster of highly recommended seafood restaurants. Arguably the best of these is the friendly *Restaurante Baixamar* (closed Mon), which is directly opposite the quay. In summer (usually Tues and Thurs), it's worth enquiring at Safari Boats (☎933 683 237, ✉safariboat@clix.pt) about their **river trips** up the Ria Formosa from just east of the fishing jetty. Most trips last for two or three hours and pass wading and sea birds with stop-offs for swimming at quiet beaches. Advance bookings are essential.

A kilometre west down the river, 4km west from Tavira, lies **PEDRAS D'EL REI** (☎281 380 600, ✉pedrasdelrei@mail.telepac.pt; ❺), a pleasant-sized holiday village with a host of facilities. Villas and apartments can be hired on a short-term basis at reasonable prices for small groups, though you'll need to book ahead in July and August. Fairly regular **buses** (Mon–Fri only) connect the resort with Tavira, most of them via Santa Luzia.

From Pedras, you cross a causeway and then catch a miniature train (daily, except in bad weather, 8am–dusk, roughly every 30min; €0.80 single) which shuttles backwards and forwards across the mud flats to the beach of **BARRIL** on the Ilha de Tavira. It's a few minutes' walk right or left to escape the tourist facilities at the terminus, and there you are: miles of beautiful, peaceful, dune-fringed beach. Take your own food and drink, though, since the relative isolation means high prices in the couple of café-bars here. The mud flats back from the beach are part of the **Parque Natural da Ria Formosa**, a nature reserve where you can watch tens of thousands of fiddler crabs, scuttling about and waving their claws at the sky.

East of Tavira: to Vila Real

Just to the east of Tavira, beyond the resort of **Cabanas**, the sand spit that protects much of the eastern Algarve from the developers starts to thin out, merging with the shoreline beach at Manta Rota, 12km away. The result is predictable: **Manta Rota** and **Altura** have been intensively developed, although the beaches at the resorts are splendid, if crowded in summer; there are more alluring sandy stops at **Praia Verde** and **Monte Gordo**. However, there is one surprise on this part of the coast: for some reason, the small hamlet of **Cacela Velha** (not to be confused with Vila Nova de Cacela, 2km inland) is – as yet – barely touched by tourism.

You can reach Cabanas, Altura and Monte Gordo by **bus** from Tavira; for Manta Rota, the only services are from Vila Real (or Monte Gordo); and for Praia Verde, the best you can do is get off any bus to Vila Real on the highway and walk down the side road. You can of course always **walk** along the beach: from Manta Rota it's around thirty minutes to Altura, another twenty minutes to Praia Verde, and forty more to Monte Gordo.

Cabanas

Six kilometres east of Tavira – past the new golf course at Benamor – lies **Cabanas**, a fairly nondescript, erstwhile fishing village which is developing into a resort in its own right thanks to its excellent sandspit beach, the Praia de Cabanas. Eight weekday **buses** (2 on Sat) run from Tavira to Cabanas (which is just 1km south of Conceição on the Tavira to Vila Real **railway** line), pulling up at the west end of the waterfront. Cabanas' other attraction is the **Quinta Alegre**, or the Happy Farm (Mon–Sat 10am–dusk, Sun 2pm–dusk; adults €5, children €2.50), reached by going through the Golden Club west of the town. This is a substantial theme park, ideal for kids of any age, complete with a mini zoo, donkey rides, crazy golf, bumper cars and Portugal's largest bouncy castle.

Most people, though, are here for the sandspit beach. There are two ferry services there, one from the east of town, the other from the west. Ten minutes' walk east of the bus stop, **ferries** shuttle passengers to the beach every fifteen minutes or so (May–Sept only; €1 return). Five minutes' walk west of the main riverfront, an all-year ferry service is also operated by the Golden Club resort (May–Sept daily every 15min; Oct–April 4 daily; €0.80 return, free to hotel guests).

Accommodation options are mainly limited to apartments and villas, although you can always ask at bars and cafés for private **rooms**. *Pastelaria Jerónimos*, opposite the eastern ferry jetty on Avenida 28 de Maio (☎281 370 649; ④), rents out decent apartments with sea-facing balconies, while on the sloping main road into town, *Pedras da Rainha* (☎281 370 181, ⓔpedrasrainha@mail.telepac.pt; ⑨), has apartments and villas (sleeping up to ten) clustered round pleasant lawns, tennis courts and a large pool, all with disabled access. Cabanas has a high number of **cafés**, **bars** and **restaurants** spreading along the riverfront and a block or two inland. Best of these is by the eastern ferry stop at Avenida 28 de Maio, the *Restaurante A Rocha* (April–Oct daily 12.30–3pm & 7–10pm), an attractive place with a breezy terrace where you can enjoy mid-priced omelettes, salads and fresh fish.

Cacela Velha

Ten kilometres from Cabanas, **CACELA VELHA** is perched on a rocky bluff overlooking the sea, surrounded by olive groves, and home to an old church and the remains of a fort. It is spectacularly pretty – a reminder of how the Algarve must have looked half a century ago. Get there while you can, as the idyllic nature of the village looks set to change with the planned construction of two golf courses, a luxury hotel and a tourist complex on the green fields immediately to the east. For the time being, the hamlet is short on facilities, with just a couple of cafés and a handful of **rooms** that are snapped up quickly in the summer. The **beach** below the village is a delight.

To get to it, follow signs to **Fabrica**, just west of the village, around 1km downhill. Here a ferry man can take you over to the beach for around €1 return, daily in summer but only during good weather the rest of the year.

To get to Cacela Velha, you need to ask to be let off the Tavira–Vila Real bus on the highway, just before Vila Nova de Cacela, from where it's a fifteen-minute walk down a side road to the village.

Manta Rota, Altura and Praia Verde

Two kilometres further along the coast at **MANTA ROTA**, a group of half a dozen restaurants, all serving platters of sardines and grilled swordfish and tuna, cluster at the entrance to a superb, broad beach. There's not much else to hang about for; the main road is a fifteen-minute walk up from the beach. The next resort east, **ALTURA**, is more developed, backed by characterless white villas and apartments facing another fantastic beach, Praia de Alagoas. Here, there's a line of beach umbrellas and beach bars, drinks kiosks and water sports on hand. Four kilometres east of Altura, **PRAIA VERDE** is far less developed, much less crowded than others along this stretch, with just one beach café. A walk up the hill to the beach car park will reward you with a splendid panoramic view along the coastline. Further east, towards Monte Gordo, the beach becomes more unkempt, backed by scrubby dunes, but the sands are much less likely to be crowded in summer.

Monte Gordo

MONTE GORDO is the last resort before the Spanish border and the most built-up of the eastern holiday towns. White hotels overlook the wide, clean sands, on which are scattered a profusion of beach **café-restaurants** with studiously similar menus and inflated prices; the *Mota* is the best bet, a huge place serving fish and grills on the sands. For something a little less expensive, try *Restaurante do Jaime* further west up the beach, which does inexpensive lunchtime snacks.

Buses from Vila Real and Tavira pull up on Rua Pedro Àlvares Cabral, by the parish church. From here it is a short walk down the main Avenida Vasco de Gama to the seafront and the casino. Just east of the casino is the **turismo** (May–Sept Mon–Fri 9.30am–7pm; Oct–April 9.30am–1pm & 2–5.30pm; ☎281 544 495), which can hand out town maps and details of **private rooms**.

If you want **accommodation** right on the beach, then the *Vasco da Gama*, Avenida Infante Dom Henrique (☎281 510 900, @vagamahotel@mail .telepac.pt; ❻), is probably your best bet, a highrise with tennis courts and kids' facilities. For something less expensive, *Pensão Monte Gordo*, Avenida Infante Dom Henrique (☎281 542 124, ☎281 542 570; ❹) is set back from the main drag just west of the casino, and offers large rooms with their own showers. Monte Gordo is also the site of the last – and largest – **campsite** (☎281 510 970, ☎ 281 511 932) on this stretch of the Algarve, a huge place set under pines near the beach on the Vila Real road.

Vila Real de Santo António

The border town and harbour of **VILA REAL DE SANTO ANTÓNIO** used to be the main bridgehead into Spain, but has declined since the opening of a road bridge over the Rio Guadiana 4km to the north in the early 1990s. Still, you may want to call in anyway, not least because it's one of the more

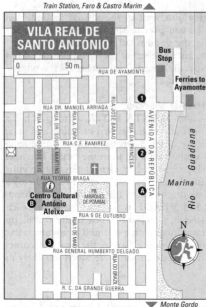

Train Station, Faro & Castro Marim

VILA REAL DE SANTO ANTÓNIO

0   50 m

Bus Stop

Ferries to Ayamonte

RUA DE AYAMONTE

RUA DR. MANUEL ARRIAGA

RUA JOSÉ BARÃO

RUA DR SOUSA MARTINS

RUA CÂNDIDO DOS REIS

RUA A. CAPA

RUA C.F. RAMIREZ

RUA DA PRINCESA

AVENIDA DA REPÚBLICA

AVENIDA DA REPÚBLICA

Rio Guadiana

RUA TEÓFILO BRAGA

Centro Cultural António Aleixo

PR. MARQUES DE POMBAL

Marina

RUA 5 DE OUTUBRO

RUA 1 DE MAIO

N

RUA GENERAL HUMBERTO DELGADO

RUA DO BRAZIL

R. C. DA GRANDE GUERRA

Monte Gordo

ACCOMMODATION		CAFÉS & RESTAURANTS	
Felix	1	Arenilha	B
Guadiana	2	Caves do Guadiana	A
Youth hostel	3		

architecturally interesting towns in the Algarve. The original settlement was demolished by a tidal wave following the earthquake of 1755, and the current town was rebuilt on a grid plan by the Marquês de Pombal using the same planning he had already pioneered in the Baixa quarter of Lisbon. Remarkably, the whole project only took five months.

The Town

The central grid built by Pombal radiates out from the handsome square that bears his name, ringed by orange trees and low, white buildings, a couple of which are pleasant outdoor cafés. Just north of the square on Rua Teófilo Braga, the former market building has been reborn as the **Centro Cultural António Aleixo** (Mon–Fri 10am–1pm & 3pm–7pm; free), an innovative space used for temporary exhibits, installations and occasionally even films. The centre also embraces the **Museu de Manuel Cabanas**, displaying the works of a local painter and wood engraver.

The surrounding streets have a certain low-key charm, bristling with linen shops, electrical retailers and grocers, and the riverside **gardens** offer fine views across to the splash of white that is Ayamonte in Spain.

Practicalities

Vila Real is the eastern terminal of the Algarve railway, and **trains** pull up at the station, five minutes north of the riverfront. **Buses** stop at the riverfront itself or at a terminus just north of the train station. The **turismo** (Mon–Fri 9.30am–1pm & 2–5.30pm; ☎281 542 100) is situated in a corner of the old market building just north of the main square on Rua Teófilo Braga, the pedestrianized drag leading inland from the riverfront Avenida da República.

Should you want to stay, **hotel** choices include the *Residencial Felix*, a block west of the bus terminal at Rua Dr. Manuel Arriaga 2 (☎281 543 791; ❶), where the eager-to-please owners oversee little rooms with wooden floors and a clean separate bathroom; and the *Hotel Guadiana* at Avenida da República 94, overlooking the gardens and river (☎281 511 482, ℱ281 511 478; ❺), which has a fine old Art Deco frontage and breakfast included in the price, though the rooms are nothing special. Alternatively, there's a **youth hostel** at Rua Dr. Sousa Martins 40 (☎ & ℱ281 544 565; dorm beds from €8.50); it's open all year round but fills up quickly in summer.

For **food and drink**, there's a line of half-a-dozen similarly priced places along the riverfront, all with outdoor seats overlooking the river. *Caves do Guadiana* (closed Tues), at Avenida da República 90, has long been considered the best in town. It's got a nice tiled, vaulted interior and you'll pay around €16 for a full meal. For less expensive fish and grilled meats, try the *Churrasqueira Arenilha*, Rua Cândido dos Reis, opposite the former market building.

Crossing the border

Two daily **buses** (9.10am & 5.15pm) run from Vila Real across the bridge to Ayamonte in Spain (15min), continuing on to Huelva for connections to Seville, the total journey taking four hours. **Coming from Spain**, two similarly timed services from Ayamonte run through Vila Real and on to Tavira and Faro. There are timetables posted at the bus terminus, and remember that Spanish time is one hour ahead.

If you just want to make a day trip to the Spanish border town – with its tapas bars and palm-lined squares – it's more fun to use the **ferry** from Vila Real's harbour to **Ayamonte** (daily every 40mins from 9am, last return 7pm, which is 8pm Spanish time; €1 each way), a lovely twenty-minute ride across the Guadiana with the forts of Castro Marim visible to the west and the impressive bridge to the north.

Inland: along the Rio Guadiana

North of Vila Real, the **Rio Guadiana** forms the border with Spain and provides a little-travelled diversion. **Buses** from Vila Real follow the N122, which runs inland of the river, with regular weekday services to **Castro Marim** and less frequent services to **Odeleite** and **Alcoutim**, each with a smattering of interest. Best of all, though, is a **boat trip** up the river itself. There are usually summer tourist charters offered in Monte Gordo or Vila Real: at around €40 per person they're not especially cheap, but you do get a barbecue lunch and plenty of swimming opportunities along the way. You should also be able to arrange river trips in Alcoutim, paying around €20 per hour for the boat – talk to the helpful turismo there (see p.532).

Castro Marim

The little village of **CASTRO MARIM**, 5km north of Vila Real (several buses daily), was once a key fortification protecting Portugal's southern coast. Marim was the first headquarters of the Order of Christ (1319) and is the site of a huge **castle** (daily: April–Oct 9am–7pm; Nov–March 9am–5pm; free), built by Afonso III in the thirteenth century. The massive ruins are all that survived the earthquake of 1755, as well as those of the smaller fort of São Sebastião across the village, but it's a pretty place with fine views of the impressive bridge to Spain. A small museum inside the castle walls (daily: May–Oct 10am–1pm & 3–6pm; Nov–April 10am–5pm; free) displays local archeological finds. The **turismo** is in Praça 1° de Maio (Mon–Fri 9.30am–1pm & 2–5.30pm; ℡281 531 232), just below the castle.

The marshy area around Castro Marim has been designated a nature reserve, the **Reserva Natural do Sapal**, so there's little danger of its being despoiled; the reserve office inside the castle has information about local walks through it (Mon–Fri 9am–12.30pm & 2–5.30pm; ℡281 531 141). One of the area's most unusual and elusive inhabitants is the extraordinary, ten-centimetre-long, swivel-eyed, opposing-toed, Mediterranean **chameleon** – a harmless, slow-moving lizard that's severely threatened elsewhere by habitat destruction.

There are various **places to eat** in the village, including the *Eira Gaio*, on Rua 25 de Abril opposite the turismo. For drinks and snacks, there are several **cafés** on Rua de São Sebastião, west of the tourist office. The best positioned is *Pastelaria Europe* on Praça 1° de Maio, with outdoor tables spilling out onto the little square opposite the tourist office.

Alcoutim

If you're feeling particularly energetic, you could walk the 15km north along the riverside road from Foz de Odeleite to **ALCOUTIM**, a beautiful route through unspoilt countryside. The village is extremely attractive, too, with a long history as a river port, dominated in turn by Greeks, Romans and Arabs who all fortified the heights with various structures; the **castle** (daily 9am–1pm & 2–5pm; €1, free on Mon) dates from the fourteenth century and offers fine views over the town and the River Guadiana. The entrance fee includes access to a small archeological **museum** by the main gates, which traces the history of the castle, its active service in the War of Restoration and the Liberal Wars, and the remnants of ealier structures on the site.

For further diversion, fishing boats ferry across the river to the **Spanish village of Sanlúcar**, a mirror image of Alcoutim, with its own ruined castle; the local boatmen will take you across for €1 each way.

A small **turismo** (Mon–Fri: May–Oct 9.30am–1pm & 2–7pm; Nov–April 9.30am–1pm & 2–5.30pm; ☎281 546 179) is located in the main square, Praça da República, right in the centre of the village. They're helpful people and can point you in the right direction for private rooms. Other **accommodation** options are the spruce modern *Pensão Afonso* (☎281 546 211; ❸), at Rua João Dias 10, just uphill from the main square, offering pleasant rooms with their own baths, and two good choices just outside the village. The smart fifty-bed **youth hostel** (☎ & ⓕ281 546 004) is around 1.5km north of the village, across the Ribeira Cadavais; cross the bridge beyond Praça da República and follow the signs. It has its own canteen, bar and launderette as well as disabled access. Double rooms from €21, ensuite €23; 4-bed dorms from €9.50. The most upmarket place in town, below (but on a separate road to) the youth hostel – head north out of Alcoutim and follow the signs – is the *Estalagem do Guadiana* (☎281 540 129, ⓕ281 546 647; closed Jan; ❺), a very swish modern inn with its own pool, tennis court and restaurant. Spacious rooms come with satellite TV, baths and fine river views.

Alcoutim's **cafés** and **restaurants** cluster around the Praça: the *Afonso* (closed Mon) is the best positioned on the square; for a full meal, *O Soeiro*, facing the river, has an upstairs restaurant serving fine local specialities such lamprey (lunches only, closed weekends) as well as a bustling downstairs café (closed Sun). For **internet** access, Casa dos Condes, the town hall with a little art gallery opposite the tourist office, has a terminal (daily 9am–1pm & 2–5pm; €3/hr). One or two **buses** a day run back down to Vila Real, and there's a twice-weekly service north to Mértola (p.489) and Beja (p.491).

The Western Algarve

The **western Algarve** stretches for a hundred kilometres from Faro to Sagres and encompasses Portugal's most intense tourist developments. The most extreme section is between Faro and Albufeira, where the beaches and coves are fronted by an almost continuous stretch of villas, apartments and hotels. Most of this stretch consists of purpose-built resorts that feature marinas, golf links and tennis centres – all fine if you've booked a holiday, but not especially inviting for casual visitors.

Albufeira itself is one of the biggest – and most enjoyable – resorts and other decent stops include **Alvor**, round **Portimão** and **Lagos**, the last of which still retains a bit of local character. All of these places are packed to the gills in summer and, particularly if you have transport, you might do better to seek a base inland at the old market towns of **Loulé** or **Silves**, and drive down to the nearest strip of beach. **Caldas de Monchique**, a nineteenth-century spa town, and the neighbouring market town of **Monchique** are other inland options, though these are a good forty minutes' drive from the sea.

The coast **west of Lagos** is a better place to escape the crowds altogether, where most of the development has been restricted by the Parque Natural do Sudouste Alentejano e Costa Vicentina, which embraces most of the coastline. As a result, erstwhile fishing villages such as Luz, Burgau and Salema retain a fair amount of charm. Beyond these villages the road cuts high above the sea, across a cliff-edged plateau, and down to **Sagres**, with its dramatic scenery and busy nightlife.

The coast **north of Sagres**, heading towards the Alentejo, is the least developed swathe of the Algarve – partly because the sea is distinctly colder and often pretty wild. If you don't mind the relative scarcity of tourist facilities, you might like to try low-key villages such as **Vila do Bispo**, **Carrapateira**, **Aljezur** and **Odeceixe**, all of which have magnificent local beaches. These attract a rather more "alternative" crowd than resorts on the Algarve proper, with plenty of beach parties, nude sunbathing and surfing.

Quinta do Lago to Vilamoura

The coast immediately northwest of Faro is unremitting holiday village territory, with little promise for anyone simply in search of a quiet beach and an unsophisticated meal. This is territory for those into "Sportugal" – as the tourist board promotes the lesiure complexes – and none too fussy about a local environment. You have to head inland for even the barest whiff of the old Algarve, best encountered at the historic market town of **Loulé**.

Loulé makes for a pleasant lunchtime or evening break for those staying on the Quarteira strip of coast. Independent travellers may find it the best place for a night away from the crowds, though it's probably more realistic to stay in Faro and see the places below by **bus**; departures are roughly hourly throughout the day.

Loulé

LOULÉ, 18km inland from Faro, has a history similar to most of the towns in southern Portugal – Roman and Moorish occupation – and **castle ruins** to match. The castle walls are the best point to begin a look around town. They have been restored as a walkway and can be visited with a ticket to the **Museu Arqueológico** (Mon–Thurs 9am–5.30pm, Sat 10am–2pm; €1.80), a museum containing an impressive range of archeological Roman, Moorish and early Portuguese finds from Loulé and the surrounding area. There are second-century anfora, ninth-century pots and the foundations of a twelfth-century Moorish house, *in situ* under a glass floor.

Between the museum and the thirteenth-century Gothic parish church nearby, a grid of whitewashed cobbled streets reveals numerous handicraft shops where you're free to watch the craftsmen at work – copperwork and lacemaking, in particular, are flourishing local industries. On Saturdays, the town is transformed as the whole region seems to arrive en masse for a busy **country market**.

Loulé's most curious sight is a beehive-shaped monument on a nearby hilltop, 2km out in the direction of Boliqueime. This is the sanctuary of **Nossa Senhora da Piedade**. At Easter, the church forms the starting point of a procession into town for Mãe Soberana, one of the Algarve's most important religious festivals.

Practicalities

The **bus terminal** (☎289 416 656) is on Rua Nossa Senhora de Fátima, a couple of minutes' walk north of the old town area; there are regular services from Quarteira and from Faro. The **turismo** (May–Sept Mon 9.30am–1pm & 2–5.30pm, Tues–Fri 9.30am–7pm, Sat 9.30am–3.30pm; Oct–April Mon 9.30am–1pm & 2–5.30pm, Tues–Fri 9.30am–5.30pm, Sat 9.30am–3pm; ☎289 463 900) is inside the castle walls next to the archeological museum, at Largo Dom Pedro I, and can help you find **accommodation**. One of the nicest places to stay is *Casa Beny*, at Rua São Domingos 13 (☎289 417 702; ❸), on the main through road virtually opposite the tourist office. It's not the quietest of spots, but the tastefully renovated town house offers neat if slightly flowery rooms, with their own TV and bathrooms. Even better is the comfortable *Loulé Jardim Hotel* at Praça Manuel de Arriaga 23 (☎289 413 094, ☎289 463 177; ❸), a block south of Rua Nossa Senhora da Piedade, which boasts a bar, a small pool and comfortable rooms with cable TV.

There's a good range of places to **eat and drink**. Just round the corner from the castle, with outdoor tables, *Café Calcina* (closed Sundays) is a great traditional café offering inexpensive snacks, with marble table tops, dark wood fittings and black and white photos of old Loulé on the walls. Among a cluster of restaurants around the parish church, the Igreja da São Francisco, *Museu do Lagar*, at Largo da Matriz 7 (closed Mon) offers moderately priced dishes such as *arroz do pato* (duck rice) and shellfish. Less expensive is *Os Tibetanos*, nearby at Rua Almeida Garrett 69 (closed Sun), a vegetarian shop and canteen serving decent if unexciting dishes such as salads and *rissóis de queijo cabra* (goat's cheese rissoles). Downhill below the castle, intimate *Bica Velha* at Rua Martim Moniz 17 (closed Sun) is a highly regarded, slightly formal restaurant offering moderate to expensive Portuguese food. Just along the same road, *A Muralha* (closed Mon & Tues lunch and all day Sun) is housed in a former bakery, with an attractive flower-filled patio and pleasant interior offering pricey and elaborate meat and seafood dishes; there's also a children's menu.

Quinta do Lago, Vale do Lobo and Almancil

The first of the resorts west of Faro, **QUINTA DO LAGO** is a vast, luxury holiday village with its own golf courses, sports complex and opulent hotels.

There's a decent beach, too, the **Praia do Anção**, reached over a wooden bridge across the western extremity of the Parque Natural da Ria Formosa; you can spot rare birds from the marked trails that lead either side of the inland waterways. Facilities are similar at **VALE DO LOBO**, next door, with a great beach backed by serious-money hotels, golf courses, a riding school, and the David Lloyd Tennis Centre.

Back on the highway, just before the otherwise drab town of **ALMANCIL**, the church of **São Laurenço** (Mon 2.30–6pm, Tues–Sat 10am–1pm & 2.30–6pm; €1) comes as a surprise amid the development. Built in the eighteenth century, it survived the earthquake of 1755 and retains its superb tiled interior depicting the life and martyrdom of St Laurence. In Almancil itself, the *Pensão Santa Teresa*, Rua do Comércio 13 (℡289 395 525, ℻289 395 364; ❹), has decent rooms with satellite TV should you wish to stay, though there is not much cause to.

Quarteira

The first proper town west of Faro is **QUARTEIRA**, 22km away, with a good weekly market and an attractive stretch of sand. In summer, a **toy train** trundles along the seafront to Vilamoura marina (see below) and back every hour or so (€1.80 per person).

Away from the seafront, development has overwhelmed most of what was once pleasant about Quarteira. The **bus terminus** (℡289 301 823) is a couple of blocks back from the beach, on Avenida Dr. Sá Carneiro, with the **turismo** on Praça do Mar by the beach (May–Sept Mon & Fri–Sun 9.30am–1pm & 2–5.30pm, Tues–Thurs 9.30am–7pm; Oct–May as above until 5.30pm; ℡289 389 209). They should be able to help with finding **accommodation** if there's no room at the very pleasant *Pensão Miramar*, at Rua Gonçalo Velho 8, off the seafront (℡289 315 225, ℻289 314 671; ❹), where some rooms have sea views, while others face a charming plant-lined internal terrace; or the similar *Pensão Romeu*, on the same street at no. 38, which lacks sea views (℡289 314 114; ❸). There's also a well-equipped **campsite** (℡289 302 821, ℻289 302 822) 1km east of town; any bus to or from Faro will stop outside it. Costs are €4.20 per person plus €3.5 per tent.

Quarteira boasts one of the Algarve's top seafood **restaurants**, *O Jacinto* at Avenida Sá Carneiro (Tues–Thurs & Fri eve; ℡289 301 887), on the north side of the main road through town; it's the best place to try Quarteira prawns, rated some of the best in the world. For something less expensive, *Rosa Branca*, at the market end of the seafront, has decently priced fish and grilled meats and outdoor tables facing the sands.

Vilamoura

Virtually merging with Quarteira but very different in feel, **VILAMOURA** is a constantly expanding resort, with a bewildering network of roads signposted to upmarket new hotels and leisure facilities, including some highly exclusive **golf courses**. The beach is impressive, and if you're not bothered by the crowds, enjoyable enough. On the outskirts, opposite the Mobil garage on the Vilamoura–Albufeira road, *Kadoc* – the Algarve's biggest **disco** – pulls in up to eight thousand revellers a night, and often hosts guest DJs from all over Europe.

The bus drops you next to the casino, one block from the beach, the **Praia da Marina**. The enormous *Vilamoura Marinotel* (℡289 389 988, ✉marinotel@mail.telepac.pt; ❾) is visible, two minutes away, overlooking the marina and is the place to stay for comforts.

Bristling with yachting hardware, the **marina** makes for an interesting stroll and is really the only other reason to stop off here; you can settle down at one of the pricey international cafés and watch the leisured set fooling around on their boats. If you fancy going on a boat yourself, to the northwest end of the marina various stalls offer **boat trips** which range from excursions to fishing trips and dolphin watching; prices start from around €25 for a two-hour trip to €50 for a full day excursion.

Just west of the marina, a tethered **balloon** (every 15 minutes May–Sept daily noon–8pm; Oct–April 10am–6pm; €15) offers the chance to peer over the town and beach from a height of 150 metres. The only historical sight in Vilamoura is just to the northwest of the marina, where the **Museu Cerra da Vila** (May–Sept Tues–Sun 10am–1pm & 3–8pm; Oct–April until 5pm; €4) displays the vestiges of a late Roman, Visigothic and Moorish colony at an archeological site with a small attached museum explaining the history of the colony. You can make out the foundations of a Roman mansion, baths and a fish-salting tank, together with well-preserved Roman mosaics laid out in a scrubby field.

Albufeira and around

Every inch a resort, **ALBUFEIRA** tops the list of package-tour destinations in the Algarve. The old centre, however, remains an unusually pretty village, with narrow, twisting lanes of whitewashed houses crisscrossing the high grey-red cliffs above a beautiful spread of beaches. But the centre is all but engulfed by hundreds of new apartment buildings strung across the hillsides that spread west around the town's new marina. If you're looking for unspoiled Portugal, this isn't it – whatever the brochures might say. Nevertheless, Albufeira is still a fun resort, attracting a varied mix of holidaymakers: an ageing, well-heeled clientele who frequent the more expensive restaurants, and a younger contingent who seem to devote themselves to consuming as much alcohol as is humanly possible.

Although the 1755 earthquake did for much of the town, there's still a Moorish feel to parts of central Albufeira, as well as the more tangible remnants of a Moorish castle – the original Arabic name of the town, *Al-Buhera*, means "Castle-on-the-Sea". There are some fine **beaches** either side of the town, too; Praia da Oura and those further east are the more developed, while the cove beaches up to the swathe of sands at Galé tend to be quieter.

Arrival and information

If you're in Albufeira on a package holiday, you might well not be staying in the town at all, but in one of the handful of small resort-villages on either side, like Montechoro, Areias de São João or Praia da Oura. All have access to their own beaches and are, in any case, within two or three kilometres of the town centre, which you can reach on regular local buses or by taxi. Everyone else will arrive in Albufeira at the **bus terminal** (☎289 589 755) on Avenida da Liberdade, at the top of town, five minutes' walk from the central Largo Eng. Duarte Pacheco, just to the west of which is the main street, Rua 5 de Outubro. Albufeira's "local" **train station** is actually 6km north of town at Ferreiras; a bus connects it with the bus terminal every 45 minutes or so (7am–8pm), or a taxi will set you back €5–7, depending on the time of day.

ALBUFEIRA

0   150 m

Bus Terminal

N

RUA DOS CALIÇOS

LARGO ENG.
D. PACHECO

A

RUA PADRE
SEMEDO AZEVEDO

RUA 1.º DE DEZEMBRO

RUA DA LIBERDADE

AVENIDA DA LIBERDADE

RUA 5 DE OUTUBRO

RUA ALVES CORREIA

RUA DA IGREJA NOVA

RUA CANDIDO DOS REIS

AVENIDA 25 DE ABRIL

RUA DOS TELHEIROS

B

C

Igreja de
Santana

R.M. BOMBARDA

DE DEUS

E F G

TR. DIOGO LEOTE

RUA DIOGO LEOTE

PR. MIGUEL
BOMBARDA

R. JOAQUIM
P. SAMORA

R. DA IGREJA VELHA

R. DO CEMITÉRIO

RUA HENRIQUE CALADO

RUA NOVA

R.S. GONÇALO DE LAGOS

H

I

AVENIDA DO TÉNIS

RUA DO TÉNIS

R. BERNARDINO DE SOUSA

LARGO CAIS HERCULANO

São
Sebastião

E LARGO
D'AYET

Museu
Arqueológico

TR. DA BATERIA

Praia da Oura

J

REGO DO MOINHO

RUA CORONEL AGUAS

RUA LATINO COELHO

K

▲ Armação de Pera

THE ALGARVE | Albufeira and around

9

RESTAURANTS		O Farol	J
Adega Dom Pipas	B	Minar	G
Bom Dia	A	A Taberna do Pescador	E
Cabaz da Praia	K	O Rei dos Frangos	C
Cantinho Algarvia	F	A Ruina	I
Casa da Fonte	D	Sotavento	H

ACCOMMODATION			
Albufeirense	2	Sol e Mar	7
Frentomar	10	Vila Bela	9
Jacques Accommodation	3	Vila Branca	6
Limas	1	Vila Recife	5
Silva	4	Villa São Vicente	8

The **turismo** (daily: May–Sept Mon–Fri 9.30am–7pm, Sat & Sun 9.30–5pm; Oct–April 9.30am–12.30pm & 2–5.30pm; ☎289 585 279) is on Rua 5 de Outubro, close to the tunnel. If you need to connect to the **internet**, head for *Augusto's* at Avenida da Liberdade 81 (Mon–Sat; €3.50/hr; ☎289 515 738), just south of the bus terminal.

Accommodation

Finding a room can be difficult in high season since most of the **hotels and pensões** are block-booked by package holiday companies. Those listed below may have "independent" vacancies, otherwise the tourist office can help you find a **private room**, though they'll charge you for any phone calls they make. Alternatively, accept the offer of a room from one of the touts at the bus station; you can always look around on your own later if it's not up to scratch.

The finely appointed (and expensive) **Camping Albufeira** (☎289 587 629, ☏289 587 633) – complete with swimming pools, restaurants, bars, shops and tennis courts – 2km to the north of town, off the N396, has regular connections from the bus station (any bus to Ferreiras passes it). Costs are €4.50 per person plus €4.20 per tent.

Pensão Albufeirense Rua da Liberdade 16–18 ☎289 512 079. Comfortable but drab with fairly reasonably priced rooms, with and without bath. ❷
Pensão Residencial Frentomar Rua Latino

Coelho ☎289 512 005. Simple, clean rooms on a quiet side road. Get one with a sea view and you will not be disappointed, though these are usually snapped up quickly. ❸

Jacques Accommodation Rua 5 de Outubro 36 ☎ 289 588 640. By far the best budget rooms in town, with large, airy rooms – each with their own bathrooms – right on the main street to the beach. Price does not include breakfast. April–Oct. ❹

Residencial Limas Rua da Liberdade 25–27 ☎ 289 514 025. Just up from the Albufeirense, with ten decent rooms in an attractive, yellow-faced building. Avoid the front ground floor rooms or it'll feel as if you're sleeping on the street. ❹

Pensão Silva Trav. André Rebelo 18, off Rua 5 de Outubro ☎ 289 512 669, ℱ 289 514 318. With the entrance on Travessa André Rebelo, this is an adequate little pension just of the main drag to the beach. Small, just-about-comfortable rooms with shower, and a toilet down the hall. Price includes breakfast. ❸

Hotel Sol e Mar Rua Bernardino de Sousa ☎ 289 580 080, ✉ hotelsolmar@mail.telepac.pt. With its entrance above the tunnel to the beach, this somewhat characterless four-star hotel streches down five floors to exit right on the beach. The rooms' balconies overlook the sands, while facilities include live entertainment, a swimming pool and a large buffet breakfast. Rates drop considerably out of season. ❻

Residencial Vila Bela Rua Coronel Águas 32 ☎ & ℱ 289 512 101. Situated on the west side of the centre (at the junction with Av do Ténis), this is an attractive *residencial* with its own bar and balconied rooms overlooking a small swimming pool and the bay. April–Oct. ❹

Residencial Vila Branca Rua do Ténis 4 ☎ 289 586 804, ℱ 289 586 592. A three-star *residencial* up in the new part of town, ten minutes from the beach. A mixed bag of modern, clean rooms with breakfast included. There's also a bar and roof terrace. ❹

Residencial Vila Recife Rua Miguel Bombarda 6 ☎ 289 583 740, ℱ 289 587 182. A huge, rambling place with its own garden and small pool. The communal areas are spotless and *azulejos*-lined, the en-suite rooms smallish but comfortable, the best with views. May–Oct. ❹

Villa São Vicente Hotel Largo Jacinto D'Ayet 4 ☎ 289 583 700, ✉ vila.s.vicent@marciano-dias .com. A modern three-star hotel attractively built in traditional style with tiled floors and whitewashed walls. It has its own small pool and a terrace facing the beach. You pay less for rooms facing the street (❺) but it is worth extra for sea views. All rooms have en-suite facilities, TVs and air conditioning. ❻

The Town

The focus of Albufeira is the **main square**, Largo Engenheiro Duarte Pacheco, a pretty, pedestrianized space with a small fountain and benches beneath palms and exotic trees. After dark, the square becomes a magnet for families and promenaders, often to the accompaniment of live performers and buskers.

From the square, Rua 5 de Outubro leads down to the town **beach** – reached through a tunnel – as good as any in the region, flanked by strange tooth-like rock formations and with a particularly fine grotto at the west end; there are usually plenty of companies offering boat rides up and down the neighbouring coastline. If it's too crowded here, a relatively short bus (or taxi) ride can open up a number of other possibilities, the best of which are detailed on p.542.

Just above the tunnel to the beach, in the old town hall, lies the **Museu Arqueológico** (Tues–Sun: mid-Sept to May 10am–5pm, June to mid-Sept 2.30–8.30pm; free) the town's archeological museum, a rather sparse but well laid out collection of artefacts gathered from the area from Neolithic times to the present. There are fragments of mosaics from a Roman villa, Visigothic rock tombs and jars, and even an Islamic silo excavated *in situ* beneath the musuem.

Albufeira's other historic sites lie up the steps to the west of the tunnel around Praça Miguel Bombarda. Here, the **Ermide de São Sebastião** is one of the region's oldest churches with a distinctive Manueline door, though most of the building was constructed in the early eighteenth century with Baroque touches. The church houses the **Museu Arte Sacra** (April–Sept Tues–Sun 2.30pm–8pm; Oct–March Tues–Sun 10.30pm–12.30pm & 2.30–5pm; free) a picturesque if uninspiring sacred art museum containing plaster images of saints; its most valuable items are a silver crown and chalice for Nossa Senhora

△ Typical cove beach, central Algarve

Ourada. Just north of this church is the **Igreja de Santana**, an attractive whitewashed eighteenth-century church with a dome. From the patio at the front there are lovely views over the distinctive filigree chimneys of the old town and across the other church spires to the sea.

Eating

Albufeira has **restaurants** to match every budget – and most tastes. As well as Portuguese restaurants, there's also a whole range of places serving pizzas, Chinese and Indian food, even fish and chips. Naturally, you tend to get what you pay for (and prices in the top restaurants are ten percent higher than resorts further east), but budget places complete with each other with bargain deals most days. The morning-after-the-night-before is well catered for in most restaurants and bars, with massive **English-style breakfasts** available until the sensible hour of 3pm.

Adega Dom Pipas Travessa dos Arcos 78. The mock olde-worlde decor and moderately priced Portuguese staples are nothing special, but the outdoor tables are in an attractive alley usually strung over with coloured ribbons.

Bom Dia Rua Alves Correira 37–39. Modest back street restaurant which offers Portuguese and international cuisine with vegetarian options; good music too.

Cabaz da Praia Praça Miguel Bombarda 7. Just up the hill from the main street and with a roof terrace overlooking the beach, this French-inspired place serves excellent but expensive meals.

Cantinho Algarvio Trav. São Gonçalo de Lagos 3a. Mid-range restaurant with a large, varied menu where you can fill up on cuts of meat and other standard Portuguese dishes.

Casa da Fonte Rua João de Deus 7 (closed Mon). Popular spot set round a beautiful Moorish-style courtyard complete with *azulejos*, lemon trees and a resident parrot. The long, averagely priced menu features the usual range of fish and meats, but get there early as the courtyard tables fill up fast.

Restaurante O Farol Cais Herculano. Simple beachside cafe-restaurant right behind the boats on the fisherman's beach. Its local and refreshingly unpretentious – though service can be excessively laid back. Generous portions of inexpensive fresh fish and grilled meats.

La Cigale Olhos de Água ☎289 501 637. Nine kilometres east of Albufeira, and right on the beach, this renowned restaurant has a lovely terrace and high-quality fare, including great seafood.

Minar Rua Diogo Cão, off Largo Cais Herculano (closed Sun lunch). Good value Indian restaurant, where you'll eat for around €15 – or €10 if you stick to the vegetarian dishes.

A Taberna do Pescador Travessa Cais Herculano. A genuinely authentic Portuguese taberna that attracts as many locals as tourists, with an outdoor terrace where most of the barbecuing takes place. The fish, seafood and meats are grilled to perfection and portions are huge and inexpensive.

O Rei dos Frangos Trav. dos Telheiros 4, off Av 25 de Abril. A first-rate inexpensive *churrasqueira* – the chicken comes smothered in *piri-piri* and there's grilled steak, swordfish and a speciality meat *cataplana*.

A Ruína Praia dos Pescadores, Largo Cais Herculano. Rustic but pricey old restaurant serving fresh fish built into the cliffs over the beach. The lower, beachside area is the best place for those with kids, as they can play in the sand while you have a meal. The waiter will show you the latest fish catch, but check on the price first as there is no menu.

Sotavento Rua São Gonçalo de Lagos 16. Behind the fishing harbour, this small tiled bar-restaurant serves an affordable selection of Portuguese and international standards.

Drinking and nightlife

At night, the focus switches to Albufeira's central, pedestrianized streets around **Rua Candido dos Reis**, the focal point of a writhing mass of humanity parading past handicraft and souvenir stalls or sitting at the rows of bars and cafes which vie with each other to play the loudest music and offer the most over the top cocktails.

Like the restaurants, Albufeira **bars** and **discos** are into promotion. There's not much to choose between them, and you may as well frequent those offering the cheapest drinks at the time – Happy Hour is an extremely flexible concept here. The other main areas for carousing are along Rua São Gonçalo de Lagos, around Largo Eng. Duarte Pacheco and Rua Alves Correira. Most bars stay open until around 3am, the discos until 6am or later in summer.

7/12 Rua São Gonçalo de Lagos 5. Central Albufeira disco on a street full of late-opening bars. The entry price of €8 includes one drink; be warned that it has a fairly strict dress code. Usually the last to close at around 6 to 7am (May–Sept, closed Mon).

Bizarro Bar Esplanada Dr Frutuosa Silva 30. This is an attractive bar high above the eastern end of the beach, with superb views over the sands from its front terrace. (Closed Sun.)

Café Latino Rua Latino Coelho 59. With spinning ceiling fans, a snooker table and a back terrace with fantastic views over the town and the beach, this is a superb spot to start off an evening with a cocktail. (Closed Mon.)

Central Station Largo Eng. Duarte Pacheco 44. Fairly tacky downstairs, serving as a café/restaurant/*gelateria* depending on the time of day. There's a big circular bar at the back and a spiral staircase leading to an upper cocktail bar with its own terrace and live music most nights.

Harry's Bar Largo Eng. Duarte Pacheco 36–37. A decidedly English mock-pub on the main square offering English breakfasts, light meals and a long list of cocktails. The drinks here – including British beers – are overpriced and it's only really worth

coming here for the nightly guitar-playing house musician.

Jardim de 1001 Noites Beco Bernardino de Sousa. An extravagant pseudo-Moorish complex with a huge courtyard by the Municipal Library. There's a bar, live entertainment most nights, Fado on Tuesdays, an art gallery and nighly *rodizio à Algarvia* – a giant buffet barbecue.

Jo Jo's Rua São Gonçalo de Lagos 1. Friendly family-run pub with British soccer and other sports on satellite TV. Serves pub-style food which always includes a vegetarian option. The owner proudly remembers the day Paul Gascoigne and his mates got hopelessly drunk here.

Kiss Rua Vasco da Gama. Out of town, at the southern end of Montechoro, this is regarded as the best club around. The club often hosts foreign guest DJs, but it tends to be overcrowded and very glitzy; watch for posters advertising events. (May–Sept daily; Oct–April Sat, Sun midnight–6am).

Portas da Vila Rua da Bateria. This high-ceilinged, cocktail and sangria bar lies just above the old fish market next to the site of the old gates to the castle.

Listings

Banks and exchange Grouped around Largo Eng. Duarte Pacheco.

Bike/motorbike hire Henrique Rent A Bike, Rua da Igreja Nova 17 ☎289 425 132 rents out bikes from €10 a day and motorbikes from €23 a day.

Bookshop The Algarve Book Centre, Rua Igreja Nova 6 (Mon–Fri 10am–6pm, Sat 10am–2pm) stocks a large range of English language books, most of them second hand.

Bullfights Take place twice weekly in the summer (usually Thurs and Sat; €25–35) at the bullring which is a five minute taxi ride to the east of the centre.

Car hire Europcar, Rua Dr Diogo Leote, ☎289 512 444, ⊕ 289 586 400; Hertz, Rua Manuel Teixeira Gomes Bloco 1, Areias de S. João, ☎289 542 920, ⊕289 589 937.

Health Centre (open 24 hours) Urbanização dos Caliços, ☎289 588 770/289 587 550. The nearest hospital is in Faro or Portimão.

Markets A lively flea market takes place to the north of the centre at Caliços on the first and third Tues of each month.

Pharmacy The most central one is Farmácia de Sousa, Rua 5 de Outubro 40.

Police ☎289 512 205.

Post office Rua 5 de Outubro; Mon–Fri 8.30am–5.30pm.

Taxi There's a taxi rank next to the bus station. To order a cab, phone ☎289 583 230.

Telephones It is easiest to make international calls from any of the numerous card phones all over town. Cards (*credifones*) can be bought from the post office and from many kiosks and shops.

Train information ☎289 571 755.

Travel agents Rua 5 de Outubro has row upon row of travel agents offering everything from tickets to local theme parks and bullfights to half day trips to inland Algarve and full day trips to Lisbon, Spain or Gibralta.

The local beaches

Immediately **east of Albufeira**, ochre-red cliffs divide the coastline into a series of bays and beaches, all reached on local buses (8–12 daily) from the bus station. You can walk to the first, **PRAIA DA OURA**, just 2km away by heading down Albufeira's beach and up along a rocky bluff along a coastal path; alternatively, head up the steps at the end of Avenida 25 de Abril and follow the road out of town; signposts point you down to the beach after 25 minutes. This, though, has been extensively developed and you might want to push on by bus to **OLHOS DE ÁGUA**, 7km further east, an erstwhile fishing village with a smaller beach (and *La Cigale* restaurant; see above). If this, too, is crowded, you can walk beyond to other more isolated coves.

At **PRAIA DA FALÉSIA**, 10km east of Albufeira and close to Vilamoura (see p.535), and twenty minutes away by bus, the character of the coastline changes to produce one long tremendous stretch of sand, backed by unbroken red cliffs, but the coast here is made up of sprawling villa complexes such as Aldeia das Açoteias, from where four daily buses depart for Vilamoura and Quarteira (see p.535).

Most development behind the beautiful rocky red headlands just to the **west of Albufeira** is set back from a series of cliff-backed cove beaches. There are no direct buses to these resorts, though the Albufeira–Portimão service drops passengers on the main road, a steep 2km walk away. The first of these, **SÃO RAFAEL**, a couple of kilometres west of Albufeira, and **CASTELO**, 1km further, spread back from small cove beaches with craggy, eroded rock faces. Five kilometres west of Albufeira, **GALÉ** is different, with more obvious development next to a giant swathe of beach, Praia de Galé. Here you'll find one of the Algarve's most exclusive and expensive hotels, the small, Moorish *Estalagem Vila Joya* (☎289 591 795, ℱ 289 591 201; ❾), which sits right above the beach and includes dinner in its (steep) prices.

Inland: São Bartolomeu de Messines and Alte

If you have your own transport, you can explore further **inland**, though it'll be difficult to get much off the beaten track. Twenty kilometres to the north of Albufeira, the small town of **SÃO BARTOLOMEU DE MESSINES** preserves a sixteenth-century parish church, remodelled in Baroque style and incorporating interior columns decorated with twisted stone rope. There are buses here from Albufeira, Portimão and Silves, with enough services to provide for a day trip.

From São Bartolomeu, it's 18km southwest to Silves, (see p.551) or only about half that to the village of **ALTE**, to the east along the winding N124 – though there is no public transport on this stretch. Tacked across the hillside, local tourist literature calls the village the prettiest in the Algarve, and consisting of a series of narrow, cobbled, mostly pedestrian streets it is certainly attractive. It is a short walk up to the local springs, Fonte Pequena and Fonte Grande, where there's a small rocky pool, artificially pumped full of water, a stream and an old mill, now converted into a **restaurant** – a delightful spot, certainly when it's not full with visiting tour groups; the springs also make a pleasant picnic stop. The **turismo** is located on the main road just below town on the Estrada da Ponte (☎289 478 666; Tues–Thurs 9am–6pm, Fri–Sat 9.30am–12.30pm & 2–6pm, Sun–Mon 9am–12.30pm & 2–5.30pm), and can give out local maps and information about private rooms. If you want to **stay**, first choice is *Casa d'Alte* (☎289 478 426; ❷), a bright, white town house next to the church: its airy front rooms have stunning views over town.

For a **drink** or snack you have a choice of the *Café Central* or the *Café Regional*, next to the church, which offer similar fare.

West towards Portimão

Heading west from Albufeira along the main N125, you'll pass through **PORCHES**, about halfway between Alcantarilha and Lagoa. This is where the most famous of the Algarve's hand-made **pottery** comes from. Thick, chunky and hand-painted, it has a good, heavy feel, and if you're looking for an attractive piece of ceramics to take home this is the place to stop. Further on, the dull town of **LAGOA** is best known for its wine; you can buy from the local producer, the Adega Cooperativo de Lagoa (Mon–Fri 9.30–11.30am & 2–5.30pm; free), on the south side of the N125 through town

Armação de Pêra

Off the main N125, 4km south of Porches, is the resort of **ARMAÇÃO DE PÊRA**, which claims the largest beach in the Algarve (not a unique claim in these parts). The area also boasts fine caves and strange rock formations to the west at **Praia da Senhora da Rocha**, which can be visited by daily summer **boat trips** which depart from the fisherman's beach. It's not the greatest looking of resorts by any means; modern high-rise buildings and apartments straggle along the town's main through-road, tempered only by the terraced gardens and cafés overlooking the central part of the sands. The remains of the town's fortified **walls** are at the eastern end of the seafront road; a terrace in front of a little white chapel provides sweeping views. The town **beach** is fine; if the main section is crowded, just head further east, beyond the fisherman's beach towards Galé where things are quieter.

Practicalities

Armação de Pêra's **bus terminal** (☎282 315 781) is at the eastern end of the town and there are regular services from Albufeira, Portimão and Silves. Walk up a block to the beach, littered with fishing boats, and then head to the right along the seafront road, which changes its name two or three times as it makes for the centre. The **turismo** is along here (Mon–Fri 9.30am–1pm & 2–5.30pm; ☎282 312 145), around ten minutes' walk from the bus station, and is good for maps and accommodation information. If you want to check your emails, the *Hotel Gharb* (see below) has a public **internet** terminal in its reception (€0.50/4min).

For **private rooms**, ask at *O Serol* restaurant, Rua da Praia (☎282 312 146; ❷), overlooking the beach near the fishing boats – you'll pass it on the way in from the bus station. If you want something more upmarket, look no further than the *Hotel Garbe* at Avenida Beira Mar 1 (☎282 315 187, Ⓔhotelgarbe@mail.telepac.pt; ❽) – just up the seafront road from the turismo – which has a pool and terrace overlooking the beach and breakfast is included in the price. The nearest **campsite**, the shady *Parque de Campismo Armacão de Pera* (☎282 312 260, Ⓕ282 315 379), is out of the centre, 1km back up the N269-1, towards highway N125. It's well equipped, with its own pool, supermarket, restaurant and gardens. Tents from €4 plus €4.50 per person. It also rents out smart bungalows for up to four people from €55 a night; price includes electricity, hot water and satellite TV.

There are countless **bars and restaurants**, all with more or less the same menus. For a bit more of a dining experience, two places that stand out are the *O Serol* restaurant itself on Rua Portas do Mar 2 (closed Wed), which sees a fair number of local people tucking into its daily fish specials; and *A Santola*, in Largo da Fortaleza – adjacent to the old walls and terrace – which serves more expensive seafood accompanied by fine views. The best budget choice is *Estrela do Mar*, Praia dos Pescadores, a simple shack right on the fishermen's beach offering bargain Portuguese staples; the *sardinhas assada* (grilled sardines) are superb.

West to Centianes

The ten kilometres or so of coast between Armação de Pêra and Centianes is flat and scrubby, fronting a series of delightful cove beaches that have somehow escaped any largescale development. The first of these, **Praia da Albondeira**, marks the start of a superb coastal footpath which stretches for 4km all the way to Praia de Benagil. Next along, **Praia da Marinha** nestles below a craggy red sandstone cliff, with the only trace of development being a seasonal beach restaurant and a tasteful villa complex a little up the hill. By car, the beach also can be reached from a turning south off the main N125, 8km west of Armação, opposite the International School. There is one weekday bus here from Lagoa.

A couple of kilometres further west, the road winds round to the next bay at **Benagil**, a tiny village consisting of a cluster of buildings with a couple of cafés above a narrow gully; the road loops down over a dried up river valley, at the bottom of which is a fine beach under high cliffs.

West of Benagil, the scenery changes again with coastal development crowding in around another appealing beach at **Praia de Centianes**, 3km away, the road lined with villas and modern apartments all the way to Carvoeiro.

Carvoeiro and Estômbar

Further to the west, the small resort of **CARVOEIRO** can be reached by bus from Lagoa. Cut into the red sea cliffs, this must once have been an attractive fishing village, but now its small cove beach has to support the prostrate bodies of hundreds of tourists shipped in to what has become an overblown and rather tacky resort. The beach is pleasant enough, though actually rockier and less impressive than many along this stretch, and most accommodation is in the form of block-booked aparments. The **tourist office** (mid-Sept to May Mon–Fri 9.30am–1pm & 2–5.30pm; June to mid-Sept daily 9.30am–7pm; ☎282 357 728), just behind the beach, can suggest **private rooms**. Out of season the town has slightly more appeal, and at least it is within range of a couple of superb neighbouring beaches, Praia de Centianes and Benagil (see above). If you want to stay here, *Hotel Carvoeiro Sol* (☎282 357 301, ✉carvoeirosol@mail.telepac.pt; ❻, up to ❼ with sea views) is the most comfortable option, a four-star concrete block right by the beach. Rooms come with small balconies, and there's also a pool, courtyard bar and a babysitting service. The best budget option is *O Castelo*, Rua da Casino 59–61 (☎ & 🖷282 357 416, ✉casteloguesthouse@clix.pt; ❸); take the road that overlooks the beach uphill above the tourist office and it's five minutes' walk. There are just three clean, modern rooms with a superb view over the beach. Price does not include breakfast.

Accessible by the coast road, a kilometre east, are the impressive rock formations of **Algar Seco**, where steps lead down low cliffs to a series of dramatic overhangs above blow holes and grottoes. By way of contrast, a few kilometres inland is **ESTÔMBAR** (a stop for slow trains on the Algarve line), an unremarkable little town that was the birthplace of the eleventh-century Moorish poet Ibn Ammâr. The town straggles down a steep hill in a confusion of narrow lanes – nothing very special, though at least it's free of tourist trappings. Its most interesting site is its church. The interior has superb eighteenth-century *azulejos* and two Manueline sculpted columns carved with exotic plants and vines.

For slides, pools and aquatic fun, take the bus from the bus station here (at 9am or 12.15pm) to the **Slide & Splash** theme park (daily May–Oct 10am–5pm; €10), just outside Estômbar, signposted off the N125 at Vale de Deus.

Portimão, Praia da Rocha and around

Portimão is one of the largest towns on the Algarve, with a population of more than thirty thousand. It has made its living from fishing since pre-Roman times and with its site on the estuary of the Rio Arade remains today a sprawling port, a major sardine-canning centre, and a base for the construction industries spawned by the tourist boom. Most visitors are just here for a day's shopping, taking time out from the resort of **Praia da Rocha**, 3km south of Portimão. This keeps a highly distinct identity of its own as a full-on resort. Just across the estuary to the east of Portimão is the more traditional village of **Ferragudo**, which has a castle right on a small beach. The coast road west of Praia da Rocha, towards Lagos, has been engulfed by a series of massive and graceless tourist developments fronting more sweeping beaches; only **Alvor**, slightly inland, retains any of its original charm.

Portimão

As a town, **PORTIMÃO** is fairly undistinguished – most of the older buildings were destroyed in the 1755 earthquake – and it is pedestrianized shopping streets and graceless concrete high-rises that dominate. Its most historic building is the **Igreja da Nossa Senhora da Conceição**, rebuilt after the earthquake, but retaining a Manueline door from the original fourteenth-century structure; the interior is more impressive, covered in sevententh-century *azulejos*. The encircling streets are pleasant enough, filled with shops catering to the day trippers selling lace, shoes, jewellery, ceramics and wicker goods; the main shopping streets are around the pedestrianized Rua Diogo Tomé and Rua da Portades de S. José. Just off the latter *rua* lies Largo 1 de Dezembro, an attractive square with seats inlaid with *azulejos* depicting historical scenes, such as the discovery of Brazil in 1500.

However, the best part of town is undoubtedly the **riverfront gardens**, which are made up of a series of squares – Largo do Duque, Praça Manuel Teixeira Gomes, and Praça Visconde de Bivar – filled with outdoor cafés beneath shady trees, right by the fishing **harbour**. At the riverfront, you'll be approached by various people offering **boat trips** along the coast to see weird and wonderful grottoes; two-hour trips cost around €15 per person. Three-hour boat trips also go up the Rio Arade to Silves (see p.551); departure times depend on the tides.

The fishing **harbour** close to the bridge has traditionally been lined with open-air restaurants, serving grilled sardine lunches, though there are plans to

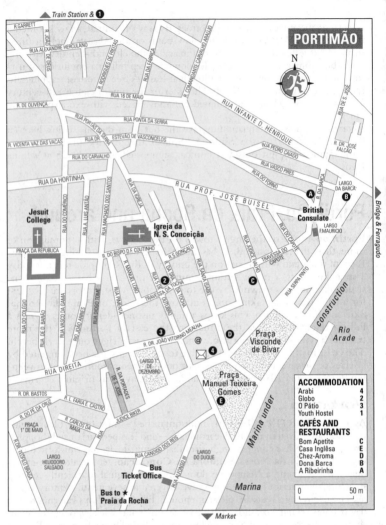

PORTIMÃO

ACCOMMODATION
Arabi	4
Globo	2
O Pátio	3
Youth Hostel	1

CAFÉS AND
RESTAURANTS
Bom Apetite	C
Casa Inglêsa	E
Chez-Aroma	D
Dona Barca	B
A Ribeirinha	A

0   50 m

extend the new marina along here and move the restaurants to the other side
of the bridge by late 2002. However, the streets just back from here – off Largo
da Barca – are Portimão's oldest: narrow, cobbled and with more than a hint of
their fishing quarter past. Other reasons to come to town are the huge **market** on the first Monday of each month, selling second-hand clothes, ceramics,
CDs and junk, held near the riverfront on the Estrada da Rocha, just southwest of town towards Praia da Rocha. On the morning of the first and third
Sunday of each month, a **flea market** laden with antiques and second-hand
bric-a-brac spreads out past the railway station in the Parque das Exposições.

Practicalities

The **train station** is inconveniently located at the northern tip of town but
the bus runs every 45 minutes (Mon–Fri) into the centre; a taxi costs about €4

or it's a fifteen-minute walk. **Buses** (including those to and from Praia da Rocha) pull up much more centrally, in the streets around the Largo do Duque, close to the river, from where it's a five-minute walk past the riverside gardens to the **quayside**, which stretches as far as the bridge over to Ferragudo. There's a **post office** in the main Praça Manuel Teixeira Gomes and the Algarve's only **British consulate** further up the quayside at Largo Francisco A. Mauricio 7–1° (☎282 417 800).

If you want to stay, Portimão has a good **Youth Hostel** at Lugar do Coca, Maravilhas (☎ & ℗282 491 804), a large modern place with its own small swimming pool, bar, canteen and sports facilities that include table tennis, snooker and tennis courts. There are eight double rooms (€20.50) and over 40 dorm rooms of four beds (€8.50). Elsewhere, the better-value **accommodation** options include *Hotel Globo*, Rua 5 de Outubro (☎282 416 350, ℗282 483 142; ❸), a good value if dull modern high-rise close to the Igreja Matriz; the characterful *Residencial O Pátio*, Rua Dr. João Vitorino Mealha 3 (☎282 424 288, ℗282 424 281; ❸), with simple rooms and a groovy bar with fur-line seats, or the spick-and-span *Pensão Arabi*, on Praça Manuel Teixeira Gomes 13 (☎282 460 250, ℗282 460 269; ❸), the main riverside square.

For **food**, the best place to head is just north of the old bridge, off Largo da Barca, where there are a few very inexpensive workers' *tascas* – like *A Ribeirinha*, Rua da Barca 15 (closed Sun) – as well as some more elaborate fish restaurants, such as the highly rated *Dona Barca*, in Largo da Barca. Otherwise, try the friendly *Bom Apetite Restaurant*, Rua Júdice Fialho 21, which serves authentic Portuguese cooking, including a splendid *arroz de marisco*. Or there's always the *Chez-Aroma*, Rua Santa Isabel 14 (May–Oct Mon–Fri only), serving a nice range of inexpensive Indonesian, Indian and Thai dishes. For something more international, *Dockside*, down in the Marina do Portimão, is of the growing number of flash modern restaurants overlooking the marina serving pricey seafood, fish and grills. For **drinks**, *Casa Inglêsa* in the main riverside Praça Manuel Teixeira Gomes is a thoroughly pleasant place with outdoor tables, a popular meeting spot for ex-pats.

Praia da Rocha

PRAIA DA ROCHA, five minutes' south of Portimão by bus, was one of the first Algarve tourist developments and it's easy to see why. The **beach** is one of the most beautiful on the entire coast: a wide expanse of sand framed by jagged sea cliffs and the walls of an old fort built in 1691, the **Fortaleza da Santa Caterina**, that once protected the mouth of the Rio Arade. The fort's terrace offers splendid views at sunset – beach and ocean on one side, Ferragudo, the river and the marina on the other. The effect, however, is spoilt by high-rise hotels, discos and a casino that sit on the clifftop behind the beach, all but swamping the *fin-de-siècle* villas. Most of the development lies channelled in a strip just two blocks wide, with the beach reached down steep steps from the elevated main street, Avenida Tomás Cabreira; from virtually every bar, restaurant and hotel terrace, all the views are of the sands and sea. There's little that is traditionally Portuguese, of course, but it is lively and brash enough to be fun at whatever time of year you visit.

Practicalities

Bus connections from Portimão are excellent, with a bus every fifteen to thirty minutes (7.30am–8.30pm); in Praia da Rocha it stops in front of the *Hotel da Rocha* (see below) on Avenida Tomás Cabreira. The **turismo** (June–Sept 9.30am–7pm; Oct–May 9.30am–12.30pm & 1–5pm; ☎282 419 132) is in the

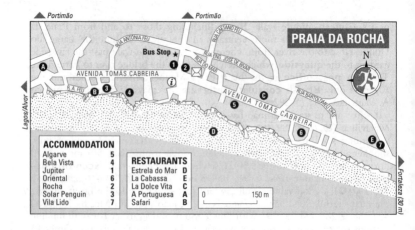

PRAIA DA ROCHA

N

ACCOMMODATION	
Algarve	5
Bela Vista	4
Jupiter	1
Oriental	6
Rocha	2
Solar Penguin	3
Vila Lido	7

RESTAURANTS	
Estrela do Mar	D
La Cabassa	E
La Dolce Vita	C
A Portuguesa	A
Safari	B

0   150 m

hut opposite. You can pick up the **return bus to Portimão** from here (every 15–30min until 11.30pm; €1.50 one way), or from the stop on Rua Eng. José de Bivar, around the back of the *Hotel da Rocha*. If you plan to do much to-ing and fro-ing between Rocha and Portimão, buy a block of ten tickets from the kiosk in Portimão, which will save you around fifty percent.

Accommodation

Finding accommodation is rarely a problem; ask at the turismo for an array of **private rooms** to rent, or try one of the following **pensões** or (expensive) **hotels**, all of which offer fine, sea-facing rooms, pools and heavily reduced winter room rates.

Hotel Algarve Av Tomás Cabreira ☎ 282 415 001, ✉ h.algarve@mail.telepac.pt. Luxurious five-star with an arm-long list of facilities including a pool and casino. ❾

Hotel Bela Vista Av Tomás Cabreira ☎ 282 450 480, ✉ inf.reservas@hotelbelavista.pt. The most stylish place to stay right on the seafront, a pseudo-Moorish mansion built in 1903 as a wedding gift by the wealthy Magalhães family; the interior is an exquisite mixture of carved wood, stained glass, and yellow, white and blue *azulejos*. ❻

Hotel Jupiter Av Tomás Cabreira ☎ 282 415 041, ✉ hoteljupiter@mail.telepac.pt. A modern hulk on the wrong (land) side of the Avenida but with all mod cons; ❺, or ❼ with sea views.

Hotel Oriental Av Tomás Cabreira ☎ 282 413 000, ⊕ 282 413 413. This hotel wins hands down for its design, a Moorish-influenced extravaganza of arches, domes and gardens, in a prime spot

overlooking the beach. ❽

Hotel da Rocha Av Tomás Cabreira ☎ 282 424 081, ⊕ 282 415 988. A slightly more affordable three-star with its own bar, restaurant and comfortable rooms. ❻

Solar Penguin Rua António Feu ☎ 282 424 308; closed mid-Nov to mid-Jan. On the cliffs above the beach, just off the main avenue, this delightful old *pensão* with a few comfortable rooms overlooking the sea is a joy; it also has a restaurant. In the antiquated lounge look out for the portrait of Queen Elizabeth which was painted by the late husband of the owner. ❸

Residencial Vila Lido Av Tomás Cabreira ☎ 282 424 127, ⊕ 282 424 246. At the eastern end of Av Tomás Cabreira, this is a beautiful blue-shuttered building in its own small grounds facing the fort; front rooms have superb views over the beach. ❺

Eating, drinking and nightlife

Restaurants are plentiful and the half a dozen down on the beach mean that you don't have to leave the sands during the day. *Estrela do Mar*, just at the bottom of the steps, sits on the beach with a terrace facing the sands and serves good value fish, salads, meat dishes and ice creams. Up in town, the *Safari*, next to the *Solar Penguin*, overlooks the beach and serves mainly Portuguese dishes, a few with an Angolan influence, with a good value tourist menu of €13. Further west along Avenida Tomás Cabreira, *A Portuguesa* (closed Sun) specializes in solid Portuguese grills backed by gentle jazzy sounds. Towards the fort on the Avenida, *La Dolce Vita* is owned and run by Italians, and the homemade pasta and pizzas are good value. However, even better Italian fare and surroundings can be had – strangely enough – at the Swedish-run *La Cabassa*, further along towards the fort in a quieter part of town. Here, they serve a mouth-watering array of authentic Italian dishes – though no pizza – for little more than you'll pay at *La Dolce Vita*.

For a civilized **drink**, the bar of the *Bela Vista* is open to the public (8.30pm–midnight). More rowdy venues include several on the Avenida: among them *On the Rocks* disco bar, *Tropicool* – the reps favourite, and *Pé de Vento*, which has live music on Wednesdays and Thursdays. The *Katedral* **disco** is housed in a futuristic building next to the *Penguin* but *Babylone* (Oct–May closed Sun), in a basement just off the Avenida, makes better cocktails; neither gets going much before midnight.

Ferragudo

FERRAGUDO, facing Portimão across the estuary, and connected by a regular bus service (hourly 7.30am–7.30pm), is very different – retaining its traditional character and with relatively few concessions to international tourism. It is centred round a strip of palm-fringed gardens which spread alongside a narrow concrete-lined riverlet up to the cobbled main square, Praça Rainha D. Leonor, a wide space dotted with cafés. The riverlet ends at the Rio Arade estuary, where there is a small fishing harbour and a few fish restaurants. South of here, the old town spreads up the side of a hill, a warren of atmospheric cobbled backstreets gathered around the town **church**; from its terrace there are great views over the estuary. Below the church – accessible from the fishing harbour or by taking the road that skirts the old town – lies the town **beach**, which gets progressively more appealing as it approaches the **Castelo de São João do Arade**, one of the only forts in Portugal that lies right behind a sandy beach. The fort, a partner to that in Praia da Rocha, is a tremendous site – built in the sixteenth century to defend Portimão against attack. Currently in private hands, there are plans to turn it into a *pousada*.

Accommodation is somewhat limited. The best option is *Quinta da Horta* (☎282 461 395, ✉art-ferragudo@clix.pt; ❸) just out of town (follow the concrete riverlet east for ten minutes and it is on the right). Run by a British artist, there is a series of spartan but tasteful studios and rooms set round a hacienda-style garden full of tropical plants. There's also a small plunge pool, a sauna, TV room and a rundown tennis court; the price includes a superb organic breakfast.

There are a number of lively bars and several **restaurants**. *Portarade*, Praça Rainha D. Leonor, has outdoor tables right on the main square. British-run and with very friendly service, the international menu features a good range of kids' meals as well as bargain salad buffets (€2.50–5) and set lunches from €2. Better value and more authentically Portuguese, however, is *O Velho Novo* on Rua Manuel Teixeira Gomes 2 (evenings only), five minutes' walk from the main square – cross the riverlet along the road signed to Belavista and it's on the left, with good value fish and meats which are grilled on an outside barbecue.

Ferragudo is close to several superb **beaches**. The town beach stretches below the castle, though more sand is to be found at **Praia Grande** round the headland, about a kilometre to the south of town, with a scattering of restaurant-bars. A large **campsite**, the *Parque Campismo de Ferragudo* (☎282 461 121), lies around 3km out of Ferragudo beyond Praia Grande, but it is only open to members of the International Camping Club. Well equipped, with a pool, kids' play area, a large supermarket and a restaurant, tents cost from €2.50, plus €4.50 per person. The campsite is around fifteen minutes' walk from two superb cove beaches, **Praia Pintadinho** and **Praia da Caneiros**, both with beachside bar-restaurants (open April–Oct).

Alvor and Quinta da Rocha

The resorts immediately west of Praia da Rocha – Vau and Praia Três Irmãos – have good beaches but little else going for them, and it is better to push on 6km west of Praia da Rocha to **ALVOR**. The ancient port here briefly achieved fame as the place that King João II died in 1495 and, though much of the town was razed in the 1755 earthquake, it still boasts a sixteenth century *Igreja Matriz* with Manueline doors, arches and pillars carved into fishing ropes and plants. It remained a sleepy fishing village until the 1960s, when tourism began to take hold, and today the old town has been outgrown by a sprawl of modern – though largely low-rise – buildings. Nevertheless, the old core around the church and the central Praça da República retains its character, while the harbour itself is a delight, lined with colourful fishing boats and aromatic fish restaurants.

The town's **turismo** is in the centre of town at Rua Dr. Alfonso Costa 51 (daily: July–Sept 9.30am–7pm; Oct–June 9.30am–1pm & 2–5.30pm; ☎282 457 540). From the tourist office, it is a short walk uphill to the vestiges of Alvor's **castle**, which dates back to the thirteenth century, now a leafy ruin housing a children's playground. From here, Rua Padre David Neto leads onto Rua Dr Frederico Romas Mendes, the main drag lined with bars and restaurants. This stretches down to the riverside square, Largo da Ribeiro, marked by a modern statue of a fish; appropriately, as this is where the old fish market stands. Here you'll find half a dozen fish restaurants, most with outdoor seating overlooking the picturesque estuary of the Rio Alvor, swooped over by seagulls and lined with beached fishing boats. It's a lovely spot; head right as you face the river and a path leads up the estuary for a tranquil walk; bear left and it is a ten-minute stroll past fishermen's huts to the expansive Praia de Alvor. This **beach** is enormous and, though it's a bit on the dull side, at least you can escape the crowds.

In season, **rooms** at Alvor are hard to come by, though there are plenty of expensive international hotels around 1km east of Alvor facing the beach. The best bet in town is *Hospedaria Buganvilia,* Rua Padre Mendes Rossio de 5 Pedro (☎282 459 412; ④), just down the hill from the turismo, a modern place above a decent restaurant. Rooms are spotless and most have balconies; there's also a roof terrace. A **campsite**, *Campismo Dourado* (☎282 459 178, ⑤282 458 002), lies around 1km north of Alvor on the N125, a pleasant, leafy place with a small shop; tents cost from €2.50, plus €3 per person.

Alvor is well catered for with restaurants and bars; there are at least a dozen Irish bars alone. One of a row of decently priced fish restaurants on the harbourfront on Largo da Ribeira, *Casa da Maré* (closed Sun) benefits from its prime position with tables spilling out onto the square. Even better is *Tasca do Margadinho* at Largo da Ribeira 9, an atmospheric old *tasca* opposite the old fish market with a basic, local feel and superbly grilled fresh fish. Down on the sands, *Restaurante Rosamar* (closed Dec) is the nearest beach restaurant and serves some tasty and unusual dishes such as sardines with rice and beans and mackerel with tomato rice.

The **Quinta da Rocha nature area** lies in the peninsula between the mouths of the rivers Alvor and Odiáxere, northwest of Alvor's huge beach. It is an extensive area which, in the parts not given over to citrus and almond groves, consists of copses, salt marshes, sandy spits and estuarine mud flats, forming a wide range of habitats for different plants and animals – including twenty-two species of **wading bird**. You can follow paths and tracks round the area by taking the turning off the main N125 opposite Mexilheira Grande.

Silves and around

Eighteen kilometres northeast of Portimão, **SILVES** – the medieval residence and capital of the Moorish kings of the al-Gharb – is one of the few inland towns in this province that really merits a detour. It has a superb castle and a highly dramatic approach, with its red ring of walls gradually revealing their course as you emerge from the wooded hills. Under the Moors, Silves was a place of grandeur, described in contemporary accounts as "of shining brightness" within its three dark circuits of guarding walls. Such glories and civilized splendours came to an end, however, in 1189, with the arrival of **Sancho I**, at the head of a mixed army of Portuguese and Crusaders. Sancho, desperately in need of extra fighting force, had recruited a rabble of "large and odious" northerners, who had already been expelled from the holy shrine of St James of Compostela for their irreligious behaviour. The army arrived at Silves toward the end of June and the thirty thousand Moors retreated to the citadel. There they remained through the long, hot summer, sustained by huge water cisterns and granaries, until September when, the water exhausted, they opened negotiations.

Sancho was ready to compromise, but the Crusaders had been recruited by the promise of plunder. The gates were opened after Sancho had negotiated guarantees for the inhabitants' personal safety and goods; all were brutally ignored by the Crusaders, who duly ransacked the town, killing some six thousand Moors in the process. Silves passed back into Moorish hands two years later, but by then the town had been irreparably weakened, and it finally fell to Christian forces in 1249.

The Town

The **Moorish Fortress** (daily: July–Aug 9am–8pm; Sept–June 9am–5.30pm; last entry 30 mins before closing time; €1.25) remains the focal point of Silves, dominating the town centre with its impressively complete set of sandstone walls and detached towers. The interior is a bit disappointing: aside from the great vaulted water cisterns – said to be haunted – there's nothing left of the old citadel, which is planted with modern gardens. However, you can circuit the walls for impressive views over the town and surrounding hills.

Silves's cathedral, or **Sé** (Mon–Fri 8.30am–6.30pm, Sun limited hours between mass; free), sits below the fortress, built on the site of the Grand Mosque. Flanked by broad Gothic towers, it has a suitably defiant, military appearance, though the Great Earthquake and centuries of impoverished restoration have left their mark within.

Opposite the Sé, it is worth a quick peer into the newer **Igreja da Misericórdia** (Mon–Fri 9.30am–1pm & 2–5.30pm; free), a sixteenth-century church with a fine Manueline doorway and hung with seven impressive religious paintings, some of them dating back to the seventeenth century.

Below the Sé, in Rua das Portas de Loulé, is the town's **Museu Arqueologia** (Mon–Sat 9am–6pm, last entry 5.45pm; €1.50). It's engaging enough, despite a lack of English-language labelling, and romps through the history of Silves from the year dot to the sixteenth century with displays of local archeological finds. At the centre of the museum is an Arab water cistern, left *in situ*, which boasts a ten-metre-deep well.

Silves' other main attraction is the **Fabrica Inglês** (daily 9am–midnight; free except during special events), by the riverfront some five minutes' walk east of the road bridge. A series of cafés, bars and fountains are clustered round a large central courtyard filled with outdoor tables below scented orange trees. It is a lovely space, most animated when it hosts the annual summer **Silves Beer Festival**, usually in July. At this time – and on Friday evenings in summer – the cafés and bars are heaving, and a spectacular light show illuminates the fountains. At other times the space seems soulless, with most of the attractions firmly closed. The one permanent attraction is the **Museu da Cortiças** (Mon–Sun 9.30am–12.45pm & 2–6.15pm; €1.25), a cork museum in the northwest corner of the complex, which won the European Industrial Museum Award in 2001. But unless you have a keen interest in the cork industry its displays are unlikely to get your pulse going. There are a few evocative black and white photos of local cork cutters, but otherwise the dull line of old cork-punching machines is about as exciting as a dentist's chair.

Strolling around the rest of Silves is a pleasure. There's a **market** (Mon–Sat 8am–1pm) on the riverfront, near the narrow thirteenth-century bridge. This is a fine place to sit outside at one of the grill-cafés (see opposite) and watch life go by.

Practicalities

The **train station** – an easy approach from either Lagos or Faro – lies 2km out of town; there is a connecting bus, but it's a pleasant walk if you're not weighed down with luggage. Arriving by **bus**, you'll be dropped on the main road, next to the market near the riverfront at the foot of town. There are two small tourist offices in Silves. The main town **turismo** is in a small kiosk below the town hall on Largo de Município (Mon–Fri 9.30am–1pm & 2–5.30pm; ☎282 442 325), which can give out details of local events. Just round the corner at Rua 25 de Abril 26–28 is a **regional tourist office** (hours as town tourist office; ☎282 442 255), in the heart of the town.

The town turismo will help arrange **private rooms**. Recommended are those at Rua Cândido dos Reis 36 (☎282 442 667; ❷), which are spotless and share the use of a kitchen and a little outdoor terrace. Alternatively, there are a couple of basic **pensões**, including the faded but central *Residencial Sousa*, Rua Samora Barros 17 (☎282 442 502; ❷), and, across the river, the somewhat poky but nicely positioned *Restaurante Residencial Ponte Romana* (☎282 443 275; ❷). More upmarket options are *Hotel Colina dos Mouros* (☎282 440 420, ☏282 440 426; ❹), a prominent modern hotel over the road bridge opposite the fortress, which has an outdoor pool, a bar and restaurant and rooms with superb views over the town. Right by the entrance to the fortress, *Estabelicimentos Dom Sancho* on Largo do Castelo (☎282 442 437; ❸) has decent rooms in a modern block above a tourist complex of shops and cafés. Price does not include breakfast.

If these are full, there are a couple of options just out of town. Around a kilometre east on the busy Messines road, after the Galp service station, *Vila Sodre* (☎282 443 441; ❸) is an attractive white villa with small, clean rooms and a small pool out the back; there is also a popular olde world restaurant downstairs. Finally, *Quinta do Rio*, at Sitio São Estevão, Apartado 217 (☎282 445 528, ⓕ282 445 528; ❸), around 5km out of town, off the road to São Bartolomeu de Messines, is a country inn with six delightful, rustic-style rooms with shaded terraces facing open country dotted with orange groves and grazing horses. The Italian owners can supply evening meals on request.

For **eating** in town, the pricey *Restaurante Marisqueira Rui*, Rua Comendador Vilarinho (☎282 442 682; closed Tues), continues to attract locals and tourists from all over the Algarve; if you manage to squeeze in – and you should try – order shellfish, the restaurant's speciality. At the other end of the price scale, and just as enjoyable in its way, is the *U Monchiqueiro Casa de Pasto* (closed Wed), with a menu that changes daily; it's the best of a handful of grill-cafés on the riverfront road in front of the market. Sit outside and tuck into *piri-piri* chicken, fries, salad and wine for around €8. The *Café Inglês* (closed Mon evening, Sat lunch and all day Sun), by the fortress, is a deslightful early twentieth-century town house which sells delicious home-made snacks, ice cream and fruit juices, as well as full meals; it also has seats outside and live music at weekends; while *Pastelaria Rosa*, in Largo do Município, is a superb old *pastelaria* with a cool *azulejos*-lined interior and a counter smothered in cakes and goodies. Outdoor tables spill onto the pretty main square next to a small fountain.

Barragem do Arade

Around 8km northeast of Silves, signed off the road to São Bartolomeu de Messines (see p.542), the **Barragem do Arade** makes a good excursion for water sports, a swim or a walk. There are various *barragems*, or resevoirs, dotted round the Algarve, many of them built by former dictator Salazar, and this is one of the area's main sources of water set amongst rolling, tree-lined hills. It's an attractive spot, popular with migrating birds, though when the water level falls its scarred sides spoil the picturesque effect.

Just as the dam itself comes into view, take the left hand fork in the road to *Café Coutada*, a café offering decent if slightly pricey drinks and meals with an outdoor terrace filled with twittering caged birds facing the water. The café can also organise **boat trips** to a scraggy, tree-lined offshore islet known as **Paradise Island**; the fee of €6.50 per person (or €5 per adult with child; children free) covers the return boat trip together with use of canoes, sun lounges and swimming in cordoned off areas of the resevoir. You can also hire jet skis.

Inland to the Serra de Monchique

Ten weekday buses – five at weekends – leave Portimão for the 24km, ninety-minute journey north to the market town of **Monchique** via **Caldas de Monchique**. Once clear of Portimão's ugly suburbs, the main road crosses the coastal plain, flanked by endless orchards of apples, pears, figs, almonds, pomegranates and citrus fruits. At Porto de Lagos the road divides, east to Silves and north into the foothills of the **Serra de Monchique**, a green and wooded mountain range of cork, chestnut and eucalyptus that provides the western Algarve with a natural northern boundary. It is ideal **hiking country**, or – with a bike or car – a superb route to take if you want to cut across afterwards to the wilder reaches of the western Algarve coast.

Caldas de Monchique

CALDAS DE MONCHIQUE, set in a ravine and surrounded by thick woods, has been a celebrated spa since Roman times. In 1495 Dom João II came here to take the waters (though he nevertheless died soon afterwards in Alvor), and in the nineteenth century the town became a favourite resort of the Spanish bourgeoisie. In 2000, virtually the entire village was purchased by the Monchique Termas company, who set about sympathetically restoring the rundown buildings round the main square into hotels and guest houses, revitalising the cafés and shops and completely modernizing the spa itself. In doing so they have transformed a somewhat ramshackle if popular spa village into a tourist village – but the results, so far at least, have been fairly successful.

The centre of Caldas de Monchique is reached by a looping, one-way side road off the main Portimão to Monchique road. Halfway down the hill on the left you'll see the cobbled, tree-shaded **main square**, fronted by the keyhole shaped pseudo-Moorish windows of the nineteenth-century former casino – now a *pensão* – and surrounded by lovely nineteenth-century buildings. The setting is as beautiful as any in the country, though the tiny village's peace and quiet is shattered daily by the busloads of day trippers who stop for a wander around and a cup of coffee.

Head downhill and you pass the **Bouvet** – a little stone building where you can sample the waters straight from the ground. The modern **thermal spa** (☎282 910 910, ✉spa@monchiquetermas.com) sits below here, on the edge of a ravine, flaunting its well-kept gardens and housing a pool, sauna, jacuzzi, Turkish bath and various specialist water treatments on the ground floor of a modern hotel. Sessions range from 40-minute "healthy leg" treatments (€36) to full weekend with accommodation and pampering (€172).

Climbing up from the spa, above the square, you can follow the stream to sit under giant eucalyptus trees – a wonderful spot for a picnic. Take along some of the local drink – *medronho* – a kind of schnapps made from the Arbutus or Strawberry Tree that grows on the surrounding hills.

Apart from the *Albergaria do Lageado* (see below), Caldas' **accommodation** is all owned by the Monchique Termas company (☎282 910 910, ✉fpguerreiro @monchiquetermas.com). It also hires out aparments overlooking the main square suitable for families, with small living rooms and kitchenettes sleeping up to four people from €90 a night. The best option is *Pensão Central* (❺), a very comfortable three-star *pension* partly set in the former casino building on the main square, though the interior is fully decked out with modern comforts including satellite TV, fridges and air conditioning. Facing the main square opposite the *Pensão Central*, *Estalagem Dom João 11* (❻) is a four-star inn in another converted nineteenth-century building, with similar facilities and marginally larger rooms. Otherwise try **Albergaria do Lageado** (☎282 912 616, ℱ282 911 310; May–Oct; ❺), just above the main square below a small chapel. This four-star inn has twenty smart rooms, each with TV and en-suite bathrooms. There's also a bar and a pool in the garden, along with an excellent restaurant where you can eat for around €15.

Other good places to **eat** include the *Restaurante Dom João II*, in a building dating from 1692, with lovely outdoor tables set out under the main square's trees. Moderate to expensive meals include interesting starters such as *morcelo* (spicy sausage) and melon with ham. For something simpler, *Bar Caldas*, on the far side of the main square below the path up to the picnic tables, is a darkened bar set in sixteenth-century former stables. Specialities include bread rolls with sausage meat inside, baked in the traditional outside oven opposite.

Not all the **buses** from Portimão call into the centre of Caldas, stopping instead on the main road just out of town before continuing up to Monchique.

Monchique and around

MONCHIQUE, 6km to the north of Caldas de Monchique, and 300m higher up the range, is a small market town whose large market on the second Friday of each month is famous for its smoked hams and furniture, especially its distinctive cross-shaped wooden chairs. There's not a great deal else to see, but it's a busy town and makes a nice enough excursion. Of the buildings, the most impressive is the **Igreja Matriz** (Mon–Sat 10am–5.30pm), the parish church, up a steep cobbled street from the main square, which has a Manueline porch and, inside, a little chapel with a facade of *azulejos*. The most evocative sight, though, is the ruined seventeenth-century monastery of **Nossa Senhora do Desterro**, which you can walk to up a wooded track – brown signs point you up here from Rua do Porto Fundo, the road leading uphill from the bus station. Only a roofless shell of this Franciscan foundation survives, apparently quite uncared for, but it's in a great position overlooking the town and shows a beautiful blend of classical Renaissance facade with Moorish-influenced vaulting.

Buses arrive at the terminal in the main square, Largo 5 de Outubro. Opposite here, Monchique's helpful **turismo** (Mon–Fri 9.30am–1pm & 2–5.30pm; ☎282 911 189) sits on a pretty, pedestrianized part of the square.

There are a couple of budget **places to stay** in town. First choice is the very welcoming *Estrela de Monchique*, Rua do Porto Fundo 46 (☎282 913 111; ❷), a stone's throw to the right of the bus terminal. Otherwise, the *Bela Vista*, on Largo 5 de Outubro (☎282 912 252; ❷) above a decent café, offers basic comforts with a communal bathroom. The front rooms have balconies facing the square, but these can be noisy. Better by far are the **inns** on the road up to Fóia (see below), though you'll need your own transport to reach them; the *Estalagem Abrigo da Montanha*, on Estrada da Fóia Estrada da Fóia (☎282 912 131, ✉abrigodamontanha@hotmail.com; ❺), has a lovely garden and views as well as a fine dining room, while, four and a half kilometres out of Monchique, on the same road, the *Quinta de São Bento* (☎ & ℻282 912 143; ❻) has just five rooms stuffed with period antiques in a home owned by the Bragança family, the former monarchs of Portugal. It is also one of the best places in this part of the Algarve for high quality, reasonably priced Portuguese cooking, featuring traditional recipes.

Monchique itself also has a handful of **restaurants** which soak up the passing tourist trade. *Restaurante A Charrete* on Rua Samora Gil 30–34 is recommended, specialising in award-winning "mountain food" – meat and fish cooked with beans, pasta and rice and the like, while *Restaurante Central,* near the church at Rua da Igreja 5, offers basic but inexpensive Portuguese cuisine in a tiny place virtually smothered under the weight of thousands of photocopied notes and postcards detailing past visitors' comments – most of them complimentary.

Fóia

Fóia, 8km west of Monchique, is – at nearly 900m – the highest of the Serra's peaks; on Mondays and Thursdays, two buses (11am and 3.30pm) make the delightful run up here from Monchique. Bristling with antennae and radio masts and capped by an ungainly modern complex of a café-restaurant, shop and a modern inn – *Estalagem de Santo António* (☎282 912 158, ℻282 912 878;

❹) – the summit itself can be an anticlimax, especially if clouds obscure the views or you have to share the experience with the midsummer crowds. Get here early if you can. On a clear day, the panoramic view of the Algarve takes in Portimão, Lagos, the foothills stretching to the Barragem da Bravura, and across west to Cabo de São Vicente. The poet Robert Southey claimed to have caught a glimpse of the hills of Sintra, beyond Lisbon, but that must have been poetic licence – or maybe the air's not as clear now as it was in 1801.

Picota

Reaching 770m, **Picota** comes second in altitude to Fóia, though it's much more interesting in terms of its botany, and easier to reach without transport. You can get to the peak from Monchique in around one and a half hours, a walk that takes in cork trees (and cork collection points), eucalyptus and pines, peach, lemon and orange orchards, and even wild goats scurrying about the heights. From Monchique, take the N266 Caldas de Monchique road, and turn left onto the N267, signposted Alferce. Picota is the second turning, signed around 800m along this road off to the right. At the top there's nothing save a rickety watchtower occupied by a solitary guardian with a pair of binoculars. From here you can see the coastline stretching all the way to Sagres, and take in another magnificent view of the Monchique mountain range.

West to the coast

Back down the road from Monchique towards Caldas, the minor N267 cuts west towards the coast, passing through the little mountain village of **MARMELETE** after 14km and continuing all the way to Aljezur (see p.570), another 20km west. In a car, it's a fine route, heading through tranquil countryside before swinging down through the hills and forests to the west coast; infrequent buses from Monchique only go as far as Marmelete.

Lagos and around

LAGOS is one of the most ancient settlements in the Algarve, founded by the Phoenicians, who were attracted to its superb natural harbour. Under the Moors it became an important trading post until its reconquest by Christian armies in 1241. Its attractions today are less the historical associations – though there are a couple of fine churches and a circuit of medieval walls – than the fact that it remains a real town: a fishing port and market centre with a sense of independence and a life of its own. Over the last few decades, it has also developed into a major resort (complete with huge marina), and attracts a range of visitors, from backpackers to moneyed second-homers – during the summer the population of 20,000 people swells to more than 200,000. Visitors come for some of the best beaches of the whole Algarve coast: to the east of the town is a long sweep of sand – Meia Praia – where there's space even in summer, while to the west is an extraordinary network of coves, sheltered by cliffs, pierced by tunnels and grottoes, and studded by weird and extravagantly weathered outcrops of purple-tinted rock.

Arrival and information

Lagos is the western terminal of the Algarve railway line and its **train station** is across the river, fifteen minutes' walk from the centre via a swing bridge in

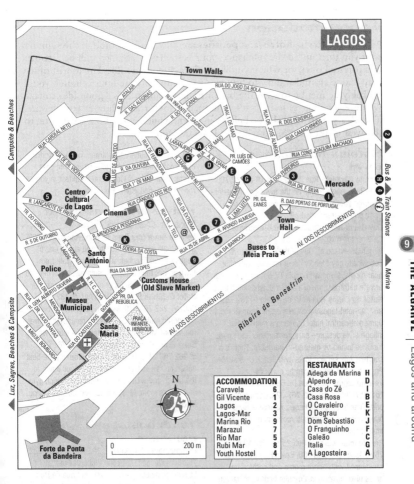

LAGOS

Town Walls

RUA DO JOGO DA BOLA

Campsite & Beaches

Centro
Cultural
de Lagos

Cinema

Santo
António

Police

Museu
Municipal

Santa
Maria

Customs House
(Old Slave Market)

Buses to
Meia Praia ★

Town
Hall

Mercado

Luz, Sagres, Beaches & Campsite

Forte da Ponta
da Bandeira

Ribeira de Bensafrim

AV. DOS DESCOBRIMENTOS

N

0   200 m

Bus & Train Stations

Marina

9

THE ALGARVE | Lagos and around

ACCOMMODATION	
Caravela	6
Gil Vicente	1
Lagos	2
Lagos-Mar	3
Marina Rio	9
Marazul	7
Rio Mar	5
Rubi Mar	8
Youth Hostel	4

RESTAURANTS	
Adega da Marina	H
Alpendre	D
Casa do Zé	I
Casa Rosa	B
O Cavaleiro	E
O Degrau	K
Dom Sebastião	J
O Franguinho	F
Galeão	C
Italia	G
A Lagosteira	A

the marina; taxis are usually available if you can't face the walk. The **bus station** is a bit closer in, a block back from the main estuary road, Avenida dos Descobrimentos, and almost opposite the bridge to the train station.

The **turismo** (June to mid-Sept Mon 9.30am–12.30pm & 2–7pm, Tues 9.30am–1.30pm & 3–7pm, Wed & Sun 9.30am–12.30pm & 2–5.30pm, Thurs–Sat 9.30am–7pm; mid-Sept to May Wed–Sat 9.30am–12.30pm & 2–5.30pm; ☎282 763 031) is inconveniently positioned at Sítio de São João, which is the first roundabout as you come into the town from the east. From the centre, it's a twenty-minute walk; just follow the signs. A taxi will cost about €3 each way.

Most of Lagos can be explored comfortably on foot, but the best way to see the outlying sights in season is on the **Toy Train**, which trundles hourly (May–Sept 10am–6pm; €3) from the marina along Avenida dos Descobrimentos and out via the beaches of Praia dona Ana and Porto de Moz to the headland at Ponta da Piedade.

Accommodation

Most of the town's **hotels** and **pensões** are fully booked through the summer so if you turn up on the offchance, your best chance of a bed will be a **room** in a private house, for which you'll pay €25–40 for a double. The tourist office may phone around and try to find you a space in a private house, though you'll probably be met by touts at the bus or train station, and it's a good idea to take whatever's going (as long as it's central), and look round later at your leisure. There's a **youth hostel** (see below) in town, while Lagos also a **campsite**, to the west of the centre, close by the Praia de Dona Ana.

Hotels and pensões in town

Pensão Caravela Rua 25 de Abril 16 ☎ 282 763 361. Reasonable rooms on the town's main pedestrianized street. Doubles come with or without bath; breakfast included. ❷

Gay Guest House/Residencial Gil Vicente Rua Gil Vicente 26 ☎ 282 081 150, ✉ ggh@netvisao.pt. One of the Algarve's few specifically gay friendly guest houses, with nine neat rooms, some with cable TV, but only one with private bathroom; there's also a downstairs bar. ❸

Hotel de Lagos Rua Nova da Aldeia ☎ 282 769 967, ✉ hotel-lagos@mail.telepac.pt. Lagos's most upmarket central hotel boasting a landscaped, village-style design – bars, restaurants and sports facilities joined by glassed-in corridors. There's a courtesy bus service to its own beach club at Meia Praia, too; but service can be surly. ❼

Pensão Lagos-Mar Rua Dr. Faria e Silva 13 ☎ 282 763 523, ☏ 282 767 324. Upmarket *pensão*, close to Praça Gil Eanes. All rooms have TV, telephone and private bathrooms and some have small balconies. ❹

Residencial Marazul Rua 25 de Abril 13 ☎ 282 769 143, ☏ 282 769 960. Beautifully decorated *residencial*, with bright rooms and communal areas tiled in *azulejos*. En-suite bedrooms vary in size, but all come with TVs and some have terraces with sea views. April–Nov. ❸

Albergaria Marina Rio Av dos Descobrimentos 388 ☎ 282 769 859, ✉ marinario@ip.pt. A large, modern inn facing the harbour across the busy *avenida* (back rooms face the bus station), the place to go for decent rooms and modern facilities, including satellite TV, a games room and a rooftop pool. ❻

Hotel Rio Mar Rua Cândido dos Reis 83 ☎ 282 770 130, ☏ 282 763 927. Smart, medium-sized hotel, tucked into a central street. Most rooms have a balcony – the best overlook the sea at the back of the hotel, others overlook a fairly quiet main street. ❹

Pensão Rubi Mar Rua da Barroca 70–1° ☎ 282 763 165, ✉ rubimar01@hotmail.com. Wonderful old *pensão* with nine spacious rooms; the best rooms have harbour views and breakfast in your room is included. Book ahead. ❸

Hotels and pensões at Praia De Don Ana

Pensão Dona Ana Praia de Dona Ana ☎ 282 762 322. Small, white *pensão* situated above one of Lagos's finest beaches, a 20-minute walk from town across the clifftops. In summer, you'll need to book well in advance for one of the 20 rooms. ❷

Hotel Golfinho Praia de Dona Ana ☎ 282 769 900, ☏ 282 769 999. Modern hotel on the cliff set a hundred metres back from the beach. Attractive rooms, fine views and a courtesy bus into town. ❹

Sol e Praia Praia de Dona Ana ☎ 282 762 026, ☏ 282 760 247. The newest and probably the best option on this stretch, close to the steps down to the beach and with facilities including a pool, gym and games room. Most rooms have coastal-facing balconies. ❺

Youth hostel and campsite

Campismo da Trindade ☎ 282 763 893, ☏ 282 762 885. Wedged up by the Clube de Futebol Esperança de Lagos on the way to Praia de Dona Ana, this is a basic and cramped campsite with a small shop. Prices are €3 per person per night, with tents starting at €3.50 per night. In season a bus marked "D. Ana/Porto de Mós" runs to the site from the bus station. On foot, follow the main Sagres road around the old town and it's about ten to fifteen minutes from the Forte Ponta da Bandeira to the site.

Pousada de Juventude de Lagos Rua de Lançarote de Freitas 50 ☎ 282 761 970, ✉ lagos@movijovem.pt. Modern, well-designed youth hostel, just up from the Centro Cultural de Lagos, with several dorms (€15) plus a few en-suite doubles (€30); be sure to book in advance. There's a nice central courtyard plus internet access and currency exchange.

The Town

Lagos was a favoured residence of Henry the Navigator, who used the town as a base for the new African trade, to which is owed the town's least proud relic – Europe's first **slave market**, whose arcades survive alongside the old **Customs House** in the **Praça da República** near the waterfront. On the other side of this square is the church of **Santa Maria**, through whose whimsical Manueline windows the youthful Dom Sebastião is said to have roused his troops before the ill-fated Moroccan expedition of 1578. Fired up by militant Catholicism, the dream-crazed king was to perish on the battlefield of Alcácer-Quibir (modern Ksar el Kbir, between Tangier and Fez) along with almost the entire Portuguese nobility. It was a disaster that enabled the Spanish to absorb Portugal for sixty years, but it did Dom Sebastião's reputation a world of good among the aggressively devout. He's commemorated in the centre of Lagos, in **Praça Gil Eanes**, by a fantastically dreadful modern statue – pink, ridiculous and looking like a flowerpot man.

Much of the old town was devastated by the 1755 earthquake, though one rare and beautiful church that survived is the **Igreja de Santo António**. Decorated around 1715, its gilt and carved interior is wildly obsessive, every last inch filled with a private fantasy of cherubic youths struggling with animals and fish. The church forms part of a visit to the **Museu Municipal** (Tues–Sun 9.30am–12.30pm & 2–5pm; €1.70) next door, worth a look if only to discover the true meaning of the word eclectic. Alongside barrowloads of Neolithic axeheads, pottery shards, statuary and local religious art are jars containing misshapen animal foetuses, a display of models of Algarvian chimneys, straw hats, lobster pots and fossils, travelogues, the 1504 town charter, and assorted muskets, swords and cannonballs.

The Praça da República, and the waterfront Avenida dos Descobrimentos, are the best vantage points for the remains of Lagos's once impregnable **walls** and fortifications, which include the squat seventeenth-century **Forte Ponta da Bandeira** (Tues–Sun 9.30am–12.30pm & 2–5pm; €1.80), guarding the entrance to the harbour. The Forte also sits opposite Lagos's small but attractive sandy **town beach**. North of here, Avenida dos Descobrimentos is usually lined with stalls selling **boat trips** to the surrounding coastline (see "Listings", p.562).

The beaches

The promontory **south** of Lagos is fringed by eroded cliff faces that shelter a series of postage stamp-sized cove-beaches. All are within easy walking distance of the old town. The easiest access on foot to the **cove-beaches** to the south and west is to follow the Avenida dos Descobrimentos up the hill (toward Sagres) and turn left just opposite the fire station, where you see signs to the tiny **Praia do Pinhão**. This is the first of the coves – around a twenty-minute walk from town. Five minutes further, across the cliffs, is the **Praia de Dona Ana** – one of the most photogenic of all the Algarve's beaches, with a restaurant, the *Mirante*, built into the cliffs. Out of season it is superb, though in summer the crowds can get overwhelming.

Beyond here, you can follow a path around the cliffs and coast to **Praia do Camilo** – sometimes a bit less crowded – and right to the **Ponta da Piedade**, a headland where a palm-bedecked lighthouse makes a great vantage point for the sunset. This marks the final point of call for the Toy Train from Lagos's marina.

Beyond the point, the coast sweeps west again and you can continue to follow paths close to the cliff's edge to the beach of **Porto do Mós**, another 45 minutes' walk away, a nice enough beach though development has spoilt the surroundings. The path then moves on as far as Luz (see p.563), another hour away; it's a splendid stretch, high above the ocean, until the obelisk above Luz comes into sight, from where you scramble down the hillside and into town.

To the **east** of Lagos, across the river and flanked by the railway line, is **Meia Praia**, a vast tract of sand that extends for 4km to the delta of the rivers Odiáxere and Arão. The beach is particularly popular with backpackers who congregate at one of the beach bars dotted along the beach. You can walk to the beach via the marina in around thirty minutes or a regular **bus service** leaves from the Avenida dos Descobrimentos and travels the length of the beach; alternatively, there's a seasonal **ferry** from Avenida dos Descobrimentos across the river, from where the beach is a short walk away.

Barragem de Bravura and Lagos Zoo

Around 15km north of Lagos lies the **Barragem de Bravura**, one of the most picturesque of the Algarve's several resevoirs. There's no public transport there but, with a car, the drive is a delight, either along the IC4 up the Ribeira da Bensafrim valley towards Aljezur – from where the *barragem* is signed off to the right – or along the coast road towards Portimão, where the *barragem* can be reached by taking the N125-9 from Odeáxere. Both roads pass through bucolic countryside, delightfully flower-filled in spring and early summer, before the landscape gets gradually more rolling as you approach the resevoir. When the resevoir comes into view, there's a car park on the left where you pull over and admire the views over the glittering waters, surrounded by densely wooded hills. A few hundred metres from the car park lies a seasonal café, *A Recanto da Barragem* (April–Oct, closed Mon), which dispenses drinks and decent snacks inside or on an outdoor terrace next to a small children's playground. Another 400m beyond the café, the road stops at the top of the dam over the river Bravura; to the south, the deep valley is little more than an overgrown stream fed by a waterfall from the dam, while behind the dam lies the deep, still green waters of the resevoir, filled with huge carp. It's an idyllic spot, and you can walk right over the top of the dam and round the edges of the resevoir on the other side along a dirt trail. Swimming, fishing and water sports, however, are prohibited.

Around 8km north of Lagos, just off the main N120 to Aljezur and close to the village of Barão de São João, **Lagos Zoo** (May–Sept daily 10am–7pm; Oct–April daily 10am–5pm; €6, children €3.50) makes an interesting hour or two's detour, especially for those with kids. The large, leafy complex houses various birds including flamingos, tucans, ibis, parrots and emus, as well as a few wallabies, monkeys and farm animals in a special children's enclosure. There's also a shop, a restaurant and an exhibition centre.

Eating

The centre of Lagos is packed with **restaurants**, most found along ruas Afonso d'Almeida and 25 de Abril. Where the Avenida dos Descobrimentos meets Rua das Portas de Portugal, there's a diverting **fish and vegetable market** (Mon–Sat mornings), in front of which is a line of good fish restaurants. Menus are of a similar standard and price almost everywhere, though Lagos does also have a couple of highly regarded places where it's worth pushing the boat out.

Adega da Marina Av dos Descobrimentos 35. A great barn of a place with rows of tables like a giant wedding party. Food consists of stonking portions of charcoal-grilled meat and fish; great house wines, too. Moderate.

Alpendre Rua António Barbosa Viana 17. One of the oldest – and more formal – restaurants in the Algarve, serving memorable smoked swordfish and decent *arroz de marisco*. The crêpes are still the best reason to come though – flambéed at your table. At least €25. Expensive.

Casa do Zé Av dos Descobrimentos. On the corner with the market, a 24-hour place where filling fish dishes are served at very fair prices. Very much a locals' choice at lunchtime, with the outdoor seating soaking up a brisk trade – daily specials at around €5.

Casa Rosa Rua do Ferrador 22. With substantial €3.50 fast food meals – though nothing particularly Portuguese – this is a backpackers' favourite; also does cocktails. Closed Mon. Inexpensive.

O Cavaleiro Rua Garret 23. Just off the Praça Luís Camões and open twenty-three hours a day, it makes a pleasant place to sit outside during the day and welcome refuelling stop in the small hours. There's an inexpensive menu of drinks, meals, snacks and pizzas.

O Degrau Rua Soeira da Costa 46 ☎282 764 716. International cuisine – including a variety of vegetarian dishes – for around €13 a head served in a comfortable and welcoming atmosphere. Book in advance during the season to avoid queuing. Closed Mon.

Dom Sebastião Rua 25 de Abril 20–22 ☎ 282 762 795. Arguably the town's finest restaurant, with outdoor seating, a traditional, cobbled-floor interior, good seafood, and a fabulous selection of appetizers. A full meal runs to about €25, though with careful selection you could get away for less.

O Franguinho Rua Luís de Azevedo 25. Bustling *churrasqueira* with a tiny, first-floor dining room. This is the place to come for fine (if greasy) chicken or *febras de porco* (grilled pork steaks). There are daily changing specials, too. Closed Mon. Inexpensive.

Galeão Rua de Laranjeira 1. A little hidden away, but offers all the Algarvian classics and superb steaks at eminently reasonable prices. Under €20; closed Sun.

Italia Rua Garrett 26–28, off Praça Luís Camões. Bright, cheery restaurant run by Italians: pizzas come from a wood-burning oven; there's Italian wine, pasta and a full menu besides. Around €10 for a pizza or pasta meal, more if you eat the meat or fish specials.

A Lagosteira Rua 1º de Maio 20. Upmarket, blue-tiled restaurant specializing in *camarão flambé* (flambéed prawns), *peixe na cataplana* (fish cooked in a circular pan) and, of course, *lagosta*: lobster. Daily specials too. Expensive.

Drinking and nightlife

There is no shortage of **bars** around town, many of them owned by expatriates – in particular Irish and British. Cocktails are extremely popular in Lagos and measures are almost universally generous; look out for the places offering two-for-one deals and special events. Most bars stay open until at least 2am, some even later if the party is in full flow.

Snack Bar Abrigo Rua Marquês de Pombal 2. With outdoor tables under the orange trees – beer, cocktails, snacks and meals all day. Closed Sun.

Eddie's Bar Rua 25 de Abril 99. Small, friendly bar with an extended Happy Hour from 5–9pm, a good selection of sounds and internet access for €4/hr. Attracts a surf/bike/skate dude kind of crowd.

Esplanade Rosa Praça Infante Dom Henrique. This kiosk café-bar opposite the Igreja Santa Maria has outdoor tables sprawling across the leafty square adjacent to Praça da Republica. Serves inexpensive pastries, pizzas, coffees, beer and ice creams.

Cervejaria Ferradura Rua de Ferradura 26A. Atmospheric *cervejaria* that is very much a local, with walls covered in soccer posters and stacks of inexpensive *petiscos* on the bar, mostly shellfish. Closed Sun.

Hideaway Trav. 1º de Maio 9, off Praça Luís de Camões. Cheap beer, more than fifty cocktails, laid-back sounds and food till 2am.

Joe's Garage Rua 1º de Maio 78. Not for the faint-hearted, this joint throngs with antipodians drinking heavily and usually dancing on the tables. To cushion your stomach, a filling plate of food costs €4 and you know it's closing time when they set fire to the bar and put it out with a fire extinguisher.

Lords Tavern Rua António Crisogono Santos 56. Near the bus station, this British-style pub offers dismal crooners most nights and sports channel TV for the big games. There's also reasonably priced, if very average, bar food.

Mullens Rua Cândido dos Reis 86. This atmospheric, cavernous *adega*, is the most appealing late-night choice in town. Inexpensive drinks including Guinness, sangria and *vinho verde* on tap, are served alongside excellent and moderately priced meals to a jazz and soul soundtrack.

Naufragio Bar Av dos Descobrimentos. Pleasant beach bar with a youthful clientele, jazzy sounds and moderately priced bar snacks. Out the back there's a great terrace facing the town beach and the Forte da Ponta da Bandeira.

Roskos Rua Cândido dos Reis 79. Down the road

from *Mullens*, an Irish bar with an 8–10pm Happy Hour and fifty serious cocktails. Open till 4am.

Bar Vivante Rua 25 Abril 105. Just before the slave market, this late-night drinking den has gaudy marble pillars and a superb "tropical" roof terrace; a good place to hit when the other bars have closed. Open till 4am.

Listings

Banks and exchange Banks are grouped around Praça Gil Eanes and you can exchange money in almost every travel agency.

Bike and motorbike rental *Eddie's Bar*, Rua 25 de Abril 99 ☎ 282 768 329, ✉ free_tours@hot-mail.com organizes mountain bike excursions. For motorbikes try Motor Ride, Rua José Afonso 23 ☎ 282 761 720, in the new town towards Ponta da Piedade, which rents out bikes from €60 a day.

Boat trips The best way to see the extraordinary rock formations is to take a boat trip out to the grottoes and sea caves along the surrounding coast. It's worth shopping around for the best deal, but most cost around €10 per person for a two-hour trip; some of them include a soft or alcoholic drink. Trips are also easy to arrange with the fishing boats that gather around the Forte Ponta da Bandeira or from one of the many stalls along Av dos Descobrimentos up towards the marina. Bom Dia (☎ 282 764 670, ✉ bomdia-cruises@ip.pt) offers sailing boat trips to the nearby grottoes from €15, which includes food on board, and also offers longer half-day trips to Sagres for €50 per person. It can also arrange dolphin "seafaris" and speed boat trips to Luz.

Bullfights These take place most Saturdays throughout the summer, usually at 5.30pm (€30) at the Praça de Touros de Lagos, out on the Portimão road. *Mbtours* offers tickets and return buses to the bullring; ☎ 282 426 045.

Buses Travel information for all destinations from

the bus terminal (☎ 282 762 944).

Car rental Try Auto Jardim, Rua Vítor da Costa Silva 18 (☎ 282 769 486; three-day minimum); Avis, Largo das Portas de Portugal 11 (☎ 282 763 691); Hertz, Rossio de São João (☎ 282 769 809, ✉ 282 760 008); LuzCar-Sociedade, Largo das Portas de Portugal 10 (☎ 282 761 016).

Doctor For an English-speaking doctor, call MediLagos ☎ 282 760 181.

Hospital Rua do Castelo dos Governadores, adjacent to the church of Santa Maria (☎ 282 763 034).

Internet *Eddie's Bar*, Rua 25 de Abril 99 (daily 4pm–2am; €4/hr).

Police Rua General Alberto Silveira (☎ 282 762 930).

Post office Next to the town hall, just off Av dos Descobrimentos; open Mon–Fri 8.30am–6pm.

Taxis There are ranks in front of the post office or call Lagos Central Taxi (☎ 282 762 469 or 282 763 587).

Telephones It's easiest to make long-distance calls at the Telecom office, next to the post office (June to mid-Sept Mon–Fri 8.30am–10pm, Sat 9am–1pm & 5pm–midnight, Sun 6–10pm; mid-Sept to May Mon–Sat 8am–6pm).

Travel agency Tickets (including bus tickets) and tours from Clubalgarve, Rua Marreiros Netto 25 (☎ 282 762 337) and Tourlagos, Rua Infante de Sagres 31 (☎ 282 767 967).

West to Sagres

Despite a certain amount of development, the coast **west of Lagos**, to Vila do Bispo and Sagres, remains one of the least spoiled parts of the Algarve, largely thanks to the Parque Natural do Sudoeste Alentejano e Costa Vicentina which prohibits largescale building on the coastline west of Burgau. As a result, the resorts – **Luz, Burgau** and **Salema** – remain largely low-rise and low key. Of these, Salema – with a superb beach and still recognizable as a former fishing village – promises most.

In summer there are frequent **bus** services from Lagos to Luz and Burgau, and a regular service to Salema. Connections are less frequent during the winter, but you should always be able to get to at least one of the villages and back in a day trip, even if it means walking to the highway on occasion to pick up the bus. You could also plan a day that involved **walking** between the villages: Burgau to Luz to Lagos, in particular, is a nice, relatively easy stretch.

Luz

Five kilometres west of Lagos, the mass of white chalets and villas that is the resort of **LUZ** pile up behind a fine, sweeping beach set below towering cliffs. In high season, visitors all but swamp the beach, but at other times it remains delightfully tranquil. The largely upmarket villas are low-rise and many have prime sea views. There's a palm-lined beachside promenade that leads from the sands up to a *miradouro* beneath the village's old fort – now a restaurant (see below) – and the church. Along the promenade there are any number of bar-restaurants with advantageous terraces. Of these, *Kiwi Pastelaria* is the best bet for inexpensive **snacks**, salads, sandwiches and croissants. For a full **meal**, *O Poço* sits in a superb raised position facing the beach, and serves moderately priced fish and seafood such as *espadarte de tamboril* (monkfish kebab). For something upmarket, *Restaurante Fortaleza da Luz*, above the west end of the beach, opposite the church, offers expensive Algarvian and international cuisine inside the old fort or on a lovely outdoor terrace facing the sea. For **accommodation**, Luz has just one hotel, *Hotel Belavista da Luz* (☏282 788 655, ⓕ 282 788 656; ❻), around 1km uphill on the road out of town towards Sagres, set in a modern pink four-star with all mod cons including a restaurant and pool, but little in way of character. The rest of Luz's accommodation consists of apartments and villas, often block-booked in summer. The main agencies are the *Ocean Club*, Rua Direita 20 (☏282 789 472, ⓦocean.club.luz@ mail.telepac; ❼) which offers superb upmarket apartments, many right on the beach. The local sports centre, *Luz Bay Club*, Rua do Jardim (☏282 789 640, ⓕ282 789 641; ❹), has less exclusive and simpler apartments with kitchenettes, TVs and balconies, some of which have views of the sea. *Luz Bay Club* also offers tennis, squash and wall tennis, a sauna and pool for a day membership fee of €11.

Campers might want to head for the large luxury *Valverde* site (☏282 789 211, ⓕ 282 789 213) close to the highway, with the full range of tourist facilities including a restaurant, bar, supermarket and kids' playground, but it's a good 1.5km or so trek from the seafront.

Incidentally, the **path back to Lagos** starts at the eastern end of the beach. At the Algarve Sports Club, follow the private road uphill and make the steep scramble up to the obelisk on the cliffs, from where a gentle path careers along the tops to Porto do Mós, Ponte das Piedade and Lagos (see p.556).

Burgau

It's another 5km or so to **BURGAU**, a resort which still displays vestiges of its former fishing village life. The cobbled main street, with its side alleys and terraces, retains some charm, running right through the village and tumbling down to a wide sweep of sand backed by crumbling cliffs. Out of season, it's truly attractive, the beach deserted and the shutters down in most of the shops and restaurants, leaving the streets to echo to your own footsteps and little else. In summer, there's no mistaking Burgau for the out-and-out resort it is, its fine beach and backstreets packed day and night.

Again, unless you're here on a pre-booked holiday, you'll find it tough to locate **accommodation** in summer, though signs scattered around the village advertise rooms in private houses. The best place to head for is *Casa Grande*

(☎282 697 416, @casagrande@mail.telepac.pt; ❸) at the top end of town on the road towards Luz, a characterful old manor run by Brits. Set in its own grounds, the giant rooms have soaring ceilings, each decorated with a motley assortment of old furniture, and there's a fine restaurant attached, the *Adega Casa Grande* (daily April–Oct).

Burgau is well served with bars and restaurants, including the *Beach Bar Burgau* with a splendid terrace-bar right on the beach (open till 2am). The food isn't all it could be (restaurant closed Mon), but it's a great spot for a late-night drink.

Not all the **buses** from Lagos and Sagres call into Burgau itself, though all pass the turn-off on the highway, from where it's a 2km walk to the village through arid farming country.

Salema

SALEMA remains one of the most popular resorts along this stretch, certainly for independent travellers who have numerous accommodation options. Just 20km west of Lagos, the turn-off from the N125 snakes down a delightful, semi-cultivated valley, the sea creeping ever closer. The bus parks just above the fishing harbour, where the slipway is cluttered with brightly coloured boats. The fairly homogenous white splodge of apartment and villa construction spreads back up the valley from the village leaving the old village to the east of the harbour largely untouched. Here, white terraced houses are divided by narrow alleys which run down on the east side. The western **beach** – a wide, rock-sheltered bay – is magnificent: in winter, the sea comes crashing right up to the edge of the village.

Most of the **accommodation** in Salema is in apartments, though there is a fair-sized hotel, *Hotel Residencial Salema,* (☎282 665 328, Ⓕ282 685 329; March–Oct only; ❹) at Rua 28 de Janeiro, with a bar and small balconies plonked rather unceremoniously by the cobbled square just back from the beach. There are cheaper rooms at *A Mare* (☎282 695 165, @johnmare@telepac.pt; ❸), on the hill above the main road into town, where the small rooms have bath, sea views and terraces with sun loungers. More upmarket – and steeply uphill – is the *Estalagem Infante do Mar* (☎282 690 100, Ⓕ282 609 109; ❺) around 1km from the seafront on the road to Figueira, a smart four-star inn with comfy rooms, most offering panoramic views over the coast, as well as a restaurant, bar and pool. Alternatives are private **rooms** in the old village – just stroll along the street and look for signs: you should be able to secure something with a terrace and kitchen. There's also a pleasantly landscaped and very well-equipped **campsite**, *Quinta dos Carriços* (☎282 695 201, Ⓕ282 695 122), 1.5km back up towards the main highway – the bus passes it on the way into the village.

Best of the **restaurants** is *Boia Bar Restaurante*, at Rua das Pescadores 101 just east of the harbour, serving everything from breakfasts to snacks, drinks and inexpensive full meals; the *caldeirada* (fish stew) for four is the speciality. There's also a special children's menu. The *Atlântico* is the best sited – right on the beach and with a cheapish menu incorporating fresh fish and all the usual dishes. *Bar Aventura*, Rua das Pescadores, is an attractive bar which offers **internet** access at €4.50 per hour.

Figueira and Raposeira

At the village of **FIGUEIRA** on the N125, around 3km northwest of Salerna (the point at which the highway most closely approaches the coast between Lagos and Sagres), there's the very welcoming *Bar Celeiro* by the bus stop.

Opposite here, a rough farm track leads off to the isolated **Praia da Figueira** (a 20–30min walk through lovely countryside), which is often more or less deserted except for a couple of nudists.

Between Figueira and Raposeira, a sign points off the main N125 to the chapel of **Nossa Senhora de Guadalupe**, reached down the old road which runs parallel to the highway. Built in the thirteenth century by the Knights Templars, and said to have been frequented by Henry the Navigator, the chapel stands in rural solitude. It is usually kept locked, but it's a pleasant place to stroll around or have a picnic.

Two other worthwhile beaches are accessible by road from the village of **RAPOSEIRA**, 3km further west, sliced through by the speeding highway. There is, though, a decent if simple café-restaurant here, the *Rodrigues* opposite the church. The turn-off to the beach ("Ingrina") is signposted at the traffic lights on the highway: go through Hortas do Tabual and take the left fork, and after 3km you'll reach **Praia do Zavial**, a rocky beach popular with surfers and with a decent café-restaurant (closed Mon). Another couple of kilometres round the bay, **Praia da Ingrina** is more sheltered and sandy, good for beach-combing amid the rock pools, with another beachside café (closed Tues). There's also a rural **campsite** (☎ & ℻282 639 242) here, 1km up from the sea, with its own bar-restaurant. There are no public transport connections with either beach from the main road.

West of Raposeira the road passes Vila do Bispo (see p.569) and the turn-off for the west coast, before heading across the flattened landscape for Sagres.

Sagres and Cabo de São Vicente

Wild and windswept, **SAGRES** and its cape were considered by the Portuguese as the far limit of the world. It was on these headlands in the fifteenth century that Prince Henry the Navigator made his residence and it was here, too, that he set up a school of navigation, gathering together the greatest astronomers, cartographers and adventurers of his age. Fernão de Magalhães (Magellan), Pedro Álvares Cabral and Vasco da Gama all studied at Sagres, and from the beach at Belixe – midway between the capes of Sagres and **São Vicente** – the first long caravels were launched, revolutionizing shipping with their wide hulls, small adaptable sails, and ability to sail close to the wind. Each year new expeditions were dispatched to penetrate a little further than their predecessors, and to resolve the great navigational enigma presented by the west coast of Africa, thereby laying the foundations of the country's overseas empire.

After Henry's death here in 1460, the centre of maritime studies was moved to Lisbon and Sagres slipped back into the obscurity from which he'd raised it. In the early 1980s, the forlorn one-street village began to attract a growing number of young backpackers and windsurfers, drawn by the string of magnificent, isolated local beaches. Now, the main highway from Lagos has put Sagres within easy reach and the inevitable trail of villas and apartments has followed. But it can still be a great place to stay, especially in winter, when the wind blows hard and there's a bleak, desolate appeal to the scenery, with hardly a tourist to be seen. Throughout the summer, by contrast, the sprawling village draws a lively alternative social scene: the young beachgoers still flock here, well catered for by an ever-growing array of rooms for rent, restaurants and bars, rubbing shoulders these days though with families in villas and guests from the *pousada*, which overlooks the village.

Sagres

Sagres village, rebuilt in the nineteenth century over the earthquake ruins of Henry's town, has nothing of architectural or historical interest. Its small sixteenth-century Fortaleza de Baleeira was damaged by Francis Drake in 1587 and further ruined in the 1755 earthquake; the rest of the town is little more than a main road – Rua Comandante Matoso – connecting the fishing harbour and Praia da Baleeira at one end with the main square, Praça da République, at the other, all backed by a new town of white villas and apartments. **Praça da République** is the main focus of the town, an attractive cobbled space lined with squat palms and whitewashed cafés, swooped over by swallows. From here, it's a short walk southeast to Sagres' best beach, Praia da Mareta (see below).

Henry the Navigator's **Fortaleza** (daily: May–Sept 10am–8.30pm; Oct–April 10am–6.30pm; €3) dominates the whole village, with Rua da Fortaleza running directly up the headland towards its massive bulk; it is better to walk this way than to follow the road signs which take you on a detour to a giant car park set well back from the fort. An immense circuit of walls – only the north side survives intact – once surrounded the vast, shelf-like promontory, high above the Atlantic.

After the formidable tunnel entrance is spread a huge pebble **Rosa dos Ventos** (wind compass), unearthed beneath a church in 1921. Wind compasses are used to measure the direction of the wind, but most are divided into 30 segments. This is unusual in that its 43-metre diameter is divided into 40 segments. No one is sure whether the compass dates back to Henry's time, though the simple, much-restored chapel of **Nossa Senhora da Graça** besides the compass is accepted as dating from the fifteenth century.

Over the last few years there has been an attempt to beef up the contents of the fortress with new buildings within the walls – a **shop, café** and **exhibition space** showing maps of Portugal and other nautical memorabilia – but, gracelessly constructed with concrete, they have done little to enhance the beauty of the site. Elsewhere, it's a pleasant enough place to wander around the walls or out to **Ponta de Sagres**, a headland with a small lighthouse beacon offering fine views along the coast.

Local beaches

However impressive the fortress, most people's days in Sagres are spent on one of the excellent nearby beaches, five of which are within easy walking distance of the village. Three of them are on the more sheltered coastline east of the fortress: one of the nicest, **Praia da Mareta** is just five minutes' walk southeast of the main square. The small **Praia da Baleeira** is by the working fishing harbour, around fifteen minutes' walk from the main square along Rua Comandante Matoso. From the cliffs above the harbour it's another five- to ten-minute walk to the longest and generally least crowded beach, the **Praia do Martinhal**, an ideal spot for windsurfing. West of the fortress, the beaches are rockier and wilder, such as **Praia do Tonel**, which is generally quieter. It's a longer walk to the beautiful **Praia de Belixe**, 2km down the road from Sagres to Cabo São Vicente, where you are usually guaranteed plenty of sand to yourself.

Whichever beach you choose, the swimming must be approached with caution – there are some very strong currents especially on the west side of the fortress. Before setting off for the more distant strands, stock up with drinks and picnic supplies as there are virtually no facilities, especially out of season. The village supermarket can oblige with most provisions, plus five-litre flagons of the local wine for evening parties.

Practicalities

Buses from Lagos stop on the main village road, just by the square, Praça da República, and continue to the harbour. The **turismo** (Tues–Sat 9.30am–1pm & 2–5.30pm; T 282 763 031) is a lonely hut a couple of minutes walk – or one bus stop – along the village road from the Praça towards the fishing harbour. On the Praça there's also a privately run information office, *Turinfo* (daily 9.30am–1pm & 2–5.30pm; T 282 620 003, F 282 620 004), which can arrange room rental, book you on a local jeep or boat tour, offer **internet** access (€3/30min) and rent out mountain **bikes** (€10/day).

Accommodation

There are places to stay in and around Sagres village, and in high season, at least, it's basically a question of turning up and seeing what you're offered. Generally, you'll be approached by people offering **rooms** (from around €30 a double) and, if you want it, access to a kitchen too. There is also a scattering of regular **pensões** and **hotels**; as with the private rooms, prices come down considerably out of season. The nearest **campsite**, *Belixe* (T 282 624 351, F 282 624 445; €4/person, from €34/tent), is 2km northwest of the village, along (and off) the main road; it is convenient for Praia de Belixe.

Hotel da Baleeira Porto da Baleeira T 282 624 212, © hotel.baleeira@mail.telepac.pt. This smart hotel is the spot for harbour views, complete with pool, restaurant and tennis courts. ❻

Residencial Dom Henrique Praça da República T 282 620 000, F 282 620 001. In a great position right on the square – there's a terrace and bar and front rooms have superb sea-facing balconies (which you pay more for). ❹

Fortaleza do Belixe Belixe T 282 624 124, W www.pousadas.pt. Small, four-room hotel, an annexe of the *pousada*, perched high on the cliff edge, 2km out of town at Belixe. ❺

Motel Gambozinhos Praia do Martinhal T 282 620 160, F 282 620 169. Also out of town, but right on the beach, this is a very attractive, simple motel with a line of low rooms and apartments set in peaceful gardens just back from the sands of Praia do Martinhal. ❹

Pousada do Infante T 282 624 222, W www.pousadas.pt. Best choice in town – if your budget will stretch to it – an attractive clifftop mansion with Moorish elements and splendid views of the fortress from its bar-terrace. ❼

Eating, drinking and nightlife

Sagres's main street, from Praça da República to the fishing harbour, is lined with restaurants and bars, catering for a range of tastes and budgets. For **breakfast**, either *Café Conchinha* or the next-door *Pastelaria Marreiros,* both on Praça da República, open at 8am. Sagres's main street, from Praça da República to the fishing harbour, is lined with restaurants and bars, catering for a range of tastes and budgets. Of the **bars**, two long-standing favourites, both packed with the youth contingent, are *A Rosa dos Ventos* (closed Mon), on the village square – lively, loud and drunken – and *The Last Chance Saloon* (closed Mon), around the corner, overlooking the Mareta beach. When it's falling down time, everyone moves on to *Polvo Dreams* (open until 2am), just off the square towards Belixe.

Atlântico Rua Comandante Matoso. Another reasonable if slightly pricey fish restaurant; a full meal will cost around €15–20.

Bossa Nova Rua da Mareta. Lively place just off the main drag noted for its pizzas, pasta, salads and imaginative vegetarian meals (closed Mon). Inexpensive.

Dromedário Rua Comandante Matoso. Nearer the square and opposite the kiosks on the main street, this is a lively bistro serving drinks and snacks all day. Moderate.

Estrela do Mar II Rua Comandante Matoso. Not a bad moderately priced fish restaurant, though dishes can be hit or miss.

A Grelha Rua Comandante Matoso. At the fishing harbour end of the road, this is a simple place with a modest menu where you can eat for around €8.

Pousada do Infante ☏ 282 624 222. If you can afford it, try and eat at the *pousada* for a total dining experience in elegant surroundings with superb

service. French–Portuguese food for around €30 a head, with coffee served on the terrace.

A Tasca Porto da Baleeira. Great grills and seafood complemented by harbour views; just down the steps to the port (Oct–April closed Sat). Moderate.

Vila Velha Rua Patrão António Faustino. Excellent upmarket restaurant near the *pousada* which serves a pleasant mix of Portuguese and Dutch dishes in a rustic-style interior (closed Mon Oct–April). Expensive.

Cabo de São Vicente

The exposed **Cabo de São Vicente** – Cape St Vincent – across the bay from Sagres, was sacred to the Romans, who called it Promontorium Sacrum and believed the sun sank hissing into the water beyond here every night. It became a Christian shrine when the relics of the martyred St Vincent arrived in the eighth century (see box below). Today the sea off this wild set of cliffs shelters the highest concentration of marine life in Portugal, including rare birds such as Bonelli's eagles, white storks, white herons, kites and rock doves.

It was almost certainly at the cape that Henry established his School of Navigation, founded a small town, and built his Vila do Infante. Today only a **lighthouse**, flanked by the ruins of a sixteenth-century Capuchin convent, are to be seen. The lighthouse is the most powerful in Europe; if he's in the mood, the lighthouse keeper gives impromptu tours of the tower. The other buildings on the cape, already vandalized by the piratical Sir Francis Drake in 1587, came crashing to the ground in the Great Earthquake of 1755, the monks staying on alone until the Liberal suppression of the monasteries in 1834.

The cape is nonetheless a dramatic and exhilarating 6km walk from Sagres, a path skirting the tremendous cliffs for much of the way. This is a wonderful spot for **birdlife** and at the right time of year you should be able to spot blue rock thrushes and peregrines nesting on the cliffs. Walking on the road is easier – it'll take less than an hour and a half, with glorious views all the way. Try to be at the cape for sunset, which is invariably gorgeous, though frequently also very windy.

St Vincent

St Vincent was born in Zaragoza in Spain in the fourth century AD and became the town's deacon during the early days of Christianity in Iberia. He was later imprisoned in Valencia and sentenced to death in 304 during the days of Christian persecution. It is said that while he was being burned alive, the room filled with flowers, light and the voices of angels, and he was proclaimed a martyr and then a saint. In the eighth century, his remains – which had somehow survived the fire – were miraculously washed up in an unmanned boat piloted by ravens at what is now Cabo de São Vicente. Perhaps more credible is the theory that Christians took whatever was left of Vincent with them to flee invading Moors, arriving at the safe outpost of the Cape where they later built a chapel to house his remains. In 1173, Afonso Henriques, Portugal's first Christian monarch, had the saint's remains moved to Lisbon. Legend has it that the faithful ravens followed to the capital, and guarded over him in the cloisters of Lisbon's Sé (cathedral), until the last one died in 1978. Today São Vicente remains Lisbon's patron saint.

Vila do Bispo and the coast to Odeceixe

Unlike the southern stretches of the Algarve, the **west coast**, stretching north from Sagres to Odeceixe, is still relatively undeveloped. There are several reasons: the coast is exposed to strong Atlantic winds; the sea can be several degrees cooler than on the south coast; and swimming is dangerous. In addition, the designation in 1995 of the stretch of coast from Burgau to Cabo de São Vicente and up through the Alentejo as a nature reserve – the Parque Natural Sudoeste Alentejano e Costa Vincentina – should go even further to protect this dramatic and rugged scenery from potentially harmful development. The nearest bases to the beaches are at the uneventful villages of **Vila do Bispo** and **Carrapateira** or the livelier **Aljezur** and **Odeceixe**, all of which have an inexpensive network of private rooms and accommodation options. Like Sagres, these resorts attract a predominantly young crowd of surfers and camper-vanners.

Vila do Bispo

VILA DO BISPO, at the junction of the west and south coast roads, is a fairly scrappy traditional little town whose kernel of old white houses centres on a lovely seventeenth-century parish **church** (summer Mon–Sat 10am–1pm & 2–6pm), every interior surface of which has been painted, tiled or gilded. The town has no other sights, but it makes a pleasant spot for a coffee or a meal in one of the bars and restaurants by the town garden, or to look out over the hills from the terrace outside the church.

If you have your own transport, the town could make a reasonable accommodation base, ideally suited for day trips to the surrounding beaches. The nearest stretch of sand, **Praia do Castelejo**, is reached via the bottom of town – from the main square, take the road downhill past the post office and bear right – along a narrow road leading 5km west. There is no public transport, but it is worth the effort: the beach is a huge swathe of sand lashed by heavy waves below dark grey cliffs, with a seasonal café to add a touch of civilisation.

Buses from Sagres or Lagos drop you right at the bottom of the village, five minutes' walk from the church. There are **rooms** advertised here and there, or try the *Pensão Mira Sagres*, Rua do Hospital 3 (☎282 639 160; ❷) – opposite the church – which has its own basic bar-restaurant downstairs. Not that Vila do Bispo lacks places to **eat**: down Rua 1º de Maio from the church, *Restaurante Correia* (closed Sat) has a decent menu and a friendly, local feel, while *Restaurante Central,* on Rua Comandante Matoso 20, just by the main square, is less characterful but offers a more upmarket fish and seafood menu. And there's a small supermarket, bakery and even a couple of **bars** that see some late-night action; the *Convivio Bistro* on the central square, Praça da República, serves a wicked range of cocktails until 2am.

Carrapateira and its beaches

Fifteen kilometres to the north of Vila do Bispo (connected by occasional weekday bus from Vila do Bispo) is the village of **CARRAPATEIRA**, which is better positioned for the beach. It's possible to get **accommodation** in a private room if you ask around the main square or at the *Bar Barroca*, or try for space at the best budget place, *Pensão das Dunas*, Rua da Padaria 9 (☎ & ℱ282 973 118; ❶), a very pretty building on the beach-side of the village which has a number of simple rooms overlooking a flower-filled courtyard; there is also one apartment (❷). *Residencial Casa Fajara* (☎282 973 184/967 095 937, ℱ282 973 186; ❺), a couple of kilometres north of Carrapateira, is the most upmarket choice: a spruce modern villa with neat gardens and its own pool beautifully positioned overlooking a wide, green valley. Smart rooms have their own terraces; there is a communal kitchen and breakfast can be supplied on request.

Carrapateira's local beach, a kilometre's walk from the *Casa Fajara*, is the **Praia da Bordeira**, a spectacular strand with dunes, a tiny river and crashing surf. The sandbanks provide shelter from the wind for a sizeable community of unauthorised community, who seem to be tolerated by the local police. There is a restaurant just back from the beach, *O Sitio do Rio* (closed Tues and Nov; ☎282 997 119) which uses largely organic produce.

Four kilometres south of Praia da Bordeira, along the coast road, lies **Praia do Amado**, which is also signed off the main road just south of Carrapateira. This fantastic, broad sandy bay backed by low hills with a couple of seasonal cafés is particularly popular with surfers. There's also a **surf school** here (☎ & ℱ282 624 560) which offers equipment hire and surf courses from €60.

Aljezur and around

Fairly regular buses run from Lagos and Portimão to the village of **Aljezur**, 16km north of Carrapeteira, which is both the prettiest and liveliest town along the west coast of the Algarve. The main coast road passes through a prosaic, modern lower town where you find banks, the post office and a range of cafés and restaurants. The more interesting **historic centre** spreads uphill beyond the bridge over the Aljezur river, a network of narrow cobbled streets reaching up through whitewashed houses to the remains of a tenth-century Moorish **castle**. It's a lovely walk with sweeping views over the valley, via a trio of dull museums; the only one worth a visit is the **Casa Museu Pintor José Cercas** (Tues–Sat 10am–1pm & 2–5.30pm), which displays the works and collections of local artist José Cercas, who lived in the house until his death in 1992. His well-observed landscapes and religious scenes are complemented by an attractive house with a pretty garden.

At the foot of the old town, the **turismo** (Mon & Fri–Sun 9.30am–1pm & 2–5.30pm, Tues–Thurs 9.30am–7pm; ☎282 998 229) in Largo do Mercado, by the river, does its best to help with private **rooms**. There are also a couple of **pensões** scattered around the vicinity: the *Hospedaria S. Sebastião* is the most central, on Rua 25 de Abril, (☎933 264 943; ❷), at the eastern end of town on the busy through-road. It offers decent-sized rooms with showers, the front ones with balconies overlooking the pretty valley opposite. One kilometre out of Aljezur in the neighbouring village of Igreja Nova – just off the Monchique road – the modern *Residencial Dom Sancho*, on Largo Igreja Nova 1 (☎282 998 119, ℱ282 998 763; ❹), overlooks a pedestrianized street. Rooms are large and comfortable and come with bath and TV; price includes breakfast. The bus from Lagos loops through Igreja Nova on its way out of Aljezur.

There are several inexpensive **cafés** and **restaurants** in Aljezur, most of them along the main through-road, Rua 25 de Abril. Here, *Primavera* (closed Sun) is a bar-café and restaurant offering all-day food and drinks on a little outdoor terrace including superb *frango no churrasco* (chargrilled chicken). At the tourist-office end of the main street, *Restaurante Ruth* (closed Sat) is a highly regarded restaurant specializing in moderately priced regional dishes such as *arroz de tamboril com camarão*.

From May to September, two buses daily run to a couple of superb beaches within a few kilometres of Aljezur. The largest of these is **Arrifana**, 10km to the southeast, a fine, sandy sweep set below high, crumbling black cliffs. The beach is popular with surfers and surf competitions are sometimes held here.

The clifftop boasts the remains of a ruined fort, just up from a half a dozen cafés and holiday villas. If you want to stay, there are private **rooms** behind the *Brisamar Café* at the top of the cliff, at Rua João Dias Mendes 43a (☎282 987 254, ☎282 767 645; ❷), with TVs and small bathrooms.

Around 4km north lies **MONTE CLÉRIGO**, 8km northwest from Aljezur, a pretty little holiday village of pink- and white-faced beach houses. A cluster of café-restaurants face a superb, family-oriented beach tucked into the foot of a river valley. There is also a decent **campsite**, *Camping Vale da Telha* at Vale da Telha (☎282 998 444; €2/person, from €2/tent), less than 1km from Monte Clérigo beach and around 4km from Arrifana.

Odeceixe

ODECEIXE, hunched on a hill and cramped by the river, is the last village before the Alentejo. Situated near the head of a delightful curving estuary, it is a fairly quiet little place. From June to September, it attracts just about every hippy and surf dude in the Algarve, drawn by the proximity of the superb beach along with some of the cheapest rooms in the region. If you hit town outside high season, though, it is very pleasant. Most of the action is centred round the main **square**, Largo 1º de Maio, from where the beach is signed to the west. Round here you'll find the post office, banks, supermarkets, café-restaurants and plenty of places letting out **rooms**. First point of call, however, should be *Residêncio do Parque* on Rua da Estrada Nacional 11 (☎282 947 117; ❶), a huge place that is probably the cheapest option in the Algarve. The rooms are a mixed bag – the best on the top floor with small balconies overlooking the valley; all are ensuite with TVs.

Reached down a verdant river valley, the beach – **Praia de Odeceixe** – lies some 4km to the west. It's a lovely walk following the river to a broad, sandy bay framed by low cliffs. It is one of the most sheltered beaches on this stretch of coast, offering superb surfing and relatively safe swimming, especially when the tide is down. A pretty cluster of traditional houses and cafés lie banked up to the south of the bay. *Restaurante Café Dorita* serves decent grills and snacks on a terrace above the beach, and also lets out simple rooms (☎282 947 581; ❶), the best with sweeping views over the waves. Shared facilities only, but book ahead in high season.

Travel details

Trains

CP, the Portuguese railway company, operates the Algarve rail line, which runs from Lagos to Vila Real de Santo António, but you may have to change at Tunes, Faro or Tavira, depending on your destination. There are five to six services with convenient connections to make the whole run from one end to the other, which takes around three hours. Train timetables for the Algarve line (free) are available from information desks at main stations. Always turn up at the station with time to spare as long queues often form at the ticket desk. The IC (Intercidades) trains are considerably faster than the stopping IR (Interregional) and

snail-like R (Regional) trains. Details of train times and routes are online at ⓦ www.cp.pt.

Faro to: Albufeira (14 daily; 15–45min); Lagos (7 daily; 1hr 40min); Monte Gordo (3–4 daily; 1hr–1hr 15min); Olhão (16 daily; 10min); Portimão (7 daily; 1hr 15min–1hr 35min); Silves (7 daily; 1hr–1hr 15min); Tavira (12–17 daily; 35–45min); Vila Real de Santo António (10–13 daily; 1hr–1hr 20min).

Lagos to: Albufeira (8 daily; 1hr 10min); Faro (7 daily; 1hr 40min); Loulé (8 daily; 1hr 25min); Portimão (10–13 daily; 15–20min); Silves (13 daily; 30–50min); Tunes (13 daily; 50min–1hr).

Tunes to: Lisbon (4 daily; 4hr 15min, add on 2hr or so for connections from Vila Real, 1hr from Faro or Lagos); Beja (3 daily; 3hr).

Buses

Up-to-date information on routes and times is available on the internet at ⊛www.eva-transportes.pt and ⊛rede-expressos.pt/index_uk.htm both of which are available in English. Currently there is no website for Frota Azul. See the text for details of other local routes.

Albufeira to: Areias de São João (8–11 daily; 10min); Armacão de Pêra (Mon–Sat 12 daily, Sun 5 daily; 15–20min); Faro (8 daily; 40min–1hr 15min); Montechoro (8–11 daily; 10min); Olhos d'Água (hourly; 10min); Portimão (Mon–Fri 11 daily, Sat & Sun 4 daily; 45min); Quarteira (Mon–Fri 15 daily, Sat & Sun 9 daily; 40min); São Bartolomeu de Messines (3–8 daily; 45min); Silves (3–7 daily; 45min); Vila Real (1 daily; 3hr).

Faro to: Albufeira (8 daily; 40min–1hr 15min); Estói (Mon–Fri 14 daily, Sat & Sun 9 daily; 25min); Loulé (Mon–Fri hourly till 7.30pm, Sat 8 daily, Sun 6 daily; 40min); Monte Gordo (Mon–Fri 9 daily, Sat & Sun 4 daily; 1hr 35min); Olhão (Mon–Fri every 15–30min, Sat & Sun roughly hourly; 20min); Quarteira (Mon–Fri hourly, Sat & Sun 3 daily; 25min); São Brás de Alportel (Mon–Fri 10 daily, Sat 9 daily, Sun 3 daily; 35min); Tavira (7–11 daily; 1hr); Vilamoura (Mon–Fri hourly, Sat & Sun 9 daily; 30–40min); Vila Real (6–9 daily; 1hr 40min).

Lagos to: Albufeira (12 daily; 1hr 15min); Aljezur (Mon–Fri 4–5 daily, Sat 1 daily, Sun 1 daily in summer; 50min); Alvor (6 daily, Sat & Sun 4 daily; 15min); Armacão de Pêra (12 daily; 45min–1hr); Burgau (8–10 daily, 4 daily on Sun in winter; 25min); Faro (8 daily; 1hr 45 min); Luz (8–10 daily, 4 daily on Sun in winter; 15min); Odeceixe (Mon–Fri 3–4 daily, Sat 1 daily; 1hr 20min); Portimão (hourly; 15min–35min); Sagres (7–11 daily; 1hr); Salema (5–8 daily; 40min); Vila do Bispo (7–11 daily; 45min).

Portimão to: Albufeira (Mon–Fri 11 daily, Sat & Sun 4 daily; 45min); Alvor (Mon–Fri hourly; Sat & Sun roughly every 2hr; 20min); Faro (8 daily; 1hr 25min–1hr 45min); Ferragudo (hourly; 10min); Lagos (hourly; 15–35min); Monchique (Mon–Fri 9 daily; Sat & Sun 5 daily; 30–45min); Praia da Rocha (every 15–20min; 5min); São Bartolomeu de Messines (4–8 daily; 1hr 15min); Silves (Mon–Fri 9 daily, Sat & Sun 7 daily; 35–45min).

Sagres to: Lagos (Mon–Fri 7–11 daily; 1hr); Salema (Mon–Fri 7–9 daily, Sat & Sun 3–4 daily; 35min); Vila do Bispo (hourly; 15min).

Vila Real de Santo António to: Albufeira (1 daily; 3hr); Alcoutim (Mon–Fri 2–3 daily, Sat 1 daily; 1hr 15min); Ayamonte, Spain (2 daily; 1hr 15min); Faro (6–9 daily; 1hr 40min); Huelva, Spain (1 daily; 1hr); Manta Rota (Mon–Fri 4–5 daily, Sat 2 daily; 30min); Monte Gordo (Mon–Fri at least half-hourly, Sat & Sun in winter 10–13 daily; 7min); Tavira (9–10 daily; 40min).

Long-distance buses

Comfortable express buses operate on longer routes, for which you'll usually have to reserve tickets in advance. There's a long-distance Linha Litoral express service which connects Lagos to Vila Real/Ayamonte once daily on weekdays, the whole route taking four hours; on the Lagos–Albufeira leg of the route, there are more like seven weekday departures and four at weekends. Several companies also operate regular daily express buses between Lisbon and the Algarve, with approximate journey times as follows: Albufeira (3hr 35min); Faro (4hr 20min); Lagos (4hr 45min); Olhão (4hr 30min); Tavira (4hr 45min); Vila Real (4hr 30min). Ask at any travel agency or bus terminal for details, though note that the Rede Expressos buses are around €4 cheaper than the EVA bus.

International buses

EVA runs a number of international buses from the Algarve, the most useful being the twice daily service from Albufueira to Huelva. Buses leave Albufueira at 7.20am and 2.30pm, continuing through Faro (8.10am/4.15pm) to Vila Real de Santo António (9.10am/5.15pm) and the Spanish border at Ayamonte. The bus stops at Huelva (11.25pm/7.30pm) for connections to Seville (1.05pm/9.40pm) where you can pick up connections to Malaga, Cádiz, Algeciras and Grenada. The full run costs around €15 single.

contexts

contexts

History

The early history of Portugal – as part of the Iberian Peninsula – has obvious parallels with that of Spain. Indeed, any geographical division is somewhat arbitrary, independent development only really occurring following Afonso Henriques' creation of a Portuguese kingdom in the twelfth century.

Early civilization

Remnants of pottery and cave burials point to tribal societies occupying the Tagus valley, as well as parts of the Alentejo and Estremadura, as early as 8000 to 7000 BC, and the recently discovered Paleolithic paintings near Vila Nova de Foz Côa in Beira Alta are thought to date back around 20,000 years (see p.337). More, however, is known of **Neolithic** Portugal and its Castro culture based on hilltop forts, a culture that was to be developed and refined after the arrival of Celtic peoples in around 700 to 600 BC. These forts, the first permanent settlements, were concentrated in northern Portugal, and particularly in the Minho, where excavations have revealed dozens of **citânias**, or fortified villages. The most impressive is at Briteiros (p.361), near Braga, with its paved streets, drainage systems and circuits of defensive walls; like many of the *citânias* it survived, remarkably unchanged, well into the Roman era. Settlements in neighbouring Trás-os-Montes, in contrast, reflect less of a defensive spirit – but all that remains of this more pastoral **Verracos** culture are the crude granite *porcas*, stone figures venerating wild sows as objects of a primitive fertility cult.

The potential for new trading outlets and the quest for metals, in particular tin for making bronze, attracted a succession of peoples from across the Mediterranean but most of their settlements lay on the eastern seaboard and so fell within "Spanish" history. The **Phoenicians**, however, established an outpost at Lisbon around 900 BC and there were probably contacts, too, with Mycenaean Greeks. In the mid-third century BC, they were followed by **Carthaginians**, who recruited Celtic tribesmen for military aid against the Roman empire. Once again, though, their influence was predominantly on the eastern seaboard and in the south; with defeat in the Second Punic War (218–202 BC) they were to be replaced by a more determined colonizing force.

Romans, Suevi and Visigoths

Entering the peninsula in 210 BC, the **Romans** swiftly subdued and colonized the Mediterranean coast and the south of Spain and Portugal. In the interior, however, they met with great resistance from the Celtiberian tribes and in 193 BC the **Lusitani** rose up in arms. Based in central Portugal, between the Tagus and Lima rivers, they were, in the words of the Roman historian Strabo, "the most powerful of the Iberian peoples, who resisted the armies of Rome for the longest period". For some fifty years, in fact, they held up the Roman advance, under the leadership of **Viriatus**, a legendary Portuguese hero and masterful exponent of the feigned retreat who, on several occasions, brought the Romans to accept his autonomous rule. He was betrayed after a successful campaign in 139 BC and within two years the Lusitani had capitulated as the legions of Decimus Junius Brutus swept through the north. Still, over a century later, their name was given to this most westerly of the Roman provinces, while in the northern Celtic villages Roman colonization can scarcely have been felt.

Integration into the Roman Empire occurred largely under Julius Caesar, who in 60 BC established a capital at Olisipo (Lisbon) and significant colonies at Ebora (Évora), Scallabis (Santarém) and Pax Julia (Beja). In 27 BC the Iberian provinces were further reorganized under Augustus, with all but the north of Portugal being governed – as Lusitania – from the great Roman city of Merida in Spanish Extremadura. The Minho formed part of a separate province, later added to northwest Spain to create Gallaecia, with an important regional centre at Bracara Augusta (Braga). In general, though, it was the south where Roman influence was deepest. Here they established huge agricultural estates (the infamous *Latifundia* which still survive in Alentejo) and changed the nature of the region's crops, as they introduced wheat, barley, olives and the vine to the area.

There are no great **Roman sites** in Portugal – at least nothing to compare with Spanish Merida, Tarragona or Italica – though both Évora (p.463) and Conímbriga (p.219) have individual monuments of interest. The mark of six centuries of Roman rule consists more in a network of roads and bridges, many of them still in use today. There is a more basic legacy, too, the Portuguese language being very heavily derived from Latin.

The **decline of the Roman Empire** in Portugal echoes its pattern elsewhere, though perhaps with greater indifference, the territory always being something of a provincial backwater. **Christianity** reached Portugal's southern coast towards the end of the first century AD and by the third century bishoprics were established at Braga, Évora, Faro and Lisbon. But the Roman state was already disintegrating and in 409 the first waves of barbarian invaders crossed the Pyrenees into Spain. Vandals, Alans, Suevi and Visigoths all passed through Portugal, though only the last two were of any real importance.

The **Suevi**, a semi-nomadic people from eastern Germany, eventually settled in the area between the Douro and Minho rivers, establishing courts at Braga and Portucale (Porto). They seem to have coexisted fairly peacefully with the Hispano-Roman nobility and were converted to Christianity by St Martin of Dume, a saint frequently found in the dedications of northern churches.

Around 585AD, however, the Suevian state disappeared, having been suppressed and incorporated into the **Visigothic** empire, a heavily Romanized yet independent force which for two centuries maintained a spurious unity and rule over most of the peninsula. The Visigothic kings, however, ruled from Toledo, supported by a small and elite aristocratic warrior-caste, so in Portugal their influence was neither great nor lasting. And by the end of the seventh century their divisions, exacerbated by an elective monarchy and their intolerance (including the first Iberian persecution of the Jews), resulted in one faction appealing for aid from Muslim North Africa. In 711 a first force of **Moors** crossed the straits into Spain and within a decade they had advanced and conquered all but the mountainous reaches of the Asturias in northern Spain.

The Moors and the Christian reconquest

In Portugal, Aveiro probably marked the northernmost point of the **Moorish advance**. The Moors met with little resistance but the dank, green hills of the Minho held little attraction for the colonizers and over the following century seem to have been severely depopulated. Most of the Moors were content to settle in the south: in the Tagus valley, in the rich wheat belts around Évora and Beja, and above all in the coastal region of **al–Gharb**. Here they established a capital at Shelb, modern Silves, and, by the middle of the ninth century, an independent kingdom, detached from the great Muslim emirate of al-Andalus which covered most of Spain.

The Moors in Portugal were a mix of ethnic races – for the most part consisting of Berbers from Morocco, but also considerable numbers of Syrians and, around Faro, a contingent of Egyptians, some of them probably Coptic Christians. In contrast to the Visigoths, the Moors were tolerant and productive, their rule a civilizing influence. Both Jews and Christians were allowed freedom of worship and their own civil laws, while under Muslim law small landholders continued to occupy and cultivate their own land. For most of these "**Moçárabes**"– Christians subject to Moorish rule – life must have improved. Roman irrigation techniques were perfected and the Moors introduced the rotation of crops and cultivation of cotton, rice, oranges and lemons. Their culture and scholarship led the world – though less from al-Gharb than from Córdoba and Seville – and they forged important trade links, many of which were to continue centuries after their fall. Perhaps still more important, **urban life** developed, with prosperous local craft industries: Lisbon, Évora, Beja and Santarém all emerged as sizeable towns.

The Christian **Reconquista** began – at least by tradition – at Covadonga in Spain in 718, when Pelayo, at the head of a small band of Visigoths, halted the advance of a Moorish expeditionary force. The battle's significance has doubtless been inflated but from the victory a tiny kingdom of the Asturias does seem to have been established. Initially only 65 by 50 kilometres in extent, it expanded over the next two centuries to take in León, Galicia and the "lands of Portucale", the latter an area roughly equivalent to the old Swabian state between the Douro and the Minho.

By the eleventh century **Portucale** had the status of a country, its governors appointed by the kings of León. In 1073 Alfonso VI came to the throne. It was to be a reign hard-pressed by a new wave of Muslim invaders – the fanatical Almoravids, who crossed over to Spain in 1086 after appeals from al-Andalus and established a new Muslim state at Seville. Like many kings of Portugal after him, Alfonso was forced to turn to European Crusaders, many of whom would stop in at the shrine of St James in Compostela. One of them, Raymond of Burgundy, married Alfonso's eldest daughter and became heir-apparent to the throne of León; his cousin Henry, married to another daughter, Teresa, was given jurisdiction over Portucale. With Henry's death Teresa became regent for her son, **Afonso Henriques**, and began to try to forge a union with Galicia. Afonso, however, had other ideas and having defeated his mother at the battle of São Mamede (1128), he established a capital at **Guimarães** and set about extending his domains to the south.

The reconquest of central Portugal was quickly achieved. Afonso's victory at

Ourique in 1139 was a decisive blow and by 1147 he had taken Santarém. In the same year Lisbon fell, after a siege in which passing Crusaders again played a vital role – though not sailing on to the Holy Land before murderously sacking the city. Many of them were English and some stayed on; Gilbert of Hastings became Archbishop. By now Afonso was dubbing himself the **first King of Portugal**, a title tacitly acknowledged by Alfonso VII (the new king of León) in 1137 and officially confirmed by the Treaty of Zamora in 1143. His kingdom spread more or less to the borders of modern Portugal, though in the south, Alentejo and the Algarve were still in Muslim hands.

For the next century and a half Afonso's successors struggled to dominate this last stronghold of the Moors. Sancho I (1185–1211) took their capital, Silves, in 1189, but his gains were not consolidated and almost everything south of the Tagus was recaptured the following year by al-Mansur, the last great campaigning vizier of al-Andalus. The overall pattern, though, was of steady expansion with occasional setbacks. Sancho II (1223–48) invaded the Alentejo and the eastern Algarve, while his successor **Afonso III** (1248–79) moved westwards, taking Faro and establishing the kingdom in pretty much its final shape.

The Burgundian kings

The reconquest of land from the Muslims also incorporated a process of **recolonization**. As it fell into the king's hands, new territory was granted to such of his subjects that he felt would be able to defend it. In this way much of the country came to be divided between the church, the Holy Orders – chief among them the Knights Templar – and a hundred or so powerful nobles (*ricos homens*). The entire kingdom had a population of under half a million, the majority of them concentrated in the north. Here, there was little displacement of the traditional feudal ties, but in the south the influx of Christian peasants blurred the distinction between serf and settler, dependent relationships coming instead to be based on the payment of rent.

Meanwhile a **political infrastructure** was being established. The land was divided into municipalities (*concelhos*), each with its own charter (*foral*). A formalized structure of consultation began, with the first **Cortes** (parliament) being held in Coimbra in 1211. At first consisting mainly of the clergy and nobility, it later came to include wealthy merchants and townsmen, a development speeded both by the need to raise taxes and by later kings' constant struggles against the growing power of the church. The capital, which Afonso Henriques had moved to Coimbra in 1139, was transferred to **Lisbon** in about 1260 by Afonso III.

The Burgundian dynasty lasted through nine kings for 257 years. In the steady process of establishing the new kingdom, one name stands out above all others, that of **Dom Dinis** (1279–1325). With the reconquest barely complete when he came to the throne, Dinis set about a far-sighted policy of stabilization and of strengthening the nation to ensure its future independence. During his reign, fifty fortresses were constructed along the frontier with Castile, while at the same time negotiations were going on, leading eventually to the Treaty of Alcañices (1297) by which Spain acknowledged Portugal's frontiers. At home Dinis established a major programme of forest planting and of agricultural reform; grain, olive oil, wine, salt, salt fish and dried fruit became staple exports to Flanders, Brittany, Catalonia and Britain. Importance, too, was attached to education and the arts: a **university**, later transferred to Coimbra, was founded at Lisbon in 1290. Dinis also helped entrench the power of the monarchy, forcing the church to accept a much larger degree of state control and, in 1319, reorganizing the Knights Templar – at the time being suppressed all over Europe – as the **Order of Christ**, still enormously powerful but now responsible directly to the king rather than to the pope.

Despite Dinis's precautions, fear of **Castilian domination** continued to play an important part in the reigns of his successors, largely owing to consistent intermarrying between the two royal families. On the death of the last of the Burgundian kings, Fernando I, power passed to his widow Leonor, who ruled as regent. Leonor, whose only daughter had married Juan I of Castile, promised the throne to the children of that marriage. In this she had the support of most of the nobility, but the merchant and peasant classes strongly opposed a Spanish ruler, supporting instead the claim of João, Grand Master of the House of Avis and a bastard heir of the Burgundian line. A popular revolt against Leonor led to two years of war with Castile, finally settled at the **Battle of Aljubarrota** (1385) in which João, backed up by a force of English archers, wiped out the much larger Castilian army.

The great abbey of **Batalha** (p.178) was built to commemorate the victory. **João I**, first king of the **House of Avis**, was crowned at Coimbra the same year, sealing relations with England through the 1386 Treaty of Windsor – an alliance which lasted into the twentieth century – and his marriage to Philippa of Lancaster, daughter of John of Gaunt, the following year.

Dom Manuel and the maritime empire

Occupying such a strategic position between the Atlantic and the Mediterranean, it was inevitable that Portuguese attention would at some stage turn to **maritime expansion**. When peace was finally made with Castile in 1411, João was able to turn his resources toward Morocco. The outpost at Ceuta fell in 1415, but successive attempts to capture Tangier were not realized until the reign of Afonso V, in 1471.

At first such overseas adventuring was undertaken partly in a crusading spirit, partly to keep potentially troublesome nobles busy. The proximity of North Africa made it a constant feature of foreign policy, giving a welcome boost to the economy of the Algarve. The first real advances in exploration, however, came about through the activities of **Prince Henry "the Navigator"**, third son of João and Philippa. As Grand Master of the Order of Christ, he turned that organization's vast resources towards marine development, founding a School of Navigation on the desolate promontory of Sagres (then regarded as the end of the world) and staffing it with Europe's leading cartographers, navigators and seamen. As well as improving the art of offshore navigation, they redesigned the caravel, making it a vessel well suited to long ocean-going journeys. **Madeira** and the **Azores** were discovered in 1419 and 1427 respectively, and by the time of Henry's death in 1460 the **Cape Verde Islands** and the **west coast of Africa** down to Sierra Leone had both been explored.

After a brief hiatus, overseas expansion received a fresh boost in the reigns of João II, Manuel I and João III. In 1487 **Bartolomeu Dias** finally made it around the southern tip of Africa, christening it "Cabo da Boa Esperança" in the hope of good things to come. Within ten years **Vasco da Gama** had sailed on past it to open up the **trade route to India**. This was the great breakthrough and the Portuguese monarchy, already doing well out of African gold, promptly became the richest in Europe, taking a fifth of the profits of all trade and controlling important monopolies on some spices. The small cargo of pepper brought back by Vasco on his first expedition was enough to pay for the trip three times over. Meanwhile Spain was opening up the New World and by the **Treaty of Tordesillas** in 1494 the two Iberian nations divided the world between them along an imaginary line 370 leagues west of the Cape Verde Islands. This not only gave Portugal the run of the Orient but also, when it was discovered in 1500, Brazil (though its exploitation would have to wait nearly 200 more years). By the mid-sixteenth century Portugal dominated **world trade**; strategic posts had been established at Goa (1510), Malacca (1511), Ormuz (1515) and Macau (1557), and the revenue from dealings with the East was backed up by a large-scale **slave trade** between West Africa and Europe and Brazil.

The reign of **Manuel I** (1495–1521) marked the apogee of Portuguese wealth and strength. It found its expression at home in the extraordinary exuberance of the **Manueline** style of architecture (see box on p.190). Notable examples can be seen in the Convento de Cristo at Tomar and the monastery and tower of Belém in Lisbon, while decorations and motifs are to be found on churches and civil buildings throughout the country.

Enormous wealth there may have been, but very little of it filtered down through the system, and in the country at large conditions barely improved. The practice of siphoning off a hefty slice of the income into the royal coffers effectively prevented the development of an entrepreneurial class and, as everywhere else in Europe, financial matters were left very much in the hands of the Jews, who were not allowed to take up most other professions.

Portugal had traditionally been considerably more tolerant than other European nations in its treatment of its **Jewish citizens** (and towards the Moorish minority who had been absorbed after the reconquest). However, popular resentment of their riches, and pressure from Spain, forced Manuel – who had initially welcomed refugees from the Spanish persecution – to order their **expulsion** in 1496. Although many chose the pragmatic course of remaining as "New Christian" converts, others fled to the Netherlands. This exodus, continued as a result of the activities of the **Inquisition** (from 1531 on), created a vacuum which left Portugal with an extensive empire based upon commerce, but deprived of much of its financial expertise. By the 1570s the economy was beginning to collapse: incoming wealth was insufficient to cover the growing costs of maintaining an empire against increasing competition, a situation exacerbated by foreign debts, falling prices and a decline in the productivity of domestic agriculture.

Spanish domination

In the end it was a combination of reckless imperialism and impecunity which brought to an end the dynasty of the House of Avis and with it, at least temporarily, Portuguese independence. **Dom Sebastião** (1557–78), obsessed with dreams of a new crusade against Morocco, set out at the head of a huge army to satisfy his fanatical fantasies. They were crushed at the battle of **Alcácer-Quibir** (1578), where the Portuguese dead numbered over eight thousand, including Sebastião and most of Portugal's nobility. The aged **Cardinal Henrique** took the throne as the closest legitimate relative and devoted his brief reign to attempting to raise the crippling ransoms for those captured on the battlefield.

The Cardinal's death without heirs in 1580 provided Spain with the pretext to renew its claim to Portugal. **Philip II** of Spain, Sebastião's uncle, defeated his rivals at the battle of Alcântara and in 1581 was crowned Felipe I of Portugal, inaugurating a period of Hapsburg rule which lasted for another sixty years. In the short term, although unpopular, the union had advantages for Portugal. Spanish wheat helped alleviate the domestic shortage and Spanish seapower helped protect the far-flung empire. Philip, moreover, studiously protected Portuguese autonomy, maintaining an entirely separate bureaucracy and spending long periods in Portugal in an attempt to win popular support. Not that he ever did – throughout his reign pretenders appeared claiming to be Sebastião miraculously saved from the Moroccan desert, tapping a strong vein of resentment among the people. And, in the long run, Spanish control proved disastrous. Association with Spain's foreign policy (part of the Armada was prepared in Lisbon) meant the enmity of the Dutch and the British, Portugal's traditional allies, losing the country an important part of its trade which was never to be regained.

Philip's successors made no attempt at all to protect Portuguese sensibilities – cynical and uninterested, they attempted to rule from Madrid while raising heavy taxes to pay for Spain's wars. The final straw was the attempt by Philip IV (Felipe III of Portugal) to conscript Portuguese troops to quell a rising in Catalonia. On December 1, 1640, a small group of conspirators stormed the palace in Lisbon and deposed the Duchess of Mantua, Governor of Portugal. By popular acclaim and despite personal reluctance, the Duke of Bragança, senior member of a family which had long been the most powerful in the country, took the throne as **João IV**.

The House of Bragança

At first the newly independent nation looked pretty shaky, deprived of most of its trade routes and with the apparently imminent threat of invasion from Spain hanging over it. As it turned out, however, the Spanish were so preoccupied with wars elsewhere that they had little choice but to accept the situation, though they did not do so formally until 1668 under the **Treaty of Lisbon**. João IV used the opportunity to rebuild old alliances and although the Portuguese were often forced into unfavourable terms, they were at least trading again. Relations with Britain had been strained during the establishment of that country's Commonwealth, especially by Oliver Cromwell's particular brand of Protestant commercialism, but were revived by the marriage of Charles II to Catherine of Bragança in 1661.

At home Portugal was developing an increasingly centralized administration. The **discovery of gold and diamonds in Brazil** during the reign of Pedro II (1683–1706) made the crown financially independent and did away with the need for the Cortes (or any form of popular representation) for most of the next century. It was **João V**, coming to the throne in 1706, who most benefited from the new riches, which he squandered in an orgy of lavish Baroque building. His massive convent at **Mafra** (see p.140), built totally without regard to expense, employed at times as many as fifty thousand workmen, virtually bankrupting the state. Meanwhile nothing was being done to revive the economy, and what little remained from João's grandiose schemes went mainly to pay for imports. The infamous **Methuen Treaty**, signed in 1703 to stimulate trade with Britain, only made matters worse: although it opened up new markets for Portuguese wine, it helped destroy the native textile industry by letting in British cloth at preferential rates.

The accession of João's apathetic son, **José I** (1750–77), allowed the total concentration of power in the hands of the king's chief minister, the **Marquês de Pombal**, who became the classic enlightened despot of eighteenth-century history. It was the **Great Earthquake of 1755** that sealed his dominance over the age; while everyone else was panicking, Pombal's policy was simple – "bury the dead and feed the living".

Pombal saw his subsequent mission as to modernize all aspects of Portuguese life, by establishing an efficient and secular bureaucracy, renewing the system of taxation, setting up export companies, protecting trade and abolishing slavery within Portugal. It was a strategy that made him many enemies among the old aristocracy and above all within the Church, whose overbearing influence he fought at every turn. Opposition, though, was dealt with ruthlessly and an assassination attempt on the king in 1758 (which some say was staged by Pombal) gave him the chance he needed to destroy his enemies. Denouncing their supposed involvement, Pombal executed the country's leading aristocrats and abolished the Jesuit order, which had long dominated education and religious life in Portugal and Brazil.

Although Pombal himself was taken to trial (and found guilty but pardoned on the grounds of old age) with the accession of Maria I (1777–1816), the majority of his labours survived him, most notably the reform of education along scientific lines and his completely rebuilt capital, Lisbon. Further development, however, was soon thwarted by a new invasion.

French occupation and the Miguelite years

With the appearance of **Napoleon** on the international scene, Portugal once more became embroiled in the affairs of Europe. The French threatened to invade unless the Portuguese supported their naval blockade of Britain, a demand that no one expected them to obey since British ports were the destination for most of Portugal's exports. Only the protection of the British fleet, especially after the victory at Trafalgar in 1805, kept the country's trade routes open. General Junot duly marched into Lisbon in November 1807.

On British advice the royal family had already gone into exile in Brazil, where they were to stay until 1821, and the war was left largely in the hands of British generals **Beresford** and **Wellington**. Having twice been driven out and twice reinvaded, the French were finally forced back into Spain in 1811 following the Battle of Buçaco (1810) and a long period of near starvation before the lines of Torres Vedras.

Britain's prize for this was the right to trade freely with **Brazil**, which, together with the declaration of that country as a kingdom in its own right, fatally weakened the dependent relationship that had profited the Portuguese treasury for so long. Past roles were reversed, with Portugal becoming effectively a colony of Brazil (where the royal family remained) and a protectorate of Britain, with General Beresford as administrator. The only active national institution was the army, many of whose officers had absorbed the constitutional ideals of revolutionary France.

In August 1820, with Beresford temporarily out of the country and King João VI still in Brazil, a group of officers called an unofficial Cortes and proceeded to draw up a new **constitution**. Inspired by the recent liberal advances in Spain, it called for an assembly – to be elected every two years by universal male suffrage – and the abolition of clerical privilege and the traditional rights of the nobility. The king, forced to choose between Portugal and Brazil, where his position looked even more precarious, came back in 1821 and accepted its terms. His queen, Carlota, and younger son **Miguel**, however, refused to take the oath of allegiance and became the dynamic behind a reactionary movement which drew considerable support in rural areas. With João VI's death in 1826, a delegation was sent to Brazil to pronounce Crown Prince Pedro the new king. Unfortunately Pedro was already Emperor of Brazil, having declared its independence some years earlier. He resolved to pass the crown to his infant daughter, with Miguel as regent provided that he swore to accept a new charter, drawn up by Pedro and somewhat less liberal than the earlier constitution. Miguel agreed, but once in power promptly tore up any agreement, abolished the charter and returned to the old, absolutist ways. This was a surprisingly popular move in Portugal, certainly in the countryside, but not with the governments of Britain, Spain, or France who backed the liberal rebels and finally put Pedro IV (who had meanwhile been deposed in Brazil) on the throne after Miguel's defeat at Évora-Monte in 1834.

The death of the monarchy

Pedro didn't survive long. The rest of the century – under the rule of his daughter Maria II (1834–53) and his grandsons Pedro V (1853–61) and Luís (1861–89) – saw almost constant struggle between those who supported the charter and those who favoured a return to the more liberal constitution of 1822. In 1846 the position deteriorated virtually to a state of **civil war** between Maria, who was fanatical in her support of her father's charter, and the radical constitutionalists. Only a further intervention by foreign powers maintained peace, imposed at the Convention of Gramido (1847).

In the second half of the century, with relative stability and the two warring factions to some extent institutionalized into a revolving two-party system, the economy began at last to recover, with the first signs of widespread industrialization and a major public works programme under the minister Fontes Pereira de Melo. The monarchy, however, was almost bankrupt and its public humiliation over possessions in Africa – Britain and Germany simply ignored the Portuguese claim to the land between Angola and Mozambique – helped strengthen growing republican feelings.

Republicanism took root particularly easily in the army and among the urban poor, fuelled by falling standards of living and growing anger at government ineptitude. **Dom Carlos** (1898–1908) attempted to rule dictatorially after 1906, alienating most sectors of the country in the process, and was assassinated, along with his eldest son, following a failed Republican coup in 1908. Finally, on October 5, 1910, the **monarchy was overthrown** once and for all by a joint revolt of the army and navy. Dom Manuel went into exile and died, in Britain, in 1932.

The "Democratic" Republic

After a provisional government of Republican Unity, **elections** took place in 1911, showing a marked swing towards Afonso Costa's **Democratic Party**, which remained the most dominant political force in the country until 1926. However, the divisions among the Republicans, the cyclical attempts at violent overthrow of the new regime by the monarchists, and the weakening of the country's economic, social and political structures kept the Republic in permanent turmoil. Political life was in chaos and the hopes, perhaps unrealistically high, of the Republic's supporters never began to be realized. There were 45 changes of government in sixteen years and several military uprisings.

The forces that had brought the Republic were supported largely by the urban and rural poor, yet new electoral laws based on a literacy test led to a smaller electorate than under the monarchy, disenfranchising most of the Republic's strongest supporters. Successive governments failed to fulfil the least aspirations. Anticlericalism had been a major plank of Costa's platform, arousing massive hostility in the countryside. Legalizing the right to strike merely gave workers a chance to voice their discontent in a massive wave of work stoppages, but the new regime proved to be less than responsive to workers' rights and the repression of union activities was a constant theme. Further fuel was given to the reaction by Portugal's economically disastrous decision to enter **World War I** on the side of the Allies in 1916 and by the vicissitudes of the postwar recession. By 1926 not even the trade unions were prepared to stand by the Republic, preferring to maintain "proletarian neutrality" in the face of what at first seemed no more significant a military intervention than any other.

Salazar and the "New State"

While the military may have known what they wanted to overthrow in 1926, they were at first divided as to whether to replace it with a new Republican government or a restored monarchy. From the infighting, a Catholic monarchist, **General Carmona**, eventually emerged as president (which he remained until his death in 1951) with the Republican constitution suspended.

In 1928 one **Dr. António de Oliveira Salazar** joined the Cabinet as Finance Minister. A professor of economics at Coimbra University, he took the post only on condition that he would control the spending and revenue of all government departments. His strict monetarist line (helped by a change in the accounting system) immediately balanced the budget for the first time since 1913 and in the short term the economic situation was visibly improved. From then on he effectively controlled the country, becoming prime minister in 1932 and not relinquishing that role until 1968.

His regime was very much in keeping with the political tenor of the 1930s and while it had few of the ideological pretensions of a **fascist** state, it had many of the trappings. Members of the National Assembly were chosen from the one permitted political association, the National Union (UN); "workers' organizations" were set up, but run by their employers; education was strictly controlled by the state to promote Catholic values; and censorship was strictly enforced. Opposition was kept in check by the PIDE – a secret police force set up with Gestapo assistance – which used systematic torture and long-term detention in camps on the Azores and Cabo Verde Islands to defuse most resistance. The army, too, was heavily infiltrated by PIDE and none of the several coups mounted against Salazar came close to success. Despite remaining formally neutral throughout the **Spanish Civil War**, Salazar had openly assisted the plotters in their preparations and later sent unofficial army units to fight with Franco. Republican refugees were deported to face certain execution at Nationalist hands.

At home Salazar succeeded in producing the infrastructure of a relatively modern economy but the results of growth were felt by only a few and agriculture, in particular, was allowed to stagnate. Internal unrest, while widespread, was surprisingly muted and apparently easily controlled; the New State's downfall, when it came, was precipitated far more by external factors. Salazar was an ardent imperialist who found himself faced with growing **colonial wars**, which proved costly and brought international disapprobation. India seized Goa and the other Portuguese possessions in 1961 and at about the same time the first serious disturbances were occurring in Angola, Mozambique and, later, in Guinea-Bissau. The regime was prepared to make only the slightest concessions, attempting to defuse the freedom movements by speeding economic development.

The government's reign came to an end in 1968 when Salazar's deck chair collapsed, and he suffered brain damage. Incapacitated, he lived for another two years, deposed as premier – though such was the fear of the man, no one ever dared tell him. His successor, **Marcelo Caetano**, attempted to prolong the regime by offering limited democratization at home. However, tensions beneath the surface were fast becoming more overt and attempts to liberalize foreign policy failed to check the growth of guerrilla activity in the remaining colonies, or of **discontent in the army**.

It was in the African-stationed army especially that opposition crystallized. There the young conscript officers came more and more to sympathize with the freedom movements they were intended to suppress and to resent the cost – in economic terms and in lives – of the hopeless struggle. From their number grew the revolutionary **Movimento das Forças Armadas** (MFA).

Revolution

By 1974 the situation in Africa was deteriorating rapidly and at home Caetano's liberalization had come to a dead end; morale, among the army and the people, was lower than ever. The **MFA**, formed originally as an officers' organization to press for better conditions, and which had become increasingly politicized, was already laying its plans for a takeover. Dismissal of two popular generals – Spínola and Costa Gomes – for refusing publicly to support Caetano, led to a first chaotic and abortive attempt on March 16. Finally, on

April 25, 1974, the plans laid by **Major Otelo Saraiva de Carvalho** for the MFA were complete and their virtually bloodless coup – known as the **Revolution of the Carnations** – went without a hitch, no serious attempt being made to defend the government.

The next two years were perhaps the most extraordinary in Portugal's history, a period of continual **revolution**, massive politicization and virtual anarchy, during which decisions of enormous importance were nevertheless made – above all the granting of independence to all of the overseas territories. At first there was little clear idea of any programme beyond the fact that the army wanted out of Africa. Though the MFA leadership was clearly to the left and at first associated with the PCP (Portuguese Communist Party), the bulk of the officers were less political and **General Spínola**, whom they had been forced to accept as a figurehead, was only marginally to the left of Caetano and strongly opposed total independence for the colonies. Spínola's dream was clearly to share the conservative nationalist policies that General de Gaulle had imposed in France, while the army was above all determined not to replace one dictator with another.

In the event their hands were forced by the massive popular response and especially by huge demonstrations on May Day. It was clear that whatever the leadership might decide, the people, especially in the cities, demanded a rapid move to the left. From the start every party was striving to project itself as the true defender of the "ideals of April 25". Provisional governments came and went but real power rested, where it had begun, with the MFA, now dominated by Saraiva de Carvalho and Vasco Gonçalves. While politicians argued around them, the army claimed to speak directly to the people, leading the country steadily left. It was a period of extraordinary contradictions, with the PCP, hoping to consolidate their position as the true revolutionary party, opposing liberalization and condemning strikes as counter-revolutionary, while ultra-conservative peasants were happily seizing their land from its owners.

Sudden **independence** and the withdrawal of Portuguese forces from the former colonies – while generally greeted in Portugal with relief – did not always work so well for the countries involved. Guinea-Bissau and Mozambique, the first to go, experienced relatively peaceful transitions, but **Angola** came to be a serious point of division between Spínola and the MFA. When independence finally came, after Spínola's resignation, the country was already in the midst of a full-scale civil war. The situation was even worse in **East Timor**, where more than ten percent of the population was massacred by invading Indonesian forces following Portuguese withdrawal. In Portugal itself the arrival of more than half-a-million colonial refugees – many of them destitute, most bitter – came to be a major problem for the regime, though their eventual integration proved one of its triumphs.

At home, the first **crisis** came in September 1974, when Spínola, with Gonçalves and Saraiva de Carvalho virtual prisoners in Lisbon's Belém Palace, moved army units to take over key positions. The MFA, however, proved too strong and Spínola was forced to resign, General Costa Gomes replacing him as president. By the summer of 1975 more general reaction was setting in and even the MFA began to show signs of disunity. The country was increasingly split, supporting the Revolution in the south, while remaining deeply conservative in the north. The Archbishop of Braga summed up the north's traditional views, declaring that the struggle against communism should be seen "not in terms of man against man, but Christ against Satan". Nevertheless the Revolution continued to advance; a coup attempt in March failed when the troops involved turned against their officers. The Council of the Revolution was formed, promptly nationalizing banking and private insurance; widespread land seizures went ahead in the Alentejo; and **elections** in the summer resulted in an impressive victory for Mário Soares' Socialist Party (PS).

On November 25, 1975, elements of the army opposed to the rightward shift in the government moved for yet another **coup**, taking over major air bases across the country. Otelo Saraiva de Carvalho, however, declined to bring his Lisbon command to their aid; nor did the hoped-for mass mobilization of the people take place. Government troops under Colonel Ramalho Eanes moved in to force their surrender and – again virtually without bloodshed – the Revolution had ended.

Democracy and Europe: the 1980s

In 1975, the ruling Socialist Party helped to shape the post-revolutionary constitution – a mildly Socialist document, though providing for a fairly powerful president. Early fears of a right-wing coup led by Spínola failed to materialize, helped by the election of **Colonel Eanes**, a man whom the army trusted, as president. He above all was a figure of stability, with enormous popular support and happy to concentrate on developing Portugal's links with Africa, Asia and Latin America and overseeing a gradual normalization process. The Socialists had effective control until 1980 when Dr. Sá Carneiro managed to create the **Democratic Alliance**, uniting the larger groupings on the right. But within a few months he died – some say suspiciously – in a plane crash.

In **elections** held on the ninth anniversary of the Revolution, April 25, 1983, Mário Soares' Socialist Party again became the largest single party in the national assembly. Soares' premiership was dogged by the unpopularity of his **economic austerity measures** (in part insisted on by the IMF) and by constant delays and breakdowns in the talks over Portuguese and Spanish **entry into the European Community**. These problems did have one positive result, however, namely closer relations with the traditionally hostile government in Madrid. But the government's economic problems led eventually to the withdrawal of Social Democratic support and to the collapse of the coalition.

Soon after the inconclusive elections of October 1985, the revolutionary leader, Lt-Colonel Otelo Saraiva de Carvalho, was arrested and put on trial in Lisbon accused of being the leader of 73 suspected terrorists in the **FP-25** urban guerrilla group. Proceedings were postponed following the shooting of one of the key witnesses and it was not until 1987 that Saraiva de Carvalho was sentenced to 15 years' imprisonment (50 others also received prison sentences). He was later conditionally released after a Supreme Court ruling that there had been irregularities at his trial. In February 1990 he renounced the armed struggle and requested an amnesty.

President Eanes, meanwhile – the other great figure at the end of the Revolution – had been forced to resign the presidency on completion of his second term in January 1986. He was replaced by former Socialist Prime Minister **Mário Soares** who, with the reluctant support of the Communists, narrowly defeated the candidate of the centre-right, becoming the first civilian president for sixty years.

Portugal's entry into the **European Community** in 1986 brought with it the most important changes since the Revolution. With the help of a massive injection of funds to modernize infrastructure and increased foreign investment, Portugal enjoyed unprecedented **economic growth**. For many Portuguese this resulted in greater material wealth, but behind the trappings of the new prosperity remained pockets of deeply entrenched poverty. Prime Minister Aníbal Cavaco Silva's early attempts to introduce an economic reform programme were hampered by his lack of a majority, but in 1987 his PSD (Social Democrats) party as returned to power in surprising numbers, enjoying the first absolute majority since the 1974 Revolution and the strength to implement real changes. The centre-right government's free enterprise drive for the removal of Socialist structures and privatization did not run unchallenged: the late 1980s were marked by **industrial unrest**.

In 1989 the socialist opposition gained control of the capital, Lisbon; the northern industrial centre, Porto; and other significant cities during municipal elections. Four years of economic growth had benefited a new yuppie class, but voters were aware of accentuated social inequality and the continued inadequacy of health and education structures. Despite this, Cavaco Silva won a convincing mandate in the elections of October 1991, when the PSD was returned to government with over fifty percent of the vote.

The 1990s

The 1990s took Portugal into the second stage of its ten-year transition phase for EC entry and into its **presidency of the European Community** in 1992, the year when (on December 31) all remaining trade and employment barriers were removed and the EC became the EU. The country adopted its EU task with considerable imagination and expense, staging a superb exhibiton of its culture – Europalia – in Brussels, and building a grand presidency HQ in the Lisbon suburb of Belém. On the domestic front, the PSD continued with privatization and forged plans for the conversion of state-run banks in preparation for joining the European Monetary System.

Dealing with **inflation** remained at the top of the government's agenda, during the early 1990s. It had to do this while coping with increased discontent over social issues: statistics show Portugal had – and still has – some of the highest **infant mortality** and **illiteracy** rates in Europe. Unemployment figures, too, hid a high proportion of underpaid and part-time workers and disguised the fact that wages failed to increase in real terms in spite of impressive economic growth.

General elections in October 1995 brought ten years of Conservative rule to an end and the moderate Socialists came into power under the enthusiastic leadership of **António Guterres**. Cavaco Silva's surprise defeat in the presidential elections of January 1996, ushered in leftwing former mayor of Lisbon, **Jorge Sampaio**, giving Portugal a head of state and prime minister from the same – Socialist – party for the first time since the 1974 Revolution.

Guterres' programme differed little from that of his conservative predecessors and caused few worries for the business world. He offered a touch more sympathy towards the social welfare budget and a tougher stance towards the European Union, but otherwise pledged to continue to liberalize and privatize the economy. In the **October 1999 general elections**, stability seemed the order of the day, with Guterres and the Socialists returned for a second consecutive mandate – the first since the revolution, with precisely fifty percent of the vote (which guaranteed the liveliest parliament for years).

On a broader stage, the late 1990s saw a huge boost in Portuguese self-esteem internationally. Lisbon's **Expo 98** was an enormous success; the following year, Portugal's last colony – Macau – was handed back to Chinese rule without the problems encountered with Hong Kong. Portugal also played a large part in the fate of former colony, **East Timor** (Timor Loro Sae). Following the 1974 revolution, the Portuguese abandoned the territory, leaving it unable to prevent its illegal annexation by Indonesia. Indonesia's bloody 24-year rule resulted in the genocide of over a third of the population, and only came to an end after a UN-organized referendum in August 1999 – for which the Portuguese had been pushing for two decades, and which voted overwhelmingly in favour of independence. Although East Timor now barely functions as an independent state, and will be reliant on international donors and the UN for many years to come, the sense of relief in Portugal was palpable – the feeling was not one of success, but of a long-standing obligation which had finally been fulfilled.

Into the new millennium

Optimism engendered by the new millennium – and by Porto being chosen as European Capital of Culture in 2001 – was tempered by new problems for the government. The country's growing **drugs problem** led to the government decriminalizing drug usage in 2001 in a controversial forward-looking approach to help drug addicts rather than attract new ones. But such social problems, exacerbated by the crisis engendered by the 2001 September 11 terrorist attacks on New York, helped explain why the country finally lost patience with António Guterres' PSP rule, and they were resoundingly trounced in local elections in December 2001. Guterres' previously unflappable and highly popular government had also been given the unenviable task of overseeing the country's currency being replaced by the Euro; just one month before it took over from the escudo, Guterres resigned. The right-of-centre Social Democrat PSD party as elected into government in March 2002 under **Manuel Durão Barroso**, who promised to cut back government spending and to tighten drugs and immigration laws.

The first Portuguese **euro** were withdrawn from a cash machine in Porto just seconds after midnight on January 2002, and on the whole the transfer to the currency seems to have been relatively painless, despite reports of panic buying beforehand to get rid of blackmarket escudos stashed under people's beds. The persistent worry, however, is that the euro might slowly push up prices in a country which still earns much less per capita than its more industrialized partners. A slightly alarming shift, too, has been the takeover of large areas of banking, real estate and the financial sectors by Spanish companies, while EU funds that have played a dominant role in Portugal's development will largely end in 2006.

Portugal's next big event is the **2004 European Football Championships**, with seven centres benefitting from upgraded stadia and a brand new stadium to be built near Almancil in the Algarve. Meanwhile, ambitious **transport plans** have seen an extension of the metro in Lisbon and a new metro in Porto, while a rail crossing over the Tejo will create a direct link with the Algarve. A new, larger international airport is also due to be built at Ota to the northwest of Lisbon by 2010. Many economists worry that the funds for such grandiose projects can never be paid back and will burden the country with permanent debts, while critics also point to the fact that investment has only benefitted the major centres, neglecting the rest of the country. The European Championships alone saw nearly £250 million of public money funnelled into one sporting event. One of Manuel Durão Barroso's first pledges was to work out which plans were really necessary and many may never come to light.

Another headache for the government continues to be the inefficiency of Portuguese **agriculture**, which employs nearly one-fifth of the workforce but produces only a fraction of the country's wealth. The opening in 2002 of the Alqueva dam – the largest man-made lake in Europe – in the Alentejo district, is a controversial attempt to bring agriculture to a previously barren area. The water should permit the farming of vegetables, but at the expense of millions of trees. Damming the Guadiana river also threatens the delicate ecosystems at the river's estuary around Castro Marim and Vila Real in the Algarve.

The good news for Portugal's economy is that **tourism**, which accounts for nearly a tenth of the country's GNP and over a quarter of all foreign invest-ment, continues to flourish. Perhaps better news still is the emerging awareness that responsible, greener tourism is the way forward, and though there are exceptions, many resorts at least pay lip-service to environmental concerns, with recycling bins and beach-cleaning the norm.

Chronology of monuments and arts

2000–1500BC ▶ **Neolithic** settlements in the north of the country. eg **Verracos culture** in Trás-os-Montes; *Porcas* (stone boars) of Bragança, Murça.

700–600 BC ▶ **Castro culture** of fortified hill-towns, or *citânias*, concentrated in the Minho; refined by the **Celtic** Iron Age influence: eg Citânia de Briteiros, near Braga. Best collection of artefacts in Museu Martins Sarmento, Guimarães.

210 BC ▶ **Romans** enter peninsula and begin colonization; northern Portugal not finally pacified until 19 BC. Conímbriga, 4th centuryBC Celtic town near Coimbra, adapted to Roman occupation (survives until 5th c AD).

60 BC ▶ Julius Caesar establishes a capital at Lisbon and towns at Beja, Évora, Santarém, etc. Walls and other remains at Idanha, in Beira Baixa; temple and aqueducts of Évora; bridges at Chaves, Ponte de Lima, Leiria and elsewhere.

4th century AD ▶ Bishoprics founded at Braga, Évora, Faro and Lisbon.

409–411 ▶ **Barbarian** invasions: Suevi settle in the north.

585 ▶ **Visigoths** incorporate Suevian state into their Iberian empire. Isolated churches, mainly in the north, include 7th-century São Pedro de Balsemão (near Lamego) and São Frutuoso at Braga.

711 ▶ **Moors** from North Africa invade and conquer peninsula within seven years. Moorish fortresses/walls survive at Silves, Lisbon, Sintra, Elvas, Mértola and Alcácer do Sal.

9th century ▶ **Al-Gharb** (Algarve) becomes an independent Moorish kingdom, governed from Silves.

868 ▶ Porto reconquered by the Christian kings of Asturias-León.

11th century ▶ Country of **Portucale** emerges and (1097) is given to Henry of Burgundy. Cluniac monks, administering pilgrimage route to Santiago, bring Romanesque architecture from France: 12th-century churches at Bravães and Tomar, and council chamber at Bragança.

1143 ▶ **Afonso Henriques** recognized as first king of Portucale at the Treaty of Zamora. Guimarães castle built.

1147 ▶ Afonso takes Lisbon and Santarém from the Moors; followed in 1162 by Beja and Évora and in 1189 (temporarily) Silves. Fortress-like Romanesque cathedrals of Lisbon, Coimbra, Évora, Braga and Porto constructed.

1212 ▶ First assembly of the Cortes (parliament) at Coimbra. Gothic architecture enters Portugal at the Cistercian abbey of Alcobaça and several churches, most notably in Coimbra.

1249 ▶ **Afonso III** completes reconquest of the Algarve.

1385 ▶ Battle of Aljubarrota: **João I** defeats Castilians to become first king of House of Avis. The great triumph of mature Portuguese Gothic – the abbey of Batalha – is built in celebration. Paço Real built at Sintra.

1415 ▶ **Infante Henriques** (Henry the Navigator) active at the Navigation School in Sagres.

1419 ▶ Madeira discovered. Flemish-influenced "Portuguese Primitive" painters include Nuno Gonçalves.

1427 ▶ Azores discovered.

1457 ▶ Cape Verde Islands discovered.

1495–1521 ▶ Reign of **Dom Manuel I** ("The Fortunate"). Late-Gothic Manueline style develops with greatest examples at Tomar, Batalha, Belém and Sintra. By 1530s Renaissance forms are introduced and merged.

1497 ▶ Vasco da Gama opens up sea route to India.

1500 ▶ Cabral discovers Brazil.

1513 ▶ Portuguese reach China.

1521–57 ▶ Reign of **João III**. Celebrated contemporary painters include Grão Vasco (see p.251).

1557–78 Reign of **Dom Sebastião**. Important sculptural school at Coimbra (1520–70) centred on French Renaissance sculptors Nicolas Chanterenne, Filipe Hodart and Jean de Rouen.

1578 ▶ Disastrous expedition to Morocco, loss of king and mass slaughter of nobility at Alcácer-Quibir.

1581–1640 ▶ **Philip II** brings Spanish (Hapsburg) rule.

1640 ▶ **João IV**, Duke of Bragança, restores independence. Severe late-Renaissance style: eg São Vicente in Lisbon designed by Felipe Terzi.

1706–50 ▶ Reign of **Dom João V**. Gold and diamonds discovered in Brazil, reached peak of wealth and exploitation in the 1740s. High Baroque including the palace-monastery of Mafra, decoration of Coimbra University Library and the simpler, more rustic Baroque style of plaster/granite witnessed in Lamego and Bom Jesus. Rococo Palace of Queluz (1752).

1755 ▶ **Great Earthquake** destroys Lisbon and parts of the Alentejo and Algarve. "Pombaline" Neoclassical style employed for rebuilding of Lisbon (Baixa) and Vila Real de Santo António in the Algarve.

1843–53 ▶ **Maria II** holds throne with German consort, Fernando II. Pena Palace folly built at Sintra.

1908 ▶ Assassination of **Carlos I** in Lisbon.

1910 ▶ Exile of **Manuel II** ("The Unfortunate") and **end of Portuguese monarchy**. Cubist painter Amadeu de Sousa Cardoso; see p.328 for museum in Amarante.

1910–26 ▶ "Democratic" Republic.

1932–68 ▶ **Salazar** dictatorship. Goa is seized by India; colonial wars in Africa.

1974 ▶ April 25 **Revolution**.

1986 ▶ Entry to European Community (EC).

1994 ▶ Lisbon is European City of Culture. Permanent gallery of modern Portuguese artists opens at Lisbon's Gulbenkian Foundation.

1998 ▶ Lisbon hosts Expo 98. Capital becomes a showcase for the work of national and international architects.

2001 ▶ Porto is European City of Culture.

2002 ▶ The escudo is replaced by the euro.

Music

Musically, Portugal is best known as the home of the passionate and elegant vocal and instrumental fado of Lisbon and Coimbra but, away from the cities, a rich variety of regionally distinct music and a wide range of traditional instruments can still be encountered. Even though social and economic change has diminished their role in everyday life you are still likely to come across traditional music during local festivals, family celebrations and public performances. This inheritance invests much of what is distinctively Portuguese in the music coming out of the country today, as it did in the "new song" movement of singer-songwriters associated with the political change of the 1974 revolution. Portuguese democracy has matured to an eclectic soundtrack: vibrant music from the country's former colonies and Lusophone variants of global pop, rock, rap, electronic dance music and jazz have developed alongside the home-grown wilful kitsch known as *pimba*.

Regional traditions

Each region of Portugal has its own characteristic songs, ensembles and instruments but the vocal and instrumental traditions survive most strongly in the rural areas away from the sea – regions like Trás-os-Montes, the Beiras and Alentejo. Villages and towns throughout Portugal have folklore troupes known as **ranchos folclóricos** who perform at festivals and sometimes on concert stages and help perpetuate the musical traditions of the country. These were encouraged by the dictatorship as exemplars of the happy colourful peasantry, and were therefore somewhat disapproved of by musicians who were opponents of the regime, but emerging from those associations some continue to exist. Recently there has also been something of an increase in the number of musicians and bands performing traditional material, using and reviving traditional instruments and combining them, and making new music with a roots heritage.

Portuguese tradition is rich with song, some of it drawing on the **oral ballad** repertoire that was once widespread across Europe. Iberia has its own specific group of ballads – the *Romanceiro* – which were sung in the royal courts from the fifteenth until the seventeenth century, but continued in the fields and villages long after that. Many other traditional songs – of love, religion or the cycles of nature – remained within living tradition into the 1970s, but with migration, changing ways of work, and mass media, the need and occasions for singing them have dwindled and many now exist only in field recordings or in the repertoire of the revival folk bands.

Singers are sometimes joined by others in a refrain, perhaps accompanied by a stringed instrument or percussion. In the south, particularly **Alentejo**, there is a long tradition of a cappella vocal groups, a vibrant Mediterranean sound comparable to that of the vocal ensembles of Corsica and Sardinia. These are generally single-sex with a lead singer who delivers the first couple of verses before being joined by harmonising lines from a second singer and then full-group vocal. Performing and recording ensembles exist, such as **Ensemble Vidigueira**, **Cantadores de Redondo**, **As Ceifeiros de Pias** or the female

Portugal is home to a remarkable variety of instruments, most of them associated with particular regional traditions.

Guitarra Portuguesa

The best-known Portuguese music is fado, and be that the Lisboa or Coimbra tradition its dominant instrument is the **guitarra**. Though sometimes called the Portuguese guitar, its body isn't "guitar-shaped": it is a variety of the European cittern, which arrived in Portugal in the eighteenth century in the form of the "English guitar" largely via the English community of Porto. Two designs evolved – the Lisbon *guitarra*, usually used for accompanying singers, and the larger body and richer bass of the version more suited to Coimbra fado, with its strong *guitarra*-virtuoso strand. Both have six pairs of steel strings tuned by knurled turn-screws on a fan-shaped metal machine head.

"Violas"

In fado, the *guitarra* is usually accompanied by a six-string guitar of the Spanish form which, like all fretted instruments of that waisted body-shape, is known in Portugal as a *viola*. Though the **viola de fado** is usually a normal Spanish guitar, there is a remarkable range of other specifically Portuguese *violas*. They are virtually always steel-strung, and most have soundboards decorated with flowing tendril-like dark wood inlays spreading from the bridge, and soundholes in a variety of shapes.

The version encountered most often, particularly in the north, is the **viola braguesa**, which has five pairs of strings and is usually played *rasgado* (a fast intricate rolling strum with an opening hand). A slightly smaller close relative, from the region of Amarante, is the **viola amarantina**, whose soundhole is usually in the form of two hearts. Other varieties include the ten- or twelve-stringed **viola campanica alentejana** which has a very deeply indented waist, almost like a figure of eight; a notable modern player is **José Barros** of the Alentejo duo **Cantesul**. Another version is the **viola beiroa**, which is distinctive in having an extra pair of strings which are played in a way similar to the high fifth string on an American banjo.

group **As Camponesas de Castro Verde**. **Vozes do Sul**, a group led by Alentejo singer-songwriter **Janita Salome**, combines the singers from some of these groups and from his own family with new arrangements on acoustic instruments.

Trás-os-Montes in the northeast – the land "behind the mountains" – is the heartland of *gaita-de-foles* (bagpipes), and the old tradition survives principally in the easternmost tip, Miranda do Douro, hard up against the Spanish border. Of the surviving handful of traditional Mirandês *gaiteiros*, two of the best are in the quartet **Galandum Galundaina**, fine musicians and singers whose activity shows signs of creating new interest. They play regularly for the *dança dos paulitos*, a stick dance for men which is strongly reminiscent of an English morris dance. Its music is provided by the standard Trás-os-Montes line-up of a *gaita* accompanied by a *bombo* (bass drum) and *caixa* (snare drum), or sometimes by a solo musician playing a three-hole whistle (*flauta pastoril*) with one hand and a small snare drum (*tamboril*) with the other.

Bombos and *caixas* also feature in other northern and central regions as the thud and snap driving various ensembles playing for ceremony or celebration such as the *zés-pereiras* of the **Minho** region, where they join flutes and

Cavaquinhos and bandolims

One popular Portuguese stringed instrument has taken root across the world. The **cavaquinho** looks like a baby viola with four strings, and is played with an ingenious fast strum akin to the braguesa's *rasgado*. It spread from Portugal to the Azores and Madeira, and travelled onwards with Portuguese migrants from the Atlantic islands to Hawaii, where it became, with very few changes, the ukulele. The Portuguese form of mandolin, the **bandolim** or *banjolim*, is much used; a particularly fine player is **Júlio Pereira**, who is also an expert exponent of cavaquinho and the range of *violas*.

Pipes

The **gaita-de-foles** is the Portuguese bagpipe, in form similar to the Scottish Highland war-pipe but closest to the *gaitas* of Spain's Galicia and Asturias. It is the main melody instrument of Trás-os-Montes music, accompanied by *bombo* and *caixa*. Each *gaita* has the tuning its player chooses, the scale in which he sings, rather than the fixed, mathematical scale developed for classical harmony that has come to prevail in much of the western world.

Percussion

A feature of Beira Baixa music, and found elsewhere too, is the **adufe**. Introduced by the Arabs a millennium ago, it is a square double-headed drum usually containing pieces of wood or pebbles which rattle. Held on edge and tapped with the fingers, it's played by women, often in groups, to accompany their singing. Also found in several traditions is the clanking **ferrinhos** (triangle), played pretty much as in Cajun music.

Bombo, *caixa*, *adufe*, *pandeiro* (small drum) and *pandeireta* (tambourine) or occasionally *cântaro com abanho* (a clay pot struck across its mouth with a leather or straw fan) provide the thump of Portuguese traditional music, while the clatter comes from the likes of the *cana* (a split cane slap-stick), **trancanholas** (wooden "bones"), *castanholas* (castañuelas), *reco-reco* or *reque-reque* (a scraped serrated stick), *conchas* (shells rubbed together), *zaclitracs* (a form of rattle) and *genebres* (a wooden xylophone hung from the neck (a feature of the *dança dos homens* (men's dance) in Beira Baixa.

sometimes clarinets and *gaitas*. Another style of Minho ensemble is the *rusga*, a variable line-up of stringed instruments such as *viola braguesa*, *cavaquinho* and perhaps violin, with accordion, flutes, clarinet, perhaps ocarina, and a clattering rhythm section.

Whatever its current vitality or otherwise, every region of Portugal has its own traditions – songs and ways of singing them, instruments, types of ensemble – and social or calendar events at which they occur. Wherever you are, you might well stumble across something interesting. For more detail, sound samplers, festival listings and links, take a look at the **website** ®www.attambur.com run by the group At Tambur.

Roots revival

In the 1970s, young performing groups began to form to devote their attention either to the performance of traditional music, or to the construction of new music with folk roots. They used material that was still being sung or played, or could be enticed from the memories of their elders. Another source of inspiration was the material preserved in the **field recordings** made by enlightened individuals earlier in the 20th century, notable among them being Michel Giacometti (1929–90), a Corsican-born Frenchman who together with Fernando Lopes Graça made field recordings throughout Portugal that were released on various labels from the late 1950s onwards.

Such revival bands form, dissolve and regroup but the number of new ones appearing seems to be increasing and several of the pioneers are still around, including **Brigada Victor Jara**, formed in Coimbra in 1975, which, while containing none of its original members, continues to be a major force. A particularly impressive and innovative more recent arrival is **Gaiteiros de Lisboa**, which makes dramatic new music with deep roots, using raw percussion, voices, *gaitas* and other reeds plus quirky invented instruments. Another such inventive project is the group **Adufe**, inspired by Japanese Taiko drumming and formed by José Salgueiro for Expo 98, which makes a dramatic show focused on four giant *adufes*.

Fado

Portugal's most famous musical form, **fado** ("fate") is currently experiencing a boom in popularity at home and abroad. It's an urban music, a thing of nighttime and bars, the origins of which are debatable but certainly involve influences from Portugal's overseas explorations. The essence of fado is *saudade* (inadequately translatable as "yearning" or "beautiful melancholy") which is carried in the lyrical and sentimental expression of a solo singer usually accompanied by the *guitarra* and *viola de fado*. There are two distinct traditions of fado: Lisbon, which is very much a vocal form, male and female, and Coimbra, which in addition to its songs has a purely instrumental, *guitarra*-led aspect and is a male-only preserve. Portuguese are often mystified as to what a non-Portuguese speaker could get from fado, since so much of its meaning is in the poetic lyrics, but the beauty of the soaring vocals over the silvery *guitarra* is certainly seductive.

By far the most famous of the fado singers, and arguably its greatest performer, was **Amália Rodrigues** who had an immeasurable impact upon the direction of the fado through her recordings. Born in 1920 in the Alfama district of Lisbon, her death in October 1999 saw three days of official mourning announced in Portugal. Though in the course of her long singing and occasional film acting career she ventured into other musical forms, her style and most celebrated recordings have become a central reference point in what people mean by fado.

Two working class districts of Lisbon – Mouraria and Alfama – are considered the birthplace of fado, and the music can still be found in both, but the main focus of fado clubs theses days, is the Bairro Alto. Some are expensive, some are tourist-traps, some are both; there's no easy guidebook pathway to the magical night in the right place – word of mouth might help but don't count on it. As with the elusive *duende* of Spain's flamenco, you may find the most memorable fado of all is performed by an unadvertised performer, and whether the performer is famous or not when you're present at a special, real moment of fado you'll know it.

It's not unusual for well-known fadistas to run their own clubs. **Maria da Fé** owns the Lisbon fado house *Sr. Vinho*, at Rua Meio Lapa 18 (☏21 397 2681, ⊛www.restsrvinho.com), where she and other notables perform. Seated at the long tables in the club *Clube de Fado* (☏021 888 2694, ⊛www.clube -de-fado.com), at Rua de S. João da Praça 94, in Alfama, you might well hear the owner **Mário Pacheco** himself, a fine *guitarrista* and the last to play with Amália, accompanying **Ana Sofia Varela**. Fado clubs are social places, with eating, drinking and informality, but during a song set in a good club the waiters don't serve, and the music is treated with due reverence.

Fado is also a thing of concert stages and international touring, and there, and on record, the band line-up may be larger and use a wider range of instruments, including sometimes piano, strings or wind instruments. This isn't a new phenomenon – Amália and others of her generation did it – but with the new confidence and public enthusiasm the elegant simplicity of the traditional lineup is the key in the work of many of today's leading young international performers such as **Mariza**, **Mísia**, **Cristina Branco**, **Kátia Guerreiro**, **Mafalda Arnauth** and male singers (currently in a minority among the new wave) **Helder Moutinho** and **Camané**. At the same time, **Dona Rosa**, unaccompanied save for her gently tinkling triangle, as stark as a rural ballad-singer, is now receiving international acclaim after years of performing her very personal fado on the streets of Lisbon.

Many performers move in and out of fado, or mix aspects of it with other genres. For example **Dulce Pontes** began in the world of rock-pop ballads, then for her second CD, *Lagrimas*, she performed fado and while she explores other genres it has remained a strong thread in her music, including on her 1999 release, *O Primeiro Canto*. The music of the equally well-known Lisbon band **Madredeus**, a manicured blend of classical guitars and keyboards surrounding the songbird vocals of Teresa Salgueiro in songs largely by band leader Pedro Ayres Magalhães, while not fado as such is, nevertheless, replete with the reflective melancholy of *saudade*.

Coimbra fado has a very different style: reflecting that city's ancient university traditions, and typically performed by students and Coimbra graduates, it's an exclusively male domain. As well as more formal songs that are less personally expressive than in Lisbon fado, there is also a strong aspect of *guitarra*-led instrumentals. The most famous Coimbra *guitarra* fadista of the latter half of the twentieth century has been **Carlos Paredes**. He has now retired from live performance, but Coimbra instrumental fado continues to evolve in skilled hands in both traditional and new combinations. Most of **Pedro Caldeira Cabral**'s compositions aren't fado as such, but they and his immense virtuosity on the *guitarra* can be seen as part of the legacy of Coimbra fado.

Nova canção and música popular

It was an attempt to update the Coimbra fado that resulted in the modern Portuguese **ballad** (the term in this context meaning a set of poetic – usually contemporary – lyrics set to music, rather than the epic story-song that is the traditional folk-ballad).

The great figure in this movement was **José Afonso**. He had a classic, soaring fado-style voice and his first recording, with Luís Góes in 1956, comprised fados from Coimbra together with a couple of his own songs. It was principally Afonso's songs, his choice of those by others, and his music drawing on regional traditional musics and fado, that during the last years of the dictatorship, became known as **nova canção** (new song). Together with the songs and performances of a gathering cast of others such as **Fausto**, **Luís Cília**, **Sérgio Godinho** and **Vitorino**, this provided a rallying point in the development not only of new Portuguese music but also of a new democratized state. In the final years of dictatorship, censorship and the restriction of performing opportunities caused some songwriters to move and record abroad, but Afonso remained, when necessary masking social and political messages with allegory.

In the years after the 1974 revolution *nova canção* broadened to a movement known as **música popular** – essentially contemporary singer-songwriter music with folk roots. As in fado, the lyrics were as significant as the music, but unlike the more personal and emotional subject matter of fado they dealt with contemporary social and cultural issues. The music drew on popular tradition, both rural and urban, as well as reflecting Latin American, European and North African influences. Though he died in 1987, Afonso's albums keep his music and ideas very much a touchstone in Portuguese musical thinking, and many of his contemporaries are still performing. Younger singers and songwriters, such as **Amélia Muge**, continue in a similar spirit of drawing on a mixture of rural and fado traditions, and you'll frequently hear songs by Afonso, Godinho and other *nova canção* leaders in the repertoire of fado singers.

Rock and pop

Although the music of the likes of **Madredeus**, **Brigada Victor Jara**, **Dulce Pontes**, **Cristina Branco**, **Misia** and **Mariza** has an identifiably Portuguese international profile, pop bands like **Coldfinger** have come onto the scene in recent years and, as they sing mainly in English, are easily marketable abroad as pop rather than world music. Among other mainstream pop groups to keep an ear out for in Portugal are **Delfins**, Santos e Pecadores, Clã and the REM-influenced **Silence 4**.

On a national level, rap singer **Pedro Abrunhosa** is idolized throughout the country. On its release, his first record, *Viagens*, broke sales records and opened the doors for many groups. One of the main achievements of his music was to make **rap** more acceptable and its decidedly jazzy feel has provided an alternative to a music scene previously dominated by FM-style hard rock. In fact Portuguese rap and hip-hop from General D, Da Weasel, Boss AC and others now dominate the underground music and club scene.

Dance music took a while to catch on, but in 1991 the first ever Portuguese house track, *Deep Sky* by Matrix Run, stimulated a wave of new interest and Lisbon has become a major clubbing destination. Although the scene is still dominated by foreign music, home-grown talent is growing in reputation, with **DJ Vibe** as the country's major exponent both at home and abroad.

You're unlikely to get through a visit to Portugal without hearing some **música pimba** – a fashionably tacky music of the sort that usually enters the charts around Christmas time. Despite the wholesale snubbing of this style by the Portuguese media, *pimba* has succeeded in conquering the whole country as well as being big in countries with large Portuguese communities.

Mixing traditional and modern elements, its success was previously limited to the provinces, but the introduction of satirical jokes and sexual references to the lyrics found new support among college students and its popularity has now spread to the main cities. Today, *pimba* is firmly established and, to some extent, its humorous and satirical style reflects a lot of the national character. The main exponent of *pimba* is the singer/songwriter **Marco Paulo**. Another seasoned performer is **Quim Barreiros**; if you get a chance to see him, take it. Even if you can't speak Portuguese, the atmosphere at the shows is contagious.

Music from former colonies

There are touring musicians and bands from all over the world to be seen in Portugal, but naturally it's a good place to encounter performers from world's biggest Lusophone country, **Brazil**. An exciting and relatively recent development in the Portuguese music scene has been the appearance of groups from the **former colonies** of Angola, Mozambique, Cabo Verde, Guinea-Bissau and São Tomé e Príncipe. Following the colonial wars and independence many African musicians settled in Lisbon, while some spend part of the year based in Portugal while they tour Europe or record.

Cabo Verde music in particular has achieved great acclaim, with the reflective, melodic fado-like *morna* – whose most internationally famous exponent is **Cesaria Évora** – and the more danceable *moradeira*. Another fine Lisbon resident Cabo Verdean singer is **Celina Pereira**. Among the **Lisbon Cabo Verdean** community, some women, such as the twelve-strong group **Voz de Africa**, gather on Sundays and at celebrations to play, sing and dance *batuc* – a social music banned in colonial times in which lively singing is accompanied by clapping, slapping on plastic-covered pillows and a dance in which two women circle and bump hips. Taking some influences from *batuc*, **Sara Tavares**, who made a reputation in her teens as a pop singer, is now turning to what she describes as her personal tradition, with roots in Cabo Verde, Portugal and elsewhere, delivering live performances of freshness, beauty and subtlety.

Soft-voiced Angolan singer-guitarist **Waldemar Bastos** was imprisoned in his native country in the 1970s, and defected to Portugal in 1982. Now an internationally esteemed performer with influences from Brazilian and Portuguese as well as Angolan forms, he runs a small restaurant with his wife in Lisbon's Barrio Alto (*Agua do Bengo*, Rua do Texeira 1) where you can dine to an Angolan-inspired soundtrack. New resident African-rooted formations arise and visiting bands arrive frequently, so it's worth keeping an eye on the posters and papers for promising-looking live shows and festivals.

Discography

This list is just a pointer to some of the recordings available, many of them internationally. Don't regard it as a shopping list: investigation of record shops in Portugal, the little ones and the shiny city chain-stores too, will turn up the many CDs that don't have international distribution, and there's a steady stream of fine new releases and re-issues. Better than any CD, though, go and experience the music live – follow that sound echoing down the street.

Tradition

Alentejo

Ensemble Vidigueira *Portugal: Voices of Alentejo* (Auvidis)
Grupo Coral e Etnográfico *As Camponesas de Castro Verde – Castro Verde: Vozes das Terras Brancas* (EMI Valentim de Carvalho), *Os Camponeses de Pias – Pias: O Cante na margem Esquerda* (EMI Valentim de Carvalho)
Vozes do Sul *Vozes do Sul* (Capella)
Various *Portugal: Musique de l'Alentejo* (Ocora)

Trás-os-Montes

Various *Musica Tradicional: Terra de Miranda* (Tecnosaga)
Various *Portugal: Trás-os-Montes: Chants du Blé et Cornemuses de Berger* (Ocora)

Estremadura

Various *Tradições Musicais da Estremadura* (Book & 3 CDs) (Tradisom)

Various regions

Various *Arquivos Sonoros* (Series of 5 CDs of Michel Giacometti & Fernando Lopes Graça's field recordings) (Strauss)
Various *Musical Traditions of Portugal* (Smithsonian/Folkways)
Various *Musical Travel: Portugal and the Islands* (Auvidis)
Various *Sons da Terra: A tradição é o que é...* (Series of 10 CDs) (Sons da Terra/Edições e Produções Musicais)
Various *Women's Voices of Portugal* (Auvidis)

Roots revival and development

Brigada Victor Jara *Danças e Folias* (Farol)
Gaiteiros de Lisboa *Bocas do Inferno* (Farol), *Invasões Bárbaras* (Farol), *Dançachamas* (Farol)
Né Ladeiras *Traz os Montes* (EMI Valentim de Carvalho)
Realejo *Cenários* (Movieplay)
Sétima Legião *Sexto Sentido* (EMI Valentim de Carvalho)
Vai de Roda *Polas Ondas* (Alba)

Fado

Lisbon fado

There are a large number of Lisbon fado CDs to be found in the better Portuguese record shops – new and historic recordings, single artist releases (including vast numbers by Amália) and compilations (which often include tracks from great singers, particularly from the past, who have no whole album extant). Here's a cross section:

João Braga *Cantar ao Fado* (Strauss)
Camané *Pelo Dia Dentro* (EMI Valentim de Carvalho)
Katia Guerreiro *Fado Maior* (Ocarina)
Mafalda Arnauth *Esta Voz Que Nos Atravessa* (EMI Valentim de Carvalho)
Mariza *Fado em Mim* (World Connection)
Mísia *Ritual* (Erato)
Helder Moutinho *Sete Fados e* *Alguns Cantos* (Ocarina)
Amália Rodrigues *The Art of Amália* (EMI Hemisphere), *The First Recordings* (EPM)
Dona Rosa *Histórias da Rua* (Jaro)
Various *Portugal: The Story Of Fado* (EMI Hemisphere)
Various *Arquivos do Fado* (Heritage) (Series of CDs; recordings from the 1920s and 1930s)

Various *Un Parfum de Fado* (Playa-sound) (Series of CDs)

Coimbra vocal fado
Fernando Machado Soares *The*

Fado of Coimbra (Auvidis)

Coimbra instrumental fado
Carlos Paredes *Guitarra Portuguesa* (EMI Valentim de Carvalho)

Nova canção and música popular

José Afonso *Cantigas do Maio* (Movieplay), *Fados de Coimbra e Outras Canções* (Movieplay), *Best of José Afonso* (Movieplay)

Sérgio Godinho *Lupa* (EMI Valentim de Carvalho)
Vitorino *Alentejanas e Amorosas* (Emi Valentim de Carvalho)

Fado-influenced developments

Fernando Lameirinhas *Live* (Munich)
Madredeus *Antologia* (EMI Valentim de Carvalho)
Amélia Muge *Todos os Dias* (Columbia)
Filipa Pais *L'Amar* (Strauss)

Carlos Paredes & Charlie Haden *– Dialogues* (Antilles)
Pedro Caldeira Cabral *Variações – Guitarra Portuguesa* (World Network)
Dulce Pontes *Caminhos* (Movieplay)
Júlio Pereira *Acústico* (Sony)

Rock/Pop

Coldfinger *Lefthand* (Nortesul)
Rádio Macau *Onde o Tempo Faz a Curva* (BMG)

Silence 4 *Only Pain is Real* (Universal)

Music from former colonies

Waldemar Bastos *Pretaluz* (Luaka Bop)
Justino Delgado *Casamenti D'Haos* (Lusafrica)
Cesaria Évora *Miss Perfumado*

(Lusafrica)
Celina Pereira *Nôs Tradições* (Lusafrica)
Various *The Soul of Cape Verde* (Tinder)

Compilations

Various *Music from the Edge of Europe: Portugal* (EMI Hemisphere). Compiled from EMI Valentim de Carvalho's catalogue. Amália Rodrigues, Carlos Paredes, Vitorino, Sérgio Godinho, Né Ladeiras, António Pinho Vargas & Maria João, Madredeus, Danças Ocultas, Lua Extravagante, Trovante et al. Fado, *guitarra, nova canção/música popular, guitarra* and jazzish, but no rural traditional music.

Various *The Rough Guide to the Music of Portugal* (World Music Network). Compiled from Movieplay's catalogue; fado, *nova canção, guitarra*, roots revival but again no traditional rural music. José Afonso, Dulce Pontes, Carlos Paredes, Vai de Roda, Carlos Zel, Vitorino, Maria Teresa de Noronha, Maria da Fé, Teresa Silva de Carvalho et al.

by Andrew Cronshaw

Books

A reliable specialist source for out-of-print books (marked "o/p" in the list below) on all aspects of Portugal is Keith Harris Books (℡020 8898 7789, ⓦwww.books-on-portugal.com). For more contemporary publications, it's worth checking the latest books available from the UK publisher Carcanet Press (℡0161/834 8730, ⓦwww.carcanet.co.uk), which has a fiction series entitled "From the Portuguese" and a non-fiction series entitled "Aspects of Portugal". Some of the titles in these series are reviewed below.

General travel writing

William Beckford *Recollections of an Excursion to the Monasteries of Alcobaça and Batalha; Travels in Spain and Portugal (1778–88)*. Highly eccentric and enormously rich, Beckford lived for some time at Sintra and travelled widely in Estremadura. His accounts, told with a fine eye for the absurd, are a lot of fun.

Lord Byron *Selected Letters and Journals.* Only a few days of Portuguese travel but memorable ones – beginning with romantic enthusiasm, ending in outright abuse.

Almeida Garrett *Travels in My Homeland.* A classic Portuguese writer, Garrett was exiled to Europe in the 1820s, came into contact with the Romantics and later returned to play a part in the liberal government of the 1830s. This is a witty, discursive narrative ramble around the country.

Paul Hyland *Backwards Out of the Big World.* A fascinating and sympathetic account of a journey through Portugal by a man who knows the country's people, history and literature as few foreigners do.

Manfredd Hamm and Werner Radasewsky *Lisbon.* The strength of this book is its wonderful photographs, which capture the atmosphere and light of the city, its people and its surroundings through all its varying moods.

★ **Marion Kaplan** *The Portuguese: the Land and its People.* Published in 1991, this is a readable, all-embracing volume, covering everything from wine to the family, poetry and the land. The style is a bit old-fashioned, but it's the best general introduction to the country available.

Rose Macaulay *They Went to Portugal.* The book covers British travellers to Portugal from the Crusaders to Byron, weaving an anecdotal history of the country in the process. The follow-up volume, *They Went to Portugal, Too*, is only available as an expensive hardback.

Fernando Pessoa *Lisbon: What the Tourist Should See (o que o turista deve ver)* (Livros Horizonte, Portugal). A somewhat dull insight into the city as Pessoa saw it. Written in English and Portuguese (but only available in Portugal), Pessoa's 1925 guidebook describes a Lisbon that is largely recognizable today.

José Saramago *Journey to Portugal.* Portugal's best-known novelist describes his journey round the country towards the end of the last century. The book is a strangely pedestrian plod which reveals little about himself or the places he visits; Saramago proves himself to be better at fiction than travel writing.

Sacheverell Sitwell *Portugal and Madeira* (o/p). Mix of art history, observation and rather pompous upper-class travelogue from the 1950s. Sitwell's great enthusiasm is Portuguese Baroque. He also "discovers" Mateus Rosé wine for the British.

★ **Anne de Stoop** *Living in Portugal.* A glossy coffee-table tome filled with beautifully evocative photographs of Portugal's sights and architectural gems, from palaces and manor houses to rural houses, *pastelarias* and restaurants.

History and politics

★ **David Birmingham** *A Concise History of Portugal.* Recommended for the casual reader; concise but providing straightforward and informative coverage from the year dot to 1991.

C.R. Boxer *The Portuguese Seaborne Empire 1415–1825.* Classic account of Portuguese imperial expansion by a prolific writer on the region.

António de Figueiredo *Portugal: Fifty Years of Dictatorship.* An illuminating study which takes as its starting-point the 1926 military coup that brought Salazar to power and goes through to the 1974 Revolution.

A.H. de Oliveira Marques *History of Portugal.* Accessible general history.

Dan L. Raby *Fascism and Resistance in Portugal.* Scholarly account of the subject.

Peter Russell *Prince Henry "the Navigator": A life.* Fascinating, if academic, biography of the fifteenth-century prince.

★ **José Hermano Saraiva** *Portugal: A Companion History.* The most recent of its kind, this is an accessible and concise history of the country written especially for non-specialist foreigners by the author of the bestselling Portuguese original. Includes useful easy-reference glossaries of historical figures and places.

Art and architecture

Patrick Bowe *Houses and Gardens of Portugal.* The excellent photos is the main reason to buy this solid volume.

Helder Carita and Homem Cardoso *Portuguese Gardens.* A huge, beautiful tome, lavishly illustrated with photos and plans, with a scholarly text.

Miles Danby *The Fires of Excellence.* Magnificent and detailed study of the Oriental architecture of Spain and Portugal, illustrated with specially commissioned photographs.

Júlio Gil and Augusto Cabrita *The Finest Castles in Portugal.* A superb illustrated survey of Portuguese castles, let down a little by a highly pedestrian translation/text.

George Kubler Portuguese Plain Architecture *1521–1706* (o/p). A well-illustrated, scholarly overview of the rather severe version of Baroque architecture that prevailed in Portugal.

Robert C. Smith *The Arts of Portugal 1500–1800* (o/p). The only detailed account of all the arts of this period, but long out of print.

Fiction

António Lobo Antunes *An Explanation of the Birds, The Natural Order of Things, Act of the Damned,* ✴ *The Return of the Caravels* and *South of Nowhere.* Psychologically astute and with a helter-skelter prose style, Antunes is considered by many to be Portugal's finest contemporary writer after Saramago. His recent *The Return of the Caravels,* a modern "take" on the Discoveries, is a good place to start.

Maria Isabel Barreno, Maria Teresa Horta and Maria Velho da Costa *New Portuguese Letters: The Three Marias.* Published (and prosecuted) in 1972, pre-Revolution Portugal, this collage of stories, letters and poems is a modern feminist parable based on the seventeenth-century "Letters of a Portuguese Nun".

José Cardoso Pires *Ballad of Dog's Beach* (o/p). Ostensibly a detective thriller but the murder described actually took place during the last years of Salazar's dictatorship and Pires' research draws upon the original secret-police files. Compelling, highly original and with acute psychological insights, it was awarded Portugal's highest literary prize and made into a film.

★ **Lídia Jorge** *The Migrant Painter of Birds.* Born near Albufeira in 1946, Lídia Jorge is one of Portugal's most respected contemporary writers. This beautifully written novel describes a girl's memories as she grows up in a small village close to the Atlantic, and in doing so poignantly captures a changing rural community.

Ray Keenoy, David Treece and Paul Hyland *The Babel Guide to the Fiction of Portugal, Brazil and Africa.* A tantalizing introduction to Portuguese literature, with a collection of reviews of the major works of Lusophone fiction since 1945.

Eugénio Lisboa (ed) *The Anarchist Banker and Other Portuguese Stories* and *Professor Pfiglzz and His Strange Companion and Other Portuguese Stories.* A fabulous two-volume collection of twentieth-century short stories, which gives more than a taste of the exuberance and talent currently proliferating in Portuguese literature. Stories by old favourites – Eça de Queiroz, Pessoa, José Régio and Miguel Torga – are included too, mostly for the first time in English.

Eugénio Lisboa and Helder Macedo (eds) *The Dedalus Book of Portuguese Fantasy.* A rich feast of literary fantasy comprising short stories by the likes of Eça de Queiroz and José de Almada Negreiros.

José Rodrigues Miguéis *Happy Easter.* A powerful and disturbing account of the distorted reality experienced by a schizophrenic, whose deprived childhood leads him to a self-destructive and tragic life in Lisbon; evocatively written and a gripping read.

Fernando Pessoa ✴ *Book of Disquiet* and *A Centenary Pessoa.* The country's best-known poet wrote *The Book of Disquiet* in prose; it's an unclassifiable text compiled from unordered fragments, that is part autobiography, part philospohical rambling. Regarded as a Modernist classic, the Penguin edition is the most complete English version. *A Centenary Pessoa* includes a selection of his prose and poetry, including his works under the pseudonym of Ricardo Reis.

Eça de Queiroz *The Sin of Father Amaro* (o/p), ✴ *Cousin Bazilio,* ✴ *The Maias* and *The Illustrious House of Ramires.* One of Portugal's greatest writers, Eça de Queirós (1845–1900) introduced realism into Portuguese fiction with *The Sin of Father Amaro,* published in 1876. Over half a dozen of his novels have been translated into English; always highly readable, they present a cynical but affectionate picture of Portuguese society in the second half of the nineteenth century. His *English Letters* (Carcanet, UK), written during his long stint as consul in England, is also well worth investigating.

Erich Maria Remarque *The Night in Lisbon*. Better known as author of *All Quiet On The Western Front*, German author Remarque writes with a similar detachment in this tale of a World War II refugee seeking an escape route from Europe. One night in Lisbon, he meets a stranger who has two tickets, and within hours their lives are inextricably linked in a harrowing and moving tale.

Mário de Sá-Carneiro *The Great Shadow* and *Lucio's Confessions*. *The Great Shadow* is a collection of short stories set against the backdrop of Lisbon in the early 1900s as the author describes his obsession with great art. Sá-Carneiro, who committed suicide at 26, writes with stunning intensity and originality about art, science, death, homosexual sex and insanity. Similar themes appear in *Lucio's Confessions*, in which a menage-a-trois between three artists ends in a death.

José Saramago ▣*All the Names*, ▣*Baltasar and Blimunda*, *Blindness*, *The History of the Seige of Lisbon*, ▣ *The Year of the Death of Ricardo Reis*, *The Gospel According to Jesus Christ*, *The Stone Raft*, *The Tale of the Unknown Island*, *Manual of Painting and Calligraphy*. Saramago won the Nobel prize for literature in 1998 and is Portugal's most famous living writer. His novels have come thick and fast and are mostly experimental, often dispensing with punctuation altogether; *Blindness* even avoided naming a single character in the book. The one to start with is

Ricardo Reis, a magnificent novel which won the *Independent* foreign fiction award. Its theme is the return of Dr. Reis, after sixteen years in Brazil, to a Lisbon where the Salazar dictatorship is imminent and where Reis wanders the streets to be confronted by the past and the ghost of the writer Fernando Pessoa. In *Baltasar and Blimunda*, Saramago mixes fact with myth in an entertaining novel set around the building of the Convent of Mafra and the construction of the world's first flying machine.

Antonio Tabucchi *Declares Pereira*, *Requiem: A Hallucination* and *Fernando Pessoa* (with Maria José de Lancastre). Tabucchi is a highly regarded Italian author and biographer of Pessoa, who lived in Portugal for many years. In *Declares Pereira* he has re-created the repressive atmosphere of Salazar's Lisbon, tracing the experiences of a newspaper editor who questions his own lifestyle under a regime which he can no longer ignore. The book has recently been made into a film by Roberto Faenza. *Requiem: A Hallucination* is an imaginative and dreamlike journey around Lisbon. The unifying theme is food and drink, and the book even contains a note on recipes at the end.

Miguel Torga *The Creation of the World* and *Tales from the Mountain*. Twice nominated for the Nobel Prize before his death in 1995, Torga lived and set his stories in the wild Trás-os-Montes region. His pseudonym "Torga" is a tough species of heather which thrives in this rural, unforgiving landscape, where the fiercely independent characters of his books battle to survive in a repressed society. Torga's harsh views of rural life in *Tales from the Mountain* led to the book being banned under the Salazar regime.

Gil Vicente *Three Discovery Plays:*

Auto da Barca do Inferno, Exortação da Guerra, Auto da Índia. Three plays from the 16th-century scribe whom some consider the Portuguese equivalent of Shakespeare, with the original archaic Portuguese versions alongside English translations, and copious notes.

⭐ **Robert Wilson** *A Small Death in Lisbon.* A policeman attempts to find the murderer of a girl found dumped near a beach on the train line to Cascais, opening up a can of worms stretching back to the last World War. The novel presents an evocative account of the seedier side of contemporary Lisbon, though its potted summary of the last War is less convincing. A gripping page-turner from a British author who lives in Portugal.

Richard Zimler *The Last Kabbalist of Lisbon.* Kabbala is a magical art based on an esoteric interpretation of the Old Testament. American author Zimler, now a resident of Porto, writes an intense and compelling story of a Jewish kabbalist attempting to discover the mystery behind his uncle's murder during the massacre of New Christians in Lisbon in 1506. Based on historical fact, the story has been a bestseller in Portugal, Italy and Brazil.

Poetry

⭐ **Luís de Camões** ⊞ *The Lusiads* and *Epic and Lyric. The Lusiads* is Portugal's great national epic. Modelled on Virgil's *Aeneid*, it celebrates the ten-month voyage of Vasco da Gama which opened the sea route to India. The Oxford Classics is a good verse translation by Landeg White. *Epic and Lyric* includes extracts from *The Lusiads* together with other shorter poems.

Sophia de Mello *Breyner Log Book: Selected Poems.* Evocative selection of translated poems from one of the country's foremost writers, winner of the 1999 Prémio Camões.

Fernando Pessoa ⊞ *Pessoa: Selected Poems.* Pessoa wrote his poetry under several different identities, which he called heteronyms. Those wanting a brief introduction to the range of his different "voices" are well served by Jonathan Griffin's elegant translations of four of them. *A Centenary Pessoa* This superlative anthology of poems, prose, letters and photographs is the most comprehensive selection of Pessoa's output yet published in English. *Fernando Pessoa*, available only in Portugal (Hazan, Portugal), is a revealing collection of documents and photographs of the author at work, with an introduction by Antonio Tabucchi.

Pedro Tamen *Honey and Poison: Selected Poems.* Lisbon law graduate Tamen is regarded as one of Portugal's leading contemporary poets; his poems of passion capture the distinctive sights and emotions of a country which has moved from dictatorship to democracy during his lifetime.

Food and wine

Rainer Horbelt and Sonja Spindler *Algarve Country Cooking* (Vista Ibérica, Portugal). A series of regional recipes based round local anecdotes and the four seasons; well translated from German and a charming insight into rural Algarve traditions.

Alex Liddell and Janet Price *Port Wine Quintas of the Douro* (o/p) Highly erudite account of the wines and history; superb photos put it beyond specialist interest.

Maite Manjon *Gastronomy of Spain and Portugal.* A comprehensive collection of classic Iberian recipes, including a glossary of Portuguese and Spanish terms and explanations of traditional cooking techniques. Particularly good on regional specialities and wines, too.

Richard Mayson *The Wines and Vineyards of Portugal.* A wide ranging account of all you need to know about Portuguese wines by a leading expert in the field.

 Edite Vieira *The Taste of Portugal* A delight to read, let alone cook from. Vieira combines snippets of history and passages from Portuguese writers (very well translated) to illustrate her dishes; highly recommended.

Wine Routes – Portugal (Publicações Dom Quixote, Portugal). Spiral-bound booklet produced by the Portuguese tourist board detailing touring routes round Portugal's various wine-growing areas. Details on individual places are sketchy, but it is attractively illustrated with excellent background information on wines, grape varieties and the wine lodges themselves.

Guides

Brian and Eileen Anderson *Landscapes of Portugal* (Sunflower Books online only; ®www .sunflowerbooks.co.uk). Regional books with maps and small photos detailing walks – covering the Algarve and Lisbon areas; there are also car tours and some practical information.

Bethan Davies and Ben Cole *Walking in Portugal.* Dependable guide to trekking in the national parks of Gerês, Serra da Estrela, Montesinho and Serra de São Mamede. An excellent supplement to our own coverage by the same authors.

Oleg Polunin and B.E. Smythies *Flowers of South-West Europe: A Field Guide.* The best available guide to the Portuguese flora.

Laurence Rose *Where to Watch Birds in Spain and Portugal.*

Comprehensive guide to some of Europe's finest and most environmentally sensitive wildlife sites, with practical information on how to get there and when to go. Interesting reading for amateurs as well as being invaluable for ardent ornithologists.

Stuart Ross *Portugal's Pousada Route* (Vista Ibérica Publicações, Portugal; Seven Hill, US, o/p). An informative book containing details about Portugal's state-owned hotels and some background history on the surrounding countryside, with photos by Marion Kaplan.

John Russell and Nuno Campos *Golf's Golden Coast* (Vista Ibérica Publicações, Portugal). An attractive, illustrated guide for anyone interested in the Algarve's clubs – of the 18-hole variety.

Residence

Jonathan Packer *Live and Work in Spain and Portugal.* Invaluable handbook packed with details on permits, business, teaching, health, schools, renting and buying property, etc. Only downside is a heavy slant towards English ex-pats.

Sue Tyson-Ward *How to Live and Work in Portugal.* Another detailed and practical guide on all aspects of living in the country, including info on how to start a business, open a bank account, find out about schools and, of course, track down ex-pat activities.

language

language

Language

If you have some knowledge of Spanish and/or French you won't have much problem reading Portuguese. Understanding it when it's spoken, though, is another matter: pronunciation is entirely different and at first even the easiest words are hard to distinguish – the sound is more like that of an East European language than of the Romance tongues in which it has its roots. If you're stuck, most people will understand Spanish (albeit reluctantly) and in the cities and tourist areas French and English are also widely spoken. Even so, it's well worth the effort to master at least the rudiments; once you've started to figure out the words it gets a lot easier very quickly.

The pronunciation guide below and the words on pp.612–613 will equip you with the basics. For more detail, check out the *Rough Guide Portuguese Phrasebook*, set out dictionary-style for easy access, with English–Portuguese and Portuguese–English sections, cultural tips for tricky situations and a handy menu reader.

Pronunciation

The chief difficulty with **pronunciation** is its lack of clarity – consonants tend to be slurred, vowels nasal and often ignored altogether.

Consonants

The **consonants** are, at least, consistent:

C is soft before E and I, hard otherwise unless it has a cedilla – açucar (sugar) is pronounced "assookar".

CH is somewhat softer than in English; chá (tea) sounds like Shah.

J is pronounced like the "s" in pleasure, as is **G** except when it comes before a "hard" vowel (A, O and U).

LH sounds like "lyuh" (Batalha).

Q is always pronounced as a "k".

S before a consonant or at the end of a word becomes "sh", otherwise it's as in English – Cascais is pronounced "Kashkaish", Sagres is "Sahgresh".

X is also pronounced "sh"– caixa (cash desk) is pronounced "kaisha".

Vowels

Vowels are worse – flat and truncated, they're often difficult for English-speaking tongues to get around. The only way to learn is to listen: accents, ã, ô or é turn them into longer, more familiar sounds.

When two vowels come together they continue to be enunciated separately except in the case of **EI** and **OU** – which sound like a and long o respectively.

E at the end of a word is silent unless it has an accent, so that carne (meat) is pronounced "karn", while café sounds much as you'd expect.

The tilde over **Ã** or **Õ** renders the pronunciation much like the French -an and -on endings only more nasal.

More common is **ÃO** (as in pão, bread – são, saint – limão, lemon), which sounds something like a strangled yelp of "Ow!" cut off in midstream.

A few key words

Even if you speak no Portuguese at all there are a **few key words** which can help you out in an enormous number of situations.

Há (the H is silent) means "there is" or "is there?" and can be used for just about anything. Thus: Há uma pensão aqui? (Is there a pension here?), Há uma camioneta para…? (Is there a bus to…?), or even Há um quarto? (Do you have a room?).

More polite and better in shops or restaurants are **Tem…?** (Do you have…?) or Queria… (I'd like…).

And of course there are the old standards **Fala Inglês?** (Do you speak English?) and **Não compreendo** (I don't understand).

Portuguese words and phrases

Basics

sim; não – yes; no
olá; bom dia – hello; good morning
boa tarde/noite – good afternoon/night
adeus, até logo – goodbye, see you later
hoje; amanhã – today; tomorrow
por favor/se faz favor – please
tudo bem? – Everything all right?
está bem – it's all right/OK
obrigado/a* – thank you
onde; que – where; what
quando; porquê – when; why
como; quanto – how; how much
não sei – I don't know
sabe . . .? – do you know . . .?
pode . . .? – could you . . .?
desculpe; com licença – sorry; excuse me
aqui; ali – here; there
perto; longe – near; far
este/a; esse/a – this; that
agora; mais tarde – now; later
mais; menos – more; less
grande; pequeno – big; little

aberto; fechado – open; closed
senhoras; homens – women; men
lavabo/quarto de banho – toilet/bathroom
banco; câmbio – bank; change
correios – post office
(dois) selos – (two) stamps
O que é isso? – What's that?
Quanto é? – How much is it?
sou Inglês/Inglesa – I am English
Americano/a – American
Irlandês/Irlandesa – Irish
Australiano/a – Australian
Canadiano/a – Canadian
Escocês/Escosesa – Scottish
Galês/Galesa – Welsh
Como se chama? – What's your name?
(chamo-me . . .) – (my name is . . .)
Como se diz isto em Português? – What's this called in Portuguese?

* Obrigado agrees with the sex of the person speaking – a woman says obrigada, a man obrigado.

Getting around

Para ir a . . .? – How do I get to . . .?
esquerda, direita, – left, right,
sempre em frente – straight ahead
Onde é a estação de camionetas? – Where is the bus station?
a paragem de autocarro para... – the bus stop for...
a estação de comboios – the railway station
Donde parte o autocarro para . . .? – Where does the bus to . . . leave from?
É este o comboio para Coimbra? – Is this the train for Coimbra?

A que horas parte? – What time does it leave?
(chega a . . .?) – (arrive at . . .?)
bilhete (para) – ticket (to)
ida e volta – round trip
Qual é a estrada para. . .? – Which is the road to . . .?
Para onde vai? – Where are you going?
Vou a.. – I'm going to...
Está bem, muito – That's great,
obrigado/a – thanks a lot
Pare aqui por favor – Stop here please

Accommodation

Há uma pensão aqui perto? - Is there a pension near here?
Queria um quarto - I'd like a room
É para uma noite (semana) - It's for one night (week)
É para uma pessoa - It's for one person (duas pessoas) - (two people)
Posso ver? - May I see/look around?
Está bem, fico com ele - OK, I'll take it
Quanto custa? - How much is it?

É caro, não o quero - It's expensive, I don't want it
Posso/podemos deixar os sacos aqui até . . ? - Can I/we leave the bags here until . . ?
Há um quarto mais barato?- Is there a cheaper room?
Com duche - With a shower
(quente/frio) - (hot/cold)
Pode-se acampar aqui? - Can we camp here?
chave - key

Days and months

domingo - Sunday
segunda-feira - Monday
terça-feira - Tuesday
quarta-feira - Wednesday
quinta-feira - Thursday
sexta-feira - Friday
sábado - Saturday
janeiro - January
fevereiro - February
março - March

abril - April
maio - May
junho - June
julho - July
agosto - August
setembro - September
outubro - October
novembro - November
dezembro - December

The time

Que horas são? - What time is it?
é/são . . . - it's . . .
A que horas? - (At) what time?
à/às . . . - at . . .
meia-noite - midnight
uma da manhã - one in the morning (1am)
uma e dez - ten past one
uma e quinze - quarter past one
uma e vinte - twenty past one
uma e meia - half past one
quinze para as duas - quarter to two

dez para as duas - ten to two
meio-dia - midday, noon
uma da tarde - one in the afternoon (1pm)
sete da tarde - seven in the evening (dezanove) - (7pm)
nove e meia da noite (vinte e uma e trinta) - half past nine (pm)
meio-dia e quinze - quarter past noon
meia-noite - midnight
meia-noite e dez - ten past midnight

Numbers

1 - um	13 - treze	60 - sessenta
2 - dois	14 - catorze	70 - setenta
3 - três	15 - quinze	80 - oitenta
4 - quatro	16 - dezasseis	90 - noventa
5 - cinco	17 - dezassete	100 - cem
6 - seis	18 - dezoito	101 - cento e um
7 - sete	19 - dezanove	200 - duzentos
8 - oito	20 - vinte	500 - quinhentos
9 - nove	21 - vinte e um	1000 - mil
10 - dez	30 - trinta	2000 - dois mil
11 - onze	40 - quarenta	
12 - doze	50 - cinquenta	

Food glossary

Basics

Arroz – Rice
Azeitonas – Olives
Manteiga – Butter
Ovos – Eggs
Pão – Bread

Pimenta – Pepper
Piri-piri – Chilli sauce
Queijo – Cheese
Sal – Salt
Salada – Salad

Soups (Sopas)

Caldo verde – Cabbage/potato broth
Canja de galinha – Chicken broth with rice and boiled egg yolks
Gaspacho – Chilled vegetable soup
Sopa à alentejana – Garlic/bread soup with poached egg on top

Sopa de feijão verde – Green bean soup
Sopa de grão – Chickpea soup
Sopa de legumes – Vegetable soup
Sopa de marisco – Shellfish soup
Sopa de peixe – Fish soup

Fish (peixe) and shellfish (mariscos)

Ameijoas – Clams
Anchovas – Anchovies
Atum – Tuna
Besugo – Sunfish
Camarões – Shrimp
Caranguejo – Crab
Carapau – Mackerel
Cherne – Sea bream
Chocos – Cuttlefish
Corvina – Meagre
Dourada – Bream
Enguia – Eel
Espada – Scabbard fish (a long, thin fish, black or white in colour)
Espadarte – Swordfish
Gambas – Prawns
Garoupa – (Like) bream
Lagosta – Lobster
Lagostim – Giant prawns
Lampreia – Lamprey (similar to eel)

Linguado – Sole
Lulas – Squid
Mexilhões – Mussels
Ostras – Oysters
Pargo – Snapper
Peixe Gale – John Dory
Perceves – Goose barnacles
Pescada – Hake
Polvo – Octopus
Robalo – Sea bass
Salmão – Salmon
Salmonete – Red mullet
Santolas – Spider crabs
Sapateiras – Common crabs
Sarda – Mackerel
Sardinhas – Sardines
Tamboril – Monkfish
Truta – Trout
Vieiras – Scallops

Meat (carne), poultry (aves) and game (caça)

Almondegas – Meatballs
Borrego – Lamb
Cabrito – Kid
Carne de porco – Pork
Carneiro – Mutton
Coelho – Rabbit
Cordoniz – Quail
Costeleta – Chop
Dobrada – Tripe
Fiambre – Boiled ham

Fígado – Liver
Frango – Young chicken
Lombo – Loin of pork
Pato – Duck
Perdiz – Partridge
Perú – Turkey
Presunto – Smoked ham
Salsicha – Sausage
Tripas – Tripe
Vitela – Veal

Vegetables (legumes) and salad (salads)

Alcachofra – Artichoke
Alface – Lettuce
Alho – Garlic
Batatas – Potatoes
Batatas fritas – French fries
Cebola – Onion
Cenoura – Carrot
Cogumelos – Mushrooms
Ervilhas – Peas

Espargos – Asparagus
Espinafre – Spinach
Favas – Broad beans
Feijão – Beans
Grão – Chickpeas
Pepino – Cucumber
Pimenta – Pepper
Salada – Salad

Fruit (fruta)

Ameixas – Plums
Ananás – Pineapple
Cerejas – Cherries
Figos – Figs
Laranja – Orange
Limão – Lemon

Maçã – Apple
Melão – Melon
Morangos – Strawberries
Pêra – Pear
Pêssego – Peach
Uvas – Grapes

In a restaurant

Acepipes – Hors d'oeuvres
Pequeno almoço – Breakfast
Almoço – Lunch
Jantar – Dinner
Mesa – Table
Ementa – Menu

Copo – Glass
Garrafa – Bottle
Faca – Knife
Garfo – Fork
Colher – Spoon
Conta – Bill

Some cooking terms

Assado/no espeto – Roasted/spit-roasted
Cozido – Boiled/stewed
Ensopado de… – Soup or stew of…
Estrelado – Fried
Frito – Fried
Fumado – Smoked
Grelhado – Grilled

Guisado – Stew
Mexido – Scrambled
Molho – Sauce
Na brasa – Charcoal-grilled
No forno – Baked
Piri-piri – With chilli sauce
Salteado – Sautéed

Specialities

Açorda (de marisco) (cooked with shellfish and spices) – Bread-based stew
Arroz de marisco – Seafood paella
Bacalhau – There are reputedly 365 ways of cooking dried salt cod, including *com batatas e grão* (with boiled potatoes and chickpeas), *à brás* (with egg, onions and potatoes), *na brasa* (roasted with sliced potatoes), *à Gomes de Sá* (sliced, with boiled eggs and potatoes), and *à minhota* (with fried potatoes)
Bife à Portuguesa – Beef steak, topped with mustard sauce and a fried egg
Caldeirada – Fish stew, with a base of onions, tomatoes and potatoes
Cataplana – Shellfish or fish cooked with strips of ham, pepper and onion
Chanfana – Casserole of lamb or kid
Cozido à portuguesa – Boiled casserole of chicken, lamb, pork, beef, sausages, offal and beans, served with rice and vegetables
Espetada mista – Mixed meat kebab
Frango no churrasco – Barbecued chicken, nearly always superb; eat with the piri-piri (chilli) sauce provided
Leitão assado – Roast suckling pig
Porco à alentejana – Pork cooked with clams, an oily and salty dish from the Alentejo
Tripas à moda do Porto – Tripe stewed with beans and vegetables

Glossary

Architectural, historical and religious terms

Afonsino Relating to the reign of Dom Afonso Henriques, first king of Portugal.

Anta Prehistoric megalith tomb.

Azulejo Glazed, painted tile (see p.90).

Capela Chapel; *capela-mor* is a chancel or sanctuary.

Capela dos ossos Ossuary.

Citânia Prehistoric/Celtic hill settlement.

Claustro Cloister.

Convento Convent, though just as often an old church.

Coro Central, often enclosed, part of church built for the choir.

Dom, dona Courtesy titles (sir, madam) usually applied to kings and queens. When used in common speech, it precedes the first name of the person referred to (e.g. Dona Maria).

Ermida Remote chapel – not necessarily a hermitage.

Fortaleza Fort.

Igreja Church; *igreja matriz* is a parish church.

Infanta Princess.

Infante Prince.

Manuelino Flamboyant, marine-influenced style of late Gothic architecture developed in the reign of Manuel I (1495–1521).

Moçárabe Moorish-Arabic (usually of architecture or a design).

Mosteiro Monastery, or just as often an old church since most orders were suppressed in 1834–38.

Mudéjar Moorish-style architecture and decoration.

Nossa senhora (n.s.) Our Lady – the Virgin Mary.

Retábulo Altarpiece – usually large, carved and heavily gilt.

Sala do capítulo Chapterhouse.

Sé Cathedral.

Torre de menagem Keep of a castle.

General vocabulary and terms

Adega Wine cellar or winery, often also a wine bar or restaurant where wine is served straight from the barrel.

Alameda Promenade.

Albergaria Upmarket inn.

Albufeira Reservoir or lagoon.

Aldeia Small village or hamlet.

Artesanato Handicraft shop.

Bairro Quarter, area (of a town); *alto* is upper, *baixo* lower.

Baixa Low; used to mean commercial/shopping centre of town.

Barragem Dam.

Cachoeira Waterfall.

Caldas Mineral springs or spa complex.

Câmara municipal Town hall.

Campo Square or field.

Casa abrigo Open house; a hut or shelter in natural and national parks for hikers and park staff (free); also "abandoned house" usually a farmhouse for rent.

Casa de pasto Cheap and simple place to eat.

Castelo Castle.

Centro comercial Shopping centre.

Chafariz Public fountain.

Churrasqueira (spelt variously) Grill house, usually serving chicken.

Cidade City.

Correios Post office, abbreviated CTT.

Cruzeiro Cross.

Dormida Room in a private house.

Eléctrico Tramcar.

Elevador Elevator or funicular railway.

Espigueiro Grain shed on stilts, common in the north.

Esplanada Seafront promenade.

Estação Station.

Estalagem One step up from an *albergaria*, usually in rural towns, formerly a coaching inn.

Estrada Road; Estrada Nacional is a main road, designated EN on maps.

Farmácia Pharmacy.

Feira Fair or market.

Festa Festival or carnival.

Fonte Fountain or spring.

Freguesia Parish (*Junta da Freguesia* is the local council).

Grutas Caves.

Horário Timetable.

Hospedaria Cheap and basic pension, usually with shared facilities (same as *casa de hóspedes*).

Ilha Island.

Jardim Garden.

Lago Lake.

Largo Square.

Mercado Market.

Miradouro Belvedere or viewpoint.

Paço Palace or country house.

Paços do concelho Town hall.

Palácio Palace or country house; *palácio real*, royal palace.

Paragem Bus stop.

Parque Park.

Parque de campismo Camping site.

Parque nacional/natural National/Natural Park or Reserve.

Pastelaria Bakery, pastry shop.

Pelourinho Stone pillory, seen in almost every northern village.

Poço Well.

Pombal Pigeon house.

Ponte Bridge.

Pousada Luxury state-run hotel, sometimes converted from a castle or monastery.

Pousada de juventude Youth hostel.

Praça Square.

Praça de touros Bullring.

Praia Beach.

Quinta Country estate, farm or villa.

Ria Narrow, open-ended lagoon where sand bars block a river's mouth.

Ribeiro Stream.

Rio River.

Romaria Pilgrimage-festival.

Sé Cathedral.

Senhor Man, Sir, or Mr.

Senhora Woman, Madam, Ms or Mrs.

Serra Mountain or mountain range.

Solar Manor house or important town mansion.

Solares de Portugal (formerly *Turismo de Habitação*). A number of organizations use this term to market accommodation in buildings, often of historical or architectural importance (see p.33).

Tasca No-frills local bar.

Termas Thermal springs or spa complex.

Tourada Bullfight.

Vila Town.

Index

and small print

Index

Map entries are in colour

E

D

INDEX

I

INDEX

627

INDEX

Twenty Years of Rough Guides

In the summer of 1981, Mark Ellingham, Rough Guides' founder, knocked out the first guide on a typewriter, with a group of friends. Mark had been travelling in Greece after university, and couldn't find a guidebook that really answered his needs.There were heavyweight cultural guides on the one hand – good on museums and classical sites but not on beaches and tavernas – and on the other hand student manuals that were so caught up with how to save money that they lost sight of the country's significance beyond its role as a place for a cool vacation. None of the guides began to address Greece as a country, with its natural and human environment, its politics and its contemporary life.

Having no urgent reason to return home, Mark decided to write his own guide. It was a guide to Greece that tried to combine some erudition and insight with a thoroughly practical approach to travellers' needs. Scrupulously researched listings of places to stay, eat and drink were matched by careful attention to detail on everything from Homer to Greek music, from classical sites to national parks and from nude beaches to monasteries. Back in London, Mark and his friends got their Rough Guide accepted by a farsighted commissioning editor at the publisher Routledge and it came out in 1982.

The Rough Guide to Greece was a student scheme that became a publishing phenomenon. The immediate success of the book – shortlisted for the Thomas Cook award – spawned a series that rapidly covered dozens of countries. The Rough Guides found a ready market among backpackers and budget travellers, but soon acquired a much broader readership that included older and less impecunious visitors. Readers relished the guides' wit and inquisitiveness as much as the enthusiastic, critical approach that acknowledges everyone wants value for money – but not at any price.

Rough Guides soon began supplementing the "rougher" information – the hostel and low-budget listings – with the kind of detail that independent-minded travellers on any budget might expect. These days, the guides – distributed worldwide by the Penguin group – include recommendations spanning the range from shoestring to luxury, and cover more than 200 destinations around the globe. Our growing team of authors, many of whom come to Rough Guides initially as outstandingly good letter-writers telling us about their travels, are spread all over the world, particularly in Europe, the USA and Australia. As well as the travel guides, Rough Guides publishes a series of dictionary phrasebooks covering two dozen major languages, an acclaimed series of music guides running the gamut from Classical to World Music, a series of music CDs in association with World Music Network, and a range of reference books on topics as diverse as the Internet, Pregnancy and Unexplained Phenomena. Visit **www.roughguides.com** to see what's cooking.

Rough Guide credits

Text editor: Lucy Ratcliffe
Series editor: Mark Ellingham
Editorial: Martin Dunford, Jonathan Buckley,
Kate Berens, Ann-Marie Shaw, Helena Smith,
Olivia Swift, Ruth Blackmore, Geoff Howard,
Claire Saunders, Gavin Thomas, Alexander
Mark Rogers, Polly Thomas, Joe Staines,
Richard Lim, Duncan Clark, Peter Buckley,
Clifton Wilkinson, Alison Murchie, Matthew
Teller, Andrew Dickson, Fran Sandham (UK);
Andrew Rosenberg, Stephen Timblin, Yuki
Takagaki, Richard Koss, Hunter Slaton, Julie
Feiner (US)
Production: Susanne Hillen, Andy Hilliard,
Link Hall, Helen Prior, Julia Bovis, Michelle
Draycott, Katie Pringle, Zoë Nobes, Rachel
Holmes, Andy Turner

Cartography: Melissa Baker, Maxine Repath,
Ed Wright, Katie Lloyd-Jones
Cover art direction: Louise Boulton
Picture research: Sharon Martins,
Mark Thomas
Online: Kelly Cross, Anja Mutic-Blessing,
Jennifer Gold, Audra Epstein,
Suzanne Welles, Cree Lawson (US)
Finance: John Fisher, Gary Singh,
Edward Downey, Mark Hall, Tim Bill
Marketing & Publicity: Richard Trillo, Niki
Smith, David Wearn, Chloë Roberts, Demelza
Dallow, Claire Southern (UK); Simon Carloss,
David Wechsler, Megan Kennedy (US)
Administration: Tania Hummel, Julie
Sanderson

Publishing information

This tenth edition published November 2002
by **Rough Guides Ltd**,
62–70 Shorts Gardens, London WC2H 9AH.
Penguin Putnam, Inc. 375 Hudson Street,
NY 10014, USA.
Distributed by the Penguin Group
Penguin Books Ltd,
80 Strand, London WC2R ORL
Penguin Putnam, Inc.
375 Hudson Street, NY 10014, USA
Penguin Books Australia Ltd,
487 Maroondah Highway, PO Box 257,
Ringwood, Victoria 3134, Australia
Penguin Books Canada Ltd,
10 Alcorn Avenue, Toronto, Ontario,
Canada M4V 1E4
Penguin Books (NZ) Ltd,
182–190 Wairau Road, Auckland 10,
New Zealand
Typeset in Bembo and Helvetica to an
original design by Henry Iles.

Printed in Italy by LegoPrint S.p.A

© Mark Ellingham, John Fisher & Graham
Kenyon 2002

No part of this book may be reproduced in
any form without permission from the
publisher except for the quotation of brief
passages in reviews.

664pp includes index
A catalogue record for this book is available
from the British Library

ISBN 1-85828-877-0

The publishers and authors have done their
best to ensure the accuracy and currency of
all the information in **The Rough Guide to
Portugal**, however, they can accept no
responsibility for any loss, injury, or
inconvenience sustained by any traveller as a
result of information or advice contained in
the guide.

Help us update

We've gone to a lot of effort to ensure that
the tenth edition of **The Rough Guide to
Portugal** is accurate and up to date.
However, things change – places get
"discovered", opening hours are notoriously
fickle, restaurants and rooms raise prices or
lower standards. If you feel we've got it
wrong or left something out, we'd like to
know, and if you can remember the address,
the price, the time, the phone number, so
much the better.
We'll credit all contributions, and send a
copy of the next edition (or any other Rough

Guide if you prefer) for the best letters.
Everyone who writes to us and isn't already a
subscriber will receive a copy of our full-
colour thrice-yearly newsletter. Please mark
letters: "**Rough Guide Portugal Update**"
and send to: Rough Guides, 62–70 Shorts
Gardens, London WC2H 9AH, or Rough
Guides, 4th Floor, 345 Hudson St, New York,
NY 10014. Or send an email to
mail@roughguides.com
Have your questions answered and tell
others about your trip at
www.roughguides.atinfopop.com

Acknowledgements

Matthew Hancock would like to thank Vitor Carriço, João Lima, Teresa Ventura and everyone at ICEP; Bob Taylor for Lisbon nightlife; Amanda Tomlin for basics; Amanda (again), Alex and Olivia for at-home support; Saphire Flash for insights into the gay scene; Luke and Paula for their usual invaluable assistance; Heritage Hotels, Hotel Dom Carlos, Lawrence's Hotel, Enatur and The Ocean Club in Luz; Daniel Albano at TAP; the superb Go magazine team; and everyone involved at Rough Guides, especially Lucy for her patient and diligent editing.

Francisca Kellett thanks Artur Jorge from the Aveiro tourist office, Marly Monteiro and her team from the Coimbra tourist office, Carla Basilio from the Serra da Estrela tourist office and Patricia Pereira from the Portugal tourist office for their invaluable help.

Josephine Quintero would like to thank Elisa Teixeira for her invaluable insight into the more sensitive aspects of Portuguese culture and lifestyle, and Kevin Hawthorn for providing equally enlightening guidance and expertise, as well as a spare bed.

Paul Smith: Thank you to my family for supporting my ambition to become a professional wastrel, Annabela Pereira in Bragança and Luis Luis in Foz Coa for going well beyond the call of duty to help, Lucy Ratcliffe for unending patience and the old man in the bar in Braga who convinced me that I too could be European.

The authors would like to thank Joe Staines for the boxes on p.80 and p.190, Rachel Holmes for typesetting, Stratigraphics for maps, Sharon Martins and Mark Thomas for picture research and Susannah Wight for proofreading.

Readers' letters

Thanks to all the readers who took the time to write in with their comments and suggestions (and apologies to anyone whose name we've misspelt or omitted):

Jackie Aitkan, Isabel Alarcão, Geraldine and Zahir Anwar, Martha d'Avila and Jim Burton, Natalie Awbery, Ooliele Ayral, Professor Paul Bardos, Bob Barnes, Anne Bartlett, Victoria Bennett, Ernst Boermans Joanna Bogumsky, Janet Borch, Ian Bouncer, W.D. Brookes, Vanessa and Shaylan Buckhart, Philippa Canton, Kiki de Carvalho, Dave Curry, Jo Dale, Kees van Draanen, Tom Eagleton, Joy and Gordon Ewen, Jonathan Mark Ezart, Sónia Fellner, A Ferreira, Stavros Fotiadis, Niels Fold, Stavros Fotiadis, Peter Gaukroger, Celia Gleeson, Mr and Mrs Gornall, S.I. Graham, Julie and Jon Green, Philip and Judy Greenword, Paul and Daniela Hagger, Vanessa Halley, Sally and Colin Hawgood, Alison and Yuri Higgins, Patrick Horan, Terence Horan, Dave Hudson, D.J. Humphrey, Rebecca Marina Illing, Sue and Alan Jackson, Keith Jay, Pete Johnson, B.D. Jones, Richard Kaplan, Ravi Kapur, M. Ladhu, John Landau, Anna Lass, Edgar Locke, Mark Long, Rieke Marien, Emma Martin, Rosemary Martin, Sue Massey, Normal Mazèl, Paula McGinley, Julia McMillan, Marius Møllersen, Rosemary Morlin, Victoria Ortiz, Carol Pardy, Joan and Des Paton, Primrose Peacock, A.E. Pegg, Anthony Pennick, S.A. Pickett, Anna Pinder, Fernando Maia Pinto, Guy and Christine Pooley, Elly Prijs, Kees Punt, Ian Ray, Chris and Janet Ridley, Lucia Rimondini, Sally and Mark Robinson, Barbara Rowlands, Jennie and Donald Rowlands, Jim Rose, B. Alex Sanders, Peter Saunders, Penelope Senior, P.L. Tan, Steve Teers, Emma Thomas, Faith and Malcolm Thomas, Charles Thuaire, Paul Tisserant, Chris Walker, Isabel Walker and David Hoare, N.C. Walker, Mark Wild, Robin Wilkinson, Steve and Linnus Williams, Vimal Williams, B.S. Wood, Jacqui Wren-Hilton, and Richard and Lisa Young.

Photo Credits

Grilled sardines © Michael Jenner
Tavira © Matthew Hancock
Stone carving in Batalha Abbey © Robert Frerck/Robert Harding
Praia de Faro © Michael Jenner
Chicken piri-piri © Simon Reddy/Travel Ink
Café, Lisbon © Paul Miles/AXIOM
Barcelos market © Louise Boulton
Spanish lynx © Ardea
Cork trees and wild flowers © Jeremy Phillips/Travel Ink

Things Not To Miss

1. View to Ribeira from Vila Nova de Gaia, Porto © Peter Wilson
2. Lagos © Peter Wilson
3. Grape harvest © Robert Harding
4. Bom Jesus do Monte © Peter Wilson
5. Fatima © Peter M. Wilson/AXIOM
6. Overview, Obidos © Jeremy Phillips/Travel Ink
7. Bacalhau shop © Peter Wilson
8. View along Douro river valley © Andrew Watson/Travel Ink
9. Gulbenkian museum, Lisbon © Peter Wilson
10. Pousadas, Palmela © Matthew Hancock
11. Barcelona v. Porto © Matthew Ashton/EMPICS Sports Photo Agency
12. Mosaics, Conimbriga © Peter Wilson
13. Tram #28, Lisbon; © Chris North/Travel Ink
14. Basilica interior, Mafra Convent © Robert Harding
15. Monsanto © Peter Wilson
16. Serra da Estrela © F. Kellett
17. Temple of Diana, Évora © Peter Wilson
18. Palacio Nacional de Pena, Sintra © Jeremy Richards/Travel Ink
19. Citania de Briteiros © Nik Wheeler/CORBIS
20. Pastéis de Belém; © Jenny Acheson/AXIOM
21. Cascais © Peter Wilson
22. Alfama, Lisbon © Peter Wilson
23. Fundaçao de Serralves, Porto © Hans Georg Roth/CORBIS
24. Algarve's sandspit beaches © Matthew Hancock
25. Corgo train line © Tony Arruza/CORBIS
26. Senhor Antonio's, Bairro Alto © Peter Wilson

27. Festa de Santo António © Peter Wilson
28. Surfer © Adam Woolfitt/CORBIS
29. Tomb of Dona Inês de Castro, Alcobaça © Peter Wilson
30. Feira de Barcelos © Matthew Hancock
31. Coimbra students © Peter Wilson
32. Convento de Cristo, Tomar © Graham Lawrence/Robert Harding
33. Monsaraz © Peter Wilson
34. Parque Natural de Montesinho © Matthew Hancock
35. Church facade, Rua Santa Catarina, Porto © Peter Wilson
36. Pinhal de Leiria © Matthew Hancock
37. Mariza © Eduardo Mota
38. Festa de São João © Peter Wilson
39. Vilharinho, Parque Nacional da Peneda-Gerês © Jeremy Phillips/Travel Ink
40. Dolphins in Sado Estuary © Pedro Narra

Black and white images

Torre de Belem © Peter Wilson (p.56)
Balconies, Rua dos Bacalhoeiros © Peter Wilson (p.087)
Igreja de Jesus, Setúbal © Peter Wilson (p.147)
Nazare © Josephine Quintero (p.154)
Cloisters, Convento de Cristo Tomar © Peter Wilson (p.191)
Bacalhau shop © Peter Wilson (p.206)
Moliceiro boat, Aveiro © Peter Wilson (p.237)
Granite house, Monsanto © Matthew Hancock (p.248)
Sortelha © F. Kellett (p.275)
Old Port © Josephine Quintero (p.284)
Barcos rabelos © Peter Wilson (p.335)
Ponte de Lima © Duncan Maxwell/Robert Harding (p.350)
Barcelos market © Peter Wilson (p.375)
Espigueiro © Peter Wilson (p.407)
Bragança citadel, Trás-os-Montes © Matthew Hancock (p.420)
Harvest inspection, Douro valley © Peter Wilson (p.429)
Azulejos, Estremoz train station © Alex Eon-Duval/Travel Ink (p.460)
Pillory, Elvas © Peter Wilson (p.481)
Tavira © Peter Wilson (p.508)
Central Algarve cove beach © Tom Teegan/Robert Harding (p.539)

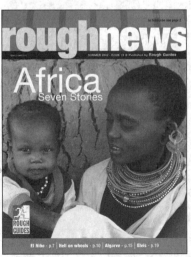

Music

Acoustic Guitar
Blues: 100 Essential CDs
Cello
Clarinet
Classical Music
Classical Music: 100 Essential CDs
Country Music
Country: 100 Essential CDs
Cuban Music
Drum'n'bass
Drums
Electric Guitar & Bass Guitar
Flute
Hip-Hop
House
Irish Music
Jazz
Jazz: 100 Essential CDs
Keyboards & Digital Piano
Latin: 100 Essential CDs
Music USA: a Coast-To-Coast Tour
Opera
Opera: 100 Essential CDs
Piano
Reading Music
Reggae
Reggae: 100 Essential CDs
Rock
Rock: 100 Essential CDs
Saxophone
Soul: 100 Essential CDs
Techno
Trumpet & Trombone
Violin & Viola
World Music: 100 Essential CDs

World Music Vol1
World Music Vol2

Reference

Children's Books, 0–5
Children's Books, 5–11
China Chronicle
Cult Movies
Cult TV
Elvis
England Chronicle
France Chronicle
India Chronicle
The Internet
Internet Radio
James Bond
Liverpool FC
Man Utd
Money Online
Personal Computers
Pregnancy & Birth
Shopping Online
Travel Health
Travel Online
Unexplained Phenomena
Videogaming
Weather
Website Directory
Women Travel

Music CDs

Africa
Afrocuba
Afro-Peru
Ali Hussan Kuban
The Alps
Americana
The Andes
The Appalachians
Arabesque
Asian Underground
Australian Aboriginal Music
Bellydance
Bhangra
Bluegrass

Bollywood
Boogaloo
Brazil
Cajun
Cajun and Zydeco
Calypso and Soca
Cape Verde
Central America
Classic Jazz
Congolese Soukous
Cuba
Cuban Music Story
Cuban Son
Cumbia
Delta Blues
Eastern Europe
English Roots Music
Flamenco
Franco
Gospel
Global Dance
Greece
The Gypsies
Haiti
Hawaii
The Himalayas
Hip Hop
Hungary
India
India and Pakistan
Indian Ocean
Indonesia
Irish Folk
Irish Music
Italy
Jamaica
Japan
Kenya and Tanzania
Klezmer
Louisiana
Lucky Dube
Mali and Guinea
Marrabenta Mozambique
Merengue & Bachata
Mexico
Native American Music
Nigeria and Ghana
North Africa

Nusrat Fateh Ali Khan
Okinawa
Paris Café Music
Portugal
Rai
Reggae
Salsa
Salsa Dance
Samba
Scandinavia
Scottish Folk
Scottish Music
Senegal & The Gambia
Ska
Soul Brothers
South Africa
South African Gospel
South African Jazz
Spain
Sufi Music
Tango
Thailand
Tex-Mex
Wales
West African Music
World Music Vol 1: Africa, Europe and the Middle East
World Music Vol 2: Latin & North America, Caribbean, India, Asia and Pacific
World Roots
Youssou N'Dour & Etoile de Dakar
Zimbabwe

Rough Guides music, reference & CDs

TAP Air Portugal
Your perfect partner

Portugal, a unique blend of history,
culture, spectacular countryside, wine and fine cuisine,
entertainment, great golf
and good weather all year round.

**TAP Air Portugal - the best way to fly.
Daily flights to Lisbon, Porto and Faro
from London Heathrow and daily to Lisbon
from Gatwick.**

Call 0870 240 0033 for information and reservations
or visit our website

www.tap-airportugal.co.uk